Lecture Notes in Computer Science 8695

Commenced Publication in 1973
Founding and Former Series Editors:
Gerhard Goos, Juris Hartmanis, and Jan van Leeuwen

T0236432

David Fleet   Tomas Pajdla   Bernt Schiele
Tinne Tuytelaars (Eds.)

Computer Vision – ECCV 2014

13th European Conference
Zurich, Switzerland, September 6-12, 2014
Proceedings, Part VII

Springer

Volume Editors

David Fleet
University of Toronto, Department of Computer Science
6 King's College Road, Toronto, ON M5H 3S5, Canada
E-mail: fleet@cs.toronto.edu

Tomas Pajdla
Czech Technical University in Prague, Department of Cybernetics
Technicka 2, 166 27 Prague 6, Czech Republic
E-mail: pajdla@cmp.felk.cvut.cz

Bernt Schiele
Max-Planck-Institut für Informatik
Campus E1 4, 66123 Saarbrücken, Germany
E-mail: schiele@mpi-inf.mpg.de

Tinne Tuytelaars
KU Leuven, ESAT - PSI, iMinds
Kasteelpark Arenberg 10, Bus 2441, 3001 Leuven, Belgium
E-mail: tinne.tuytelaars@esat.kuleuven.be

Videos to this book can be accessed at
http://www.springerimages.com/videos/978-3-319-10583-3

ISSN 0302-9743   e-ISSN 1611-3349
ISBN 978-3-319-10583-3   e-ISBN 978-3-319-10584-0
DOI 10.1007/978-3-319-10584-0
Springer Cham Heidelberg New York Dordrecht London

Library of Congress Control Number: 2014946360

LNCS Sublibrary: SL 6 – Image Processing, Computer Vision, Pattern Recognition,
and Graphics

Typesetting: Camera-ready by author, data conversion by Scientific Publishing Services, Chennai, India

Printed on acid-free paper

Springer is part of Springer Science+Business Media (www.springer.com)

Foreword

The European Conference on Computer Vision is one of the top conferences in computer vision. It was first held in 1990 in Antibes (France) with subsequent conferences in Santa Margherita Ligure (Italy) in 1992, Stockholm (Sweden) in 1994, Cambridge (UK) in 1996, Freiburg (Germany) in 1998, Dublin (Ireland) in 2000, Copenhagen (Denmark) in 2002, Prague (Czech Republic) in 2004, Graz (Austria) in 2006, Marseille (France) in 2008, Heraklion (Greece) in 2010, and Florence (Italy) in 2012. Many people have worked hard to turn the 2014 edition into as great a success. We hope you will find this a mission accomplished.

The chairs decided to adhere to the classic single-track scheme. In terms of the time ordering, we decided to largely follow the Florence example (typically starting with poster sessions, followed by oral sessions), which offers a lot of flexibility to network and is more forgiving for the not-so-early-birds and hard-core gourmets.

A large conference like ECCV requires the help of many. They made sure there was a full program including the main conference, tutorials, workshops, exhibits, demos, proceedings, video streaming/archive, and Web descriptions. We want to cordially thank all those volunteers! Please have a look at the conference website to see their names (http://eccv2014.org/people/). We also thank our generous sponsors. Their support was vital for keeping prices low and enriching the program. And it is good to see such a level of industrial interest in what our community is doing!

We hope you will enjoy the proceedings ECCV 2014.

Also, willkommen in Zürich!

September 2014

Marc Pollefeys
Luc Van Gool
General Chairs

Preface

Welcome to the proceedings of the 2014 European Conference on Computer Vision (ECCV 2014) that was in Zurich, Switzerland. We are delighted to present this volume reflecting a strong and exciting program, the result of an extensive review process. In total, we received 1,444 paper submissions. Of these, 85 violated the ECCV submission guidelines and were rejected without review. Of the remainder, 363 were accepted (26,7%): 325 as posters (23,9%) and 38 as oral presentations (2,8%). This selection process was a combined effort of four program co-chairs (PCs), 53 area chairs (ACs), 803 Program Committee members and 247 additional reviewers.

As PCs we were primarily responsible for the design and execution of the review process. Beyond administrative rejections, we were not directly involved in acceptance decisions. Because the general co-chairs were permitted to submit papers, they played no role in the review process and were treated as any other author.

Acceptance decisions were made by the AC Committee. There were 53 ACs in total, selected by the PCs to provide sufficient technical expertise, geographical diversity (21 from Europe, 7 from Asia, and 25 from North America) and a mix of AC experience (7 had no previous AC experience, 18 had served as AC of a major international vision conference once since 2010, 8 had served twice, 13 had served three times, and 7 had served 4 times).

ACs were aided by 803 Program Committee members to whom papers were assigned for reviewing. There were 247 additional reviewers, each supervised by a Program Committee member. The Program Committee was based on suggestions from ACs, and committees from previous conferences. Google Scholar profiles were collected for all candidate Program Committee members and vetted by PCs. Having a large pool of Program Committee members for reviewing allowed us to match expertise while bounding reviewer loads. No more than nine papers were assigned to any one Program Committee member, with a maximum of six to graduate students.

The ECCV 2014 review process was double blind. Authors did not know the reviewers' identities, nor the ACs handling their paper(s). We did our utmost to ensure that ACs and reviewers did not know authors' identities, even though anonymity becomes difficult to maintain as more and more submissions appear concurrently on arXiv.org.

Particular attention was paid to minimizing potential conflicts of interest. Conflicts of interest between ACs, Program Committee members, and papers were based on authorship of ECCV 2014 submissions, on their home institutions, and on previous collaborations. To find institutional conflicts, all authors,

Program Committee members, and ACs were asked to list the Internet domains of their current institutions. To find collaborators, the DBLP (www.dblp.org) database was used to find any co-authored papers in the period 2010–2014.

We initially assigned approximately 100 papers to each AC, based on affinity scores from the Toronto Paper Matching System and authors' AC suggestions. ACs then bid on these, indicating their level of expertise. Based on these bids, and conflicts of interest, approximately 27 papers were assigned to each AC, for which they would act as the primary AC. The primary AC then suggested seven reviewers from the pool of Program Committee members (in rank order) for each paper, from which three were chosen per paper, taking load balancing and conflicts of interest into account.

Many papers were also assigned a secondary AC, either directly by the PCs, or as a consequence of the primary AC requesting the aid of an AC with complementary expertise. Secondary ACs could be assigned at any stage in the process, but in most cases this occurred about two weeks before the final AC meeting. Hence, in addition to their initial load of approximately 27 papers, each AC was asked to handle three to five more papers as a secondary AC; they were expected to read and write a short assessment of such papers. In addition, two of the 53 ACs were not directly assigned papers. Rather, they were available throughout the process to aid other ACs at any stage (e.g., with decisions, evaluating technical issues, additional reviews, etc.).

The initial reviewing period was three weeks long, after which reviewers provided reviews with preliminary recommendations. Three weeks is somewhat shorter than normal, but this did not seem to cause any unusual problems. With the generous help of several last-minute reviewers, each paper received three reviews.

Authors were then given the opportunity to rebut the reviews, primarily to identify any factual errors. Following this, reviewers and ACs discussed papers at length, after which reviewers finalized their reviews and gave a final recommendation to the ACs. Many ACs requested help from secondary ACs at this time.

Papers, for which rejection was clear and certain, based on the reviews and the AC's assessment, were identified by their primary ACs and vetted by a shadow AC prior to rejection. (These shadow ACs were assigned by the PCs.) All papers with any chance of acceptance were further discussed at the AC meeting. Those deemed "strong" by primary ACs (about 140 in total) were also assigned a secondary AC.

The AC meeting, with all but two of the primary ACs present, took place in Zurich. ACs were divided into 17 triplets for each morning, and a different set of triplets for each afternoon. Given the content of the three (or more) reviews along with reviewer recommendations, rebuttals, online discussions among reviewers and primary ACs, written input from and discussions with secondary ACs, the

AC triplets then worked together to resolve questions, calibrate assessments, and make acceptance decisions.

To select oral presentations, all strong papers, along with any others put forward by triplets (about 155 in total), were then discussed in four panels, each comprising four or five triplets. Each panel ranked these oral candidates, using four categories. Papers in the two top categories provided the final set of 38 oral presentations.

We want to thank everyone involved in making the ECCV 2014 Program possible. First and foremost, the success of ECCV 2014 depended on the quality of papers submitted by authors, and on the very hard work of the reviewers, the Program Committee members and the ACs. We are particularly grateful to Kyros Kutulakos for his enormous software support before and during the AC meeting, to Laurent Charlin for the use of the Toronto Paper Matching System, and Chaohui Wang for help optimizing the assignment of papers to ACs. We also owe a debt of gratitude for the great support of Zurich local organizers, especially Susanne Keller and her team.

September 2014

David Fleet
Tomas Pajdla
Bernt Schiele
Tinne Tuytelaars

Organization

General Chairs

Luc Van Gool	ETH Zurich, Switzerland
Marc Pollefeys	ETH Zurich, Switzerland

Program Chairs

Tinne Tuytelaars	KU Leuven, Belgium
Bernt Schiele	MPI Informatics, Saarbrücken, Germany
Tomas Pajdla	CTU Prague, Czech Republic
David Fleet	University of Toronto, Canada

Local Arrangements Chairs

Konrad Schindler	ETH Zurich, Switzerland
Vittorio Ferrari	University of Edinburgh, UK

Workshop Chairs

Lourdes Agapito	University College London, UK
Carsten Rother	TU Dresden, Germany
Michael Bronstein	University of Lugano, Switzerland

Tutorial Chairs

Bastian Leibe	RWTH Aachen, Germany
Paolo Favaro	University of Bern, Switzerland
Christoph Lampert	IST Austria

Poster Chair

Helmut Grabner	ETH Zurich, Switzerland

Publication Chairs

Mario Fritz	MPI Informatics, Saarbrücken, Germany
Michael Stark	MPI Informatics, Saarbrücken, Germany

Demo Chairs

Davide Scaramuzza University of Zurich, Switzerland
Jan-Michael Frahm University of North Carolina at Chapel Hill,
         USA

Exhibition Chair

Tamar Tolcachier University of Zurich, Switzerland

Industrial Liaison Chairs

Alexander Sorkine-Hornung Disney Research Zurich, Switzerland
Fatih Porikli ANU, Australia

Student Grant Chair

Seon Joo Kim Yonsei University, Korea

Air Shelters Accommodation Chair

Maros Blaha ETH Zurich, Switzerland

Website Chairs

Lorenz Meier ETH Zurich, Switzerland
Bastien Jacquet ETH Zurich, Switzerland

Internet Chair

Thorsten Steenbock ETH Zurich, Switzerland

Student Volunteer Chairs

Andrea Cohen ETH Zurich, Switzerland
Ralf Dragon ETH Zurich, Switzerland
Laura Leal-Taixé ETH Zurich, Switzerland

Finance Chair

Amael Delaunoy ETH Zurich, Switzerland

Conference Coordinator

Susanne H. Keller ETH Zurich, Switzerland

Area Chairs

Lourdes Agapito	University College London, UK
Sameer Agarwal	Google Research, USA
Shai Avidan	Tel Aviv University, Israel
Alex Berg	UNC Chapel Hill, USA
Yuri Boykov	University of Western Ontario, Canada
Thomas Brox	University of Freiburg, Germany
Jason Corso	SUNY at Buffalo, USA
Trevor Darrell	UC Berkeley, USA
Fernando de la Torre	Carnegie Mellon University, USA
Frank Dellaert	Georgia Tech, USA
Alexei Efros	UC Berkeley, USA
Vittorio Ferrari	University of Edinburgh, UK
Andrew Fitzgibbon	Microsoft Research, Cambridge, UK
JanMichael Frahm	UNC Chapel Hill, USA
Bill Freeman	Massachusetts Institute of Technology, USA
Peter Gehler	Max Planck Institute for Intelligent Systems, Germany
Kristen Graumann	University of Texas at Austin, USA
Wolfgang Heidrich	University of British Columbia, Canada
Herve Jegou	Inria Rennes, France
Fredrik Kahl	Lund University, Sweden
Kyros Kutulakos	University of Toronto, Canada
Christoph Lampert	IST Austria
Ivan Laptev	Inria Paris, France
Kyuong Mu Lee	Seoul National University, South Korea
Bastian Leibe	RWTH Aachen, Germany
Vincent Lepetit	TU Graz, Austria
Hongdong Li	Australian National University
David Lowe	University of British Columbia, Canada
Greg Mori	Simon Fraser University, Canada
Srinivas Narasimhan	Carnegie Mellon University, PA, USA
Nassir Navab	TU Munich, Germany
Ko Nishino	Drexel University, USA
Maja Pantic	Imperial College London, UK
Patrick Perez	Technicolor Research, Rennes, France
Pietro Perona	California Institute of Technology, USA
Ian Reid	University of Adelaide, Australia
Stefan Roth	TU Darmstadt, Germany
Carsten Rother	TU Dresden, Germany
Sudeep Sarkar	University of South Florida, USA
Silvio Savarese	Stanford University, USA
Christoph Schnoerr	Heidelberg University, Germany
Jamie Shotton	Microsoft Research, Cambridge, UK

Kaleem Siddiqi	McGill, Canada
Leonid Sigal	Disney Research, Pittsburgh, PA, USA
Noah Snavely	Cornell, USA
Raquel Urtasun	University of Toronto, Canada
Andrea Vedaldi	University of Oxford, UK
Jakob Verbeek	Inria Rhone-Alpes, France
Xiaogang Wang	Chinese University of Hong Kong, SAR China
Ming-Hsuan Yang	UC Merced, CA, USA
Lihi Zelnik-Manor	Technion, Israel
Song-Chun Zhu	UCLA, USA
Todd Zickler	Harvard, USA

Program Committee

Gaurav Aggarwal	Joao Barreto	Kristin Branson
Amit Agrawal	Jonathan Barron	Steven Branson
Haizhou Ai	Adrien Bartoli	Francois Bremond
Ijaz Akhter	Arslan Basharat	Michael Bronstein
Karteek Alahari	Dhruv Batra	Gabriel Brostow
Alexandre Alahi	Luis Baumela	Michael Brown
Andrea Albarelli	Maximilian Baust	Matthew Brown
Saad Ali	Jean-Charles Bazin	Marcus Brubaker
Jose M. Alvarez	Loris Bazzani	Andres Bruhn
Juan Andrade-Cetto	Chris Beall	Joan Bruna
Bjoern Andres	Vasileios Belagiannis	Aurelie Bugeau
Mykhaylo Andriluka	Csaba Beleznai	Darius Burschka
Elli Angelopoulou	Moshe Ben-ezra	Ricardo Cabral
Roland Angst	Ohad Ben-Shahar	Jian-Feng Cai
Relja Arandjelovic	Ismail Ben Ayed	Neill D.F. Campbell
Ognjen Arandjelovic	Rodrigo Benenson	Yong Cao
Helder Araujo	Ryad Benosman	Barbara Caputo
Pablo Arbelez	Tamara Berg	Joao Carreira
Vasileios Argyriou	Margrit Betke	Jan Cech
Antonis Argyros	Ross Beveridge	Jinxiang Chai
Kalle Astroem	Bir Bhanu	Ayan Chakrabarti
Vassilis Athitsos	Horst Bischof	Tat-Jen Cham
Yannis Avrithis	Arijit Biswas	Antoni Chan
Yusuf Aytar	Andrew Blake	Manmohan Chandraker
Xiang Bai	Aaron Bobick	Vijay Chandrasekhar
Luca Ballan	Piotr Bojanowski	Hong Chang
Yingze Bao	Ali Borji	Ming-Ching Chang
Richard Baraniuk	Terrance Boult	Rama Chellappa
Adrian Barbu	Lubomir Bourdev	Chao-Yeh Chen
Kobus Barnard	Patrick Bouthemy	David Chen
Connelly Barnes	Edmond Boyer	Hwann-Tzong Chen

Tsuhan Chen
Xilin Chen
Chao Chen
Longbin Chen
Minhua Chen
Anoop Cherian
Liang-Tien Chia
Tat-Jun Chin
Sunghyun Cho
Minsu Cho
Nam Ik Cho
Wongun Choi
Mario Christoudias
Wen-Sheng Chu
Yung-Yu Chuang
Ondrej Chum
James Clark
Brian Clipp
Isaac Cohen
John Collomosse
Bob Collins
Tim Cootes
David Crandall
Antonio Criminisi
Naresh Cuntoor
Qieyun Dai
Jifeng Dai
Kristin Dana
Kostas Daniilidis
Larry Davis
Andrew Davison
Goksel Dedeoglu
Koichiro Deguchi
Alberto Del Bimbo
Alessio Del Bue
Hervé Delingette
Andrew Delong
Stefanie Demirci
David Demirdjian
Jia Deng
Joachim Denzler
Konstantinos Derpanis
Thomas Deselaers
Frederic Devernay
Michel Dhome

Anthony Dick
Ajay Divakaran
Santosh Kumar Divvala
Minh Do
Carl Doersch
Piotr Dollar
Bin Dong
Weisheng Dong
Michael Donoser
Gianfranco Doretto
Matthijs Douze
Bruce Draper
Mark Drew
Bertram Drost
Lixin Duan
Jean-Luc Dugelay
Enrique Dunn
Pinar Duygulu
Jan-Olof Eklundh
James H. Elder
Ian Endres
Olof Enqvist
Markus Enzweiler
Aykut Erdem
Anders Eriksson
Ali Eslami
Irfan Essa
Francisco Estrada
Bin Fan
Quanfu Fan
Jialue Fan
Sean Fanello
Ali Farhadi
Giovanni Farinella
Ryan Farrell
Alireza Fathi
Paolo Favaro
Michael Felsberg
Pedro Felzenszwalb
Rob Fergus
Basura Fernando
Frank Ferrie
Sanja Fidler
Boris Flach
Francois Fleuret

David Fofi
Wolfgang Foerstner
David Forsyth
Katerina Fragkiadaki
Jean-Sebastien Franco
Friedrich Fraundorfer
Mario Fritz
Yun Fu
Pascal Fua
Hironobu Fujiyoshi
Yasutaka Furukawa
Ryo Furukawa
Andrea Fusiello
Fabio Galasso
Juergen Gall
Andrew Gallagher
David Gallup
Arvind Ganesh
Dashan Gao
Shenghua Gao
James Gee
Andreas Geiger
Yakup Genc
Bogdan Georgescu
Guido Gerig
David Geronimo
Theo Gevers
Bernard Ghanem
Andrew Gilbert
Ross Girshick
Martin Godec
Guy Godin
Roland Goecke
Michael Goesele
Alvina Goh
Bastian Goldluecke
Boqing Gong
Yunchao Gong
Raghuraman Gopalan
Albert Gordo
Lena Gorelick
Paulo Gotardo
Stephen Gould
Venu Madhav Govindu
Helmut Grabner

Roger Grosse
Matthias Grundmann
Chunhui Gu
Xianfeng Gu
Jinwei Gu
Sergio Guadarrama
Matthieu Guillaumin
Jean-Yves Guillemaut
Hatice Gunes
Ruiqi Guo
Guodong Guo
Abhinav Gupta
Abner Guzman Rivera
Gregory Hager
Ghassan Hamarneh
Bohyung Han
Tony Han
Jari Hannuksela
Tatsuya Harada
Mehrtash Harandi
Bharath Hariharan
Stefan Harmeling
Tal Hassner
Daniel Hauagge
Søren Hauberg
Michal Havlena
James Hays
Kaiming He
Xuming He
Martial Hebert
Felix Heide
Jared Heinly
Hagit Hel-Or
Lionel Heng
Philipp Hennig
Carlos Hernandez
Aaron Hertzmann
Adrian Hilton
David Hogg
Derek Hoiem
Byung-Woo Hong
Anthony Hoogs
Joachim Hornegger
Timothy Hospedales
Wenze Hu

Zhe Hu
Gang Hua
Xian-Sheng Hua
Dong Huang
Gary Huang
Heng Huang
Sung Ju Hwang
Wonjun Hwang
Ivo Ihrke
Nazli Ikizler-Cinbis
Slobodan Ilic
Horace Ip
Michal Irani
Hiroshi Ishikawa
Laurent Itti
Nathan Jacobs
Max Jaderberg
Omar Javed
C.V. Jawahar
Bruno Jedynak
Hueihan Jhuang
Qiang Ji
Hui Ji
Kui Jia
Yangqing Jia
Jiaya Jia
Hao Jiang
Zhuolin Jiang
Sam Johnson
Neel Joshi
Armand Joulin
Frederic Jurie
Ioannis Kakadiaris
Zdenek Kalal
Amit Kale
Joni-Kristian
    Kamarainen
George Kamberov
Kenichi Kanatani
Sing Bing Kang
Vadim Kantorov
Jörg Hendrik Kappes
Leonid Karlinsky
Zoltan Kato
Hiroshi Kawasaki

Verena Kaynig
Cem Keskin
Margret Keuper
Daniel Keysers
Sameh Khamis
Fahad Khan
Saad Khan
Aditya Khosla
Martin Kiefel
Gunhee Kim
Jaechul Kim
Seon Joo Kim
Tae-Kyun Kim
Byungsoo Kim
Benjamin Kimia
Kris Kitani
Hedvig Kjellstrom
Laurent Kneip
Reinhard Koch
Kevin Koeser
Ullrich Koethe
Effrosyni Kokiopoulou
Iasonas Kokkinos
Kalin Kolev
Vladimir Kolmogorov
Vladlen Koltun
Nikos Komodakis
Piotr Koniusz
Peter Kontschieder
Ender Konukoglu
Sanjeev Koppal
Hema Koppula
Andreas Koschan
Jana Kosecka
Adriana Kovashka
Adarsh Kowdle
Josip Krapac
Dilip Krishnan
Zuzana Kukelova
Brian Kulis
Neeraj Kumar
M. Pawan Kumar
Cheng-Hao Kuo
In So Kweon
Junghyun Kwon

Junseok Kwon
Simon Lacoste-Julien
Shang-Hong Lai
Jean-François Lalonde
Tian Lan
Michael Langer
Doug Lanman
Diane Larlus
Longin Jan Latecki
Svetlana Lazebnik
Laura Leal-Taixé
Erik Learned-Miller
Honglak Lee
Yong Jae Lee
Ido Leichter
Victor Lempitsky
Frank Lenzen
Marius Leordeanu
Thomas Leung
Maxime Lhuillier
Chunming Li
Fei-Fei Li
Fuxin Li
Rui Li
Li-Jia Li
Chia-Kai Liang
Shengcai Liao
Joerg Liebelt
Jongwoo Lim
Joseph Lim
Ruei-Sung Lin
Yen-Yu Lin
Zhouchen Lin
Liang Lin
Haibin Ling
James Little
Baiyang Liu
Ce Liu
Feng Liu
Guangcan Liu
Jingen Liu
Wei Liu
Zicheng Liu
Zongyi Liu
Tyng-Luh Liu

Xiaoming Liu
Xiaobai Liu
Ming-Yu Liu
Marcus Liwicki
Stephen Lombardi
Roberto Lopez-Sastre
Manolis Lourakis
Brian Lovell
Chen Change Loy
Jiangbo Lu
Jiwen Lu
Simon Lucey
Jiebo Luo
Ping Luo
Marcus Magnor
Vijay Mahadevan
Julien Mairal
Michael Maire
Subhransu Maji
Atsuto Maki
Yasushi Makihara
Roberto Manduchi
Luca Marchesotti
Aleix Martinez
Bogdan Matei
Diana Mateus
Stefan Mathe
Yasuyuki Matsushita
Iain Matthews
Kevin Matzen
Bruce Maxwell
Stephen Maybank
Walterio Mayol-Cuevas
David McAllester
Gerard Medioni
Christopher Mei
Paulo Mendonca
Thomas Mensink
Domingo Mery
Ajmal Mian
Branislav Micusik
Ondrej Miksik
Anton Milan
Majid Mirmehdi
Anurag Mittal

Hossein Mobahi
Pranab Mohanty
Pascal Monasse
Vlad Morariu
Philippos Mordohai
Francesc Moreno-Noguer
Luce Morin
Nigel Morris
Bryan Morse
Eric Mortensen
Yasuhiro Mukaigawa
Lopamudra Mukherjee
Vittorio Murino
David Murray
Sobhan Naderi Parizi
Hajime Nagahara
Laurent Najman
Karthik Nandakumar
Fabian Nater
Jan Neumann
Lukas Neumann
Ram Nevatia
Richard Newcombe
Minh Hoai Nguyen
Bingbing Ni
Feiping Nie
Juan Carlos Niebles
Marc Niethammer
Claudia Nieuwenhuis
Mark Nixon
Mohammad Norouzi
Sebastian Nowozin
Matthew O'Toole
Peter Ochs
Jean-Marc Odobez
Francesca Odone
Eyal Ofek
Sangmin Oh
Takahiro Okabe
Takayuki Okatani
Aude Oliva
Carl Olsson
Bjorn Ommer
Magnus Oskarsson
Wanli Ouyang

Geoffrey Oxholm
Mustafa Ozuysal
Nicolas Padoy
Caroline Pantofaru
Nicolas Papadakis
George Papandreou
Nikolaos
    Papanikolopoulos
Nikos Paragios
Devi Parikh
Dennis Park
Vishal Patel
Ioannis Patras
Vladimir Pavlovic
Kim Pedersen
Marco Pedersoli
Shmuel Peleg
Marcello Pelillo
Tingying Peng
A.G. Amitha Perera
Alessandro Perina
Federico Pernici
Florent Perronnin
Vladimir Petrovic
Tomas Pfister
Jonathon Phillips
Justus Piater
Massimo Piccardi
Hamed Pirsiavash
Leonid Pishchulin
Robert Pless
Thomas Pock
Jean Ponce
Gerard Pons-Moll
Ronald Poppe
Andrea Prati
Victor Prisacariu
Kari Pulli
Yu Qiao
Lei Qin
Novi Quadrianto
Rahul Raguram
Varun Ramakrishna
Srikumar Ramalingam
Narayanan Ramanathan

Konstantinos
    Rapantzikos
Michalis Raptis
Nalini Ratha
Avinash Ravichandran
Michael Reale
Dikpal Reddy
James Rehg
Jan Reininghaus
Xiaofeng Ren
Jerome Revaud
Morteza Rezanejad
Hayko Riemenschneider
Tammy Riklin Raviv
Antonio Robles-Kelly
Erik Rodner
Emanuele Rodola
Mikel Rodriguez
Marcus Rohrbach
Javier Romero
Charles Rosenberg
Bodo Rosenhahn
Arun Ross
Samuel Rota Bul
Peter Roth
Volker Roth
Anastasios Roussos
Sebastien Roy
Michael Rubinstein
Olga Russakovsky
Bryan Russell
Michael S. Ryoo
Mohammad Amin
    Sadeghi
Kate Saenko
Albert Ali Salah
Imran Saleemi
Mathieu Salzmann
Conrad Sanderson
Aswin
    Sankaranarayanan
Benjamin Sapp
Radim Sara
Scott Satkin
Imari Sato

Yoichi Sato
Bogdan Savchynskyy
Hanno Scharr
Daniel Scharstein
Yoav Y. Schechner
Walter Scheirer
Kevin Schelten
Frank Schmidt
Uwe Schmidt
Julia Schnabel
Alexander Schwing
Nicu Sebe
Shishir Shah
Mubarak Shah
Shiguang Shan
Qi Shan
Ling Shao
Abhishek Sharma
Viktoriia Sharmanska
Eli Shechtman
Yaser Sheikh
Alexander Shekhovtsov
Chunhua Shen
Li Shen
Yonggang Shi
Qinfeng Shi
Ilan Shimshoni
Takaaki Shiratori
Abhinav Shrivastava
Behjat Siddiquie
Nathan Silberman
Karen Simonyan
Richa Singh
Vikas Singh
Sudipta Sinha
Josef Sivic
Dirk Smeets
Arnold Smeulders
William Smith
Cees Snoek
Eric Sommerlade
Alexander
    Sorkine-Hornung
Alvaro Soto
Richard Souvenir

Anuj Srivastava
Ioannis Stamos
Michael Stark
Chris Stauffer
Bjorn Stenger
Charles Stewart
Rainer Stiefelhagen
Juergen Sturm
Yusuke Sugano
Josephine Sullivan
Deqing Sun
Min Sun
Hari Sundar
Ganesh Sundaramoorthi
Kalyan Sunkavalli
Sabine Süsstrunk
David Suter
Tomas Svoboda
Rahul Swaminathan
Tanveer
  Syeda-Mahmood
Rick Szeliski
Raphael Sznitman
Yuichi Taguchi
Yu-Wing Tai
Jun Takamatsu
Hugues Talbot
Ping Tan
Robby Tan
Kevin Tang
Huixuan Tang
Danhang Tang
Marshall Tappen
Jean-Philippe Tarel
Danny Tarlow
Gabriel Taubin
Camillo Taylor
Demetri Terzopoulos
Christian Theobalt
Yuandong Tian
Joseph Tighe
Radu Timofte
Massimo Tistarelli
George Toderici
Sinisa Todorovic

Giorgos Tolias
Federico Tombari
Tatiana Tommasi
Yan Tong
Akihiko Torii
Antonio Torralba
Lorenzo Torresani
Andrea Torsello
Tali Treibitz
Rudolph Triebel
Bill Triggs
Roberto Tron
Tomasz Trzcinski
Ivor Tsang
Yanghai Tsin
Zhuowen Tu
Tony Tung
Pavan Turaga
Engin Türetken
Oncel Tuzel
Georgios Tzimiropoulos
Norimichi Ukita
Martin Urschler
Arash Vahdat
Julien Valentin
Michel Valstar
Koen van de Sande
Joost van de Weijer
Anton van den Hengel
Jan van Gemert
Daniel Vaquero
Kiran Varanasi
Mayank Vatsa
Ashok Veeraraghavan
Olga Veksler
Alexander Vezhnevets
Rene Vidal
Sudheendra
  Vijayanarasimhan
Jordi Vitria
Christian Vogler
Carl Vondrick
Sven Wachsmuth
Stefan Walk
Chaohui Wang

Jingdong Wang
Jue Wang
Ruiping Wang
Kai Wang
Liang Wang
Xinggang Wang
Xin-Jing Wang
Yang Wang
Heng Wang
Yu-Chiang Frank Wang
Simon Warfield
Yichen Wei
Yair Weiss
Gordon Wetzstein
Oliver Whyte
Richard Wildes
Christopher Williams
Lior Wolf
Kwan-Yee Kenneth
  Wong
Oliver Woodford
John Wright
Changchang Wu
Xinxiao Wu
Ying Wu
Tianfu Wu
Yang Wu
Yingnian Wu
Jonas Wulff
Yu Xiang
Tao Xiang
Jianxiong Xiao
Dong Xu
Li Xu
Yong Xu
Kota Yamaguchi
Takayoshi Yamashita
Shuicheng Yan
Jie Yang
Qingxiong Yang
Ruigang Yang
Meng Yang
Yi Yang
Chih-Yuan Yang
Jimei Yang

Bangpeng Yao
Angela Yao
Dit-Yan Yeung
Alper Yilmaz
Lijun Yin
Xianghua Ying
Kuk-Jin Yoon
Shiqi Yu
Stella Yu
Jingyi Yu
Junsong Yuan
Lu Yuan
Alan Yuille
Ramin Zabih
Christopher Zach

Stefanos Zafeiriou
Hongbin Zha
Lei Zhang
Junping Zhang
Shaoting Zhang
Xiaoqin Zhang
Guofeng Zhang
Tianzhu Zhang
Ning Zhang
Lei Zhang
Li Zhang
Bin Zhao
Guoying Zhao
Ming Zhao
Yibiao Zhao

Weishi Zheng
Bo Zheng
Changyin Zhou
Huiyu Zhou
Kevin Zhou
Bolei Zhou
Feng Zhou
Jun Zhu
Xiangxin Zhu
Henning Zimmer
Karel Zimmermann
Andrew Zisserman
Larry Zitnick
Daniel Zoran

Additional Reviewers

Austin Abrams
Hanno Ackermann
Daniel Adler
Muhammed Zeshan
  Afzal
Pulkit Agrawal
Edilson de Aguiar
Unaiza Ahsan
Amit Aides
Zeynep Akata
Jon Almazan
David Altamar
Marina Alterman
Mohamed Rabie Amer
Manuel Amthor
Shawn Andrews
Oisin Mac Aodha
Federica Arrigoni
Yuval Bahat
Luis Barrios
John Bastian
Florian Becker
C. Fabian
  Benitez-Quiroz
Vinay Bettadapura
Brian G. Booth

Lukas Bossard
Katie Bouman
Hilton Bristow
Daniel Canelhas
Olivier Canevet
Spencer Cappallo
Ivan Huerta Casado
Daniel Castro
Ishani Chakraborty
Chenyi Chen
Sheng Chen
Xinlei Chen
Wei-Chen Chiu
Hang Chu
Yang Cong
Sam Corbett-Davies
Zhen Cui
Maria A. Davila
Oliver Demetz
Meltem Demirkus
Chaitanya Desai
Pengfei Dou
Ralf Dragon
Liang Du
David Eigen
Jakob Engel

Victor Escorcia
Sandro Esquivel
Nicola Fioraio
Michael Firman
Alex Fix
Oliver Fleischmann
Marco Fornoni
David Fouhey
Vojtech Franc
Jorge Martinez G.
Silvano Galliani
Pablo Garrido
Efstratios Gavves
Timnit Gebru
Georgios Giannoulis
Clement Godard
Ankur Gupta
Saurabh Gupta
Amirhossein Habibian
David Hafner
Tom S.F. Haines
Vladimir Haltakov
Christopher Ham
Xufeng Han
Stefan Heber
Yacov Hel-Or

David Held
Benjamin Hell
Jan Heller
Anton van den Hengel
Robert Henschel
Steven Hickson
Michael Hirsch
Jan Hosang
Shell Hu
Zhiwu Huang
Daniel Huber
Ahmad Humayun
Corneliu Ilisescu
Zahra Iman
Thanapong Intharah
Phillip Isola
Hamid Izadinia
Edward Johns
Justin Johnson
Andreas Jordt
Anne Jordt
Cijo Jose
Daniel Jung
Meina Kan
Ben Kandel
Vasiliy Karasev
Andrej Karpathy
Jan Kautz
Changil Kim
Hyeongwoo Kim
Rolf Koehler
Daniel Kohlsdorf
Svetlana Kordumova
Jonathan Krause
Till Kroeger
Malte Kuhlmann
Ilja Kuzborskij
Alina Kuznetsova
Sam Kwak
Peihua Li
Michael Lam
Maksim Lapin
Gil Levi
Aviad Levis
Yan Li

Wenbin Li
Yin Li
Zhenyang Li
Pengpeng Liang
Jinna Lie
Qiguang Liu
Tianliang Liu
Alexander Loktyushin
Steven Lovegrove
Feng Lu
Jake Lussier
Xutao Lv
Luca Magri
Behrooz Mahasseni
Aravindh Mahendran
Siddharth Mahendran
Francesco Malapelle
Mateusz Malinowski
Santiago Manen
Timo von Marcard
Ricardo Martin-Brualla
Iacopo Masi
Roberto Mecca
Tomer Michaeli
Hengameh Mirzaalian
Kylia Miskell
Ishan Misra
Javier Montoya
Roozbeh Mottaghi
Panagiotis Moutafis
Oliver Mueller
Daniel Munoz
Rajitha Navarathna
James Newling
Mohamed Omran
Vicente Ordonez
Sobhan Naderi Parizi
Omkar Parkhi
Novi Patricia
Kuan-Chuan Peng
Bojan Pepikj
Federico Perazzi
Loic Peter
Alioscia Petrelli
Sebastian Polsterl

Alison Pouch
Vittal Premanchandran
James Pritts
Luis Puig
Julian Quiroga
Vignesh Ramanathan
Rene Ranftl
Mohammad Rastegari
S. Hussain Raza
Michael Reale
Malcolm Reynolds
Alimoor Reza
Christian Richardt
Marko Ristin
Beatrice Rossi
Rasmus Rothe
Nasa Rouf
Anirban Roy
Fereshteh Sadeghi
Zahra Sadeghipoor
Faraz Saedaar
Tanner Schmidt
Anna Senina
Lee Seversky
Yachna Sharma
Chen Shen
Javen Shi
Tomas Simon
Gautam Singh
Brandon M. Smith
Shuran Song
Mohamed Souiai
Srinath Sridhar
Abhilash Srikantha
Michael Stoll
Aparna Taneja
Lisa Tang
Moria Tau
J. Rafael Tena
Roberto Toldo
Manolis Tsakiris
Dimitrios Tzionas
Vladyslav Usenko
Danny Veikherman
Fabio Viola

Minh Vo
Christoph Vogel
Sebastian Volz
Jacob Walker
Li Wan
Chen Wang
Jiang Wang
Oliver Wang
Peng Wang
Jan Dirk Wegner
Stephan Wenger
Scott Workman
Chenglei Wu

Yuhang Wu
Fan Yang
Mark Yatskar
Bulent Yener
Serena Yeung
Kwang M. Yi
Gokhan Yildirim
Ryo Yonetani
Stanislav Yotov
Chong You
Quanzeng You
Fisher Yu
Pei Yu

Kaan Yucer
Clausius Zelenka
Xing Zhang
Xinhua Zhang
Yinda Zhang
Jiejie Zhu
Shengqi Zhu
Yingying Zhu
Yuke Zhu
Andrew Ziegler

Table of Contents

Motion and 3D Scene Analysis

Person Re-Identification
Using Kernel-Based Metric Learning Methods⋆

Fei Xiong, Mengran Gou, Octavia Camps, and Mario Sznaier

Dept. of Electrical and Computer Engineering,
Northeastern University, Boston, MA 02115
{fxiong,mengran,camps,msznaier}@coe.neu.edu
http://robustsystems.coe.neu.edu

Abstract. Re-identification of individuals across camera networks with limited or no overlapping fields of view remains challenging in spite of significant research efforts. In this paper, we propose the use, and extensively evaluate the performance, of four alternatives for re-ID classification: regularized Pairwise Constrained Component Analysis, kernel Local Fisher Discriminant Analysis, Marginal Fisher Analysis and a ranking ensemble voting scheme, used in conjunction with different sizes of sets of histogram-based features and linear, χ^2 and RBF-χ^2 kernels. Comparisons against the state-of-art show significant improvements in performance measured both in terms of Cumulative Match Characteristic curves (CMC) and Proportion of Uncertainty Removed (PUR) scores on the challenging VIPeR, iLIDS, CAVIAR and 3DPeS datasets.

1 Introduction

Surveillance systems for large public spaces (i.e. airport terminals, train stations, etc.) use networks of cameras to maximize their coverage area. However, due to economical and infrastructural reasons, these cameras often have very little or no overlapping field of view. Thus, recognizing individuals across cameras is a critical component when tracking in the network.

The task of re-identification (re-ID) can be formalized as the problem of matching a given *probe* image against a *gallery* of candidate images. As illustrated in Figure 1(a), this is a very challenging task since images of the same individual can be very different due to variations in pose, viewpoint, and illumination. Moreover, due to the (relatively low) resolution and the placement of the cameras, different individuals may appear very similar and with little or none visible faces, preventing the use of biometric and soft-biometric approaches [9,24].

A good overview of existing re-ID methods can be found in [7,10,13,23,29] and references therein. The three most important aspects in re-ID are i) the features used, ii) the matching procedure, and iii) the performance evaluation.

⋆ Electronic supplementary material -Supplementary material is available in the online version of this chapter at http://dx.doi.org/10.1007/978-3-319-10584-0_1. Videos can also be accessed at http://www.springerimages.com/videos/978-3-319-10583-3

D. Fleet et al. (Eds.): ECCV 2014, Part VII, LNCS 8695, pp. 1–16, 2014.
© Springer International Publishing Switzerland 2014

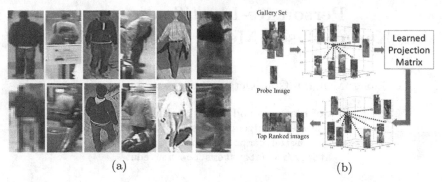

(a)   (b)

Fig. 1. The re-ID problem. (a) Challenges (left to right): low resolution, occlusion, viewpoint, pose, and illumination variations and similar appearance of different people. (b) Projecting the data improves classification performance.

Most re-ID approaches use appearance-based features that are viewpoint quasi-invariant [2,3,5,11,12,14,25] such as color and texture descriptors. However, the number and support of features used varies greatly across approaches making it difficult to compare their impact on performance. Using standard metrics such as Euclidean distance to match images based on this type of features results in poor performance due to the large variations in pose and illumination and limited training data. Thus, recent approaches [18,20,21,29,31] design classifiers to learn specialized metrics (see Figure 1(b)), that enforce features from the same individual to be closer than features from different individuals. Yet, state-of-the-art performance remains low, slightly above 30% for the best match. Performance is often reported on standard datasets that bring in different biases. Moreover, the number of datasets and the experimental evaluation protocols used vary greatly across approaches, making difficult to compare them.

This paper focuses on all aspects of the problem, feature extraction, distance learning for re-ID classification, and performance evaluation. In particular:

- We explore the effect of the size and location of support regions for commonly used histogram-based feature vectors may have on classification performance.
- We propose four kernel-based distance learning approaches to improve re-ID classification accuracy when the data space is under-sampled: regularized Pairwise Constrained Component Analysis (rPCCA), kernel Local Fisher Discriminant Classifier (kLFDA), Marginal Fisher Analysis (MFA) [26], and a ranking ensemble voting (REV) scheme.
- We provide a comprehensive performance evaluation using four sets of features, three kernels (linear, χ^2 and RBF-χ^2) and four challenging re-ID datasets: VIPeR [14], CAVIAR [8], 3DPeS [4] and iLIDS [30]. Using this protocol, we compare the proposed methods against four state-of-the-art methods: Pairwise Constrained Component Analysis (PCCA) [20], Local Fisher Discriminant Analysis (LDFA) [21], SVMML [18] and KISSME [15].

Our experiments not only allow us to compare previously published classification techniques using a common set of features and datasets (an experiment that to the best of our knowledge has not been reported so far) but also show that the classification methods proposed here result in a significant improvement in performance over the state-of-the-art.

2 Related Work

Re-ID data samples consist of images of individuals, cropped such that the target occupies most of the image. The most commonly used features are inspired on a "bag-of-words" approach and are histograms based using local support regions within the target's bounding box [10]. Yet, the number of support regions and the dimension of the feature vector can vary widely. For example, Mignon and Jurie [20] use feature vectors of dimension 2,676 while [21] use feature vectors of dimension 22,506. In our experiments we evaluate the effect of these choices on re-ID accuracy performance. As shown in our experiments, using too many of these features can decrease performance.

Most re-ID approaches can be formalized as a supervised metric/distance learning algorithm where a projection matrix $\mathbf{P}$ is sought so that the projected Mahalanobis-like distance $D_{\mathbf{M}}(\mathbf{x}_{i_k}, \mathbf{x}_{j_k}) = (\mathbf{x}_i - \mathbf{x}_j)^T \mathbf{M}(\mathbf{x}_i - \mathbf{x}_j)$, where $\mathbf{M} = \mathbf{P}^T \mathbf{P}$, is small when feature vectors $\mathbf{x}_{i_k}$ and $\mathbf{x}_{j_k}$ represent the same person and large otherwise.

The best reported performance on the VIPeR dataset [18] was achieved using an adaptive boundary approach that jointly learns the distance metric and an adaptive thresholding rule. However, a drawback of this approach is that it scales poorly since its computational complexity is $O(d^2)$ where d is the dimension of the feature vector $\mathbf{x}_{i_k}$. An alternative approach is to use a logistic function to approximate the hinge loss so that the global optimum still can be achieved by iteratively gradient search along $\mathbf{P}$ as in Pairwise Constrained Component Analysis (PCCA) [20] and in (PRDC) [29]. However, these methods are prone to over fitting. We propose to address this problem by introducing a regularization term that uses the additional degrees of freedom available in the problem to maximize the inter-class margin.

The state-of-the-art performance on the CAVIAR and the 3DPeS datasets was achieved by using a Local Fisher Discriminant Classifier (LFDA) as proposed by Pedagadi et al. [21]. While this approach has a closed form solution for the Mahalanobis matrix, it requires an eigenanalysis of a $d \times d$ scatter matrix. For large d, [21] proposed to first reduce the dimensionality of the data using principal component analysis (PCA). However, PCA can eliminate discriminant features defeating the benefits of LFDA. We propose instead to use a kernel approach to preserve discriminant features while reducing the dimension of the problem to a $N \times N$ eigendecomposition, where $N << d$ is the number of images.

2.1 Notation

For the sake of clarity, we list the notation used in this paper here. $\mathbf{x}_i \in \mathbf{R}^d$ is a feature vector representing the ith image. $l_i \in \{1, \cdots, c\}$ is the *identity label* for the ith image. A pair of samples $(\mathbf{x}_{i_k}, \mathbf{x}_{j_k})$ has associated a *class label* $y_k = 1$ if

$l_i = l_j$ and $y_k = -1$, otherwise. $N << d$, N_c and $N' \leq N^2$ represent the total number of samples, the number of images with label c, and the number of pairs of images used, respectively[1]. $\phi(\mathbf{x})$ is a mapping from feature to Kernel space.

3   Proposed Methods

In this section we propose four possible approaches towards increasing accuracy performance. The first approach, rPCCA, is a new iterative procedure that intro-duces a regularization term to maximize the inter-class margin to the hinge loss PCCA approach. The second approach, kLDFA, is a new closed-form method that uses a kernel trick to handle large dimensional feature vectors while maximizing a Fischer optimization criteria. The third approach is to use the Marginal Fisher Analysis method introduced in [26] which to best of our knowledge has not been used for re-ID before. Finally, we also propose a new ensemble approach where the results of multiple classifiers are combined to exploit their individual strengths.

3.1   Regularized PCCA (rPCCA)

In [20] Mignon and Jurie proposed to use PCCA with an approximation to the hinge loss to learn the projected metric. Their motivation was that the projected distances between samples from the same class should be smaller than a given threshold T while the distances between inter-class samples should be larger than T. To this effect, without loss of generality, they set $T = 1$ and then approximated the hinge loss with the generalized logistic loss function [27] $\ell_\beta(x) = \frac{1}{\beta}log(1 + e^{\beta x})$ to form the objective function:

$$\min_{\mathbf{P}} E(\mathbf{P}) = \sum_{k=1}^{N'} \ell_\beta(y_k(D_{\mathbf{P}}^2(\mathbf{x}_{i_k}, \mathbf{x}_{j_k}) - 1)) \tag{1}$$

where $\mathbf{P}$ is a $d' \times d$ matrix ($d' < d$) that is found using a gradient descent-based method. Additionally, it is possible to use a "kernel trick" to improve classification when the data is not linearly separable. In this case, a projection $d' \times N$ matrix $\mathbf{Q}$ is applied to the feature vectors in the kernel space $\mathbf{P} = \mathbf{Q}\phi^T(\mathbf{X})$ and the objective function becomes:

$$E(\mathbf{Q}) = \sum_{k=1}^{N'} \ell_\beta[y_k((\mathbf{e}_{i_k} - \mathbf{e}_{j_k})^T \mathbf{K} \mathbf{Q}^T \mathbf{Q} \mathbf{K}(\mathbf{e}_{i_k} - \mathbf{e}_{j_k}) - 1)] \tag{2}$$

where $\mathbf{K} = \phi(\mathbf{X})^T \phi(\mathbf{X})$ is the $N \times N$ kernel matrix and $\mathbf{e}_i$ is the ith vector of the canonical basis in $\mathbf{R}^N$ – i.e. a unit vector with 1 at position i. Using trace,

$$E(\mathbf{Q}) = \sum_{k=1}^{N'} \sum \ell_\beta y_k \text{trace}[\mathbf{Q}\mathbf{K}(\mathbf{e}_{ik} - \mathbf{e}_{jk})(\mathbf{e}_{ik} - \mathbf{e}_{jk})^T \mathbf{K} \mathbf{Q}^T] - 1 \tag{3}$$

and the gradient of the new objective function $E(\mathbf{Q})$ is:

---

[1] We will use all possible positive pairs but only a fraction of the negative ones.

$$\frac{\partial E}{\partial Q} = 2Q \sum_{k=1}^{N'} y_k \sigma_\beta (y_k (D_{\mathbf{P}}^2(\mathbf{x}_{i_k}, \mathbf{x}_{j_k}) - 1)) \mathbf{K} \mathbf{C}_k \mathbf{K} \tag{4}$$

where $\sigma_\beta(x) = (1 + e^{-\beta x})^{-1}$ for $\beta = 1$ and $\mathbf{C}_k = (\mathbf{e}_{i_k} - \mathbf{e}_{j_k})(\mathbf{e}_{i_k} - \mathbf{e}_{j_k})^T$. The matrix $\mathbf{K}$ is full rank since $\phi(\mathbf{X})$ is $D \times N$ and $D > d >> N$. Then, one can multiply the gradient with a preconditioner $\mathbf{K}^{-1}$ and iteratively solve the problem by updating $\mathbf{Q}$ using the expression

$$\mathbf{Q}_{t+1} = \mathbf{Q}_t(\mathbf{I} - 2\eta \sum_{k=1}^{N'} \mathcal{L}_k^t \mathbf{K} \mathbf{C}_k) \tag{5}$$

where η is the learning rate and where $\mathcal{L}_k^t$ denotes the value of $y_k \sigma_\beta(y_k(D_{\mathbf{P}}^2(\mathbf{x}_{i_k}, \mathbf{x}_{j_k}) - 1))$ at time t. It can be easily shown that the effect of this preconditioning step is that using changes in direction of $\mathbf{Q}$ results in the desired optimal change in direction of $\mathbf{P}$. Furthermore, it should be noted that updating $\mathbf{Q}$ uses $\mathbf{K}$ but does not require to compute its inverse.

PCCA can result in poor classification performance due to large variations among samples and limited training data. We propose to address this problem by using the additional degrees of freedom available in the problem to maximize the inter-class margin. To this effect, motivated by the objective functions used on SVMs, we propose the *regularized* PCCA (rPCCA) objective function with a regularization term penalizing the Frobenius norm of $\mathbf{P}$:

$$E(\mathbf{P}) = \sum_{k=1}^{N'} \ell_\beta(y_k(D_{\mathbf{P}}^2(\mathbf{x}_{i_k}, \mathbf{x}_{j_k}) - 1)) + \lambda \|\mathbf{P}\|_F^2 \tag{6}$$

where λ is the regularization parameter. Briefly, the intuition behind this new objective function is to treat each of the rows $\mathbf{p}_i$ of $\mathbf{P}$ as the separating hyperplane in an SVM and use the fact that the classification margin is precisely given by $(\|\mathbf{p}_i\|_2)^{-1}$. Substituting $\mathbf{P}$ with $\mathbf{Q}\phi^T(\mathbf{X})$, the derivative of the regularized objective function with respect to $\mathbf{Q}$ becomes:

$$\frac{\partial E}{\partial Q} = 2Q(\sum_{k=1}^{N'} \mathcal{L}_k^t \mathbf{K} \mathbf{C}_k + \lambda \mathbf{I})\mathbf{K} \tag{7}$$

Similarly to PCCA, the global optimum can be achieved by multiplying the gradient with the preconditioner $\mathbf{K}^{-1}$ and iteratively updating the matrix $\mathbf{Q}$.

3.2 Kernel LFDA (kLDFA)

A drawback of using LFDA is that it requires solving a generalized eigenvalue problem of very large scatter $d \times d$ matrices. For example, in [21] the authors use feature vectors with $d = 22506$ features. To circumvent this problem, [21] proposed to exploit the redundancy among the features by performing a preprocessing step where principal component analysis (PCA) is used to reduce the dimensionality of the data. However, a potential difficulty here is that this unsupervised dimensionality reduction step, when applied to relatively small datasets, can result in an undesirable compression of the most discriminative features. To avoid this problem, we propose to use a kernel approach, based on the method introduced in [22] in the context of supervised dimensionality reduction. The benefits of this approach are twofold: it avoids performing an eigenvalue decomposition of the large scatter matrices and it can exploit the flexibility in choosing the kernel to improve the classification accuracy.

The proposed *kernel* LDFA (kLDFA) method finds a projection matrix $\mathbf{P} \in \mathbf{R}^{d' \times d}$ to maximize the 'between-class' scatter while minimizing the 'within-class' scatter for *similar* samples using the Fisher discriminant objective:

$$\mathbf{P} = \max_{\mathbf{P}}(\mathbf{PS^wP})^{-1}\mathbf{P}^T\mathbf{S^bP} \tag{8}$$

where the *within* and *between* scatter matrices are $\mathbf{S^w} = \frac{1}{2}\phi(\mathbf{X})\tilde{\mathbf{S}}^\mathbf{w}\phi(\mathbf{X})^T$ and $\mathbf{S^b} = \frac{1}{2}\phi(\mathbf{X})\tilde{\mathbf{S}}^\mathbf{b}\phi(\mathbf{X})^T$ where $\tilde{\mathbf{S}}^\mathbf{w} = \sum_{i,j=1}^{N} \mathbf{A}_{i,j}^w(\mathbf{e}_i - \mathbf{e}_j)(\mathbf{e}_i - \mathbf{e}_j)^T$ and $\tilde{\mathbf{S}}^\mathbf{b} = \sum_{i,j=1}^{N} \mathbf{A}_{i,j}^b(\mathbf{e}_i - \mathbf{e}_j)(\mathbf{e}_i - \mathbf{e}_j)^T$. Then, representing the projection matrix with the data samples in the kernel space $\mathbf{P} = \mathbf{Q}\phi^T(\mathbf{X})$, the kLFDA problem is formulated as:

$$\mathbf{Q} = \max_{\mathbf{Q}}(\mathbf{QK}\tilde{\mathbf{S}}^\mathbf{w}\mathbf{KQ})^{-1}\mathbf{QK}\tilde{\mathbf{S}}^\mathbf{b}\mathbf{KQ} \tag{9}$$

Since the within class scatter matrix $\tilde{\mathbf{S}}^\mathbf{w}$ is usually rank deficient, a regularized $\hat{\mathbf{S}}^\mathbf{w}$ defined below is used instead:

$$\hat{\mathbf{S}}^\mathbf{w} = (1-\alpha)\tilde{\mathbf{S}}^\mathbf{w} + \frac{\alpha}{N}trace(\tilde{\mathbf{S}}^\mathbf{w})\mathbf{I} \tag{10}$$

3.3   Marginal Fisher Analysis(MFA)

Marginal Fisher Analysis (MFA) was proposed in [26] as yet another graph embedding dimension reduction method. Similarly to kLDFA and LDFA, it has a closed form solution given by a general eigenvalue decomposition. However, in contrast to LDFA, its special discriminant objective allows to maximize the marginal discriminant even when the assumption of a Gaussian distribution for each class is not true. Moreover, the results in [26] showed that the learned discriminant components have larger margin between classes, similar to a SVM. The scatter matrices for MFA are defined as:

$$\tilde{\mathbf{S}}^\mathbf{w} = (\mathbf{D^w} - \mathbf{W^w}) \text{ and } \tilde{\mathbf{S}}^\mathbf{b} = (\mathbf{D^b} - \mathbf{W^b}) \tag{11}$$

where $\mathbf{D^b}_{ii} = \sum_j \mathbf{W^b}_{ij}$, $\mathbf{D^w}_{ii} = \sum_j \mathbf{W^w}_{ij}$ as well as the sparse matrices $\mathbf{W^w}$ and $\mathbf{W^b}$ are defined as: $\mathbf{W}_{ij}^w = 1$ if and only if $\mathbf{x}_i$ or $\mathbf{x}_j$ is the k_w nearest within class neighbor of other; and $\mathbf{W}_{ij}^b = 1$ if and only if $\mathbf{x}_i$ or $\mathbf{x}_j$ is the k_b nearest between class neighbor of other.

3.4   Ranking Ensemble Voting

Classification accuracy is affected by the method used to learn the projected metric, the kernel used and the features used to represent the data. Thus, it is possible to design an ensemble of classifiers that use different kernels and sets of features. Then, given a test image and a gallery of candidate matches, each of these classifiers will produce, in principle, a different ranking among the candidates which, in turn, could be combined to produce a single and better ranking. That is, instead of tuning for the best set of parameters through cross-validation, one could independently run different ranking classifiers and merge the results. In this paper, we will consider two alternative ways on how to combine the results from the individual rankings into a ranking ensemble voting (REV) scheme; *"Ensemble 1"*: adding the rankings in a simple voting scheme; or *"Ensemble 2"*: assuming that the output of a ranking algorithm represents the probability of the rth closest reference image is the correct match, given the ranking algorithm $\mathcal{R}_m$, $p(r|\mathcal{R}_m)$; $m = 1,\ldots,N_r$, for each of the N_r algorithms. Then, assuming conditional independence among the different algorithms we have $p(r) = \prod_{i=1}^{N_r} p(r|\mathcal{R}_i)$.

4   Experiments

In this section we describe the set of experiments used to evaluate the proposed methods as well as the choice of features and kernels. In particular, we compared the performance of rPCCA, kLFDA, MFA and REV, against the current state-of-art PCCA, LFDA, SVMML and KISSME, using four different sets of features, three different kernels, and four different datasets, as described below.

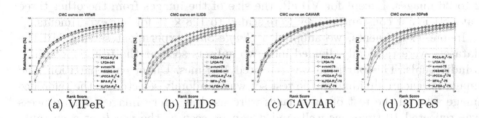

(a) VIPeR   (b) iLIDS   (c) CAVIAR   (d) 3DPeS

Fig. 2. Best CMC curves for each method on four datasets

4.1   Datasets and Experimental Protocol

All the algorithms were evaluated using the four most challenging and commonly used throughout the literature datasets. The **VIPeR** dataset [14] is composed of 1264 images of 632 individuals, with 2 images of 128 × 48 pixels per individual. The images are taken from horizontal viewpoints but in widely different directions. The **iLIDS** dataset [30] has 476 images of 119 pedestrians. The number of images for each individual varies from 2 to 8. Since this dataset was collected at an airport, the images often have severe occlusions caused by people and luggage. The **CAVIAR** dataset [8] contains 1220 images of 72 individuals from 2 cameras in a shopping mall. Each person has 10 to 20 images. The image sizes

Table 1. CMC at $r = 1, 5, 10, 20$ and PUR scores on VIPeR with $p = 316$ test individuals (highest scores in red)

		PCCA			LFDA	SVMML	KISSME	rPCCA			kLFDA			MFA		
														VIPeR		
	r	L	χ^2	R_{χ^2}	w/o	w/o	w/o	L	χ^2	R_{χ^2}	L	χ^2	R_{χ^2}	L	χ^2	R_{χ^2}
6	1	14.3	16.7	19.6	19.7	27.0	23.8	19.1	19.9	22.0	20.6	28.1	32.3	21.1	28.4	32.2
	5	40.5	46.0	51.5	46.7	60.9	52.9	48.3	50.6	54.8	46.2	60.0	65.8	48.7	60.1	66.0
	10	57.5	62.6	68.2	62.1	75.4	67.1	64.9	67.8	71.0	60.8	75.0	79.7	63.9	74.8	79.7
	20	74.7	79.6	82.9	77.0	87.3	80.5	80.9	83.2	85.3	75.9	87.8	90.9	78.9	87.7	90.6
	PUR	36.1	39.6	42.9	38.2	47.6	42.1	41.0	42.7	44.8	37.5	48.4	52.5	39.9	48.3	52.4
14	1	15.0	17.0	19.7	20.0	25.3	22.6	19.3	19.7	21.1	21.2	28.9	31.8	20.9	28.7	32.2
	5	41.5	46.1	50.7	46.9	58.3	51.0	47.8	49.6	52.9	47.1	60.4	64.8	49.3	59.7	65.5
	10	58.2	63.1	67.2	61.9	73.0	65.1	64.5	65.9	69.2	61.3	74.7	79.1	63.9	74.4	79.0
	20	75.9	79.2	82.5	76.2	85.1	78.3	80.6	81.5	83.6	76.2	87.1	90.3	78.2	86.6	90.3
	PUR	36.8	39.5	42.2	38.0	45.4	40.5	40.7	41.8	43.5	38.0	48.3	51.9	39.8	47.9	52.0
75	1	18.3	18.4	16.4	21.5	30.1	25.2	21.1	20.5	20.5	23.3	30.3	30.9	23.6	29.6	31.1
	5	46.9	46.4	45.0	49.6	63.2	54.2	51.1	50.5	51.3	52.8	63.5	64.4	52.1	63.0	65.2
	10	63.7	63.4	61.4	64.6	77.4	68.4	67.5	67.4	67.7	68.3	77.9	79.3	67.4	77.3	79.6
	20	80.2	79.3	77.0	79.1	88.1	81.6	82.9	82.4	82.3	82.4	89.8	90.6	81.5	88.9	90.6
	PUR	40.1	39.9	37.9	40.2	49.4	43.2	42.7	42.5	42.6	43.2	51.0	51.9	42.6	50.3	52.0
341	1	16.2	15.2	11.8	21.4	28.0	25.8	19.2	19.0	16.8	23.6	27.0	24.5	22.7	27.3	24.8
	5	43.5	41.5	35.5	49.6	61.5	56.2	49.4	48.4	45.1	54.4	60.1	56.0	53.8	60.2	56.9
	10	59.0	57.0	51.1	65.2	76.7	70.1	65.5	64.7	60.9	70.1	75.3	72.1	69.1	75.2	72.3
	20	75.6	73.3	68.4	79.5	88.2	82.9	80.8	80.3	77.2	84.0	88.6	86.8	83.3	88.8	86.3
	PUR	37.2	35.7	32.0	40.8	48.7	44.4	41.3	40.9	38.6	44.4	48.9	46.7	43.9	48.8	46.7

of this dataset vary significantly (from 141×72 to 39×17). Finally, the **3DPeS** dataset [4] includes 1011 images of 192 individuals captured from 8 outdoor cameras with significantly different viewpoints. In this dataset each person has 2 to 26 images. Except for VIPeR, the size of the images from the other three datasets is not constant so they were scaled to 128×48 for our experiments.

In our experiments, we adopted a *Single-Shot* experiment setting. All the datasets were randomly divided into two subsets so that the test set contains p individuals. This partition was repeated 10 times. Under each partition, one image for each individual in the test set was randomly selected as the reference image set and the rest of the images were used as query images. This process was repeated 10 times, as well, and it can be seen as the *recall* at each rank. The rank of the correct match was recorded and accumulated to generate the match characteristic $M(r)$.

For easy comparison with other algorithms, we report the widely used accumulated $M(r)$, Cumulative Match Characteristic (CMC) performance curves, averaged across the experiments. In addition, we also report the *proportion of uncertainty removed* (PUR) [21] scores:

$$\text{PUR} = \frac{\log(N) + \sum_{r=1}^{N} M(r) \log(M(r))}{\log(N)} \tag{12}$$

where N is the size of the gallery set. This score compares the uncertainty under random selection among a gallery of images and the uncertainty after using a ranking method. Finally, since the first few retrieved images can be quickly inspected by a human, higher scores at rank $r \geq 1$ are preferred.

Table 2. CMC at $r = 1, 5, 10, 20$ and PUR scores on iLIDS with $p = 60$ test individuals (highest scores shown in red)

		iLIDS																	
		PCCA			LFDA	SVMML	KISSME	rPCCA			kLFDA			MFA		
	r	L	χ^2	$R_{\chi 2}$	w/o	w/o	w/o	L	χ^2	$R_{\chi 2}$	L	χ^2	$R_{\chi 2}$	L	χ^2	$R_{\chi 2}$
	1	21.7	23.0	24.1	32.2	20.8	28.0	25.5	26.6	28.0	32.3	36.5	36.9	30.5	32.6	32.1
	5	49.7	51.1	53.3	56.0	49.1	54.2	53.8	54.3	56.5	57.2	64.1	65.3	53.9	58.5	58.8
6	10	65.0	67.0	69.2	68.7	65.4	67.9	68.4	69.7	71.8	70.0	76.5	78.3	66.3	71.5	72.2
	20	81.4	83.3	84.8	81.6	81.7	81.6	83.0	84.5	85.9	83.9	88.5	89.4	80.4	84.8	85.9
	PUR	21.3	22.8	24.4	26.6	20.9	24.7	24.2	25.4	27.0	27.9	33.7	34.9	24.8	28.8	29.1
	1	23.9	24.5	25.7	32.0	20.3	29.4	27.8	28.0	29.6	33.3	37.8	37.4	30.7	34.2	33.7
	5	53.0	53.2	54.0	54.2	48.6	54.9	55.3	56.0	57.3	57.5	64.8	64.8	54.0	58.9	59.5
14	10	68.3	68.8	69.6	66.4	64.5	68.8	70.2	70.4	71.7	70.1	76.6	77.3	66.2	71.1	72.0
	20	83.9	84.9	84.4	80.5	80.9	82.1	84.6	85.3	85.9	83.5	88.6	89.1	80.7	85.3	86.0
	PUR	23.9	24.5	25.1	25.7	20.3	25.8	26.1	26.6	27.8	28.3	34.7	34.8	25.1	29.9	30.0
	1	24.0	23.8	24.0	33.8	22.3	28.5	28.4	28.9	29.2	34.1	38.0	36.2	30.3	33.7	32.1
	5	53.6	52.9	51.7	57.4	51.1	55.3	57.0	57.1	57.2	60.4	65.1	63.5	56.2	59.3	57.4
75	10	69.1	68.6	67.1	69.7	66.7	68.7	71.4	71.4	71.1	73.5	77.4	76.1	68.9	71.7	70.5
	20	84.4	84.1	82.8	82.8	83.0	83.4	85.8	85.7	85.4	86.5	89.2	89.2	83.6	86.5	85.9
	PUR	24.4	24.2	23.4	28.1	22.4	25.9	27.3	27.6	27.6	30.8	35.4	33.9	26.7	30.3	28.9
	1	21.4	21.4	20.2	32.7	21.4	28.4	26.0	26.6	25.9	32.2	34.2	30.5	29.2	30.2	26.8
	5	49.1	48.5	45.1	56.7	49.6	55.7	53.3	53.4	52.5	59.9	61.5	57.3	55.1	55.3	50.3
341	10	65.5	64.9	61.1	69.0	65.5	68.9	68.9	68.7	67.7	73.8	74.8	71.8	69.3	69.3	64.8
	20	82.1	81.3	78.4	82.3	82.8	83.4	84.5	84.3	83.0	86.5	87.7	85.6	83.8	84.3	82.1
	PUR	21.5	21.1	18.7	27.3	21.6	26.1	24.7	25.0	24.1	30.2	31.8	28.4	26.3	27.0	23.4

4.2 Features, Kernels and Implementation Details

In [20], PCCA was applied to feature vectors made of 16-bins histograms from the RGB, YUV and HSV color channels, as well as texture histograms based on Local Binary Patterns extracted from 6 non-overlapping horizontal bands[2]. In the sequel we will refer to these features as the *band* features.

On the other hand, the authors in [21] applied LDFA to a set of feature vectors consisting of 8-bins histograms and 3 moments extracted from 6 color channels (RGB and HSV) over a set of 341 dense overlapping 8×8 pixel regions, defined every 4 pixels in both the horizontal and vertical directions, resulting in 11,253 dimensional vectors. These vectors were then compressed into 100 dimensional vectors using PCA before applying LDFA. In the sequel, we will refer to these features as the *block* features.

Even though the authors of [20] and [21] reported performance analysis using the same datasets, they used different sets of features to characterize the sample images. Thus, it is difficult to conclude whether the differences on the reported performances are due to the classification methods or to the feature selection. Therefore, in order to fairly evaluate the benefits of each algorithm and the effect of the choice of features, in our experiments we tested each of the algorithms using the *same* set of features. Moreover, while both band and block features are extracted within rectangular or square regions, their size and location are very different. Thus, to evaluate how these regions affect the re-identification accuracy, we run experiments varying their size and position. In addition to the

---

[2] Since the parameters for the LBP histogram and horizontal bands were not given in [20], we found values that provide even better matching accuracy than in [20].

Table 3. CMC at $r = 1, 5, 10, 20$ and PUR scores on CAVIAR with $p = 36$ test individuals (highest scores shown in red)

						CAVIAR										
		PCCA			LFDA	SVMML	KISSME	rPCCA			kLFDA			MFA		
	r	L	χ^2	R_{χ^2}	w/o	w/o	w/o	L	χ^2	R_{χ^2}	L	χ^2	R_{χ^2}	L	χ^2	R_{χ^2}
	1	25.7	29.1	33.4	31.7	25.8	31.4	28.8	30.4	34.0	31.5	36.2	35.9	33.8	37.7	38.4
	5	57.9	62.5	67.2	56.1	61.4	61.9	61.3	63.6	67.5	55.4	64.0	63.6	62.0	67.2	69.0
6	10	75.8	79.7	83.1	70.4	78.6	77.8	78.0	80.4	83.4	69.5	78.7	77.9	77.2	82.1	83.6
	20	92.0	94.2	95.7	86.9	93.6	92.5	93.2	94.5	95.8	86.1	92.2	91.2	92.1	94.6	95.1
	PUR	21.5	25.5	29.8	20.7	23.7	24.9	24.3	26.5	30.3	20.2	27.5	26.9	25.6	30.7	32.0
	1	28.8	30.7	33.9	33.4	26.5	32.9	30.6	31.8	34.6	33.6	38.5	37.9	35.3	39.0	38.9
	5	62.3	64.8	67.8	58.8	62.1	64.0	64.0	65.9	68.5	59.1	66.7	67.0	63.8	68.6	69.7
14	10	79.1	81.4	83.5	73.0	79.5	79.8	80.4	82.1	83.9	73.1	80.7	81.0	78.6	83.0	83.7
	20	94.0	94.9	95.6	88.4	94.2	93.4	94.5	95.0	95.8	88.5	93.3	92.7	92.8	94.8	94.9
	PUR	25.2	27.5	30.3	22.9	24.6	26.9	26.7	28.4	31.0	23.1	30.1	29.7	27.3	32.0	32.5
	1	31.9	32.9	33.2	35.2	28.8	34.1	33.0	34.1	35.1	35.7	39.1	39.1	36.6	40.2	39.4
	5	65.2	66.3	65.9	59.9	63.1	64.9	66.0	67.1	67.2	62.6	66.8	68.4	65.5	70.2	69.7
75	10	81.6	82.4	81.9	73.7	79.8	80.1	82.0	82.9	83.1	77.0	80.9	82.4	80.2	83.9	83.7
	20	95.3	95.5	95.2	88.8	93.9	93.0	95.4	95.5	95.6	91.4	93.4	94.3	93.3	95.1	95.0
	PUR	28.2	29.1	28.8	24.2	25.5	27.5	29.0	29.9	30.4	26.4	30.5	31.6	28.8	33.4	32.7
	1	30.8	31.3	30.4	35.1	28.9	34.9	32.5	33.0	33.4	34.7	37.7	36.4	34.9	37.8	36.3
	5	63.5	64.1	62.2	59.4	62.5	64.7	64.9	65.3	64.4	62.0	65.9	65.6	64.5	67.9	66.4
341	10	80.2	80.5	79.1	73.1	79.2	79.7	81.2	81.6	80.6	76.6	80.5	80.6	79.7	82.4	81.6
	20	94.6	94.7	93.6	88.2	93.3	93.3	94.9	95.0	94.3	91.2	93.6	93.6	93.3	94.6	94.2
	PUR	26.7	27.1	25.4	23.8	25.0	27.8	28.0	28.4	27.8	25.7	29.6	29.0	27.7	31.1	29.5

band and block features described above, we used a set of features extracted from 16×16 and 32×32 pixels overlapping square regions, similar to the ones used in the block features, but defined with a step half of the width/height of the square regions in both directions. Thus, a total of 75 and 14 regions were selected in these two feature sets. The feature vectors were made of 16-bins histogram of 8 color channels extracted on these image patches. To represented the texture patterns, 8-neighbors of radius 1 and 16-neighbors of radius 2 uniform LBP histograms were also computed for each region. Finally, the histograms were normalized with the ℓ_1 norm in each channel and concatenated to form the feature for each image.

The projected feature space dimensionality was set to $d' = 40$ for the PCCA algorithm. To be fair, we also used $d' = 40$ with rPCCA. The parameter in the generalized logistic loss function was set to 3 for both PCCA and rPCCA. Since we could not reproduce the reported results of LFDA using their parameters setting, we set the projected feature space as 40 and the regularizing weight β as 0.15 for LFDA[3]. In kLFDA, we used the same d' and set the regularizing weight to 0.01. For MFA, we used all positives pairs of each person for the within class sets and set k_b to 12, $\beta = 0.01$, and $d' = 30$. Since SVMML in [18] used different features, we also tuned the parameters to achieve results as good as possible. The two regularized parameters of A and B were set to 10^{-8} and 10^{-6}, respectively. Since KISSME is very sensitive to the PCA dimensions, we chose the dimension for each dataset that gives best PUR and rank 1 CMC score, which are 77, 45, 65 and 70 for VIPeR, iLIDS, CAVIAR and 3DPeS, respectively. In the training

---

[3] It was set as 0.5 in [21]. However, we could not reproduce their reported results with this parameter.

Table 4. CMC at $r = 1, 5, 10, 20$ and PUR scores on 3DPeS with $p = 95$ test individuals (highest scores shown in red)

		3DPeS														
		PCCA			LFDA	SVMML	KISSME	rPCCA			kLFDA			MFA		
	r	L	χ^2	R_{χ^2}	w/o	w/o	w/o	L	χ^2	R_{χ^2}	L	χ^2	R_{χ^2}	L	χ^2	R_{χ^2}
	1	33.4	36.4	39.7	39.1	27.7	34.2	39.2	40.4	43.5	38.8	48.4	48.7	35.9	42.3	41.8
	5	63.5	66.3	68.4	61.7	58.5	58.7	68.3	69.5	71.6	62.0	72.5	73.7	58.5	65.3	65.5
6	10	75.8	78.1	79.6	71.8	72.1	69.6	79.7	80.5	81.8	72.6	82.1	83.1	69.3	75.2	75.7
	20	86.9	88.6	89.5	82.6	84.1	80.2	89.3	90.0	91.0	82.7	89.9	90.7	79.9	84.8	85.2
	PUR	37.7	40.4	42.7	36.4	32.9	32.9	42.5	43.6	46.0	36.7	47.6	48.5	33.2	40.0	40.1
	1	37.3	39.8	42.2	43.2	31.8	39.4	41.9	44.0	46.2	44.1	51.9	52.2	40.0	45.6	45.0
	5	67.4	69.6	71.1	65.3	63.0	63.1	71.3	72.6	74.7	66.5	75.1	75.9	62.6	69.0	68.3
14	10	79.4	80.9	82.1	75.0	75.6	73.1	82.2	82.9	84.2	75.8	83.6	84.6	72.9	78.4	78.1
	20	89.3	89.8	90.5	84.3	86.1	82.2	90.6	91.0	91.5	84.7	90.9	91.5	82.9	87.1	86.9
	PUR	41.4	43.4	45.1	40.1	36.5	37.0	45.2	46.6	48.7	41.3	50.5	51.3	37.4	43.7	43.2
	1	40.7	41.6	40.2	45.5	34.7	41.3	46.9	47.3	47.6	47.6	54.0	52.4	42.4	48.4	46.3
	5	70.3	70.5	68.4	69.2	66.4	66.2	74.5	75.0	74.6	71.8	77.7	77.1	66.8	72.4	70.5
75	10	81.5	81.3	79.6	78.0	78.8	76.3	84.4	84.5	84.1	81.1	85.9	85.7	76.5	81.5	80.0
	20	90.7	90.4	89.3	86.1	88.5	85.3	91.8	91.9	91.7	88.8	92.4	92.4	86.0	89.8	89.1
	PUR	44.5	44.6	42.7	43.2	39.7	40.1	49.1	49.3	49.1	46.4	53.5	52.5	41.2	47.6	45.6
	1	37.9	38.4	33.8	44.8	34.4	40.5	45.2	45.2	43.8	46.8	51.6	48.2	41.8	46.0	42.0
	5	67.2	66.9	61.8	68.6	65.9	66.2	72.8	72.6	70.5	72.5	76.4	73.9	66.6	70.6	66.5
341	10	79.0	78.5	74.2	77.7	77.8	76.1	82.5	82.4	80.8	81.8	84.9	83.1	76.8	80.1	77.1
	20	89.1	88.5	85.4	86.0	87.8	85.7	90.8	90.6	89.5	89.5	92.0	91.0	86.2	89.0	86.3
	PUR	41.5	41.1	36.2	42.7	38.9	40.1	47.0	46.9	44.7	46.8	51.7	48.6	41.0	45.6	41.4

process for PCCA, rPCCA and KISSME, the number of negative pairs was set to 10 times the number of positive pairs. Finally, we tested three kernels with each algorithm and feature set: a linear, a χ^2 and a $RBF - \chi^2$ kernel which are denoted with L, χ^2 and R_{χ^2}, respectively.

4.3   Performance Analysis

For both, the VIPeR and iLIDS datasets, the test sets were randomly selected using half of the available individuals. Specifically, there are $p = 316$, $p = 60$, $p = 36$, and $p = 95$ individuals in each of the test sets for the VIPeR, iLIDS, CAVIAR, and 3DPeS datasets, respectively. Figure 2 shows the best CMC curves for each algorithm on the four datasets. The results are also summarized in Tables 1 to 4, along with the PUR scores for all the experiments. The experiments show that the VIPeR dataset is more difficult than the iLIDS dataset. This can be explained by observing that VIPeR has only two images per individual, resulting in much lower $r = 1$ CMC scores. On the other hand, the overall PUR score is higher for the VIPeR set, probably because the iLIDS set has less than half of the images than VIPeR has.

The highest CMC and PUR scores in every experiment at every ranking were highlighted in red in the given table. The highest CMC and PUR scores were achieved using the proposed methods with either a χ^2 or a R_{χ^2} kernel. The proposed approaches achieve as much as 19.6% at $r = 1$ and a 10.3% PUR score improvement on the VIPeR dataset, 14.6% at $r = 1$ and a 31.2% PUR score improvement on the iLIDS dataset, 15.0% at $r = 1$ and a 7.4% PUR score improvement on the CAVIAR dataset and 22.7% at $r = 1$ and a 13.6% PUR score improvement on the 3DPeS dataset, when using band features (6 bands).

Table 5. The best reported CMC scores in the existing literature

	VIPeR		iLIDS		CAVIAR		3DPeS	
	SVMML [18]	kLFDA	PRDC [31]	kLFDA	LFDA [21]	MFA	LFDA [21]	kLFDA
$r = 1$	30.0	32.3	37.83	38.0	32.0	40.2	33.43	54.0
$r = 5$	65.0	65.8	63.7	65.1	56.3	70.2		77.7
$r = 10$	80.0	79.7	75.09	77.4	70.7	83.9	69.98	85.9
$r = 20$	91.0	90.9	88.35	89.2	87.4	95.1		92.4
PUR		52.5		35.4	21.2	33.4	34.85	53.5

In general, rPCCA performed better than LFDA which, in turn, performed better than PCCA. The better performance of rPCCA over PCCA and LFDA shows that the regularizer term $\|\mathbf{P}\|_F$ plays a significant role in preventing over-fitting of noisy data. However, the best performance is achieved by kLFDA because this approach does a better job at selecting the features by avoiding the PCA pre-processing step while taking advantage of the locally scaled affinity matrix.

It should be noted that using 6, 14, 75 and 341 regions results in similar performance, but using 341 results in slightly lower PUR scores. Moreover, the RBF-χ^2 kernel does not help improving the matching accuracy when the regions are small. It was observed in our experiments that the χ^2 distance of the positive and negative pairs were distributed within a small range around 1 and that the kernel mapping of these values were hard to distinguish. A possible explanation for this effect, is that the histograms are noisier and sparser when the base regions are small.

For sake of completeness, we also compared the best performance for the proposed algorithms against the best results as reported in the existing literature (even though as pointed above, the values reported elsewhere do not use the same set of features or experimental protocol) [1, 2, 6, 11, 16–21, 28, 29, 31] in Table 5.

Our algorithm matches the best reported results for the VIPeR and iLIDS datasets, even though the reported PRDC [31] ranking was obtained under easier experiment settings[4]. Note that both SVMML[5] [18] and PRDC require an iterative optimization which is very expensive on both computation and memory. In comparison, computing the closed-form solution for the proposed kLFDA and MFA algorithms is much cheaper. When using a 3.8Hz Intel quad-core computer with 16GB RAM, the average training times for VIPeR, using 6 patches with a linear kernel are 0.24s, 0.22s and 155.86s for kLFDA, MFA and SVMML, respectively. While average training times for the iLIDS are 0.07s, 0.04s and 155.6s for kLFDA, MFA and PRDC, respectively. In the experiments on the CAVIAR and 3DPeS datasets, our ranking is more accurate than LFDA algorithm[6].

---

[4] Only 50 individuals were selected as test, while our test set is composed of 60 individuals. Thus, the ranking accuracy is computed in an easier experiment setting.

[5] The ranking accuracy was read from the figure.

[6] The CAVIAR ranking reported in [21] was obtained by using the mean of the features from the sample person in the test set as the reference feature. We believe this is equivalent to knowing the ground truth before ranking. Hence we report the result in Table 5 via following our protocol but using the same features as in [21].

Finally, Table 6 shows the results for ranking ensembles voting using different learning algorithms, feature sets, kernels, and aggregating methods. Since the features extracted from 8×8 pixels regions provided the worst performance for almost all the algorithms, we do not use this set of features in the ensemble. Therefore, for each metric learning algorithm, we created an ensemble with 9 ranking algorithms, combining 3 kernels (if applicable) and 3 feature sets, which were used to vote for a final ranking. The best performances of the individual ranking case for each of the metric learning methods from Tables 1 to 4 are also shown (with a gray background) for easy comparison. The experimental results show that the ensemble methods produced different level of improvements for each dataset and in general "Ensemble 1" results in larger gains. For single ensemble metric learning algorithm, the performance of ensemble rPCCA improved from 1.56% to 7.91% across all four datasets whereas the ensemble kLFDA benefited much less. The performance on iLIDS datasets improved on all experiments whereas the ones on 3DPeS decreased for ensemble kLFDA and MFA. Since the images in the iLIDS dataset have severe occlusions, using an ensemble of different feature sets is beneficial with this dataset. The highest improvement is all algorithms ensemble on CAVIAR dataset, the rank1 score increased 4.73% and the PUR score increased 8.08% These results suggest that combining different feature grids can improve the performance.

Table 6. CMC scores of ensembles of rPCCA, kLFDA, MFA on all four datasets. The columns with gray background show the performance of the best ranking algorithm in this category (highest scores shown in red).

	r	VIPeR	Ensb 1	Ensb 2	iLIDS	Ensb 1	Ensb 2	CAVIAR	Ensb 1	Ensb 2	3DPeS	Ensb 1	Ensb 2
rPCCA	1	22.0	23.7	23.9	29.6	32.6	32.7	34.6	37.3	37.4	47.3	49.8	50.0
	5	54.8	55.3	55.7	57.3	59.4	59.8	68.5	69.5	70.0	75.0	76.1	76.6
	10	71.0	71.7	72.3	71.7	73.3	73.5	83.9	84.6	84.7	84.5	85.4	85.5
	20	85.3	85.4	86.0	85.9	86.8	86.9	95.8	96.2	96.3	91.9	92.6	92.4
	PUR	44.8	45.5	44.7	27.8	29.9	30.0	31.0	32.7	32.8	49.3	51.1	51.3
kLFDA	1	32.3	32.8	31.8	38.0	40.2	40.3	39.1	39.4	39.1	54.0	53.1	52.6
	5	65.8	65.5	64.6	65.1	66.0	66.7	68.4	67.2	66.9	77.7	76.1	76.2
	10	79.7	79.1	78.4	77.4	78.1	78.1	82.4	81.5	81.0	85.9	84.7	84.7
	20	90.9	90.0	89.3	89.2	89.6	89.6	94.3	93.8	93.6	92.4	91.4	91.5
	PUR	52.5	51.9	49.6	35.4	36.7	36.7	31.6	31.0	30.6	53.5	51.8	51.6
MFA	1	32.2	34.1	33.2	33.7	36.8	37.0	40.2	41.5	41.4	48.4	48.2	47.9
	5	66.0	66.5	66.1	59.3	61.3	61.7	70.2	70.8	70.7	72.4	71.3	71.2
	10	79.7	80.1	79.7	71.7	73.8	73.6	83.9	85.0	84.9	81.5	80.9	80.7
	20	90.6	90.3	89.8	86.5	87.3	87.5	95.1	95.4	95.4	89.8	89.0	88.7
	PUR	52.4	52.8	50.9	30.3	32.3	32.5	33.4	34.4	34.4	47.6	46.6	46.3
kLFDA + rPCCA + MFA	1	32.3	33.9	32.7	38.0	39.4	39.0	40.2	41.8	41.5	54.0	54.2	53.2
	5	65.8	67.0	66.1	65.1	65.0	65.1	70.2	72.0	71.7	77.7	77.7	77.5
	10	79.7	80.5	79.6	77.4	76.9	77.5	83.9	85.8	85.5	85.9	86.1	85.8
	20	90.9	90.6	88.4	89.2	89.0	88.7	95.1	96.4	96.2	92.4	92.8	92.3
	PUR	52.5	53.1	49.0	35.4	35.6	35.1	33.4	35.7	35.3	53.5	53.8	52.7
All	1	32.3	35.1	36.1	38.0	39.8	39.4	40.2	42.1	41.7	54.0	54.1	53.4
	5	65.8	68.2	68.7	65.1	65.3	65.2	70.2	72.2	72.0	77.7	77.7	77.4
	10	79.7	81.3	80.1	77.4	77.1	77.4	83.9	86.2	85.9	85.9	86.0	85.9
	20	90.9	91.1	85.6	89.2	89.2	88.4	95.1	96.5	96.4	92.4	92.6	92.0
	PUR	52.5	53.9	48.8	35.4	35.9	35.1	33.4	36.1	35.6	53.5	53.6	52.6

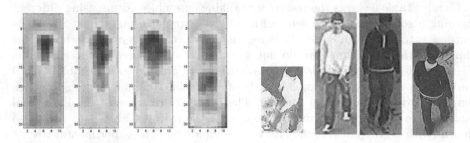

Fig. 3. The kLFDA projection weight map for 3DPeS, CAVIAR, iLIDS and VIPeR

Fig. 4. View point variation in 3DPeS

4.4   Dataset Analysis

Figure 3 shows a heat map illustrating the projection weight map for each of the datasets when using kLDFA with 341 patches and a linear kernel. There, it is seen that the upper body features are the most discriminant ones in all four datasets. This is expected since the bounding-boxes of the samples are reasonably accurate and the torsos are relatively well aligned. On the other hand, the feature projection weights at the bottom of the sample are different across the four datasets. This can be explained by the fact that the viewpoint variations in the 3DPeS dataset are the most severe among all the datasets. As shown in Figure 4, when looking from a top view the legs for the pedestrians occupy fewer pixels and their locations change more than when seen from an horizontal viewpoint as is the case for the VIPeR samples.

Moreover, the projection weights for the VIPeR dataset are larger for patches in the background than for the other three datasets. This reflects the fact that the VIPeR samples were taken in three different scenes, walk way through a garden, play ground and street side way with distinctive backgrounds and that the two images for each person were always taken in the same scene.

5   Conclusion

We proposed and evaluated the performance of four alternatives for re-ID classification: rPCCA, kLFDA, MFA and two ranking ensemble voting (REV) schema, used in conjunction with sets of histogram-based features and linear, χ^2 and RBF-χ^2 kernels. Comparison against four state-of-the-art approaches (PCCA, LDFA, SVMML and KISSME) showed consistently better performance and up to a 19.6%, 14.6%, 15.0% and 22.7% accuracy improvements at rank 1 and 10.3%, 31.2%, 7.4% and 13.6% PUR scores improvements, on the VIPeR, iLIDS, CAVIAR and 3DPeS datasets, respectively, when using 6 bands as support regions for the extracted features and using an RBF-χ^2 kernel with the kLFDA and MFA approaches. With the *Ensemble 1* voting schema, we can further increase accuracy by 8.7%, 4.7%, 4.7% at rank 1 and by 2.7%, 1.4%, 8.1% at PUR on the VIPeR, iLIDS, CAVIAR datasets, respectively.

References

1. An, L., Kafai, M., Yang, S., Bhanu, B.: Reference-based person re-identification. In: 2013 10th IEEE International Conference on Advanced Video and Signal Based Surveillance (AVSS), pp. 244–249 (August 2013)
2. Bak, S., Corvee, E., Brémond, F., Thonnat, M.: Person re-identification using spatial covariance regions of human body parts. In: 2010 Seventh IEEE International Conference on Advanced Video and Signal Based Surveillance (AVSS), pp. 435–440. IEEE (2010)
3. Bak, S., Corvee, E., Bremond, F., Thonnat, M.: Multiple-shot human re-identification by mean riemannian covariance grid. In: 2011 8th IEEE International Conference on Advanced Video and Signal-Based Surveillance (AVSS), pp. 179–184. IEEE (2011)
4. Baltieri, D., Vezzani, R., Cucchiara, R.: 3dpes: 3d people dataset for surveillance and forensics. In: Proceedings of the 1st International ACM Workshop on Multimedia access to 3D Human Objects, Scottsdale, Arizona, USA, pp. 59–64 (November 2011)
5. Bauml, M., Stiefelhagen, R.: Evaluation of local features for person re-identification in image sequences. In: 2011 8th IEEE International Conference on Advanced Video and Signal-Based Surveillance (AVSS), pp. 291–296. IEEE (2011)
6. Bazzani, L., Cristani, M., Murino, V.: Symmetry-driven accumulation of local features for human characterization and re-identification. Computer Vision and Image Understanding 117(2), 130–144 (2013)
7. Bedagkar-Gala, A., Shah, S.K.: A survey of approaches and trends in person re-identification. In: Image and Vision Computing (2014)
8. Cheng, D.S., Cristani, M., Stoppa, M., Bazzani, L., Murino, V.: Custom pictorial structures for re-identification. In: British Machine Vision Conference (BMVC), pp. 1–68 (2011)
9. Dantcheva, A., Dugelay, J.L.: Frontal-to-side face re-identification based on hair, skin and clothes patches. In: 2011 8th IEEE International Conference on Advanced Video and Signal-Based Surveillance (AVSS), pp. 309–313 (August 2011)
10. Doretto, G., Sebastian, T., Tu, P., Rittscher, J.: Appearance-based person reidentification in camera networks: problem overview and current approaches. Journal of Ambient Intelligence and Humanized Computing 2(2), 127–151 (2011)
11. Farenzena, M., Bazzani, L., Perina, A., Murino, V., Cristani, M.: Person re-identification by symmetry-driven accumulation of local features. In: 2010 IEEE Conference on Computer Vision and Pattern Recognition (CVPR), pp. 2360–2367. IEEE (2010)
12. Gheissari, N., Sebastian, T., Hartley, R.: Person reidentification using spatiotemporal appearance. In: CVPR (2006)
13. Gong, S., Cristani, M., Yan, S., Loy, C.C.: Person Re-Identification. Springer, London (2014)
14. Gray, D., Tao, H.: Viewpoint invariant pedestrian recognition with an ensemble of localized features. In: Forsyth, D., Torr, P., Zisserman, A. (eds.) ECCV 2008, Part I. LNCS, vol. 5302, pp. 262–275. Springer, Heidelberg (2008)
15. Kostinger, M., Hirzer, M., Wohlhart, P., Roth, P.M., Bischof, H.: Large scale metric learning from equivalence constraints. In: 2012 IEEE Conference on Computer Vision and Pattern Recognition (CVPR), pp. 2288–2295. IEEE (2012)
16. Kuo, C.-H., Khamis, S., Shet, V.: Person re-identification using semantic color names and rankboost. In: IEEE Workshop on Applications of Computer Vision, vol. 0, pp. 281–287 (2013)

17. Li, W., Wang, X.: Locally aligned feature transforms across views. In: 2013 IEEE Conference on Computer Vision and Pattern Recognition (CVPR), pp. 3594–3601 (June 2013)
18. Li, Z., Chang, S., Liang, F., Huang, T.S., Cao, L., Smith, J.R.: Learning locally-adaptive decision functions for person verification. In: 2013 IEEE Conference on Computer Vision and Pattern Recognition (CVPR), pp. 3610–3617. IEEE (2013)
19. Loy, C.C., Liu, C., Gong, S.: Person re-identification by manifold ranking. In: IEEE International Conference on Image Processing, vol. 20 (2013)
20. Mignon, A., Jurie, F.: Pcca: A new approach for distance learning from sparse pairwise constraints. In: 2012 IEEE Conference on Computer Vision and Pattern Recognition (CVPR), pp. 2666–2672. IEEE (2012)
21. Pedagadi, S., Orwell, J., Velastin, S., Boghossian, B.: Local fisher discriminant analysis for pedestrian re-identification. In: 2013 IEEE Conference on Computer Vision and Pattern Recognition (CVPR), pp. 3318–3325. IEEE (2013)
22. Sugiyama, M.: Local fisher discriminant analysis for supervised dimensionality reduction. In: 23rd International Conference on Machine Learning, pp. 905–912. ACM (2006)
23. Vezzani, R., Baltieri, D., Cucchiara, R.: People reidentification in surveillance and forensics: A survey. ACM Computing Surveys (CSUR) 46(2), 29 (2013)
24. Wang, L., Tan, T., Ning, H., Hu, W.: Silhouette analysis-based gait recognition for human identification. IEEE Transactions on Pattern Analysis and Machine Intelligence 25(12), 1505–1518 (2003)
25. Wang, X., Doretto, G., Sebastian, T., Rittscher, J., Tu, P.: Shape and appearance context modeling. In: CVPR (2007)
26. Yan, S., Xu, D., Zhang, B., Zhang, H.J., Yang, Q., Lin, S.: Graph embedding and extensions: a general framework for dimensionality reduction. IEEE Transactions on Pattern Analysis and Machine Intelligence 29(1), 40–51 (2007)
27. Zhang, T., Oles, F.: Text categorization based on regularized linear classification methods. Information Retrieval 4, 5–31 (2001)
28. Zhao, R., Ouyang, W., Wang, X.: Person re-identification by salience matching. In: ICCV (2013)
29. Zheng, W., Gong, S., Xiang, T.: Re-identification by relative distance comparison. PAMI 35(3), 653–668 (2013)
30. Zheng, W.S., Gong, S., Xiang, T.: Associating groups of people. In: BMVC (2009)
31. Zheng, W.S., Gong, S., Xiang, T.: Person re-identification by probabilistic relative distance comparison. In: 2011 IEEE Conference on Computer Vision and Pattern Recognition (CVPR), pp. 649–656. IEEE (2011)

Saliency in Crowd

Ming Jiang, Juan Xu, and Qi Zhao*

Department of Electrical and Computer Engineering
National University of Singapore, Singapore
eleqiz@nus.edu.sg

Abstract. Theories and models on saliency that predict where people look at focus on regular-density scenes. A crowded scene is characterized by the co-occurrence of a relatively large number of regions/objects that would have stood out if in a regular scene, and what drives attention in crowd can be significantly different from the conclusions in the regular setting. This work presents a first focused study on saliency in crowd. To facilitate saliency in crowd study, a new dataset of 500 images is constructed with eye tracking data from 16 viewers and annotation data on faces (the dataset will be publicly available with the paper). Statistical analyses point to key observations on features and mechanisms of saliency in scenes with different crowd levels and provide insights as of whether conventional saliency models hold in crowding scenes. Finally a new model for saliency prediction that takes into account the crowding information is proposed, and multiple kernel learning (MKL) is used as a core computational module to integrate various features at both low- and high-levels. Extensive experiments demonstrate the superior performance of the proposed model compared with the state-of-the-art in saliency computation.

Keywords: visual attention, saliency, crowd, multiple kernel learning.

1 Introduction

Humans and other primates have a tremendous ability to rapidly direct their gaze when looking at a visual scene, and to select visual information of interest. Understanding and simulating this mechanism has both scientific and economic impact [21,36,7,31].

Existing saliency models are generally built on the notion of "standing out", i.e., regions [17,25] or objects [8,26] that stand out from their neighbors are salient. The intuition has been successfully validated in both the biological and computational domains, yet the focus in both communities is regular-density scenarios. When a scene is crowded, however, there is a relatively large number of regions/objects of interest that would compete for attention. The mechanism that determines saliency in this setting can be quite different from the conventional principles, and saliency algorithms that completely ignore the crowd information may not be the optimal in crowded scenes.

There is hardly any work that explicitly models saliency in crowd, yet the problem has remarkable societal significance. Crowd is prevalent [24,22] and saliency in crowd has direct applications to a variety of important problems like security, population monitoring, urban planning, and so on. In many applications, automatic systems to monitor

---

* Corresponding author.

D. Fleet et al. (Eds.): ECCV 2014, Part VII, LNCS 8695, pp. 17–32, 2014.

crowded scenes can be more important than regular scenes as criminal or terrorist attacks often happen with a crowd of people. On the other hand, crowded scenes are more challenging to human operators, due to the limited perceptual and cognitive processing capacity.

This paper presents a focused study on saliency in crowd. Given the evolutionary significance as well as prevalence in real-world problems, this study focuses on humans (faces). In particular, we identify key features that contribute to saliency in crowd and analyze their roles with varying crowd densities. A new framework is proposed that takes into account crowd density in saliency prediction. To effectively integrate information from multiple features at both low- and high-levels, we propose to use multiple kernel learning (MKL) to learn a more robust discrimination between salient and non-salient regions. We have also constructed a new eye tracking dataset for saliency in crowd analysis. The dataset includes images with a wide range of crowding densities (defined by the number of faces), eye tracking data from 16 viewers, and bounding boxes on faces as well as annotations on face features.

The main contributions of the paper are summarized as follows:

1. Features (on faces) are identified and analyzed in the context of saliency in crowd.
2. A new framework for saliency prediction is proposed which takes into account crowding information and is able to adapt to crowd levels. Multiple kernel learning (MKL) is employed as a core computational method for feature integration.
3. A new eye tracking dataset is built for crowd estimation and saliency in crowd computation.

Fig. 1. Examples of image stimuli and eye tracking data in the new dataset. Note that despite the rich (and sometimes seemingly overwhelming) visual contents in crowded scenes, fixations between subjects are quite consistent, indicating a strong commonality in viewing patterns.

2   Related Work

2.1   Visual Saliency

There is an abundant literature in visual saliency. Some of the models [17,5,28] are inspired by neural mechanisms, e.g., following a structure rooted in the Feature Integration Theory (FIT) [35]. Others use probabilistic models to predict where humans look at. For example, Itti and Baldi [16] hypothesized that the information-theoretical concept of spatio-temporal surprise is central to saliency, and computed saliency using Bayesian statistics. Vasconcelos et al. [11,23] quantified saliency based on a discriminant center-surround hypothesis. Raj et al. [30] derived an entropy minimization algorithm to select fixations. Seo and Milanfer [32] computed saliency using a "self-resemblance" measure, where each pixel of the saliency map indicates the statistical likelihood of saliency of a feature matrix given its surrounding feature matrices. Bruce and Tsotsos [2] presented a model based on "self-information" after Independent Component Analysis (ICA) decomposition [15] that is in line with the sparseness of the response of cortical cells to visual input [10]. In Harel et al.'s work [13], an activation map within each feature channel is generated based on graph computations.

A number of recent models employed data-driven methods and leveraged human eye movement data to learn saliency models. In these models, saliency is formulated as a classification problem. Kienzle et al. [20] aimed to learn a completely parameter-free model directly from raw data (13×13 patches) using support vector machine (SVM) [3] with Gaussian radial basis functions (RBF). Judd et al. [19] and Xu et al. [42] learned saliency with low-, mid-, and high-level features using linear SVM [9]. Zhao and Koch [39,40] employed least-square regression and AdaBoost to infer weights of biologically-inspired features and to integrate them for saliency prediction. Jiang et al. [43] proposed a sparse coding approach to learn a discriminative dictionary for saliency prediction.

Among all the methods, also relevant to the proposed work is the role of faces in saliency prediction. In 2007, Cerf et al. [5] first demonstrated quantitatively the importance of faces in gaze deployment. It has been shown that faces attract attention strongly and rapidly, independent of tasks [5,4]. In their works as well as several subsequent models [13,19,39,40], a face detector was added to saliency models as a separate visual cue, and combined with other low-level features in a linear or nonlinear manner. Saliency prediction performance has been significantly boosted with the face channel, though only frontal faces with reasonably large sizes were detected [37].

2.2   Saliency and Crowd Analysis

While visual saliency has been extensively studied, few efforts have been spent in the context of crowd. Given the specialty of crowded scenes, the vast majority works in saliency are not directly applicable to crowded scenes. The most relevant works relating to both topics (i.e., *saliency* and *crowd*) are those which applied bottom-up saliency models for anomaly detection in crowded scenes. For example, Mancas et al. [24] used motion rarity to detect abnormal events in crowded scenes. Mahadevan et al. [22] used a spatial-temporal saliency detector based on a mixture of dynamic textures for the same purpose. The model achieves state-of-the-art anomaly detection results and also works well in densely crowded scenes.

Note that although similar in name (with key words of *saliency* and *crowd*), the works mentioned above are inherently different from the proposed one. They applied saliency models to crowded scenes for anomaly detection while we aim to find key features and mechanisms in attracting attention in crowd. In a sense the previous models focused on the application of suitable bottom-up saliency algorithms to crowd while ours aims to investigate mechanisms underlying saliency in crowd and develop new features and algorithms for this topic. Furthermore, previous works relied heavily on motion and have no or limited predictability power with static scenes, while we aim to look at underlying low- and high-level appearance features, and the model is validated with static images.

3   Dataset and Statistical Analysis

3.1   Dataset Collection

A large eye tracking dataset was constructed for saliency in crowd study (examples shown in Fig. 1). In particular, we collected a set of 500 natural crowd images with a diverse range of crowd densities. The images comprised indoor and outdoor scenes from Flickr and Google Images. They were cropped and/or scaled to a consistent resolution of 1024×768. In all images, human faces were manually labeled with rectangles, and two attributes were annotated on each face: *pose* and *partial occlusion*. Pose has three categories: *frontal* if the angle between the face's viewing and the image plane is roughly less than $45°$, *profile* if the angle is roughly between $45°$ and $90°$, and *back* otherwise. The second attribute was annotated as *partial occluded* if a face is partially occluded. Note that if a face is completely occluded, it is not labeled.

Sixteen students (10 male and 6 female, between the ages of 20 and 30) with corrected or uncorrected normal eyesight free-viewed the full set of images. These images were presented on a 22-inch LCD monitor (placed 57cm from the subjects), and eye movements of the subjects were recorded using an Eyelink 1000 (SR Research, Osgoode, Canada) eye tracker, at a sample rate of 1000Hz. The screen resolution was set to 1680×1050, and the images were scaled to occupy the full screen height when presented on the display. Therefore, the visual angle of the stimuli was about $38.8° \times 29.1°$, and each degree of visual angle contained about 26 pixels in the 1024×768 image.

In the experiments, each image was presented for 5 seconds and followed by a drift correction. The images were separated into 5 blocks of 100 each. Before each block, a 9-point target display was used for calibration and a second one was used for validation. After each block subjects took a 5 minute break.

3.2   Statistics and Observations

The objective of the work and the dataset is to provide a benchmark for saliency studies in crowded scenes. Due to the significant role of faces, we define "crowd" based on the number of faces in a scene, and the dataset includes a wide range of crowding levels, from a relatively low density ($3 - 10$ faces per image) to a very high density (up to 268 faces per image). The varying levels of crowding in the dataset allows an objective and comprehensive assessment of whether and how eye movement patterns are modulated by crowd levels. Fig. 2(a) shows the distribution of the numbers of faces per image. To better quantify the key factors with respect to crowd levels, we sorted the images by their numbers of faces, and evenly partitioned all images into 4 crowd levels (namely, low, mid, high and very high, Fig. 2(b)).

With eye tracking experiments, we collected 15.79 ± 0.97 (mean$\pm$SD) eye fixations from each subject for each image. To analyze the fixation distribution, we constructed a fixation map of each image, by convolving a fovea-sized (i.e. $\sigma = 26$ pixels) Gaussian kernel over the successive fixation locations of all subjects and normalizing it to sum 1, which can be considered as a probability density function of eye fixations.

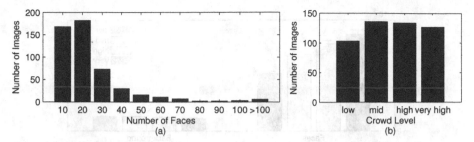

Fig. 2. (a) Histogram of face numbers per image. (b) Number of images for each crowd level.

In the following, we report key observations on where people look at in crowd:

Observation 1: Faces attract attention strongly, across all crowd levels. Furthermore, the importance of faces in saliency decreases as crowd level increases.

Consistent with previous findings [33,19,4,39], the eye tracking data display a center bias. Fig. 3(a) shows the distribution of all human fixations for all the 500 images, where 40.60% of the eye fixations are in the center 16% area, and 68.99% fixations are in the center 36% area. Note that 68.58% fixations are in the upper half of the images, in line with the distribution of the labeled faces (see Fig. 3(b)), suggesting that humans consistently fixate at faces despite the presence of whole bodies.

0.037	0.073	0.094	0.14	0.17	0.16	0.13	0.14	0.1	0.065
0.17	0.58	0.6	0.73	0.81	0.76	0.66	0.68	0.53	0.23
0.41	1.2	1.5	1.7	2.5	2.2	1.9	1.6	1.3	0.58
0.7	1.7	2.2	3	3.8	3.8	3	2.7	1.9	0.88
0.68	1.9	2.1	3	4.3	3.5	3	2.4	1.7	0.83
0.53	1.2	1.2	1.9	2.6	2.4	1.8	1.5	1.3	0.65
0.28	0.68	0.74	1.1	1.3	1.3	0.98	0.81	0.64	0.28
0.14	0.36	0.42	0.55	0.73	0.7	0.57	0.45	0.4	0.18
0.067	0.18	0.2	0.32	0.43	0.4	0.38	0.3	0.25	0.1
0.031	0.059	0.078	0.13	0.16	0.16	0.16	0.12	0.086	0.025

(a)

0.37	0.34	0.33	0.41	0.49	0.43	0.4	0.51	0.41	0.47
0.62	0.89	0.78	1	1.1	0.99	0.96	0.94	0.99	0.87
1.2	1.6	1.9	1.9	2.1	2.1	2	1.9	1.7	1.6
2.1	2.6	2.3	2.8	2.5	3	2.8	2.6	2.4	1.9
1.6	2	2	2.2	2.2	2.3	2.4	2.1	1.9	1.7
1.1	1.6	1.2	1.4	1.3	1.4	1.4	1.2	1.3	0.97
0.49	0.58	0.71	0.56	0.63	0.52	0.52	0.48	0.61	0.37
0.28	0.19	0.31	0.24	0.19	0.2	0.28	0.29	0.22	0.3
0.2	0.13	0.15	0.13	0.14	0.19	0.19	0.18	0.1	0.13
0.072	0.051	0.13	0.092	0.051	0.1	0.1	0.092	0.12	0.13

(b)

Fig. 3. Distributions of (a) all eye fixations, and (b) all faces in the dataset. The number in each histogram bin represents the percentage of fixations or faces.

We further investigated the importance of faces by comparing the mean fixation densities on faces and on the background. From Fig. 4, we observe that (1) faces attract attention more than non-face regions, consistent across all crowd levels, and (2) the importance of faces in saliency decreases with the increase of crowd densities.

Observation 2: The number of fixations do not change (significantly) with crowd density. The entropy of fixations increases with the crowd level, consistent with the entropy of faces in a scene.

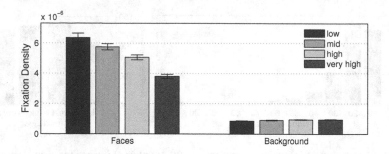

Fig. 4. Fixation densities averaged over the stimuli under the four crowd levels. Error bars indicate the standard error of the mean.

We then analyzed two global eye fixation parameters (i.e., *number* and *entropy*). Fig. 5(a) illustrates that the number of fixations does not increase with the crowd level, indicating that only a limited number of faces can be fixated at despite the larger number of faces in a crowded scene. Similarly we measured the entropy of the face as well as fixation distributions to analyze their randomness in different crowd densities. Formally, entropy is defined as $S = -\sum_{i=1}^{n} p_i log_2(p_i)$ where the vector $\mathbf{p} = (p_1, \ldots, p_n)$ is a histogram of $n = 256$ bins representing the distribution of values in each map. To measure the entropy of the original image in terms of face distributions, we constructed a face map for each image, i.e., plotting the face centers in a blank map and convolving it using a Gaussian kernel the same way as generating the fixation map. Fig. 5(b) shows that as a scene gets more crowded, the randomness of both the face map and the fixation map increases.

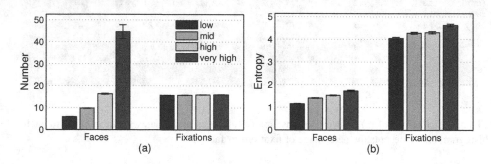

Fig. 5. (a) Numbers of faces and fixations averaged over the stimuli under the four crowd levels. (b) Entropies of faces and fixations averaged over the stimuli under the four crowd levels. Error bars indicate the standard error of the mean.

Observation 3: Crowd density modulates the correlation of saliency and features.

From Observations 1 and 2, we know that faces attract attention, yet in crowding scenarios, not all faces attract attention. There is a processing bottleneck that allows only a limited number of entities for further processing. What, then, are the driving factors in determining which faces (or non-face regions) are the most important in crowd?

Furthermore, are these factors change with crowd density? While there is no previous works that systematically study these problems in the context of saliency in crowd, we aim to make a first step in this exploration. In particular, we first define a number of relevant features in the context of crowd.

Face Size. Size describes an important object-level attribute, yet it is not clear how it affects saliency - whether large or small objects tend to attract attention. In this work, we measure the face size with $d_i = \sqrt{h_i \times w_i}$, where h_i and w_i are the height and width of the i-th face.

Face Density. This feature describes the local face density around a particular face. Unlike regular scenes where faces are sparse and mostly with low local density, in a crowded scene, local face density can vary significantly in a same scene. Formally, for each face, its local face density is computed as follows:

$$f_i = \sum_{k \neq i} \frac{1}{\sqrt{2\pi}\sigma} \exp\left(\left((x_k - x_i)^2 + (y_k - y_i)^2\right)/2\sigma^2\right), \qquad (1)$$

where (x_i, y_i) is the center coordinate of the i-th face, and σ is set to 2 degrees of visual angle.

Face Pose. Several recent works showed that faces attract attention [4,39,40], yet they all focused on frontal faces. While frontal faces are predominantly important in many regular images due to for example, photographers' preference; in a crowding setting, faces with various poses frequently appear in one scene, and to which extent pose affects saliency is.

Face Occlusion. In crowded scenes, occlusion becomes more common. While studies [18] show that humans are able to fixate on faces even though they are fully occluded, the way occlusion affects saliency has not been studied.

We then analyzed how each of the features affects saliency with varying crowd levels. Fig. 6 illustrates the saliency values (ground truth, from fixation maps) of faces with different feature values for all 4 crowd groups, and the following observations were made:

Observation 3.1 Saliency increases with face size, across all crowd levels. Intuitively in natural images, a larger size suggests a closer distance to the viewer thus is expected to be more salient. For faces of similar sizes, saliency decreases as crowd density increases.

Observation 3.2 Saliency decreases with local face density, across all crowd levels, suggesting that isolated faces attract more attention than locally crowded ones. In the same local density category, saliency decreases with global crowd density.

Observation 3.3 Generally frontal faces attract attention most strongly, followed by profile faces, and then back-view faces. Note that the "difference" of saliency values of the three face categories drop monotonically with the crowd density, and for the highly crowded group, saliency with different poses are similar indicating little contribution of pose in determining saliency there. In addition, within each pose category, saliency decreases with crowd levels.

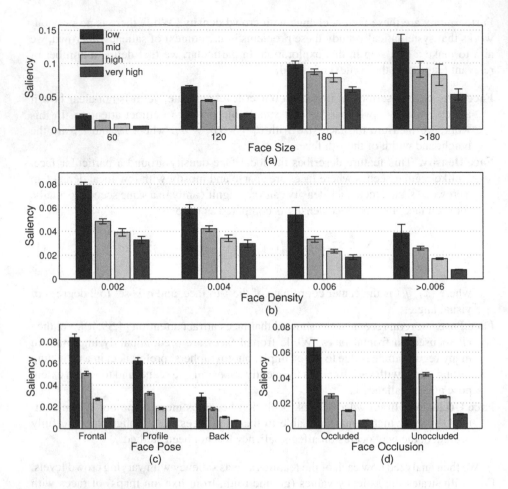

Fig. 6. Average saliency values (ground truth, from fixation maps) of faces change with (a) size, (b) density, (c) pose and (d) occlusion, modulated by the crowd levels. Error bars indicate the standard error of the mean.

Observation 3.4 Although humans still fixate consistently on (partially) occluded faces, unoccluded faces attract attention more strongly, across all crowd levels. The saliency for both occluded and unoccluded categories decreases with crowd density.

To summarize, for all individual features, saliency on face regions decreases as crowd density increases, in consistent with Observation 2. In addition, crowd density modulates the correlation between saliency and features. The general trend is that larger faces are more salient; frontal faces are more salient than profile ones, and back-view ones are the least salient (though saliency with different poses are similar in the most crowded group); and occluded faces are less salient than unoccluded ones. The varying importance with respect to the features is largely due to the details contained in the face regions as well as ecological reasons like experiences and genetic factors. Note that, however, the ways/parameters that characterize the trends vary significantly with different crowd levels.

4   Computational Model

In this section, we propose a computational model based on Support Vector Machine (SVM) learning to combine features automatically extracted from crowd images for saliency prediction at each pixel.

4.1   Face Detection and Feature Extraction

Section 3 suggests an important role of various face features in determining saliency, especially in the context of crowd. Despite the success in face detection, automatically detecting all the face features remains challenging in the literature. We in this work employ a part-based face detector [41] that is able to provide pose information besides the location and size of the faces. In particular, with its output face directions $\alpha \in [-90°, 90°]$, we consider faces with $|\alpha| \leq 45°$ as frontal faces and the others as profile faces. We expect that with the constant progress in face detection, more attributes like back-view, occlusion, can also be incorporated in the computational model.

With a wide range of sizes and different poses in crowd, the number of detected faces is always smaller than the ground truth, thus the partition of the crowd levels needs to be adjusted to the face detection results. As introduced in Section 3, the way we categorize crowd levels is data-driven and not specific to any number of faces in a scene, thus the generalization is natural.

Our model combines low-level center-surround contrast and high-level semantic face features for saliency prediction in crowd. For each image, we pre-compute feature maps for every pixel of the image resized to 256×192. In particular, we generate three simple biologically plausible low-level feature maps (i.e., intensity, color, and orientation) following Itti et al.'s approach [17]. Moreover, while Observation 1 emphasizes the importance of face in saliency prediction, Observation 2 implies that a single feature map on faces is not sufficient since only a limited number of faces are looked at despite a larger number of faces present in crowded scenes. It points to the importance of new face features that can effectively distinguish salient faces from the many faces. According to Observation 3 and the availability of face features from current face detectors (detailed below), we propose to include in the model four new feature maps on faces (size, density, frontal faces and profile faces). The face feature maps are generated by placing a 2D Gaussian component at the center of each face, with a fixed width of ($\sigma = 1°$ of visual field, 24 pixels). For size and density maps, the magnitude of each Gaussian component is the corresponding feature value computed as described in Observation 3, while for the two maps of frontal and profile faces, all Gaussian components have the same magnitude.

4.2   Learning a Saliency Model with Multiple Kernels

To predict saliency in crowd, we learn a classifier from our images with eye-tracking data, using a 10-fold cross validation (i.e. 450 training images and 50 test images).

From the top 20% and bottom 70% regions in a ground truth saliency map, we randomly sample 10 pixels respectively, yielding a training set of 4500 positive samples and 4500 negative samples. The values at each selected pixel in the seven feature maps are concatenated into a feature vector. All the training samples are normalized to have a zero mean and a unit variance. The same parameters are used to normalize the test images afterwards. This sampling and normalization approach is consistent with the implementation in the MIT model [19] that learns a linear support vector machine (SVM) classifier for feature integration.

In this paper, instead of learning an ordinary linear SVM model, we propose to use multiple kernel learning (MKL) [6] that is able to combine features at different levels in a well founded way that chooses the most appropriate kernels automatically. The MKL framework aims at removing assumptions of kernel functions and eliminating the burdensome manual parameter tuning in the kernel functions of SVMs. Formally, the MKL defines a convex combination of m kernels. The output function is formulated as follows:

$$s(\boldsymbol{x}) = \sum_{k=1}^{m} [\beta_k \langle \boldsymbol{w}_k, \Phi_k(\boldsymbol{x}) \rangle + b_k] \tag{2}$$

where $\Phi_k(\boldsymbol{x})$ maps the feature data $\boldsymbol{x}$ using one of m predefined kernels including Gaussian ($\sigma = 0.05, 0.1, 0.2, 0.4$) and polynomial kernels (degree $= 1, 2, 3$), with an L1 sparsity constraint. The goal is to learn the mixing coefficients $\boldsymbol{\beta} = (\beta_k)$, along with $\boldsymbol{w} = (\boldsymbol{w}_k)$, $\boldsymbol{b} = (b_k)$, $k = 1, \ldots, m$. The resulting optimization problem becomes:

$$\min_{\boldsymbol{\beta}, \boldsymbol{w}, \boldsymbol{b}, \xi} \frac{1}{2}\Omega(\boldsymbol{\beta}) + C \sum_{i=1}^{N} \xi_i \tag{3}$$

$$\text{s.t.} \quad \forall i : \xi_i = l\left(s(\boldsymbol{x}^{(i)}), y^{(i)}\right) \tag{4}$$

where $(\boldsymbol{x}^{(i)}, y^{(i)})$, $i = 1, \ldots, N$ are the training data and N is the size of the training set. Specifically, $\boldsymbol{x}^{(i)}$ is the feature vector concatenating all feature values (from the feature maps) at a particular image pixel, and the training label $y^{(i)}$ is $+1$ for a salient point, or -1 for a non-salient point.

In Eq. 4, C is the regularization parameter and l is a convex loss function, and $\Omega(\boldsymbol{\beta})$ is an L1 regularization parameter to encourage a sparse $\boldsymbol{\beta}$, so that a small number of crowd levels are selected. This problem can be solved by iteratively optimizing $\boldsymbol{\beta}$ with fixed $\boldsymbol{w}$ and $\boldsymbol{b}$ through linear programming, and optimizing $\boldsymbol{w}$ and $\boldsymbol{b}$ with fixed $\boldsymbol{\beta}$ through a generic SVM solver.

Observation 3 provides a key insight that crowd level modulates the correlation between saliency and the features. To account for this, we learn an MKL classifier for each crowd level, and the use of MKL automatically adapts both the feature weights and the kernels to each crowd level. In this work, the crowd levels are categorized based on the number of faces detected. In practice, the number of detected faces is normally smaller than the ground truth due to a wide range of sizes/poses in crowd, thus the partition of

the crowd levels needs to be adjusted to the face detection results. The way we categorize crowd levels is data-driven and not specific to any number of faces in a scene, thus
the generalization is natural.

5 Experimental Results

Extensive and comparative experiments were carried out and reported in this section.
We first introduce experimental paradigm with the choice of face detection algorithms
and implementation details, followed by metrics to evaluate and compare the models.
Qualitative as well as quantitative comparative results are then shown to demonstrate
the effective of the algorithm to predict saliency in crowd.

5.1 Evaluation Metrics

In the saliency literature, there are several widely used criteria to quantitatively evaluate the performance of saliency models by comparing the saliency prediction with eye
movement data. One of the most common evaluation metrics is the area under the receiver operator characteristic (ROC) curve (i.e. AUC) [34]. However, the AUC as well
as many other metrics are significantly affected by the center bias effect [33], so the
Shuffled AUC [38] is then introduced to address this problem. Particularly, to calculate
the Shuffled AUC, negative samples are selected from human fixational locations from
all images in a dataset (except the test image), instead of uniformly sampling from all
images.

In addition, the Normalized Scanpath Saliency (NSS) [29] and the Correlation Coefficient (CC) [27] are also used to measure the statistical relationship between the
saliency prediction and the ground truth. NSS is defined as the average saliency value
at the fixation locations in the normalized predicted saliency map which has zero mean
and unit standard deviation, while the CC measures the linear correlation between the
saliency map and the ground truth map. The three metrics are complementary, and provide a relatively objective evaluation of the various models.

5.2 Performance Evaluation

We perform qualitative and quantitative evaluation of our models with a single MKL
classifier (SC-S) and a combination of multiple classifiers (SC-M) for different crowd-
levels, in comparison with six classic/state-of-the-art saliency models that are publicly
available.

Two of the comparative models are bottom-up ones combined with object detectors
(i.e. MIT [19] and SMVJ [5], while the others are purely bottom-up, including the Itti
et al.'s model implemented by Harel, the Graph Based Visual Saliency (GBVS) model
[13], the Attention based on Information Maximization (AIM) model [2], the Saliency
Using Natural statistics (SUN) model [38], the Adaptive Whitening Saliency (AWS)
model [12], and the Image Signature (IS) model [14]. For a fair comparison, the Viola-
Jones face detector used in the MIT and SMVJ models is replaced with [41]. We also
compare with the face detector as a baseline saliency model. Moreover, since the MIT

saliency model and our models are both data-driven, we test them on the same training and test image sets, and the parameters used for data sampling and SVM learning are also the same. In addition, the "distance to center" channel in the MIT model is discarded to make it fair with respect to this spatial bias. Finally, all the saliency maps are smoothed with the same Gaussian kernel.

Fig. 7 shows the quantitative evaluation following Borji's implementations [1]. Further, in Fig. 8, we illustrate the ROC curves for the Shuffled AUC computation of the compared models. Four key observations are made:

1. Models with face detectors perform generally better than those without face detectors.
2. The face detector itself does not perform well enough. It only predicts a small region in the images (where the faces are detected) as salient, and the saliency of non-faces is considered to be zero. Since most of the predictions are zero, in the ROC curve for the face detector, both true positive rate and false positive rate are generally low, and there are missing samples in the right side of the curve.
3. The proposed models outperform all other models in predicting saliency in crowd (with all three metrics), suggesting the usefulness of the new face related features. The comparative models (i.e. SMVJ and MIT) use the same face detector. By combining low-level features and the face detector, SMVJ and MIT perform better than most low-level models.
4. The better performance of SC-M compared with SC-S demonstrates the effectiveness of considering different crowd levels in modeling. In fact, besides the richer set of face features, the proposed models use only three conventional low-level features, so there is still a large potential in our models to achieve higher performance with more features.

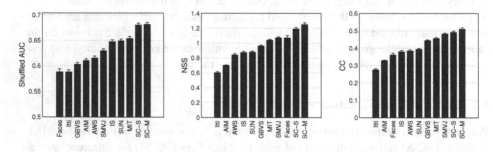

Fig. 7. Quantitative comparison of models. The prediction accuracy is measured with Shuffled AUC, NSS and CC scores. The bar values indicate the average performance over all stimuli. The error bars indicate the standard error of the mean.

For a qualitative assessment, Fig. 9 illustrates saliency maps from the proposed models and the comparative ones. First, as illustrated in the human fixation maps (2nd column), faces consistently and strongly attract attention. Models with face detectors (SC-M, SC-S, MIT and SMVJ) generally outperform those without face detectors (GBVS, IS, SUN, AIM and Itti). Compared with the MIT model that performs the best among all comparative models, our models use fewer low-, mid-, and high-level

ROC Curves

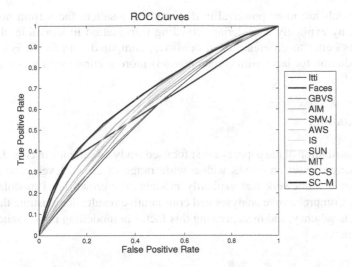

Fig. 8. ROC curves of the compared models. Bold lines represent models incorporating the face detector.

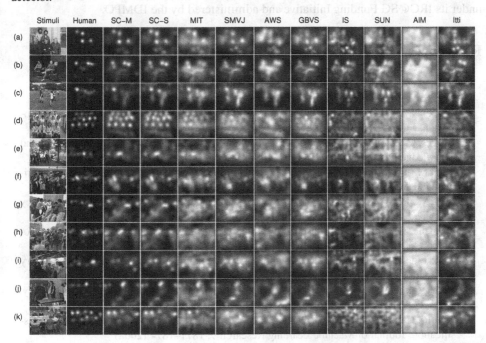

Fig. 9. Qualitative results of the proposed models and the state-of-the-art models over the crowd dataset

features, yet still perform better, demonstrating the importance of face related features in the context of crowd. Second, in scenes with relatively high crowd densities, e.g. images (f-h), there is a large variance in face size, local density, and pose, so the proposed models are more powerful in distinguishing salient faces from non-salient ones. Third, by explicitly considering crowding information in modeling, the SC-M model adapts better to different crowd densities, compared with SC-S. For example saliency prediction for faces with certain poses is more accurate with SC-M (e.g., images (c) and (i)).

6   Conclusions

The main contribution of the paper is a first focused study on saliency in crowd. It builds an eye tracking dataset on scenes with a wide range of crowd levels, and proposes a computational framework that explicitly models how crowd level modulates gaze deployment. Comprehensive analyses and comparative results demonstrate that crowd density affects saliency, and incorporating this factor in modelling boosts saliency prediction accuracy.

Acknowledgement. This research was supported by he Singapore Ministry of Education Academic Research Fund Tier 1 (No.R-263-000-A49-112) and the Singapore NRF under its IRC@SG Funding Initiative and administered by the IDMPO.

References

1. Borji, A.: Evaluation measures, https://sites.google.com/site/saliencyevaluation/evaluation-measures
2. Bruce, N., Tsotsos, J.: Saliency, attention, and visual search: An information theoretic approach. Journal of Vision 9(3), 5 (2009)
3. Burges, C.: A tutorial on support vector machines for pattern recognition. Data Mining and Knowledge Discovery 2(2), 121–167 (1998)
4. Cerf, M., Frady, E., Koch, C.: Faces and text attract gaze independent of the task: Experimental data and computer model. Journal of Vision 9(12), 10 (2009)
5. Cerf, M., Harel, J., Einhäuser, W., Koch, C.: Predicting human gaze using low-level saliency combined with face detection. In: NIPS (2008)
6. Chapelle, O., Vapnik, V., Bousquet, O., Mukherjee, S.: Choosing multiple parameters for support vector machines. Machine Learning 46(1-3), 131–159 (2002)
7. Chikkerur, S., Serre, T., Tan, C., Poggio, T.: What and where: a bayesian inference theory of attention. Vision Research 50(22), 2233–2247 (2010)
8. Einhäuser, W., Spain, M., Perona, P.: Objects predict fixations better than early saliency. Journal of Vision 8(14), 18 (2008)
9. Fan, R., Chang, K., Hsieh, C., Wang, X., Lin, C.: Liblinear: A library for large linear classification. Journal of Machine Learning Research 9, 1871–1874 (2008)
10. Field, D.J.: What is the goal of sensory coding? Neural Computation 6, 559–601 (1994)
11. Gao, D., Mahadevan, V., Vasconcelos, N.: The discriminant center-surround hypothesis for bottom-up saliency. In: NIPS (2007)
12. Garcia-Diaz, A., Fdez-Vidal, X.R., Pardo, X.M., Dosil, R.: Saliency from hierarchical adaptation through decorrelation and variance normalization. Image and Vision Computing 30(1), 51–64 (2012)
13. Harel, J., Koch, C., Perona, P.: Graph-based visual saliency. In: NIPS (2007)

14. Hou, X., Harel, J., Koch, C.: Image signature: Highlighting sparse salient regions. T-PAMI 34(1), 194–201 (2012)
15. Hyvarinen, A., Oja, E.: Independent component analysis: algorithms and applications. Neural Networks 13(4-5), 411–430 (2000)
16. Itti, L., Baldi, P.: Bayesian surprise attracts human attention. In: NIPS (2006)
17. Itti, L., Koch, C., Niebur, E.: A model for saliency-based visual attention for rapid scene analysis. T-PAMI 20(11), 1254–1259 (1998)
18. Judd, T.: Learning to predict where humans look,
    http://people.csail.mit.edu/tjudd/WherePeopleLook/index.html
19. Judd, T., Ehinger, K., Durand, F., Torralba, A.: Learning to predict where humans look. In: ICCV (2009)
20. Kienzle, W., Wichmann, F., Scholkopf, B., Franz, M.: A nonparametric approach to bottom-up visual saliency. In: NIPS (2006)
21. Koch, C., Ullman, S.: Shifts in selective visual attention: towards the underlying neural circuitry. Human Neurobiology 4(4), 219–227 (1985)
22. Li, W., Mahadevan, V., Vasconcelos, N.: Anomaly detection and localization in crowded scenes. T-PAMI 36(1), 18–32 (2014)
23. Mahadevan, V., Vasconcelos, N.: Spatiotemporal saliency in highly dynamic scenes. T-PAMI 32(1), 171–177 (2010)
24. Mancas, M.: Attention-based dense crowds analysis. In: WIAMIS (2010)
25. Margolin, R., Tal, A., Zelnik-Manor, L.: What makes a patch distinct? In: CVPR (2013)
26. Nuthmann, A., Henderson, J.: Object-based attentional selection in scene viewing. Journal of Vision 10(8), 20 (2010)
27. Ouerhani, N., Von Wartburg, R., Hugli, H., Muri, R.: Empirical validation of the saliency-based model of visual attention. Electronic Letters on Computer Vision and Image Analysis 3(1), 13–24 (2004)
28. Parkhurst, D., Law, K., Niebur, E.: Modeling the role of salience in the allocation of overt visual attention. Vision Research 42(1), 107–123 (2002)
29. Peters, R., Iyer, A., Itti, L., Koch, C.: Components of bottom-up gaze allocation in natural images. Vision Research 45(18), 2397–2416 (2005)
30. Raj, R., Geisler, W., Frazor, R., Bovik, A.: Contrast statistics for foveated visual systems: Fixation selection by minimizing contrast entropy. Journal of the Optical Society of America A 22(10), 2039–2049 (2005)
31. Rudoy, D., Goldman, D.B., Shechtman, E., Zelnik-Manor, L.: Learning video saliency from human gaze using candidate selection. In: CVPR (2013)
32. Seo, H., Milanfar, P.: Static and space-time visual saliency detection by self-resemblance. Journal of Vision 9(12), 15 (2009)
33. Tatler, B.W.: The central fixation bias in scene viewing: Selecting an optimal viewing position independently of motor biases and image feature distributions. Journal of Vision 7(14), 4 (2007)
34. Tatler, B.W., Baddeley, R., Gilchrist, I.: Visual correlates of fixation selection: Effects of scale and time. Vision Research 45(5), 643–659 (2005)
35. Treisman, A.M., Gelade, G.: A feature-integration theory of attention. Cognitive Psychology 12(1), 97–136 (1980)
36. Treue, S.: Neural correlates of attention in primate visual cortex. Trends in Neurosciences 24(5), 295–300 (2001)
37. Viola, P., Jones, M.: Rapid object detection using a boosted cascade of simple features. In: CVPR (2001)
38. Zhang, L., Tong, M., Marks, T., Shan, H., Cottrell, G.: Sun: A bayesian framework for saliency using natural statistics. Journal of Vision 8(7), 32 (2008)

39. Zhao, Q., Koch, C.: Learning a saliency map using fixated locations in natural scenes. Journal of Vision 11(3), 9 (2011)
40. Zhao, Q., Koch, C.: Learning visual saliency by combining feature maps in a nonlinear manner using adaboost. Journal of Vision 12(6), 22 (2012)
41. Zhu, X., Ramanan, D.: Face detection, pose estimation, and landmark localization in the wild. In: CVPR (2012)
42. Xu, J., Jiang, M., Wang, S., Kankanhalli, M.S., Zhao, Q.: Predicting human gaze beyond pixels. Journal of Vision 14(1), 28 (2014)
43. Jiang, M., Song, M., Zhao, Q.: Leveraging Human Fixations in Sparse Coding: Learning a Discriminative Dictionary for Saliency Prediction. In: SMC (2013)

Webpage Saliency

Chengyao Shen[1,2] and Qi Zhao[2,*]

[1] Graduate School for Integrated Science and Engineering
[2] Department of Electrical and Computer Engineering,
National University of Singapore, Singapore
eleqiz@nus.edu.sg

Abstract. Webpage is becoming a more and more important visual input to us. While there are few studies on saliency in webpage, we in this work make a focused study on how humans deploy their attention when viewing webpages and for the first time propose a computational model that is designed to predict webpage saliency. A dataset is built with 149 webpages and eye tracking data from 11 subjects who free-view the webpages. Inspired by the viewing patterns on webpages, multi-scale feature maps that contain object blob representation and text representation are integrated with explicit face maps and positional bias. We propose to use multiple kernel learning (MKL) to achieve a robust integration of various feature maps. Experimental results show that the proposed model outperforms its counterparts in predicting webpage saliency.

Keywords: Web Viewing, Visual Attention, Multiple Kernel Learning.

1 Introduction

With the wide spread of Internet in recent decades, webpages have become a more and more important source of information for an increasing population in the world. According to the *Internet World States*, the number of internet users has reached 2.4 billion in 2012. A recent survey conducted on US-based web users in May 2013 also showed that an average user spends 23 hours a week online [25]. This trend of increasing time spent on web has greatly reshaped people's life style and companies' marketing strategy. Thus, the study of how users' attention is deployed and directed on a webpage is of great research and commercial value.

The deployment of human attention is usually driven by two factors: a bottom-up factor that is memory-free and biased by the conspicuity of a stimuli, and a top-down factor which is memory-dependent and with variable selective criteria [16]. The saliency of stimuli is the distinct perceptual quality by which the stimuli stand out relative to their neighbors. It is typically computed based on low-level image statistics, namely luminance contrast, color contrast, edge density, and orientation (also motion and flickr in video) [16,4]. Recent studies show that text, face, person, animals and other specific objects also contribute much to the saliency of a stimulus [18,5,9,28,29].

---

* Corresponding author.

D. Fleet et al. (Eds.): ECCV 2014, Part VII, LNCS 8695, pp. 33–46, 2014.

Compared with natural images, webpage has its own characteristics that make a direct application of existing saliency models ineffective. For example, webpages are usually rich in visual media, such as text, pictures, logos and animations [21]. From the classical low-level feature based saliency point of view, a webpage is thus full of salient stimuli and competition arises everywhere, which makes an accurate prediction of eye fixations difficult. Besides, studies show that people's web-viewing behavior is different from that on natural images and reveals several distinct patterns such as F-bias to scan top-left region at the start [19,4] and banner blindness to avoid banner-like advertisement [6,12,14]. These differentiating factors suggest new ways for webpage saliency.

1.1   Visual Attention Models on Webpages

Up to now, there is no report on webpage saliency models in the literature. There are, however, several conceptual models and computational models based on non-image information that investigate into the user viewing behaviors on different webpages.

For conceptual models, Faraday's visual scanning model [10] represents the first framework that gave a systematic evaluation of visual attention on webpages. This model identified six "salient visual elements"(SAE) in a hierarchy (motion, size, image, color, text-style, and position) that direct our attention in webpages and provided a description of how these elements are scanned by a user. A later research by Grier *et al.* [12] showed that Faraday's model is oversimplified for complex web-viewing behaviors (e.g., the salience order of SAE selected by the model might be inaccurate). Based on Faradays model, Grier *et al.* described three heuristics ("top left corner of the main content area is dominant, "overly salient items do not contain information, "information of similar type will be grouped together) from their observation and they further proposed a three stage EHS (Expected Location, Heuristic Search, Systematic Search) theory that explains the viewing behavior on webpages. These conceptual models give us a good foundation on developing a computational algorithm to predict webpage saliency.

For the computational models based on non-image information, the model from Buscher *et al.* [4] that utilized HTML-induced document object model (DOM) is among the most prominent. In [4], the authors first collected data when users were engaged in information foraging and page recognition tasks on 361 webpages from 4 categories (cars, diabetes, kite surfing, wind energy). They then performed a linear regression on features extracted from DOM and generated a model for predicting visual attention on webpages using decision trees. Their linear regression showed that size of the DOM is the most decisive factor and their decision tree get a precision of 75% and a recall of 53% in predicting the eye fixations on webpages. From their data, they also observed that the first few fixations (i.e., during the first second of each page view) are consistent in both tasks. Other models in this category either focus on a specific type of webpages [7] that does not generalize well, or based themselves on text semantics [22,23] thus quite different from the goal in this work.

The only work we found sharing a similar goal with ours is from Still and Masciocchi [21]. The referred work, however, simply applied the classic Itti-Koch model [16] to predict the web-viewing entry points while we investigate features and mechanisms underlying webpage saliency and propose a dedicated model for saliency prediction in this context.

1.2 Motivations and Contributions

In this study, we aim to develop a saliency model that is purely based on visual features to predict the eye fixation deployment on webpages. To achieve this, we first collect eye tracking data from 11 subjects on 149 webpages and analyzed the data to get ground truth fixation maps for webpage saliency. We then extract various visual features on webpages with multi-scale filters and face detectors. After feature extraction, we integrate all these feature maps incorporating positional bias with multiple kernel learning (MKL) and use this integrated map to predict eye fixation on webpages. Comparative results demonstrate that our model outperforms existing saliency models. Besides the scientific question of how humans deploy attention when viewing webpage, computational models that mimic human behavior will have general applicability to a number of tasks like guiding webpage design, suggesting ad placement, and so on.

The main contributions of our research include:

1. We collect an eye fixation dataset from 11 subjects on 149 webpages which is the first dataset on webpage saliency according to our knowledge.
2. We propose a new computational model for webpage saliency by integrating multi-scale feature maps, face map and positional bias, in a MKL framework. The model is the first one for webpage saliency that is purely based on visual features.

2 Webpage Saliency Dataset

Since there is no publicly available eye tracking dataset on webpages, we create one dataset and plan to make it public to facilitate further research on webpage saliency. In the following, we describe the stimuli, data collection procedure, and data analysis for the dataset.

2.1 Stimuli

149 screenshots of webpages rendered in Chrome browser in full screen mode were collected from various sources on the Internet in the resolution of 1360 by 768 pixels. These webpages were categorized as pictorial, text and mixed according to the different composition of text and pictures and each category contains around 50 images. Examples of webpage in each category are shown in Figure 1 and the following criteria were used during the collection of webpage image samples:

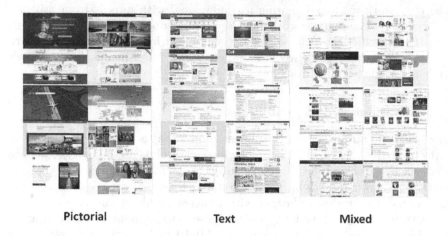

Pictorial   Text   Mixed

Fig. 1. Examples of webpages in our dataset

- **Pictorial:** Webpages occupied by one dominant picture or several large thumbnail pictures and usually with less text. Examples in this category include photo sharing websites and company websites that put their products in the homepages.
- **Text:** Webpages containing informative text with high density Examples include wikipedia, news websites, and academic journal websites.
- **Mixed:** Webpages with a mix of thumbnail pictures and text in middle density. Examples are online shopping websites and social network sites.

The collected samples consisted of webpages from various domains. This was done to suppress the subjects's prior familiarity of the layout of the webpage as well as to prevent the subjects from developing familiarity during the experiment, so as to reduce personal bias or top-down factors.

2.2 Eye Tracking Data Collection

Subjects. 11 students (4 males and 7 females) in the age range of 21 to 25 participated in data collection. All participants had normal vision or corrective visual apparatus during the experiment and all of them were experienced Internet users.

Apparatus and Eye Tracking. Subjects were seated in a dark room with their head positioned on a chin and forehead rest, 60 cm from the computer screen. The resolution of the screen was 1360×768 pixels. Stimuli were placed across the entire screen and were presented using MATLAB (MathWorks, Natick, Massachusetts, USA) with the Psychtoolbox 3 [2]. Eye movement data were monocularly recorded using a noninvasive Eyelink 1000 system with a sampling rate of 1000 Hz. Calibration was done using the 9-point grid method.

Procedure. For each trial, an image was presented in random order for 5 seconds. Subjects were instructed to free-view the webpages and were informed that they had 5 seconds for each webpage. Each trial will follow by a drift correction where the subject would have to fixate at the center and initiate the next trial via a keyboard press.

2.3   Dataset Analysis

We analyze the eye fixation data collected from 11 subjects by visualizing their fixation heat maps. The fixation heat map was generated by convolving a 2D Gaussian filter on fixation points gathered from all the images in the dataset or in one particular category. In this work, a gaussian filter with a standard deviation of 25 pixels is used to smooth the fixation point and to generate a map. This size approximates the size of foveal region in human eye (1 visual degree approximates 50 pixels in our experimental setup).

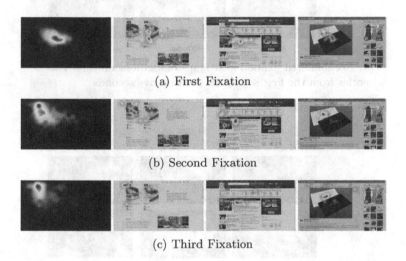

(a) First Fixation

(b) Second Fixation

(c) Third Fixation

Fig. 2. Fixation heat maps of the first, second, and third fixations over all the webpage images (1st column) and the position distributions of the first, second and third fixations on three example images from the dataset

Figure 2 visualizes the distributions of the first three fixations on all the webpages and on three individual webpages. Figure 3 illustrates category-wise fixation heat maps in first five seconds. From the figures we made the following observations: From the figures we made the following observations:

- **Positional Bias:** The positional bias on top-left region is evident in the visualization. From Figure 2, we observe that most of the first, second and third fixations fall in this region. More specifically, the first fixations tend to locate in the centre position that is slightly toward top-left corner and

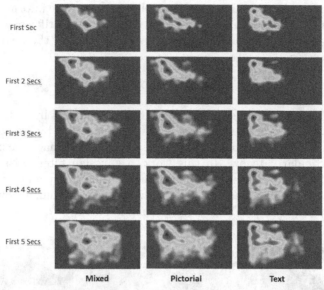

First Sec

First 2 Secs

First 3 Secs

First 4 Secs

First 5 Secs

Mixed   Pictorial   Text

(a) Accumulated fixation heat maps of fixations on three categories from the first second to the first five seconds

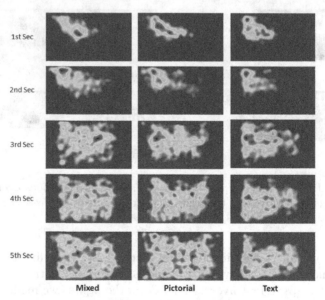

1st Sec

2nd Sec

3rd Sec

4th Sec

5th Sec

Mixed   Pictorial   Text

(b) Fixation heat maps on three categories with a second-by-second visualization

Fig. 3. Fixation heat maps on three categories of webpages

the second and third fixations usually fall on the trajectory from center to top-left corner. From Figure 3, we can further observe that this top-left bias is common in all the three categories at first three seconds. These findings are in line with the F-bias described in [19,12,4]

- **Object and Text Preference:** By looking into the eye fixation distributions on each individual webpage, we found that the first several fixations usually fall on large texts, logos, faces and objects that near the center or the top-left regions (Figure 2, 2rd to 4th columns).
- **Category Difference:** From Figure 3, we observe that, in all categories, fixations tend to cluster at the center and top-left region in the first two seconds and start to diversify after the 3rd second. Webpages from the 'Text' category display a preference of the middle left and bottom left regions in 4th and 5th second while the fixations on the other two categories are more evenly distributed across all the locations.

3   The Saliency Model

Data analysis from Section 2.3 suggest the following for computational modeling of web saliency: 1. positional bias is evident in the eye fixation distribution on webpages. 2. Face, object, text and website logo are important in predicting eye fixations on webpages. In this work, we propose a saliency model following the classic Itti-Koch saliency model [16,17], which is one of the seminal works in the computational modeling of visual attention. We show below how in-depth analysis of the low-level feature cues and proper feature integration can effectively highlight important regions in webpages.

3.1   Multi-scale Feature Maps

The original Itti-Koch saliency model [16,17] computes multi-scale intensity, color, and orientation feature maps from an image using pyramidal center-surround computation and gabor filters and then combines these maps into one saliency map after normalization. In our model, we further optimize this multi-scale representation by adding a thresholded center-surround filter to eliminate the edge artifacts in the representation. The edge artifacts are the scattered responses surrounding objects caused by center-surround/gabor filtering (especially for filters of low spatial frequency.). The additional thresholded center-surround filter is mostly to inhibit these false alarms and make the responses concentrated on the objects. The resulting model is able to capture higher-level concepts like object blobs and text, as illustrated in Figure 4.

Object Representation. Object blobs on webpages usually have large contrast in intensity and color to their backgrounds. In our experiments we found that object blobs could be well represented by the intensity and color maps in low spatial frequency, as shown in Figure 4(a).

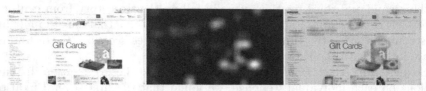

(a) Object representation from intensity and color maps in low spatial frequency.

(b) Text representation from four orientation feature maps in high spatial frequency.

Fig. 4. Object blob and text representations from different feature maps. Left: input image, Middle: integrated feature map, Right: heat map overlay of input image and integrated feature map.

Text Representation. Texts are usually in high spatial frequency and with large responses in all the orientation as they contain edges in each orientation. Based on this, the text representation can be derived from orientation feature maps. By integrating orientation feature maps in high spatial frequency, we found that almost all the texts can be encoded (Figure 4(b)).

In our implementation, we used Derrington-Krauskopf-Lennie (DKL) color space [8] to extract intensity, color and orientation features from webpage images. The DKL color space is defined physiologically using the relative excitations of the three types of retinal cones and its performance on saliency prediction is superior to RGB color space.

For the computation of multi-scale feature maps, we use six levels of pyramid images and we apply center surround filters and gabor filters with orientations of $0°, 45°, 90°, 135°$ on the input image. In this way a total of 42 multi-scale feature maps are yielded on the seven channels (The DKL color space generates 3 feature maps: 1 intensity and 2 color maps, and center-surround filters are applied on these 3 channels. In addition, 4 orientation filters on the intensity map result 4 orientation maps, Thus 6 levels of image pyramid lead to a total of 42 feature maps). Based on the fact that different feature maps in different spatial frequency might encode different representations, we treat each feature map separately with MKL regression for feature integration thus each feature map would have a different contribution to the final saliency map.

3.2 Face Detection

From data analyses above, we found that in viewing webpages, human related features like eye, face and upper body also attract attention strongly, consistent with the literature [18,5,9,28,29]. We thus generate a separate face map by face and upper body detection. The upper body detector is used here to increase the robustness of face detection under different scenarios. The two detectors are based on cascaded object detector with Viola-Jones detection algorithm[26] implemented in Matlab Computer Vision System Toolbox. An scaling step of 1.02 on the input and a merging threshold of 20 and 30 are used for the face detector and the upper body detector to ensure correct detections and suppress false alarms. The face map is then generated by convolving the detection results with a Gaussian kernel.

3.3   Positional Bias

The positional bias in webpage saliency include center bias and top-left bias. In our implementation, the accumulated fixation map of all the webpages over 5 seconds is used as the positional bias and it is treated as one independent map in regression.

3.4   Feature Integration with Multiple Kernel Learning

We use multiple kernel learning (MKL) for regression and all the feature maps are integrated to predict eye fixations on webpage. MKL is a method that combines multiple kernels of support vector machines (SVMs) instead of one. Suppose we have N training pairs $\{(\mathbf{x}_i, y_i)\}_{i=1}^{N}$, where $\mathbf{x}_i$ denotes a feature vector that contains the values of each feature map on one particular position and $y_i \in \{-1, 1\}$ represents whether there is an eye fixation on the same position. An SVM model on them defines a discriminant function as:

$$f_m(\mathbf{x}) = \sum_{i=1}^{N} \alpha_{mi} y_i k_m(\mathbf{x}_i, \mathbf{x}) + b_m \tag{1}$$

where α represents dual variables, b is the bias and $k(\mathbf{x}_i, \mathbf{x})$ is the kernel. m is a subscript for each set of kernel in a standard SVM.

In its simplest form MKL considers a combination of M kernels as

$$k(\mathbf{x}_i, \mathbf{x}) = \sum_{m=1}^{M} \beta_m k_m(\mathbf{x}_i, \mathbf{x})$$

$$\text{s.t. } \beta_m > 0, \sum_{m=1}^{M} \beta_m = 1 \tag{2}$$

Then our final discriminant function on a vectorized input image $\mathbf{x}$ is

$$f(\mathbf{x}) = \sum_{m=1}^{M} \sum_{i=1}^{N} \alpha_{mi} y_i \beta_m k_m(\mathbf{x}_i, \mathbf{x}) + b_m \tag{3}$$

We utilized simpleMKL algorithm [20] in our model to solve this MKL problem and the probability of eye fixations on each position, or the final saliency map S, can then be obtained by

$$S = g \circ \max(f(\mathbf{x}), 0) \tag{4}$$

Where g is a gaussian mask that is used to smooth the saliency map.

4   Experiments

To verify our model in predicting eye fixations on webpage, we apply it to our webpage saliency dataset under different feature settings and then compare our results with the state-of-the-art saliency models. For a fair comparison and a comprehensive assessment, the fixation prediction results of all the models were measured by three similarity metrics and all the evaluation scores presented in this section are obtained as the highest score by varying the smooth parameter (standard deviation of a Gaussian mask) from $1\% - 5\%$ of the image width in a step of 0.05%.

4.1   Similarity Metrics

The similarity metrics we use include Linear Correlation Coefficient (CC), Normalized Scanpath Saliency (NSS) and shuffled Area Under Curve (sAUC), whose codes and descriptions are available online[1][1].

CC measures the linear correlations between the estimated saliency map and the ground truth fixation map. The more CC close to 1, the better the performance of the saliency algorithm.

AUC is the most widely used score for saliency model evaluation. In the computation of AUC, the estimated saliency map is used as a binary classifier to separate the positive samples (human fixations) from the negatives (uniform non-fixation region for classical AUC, and fixations from other images for sAUC). By varying the threshold on the saliency map, a Receiver Operating Characteristics (ROC) curve can then be plotted as the true positive rate vs. false negative rate. AUC is then calculated as the area under this curve. For the AUC score, 1 means perfect predict while 0.5 indicates chance level. Shuffled AUC (sAUC) could eliminate the influence of positional bias since the negatives are from fixations of other images and it generates a score of 0.5 on any positional bias.

NSS measures the average of the response values at fixation locations along the scanpath in the normalized saliency map. The larger the NSS score, the more corresponding between predictions and ground truths.

All these three metrics have their advantages and limitations and a model that performs well should have relatively high score in all these three metrics.

---

[1] https://sites.google.com/site/saliencyevaluation/evaluation-measures

4.2   Experimental Setup

To train the MKL, the image sample set was randomly divided into 119 training images and 30 testing images and the final results were tested iteratively with different training and testing sets separation. We collect positive samples and negative samples from all the webpage images in our dataset. For each image, positively labeled feature vectors from 10 eye fixation locations in eye fixation position map and 10 negatively labeled feature vectors from the image regions with saliency values below 50% of the max saliency value in the scene to yield a training set of 2380 training samples and 600 testing samples for training and validation. An MKL with a set of gaussian kernels and polynomial kernels is then trained as a binary-class regression problem based on these positive and negative samples.

4.3   Results and Performance

We first test our model in different feature settings including multi-scale feature maps with and without regression, face map, and positional bias. From Table 1, we could see that MKL regression and face map could greatly improve the model's performance on eye fixation prediction with all the three similarity metrics. However, the positional bias improve the performance in CC and NSS but does not improve sAUC, largely due to the design of sAUC that compensates positional bias itself [24,27].

Table 1. The performance of our model under different feature settings

Feature Settings	CC	sAUC	NSS
Multiscale (no MKL)	0.2446	0.6616	0.8579
Multiscale	0.3815	0.7020	1.2000
Multiscale+Position	0.4433	0.6754	1.3895
Multiscale+Face	0.3977	**0.7206**	1.2475
Multiscale+Face+Position	**0.4491**	0.6824	**1.3982**

Table 2. The performance of our model on three different categories in the webpage saliency dataset

Feature Settings	CC	sAUC	NSS
Pictorial	0.4047	0.7121	1.2923
Text	0.3746	0.6961	1.1824
Mixed	0.3851	0.7049	1.1928

We also test our model on each category in the webpage saliency data and train a MKL on the images inside the category with multi-scale feature maps and face map. From Table 2, we could see that the performance on all the three categories are close, however, the performance on Text is a bit smaller than that on Pictorial and the performance on Mixed is between them. This results indicate that text might be a difficult part to predict saliency. Besides, we also observe that almost all the scores in Table 2 is slightly smaller than the Multiscale+Face in Table 1, which may result from the fewer images got in each category for training.

Then, we compare our model (Multiscale+Face) with other saliency models on the webpage saliency dataset. These saliency models include GBVS [13], AIM [3], SUN [27], Image Signature [15], AWS[11] and Judd's saliency model with both a face detector and a learning mechanism [18]. All the evaluation scores presented here are also obtained as the highest score by varying the smooth parameter for a fair comparion. From the prediction results listed in Table 3, we could see that our model outperforms of all the other saliency models with all the three similarity metrics.

For a qualitative assessment, we also visualize human fixation maps and saliency maps generated from different saliency algorithms on 9 images randomly selected from our webpage saliency dataset in Figure 5. From the visualization, we could see that our model predicts important texts like title or logo to be more salient than other objects and the background. It highlights all the regions where evident texts and objects locate.

Table 3. The performance of different saliency models on the webpage saliency dataset

Measure	GBVS [13]	AIM [3]	AWS [11]	Signature [15]	SUN [27]	Judd *et. al.* [18]	Our Model
CC	0.1902	0.2625	0.2643	0.2388	0.3137	0.3543	**0.3977**
sAUC	0.5540	0.6566	0.6599	0.6230	0.7099	0.6890	**0.7206**
NSS	0.6620	0.9104	0.9216	0.8284	1.1020	1.0953	**1.2475**

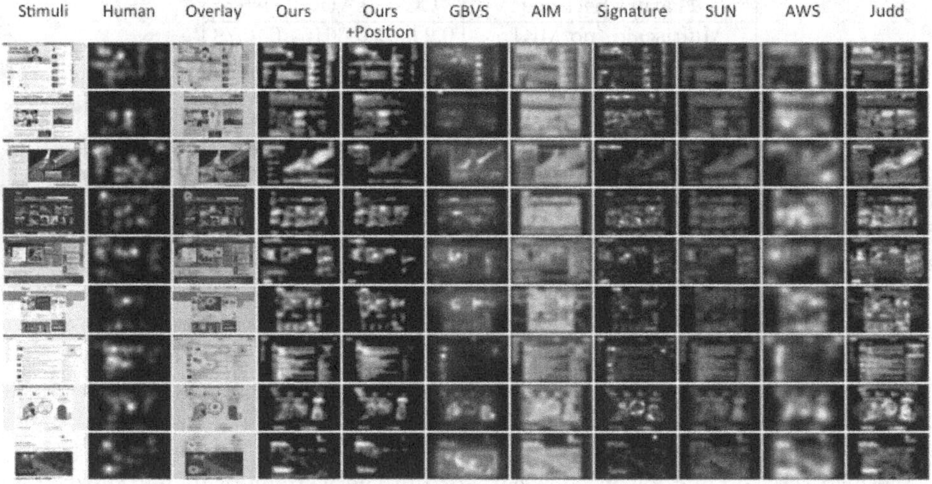

Fig. 5. Qualitative comparisons of the proposed models and the state-of-the-art on the webpage saliency dataset

5   Conclusion

Despite the abundant literature in saliency modeling that predicts where humans look at in a visual scene, there are few studies on saliency in webpages, and we in this work make a first step to the exploration on this topic. Particularly, we build a webpage saliency dataset with 149 webpages from a variety of web sources and collect eye tracking data from 11 subjects free-viewing the images. A saliency model is learned by integrating multi-scale low-level feature representations as well as priors observed web-viewing behavior. MKL is used as the computational technique for a robust integration of features, without assumption of kernel functions. Experiments demonstrate the increased performance of the proposed method, compared with the state-of-the-art in saliency prediction. As far as we know, this is the first computational visual saliency model to predict human attention deployment on webpages, and we expect development along this line to have large commercial values in webpage design and marketing strategy.

Acknowledgement. The authors would like to thank Tong Jun Zhang for his help in data collection and model implementation. The work is supported by the Singapore Ministry of Education Academic Research Fund Tier 1 (No.R-263-000-A49-112).

References

1. Borji, A.: Boosting bottom-up and top-down visual features for saliency estimation. In: 2012 IEEE Conference on Computer Vision and Pattern Recognition (CVPR), pp. 438–445. IEEE (2012)
2. Brainard, D.H.: The psychophysics toolbox. Spatial Vision 10(4), 433–436 (1997)
3. Bruce, N., Tsotsos, J.: Saliency, attention, and visual search: An information theoretic approach. Journal of Vision 9(3) (2009)
4. Buscher, G., Cutrell, E., Morris, M.R.: What do you see when you're surfing?: using eye tracking to predict salient regions of web pages. In: Proceedings of the SIGCHI Conference on Human Factors in Computing Systems, pp. 21–30. ACM (2009)
5. Cerf, M., Harel, J., Einhäuser, W., Koch, C.: Predicting human gaze using low-level saliency combined with face detection. Advances in Neural Information Processing Systems 20 (2008)
6. Cho, C.H., Cheon, H.J.: Why do people avoid advertising on the internet? Journal of Advertising, 89–97 (2004)
7. Cutrell, E., Guan, Z.: What are you looking for?: an eye-tracking study of information usage in web search. In: Proceedings of the SIGCHI Conference on Human Factors in Computing Systems, pp. 407–416. ACM (2007)
8. Derrington, A.M., Krauskopf, J., Lennie, P.: Chromatic mechanisms in lateral geniculate nucleus of macaque. The Journal of Physiology 357(1), 241–265 (1984)
9. Einhäuser, W., Spain, M., Perona, P.: Objects predict fixations better than early saliency. Journal of Vision 8(14) (2008)
10. Faraday, P.: Visually critiquing web pages. In: Multimedia' 89, pp. 155–166. Springer (2000)

11. Garcia-Diaz, A., Leborán, V., Fdez-Vidal, X.R., Pardo, X.M.: On the relationship between optical variability, visual saliency, and eye fixations: A computational approach. Journal of Vision 12(6), 17 (2012)
12. Grier, R., Kortum, P., Miller, J.: How users view web pages: An exploration of cognitive and perceptual mechanisms. In: Human Computer Interaction Research in Web Design and Evaluation, pp. 22–41 (2007)
13. Harel, J., Koch, C., Perona, P.: Graph-based visual saliency. Advances in Neural Information Processing Systems 19, 545 (2007)
14. Hervet, G., Guérard, K., Tremblay, S., Chtourou, M.S.: Is banner blindness genuine? eye tracking internet text advertising. Applied Cognitive Psychology 25(5), 708–716 (2011)
15. Hou, X., Harel, J., Koch, C.: Image signature: Highlighting sparse salient regions. IEEE Transactions on Pattern Analysis and Machine Intelligence 34(1), 194–201 (2012)
16. Itti, L., Koch, C.: A saliency-based search mechanism for overt and covert shifts of visual attention. Vision Research 40(10), 1489–1506 (2000)
17. Itti, L., Koch, C.: Computational modelling of visual attention. Nature Reviews Neuroscience 2(3), 194–203 (2001)
18. Judd, T., Ehinger, K., Durand, F., Torralba, A.: Learning to predict where humans look. In: 2009 IEEE 12th International Conference on Computer Vision, pp. 2106–2113. IEEE (2009)
19. Nielsen, J.: F-shaped pattern for reading web content (2006)
20. Rakotomamonjy, A., Bach, F.R., Canu, S., Grandvalet, Y.: Simplemkl. Journal of Machine Learning Research 9(11) (2008)
21. Still, J.D., Masciocchi, C.M.: A saliency model predicts fixations in web interfaces. In: 5 th International Workshop on Model Driven Development of Advanced User Interfaces (MDDAUI 2010), p. 25 (2010)
22. Stone, B., Dennis, S.: Using lsa semantic fields to predict eye movement on web pages. In: Proc. 29th Cognitive Science Society Conference, pp. 665–670 (2007)
23. Stone, B., Dennis, S.: Semantic models and corpora choice when using semantic fields to predict eye movement on web pages. International Journal of Human-Computer Studies 69(11), 720–740 (2011)
24. Tatler, B.W.: The central fixation bias in scene viewing: Selecting an optimal viewing position independently of motor biases and image feature distributions. Journal of Vision 7(14), 4 (2007)
25. Social usage involves more platforms, more often, http://www.emarketer.com/Article/SocialUsage-Involves-More-Platforms-More-Often/1010019
26. Viola, P., Jones, M.: Rapid object detection using a boosted cascade of simple features. In: Proceedings of the 2001 IEEE Computer Society Conference on Computer Vision and Pattern Recognition, CVPR 2001, vol. 1, p. I–511. IEEE (2001)
27. Zhang, L., Tong, M., Marks, T., Shan, H., Cottrell, G.: Sun: A bayesian framework for saliency using natural statistics. Journal of Vision 8(7) (2008)
28. Zhao, Q., Koch, C.: Learning a saliency map using fixated locations in natural scenes. Journal of Vision 11(3) (2011)
29. Zhao, Q., Koch, C.: Learning visual saliency. In: 2011 45th Annual Conference on Information Sciences and Systems (CISS), pp. 1–6. IEEE (2011)

Deblurring Face Images with Exemplars

Jinshan Pan[1,*], Zhe Hu[2,*], Zhixun Su[1], and Ming-Hsuan Yang[2]

[1] Dalian University of Technology, Dalian, China
[2] University of California, Merced, USA

Abstract. The human face is one of the most interesting subjects involved in numerous applications. Significant progress has been made towards the image deblurring problem, however, existing generic deblurring methods are not able to achieve satisfying results on blurry face images. The success of the state-of-the-art image deblurring methods stems mainly from implicit or explicit restoration of salient edges for kernel estimation. When there is not much texture in the blurry image (e.g., face images), existing methods are less effective as only few edges can be used for kernel estimation. Moreover, recent methods are usually jeopardized by selecting ambiguous edges, which are imaged from the same edge of the object after blur, for kernel estimation due to local edge selection strategies. In this paper, we address these problems of deblurring face images by exploiting facial structures. We propose a maximum a posteriori (MAP) deblurring algorithm based on an exemplar dataset, without using the coarse-to-fine strategy or ad-hoc edge selections. Extensive evaluations against state-of-the-art methods demonstrate the effectiveness of the proposed algorithm for deblurring face images. We also show the extendability of our method to other specific deblurring tasks.

1 Introduction

The goal of image deblurring is to recover the sharp image and the corresponding blur kernel from one blurred input image. The process under a spatially-invariant model is usually formulated as

$$B = I * k + \varepsilon, \tag{1}$$

where I is the latent sharp image, k is the blur kernel, B is the blurred input image, $*$ is the convolution operator, and ε is the noise term. The single image deblurring problem has attracted much attention with significant advances in recent years [5,15,20,3,22,12,13,6,24]. As image deblurring is an ill-posed problem, additional information is required to constrain the solutions. One common approach is to utilize prior knowledge from the statistics of natural images, such as heavy-tailed gradient distributions [5,15,20,14], L_1/L_2 prior [13], and sparsity constraints [1]. While these priors perform well for generic cases, they are not designed to capture image properties for specific object classes, e.g., text and

---

* Both authors contributed equally to this work.

D. Fleet et al. (Eds.): ECCV 2014, Part VII, LNCS 8695, pp. 47–62, 2014.

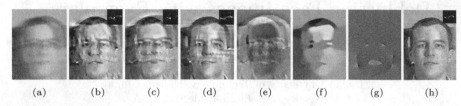

(a)   (b)   (c)   (d)   (e)   (f)   (g)   (h)

Fig. 1. A challenging example. (a) Blurred face image. (b)-(d) are the results of Cho and Lee [3], Krishnan et al. [13], and Xu et al. [24]. (e)-(f) are the intermediate results of Krishnan et al. [13] and Xu et al. [24]. (g) Our predicted salient edges visualized by Poisson reconstruction. (h) Our results (with the support size of 75×75 pixels).

face images. The methods that exploit specific object properties are likely to perform well, e.g., text images [2,19] and low-light images [10]. As the human face is one of the most interesting objects that finds numerous applications, we focus on face image deblurring in this work.

The success of state-of-the-art image deblurring methods hinges on implicit or explicit extraction of salient edges for kernel estimation [3,22,12,24]. Those algorithms employ sharp-edge prediction steps, mainly based on local structure, while not considering the structural information of an object class. This inevitably brings ambiguity to salient-edge selection if only considering local appearance, since multiple blurred edges from the same latent edge could be selected for kernel estimation. Moreover, for blurred images with less texture, the edge prediction step is less likely to provide robust results and usually requires parameter tuning, which would downgrade the performance of these methods. For example, face images have similar components and skin complexion with less texture than natural images, and existing deblurring methods do not perform well on face images. Fig. 1(a) shows a challenging face example which contains scarce texture due to large motion blur. For such images, it is difficult to restore a sufficient number of sharp edges for kernel estimation using the state-of-the-art methods. Fig. 1(b) and (c) show that the state-of-the-art methods based on sparsity prior [13] and explicit edge prediction [3] do not deblur this image well.

In this work, we propose an exemplar-based method for face image deblurring to address the above-mentioned issues. To express the structural information, we collect an exemplar dataset of face images and extract important structures from exemplars. For each test image, we compare it with the exemplars' structure and find the best matched one. The matched structure is used to reconstruct salient edges and guide the kernel estimation process. The proposed method is able to extract good facial structures (Fig. 1(g)) for kernel estimation, and better restore this heavily blurred image (Fig. 1(h)). We will also demonstrate its ability to extend to other objects.

2   Related Work

Image deblurring has been studied extensively and numerous algorithms have been proposed. In this section we discuss the most relevant algorithms and put this work in proper context.

Since blind deblurring is an ill-posed problem, it requires certain assumptions or prior knowledge to constrain the solution space. Early approaches, e.g., [25], usually use the assumptions of simple parametric blur kernels to deblur images, which cannot deal with complex motion blur. As image gradients of natural images can be described well by a heavy-tailed distribution, Fergus et al. [5] use a mixture of Gaussians to learn the prior for deblurring. Similarly, Shan et al. [20] use a parametric model to approximate the heavy-tailed prior of natural images. In [1], Cai et al. assume that the latent images and kernels can be sparsely represented by an over-complete dictionary based on wavelets. On the other hand, it has been shown that the most favorable solution for a MAP deblurring method with sparse prior is usually a blurred image rather than a sharp one [14]. Consequently, an efficient approximation of marginal likelihood deblurring method is proposed in [15]. In addition, different sparsity priors have been introduced for image deblurring. Krishnan et al. [13] present a normalized sparsity prior and Xu et al. [24] use L_0 constraint on image gradients for kernel estimation. Recently, non-parametric patch priors that model appearance of image edges and corners have also been proposed [21] for blur kernel estimation. We note that although the use of sparse priors facilitates kernel estimation, it is likely to fail when the blurred images do not contain rich texture.

In addition to statistical priors, numerous blind deblurring methods explicitly exploit edges for kernel estimation [3,22,12,4]. Joshi et al. [12] and Cho et al. [4] directly use the restored sharp edges from a blurred image for kernel estimation. In [3], Cho and Lee utilize bilateral filter together with shock filter to predict sharp edges. The blur kernel is determined by alternating between restoring sharp edges and estimating the blur kernel in a coarse-to-fine manner. As strong edges extracted from a blurred image are not necessarily useful for kernel estimation, Xu and Jia [22] develop a method to select informative ones for deblurring. Despite demonstrated success, these methods rely largely on heuristic image filtering methods (e.g., shock and bilateral filters) for restoring sharp edges, which are less effective for objects with known geometric structures.

For face image deblurring, there are a few algorithms proposed to boost recognition performance. Nishiyama et al. [17] learn subspaces from blurred face images with known blur kernels for recognition. As the set of blur kernels is pre-defined, the application domain of this approach is limited. Zhang et al. [26] propose a joint image restoration and recognition method based on sparse representation prior. However, this method is most effective for well-cropped face images with limited alignment errors and simple motion blurs.

Recently, HaCohen et al. [8] propose a deblurring method which uses a sharp reference example for guidance. The method requires a reference image with the same content as the input and builds up dense correspondence for reconstruction. It has shown decent results on deblurring specific images, however, the usage of the same-content reference image restrains its applications. Different from this method, we do not require the exemplar to be similar to the input. The blurred face image can be of different identity and background compared to any exemplar images. Moreover, our method only needs the matched contours that encode the

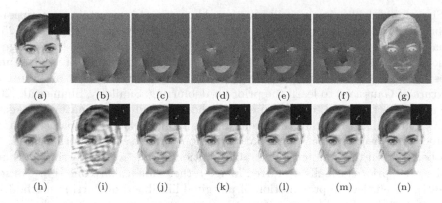

Fig. 2. The influence of salient edges in kernel estimation. (a) True image and kernel. (h) Blurred image. (b)-(f) are extracted salient edges from the clear images visualized by Poisson reconstruction. (g) shows the ground truth edges of (a). (i)-(n) are the results by using edges (b)-(g), respectively.

global structure of the exemplar for kernel estimation, instead of using dense corresponding pixels. In this sense, our method is more general on the object deblurring task with less constraints.

3 Proposed Algorithm

As the kernel estimation problem is non-convex [5,15], most state-of-the-art deblurring methods use coarse-to-fine approaches to refine the estimated kernels. Furthermore, explicit or implicit edge selections are adopted to constrain and converge to feasible solutions. Notwithstanding demonstrated success in deblurring images, these methods are less effective for face images that contain fewer textures. To address these issues, we propose an exemplar-based algorithm to estimate blur kernels for face images. The proposed method extracts good structural information from exemplars to facilitate estimating accurate kernels.

3.1 Structure of Face Images

We first determine the types and number of salient edges for kernel estimation within the context of face deblurring. For face images, the salient edges that capture the object structure could come from the lower face contour, mouth, eyes, nose, eyebrows and hair. As human eyebrows and hair have small edges which could jeopardize the performance [22,11], combined with their large variation, we do not take them into consideration as useful structures. Fig. 2 shows several components extracted from a clear face image as approximations of the latent image for kernel estimation (the extraction step will be described later). We test those edges by posing them as the predicted salient edges in the deblurring framework and estimate the blur kernels according to [15] by

$$k^* = \arg\min_k \|\nabla S * k - \nabla B\|_2^2 + \alpha \|k\|^{0.5}, \tag{2}$$

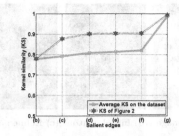

Fig. 3. The relationship between extracted salient edges and kernel estimation accuracy("KS" is the abbreviation of kernel similarity). The notation (b)-(g) for salient edges represent the 6 edge status as Fig. 2(b)-(g).

where ∇S is the gradients of the salient edges extracted from an exemplar image as shown in Fig. 2(b)-(g), ∇B is the gradient computed from the blurred input (Fig. 2(h)), k is the blur kernel, and α is a weight (e.g., 0.005 in this work) for the kernel constraint. The sparse deconvolution method [15] with a hyper-Laplacian prior $L_{0.8}$ is employed to recover the images (Fig. 2(i)-(n)). The results show that the deblurred result using the above-mentioned components (e.g., Fig. 2(l) and (m)), is comparable to that using the ground truth edges (Fig. 2(n)), which is the ideal case for salient edge prediction.

To validate the above-mentioned point, we collect 160 images generated from 20 images (10 images from CMU PIE dataset [7] and 10 images from the Internet) convolving with 8 blur kernels and extract their corresponding edges from different component combination (i.e., Fig. 2(b)-(g)). We conduct the same experiment as Fig. 2, and compute the average accuracy of the estimated kernels in terms of kernel similarity [11]. The curve in Fig. 3 depicts the relationship between the edges of facial components and the accuracy of the estimated kernel. As shown in the figure, the metric tends to converge as all the mentioned components (e.g., Fig. 2(e)) are included, and the set of those edges is sufficient (kernel similarity value of 0.9 in Fig. 3) for accurate kernel estimation.

For real-world applications, the ground-truth edges are not available. Recent methods adopt thresholding or similar techniques to select salient edges for kernel estimation and this inevitably introduces some incorrect edges from a blurred image. Furthermore, the edge selection strategies, either explicitly or implicitly, consider only local edges rather than structural information of a particular object class, e.g., facial components and contour. In contrast, we consider the geometric structures of a face image for kernel estimation. From the experiments with different facial components, we determine that the set of lower face contour, mouth and eyes is sufficient to achieve high-quality kernel estimation and deblurred results. More importantly, these components can also be robustly extracted [28] unlike the other parts (e.g., eyebrows or nose in Fig. 2(a)). Thus, we use these three components as the informative structures for face image deblurring.

(a) Input image   (b) Initial contour   (c) Refined contour

Fig. 4. Extracted salient edges (See Sec. 3.2 for details)

3.2   Exemplar Structures

We collect 2, 435 face images from the CMU PIE dataset [7] as our exemplars. The selected face images are from different identities with variant facial expressions and poses. For each exemplar, we extract the informative structures (i.e., lower face contour, eyes and mouth) as discussed in Sec. 3.1. We manually locate the initial contours of the informative components (Fig. 4(b)), and use the guided filter [9] to refine the contours. The optimal threshold, computed by the Otsu method [18], is applied to each filtered image for the refined contour mask $\mathcal{M}$ of the facial components (Fig. 4(c)). Thus, a set of 2, 435 exemplar structures are generated as the potential facial structure for kernel estimation.

Given a blurred image B, we search for its best matched exemplar structure. We use the maximum response of normalized cross-correlation as the measure to find the best candidate based on their gradients

$$v_i = \max_t \left\{ \frac{\sum_x \nabla B(x) \nabla T_i(x+t)}{\|\nabla B(x)\|_2 \|\nabla T_i(x+t)\|_2} \right\}, \tag{3}$$

where i is the index of the exemplar, $T_i(x)$ is the i-th exemplar, and t is the possible shift between image gradients $\nabla B(x)$ and $\nabla T_i(x)$. If $\nabla B(x)$ is similar to $\nabla T_i(x)$, v_i is large; otherwise, v_i is small. To deal with different scales, we resize each exemplar with sampled scaling factors in the range $[1/2, 2]$ before performing (3). Similarly, we handle rotated faces by testing the rotation angle in [-10, 10] degree.

We denote the predicted salient edges used for kernel estimation as ∇S and it is defined as

$$\nabla S = \nabla S_{i^*}, \tag{4}$$

where $i^* = \arg\max_i v_i$, and $\nabla S_{i^*}(x)$ is computed as

$$\nabla S_{i^*}(x) = \begin{cases} \nabla T_{i^*}(x), & \text{if } x \in \{x | \mathcal{M}_{i^*}(x) = 1\}, \\ 0, & \text{otherwise.} \end{cases} \tag{5}$$

Here $\mathcal{M}_{i^*}$ is the contour mask for i^*-th exemplar. In the experiments, we find that using the edges of exemplars $\nabla T_{i^*}(x)$ as the predicted salient edges performs similarly as that of the input image $\nabla B(x)$, which can be found in Sec. 4. The reason is that $\nabla T_{i^*}(x)$ and $\nabla B(x)$ share similar structures due to the matching step, thus the results using either of them as the guidance are similar.

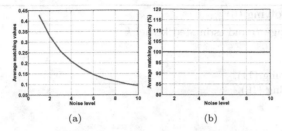

(a)   (b)

Fig. 5. The influence of noise on the proposed matching criterion

We conduct experiments with the quantitative accuracy to verify the effectiveness and robustness of our matching criterion. We collect 100 clear images on 50 identities, with 2 images for each. The images from the same person are different in terms of facial expression and background. In the test phase, we blur one image with random noise as the test image, and pose the others as exemplars. If the matched exemplar is the image from the same person, we mark the matching successful. We perform the test on each images with 8 blur kernels and 11 noise levels (0-10%) and show the matching accuracy in Fig. 5(b). We note that although noise will decrease the average matching values (see Fig. 5(a)), it does not affect the matching accuracy (Fig. 5(b)).

3.3   Kernel Estimation from Exemplar Structure

After obtaining salient edges ∇S, we estimate the blur kernel by alternately solving

$$\min_{I} \|I * k - B\|_2^2 + \lambda \|\nabla I\|_0 \tag{6}$$

and

$$\min_{k} \|\nabla S * k - \nabla B\|_2^2 + \gamma \|k\|_2^2, \tag{7}$$

where λ and γ are parameters for the regularization terms. Here the L_0-norm is employed to restore I and effectively remove some ringing artifacts in I as shown by [23]. In (7), the L_2-norm based regularization is employed to stabilize the blur kernel estimation with a fast solver.

For (6), we employ the half-quadratic splitting L_0 minimization method [23] to solve it. We introduce auxiliary variables $\mathbf{w} = (w_x, w_y)^\top$ corresponding to ∇I and rewrite (6) as

$$\min_{I,\mathbf{w}} \|I * k - B\|_2^2 + \beta \|\mathbf{w} - \nabla I\|_2^2 + \lambda \|\mathbf{w}\|_0, \tag{8}$$

where β is a scalar weight and increases by a factor of 2 over iterations. When β is close to ∞, the solution of (8) approaches that of (6).

We note that (8) can be efficiently solved through alternately minimizing I and $\mathbf{w}$ independently. At each iteration, the solution of I can be obtained by

$$\min_{I} \|I * k - B\|_2^2 + \beta \|\mathbf{w} - \nabla I\|_2^2, \tag{9}$$

Algorithm 1. Solving (6)

Input: Blur image B and estimated kernel k.
$I \leftarrow B$, $\beta \leftarrow 2\lambda$.
repeat
    solve for **w** using (11).
    solve for I using (10).
    $\beta \leftarrow 2\beta$.
until $\beta > 1e^5$
Output: Latent image I.

Algorithm 2. Blur kernel estimation algorithm

Input: Blur image B and predicted salient edges ∇S.
for $l = 1 \rightarrow n$ **do**
    solve for k using (7).
    solve for I using Algorithm 1.
    $\nabla S \leftarrow \nabla I$.
end for
Output: Blur kernel k and intermediate latent image I.

---

which has a closed-form solution computed in the frequency domain by

$$I = \mathcal{F}^{-1}\left(\frac{\overline{\mathcal{F}(k)}\mathcal{F}(B) + \beta(\overline{\mathcal{F}(\partial_x)}\mathcal{F}(w_x) + \overline{\mathcal{F}(\partial_x)}\mathcal{F}(w_y))}{\overline{\mathcal{F}(k)}\mathcal{F}(k) + \beta(\overline{\mathcal{F}(\partial_x)}\mathcal{F}(\partial_x) + \overline{\mathcal{F}(\partial_y)}\mathcal{F}(\partial_y))} \right). \tag{10}$$

Here $\mathcal{F}(\cdot)$ and $\mathcal{F}^{-1}(\cdot)$ denote the Discrete Fourier Transform (DFT) and inverse DFT, respectively, ∂_x and ∂_y denote the vertical and horizontal derivative operators, and the $^-$ is the complex conjugate operator.

Given I, the solution of **w** in (8) can be obtained by

$$\mathbf{w} = \begin{cases} \nabla I, & |\nabla I|^2 \geqslant \frac{\lambda}{\beta}, \\ 0, & \text{otherwise.} \end{cases} \tag{11}$$

The main steps for solving (6) are shown in Algorithm 1.

Based on the above analysis, the main steps for the proposed kernel estimation algorithm are summarized in Algorithm 2. We use the conjugate gradient method to solve the least square problem (7).

3.4 Recovering Latent Image

Once the blur kernel is determined, the latent image can be estimated by a number of non-blind deconvolution methods. In this paper, we use the method with a hyper-Laplacian prior $L_{0.8}$ [16] to recover the latent image.

3.5 Analysis and Discussion

The initial predicted salient edges ∇S play a critical role in kernel estimation. We use an example to demonstrate the effectiveness of the proposed algorithm

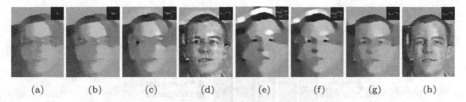

Fig. 6. Results without and with predicted salient edges ∇S. (a)-(c) denote the 1st, 2nd, and 9th iteration intermediate results, respectively, with edge selection method [3] to predict salient edges ∇S in Algorithm 2. (d) Deblurred result with edge selection method [3] to predict salient edges ∇S in Algorithm 2. (e)-(g) denote the 1st, 2nd, and 9th iteration intermediate results, respectively, using our method to predict salient edges ∇S in Algorithm 2. (h) Our deblurred result. The blurred image in this figure is the same as that of Fig. 1.

for predicting initial salient edges ∇S. Fig. 6 shows that the deblurred result using the edge selection method [3] is unsatisfactory as it introduces artifacts by selecting ambiguous edges. However, the proposed method using the facial structure does not introduce ambiguous edges and thus avoids the misleading kernel estimation. Fig. 6(e)-(g) also demonstrate that the correct predicted salient edges ∇S lead to fast convergence.

We note that the proposed algorithm does not require coarse-to-fine kernel estimation strategies or ad-hoc edge selections. The coarse-to-fine strategy can be viewed as the initialization for the finer levels, which both constrains the solution and reduces the computational load. Recent results of several state-of-the-art methods [3,13,24] show that good salient edges at the initial stage are important for kernel estimation. If good initial edges can be obtained, it is not necessary to use coarse-to-fine strategies and specific edge selection, thereby simplifying the kernel estimation process significantly. Our method acts on the original scale only and exploits the exemplar-based structure information to regularize the solution. Benefiting from the facial structure, the proposed method performs well from the beginning without a coarse-to-fine strategy and achieves fast convergence. In the method [3], blur kernels are estimated in a coarse-to-fine manner based on an ad-hoc edge selection strategy. However, it is difficult to select salient edges from severely blurred images without exploiting any structural information (Fig. 6(a)). Comparing to the intermediate results using L_0 prior (Fig. 1(f)), our method maintains the facial components well (Fig. 6(g)), which boosts the performance of kernel estimation and the image restoration.

Robustness of Exemplar Structures: We use (3) to find the best matched exemplar in gradient space. If the face contour in the latent image is salient, it would present more saliently than other edges after blur. Thus the matched exemplar should share similar parts of the contours with the input, although not perfectly (e.g., Fig. 1(g)). Moreover, the shared contours encode global structures and do not contain many false salient edges caused by blur. We also note that most mismatched contours caused by facial expressions correspond to the small gradients in blurred images. In this situation, these components exert little

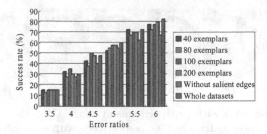

Fig. 7. Robustness to the size of dataset

effect on the kernel estimation according to the edge based methods [3,22]. To alleviate the problem, we update exemplar edges during the iteration to increase its reliability as shown in Fig. 6(e)-(g). For these reasons, along with the fact that a few correct contours would lead to high-quality kernel estimation, the matched exemplar guides kernel estimation well.

Robustness to Dataset: Large dataset will provide reliable results in an exemplar-based method. However, since our method only requires partial matched contours as the initialization, it does not require a huge dataset for good results. To test the sensitivity, we evaluate our method with different numbers of exemplars. We use the k-means method on the exemplar dataset, and choose 40, 80, 100, and 200 clustering centers as the new exemplar datasets, respectively. Similar to [14], we generate 40 blurred images consisting of 5 images (of different identities as the exemplars) with 8 blur kernels for test. The cumulative error ratio [14] is used to evaluate the method. Fig. 7 shows that the proposed method can provide good results with very few exemplars (e.g., 40). With the increasing size of the exemplar dataset, the estimated results do not change significantly, which demonstrates the robustness of our method to the size of dataset.

Robustness to Noise: If the blurred image contains severe noise, several edge selection methods [3,22] and other state-of-the-art methods (e.g., [15,13,24]) may not provide reliable edge information for kernel estimation. However, our method will not be affected much due to the robustness of our matching criterion (See analysis in Sec. 3.2). We will show some examples in Sec. 4.

4   Experimental Results

In all the experiments, the parameters λ, γ and n are set to be 0.002, 1 and 50, respectively. We implement Algorithm 2 in MATLAB, and it takes about 27 seconds to process a blurred image of 320×240 pixels on an Intel Xeon CPU with 12 GB RAM. The MATLAB code and dataset are available at http://eng.ucmerced.edu/people/zhu/eccv14_facedeblur. As the method of [8] requires a reference image with same content as the blurred image which is not practical, we do not compare to [8] in this section, but we provide some comparisons in the supplementary material.

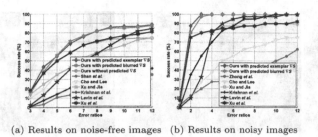

(a) Results on noise-free images   (b) Results on noisy images

Fig. 8. Quantitative comparisons with several state-of-the-art single-image blind deblurring methods: Shan et al. [20], Cho and Lee [3], Xu and Jia [22], Krishnan et al. [13], Levin et al. [15], Zhong et al. [27], and Xu et al. [24].

Synthetic Dataset: For quantitative evaluations, we collect a dataset of 60 clear face images and 8 ground truth kernels in a way similar to [14] to generate a test set of 480 blurred inputs. We evaluate the proposed algorithm against state-of-the-art methods based on edge selection [3,22] and sparsity prior [20,13,15,24] using the error metric proposed by Levin et al. [14]. Fig. 8 shows the cumulative error ratio where higher curves indicate more accurate results. The proposed algorithm generates better results than state-of-the-art methods for face image deblurring. The results show the advantages of using the global structure as the guidance comparing with those using local edge selection methods [3,22,24]. We also test different strategies for computing the predicted edges ∇S: 1) using the edges of exemplars $\nabla T_{i*}(x)$ as ∇S (original); 2) using the edges of the input image $\nabla B(x)$ as ∇S; 3) not using ∇S at all. The first two approaches perform similarly as $\nabla B(x)$ and the matched $\nabla T_{i*}(x)$ share partial structures, which also demonstrates the effectiveness of our matching step. Compared to the results without predicted edges ∇S, the ones using the predicted edges are significantly improved as shown in Fig. 8(a). It is noted that our method without predicted ∇S does not use coarse-to-fine strategy and generates similar results to [24], which indicates that the coarse-to-fine strategy does not help the kernel estimation much on face images with few textures.

To test the robustness to noise, we add 1% random noise to the test images and present the quantitative comparisons in Fig. 8(b). Compared to other state-of-the-arts methods, our method is robust to noise. We note that the results on noise images are of higher curve than that of noise-free images. The reason is that a noisy input increases the denominator value of the measure [14]. Thus the error ratios from noisy images are usually smaller than those from noise-free images, under the same blur kernel.

We show one example from the test dataset in Fig. 9 for discussion. The sparsity-prior-based methods [20,13] generate deblurred images with significant artifacts as the generic priors are not effective for kernel estimation when blurred images do not contain rich texture. Edge based methods [3,22] do not perform well for face deblurring as the assumption that there exists a sufficient number of sharp edges in the latent images does not hold. Compared to the method [24] based on an L_0-regularized method, the results by our method contain fewer

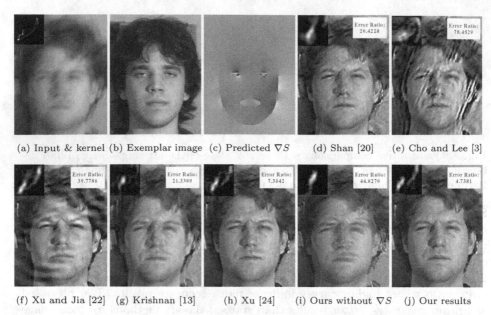

(a) Input & kernel (b) Exemplar image (c) Predicted ∇S (d) Shan [20]   (e) Cho and Lee [3]

(f) Xu and Jia [22] (g) Krishnan [13]   (h) Xu [24]   (i) Ours without ∇S (j) Our results

Fig. 9. An example from the synthesized test dataset

visual artifacts with lower error. Although the best matched exemplar is from a different person (the identities of exemplar and test sets are not overlapped) with different facial expressions, the main structures of Fig. 9(a) and (b) are similar, e.g., the lower face contours and upper eye contours. This also indicates that our approach via (3) is able to find the image with similar structure. The results shown in Fig. 9(i) and (j) demonstrate that the predicted salient edges significantly improve the accuracy of kernel estimation, while the kernel estimation result without predicted salient edges looks like a delta kernel. Although our method is also MAP-based, the predicted salient edges based on the matched exemplar provide good initialization for kernel estimation such that the delta kernel solution (e.g., Fig. 9(i)) is not preferred.

Real Images: We have evaluated the proposed algorithm on real blurred images and show some comparisons with the state-of-the-art deblurring methods. In this example, the input image (Fig. 10(a)) contains some noise and several saturated pixels. The results of [20,3,22,13,27] are not favorable with obvious noise and ringing artifacts. The proposed method generates a deblurred result with fewer visual artifacts and finer details compared with other methods despite the best matched exemplar visually bearing partial resemblance to the input image.

Fig. 11(a) shows another example of a real captured image. The edge selection methods [3,22] do not perform well as ambiguous edges are selected for kernel estimation. Similarly, the sparsity prior based methods [20,13,24] do not perform well with unpleasant artifacts, while our method generates decent results.

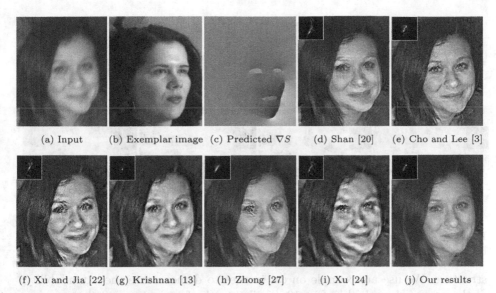

(a) Input   (b) Exemplar image (c) Predicted ∇S (d) Shan [20]   (e) Cho and Lee [3]

(f) Xu and Jia [22]   (g) Krishnan [13]   (h) Zhong [27]   (i) Xu [24]   (j) Our results

Fig. 10. Real captured example with some noise and saturated pixels. The support size is 35×35 pixels.

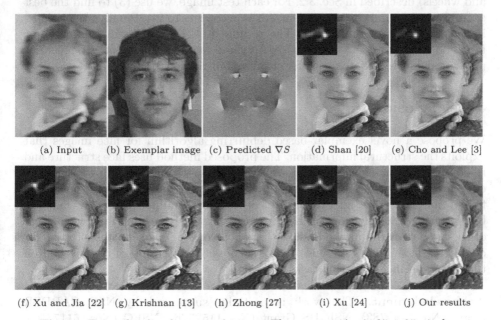

(a) Input   (b) Exemplar image (c) Predicted ∇S (d) Shan [20]   (e) Cho and Lee [3]

(f) Xu and Jia [22]   (g) Krishnan [13]   (h) Zhong [27]   (i) Xu [24]   (j) Our results

Fig. 11. Example of real captured image. The support size is 25×25 pixels.

4.1 Extension of the Proposed Method

In this work, we focus on face image deblurring, as it is of great interest with numerous applications. However, our exemplar-based method can be applied to other deblurring tasks by simply preparing exemplars with the extracted

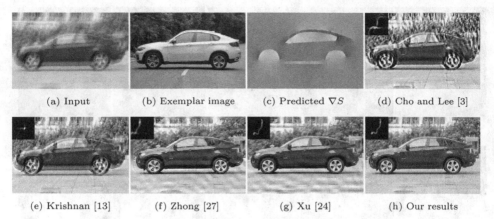

| (a) Input | (b) Exemplar image | (c) Predicted ∇S | (d) Cho and Lee [3] |
| (e) Krishnan [13] | (f) Zhong [27] | (g) Xu [24] | (h) Our results |

Fig. 12. Our exemplar-based method on car image. Our method generates the deblurred result with fewer ringing artifacts.

structure. We use an example on car images to demonstrate the extendability of the proposed method in Fig. 12. Similar to the face images, we first prepare some exemplar images and extract the main structures (e.g., car body, windows and wheels) described in Sec. 3.2. For each test image, we use (3) to find the best exemplar image and compute salient edges according to (4). Finally, Algorithm 2 is used to generate the results. The results of [3,13,24,27] still contain some blur and ringing artifacts. Compared to these methods, our method generates pleasant deblurred results with fewer noise and ringing artifacts.

5   Conclusion

We propose a novel exemplar-based deblurring algorithm for face images that exploits the structural information. The proposed method uses face structure and reliable edges from exemplars for kernel estimation without resorting to complex edge predictions. Our method generates good initialization without coarse-to-fine optimization strategies to enforce convergence, and performs well when the blurred images do not contain rich textures. Extensive evaluations with state-of-the-art deblurring methods show that the proposed algorithm is effective for deblurring face images. We also show the possible extension of our method on the other specific deblurring tasks.

Acknowledgment. The work is partially supported by NSF CAREER Grant (No. 1149783), NSF IIS Grant (No. 1152576), NSFC (Nos. 61173103, 61300086, and 91230103), and National Science and Technology Major Project (2013ZX04005021).

References

1. Cai, J.F., Ji, H., Liu, C., Shen, Z.: Framelet based blind motion deblurring from a single image. IEEE Trans. Image Process. 21(2), 562–572 (2012)
2. Cho, H., Wang, J., Lee, S.: Text image deblurring using text-specific properties. In: Fitzgibbon, A., Lazebnik, S., Perona, P., Sato, Y., Schmid, C. (eds.) ECCV 2012, Part V. LNCS, vol. 7576, pp. 524–537. Springer, Heidelberg (2012)
3. Cho, S., Lee, S.: Fast motion deblurring. ACM Trans. Graph. 28(5), 145 (2009)
4. Cho, T.S., Paris, S., Horn, B.K.P., Freeman, W.T.: Blur kernel estimation using the radon transform. In: CVPR, pp. 241–248 (2011)
5. Fergus, R., Singh, B., Hertzmann, A., Roweis, S.T., Freeman, W.T.: Removing camera shake from a single photograph. ACM Trans. Graph. 25(3), 787–794 (2006)
6. Goldstein, A., Fattal, R.: Blur-kernel estimation from spectral irregularities. In: Fitzgibbon, A., Lazebnik, S., Perona, P., Sato, Y., Schmid, C. (eds.) ECCV 2012, Part V. LNCS, vol. 7576, pp. 622–635. Springer, Heidelberg (2012)
7. Gross, R., Matthews, I., Cohn, J.F., Kanade, T., Baker, S.: Multi-pie. In: FG, pp. 1–8 (2008)
8. HaCohen, Y., Shechtman, E., Lischinski, D.: Deblurring by example using dense correspondence. In: ICCV, pp. 2384–2391 (2013)
9. He, K., Sun, J., Tang, X.: Guided image filtering. In: Daniilidis, K., Maragos, P., Paragios, N. (eds.) ECCV 2010, Part I. LNCS, vol. 6311, pp. 1–14. Springer, Heidelberg (2010)
10. Hu, Z., Cho, S., Wang, J., Yang, M.-H.: Deblurring low-light images with light streaks. In: CVPR, pp. 3382–3389 (2014)
11. Hu, Z., Yang, M.-H.: Good regions to deblur. In: Fitzgibbon, A., Lazebnik, S., Perona, P., Sato, Y., Schmid, C. (eds.) ECCV 2012, Part V. LNCS, vol. 7576, pp. 59–72. Springer, Heidelberg (2012)
12. Joshi, N., Szeliski, R., Kriegman, D.J.: PSF estimation using sharp edge prediction. In: CVPR, pp. 1–8 (2008)
13. Krishnan, D., Tay, T., Fergus, R.: Blind deconvolution using a normalized sparsity measure. In: CVPR, pp. 2657–2664 (2011)
14. Levin, A., Weiss, Y., Durand, F., Freeman, W.T.: Understanding and evaluating blind deconvolution algorithms. In: CVPR, pp. 1964–1971 (2009)
15. Levin, A., Weiss, Y., Durand, F., Freeman, W.T.: Efficient marginal likelihood optimization in blind deconvolution. In: CVPR, pp. 2657–2664 (2011)
16. Levin, A., Fergus, R., Durand, F., Freeman, W.T.: Image and depth from a conventional camera with a coded aperture. ACM Trans. Graph. 26(3), 70 (2007)
17. Nishiyama, M., Hadid, A., Takeshima, H., Shotton, J., Kozakaya, T., Yamaguchi, O.: Facial deblur inference using subspace analysis for recognition of blurred faces. IEEE Trans. Pattern Anal. Mach. Intell. 33(4), 838–845 (2011)
18. Otsu, N.: A threshold selection method from gray-level histograms. IEEE Trans. Syst., Man, and Cybern. 9(9), 62–66 (1979)
19. Pan, J., Hu, Z., Su, Z., Yang, M.-H.: Deblurring text images via L_0-regularized intensity and gradient prior. In: CVPR, pp. 2901–2908 (2014)
20. Shan, Q., Jia, J., Agarwala, A.: High-quality motion deblurring from a single image. ACM Trans. Graph. 27(3), 73 (2008)
21. Sun, L., Cho, S., Wang, J., Hays, J.: Edge-based blur kernel estimation using patch priors. In: ICCP, pp. 1–8 (2013)
22. Xu, L., Jia, J.: Two-phase kernel estimation for robust motion deblurring. In: Daniilidis, K., Maragos, P., Paragios, N. (eds.) ECCV 2010, Part I. LNCS, vol. 6311, pp. 157–170. Springer, Heidelberg (2010)

23. Xu, L., Lu, C., Xu, Y., Jia, J.: Image smoothing via L_0 gradient minimization. ACM Trans. Graph. 30(6), 174 (2011)
24. Xu, L., Zheng, S., Jia, J.: Unnatural L_0 sparse representation for natural image deblurring. In: CVPR, pp. 1107–1114 (2013)
25. Yitzhaky, Y., Mor, I., Lantzman, A., Kopeika, N.S.: Direct method for restoration of motion-blurred images. J. Opt. Soc. Am. A 15(6), 1512–1519 (1998)
26. Zhang, H., Yang, J., Zhang, Y., Huang, T.S.: Close the loop: joint blind image restoration and recognition with sparse representation prior. In: ICCV, pp. 770–777 (2011)
27. Zhong, L., Cho, S., Metaxas, D., Paris, S., Wang, J.: Handling noise in single image deblurring using directional filters. In: CVPR, pp. 612–619 (2013)
28. Zhu, X., Ramanan, D.: Face detection, pose estimation, and landmark localization in the wild. In: CVPR, pp. 2879–2886 (2012)

Sparse Spatio-spectral Representation for Hyperspectral Image Super-resolution

Naveed Akhtar, Faisal Shafait, and Ajmal Mian

School of Computer Science and Software Engineering,
The University of Western Australia,
35 Stirling Highway, 6009 Crawley WA
naveed.akhtar@research.uwa.edu.au,
{faisal.shafait,ajmal.mian}@uwa.edu.au

Abstract. Existing hyperspectral imaging systems produce low spatial resolution images due to hardware constraints. We propose a sparse representation based approach for hyperspectral image super-resolution. The proposed approach first extracts distinct reflectance spectra of the scene from the available hyperspectral image. Then, the signal sparsity, non-negativity and the spatial structure in the scene are exploited to explain a high-spatial but low-spectral resolution image of the same scene in terms of the extracted spectra. This is done by learning a sparse code with an algorithm G-SOMP+. Finally, the learned sparse code is used with the extracted scene spectra to estimate the super-resolution hyperspectral image. Comparison of the proposed approach with the state-of-the-art methods on both ground-based and remotely-sensed public hyperspectral image databases shows that the presented method achieves the lowest error rate on all test images in the three datasets.

Keywords: Hyperspectral, super-resolution, spatio-spectral, sparse representation.

1 Introduction

Hyperspectral imaging acquires a faithful representation of the scene radiance by integrating it against several basis functions that are well localized in the spectral domain. The spectral characteristics of the resulting representation have proven critical in numerous applications, ranging from remote sensing [6], [3] to medical imaging [16]. They have also been reported to improve the performance in computer vision tasks, such as, tracking [23], segmentation [25], recognition [29] and document analysis [18]. However, contemporary hyperspectral imaging lacks severely in terms of spatial resolution [16], [13]. The problem stems from the fact that each spectral image acquired by a hyperspectral system corresponds to a *very narrow* spectral window. Thus, the system must use long exposures to collect enough photons to maintain a good signal-to-noise ratio of the spectral images. This results in low spatial resolution of the hyperspectral images.

Normally, spatial resolution can be improved with high resolution sensors. However, this solution is not too effective for hyperspectral imaging, as it further

D. Fleet et al. (Eds.): ECCV 2014, Part VII, LNCS 8695, pp. 63–78, 2014.

reduces the density of the photons reaching the sensor. Keeping in view the hardware limitations, it is highly desirable to develop software based techniques to enhance the spatial resolution of hyperspectral images. In comparison to the hyperspectral systems, the low spectral resolution imaging systems (e.g. RGB cameras) perform a gross quantization of the scene radiance - loosing most of the spectral information. However, these systems are able to preserve much finer spatial information of the scenes. Intuitively, images acquired by these systems can help in improving the spatial resolution of the hyperspectral images.

This work develops a sparse representation [24] based approach for hyperspectral image super-resolution, using a high-spatial but low-spectral resolution image (henceforth, only called the *high spatial resolution image*) of the same scene. The proposed approach uses the hyperspectral image to extract the reflectance spectra related to the scene. This is done by solving a constrained sparse representation problem using the hyperspectral image as the input. The basis formed by these spectra is transformed according to the spectral quantization of the high spatial resolution image. Then, the said image and the transformed basis are fed to a simultaneous sparse approximation algorithm G-SOMP+. Our algorithm is a generalization of Simultaneous Orthogonal Matching Pursuit (SOMP) [28] that additionally imposes a non-negativity constraint over its solution space. Taking advantage of the spatial structure in the scene, G-SOMP+ efficiently learns a sparse code. This sparse code is used with the reflectance spectra of the scene to estimate the super-resolution hyperspectral image. We test our approach using the hyperspectral images of objects, real-world indoor and outdoor scenes and remotely sensed hyperspectral image. Results of the experiments show that the proposed approach consistently performs better than the existing methods on all the data sets.

This paper is organized as follows. Section 2 reviews the previous literature related to the proposed approach. We formalize our problem in Section 3. The proposed solution is described in Section 4 of the paper. In Section 5, we give the results of the experiments that have been performed to evaluate the approach. We dedicate Section 6 for the discussion on the results and the parameter settings. The paper concludes with a brief summary in Section 7.

2   Related Work

Hardware limitations have lead to a notable amount of research in software based techniques for high spatial resolution hyperspectral imaging. The software based approaches that use image fusion [31] as a tool, are particularly relevant to our work. Most of these approaches have originated in the remote sensing literature because of the early introduction of hyperspectral imaging in the airborne/spaceborne observatory systems. In order to enhance the spatial resolution of the hyperspectral images these approaches usually fuse a hyperspectral image with a high spatial resolution pan-chromatic image. This process is known as pan-sharpening [5]. A popular technique ([9], [2], [14], [20]) uses a linear transformation of the color coordinates to improve the spatial resolution of hyperspectral images. Exploiting the fact that human vision is more sensitive to luminance, this technique fuses the luminance component of a high resolution image with the hyperspectral image. Generally, this improves the spatial resolution of the hyperspectral image, however the resulting image is sometimes spectrally distorted [10].

In spatio-spectral image fusion, one class of methods exploits unmixing ([22], [35]) for improving the spatial resolution of the hyperspectral images. These methods only perform well for the cases when the spectral resolutions of the two images are not too different. Furthermore, their performance is compromised in highly mixed scenarios [13]. Zurita-Milla et al. [36] employed a sliding window strategy to mitigate this issue. Image filtering is also used for interpolating the spectral images to improve the spatial resolution [19]. In this case, the implicit assumption of smooth spatial patterns in the scenes often produces overly smooth images.

More recently, matrix factorization has played an important role in enhancing the spatial resolution of the ground based and the remote sensing hyperspectral imaging systems ([16], [13], [32], [34]). Kawakami et al. [16] have proposed to fuse a high spatial resolution RGB image with a hyperspectral image by decomposing each of the two images into two factors and constructing the desired image from the complementary factors of the two decompositions. A very similar technique has been used by Huang et al. [13] for remote sensing data. The main difference between [16] and [13] is that the latter uses a spatially down-sampled version of the high spatial resolution image in the matrix factorization process. Wycoff et al. [32] have proposed an algorithm based on Alternating Direction Method of Multipliers (ADMM) [7] for the factorization of the matrices and later using it to fuse the hyperspectral image with an RGB image. Yokoya et al. [34] have proposed a coupled matrix factorization approach to fuse multi-spectral and hyperspectral remote sensing images to improve the spatial resolution of the hyperspectral images.

The matrix factorization based methods are closely related to our approach. However, our approach has major differences with each one of them. Contrary to these methods, we exploit the spatial structure in the high spatial resolution image for the improved performance. The proposed approach also takes special care of the physical significance of the signals and the processes related to the problem. This makes our formalization of the problem and its solution unique. We make use of the non-negativity of the signals, whereas [16] and [13] do not consider this notion at all. In [32] and [34] the authors do consider the non-negativity of the signals, however their approaches require the down sampling matrix that converts the high resolution RGB image to the corresponding bands of the low resolution hyperspectral image. Our approach does not impose any such requirement.

3   Problem Formulation

We seek estimation of a super-resolution hyperspectral image $\mathbf{S} \in \mathbb{R}^{M \times N \times L}$, where M and N denote the spatial dimensions and L represents the spectral dimension, from an acquired hyperspectral image $\mathbf{Y}_h \in \mathbb{R}^{m \times n \times L}$ and a corresponding high spatial (but low spectral) resolution image of the same scene $\mathbf{Y} \in \mathbb{R}^{M \times N \times l}$. For our problem, $m \ll M, n \ll N$ and $l \ll L$, which makes the problem severely ill-posed. We consider both of the available images to be linear mappings of the target image:

$$\mathbf{Y} = \Psi(\mathbf{S}), \quad \mathbf{Y}_h = \Psi_h(\mathbf{S}) \tag{1}$$

where, $\Psi : \mathbb{R}^{M \times N \times L} \rightarrow \mathbb{R}^{M \times N \times l}$ and $\Psi_h : \mathbb{R}^{M \times N \times L} \rightarrow \mathbb{R}^{m \times n \times L}$.

A typical scene of the ground based imagery as well as the space-borne/airborne imagery contains only a small number of distinct materials [4], [17]. If the scene contains q materials, the linear mixing model (LMM) [15] can be used to approximate a pixel $\mathbf{y}_h \in \mathbb{R}^L$ of $\mathbf{Y}_h$ as

$$\mathbf{y}_h \approx \sum_{\omega=1}^{c} \varphi_\omega \alpha_\omega \ , \ c \leq q \tag{2}$$

where, $\varphi_\omega \in \mathbb{R}^L$ denotes the reflectance of the ω-th distinct material in the scene and α_ω is the *fractional abundance* (i.e. proportion) of that material in the area corresponding to the pixel. We rewrite (2) in the following matrix form:

$$\mathbf{y}_h \approx \boldsymbol{\Phi}\boldsymbol{\alpha} \tag{3}$$

In (3), the columns of $\boldsymbol{\Phi} \in \mathbb{R}^{L \times c}$ represent the reflectance vectors of the underlying materials and $\boldsymbol{\alpha} \in \mathbb{R}^c$ is the coefficient vector. Notice that, when the scene represented by a pixel $\mathbf{y}_h$ also includes the area corresponding to a pixel $\mathbf{y} \in \mathbb{R}^l$ of $\mathbf{Y}$, we can approximate $\mathbf{y}$ as

$$\mathbf{y} \approx (\mathbf{T}\boldsymbol{\Phi})\boldsymbol{\beta} \tag{4}$$

where, $\mathbf{T} \in \mathbb{R}^{l \times L}$ is a transformation matrix and $\boldsymbol{\beta} \in \mathbb{R}^c$ is the coefficient vector. In (4), $\mathbf{T}$ is a highly rank deficient matrix that relates the spectral quantization of the hyperspectral imaging system to the high spatial resolution imaging system. Using the associativity between the matrices:

$$\mathbf{y} \approx \mathbf{T}(\boldsymbol{\Phi}\boldsymbol{\beta}) \approx \mathbf{Ts} \tag{5}$$

where, $\mathbf{s} \in \mathbb{R}^L$ denotes the pixel in the target image $\mathbf{S}$. Equation (5) suggests, if $\boldsymbol{\Phi}$ is known, the super-resolution hyperspectral image can be estimated using an appropriate coefficient matrix without the need of computing the inverse (i.e. pseudo-inverse) of $\mathbf{T}$, which is a highly rank deficient matrix.

4   Proposed Solution

Let $\mathcal{D}$ be a finite collection of unit-norm vectors in $\mathbb{R}^L$. In our settings, $\mathcal{D}$ is the *dictionary* whose elements (i.e. the *atoms*) are denoted by φ_ω, where ω ranges over an index set Ω. More precisely, $\mathcal{D} \overset{\text{def}}{=} \{\varphi_\omega : \omega \in \Omega\} \subset \mathbb{R}^L$. Considering (3)-(5), we are interested in forming the matrix $\boldsymbol{\Phi}$ from $\mathcal{D}$, such that

$$\bar{\mathbf{Y}}_h \approx \boldsymbol{\Phi}\mathbf{A} \tag{6}$$

where, $\bar{\mathbf{Y}}_h \in \mathbb{R}^{L \times mn}$ is the matrix formed by concatenating the pixels of the hyperspectral image $\mathbf{Y}_h$ and $\mathbf{A}$ is the coefficient matrix with α_i as its ith column. We propose to draw $\boldsymbol{\Phi}$ from $\mathbb{R}^{L \times k}$, such that $k > q$; see (2). This is because, the LMM in (2) approximates a pixel assuming *linear* mixing of the material reflectances. In the real world, phenomena like multiple light scattering and existence of intimate material mixtures also cause non-linear mixing of the spectral signatures [15]. This usually alters the reflectance spectrum of a material or results in multiple distinct reflectance spectra of the same material in the scene. The matrix $\boldsymbol{\Phi}$ must also account for these spectra. Henceforth, we use the term *dictionary* for the matrix $\boldsymbol{\Phi}^1$.

According to the model in (6), each column of $\bar{\mathbf{Y}}_h$ is constructed using a very small number of dictionary atoms. Furthermore, the atoms of the dictionary are non-negative vectors as they correspond to reflectance spectra. Therefore, we propose to solve the following constrained sparse representation problem to learn the proposed dictionary $\boldsymbol{\Phi}$:

$$\min_{\boldsymbol{\Phi},\mathbf{A}} ||\mathbf{A}||_1 \text{ s.t. } ||\bar{\mathbf{Y}}_h - \boldsymbol{\Phi}\mathbf{A}||_F \leq \eta, \varphi_\omega \geq 0, \forall \omega \in \{1, ..., k\} \tag{7}$$

where, $||.||_1$ and $||.||_F$ denote the element-wise l_1 norm and the Forbenious norm of the matrices respectively, and η represents the modeling error. To solve (7) we use the online dictionary learning approach proposed by Mairal et al. [21] with an additional non-negativtiy constraint on the dictionary atoms - we refer the reader to the original work for details.

Once $\boldsymbol{\Phi}$ is known, we must compute an appropriate coefficient matrix $\mathbf{B} \in \mathbb{R}^{k \times MN}$; as suggested by (5), to estimate the target image $\mathbf{S}$. This matrix is computed using the learned dictionary and the image $\mathbf{Y}$ along with two important pieces of prior information. a) In the high spatial resolution image, nearby pixels are likely to represent the same materials in the scene. Hence, they should be well approximated by a small group of the same dictionary atoms. b) The elements of $\mathbf{B}$ must be non-negative quantities because they represent the fractional abundances of the spectral signal sources in the scene. It is worth mentioning that we could also use (b) for $\mathbf{A}$ in (7), however, there we were interested only in $\boldsymbol{\Phi}$. Therefore, a non-negativity constraint over $\mathbf{A}$ was unnecessary. Neglecting this constraint in (7) additionally provides computational advantages in solving the optimization problem.

Considering (a), we process the image $\mathbf{Y}$ in terms of small disjoint spatial patches for computing the coefficient matrix. We denote each of the image patch by $\mathbf{P} \in \mathbb{R}^{M_P \times N_P \times l}$ and estimate its corresponding coefficient matrix

---

[1] Formally, $\boldsymbol{\Phi}$ is the *dictionary synthesis matrix* [28]. However, we follow the convention of the previous literature in dictionary learning (e.g. [1], [27]), which rarely distinguishes the synthesis matrix from the dictionary.

$\mathbf{B}_P \in \mathbb{R}^{k \times M_P N_P}$ by solving the following constrained simultaneous sparse approximation problem:

$$\min_{\mathbf{B}_P} ||\mathbf{B}_P||_{row\_0} \text{ s.t. } ||\bar{\mathbf{P}} - \widetilde{\boldsymbol{\Phi}} \mathbf{B}_P||_F \leq \varepsilon, \ \boldsymbol{\beta}_{p_i} \geq \mathbf{0} \ \forall i \in \{1, ..., M_P N_P\} \qquad (8)$$

where, $\bar{\mathbf{P}} \in \mathbb{R}^{l \times M_P N_P}$ is formed by concatenating the pixels in $\mathbf{P}$, $\widetilde{\boldsymbol{\Phi}} \in \mathbb{R}^{l \times k}$ is the transformed dictionary i.e. $\widetilde{\boldsymbol{\Phi}} = \mathbf{T}\boldsymbol{\Phi}$; see (4), and $\boldsymbol{\beta}_{p_i}$ denotes the ith column of the matrix $\mathbf{B}_p$. In the above objective function, $||.||_{row\_0}$ denotes the row-l_0 quasi-norm [28] of the matrix, which represents the cardinality of its row-support[2]. Formally,

$$||\mathbf{B}_p||_{row\_0} \stackrel{\text{def}}{=} \left| \bigcup_{i=1}^{M_P N_p} \text{supp}(\boldsymbol{\beta}_{p_i}) \right|$$

where, supp(.) indicates the support of a vector and $|.|$ denotes the cardinality of a set. Tropp [27] has argued that (8) is an NP-hard problem without the non-negativity constraint. The combinatorial complexity of the problem does not change with the non-negativity constraint over the coefficient matrix. Therefore, the problem must either be relaxed [27] or solved by the greedy pursuit strategy [28]. We prefer the latter because of its computational advantages [8] and propose a simultaneous greedy pursuit algorithm, called G-SOMP+, for solving (8). The proposed algorithm is a generalization of a popular greedy pursuit algorithm Simultaneous Orthogonal Matching Pursuit (SOMP) [28], which additionally constrains the solution space to non-negative matrices. Hence, we denote it as G-SOMP+. Here, the notion of 'generalization' is similar to the one used in [30] that allows selection of multiple dictionary atoms in each iteration of Orthogonal Matching Pursuit (OMP) [26] to generalize OMP.

G-SOMP+ is given below as Algorithm 1. The algorithm seeks an approximation of the input matrix $\bar{\mathbf{P}}$ - henceforth, called the *patch* - by selecting the dictionary atoms $\tilde{\varphi}_\xi$ indexed in a set $\Xi \subset \Omega$, such that, $|\Xi| \ll |\Omega|$ and every $\tilde{\varphi}_\xi$ contributes to the approximation of the *whole* patch. In its ith iteration, the algorithm first computes the cumulative correlation of each dictionary atom with the residue of its current approximation of the patch (line 5 in Algorithm 1) - the patch itself is considered as the residue for initialization. Then, it identifies L (an algorithm parameter) dictionary atoms with the highest cumulative correlations. These atoms are added to a subspace indexed in a set Ξ^i, which is empty at initialization. The aforementioned subspace is then used for a non-negative least squares approximation of the patch (line 8 in Algorithm 1) and the residue is updated. The algorithm stops if the updated residue is more than a fraction γ of the residue in the previous iteration. Note that, the elements of the set Ξ in G-SOMP+ also denote the row-support of the coefficient matrix. This is because, a dictionary atom can only participate in the patch approximation if the corresponding row of the coefficient matrix has some non-zero element in it. G-SOMP+ has three major differences from SOMP. 1) Instead of integrating the

---

[2] Set of indices for the non-zero rows of the matrix.

Algorithm 1. G-SOMP+

Initializaiton:

1: Iteration: $i = 0$
2: Initial solution: $\mathbf{B}^0 = \mathbf{0}$
3: Initial residue: $\mathbf{R}^0 = \bar{\mathbf{P}} - \widetilde{\boldsymbol{\Phi}}\mathbf{B}^0 = \bar{\mathbf{P}}$
4: Initial index set: $\Xi^0 = \emptyset = \text{row-supp}\{\mathbf{B}^0\}$, $\text{row-supp}\{\mathbf{B}\} = \{1 \le t \le k : \boldsymbol{\beta}^t \ne \mathbf{0}\}$,
   where $\boldsymbol{\beta}^t$ is the tth row of $\mathbf{B}$.

Main Iteration: Update iteration: $i = i + 1$

5:    Compute $b_j = \sum_{\tau=1}^{M_P N_P} \frac{\widetilde{\boldsymbol{\Phi}}_j^T \mathbf{R}_\tau^{i-1}}{\|\mathbf{R}_\tau^{i-1}\|_2^2}$, $\forall j \in \{1, ..., k\}$, where, $\mathbf{X}_z$ denotes the zth
      column of the matrix $\mathbf{X}$.
6:    $\mathcal{N} = \{$indices of $\widetilde{\boldsymbol{\Phi}}$'s atoms corresponding to the L largest $b_j\}$
7:    $\Xi^i = \Xi^{i-1} \cup \mathcal{N}$
8:    $\mathbf{B}^i = \min \|\widetilde{\boldsymbol{\Phi}}\mathbf{B} - \bar{\mathbf{P}}\|_F^2$ s.t. $\text{row-supp}\{\mathbf{B}\} = \Xi^i$, $\boldsymbol{\beta}^t \ge 0, \forall t$
9:    $\mathbf{R}^i = \bar{\mathbf{P}} - \widetilde{\boldsymbol{\Phi}}\mathbf{B}^i$
10:   If $\|\mathbf{R}^i\|_F > \gamma \|\mathbf{R}^{i-1}\|_F$ stop, otherwise iterate again.

---

absolute correlations, it sums the correlations between a dictionary atom and the residue vectors (line 5 of Algorithm 1). 2) It approximates the patch in each iteration with the *non-negative* least squares method, instead of using the standard least squares approximation. 3) It selects L dictionary atoms in each iteration instead of a single dictionary atom. In the above mentioned difference, (1) and (2) impose the non-negativety constraint over the desired coefficient matrix. On the other hand, (3) primarily aims at improving the computation time of the algorithm. G-SOMP+ also uses a different stopping criterion than SOMP, that is controlled by γ - the residual decay parameter. We defer further discussion on (3) and the stopping criterion to Section 6. G-SOMP+ has been proposed specifically to solve the constrained simultaneous sparse approximation problem in (8). Therefore, it is able to approximate a patch better than a generic greedy pursuit algorithm (e.g. SOMP).

Solving (8) for each image patch results in the desired coefficient matrix $\mathbf{B}$ that is used with $\boldsymbol{\Phi}$ to compute $\hat{\bar{\mathbf{S}}} \in \mathbb{R}^{L \times MN}$, which is the estimate of the super-resolution hyperspectral image $\bar{\mathbf{S}} \in \mathbb{R}^{L \times MN}$ (in matrix form).

$$\hat{\bar{\mathbf{S}}} = \boldsymbol{\Phi}\mathbf{B} \tag{9}$$

Fig. 1 pictorially summarizes the proposed approach.

5   Experimental Results

We have evaluated our approach[3] using ground based hyperspectral images as well as remotely sensed data. For the ground based images, we have conducted

---

[3] Source code/demo available at http://www.csse.uwa.edu.au/~ajmal/code/ HSISuperRes.zip

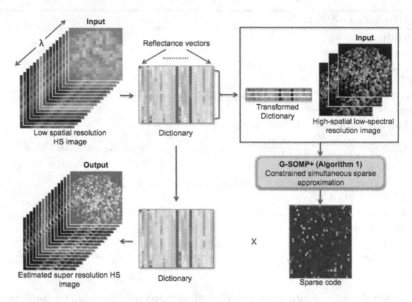

Fig. 1. Schematic of the proposed approach: The low spatial resolution hyperspectral (HS) image is used for learning a dictionary whose atoms represent reflectance spectra. This dictionary is transformed and used with the high-spatial but low-spectral resolution image to learn a sparse code by solving a constrained simultaneous sparse approximation problem. The sparse code is used with the original dictionary to estimate the super-resolution HS image.

experiments with two different public databases. The first database [33], called the CAVE database, consists of 32 hyperspectral images of everyday objects. The 512×512 spectral images of the scenes are acquired at a wavelength interval of 10 nm in the range $400 - 700$ nm. The second is the Harvard database [11], which consists of hyperspectral images of 50 real-world indoor and outdoor scenes. The 1392×1040 spectral images are sampled at every 10 nm from 420 to 720 nm. Hyperspectral images of the databases are considered as the ground truth for the super-resolution hyperspectral images. We down-sample a ground truth image by averaging over 32×32 disjoint spatial blocks to simulate the low spatial resolution hyperspectral image $\mathbf{Y}_h$. From the Harvard database, we have only used 1024×1024 image patches to match the down-sampling strategy. Following [32], a high spatial (but low spectral) resolution image $\mathbf{Y}$ is created by integrating a ground truth image over the spectral dimension, using the Nikon D700 spectral response[4] - which makes $\mathbf{Y}$ a simulated RGB image of the same scene. Here, we present the results on eight representative images from each database, shown in Fig. 2. We have selected these images based on the variety of the scenes. Results on further images are provided in the supplementary. For our experiments, we initialize the dictionary $\boldsymbol{\Phi}$ with random pixels from $\mathbf{Y}_h$.

---

[4] https://www.maxmax.com/spectral_response.htm

Fig. 2. RGB images from the databases. First row: Images from the CAVE database [33]. Second row: Images from the Harvard database [11].

Thus, the inherent smoothness of the pixels serves as an implicit loose prior on the dictionary.

Fig. 3 shows the results of using our approach for estimating the super-resolution hyperspectral images of 'Painting' and 'Peppers' (see Fig. 2). The top row shows the input 16×16 hyperspectral images at 460, 540 and 620 nm. The ground truth images at these wavelengths are shown in the second row, which are clearly well approximated in the estimated images shown in the third row. The fourth row of the figure shows the difference between the ground truth images and the estimated images. The results demonstrate a successful estimation of the super-resolution spectral images. Following the protocol of [16] and [32], we have used Root Mean Square Error (RMSE) as the metric for further quantitative evaluation of the proposed approach and its comparison with the existing methods. Table 1 shows the RMSE values of the proposed approach and the existing methods for the images of the CAVE database [33]. Among the existing approaches we have chosen the Matrix Factorization method (MF) in [16], the Spatial and Spectral Fusion Model (SASFM) [13], the ADMM based method [32] and the Coupled Matrix Factorization method (CMF) [34] for the comparison. Most of these matrix factorization based approaches have been shown to outperform the other techniques discussed in Section 2. To show the difference in the performance, Table 1 also includes some results from the Component Substitution Method (CSM) [2] - taken directly from [16]. We have used our own implementations of MF and SASFM because of unavailability of the public codes from the authors. To ensure an un-biased comparison, we take special care that the results achieved by our implementations are either the same or better than the results reported originally by the authors on the same images. Needless to mention, we follow the same experimental protocol as the previous works. The results of CSM and ADMM are taken directly form [32]. Note that, these algorithms also require *a priori* knowledge of the spatial transform between the hyperspectral image and the high resolution image, because of which they are highlighted in red in the table. We have also experimented by replacing G-SOMP+ in the our approach with SOMP; its non-negative variant SOMP+ and its generalization G-SOMP. The means of the RMSEs computed over the complete CAVE database are 4.97, 4.62 and 4.10 when we replace G-SOMP+

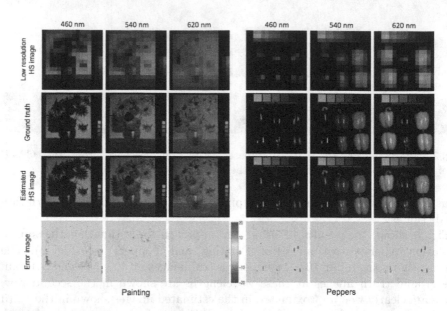

Fig. 3. Spectral images for Painting (Left) and Peppers (Right) at 460, 540 and 620 nm. Top row: 16×16 low spatial resolution hyperspectral (HS) images. Second row: 512×512 ground truth images. Third row: Estimated 512×512 HS images. Fourth row: Corresponding error images, where the scale is in the range of 8 bit images.

with SOMP, SOMP+ and G-SOMP respectively, in our approach. This value is 2.29 for G-SOMP+.

For the proposed approach, we have used 75 atoms in the dictionary and let $L = 20$ for each iteration of G-SOMP+, which processes 8×8 image patches. We have chosen $\eta = 10^{-5}$ in (7) and the residual decay parameter of G-SOMP+, $\gamma = 0.99$. We have optimized these parameter values, and the parameter settings of MF and SASFM, using a separate training set of 30 images. The training set comprises 15 images selected at random from each of the used databases. We have used the same parameter settings for all the results reported here and in the supplementary material. We defer further discussion on the parameter value selection for the proposed approach to Section 6.

Results on the images from the Harvard database [11] are shown in Table 2. In this table, we have compared the results of the proposed approach only with MF and SASFM because, like our approach, only these two approaches do not require the knowledge of the spatial transform between the input images. The table shows that the proposed approach consistently performs better than others. We have also experimented with the hyperspectral data that is remotely sensed by the NASA's Airborne Visible and Infrared Imaging Spectrometer (AVIRIS) [12]. AVIRIS samples the scene reflectance in the wavelength range 400 - 2500 nm at a nominal interval of 10 nm. We have used a hyperspectral image taken over

Table 1. Benchmarking on CAVE database [33]: The reported RMSE values are in the range of 8 bit images. The best results are shown in bold. The approaches highlighted in red also require the knowledge of spatial transform between the input images, which restrict their practical applicability.

Method	CAVE database [33]							
	Beads	Sponges	Spools	Painting	Pepper	Photos	Cloth	Statue
CSM [2]	28.5	19.9	-	12.2	13.7	13.1	-	-
MF [16]	8.2	3.7	8.4	4.4	4.6	3.3	6.1	2.7
SASFM [13]	9.2	5.3	6.1	4.3	6.3	3.7	10.2	3.3
ADMM [32]	6.1	2.0	5.3	6.7	2.1	3.4	9.5	4.3
CMF [34]	6.6	4.0	15.0	26.0	5.5	11.0	20.0	16.0
Proposed	**3.7**	**1.5**	**3.8**	**1.3**	**1.3**	**1.8**	**2.4**	**0.6**

Table 2. Benchmarking on Harvard database [11]: The reported RMSE values are in the range of 8 bit images. The best results are shown in bold.

Method	Harvard database [11]							
	Img 1	Img b5	Img b8	Img d4	Img d7	Img h2	Img h3	Img f2
MF [16]	3.9	2.8	6.9	3.6	3.9	3.7	2.1	3.1
SASFM [13]	4.3	2.6	7.6	4.0	4.0	4.1	2.3	2.9
Proposed	**1.2**	**0.9**	**2.8**	**0.8**	**1.2**	**1.6**	**0.5**	**0.9**

the Cuprite mines, Nevada[5]. The image has dimensions $512 \times 512 \times 224$, where 224 represents the number of spectral bands in the image. Following [15], we have removed the bands 1-2, 105-115, 150-170 and 223-224 of the image because of extremely low SNR and water absorptions in those bands. We perform the down-sampling on the image as before and construct $\mathbf{Y}$ by directly selecting the 512×512 spectral images from the ground truth image, corresponding to the wavelengths 480, 560, 660, 830, 1650 and 2220 nm. These wavelengths correspond to the visible and mid-infrared range spectral channels of USGS/NASA Landsat 7 satellite[6]. We adopt this strategy of constructing $\mathbf{Y}$ from Huang et al. [13]. Fig. 4 shows the results of our approach for the estimation of the super-resolution hyperspectral image at 460, 540, 620 and 1300 nm. For this data set, the RMSE values for the proposed approach, MF [16] and SASFM [13] are 1.12, 3.06 and 3.11, respectively.

6 Discussion

G-SOMP+ uses two parameters. L: the number of dictionary atoms selected in each iteration, and γ: the residual decay parameter. By selecting more dictionary

---

[5] Available at http://aviris.jpl.nasa.gov/data/free_data.html

[6] http://www.satimagingcorp.com/satellite-sensors/landsat.html

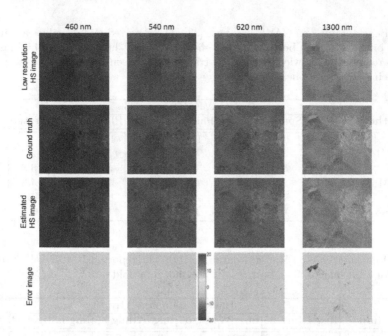

Fig. 4. Spectral images for AVIRIS data at 460, 540, 620 and 1300 nm. Top row: 16×16 low spatial resolution hyperspectral (HS) image. Second row: 512×512 ground truth image. Third row: Estimated 512×512 HS image. Fourth row: Corresponding error image, with the scale is in the range of 8 bit images.

atoms in each iteration, G-SOMP+ computes the solution more quickly. The processing time of G-SOMP+ as a function of L, is shown in Fig. 5a. Each curve in Fig. 5 represents the mean values computed over a separate training data set of 15 images randomly selected from the database, whereas the dictionary used by G-SOMP+ contained 75 atoms. Fig. 5a shows the timings on an Intel Core i7-2600 CPU at 3.4 GHz with 8 GB RAM. Fig. 5b shows the RMSE values on the training data set as a function of L. Although, the error is fairly small over the complete range of L, the values are particularly low for $L \in \{15, ..., 25\}$, for both of the databases. Therefore, we have chosen $L = 20$ for all the test images in our experiments. Incidentally, the number of distinct spectral sources in a typical remote sensing hyperspectral image is also considered to be close to 20 [17]. Therefore, we have used the same value of the parameter for the remote sensing test image.

Generally, it is hard to know *a priori* the exact number of iterations required by a greedy pursuit algorithm to converge. Similarly, if the residual error (i.e. $||\mathbf{R}^i||_F$ in Algorithm 1) is used as the stopping criterion, it is often difficult to select a single best value of this parameter for all the images. Fig. 5b shows that the RMSE curves rise for the higher values of L after touching a minimum value. In other words, more than the required number of dictionary atoms adversely affect the signal approximation. We use this observation to decide on the

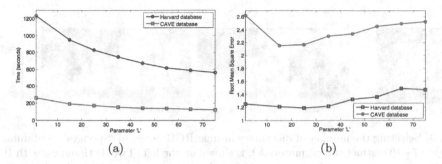

(a)   (b)

Fig. 5. Selection of the G-SOMP+ parameter L: The values are the means computed over 15 separate training images for each database: a) Processing time of G-SOMP+ in seconds as a function of L. The values are computed on an Intel Core i7-2600 CPU at 3.4 GHz with 8 GB RAM. b) RMSE of the estimated images by G-SOMP+ as a function of L.

stopping criterion of G-SOMP+. Since the algorithm selects a constant number of atoms in each iteration, it stops if the approximation residual in its current iteration is more than a fraction γ of the residual in the previous iteration. As the approximation residual generally decreases rapidly before increasing (or becoming constant in some cases), we found that the performance of G-SOMP+ on the training images was mainly insensitive for $\gamma \in [0.75, 1]$. From this range, we have selected $\gamma = 0.99$ for the test images in our experiments.

Our approach uses the online-dictionary learning technique [21] to solve (7). This technique needs to know the total number of dictionary atoms to be learned *a priori*. In Section 4, we have argued to use more dictionary atoms than the number of distinct materials in the scene. This results in a better separation of the spectral signal sources in the scene. Fig. 6 illustrates this notion. The figure shows an RGB image of 'Sponges' on the left. To extract the reflectance spectra, we learn two different dictionaries with 10 and 50 atoms, respectively, using the 16×16 hyperspectral image of the scene. We cluster the atoms of these dictionaries based on their correlation and show the arranged dictionaries in Fig. 6. From the figure, we can see that the dictionary with 10 atoms is not able to clearly distinguish between the reflectance spectra of the blue (C1) and the green (C2) sponge, whereas 10 seems to be a reasonable number representing the distinct materials in the scene. On the other hand, the dictionary with 50 atoms has learned two separate clusters for the two sponges.

The results reported in Fig. 5 are relatively insensitive to the number of dictionary atoms in the range of 50 to 80. In all our experiments, the proposed approach has learned a dictionary with 75 atoms. We choose a larger number to further incorporate the spectral variability of highly mixed scenes.

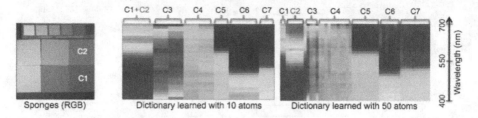

Fig. 6. Selecting the number of dictionary atoms: RGB image of 'Sponges', containing roughly 7 − 10 distinct colors (materials), is shown on the left. Two dictionaries, with 10 and 50 atoms, are learned for the scene. After clustering the spectra (i.e. the dictionary atoms) into seven clusters (C1 - C7), it is visible that the dictionary with 50 atoms learns distinct clusters for the blue (C1) and the green (C2) sponges, whereas the dictionary with 10 atoms is not able to clearly distinguish between these sponges.

7   Conclusion

We have proposed a sparse representation based approach for hyperspectral image super-resoltuion. The proposed approach fuses a high spatial (but low spectral) resolution image with the hyperspectral image of the same scene. It uses the input low resolution hyperspectral image to learn a dictionary by solving a constrained sparse optimization problem. The atoms of the learned dictionary represent the reflectance spectra related to the scene. The learned dictionary is transformed according to the spectral quantization of the input high resolution image. This image and the transformed dictionary are later employed by an algorithm G-SOMP+. The proposed algorithm efficiently solves a constrained simultaneous sparse approximation problem to learn a sparse code. This sparse code is used with the originally learned dictionary to estimate the super-resolution hyperspectral image of the scene. We have tested our approach using the hyperspectral images of objects, real-world indoor and outdoor scenes and a remotely sensed hyeprspectral image. Results of the experiments demonstrate that by taking advantage of the signal sparsity, non-negativity and the spatial structure in the scene, the proposed approach is able to consistently perform better than the existing state of the art methods on all the data sets.

Acknowledgements. This research was supported by ARC Discovery Grant DP110102399.

References

1. Aharon, M., Elad, M., Bruckstein, A.: K-svd: An algorithm for designing overcomplete dictionaries for sparse representation. IEEE Trans. Signal Process. 54(11), 4311–4322 (2006)

2. Aiazzi, B., Baronti, S., Selva, M.: Improving component substitution pansharpening through multivariate regression of MS +Pan data. IEEE Trans. Geosci. Remote Sens. 45(10), 3230–3239 (2007)
3. Akhtar, N., Shafait, F., Mian, A.: Repeated constrained sparse coding with partial dictionaries for hyperspectral unmixing. In: IEEE Winter Conference on Applications of Computer Vision, pp. 953–960 (2014)
4. Akhtar, N., Shafait, F., Mian, A.: SUnGP: A greedy sparse approximation algorithm for hyperspectral unmixing. In: Int. Conf. on Pattern Recognition (2014)
5. Alparone, L., Wald, L., Chanussot, J., Thomas, C., Gamba, P., Bruce, L.: Comparison of pansharpening algorithms: Outcome of the 2006 GRS-S data-fusion contest. IEEE Trans. Geosci. Remote Sens. 45(10), 3012–3021 (2007)
6. Bioucas-Dias, J., Plaza, A., Camps-Valls, G., Scheunders, P., Nasrabadi, N., Chanussot, J.: Hyperspectral remote sensing data analysis and future challenges. IEEE Geosci. Remote Sens. Mag. 1, 6–36 (2013)
7. Boyd, S., Parikh, N., Chu, E., Peleato, B., Eckstein, J.: Distributed optimization and statistical learning via the alternating direction method of multipliers. Found. Trends Mach. Learn. 3(1), 1–122 (2011)
8. Bruckstein, A., Elad, M., Zibulevsky, M.: On the uniqueness of nonnegative sparse solutions to underdetermined systems of equations. IEEE Trans. Inf. Theory 54(11), 4813–4820 (2008)
9. Carper, W.J., Lilles, T.M., Kiefer, R.W.: The use of intensity-hue-saturation transformations for merging SOPT panchromatic and multispectrl image data. Photogram. Eng. Remote Sens. 56(4), 459–467 (1990)
10. Cetin, M., Musaoglu, N.: Merging hyperspectral and panchromatic image data: Qualitative and quantitative analysis. Int. J. Remote Sens. 30(7), 1779–1804 (2009)
11. Chakrabarti, A., Zickler, T.: Statistics of real-world hyperspectral images. In: IEEE Conf. on Computer Vision and Pattern Recognition (CVPR), pp. 193–200 (2011)
12. Green, R.O., Eastwood, M.L., Sarture, C.M., Chrien, T.G., Aronsson, M., Chippendale, B.J., Faust, J.A., Pavri, B.E., Chovit, C.J., Solis, M., Olah, M.R., Williams, O.: Imaging spectroscopy and the airborne visible/infrared imaging spectrometer (AVIRIS). Remote Sensing of Environment 65(3), 227–248 (1998)
13. Huang, B., Song, H., Cui, H., Peng, J., Xu, Z.: Spatial and spectral image fusion using sparse matrix factorization. IEEE Trans. Geosci. Remote Sens. 52(3), 1693–1704 (2014)
14. Imai, F.H., Berns, R.S.: High resolution multispectral image archives: a hybrid approach. In: Color Imaging Conference, pp. 224–227 (1998)
15. Iordache, M.D., Bioucas-Dias, J., Plaza, A.: Sparse unmixing of hyperspectral data. IEEE Trans. Geosci. Remote Sens. 49(6), 2014–2039 (2011)
16. Kawakami, R., Wright, J., Tai, Y.W., Matsushita, Y., Ben-Ezra, M., Ikeuchi, K.: High-resolution hyperspectral imaging via matrix factorization. In: IEEE Conf. on Computer Vision and Pattern Recognition (CVPR), pp. 2329–2336 (2011)
17. Keshava, N., Mustard, J.F.: Spectral unmixing. IEEE Signal Process. Mag. 19(1), 44–57 (2002)
18. Khan, Z., Shafait, F., Mian, A.: Hyperspectral imaging for ink mismatch detection. In: Int. Conf. on Document Analysis and Recognition (ICDAR), p. 877 (2013)
19. Kopf, J., Cohen, M.F., Lischinski, D., Uyttendaele, M.: Joint bilateral upsampling. ACM Trans. Graph. 26(3) (July 2007)
20. Koutsias, N., Karteris, M., Chuvieco, E.: The use of intensity hue saturation transformation of Landsat 5 Thematic Mapper data for burned land mapping. Photogram. Eng. Remote Sens. 66(7), 829–839 (2000)

21. Mairal, J., Bach, F., Ponce, J., Sapiro, G.: Online dictionary learning for sparse coding. In: Int. Conf. on Machine Learning, ICML 2009, pp. 689–696 (2009)
22. Minghelli-Roman, A., Polidori, L., Mathieu-Blanc, S., Loubersac, L., Cauneau, F.: Spatial resolution improvement by merging MERIS-ETM images for coastal water monitoring. IEEE Geosci. Remote Sens. Lett. 3(2), 227–231 (2006)
23. Nguyen, H.V., Banerjee, A., Chellappa, R.: Tracking via object reflectance using a hyperspectral video camera. In: IEEE Conf. on Computer Vision and Pattern Recognition Workshops (CVPRW), pp. 44–51 (2010)
24. Olshausen, B.A., Fieldt, D.J.: Sparse coding with an overcomplete basis set: a strategy employed by v1. Vision Research 37, 3311–3325 (1997)
25. Tarabalka, Y., Chanussot, J., Benediktsson, J.A.: Segmentation and classification of hyperspectral images using minimum spanning forest grown from automatically selected markers. IEEE Trans. Syst., Man, Cybern., Syst. 40(5), 1267–1279 (2010)
26. Tropp, J., Gilbert, A.: Signal recovery from random measurements via orthogonal matching pursuit. IEEE Trans. Inf. Theory 53(12), 4655–4666 (2007)
27. Tropp, J.A.: Algorithms for simultaneous sparse approximation. part ii: Convex relaxation. Signal Processing 86(3), 589–602 (2006)
28. Tropp, J.A., Gilbert, A.C., Strauss, M.J.: Algorithms for simultaneous sparse approximation. part i: Greedy pursuit. Signal Processing 86(3), 572–588 (2006)
29. Uzair, M., Mahmood, A., Mian, A.: Hyperspectral face recognition using 3D-DCT and partial least squares. In: British Machine Vision Conf (BMVC), pp. 57.1–57.10 (2013)
30. Wang, J., Kwon, S., Shim, B.: Generalized orthogonal matching pursuit. IEEE Trans. Signal Process. 60(12), 6202–6216 (2012)
31. Wang, Z., Ziou, D., Armenakis, C., Li, D., Li, Q.: A comparative analysis of image fusion methods. IEEE Trans. Geosci. Remote Sens. 43(6), 1391–1402 (2005)
32. Wycoff, E., Chan, T.H., Jia, K., Ma, W.K., Ma, Y.: A non-negative sparse promoting algorithm for high resolution hyperspectral imaging. In: IEEE Int. Conf. Acoustics, Speech and Signal Processing (ICASSP), pp. 1409–1413 (2013)
33. Yasuma, F., Mitsunaga, T., Iso, D., Nayar, S.: Generalized Assorted Pixel Camera: Post-Capture Control of Resolution, Dynamic Range and Spectrum. Tech. rep., Department of Computer Science, Columbia University CUCS-061-08 (November 2008)
34. Yokoya, N., Yairi, T., Iwasaki, A.: Coupled nonnegative matrix factorization unmixing for hyperspectral and multispectral data fusion. IEEE Trans. Geosci. Remote Sens. 50(2), 528–537 (2012)
35. Zhukov, B., Oertel, D., Lanzl, F., Reinhackel, G.: Unmixing-based multisensor multiresolution image fusion. IEEE Trans. Geosci. Remote Sens. 37(3), 1212–1226 (1999)
36. Zurita-Milla, R., Clevers, J.G., Schaepman, M.E.: Unmixing-based Landsat TM and MERIS FR data fusion. IEEE Trans. Geosci. Remote Sens. 5(3), 453–457 (2008)

Hybrid Image Deblurring
by Fusing Edge and Power Spectrum Information

Tao Yue[1], Sunghyun Cho[2,*], Jue Wang[2], and Qionghai Dai[1]

[1] Tsinghua University, China
[2] Adobe Research, USA

Abstract. Recent blind deconvolution methods rely on either salient edges or the power spectrum of the input image for estimating the blur kernel, but not both. In this work we show that the two methods are inherently complimentary to each other. Edge-based methods work well for images containing large salient structures, but fail on small-scale textures. Power-spectrum-based methods, on the contrary, are efficient on textural regions but not on structural edges. This observation inspires us to propose a hybrid approach that combines edge-based and power-spectrum-based priors for more robust deblurring. Given an input image, our method first derives a structure prediction that coincides with the edge-based priors, and then extracts dominant edges from it to eliminate the errors in computing the power-spectrum-based priors. These two priors are then integrated in a combined cost function for blur kernel estimation. Experimental results show that the proposed approach is more robust and achieves higher quality results than previous methods on both real world and synthetic examples.

1 Introduction

Blind image deblurring, i.e. estimating both the blur kernel and the latent sharp image from an observed blurry image is a significantly ill-posed problem. It has been extensively studied in recent years, and various image priors have been explored in recent approaches for alleviating the difficulty. The problem however remains unsolved. In particular, as we will show later, although each individual method performs well in certain situations, none of them can reliably produce good results in all cases.

Among recent deblurring approaches, edge-based methods and power-spectrum-based ones have shown impressive performance [1, 2, 3, 4, 5, 6, 7, 8, 9, 10, 11]. *Edge-based methods* recover the blur kernel mainly from salient image edges, assuming the blurry edges extracted from the input image correspond to sharp, step-like edges in the latent image. *Power-spectrum-based methods* make the white random distribution assumption on the gradient of the latent image, so that the kernel's power spectrum can be recovered from the blurred image in a closed form. Phase retrieval methods can then be applied to recover the final blur kernel from its power spectrum.

The underlying assumptions of both approaches however do not hold in some common situations. For instance, edge-based methods may fail on images where strong edges are lacking or difficult to extract and analyze. On the other hand, the power-spectrum-based methods can handle small-scale textures well, but may be negatively

---

* Sunghyun Cho is currently with Samsung Electronics.

D. Fleet et al. (Eds.): ECCV 2014, Part VII, LNCS 8695, pp. 79–93, 2014.

affected by strong edges and tend to produce erroneous kernel components when they are abundant. Given that the failure modes of these two approaches are complimentary to each other, in order to achieve better robustness and a wider application range, we propose a hybrid method that simultaneously utilizes both the strong edges and the power spectrum information extracted from an input image for blur kernel estimation. Specifically, we detect and separate the input image into two components favored by each method, and develop an optimization process that takes into account both types of information for reliable blur kernel estimation. We conduct thorough experiments to show that the proposed method is indeed more robust and achieves higher quality results in general than previous approaches that use only one source of information.

The main contributions of the proposed approach include: (1) a modified blur kernel power spectrum estimation approach that eliminates the negative impact from structural image edges; and (2) a hybrid kernel estimation method that effectively integrates edge and power spectrum information.

1.1 Related Work

Strong edges are important components in nature images, and have been heavily explored for image deblurring. Existing approaches either extract strong edges explicitly and use them for kernel estimation [1, 2, 3, 4, 5], or use them implicitly by incorporating them into regularization terms [6, 7, 8]. In explicit methods, Jia [1] recovers the blur kernel from transparency on blurry edges. Joshi et al. [2] utilize sub-pixel differences of Gaussian edge detectors to detect edges from blurry image and predict their sharp version. Cho and Lee [4] propose to use simple image filters to predict sharp edges in the latent image from blurry ones in the input for kernel estimation. This method is further improved by Xu and Jia [12] by using better edge prediction and selection methods. Zhong et al. [13] estimate 1D profiles of the kernel from edges and reconstruct the kernel by inverse Radon transform. More recently Sun et al. [9] improve Cho and Lee [4]'s method by predicting sharp edges using patch-based data driven methods. In implicit methods, Fergus et al. [14] use the heavy-tail prior of image gradients and marginalize the joint distribution over all possible sharp images. Shan et al. [6] use sparse priors to suppress insignificant structures for kernel estimation. Krishnan et al. [7] instead propose to use L_1/L_2 regularizer for edge selection. Recently, Xu et al. [8] propose to use L_0 sparse representation for the same purpose.

Power-spectrum-based methods try to recover the blur kernel directly from the input image without alternatingly estimating the blur kernel and the latent sharp image, by using the fact that the gradients of natural images are approximately uncorrelated. Yitzhaky et al. [15] handle 1D motion blur by analyzing the characteristics of the power spectrum of the blurred image along the blur direction. Similarly Hu et al. [10] use an eight-point Laplacian whitening method to whiten the power spectrum of the image gradients and use it for estimating a 2D blur kernel. To deal with the irregularities of strong edges, Goldstein et al. [11] use a power-law model as well as a dedicated spectral whitening formula for achieving more robust kernel estimation.

For spectrum-based methods, phase retrieval is a key step to recover the blur kernel from the estimated power spectrum. It is a well studied problem in optical imaging field such as electron microscopy, wave front sensing, astronomy, crystallography,

etc. Fienup [16] compare the classical phase retrieval algorithms and report the stagnate problem of the existing algorithms. He and Wackerman [17] discuss the stagnate
problem in detail and propose several solutions to overcome different kinds of stagnate. Luke [18] proposes a Relaxed Averaged Alternating Reflection (RAAR) algorithm which is later adopted by Goldstein and Fattal's approach [11]. Osherovich [19]
recently proposes a method that achieves fast and accurate phase retrieval from a rough
initialization.

2   Overview

2.1   Blur Model

To model the camera shake in a blurred image, we use a conventional convolution based
blur model:

$$b = k * l + n, \tag{1}$$

where b is a blurred image, k is a blur kernel, l is a latent image, and n is noise. $*$ is
the convolution operator. We assume that n follows an i.i.d. Gaussian distribution with
zero mean. We treat b, k, l, and n as vectors, i.e., b is a vector consisting of pixel values
of a blurred image. Eq. (1) can be also expressed as:

$$b = Kl + n = Lk + n, \tag{2}$$

where K and L are convolution matrices corresponding to the blur kernel k and the
latent image l, respectively.

2.2   Framework

Given that edge-based and power-spectrum-based methods have different advantages,
combining them together seems to be a natural idea. However, doing it properly is not
trivial. Directly combining the objective functions in both methods together may make
the hybrid algorithm to perform worse than either one. That is because the salient edges
and the power spectrum are only preferred by one method and may seriously deteriorate
the other. In fact, both edge-based and power-spectrum-based methods have their own
dedicated operations to remove the influence of undesired image information. For instance, bilateral and shock filterring are used in Cho and Lee's method [4] for removing
small edges being considered for kernel estimation, and directional whitening has been
used in Goldstein and Fattal's approach [11] for minimizing the influence of strong
edges on computing the power spectrum. In this paper, we propose a framework that
explicitly considers both the helpful and harmful image components of each method, so
that the hybrid approach can perform better than each individual method.

The flowchart of the proposed hybrid approach is shown in Fig. 1. We adopt the
widely-used multi-scale framework which has shown to be effective for kernel estimation, especially for edge-based methods [6, 7, 8, 9, 12]. In each scale, a latent image
composed of only strong edges is predicted by image filtering operations as done in [4].
We use the same filtering operations and parameter settings to Cho and Lee's method

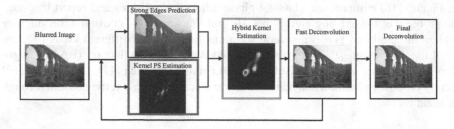

Fig. 1. The flowchart of the proposed hybrid deblurring method

for this step. We refer the readers to [4] for details. The power spectrum of the kernel is estimated by compensating the initial power spectrum computed from the blurry image using the extracted edges in the latent image. The blur kernel is estimated then by optimizing a hybrid objective function that contains both edge and power spectrum terms. In each iteration, the latent image is computed fast by the deconvolution method with L_2 regularization term [4]. Finally, a state-of-the-art non-blind deconvolution algorithm with hyper-Laplacian priors [20] are applied to generate the final deblurred image.

In Sec. 3 and Sec. 4, we will describe the kernel power spectrum estimation and hybrid kernel estimation steps in more detail, which are our main technical contributions.

3   Kernel Power Spectrum Estimation

In this step, we estimate the power spectrum of the blur kernel from the input image, with the help of the current estimate of the latent image to reduce estimation errors caused by strong edges. The power spectrum estimated in this step will be used as a constraint in the blur kernel estimation process in Sec. 4.

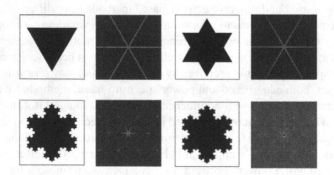

Fig. 2. The autocorrelation maps of Koch snowflake fractal images with 1st, 2nd, 4th and 6th iterations, from top-left to bottom-right, respectively. The edges with large gradient magnitude are regarded as good edges for edge-based methods. However, for spectrum based methods the straightness is more important. We can see that all the synthetic images have the same gradient magnitude, while they have totally different pattern in spectrum domain

According to the power law of natural images [11], which assumes that natural images have fractal-like structures (as shown in Fig. 2), the power spectrum of a sharp image follows an exponential-like distribution. In other words, the autocorrelation of the gradient map of a natural sharp image can be approximated by a delta function:

$$(d * l) \otimes (d * l) \approx \delta, \tag{3}$$

where d is a derivative filter and $\otimes$ is the correlation operator. Given a blurry input image b, by adopting Eq. (1), we have:

$$(d * b) \otimes (d * b) = (d * (k * l + n)) \otimes (d * (k * l + n))$$
$$\approx k \otimes k * \delta + c_n \delta, \tag{4}$$

where c_n is the magnitude coefficient that can be computed as $c_n = 2\sigma_r^2$, and σ_r^2 is the variance of noise n. In the frequency domain, Eq. (4) becomes:

$$\mathcal{F}(d)\overline{\mathcal{F}(d)}\mathcal{F}(b)\overline{\mathcal{F}(b)} \approx |\mathcal{F}(k)|^2 + c_n, \tag{5}$$

where $\mathcal{F}(\cdot)$ denotes Fourier transform and $\overline{(\cdot)}$ is the complex conjugate. Therefore, the power spectrum of the blur kernel k can be approximated as:

$$|\mathcal{F}(k)| \approx \sqrt{\mathcal{F}(d)\overline{\mathcal{F}(d)}\mathcal{F}(b)\overline{\mathcal{F}(b)} - c_n}. \tag{6}$$

In practice, the power spectrum assumption in Eq. (3) may fail for images that contain strong edges (see Fig. 3(f)). On the other hand, not all strong edges will violate the assumption, and our observation is that only *straight lines* have a strong effect on it. To illustrate this finding, we show the autocorrelation maps of the gradients of Koch snowflake fractal images with different iterations in Fig. 2. It is obvious that the straight edges affect the power spectrum assumption significantly, and as the fractal grows the autocorrelation map follows the assumption better and better.

Therefore, to avoid bad effects from such straight lines, our method detects strong straight lines explicitly at each iteration, and remove the effect of them when computing the power spectrum. Specifically, we detect the straight lines from the current estimate of the latent image l using EDLine [21], and remove lines that are shorter than the blur kernel size. A dilation operation is applied on the detected line maps to generate a straight line mask.

Given the straight line mask, we can decompose the image l into two components as:

$$l = l_s + l_d, \tag{7}$$

where l_s is the structure component derive by masking l with the straight line mask, and l_d is the rest detail component. Eq. (4) then becomes:

$$(d * b) \otimes (d * b) \approx k \otimes k * ((d * l_s) \otimes (d * l_s) + c_d \delta) + c_n \delta, \tag{8}$$

where c_d is the magnitude coefficient of the detail component. Because the Fourier transform of impulse δ is a constant, c_d can be approximated as:

$$c_d = \frac{1}{N} \sum_{\omega_1, \omega_2} \mathcal{F}(d)\overline{\mathcal{F}(d)}\mathcal{F}(l_d)\overline{\mathcal{F}(l_d)}, \tag{9}$$

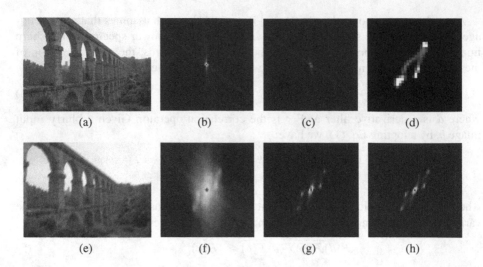

Fig. 3. Estimating the power spectrum of the blur kernel on a synthetic example. (a) latent image; (e) synthetically blurred input image; (b) power spectrum of (a); (f) power spectrum of kernel estimated from Eq. (6); (c) our estimated power-spectrum correction term (Denominator in Eq. 10); (g) corrected power spectrum map from Eq. (10); (d) the ground truth blur kernel; (h) the autocorrelation map of the ground truth kernel. Note that the corrected power spectrum in (g) is much closer to (h) compared with the original power spectrum in (f).

where (ω_1, ω_2) is the index of the 2D Fourier transform, and N is the number of elements in $\mathcal{F}(l_d)$. By applying Fourier transforms to Eq. (8), we can derive a new approximation for the power spectrum of the kernel K as:

$$|\mathcal{F}(k)| = \sqrt{\frac{\mathcal{F}(d)\overline{\mathcal{F}(d)}\mathcal{F}(b)\overline{\mathcal{F}(b)} - c_n}{\mathcal{F}(d)\overline{\mathcal{F}(d)}\mathcal{F}(l_s)\overline{\mathcal{F}(l_s)} + c_d}}. \tag{10}$$

Fig. 3 shows an example of kernel power spectrum estimation on a synthetic example. It shows that the strong structural edges in the input image can significantly affect the power spectrum estimation, while our corrected power spectrum is much closer to the ground truth.

4   Hybrid Kernel Estimation

We now describe how to incorporate the estimated kernel power spectrum and the extracted strong edges into a unified framework for blur kernel estimation.

4.1   The Formulation

Our optimization objective for kernel estimation contain a few terms. First, following previous work, we adopt a data term which is derived from the linear blur model in Eq. (1):

$$E_d(k) = \|p_x * k - b_x\|^2 + \|p_y * k - b_y\|^2, \tag{11}$$

where p_x and p_y are gradient maps of latent sharp image, b_x and b_y are gradient maps of the input image b along the x and y directions, respectively.

Given the power spectrum information of the blur kernel, the magnitude of the Fourier transform of the blur kernel, which is equivalent to the power spectrum, can be constrained as:

$$E_s(k) = \left\| |\mathcal{F}(k)| - |\mathcal{F}(k_s)| \right\|^2, \tag{12}$$

where $\mathcal{F}(k_s)$ is computed as in Eq. (10). Our energy function for kernel estimation then can be formulated as:

$$E(k) = E_d(k) + \alpha E_s(k) + \beta\|k\|_1 + \gamma\|\nabla k\|_2^2, \tag{13}$$

where α, β and γ are the weights for the power-spectrum-based, kernel sparsity and smoothness constraints respectively. In this paper, the weight of spectrum term α is set adaptively, and the rest parameters are set empirically by, $\beta = 150/(mn)$ and $\gamma = 0.2/max(m, n)$, where m, n are kernel size in x, y direction.

4.2 Optimization

To minimize the proposed energy function in Eq. (13), the phase retrieval problem need to be solved. Traditional phase retrieval algorithms [16, 17, 18] suffer from the well-known stagnation problem. Surprisingly, we found that a rough initialization of phase information provided by structural edges can greatly alleviate this problem. We empirically tested several phase retrieval methods, and found that even the simplest gradient descent method (error reduction) which has been shown to seriously suffer from stagnation can produce promising result in our framework. Therefore, we adopt this method for phase retrieval in our system.

Specifically, The gradient of the power-spectrum-based constraint term is derived as:

$$\frac{d\left\| |\mathcal{F}(k)| - |\mathcal{F}(k_s)| \right\|^2}{dk} = 2(k - k'), \tag{14}$$

where

$$k' = \mathcal{F}^{-1}\left(|\mathcal{F}(k_s)|e^{i\theta} \right). \tag{15}$$

Here, $e^{i\theta}$ is the phase of the Fourier transform of the kernel k. For the detailed derivation, we refer the readers to [16]. The gradient of Eq. (13) becomes:

$$\begin{aligned}
\frac{dE(k)}{dk} = &2P_x^T P_x k + 2P_x^T P_x + \\
&2P_y^T P_y k + 2P_y^T b_y + \\
&2\alpha(k - k') + 2\beta W k + 2\gamma L k,
\end{aligned} \tag{16}$$

where k is kernel in vector form, and L is Laplace operator, W is a diagonal matrix whose entries are defined by

$$W_{i,i} = \begin{cases} \frac{1}{k_i} & \text{if } k_i \neq 0 \\ 0 & \text{if } k_i = 0 \end{cases}, \tag{17}$$

where k_i is the i-th elements of kernel k. Finally, we set the descent direction g as $g = -dE(k)/dk$.

After determining the decent direction g, the optimal step length ζ is computed by minimizing Eq. (13) with respect to the step length ζ. Then, by finding the zero of $dE(k + \zeta g)/d\zeta$, we can derive the optimal ζ as:

$$\zeta = \frac{g^T g}{g^T \left(P_x^T P_x + P_y^T P_y + \alpha I + \beta W + \gamma L\right) g}. \tag{18}$$

In our implementation, the iterative procedure will be terminated when the update step size ζ is smaller than 10^{-7} or the iteration number is larger than 300.

4.3   Adaptive Weighting

The weight α in Eqn. 13 is an important parameter that determines the relative importance of the power-spectrum-based term versus the edge-based ones. Ideally, it should be adaptively selected for a specific input image, based on which type of information can be extracted more reliably. The optimal weight thus depends on various factors of the input image, including the distributions and characteristics of the structural edges and textured regions, as well as the underlying blur kernel. However, given that we do not know the blur kernel beforehand, it is difficult to derive an analytic solution for determining the optimal α at the beginning of optimizing process. To alleviate this problem, we propose a machine learning approach to predict good α from low-level image features including both structure and texture descriptors. In particular, considering the characteristics of edge-based and spectrum-based methods, we extract the following two features:

1. Distributions of strong edges in different directions. We extract the straight line mask from the input image as described in Sec. 3, and compute the histogram of edge pixels in the extracted straight lines in different edge direction bins. In our implementation we divide the edge directions into 8 bins, resulting in a 8-dimensions vector that describes the richness of the strong edges that can be extracted from the input image. Intuitively, a balanced histogram usually means that strong edges exist in different directions, providing good constraints for solving the blur kernel reliably.
2. The richness of image details. We exclude the pixels inside the straight line mask and use the rest of pixels to compute a gradient magnitude histogram. This is under the consideration that if more pixels have large gradient magnitudes, then the input image probably contains rich texture details that are beneficial to the power-spectrum-based component. In our implementation we use a 8-bin histogram.

The complete feature vector for an input image thus have 16 dimensions. To train a regression model for predicting α, we used the 640-image dataset proposed by Sun et al. [9] as the training dataset, which contains the blurred input image and the ground truth latent image for each example. According to our experiments, the algorithm is not very sensitive for small changes of α. Thus, for each test image, we deblurred it using

| Ground Truth | Cho & Lee | Goldstein & Fattal | Sun *et al.* -Nat | Our |

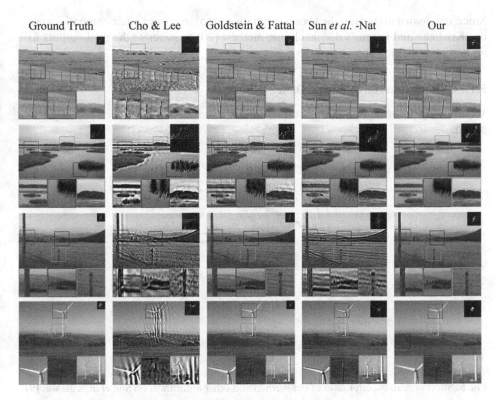

Fig. 4. Qualitative comparisons on four images from Sun *et al.*'s dataset [9]. From left to right: ground truth image and kernel, latent image and kernel estimated by Cho and Lee [4], Goldstein and Fattal [11], Sun *et al.* [9] and proposed method, respectively.

our method with 5 different settings of α: $\alpha = 0.1, 1, 10, 100, 1000$, and chose the one with the best deblurring quality as the target α value. In practice we found this discrete set of α weights can well represent the reasonable range of this parameter. We used the SVM as the classification model to label each input image with an α value. 480 images were randomly selected from the whole dataset for training and the remaining 160 images were used for testing. On the test dataset, the mean SSIM achieved by our method using the α weights predicted by the SVM model is 0.8195, while the mean SSIM achieved by using the ground truth α weights is 0.8241, just slightly higher than the trained model. This suggests that the proposed learning approach can effectively select good α values given an input blurry image.

5 Experiment Results

To evaluate the proposed method, we have applied it on both synthetic and real test datasets that have been proposed in previous work. We also compare our approach with state-of-the-art single image deblurring methods, both qualitatively and quantitatively.

Since our contribution is in the kernel estimation step, to ensure a fair comparison, we use Krishnan and Fergus's deconvolution method [20] to generate the final outputs for all kernel estimation approaches.

5.1 Comparisons on Synthetic Data

We first apply our algorithm on some synthetic datasets that have been recently proposed.

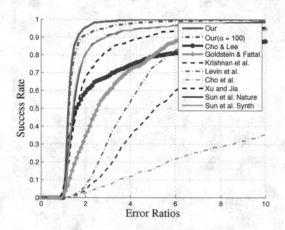

Fig. 5. Success ratio vs. error ratio of our method and other algorithms on Sun *et al.*'s dataset [9]

***Sun* et al.'s Dataset [9].** This dataset contains 640 images generated from 80 high quality nature images and 8 blur kernels. Fig. 4 shows some qualitative comparisons between our method and other state-of-the-art algorithms. It suggest that our methods achieves higher quality results than either edge-base (Cho and Lee [4] and Xu and Jia [12]) methods or power-spectrum-based (Goldstein and Fattal [11]) ones. Fig. 5 shows the cumulative distrutribution of error ratio metric (ratio between SSD errors of images deblurred from estimated and ground truth kenrels, see [22] for details) on this dataset, which also suggests that our method performs the best on this large scale dataset. We also tested our algorithm with different constant spectrum weights (α), and it achieved the best performance when $\alpha = 100$ on this dataset, which is better than previous algorithms, but still worse than using adaptive weights proposed in Sec. 4.3.

***Levin* et al.'s Dataset [22].** This dataset has 32 images generated from 4 small size images (255×255 pixels) and 8 blur kernels (kernels' supports varys from 10~25 pixels). All the kernels estimated by Cho and Lee [4], Goldstein and Fattal [11] and proposed methods are shown in Fig. 6(a)(b)(c) respectively. Notice that the power-spectrum-based method does not perform well on this dataset, as some of the kernels shown in Fig. 6(b) contain large errors. This is because the corresponding images in this dataset do not contain enough image texture for reliable kernel estimation. Our hybrid method correctly handles this situation, and generates results that are mostly similar but slightly better to those of the edge-based method [4].

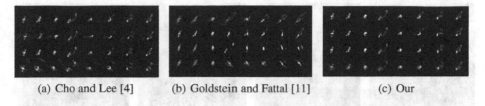

(a) Cho and Lee [4]   (b) Goldstein and Fattal [11]   (c) Our

Fig. 6. Kernels estimated by by Cho and Lee [4], Goldstein and Fattal [11] and proposed methods on Levin *et al.*'s dataset [22]

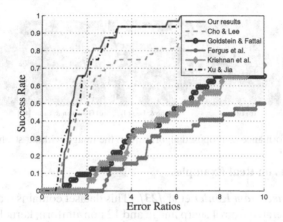

Fig. 7. Error ratios of different methods on Levin *et al.*'s dataset [22]

Fig. 7 shows the cumulative distributions of error ratio on this dataset. Note that the success rates in this plot are lower than those in the original plot [22]. This is because we found that since the kernel sizes are relatively large with respect to the image sizes in this dataset, the border artifacts are serious, and the SSD error mainly occurs in the border region. To eliminate the influence of border artifacts introduced by deconvolution methods, we cut off the border region in the error ratio calculation.

As shown in Eq. (13), our hybrid method contains edge-based terms that are similar to those in Cho and Lee's method [4], and a power spectrum term similar to the one in Goldstein and Fattal's method [11]. The hybrid method performs better than both individual methods on this dataset, showing the advantage of this fusion strategy.

Image without Strong Edges. To better understand the effectiveness of the spectrum component of the proposed method, we apply it on a texture image shown in Fig. 9(a,b). The results estimated by Cho and Lee [4], Goldstein and Fattal [11] and our method are shown in Fig. 9(c), (d) and (e), respectively. It is not a surprise that the edge-based method (Cho and Lee [4]) completely fails on this image, since it contains no strong edges. On the other hand, both Goldstein and Fattal [11] and our method produce good results given that the blur kernel can be well extracted from the power spectrum information.

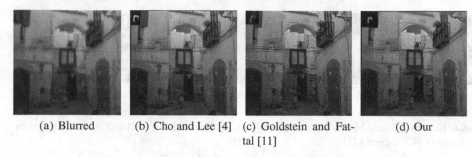

(a) Blurred   (b) Cho and Lee [4]   (c) Goldstein and Fat-   (d) Our
                                            tal [11]

Fig. 8. Qualitative Comparisons of one image from dataset [23]

(a) Ground Truth   (b) Blurred   (c) Cho & Lee [4]   (d) Goldstein & Fattal [11]   (e) Our

Fig. 9. Performance of proposed algorithm on the image without strong edges

5.2 Comparisons on Real Examples

Non-uniform Dataset from Köhler et al. *[23].* This dataset contains real blurry images
systematically generated from 4 sharp image and 12 non-uniform kernels. The quantitative comparison results on this dataset is shown in Table. 1. It suggests that the proposed
method consistently achieves better performance than the state-of-the-art image deblurring algorithms, including uniform and non-uniform, edge-based and spectrum-based
methods.

In this dataset, the spectrum-based method [11] performs much worse than other
methods. This is because the stagnate and robustness problem of the phase retrieval
algorithm is much more severe when the blur kernel is large. Because our algorithm
can take advantage of the phase information estimated from structural image edges, the
phase retrieval algorithm works much better in our method, which in turn improves the
performance of the hybrid kernel estimation.

Table 1. Quantative comparsion on Köhler *et al.*'s dataset [23]

Methods	Image 01		Image 02		Image 03		Image 04		Total	
	PSNR	SSIM	PSNR	SSIM	PSNR	SSIM	PSNR	SSIM	PSNR	SSIM
Whyte *et al.* [24]	27.5475	0.7359	22.8696	0.6796	28.6112	0.7484	24.7065	0.6982	25.9337	0.7155
Hirsch *et al.* [25]	26.7232	0.7513	22.5867	0.7290	26.4155	0.7405	23.5364	0.7060	24.8155	0.7317
Shan *et al.* [6]	26.4253	0.7001	20.5950	0.5872	25.8819	0.6920	22.3954	0.6486	23.8244	0.6570
Fergus *et al.* [14]	22.7770	0.6858	14.9354	0.5431	22.9687	0.7153	14.9084	0.5540	18.8974	0.6246
Krishnan *et al.* [7]	26.8654	0.7632	21.7551	0.7044	26.6443	0.7768	22.8701	0.6820	24.5337	0.7337
Goldstein & Fattal [11]	25.9454	0.7024	21.3887	0.6836	24.2768	0.6989	23.3397	0.6820	23.7377	0.6917
Cho & Lee [4]	28.9093	0.8156	24.2727	0.8008	29.1973	0.8067	26.6064	0.8117	27.2464	0.8087
Xu & Jia [12]	29.4054	0.8207	**25.4793**	0.8045	29.3040	0.8162	26.7601	0.7967	27.7372	0.8095
Our	**30.1340**	**0.8819**	25.4749	**0.8439**	**30.1777**	**0.8740**	**26.7661**	**0.8117**	**28.1158**	**0.8484**

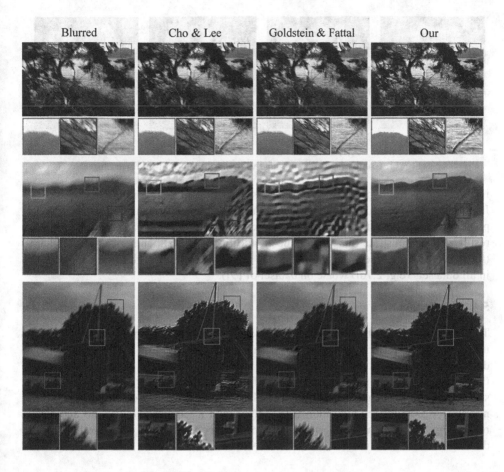

| Blurred | Cho & Lee | Goldstein & Fattal | Our |

Fig. 10. Comparisons on real-world examples

Real-World Examples. Fig. 10 shows three real-world blurry images with unknown blur parameters, and the deblurring results of Cho and Lee [4], Goldstein and Fattal [11] and the proposed approach. It suggest that previous edge-based and power-spectrum-based methods cannot achieve satisfactory results on these examples. In contrast, our approach is able to generate much higher quality results on these examples.

5.3 The Contribution of the Two Priors

One may wonder how much contribution each prior has in the hybrid approach. Given that most natural images contain some amount of sharp or strong edges, edge information is more universal, thus the edge prior plays a more dominant role in determining the blur kernel. Our approach reveals that the true merit of the power-spectrum prior is its ability to augment edge-based information. When edge-based methods fail badly, such as the examples in the 3rd and 4th rows of Fig. 4, power-spectrum prior leads to significant improvements. In these examples, although strong edges exist, they concentrate in few directions, making kernel estimation ill-posed. The complementary

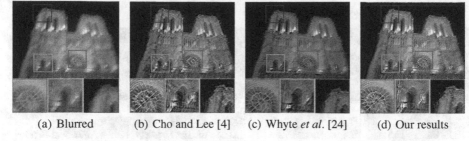

|(a) Blurred|(b) Cho and Lee [4]|(c) Whyte *et al.* [24]|(d) Our results|

Fig. 11. Comparisons on an image with significant non-uniform blur

information from the power spectrum makes kernel estimation possible in these cases. In other cases where edge-based methods generate reasonable results, incorporating the power-spectrum prior further improves the kernel accuracy and leads to higher quality results. To demonstrate this we conducted additional experiments by setting alpha=0 (meaning no power-spectrum at all), and the quantitative results are significantly worse in all data sets (e.g. 2.7dB worse on dataset of [9]).

5.4 Limitation

The main limitation of the proposed approach is that it cannot handle significant non-uniform blur well, because the power spectrum prior is based on global statistics that does not consider spatially-varying blur. In Fig. 11 we apply our algorithm on one of the images that contain significant non-uniform blur in Whyte *et al.*'s dataset [24]. It shows that the result generated by our method (Fig. 11(d)) is worse than that of the non-uniform deblurring algorithm (Fig. 11(c)), and is comparable to Cho and Lee's result (Fig. 11(b)). This suggests that the power spectrum term does not help when dealing with non-uniform blur.

6   Conclusion

We propose a new hybrid deblurring approach that restores blurry images by the aid of both edge-based and power-spectrum-based priors. Our approach extracts the strong edges from the image, and use them for estimating a more accurate power spectrum of the kernel. Both the edges and the improved power spectrum of the blur kernel are then combined in an optimization framework for kernel estimation. Experimental results show that our method achieves better performance than either edge-based or power-spectrum-based methods.

Acknowledgements. This work was supported by the Project of NSFC (No. 61327902, 61035002 and 61120106003).

References

1. Jia, J.: Single Image Motion Deblurring Using Transparency. In: CVPR (2007)
2. Joshi, N., Szeliski, R., Kriegman, D.J.: PSF estimation using sharp edge prediction. In: CVPR (2008)

3. Money, J.H., Kang, S.H.: Total variation minimizing blind deconvolution with shock filter reference. Image and Vision Computing 26(2), 302–314 (2008)
4. Cho, S., Lee, S.: Fast motion deblurring. ACM Transactions on Graphics 28(5), 1 (2009)
5. Cho, T.S., Paris, S., Horn, B.K.P., Freeman, W.T.: Blur kernel estimation using the radon transform. In: CVPR (2011)
6. Shan, Q., Jia, J., Agarwala, A.: High-quality motion deblurring from a single image. ACM Transactions on Graphics 27(3), 1 (2008)
7. Krishnan, D., Tay, T., Fergus, R.: Blind deconvolution using a normalized sparsity measure. In: CVPR (2011)
8. Xu, L., Zheng, S., Jia, J.: Unnatural L 0 Sparse Representation for Natural Image Deblurring. In: CVPR (2013)
9. Sun, L., Cho, S., Wang, J., Hays, J.: Edge-based blur kernel estimation using patch priors. In: ICCP (2013)
10. Hu, W., Xue, J.: PSF Estimation via Gradient Domain Correlation. IEEE Trans. on Image Process 21(1), 386–392 (2012)
11. Goldstein, A., Fattal, R.: Blur-Kernel Estimation from Spectral Irregularities. In: Fitzgibbon, A., Lazebnik, S., Perona, P., Sato, Y., Schmid, C. (eds.) ECCV 2012, Part V. LNCS, vol. 7576, pp. 622–635. Springer, Heidelberg (2012)
12. Xu, L., Jia, J.: Two-phase kernel estimation for robust motion deblurring. In: Daniilidis, K., Maragos, P., Paragios, N. (eds.) ECCV 2010, Part I. LNCS, vol. 6311, pp. 157–170. Springer, Heidelberg (2010)
13. Zhong, L., Cho, S., Metaxas, D., Paris, S., Wang, J.: Handling Noise in Single Image Deblurring using Directional Filters. In: CVPR (2013)
14. Fergus, R., Singh, B., Hertzmann, A., Roweis, S.T., Freeman, W.T.: Removing camera shake from a single photograph. ACM Transactions on Graphics 25(3), 787 (2006)
15. Yitzhaky, Y., Mor, I., Lantzman, A., Kopeika, N.S.: Direct method for restoration of motion-blurred images. JOSA A 15(6), 1512–1519 (2000)
16. Fienup, J.R.: Phase retrieval algorithms: a comparison. Applied Optics 21(15), 2758–2769 (1982)
17. Fienup, J., Wackerman, C.: Phase-retrieval stagnation problems and solutions. JOSA A 3(11), 1897–1907 (1986)
18. Luke, D.R.: Relaxed averaged alternating reflections for diffraction imaging. Inverse Problems 21(1), 37–50 (2005)
19. Osherovich, E.: Numerical methods for phase retrieval. PhD thesis
20. Krishnan, D., Fergus, R.: Fast Image Deconvolution using Hyper-Laplacian Priors. In: NIPS (2009)
21. Akinlar, C., Topal, C.: EDLines: A real-time line segment detector with a false detection control. Pattern Recognition Letters 32(13), 1633–1642 (2011)
22. Levin, A., Weiss, Y., Durand, F., Freeman, W.: Understanding and evaluating blind deconvolution algorithms. In: CVPR (2009)
23. Köhler, R., Hirsch, M., Mohler, B., Schölkopf, B., Harmeling, S.: Recording and playback of camera shake: Benchmarking blind deconvolution with a real-world database. In: Fitzgibbon, A., Lazebnik, S., Perona, P., Sato, Y., Schmid, C. (eds.) ECCV 2012, Part VII. LNCS, vol. 7578, pp. 27–40. Springer, Heidelberg (2012)
24. Whyte, O., Sivic, J., Zisserman, A., Ponce, J.: Non-uniform deblurring for shaken images. International Journal of Computer (2012)
25. Hirsch, M., Schuler, C., Harmeling, S., Schölkopf, B.: Fast removal of non-uniform camera shake. In: ICCV (2011)

Affine Subspace Representation for Feature Description

Zhenhua Wang, Bin Fan, and Fuchao Wu

National Laboratory of Pattern Recognition, Institute of Automation
Chinese Academy of Sciences, 100190, Beijing, China
{wzh,bfan,fcwu}@nlpr.ia.ac.cn

Abstract. This paper proposes a novel Affine Subspace Representation (ASR) descriptor to deal with affine distortions induced by viewpoint changes. Unlike the traditional local descriptors such as SIFT, ASR inherently encodes local information of multi-view patches, making it robust to affine distortions while maintaining a high discriminative ability. To this end, PCA is used to represent affine-warped patches as PCA-patch vectors for its compactness and efficiency. Then according to the subspace assumption, which implies that the PCA-patch vectors of various affine-warped patches of the same keypoint can be represented by a low-dimensional linear subspace, the ASR descriptor is obtained by using a simple subspace-to-point mapping. Such a linear subspace representation could accurately capture the underlying information of a keypoint (local structure) under multiple views without sacrificing its distinctiveness. To accelerate the computation of ASR descriptor, a fast approximate algorithm is proposed by moving the most computational part (*i.e.*, warp patch under various affine transformations) to an offline training stage. Experimental results show that ASR is not only better than the state-of-the-art descriptors under various image transformations, but also performs well without a dedicated affine invariant detector when dealing with viewpoint changes.

1   Introduction

Establishing visual correspondences is a core problem in computer vision. A common approach is to detect keypoints in different images and construct keypoints' local descriptors for matching. The challenge lies in representing keypoints with discriminative descriptors, which are also invariant to photometric and geometric transformations.

Numerous methods have been proposed in the literature to tackle such problems in a certain degree. The scale invariance is often achieved by estimating the characteristic scales of keypoints. The pioneer work is done by Lindeberg [11], who proposes a systematic methodology for automatic scale selection by detecting the keypoints in multi-scale representations. Local extremas over scales of different combinations of γ-normalized derivatives indicate the presence of characteristic local structures. Lowe [13] extends the idea of Lindeberg by selecting scale invariant keypoints in Difference-of-Gaussian (DoG) scale space. Other alternatives are SURF [4], BRISK [10], Harris-Laplacian and Hessian-Laplacian [16]. Since these methods are not designed for affine invariance, their performances drop quickly under significant viewpoint changes. To deal with the distortion induced by viewpoint changes, some researchers propose to

D. Fleet et al. (Eds.): ECCV 2014, Part VII, LNCS 8695, pp. 94–108, 2014.

detect regions covariant to the affine transformations. Popular methods include Harris-Affine [16], Hessian-Affine [15], MSER [14], EBR and IBR [21]. They estimate the shapes of elliptical regions and normalize the local neighborhoods into circular regions to achieve affine invariance. Since the estimation of elliptical regions are not accurate, ASIFT [19] proposes to simulate all image views under the full affine space and match the SIFT features extracted in all these simulated views to establish correspondences. It improves the matching performance at the cost of a huge computational complexity.

This paper aims to tackle the affine distortion by developing a novel Affine Subspace Representation (ASR) descriptor, which effectively models the inherent information of a local patch among multi-views. Thus it can be combined with any detector to match images with viewpoint changes, while traditional methods usually rely on an affine-invariant detector, such as Harris-Affine + SIFT. Rather than estimating the local affine transformation, the main innovation of this paper lies in directly building descriptor by exploring the local patch information under multiple views. Firstly, PCA (Principle Component Analysis) is applied to all the warped patches of a keypoint under various viewpoints to obtain a set of patch representations. These representations are referred to as *PCA-patch vectors* in this paper. Secondly, each set of PCA-patch vectors is represented by a low-dimensional linear subspace under the assumption that PCA-patch vectors computed from various affine-warped patches of the same keypoint span a linear subspace. Finally, the proposed Affine Subspace Representation (ASR) descriptor is obtained by using a subspace-to-point mapping. Such a linear subspace representation could efficiently capture the underlying local information of a keypoint under multiple views, making it capable of dealing with affine distortions. The workflow our method is summarized in Fig. 1, each step of which will be elaborated in Section 3. To speedup the computation, a fast approximate algorithm is proposed by removing most of its computational cost to an offline learning stage (the details will be introduced in Section 3.3). This is the second contribution of this paper. Experimental evaluations on image matching with various transformations have demonstrated that the proposed descriptors can achieve state-of-the-art performance. Moreover, when dealing with images with viewpoint changes, ASR performs rather well without a dedicated affine detector, validating the effectiveness of the proposed method.

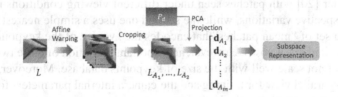

Fig. 1. The workflow of constructing ASR descriptor

The rest of this paper is organized as follows: Section 2 gives an overview of related works. The construction of the proposed ASR descriptor as well as its fast computation algorithm are elaborated in Section 3. Some details in implementation is given in Section 4. Experimental evaluations are reported in Section 5 and finally we conclude the paper in Section 6.

2   Related Work

Lindeberg and Garding [12] presented a methodology for reducing affine shape distortion. The suggested approach is to adapt the shape of smoothing kernel to the local image structure by measuring the second moment matrix. They also developep a method for extracting blob-like affine features with an iterative estimation of local structures. Based on the work of Lindeberg, Baumberg [3] adapted the local shapes of keypoints at fixed scales and locations , while Mikolajczyk and Schmid [16] iteratively estimated the affine shape as well as the location and scale. Tuytelaars and Van Gool [21] proposed two affine invariant detectors. The geometry-based method detects Harris corners and extracts edges close to such keypoints. Several functions are then chosen to determine a parallelogram spanned by the nearby two edges of the keypoint. The intensity-based method extracts local extremas in intensity as anchor points. An intensity function along rays emanating from these anchor points is used to select points where this function reaches an extremum. All these selected points are linked to enclose an affine covariant region which is further replaced by an ellipse having the same shape moments up to the second moments. Matas *et al.* [14] developed an efficient affine invariant detector based on the concept of extremal regions. The proposed maximally stable extremal regions are produced by a watershed algorithm and their boundaries are used to fit elliptical regions.

Since the accuracy of affine shape estimation is not guaranteed, Morel and Yu [19] presented a new framework for affine invariant image matching named ASIFT. They simulated all possible affine distortion caused by the change of camera optical axis orientation from a frontal position, and extract SIFT features on all these simulated views. The SIFT features on all simulated views are matched to find correspondences. Since ASIFT has to compute SIFT on lots of simulated views and make use of an exhaustive search on all possible views, it suffers a huge computational complexity. Although a similar view simulation method of ASIFT is used in our method, here it is for a totally different purpose: warping local patch of a keypoint under multiple views to extract PCA-patch vectors for keypoint description. Therefore, our method does not suffer from the huge computational burden as in ASIFT. Hintersoisser *et al.* [9] proposed two learning based methods to deal with full perspective transformation. The first method trains a Fern classifier [20] with patches seen under different viewing conditions in order to deal with perspective variations, while the second one uses a simple nearest neighbors classifier on a set of "mean patches"that encodes the average of the keypoints appearance over a limited set of poses. However, an important limitation of these two methods is that they can not scale well with the size of keypoints database. Moreover, they both need a fronto-parallel view for training and the camera internal parameters for computing the camera pose relative to the keypoint.

The most related work to this paper is SLS [8], which describes each pixel as a set of SIFT descriptors extracted at multiple scales. Our work extends SLS to deal with affine variations. Moreover, we propose to use PCA-patch vector as a compact intermediate representation of the warped patch instead of SIFT. The main advantages are two-folds: (a) fast, because PCA-patch vector is fast to compute while computing SIFT is much slower; (b) since computing PCA vector is a linear operation, it leads to the proposed fast algorithm.

3 Our Approach

3.1 Multiple View Computation

As the projective transformation induced by camera motion around a smooth surface can be locally approximated by an affine transformation, we locally model the apparent deformations arising from the camera motions by affine transformations. In order to deal with affine distortions, we propose to integrate local patch information under various affine transformations for feature description rather than estimating the local affine transformation (e.g., [21,16]).

Since we employ scale-invariant detector to select keypoints, we first extract a local patch at the given scale around each keypoint and then resize it to a uniform size of $s_l \times s_l$. To deal with linear illumination changes, the local patch is usually normalized to have zero mean and unit variance. Here we skip this step since the subsequent computation of linear subspace is invariant to linear illumination changes.

The local patch is aligned by the local dominant orientation to achieve invariance to in-plane rotation. In order to efficiently estimate such orientations, we sample some pattern points in the local patch similar to BRISK [10]. The dominant orientation is then estimated by the average gradient direction of all the sampling points:

$$\bar{g} = (1/n_p \sum_{i=1}^{n_p} g_x(\mathbf{p_i}), 1/n_p \sum_{i=1}^{n_p} g_y(\mathbf{p_i})), \tag{1}$$

where n_p is the number of sampling points, $\bar{g}$ is the average gradients, $g_x(\mathbf{p_i})$ and $g_y(\mathbf{p_i})$ are the x-directional and y-directional gradients of ith sampling point $\mathbf{p_i}$ respectively. Since there are only a few sample points, e.g., $n_p = 60$ in our experiments, the orientation can be estimated very fast.

Let L be the aligned reference patch around a keypoint at a given scale, the warped patch under an affine transformation A is computed by:

$$L_A = w(L, A), \tag{2}$$

where $w(\cdot, A)$ is the warping function using transformation A. To avoid the case that some parts of the warped patch may not visible in the reference patch, we take the reference patch a little larger in practice. Hence, Eq. (2) can be re-written as:

$$L_A = p(w(L, A)), \tag{3}$$

where $p(\cdot)$ is a function that extracts a small central region from the input matrix.

To encode the local information of each L_A, we propose to use a simple PCA based representation for its compactness and efficiency. By using PCA, the local patch is projected into the eigenspace and the largest n_d principal component coordinates are taken to represent the patch, i.e., the PCA-patch vector. Mathematically, the PCA-patch vector $\mathbf{d_A}$ for L_A can be computed as :

$$\mathbf{d_A} = P_d^T vec(L_A) = f(L_A), \tag{4}$$

where P_d is the learned PCA projection matrix, $vec(\cdot)$ denotes vectorization of a matrix, and $f(\cdot) = P_d^T vec(\cdot)$. By substituting Eq. (3), Eq. (4) can be rewritten as:

$$\mathbf{d_A} = f(p(w(L, A))). \tag{5}$$

The idea of using PCA for feature description is not novel, e.g., PCA-SIFT descriptor in [24] and GLOH descriptor in [17]. Here we only use such a technique to effectively generate a set of compact vectors as the intermediate representations. Further representation of the keypoint will be explored based on these intermediate representations.

3.2 Subspace Representation

Suppose there are m parameterized affine transformations to warp a local patch, we can get a PCA-patch vector set $\mathcal{D} = \{\mathbf{d_{A_m}}\}$ for a keypoint by the above approach. Inspired by Hassner et al.[8] who dealt with scale invariant matching by using a linear subspace representation of SIFT descriptors extracted on multiple scales, we proposed to construct a subspace model to represent the PCA-patch vectors extracted on multiple views.

The key observation is that the PCA-patch vectors extracted under various affine transformations of a same keypoint approximately lie on a low-dimensional linear subspace. To show this point, we conducted statistical analysis on the reconstruction loss rates[1] of PCA-patch vectors for about 20,000 keypoints detected from images randomly downloaded from the Internet. For each keypoint, its PCA-patch vector set is computed and used to estimate a subspace by PCA. Then the reconstruction loss rates of each set by using different numbers of subspace basis are recorded. Finally, the loss rates of all PCA-patch vector sets are averaged. Fig. 2 shows how the averaged loss rate is changed with different subspace dimensions. It can be observed that a subspace of 8 dimensions is enough to approximate the 24 dimensional PCA-patch vector set with 90% information kept in average. Therefore, we choose to use a n_s-dimensional linear subspace to represent $\mathcal{D}$. Mathematically,

$$[\mathbf{d}_{A_1}, \cdots, \mathbf{d}_{A_m}] \approx [\widehat{\mathbf{d}}_1, \cdots, \widehat{\mathbf{d}}_{n_s}] \begin{bmatrix} b_{11}, \cdots, b_{1m} \\ \vdots \ddots \vdots \\ b_{n_s1}, \cdots, b_{n_sm} \end{bmatrix}, \tag{6}$$

where $\widehat{\mathbf{d}}_1, \cdots, \widehat{\mathbf{d}}_{n_s}$ are basis vectors spanning the subspace and b_{ij} are the coordinates in the subspace. By simulating enough affine transformations, the basis $\widehat{\mathbf{d}}_1, \cdots, \widehat{\mathbf{d}}_{n_s}$ can be estimated by PCA.

Let $\mathcal{D}_k$ and $\mathcal{D}_{k'}$ be the PCA-patch vector sets of keypoints k and k' respectively, the distance between $\mathcal{D}_k$ and $\mathcal{D}_{k'}$ can be measured by the distance between corresponding subspaces $\mathbb{D}_k$ and $\mathbb{D}_{k'}$. As shown in [5], all the common distances between two subspaces are defined based on the principal angles. In our approach, we use the Projection Frobenius Norm defined as:

$$dist(\mathbb{D}_k, \mathbb{D}_{k'}) = \|\sin \boldsymbol{\psi}\|_2 = \frac{1}{\sqrt{2}} \left\| \widehat{D}_k \widehat{D}_k^T - \widehat{D}_{k'} \widehat{D}_{k'}^T \right\|_F, \tag{7}$$

---

[1] It is defined as the rate between reconstruction error and the original data, while the reconstruction error is the squared distance between the original data and its reconstruction by PCA.

where $\sin\psi$ is a vector of sines of the principal angles between subspaces $\mathbb{D}_k$ and $\mathbb{D}_{k'}$, $\widehat{D}_k$ and $\widehat{D}_{k'}$ are matrixes whose columns are basis vectors of subspaces $\mathbb{D}_k$ and $\mathbb{D}_{k'}$ respectively.

To obtain a descriptor representation of the subspace, similar to [8] we employ the subspace-to-point mapping proposed by Basri *et al.* [2]. Let $\widehat{D}$ be the matrix composed of orthogonal basis of subspace $\mathbb{D}$, the proposed ASR descriptor can be obtained by mapping the projection matrix $Q = \widehat{D}\widehat{D}^T$ into vectors. Since Q is symmetric, the mapping $h(Q)$ can be defined as rearranging the entries of Q into a vector by taking the upper triangular portion of Q, with the diagonal entries scaled by $1/\sqrt{2}$. Mathematically, the ASR descriptor $\mathbf{q}$ is

$$\mathbf{q} = h(Q) = (\frac{q_{11}}{\sqrt{2}}, q_{12}, \cdots, q_{1n_d}, \frac{q_{22}}{\sqrt{2}}, q_{23}, \cdots, \frac{q_{n_d n_d}}{\sqrt{2}}), \tag{8}$$

where q_{ij} are elements of Q, and n_d is the dimension of the PCA-patch vector. Thus the dimension of $\mathbf{q}$ is $n_d * (n_d + 1)/2$.

By such mapping, it is worth noting that the Projection Frobenius Norm distance between subspaces $\mathbb{D}_k$ and $\mathbb{D}_{k'}$ is equal to the Euclidean distance between the corresponding ASR descriptors $\mathbf{q}_k$ and $\mathbf{q}_{k'}$:

$$dist(\mathbb{D}_k, \mathbb{D}_{k'}) = \|\mathbf{q}_k - \mathbf{q}_{k'}\|_2. \tag{9}$$

It is worth noting that ASR is inherently invariant to linear illumination changes. Suppose $\mathcal{D} = \{\mathbf{d}_{A_m}\}$ is the set of PCA-patch vectors for a keypoint, while $\mathcal{D}' = \{\mathbf{d}_{A_m}'\}$ is its corresponding set after linear illumination changes. For each element in $\mathcal{D}$, $\mathbf{d}_{A_m} = a \times \mathbf{d}_{A_m}' + b$ where a and b parameterize the linear illumination changes. Let $cov(\mathcal{D})$ and $cov(\mathcal{D}')$ be their covariant matrixes, it is easy to verify that $cov(\mathcal{D}) = a^2 \times cov(\mathcal{D}')$. Therefore, they have the same eigenvectors. Since it is the eigenvectors used for ASR construction, the obtained ASR for $\mathcal{D}$ and $\mathcal{D}'$ will be identical.

3.3   Fast Computation

Due to the high computational burden of warping patches, it would be very inefficient to compute a set of PCA-patch vectors extracted under various affine transformations by utilizing Eq. (5) directly.

In [9], Hinterstoisser *et al.* proposed a method to speed up the computation of warped patches under different camera poses based on the linearity of warping function. We found that their method could be easily extended to speed up the computation of any linear descriptor of the warped patches. According to this observation, we develop a fast computation method of $\mathbf{d}_A$ at the cost of a little accuracy degradation in this section.

Similar to [9], we firstly approximate L by its principal components as:

$$L \approx \overline{L} + \sum_{i=1}^{n_l} a_i L_i, \tag{10}$$

where n_l is the number of principal components, L_i and a_i are the principal components and the projection coordinates respectively.

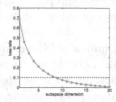

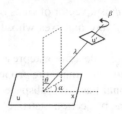

Fig. 2. Averaged loss rate as a function of the subspace dimension. The patch size is 21×21 and the dimension of PCA-patch vector is 24.

Fig. 3. Geometric interpretation of the decomposition in Eq. (15). See text for details.

Then, by substituting Eq. (10) into Eq. (5), it yields:

$$\mathbf{d}_A \approx f(p(w(\overline{L} + \sum_{i=1}^{n_l} a_i L_i, A))). \qquad (11)$$

Note that the warping function $w(\cdot, A)$ is essentially a permutation of the pixel intensities between the reference patch and the warped patch. It implies that $w(\cdot, A)$ is actually a linear transformation. Since $p(\cdot)$ and $f(\cdot)$ are also linear functions, Eq. (11) can be re-written as:

$$\mathbf{d}_A \approx f(p(w(\overline{L}, A))) + \sum_{i=1}^{n_l} a_i f(p(w(L_i, A))) = \overline{\mathbf{d}}_A + \sum_{i=1}^{n_l} a_i \mathbf{d}_{i,A}, \qquad (12)$$

where

$$\begin{aligned} \overline{\mathbf{d}}_A &= f(p(w(\overline{L}, A))) \\ \mathbf{d}_{i,A} &= f(p(w(L_i, A))) \end{aligned} \qquad (13)$$

Fig. 4 illustrates the workflow of such a fast approximated algorithm.

Although the computation of $\overline{\mathbf{d}}_A$ and $\mathbf{d}_{i,A}$ is still time consuming, it can be previously done in an offline learning stage. At run time, we simply compute the projection coordinates $\mathbf{a} = (a_1, \cdots, a_{n_l})^T$ of the reference patch L by

$$\mathbf{a} = P_l^T vec(L), \qquad (14)$$

where P_l is the learned projection matrix consisting of L_i. Then, $\mathbf{d_A}$ can be computed by a linear combination of $\mathbf{d}_{i,A}$ and $\overline{\mathbf{d}}_A$.

Obviously, this approach combines the patch warping and representation into one step, and moves most of the computational cost to the offline learning stage. Compared to the naive way in Eq. (5), it significantly reduces the running time. We refer to ASR descriptor computed by such a fast approximate algorithm as ASR-fast descriptor, while the original one is referred to as ASR-naive descriptor.

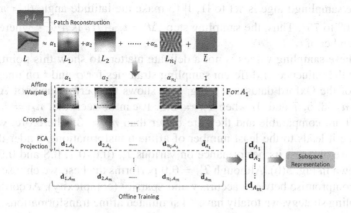

Fig. 4. Fast computation strategy for constructing ASR descriptor

4 Notes on Implementation

4.1 Parameterization of Affine Transformation

As shown in [19], any 2D affine transformation A with strictly positive determinant which is not a similarity has a unique decomposition:

$$A = \lambda R(\alpha)T(t)R(\beta) = \lambda \begin{bmatrix} \cos\alpha & -\sin\alpha \\ \sin\alpha & \cos\alpha \end{bmatrix} \begin{bmatrix} t & 0 \\ 0 & 1 \end{bmatrix} \begin{bmatrix} \cos\beta & -\sin\beta \\ \sin\beta & \cos\beta \end{bmatrix}, \quad (15)$$

where $\lambda > 0$, R is a rotation matrix, $\alpha \in [0, \pi)$, $\beta \in [0, 2\pi)$, T is a diagonal matrix with $t > 1$.

Fig. 3 gives a geometric interpretation of this decomposition: u is the object plane, u' is the image plane, α (longitude) and $\theta = \arccos 1/t$ (latitude) are the camera viewpoint angles, β is the camera in-plane rotation, and λ is the zoom parameter. The projective transformation from image plane u' to object plane u can be approximated by the affine transformation in Eq. (15).

Since the scale parameter λ can be estimated by scale-invariant detectors and the in-plane rotation β can be aligned by local dominant orientation, we only sample the longitude angle α and the tilt t.

For α, the sampling range is $[0, \pi)$ as indicated by the decomposition in Eq. (15). The sampling step $\Delta\alpha = \alpha_{k+1} - \alpha_k$ is determined by considering the overlap between the corresponding ellipses of adjacent samplings. More specifically, for an affine transformation $A_{t,\alpha}$ with tilt t and longitude α, the corresponding ellipse is $e_{t,\alpha} = A_{t,\alpha}^T A_{t,\alpha}$. Let $\varepsilon(e_{t,\alpha}, e_{t,\alpha+\Delta\alpha})$ denotes the overlap rate between $e_{t,\alpha}$ and $e_{t,\alpha+\Delta\alpha}$, it can be proved that $\varepsilon(e_{t,\alpha}, e_{t,\alpha+\Delta\alpha})$ is a decreasing function of $\Delta\alpha$ when $t > 1 \wedge \Delta\alpha \in [0, \pi/2)$. We can choose the sampling step $\Delta\alpha$ as the max value that satisfies $\varepsilon(e_{t,\alpha}, e_{t,\alpha+\Delta\alpha}) > T_o$ where T_o is a threshold that controls the minimal overlap rate required for the corresponding ellipses of adjacent samplings. The larger T_o is, the more α will be sampled.

For t, the sampling range is set to $[1, 4]$ to make the latitude angle $\theta = \arccos 1/t$ range from $0°$ to $75°$. Thus, the sampling step $\Delta t = t_{k+1}/t_k$ is $4^{\frac{1}{n_t-1}}$ where n_t is the sampling number of t.

Setting these sampling values is not a delicate matter. To show this point, we have investigated the influence of different sampling strategies for α and t on image pair of *'trees 1-2'* of the Oxford dataset [1]. Fig. 5(a) shows the performance of ASR-naive by varying n_t (3, 5, 7 and 9) when $T_o = 0.8$. It can be seen that $n_t = 5$, $n_t = 7$ and $n_t = 9$ are comparable and they are better than $n_t = 3$. Therefore, we choose $n_t = 5$ since it leads to the least number of affine transformations. Under the choice of $n_t = 5$, we also test its performance on various T_o (0.6, 0.7, 0.8 and 0.9) and the result is shown in Fig. 5(b). Although $T_o = 0.9$ performs the best, we choose $T_o = 0.8$ to make a compromise between accuracy and sparsity (complexity). According to the above sampling strategy, we totally have 44 simulated affine transformations. Note that the performance is robust to these values in a wide range. Similar observations can be obtained in other test image pairs.

4.2   Offline Training

From Section 3, it can be found there are three cases in which PCA is utilized:

(1) PCA is used for raw image patch representation to obtain a PCA-patch vector for each affine-warped image patches.
(2) PCA is used to find subspace basis of a set of PCA-patch vectors for constructing ASR descriptor.
(3) PCA is used to find principal components to approximate a local image patch L for fast computation (c.f. Eq. (10)).

In cases of (1) and (3), several linear projections is required. More specifically, n_d principal projections are used for PCA-patch vector computation and n_l principal components are used to approximate a local image patch. These PCA projections are learned in an offline training stage. In this stage, the PCA projection matrix P_d in Eq. (4), $\mathbf{d}_{i,A}$ and $\overline{\mathbf{d}}_A$ in Eq. (13) are computed by using about $2M$ patches detected on 17125 training images provided by PASCAL VOC 2012. Thus the training images are significantly different from those used for performance evaluation in Section 5.

5   Experiments

In this section, we conduct experiments to show the effectiveness of the proposed method. Firstly, we study the potential impact of different parameter settings on the performance of the proposed method. Then, we test on the widely used Oxford dataset [1] to show its superiority to the state-of-the-art local descriptors. With the image pairs under viewpoint changes in this dataset, we also demonstrate that it is capable of dealing with affine distortion without an affine invariant detector, and is better than the traditional method, e.g., building SIFT descriptor on Harris Affine region. To further show its performance in dealing with affine distortion, we conduct experiments on a larger dataset (Caltech 3D Object Dataset [18]), containing a large amount of images of different 3D objects captured from different viewpoints. The detailed results are reported in the following subsections.

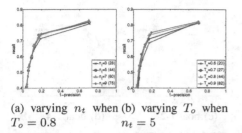

(a) varying n_t when (b) varying T_o when
$T_o = 0.8$ $\qquad\qquad n_t = 5$

Fig. 5. Performance comparison of ASR descriptor on DoG keypoints under different sampling strategies. The number of simulated affine transformations is enclosed in the parenthesis.

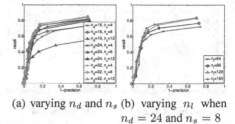

(a) varying n_d and n_s (b) varying n_l when
$\qquad\qquad n_d = 24$ and $n_s = 8$

Fig. 6. Performance comparison of ASR descriptor on DoG keypoints under different parameter configurations by varying n_d, n_s and n_l

5.1 Parameters Selection

In addition to T_o and n_t for sampling affine transformations, our method has several other parameters listed in Table 1. We have investigated the effect of different parameter settings on image pair of *'trees 1-2'* in the Oxford dataset [1]. We simply tried several combinations of these parameters and compared the matching performance among them. The result is shown in Fig. 6. Fig. 6(a) is obtained by computing ASR-naive under different n_d (16, 24 and 32) and n_s (4, 8 and 12). It is found that the configuration of $(n_d = 32, n_s = 8)$ obtains the best result. For a trade off between the performance and descriptor dimension, we choose $(n_d = 24, n_s = 8)$, leading to ASR with $24 * (24 + 1)/2 = 300$ dimensions. Under the choice of $(n_d = 24, n_s = 8)$, we investigate the fast approximate algorithm by computing ASR-fast under different n_l (64, 96, 128 and 160). Fig. 6(b) shows that $n_l = 160$ obtains the best result. A typical setting of all parameters is given in Table 1 and kept unchanged in the subsequent experiments.

Table 1. Parameters in ASR descriptor and their typical settings

parameter	description	typical value
n_p	pattern number for dominant orientation estimation	60
n_l	number of orthogonal basis for approximating local patch	160
s_l	size of local patch	21
n_d	dimension of the PCA-patch vector	24
n_s	dimension of the subspace that PCA-patch vector set $\mathcal{D}$ lies on	8

5.2 Evaluation on Oxford Dataset

To show the superiority of our method, we conduct evaluations on this benchmark dataset based on the standard protocol [17], using the nearest neighbor distance ratio (NNDR) matching strategy. For comparison, the proposed method is compared with SIFT [13] and DAISY [23] descriptors, which are the most popular ones representing the state-of-the-art. The results of other popular descriptors (SURF, ORB, BRISK etc.) are not reported as they are inferior to that of DAISY. In this experiment, keypoints are

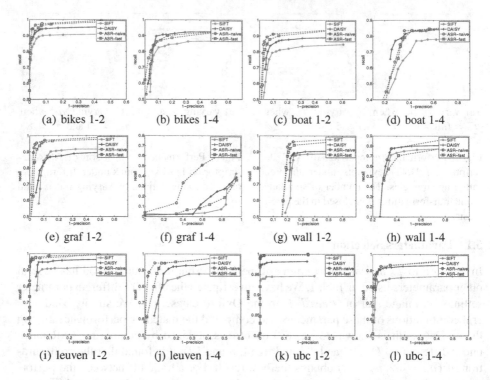

(a) bikes 1-2   (b) bikes 1-4   (c) boat 1-2   (d) boat 1-4

(e) graf 1-2   (f) graf 1-4   (g) wall 1-2   (h) wall 1-4

(i) leuven 1-2   (j) leuven 1-4   (k) ubc 1-2   (l) ubc 1-4

Fig. 7. Experimental results for different image transformations on DoG keypoints: (a)-(b) image blur, (c)-(d) rotation and scale change, (e)-(h) viewpoint change, (i)-(j) illumination change and (k)-(l) JPEG compression.

detected by DoG [13] which is the most representative and widely used scale invariant detector. Due to space limit, only the results of two image pairs (the 1st vs. the 2nd and the 1st vs. the 4th) for each image sequence are shown, which represent small and large image transformations respectively.

As shown in Fig. 7, it is clear that ASR-fast performs comparable to ASR-naive in all cases except '*graf 1-4*' (Fig. 7(f)). This demonstrates the fact that the proposed fast computation strategy in Eq. (12) can well approximate the naive computation of PCA-patch vector set. The performance degradation in '*graf 1-4*' can be explained by the difference in patch alignment. Since ASR-fast does not generate the warped patches directly, it simply aligns the reference patch before computing the PCA-patch vector set. This strategy could be unreliable under large image distortions since all the PCA-patch vectors extracted under various affine transformations depend on the orientation estimated on reference patch. ASR-naive avoids this by computing the dominant orientation on each warped patch and aligning it separately. In other words, the inferior performance of ASR-fast is because that the PCA-patch vector (*i.e.*, the intermediate representation) relies on robust orientation estimation, but *does not* imply that ASR-fast is not suitable for viewpoint changes. Therefore, if we can use an inherent rotation invariant intermediate representation (such as the one in similar spirit to the intensity

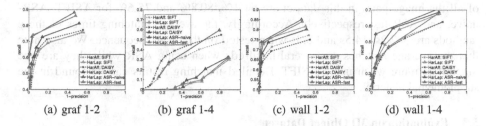

(a) graf 1-2   (b) graf 1-4   (c) wall 1-2   (d) wall 1-4

Fig. 8. Experimental results on image sequences containing viewpoint changes

order based methods [6,7,22]), ASR-fast is expected to be as good as ASR-naive. We would leave this for our future work.

According to Fig. 7, both ASR-naive and ASR-fast are consistently better than SIFT in all cases and outperform DAISY in most cases. The superior performance of the proposed method can be attributed to the effective use of local information under various affine transformation. For all cases of viewpoint changes especially in 'graf 1-4', ASR-naive outperforms all competitors by a large margin, which demonstrates its ability of dealing with affine distortions.

To further show ASR's ability in dealing with affine distortions without a dedicated affine detector, we use image pairs containing viewpoint changes to compare ASR with traditional methods, i.e., build local descriptor on top of affine invariant regions. In this experiment, Harris-Affine (HarAff) is used for interest region detection and SIFT/DAISY descriptors are constructed on these interest regions. For a fair comparison, ASR is build on top of Harris-Laplace (HarLap) detector since Harris-Affine regions are build up on Harris-Laplace regions by an additional affine adaptive procedure. Therefore, such a comparison ensures a fair evaluation for two types of affine invariant image matching methods, i.e., one based on affine invariant detectors, while the other based on affine robust descriptors.

The results are shown in Fig. 8. To show the affine adaptive procedure is necessary for dealing with affine distortions if the used descriptor does not account for this aspect, the results of HarLap:SIFT and HarLap:DAISY are also supplied. It is clear that HarAff:SIFT (HarAff:DAISY) is better than HarLap:SIFT (HarAff:DAISY). By using the same detector, HarLap:ASR-naive significantly outperforms HarLap:SIFT and HarLap:DAISY. It is also comparable to HarAff:DAISY and HarAff:SIFT in 'graf 1-4', and even better than them in all other cases. This demonstrate that by considering affine distortions in feature description stage, ASR is capable of matching images with viewpoint changes without a dedicated affine invariant detector. The failure of HarLap:ASR-fast is due to the unreliable orientation estimation as explained before.

Another excellent method to deal with affine invariant image matching problem is ASIFT. However, ASIFT can not be directly compared to the proposed method. This is because that ASIFT is an image matching framework while the propose method is a feature descriptor. Therefore, in order to give the reader a picture of how our method performs in image matching compared to ASIFT, we use ASR descriptor combined with DoG detector for image matching and the NNDR threshold is set to 0.8. The matching results are compared to those obtained by ASIFT when the matching threshold equals to 0.8. ASIFT is downloaded from the authors' website. The average matching precisions of all the image pairs in this dataset are 64.4%, 80.8% and 75.6% for ASIFT, ASR-naive, and ASR-fast respectively. Accordingly, the average matching times of these methods are 382.2s, 14.5s and 8.3s when tested on the 'wall' sequence. We also note that the average matches are several hundreds when using ASR while they are one magnitude more when using ASIFT. Detailed matching results can be found in the supplemental material.

5.3 Evaluation on 3D Object Dataset

To obtain a more thoroughly study of dealing with affine distortions, we have also evaluated our method on the 3D object dataset [18], which has lots of images of 100 3D objects captured under various viewpoints. We use the same evaluation protocol as [18]. The ROC curves are obtained by varying the threshold T_{app} on the quality of the appearance match , while the stability curves are obtained at fixed false alarm rate of $1.5 * 10^{-6}$.

As previous experimental setting, we use Harris-Laplace (HarLap) detector to produce scale invariant regions and then compute ASR descriptors for matching. For comparison, the corresponding Harris-Affine (HarAff) detector is used to produce affine invariant regions and SIFT/DAISY descriptors are computed based on them.

Fig. 9 shows the results averaged on all objects in the dataset when the viewing angle is varied from 5° to 45°. It can be observed that HarLap:ASR-naive performs best, and HarLap:ASR-fast is comparable to HarAff:SIFT and HarAff:DAISY. This further demonstrates that the subspace representation of PCA-patch vectors extracted under various affine transformations is capable of dealing with affine distortion.

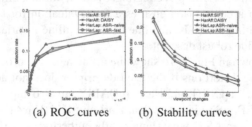

(a) ROC curves   (b) Stability curves

Fig. 9. Performance of different methods for 3D Object Dataset

5.4 Timing Result

In this section, we conduct time test on a desktop with an Intel Core2 Quad 2.83GHz CPU. We first test the time cost for each components of ASR, and the detailed results are given in Table 2. It can be found that most of construction time in ASR is spent on patch warping. It is worthy to note that by using the fast approximate algorithm, ASR-fast does not compute the warped patch directly and so largely reduce its time by about 75%. For comparison, we also report the time costs for SIFT and DAISY. Note that these timing results are averaged over 100 runs, each of which computes about 1000 descriptors on image 'wall 1'. It is clear that ASR-fast is faster than SIFT and DAISY, while ASR-naive is slower than SIFT but still comparable to DAISY.

Table 2. Timing costs for constructing different descriptors

	ASR-naive	ASR-fast	SIFT	DAISY
patch warping[ms]	2.98	0.00	-	-
patch representation[ms]	0.71	0.64	-	-
subspace representation[ms]	0.49	0.49	-	-
total time[ms]	4.18	1.13	2.09	3.8

6   Conclusion

In this paper, we have proposed the Affine Subspace Representation (ASR) descriptor. The novelty lies in three aspects: 1) dealing with affine distortion by integrating local information under multiple views, which avoids the inaccurate affine shape estimation, 2) a fast approximate algorithm for efficiently computing the PCA-patch vector of each warped patch, and 3) the subspace representation of PCA-patch vectors extracted under various affine transformations of the same keypoint.

Different from existing methods, ASR effectively exploits the local information of a keypoint by integrating the PCA-patch vectors of all warped patches. The use of multiple views' information makes it is capable of dealing with affine distortions to a certain degree while maintaining high distinctiveness. What is more, to speedup the computation, a fast approximate algorithm is proposed at a little cost of performance degradation. Extensive experimental evaluations have demonstrated the effectiveness of the proposed method.

Acknowledgment. This work is supported by the National Nature Science Foundation of China (No.91120012, 61203277, 61272394) and the Beijing Nature Science Foundation (No.4142057).

References

1. http://www.robots.ox.ac.uk/~vgg/research/affine/
2. Basri, R., Hassner, T., Zelnik-Manor, L.: Approximate nearest subspace search. PAMI 33(2), 266–278 (2011)
3. Baumberg, A.: Reliable feature matching across widely separated views. In: Proc. of CVPR, vol. 1, pp. 774–781. IEEE (2000)
4. Bay, H., Tuytelaars, T., Van Gool, L.: SURF: Speeded up robust features. In: Leonardis, A., Bischof, H., Pinz, A. (eds.) ECCV 2006, Part I. LNCS, vol. 3951, pp. 404–417. Springer, Heidelberg (2006)
5. Edelman, A., Arias, T.A., Smith, S.T.: The geometry of algorithms with orthogonality constraints. SIAM Journal on Matrix Analysis and Applications 20(2), 303–353 (1998)
6. Fan, B., Wu, F., Hu, Z.: Aggregating gradient distributions into intensity orders: A novel local image descriptor. In: Proc. of CVPR, pp. 2377–2384 (2011)
7. Fan, B., Wu, F., Hu, Z.: Rotationally invariant descriptors using intensity order pooling. PAMI 34(10), 2031–2045 (2012)
8. Hassner, T., Mayzels, V., Zelnik-Manor, L.: On sifts and their scales. In: Proc. of CVPR (2012)

9. Hinterstoisser, S., Lepetit, V., Benhimane, S., Fua, P., Navab, N.: Learning real-time perspective patch rectification. IJCV, 1–24 (2011)
10. Leutenegger, S., Chli, M., Siegwart, R.Y.: Brisk: Binary robust invariant scalable keypoints. In: Proc. of ICCV, pp. 2548–2555 (2011)
11. Lindeberg, T.: Feature detection with automatic scale selection. IJCV 30(2), 79–116 (1998)
12. Lindeberg, T., Gårding, J.: Shape-adapted smoothing in estimation of 3-d shape cues from affine deformations of local 2-d brightness structure. Image and Vision Computing 15(6), 415–434 (1997)
13. Lowe, D.: Distinctive image features from scale-invariant keypoints. IJCV 60(2), 91–110 (2004)
14. Matas, J., Chum, O., Urban, M., Stereo, T.P.: Robust wide baseline stereo from maximally stable extremal regions. In: Proc. of BMVC, pp. 414–431 (2002)
15. Mikolajczyk, K., Tuytelaars, T., Schmid, C., Zisserman, A., Matas, J., Schaffalitzky, F., Kadir, T., Gool, L.: A comparison of affine region detectors. IJCV 65(1), 43–72 (2005)
16. Mikolajczyk, K., Schmid, C.: Scale & affine invariant interest point detectors. IJCV 60, 63–86 (2004)
17. Mikolajczyk, K., Schmid, C.: A performance evaluation of local descriptors. PAMI 27(10), 1615–1630 (2005)
18. Moreels, P., Perona, P.: Evaluation of features detectors and descriptors based on 3d objects. International Journal of Computer Vision 73(3), 263–284 (2007)
19. Morel, J.-M., Yu, G.: Asift: A new framework for fully affine invariant image comparison. SIAM Journal on Imaging Sciences, 438–469 (2009)
20. Ozuysal, M., Calonder, M., Lepetit, V., Fua, P.: Fast keypoint recognition using random ferns. PAMI 32(3), 448–461 (2010)
21. Tuytelaars, T., Van Gool, L.: Matching widely separated views based on affine invariant regions. IJCV 59, 61–85 (2004)
22. Wang, Z., Fan, B., Wu, F.: Local intensity order pattern for feature description. In: Proc. of ICCV, pp. 603–610 (2011)
23. Winder, S., Hua, G., Brown, M.: Picking the best daisy. In: Proc. of CVPR, pp. 178–185 (2009)
24. Yan, K., Sukthankar, R.: Pca-sift: A more distinctive representation for local image descriptors. In: Proc. of CVPR, pp. 506–513 (2004)

A Generative Model for the Joint Registration of Multiple Point Sets*

Georgios D. Evangelidis[1], Dionyssos Kounades-Bastian[1,2], Radu Horaud[1], and Emmanouil Z. Psarakis[2]

[1] INRIA Grenoble Rhône-Alpes, France
[2] CEID, University of Patras, Greece

Abstract. This paper describes a probabilistic generative model and its associated algorithm to jointly register multiple point sets. The vast majority of state-of-the-art registration techniques select one of the sets as the "model" and perform pairwise alignments between the other sets and this set. The main drawback of this mode of operation is that there is no guarantee that the model-set is free of noise and outliers, which contaminates the estimation of the registration parameters. Unlike previous work, the proposed method treats all the point sets on an equal footing: they are realizations of a Gaussian mixture (GMM) and the registration is cast into a clustering problem. We formally derive an EM algorithm that estimates both the GMM parameters and the rotations and translations that map each individual set onto the "central" model. The mixture means play the role of the registered set of points while the variances provide rich information about the quality of the registration. We thoroughly validate the proposed method with challenging datasets, we compare it with several state-of-the-art methods, and we show its potential for fusing real depth data.

Keywords: point set registration, joint registration, expectation maximization, Gaussian mixture model.

1 Introduction

Registration of point sets is an essential methodology in computer vision, computer graphics, robotics, and medical image analysis. To date, while the vast majority of techniques deal with two sets, e.g., [4,10,26,23,15,18], the multiple-set registration problem has comparatively received less attention, e.g., [30,28]. There are many practical situations when multiple-set registration is needed, nevertheless the problem is generally solved by applying pairwise registration repeatedly, either sequentially [6,20,17], or via a *one-versus-all* strategy [3,7,16].

Regardless of the particular pairwise registration algorithm that is being used, their use for multiple-set registration has limited performance. On the one hand, sequential register-then-integrate strategies suffer from error propagation while

---

* This work has received funding from Agence Nationale de la Recherche under the MIXCAM project number ANR-13-BS02-0010-01.

D. Fleet et al. (Eds.): ECCV 2014, Part VII, LNCS 8695, pp. 109–122, 2014.

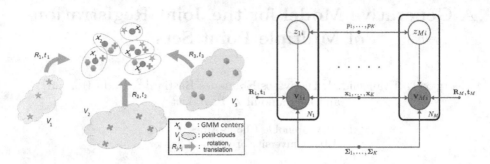

Fig. 1. The proposed generative model for joint registration of multiple point clouds (left) and the associated graphical model (right). Unlike pairwise registration strategies, the proposed model simultaneously registers an arbitrary number of point clouds with partial or total overlap and optimally estimates both the GMM and registration parameters. Hence, the solution is not biased towards a particular cloud.

they are optimal only locally, i.e., between point-set pairs. On the other hand, one-versus-all registration apparently leads to a biased estimator since one of the sets governs the registration and the solution is optimal only for this reference set. Therefore, an unbiased solution that evenly distributes the errors across all point sets is particularly desirable.

In this paper we propose a generative approach to the problem of joint registration of multiple 3D point sets. An arbitrary number of point sets are assumed to be generated from the *same* Gaussian mixture model (GMM). More precisely, an observed point i from set j, once rotated ($\mathbf{R}_j$) and translated ($\mathbf{t}_j$), is generated from the k-th component of a GMM, e.g., Fig. 1. Therefore, the GMM parameters are conditioned by the registration parameters (rotations and translations). This can be cast into a maximum likelihood formulation that is efficiently solved via an expectation conditional maximization (ECM) algorithm that jointly and optimally estimates all the GMM and registration parameters.

Unlike existing approaches to point registration that constrain the GMM means to coincide with the points of one set, the parameters of the proposed mixture model are not tight to a particular set. Existing approaches have the danger that noise and outliers, inherently present in the point set chosen to be the GMM means, contaminates the solution in an irrevocable way. It is well known that noisy data and outliers can be very robustly handled with GMMs by including a uniform component [1]. This has already been proposed in the framework of pairwise registration [23,15], in which case one set is supposed to be "bad" while the other one is supposed to be "perfect". In the proposed model all the sets are treated similarly and the GMM means are obtained by averaging over several transformed points belonging to different sets. Therefore, the proposed approach puts all the data on an equal footing and hence it is more robust. This is particularly beneficial when the task is to align a large number of point clouds, e.g., gathered with a depth camera.

The remainder of this paper is organized as follows: Section 2 discusses the related work. Section 3 formulates the problem in a generative probabilistic framework while Section 4 presents the proposed formulation and the associated algorithm. Experiments are presented in Section 5 and Section 6 concludes the paper.

2 Related Work

Modern point registration methods adopt soft assignment strategies, thus generalizing ICP [4]. In all these methods one set is the "model" and the other set is the "data" [29,11,9,23,15], to cite just a few. This non-symmetric treatment leads to biased solutions. Alternatively, [18,14] consider two GMMs, one for each point set and the rigid transformation is applied to one of these mixtures. This leads to a non-linear optimization problem, hence requiring proper initialization. Moreover, outliers are not explicitly taken into account by these methods.

Multiple point-set registration is often solved using a sequential pairwise registration strategy [6,20,17,24,8]. Whenever an additional set is available, the model parameters are updated using either ICP or a probabilistic scheme. In addition to the drawbacks associated with pairwise registration, this incremental mode of operation is subject to error propagation. Another possible strategy is to register pairs of views and subsequently to refine the registration parameters by solving an optimization problem that updates the parameters with respect to a reference set [3]. [16] starts with pairwise registrations to build a connected graph of overlapping sets, while a global optimization step over this graph representation eliminates matches that are not globally consistent. Similarly and more efficiently, [7] and [25] globally refine the registration between overlapping sets by working only in the transformation space. Despite the global refinement step, these methods suffer from the same limitation, namely one of the point sets is chosen as a reference set and hence the final parameters are biased.

Multiple point-set registration was also addressed in [30,28]. Both these methods estimate a transformation for each point set, such that the transformed sets can be jointly registered. Starting from some *known* point correspondences between the sets, [30] estimates the transformation parameters through the minimization of a criterion that relates *any* two overlapping sets, and optionally integrates confidence of points. Since point correspondences are provided by pairwise ICP, this approach is referred to as multi-set ICP. As with pairwise ICP, one-to-one correspondences lead to the aforementioned limitations. Notice that the same formulation but with a different optimization method is proposed in [19], and was recently extended in [21] to deal with unknown correspondences. As in [30], [2] registers matched shapes by estimating transformations (one per shape) of an unknown reference shape. [28] shares a lot of similarities with [18] in the sense that it represents each point set as a GMM and the transformations are applied to these mixtures rather than to individual points. The model parameters are estimated by minimizing the Jensen-Shannon divergence. A by-product of the algorithm is a probabilistic atlas defined by a convex combination of the mixtures. To the best of our knowledge, this is the only method that achieves joint multiple-set registration without recourse to a pairwise strategy. However the GMM representation of a point set inherently encapsulates the set's noisy and outlier observations, and hence the registration of point sets with different amounts of noise and of outliers is problematic, as well as sets with large non overlapping regions.

3   Problem Formulation

Let $\mathbf{V}_j = [\mathbf{v}_{j1} \ldots \mathbf{v}_{ji} \ldots \mathbf{v}_{jN_j}]$ be a $\mathbb{R}^{3 \times N_j}$ matrix of N_j points associated with the j-th point set and let M be the number of sets. We denote with $\mathbf{V} = \{\mathbf{V}_j\}_{j=1}^M$ the union of all the data points. It is assumed that there is a rigid transformation $\phi_j : \mathbb{R}^3 \to \mathbb{R}^3$ that maps a point set j onto a scene-centered model. The objective is to estimate the set-to-scene transformations under the constraint that the sets are jointly registered. It is assumed that the point sets are rigidly-transformed realizations of an unknown "central" GMM. Hence, one can write

$$P(\mathbf{v}_{ji}) = \sum_{k=1}^K p_k \mathcal{N}\big(\phi_j(\mathbf{v}_{ji})|\mathbf{x}_k, \mathbf{\Sigma}_k\big) + p_{K+1}\mathcal{U}(a - b), \tag{1}$$

where $\phi(\mathbf{v}_{ji}) = \mathbf{R}_j\mathbf{v}_{ji} + \mathbf{t}_j$ (a 3×3 rotation matrix $\mathbf{R}_j$ and a 3×1 translation vector $\mathbf{t}_j$), p_k are the mixing coefficients $\sum_{k=1}^{K+1} p_k = 1$, $\mathbf{x}_k$ and $\mathbf{\Sigma}_k$ are the means and covariance matrices, and $\mathcal{U}$ is the uniform distribution parameterized by $a - b$. Here we take $a - b = h$, where h is the volume of the 3D convex hull encompassing the data [15]. We now define γ as the ratio between outliers and inliers, that is,

$$p_{K+1} = \gamma \sum_{k=1}^K p_k. \tag{2}$$

This allows to balance the outlier/inlier proportion by choosing γ. To summarize, the model parameters are

$$\Theta = \big(\{p_k, \mathbf{x}_k, \mathbf{\Sigma}_k\}_{k=1}^K, \{\mathbf{R}_j, \mathbf{t}_j\}_{j=1}^M\big). \tag{3}$$

We stress that the deterministic nature of ϕ_j does not affect the statistical properties of the mixture model. Fig. 1 shows a graphical representation of the proposed model.

This problem can be solved in the framework of expectation-maximization. In particular, we define hidden variables $\mathcal{Z} = \{z_{ji}|j = 1 \ldots M, i = 1 \ldots N_j\}$ such that $z_{ji} = k$ assigns observation $\phi_j(\mathbf{v}_{ji})$ to the k-th component of the mixture model, and we aim to maximize the expected complete-data log-likelihood

$$\mathcal{E}(\Theta|\mathbf{V}, \mathcal{Z}) = \mathbb{E}_{\mathcal{Z}}[logP(\mathbf{V}, \mathcal{Z}; \Theta)|\mathbf{V}] = \sum_{\mathcal{Z}} P(\mathcal{Z}|\mathbf{V}, \Theta) \log(P(\mathbf{V}, \mathcal{Z}; \Theta)) \tag{4}$$

in order to estimate the parameters Θ.

4   Joint Multiple-Set Registration

Assuming that the observed data $\mathbf{V}$ are independent and identically distributed, it is straightforward to write (4) as

$$\mathcal{E}(\Theta|\mathbf{V},\mathcal{Z}) = \sum_{j,i,k} \alpha_{jik}\Big(\log p_k + \log P(\phi_j(\mathbf{v}_{ji})|z_{ji} = k; \Theta)\Big) \tag{5}$$

where $\alpha_{jik} = P(z_{ji} = k|\mathbf{v}_{ji}; \Theta)$ are the posteriors. By replacing the standard expressions of the likelihoods [5] and by ignoring constant terms, (5) can be written as an objective function of the form

$$f(\Theta) = -\frac{1}{2}\sum_{j,i,k} \alpha_{jik}\Big(\|\phi_j(\mathbf{v}_{ji}) - \mathbf{x}_k\|^2_{\boldsymbol{\Sigma}_k} + \log|\boldsymbol{\Sigma}_k| - 2\log p_k\Big)$$
$$+ \log p_{K+1}\sum_{j,i}\alpha_{ji(K+1)} \tag{6}$$

where $|\cdot|$ denotes the determinant and $\|y\|^2_A = y^\top A^{-1}y$. Therefore, one has to solve the following constrained optimization problem:

$$\begin{cases} \max_{\Theta} & f(\Theta) \\ \text{s.t.} & \mathbf{R}_j^\top \mathbf{R}_j = \mathbf{I}, \quad |\mathbf{R}_j| = 1, \forall j = 1\dots M. \end{cases} \tag{7}$$

Direct optimization of $f(\Theta)$ via a closed-form solution is difficult owing to the induced non-linearities. Therefore, we adopt an expectation conditional maximization (ECM) scheme to solve (7). ECM is more broadly applicable than EM, while it is well suited for our problem owing to the extended parameter set. Notice that ECM replaces the M-step of EM with a series of conditional maximization (CM) steps, that is, an M-substep for each parameter. We will refer to this algorithm as *joint registration of multiple point clouds* (JR-MPC); its outline is given in Algorithm 1. JR-MPC maximizes $f(\Theta)$, and hence $\mathcal{E}(\Theta|\mathbf{V},\mathcal{Z})$, sequentially with respect to each parameter, by clamping the remaining ones to their current values. Commonly, such an iterative process leads to a stepwise maximization of the observed-data likelihood as well [22]. At each iteration, we first estimate the transformation parameters, given the current GMM parameters, and then we estimate the new GMM parameters, given the new transformation parameters. It is of course possible to adopt a reverse order, in particular when a rough alignment of the point sets is provided. However, we consider no prior information on the rigid transformations, so that the pre-estimation of the registration parameters favors the estimation of the GMM means, $\mathbf{x}_k$, that should be well distributed in space.

Now that our objective function is specified, we are going to present in detail each step of JR-MPC. We restrict the model to isotropic covariances, i.e., $\boldsymbol{\Sigma}_k = \sigma_k^2\mathbf{I}$, since it leads to a more efficient algorithm, while experiments with non-isotropic covariance [15] showed that there is no significant accuracy gain.

Algorithm 1. Joint Registration of Multiple Point Clouds (JR-MPC)

Require: Initial parameter set Θ^0
1:   $q \leftarrow 1$
2: **repeat**
3:     *E-step*: Use Θ^{q-1} to estimate posterior probabilities $\alpha_{jik}^q = P(z_{ji} = k | \mathbf{v}_{ji}; \Theta^{q-1})$
4:     *CM-step-A*: Use α_{jik}^q, $\mathbf{x}_k^{q-1}$ and $\mathbf{\Sigma}_k^{q-1}$ to estimate $\mathbf{R}_j^q$ and $\mathbf{t}_j^q$.
5:     *CM-step-B*: Use α_{jik}^q, $\mathbf{R}_j^q$ and $\mathbf{t}_j^q$ to estimate the means $\mathbf{x}_k^q$.
6:     *CM-step-C*: Use α_{jik}^q, $\mathbf{R}_j^q$, $\mathbf{t}_j^q$ and $\mathbf{x}_k^q$ to estimate the covariances $\mathbf{\Sigma}_k^q$.
7:     *CM-step-D*: Use α_{jik}^q to estimate the priors p_k^q.
8:     $q \leftarrow q + 1$
9: **until** Convergence
10: **return** Θ^q

E-step: By using the definitions for the likelihood and prior terms, and the decomposition of the marginal distribution, $P(\phi_j(\mathbf{v}_{ji})) = \sum_{s=1}^{K+1} p_s P(\phi_j(\mathbf{v}_{ji})|z_{ji} = s)$, the posterior probability α_{jik} of $\mathbf{v}_{ij}$ to be an *inlier* can be computed by

$$\alpha_{jik} = \frac{p_k \sigma_k^{-3} \exp\left(-\frac{1}{2\sigma_k^2} \|\phi_j(\mathbf{v}_{ji}) - \mathbf{x}_k\|^2\right)}{\sum\limits_{s=1}^{K} \left[p_s \sigma_s^{-3} \exp\left(-\frac{1}{2\sigma_s^2} \|\phi_j(\mathbf{v}_{ji}) - \mathbf{x}_s\|^2\right) \right] + \beta}, \quad k = 1, \ldots, K, \quad (8)$$

where $\beta = \gamma/h(\gamma + 1)$ accounts for the outlier term, while the posterior to be an *outlier* is simply given by $\alpha_{ji(K+1)} = 1 - \sum_{k=1}^{K} \alpha_{jik}$. As shown in Alg. 1, the posterior probability at the q-th iteration, α_{jik}^q, is computed from (8) using the parameter set Θ^{q-1}.

CM-step-A: This step estimates the transformations ϕ_j that maximize $f(\Theta)$, given current values for α_{jik}, $\mathbf{x}_k$, $\mathbf{\Sigma}_k$. Notice that this estimation can be carried out independently for each set j, since ϕ_j associates each point set with the common set of GMM means.

By setting the GMM parameters to their current values, we reformulate the problem to estimate the roto-translations. It can be easily shown that the maximizers $\mathbf{R}_j^*$, $\mathbf{t}_j^*$ of $f(\Theta)$ coincide with the minimizers of the following constrained optimization problems

$$\begin{cases} \min\limits_{\mathbf{R}_j, \mathbf{t}_j} & \|(\mathbf{R}_j \mathbf{W}_j + \mathbf{t}_j \mathbf{e}^\top - \mathbf{X})\mathbf{\Lambda}_j\|_F^2 \\ \text{s.t.} & \mathbf{R}_j^\top \mathbf{R}_j = \mathbf{I}, \ |\mathbf{R}_j| = 1 \end{cases} \quad (9)$$

where $\mathbf{\Lambda}_j$ is a $K \times K$ diagonal matrix with elements $\lambda_{jk} = \frac{1}{\sigma_k}\sqrt{\sum_{i=1}^{N_j} \alpha_{jik}}$, $\mathbf{X} = [\mathbf{x}_1, \ldots, \mathbf{x}_K]$, $\mathbf{e}$ is a vector of ones, $\|\cdot\|_F$ denotes the Frobenius norm, and $\mathbf{W}_j = [\mathbf{w}_{j1}, \ldots, \mathbf{w}_{jK}]$, with $\mathbf{w}_{jk}$, is a virtual 3D point given by

$$\mathbf{w}_{jk} = \frac{\sum_{i=1}^{N_j} \alpha_{jik} \mathbf{v}_{ji}}{\sum_{i=1}^{N_j} \alpha_{jik}}, \quad (10)$$

or the weighted average of points in point set j, being the weights proportional to the posterior probabilities in terms of the k-th component. The above problem is an extension of the problem solved in [27] as here we end up with a weighted case due to Λ_j. The problem still has an analytic solution. In specific, the optimal rotation is given by

$$\mathbf{R}_j^* = \mathbf{U}_j^L \mathbf{S}_j \mathbf{U}_j^{R^\top}, \tag{11}$$

where $\mathbf{U}_j^L$ and $\mathbf{U}_j^R$ are the left and right matrices obtained from the singular value decomposition of matrix $\mathbf{X}\Lambda_j \mathbf{P}_j \Lambda_j \mathbf{W}_j^\top$, with $\mathbf{P}_j = \mathbf{I} - \frac{\Lambda_j \mathbf{e}(\Lambda_j \mathbf{e})^\top}{(\Lambda_j \mathbf{e})^\top \Lambda_j \mathbf{e}}$ being a projection matrix, and $\mathbf{S}_j = \mathrm{diag}(1, 1, |\mathbf{U}_j^L||\mathbf{U}_j^R|)$. Once the optimum rotation is known, the optimum translation is computed by

$$\mathbf{t}_j^* = \frac{-1}{tr(\Lambda_j^2)}(\mathbf{R}_j^* \mathbf{W}_j - \mathbf{X})\Lambda_j^2 \mathbf{e}. \tag{12}$$

Note that ϕ_j aligns the GMM means $\{\mathbf{x}_k\}_{k=1}^K$ with the virtual points $\{\mathbf{w}_{jk}\}_{k=1}^K$. Hence, our method deals with point sets of different cardinalities and the number of components K in the GMM can be chosen independently of the cardinality of the point sets.

CM-step-B and CM-step-C: These steps estimate the GMM means and variances given the current estimates of the rigid transformations and of the posteriors. By setting $\partial f/\partial \mathbf{x}_k = 0$, $k = 1 \ldots, K$, we easily obtain the optimal means. Then, we replace these values and obtain optimal variances by setting $\partial f/\partial \sigma_k = 0$. This leads to the following formulas for the means and the variances

$$\mathbf{x}_k^* = \frac{\sum_{j=1}^M \sum_{i=1}^{N_j} \alpha_{jik}(\mathbf{R}_j^* \mathbf{v}_{ji} + \mathbf{t}_j^*)}{\sum_{j=1}^M \sum_{i=1}^{N_j} \alpha_{jik}}, \quad \sigma_k^{*2} = \frac{\sum_{j=1}^M \sum_{i=1}^{N_j} \alpha_{jik}\|\mathbf{R}_j^* \mathbf{v}_{ji} + \mathbf{t}_j^* - \mathbf{x}_k^*\|_2^2}{3\sum_{j=1}^M \sum_{i=1}^{N_j} \alpha_{jik}} + \epsilon^2,$$

$$\tag{13}$$

with ϵ^2 being a very low positive value to efficiently avoid singularities [15].

CM-step-D: This step estimates the priors p_k. From (2) we obtain $\sum_{k=1}^K p_k = 1/(1 + \gamma)$. By neglecting the terms in (6) that do not depend on the priors and by using a Lagrange multiplier, the dual objective function becomes

$$f_L(p_1, \ldots, p_K, \mu) = \sum_{k=1}^K \left(\log p_k \sum_{i,j} \alpha_{jik} \right) + \mu \left(\sum_{k=1}^K p_k - \frac{1}{1+\gamma} \right). \tag{14}$$

Setting $\partial f_L/\partial p_k = 0$ yields the following optimal priors

$$p_k^* = \frac{\sum_{j,i} \alpha_{jik}}{\mu}, \quad k = 1 \ldots K \quad \text{and} \quad p_{K+1}^* = 1 - \sum_{k=1}^K p_k^*, \tag{15}$$

with $\mu = (\gamma + 1)(N - \sum_{j,i} \alpha_{ji(K+1)})$ and $N = \sum_j N_j$ being the cardinality of $\mathbf{V}$. Note that if $\gamma \to 0$, which means that there is no uniform component in the mixture, then $\mu \to N$, which is in agreement with [5]. Based on the pseudocode of Alg. 1, the above steps are iterated until a convergence criterion is met, e.g., a sufficient number of iterations or a bound on the improvement of $f(\Theta)$.

5 Experiments with Synthetic and Real Data

For quantitative evaluation, we experiment with the 3D models "Bunny", "Lucy" and "Armadillo" from the Stanford 3D scanning repository[1]. We use fully viewed models in order to synthesize multiple point sets, as follows. The model point coordinates are shifted at the origin, the points are downsampled and then rotated in the xz-plane; points with negative z coordinates are rejected. This way, only a part of the object is viewed in each set, the point sets do not fully overlap, and the extent of the overlap depends on the rotation angle, as in real scenarios. It is important to note that the downsampling is different for each set, such different points are present in each set and the sets have different cardinalities (between 1000 and 2000 points). We add Gaussian noise to point coordinates based on a predefined signal-to-noise ratio (SNR), and more importantly, we add outliers to each set which are uniformly distributed around five randomly chosen points of the set.

For comparison, we consider the 3D rigid registration algorithms ICP [4], CPD [23], ECMPR [15], GMMReg [18] and the simultaneous registration algorithm of [30] abbreviated here as SimReg. Note that CPD is exactly equivalent to ECMPR when it comes to rigid registration and that SimReg internally uses an ICP framework. Other than SimReg, the rest are pairwise registration schemes that register the first point set with each of the rest. Sequential ICP (seqICP) does the known register–then–integrate cycle. Although GMMReg is the version of [28] for two point sets, the authors provide the code only for the pairwise case. We choose GMMReg for comparison since, as showed in [18], Levenberg-Marquardt ICP [10] performs similarly with GMMReg, while [28] shows that GMMReg is superior to Kernel Correlation [26].

As far as the registration error is concerned, we use the root–mean–square error (RMSE) of rotation parameters since translation estimation is not challenging. For all algorithms, we implicitly initialise the translations by transferring the centroids of the point clouds into the same point, while identity matrices initialize the rotations. The only exception is the SimReg algorithm which fails without a good starting point, thus the transformations are initialized by pairwise ICP. GMMReg is kind of favored in the comparison, since it uses a two-level optimization process and the first level helps the algorithm to initialize itself. Notice that both SimReg and the proposed method provide rigid transformations for *every* point set, while ground rotations are typically expressed in terms

---

[1] https://graphics.stanford.edu/data/3Dscanrep/3Dscanrep.html

of the first set. Hence, the product of estimations $\hat{R}_1^\top \hat{R}_j$ is compared with the ground rotation R_j, and the error is $\|\hat{R}_1^\top \hat{R}_j - R_j\|_F$.

We consider a tractable case of jointly registering four point sets, the angle between the first set and the other sets being $10°$, $20°$ and $30°$ respectively. Since JR-MPC starts from a completely unknown GMM, the initial means $\mathbf{x}_k$ are distributed on a sphere that spans the convex hull of the sets. The variances σ_k are initialized with the median distance between $\mathbf{x}_k$ and all the points in $\mathbf{V}$. For our experiments, we found that updating priors do not drastically improve the registration, thus we fix the priors equal to $1/(K+1)$ and $\gamma = 1/K$, while h is chosen to be the volume of a sphere whose radius is 0.5; the latter is not an arbitrary choice since the point coordinates are normalized by the maximum distance between points of the convex hull of $\mathbf{V}$. CPD and ECMPR deal with the outliers in the same way. The number of the components, K, is here equal to 60% of the mean cardinality. We use 100 iterations for all algorithms excepting GMMReg, whose implementation performs 10 and 100 function evaluations for the first and second optimization levels respectively.

Fig. 2 shows the final log-RMSE averaged over 100 realisations and all views as a function of outlier percentage for each 3D model. Apparently, ICP and SimReg are more affected by the presence of outliers owing to one-to-one correspondences. CPD and GMMReg are affected in the sense that the former assigns outliers to any of the GMM components, while the latter clusters together outliers. The proposed method is more robust to outliers and the registration is successful even with densely present outliers. The behavior of the proposed algorithm in terms of the outliers is discussed in detail below and showed on Fig. 4. To visualize the convergence rate of the algorithms, we show curves for a typical setting ($SNR = 10dB$ and 20% outliers). Regarding GMMReg, we just plot a line that shows the error in steady state. There is a performance variation as the model changes. "Lucy" is more asymmetric than "Bunny" and "Armadillo", thus a lower floor is achieved. Unlike the competitors, JR-MPC may show a minor perturbation in the first iterations owing to the joint solution and the random initialization of the means $\mathbf{x}_k$. However, the estimation of each transformation benefits from the proposed joint solution, in particular when the point sets contain outliers, and JR-MPC attains the lowest floor.

It is also important to show the estimation error between non overlapping sets. This also shows how biased each algorithm is. Based on the above experiment (SNR=10db, 20% outliers), Table 1 reports the average rotation error for the pairs (V_2, V_3) and (V_3, V_4), as well as the standard deviation of these two errors as a measure of bias. All but seqICP do not estimate these direct mappings. The proposed scheme, not only provides the lowest error, but it also offers the most symmetric solution.

A second experiment evaluates the robustness of the algorithms in terms of rotation angle between two point sets, hence the degree of overlap. This also allows us to show how the proposed algorithm deals with the simple case of two point sets. Recall that JR-MPC does not reduce to CPD/ECMPR in the two-set case, but rather it computes the poses of the two sets with respect to the

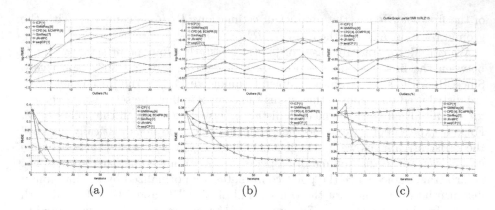

(a)   (b)   (c)

Fig. 2. *Top:* log-RMSE as a function of outlier percentage when SNR=10dB. *Bottom:* The learning curve of algorithms for a range of 100 iterations when the models are disturbed by SNR=10dB and 20% outliers. (a) "Lucy", (b) "Bunny" (c) "Armadillo".

Table 1. Registration error of indirect mappings. For each model, the two first columns show the rotation error of $V_2 \rightarrow V_3$ and $V_3 \rightarrow V_4$ respectively, while the third column shows the standard deviation of these two errors ($SNR = 10db$, 30% outliers).

	Bunny			Lucy			Armadillo		
ICP [4]	0.329	0.423	0.047	0.315	0.297	0.009	0.263	0.373	0.055
GMMReg [18]	0.364	0.303	0.030	0.129	0.110	0.009	0.228	0.167	0.031
CPD [23], ECMPR [15]	0.214	0.242	0.014	0.144	0.109	0.017	0.222	0.204	0.009
SimReg [30]	0.333	0.415	0.041	0.354	0.245	0.055	0.269	0.301	0.016
JR-MPC	0.181	0.165	**0.008**	0.068	0.060	**0.004**	0.147	0.147	**0.000**

"central" GMM. Fig. 3 plots the average RMSE over 50 realizations of "Lucy" and "Armadillo", when the relative rotation angle varies from $-90°$ to $90°$. As for an acceptable registration error, the proposed scheme achieves the widest and shallowest basin for "Lucy", and competes with GMMReg for "Armadillo". Since "Armadillo" consists of smooth and concave surface parts, the performance of the proposed scheme is better with multiple point sets than the two-set case, hence the difference with GMMReg. The wide basin of GMMReg is also due to its initialization.

As mentioned, a by-product of the proposed method is the reconstruction of an outlier-free model. In addition, we are able to detect the majority of the outlying points based on the variance of the component they most likely belong to. To show this effect, we use the results of one realization of the first experiment with 30% outliers. Fig 4 shows in (a) and (b) two out of four point sets, thereby one verifies the distortion of the point sets, as well as how different the sets may be, e.g., the right hand is missing in the first set. The progress of $\mathbf{x}_k$ estimation is shown in (d-f). Apparently, the algorithm starts by reconstructing the scene model (observe the presence of the right hand). Notice the size increment of the hull of the points $\mathbf{x}_k$, during the progress. This is because the posteriors in

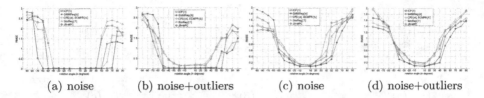

(a) noise   (b) noise+outliers   (c) noise   (d) noise+outliers

Fig. 3. RMSE as a function of the overlap (rotation angle) when two point sets are registered (SNR=20dB, 30% outliers) (a),(b) "Lucy" (c), (d) "Armadillo"

the first iteration are very low and make the means $\mathbf{x}_k$ shrink into a very small cell. While the two point sets are around the points $(0,0,0)$ and $(40,40,40)$, we build the scene model around the point $(5,5,5)$. The distribution of the final deviations σ_k is shown in (c). We get the same distribution with any model and any outlier percentage, as well as when registering real data. Although one can fit a pdf here, e.g., Rayleigh, it is convenient enough to split the components using the threshold $T_\sigma = 2 \times median(\mathcal{S})$, where $\mathcal{S} = \{\sigma_k | k = 1, \ldots K\}$. Accordingly, we build the scene model and we visualize the binary classification of points $\mathbf{x}_k$. Apparently, whenever components attract outliers, even not far from the object surface, they tend to spread their hull by increasing their scale. Based on the above thresholding, we can detect such components and reject points that are assigned with high probability to them, as shown in (g). Despite the introduction of the uniform component that prevents the algorithm from building clusters away from the object surface, locally dense outliers are likely to create components outside the surface. In this example, most of the point sets contain outliers above the shoulders, and the algorithm builds components with outliers only, that are post-detected by their variance. The integrated surface is shown in (h) and (i) when "bad" points were automatically removed. Of course, the surface can be post-processed, e.g., smoothing, for a more accurate representation, but this is beyond of our goal.

We report here CPU times obtained with unoptimized Matlab implementations of the algorithms. ICP, CPD (ECMPR), SimReg, and JR-MPC require 14.7s, 40.6s, 24.6s, and 20.9s respectively to register four point sets of 1200 points, on an average. The C++ implementation of GMMReg requires 6.7s. JR-MPC runs faster than repeating CPD(ECMPR) since only one GMM is needed and the number of components is less than the number of points. Of course, ICP is the most efficient solution. However, SimReg needs more time as it enables every pair of overlapping point sets.

We also tested our method with real depth data captured from a time-of-flight (TOF) camera that is rigidly attached to two color cameras. Once calibrated [13,12], this sensor provides 3D point clouds with associated color information. We gathered ten point clouds by manually moving the sensor in front of a scene, e.g., Fig. 5. Multiple-set registration was performed with all the above methods. While only depth information is used for the registration, the use of color information helps the final assessment and also shows the potential for fusing RGB-D data.

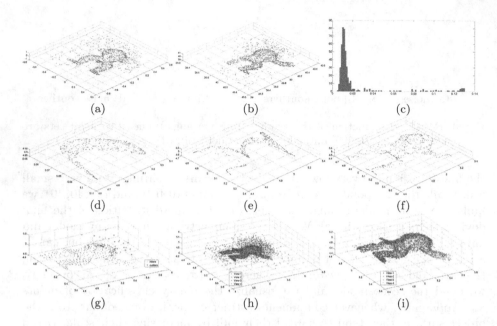

Fig. 4. (a),(b) Two point sets (out of four) with outliers; (c) distribution of estimated variances; instances of GMM means after (d) 5, (e) 15, and (f) 30 iterations; (g) the splitting of model points into inliers and outliers; joint-registration of four point sets (h) before and (i) after removing "bad" points (*best viewed on-screen*)

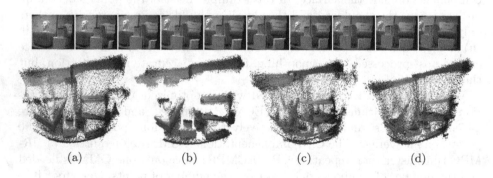

Fig. 5. The integrated point clouds from the joint registration of 10 TOF images that record a static scene. *Top*: color images that roughly show the scene content of each range image (occlusions due to cameras baseline cause some texture artefacts). *Bottom*: top-view of joint registration obtained from (a) JR-MPC, (b) JR-MPC+outlier rejection, (c) sequential ICP and (d) SimReg.

Fig. 5 shows the results obtained with JR-MPC before (a) and after (b) rejecting outliers, seqICP (c) and SimReg (d). The proposed method successfully register the point clouds, while it automatically removes most of the jump-edge errors contained in range images. SimReg registers the majority of point sets, but it fails to register a few sets that appear flipped in the integrated view. Using the 5-th set as a reference for symmetry reasons, CDP/ECMPR and ICP also fail to register all the clouds while GMMReg yields low performance with too many misalignments. SeqICP causes weak misalignments, since it estimates weak geometric deformations between successive captures. However, the registration is not very accurate and further processing may be necessary, e.g., [17]. We refer the reader to the supplementary material for the integrated set of all the algorithms, viewed by several viewpoitns.

6   Conclusions

We presented a probabilistic generative model and its associated algorithm to jointly register multiple point sets. The vast majority of state-of-the-art techniques select one of the sets as the model and attempt to align the other sets onto this model. However, there is no guarantee that the model set is free of noise and outliers and this contaminates the estimation of the registration parameters. Unlike previous work, the proposed method treats all the point sets on an equal footing: they are realizations of a GMM and the registration is cast into a clustering problem. We formally derive an expectation-maximization algorithm that estimates the GMM parameters as well as the rotations and translations between each individual set and a "central" model. In this model the GMM means play the role of the registered points and the variances provide rich information about the quality of the registration. We thoroughly validated the proposed method with challenging datasets, we compared it with several state-of-the-art methods, and we showed its potential for fusing real depth data.

Supplementary Material. Datasets, code and videos are publicly available at https://team.inria.fr/perception/research/jrmpc/

References

1. Banfield, J.D., Raftery, A.E.: Model-based Gaussian and non-Gaussian clustering. Biometrics 49(3), 803–821 (1993)
2. Bartoli, A., Pizzaro, D., Loog, M.: Stratified generalized procrustes analysis. IJCV 101(2), 227–253 (2013)
3. Bergevin, R., Soucy, M., Gagnon, H., Laurendeau, D.: Towards a general multiview registration technique. IEEE-TPAMI 18(5), 540–547 (1996)
4. Besl, P.J., McKay, N.D.: A method for registration of 3-D shapes. IEEE TPAMI 14, 239–256 (1992)
5. Bishop, C.M.: Pattern Recognition and Machine Learning. Springer (2006)
6. Blais, G., D. Levine, M.: Registering multiview range data to create 3d computer objects. IEEE-TPAMI 17(8), 820–824 (1995)
7. Castellani, U., Fusiello, A., Murino, V.: Registration of multiple acoustic range views for underwater scene reconstruction. CVIU 87(1-3), 78–89 (2002)
8. Chen, Y., Medioni, G.: Object modelling by registration of multiple range images. IVC 10(3), 145–155 (1992)
9. Chui, H., Rangarajan, A.: A new point matching algorithm for non-rigid registration. CVIU 89(2-3), 114–141 (2003)

10. Fitzgibbon, A.W.: Robust registration of 2D and 3D point sets. IVC 21(12), 1145–1153 (2001)
11. Granger, S., Pennec, X.: Multi-scale EM-ICP: A fast and robust approach for surface registration. In: Heyden, A., Sparr, G., Nielsen, M., Johansen, P. (eds.) ECCV 2002, Part IV. LNCS, vol. 2353, pp. 418–432. Springer, Heidelberg (2002)
12. Hansard, M., Horaud, R., Amat, M., Evangelidis, G.: Automatic detection of calibration grids in time-of-flight images. CVIU 121, 108–118 (2014)
13. Hansard, M., Horaud, R., Amat, M., Lee, S.: Projective alignment of range and parallax data. In: CVPR (2011)
14. Hermans, J., Smeets, D., Vandermeulen, D., Suetens, P.: Robust point set registration using em-icp with information-theoretically optimal outlier handling. In: CVPR (2011)
15. Horaud, R., Forbes, F., Yguel, M., Dewaele, G., ZhangI, J.: Rigid and articulated point registration with expectation conditional maximization. IEEE-TPAMI 33(3), 587–602 (2011)
16. Huber, D.F., Hebert, M.: Fully automatic registration of multiple 3d data sets. IVC 21(7), 637–650 (2003)
17. Izadi, S., Kim, D., Hilliges, O., Molyneaux, D., Newcombe, R., Kohli, P., Shotton, J., Hodges, S., Freeman, D., Davison, A., Fitzgibbon, A.: Kinectfusion: Real-time 3d reconstruction and interaction using a moving depth camera. In: ACM Symposium on UIST (2011)
18. Jian, B., Vemuri, B.C.: Robust point set registration using gaussian mixture models. IEEE-TPAMI 33(8), 1633–1645 (2011)
19. Krishnan, S., Lee, P.Y., Moore, J.B.: Optimisation-on-a-manifold for global registration of multiple 3d point sets. Int. J. Intelligent Systems Technologies and Applications 3(3/4), 319–340 (2007)
20. Masuda, T., Yokoya, N.: A robust method for registration and segmentation of multiple range images. CVIU 61(3), 295–307 (1995)
21. Mateo, X., Orriols, X., Binefa, X.: Bayesian perspective for the registration of multiple 3d views. CVIU 118, 84–96 (2014)
22. Meng, X.L., Rubin, D.B.: Maximum likelihood estimation via the ECM algorithm: a general framework. Biometrika 80, 267–278 (1993)
23. Myronenko, A., Song, X.: Point-set registration: Coherent point drift. IEEE-TPAMI 32(12), 2262–2275 (2010)
24. Newcombe, R.A., Izadi, S., Hilliges, O., Molyneaux, D., Kim, D., Davison, A.J., Kohli, P., Shotton, J., Hodges, S., Fitzgibbon, A.: Kinectfusion: Real-time dense surface mapping and tracking. In: IEEE ISMAR (2011)
25. Torsello, A., Rodola, E., Albarelli, A.: Multiview registration via graph diffusion of dual quaternions. In: CVPR (2011)
26. Tsin, Y., Kanade, T.: A correlation-based approach to robust point set registration. In: Pajdla, T., Matas, J(G.) (eds.) ECCV 2004, Part III. LNCS, vol. 3023, pp. 558–569. Springer, Heidelberg (2004)
27. Umeyama, S.: Least-squares estimation of transformation parameters between two point patterns. IEEE-TPAMI 13(4), 376–380 (1991)
28. Wang, F., Vemuri, B.C., Rangarajan, A., Eisenschenk, S.J.: Simultaneous nonrigid registration of multiple point sets and atlas construction. IEEE-TPAMI 30(11), 2011–2022 (2008)
29. Wells III, W.M.: Statistical approaches to feature-based object recognition. IJCV 28(1/2), 63–98 (1997)
30. Williams, J., Bennamoun, M.: Simultaneous registration of multiple corresponding point sets. CVIU 81(1), 117–142 (2001)

Change Detection in the Presence of Motion Blur and Rolling Shutter Effect

Vijay Rengarajan Angarai Pichaikuppan,
Rajagopalan Ambasamudram Narayanan, and Aravind Rangarajan

Department of Electrical Engineering
Indian Institute of Technology Madras, Chennai 600036, India
{ee11d035,raju,aravind}@ee.iitm.ac.in

Abstract. The coalesced presence of motion blur and rolling shutter effect is unavoidable due to the sequential exposure of sensor rows in CMOS cameras. We address the problem of detecting changes in an image affected by motion blur and rolling shutter artifacts with respect to a reference image. Our framework bundles modelling of motion blur in global shutter and rolling shutter cameras into a single entity. We leverage the sparsity of the camera trajectory in the pose space and the sparsity of occlusion in spatial domain to propose an optimization problem that not only registers the reference image to the observed distorted image but detects occlusions as well, both within a single framework.

1 Introduction

Change detection in images is a highly researched topic in image processing and computer vision due to its ubiquitous use in a wide range of areas including surveillance, tracking, driver assistance systems and remote sensing. The goal of change detection is to identify regions of difference between a pair of images. Seemingly a straightforward problem at first look, there are many challenges due to sensor noise, illumination changes, motion, and atmosphere distortions. A survey of various change detection approaches can be found in Radke et al. [14]. One of the main problems that arises in change detection is the presence of motion blur. It is unavoidable due to camera shake during a long exposure especially when a lowly lit scene is being captured. The same is also true if the capturing mechanism itself is moving, for example in drone surveillance systems.

In the presence of motion blur, traditional feature-based registration and occlusion detection methods cannot be used due to photometric inconsistencies as pointed out by Yuan et al. [23]. It is possible to obtain a sharp image from the blurred observation through many of the available deblurring methods before sending to the change detection pipeline. Non-uniform deblurring works, which employ homography-based blur model, include that of Gupta et al. [6], Whyte et al. [20], Joshi et al. [8], Tai et al. [18] and Hu et al. [7]. Paramanand and Rajagopalan [12] estimate camera motion due to motion blur and the depth map of static scenes using a blurred/unblurred image pair. Cho et al. [3] estimate homographies in the motion blur model posed as a set of image registration problems. A filter flow problem computing a space-variant linear filter that encompasses

D. Fleet et al. (Eds.): ECCV 2014, Part VII, LNCS 8695, pp. 123–137, 2014.

(a)   (b)

Fig. 1. (a) Reference image with no camera motion, (b) Distorted image with rolling shutter and motion blur artifacts

a wide range of tranformations including blur, radial distortion, stereo and optical flow is developed by Seitz and Baker [16]. Wu et al. [22] develop a sparse approximation framework to solve the target tracking problem in the presence of blur.

Contemporary CMOS sensors employ an electronic rolling shutter (RS) in which the horizontal rows of the sensor array are scanned at different times. This behaviour results in deformations when capturing dynamic scenes and when imaging from moving cameras. One can observe that the horizontal and vertical lines in Fig. 1(a) have become curved in Fig. 1(b). The very study of RS cameras is a growing research area. Ait-Aider et al. [1] compute the instantaneous pose and velocity of an object captured using an RS camera assuming known 2D-3D point correspondences. Liang et al. [9] rectify the RS effect between successive frames in a video by estimating a global motion and then interpolating motion for every row using a Bézier curve. Cho et al. [4] model the motion as an affine change with respect to row index. Baker et al. [2] remove the RS wobble from a video by posing it as a temporal super-resolution problem. Ringaby and Forssén [15] model the 3D rotation of the camera as a continuous curve to rectify and stabilise video from RS cameras. Grundmann et al. [5] have proposed an algorithm based on homography mixtures to remove RS effect from streaming uncalibrated videos. All these papers consider only the presence of RS deformations and the motion blur is assumed to be negligible. They typically follow a feature-based approach to rectify the effect between adjacent frames of a video.

In reality, it is apparent that both rolling shutter and motion blur issues will be present due to non-negligible exposure time. Fig. 1(b) exhibits geometric distortion due to rolling shutter effect and photometric distortion due to motion blur. Hence it is imperative to consider both the effects together in the image formation model. Meilland et al. [11] formulate a unified approach to estimate both rolling shutter and motion blur, but assume uniform velocity of the camera across the image. They follow a dense approach of minimisation of intensity errors to estimate camera motion between two consecutive frames of a video. In this paper, we remove the assumption of uniform camera velocity, and propose a general model that combines rolling shutter and motion blur effects. In the application of change detection, it is customary to rectify the observed image first and then to detect the occluded regions. Instead of following this rectify-difference pipeline, we follow a distort-difference pipeline, in which we first distort the reference image to register it with the observation followed by change detection. In the presence of motion blur, this pipeline has been shown to be simple and effective by Vageeswaran et al. [19] in face recognition and by Punnappurath et al. [13] for the application of image registration in blur. We assume that the reference image is free from blur and rolling-shutter artifacts as is often the case in aerial imagery, where the reference is captured beforehand under conducive conditions. Throughout this paper, we consider the scene to be sufficiently far away from the camera so that planarity can be invoked.

Our main contributions in this paper are:

- To the best of our knowledge, the work described in this paper is the first of its kind to perform registration between a reference image and an image captured at a later time but distorted with *both* rolling shutter and motion blur artifacts, and to also simultaneously detect occlusions in the distorted image, all within a *single* framework. We thus efficiently account for both geometric and photometric distortions under one roof.
- Unlike existing works, we do not assume uniform velocity of camera motion during image exposure. Instead, we pose an optimisation problem with sparsity and partial non-negativity constraints to solve simultaneously for camera motion and occlusion for each row in the image.

2   Motion Blur in RS Cameras

In this section, we first explain the working of rolling shutter mechanism followed by a description of our combined motion blur and rolling shutter model.

Fig. 2 shows the mechanism by which sensors are exposed in RS and global shutter (GS) cameras. A GS camera exposes all the pixels at the same time. Fig. 2(a) illustrates this operation by showing same start and end exposure times for each row of the sensor array. The rows of an RS camera sensor array, on the other hand, are not exposed simultaneously. Instead, the exposure of consecutive rows starts sequentially with a delay as shown in Fig. 2(b), where t_e represents the exposure time of a single row and t_d represents the inter-row exposure delay with $t_d < t_e$. Both these values are same for all rows during image capture. The sequential capture causes the vertical line in the left of Fig. 1(a) to get displaced by different amounts in different rows due to camera motion which results in a curved line in Fig. 1(b). We will ignore the reset and read-out times in this discussion.

We now explain our *combined* motion blur and rolling shutter model. Let the number of rows of the image captured be M. Assuming the exposure starts at $t = 0$ for the first row, the ith row of the image is exposed during the time interval $[(i - 1)t_d, (i - 1)t_d + t_e]$. The total exposure time of the image T_e is $(M - 1)t_d + t_e$. Thus the camera path observed by each row in their exposure times is unique. If the camera moves according to $\mathbf{p}(t)$ for $0 \leq t \leq T_e$, then the

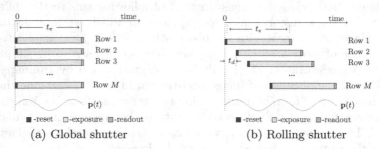

(a) Global shutter   (b) Rolling shutter

Fig. 2. Exposure mechanism of global shutter and rolling shutter cameras

ith row is blinded to the whole time except for $(i-1)t_d \leq t \leq (i-1)t_d + t_e$. Here $\mathbf{p}(t)$ is a vector with six degrees of freedom corresponding to 3D camera translations and 3D camera rotations. Let $\mathbf{f}$ and $\mathbf{g}$ represent respectively, the images captured by the RS camera without and with camera motion. We denote the ith row of any image with a superscript (i). Each row of $\mathbf{g}$ is an averaged version of the corresponding rows in warped versions of $\mathbf{f}$ due to the camera motion in its exposure period. We have

$$\mathbf{g}^{(i)} = \frac{1}{t_e} \int_{(i-1)t_d}^{(i-1)t_d+t_e} \mathbf{f}_{\mathbf{p}(t)}^{(i)} \, dt, \text{ for } i = 1 \text{ to } M, \tag{1}$$

where $\mathbf{f}_{\mathbf{p}(t)}^{(i)}$ is the ith row of the warped version of $\mathbf{f}$ due to the camera pose $\mathbf{p}(t)$ at a particular time t.

We discretise this model of combined rolling shutter and motion blur in (1) with respect to a finite camera pose space $\mathcal{S}$. We assume that the camera can undergo only a finite set of poses during the total exposure time, and this is represented by $\mathcal{S} = \{\tau_k\}_{k=1}^{|\mathcal{S}|}$. Hence we write (1) equivalently as,

$$\mathbf{g}^{(i)} = \sum_{\tau_k \in \mathcal{S}} \omega_{\tau_k}^{(i)} \mathbf{f}_{\tau_k}^{(i)} \tag{2}$$

where $\mathbf{f}_{\tau_k}^{(i)}$ is the ith row of the warped reference image $\mathbf{f}_{\tau_k}$ due to camera pose τ_k. Pose weight $\omega_{\tau_k}^{(i)}$ denotes the fraction of exposure time t_e, that the camera has spent in the pose τ_k during the exposure of ith row. Since the pose weights represent time, we have $\omega_{\tau_k} \geq 0$ for all τ_k. When the exposure times of $\mathbf{f}^{(i)}$ and $\mathbf{g}^{(i)}$ are same, then by conservation of energy, we have $\sum_{\tau_k \in \mathcal{S}} \omega_{\tau_k}^{(i)} = 1$ for each i. In this paper, we follow a projective homography model for planar scenes [6,8,20,7,12]. We denote camera translations and rotations by $(\mathbf{T}_k, \mathbf{R}_k)$ and the corresponding motion in the image plane by $(\mathbf{t}_k, \mathbf{r}_k)$.

In fact, our model is general enough that it encompasses both GS and RS camera acquisition mechanisms with and without motion blur (MB) as shown in Table 1. Here $\boldsymbol{\omega}^{(i)}$ is the pose weight vector of the ith row with each of its elements $\omega_{\tau_k}^{(i)}$ representing a number between 0 and 1, which is the weight for the τ_kth pose in the ith row. Fig. 3 showcases images with different types of distortions.

Table 1. Generalised motion blur model for GS and RS cameras

Type	Inter-row delay	Pose weight vector $(1 \leq i \leq M)$
GS	$t_d = 0$	$\omega_{\tau_k}^{(i)} = \begin{cases} 1 & \text{for } k = k_0 \\ 0 & \text{otherwise} \end{cases}$ where k_0 is independent of i
GS+MB	$t_d = 0$	Same $\boldsymbol{\omega}^{(i)}$ for all i
RS	$t_d \neq 0$	$\omega_{\tau_k}^{(i)} = \begin{cases} 1 & \text{for } k = k_i \\ 0 & \text{otherwise} \end{cases}$
RS+MB	$t_d \neq 0$	Different $\boldsymbol{\omega}^{(i)}$ for each i

GS   GS+MB   RS   RS+MB

Fig. 3. Various types of distortions as listed in Table 1

3 Image Registration and Occlusion Detection

Given the reference image and the distorted image affected by rolling shutter and
motion blur (denoted by RSMB from now on) with occlusions, we simultaneously register the reference image with the observed image and detect occlusions
present in the distorted image.

Let us first consider the scenario of registering the reference image to the
RSMB image without occlusions. We can represent the rows of the RSMB image
as linear combinations of elements in a dictionary formed from the reference
image. The relationship between them as matrix-vector multiplication from (2)
is given by

$$\mathbf{g}^{(i)} = \mathbf{F}^{(i)} \boldsymbol{\omega}^{(i)} \quad i = 1, 2, \ldots, M, \qquad (3)$$

where $\mathbf{g}^{(i)} \in \mathbb{R}^{N \times 1}$ is the ith row of the RSMB image stacked as a column
vector and N is the width of RSMB and reference images. Each column of
$\mathbf{F}^{(i)} \in \mathbb{R}^{N \times |\mathcal{S}|}$ contains the ith row of a warped version of the reference image $\mathbf{f}$,
for a pose $\boldsymbol{\tau}_k \in \mathcal{S}$, where $\mathcal{S}$ is the discrete pose space we define, and $|\mathcal{S}|$ is the
number of poses in it. Solving for the column vector $\boldsymbol{\omega}^{(i)}$ amounts to registering
every row of the reference image with the distorted image.

In the presence of occlusion, the camera observes a distorted image of the
clean scene with occluded objects. We model the occlusion as an additive term
to the observed image $\mathbf{g}$ (Wright et al. [21]), as $\mathbf{g}_{occ}^{(i)} = \mathbf{g}^{(i)} + \boldsymbol{\chi}^{(i)}$, where $\mathbf{g}_{occ}^{(i)}$
is the ith row of the RSMB image with occlusions, $\boldsymbol{\chi}^{(i)}$ is the occlusion vector
which contains non-zero values in its elements where there are changes in $\mathbf{g}_{occ}^{(i)}$
compared to $\mathbf{g}^{(i)}$. Since the occluded pixels can have intensities greater or less

than the original intensities, $\chi^{(i)}$ can take both positive and negative values. We compactly write this using a combined dictionary $\mathbf{B}^{(i)}$ as

$$\mathbf{g}_{\text{occ}}^{(i)} = \begin{bmatrix} \mathbf{F}^{(i)} \ \mathbf{I}_N \end{bmatrix} \begin{bmatrix} \boldsymbol{\omega}^{(i)} \\ \boldsymbol{\chi}^{(i)} \end{bmatrix} = \mathbf{B}^{(i)} \boldsymbol{\xi}^{(i)}, \quad i = 1, 2, \ldots, M. \tag{4}$$

Here $\mathbf{I}_N$ is an $N \times N$ identity matrix, $\mathbf{B}^{(i)} \in \mathbb{R}^{N \times (|\mathcal{S}|+N)}$ and $\boldsymbol{\xi}^{(i)} \in \mathbb{R}^{(|\mathcal{S}|+N)}$. We can consider the formulation in (4) as a representation of the rows of the RSMB image in a two-part dictionary, the first part being the set of projective transformations to account for the motion blur and the second part accounting for occlusions.

To solve for $\boldsymbol{\omega}^{(i)}$ and $\boldsymbol{\chi}^{(i)}$ is a data separation problem in the spirit of morphological component analysis (Starck et al. [17]). To solve the under-determined system in (4), we impose priors on pose and occlusion weights leveraging their sparseness. We thus formulate and solve the following optimisation problem to arrive at the desired solution.

$$\widetilde{\boldsymbol{\xi}}^{(i)} = \arg\min_{\boldsymbol{\xi}^{(i)}} \left\{ \|\mathbf{g}_{\text{occ}}^{(i)} - \mathbf{B}^{(i)} \boldsymbol{\xi}^{(i)}\|_2^2 + \lambda_1 \|\boldsymbol{\omega}^{(i)}\|_1 + \lambda_2 \|\boldsymbol{\chi}^{(i)}\|_1 \right\} \tag{5}$$

$$\text{subject to } \boldsymbol{\omega}^{(i)} \succeq 0$$

where λ_1 and λ_2 are non-negative regularisation parameters and $\succeq$ denotes non-negativity of each element of the vector. ℓ_1-constraints impose sparsity on camera trajectory and occlusion vectors by observing that (i) camera can move only so much in the whole space of 6D camera poses, and (ii) occlusion is sparse in all rows in spatial domain. To enforce different sparsity levels on camera motion and occlusion, we use two ℓ_1 regularisation parameters λ_1 and λ_2 with different values. We also enforce non-negativity for the pose weight vector $\boldsymbol{\omega}^{(i)}$. Our formulation elegantly imposes non-negativity only on the pose weight vector.

An equivalent formulation of (5) and its illustration is shown in Fig. 4. We modify the *nnLeastR* function provided in the SLEP package (Liu et al. [10]) to account for the partial non-negativity of $\boldsymbol{\xi}^{(i)}$ and solve (5). Observe that when $\boldsymbol{\xi}^{(i)} = \boldsymbol{\omega}^{(i)}$ and $\mathbf{B}^{(i)} = \mathbf{F}^{(i)}$, (5) reduces to the problem of image registration in the presence of blur.

In our model, the static occluder is elegantly subsumed in the reference image $\mathbf{f}$. It is possible to obtain the exact occlusion mask in $\mathbf{f}$ (instead of the blurred occluder region) as a forward problem, by inferring which pixels in $\mathbf{f}$ contribute to the blurred occlusion mask in $\mathbf{g}$, since the pose space weights $\boldsymbol{\omega}$ of the camera motion are known. Our framework is general, and it can detect occluding objects in the observed image as well as in the reference image (which are missing in the observed image). Yet another important benefit of adding the occlusion vector to the observed image is that it enables detection of even independently moving objects.

3.1 Dynamically Varying Pose Space

Building $\{\mathbf{F}^{(i)}\}_{i=1}^M$ in (5) is a crucial step in our algorithm. If the size of the pose space $\mathcal{S}$ is too large, then storing this matrix requires considerable memory

Equivalent formulation of (5):

$$\min_{\boldsymbol{\xi}^{(i)}} \left\{ \lambda_1 \|\widehat{\boldsymbol{\xi}}^{(i)}\|_1 \right\}$$

subject to
$$\begin{cases} \|\mathbf{g}_{occ}^{(i)} - \widehat{\mathbf{B}}^{(i)}\widehat{\boldsymbol{\xi}}^{(i)}\|_2^2 \le \epsilon, \\ \mathbf{C}\widehat{\boldsymbol{\xi}}^{(i)} \succeq 0, \end{cases}$$

where $\widehat{\mathbf{B}}^{(i)} = \left[\mathbf{F}^{(i)} \frac{\lambda_1}{\lambda_2} \mathbf{I}_N \right]$,

$$\mathbf{C} = \begin{bmatrix} \mathbf{I}_{|S|} & \mathbf{0} \\ \mathbf{0} & \mathbf{0} \end{bmatrix} \text{ and } \widehat{\boldsymbol{\xi}} = \begin{bmatrix} \boldsymbol{\omega} \\ \frac{\lambda_2}{\lambda_1} \boldsymbol{\chi} \end{bmatrix}.$$

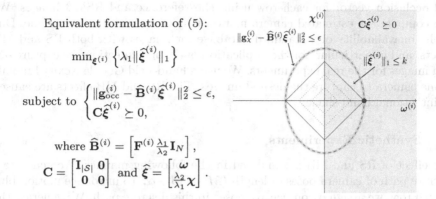

Fig. 4. Illustration of the constraints in our optimisation framework in two dimensions

and solving the optimisation problem becomes computationally expensive. We also leverage the continuity of camera motion in the pose space. We note the fact that the camera poses that a row observes during its exposure time will be in the neighbourhood of that of its previous row, and so we dynamically vary the search space for every row. While solving (5) for the ith row, we build $\mathbf{F}^{(i)}$ on-the-fly for the restricted pose space which is exclusive to each row.

Let $N(\boldsymbol{\tau}, \mathbf{b}, \mathbf{s}) = \{\boldsymbol{\tau} + q\mathbf{s} : \boldsymbol{\tau} - \mathbf{b} \preceq \boldsymbol{\tau} + q\mathbf{s} \preceq \boldsymbol{\tau} + \mathbf{b}, q \in \mathbb{Z}\}$ denote the neighbourhood of poses around a particular 6D pose vector $\boldsymbol{\tau}$, where $\mathbf{b}$ is the bound around the pose vector and $\mathbf{s}$ is the step-size vector. We start by solving (5) for the middle row $M/2$. Since there is no prior information about the camera poses during the time of exposure of the middle row, we assume a large pose space around the origin (zero translations and rotations), i.e. $\mathcal{S}^{(M/2)} = N(\mathbf{0}, \mathbf{b}_0, \mathbf{s}_0)$ where $\mathbf{b}_0$ and $\mathbf{s}_0$ are the bound and the step-size for the middle row, respectively. We build the matrix $\mathbf{F}^{(M/2)}$ based on this pose space. We start with the middle row since there is a possibility that the first and last rows of the RSMB image may contain new information and may result in a wrong estimate of the weight vector. Then we proceed as follows: for any row $i < M/2 - 1$, we build the matrix $\mathbf{F}^{(i)}$ only for the neighbourhood $N(\boldsymbol{\tau}_c^{(i+1)}, \mathbf{b}, \mathbf{s})$, and for any row $i > M/2 + 1$, we use only the neighbourhood $N(\boldsymbol{\tau}_c^{(i-1)}, \mathbf{b}, \mathbf{s})$ where $\boldsymbol{\tau}_c^{(i)}$ is the centroid pose of the ith row, which is given by

$$\boldsymbol{\tau}_c^{(i)} = \frac{\sum_{\boldsymbol{\tau}_k} \omega_{\boldsymbol{\tau}_k}^{(i)} \boldsymbol{\tau}_k}{\sum_{\boldsymbol{\tau}_k} \omega_{\boldsymbol{\tau}_k}^{(i)}}. \tag{6}$$

4   Experimental Results

To evaluate the performance of our technique, we show results for both synthetic and real experiments. For synthetic experiments, we simulate the effect of RS and MB for a given camera path. We estimate the pose weight vector and occlusion vector for each row using the reference and RSMB images. We also compare the estimated camera motion trajectory with the actual one. Due to the unavailability of a standard database for images with both RS and MB effects, and in particular, for the application of change detection, we capture our own images for the real experiments. We use a hand-held Google Nexus 4 mobile phone camera to capture the desired images. The RS and MB effects are caused by intentional hand-shake.

4.1   Synthetic Experiments

The effect of RS and MB is simulated in the following manner. We generate a discrete path of camera poses of length $(M-1)\beta + \alpha$. To introduce motion blur in each row, we assign α consecutive poses in this discrete path. We generate the motion blurred row of the RSMB image by warping and averaging the row of the reference image according to these poses. Since the row index is synonymous with time, a generated camera path with continuously changing slope corresponds to non-uniform velocity of the camera. The RS effect is arrived by using different sets of α poses for each row along the camera path. For the ith row, we assign α consecutive poses with index from $(i-1)\beta + 1$ to $(i-1)\beta + \alpha$ in the generated discrete camera path. Thus each row would see a unique set of α poses with β index delay with respect to the previous row. The centroid of poses corresponding to each row will act as the actual camera path against which our estimates are compared.

In the first experiment, we simulate a scenario where RS and MB degradations happen while imaging from an aerial vehicle. We first add occluders to the reference image (Compare Figs. 5(a) and (b)). The images have 245 rows and 345 columns. While imaging a geographical region from a drone, RS effect is unavoidable due to the motion of the vehicle itself. Especially it is difficult to maintain a straight path while controlling the vehicle. Any drift in the flying direction results in in-plane rotations in the image. We introduce different sets of in-plane rotation angles to each row of the image to emulate flight drifts. We generate a camera motion path with non-uniform camera velocity for in-plane rotation R_z. We use $\alpha = 20$ and $\beta = 3$ while assigning multiple poses to each row as discussed earlier. The centroid of R_z poses for each row is shown as a continuous red line in Fig. 5(d) which is the actual camera path. Geometrical misalignment between the reference and RSMB images in the flying direction (vertical axis) is added as a global t_y shift which is shown as a dotted red line in Fig. 5(d). The RSMB image thus generated is shown in Fig. 5(c). Though we generate a sinusoidal camera path in the experiment, its functional form is not used in our algorithm.

We need to solve (5) to arrive at the registered reference and occlusion images. Since there is no prior information about possible camera poses, we assume a large initial pose space around the origin while solving for the middle row: x-translation $t_x = N(0, 10, 1)$ pixels, y-translation $t_y = N(0, 10, 1)$ pixels, scale $t_z = N(1, 0.1, 0.1)$, rotations $R_x = N(0, 2, 1)°$, $R_y = N(0, 2, 1)°$ and $R_z = N(0, 8, 1)°$. The columns of $\mathbf{F}^{(M/2)}$ contain the middle rows of the

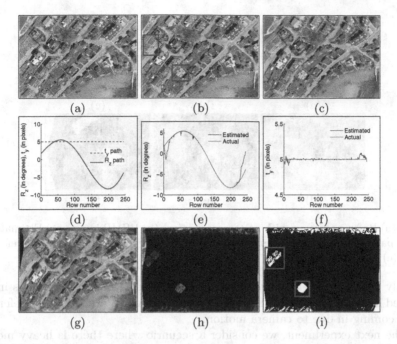

Fig. 5. (a) Reference image with no camera motion, (b) Reference image with added occlusions, (c) RSMB image, (d) Simulated camera path, (e) Estimated R_z camera path (blue) overlaid on simulated camera path (red), (f) Estimated t_y camera path (blue) overlaid on simulated camera path (red), (g) Registered reference image, (h) Occlusion image, and (i) Thresholded occlusion image

warps of the reference image $\mathbf{f}$ for all these pose combinations. For the remaining rows, the search neighbourhood is chosen around the centroid pose of its neighbouring row. Since the camera would move only so much between successive rows, we choose a relatively smaller neighbourhood: $N(t_{cx}, 3, 1)$ pixels, $N(t_{cy}, 3, 1)$ pixels, $N(t_{cz}, 0.1, 0.1)$, $N(R_{cx}, 2, 1)°$, $N(R_{cy}, 2, 1)°$ and $N(R_{cz}, 2, 1)°$. Here $[t_{cx}, t_{cy}, t_{cz}, R_{cx}, R_{cy}, R_{cz}]$ is the centroid pose vector of the neighbouring row as discussed in Section 3.1. Since we work in [0–255] intensity space, we use $255 \times \mathbf{I}_N$ in place of $\mathbf{I}_N$ in (4). The camera trajectory experienced by each row is very sparse in the whole pose space and hence we set a large λ_1 value of 5×10^3. We set $\lambda_2 = 10^3$ since the occlusion will be comparatively less sparse in each row, if present. We empirically found out that these values work very well for most images and different camera motions as well.

On solving (5) for each $1 \leq i \leq M$, we get the estimated pose weight vectors $\{\widetilde{\boldsymbol{\omega}}^{(i)}\}_{i=1}^{M}$ and occlusion vectors $\{\widetilde{\boldsymbol{\chi}}^{(i)}\}_{i=1}^{M}$. We form the registered reference image using $\{\mathbf{F}^{(i)}\widetilde{\boldsymbol{\omega}}^{(i)}\}_{i=1}^{M}$ and the occlusion image using $\{255\,\mathbf{I}_N\widetilde{\boldsymbol{\chi}}^{(i)}\}_{i=1}^{M}$. These are shown in Figs. 5(g) and (h), respectively. Fig. 5(i) shows the thresholded binary image with occlusion regions marked in red. The estimated camera trajectories for R_z and t_y are shown in Figs. 5(e) and (f). Note that the trajectories are

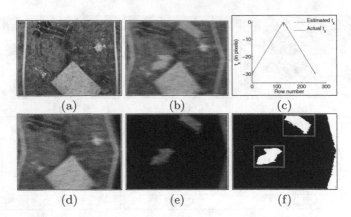

Fig. 6. (a) Reference image with no camera motion, (b) RSMB image, (c) Estimated t_x camera path (blue) overlaid on simulated camera path (red), (d) Registered reference image, (e) Occlusion image, and (f) Thresholded occlusion image

correctly estimated by our algorithm. The presence of boundary regions in the occluded image is because of the new information, which are not in the reference image, coming in due to camera motion.

In the next experiment, we consider a scenario where there is heavy motion blur along with the RS effect. An image of a synthetic grass-cover with objects is shown in Fig. 6(a). After adding occluders, we distort the reference image to create an image which is heavily blurred with zig-zag horizontal translatory RS effect. The RSMB image is shown in Fig. 6(b). The camera path simulated is shown in Fig. 6(c) in red. The algorithm parameters are the same as that for the previous experiment. The two output components of our algorithm, the registered and occlusion images, are shown respectively in Figs. 6(d) and (e). Boxed regions in the thresholded image in Fig. 6(f) show the effectiveness of our framework. The estimated camera trajectory is shown in blue in Fig. 6(c). More synthetic examples are available at http://www.ee.iitm.ac.in/ipcvlab/research/changersmb.

4.2   Real Experiments

In the first scenario, the reference image is a scene with horizontal and vertical lines, and static objects as shown in Fig. 7(a). This is captured with a static camera. We then added an occluder to the scene. With the camera at approximately the same position, we recorded a video of the scene with free-hand camera motion. The purpose of capturing a video (instead of an image) is to enable comparisons with the state-of-the-art as will become evident subsequently. From the video, we extracted a frame with high RS and MB artifacts and this is shown in Fig. 7(b). Our algorithm takes only these *two images* as input. We perform geometric and photometric registration, and change detection simultaneously by solving (5). To register the middle row, we start with a large pose

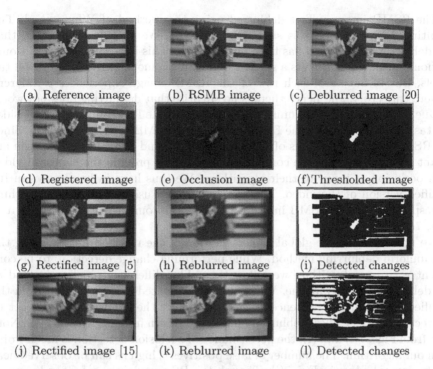

(a) Reference image   (b) RSMB image   (c) Deblurred image [20]

(d) Registered image   (e) Occlusion image   (f)Thresholded image

(g) Rectified image [5]   (h) Reblurred image   (i) Detected changes

(j) Rectified image [15]   (k) Reblurred image   (l) Detected changes

Fig. 7. (a)-(b): Reference and RSMB images (inputs to our algorithm), (c): RSMB image deblurred using Whyte et al. [20], (d)-(f): Proposed method using combined RS and MB model, (g)-(i): Rectify RS effect from video using Grundmann et al. [5], then estimate the kernel [20] and reblur the reference image, and detect changes, (j)-(l) Rectify-blur estimation pipeline using Ringaby and Forssén [15]

space: $t_x, t_y = N(0, 8, 1)$ pixels, $t_z = N(1, 0.1, 0.1)$, $R_x, R_y = N(0, 6, 1)°$, and $R_z = N(0, 10, 1)°$. The regularization parameters are kept the same as used for synthetic experiments. The relatively smaller pose space adaptively chosen for other rows is: $N(t_{cx}, 3, 1)$ pixels, $N(t_{cy}, 3, 1)$ pixels, $N(t_{cz}, 0.1, 0.1)$, $N(R_{cx}, 1, 1)°$, $N(R_{cy}, 1, 1)°$ and $N(R_{cz}, 1, 1)°$. The registered reference image is shown in Fig. 7(d). The straight lines of the reference image are correctly registered as curved lines since we are forward warping the reference image by incorporating RS. The presence of motion blur is also to be noted. This elegantly accounts for both geometric and photometric distortions during registration. Figs. 7(e) and (f) show the occlusion image and its thresholded version respectively.

We compare our algorithm with a serial framework which will rectify the RS effect and account for MB independently. We use the state-of-the-art method of Whyte et al. [20] for non-uniform motion blur estimation, and recent works of Grundmann et al. [5] and Ringaby and Forssén [15] for RS rectification. Since the code of the combined RS and MB approach by Meilland et al. [11] hasn't been shared with us, we are unable to compare our algorithm with their method.

The RSMB image is first deblurred using the method of Whyte et al. The resulting deblurred image is shown in Fig. 7(c). We can clearly observe that the deblurring effort itself has been unsuccessful. This is because the traditional motion blur model considers a single global camera motion trajectory for all the pixels. But in our case, each row of the RSMB image experiences a different camera trajectory, and hence there is no surprise that deblurring does not work.

Due to the failure of non-uniform deblurring on the RSMB image, we consider the task of first rectifying the RS effect followed by MB kernel estimation. Since the RS rectification methods of Grundmann et al. and Ringaby and Forssén are meant for videos, to let the comparison be fair, we provide the captured video with occlusion as input to their algorithms. We thus have in hand now, an RS rectified version of the video. The rectified frames using these two algorithms corresponding to the RSMB image we had used in our algorithm are shown in Figs. 7(g) and (j).

We now estimate the global camera motion of the rectified images using the non-uniform deblurring method. While performing change detection, to be consistent with our algorithm, we follow the reblur-difference pipeline instead of the deblur-difference pipeline. We apply the estimated camera motion from the rectified frame on the reference image, and detect the changes with respect to the rectified frame. These reblurred images are shown in Figs. 7(h) and (k). Note that from Figs. 7(i) and (l), the performance of occlusion detection is much worse than our algorithm. The number of false positives is high as can be observed near the horizontal edges in Fig. 7(i). Though the RS rectification of Grundmann et al. works reasonably well to stabilise the video, the rectified video is not equivalent to a global shutter video especially in the presence of motion blur. The camera motion with non-uniform velocity renders invalid the notion of having a global non-uniform blur kernel. The RS rectification of Ringaby et al. is worse than that of Grundmann et al., and hence the change detection suffers heavily as shown in Fig. 7(l). Hence it is amply evident that the state-of-the-art algorithms cannot handle these two effects together, and that an integrated approach is indispensable. To further confirm the efficacy of our method, we show more results.

| (a) | (b) | (c) | (d) |

Fig. 8. (a) Reference image with no camera motion, (b) RSMB image with prominent curves due to y-axis camera rotation, (c) Reference image registered to RSMB image, and (d) Thresholded occlusion image

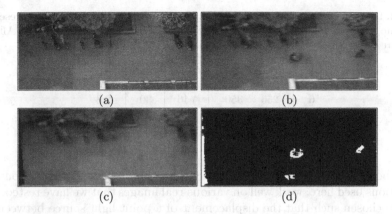

Fig. 9. (a) Reference image, (b) RSMB image, (c) Registered image, and (d) Thresholded occlusion image

In the next example, we capture an image from atop a tall building looking down at the road below. The reference image in Fig. 8(a) shows straight painted lines and straight borders of the road. The RSMB image is captured by rotating the mobile phone camera prominently around the y-axis (vertical axis). This renders the straight lines curved as shown in Fig. 8(b). Our algorithm works quite well to register the reference image with the RSMB image as shown in Fig. 8(c). The occluding objects, both the big vehicles and smaller ones, have been detected correctly as shown in Fig. 8(d). We do note here that one of the small white columns along the left edge of the road in the row where the big van runs, is detected as a false occlusion.

Figs. 9(a) and (b) show respectively, the reference image and the distorted image with prominent horizontal RS and MB effects. Figs. 9(c) and (d) show our registered and thresholded occlusion images, respectively. We can observe that the shear effect due to RS mechanism is duly taken care of in registration and the occluding objects are also correctly detected. The parapet in the bottom right of the image violates our planar assumption and hence its corner shows up wrongly as an occlusion.

4.3 Algorithm Complexity and Run-Time

We use a gradient projection based approach to solve the ℓ_1-minimisation problem (5) using SLEP [10]. It requires a sparse matrix-vector multiplication with order less than $O(N(|\mathcal{S}| + N))$ and a projection onto a subspace with order $O(|\mathcal{S}| + N)$ in each iteration with convergence rate of $O(1/k^2)$ for the kth iteration. Here N is the number of columns and $|\mathcal{S}|$ is the cardinality of the pose space (which is higher for the middle row). Run-times for our algorithm using an unoptimised MATLAB code without any parallel programming on a 3.4GHz PC with 16GB RAM are shown in Table 2. We do note here that, since the motion blur estimation of rows in the top-half and bottom-half are independent, they can even be run in parallel.

Table 2. Run-times of our algorithm for Figs. 5 to 9, with $t_{total}, t_{mid}, t_{other}$ representing total time, time for middle row, and average time for other rows respectively. All time values are in seconds.

Fig.	Rows × Cols	t_{total}	t_{mid}	t_{other}
5	245 × 345	712	28	2.8
6	256 × 350	746	30	2.8
7	216 × 384	644	29	2.9
8	167 × 175	404	34.5	2.2
9	147 × 337	317	29	2.0

The bounds of the camera pose space and the step sizes of rotations and translations used here, work well on various real images that we have tested. Step sizes are chosen such that the displacement of a point light source between two different warps is at least one pixel. Decreasing the step sizes further increases the complexity, but provides little improvement for practical scenarios. The large bounding values for the middle row used suffice for most real cases. However, for extreme viewpoint changes, those values can be increased further, if necessary. We have observed that the given regularisation values (λ_1 and λ_2) work uniformly well in all our experiments.

5   Conclusions

Increased usage of CMOS cameras forks an important branch of image formation model, namely the rolling shutter effect. The research challenge is escalated when the RS effect entwines with the traditional motion blur artifacts that have been extensively studied in the literature for GS cameras. The combined effect is thus an important issue to consider in change detection. We proposed an algorithm to perform change detection between a reference image and an image affected by rolling shutter as well as motion blur. Our model advances the state-of-the-art by elegantly subsuming both the effects within a single framework. We proposed a sparsity-based optimisation framework to arrive at the registered reference image and the occlusion image simultaneously. The utility of our method was adequately demonstrated on both synthetic and real data.

As future work, it would be interesting to consider the removal of both motion blur and rolling shutter artifacts given a single distorted image, along the lines of classical single image non-uniform motion deblurring algorithms.

References

1. Ait-Aider, O., Andreff, N., Lavest, J.M., Martinet, P.: Simultaneous object pose and velocity computation using a single view from a rolling shutter camera. In: Leonardis, A., Bischof, H., Pinz, A. (eds.) ECCV 2006, Part II. LNCS, vol. 3952, pp. 56–68. Springer, Heidelberg (2006)
2. Baker, S., Bennett, E., Kang, S.B., Szeliski, R.: Removing rolling shutter wobble. In: Proc. CVPR, pp. 2392–2399. IEEE (2010)

3. Cho, S., Cho, H., Tai, Y.-W., Lee, S.: Registration based non-uniform motion deblurring. In: Computer Graphics Forum, vol. 31, pp. 2183–2192. Wiley Online Library (2012)
4. Cho, W.H., Kim, D.W., Hong, K.S.: CMOS digital image stabilization. IEEE Trans. Consumer Electronics 53(3), 979–986 (2007)
5. Grundmann, M., Kwatra, V., Castro, D., Essa, I.: Calibration-free rolling shutter removal. In: Proc. ICCP, pp. 1–8. IEEE (2012)
6. Gupta, A., Joshi, N., Lawrence Zitnick, C., Cohen, M., Curless, B.: Single image deblurring using motion density functions. In: Daniilidis, K., Maragos, P., Paragios, N. (eds.) ECCV 2010, Part I. LNCS, vol. 6311, pp. 171–184. Springer, Heidelberg (2010)
7. Hu, Z., Yang, M.-H.: Fast non-uniform deblurring using constrained camera pose subspace. In: Proc. BMVC, pp. 1–11 (2012)
8. Joshi, N., Kang, S.B., Zitnick, C.L., Szeliski, R.: Image deblurring using inertial measurement sensors. ACM Trans. Graphics 29(4), 30 (2010)
9. Liang, C.-K., Chang, L.-W., Chen, H.H.: Analysis and compensation of rolling shutter effect. IEEE Trans. Image Proc. 17(8), 1323–1330 (2008)
10. Liu, J., Ji, S., Ye, J.: SLEP: Sparse Learning with Efficient Projections. Arizona State University (2009), http://www.public.asu.edu/~jye02/Software/SLEP
11. Meilland, M., Drummond, T., Comport, A.I.: A unified rolling shutter and motion blur model for 3D visual registration. In: Proc. ICCV (2013)
12. Paramanand, C., Rajagopalan, A.N.: Shape from sharp and motion-blurred image pair. Intl. Jrnl. of Comp. Vis. 107(3), 272–292 (2014)
13. Punnappurath, A., Rajagopalan, A.N., Seetharaman, G.: Registration and occlusion detection in motion blur. In: Proc. ICIP (2013)
14. Radke, R.J., Andra, S., Al-Kofahi, O., Roysam, B.: Image change detection algorithms: A systematic survey. IEEE Trans. Image Proc. 14(3), 294–307 (2005)
15. Ringaby, E., Forssén, P.E.: Efficient video rectification and stabilisation for cellphones. Intl. Jrnl. Comp. Vis. 96(3), 335–352 (2012)
16. Seitz, S.M., Baker, S.: Filter flow. In: Proc. ICCV, pp. 143–150. IEEE (2009)
17. Starck, J.-L., Moudden, Y., Bobin, J., Elad, M., Donoho, D.L.: Morphological component analysis. In: Optics & Photonics 2005, pp. 59140Q–59140Q. International Society for Optics and Photonics (2005)
18. Tai, Y.-W., Tan, P., Brown, M.S.: Richardson-lucy deblurring for scenes under a projective motion path. IEEE Trans. Patt. Anal. Mach. Intell. 33(8), 1603–1618 (2011)
19. Vageeswaran, P., Mitra, K., Chellappa, R.: Blur and illumination robust face recognition via set-theoretic characterization. IEEE Trans. Image Proc. 22(4), 1362–1372 (2013)
20. Whyte, O., Sivic, J., Zisserman, A., Ponce, J.: Non-uniform deblurring for shaken images. Intl. Jrnl. Comp. Vis. 98(2), 168–186 (2012)
21. Wright, J., Yang, A.Y., Ganesh, A., Sastry, S.S., Ma, Y.: Robust face recognition via sparse representation. IEEE Trans. Patt. Anal. Mach. Intell. 31(2), 210–227 (2009)
22. Wu, Y., Ling, H., Yu, J., Li, F., Mei, X., Cheng, E.: Blurred target tracking by blur-driven tracker. In: Proc. ICCV, pp. 1100–1107. IEEE (2011)
23. Yuan, L., Sun, J., Quan, L., Shum, H.-Y.: Blurred/non-blurred image alignment using sparseness prior. In: Proc. ICCV, pp. 1–8. IEEE (2007)

An Analysis of Errors in Graph-Based Keypoint Matching and Proposed Solutions

Toby Collins, Pablo Mesejo, and Adrien Bartoli

ALCoV-ISIT, UMR 6284 CNRS/Université d'Auvergne, Clermont-Ferrand, France

Abstract. An error occurs in graph-based keypoint matching when keypoints in two different images are matched by an algorithm but do not correspond to the same physical point. Most previous methods acquire keypoints in a black-box manner, and focus on developing better algorithms to match the provided points. However to study the complete performance of a matching system one has to study errors through the whole matching pipeline, from keypoint detection, candidate selection to graph optimisation. We show that in the full pipeline there are six different types of errors that cause mismatches. We then present a matching framework designed to reduce these errors. We achieve this by adapting keypoint detectors to better suit the needs of graph-based matching, and achieve better graph constraints by exploiting more information from their keypoints. Our framework is applicable in general images and can handle clutter and motion discontinuities. We also propose a method to identify many mismatches a posteriori based on Left-Right Consistency inspired by stereo matching due to the asymmetric way we detect keypoints and define the graph.

1 Introduction

Nonrigid keypoint-based image matching is the task of finding correspondences between keypoints detected in two images that are related by an unknown nonrigid transformation. This lies at the heart of several important computer vision problems and applications including nonrigid registration, object recognition and nonrigid 3D reconstruction. Graph-based methods solve this with a discrete optimisation on graphs whose edges encode geometric constraints between keypoints. This is NP hard in general and current research involves finding good approximate solutions [1–3] or better ways to learn the graph's parameters [4–6]. Most methods tend to treat the underlying keypoint detector as a black box, however to improve the overall performance of a graph matching system one should design or adapt the keypoint detector to also reduce errors and ease the matching problem. We show that there are six types of errors that cause mismatches which occur throughout the whole matching pipeline from keypoint detection to graph optimisation. We then give a general framework for reducing these errors and show this greatly improves the end performance. This includes a method for detecting mismatches a posteriori that is based on the Left-Right Consistency (LRC) test [7, 8] originating in stereo matching. Although simple, this has not

D. Fleet et al. (Eds.): ECCV 2014, Part VII, LNCS 8695, pp. 138–153, 2014.

been used in graph-matching before because many prior formulations are symmetric (*i.e.* if the roles of the two images are reversed the solution remains the same). We argue that, to reduce errors, an asymmetric approach (where keypoints sets in either image are significantly different) has many advantages, and it also permits using the LRC[1].

Previous Work. Graph-based keypoint matching is typically formulated as a quadratic binary assignment problem [2, 6, 9–16]. This can represent constraints on individual matches (*i.e.* unary terms) and pairs of matches (*i.e.* pairwise terms). Some works have incorporated higher-order constraints [13, 14] to handle the fact that pairwise constraints, such as preserving 2D Euclidean distances between points [6, 15] are not invariant to deformation and viewpoint change. However increasing the order to third and beyond increases exponentially the cost to compute and store the graph's terms. Thus second-order graphs remain the dominant approach. A limitation of many previous works is that they enforce all nodes in the graph to have a match. In some works this is done explicitly by using a permutation assignment matrix [9, 17]. In the others this is done implicitly because their cost function is always reduced by making a match [10–14, 16, 4]. Works that deal with unmatchable keypoints include [6, 18, 19, 15]. [6] allows keypoints to be assigned to an unmatchable state in a Markov Random Field (MRF)-based energy function. However reported results required ground-truth training images of the scene to learn the right weighting of the energy terms, which limits applicability. Unmatchable keypoints are found in [18, 15] by detecting those which have poor geometric compatibility with high-confidence matches. [15] requires a fully-connected graph and is very computationally demanding for large keypointsets. [18] iteratively computes correspondence subspace from high-confident matches and uses this as a spatial prior for other points. This was shown to work well for smooth deformable surfaces but may have difficulty with motion discontinuous or cluttered scenes. Other approaches are the *Hard Matching with Outlier Detection* (HMOD) methods [20–23]. These match keypoints using only their texture descriptors, and because many of these matches will be false, use a secondary stage of detecting mismatches by computing their agreement with a deformation model fitted from the matches that are considered correct.

2   Types of Errors in Graph-Based Keypoint Matching

We define $\mathcal{R} = \{r_1, ..., r_m\}$ and $\mathcal{T} = \{t_1, ..., t_n\}$ to be the keypoint-sets for the two images, which we refer to as the *reference* and *target* images respectively. Without loss of generality let $m \geq n$. The goal of keypoint matching is to find, if it exists, a correct correspondence for each member of $\mathcal{T}$ in $\mathcal{R}$ (Fig. 1). Because keypoint detectors localise keypoints with some margin of error, a soft criteria is required to distinguish correct from incorrect correspondences. This means that for any member of $\mathcal{T}$ there may exist multiple correct matches in $\mathcal{R}$. We define

---

[1] Source code is available at http://isit.u-clermont1.fr/~ab/Research/

$\mathcal{S}_i \subset \mathcal{R}$ to be all correct matches for a keypoint t_i. We define t_i to be a *matchable keypoint* if $\mathcal{S}_i$ is non-empty. We define t_i to be an *unmatchable keypoint* if $\mathcal{S}_i$ is empty. We define the *visible keypoint-set* $\mathcal{V} \subseteq \mathcal{T}$ to be all keypoints in $\mathcal{T}$ that are visible in the reference image (but are not necessarily in $\mathcal{R}$). In this paper we tackle problems where $\mathcal{T}$ and $\mathcal{R}$ are large unfiltered keypoint-sets generated by a keypoint detector such as SIFT [24] or SURF [25]. For typical images m and n will be $O(10^2 \to 10^5)$. To keep the costs of graph-based matching manageable in terms of *(i)* storage, *(ii)* time to compute the graph's constraints and *(iii)* time to find the solution, the possible members of $\mathcal{R}$ that t_i can be matched to should be pruned significantly. This has been done previously by taking the p members in $\mathcal{R}$ that have the most similar descriptors, with p being small (*e.g.* $O(10^1)$). We define a keypoint's *candidate match set* $\mathcal{C}(t_i) \subset \mathcal{R}$ to be the pruned set for t_i. We define the output of a matching system by the assignment vector $\mathbf{s} \in \{0, 1, ...m\}^n$, where $\mathbf{s}(i) \neq 0$ means that t_i is matched to $r_{\mathbf{s}(i)} \in \mathcal{C}(t_i)$, and $\mathbf{s}(i) = 0$ means that t_i is unmatched and in the *unmatchable state*. In all prior works in graph-based keypoint matching performance is evaluated by measuring the number of correct matches made between $\mathcal{T}$ and $\mathcal{R}$. This does not tell us the whole story for the complete performance of the system, nor does it provide a breakdown of where the error occurred. For a visible keypoint $t_i \in \mathcal{V}$ a matching system will fail to establish a correct correspondence in the reference image according to four types of errors (Fig. 1). These are as follows:

- *Detection Error*: $E_d(t_i \in \mathcal{V}) \overset{\text{def}}{=} (\mathcal{S}_i = \emptyset)$. t_i is visible in the reference image but there was no correct correspondence detected in the reference image.
- *Candidate Pruning Error*: $E_{cp}(t_i \in \mathcal{V}) \overset{\text{def}}{=} (\mathcal{S}_i \neq \emptyset, \mathcal{C}_i \cap \mathcal{S}_i = \emptyset)$. There is no detection error but the keypoint's candidates do not contain a correct correspondence.
- *Candidate Selection Error*: $E_{cs}(t_i \in \mathcal{V}) \overset{\text{def}}{=} (\mathcal{S}_i \neq \emptyset, \mathcal{C}_i \cap \mathcal{S}_i \neq \emptyset, \mathbf{s}_i \neq 0, \mathbf{s}_i \notin \mathcal{S}_i)$. There is neither a detection nor candidate pruning error, but $\mathbf{s}_i$ selects a wrong correspondence in the candidate-set.
- *Unmatched Error*: $E_u(t_i \in \mathcal{V}) \overset{\text{def}}{=} (\mathcal{S}_i \neq \emptyset, \mathcal{C}_i \cap \mathcal{S}_i \neq \emptyset, \mathbf{s}_i = 0)$. There is neither a detection nor candidate pruning error, but the keypoint is unmatched.

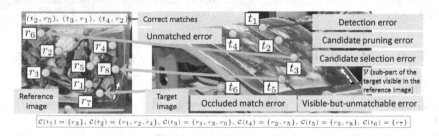

Fig. 1. The six types of errors in graph-based matching. Reference and target keypoint-sets are illustrated by circles and candidate matches are given at the bottom. Orange arrows illustrate matches made by a matching algorithm. Best viewed in colour.

We can aggregate these errors into what we call a *visible-keypoint match error*: $E_v(t_i \in \mathcal{V}) = (E_d(t_i) \vee E_{cp}(t_i) \vee E_{cs}(t_i) \vee E_u(t_i))$. A matching system can make two other types of errors which involve matching keypoints that have no match in $\mathcal{R}$. The first is an *occluded match error*: $E_{oc}(t_i \notin \mathcal{V}) = (\mathbf{s}_i \neq 0)$. The second is what we call a *visible-but-unmatchable error*: $E_{vu}(t_i \in \mathcal{V}) = (E_d \vee E_{cp})$, $\mathbf{s}_i \neq 0$. We can also combine E_{oc} and E_{vu} into what we call an *unmatchable-keypoint error*: $E_u(t_i) = E_{oc}(t_i) \vee E_{vu}(t_i)$. Developing a good graph-based matching system is very challenging because it must simultaneously reduce unmatchable keypoint errors yet try to match as many visible keypoints as possible. For visible keypoint matching errors, we will show that errors in detection and candidate pruning tend to have a compounding effect: not only does a visible keypoint become unmatchable, but also geometric constraints are lost between it and its neighbours in the graph. When this occurs too frequently the graph is weakened, which can then lead to more candidate selection errors.

How might one reduce visible-keypoint match errors? Current research in keypoint detection involves reducing the so-called *repeatability error* [26]. A repeatability error occurs when a keypoint detector fails to find the same two keypoints in both images. Thus perfect repeatability implies $\mathcal{V} = \mathcal{V}'$, but this is different from perfect detection error (which is what we want), which implies $\mathcal{V} \subseteq \mathcal{V}'$. *To improve matching performance, we should design or adapt keypoint detectors to reduce detection and candidate pruning errors.* The challenge here is how to incorporate this into graph matching efficiently. For example, one could reduce detection errors by having keypoints positioned densely in scale-space in the reference image. This requires an expensive dense computation of keypoint descriptors, and heavy candidate pruning. Reducing candidate selection errors has been the main objective in prior graph matching papers, and this has mainly been used as the evaluation criteria. This ignores the other types of errors we have listed. We now propose the first matching framework designed to reduce *all* types of errors. We call this framework Graph-based Affine Invariant Matching (GAIM), and its main contributions are:

1. To reduce detection and candidate pruning errors by constructing $\mathcal{R}$ using a redundant set keypoints. We do this so that even if there is large deformation between the two images, there is a high likelihood of a correct correspondence in $\mathcal{R}$ with a similar descriptor (§3.1).
2. To reduce candidate selection errors by constructing *second-order* graph-constraints that are fast to evaluate and *deformation invariant* (§3.3). To achieve this we show that one can obtain automatically an estimate of the local affine transform for each candidate match from our solution to point 1. These can then be used to enforce piecewise smooth matches. We show that this reduces assignment errors compared with the most common second-order constraint, which is to preserve Euclidean distance [6, 2].
3. To handle unmatchable keypoints with a robust graph cost function, and show that many can be effectively detected *a posteriori* using an LRC procedure adapted to graph matching (§3.4).

3   Proposed Framework: GAIM

3.1   Reference Keypoint-Set Construction to Reduce Detection and Candidate Pruning Errors

We use the fact that keypoint detectors trigger at different image positions in scale-space depending to a large part on deformation and viewpoint change. Thus, rather than attempting to make a keypoint's descriptor affine-invariant (*e.g.* [26]) we construct $\mathcal{R}$ by simulating many deformations of the reference image, and for each simulation we harvest keypoints and add them into $\mathcal{R}$. Although the deformation space is enormous, most deformations can be well-approximated locally by an affine transformation. Thus we only need to simulate global affine deformations of the reference image (Fig. 2). We do not simulate all of its six DoFs because keypoint methods such as SIFT are reasonably invariant to 2D translation, isotropic scale and rotation. Thus we simulate deformations by varying the remaining two DoFs (shear and aspect ratio). A similar strategy was proposed in [27] to make SIFT affine invariant. However, our goal is different because we want to have asymmetric keypoints (where all keypoints in $\mathcal{V}$ have a correspondence in $\mathcal{R}$, but not necessarily all keypoints in $\mathcal{R}$ have a correspondence in $\mathcal{V}$). We also want to obtain an estimate of the affine transform between t_i and its candidate matches, as we will include these in the graph's cost. In [27] the affine transforms were not inferred. We uniformly quantise shear in the range $[-1.0 : 1.0]$ and anisotopic scale in the range $[-0.25 : 4.0]$. We use x intervals that we experimentally vary from 3 to 8. We denote the simulated image set by $\mathcal{I}_s$, $s \in [1...S]$, and its simulated affine transform by $\mathbf{A}_s$. We represent each keypoint $r_k \in \mathcal{R}$ by $r_k = (y_k, \mathbf{q}_k, \mathbf{d}_k, \sigma_k, \theta_k, \mathbf{p}_k)$. We use y_k to denote the index of the simulated reference image from which r_k was harvested. We use $\mathbf{q}_k \in \mathbb{R}^2$ to denote the 2D position of the keypoint in $\mathcal{I}_{y_k}$ and $\mathbf{d}_k \in \mathbb{R}^d$ denotes its descriptor (using SIFT we have $d = 128$). We use $\mathbf{p}_k \in \mathbb{R}^2$ to denote its 2D position in the reference image. This is given by $\mathbf{p}_k = w(\mathbf{A}_{\sigma_k}^{-1}, \mathbf{q}_k)$ where $w(\mathbf{A}, \cdot) : \mathbb{R}^2 \to \mathbb{R}^2$ transforms a 2D point by an affine transform $\mathbf{A}$. We use $\sigma_k \in \mathbb{R}^+$ and $\theta_k \in [0; 2\pi]$ to denote the scale and orientation of the keypoint in $\mathcal{I}_{y_k}$ respectively.

3.2   Target Keypoint-Set, Candidate-Sets, and Graph Construction

We construct $\mathcal{T}$ by running the keypoint detector on the target image with the same parameters as used to construct $\mathcal{R}$. Unless otherwise stated we rescale the images to a default image diagonal resolution of 1,000 pixels before running the detector. For any keypoint that have multiple descriptors due to multiple orientation estimates, we use the descriptor that corresponds to the strongest orientation. However in $\mathcal{R}$ multiple descriptors are kept. We denote each keypoint $t_i \in \mathcal{T}$ by $t_i = (\tilde{\mathbf{p}}_i, \tilde{\mathbf{d}}_i, \tilde{\sigma}_i, \tilde{\theta}_i)$, which holds its 2D position, descriptor, scale and orientation respectively. We construct $\mathcal{C}(t_i)$ by running an Approximate Nearest Neighbour (ANN) search over $\mathcal{R}$. Currently we use FLANN [28] with default parameters with a forest of 8 KD trees. We modify the search to account for the fact that due to the redundancy in $\mathcal{R}$, several keypoints are often returned as nearest neighbours but they are approximately at the same position in the reference image. If this occurs then slots in the candidate-set are wasted. We deal with this in a simple manner by sequentially selecting as a candidate the keypoint in $\mathcal{R}$ with the closest descriptor from the ANN method, then eliminating keypoints which are approximately at the same image location (we use a default threshold of 5 pixels). The graph is then constructed that connects spatial neighbours in $\mathcal{T}$. In our experiments this is done with a simple Delaunay triangulation. We handle the fact that edges may cross motion discontinuities by including robustness into the graph's cost function. Because the geometric constraints are defined locally a natural way to express matching constraints is with a MRF. We use a second-order MRF of the form:

$$E(\mathbf{s}) = \sum_{i \in [1...|\mathcal{T}|]} U_i(\mathbf{s}(i)) + \lambda \sum_{(i,j) \in \mathcal{E}} P_{ij}(\mathbf{s}(i), \mathbf{s}(j))) \tag{1}$$

The first-order term $U_i \in \mathbb{R}$ is used to penalise matches with dissimilar descriptors. We use the standard unary term $U_i(\mathbf{s}(i) > 0) \stackrel{\text{def}}{=} \|\mathbf{d}_{\mathbf{s}(i)} - \tilde{\mathbf{d}}_i\|_1$. The 2nd-order term $P_{ij} \in \mathbb{R}$ enforces geometric consistency. The term λ balances the influence of P_{ij}, and can be set by hand or learned from training images.

3.3   Second-Order Deformation-Invariant Graph Constraints

We now show how the full-affine transform $\mathbf{A}_i^k$ that maps the local region in the target image about a keypoint t_i to the local region about a candidate match r_k in the reference image can be computed very cheaply (Fig. 2). Unlike affine normalisation [26] this requires no optimisation. We achieve this by making the following assumption. Suppose t_i and r_k is a correct correspondence. Because their descriptors are close (since r_k was selected as a candidate match), the local transform between the simulated image $\mathcal{I}_{y_k}$ and the target image at these points is likely to not have undergone much anisotropic scaling or shearing, and can be approximated by a similarity transform $\mathbf{S}_i^k$. We obtain $\mathbf{S}_i^k$ from the keypoint detector: $\mathbf{S}_i^k \approx \begin{bmatrix} \sigma_k \mathbf{R}(\theta_k) & \mathbf{q}_k \\ \mathbf{0}^\top & 1 \end{bmatrix} \begin{bmatrix} \tilde{\sigma}_i \mathbf{R}(\tilde{\theta}_i) & \tilde{\mathbf{p}}_i \\ \mathbf{0}^\top & 1 \end{bmatrix}^{-1}$ where $\mathbf{R}(\theta)$ is a 2D rotation by an angle θ. $\mathbf{A}_i^k$ is then given by composing this transform with $\mathbf{A}_{y_i}^{-1}$ as $\mathbf{A}_i^k \approx \mathbf{A}_{y_i}^{-1} \mathbf{S}_i^k$ (Fig. 2). There are two points to note. The first is that we are exploiting the fact that the keypoint is *not* fully affine invariant to give us $\mathbf{A}_i^k$. Two of its DoFs come from the simulated deformation transform $\mathbf{A}_{y_i}$ (shear and aspect ratio) and four come from the keypoint's built-in invariance to give $\mathbf{S}_i^k$. The second is that computing it is virtually free given any candidate match. We then use these affine transforms to construct P_{ij} in a way which makes the graph invariant to local affine deformation. By enforcing this robustly we can encourage matches that can be explained by a piecewise smooth deformation. This writes as follows:

$$P_{ij}(\mathbf{s}(i) > 0, \mathbf{s}(j) > 0) \stackrel{\text{def}}{=} \min \left[\left\| w(\mathbf{A}_i^{\mathbf{s}(i)}, \tilde{\mathbf{p}}_j) - \mathbf{p}_{\mathbf{s}(j)} \right\|_2, \left\| w(\mathbf{A}_j^{\mathbf{s}(j)}, \tilde{\mathbf{p}}_i) - \mathbf{p}_{\mathbf{s}(i)} \right\|_2, \tau \right] \tag{2}$$

The first term in Eq. (2) penalises a pair of matches if $\mathbf{A}_i^{\mathbf{s}(i)}$ (the affine transform between t_i and $r_{\mathbf{s}(i)}$) cannot predict well $\mathbf{p}_{\mathbf{s}(j)}$ (the 2D position of $r_{\mathbf{s}(j)}$). Because we also have $\mathbf{A}_j^{\mathbf{s}(j)}$, the second term is similar but made by switching the roles of i and j. We take the minimum of these two terms to improve robustness, which allows tolerance if either $\mathbf{A}_i^{\mathbf{s}(i)}$ or $\mathbf{A}_j^{\mathbf{s}(j)}$ is estimated wrongly. The term τ is a constant which truncates the pairwise term. This is used to provide robustness. Currently we set τ manually using a small dataset of training images (see §4).

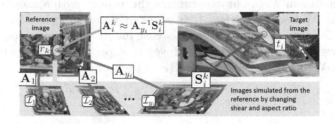

Fig. 2. Full affine transform $\mathbf{A}_i^k$ for a candidate match using simulation (for shear and aspect ratio) and keypoint-invariance (scale, rotation and translation)

3.4   Detecting Unmatchable Keypoints *a posteriori*

The unmatchable state is difficult to handle as a graph constraint. To define the unary term $U_i(\mathbf{s}(i) = 0)$ we would require to associate some cost (otherwise the graph would prefer a solution with all nodes in the unmatchable state [29]). Balancing this cost ideally is non-trivial because $\mathcal{V}$ can vary significantly between image pairs depending on clutter, different backgrounds and surface self-occlusions. We also do not usually know *a priori* the expected number of detection and candidate pruning errors, as these vary between scenes and imaging conditions. We face the same difficulty with defining the pairwise terms involving the unmatchable state. To address this problem we note that our matching framework *is not a symmetric process*. When searching for matches, only the detected keypoints in the target image are matched. If the role of the reference and target images is reversed, a second set of matches would be found, and this should be consistent with the first set. This is the so-called LRC test [7, 8] applied to graph-based keypoint matching. We note that the LRC is also equivalent to the uniqueness constraint which ensures each point in one image can match at most one point in the other image [7].

Our solution to handle the unmatchable state and the uniqueness constraint is to apply the LRC constraint (Fig. 3). First the MRF is defined in the target image *without* utilising the unmatchable state (we call this the *target MRF*). The robustness of the graph's terms are used to prevent unmatchable keypoints adversely affecting the solution. The target MRF is then solved and we denote its solution by $\hat{\mathbf{s}}$ and the matched pairs by $\mathcal{M}_T = \{(t_i, r_{\hat{\mathbf{s}}(i)})\}$, $i \in \{1...n\}$ (Fig. 3, top right). We then form the set $\mathcal{R}' \overset{\text{def}}{=} \{r_{\hat{\mathbf{s}}(i)}\} \subset \mathcal{R}$, $i \in \{1...n\}$, and define a second MRF called the *reference MRF* using $\mathcal{R}'$ as its nodes. Duplicates or near-duplicates may exist in $\mathcal{R}'$ because two keypoints in $\mathcal{T}$ may have been matched to approximately the same location in the reference image. We detect these using agglomerative clustering (we use a cluster threshold of 5 pixels), and collapse reference MRF nodes to have one node per cluster. A new MRF is then constructed using the cluster centres and their neighbours. Then the target image is treated as the reference image and the reverse match is computed (Fig. 3, bottom left). We denote its solution by $\mathcal{M}_T = \{(r_{\hat{s}(i)}, t_i')\}$. The LRC is then applied by ensuring that t_i and t_i' are close, and we assign t_i to the unmatchable state if $\|\tilde{\mathbf{p}}_i' - \tilde{\mathbf{p}}_i\|_2 \geq \tau_c$. We use a default threshold of $\tau_c = 15$ pixels.

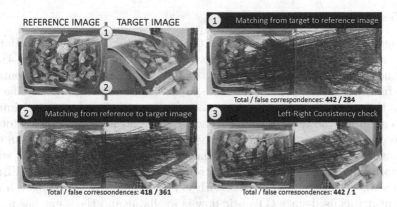

Fig. 3. Proposed Left-Right Consistency test for keypoint-based graph-matching

4   Experimental Evaluation

We divide the experimental evaluation into three parts. The first part evaluates GAIM for reducing detection and candidate pruning errors. The second part evaluates GAIM for reducing assignment errors. The third part evaluates our method for detecting incorrect matches after graph optimisation. We compare against two state-of-the-art HMOD methods: PB12 [21] and TCCBS12 [22]. Because we deal with such large keypoint-sets ($O(n) \approx 10^3$ and $O(m) \approx 10^4$), most factorisation-based methods are unsuitable to tackle the problem. As a baseline graph-based method we use [6] which can handle large m and n via candidate match pruning. We use the naming scheme F/G/O/M to describe a graph matching method configuration. This denotes a method that computes keypoints with a method F, computes graph constraints with a method G, optimises the graph with an MRF optimiser O, and performs mismatch detection *a posterior* with a method M. In our experiments F is either SIFT, AC-SIFT (Affine-Covariant SIFT), or Gx-SIFT (our proposed asymmetric method by adapting SIFT in §3.1, where x denotes the number of synthesised views plus the original image). SIFT and AC-SIFT are computed with VLFeat's implementation [30]. We use SIFT because it is still very popular, has matching accuracy that is competitive with state-of-the-art, and currently supports switching between standard and affine-Covariant versions of the descriptor. G is either GAIM (our proposed graph constraint) or RE (which stands for Robust Euclidean). RE is the Euclidean distance-preserving constraint from [6] but made robust by introducing the truncation term τ. This allows a fair comparison with our constraint, and we manually tune τ using the same training images. For O we use fast methods known to work well on correspondence problems. These are AE (α-expansion [31] with QPBO [32, 33]) or BP (loopy Belief Propagation). M is either PB12 [21], TCCBS12 [22] or LRC+ (our proposed Left-Right Consistency test). We use GAIM to be shorthand for G26-SIFT/GAIM/AE/LRC+.

4.1   Test Datasets

We evaluate using public datasets from the deformable surface registration literature, and some new challenging datasets that we have created (Fig. 4). We divide the datasets into 6 groups (Fig. 4). Group 1 involves 8 representative images from CVLAB's paper-bend and paper-crease sequences [34]. The first frame is the reference image and five other frames were used as target images. We also swapped the roles of the reference and target images, giving a total of 20 reference/target pairs. Group 2 involves 8 reference/target pairs of an open deforming book with strong viewpoint change and optic blur that we shot with a 720p smartphone. Group 3 involves 8 reference/target pairs taken from CVLAB's multiview 3D reconstruction dataset with GT computed by [35]. This is a rigid scene, but it was used since GT optic flow is available and the scene has motion and surface discontinuities. Although the epipolar constraint is available due to rigidity, we did not allow methods to use this constraint. Group 4 involves 16 reference/target pairs from CVLAB's cardboard dataset [36] that we constructed in a similar manner to Group 1. This is challenging due to texture sparseness and local texture ambiguity. Groups 5 and 6 involve 20 reference/target pairs taken from Oxford's wall and graffiti datasets respectively. We used the first frame as reference image, and the target images were generated from the first and third frames by applying randomised synthetic deformations to them using perspective and TPS transformations. In total there are 92 reference/target pairs. We trained λ and τ by hand on a training set comprising CVLAB's bedsheet and cushion datasets [34]. GT optic-flow is not provided for Groups 1,2 and 4. We computed this carefully using an interactive warping tool. All images were scaled to a resolution with diagonal 1,000 pixels and a match was considered correct if it agreed to the optic flow by less than 12 pixels.

4.2   Experiment 1: Reduction of Candidate-Set Errors

The first source of errors in graph-based keypoint matching is a candidate-set error, which is when either a detection error or a candidate pruning error occurs (see §2). In Fig. 5 we plot the mean candidate-set error rate as a function of the candidate-set size p for SIFT, AC-SIFT and Gx-SIFT, with p varying from 1 to 200 and x varying from 10 to 65. In solid lines we plot the error rates when using the default detection parameters for building $\mathcal{R}$ and $\mathcal{T}$. Across all datasets we

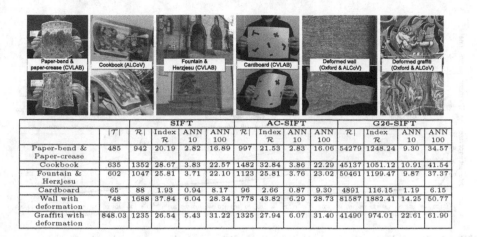

	$|\mathcal{T}|$	SIFT				AC-SIFT				G26-SIFT			
		$\mathcal{R}|$	Index $\mathcal{R}$	ANN 10	ANN 100	$\mathcal{R}|$	Index $\mathcal{R}$	ANN 10	ANN 100	$\mathcal{R}|$	Index $\mathcal{R}$	ANN 10	ANN 100
Paper-bend & Paper-crease	485	942	20.19	2.82	16.89	997	21.53	2.83	16.06	54279	1248.24	9.30	34.57
Cookbook	635	1352	28.67	3.83	22.57	1482	32.84	3.86	22.29	45137	1051.12	10.91	41.54
Fountain & Herzjesu	602	1047	25.81	3.71	22.10	1123	25.81	3.76	23.02	50461	1199.47	9.87	37.37
Cardboard	65	88	1.93	0.94	8.17	96	2.66	0.87	9.30	4891	116.15	1.19	6.15
Wall with deformation	748	1688	37.84	6.04	28.34	1778	43.82	6.29	28.73	81587	1882.41	14.25	50.77
Graffiti with deformation	848.03	1235	26.54	5.43	31.22	1325	27.94	6.07	31.40	41490	974.01	22.61	61.90

Fig. 4. Top: The six groups of test images used in evaluation. In total we test 92 reference/target image pairs. Bottom: average size of $\mathcal{R}$ and $\mathcal{T}$ and time (in ms) to construct, indexing and ANN querying $\mathcal{R}$ on an i7-3820 PC with FLANN [37] with a default maximum search depth of 15. Although the time to index G26-SIFT is considerably lager (taking a second or more) the time to query is only approximately a factor of two/three slower than SIFT and AC-SIFT. In tracking tasks where indexing only needs to be done once the benefits of using Gx-SIFT are very strong.

find a clear advantage in using Gx-SIFT. The benefits in a larger x is stronger for smaller p. For $p > 100$ we see no real benefit in G8-SIFT over G26-SIFT in any testset. For SIFT and AC-SIFT one might expect lower error rates by keeping in $\mathcal{R}$ all detections without filtering those with low edge and scale-space responses (and so to potentially reduce detection errors). In dashed we show the error rates when $\mathcal{R}$ was constructed without the post-filtering. However there is no clear error reduction in general, and in some cases this actually increased the error. The large improvement in using Gx-SIFT tells us that a major cause for candidate-set errors are the lack of viewpoint and local deformation invariance. Despite AC-SIFT being designed to handle this, the results show that it lags quite far behind Gx-SIFT.

4.3   Experiment 2: Reduction of Candidate Selection Errors

After detection and candidate pruning the next source of errors are candidate selection errors (we refer the reader to §2 for the formal definition). We compared 10 matching configurations. These are listed in the first row of Fig. 6. For our proposed keypoint detection method we use G26-SIFT. Our proposed matching configurations in full is G26-SIFT/GAIM/BP & AE. Because AC-SIFT also provides local affine transforms between candidate matches we also test the configuration AC-SIFT/GAIM by using the affine transforms from AC-SIFT in Eq. (2). In all experiments we use a default value of $p = 90$. The results

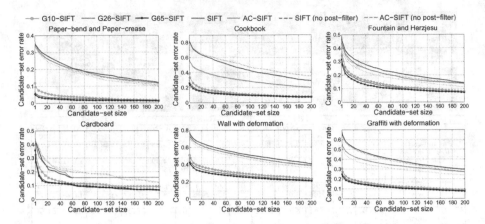

Fig. 5. Candidate-set error rate versus candidate-set size across the six test-sets. For a fair comparison all methods use the same detected keypoints in the target image.

on the test sets are shown in rows 1 and 2 of Fig. 6. The best results are obtained by the four configurations on the left (*i.e.* the ones where the reference keypoint-set was built using G26-SIFT keypoints). This result is important because it tells us that when we use keypoints with higher candidate-set errors (*i.e.* SIFT and AC-SIFT), this weakens the graph and causes keypoints that do not have candidate-set errors to be matched incorrectly. With the exception of Cardboard, there is a clear performance improvement with using GAIM constraints over RE. We believe the reason is because in Cardboard there is *(i)* little scale change between the views and *(ii)* the texture is much sparser than other datasets, which means that the local affine model used by GAIM has to be valid between distant surface points. There is little difference in the performance of G26-SIFT/GAIM/BP and G26-SIFT/GAIM/AE, which indicates both graph optimisers tend to find the same solution (although more tests are required). With respect to AC-SIFT, although this performs significantly worse than G26-SIFT we do see a performance improvement with using GAIM graph constraints over RE. We also measure the visible keypoint match error rates for each configuration. Recall from §2 that a visible keypoint match error occurs when a keypoint is visible in the target image, but the graph's solution does provide a correct correspondence. This is a combination of both candidate-set and assignment errors. The results are shown in rows 3 and 4 of Fig. 6.

4.4   Experiment 3: Complete Performance Evaluation

We now evaluate the complete performance of our approach, and show that unmatchable keypoints can be successfully detected *a posteriori* using the LRC. Space limitations prevent a full performance breakdown, so we present here the complete system recall/precision performance. This is given by the proportion of matches that a method computes correctly versus the proportion of visible

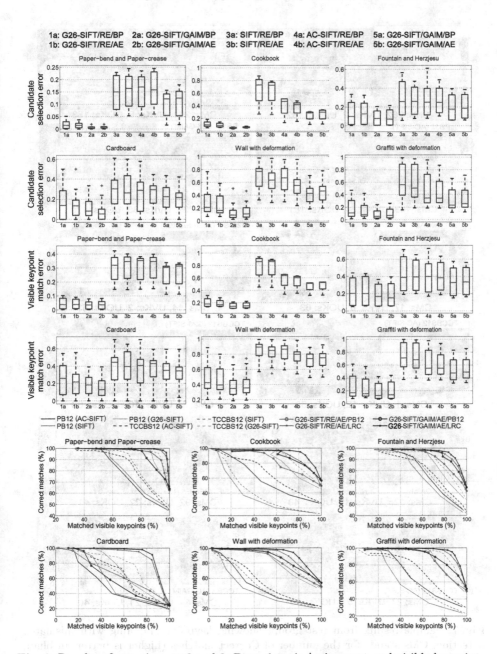

Fig. 6. Results of experiments 2 and 3. Rows 1 to 4: Assignment and visible keypoint match errors for 10 graph matching configurations. Rows 5, 6: Complete matching performance (including mis-match detection) of best-performing configurations and HMOD methods.

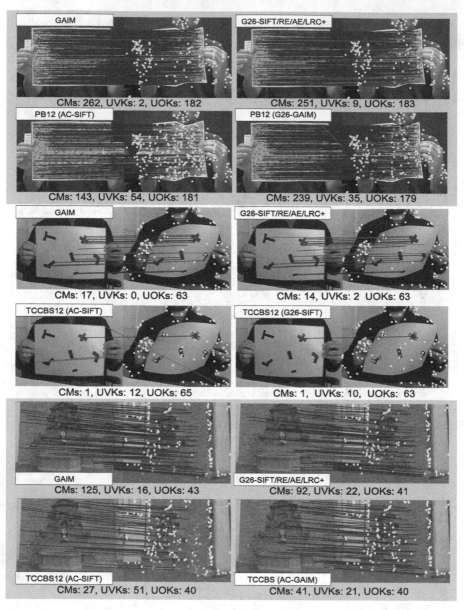

Fig. 7. Sample results from test groups showing keypoint matching with mismatch detection. CMs stands for the number of Correct matches (higher is better, in blue), UVKs stands for the number of Unmatched Visible Keypoints (lower is better, in green) and UOKs stands for the number of unmatched occluded keypoints (higher is better, in yellow). In red are false matches. In each target image we show the Region-Of-Interest (ROI) within which we had GT optic flow. To ease evaluation we restricted $\mathcal{R}$ to be keypoints within the ROI. Therefore any keypoint in the target image that does not have a correct match in the ROI is an occluded keypoint. No ROI was used to filter keypoints in the target images.

keypoints that have been matched. We compare against PB12 and TCCBS12 using hard matches from G26-SIFT, AC-SIFT and SIFT. We also investigate if PB12 and TCCBS12 can detect incorrect matches given the solution of a graph-based method. This is an interesting test and has not been done in the literature. We plot these results in rows 5 and 6 in Fig. 6. The trend we see is that the HMOD methods perform significantly better with G26-SIFT, and the reason is that many more hard matches are correct with G26-SIFT than with SIFT or AC-SIFT. For both G26-SIFT/RE/AE and G26-SIFT/GAIM/AE the performance when using PB12 to detect incorrect matches in their outputs is not significantly greater than hard matching using G26-SIFT, and in some instances is worse. The reason for this is because incorrect matches outputted by a graph method tend spatially correlated, and this makes them hard to distinguish from correct matches. The best performing method across all test sets is G26-SIFT/GAIM/AE/LRC. In Fig. 7 we give some representative visual results of the methods.

5 Conclusions

We have given a comprehensive breakdown of errors in graph-based keypoint matching into six different types. These errors occur at various stages of matching; from keypoint detection, candidate selection to final graph optimisation. In previous works keypoint detectors have been used in a rather black-box style, however there is a deep interplay between the keypoint detector and graph-based matching that should not be ignored. We hope the results of this paper will stimulate the design of new keypoint methods that specifically reduce candidate-set errors in graph-matching rather than the commonly used repeatability metric. We have presented the first matching system that has been designed to reduce all six error types. Candidate-set errors have been considerably reduced by Gx-SIFT features. These also provide automatic information about a keypoint's local affine transform that can be used as a second-order deformation invariant matching constraint. This produces lower candidate-selection errors than the commonly-used euclidean distance-preserving constraint. We have provided a method to detect mismatches *a posteriori* using a Left-Right Consistency procedure adapted to asymmetric deformable graph matching, and shown that the full framework outperforms state-of-the-art HMOD methods.

Acknowledgments. This research has received funding from the EU's FP7 through the ERC research grant 307483 FLEXABLE.

References

1. Conte, D., Foggia, P., Sansone, C., Vento, M.: Thirty years of Graph Matching in Pattern Recognition. Int. J. Pattern Recogn., 265–298 (2004)
2. Leordeanu, M., Hebert, M., Sukthankar, R.: An integer projected fixed point method for graph matching and MAP inference. In: Neural Information Processing Systems (NIPS), pp. 1114–1122 (2009)

3. Cho, M., Lee, J., Lee, K.M.: Reweighted Random Walks for Graph Matching. In: Daniilidis, K., Maragos, P., Paragios, N. (eds.) ECCV 2010, Part V. LNCS, vol. 6315, pp. 492–505. Springer, Heidelberg (2010)

4. Caetano, T.S., McAuley, J.J., Cheng, L., Le, Q.V., Smola, A.J.: Learning graph matching. IEEE T. Pattern Anal. 31, 1048–1058 (2009)

5. Leordeanu, M., Sukthankar, R., Hebert, M.: Unsupervised learning for graph matching. Int. J. Comput. Vision 96, 28–45 (2012)

6. Torresani, L., Kolmogorov, V., Rother, C.: Feature Correspondence Via Graph Matching: Models and Global Optimization. In: Forsyth, D., Torr, P., Zisserman, A. (eds.) ECCV 2008, Part II. LNCS, vol. 5303, pp. 596–609. Springer, Heidelberg (2008)

7. Faugeras, O., Hotz, B., Mathieu, H., Viville, T., Zhang, Z., Fua, P., Thron, E., Robotvis, P.: Real time correlation-based stereo: Algorithm, implementations and applications (1996)

8. Kowdle, A., Gallagher, A., Chen, T.: Combining monocular geometric cues with traditional stereo cues for consumer camera stereo. In: Fusiello, A., Murino, V., Cucchiara, R. (eds.) ECCV 2012 Ws/Demos, Part II. LNCS, vol. 7584, pp. 103–113. Springer, Heidelberg (2012)

9. Umeyama, S.: An eigendecomposition approach to weighted graph matching problems. IEEE Trans. Pattern Anal. Mach. Intell. 10, 695–703 (1988)

10. Cho, M., Alahari, K., Ponce, J.: Learning graphs to match. In: International Conference on Computer Vision (ICCV) (2013)

11. Zhou, F., la Torre, F.D.: Deformable graph matching. In: Conference on Computer Vision and Pattern Recognition (CVPR), pp. 2922–2929 (2013)

12. Zaslavskiy, M., Bach, F., Vert, J.-P.: A path following algorithm for graph matching. In: Elmoataz, A., Lezoray, O., Nouboud, F., Mammass, D. (eds.) ICISP 2008 2008. LNCS, vol. 5099, pp. 329–337. Springer, Heidelberg (2008)

13. Chertok, M., Keller, Y.: Efficient high order matching. IEEE Trans. Pattern Anal. Mach. Intell. 32, 2205–2215 (2010)

14. Duchenne, O., Bach, F., Kweon, I.S., Ponce, J.: A tensor-based algorithm for high-order graph matching. IEEE Trans. Pattern Anal. Mach. Intell. 33, 2383–2395 (2011)

15. Leordeanu, M., Hebert, M.: A spectral technique for correspondence problems using pairwise constraints. In: International Conference on Computer Vision (ICCV), pp. 1482–1489 (2005)

16. Gold, S., Rangarajan, A.: A graduated assignment algorithm for graph matching. IEEE Trans. Pattern Anal. Mach. Intell. 18, 377–388 (1996)

17. Scott, G.L., Longuet-Higgins, H.C.: An Algorithm for Associating the Features of Two Images. Royal Society of London Proceedings Series B 244, 21–26 (1991)

18. Hamid, R., DeCoste, D., Lin, C.J.: Dense non-rigid point-matching using random projections. In: CVPR, pp. 2914–2921. IEEE (2013)

19. Albarelli, A., Rodolà, E., Torsello, A.: Imposing semi-local geometric constraints for accurate correspondences selection in structure from motion: A game-theoretic perspective. Int. J. Comput. Vision 97, 36–53 (2012)

20. Pilet, J., Lepetit, V., Fua, P.: Fast non-rigid surface detection, registration and realistic augmentation. Int. J. Comput. Vision 76, 109–122 (2008)

21. Pizarro, D., Bartoli, A.: Feature-Based Deformable Surface Detection with Self-Occlusion Reasoning. Int. J. Comput. Vision 97, 54–70 (2012)

22. Tran, Q.-H., Chin, T.-J., Carneiro, G., Brown, M.S., Suter, D.: In defence of RANSAC for outlier rejection in deformable registration. In: Fitzgibbon, A., Lazeb-nik, S., Perona, P., Sato, Y., Schmid, C. (eds.) ECCV 2012, Part IV. LNCS, vol. 7575, pp. 274–287. Springer, Heidelberg (2012)
23. Chui, H., Rangarajan, A.: A new point matching algorithm for non-rigid registra-tion. Comput. Vis. Image Underst. 89, 114–141 (2003)
24. Lowe, D.G.: Distinctive image features from scale-invariant keypoints. Int. J. Com-put. Vision 60, 91–110 (2004)
25. Bay, H., Ess, A., Tuytelaars, T., Van Gool, L.: Speeded-up robust features (SURF). Comput. Vis. Image Underst. 110, 346–359 (2008)
26. Mikolajczyk, K., Schmid, C.: Scale & affine invariant interest point detectors. Int. J. Comput. Vision 60, 63–86 (2004)
27. Morel, J.M., Yu, G.: ASIFT: A New Framework for Fully Affine Invariant Image Comparison. SIAM J. Imaging Sci. 2, 438–469 (2009)
28. Muja, M., Lowe, D.G.: Scalable nearest neighbor algorithms for high dimensional data. IEEE Transactions on Pattern Analysis and Machine Intelligence 36 (2014)
29. Torresani, L., Hertzmann, A., Bregler, C.: Nonrigid structure-from-motion: Es-timating shape and motion with hierarchical priors. IEEE Trans. Pattern Anal. Mach. Intell. 30(5), 878–892 (2008)
30. Vedaldi, A., Fulkerson, B.: VLFeat: An open and portable library of computer vision algorithms (2008), http://www.vlfeat.org/
31. Boykov, Y., Veksler, O., Zabih, R.: Fast approximate energy minimization via graph cuts. IEEE Trans. Pattern Anal. Mach. Intell. 23, 1222–1239 (2001)
32. Rother, C., Kolmogorov, V., Lempitsky, V.S., Szummer, M.: Optimizing binary MRFs via extended roof duality. In: Conference on Computer Vision and Pattern Recognition (CVPR), pp. 1–8 (2007)
33. Hammer, P., Hansen, P., Simeone, B.: Roof duality, complementation and persis-tency in quadratic optimization. Mathematical Programming 28, 121–155 (1984)
34. Salzmann, M., Hartley, R., Fua, P.: Convex optimization for deformable surface 3-d tracking. In: International Conference on Computer Vision (ICCV), pp. 1–8 (2007)
35. Strecha, C., Bronstein, A.M., Bronstein, M.M., Fua, P.: LDAHash: Improved matching with smaller descriptors. In: EPFL-REPORT-152487 (2010)
36. Salzmann, M., Urtasun, R., Fua, P.: Local deformation models for monocular 3d shape recovery. In: Conference on Computer Vision and Pattern Recognition (CVPR) (2008)
37. Bartoli, A.: Maximizing the predictivity of smooth deformable image warps through cross-validation. Journal of Mathematical Imaging and Vision 31(2-3), 133–145 (2008)

OpenDR: An Approximate
Differentiable Renderer[*]

Matthew M. Loper and Michael J. Black

Max Planck Institute for Intelligent Systems, Tübingen, Germany
{mloper,black}@tue.mpg.de

Abstract. Inverse graphics attempts to take sensor data and infer 3D
geometry, illumination, materials, and motions such that a graphics renderer could realistically reproduce the observed scene. Renderers, however, are designed to solve the forward process of image synthesis. To
go in the other direction, we propose an approximate *differentiable renderer (DR)* that explicitly models the relationship between changes in
model parameters and image observations. We describe a publicly available *OpenDR* framework that makes it easy to express a forward graphics model and then automatically obtain derivatives with respect to the
model parameters and to optimize over them. Built on a new auto-
differentiation package and OpenGL, OpenDR provides a local optimization method that can be incorporated into probabilistic programming
frameworks. We demonstrate the power and simplicity of programming
with OpenDR by using it to solve the problem of estimating human body
shape from Kinect depth and RGB data.

Keywords: Inverse graphics, Rendering, Optimization, Automatic Differentiation, Software, Programming.

1 Introduction

Computer vision as *analysis by synthesis* has a long tradition [9,24] and remains
central to a wide class of generative methods. In this top-down approach, vision
is formulated as the search for parameters of a model that is *rendered* to produce
an image (or features of an image), which is then compared with image pixels
(or features). The model can take many forms of varying realism but, when
the model and rendering process are designed to produce realistic images, this
process is often called *inverse graphics* [3,33]. In a sense, the approach tries to
reverse-engineer the physical process that produced an image of the world.

We define an observation function $f(\Theta)$ as the forward rendering process
that depends on the parameters Θ. The simplest optimization would solve for
the parameters minimizing the difference between the rendered and observed
image intensities, $E(\Theta) = \|f(\Theta) - I\|^2$. Of course, we will specify much more
sophisticated functions, including robust penalties and priors, but the basic idea

---

[*] Electronic supplementary material -Supplementary material is available in the online
version of this chapter at http://dx.doi.org/10.1007/978-3-319-10584-0_11.
Videos can also be accessed at http://www.springerimages.com/videos/978-3-
319-10583-3

D. Fleet et al. (Eds.): ECCV 2014, Part VII, LNCS 8695, pp. 154–169, 2014.
© Springer International Publishing Switzerland 2014

remains – minimize the difference between the synthesized and observed data. While much has been written about this process and many methods fall under this rubric, few methods literally adopt the inverse graphics approach. High dimensionality makes optimizing an objective like the one above a challenge; renderers have a large output space, and realistic renderers require a large input parameter space. Fundamentally, the forward rendering function is complex, and optimization methods that include it are often purpose-built with great effort. Put succinctly, *graphics renderers are not usually built to be inverted.*

Here we fully embrace the view of vision as inverse graphics and propose a framework to make it more practical. Realistic graphics engines are available for rendering the forward process and many discriminative approaches exist to recover scene properties directly from images. Neither explicitly models how the observables (pixels or features) smoothly change with model parameters. These derivatives are essential for optimization of high-dimensional problems and constructing these derivatives by hand for each application is onerous. Here we describe a general framework based on differentiating the render. We define a *differentiable renderer (DR)* as a process that (1) supplies pixels as a function of model parameters to simulate a physical imaging system and (2) supplies derivatives of the pixel values with respect to those parameters. To be practical, the DR also has to be fast; this means it must have hardware support. Consequently we work directly with OpenGL. Because we make it publicly available, we call our framework *OpenDR* (http://open-dr.org).

Since many methods formulate generative models and differentiate them, why has there been no general DR framework until now? Maybe it is because rendering seems like it is not differentiable. At some level this is true, but the question is whether it matters in practice. All renderers are approximate and our DR is no exception. We describe our approximations in Sections 3 and 4 and argue that, in practice, "approximately differentiable" is actually very useful.

Our goal is not rendering, but inverse rendering: we wish to specify and minimize an objective, in which the renderer is only one part. To that end, our DR is built upon a new autodifferentiation framework, called Chumpy, in Python that makes programming compact and relatively easy. Our public autodiff framework makes it easy to extend the basic features of OpenDR to address specific problems. For example, instead of specifying input geometry as vertices, one might parameterize the vertices in a shape space; or in the output, one might want a Laplacian pyramid of pixels, or edges, or moments, instead of the raw pixel values. While autodifferentiation does not remove the need to write these functions, it does remove the need to differentiate them by hand.

Using this we define the OpenDR framework that supports a wide range of real problems in computer vision. The OpenDR framework provides a compact and efficient way of expressing computer vision problems without having to worry about how to differentiate them. This is the first publicly-available framework for differentiating the image generation process.

To evaluate the OpenDR, and to illustrate how to use it, we present two examples. The first is a simple "hello world" example, which serves to illustrate the basic ideas of the OpenDR. The second, more complex, example involves fitting an articulated and deformable model of 3D human body shape to image and range data from a Kinect. Here we optimize 3D body shape, pose, lighting, albedo, and camera parameters. This is a complex and rich generative model and optimizing it would generally be challenging; with OpenDR, it is straightforward to express and optimize.

While differentiating the rendering process does not solve the computer vision problem, it does address the important problem of local refinement of model parameters. We see this as piece of the solution that is synergistic with stochastic approaches for probabilistic programming [22]. We have no claim of novelty around vision as inverse graphics. Our novelty is in making it practical and easy to solve a fairly wide class of such problems. We believe the OpenDR is the first generally available solution for differentiable rendering and it will enable people to push the analysis-by-synthesis approach further.

2   Related Work

The view of vision as *inverse graphics* is nearly as old as the field itself [3]. It appears in the work of Grenander on *analysis by synthesis* [9], in physics-based approaches [13], in regularization theory [5,32], and even as a model for human perception [18,24,27]. This approach plays an important role in Bayesian models and today the two notions are tightly coupled [19]. In the standard Bayesian formulation, the likelihood function specifies the forward rendering process, while the prior constrains (or regularizes) the space of models or parameters [19]. Typically the likelihood does not involve an actual render in the standard graphics sense. In graphics, "inverse rendering" typically refers to recovering the illumination, reflectance, and material properties from an image (e.g. the estimation of BRDFs); see [26] for a review. When we talk about inverting the rendering process we mean something more general, involving the recovery of object shape, camera parameters, motion, and illumination.

The theory of inverse graphics is well established, but what is missing is the direct connection between rendering and optimization from images. Graphics is about synthesis. Inference is about going from observations to models (or parameters). *Differentiable rendering* connects these in a concrete way by explicitly relating changes in the observed image with changes in the model parameters.

Stochastic Search and Probabilistic Programming. Our work is similar philosophy to Mansinghka et al. [22]. They show how to write simple probabilistic graphics programs that describe the generative model of a scene and how this relates to image observations. They then use automatic and approximate stochastic inference methods to infer the parameters of the scene model from observations. While we share the goal of automatically inverting graphics models of scenes, our work is different and complimentary. They address the stochastic search problem while we address the deterministic refinement problem. While stochastic sampling is a good way to get close to a solution, it is typically not a good way to refine a solution. A full solution is likely to incorporate both of these elements of search and refinement, where the refinement stage can use richer models, deterministic optimization, achieve high accuracy, and be more efficient.

Our work goes beyond [22] in other ways. They exploit a very general but computationally inefficient Metropolis-Hastings sampler for inference that will not scale well to more complex problems. While their work starts from the premise of doing inference with a generic graphics rendering engine, they do not cope with 3D shape, illumination, 3D occlusion, reflectance, and camera calibration; that is, they do no render graphics scenes as we typically think of them. None of this is to diminish the importance of that work, which lays out a framework for probabilistic scene inference. This is part of a more general trend in probabilistic programming where one defines the generative graphical model and lets a generic solver do the inference [8,23,37]. Our goal is similar but for deterministic inference. Like them we offer a simple programming framework in which to express complex models.

Recently Jampani et al. [15] define a generic sampler for solving inverse graphics problems. They use discriminative methods (bottom up) to inform the sampler and improve efficiency. Their motivation is similar to ours in that they want to enable inverse graphics solutions with simple generic optimization methods. Their goal differs however in that they seek a full posterior distribution over model parameters, while we seek a local optimum. In general, their method is complimentary to ours and the methods could be combined.

Differentiating Graphics Models. Of course we are not the first to formulate a generative graphics model for a vision problem, differentiate it, and solve for the model parameters. This is a tried-and-true approach in computer vision. In previous work, however, this is done as a "one off" solution and differentiating the model is typically labor intensive. For a given model of the scene and particular image features, one defines an observation error function and differentiates this with respect to the model parameters. Solutions obtained for one model are not necessarily easily applied to another model. Some prominent examples follow.

Face Modeling: Blanz and Vetter [6] define a detailed generative model of human faces and do analysis by synthesis to invert the model. Their model includes 3D face shape, model texture, camera pose, ambient lighting, and directional lighting. Given model parameters they synthesize a realistic face image and compare it with image pixels using sum-of-squared differences. They explicitly compute derivatives of their objective function and use a stochastic gradient descent method for computational reasons and to help avoid local optima.

3D Shape Estimation: Jalobeanu et al. [14] estimate underlying parameters (lighting, albedo, and geometry) of a 3D planetary surface with the use of a differentiated rendering process. They point out the importance of accurate rendering of the image and the derivatives and work in *object space* to determine visibilities for each pixel using computational geometry. Like us, they define a differentiable rendering process but with a focus on Bayesian inference.

Smelyansky et al. [29] define a "fractional derivative renderer" and use it to compute camera parameters and surface shape together in a stereo reconstruction problem. Like [14], they use geometric modeling to account for the fractional contributions of different surfaces to a pixel. While accurate, such a purely geometric approach is potentially slow.

Bastian [2] also argues that working in object space avoids problems of working with pixels and, in particular, that occlusions are a problem for differentiable rendering. He suggests super-sampling the image as one solution to approximate a differentiable render. Instead he uses MCMC sampling and suggests that sampling could be used in conjunction with a differentiable renderer to avoid problems due to occlusion. See also [34], which addresses similar issues in image modeling with a continuous image representation.

It is important to remember that any render only produces an approximation of the scene. Consequently any differentiable render will only produce approximations of the derivatives. This is true whether one works in object space or pixel space. The question is how good is the approximation and how practical is it to obtain? We argue below that pixel space provides the better tradeoff.

Human Pose and Shape: Sminchisecu [31] formulates the articulated 3D human tracking problem from monocular video. He defines a generative model of edges, silhouettes and optical flow and derives approximations of these that are differentiable. In [30] Sminchisescu and Telea define a generic programming framework in which ones specifies models and relates these to image observations. This framework does not automatically differentiate the rendering process.

de La Gorce et al. [20] recover pose, shape, texture, and lighting position in a hand tracking application. They formulate the problem as a forward graphics synthesis problem and then differentiate it, paying special attention to obtaining derivatives at object boundaries; we adopt a similar approach. Weiss et al. [36] estimate both human pose and shape using range data from Kinect and an edge term corresponding to the boundary of the human body. They formulate a differentiable silhouette edge term and mention that it is sometimes not differentiable, but that this occurs at only finitely many points, which can be ignored.

The above methods all render a model of the world and differentiate some image error with respect to the model parameters. Despite the fact that they all can be seen as inverse rendering, in each case the authors formulate an objective and then devise a way to approximately differentiate it. Our key insight is that, instead of differentiating each problem, we *differentiate the render*. Then any problem that can be posed as rendering is, by construction, (approximately) differentiable. To formulate a new problem, one writes down the forward process (as expressed by the rendering system), the derivatives are given automatically, and optimization is performed by one of several local optimization methods. This approach of differentiating the rendering process provides a general solution to many problems in computer vision.

3   Defining Our Forward Process

Let $f(\Theta)$ be the rendering function, where Θ is a collection of all parameters used to create the image. Here we factor Θ into vertex locations V, camera parameters C, and per-vertex brightness A: therefore $\Theta = \{V, C, A\}$. Inverse graphics is inherently approximate, and it is important to establish our approximations in both the forward process and its differentiation. Our forward model makes the following approximations:

Appearance (A): Per-pixel surface appearance is modeled as product of mipmapped texture and per-vertex brightness, such that brightness combines the effects of reflectance and lighting. Spherical harmonics and point light sources are available as part of OpenDR; other direct lighting models are easy to construct. Global illumination, which includes interreflection and all the complex effects of lighting, is not explicitly supported.

Geometry (V): We assume a 3D scene to be approximated by triangles, parameterized by vertices V, with the option of a background image (or depth image for the depth renderer) to be placed behind the geometry. There is no explicit limit on the number of objects, and the DR does not even "know" whether it is rendering one or more objects; its currency is triangles, not objects.

Camera (C): We approximate continuous pixel intensities by their sampled central value. We use the pinhole-plus-distortion camera projection model from OpenCV. Its primary difference compared with other projections is in the details of the image distortion model [7], which are in turn derived from [11].

Our approximations are close to those made by modern graphics pipelines. One important exception is appearance: modern graphics pipelines support per-pixel assignment on surfaces according to user-defined functions, whereas here we support *per-vertex* user-defined functions (with colors interpolated between vertices). While we also support texture mapping, we do not yet support differentiation with respect to intensity values on the texture map. Unlike de La Gorce [20], we do not support derivatives with respect to texture; whereas they use bilinear interpolation, we would require trilinear interpolation because of our use of mipmapping. This is future work.

We emphasize that, if the OpenDR proves useful, users will hopefully expand it, relaxing many of these assumptions. Here we describe the initial release.

4   Differentiating Our Forward Process

To describe the partial derivatives of the forward process, we introduce U as an intermediate variable indicating 2D projected vertex coordinate positions. Differentiation follows the chain rule as illustrated in Fig. 1. Our derivatives may be grouped into the effects of appearance ($\frac{\partial f}{\partial A}$), and changes in projected coordinates ($\frac{\partial U}{\partial C}$ and $\frac{\partial U}{\partial V}$), and the effects of image-space deformation ($\frac{\partial f}{\partial U}$).

4.1   Differentiating Appearance

Pixels projected by geometry are colored by the product of texture T and appearance A; therefore $\frac{\partial f}{\partial A}$ can be quickly found by rendering the texture-mapped geometry with per-vertex colors set to 1.0, and weighting the contribution of surrounding vertices by rendered barycentric coordinates. Partials $\frac{\partial A}{\partial V}$ may be zero (if only ambient color is required), may be assigned to built-in spherical harmonics or point light sources, or may be defined directly by the user.

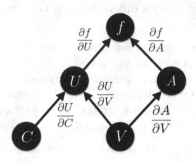

Fig. 1. Partial derivative structure of the renderer

4.2 Differentiating Projection

Image values relate to 3D coordinates and camera calibration parameters via 2D coordinates; that is, where U indicates 2D coordinates of vertices,

$$\frac{\partial f}{\partial V} = \frac{\partial f}{\partial U}\frac{\partial U}{\partial V}, \qquad \frac{\partial f}{\partial C} = \frac{\partial f}{\partial U}\frac{\partial U}{\partial C}.$$

Partials $\frac{\partial U}{\partial V}$ and $\frac{\partial U}{\partial C}$ are straightforward, as projection is well-defined. Conveniently, OpenCV provides $\frac{\partial U}{\partial C}$ and $\frac{\partial U}{\partial V}$ directly.

4.3 Differentiating Intensity with Respect to 2D Image Coordinates

In order to estimate $\frac{\partial f}{\partial U}$, we first segment our pixels into occlusion boundary pixels and interior pixels, as inspired by [20]. The change induced by boundary pixels is primarily due to the replacement of one surface with another, whereas the change induced by interior pixels relates to the image-space projected translation of the surface patch. The assignment of boundary pixels is obtained with a rendering pass by identifying pixels on edges which (a) pass a depth test (performed by the renderer) and (b) join triangles with opposing normals: one triangle facing towards the camera, one facing away. We consider three classifications for a pixel: interior, interior/boundary, and many-boundary.

Interior: a pixel contains no occlusion boundaries. Because appearance is a product of interpolated texture and interpolated color, intensity changes are piecewise smooth with respect to geometry changes. For interior pixels, we use the image-space first-order Taylor expansion approach adopted by [17]. To understand this approach, consider a patch translating right in image space by a pixel: each pixel becomes replaced by its lefthand neighbor, which is similar to the application of a Sobel filter. Importantly, we do not allow this filtering to cross or include boundary pixels (a case not handled by [17] because occlusion was not modeled).

Specifically, on pixels not neighboring an occlusion boundary, we perform horizontal filtering with the kernel $\frac{1}{2}[-1, 0, 1]$. On pixels neighboring an occlusion boundary on the left, we use $[0, -1, 1]$ for horizontal filtering; with pixels neighboring occlusion boundaries on the right, we use $[-1, 1, 0]$; and with occlusion boundaries on both sides we approximate derivatives as being zero. With vertical filtering, we use the same kernels transposed.

Interior/Boundary: a pixel is intersected by one occlusion boundary. For the interior/boundary case, we use image-space filtering with kernel $\frac{1}{2}[-1, 0, 1]$ and its transpose. This approximates one difference (that between the foreground boundary and the surface behind it) with another (that between the foreground boundary and a pixel neighboring the surface behind it). Instead of "peeking" behind an occluding boundary, we are using a neighboring pixel as a surrogate and assuming that the difference is not too great. In practical terms, the boundary gradient is almost always much larger than the gradient of the occluded background surface patch, and therefore dominates the direction taken during optimization.

Many-Boundary: more than one occlusion boundary is present in a pixel. While object space methods provide exact derivatives for such pixels at the expense of modeling all the geometry, we treat this as an interior/boundary case. This is justified because very few pixels are affected by this scenario and because the exact object-space computation would be prohibitively expensive.

To summarize, the most significant approximation of the differentiation process occurs boundary pixels where we approximate one difference (nearby pixel minus occluded pixel) with another (nearby pixel minus almost-occluded pixel). We find this works in practice, but it is important to recognize that better approximations are possible [20].

As an implementation detail, our approach requires one render pass when a raw rendered image is requested, and an additional three passes (for boundary identification, triangle identification, and barycentric coordinates) when derivatives are requested. Each pass requires read back from the GPU.

4.4   Software Foundation

Flexibility is critical to the generality of a differentiable renderer; custom functions should be easy to design without requiring differentiation by hand. To that end, we use automatic differentiation [10] to compute derivatives given only a specification of the forward process, without resorting to finite differencing methods. As part of the OpenDR release we include a new automatic differentiation framework (Chumpy). This framework is essentially Numpy [25], which is a numerical package in Python, made differentiable. By sharing much of the API of Numpy, this allows the forward specification of problems with a popular API. This in turn allows the forward specification of models not part of the renderer, and allows upper layers of the renderer to be specified minimally. Although alternative auto-differentiation frameworks were considered [4,35,21], we wrap Numpy for its ease-of-use. Our overall system depends on Numpy [25], Scipy [16], and OpenCV [7].

5 Programming in OpenDR: Hello World

First we illustrate construction of a renderer with a texture-mapped 3D mesh of Earth. In Sec. 3, we introduced f as a function of $\{V, A, U\}$; in Fig. 2, V, A, U and f are constructed in turn. While we use spherical harmonics and a static set of vertices, anything expressible in Chumpy can be assigned to these variables, as long the dimensions make sense: given N vertices, then V and A must be $N \times 3$, and U must be $N \times 2$.

```
from opendr.simple import *
w, h = 320, 240

import numpy as np
m = load_mesh('nasa_earth.obj')

# Create V, A, U, f: geometry, brightness, camera, renderer
V = ch.array(m.v)
A = SphericalHarmonics(vn=VertNormals(v=V, f=m.f),
                       components=[3.,1.,0.,0.,0.,0.,0.,0.,0.],
                       light_color=ch.ones(3))
U = ProjectPoints(v=V, f=[300,300.], c=[w/2.,h/2.], k=ch.zeros(5),
                  t=ch.zeros(3), rt=ch.zeros(3))
f = TexturedRenderer(vc=A, camera=U, f=m.f, bgcolor=[0.,0.,0.],
                     texture_image=m.texture_image, vt=m.vt, ft=m.ft,
                     frustum={'width':w, 'height':h, 'near':1,'far':20})
```

Fig. 2. Constructing a renderer in OpenDR

Figure 3 shows the code for optimizing a model of Earth to match image evidence. We reparameterize V with translation and rotation, express the error to be minimized as a difference between Gaussian pyramids, and find a local minimum of the energy function with simultaneous optimization of translation, rotation, and light parameters. Note that a Gaussian pyramid can be written as a linear filtering operation and is therefore simply differentiable. The process is visualized in Fig. 4.

In this example, there is only one object; but as mentioned in Sec. 3, there is no obvious limit to the number of objects, because geometry is just a collection of triangles whose vertices are driven by a user's parameterization. Triangle face connectivity is required but may be disjoint.

Image pixels are only one quantity of interest. Any differentiable operation applied to an image can be applied to the render and hence we can minimize the difference between functions of images. Figure 5 illustrates how to minimize the difference between image edges and rendered edges. For more examples, the `opendr.demo()` function, in the software release, shows rendering of image moments, silhouettes, and boundaries, all with derivatives with respect to inputs.

```
# Parameterize the vertices
translation, rotation = ch.array([0,0,4]), ch.zeros(3)
f.v = translation + V.dot(Rodrigues(rotation))

# Create the energy
difference = f - load_image('earth_observed.jpg')
E = gaussian_pyramid(difference, n_levels=6, normalization='SSE')

# Minimize the energy
light_parms = A.components
ch.minimize(E, x0=[translation])
ch.minimize(E, x0=[translation, rotation, light_parms])
```

Fig. 3. Minimizing an objective function given image evidence. The derivatives from the renderer are used by the minimize method. Including a translation-only stage typically speeds convergence.

Fig. 4. Illustration of optimization in Figure 3. In order: observed image of earth, initial absolute difference between the rendered and observed image intensities, final difference, final result.

6   Experiments

Run-time depends on many user-specific decisions, including the number of pixels, triangles, underlying parameters and model structure. Figure 6 illustrates the effects of resolution on run-time in a simple scenario on a 3.0 GHz 8-core 2013 Mac Pro. We render a subdivided tetrahedron with 1024 triangles, lit by spherical harmonics. The mesh is parameterized by translation and rotation, and timings are according to those 6 parameters. The figure illustrates the overhead associated with differentiable rendering.

```
rn = TexturedRenderer(...)
edge_image = rn[:,1:,:] - rn[:,:-1,:]
ch.minimize(ch.sum((edge_image - my_edge_image)**2.),
            x0=[rn.v], method='bfgs')
```

Fig. 5. Optimizing a function of the rendered image to match a function of image evidence. Here the function is an edge filter.

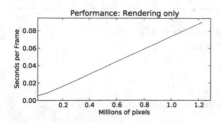
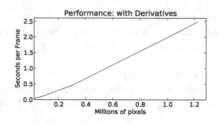

Fig. 6. Rendering performance versus resolution. For reference, 640x480 is 0.3 million pixels. Left: with rendering only. Right: with rendering and derivatives.

Fig. 7. Differentiable rendering versus finite differencing. Left: a rotating quadrilateral. Middle: OpenDR's predicted change in pixel values with respect to in-plane rotation. Right: finite differences recorded with a change to in-plane rotation.

Finite differences on original parameters are sometimes faster to compute than analytic differences. In the experiment shown in Fig. 6, at 640x480, it is 1.75 times faster to compute forward finite differencing on 6 parameters than to find analytic derivatives according to our approach. However, if derivatives with respect to all 514 vertices are required, then forward finite differencing becomes approximately 80 times slower than computing derivatives with our approach.

More importantly, the correct finite differencing epsilon is pixel-dependent. Figure 7 shows that the correct epsilon for finite-differencing can be spatially varying: the chosen epsilon is too small for some pixels and too large for others.

6.1 Body Shape from Kinect

We now address a body measurement estimation problem using the Kinect as an input device. In an analysis-by-synthesis approach, many parameters must be estimated to effectively explain the image and depth evidence. We effectively estimate thousands of parameters (per-vertex albedo being the biggest contributor) by minimizing the contribution of over a million residuals; this would be impractical with derivative-free methods.

Subjects were asked to form an A-pose or T-pose in two views separated by 45 degrees; then a capture was performed without the subject in view. This generates three depth and three color images, with most of the state, except pose, assumed constant across the two views.

Our variables and observables are as follows:

- **Latent Variables:** lighting parameters A_L, per-vertex albedo A_C, color camera translation T, and body parameters B: therefore $\Theta = \{A_L, A_C, T, B\}$.

– **Observables:** depth images $D_{1...n}$ and color images $I_{1...n}$, $n = 3$.

Appearance, A, is modeled here as a product of per-vertex albedo, A_C, and spherical harmonics parameterized by A_L: $A = A_C H(A_L, V)$, where $H(A_L, V)$ gives one brightness to each vertex according to the surface normal. Vertices are generated by a BlendSCAPE model [12], controlled by pose parameters $P_{1..n}$ (each of n views has a slightly different pose) and shape parameters S (shared across views) which we concatenate to form B.

To use depth and color together, we must know the precise extrinsic relationship between the sensors; due to manufacturing variance, the camera axes are not perfectly aligned. Instead of using a pre-calibration step, we pose the camera translation estimation as part of the optimization, using the human body itself to find the translation, T, between color and depth cameras.

Our data terms includes a color term E_C, a depth term E_D, and feet-to-floor contact term E_F. Our regularization terms include a pose prior E_P, a shape prior E_S (both Gaussian), and smoothness prior E_Q on per-vertex albedo:

$$E = E_C + E_D + E_F + E_P + E_S + E_Q. \tag{1}$$

The color term accumulates per-pixel error over images

$$E_C(I, A_L, A_C, T, B) = \sum_i \sum_u \|I_{iu} - \tilde{I}_{iu}(A_L, A_C, T, B)\|^2 \tag{2}$$

where $\tilde{I}_{ui}$ is the simulated pixel intensity of image-space position u for view i.

The depth term is similar but, due to sensor noise, is formulated robustly

$$E_D(D, T, B) = \sum_i \sum_u \|D_{iu} - \tilde{D}_{iu}(T, B)\|^\rho \tag{3}$$

where the parameter ρ is adjusted from 2 to 1 over the course of an optimization.

The floor term E_F minimizes differences between foot vertices of the model and the ground

$$E_F(D, B) = \sum_k \|r(B, D_b, k)\|^2 \tag{4}$$

where $r(B, D_b, k)$ indicates the distance between model footpad vertex k and a mesh D_b constructed from the background shot,

The albedo smoothness term E_Q penalizes squared differences between the log albedo of neighboring mesh vertices

$$E_Q = \sum_e \|\log(b(e, 0)) - \log(b(e, 1))\|^2 \tag{5}$$

where $b(e, 0)$ denotes the albedo of the first vertex on edge e, and $b(e, 1)$ denotes the albedo of the other vertex on edge e.

Finally, shape and pose parameter priors, $E_S(S)$ and $E_P(P)$, penalize the squared Mahalanobis distance from the mean body shape and pose learned during BlendSCAPE training.

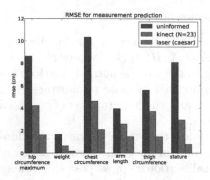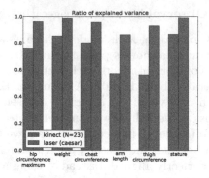

Fig. 8. Accuracy of measurement prediction for Kinect-based fitting compared to measurements from CAESAR scans or guessing the mean (uninformed). Left: root mean squared error (RMSE) in cm. Right: percentage of explained variance.

Fig. 9. Reconstruction of two subjects (top and bottom). **First column:** original captured images, with faces blurred for anonymity. **Second column:** simulated images after convergence. **Third column:** captured point cloud together with estimated body model. **Fourth column:** estimated body shown on background point cloud. More examples can be found in the supplemental materials.

Initialization for the position of the simulated body could be up to a meter away from the real body and still achieve convergence. Without the use of Gaussian pyramids or background images, initialization would require more precision (while we did not use it, initialization could be obtained with the pose information available from the Kinect API).

Male and female body models were each trained from approximately 2000 scans from the CAESAR [28] dataset. This dataset comes with anthropometric measurements for each subject; similar to [1], we use regularized linear regression to predict measurements from our underlying body shape parameters. To evaluate accuracy of the recovered body models, we measured RMSE and percentage of explained variance of our predictions as shown in Fig. 8. For comparison, Fig. 8 also shows the accuracy of estimating measurements directly from 3803 meshes accurately registered to the CAESAR laser scans. Although these two settings (23 subjects by Kinect and 3803 subjects by laser scan) differ in both subjects and method, and we do not expect Kinect scans to be as accurate, Fig. 8 provides an indication of how well the Kinect-based method works.

Figure 9 shows some representative results from our Kinect fitter; see the supplemental material for more. While foot posture on the male is slightly wrong, the effects of geometry, lighting and appearance are generally well-estimated. Obtaining this result was made significantly easier with a platform that includes a differentiable renderer and a set of building blocks to compose around it.

Each fit took around 7 minutes on a 3.0 GHz 8-core 2013 Mac Pro.

7 Conclusions

Many problems in computer vision have been solved by effectively differentiating through the rendering process. This is not new. What is new is that we provide an easy to use framework for both renderer differentiation and objective formulation. This makes it easy in Python to define a forward model and optimize it. We have demonstrated this with a challenging problem of body shape estimation from image and range data. By releasing the OpenDR with an open-source license (see http://open-dr.org), we hope to create a community that is using and contributing to this effort. The hope is that the this will push forward research on vision as inverse graphics by providing tools to make working on this easier.

Differentiable rendering has its limitations. When using differences between RGB Gaussian pyramids, the fundamental issue is overlap: if a simulated and observed object have no overlap in the pyramid, the simulated object will not record a gradient towards the observed one. One can use functions of the pixels that have no such overlap restriction (e.g. moments) to address this but the fundamental limitation is one of visibility: a real observed feature will not pull on simulated features that are entirely occluded because of the state of the renderer.

Consequently, differentiable rendering is only one piece of the puzzle: we believe that informed sampling [15] and probabilistic graphics programming [22] are also essential to a serious application of inverse rendering. Despite this, we hope many will benefit from the OpenDR platform.

Future exploration may include increasing image realism by incorporating global illumination. It may also include more features of modern rendering pipelines (for example, differentiation through a fragment shader). We are also interested in the construction of an "integratable renderer" for posterior estimation; although standard sampling methods can be used to approximate such an integral, there may be graphics-related techniques to integrate in a more direct fashion within limited domains.

Acknowledgements. We would like to thank Eric Rachlin for discussions about Chumpy and Gerard Pons-Moll for proofreading.

References

1. Allen, B., Curless, B., Popović, Z.: The space of human body shapes: Reconstruction and parameterization from range scans. ACM Trans. Graph. 22(3), 587–594 (2003)
2. Bastian, J.W.: Reconstructing 3D geometry from multiple images via inverse rendering. Ph.D. thesis, University of Adelaide (2008)
3. Baumgart, B.G.: Geometric modeling for computer vision. Tech. Rep. AI Lab Memo AIM-249, Stanford University (Oct 1974)
4. Bergstra, J., Breuleux, O., Bastien, F., Lamblin, P., Pascanu, R., Desjardins, G., Turian, J., Warde-Farley, D., Bengio, Y.: Theano: a CPU and GPU math expression compiler. In: Proceedings of the Python for Scientific Computing Conference (SciPy) (June 2010)
5. Bertero, M., Poggio, T., Torre, V.: Ill-posed problems in early vision. Proc. IEEE 76(8), 869–889 (1988)
6. Blanz, V., Vetter, T.: A morphable model for the synthesis of 3D faces. In: Proceedings of the 26th Annual Conference on Computer Graphics and Interactive Techniques, SIGGRAPH 1999, pp. 187–194. ACM Press/Addison-Wesley Publishing Co., New York (1999)
7. Bradski, G., Kaehler, A.: Learning OpenCV. O'Reilly Media Inc. (2008), http://oreilly.com/catalog/9780596516130
8. Goodman, N., Mansinghka, V., Roy, D., Bonawitz, K., Tenenbaum, J.: Church: A language for generative models. In: McAllester, D.A., Myllymäki, P. (eds.) Proc. Uncertainty in Artificial Intelligence (UAI), pp. 220–229 (July 2008)
9. Grenander, U.: Lectures in Pattern Theory I, II and III: Pattern Analysis, Pattern Synthesis and Regular Structures. Springer, Heidelberg (1976–1981)
10. Griewank, A.: Evaluating Derivatives: Principles and Techniques of Algorithmic Differentiation. Frontiers in Appl. Math., vol. 19. SIAM, Philadelphia (2000)
11. Heikkila, J., Silven, O.: A four-step camera calibration procedure with implicit image correction. In: Proceedings of 1997 IEEE Computer Society Conference on Computer Vision and Pattern Recognition, pp. 1106–1112 (June 1997)
12. Hirshberg, D.A., Loper, M., Rachlin, E., Black, M.J.: Coregistration: Simultaneous alignment and modeling of articulated 3D shape. In: Fitzgibbon, A., Lazebnik, S., Perona, P., Sato, Y., Schmid, C. (eds.) ECCV 2012, Part VI. LNCS, vol. 7577, pp. 242–255. Springer, Heidelberg (2012)
13. Horn, B.: Understanding image intensities. Artificial Intelligence 8, 201–231 (1977)
14. Jalobeanu, A., Kuehnel, F., Stutz, J.: Modeling images of natural 3D surfaces: Overview and potential applications. In: Conference on Computer Vision and Pattern Recognition Workshop, CVPRW 2004, pp. 188–188 (June 2004)
15. Jampani, V., Nowozin, S., Loper, M., Gehler, P.V.: The informed sampler: A discriminative approach to Bayesian inference in generative computer vision models. CoRR abs/1402.0859 (February 2014), http://arxiv.org/abs/1402.0859
16. Jones, E., Oliphant, T., Peterson, P., et al.: SciPy: Open source scientific tools for Python (2001), http://www.scipy.org/
17. Jones, M.J., Poggio, T.: Model-based matching by linear combinations of prototypes. In: A.I. Memo 1583, pp. 1357–1365. MIT (1996)
18. Kersten, D.: Inverse 3-D graphics: A metaphor for visual perception. Behavior Research Methods, Instruments & Computers 29(1), 37–46 (1997)
19. Knill, D.C., Richards, W.: Perception as Bayesian Inference. The Press Syndicate of the University of Cambridge, Cambridge (1996)

20. Gorce, M.d.L., Paragios, N., Fleet, D.J.: Model-based hand tracking with texture, shading and self-occlusions. In: 2008 IEEE Computer Society Conference on Computer Vision and Pattern Recognition (CVPR 2008), Anchorage, Alaska, USA, June 24-26. IEEE Computer Society (2008)
21. Lee, A.D.: ad: a python package for first- and second-order automatic differentation (2012), http://pythonhosted.org/ad/
22. Mansinghka, V., Kulkarni, T.D., Perov, Y.N., Tenenbaum, J.: Approximate Bayesian image interpretation using generative probabilistic graphics programs. In: Burges, C., Bottou, L., Welling, M., Ghahramani, Z., Weinberger, K. (eds.) Advances in Neural Information Processing Systems 26, pp. 1520–1528 (2013)
23. Minka, T., Winn, J., Guiver, J., Knowles, D.: Infer.NET 2.4. Microsoft Research Cambridge (2010), http://research.microsoft.com/infernet.
24. Mumford, D.: Neuronal architectures for pattern-theoretic problems. In: Koch, C., Davis, J.L. (eds.) Large-scale Neuronal theories of the Brain, pp. 125–152. Bradford (1994)
25. Oliphant, T.E.: Python for scientific computing. Computing in Science and Engineering 9(3), 10–20 (2007)
26. Patow, G., Pueyo, X.: A survey of inverse rendering problems. Computer Graphics Forum 22(4), 663–687 (2003)
27. Richards, W.: Natural Computation. The MIT Press (A Bradford Book), Cambridge (1988)
28. Robinette, K., Blackwell, S., Daanen, H., Boehmer, M., Fleming, S., Brill, T., Hoeferlin, D., Burnsides, D.: Civilian American and European Surface Anthropometry Resource (CAESAR) final report. Tech. Rep. AFRL-HE-WP-TR-2002-0169, US Air Force Research Laboratory (2002)
29. Smelyansky, V.N., Morris, R.D., Kuehnel, F.O., Maluf, D.A., Cheeseman, P.: Dramatic improvements to feature based stereo. In: Heyden, A., Sparr, G., Nielsen, M., Johansen, P. (eds.) ECCV 2002, Part II. LNCS, vol. 2351, pp. 247–261. Springer, Heidelberg (2002)
30. Sminchisescu, C., Telea, A.: A framework for generic state estimation in computer vision applications. In: International Conference on Computer Vision Systems (ICVS), pp. 21–34 (2001)
31. Sminchisescu, C.: Estimation algorithms for ambiguous visual models: Three dimensional human modeling and motion reconstruction in monocular video sequences. Ph.D. thesis, Inst. National Polytechnique de Grenoble (July 2002)
32. Terzopoulos, D.: Regularization of inverse visual problems involving discontinuities. IEEE PAMI 8(4), 413–424 (1986)
33. Terzopoulos, D.: Physically-based modeling: Past, present, and future. In: ACM SIGGRAPH 89 Panel Proceedings, pp. 191–209 (1989)
34. Viola, F., Fitzgibbon, A., Cipolla, R.: A unifying resolution-independent formulation for early vision. In: 2012 IEEE Conference on Computer Vision and Pattern Recognition (CVPR), pp. 494–501 (June 2012)
35. Walter, S.F.: Pyadolc 2.4.1 (2012), https://github.com/b45ch1/pyadolc
36. Weiss, A., Hirshberg, D., Black, M.: Home 3D body scans from noisy image and range data. In: Int. Conf. on Computer Vision (ICCV), pp. 1951–1958. IEEE, Barcelona (2011)
37. Wood, F., van de Meent, J.W., Mansinghka, V.: A new approach to probabilistic programming inference. In: Artificial Intelligence and Statistics (2014)

A Superior Tracking Approach:
Building a Strong Tracker through Fusion

Christian Bailer[1], Alain Pagani[1], and Didier Stricker[1,2]

[1] German Research Center for Artificial Intelligence, Kaiserslautern, Germany
{Christian.Bailer,Alain.Pagani,Didier.Stricker}@dfki.de
[2] University of Kaiserslautern, Germany

Abstract. General object tracking is a challenging problem, where each tracking algorithm performs well on different sequences. This is because each of them has different strengths and weaknesses. We show that this fact can be utilized to create a fusion approach that clearly outperforms the best tracking algorithms in tracking performance. Thanks to dynamic programming based trajectory optimization we cannot only outperform tracking algorithms in accuracy but also in other important aspects like trajectory continuity and smoothness. Our fusion approach is very generic as it only requires frame-based tracking results in form of the object's bounding box as input and thus can work with arbitrary tracking algorithms. It is also suited for live tracking. We evaluated our approach using 29 different algorithms on 51 sequences and show the superiority of our approach compared to state-of-the-art tracking methods.

Keywords: Object Tracking, Data Fusion.

1 Introduction

Visual object tracking is an important problem in computer vision, which has a wide range of applications such as surveillance, human computer interaction and interactive video production. Nowadays, the problem can be robustly solved for many specific scenarios like car tracking [18] or person tracking [2,27]. However, object tracking in the general case i.e. when arbitrary objects in arbitrary scenarios shall be tracked can still be considered as widely unsolved. The possible challenges that can occur in an unknown scenario are too various and too numerous to consider them all with reasonable effort within one approach – at least with todays capabilities. Classical challenges are for example illumination changes, shadows, translucent/opaque and complete occlusions, 2D/3D rotations, deformations, scale changes, low resolution, fast motion, blur, confusing background and similar objects in the scene.

As the evaluation in [29] and our comparison in Table 1 shows, each tracking algorithm performs well on different sequences. An on average good algorithm might fail for a sequence where an on average bad algorithm performs very well. For example in Table 1 the on average best algorithm SCM [35] fails in the

D. Fleet et al. (Eds.): ECCV 2014, Part VII, LNCS 8695, pp. 170–185, 2014.

lemming sequence, while the on average second worst algorithm SMS [8] outperforms every other algorithm on this sequence. This shows that different tracking algorithms master different challenges that can occur in general object tracking and that an approach which combines the strengths of different algorithms while avoiding their weaknesses could outperform each single algorithm by far.

A possibility for this combination is the fusion of the tracking results of different algorithms into one result. In this paper we show that we can actually clearly outperform single algorithms with this approach. Furthermore, we show that our fusion approach can generate good results for many more sequences than the globally best tracking algorithm. Moreover, our fusion approach often outperforms even the best tracking algorithm on a sequence by up to 12% in *success score* in our tests. Thanks to trajectory optimization our fusion result is also continuous and smooth as expected from standard tracking algorithms – we even outperform tracking algorithms in this regard. For the best results trajectory optimization has to run offline, but we can also obtain very good results with pure online fusion. Online means that only tracking results of the current and past frames can be considered to create the fusion result for the current frame. This makes it suitable for live tracking. In offline fusion the tracking result for a whole sequence is known beforehand. Moreover, we present a short runtime evaluation and we show the robustness of our approach towards bad tracking results. Our approach is very generic and can fuse arbitrary tracking results. As input it needs only tracking results in the form of rectangular boxes.[1]

2   Related Work

In this section we give a general overview of fusion approaches for object tracking. For an overview of common object tracking algorithms we refer to recent state of the art review articles [32,6] and general tracker evaluation articles [29,30].

Fusion of tracking algorithms can be performed actively with feedback to the tracking algorithms or passively without feedback. As tracking algorithms are usually not designed to receive feedback and to be corrected active fusion requires specific tracking methods that work hand in hand with the fusion approach. One such approach is PROST [25] which combines optical flow tracking, template tracking and a tracking by detection algorithm in a very specific way. Thus, the three component algorithms can only be replaced very similar methods. Further active fusion approaches are VTD [19] and VTS [20]. These also require special tracking algorithms which fit into the proposed probability model and the tracking algorithms need to be defined by an appropriate appearance and motion model to be compatible with their approach. It is also possible to integrate common tracking algorithms into an active model. However, active fusion with many tracking algorithms is extremely complex as the fusion approach has to consider the specifics of each algorithm. Furthermore, feedback in the form of position correction is problematic as it forces tracking algorithms to follow one truth that might be incorrect and thus leads to permanent tracking failure.

---

[1] However, optional labeled training data can improve the results of our approach.

In contrast, passive approaches work with arbitrary tracking algorithms as long as these provide outputs that are compatible with the fusion approach. To our knowledge, the only existing passive approach is part of our previous work [4]. In this work the aim was to create a user guided tracking framework that produces high quality tracking results with as little user input as possible. The framework allows the user to select the object in different frames and to track the sequence with several different tracking algorithms. One feature to keep the effort small was a fusion approach that allows the user to check one fused result instead of several tracking results. In the fusion part of [4], we first search the biggest group of tracking result boxes that have all an overlap above a threshold to each other and then we average these boxes. If there are two groups with the same size we prefer the group with the greater overlap to each other.

3 Fusion of Tracking Results

In this section we describe our fusion approach. The input for our approach are M tracking results T_j, $j \in [1...M]$ for an object in a sequence. Each tracking result consist out of N bounding boxes $b_{i,j}$, $i \in [1...N]$ – one for each frame i in the sequence. For online/live tracking N is incremented for each new frame. Each tracking result T_j is considered to be created by a different tracking algorithm j. The fusion result of our approach that we call T^* also consists of one rectangular box for each frame. Our fusion approach works online, but some parts provide a better performing offline version as well (if mentioned).

3.1 The Basic Approach

A common approach in data fusion is majority voting. Our previous work [4] is also based on this idea. However, in tracking this requires a threshold parameter that defines if two result boxes vote for the same position. In our experiments, such thresholds showed to be very sequence dependent. Instead our approach is based on the idea of attraction fields, which does not need thresholds. The closer a fusion candidate is to a tracking result box the stronger it is attracted by it. The sum of attractions for all tracking results can be seen as an energy function that we want to maximize to find the fusion result. Attraction is computed in a 4 dimensional space to consider not only the object position but also the object size. The 4 dimensions are the x and y position of the box center and the box's width w and height h. The distance d between two boxes b and c is computed as:

$$d(b,c) = \left\| (d_x(b,c), d_y(b,c), d_w(b,c), d_h(b,c))^T \right\|_2 \tag{1}$$

$$= \left\| \left(2\frac{c_x - b_x}{c_w + b_w}, 2\frac{c_y - b_y}{c_h + b_h}, 2\alpha\frac{c_w - b_w}{c_w + b_w}, 2\alpha\frac{c_h - b_h}{c_h + b_h} \right)^T \right\|_2 \tag{2}$$

α is a constant which determines the influence of scale to the distance. It has no influence if the two boxes have the same size. The attraction function (or energy) for a candidate box c in a frame i defined as:

$$a_i(c) = \sum_{j \in M} \frac{1}{d(b_{i,j}, c)^2 + \sigma} \tag{3}$$

σ is a constant that not only avoids infinite attraction for a zero distance, but also reduces attraction increase close to zero. This prevents a perfect match to a box $b_{i,j}$ from getting a higher overall attraction than a position with good agreement to many close-by boxes. Thus, a well chosen σ is useful for noise reduction. In order to find the fusion result box $c_i^* \in T^*$ that gets the greatest attraction for a frame i we first test all tracking result boxes $R_i := \{b_{i,1}...b_{i,M}\}$ for how much attraction they get and keep the one with the greatest attraction. Then we perform gradient ascent starting from that box to determine c_i^*.

3.2 Tracker Weights

Different tracking algorithms perform on average different well and it is reasonable to trust algorithms more if they perform on average better. We can consider this by adding weights to tracking algorithms, if ground truth labeling for some sequences is available to determine the weights. If we call G_s^i the ground truth labeling for a sequence s at frame i, the weight w_j for a tracking algorithm j is determined as:

$$w_j = \sum_{s \in S} \sum_{i \in N} \frac{1}{d(G_i^s, b_{i,j}^s)^2 + \sigma} \tag{4}$$

S is the set of all sequences from which we determine weights. Normalization is not necessary as long as all w_j are determined on the same frames of the same sequences. The weighted attraction function is then:

$$a_i^w(c) = \sum_{j \in M} \frac{w_j^2}{d(b_{i,j}, c)^2 + \sigma} \tag{5}$$

3.3 Trajectory Optimization

The current approach is computed on a frame by frame basis and thus ignores possible discontinuities in the tracking trajectory. As the correct trajectory likely does not have such discontinuities it is desirable to avoid them and to find a continuous trajectory. To this aim we define the energy function E_T for the whole trajectory T as an extension of the frame-based energy of Equation (5):

$$E_T = \sum_{i \in N} \overline{a_i^w}(c_i) + \beta p(c_{i-1}, c_i), c_i \in R_i := \{b_{i,1}...b_{i,M}\}, T := \{c_1...c_N\} \tag{6}$$

where c_i is the fusion candidate box for a frame i on the trajectory candidate T. β weights the importance of continuity versus the best local score. Trajectory optimization cannot determine energies for boxes which do not belong to a tracking result. Thus for a valid trajectory T, the boxes $c_i \in T$ must be chosen from the set of tracking result boxes R_i. $\overline{a_i^w}$ is the normalized attraction that can, like a_i^w, be defined for single frames as:

$$\overline{a_i^w}(c) = \frac{a_i^w(c)}{\max\limits_{b_{i,j} \in R_i} a_i^w(b_{i,j})}, \quad R_i := \{b_{i,1}...b_{i,M}\} \tag{7}$$

The normalization ensures that the algorithm considers each frame with the same attention and does not favor simple frames with a concentration of attraction. If weights are not available $\overline{a_i^w}$ can also be replaced by the corresponding $\overline{a_i}$ by using a_i (Equation 3) instead of a_i^w. The function p is a function designed in order to penalize tracking result switches in a frame. It is 1 in frames where the trajectory T keeps following one tracking result T_j and close to 1 if the tracking result which T follows is changed but the trajectories of the old and new results are very close to each other in the corresponding frame. For discontinuities i.e. a leap to a distant trajectory it is close to zero. The function is defined as:

$$p(c_{i-1}, c_i) = \frac{\sigma}{d(c_i^{\times}, c_i)^2 + \sigma}, \quad c_{i-1} = b_{i-1,j} \Leftrightarrow c_i^{\times} = b_{i,j} \tag{8}$$

$c_i^{\times}$ is the bounding box following c_{i-1} in the tracking result T_j where c_{i-1} is originating from, while c_i can belong to another tracking result on a tracking result switch in the frame. We do not use any motion model like e.g. a Kalman filter in p as we expect from the tracking algorithms themselves already to have motion models i.e. by choosing an algorithm we indirectly also choose a motion model. Instead we determine the cost of switching the tracking algorithm in a frame with our normalized distance d between the trajectories of two algorithms. To find the trajectory T^* that maximizes E_T within a reasonable time we use a dynamic programing based approach with $N \times M$ energy fields determined as:

$$E(0, j) = \overline{a_i^w}(b_{0,j}) \tag{9}$$
$$E(i, j) = \overline{a_i^w}(b_{i,j}) + \max\limits_{j_2 \in M} p(b_{i-1,j_2}, b_{i,j}) + E(i-1, j_2) \tag{10}$$

Energy fields have to be calculated in increasing frame order starting with frame 0. All costs fields for a frame can be calculated in parallel. For online trajectory optimization T^* consists of the boxes with the highest energy in each frame. For the offline version the last frame is determined in the same way. The full offline trajectory of T^* can then be found by replacing "max" with "arg max" in Equation (10) to calculate $W(f, i)$. $W(f, i)$ can then be used as a lookup table for the way back on T^* starting from the last frame.

After finding the best trajectory, gradient ascent as described in Section 3.1 is performed here es well with Equation (5). We limit the maximal descent distance as we only want to use it for noise removal and not to destroy our found trajectory. The descent is limited to:

$$maxDescent = \delta \frac{b_w + b_h}{2} \tag{11}$$

with b_w and b_h being the width and height of a box $c_i \in T^*$ and $\delta = 0.05$.

3.4   Tracking Algorithm Removal

It might be advantageous to remove bad tracking results before fusion as they may disturb the fusion process more than they support it. In this section we present two removal approaches. A local one which removes different tracking algorithms for each sequence independently and a global one that removes tracking algorithms for all sequences at once.

The Local Approach: The idea behind the local approach is that there are only a few good tracking results for each sequence and we can identify them by looking at the average attraction a tracking result gets in a sequence. To this aim we calculate the performance P_j for each tracking result j in a sequence:

$$P_j = \sum_{i \in N} a_i^w(b_{i,j}) \tag{12}$$

Then we exclude the γ worst results with the smallest value P_j from the fusion. γ is a global parameter which is set equally for all sequences. $\gamma = |T| - 1$ is a special case which forces our approach to pick a single best tracking result for a sequence. Local removal can be used offline as well as online. In the online version all P_j must be recalculated every frame as N grows with each new frame.

The Global Approach: The global removal approach has the advantage that algorithms are removed permanently i.e. we do not need them for tracking anymore. To find candidates for global removal we first divide a training dataset into 10 parts of similar number of sequences and then perform experiments with all 10 permutations of 9 different parts, each. First we calculate for each experiment the success rate (see Section 4). Then we test for each experiment the removal of single tracking algorithms starting with the algorithm with the smallest w_j and proceeding in increasing order. If the success rate raises through removal of an algorithm, it will stay removed. Otherwise it will be added again. Algorithms that are removed in at least 7 experiments will be removed permanently. The reason why we do not simply use only the full training set to determine removal is that the removal procedure is extremely instable. For many algorithms the exchange of one or very few sequences already makes a big difference. Only if we perform several experiments we can identify algorithms that can be removed safely. Global removal is compatible with all online and offline fusion approaches, but requires in contrast to local removal labeled training data.

4   Evaluation Data and Methodology

To evaluate our fusion approach we use tracking results and ground truth data provided by Wu et al. [30]. They provide tracking results for 29 different online tracking algorithms on 51 different sequences with 32 different initializations on each sequence which are in total 47,328 tracking results. 20 initializations are used for "temporal robustness initialization" (TRE) of the tracking algorithms.

This means that the tracking algorithms are not only initialized in the first frame of each sequence but at 20 different temporal positions in each sequence. The first initialization of TRE starts from the first frame, which is the classical approach in object tracking. It is used for "one-pass evaluation" (OPE). The other 12 initializations they used for "spatial robustness evaluation" (SRE). This means that the initial tracking box is compared to the ground truth either scaled (scale factors: 0.8, 0.9, 1.1, 1.2), shifted (left, right, up and downwards shift) or shifted and scaled by the factor 1.1 at the same time. Nevertheless, SRE is evaluated with the unmodified ground truth. The authors argue that SRE is interesting because tracking initialization may be performed by an object detector that is not as accurate as a human initialization. In their work, Wu et al. [30] utilized OPE, TRE and SRE as independent datasets for a detailed evaluation of all 29 tracking algorithms. To take advantage of their whole data we will evaluate our fusion approaches also on these datasets. To our knowledge, there are only very few offline tracking algorithms in single object tracking. As a result, the best performing algorithms are usually almost all online. Therefore, we use these datasets created by online algorithms also to evaluate our offline approaches.

Evaluation Methodologies: For comparability we also use the same evaluation methodologies: a precision and a success plot. *Precision* measures the center location error in pixel space between the tracking box and the ground truth data. It is used already for a long time for evaluation in object tracking, but has some drawbacks. First of all, it does not normalize for object pixel size. A negligible center location error for a big object in a high resolution sequence can mean tracking failure for a small object. Secondly, the error can still increase if the object is already lost. Furthermore, it does not consider whether the object size is determined correctly. By using a precision plot which thresholds precision (it shows the percentage of frames that are below an error threshold) the problem of increasing error on object loss can be reduced but not completely solved. Anyhow, we think it is sufficient to compare location accuracy without scale accuracy for the provided dataset as the variability of object sizes stays within an acceptable limit. A measure that does not suffer from these problems is *success* which measures the overlap between a tracking and a ground truth box:

$$O(a, b) = \frac{|a \cap b|}{|a \cup b|} \tag{13}$$

The overlap is the intersection divided by the union of the two box regions. Overlap is normalized for object pixel size, penalizes if the size of a tracking box is different to the ground truth and the error will not increase if the object is lost. The successes plot measures the percentage of frames that have an overlap above a threshold. We call the area under curve (AUC) of the success plot *success score*. The success score is at the same time also the average overlap over all frames. To make sure that tracking result fusion is performed without influence from its ground truth data we determine the weights w_j and global algorithm removal in a cross validation manner, where we optimize for success score. The parameters α, β and σ we set to 4, 20 and 0.03, respectively, for all our tests. These parameters showed to be very robust i.e. the best values for them are very similar for OPE, TRE and SRE and our approach still shows a similar performance if we vary the values of these parameters in a relativity big range (supplemental material Fig.3). In our tests γ showed to be less robust and dataset dependent. To still prove its usefulness we optimize it for each dataset with cross validation. For SRE we use OPE to find γ, the weights w_j and to perform global algorithm removal. This simulates the effect of good training data but bad initializations from an object detector on real data. Cross validation is applied here as well.

5   Results

In this section we present and discuss the evaluation results for our fusion approach. Further results and details can be found in our supplemental material. Success and precision plots can be seen in Figure 1 for OPE and Figure 2 for SRE and TRE. These plots contain different curves:

- The five best and two worst tracking algorithms according to [30].[2]
- The average of the curves of all 29 tracking algorithms.
- The fusion result of our previous work [4].
- Fusion results for our basic approach (Section 3.1), weighted approach (Section 3.2), trajectory optimization approach (Section 3.3) and for local and global removal (Section 3.4) based on our trajectory optimization approach for fusion. Due to space constraints we only show the offline versions of trajectory optimization and local removal as they provide slightly better results than the online versions and as they are sufficient for many practical applications.
- The "Best algorithm for each sequence" curve. It is determined by choosing always the best performing tracking algorithm for each sequence according to the success score. Note that this curve is not attainable without knowing the ground truth, and is only given as reference.
- The "Upper bound" curve. It is determined by taking for each frame in each sequence always the best tracking result box with the biggest overlap to the ground truth. Here again, this curve is not attainable without knowing the ground truth, and is only given as reference.

The numbers in brackets in the figures show, similar to [30], the value at location error threshold = 20 for the precision plot and the success score (AUC) for the success plot.[3] We show results of individual tracking algorithms as dashed lines in color and results of our fusion approaches as solid lines. Further lines are doted. Gray lines are not attainable without knowing the ground truth. Getting close to the "Upper bound" curve is very unrealistic for a fusion approach, as with a large amount of tracking results it is likely that there are results close to the ground truth only by chance. Nevertheless, it shows that there is at least a theoretical potential to get above the "Best algorithm for each sequence" curve.

---

[2] For plots of all 29 tracking algorithms we refer to the supplemental material of [30].

[3] Numbers differ slightly from [30] as we calculated them exactly by average overlap.

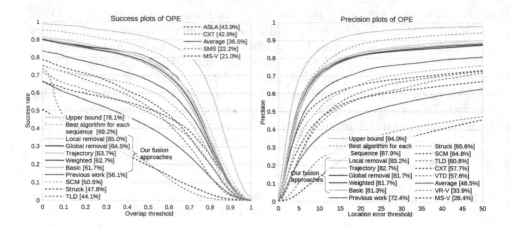

Fig. 1. Fusion results of OPE. Best viewed in color. See text for details.

Success and Precision Performance: As can be seen in Figure 1 and 2 our basic approach clearly outperforms the best tracking algorithm as well as our previous work [4] in all success and precision plots. Such good results are remarkable, given the fact that the fusion result is also influenced by many tracking algorithms that perform clearly worse than the best tracking algorithm. In every plot the weighted approach outperforms the basic approach and the trajectory optimization approach again outperforms the weighted approach. Global removal outperforms trajectory optimization in success score – for what it was optimized. However, in the success and precession plots the performance varies depending on the position. The performance for local removal differs for the three datasets.

OPE: On OPE local removal outperforms all other fusion approaches. The curve for local removal is even close to the "Best algorithm for each sequence" curve.[4] For a threshold lower than 5 pixels the curves in the precision plot are even almost the same. In the success plot which additionally considers scale correctness the approach does not get that close. This is likely because scale is often not correctly determined when position is determined correctly. We believe that this happens because many tracking algorithms are not able to determine the scale and thus they all vote for the scale of initialization.

SRE: On SRE local removal slightly underperforms the trajectory optimization approach. As reason we found that surprisingly the best γ for SRE is only 2, which is probably related to the poor initializations in SRE. However, as we take γ for SRE from OPE a γ of around 17 is used in cross validation.

TRE: On TRE tracking algorithms are mostly initialized in the middle or at the end of a sequence, which results in very short tracking results. Because of this, the difference between the best tracking algorithms and the "Average" tracking

---

[4] It is not outperformed because of a few sequences where fusion fails. See Table 1.

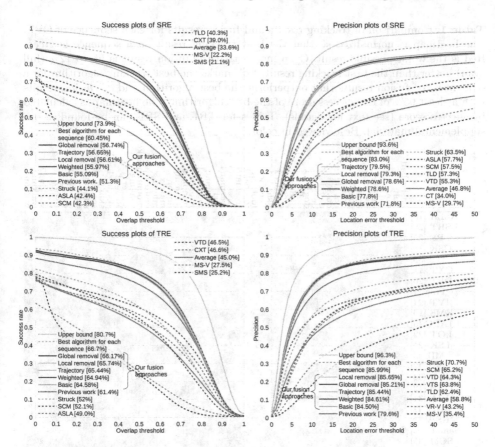

Fig. 2. Fusion results of SRE and TRE. Best viewed in color. See text for details.

algorithm curve is clearly smaller than on OPE, as good algorithms can take less advantage from short results. Similarly, the gain for our weighted, trajectory optimization and local removal approach is smaller. On the other hand, our basic approach and global removal approach seem not to be negatively affected by the short sequence effect as there is an advantage similar to OPE. As a result, our approaches are even very close to the "Best algorithm for each sequence" curve and even outperform it at some locations. The best γ for TRE is 14.

Performance on Single Sequences: Table 1 shows the performance of our fusion approach on single sequences of OPE (SRE and TRE in supplemental material). Our previous work [4] outperforms the best tracking algorithm only in 3 sequences while already our basic approach outperforms the best tracking algorithm in 11 sequences. The weighted approach, trajectory approach and global and local removal approaches outperform the best algorithm even in 15, 20, 18 and 22 sequences, respectively. Our previous work [4] has at least 95%

Table 1. Comparison of tracking results and fusion results for each sequence of OPE. The heatmap is normalized so that the best tracking result on a sequence is green. Red is the worst possible result. Cyan means that the fusion result is up to 12% (full cyan) better than the best tracking result. "x" marks the best tracking algorithm for a sequence, "o" fusion results that outperform the best algorithm and "." fusion results with at least 95% of the success score of the best algorithm. The heatmap is calculated by success score (see text for details). Tables for TRE and SRE can be found in our supplemental material. Best viewed in color.

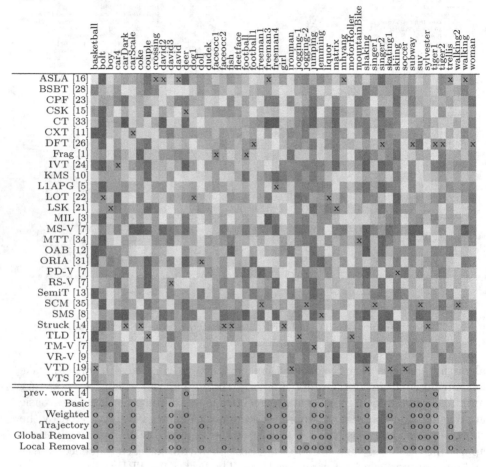

of the success score of the best tracking algorithm in 12 sequences, our basic approach in 25, the weighted approach in 27, the trajectory approach in 33 and the global and local removal approaches in 35 and 34 sequences, respectively. This shows that our fusion approaches can provide for most sequences results very close or even better than the best tracking algorithm. Hereby, we can also clearly outperform our previous work [4] and our extended approaches clearly outperform our basic approach. Furthermore, our approaches often not only outperform the best tracking algorithm, but they are even up to 12% (18% SRE,

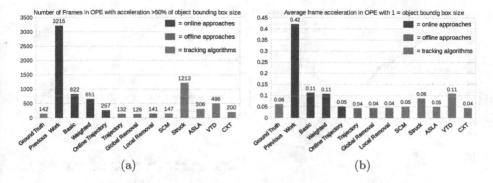

Fig. 3. Trajectory continuity evaluation on the OPE dataset. See text for details.

33% TRE) better in success score. However, there are also sequences like *skiing* and *singer2* where fusion performs poorly. The reason is probably that there are few algorithms that clearly outperform all other algorithms (*skiing*: 1 algorithm, *singer2*: 2 algorithms). Fusion cannot deal very well with such situations where very few algorithms outperform all others. The sequences where fusion performs poorly are the reason why our approach does not outperform the "Best algorithm for each sequence" curve in Figure 1.

Continuity and Smoothness of Trajectory: A good tracking trajectory should be continuous and smooth. Figure 3(a) show the number of frames on all sequences of OPE where there is a per frame acceleration greater than half of the size of the object bounding box. This happens even in the ground truth as there are a few sequences with extreme accelerations (in 0.48% of all frames). However, high accelerations that are not in the ground truth and thus not in the object trajectory can be considered as outliers or discontinuities. As expected, the frame based approaches show many discontinuities in their trajectories. Nevertheless, our basic and weighted approach perform much better than our previous work [4], but show still many discontinuities. Our trajectory optimization approach shows here its greatest strength. Thanks to its ability to consider past frames, online trajectory optimization performs much better than the other online approaches. For the offline version the numbers are even very close to the numbers of the ground truth. Our removal approaches which use offline trajectory optimization for fusion show similar results. The trajectories of some tracking algorithms like SCM and CXT also show only a few discontinuities. In contrast, Struck and VTD have by far too many discontinuities.

This shows that our trajectory optimization approach not only provides a trajectory continuity, which is similar to that of tracking algorithms, but even outperforms most of them in this regard. Figure 3(b) shows the average acceleration. Our trajectory optimization approaches (online and offline) have here even a smaller value than the ground truth. This shows that the trajectories of our trajectory optimization approaches are in general even smoother in velocity

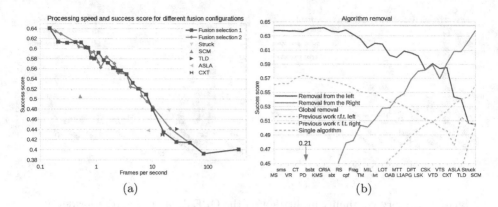

Fig. 4. a): Processing speed, success score comparison for different tracking algorithms and fusion selections. b): The performance with removal of the worst or best tracking algorithms, compared to our global removal approach. All solid non dashed results are created with our trajectory optimization approach. See text for more details.

than the ground truth. This does not mean that they are better, but we think error by smoothness is preferable over many other error source.

Processing Speed: A possible drawback of a fusion approach could be its high runtime as it requires several tracking algorithms to run. As processing speed for tracking algorithms we take the average frame per second numbers from [30]. Figure 4(a) shows the processing speed of our approach with different subsets of algorithms. We construct the subsets by selecting algorithms in two different ways. Starting with one algorithm, we build the next subset by adding the next best algorithm to the set. The next best algorithm is the one with the greatest

$$\text{frames per second} \times \text{success score}^X \tag{14}$$

that is not yet in the set. We use $X = 2$ and $X = 4$ for the two selections, respectively (See supplemental material for more details). Concerning processing speed we cannot outperform fast and good tracking algorithms like TLD [17] and Struck [14] as there are only few faster algorithms in the dataset that mostly do not perform very well. Perhaps, with more very fast algorithms it might be possible. However, for a processing speed of ten frames per second or less fusion clearly outperforms every tracking algorithm.

Removal: Figure 4(b) shows the removal of the best (from right) or worst (from left) tracking algorithms. We perform this test with our trajectory optimization approach and with our previous work [4] for comparison. Although, the worst algorithms perform really poor, fusion only slightly suffers from them and still benefits from relatively bad algorithms like ORIA [31]. This interesting effect is true for both fusion approaches. However, our previous work needs a minimal number of tracking results to get a stable result probably because it uses majority voting. It performs worse than the best tracking algorithm SCM [35] when fusing the best 6 tracking algorithms. To avoid suffering from bad tracking results global removal can be used. It outperforms the peak of removal from the left. Removal from the right shows that the best algorithm SCM [35] (success score 0.505) can already be outperformed with the 15 worst algorithms that all have a performance below the average (best is IVT [24] with success score 0.358).

We also determined the probabilities that algorithms are removed by global removal. In doing so, we discovered that some algorithms like SMS, Frag and LOT are very removal resistant while others like CSK and VTS can be easily removed despite better average performance. We think easily removed algorithms cannot utilize their strengths in fusion as these are already widely covered by other algorithms, but their weaknesses still harm. On the other hand, removal resistant algorithms likely provide more original/unique strengths that are more useful for fusion. We think that the probabilities are not only interesting for evaluating the usefulness of tracking algorithms for fusion, but they are also an interesting way of estimating the originality/diversity of tracking algorithms. For the probabilities and a more detailed discussion see our supplemental material.

6 Conclusions

In this paper we presented a new tracking fusion approach that merges the results of an arbitrary number of tracking algorithms to produce a better tracking result. Our method is based on the notion of attraction, and the result that maximizes the attraction of all the trackers is chosen as global tracking result. We presented different variants of the method, including a weighted combination of trackers and an approach that favors continuous trajectories throughout the sequence. The latter method is solved using dynamic programming. In a complete evaluation we showed that our method clearly outperforms current state of the art tracking algorithms. On most tested sequences, our method even produces better results that the best algorithm for that specific sequence. We introduced further improvements using tracker removal techniques that remove tracking results before fusion either locally or globally. In addition we presented two new criteria for evaluating trackers. One measures originality/diversity in the behavior by utilizing global removal. The other one measures the continuity of the trajectory. We showed that our approach outperforms existing algorithms in continuity – most of them even with online fusion.

We think that the awareness that fusion of tracking algorithms actually improves the tracking performance will help to improve tracking methods in general. It shows that the combination of several good tracking ideas can clearly outperform single ideas if the methods are combined in the right way. In our future work we will investigate this property further to write generic object tracking algorithms that work well in general.

Acknowledgements. This work was partially funded by the Eurostars-Project VIDP under contract number E!5558 (FKZ 01AE1103B, BMBF 01QE1103B) and by the BMBF project DENSITY (01IW12001).

References

1. Adam, A., Rivlin, E., Shimshoni, I.: Robust fragments-based tracking using the integral histogram. In: 2006 IEEE Computer Society Conference on Computer Vision and Pattern Recognition, pp. 798–805. IEEE (2006)
2. Andriluka, M., Roth, S., Schiele, B.: People-tracking-by-detection and people-detection-by-tracking. In: IEEE Conference on Computer Vision and Pattern Recognition, CVPR 2008, pp. 1–8. IEEE (2008)
3. Babenko, B., Yang, M.H., Belongie, S.: Visual tracking with online multiple instance learning. In: IEEE Conference on Computer Vision and Pattern Recognition, CVPR 2009, pp. 983–990. IEEE (2009)
4. Bailer, C., Pagani, A., Stricker, D.: A user supported tracking framework for interactive video production. In: Proceedings of the 10th European Conference on Visual Media Production (CVMP). ACM (2013)
5. Bao, C., Wu, Y., Ling, H., Ji, H.: Real time robust l1 tracker using accelerated proximal gradient approach. In: 2012 IEEE Conference on Computer Vision and Pattern Recognition (CVPR), pp. 1830–1837. IEEE (2012)
6. Chate, M., Amudha, S., Gohokar, V., et al.: Object detection and tracking in video sequences. Aceee International Journal on Signal & Image Processing 3(1) (2012)
7. Collins, R., Zhou, X., Teh, S.K.: An open source tracking testbed and evaluation web site. In: IEEE International Workshop on Performance Evaluation of Tracking and Surveillance, pp. 17–24 (2005)
8. Collins, R.T.: Mean-shift blob tracking through scale space. In: Proceedings of 2003 IEEE Computer Society Conference on Computer Vision and Pattern Recognition, vol. 2, p. II-234. IEEE (2003)
9. Collins, R.T., Liu, Y., Leordeanu, M.: Online selection of discriminative tracking features. IEEE Transactions on Pattern Analysis and Machine Intelligence 27(10), 1631–1643 (2005)
10. Comaniciu, D., Ramesh, V., Meer, P.: Kernel-based object tracking. IEEE Transactions on Pattern Analysis and Machine Intelligence 25(5), 564–577 (2003)
11. Dinh, T.B., Vo, N., Medioni, G.: Context tracker: Exploring supporters and distracters in unconstrained environments. In: 2011 IEEE Conference on Computer Vision and Pattern Recognition (CVPR), pp. 1177–1184. IEEE (2011)
12. Grabner, H., Grabner, M., Bischof, H.: Real-time tracking via on-line boosting. BMVC 1, 6 (2006)
13. Grabner, H., Leistner, C., Bischof, H.: Semi-supervised on-line boosting for robust tracking. In: Forsyth, D., Torr, P., Zisserman, A. (eds.) ECCV 2008, Part I. LNCS, vol. 5302, pp. 234–247. Springer, Heidelberg (2008)
14. Hare, S., Saffari, A., Torr, P.H.: Struck: Structured output tracking with kernels. In: 2011 IEEE International Conference on Computer Vision (ICCV), pp. 263–270. IEEE (2011)
15. Henriques, J.F., Caseiro, R., Martins, P., Batista, J.: Exploiting the circulant structure of tracking-by-detection with kernels. In: Fitzgibbon, A., Lazebnik, S., Perona, P., Sato, Y., Schmid, C. (eds.) ECCV 2012, Part IV. LNCS, vol. 7575, pp. 702–715. Springer, Heidelberg (2012)
16. Jia, X., Lu, H., Yang, M.-H.: Visual tracking via adaptive structural local sparse appearance model. In: 2012 IEEE Conference on Computer Vision and Pattern Recognition (CVPR), pp. 1822–1829. IEEE (2012)
17. Kalal, Z., Matas, J., Mikolajczyk, K.: Pn learning: Bootstrapping binary classifiers by structural constraints. In: 2010 IEEE Conference on Computer Vision and Pattern Recognition (CVPR), pp. 49–56. IEEE (2010)

18. Koller, D., Weber, J., Malik, J.: Robust multiple car tracking with occlusion reasoning. Springer (1994)
19. Kwon, J., Lee, K.M.: Visual tracking decomposition. In: 2010 IEEE Conference on Computer Vision and Pattern Recognition (CVPR), pp. 1269–1276. IEEE (2010)
20. Kwon, J., Lee, K.M.: Tracking by sampling trackers. In: 2011 IEEE International Conference on Computer Vision (ICCV), pp. 1195–1202. IEEE (2011)
21. Liu, B., Huang, J., Yang, L., Kulikowsk, C.: Robust tracking using local sparse appearance model and k-selection. In: 2011 IEEE Conference on Computer Vision and Pattern Recognition (CVPR), pp. 1313–1320. IEEE (2011)
22. Oron, S., Bar-Hillel, A., Levi, D., Avidan, S.: Locally orderless tracking. In: 2012 IEEE Conference on Computer Vision and Pattern Recognition (CVPR), pp. 1940–1947. IEEE (2012)
23. Pérez, P., Hue, C., Vermaak, J., Gangnet, M.: Color-based probabilistic tracking. In: Heyden, A., Sparr, G., Nielsen, M., Johansen, P. (eds.) ECCV 2002, Part I. LNCS, vol. 2350, pp. 661–675. Springer, Heidelberg (2002)
24. Ross, D.A., Lim, J., Lin, R.S., Yang, M.H.: Incremental learning for robust visual tracking. International Journal of Computer Vision 77(1-3), 125–141 (2008)
25. Santner, J., Leistner, C., Saffari, A., Pock, T., Bischof, H.: Prost: Parallel robust online simple tracking. In: 2010 IEEE Conference on Computer Vision and Pattern Recognition (CVPR), pp. 723–730. IEEE (2010)
26. Sevilla-Lara, L., Learned-Miller, E.: Distribution fields for tracking. In: 2012 IEEE Conference on Computer Vision and Pattern Recognition (CVPR), pp. 1910–1917. IEEE (2012)
27. Shu, G., Dehghan, A., Oreifej, O., Hand, E., Shah, M.: Part-based multiple-person tracking with partial occlusion handling. In: 2012 IEEE Conference on Computer Vision and Pattern Recognition (CVPR), pp. 1815–1821. IEEE (2012)
28. Stalder, S., Grabner, H., Van Gool, L.: Beyond semi-supervised tracking: Tracking should be as simple as detection, but not simpler than recognition. In: 2009 IEEE 12th International Conference on Computer Vision Workshops (ICCV Workshops), pp. 1409–1416. IEEE (2009)
29. Wang, Q., Chen, F., Xu, W., Yang, M.H.: An experimental comparison of online object-tracking algorithms. In: SPIE Optical Engineering+ Applications, pp. 81381A–81381A. International Society for Optics and Photonics (2011)
30. Wu, Y., Lim, J., Yang, M.H.: Online object tracking: A benchmark. In: 2013 IEEE Conference on Computer Vision and Pattern Recognition (CVPR), pp. 2411–2418. IEEE (2013)
31. Wu, Y., Shen, B., Ling, H.: Online robust image alignment via iterative convex optimization. In: 2012 IEEE Conference on Computer Vision and Pattern Recognition (CVPR), pp. 1808–1814. IEEE (2012)
32. Yang, H., Shao, L., Zheng, F., Wang, L., Song, Z.: Recent advances and trends in visual tracking: A review. Neurocomputing 74(18), 3823–3831 (2011)
33. Zhang, K., Zhang, L., Yang, M.-H.: Real-time compressive tracking. In: Fitzgibbon, A., Lazebnik, S., Perona, P., Sato, Y., Schmid, C. (eds.) ECCV 2012, Part III. LNCS, vol. 7574, pp. 864–877. Springer, Heidelberg (2012)
34. Zhang, T., Ghanem, B., Liu, S., Ahuja, N.: Robust visual tracking via multi-task sparse learning. In: 2012 IEEE Conference on Computer Vision and Pattern Recognition (CVPR), pp. 2042–2049 (2012)
35. Zhong, W., Lu, H., Yang, M.H.: Robust object tracking via sparsity-based collaborative model. In: 2012 IEEE Conference on Computer Vision and Pattern Recognition (CVPR), pp. 1838–1845. IEEE (2012)

Training-Based Spectral Reconstruction
from a Single RGB Image

Rang M.H. Nguyen, Dilip K. Prasad, and Michael S. Brown

School of Computing, National University of Singapore

Abstract. This paper focuses on a training-based method to reconstruct a scene's spectral reflectance from a single RGB image captured by
a camera with known spectral response. In particular, we explore a new
strategy to use training images to model the mapping between camera-
specific RGB values and scene reflectance spectra. Our method is based
on a radial basis function network that leverages RGB white-balancing
to normalize the scene illumination to recover the scene reflectance. We
show that our method provides the best result against three state-of-art
methods, especially when the tested illumination is not included in the
training stage. In addition, we also show an effective approach to recover
the spectral illumination from the reconstructed spectral reflectance and
RGB image. As a part of this work, we present a newly captured, publicly
available, data set of hyperspectral images that are useful for addressing
problems pertaining to spectral imaging, analysis and processing.

1 Introduction

A scene visible to the human eye is composed of the scene's spectral reflectance
and the scene spectral illumination which spans visible wavelengths. Commodity
cameras use filters on their sensors to convert the incoming light spectra into
three color channels (denoted as Red, Green, and Blue). While only three color
channels are needed to reproduce the *perceptual* quality of the scene, the projective nature of the imaging process results in a loss of the spectral information.

Directly capturing spectral information from specialized hyperspectral cameras remains costly. The goal of this work is to reconstruct a scene's spectral
properties, i.e. scene reflection and illumination, from a single RGB image (see
Figure 1). This is done by learning a mapping between spectral responses and
their corresponding RGB values for a given make and model of a camera.

Prior work in this area follow a similar training-based approach, but attempt
to find a mapping using RGB images where the effects of different illumination
are included in the learning process. This makes these approaches sensitive to
input images captured under illuminations which were not present in the training
data.

Contribution. We introduce a new strategy that learns a non-linear mapping
based on a radial basis function network between the training-data and RGB images. Our approach uses a white-balance step to provide an approximate normalization of the illumination in the RGB images to improve the learned mapping

D. Fleet et al. (Eds.): ECCV 2014, Part VII, LNCS 8695, pp. 186–201, 2014.

Training dataset

Fig. 1. Our approach takes in an input RGB image and then estimates both the spectral reflectance and the overall spectral illumination based on pre-computed training dataset

between the RGB images and spectral reflectances. This white-balance step also helps in making our approach robust to input images captured under illuminations not in our training data. Moreover, we propose a technique to estimate the illumination given our estimated spectral reflectance. Our experimental results demonstrate our approach is superior to prior methods. An additional contribution of our work is a publicly available spectral image dataset of dozens of real-world scenes taken under a number of illuminations.

2   Related Work

The need to reconstruct the spectral properties of scene reflectance (and illumination) from a three channel device or a standard color space (such as CIE-XYZ) was recognized as early as 1980s [14,15,20,21,24]. Several works targeted the reconstruction of the spectral properties of standard color samples such as the Munsell Book of Colors [2,8,10,11,15,20,24], OSA UCS [11], Swedish Natural Color System [11], and Pantone dataset [17]. Additionally, [15] considered the spectral reflectances of natural objects also.

Virtually all methods rely on the use of training-data to learn a mapping between RGB images and the corresponding spectra. For many years, a linear model was considered sufficient for this problem. It was determined using statistical analysis on standard color samples that a few (typically 3-10) basis functions are sufficient to represent the spectral reflectances [15,20,24,32]. Further, in general, basis functions were assumed to be continuous and band limited [20,24]. Most methods considered either PCA bases [2,3,11,15,17,20,30] or the Karhunen-Loeve transformation [8,10,24,25,28,32] (also called matrix R approach) which were typically pre-learnt using a few hundred to a little more than thousand spectral samples. Interestingly, [11] consider two types of PCA bases - one with least squares fit and another with assumption that the tristimulus function of the sensor and the illumination are known. The latter approach is more accurate although it is restricted in application since illumination is generally unknown.

An interesting statistical approach was used in [22] where the bases were chosen not to minimize the error in spectral reflectance representation alone, but to minimize the error in predicting the sensor response as well such that the spectral response function of the sensor plays a role in determining the suitable bases. In the work of Abed et al. [1], a tessellation of the scatter RGB points and their reflectance spectra of a standard color chart (for a given illumination) was used as a nearest-neighbor look-up table. Then, in the general case of a scene in the same illumination, the reflectance of the nodes of the polytope that encloses the scene's RGB point are used to interpolate the reflectance at that point.

Recently, the need of non-linear mappings was recognized [4,26,29], though such a requirement was indicated earlier in [22]. Further, it was recognized by some researchers that while PCA itself may be insufficient for accurate reconstruction of spectral reflectance, splitting the color space into overlapping subspaces of 10 different hues [3,30] and low-chromaticity sub-space [30] and then using PCA on each subspace performs better. Similarly, Agahian et al. [2] proposed to put weighted coefficients for each spectral reflectance in the dataset before computing PCA. Some works [9,11] highlight that illumination has a direct and important role in the ability to reconstruct the spectral reflectances. Using Bayesian decision theory, Brainard and Freeman [5] reconstructed both spectral reflectance and illumination information for color constancy. Lenz et al. [18] statistically approximated the logarithm of the reflectance spectra of Munsell and NCS color chips instead of the usual reflectance spectra themselves. Further they computed approximate distribution of the illuminant and showed its utility for color constancy.

In our work, we consider a novel non-linear mapping strategy for modeling the mapping between camera-specific RGB values and scene reflectance spectra. Specifically, we use a radial basis function network for modeling the mapping. Our model for spectral reflectances is made illumination independent by using RGB white-balancing to normalize the scene illumination before reconstructing the spectral reflectance.

The remainder of this paper is organized as follows: Sections 3 and 4 present our approaches for spectral reflectance and illumination reconstruction, respectively; Section 5 presents the details of our spectral image dataset; Section 6 describes reconstruction results using three commercial cameras; Section 7 concludes the paper.

3   Scene Reflectance Reconstruction

As discussed in previous section, most of the methods for reconstructing reflectance are not clear how to deal with different illuminations. For example, consider we have two different spectral reflectances $R_1(\lambda)$ and $R_2(\lambda)$ illuminated by two different spectral illuminations $L_1(\lambda)$ and $L_2(\lambda)$ respectively. It is possible that under a certain observer $C_c(\lambda)$ (where $c = r, g, b$), these two spectral reflectances share the same RGB values as described in Eq. 1. This metamer problem can be expressed as:

$$\int_\lambda L_1(\lambda)R_1(\lambda)C_c(\lambda)\,\mathrm{d}\lambda = \int_\lambda L_2(\lambda)R_2(\lambda)C_c(\lambda)\,\mathrm{d}\lambda. \tag{1}$$

From the above equation, we see it is difficult to determine whether the reflectance is $R_1(\lambda)$ or $R_2(\lambda)$ when information about illumination is not available. Therefore, one mapping for all illuminations can not handle this case. One straightforward solution is to build a mapping for each illumination. This approach will be the best in terms of reconstruction accuracy. However, it requires not only a huge effort to calibrate mappings over all illuminations but also known illumination of a new scene for reconstructing its reflectance. This approach is impractical for most applications.

In our approach, the illumination in the RGB is normalized before it is used for learning. The RGB images have been corrected using conventional white-balancing method. The details are discussed in Section 3.2. The following are four assumptions made in our approach:

- The mapping is specific to the camera and one mapping for a camera can be used for any spectral reflectance.
- The color matching functions of the camera are known.
- The scene is illuminated by a uniform illumination.
- The white balancing algorithm gives good performance for images taken under a variety of illuminations.

3.1   Pre-requisites

In this paper, we do not use RGB images taken directly from the camera. Instead, we synthesize RGB images from hyperspectral images using known camera's sensitivity functions. Computing the RGB images in this manner gives us two main advantages. Firstly, it removes the need to create a dataset of the images captured using the chosen camera for the same scenes as captured by the spectral camera. This method can be used for any commercial camera so far as its sensitivity functions are known. Note however that it is possible to use a given camera, however, care will be needed to ensure spatial scene correspondence between the RGB image and spectral image. This will likely limit the training data to planar scenes for accurate correspondence.

Color Matching Functions. The color matching functions are generally measured using sophisticated instruments. However, recent methods were proposed to reconstruct the color matching functions using standard colorcharts and illuminations satisfying certain practical requirements (for more details, see [16,27]). Alternatively, existing datasets such as [31] can be used if the chosen camera is a part of these datasets. Irrespective of the method used, measurement/estimation of the color matching functions is a one time process and the color matching functions can be stored for further use.

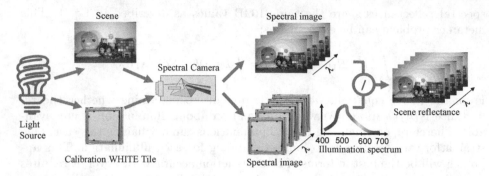

Fig. 2. This figure shows how to obtain scene reflectance and spectral illumination using a hyperspectral camera. First, a spectral image is captured from the real scene. Then, a calibration white tile is used to measure the illumination spectrum. Finally, the scene reflectance is obtained by dividing the spectral image by the illumination spectrum.

Illuminations. To obtain the illumination spectrum, we use a calibration white tile supplied with the spectral camera to capture a spectral image of the white tile illuminated by the light source (see Figure 2). We represent the spectral image captured using white tile as $S_W(\lambda, x)$, where λ is the wavelength, x is the pixel index, W denotes the white tile, and S denotes the spectral intensity captured using the spectral camera. The spectral illumination $L(\lambda)$ is computed as the average of the spectral information at all the pixels as follows:

$$L(\lambda) = \frac{1}{N} \sum_{x=1}^{N} S_W(\lambda, x) \tag{2}$$

where N is the total number of pixels.

Spectral Reflectances. After obtaining the spectral illumination, the spectral reflectance $R(\lambda, x)$ corresponding to each pixel in the spectral image $S(\lambda, x)$ can be computed directly as follows:

$$R(\lambda, x) = S(\lambda, x)/L(\lambda) \tag{3}$$

3.2   Training Stage

As discussed in the previous section, most existing methods consider computing mappings between RGB images under different illuminations and their reflectances (see Figure 3-(A)). While our approach considers a mapping between RGB images under canonical illumination (using white-balancing) and their reflectances. The training process for our model is shown in Figure 3-(B). Our approach has three steps: synthesizing the RGB image, white-balancing the RGB image, and computing the mapping.

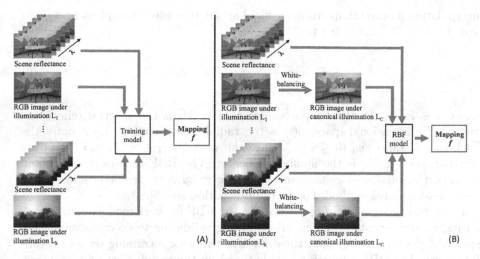

Fig. 3. This figure shows the training process for reflectance reconstruction for previous approaches and our approach. (A) shows that previous approaches consider the mapping f of RGB image to spectral reflectances. (B) shows that our approach considers the mapping f of RGB white-balanced image to the spectral reflectances.

Firstly, synthesized the RGB images corresponding to scenes and illuminations in spectral images can be formed by using the intrinsic image model as:

$$I_c(x) = \int_\lambda L(\lambda)R(\lambda, x)C_c(\lambda)\,\mathrm{d}\lambda \qquad (4)$$

where $L(\lambda)$ is the illumination spectrum, $R(\lambda, x)$ is the scene reflectance for the pixel x, $C_c(\lambda)$ is the color matching function for the cth color channel, and $c = r, g, b$ is the color channel.

After forming the RGB image $I_c(x)$, we obtain a white balanced image $\widehat{I}_c(x)$ as follows:

$$\widehat{I}_c(x) = \mathrm{diag}\left(\frac{1}{t_\mathrm{r}}, \frac{1}{t_\mathrm{g}}, \frac{1}{t_\mathrm{b}}\right) I_c(x) \qquad (5)$$

where $\mathbf{t} = [t_\mathrm{r}, t_\mathrm{g}, t_\mathrm{b}]$ is the white balancing vector obtained by a chosen white balancing algorithm. For the white-balancing step, we have used shades of grey (SoG) method [12] that uses the Minkowsky norm of order 5. We note that several other methods are known for white balancing [7,13]. Here, we have chosen SoG for its simplicity, low computational requirement and proven efficacy over various datasets[1].

Next, a mapping f is learnt between the white balanced RGB images $\widehat{I}_c(x)$ and their spectral reflectances. Because we cannot guarantee the uniformity of the spectral and RGB samples, we use scatter point interpolation based on a radial basis function (RBF) network for mapping. RBF network is a popular

---

[1] http:/www.colorconstancy.com/

interpolation method in multidimensional space. It is used to implement a mapping $f : \mathbb{R}^3 \to \mathbb{R}^P$ according to

$$f(x) = w_0 + \sum_{i=1}^{M} w_i \phi(\|x - c_i\|) \tag{6}$$

where $x \in \mathbb{R}^3$ is the RGB input value, $f(x) \in \mathbb{R}^P$ is the spectral reflectance value in P-dimensional space, $\phi(.)$ is the radial basis function, $\|.\|$ denotes the Euclidean distance, w_i ($0 \le i \le M$) are the weights, $c_i \in \mathbb{R}^3$ ($1 \le i \le M$) are the RBF centers, M is the number of center. The RBF centers c_i are chosen by the orthogonal least squares method. The weights w_i are determined using linear least squares method. For more information see [6].

To control the number of centers M for the RBF network model against overfitting, we use repeated random sub-sampling validation to do cross-validation. Specifically, we randomly split the data into two sets: a training set and a validation set. The RBF network model is fitted by the training set and its generalization ability is assessed by the validation set. We ran this procedure several times on our data and found that the number of centers M which gave the best result for validation set was within $45 - 50$.

3.3 Reconstruction Stage

Once the training is performed, the mapping can be saved and used offline for spectral reflectance reconstruction. To reconstruct spectral reflectance for a new RGB image, this image must be white-balanced to transform the image to the normalized illumination space $\widehat{I}_{rgb}(x)$. The learned mapping f is used to map the white-balanced image to the spectral reflectance image as in Eq. 7.

$$R(\lambda, x) = f(\widehat{I}_{rgb}(x)) \tag{7}$$

4 Spectral Illumination Reconstruction

In theory, the spectral illumination $L(\lambda)$ can be solved from Eq. 4 when given the spectral reflectance $R(\lambda, x)$ (estimated in Section 3.3), camera sensitivity functions $C_c(\lambda)$ (given) and RGB values $I_c(x)$ (input). This equation can be written into product of matrices as follows:

$$I_{rgb} = C \text{diag}(L) R \tag{8}$$

where I_{rgb} is a matrix of $3 \times N$, C is a matrix of $3 \times P$, L is a vector of $P \times 1$, R is a matrix of $P \times N$, P is the number of spectral bands, and N is the number of pixels.

To solve the vector L, Eq. 8 needs to be rewritten as follows:

$$I = TL \tag{9}$$

where $I = [I_r, I_g, I_b]^\top$ is a vector of $3N \times 1$, $T = [\mathrm{diag}(C_r)R, \mathrm{diag}(C_g)R, \mathrm{diag}(C_b)R]^\top$ is a matrix of $3N \times P$.

This means that the spectral illumination $L(\lambda)$ can be solved in a linear least squares manner. However, in practice the noise in $I_c(x)$ and the inaccuracy in estimation of $R(x, \lambda)$ impedes the reconstruction of $L(\lambda)$. As a result, it is necessary to include additional non-negative and smoothness constraints into the optimization function before solving $L(\lambda)$ as Eq. 10. This step is similar with work proposed by Park et al. [23] and can be expressed as follows:

$$L = \arg\min_L \left(||TL - I||_2^2 + \alpha ||WL||_2^2 \right)$$
$$\text{s.t } L \geq 0 \tag{10}$$

where $||.||_2$ denotes $l^2\text{-}norm$, the term α is a weight for the smoothness constraint, and W is the first-derivative matrix defined as follows:

$$W = \begin{vmatrix} 0 & 0 & \ldots & 0 & 0 \\ 1 & -1 & \ldots & 0 & 0 \\ & & \ldots & & \\ 0 & 0 & \ldots & 1 & -1 \end{vmatrix} \tag{11}$$

We additionally use PCA basis functions to allow $L(\lambda)$ to fall in a definite subspace. Therefore, spectral illumination $L(\lambda)$ can be described as

$$L(\lambda) = \sum_{i=1}^{M} a_i B_i(\lambda) \tag{12}$$

where $B_i(\lambda)$ are the basis functions, a_i are the corresponding coefficients, and M is the number of basis functions. Eq. 12 can be rewritten into product of matrices as follows:

$$L = Ba$$

where $\mathbf{a} = [a_i]_{i=1}^M$ is the vector of the coefficients, and $B = [B_i]_{i=1}^M$ is the matrix of the basis functions.

Thus, the optimization function in Eq. 10 becomes:

$$\mathbf{a} = \arg\min_{\mathbf{a}} \left(||TB\mathbf{a} - I||_2^2 + \alpha ||WB\mathbf{a}||_2^2 \right)$$
$$\text{s.t } B\mathbf{a} \geq 0 \tag{13}$$

Eq. 13 is a convex optimization and the global solution can be easily obtained. To make it more robust against noise from T and I (as discussed above), the optimization step in Eq. 13 should be run several times, and for each time, noise samples are removed from T and I. To determine them, the spectral illumination L is estimated and the error for each pixel is computed as in Eq. 14 at each time.

$$\epsilon(x) = ||C\mathrm{diag}(L)R(x) - I_{rgb}(x)||_2 \tag{14}$$

where x is the pixel in the image. The noise samples are determined by comparing with standard deviation. Then T and I are updated by removing these noise samples for the next run.

Fig. 4. This figure shows some hyperspectral images from our dataset. For visualization, these hyperspectral images are rendered to RGB images by using sensitivity functions of Canon 1D Mark III. There are a total of 64 spectral images and their corresponding illumination spectra in our dataset.

5   Dataset of Hyperspectral Images

Our dataset contains spectral images and illumination spectra taken using Specim's PFD-CL-65-V10E (400 nm to 1000 nm) spectral camera[2]. We have used an OLE23 fore lens (400 nm to 1000 nm), also from Specim. For light sources, we have considered natural sunlight and shade conditions. Additionally, we considered artificial wideband lights using metal halide lamps of different color temperatures - 2500 K, 3000 K, 3500 K, 4300K, 6500K and a commercial off-the-shelf LED E400 light. For the natural light sources, we have taken outdoor images of natural objects (plants, human beings, etc.) as well as man made objects. Further, a few images of buildings at very large focal length were also taken. The images corresponding to the other light sources have manmade objects as their scene content. For each spectral image, a total of 31 bands were used for imaging (400 nm to 700 nm at a spacing of about 10 nm). Figure 4 shows some samples from our dataset.

There are a total of 64 spectral images and their corresponding illumination spectra. We use 24 images with color charts as the test images for the reconstruction stage. This is because explicit ground truth of their spectral reflectances are available and thus the accuracy of reconstruction can be better assessed. These images are referred to as the *test images*. We have used the remaining 40 images as *training images*.

---

[2] http://www.specim.fi/index.php/products/industrial/spectral-cameras/vis-vnir/

In addition, we also used the dataset of illumination spectra from Barnard's website[3]. This dataset consists of 11 different spectral illuminations. We used these spectral illumination to synthetically generate more hyperspectral images from spectral reflectance captured by our hyperspectral camera. These hyperspectral images were used to test performance of all methods.

6 Experimental Results

In order to compare the different methods and verify their accuracy, we consider three cameras: Canon 1D Mark III, Canon 600D, and Nikon D40, whose color matching functions are available in the dataset of [31]. We first trained all methods from samples from our training images. Because the total number of pixels from 40 training images is too large and most of them are similar together, we sub-sampled each training image by using k-means clustering [19] and collected around 16,000 spectral reflectances from all the images for the training step. For the PCA method, three principal components are computed from this set of spectral reflectances. For weighted PCA proposed by Agahian et al. [2] and Delaunay interpolation proposed by Abed et al. [1], all 16,000 pairs of spectral reflectances and their corresponding RGB values are stored. Matlab code and spectral datasets used in this paper will be available online[4].

To verify the quantitative performance for the spectral reflectance reconstruction, we use two types of measurements: the goodness-of-fit coefficient (GFC) as in Eq. 15 to measure the similarity, and root mean square error (RMSE) as in Eq. 16 to measure the error.

$$s_R = \frac{1}{N} \sum_x \frac{|\sum_\lambda R(\lambda, x) \widehat{R}(\lambda, x)|}{\sqrt{\sum_\lambda [R(\lambda, x)]^2} \sqrt{\sum_\lambda [\widehat{R}(\lambda, x)]^2}} \tag{15}$$

$$\epsilon_R = \sqrt{\frac{\sum_x \|R(\lambda, x) - \widehat{R}(\lambda, x)\|_2^2}{N}} \tag{16}$$

where $R(x, \lambda)$ and $\widehat{R}(x, \lambda)$ are the actual and reconstructed spectral reflectances, N are the number of pixels in the image, and $\|.\|_2$ is l^2-norm.

We compare our method against other three methods: traditional PCA, Agahian et al. [2], and Abed et al. [1] method. Firstly, the RGB test images for reconstruction are formed using the intrinsic image model in Eq. 4. We reconstruct reflectances of 24 images (size of 1312 × 1924). The average time to reconstruct the whole image required by the four methods are presented in Table 1. We also test our method without using white-balance step to analyze the contribution of each steps in our framework.

---

[3] http://www.cs.sfu.ca/~colour/data/colour_constancy_synthetic_test_data/index.html

[4] http://www.comp.nus.edu.sg/~whitebal/spectral_reconstruction/index.html

In order to investigate the impact of illumination on the reconstruction performance, we test all the five methods on two test conditions. The first test condition considers images taken under illuminations that were *present* in the training images also. Table 2 shows the similarity and error measurement respectively under illumination *present* in training data. The second test condition considers images taken under illuminations that were *not* present in the training images. Table 3 shows the similarity and error measurement respectively under illumination *not* present in training data. The results show that our method provides the best result for spectral reflectance reconstruction in terms of both similarity and error for both test conditions. It is clear that white-balance step is important especially when the illumination is not present in training data. Moreover, RBF has better performance than other technique and much more compact than Delaunay interpolation and weighted PCA.

Table 1. This table shows the *average* time for each method to reconstruct spectral reflectances from a whole image of size 1312×1924

Methods	PCA	Agahian [2]	Abed [1]	Our
Time (s)	1.14	144.30	23.14	8.56

In addition, we also compare the actual reconstruction results for eight color patches in the color chart in Figure 5 for Canon 1D Mark III. The images are taken under indoor illumination using metal halide lamp of 4300K color temperature (spectrum in Figure 6). The ground truth of the spectral reflectances are obtained from the hyperspectral camera. The quantitative results of these patches for all methods are shown in Table 4. Again, it can be seen that our method performs better than the others methods. *Additional results are shown in the supplementary material.*

Our method also obtains good results for recovering spectral illumination. The reconstructed spectra of six illuminations are also shown in Figure 6 along with the ground truth ones. Three top illuminations are metal halide lamp 2500K, metal halide lamp 4300K and sunlight from our dataset. Three bottom illuminations are Sylvania 50MR16Q, Solux 3500K and Solux 4700K from Barnard's website. Our accuracies of the recovered spectral illumination are within $0.94 - 0.99$ in term of similarity measurement (goodness-of-fit coefficient).

We also test our method in terms of RGB accuracy. The reconstructed spectral reflectance and illumination are projected back onto the same camera sensitivity functions to measure the error in RGB space. Table 5 shows the mean values of similarity measurements s_R and error measurement ϵ_R. Our result is almost the same with the input RGB with only small errors. In addition, Figure 7 show an example of relighting application for our work. Our relit image is close to the ground truth image captured under the target illumination.

Table 2. This table shows the reflectance reconstruction results of three commercial cameras: Canon 1D Mark III, Canon 600D, and Nikon D40. he mean values of similarity measurements s_R in Eq. 15 and error measurement ϵ_R in Eq. 16 are shown. In this experiment, we test all five methods under illuminations *present* in the training data.

	Canon 1D Mark III		Canon 600D		Nikon D40	
	s_R	ϵ_R	s_R	ϵ_R	s_R	ϵ_R
PCA	0.8422	0.0957	0.8340	0.0966	0.8438	0.0947
Agahian [2]	0.8743	0.1139	0.8757	0.1079	0.8837	0.1008
Abed [1]	0.9715	0.0350	0.9707	0.0356	0.9723	0.0347
Ours w/o WB	0.9736	0.0315	0.9742	0.0313	0.9743	0.0320
Ours	**0.9802**	**0.0311**	**0.9811**	**0.0312**	**0.9805**	**0.0313**

Table 3. This table shows the reflectance reconstruction results of three commercial cameras: Canon 1D Mark III, Canon 600D, and Nikon D40. he mean values of similarity measurements s_R in Eq. 15 and error measurement ϵ_R in Eq. 16 are shown. In this experiment, we test all five methods under illuminations *not* present in the training data. These spectral illuminations are downloaded from the dataset in Barnard's website.

	Canon 1D Mark III		Canon 600D		Nikon D40	
	s_R	ϵ_R	s_R	ϵ_R	s_R	ϵ_R
PCA	0.8528	0.0873	0.8438	0.0896	0.8568	0.0856
Agahian [2]	0.8971	0.0791	0.8941	0.0793	0.8973	0.0773
Abed [1]	0.9293	0.0796	0.9107	0.0867	0.9281	0.0815
Ours w/o WB	0.9529	0.0722	0.9393	0.0727	0.9434	0.0702
Ours	**0.9805**	**0.0315**	**0.9812**	**0.0315**	**0.9810**	**0.0314**

Table 4. This table shows the reconstruction result (in RMSE) of colorchecker's reflectance using Canon 1D Mark III under indoor illumination using metal halide lamp of 4300K color temperature

	(a)	(b)	(c)	(d)	(e)	(f)	(g)	(h)
PCA	0.0464	0.0517	0.0360	0.0321	0.0597	0.0560	0.0366	0.0668
Agahian [2]	0.0470	0.0286	0.0328	0.0252	0.0511	0.0457	0.0350	0.0832
Abed [1]	0.0465	0.0845	0.0382	0.0225	0.0908	0.0507	0.0603	0.0721
Ours w/o WB	0.0367	0.0516	0.0553	0.0330	0.0474	0.0375	0.0723	**0.0292**
Ours	**0.0228**	**0.0260**	**0.0210**	**0.0117**	**0.0229**	**0.0226**	**0.0271**	0.0416

Table 5. This table shows colorimetric accuracy of our spectral reconstruction for three commercial cameras: Canon 1D Mark III, Canon 600D, and Nikon D40. The mean values of similarity measurements s_R in Eq. 15 and error measurement ϵ_R in Eq. 16 are shown.

Canon 1D Mark III		Canon 600D		Nikon D40	
s_R	ϵ_R	s_R	ϵ_R	s_R	ϵ_R
0.9967	0.0146	0.9969	0.0139	0.9929	0.0169

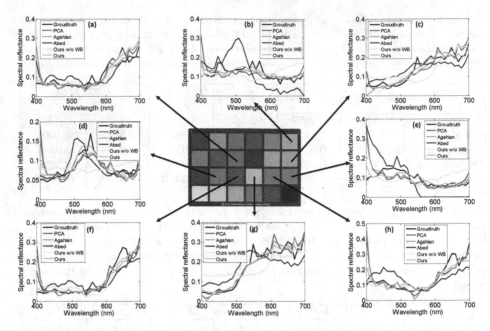

Fig. 5. This figure shows the reconstruction result of colorchecker's reflectance using Canon 1D Mark III under indoor illumination using metal halide lamp of 4300K color temperature. The quantitative errors of all patches are shown in Table 4.

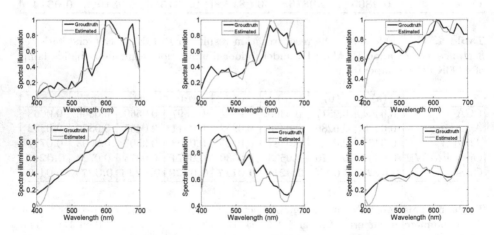

Fig. 6. This figure shows the reconstruction result for six illuminations. Three top illuminations are metal halide lamp 2500K, metal halide lamp 4300K and sunlight from our dataset. Three bottom illuminations are Sylvania 50MR16Q, Solux 3500K and Solux 4700K from Barnard's website.

Image captured under incandescent   Relit image to fluorescent   Ground truth image under fluorescent   Error map

Fig. 7. This figure shows an example of relighting application

7   Discussion and Concluding Remarks

We have presented a new approach to reconstruct a spectral reflectance image from a single RGB image which is useful for several computer vision tasks, e.g. to relight the scene with a new illumination or to obtain the image under a new observer (camera). Our approach is based on a radial basis function network using white-balancing as an intermediate step. Despite the mathematical loss of the spectral data in a RGB camera, we show that the spectral reflectance can be reconstructed with low RMSE errors and high goodness-of-fit coefficients. Our method improved reconstruction performance compared with previous works, especially when the tested illumination is not included in the training data. This indicates that our method is not severely dependent on the availability of illumination information directly or indirectly. This is a result of using RGB white balancing which indirectly normalizes the illumination component in the image.

In addition, we have also proposed an effective method to recover the spectral illumination from a single RGB image and its scene's spectral reflectance (estimated from previous step). As part of this work, we have generated a much needed set of hyperspectral images that is suitable for exploring this research as well as other aspects of spectral imaging, analysis, and processing.

A limitation of our work is the assumption that a scene is illuminated by an uniform illumination. For many scene this is not the case. Moreover, although our approach can handle well the reflectance and illumination which have smooth spectra, our approach like other approaches still has poor results in case of spiky spectra. Spectral reconstruction under very narrow band illuminations or severely spiky illuminations will be interesting and challenging areas for future investigation. Another interesting areas to explore in the future will be intrinsic video and retinal imaging (where some retinal tissues can be fluorescent).

Acknowledgement. This study was funded by A*STAR grant no. 1121202020. We sincerely thank Mr. Looi Wenhe (Russell) for his help in capturing spectral images of our dataset.

References

1. Abed, F.M., Amirshahi, S.H., Abed, M.R.M.: Reconstruction of reflectance data using an interpolation technique. J. Opt. Soc. Am. A 26(3), 613–624 (2009)
2. Agahian, F., Amirshahi, S.A., Amirshahi, S.H.: Reconstruction of reflectance spectra using weighted principal component analysis. Color Research & Application 33(5), 360–371 (2008)
3. Ayala, F., Echávarri, J.F., Renet, P., Negueruela, A.I.: Use of three tristimulus values from surface reflectance spectra to calculate the principal components for reconstructing these spectra by using only three eigenvectors. J. Opt. Soc. Am. A 23(8), 2020–2026 (2006)
4. Barakzehi, M., Amirshahi, S.H., Peyvandi, S., Afjeh, M.G.: Reconstruction of total radiance spectra of fluorescent samples by means of nonlinear principal component analysis. J. Opt. Soc. Am. A 30(9), 1862–1870 (2013)
5. Brainard, D.H., Freeman, W.T.: Bayesian color constancy. J. Opt. Soc. Am. A 14(7), 1393–1411 (1997)
6. Chen, S., Cowan, C.F., Grant, P.M.: Orthogonal least squares learning algorithm for radial basis function networks. IEEE Transactions on Neural Networks 2(2), 302–309 (1991)
7. Cheng, D., Prasad, D.K., Brown, M.S.: Illuminant estimation for color constancy: why spatial-domain methods work and the role of the color distribution. J. Opt. Soc. Am. A 31(5), 1049–1058 (2014)
8. Cohen, J.: Dependency of the spectral reflectance curves of the munsell color chips. Psychonomic Science (1964)
9. Connah, D., Westland, S., Thomson, M.G.: Recovering spectral information using digital camera systems. Coloration Technology 117(6), 309–312 (2001)
10. Eslahi, N., Amirshahi, S.H., Agahian, F.: Recovery of spectral data using weighted canonical correlation regression. Optical Review 16(3), 296–303 (2009)
11. Fairman, H.S., Brill, M.H.: The principal components of reflectances. Color Research & Application 29(2), 104–110 (2004)
12. Finlayson, G.D., Trezzi, E.: Shades of gray and colour constancy. In: Color and Imaging Conference, vol. 2004, pp. 37–41 (2004)
13. Gijsenij, A., Gevers, T., van de Weijer, J.: Computational color constancy: Survey and experiments. IEEE Transactions on Image Processing 20(9), 2475–2489 (2011)
14. Hall, R., Hall, R.: Illumination and color in computer generated imagery, vol. 7. Springer, New York (1989)
15. Jaaskelainen, T., Parkkinen, J., Toyooka, S.: Vector-subspace model for color representation. J. Opt. Soc. Am. A 7(4), 725–730 (1990)
16. Jiang, J., Liu, D., Gu, J., Susstrunk, S.: What is the space of spectral sensitivity functions for digital color cameras? In: IEEE Workshop on Applications of Computer Vision, pp. 168–179 (2013)
17. Laamanen, H., Jetsu, T., Jaaskelainen, T., Parkkinen, J.: Weighted compression of spectral color information. J. Opt. Soc. Am. A 25(6), 1383–1388 (2008)
18. Lenz, R., Meer, P., Hauta-Kasari, M.: Spectral-based illumination estimation and color correction. Color Research & Application 24, 98–111 (1999)
19. MacQueen, J.: Some methods for classification and analysis of multivariate observations. In: Proceedings of the fifth Berkeley Symposium on Mathematical Statistics and Probability, California, USA, vol. 1, pp. 281–297 (1967)
20. Maloney, L.T.: Evaluation of linear models of surface spectral reflectance with small numbers of parameters. J. Opt. Soc. Am. A 3(10), 1673–1683 (1986)

21. Maloney, L.T., Wandell, B.A.: Color constancy: a method for recovering surface spectral reflectance. J. Opt. Soc. Am. A 3(1), 29–33 (1986)
22. Marimont, D.H., Wandell, B.A.: Linear models of surface and illuminant spectra. J. Opt. Soc. Am. A 9(11), 1905–1913 (1992)
23. Park, J.I., Lee, M.H., Grossberg, M.D., Nayar, S.K.: Multispectral imaging using multiplexed illumination. In: International Conference on Computer Vision, pp. 1–8 (2007)
24. Parkkinen, J.P., Hallikainen, J., Jaaskelainen, T.: Characteristic spectra of munsell colors. J. Opt. Soc. Am. A 6(2), 318–322 (1989)
25. Peyvandi, S., Amirshahi, S.H.: Generalized spectral decomposition: a theory and practice to spectral reconstruction. J. Opt. Soc. Am. A 28(8), 1545–1553 (2011)
26. Peyvandi, S., Amirshahi, S.H., Hernández-Andrés, J., Nieves, J.L., Romero, J.: Spectral recovery of outdoor illumination by an extension of the bayesian inverse approach to the gaussian mixture model. J. Opt. Soc. Am. A 29(10), 2181–2189 (2012)
27. Prasad, D.K., Nguyen, R., Brown, M.S.: Quick approximation of camera's spectral response from casual lighting. In: IEEE International Conference on Computer Vision Workshops, pp. 844–851 (2013)
28. Romero, J., Garcia-Beltran, A., Hernández-Andrés, J.: Linear bases for representation of natural and artificial illuminants. J. Opt. Soc. Am. A 14(5), 1007–1014 (1997)
29. Sharma, G., Wang, S.: Spectrum recovery from colorimetric data for color reproductions. In: Color Imaging: Device-Independent Color, Color Hardcopy, and Applications VII. Proc. SPIE, vol. 4663, pp. 8–14 (2002)
30. Zhang, X., Xu, H.: Reconstructing spectral reflectance by dividing spectral space and extending the principal components in principal component analysis. J. Opt. Soc. Am. A 25(2), 371–378 (2008)
31. Zhao, H., Kawakami, R., Tan, R.T., Ikeuchi, K.: Estimating basis functions for spectral sensitivity of digital cameras. In: Meeting on Image Recognition and Understanding, vol. 1 (2009)
32. Zhao, Y., Berns, R.S.: Image-based spectral reflectance reconstruction using the matrix r method. Color Research & Application 32(5), 343–351 (2007)

On Shape and Material Recovery from Motion

Manmohan Chandraker

NEC Labs America, Cupertino, USA

Abstract. We present a framework for the joint recovery of the shape
and reflectance of an object with dichromatic BRDF, using motion cues.
We show that four (small or differential) motions of the object, or three
motions of the camera, suffice to yield a linear system that decouples
shape and BRDF. The theoretical benefit is that precise limits on shape
and reflectance recovery using motion cues may be derived. We show
that shape may be recovered for unknown isotropic BRDF and light
source. Simultaneous reflectance estimation is shown ambiguous for general isotropic BRDFs, but possible for restricted BRDFs representing
commong materials like metals, plastics and paints. The practical benefit of the decoupling is that joint shape and BRDF recovery need not
rely on alternating methods, or restrictive priors. Further, our theory
yields conditions for the joint estimability of shape, albedo, BRDF and
directional lighting using motion cues. Surprisingly, such problems are
shown to be well-posed even for some non-Lambertian material types.
Experiments on measured BRDFs from the MERL database validate
our theory.

1   Introduction

Shape and lighting interact in complex ways through the bidirectional reflectance
distribution function (BRDF) to produce the variety of images around us. Shape
recovery with unknown BRDF and lighting is traditionally considered hard, while
their joint recovery is deemed severely ill-posed. This paper presents a framework
for understanding how cues from object or camera motion govern shape, BRDF
and lighting recovery. Our theory leads to several surprising results – for instance,
we show that a few (three or four) motions allow shape recovery with unknown
isotropic BRDF and lighting, allow simultaneous shape and BRDF recovery for
common materials like metals or plastics, or lead to a well-posed problem for joint
recovery of shape, reflectance and directional lighting for such materials.

The appearance of many real-world materials is governed by a dichromatic
model, which consists of a diffuse albedo and a non-diffuse reflectance that is
a function of surface orientation, lighting and viewpoint. In Section 4, we show
that change in image intensties for isotropic dichromatic materials, for both the
cases of object and camera motion, may be linearly related to entities associated
with shape, reflectance and lighting. We call these differential flow and stereo
relations, respectively, following prior works for monochromatic materials [8,5].

A direct consequence of this linearity is that shape and reflectance terms are
neatly decoupled by motion cues over an image sequence. In Sec. 5 and 6, we

D. Fleet et al. (Eds.): ECCV 2014, Part VII, LNCS 8695, pp. 202–217, 2014.

Table 1. Summary of the theoretical results of this paper. We establish conditions when shape, shape + BRDF and shape + BRDF + lighting estimation problems are well-posed for dichromatic BRDFs, using motion cues resulting from either object or camera motion. Green indicates well-posed estimation, pink indicates ill-posed, while gray indicates ill-posed but solvable under mild regularization. More constrained BRDF or restrictive input conditions yield better-posed estimations, so the top to bottom variation is largely green to gray to pink. For reference, BRDF estimation results from [7], with known shape and single image, are also shown ("?" denotes conjectured, but not proved). Motion cues can recover unknown shape, as well as estimate BRDF and determine BRDF estimability under a wider set of conditions.

BRDF Type	Knowns Albedo	Knowns Light	Object Motion Shape	Object Motion + BRDF	Object Motion + Light	Camera Motion Shape	Camera Motion + BRDF	Camera Motion + Light	[7] BRDF
1-lobe	✓	✓	Prop. 3	Prop. 5	–	Prop. 4	Prop. 7	–	
1-lobe	✓	✗	Prop. 3	Sec. 7(c)		Prop. 4	Prop. 9		
1-lobe	✗	✓	Prop. 3	Prop. 5	–	Prop. 4	Prop. 7	–	?
1-lobe	✗	✗	Prop. 3	Sec. 7(a)		Prop. 4	Prop. 9		
2-lobe	✓	✓	Prop. 3	Cor. 2	–	Prop. 4	Prop. 7	–	
2-lobe	✓	✗	Prop. 3	Sec. 7(d)		Prop. 4	Sec. 7		
2-lobe	✗	✓	Prop. 3	Prop. 6	–	Prop. 4	Prop. 7	–	?
2-lobe	✗	✗	Prop. 3	Prop. 8		Prop. 4	Sec. 7		
K-lobe	✓	✓	Prop. 3	Cor. 3	–	Prop. 4	Sec. 6.2	–	?
K-lobe	✓	✗	Prop. 3	Sec. 7(e)		Prop. 4	Sec. 7		?
K-lobe	✗	✓	Prop. 3	Prop. 6	–	Prop. 4	Sec. 6.2	–	?
K-lobe	✗	✗	Prop. 3	Prop. 8		Prop. 4	Sec. 7		?

show that four differential object motions, or three camera motions, suffice to recover surface depth and in many cases, the unknown BRDF as well. This is surprising, since the BRDF can encode complex interactions between shape and lighting. The immediate practical benefit is that we may recover both shape and reflectance without resort to unstable alternating methods, iterative optimization, or restrictive priors on geometry and reflectance.

A theoretical benefit is that our analysis relates the precise extent of shape and BRDF recovery to the hardness of estimation conditions. In Sec. 6 and 7, we relate the well-posedness of shape and reflectance recovery to BRDF complexity, as well as to input conditions such as knowledge of lighting or uniform albedo. In the general isotropic case, we show that BRDF may not be estimated using motion cues alone, which justifies several works that impose priors for reflectance recovery. However, when the BRDF depends on one or more angles about the normal – for example, half-angle BRDFs for many metals, plastics or paints – we show that both shape and BRDF may be unambiguously recovered.

Finally, we analyze the well-posedness of joint recovery problems where shape, albedo, reflectance functions, lighting and reflection directions are all unknown. We show in Sec. 7 that the problem is well-posed even for some non-Lambertian materials (for example, half-angle BRDFs) under camera motion and only mildly ill-posed under object motion. This is contrary to conventional belief that such problems are severely ill-posed. Our theoretical results are summarized in Tab. 1.

2   Related Work

Motion cues for shape recovery have been extensively studied within the purviews of optical flow [11,13] and multiview stereo [21]. It is well-known from early works that a Lambertian reflectance has limitations [15,23]. Several approaches have been proposed for shape recovery with general BRDFs, such as Helmholtz reciprocity for stereo by Zickler et al. [25], intensity profiles for photometric stereo by Sato et al. [20] and specular flow for mirror surfaces by Canas et al. [4].

Our shape recovery results are closely related to prior works of Chandraker et al. for light source [6], object [8] and camera motions [5], which assume a monochromatic BRDF. The theory of this paper generalizes to dichromatic BRDFs and goes further to analyze the problem of BRDF estimation too.

For BRDF estimation, parametric models have a long history [3,22] and we refer the reader to [16] for an empirical comparison. Non-parametric [19,18] and data-driven [14] approaches are popular for their representation power, but require a large amount of data or rely on complex estimation whose properties are hard to characterize. Semiparametric models have also been proposed for BRDF editing [12] and estimation [7]. Our work extends such methods to unknown shape and characterizes how motion cues provide additional information.

Joint recovery of two or more elements among shape, BRDF and illumination have also attracted significant interest. Shape and illumination have been estimated under the Lambertian assumption by imposing priors [2]. Goldman et al. use a set of basis materials in photometric stereo to recover shape and reflectance [10]. Alldrin et al. alternatingly optimize over shape and material to recover both under light source motion [1], as do Zhang et al. for shape, motion and lighting for Lambertian reflectance [24]. An alternating method to estimate shape and isotropic BRDF under natural illumination is proposed in [17]. This paper shows that motion cues decouple shape and reflectance, so they may be estimated simultaneously, rather than in an alternating fashion.

Our focus is on establishing limits to shape and reflectance recovery using motion cues, regardless of estimation method. Some works like [7] derive conditions on well-posedness of BRDF estimation using a single image, with known shape. As discussed in Sec. 7, our theory not only supports the conclusions of [7], but also generalizes it both to unknown shape and to show how motion cues may sometimes enable BRDF estimation that is ill-posed for single images.

3   Preliminaries

Assumptions and Setup. We assume that the lighting is directional and distant, while the BRDF is isotropic and homogeneous (or having slow spatial variation). Global illumination effects like interreflections and shadows are assumed negligible. The origin of 3D coordinates is defined as the principal point on the image plane. So, the camera center is $(0, 0, -f)^\top$, where f is the focal length. The image of a 3D point $\mathbf{x} = (x, y, z)^\top$ is given by a point $\mathbf{u} = (u, v)^\top$ on the image plane, with

$$(1 + \beta z)u = x, \qquad (1 + \beta z)v = y, \qquad \text{where } \beta = f^{-1}. \qquad (1)$$

Motion Field. In the case of object motion, we assume the object undergoes rotation $\mathbf{R}$ and translation $\boldsymbol{\tau}$ relative to camera. For a camera motion $\{\mathbf{R}^\top, -\mathbf{R}^\top\boldsymbol{\tau}\}$, the object and lighting are equivalently assumed to undergo a relative motion of $\{\mathbf{R}, \boldsymbol{\tau}\}$. In either case, for differential motion, we approximate $\mathbf{R} \approx \mathbf{I} + [\boldsymbol{\omega}]_\times$, where $\boldsymbol{\omega} = (\omega_1, \omega_2, \omega_3)^\top$ and $[\cdot]_\times$ denotes the cross-product operator.

The motion field $\boldsymbol{\mu}$ is the image velocity, that is, $\boldsymbol{\mu} = (\dot{u}, \dot{v})^\top$. Substituting from (1), with α_i known functions having forms shown in [9], we obtain

$$\boldsymbol{\mu} = (1+\beta z)^{-1} \left[\alpha_1(1+\beta z) + (\alpha_2 + \omega_2 z), \; \alpha_3(1+\beta z) + (\alpha_4 - \omega_1 z)\right]^\top. \quad (2)$$

Image Formation. For surface normal $\mathbf{n}$, light source $\mathbf{s}$ and viewing direction $\mathbf{v}$, the dichromatic imaging model at a surface point $\mathbf{x}$ is

$$I(\mathbf{u}, t) = \sigma(\mathbf{x})\mathbf{n}^\top \mathbf{s} + \rho(\mathbf{x}, \mathbf{n}, \mathbf{s}, \mathbf{v}), \quad (3)$$

where σ is the diffuse albedo and ρ is the BRDF. Such models closely approximate real-world materials [16]. Parametric models like Torrance-Sparrow are often used to model ρ, but this work considers the form of ρ unknown.

4   Differential Relations for Dichromatic BRDFs

We now derive differential relations between shape and reflectance, induced by motion. We present intuitions here and refer the reader to [9] for details.

4.1   Object Motion

Consider the setup where the camera and lighting are fixed, while the object moves relative to the camera. Since the light position $\mathbf{s}$ does not change with time, we may write the BRDF of a point as a function of its position and normal, that is, $\rho(\mathbf{x}, \mathbf{n})$. Taking the total derivative on both sides of (3), we get

$$I_u\dot{u} + I_v\dot{v} + I_t = \sigma\frac{d}{dt}(\mathbf{n}^\top\mathbf{s}) + (\mathbf{n}^\top\mathbf{s})\frac{d\sigma}{dt} + \frac{d}{dt}\rho(\mathbf{x}, \mathbf{n}). \quad (4)$$

Since albedo is intrinsically defined on surface coordinates, its total derivative in 3D coordinates vanishes. For rigid body motion, change in normal is given by $\dot{\mathbf{n}} = \boldsymbol{\omega} \times \mathbf{n}$, while change in position is the linear velocity, $\dot{\mathbf{x}} = \boldsymbol{\nu}$. Using chain rule differentiation and recognizing $\boldsymbol{\mu} = (\dot{u}, \dot{v})^\top$ as the motion field, we have

$$(\nabla I)^\top \boldsymbol{\mu} + I_t = (\sigma\mathbf{s} + \nabla_\mathbf{n}\rho)^\top (\boldsymbol{\omega} \times \mathbf{n}) + (\nabla_\mathbf{x}\rho)^\top \boldsymbol{\nu}. \quad (5)$$

In our setup, the BRDF is homogeneous and lighting is distant, thus, $\nabla_\mathbf{x}\rho$ is negligible. Thus, we obtain the following relation:

$$\boxed{(\nabla_\mathbf{u} I)^\top \boldsymbol{\mu} + I_t = [\mathbf{n} \times (\sigma\mathbf{s} + \nabla_\mathbf{n}\rho)]^\top \boldsymbol{\omega}.} \quad (6)$$

Similar to [8], we call this the *differential flow relation*. However, note that the above is a relation for dichromatic BRDFs given by (3), while [8] assumes a monochromatic model. For now, we make an observation which will be used later:

Proposition 1. *For an object with dichromatic BRDF undergoing differential motion, a differential flow relation exists that is linear in entities that depend on shape (motion field and surface normals), reflectance and lighting.*

4.2 Camera Motion

Next, a similar analysis for the case of camera motion shows the existence of a *differential stereo relation* (see [9] for a derivation from first principles):

$$(\nabla_{\mathbf{u}} I)^{\top} \boldsymbol{\mu} + I_t = (\mathbf{n} \times \nabla_{\mathbf{n}}\rho + \mathbf{s} \times \nabla_{\mathbf{s}}\rho)^{\top} \boldsymbol{\omega}. \tag{7}$$

We again observe a similarity to the monochromatic case of [5], while noting:

Proposition 2. *For an object with dichromatic BRDF observed by a camera undergoing differential motion, a differential stereo relation exists that is linear in entities that depend on shape, reflectance and lighting.*

The above linearities ensconced within the differential flow and stereo relations play a key role in understanding the limits of both shape and reflectance recovery using motion cues. The following sections are devoted to exploring those limits.

5 Shape Recovery

In this section, we establish shape recovery from motion cues, with unknown dichromatic BRDF. Further, we may assume the lighting to also be unknown.

5.1 Object Motion

Substituting the motion field (2) into the differential flow relation (6), we obtain

$$(p + \beta q)z + (q + r) = (1 + \beta z)\boldsymbol{\omega}^{\top}\boldsymbol{\pi}, \tag{8}$$

where $p = I_u\omega_2 - I_v\omega_1$, $q = \alpha_1 I_u + \alpha_3 I_v + I_t$ and $r = \alpha_2 I_u + \alpha_4 I_v$ are known and

$$\boldsymbol{\pi} = \mathbf{n} \times (\sigma\mathbf{s} + \nabla_{\mathbf{n}}\rho). \tag{9}$$

We are now in a position to state the following:

Proposition 3. *Four or more differential motions of a surface with unknown dichromatic BRDF, under unknown light direction, suffice to yield surface depth.*

Proof. For $m \geq 4$, let known motions $\{\boldsymbol{\omega}^i, \boldsymbol{\tau}^i\}$, where $\boldsymbol{\omega}^i$ span $\mathbb{R}^3$, relate images $I_1, \cdots, I_m$ to I_0. From (8), we have a sequence of differential flow relations

$$(p^i + \beta q^i)z - (1 + \beta z)\boldsymbol{\pi}^{\top}\boldsymbol{\omega}^i + (q^i + r^i) = 0, \quad \text{for } i = 1, \cdots, m. \tag{10}$$

Let $\mathbf{c}^i = [p^i + \beta q^i, -\omega_1^i, -\omega_2^i, -\omega_3^i]^{\top}$ be rows of the $m \times 4$ matrix $\mathbf{C} = [\mathbf{c}^1, \cdots, \mathbf{c}^m]^{\top}$. Let $\mathbf{q} = [q^1, \cdots, q^m]^{\top}$ and $\mathbf{r} = [r^1, \cdots, r^m]^{\top}$. Define $\boldsymbol{\epsilon} = -\mathbf{C}^+(\mathbf{q} + \mathbf{r})$, where $\mathbf{C}^+$ is the Moore-Penrose pseudoinverse of $\mathbf{C}$ and let $\boldsymbol{\epsilon}' = (\epsilon_2, \epsilon_3, \epsilon_4)^{\top}$. Then, we have

$$z = \epsilon_1 \tag{11}$$

$$(1 + \beta z)\boldsymbol{\pi} = \boldsymbol{\epsilon}'. \tag{12}$$

Thus, from (11), we have obtained the surface depth. □

5.2 Camera Motion

We again start by observing that substituting the motion field (2) in the differential stereo relation (7) leads to an equation of the form (8). However, note that the definition of $\boldsymbol{\pi}$ is different for the case of camera motion. Indeed, an isotropic BRDF may be written as $\rho(\mathbf{n}, \mathbf{s}, \mathbf{v}) = \bar{\rho}(\mathbf{n}^\top\mathbf{s}, \mathbf{s}^\top\mathbf{v}, \mathbf{n}^\top\mathbf{v})$, whereby

$$\boldsymbol{\pi} = \mathbf{n} \times \nabla_\mathbf{n}\rho + \mathbf{s} \times \nabla_\mathbf{s}\rho = \bar{\rho}_{\mathbf{n}^\top\mathbf{v}}(\mathbf{n} \times \mathbf{v}) + \bar{\rho}_{\mathbf{s}^\top\mathbf{v}}(\mathbf{s} \times \mathbf{v}), \tag{13}$$

thus, $\boldsymbol{\pi}^\top\mathbf{v} = \pi_3 = 0$, as [5]. Using $m \geq 3$ differential motions $\{\boldsymbol{\omega}^i, \boldsymbol{\tau}^i\}$, one may define the $m \times 3$ matrix $\tilde{\mathbf{C}} = [\tilde{\mathbf{c}}^1, \cdots, \tilde{\mathbf{c}}^m]^\top$ with rows $\tilde{\mathbf{c}}^i = [-(p'^i + \beta q'^i), \omega_1^i, \omega_2^i]^\top$. Then, the system of m differential stereo relations (10) may be solved to obtain

$$[z, (1 + \beta z)\pi_1, (1 + \beta z)\pi_2]^\top = \tilde{\boldsymbol{\epsilon}}, \tag{14}$$

where $\tilde{\boldsymbol{\epsilon}} = (\tilde{\epsilon}_1, \tilde{\epsilon}_2, \tilde{\epsilon}_3)^\top = \tilde{\mathbf{C}}^+(\mathbf{q}+\mathbf{r})$, with $\mathbf{q}$ and $\mathbf{r}$ as defined previously. It follows that $z = \tilde{\epsilon}_1$ yields the surface depth. Thus, we have shown:

Proposition 4. *Three or more differential motions of the camera suffice to yield depth of a surface with unknown dichromatic BRDF and unknown light direction.*

We observe that even with the assumption of a dichromatic BRDF, the shape recovery results of Prop. 3 and 4 are similar to the monochromatic cases of [8,5]. Indeed, although the images are not logarithmic here and the definitions of $\boldsymbol{\pi}$ are different from [8,5], the overall forms of the differential flow and stereo relations exhibit similar linearities. Intuitively, this leads to similar shape recovery results.

But more importantly, we note an additional benefit of the linear relationship between shape and BRDF in the differential flow and stereo relations. Namely, in (12) and (14), we also obtain information about the BRDF in the form of $\boldsymbol{\pi}$. Our focus for the remainder of the paper will be on how the differential flow and stereo relations aid understanding of reflectance recovery.

5.3 Experimental Validation

We use real measured BRDFs from the MERL database [14] to illustrate shape recovery in Fig. 1. For the `colonial-maple-223` material, images such as Fig. 1(a) are observed under five differential motions of the object. Image derivatives are computed using a smoothing filter to account for noise in the measured BRDF data. The shape recovered using Prop. 3 is shown in Fig. 1(b). Similarly, for the `natural-209` material, images are observed under five differential motions of the camera (Fig. 1(c)) and the shape recovered using Prop. 4 is shown in Fig. 1(d).

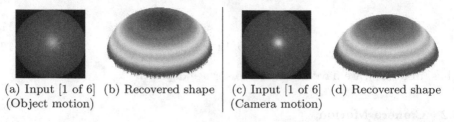

(a) Input [1 of 6]   (b) Recovered shape   (c) Input [1 of 6]   (d) Recovered shape
(Object motion)   (Camera motion)

Fig. 1. (a) One of six images using five object motions, with `colonial-maple-223` material (unknown BRDF) and unknown lighting. (b) Shape recovered using Proposition 3. (c) One of six images using five camera motions, with `natural-209` material (unknown BRDF) and unknown lighting. (d) Shape recovered using Proposition 4.

6 Shape and Reflectance Recovery

We now consider the problem of simultaneous shape and reflectance recovery. For both the cases of object and camera motion, in addition to the shape, we have obtained information about the reflectance in (12) and (14):

$$\text{Object: } \boldsymbol{\pi} = \frac{1}{1 + \beta\epsilon_1}(\epsilon_2, \epsilon_3, \epsilon_4)^\top, \qquad \text{Camera: } \boldsymbol{\pi} = \frac{1}{1 + \beta\tilde{\epsilon}_1}(\tilde{\epsilon}_2, \tilde{\epsilon}_3, 0)^\top. \quad (15)$$

It is interesting that shape and reflectance may be decoupled using motion cues, despite the complex interactions enabled by an unknown dichromatic BRDF. We now show how the linearity of differential flow and stereo allows us to impose limits on the extent to which BRDF may be recovered using motion cues. In this section, we will assume a known light source direction.

6.1 Object Motion

Using $m \geq 4$ motions of an object, we may always obtain the shape using Proposition 3. We will now explore the extent to which BRDF may be recovered.

General Isotropic BRDF. For an isotropic BRDF, image formation depends on the three angles between surface normal, camera and lighting directions:

$$I = \sigma \mathbf{n}^\top \mathbf{s} + \rho(\theta, \phi, \psi), \text{ where } \theta = \mathbf{n}^\top \mathbf{s}, \ \phi = \mathbf{s}^\top \mathbf{v} \text{ and } \psi = \mathbf{n}^\top \mathbf{v}. \quad (16)$$

Using (9) to define $\boldsymbol{\pi}$ and substituting in (12), we have the following relation:

$$(1 + \beta z)\mathbf{n} \times [(\sigma + \rho_\theta)\mathbf{s} + \rho_\psi \mathbf{v}] = \boldsymbol{\epsilon}', \quad (17)$$

where $\rho_\phi = 0$ since ϕ remains unchanged for object motion. Further, the albedo and BRDF-derivative along the θ direction, ρ_θ, cannot be disambiguated. This can also be intuitively understood since ρ is an arbitrary function and may ambiguously incorporate any information about θ that is included in the diffuse term. Thus, only BRDF variation along ψ is captured by object motion.

Even though estimation of a dichromatic BRDF from object motion is ambiguous in the fully general case, we show that it is unique for more restricted BRDFs exhibited by several real-world materials.

Single-Lobe Dichromatic Reflectance. For many materials, the reflectance depends predominantly on the angle between the surface normals and a single reflection direction, **r**. Most commonly, such as with metals, plastics and many paints, the reflection direction is aligned with the half-angle between the source and viewing directions. This observation has also been used to propose parametric models like Blinn-Phong [3] and (simplified) Torrance-Sparrow [22]. For many materials in the MERL dataset, empirical studies have found a single lobe BRDF to be sufficiently descriptive [16,7]. For such materials, we show:

Proposition 5. *Four or more differential motions of an object with single-lobe dichromatic BRDF suffice to uniquely determine its shape, albedo and reflectance.*

Proof. The image formation for an object with single-lobe BRDF is given by $I = \sigma \mathbf{n}^\top \mathbf{s} + \rho(\eta)$, where $\eta = \mathbf{n}^\top \mathbf{r}$. Substituting in (9), we obtain

$$\boldsymbol{\pi} = \mathbf{n} \times (\sigma \mathbf{s} + \nabla_{\mathbf{n}} \rho) = \mathbf{n} \times (\sigma \mathbf{s} + \rho_\eta \mathbf{r}). \tag{18}$$

Given images under four or more differential motions, Proposition 3 and (15) guarantee the existence of a relation between depth and reflectance:

$$(1 + \beta \epsilon_1) [\mathbf{n}(\epsilon_1) \times (\sigma \mathbf{s} + \rho_\eta \mathbf{r})] = \boldsymbol{\epsilon}', \tag{19}$$

where the normals $\mathbf{n}(\epsilon_1)$ are obtained from the derivatives of surface depth estimated in (11). Thus, the above is a rank 2 system of three linear equations in the two unknowns σ and ρ_η, which may both be recovered. Finally, we note that for most materials, reflection vanishes around grazing angles (indeed, the non-diffuse component of half-angle BRDFs is often super-linear). Thus, $\rho(0) = 0$, whereby ρ_η may be integrated to recover the BRDF function ρ.   □

Thus, we have shown that for a large class of dichromatic materials, motion cues alone can determine all of shape, albedo and BRDF. Intuitively, the linear separability of shape and reflectance established by Proposition 1 allows us to determine conditions when BRDF is recoverable. Further, it also allows us to determine when BRDF estimation is ambiguous, as discussed next.

Degeneracy. The result of Proposition 5 relies on the direction **r** being distinct from the light source **s**, otherwise (19) reduces to: $(1 + \beta \epsilon_1) [\mathbf{n}(\epsilon_1) \times (\sigma + \rho_\eta)\mathbf{s}] = \boldsymbol{\epsilon}'$. Clearly, in this case, one may not independently recover both albedo σ and the BRDF-derivative ρ_η. For most materials, it is indeed the case that $\mathbf{r} \neq \mathbf{s}$ (for instance, **r** is often the half-angle). However, there are two important exceptions. First, an object with arbitrary isotropic BRDF observed under colocated illumination follows an image formation model given by $I = \sigma \mathbf{n}^\top \mathbf{s} + \bar{\rho}(\mathbf{n}^\top \mathbf{s})$ (since $\mathbf{s} = \mathbf{v}$ and $\|\mathbf{s}\| = 1$, there exists a function $\bar{\rho}$ such that $\rho(\mathbf{n}^\top \mathbf{s}, \mathbf{s}^\top \mathbf{v}, \mathbf{n}^\top \mathbf{v}) = \bar{\rho}(\mathbf{n}^\top \mathbf{s}))$. Second, retroreflective materials such as those used to enhance visibility of road signs reflect light back towards the source direction. Thus, we may state:

Corollary 1. *Albedo and reflectance cannot be disambiguated using motion cues for an object with retroreflective BRDF or one observed under colocated lighting.*

Multi-lobe Reflectance. For some materials, the image may be explained by reflection along two or more angles with respect to the surface normal. That is,

$$I = \sigma \mathbf{n}^\top \mathbf{s} + \rho(\eta_1, \cdots, \eta_K), \text{ where } \eta_i = \mathbf{n}^\top \mathbf{r}_i, \text{ for } i = 1, \cdots, K, \quad (20)$$

where $K \geq 2$. Empirical studies like [16,7] show that accounting for BRDF dependence on a second direction besides the half-angle leads to a better approximation for materials like veneer paints and fabrics. We will refer to directions η_i as lobes.

Unknown Albedo. Given four or more differential motions, shape may be recovered for such BRDFs using Proposition 3. Substituting from (20) into the expression for $\boldsymbol{\pi}$ in (9) and using (15), we obtain a relation between depth and reflectance:

$$(1 + \beta\epsilon_1)\,\mathbf{n}(\epsilon_1) \times \left(\sigma\mathbf{s} + \sum_{i=1}^{K} \rho_{\eta_i} \mathbf{r}_i\right) = \epsilon', \quad (21)$$

which is a system of three linear equations in $K+1$ unknowns $\{\sigma, \rho_{\eta_1}, \cdots, \rho_{\eta_K}\}$. For $K > 2$, clearly the system (21) is underdetermined and no unique solution is possible. For $K = 2$, the above is a system of three linear equations in three unknowns σ, ρ_{η_1} and ρ_{η_2}. However, note that the 3×3 matrix associated with the system in (21), $\mathbf{A} = (\mathbf{n} \times \mathbf{s}, \mathbf{n} \times \mathbf{r}_1, \mathbf{n} \times \mathbf{r}_2)$, is rank-deficient. Thus, we state:

Proposition 6. *A K-lobe BRDF may not be recovered using object motion alone for an object with unknown albedo when $K \geq 2$ (although shape may be recovered).*

It is interesting that the above ambiguity also affects important classes of parametric BRDFs. An example is the Torrance-Sparrow model ignoring geometric attenuation and Fresnel terms, for which image formation may be expressed as

$$I = \sigma \mathbf{n}^\top \mathbf{s} + \rho(\mathbf{n}^\top \mathbf{h}, \mathbf{n}^\top \mathbf{v}), \text{ with } \rho \sim (\mathbf{n}^\top \mathbf{v})^{-1} \exp\left(-\lambda^2(\cos^{-1}\mathbf{n}^\top \mathbf{h})^2\right), \quad (22)$$

where λ is a surface roughness parameter.

Known Albedo. We now consider the important case of known albedo. Note that uniform albedo, which is a common assumption in BRDF acquisition and estimation settings like [14,16], reduces to known albedo when the non-diffuse components of a dichromatic BRDF are super-linear and rapidly diminish away from the lobe directions, as is true for most materials. Since the matrix $\mathbf{A}$ defined above is rank 2, the remaining unknowns ρ_{η_1} and ρ_{η_2} may still be recovered when the albedo is known. Thus, we have:

Corollary 2. *With known albedo, both shape and a BRDF with up to two lobes may be recovered using four or more differential motions of the object.*

Finally, we note that with $K \geq 3$ lobes, even with known albedo, the above rank 2 system of equations is underdetermined, so we state:

Corollary 3. *Object motion cannot disambiguate the estimation of a BRDF with $K \geq 3$ lobes, even with known albedo (although shape may still be recovered).*

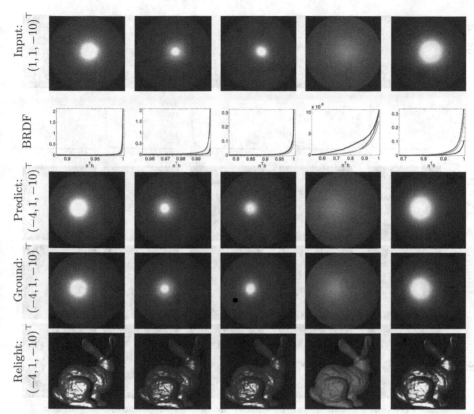

blue-metal-pt2 red-metal-pt violet-acrylic dark-blue-pt gold-metal-pt

Fig. 2. (Row 1) One of six input images from five small object motions for MERL database BRDFs. (Row 2) BRDF recovered in each color channel. (Row 3) Predicted appearance for a novel light direction. (Row 4) Ground truth appearance for the novel lighting. (Row 5) A novel geometry relighted using the estimated BRDF. Percentage image errors of row 3 relative to row 4 are 5.8%, 2.1%, 1.8%, 4.7% and 7.8%, respectively.

We also note that several interesting relationships exist between the above results and [7], where uniqueness conditions for BRDF estimation are established in a single image setting, with known shape and uniform albedo. The results of our theory further support the conclusions of [7] and extend them to a multiple image setting. A discussion of those relationships is presented in Section 7.

Experimental Validation. We validate our theory using real measured BRDFs from the MERL database [14]. In the top row of Figure 3, we show one of six input images, corresponding to five differential object motions. Spatial and temporal image derivatives are computed, following which depth and π are determined by Prop. 3. From π, the BRDF is estimated using the theory of this section.

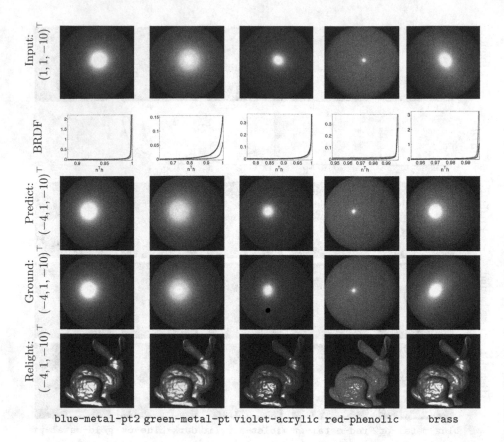

blue-metal-pt2 green-metal-pt violet-acrylic red-phenolic   brass

Fig. 3. (Row 1) One of six input images from five small camera motions for MERL database BRDFs. (Row 2) BRDF recovered in each color channel. (Row 3) Predicted appearance for a novel light direction. (Row 4) Ground truth appearance for the novel lighting. (Row 5) A novel geometry relighted using the estimated BRDF. Note the reasonable approximation obtained even for the anisotropic **brass** material. Percentage image errors of row 3 relative to row 4 are 3.4%, 2.9%, 1.6%, 4.8% and 15.8%, respectively.

The second row shows the estimated BRDF curves in each color channel. Notice the qualitative accuracy of the estimation, as more specular materials have curves with sharper rise. With the recovered shape and BRDF, appearance is predicted from a novel lighting direction, shown in the third row. It is found to closely match the ground truth, as shown in the fourth row. The final row shows a novel geometry relighted using the estimated BRDF, from a novel lighting direction. Further experiments are included in [9].

6.2 Camera Motion

We now briefly study the case of camera motion, while refering the reader to [9] for details. We have seen in (15) that $m \geq 3$ motions determine the entity π that encodes BRDF-derivatives. We specify what BRDF information may be recovered from π, given its form in (7):

$$\pi = \mathbf{n} \times \nabla_{\mathbf{n}}\rho + \mathbf{s} \times \nabla_{\mathbf{s}}\rho. \tag{23}$$

Recall from (13) that for any isotropic BRDF where $\rho(\mathbf{n}, \mathbf{s}, \mathbf{v}) = \bar{\rho}(\mathbf{n}^{\top}\mathbf{s}, \mathbf{s}^{\top}\mathbf{v}, \mathbf{n}^{\top}\mathbf{v})$, the BRDF-derivative $\bar{\rho}_{\mathbf{n}^{\top}\mathbf{s}}$ vanishes. Thus, a full isotropic BRDF may not be recovered using camera motion. However, one may still recover restricted forms of isotropic BRDFs, such as the K-lobe model, as shown next.

It also follows from (13) that $\pi^{\top}\mathbf{v} = \pi_3 = 0$. Thus, only two independent constraints on the BRDF are available through differential motion of the camera. Consider a K-lobe image formation $I = \sigma\mathbf{n}^{\top}\mathbf{s} + \rho(\eta_1, \cdots, \eta_K)$, where $\eta_i = \mathbf{n}^{\top}\mathbf{r}_i$. From the linearity of differentiation, π_j are of the form $\sum_{i=1}^{K} \rho_{\eta_i} f_i^j(\mathbf{n}, \mathbf{s}, \mathbf{r}_i)$, for some analytic functions f_i^j and $j = 1, 2$. Clearly, for $K > 2$, one may not determine all the ρ_{η_i}, since only two constraints on π are available. Further, note that there is no dependence of π on σ, unlike the case of object motion. Thus, for $K = 2$, when $\mathbf{r}_1$ and $\mathbf{r}_2$ are independent and "general" (that is, with no special dependencies for f_i), both ρ_{η_1} and ρ_{η_2} may be determined. Thus, the BRDF ρ can be recovered by integration. For known lighting, the albedo may subsequently be estimated by subtracting the non-diffuse component. Thus, we have:

Proposition 7. *Three or more differential motions of the camera suffice to uniquely determine the shape, albedo and reflectance of an object with a general K-lobe dichromatic BRDF, for $K \leq 2$.*

An important exception is the case of retroreflection, when one may have $\eta_i = \mathbf{n}^{\top}\mathbf{s}$. From the symmetry of the expression for π in (23), it follows that $\rho_{\eta_i} = 0$. Consequently, the BRDF may not be uniquely determined in this case.

Experimental Validation. To show that BRDF estimation is possible using camera motion, we again use measured real BRDFs from the MERL dataset. As before, the top row of Figure 3, shows one of six input images, corresponding to five differential motions of the camera. Depth and BRDF are estimated using the theories of Sections 5.2 and 6.2. Compare the similarities in BRDF curves to those recovered using object motion, for the repeated materials blue-metallic-paint2 and violet-acrylic. Appearance from a novel lighting direction is accurately predicted in the third row and a novel geometry is relighted in the fifth row.

The final column in Figure 3 shows results for the brass material. From the elongated shape of the specular lobe in the input images, it is clear that the material is anisotropic. However, the estimation using camera motion still yields an isotropic BRDF whose appearance is a good approximation to the original. Further experiments are included in [9].

7   Discussion: Shape, Reflectance and Lighting Recovery

We now consider the problem of jointly recovering shape, reflectance and lighting using motion cues (for convenience, "light direction" in this section also refers to the reflection directions). We show that the linear separability of shape, reflectance and lighting imposed by Propositions 1 and 2 allows a characterization of the hardness of such joint recovery problems. Further, we show how our theory is consistent with prior works like [24,7] and also extends them.

Object Motion. For a BRDF dependent on K reflection directions, image formation is given by (20) and shape recovered as $z = \epsilon_1$ using Proposition 3. Three additional equations of the form (21) are available relating the remaining unknowns $\{\sigma, \rho_{\eta_1}, \cdots, \rho_{\eta_K}, \mathbf{s}, \mathbf{r}_1, \cdots, \mathbf{r}_K\}$, reproduced here for convenience:

$$[\mathbf{n}(\epsilon_1)]_\times \left(\sigma\mathbf{s} + \sum_{i=1}^{K} \rho_{\eta_i}\mathbf{r}_i\right) = \frac{\epsilon'}{1 + \beta\epsilon_1}. \tag{24}$$

Since $[\mathbf{n}(\epsilon_1)]_\times$ is skew-symmetric, only two of the three relations in (24) are independent. Thus, for N pixels (or more precisely, N independent normals), we have $2N$ equations in $(K+1)(N+2)$ unknowns (N unknowns for each of albedo and BRDF-derivatives, two unknowns for each direction). Clearly, the system of equations (24) is underdetermined for any $K \geq 1$. Thus, we may state:

Proposition 8. *With unknown albedo and non-Lambertian dichromatic BRDF, the problem of joint recovery of shape, reflectance and lighting using object motion is underconstrained.*

Despite this apparently negative result, our framework is fruitful for understanding and extending several prior works on shape and reflectance recovery:

(a) First, it matches intuition that joint recovery problems are hard in general cases. For example, estimating even a one-lobe dichromatic BRDF with unknown albedo and light source is ambiguous in a single-image setup [7]. Our theory shows that it stays ambiguous even with object motion.

(b) Second, we observe that for Lambertian surfaces ($K = 0$), we have $2N$ equations in $N + 2$ unknowns, so such joint recovery is well-posed, which validates the solutions obtained by prior works like [24].

(c) Third, for uniform albedo and unknown lighting, reflectance may be recovered for single-lobe dichromatic BRDFs, since we have $2N$ equations in $N + 5$ unknowns. This shows that motion cues can help reflectance recovery beyond the single-image setup of [7], where uniqueness may be shown only for the case of known albedo and known lighting.

(d) Next, for the case of uniform albedo and known lighting, reflectance recovery for a dichromatic BRDF with $K = 2$ lobes is mildly ill-posed, since we have $2N$ equations in $2N + 5$ unknowns. Thus, mild external constraints or regularization suffice to recover BRDF in such cases. Additional conditions are imposed in [7] by assuming non-negative and monotonic functions, while estimation is regularized by performing a smooth regression.

(e) Finally, it is conjectured in prior works like [16,7] that BRDF estimation is ill-posed for $K > 2$, even with known shape and lighting. Indeed, when considering motion cues, while object shape may be recovered for such BRDFs, the reflectance recovery involves $2N$ equations in $3N + 5$ unknowns, which is severely ill-posed. Thus, our theory establishes that even motion cues cannot unambiguously recover such BRDFs.

Camera Motion. Considering image formation in (20) dependent on a K-lobe BRDF, shape may always be recovered using Proposition 4. By definition in (23), π is independent of albedo. As in Section 6.2, from the definitions of π in (15) and (23), the relations for camera motion corresponding to (24) are of the form

$$\sum_{i=1}^{K} \rho_{\eta_i} f_i^j(\mathbf{n}(\tilde{\epsilon}_1), \mathbf{s}, \mathbf{r}_i) = \frac{\tilde{\epsilon}_{j+1}}{1 + \beta \tilde{\epsilon}_1}, \text{ for known functions } f_i^j \text{ and } j = 1, 2. \quad (25)$$

Since $\pi_3 = 0$ by definition in (15), only two independent relations are available. Thus, for N pixels, we have $2N$ equations in $K(N + 2) + 2$ unknowns.

Proposition 9. *With unknown albedo and a K-lobe dichromatic BRDF, the problem of joint recovery of shape, reflectance and lighting using camera motion is well-posed for $K \leq 1$ and ill-posed for $K > 1$.*

This is a surprising result, since joint recovery of shape, reflectance and lighting has traditionally been considered hard. The above shows that even beyond the traditionally studied Lambertian cases, for many common materials like metals and plastics whose BRDF shows a strong half-angle dependence ($K = 1$), there are enough constraints available to solve such joint recovery problems.

For a BRDF with two lobes, we have $2N + 6$ unknowns, so the system (25) is only mildly ill-posed and may be solved for shape, relfectance and lighting under regularization. Finally, we note that the problem is severely ill-posed for $K > 2$.

8   Conclusions and Future Work

We have presented a framework that helps understand the extent to which object or camera motion cues enable recovery of shape, reflectance and lighting. The theoretical results of Sec. 5, 6 and 7 are summarized in Table 1. These results reflect the intrinsic difficulty of shape and reflectance recovery from motion cues, independent of choice of estimation method. Our framework yields some surprising results on shape and reflectance recovery. In particular, we show both theoretically and in experiments that motion cues can decouple shape and BRDF, allowing both to be simultaneously (rather than alternatingly) estimated for many common materials. Even more unexpectedly, it can be shown that under camera motion, joint recovery of shape, albedo, reflectance functions, lighting and reflection directions is well-posed for some materials (and only mildly ill-posed under object motion). Our future work will explore estimation algorithms that exploit this well-posedness for joint recovery of shape, reflectance and lighting.

Acknowledgments. We thank Ravi Ramamoorthi for helpful discussions and Shen Tian for help with preparing the figures.

References

1. Alldrin, N., Zickler, T., Kriegman, D.: Photometric stereo with non-parametric and spatially-varying reflectance. In: CVPR (2008)
2. Barron, J.T., Malik, J.: Shape, albedo, and illumination from a single image of an unknown object. In: CVPR, pp. 334–341 (2012)
3. Blinn, J.F., Newell, M.E.: Texture and reflection in computer generated images. Comm. ACM 19, 542–547 (1976)
4. Canas, G.D., Vasilyev, Y., Adato, Y., Zickler, T., Gortler, S.J., Ben-Shahar, O.: A linear formulation of shape from specular flow. In: ICCV, pp. 191–198 (2009)
5. Chandraker, M.: What camera motion reveals about shape with unknown BRDF. In: CVPR, pp. 2179–2186 (2014)
6. Chandraker, M., Bai, J., Ramamoorthi, R.: On differential photometric reconstruction for unknown, isotropic BRDFs. PAMI 35(12), 2941–2955 (2013)
7. Chandraker, M., Ramamoorthi, R.: What an image reveals about material reflectance. In: ICCV, pp. 1076–1083 (2011)
8. Chandraker, M., Reddy, D., Wang, Y., Ramamoorthi, R.: What object motion reveals about shape with unknown BRDF and lighting. In: CVPR, pp. 2523–2530 (2013)
9. Chandraker, M.: On joint shape and material recovery from motion cues. Tech. rep., NEC Labs America (2014)
10. Goldman, D.B., Curless, B., Hertzmann, A., Seitz, S.M.: Shape and spatially-varying BRDFs from photometric stereo. PAMI 32(6), 1060–1071 (2010)
11. Horn, B., Schunck, B.: Determining optical flow. Art. Intell. 17, 185–203 (1981)
12. Lawrence, J., Ben-Artzi, A., Decoro, C., Matusik, W., Pfister, H., Ramamoorthi, R., Rusinkiewicz, S.: Inverse shade trees for non-parametric material representation and editing. In: ACM ToG (SIGGRAPH), pp. 735–745 (2006)
13. Lucas, B., Kanade, T.: An iterative image registration technique with an application to stereo vision. In: Image Understanding Workshop, pp. 121–130 (1981)
14. Matusik, W., Pfister, H., Brand, M., McMillan, L.: A data-driven reflectance model. ToG 22(3), 759–769 (2003)
15. Nagel, H.H.: On a constraint equation for the estimation of displacement rates in image sequences. PAMI 11(1), 13–30 (1989)
16. Ngan, A., Durand, F., Matusik, W.: Experimental analysis of BRDF models. In: EGSR, pp. 117–126 (2005)
17. Oxholm, G., Nishino, K.: Shape and reflectance from natural illumination. In: Fitzgibbon, A., Lazebnik, S., Perona, P., Sato, Y., Schmid, C. (eds.) ECCV 2012, Part I. LNCS, vol. 7572, pp. 528–541. Springer, Heidelberg (2012)
18. Romeiro, F., Zickler, T.: Blind reflectometry. In: Daniilidis, K., Maragos, P., Paragios, N. (eds.) ECCV 2010, Part I. LNCS, vol. 6311, pp. 45–58. Springer, Heidelberg (2010)
19. Romeiro, F., Vasilyev, Y., Zickler, T.: Passive reflectometry. In: Forsyth, D., Torr, P., Zisserman, A. (eds.) ECCV 2008, Part IV. LNCS, vol. 5305, pp. 859–872. Springer, Heidelberg (2008)
20. Sato, I., Okabe, T., Yu, Q., Sato, Y.: Shape reconstruction based on similarity in radiance changes under varying illumination. In: ICCV, pp. 1–8 (2007)

21. Seitz, S., Curless, B., Diebel, J., Scharstein, D., Szeliski, R.: A comparison and evaluation of multiview stereo algorithms. In: CVPR, pp. 519–526 (2006)
22. Torrance, K.E., Sparrow, E.M.: Theory for off-specular reflection from roughened surfaces. JOSA 57, 1105–1112 (1967)
23. Verri, A., Poggio, T.: Motion field and optical flow: Qualitative properties. PAMI 11(5), 490–498 (1989)
24. Zhang, L., Curless, B., Hertzmann, A., Seitz, S.: Shape from motion under varying illumination. In: ICCV, pp. 618–625 (2003)
25. Zickler, T., Belhumeur, P., Kriegman, D.: Helmholtz stereopsis: Exploiting reciprocity for surface reconstruction. IJCV 49(2/3), 1215–1227 (2002)

Intrinsic Image Decomposition
Using Structure-Texture Separation
and Surface Normals

Junho Jeon[1], Sunghyun Cho[2,*], Xin Tong[3], and Seungyong Lee[1]

[1] POSTECH
[2] Adobe Research
[3] Microsoft Research Asia

Abstract. While intrinsic image decomposition has been studied extensively during the past a few decades, it is still a challenging problem. This is partly because commonly used constraints on shading and reflectance are often too restrictive to capture an important property of natural images, i.e., rich textures. In this paper, we propose a novel image model for handling textures in intrinsic image decomposition, which enables us to produce high quality results even with simple constraints. We also propose a novel constraint based on surface normals obtained from an RGB-D image. Assuming Lambertian surfaces, we formulate the constraint based on a locally linear embedding framework to promote local and global consistency on the shading layer. We demonstrate that combining the novel texture-aware image model and the novel surface normal based constraint can produce superior results to existing approaches.

Keywords: intrinsic image decomposition, structure-texture separation, RGB-D image.

1 Introduction

Intrinsic image decomposition is a problem to decompose an image I into its shading layer S and reflectance layer R based on the following model:

$$I(p) = S(p) \cdot R(p) \qquad (1)$$

where p is a pixel position. Shading $S(p)$ at p depicts the amount of light reflected at p, and reflectance $R(p)$ depicts the intrinsic color of the material at p, which is invariant to illumination conditions.

Intrinsic image decomposition has been extensively studied in computer vision and graphics communities because it can benefit many computer graphics and vision applications, such as image relighting [1, 2] and material property editing [3]. Since Land and McCann first introduced Retinex algorithm in 1971 [4], various approaches have been introduced for the last a few decades [5–7]. However, intrinsic image decomposition is still challenging because it is a significantly

---

* Sunghyun Cho is now with Samsung Electronics.

D. Fleet et al. (Eds.): ECCV 2014, Part VII, LNCS 8695, pp. 218–233, 2014.

ill-posed problem where there are two unknowns $S(p)$ and $R(p)$ for one observed data $I(p)$ at each pixel p.

To overcome the ill-posedness, previous methods use constraints, or priors, on shading and reflectance. Shading has been often assumed to be locally smooth, while reflectance assumed to be piecewise constant [4]. While these assumptions work well on simple cases such as Mondrian-like images consisting of patches with constant reflectance, they fail on most natural images. One important characteristic of natural images is their rich textures. Such textures may be due to the reflectance layer (e.g., a flat surface with dotted patterns), or the shading layer (e.g., a surface with bumps and wrinkles causing a shading pattern). Thus, enforcing simple constraints on either or both shading or reflectance layers with no consideration on textures may cause erroneous results.

In this paper, we propose a novel intrinsic image decomposition model, which explicitly models a separate texture layer T, in addition to the shading layer S and the reflectance layer R. By explicitly modeling textures, S and R in our model depict only textureless base components. As a result, we can avoid ambiguity caused by textures, and use simple constraints on S and R effectively.

To further constrain the problem, we also propose a novel constraint based on surface normal vectors obtained from an RGB-D image. We assume that illumination changes smoothly, and surfaces are Lambertian, i.e., shading of a surface can be determined as a dot product of a surface normal and the light direction. Based on this assumption, our constraint is designed to promote both *local* and *global* consistency of the shading layer based on a locally linear embedding (LLE) framework [8]. For robustness against noise and efficient computation, we sparsely sample points for the surface normal constraint based on local variances of surface normals. This sparse sampling works effectively thanks to our explicit texture modeling. Our shading and reflectance layers do not have any textures, so information from sampled positions can be effectively propagated to their neighbors during the optimization process.

2 Related Work

2.1 Intrinsic Image Decomposition

Intrinsic image decomposition is a long-standing problem in computer vision. The "Retinex" algorithm was first proposed by Land and McCann in 1971 [4]. The algorithm assumes Mondrian-like images consisting of regions of constant reflectances, where large image gradients are typically caused by reflectance changes, and small gradients are caused by illumination. This algorithm was extended to 2D color images by analyzing derivatives of chromaticity [6].

To overcome the fundamental ill-posedness of the problem, several approaches have been introduced utilizing additional information, such as multiple images [2, 9–11], depth maps [12–14], and user interaction [15]. Lee et al. [12] proposed a method, which takes a sequence of RGB-D video frames acquired from a Kinect camera, and proposed constraints on depth information and temporal consistency. In the setting of single input frame, their temporal constraint cannot be used. Barron and Malik [13] proposed joint estimation of a denoised depth map and spatially-varying illumination. However, due to the lack of proper texture handling, textures which should belong to either shading or reflectance layer may appear in the other layer, as shown in Sec. 6.

Recently, Chen and Koltun [14] showed that high quality decomposition results can be obtained by properly constraining shading components using surface normals without joint estimation of a denoised depth map. Specifically, they find a set of nearest neighbors for each pixel based on their spatial positions and normals, and then constrain the shading component of each pixel to be similar to those of its neighbors. While our surface normal based constraint is similar to theirs, there are three different aspects. First, our constraint is derived from the Lambertian surface assumption, which is more physically meaningful. Second, our constraint uses not only spatially close neighbors but also distant neighbors, so we can obtain more globally consistent results. Third, due to our confidence-based sparse sampling, our method can be more efficient and robust to noise.

Another relevant work to ours is Kwatra et al.'s shadow removal approach for aerial photos [16], which decomposes an aerial image into shadow and texture components. Based on the properties of shadows and textures in aerial images, they define entropy measures for shadows and textures, and minimize them for decomposition. While their work also explicitly considers textures as we do, their work focuses on removal of smooth shadows, such as shadows cast by clouds in aerial images, so it is not suitable for handling complex shadings which are often observed in natural images.

2.2   Texture Separation

Structure-texture separation has also been an important topic and extensively studied. Edge-preserving smoothing has been a popular direction, such as aniso-tropic filtering [17], total variation [18], bilateral filtering [19], nonlocal means filtering [20], weighted least squares filtering [21], and L^0 smoothing [22]. By applying edge-preserving smoothing to an image, small scale textures can be separated from structure components. However, as these approaches rely on local contrasts to distinguish structures and textures, they may fail to properly capture low contrast structures or high contrast textures.

Other approaches have also been proposed to separate textures regardless of their contrasts. Subr et al. [23] estimate envelopes of local minima and maxima, and average the envelopes to capture oscillatory components. Xu et al. [24] proposed a relative total variation measure, which takes account of inherent variation in a local window. Recently, Karacan et al. [25] proposed a simple yet powerful method, which is based on region covariance matrices [26] and nonlocal means filtering [20]. In our work, we adopt Karacan et al.'s approach to separate textures from shading and reflectance components, as it preserves underlying smooth intensity changes.

3   Image Model and Overall Framework

We define a novel model for intrinsic image decomposition as:

$$I(p) = B(p) \cdot T(p) = S_B(p) \cdot R_B(p) \cdot T(p), \tag{2}$$

where $B(p) = S_B(p) \cdot R_B(p)$ is a base layer, and $S_B(p), R_B(p)$ and $T(p)$ are shading, reflectance and texture components at a pixel p, respectively. Note that S_B and R_B are different from S and R in Eq. (1) as S_B and R_B contain no textures. Based on this model, we can safely assume that R_B is a Mondrian-like image, which is piecewise constant. We also assume that illumination changes smoothly across the entire image, thus S_B is also piecewise smooth with no oscillating variations. Under these assumptions, we will define constraints and energy functions in the following sections, which will be used to decompose an image I into S_B, R_B and T.

The overall process of our method, which consists of two steps, can be summarized as follows. In the first step, we decompose an input RGB image I into a base layer B and a texture layer T. In the second step, the base layer B is further decomposed into a reflectance layer R_B and a shading layer S_B based on the surface normal constraint and other simple constraints. While we use simple constraints similar to previous decomposition methods assuming Mondrian-like images, the constraints can work more effectively as our input for decomposition is B, instead of I, from which textures have been removed. In addition, our global constraint based on surface normals promotes overall consistency of the shading layer, which is hard to achieve by previous methods. Experimental results and comparisons in Sec. 6 demonstrate the effectiveness of our method.

4   Decomposition of B and T

In this step, we decompose an input image I into a base layer B and a texture layer T. Texture decomposition has been studied extensively for long time, and several state-of-the-art approaches are available. Among them, we adopt the region covariance based method of Karacan et al. [25], which performs nonlocal means filtering with patch similarity defined using a region covariance descriptor [26]. This method is well-suited for our purpose as it preserves the smoothly varying shading information in the filtering process. We also tested other methods, such as [22, 24], which are based on total variation, but we found that they tend to suppress all small image gradients, including those from shading. Fig. 1 shows that the region covariance based method successfully removes textures on the cushion and the floor while preserving shading on the sofa.

5   Decomposition of S and R

After obtaining B, we decompose it into S_B and R_B by minimizing the following energy function:

$$f(S_B, R_B) = f^N(S_B) + \lambda^P f^P(S_B) + \lambda^R f^R(R_B) \tag{3}$$

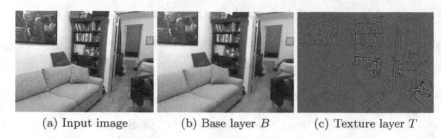

(a) Input image   (b) Base layer B (c) Texture layer T

Fig. 1. Decomposition of B and T

subject to $B(p) = S_B(p) \cdot R_B(p)$. In Eq. (3), $f^N(S_B)$ is a surface normal based constraint on S_B, $f^P(S_B)$ is a local propagation constraint on S_B, and $f^R(R_B)$ is a piecewise constant constraint on R_B. In the following, we will describe each constraint in more detail.

5.1   Surface Normal Based Shading Constraint $f^N(S_B)$

LLE-Based Local Consistency. To derive the surface normal based shading constraint, we first assume that surfaces are Lambertian. On a Lambertian surface, shading S and a surface normal N at p have the following relation:

$$S(p) = i_L \cdot \langle L(p), N(p) \rangle, \tag{4}$$

where i_L is an unknown light intensity, $L(p)$ is the lighting direction vector at p, and $\langle L(p), N(p) \rangle$ is the inner product of $L(p)$ and $N(p)$.

As we assume that illumination changes smoothly, we can also assume that i_L and L are constant in a local window. We can express a surface normal at p as a linear combination of normals at its neighboring pixels $q \in \mathcal{N}_l(p)$, i.e. $N(p) = \sum_{q \in \mathcal{N}_l(p)} w_{pq}^N N(q)$ where w_{pq}^N is a linear combination weight. Then, $S(p)$ can also be expressed as the same linear combination of the neighbors $S(q)$:

$$S(p) = i_L \cdot \left\langle L, \sum_{q \in \mathcal{N}_l(p)} w_{pq}^N N(q) \right\rangle = \sum_{q \in \mathcal{N}_l(p)} w_{pq}^N \left(i_L \cdot \langle L, N(q) \rangle \right) = \sum_{q \in \mathcal{N}_l(p)} w_{pq}^N S(q). \tag{5}$$

Based on this relation, we can define a local consistency constraint $f_l^N(S_B)$ as:

$$f_l^N(S_B) = \sum_{p \in \mathcal{P}_N} \left(S_B(p) - \sum_{q \in \mathcal{N}_l(p)} w_{pq}^N S_B(q) \right)^2, \tag{6}$$

where $\mathcal{P}_N$ is a set of pixels. Note that we could derive this constraint without having to know the value of the light intensity i_L.

Interestingly, Eq. (5) can be interpreted as a LLE representation [8]. LLE is a data representation, which projects a data point from a high dimensional space onto a low dimensional space by representing it as a linear combination of its neighbors in the feature space. Adopting the LLE approach, we can calculate the linear combination weights $\{w_{pq}^N\}$ by solving:

$$\operatorname*{argmin}_{\{w_{pq}^N\}} \sum_{p \in \mathcal{P}_N} \left\| N(p) - \sum_{q \in \mathcal{N}_l(p)} w_{pq}^N N(q) \right\|^2, \tag{7}$$

subject to $\sum_{q \in \mathcal{N}_l(p)} w_{pq}^N = 1$.

To find $\mathcal{N}_l(p)$, we build a 6D vector for each pixel as $[x(p), y(p), z(p), n_x(p),$ $n_y(p), n_z(p)]^T$, where $[x(p), y(p), z(p)]^T$ is the 3D spatial location obtained from the input depth image, and $[n_x(p), n_y(p), n_z(p)]^T$ is the surface normal at p. Then, we find the k-nearest neighbors using the Euclidean distance between the feature vectors at p and other pixels.

Global Consistency. While a locally consistent shading result can be obtained with $f_l^N(S_B)$, the result may be still globally inconsistent. Imagine that we have two flat regions, which are close to each other, but their depths are slightly different. Then, for each pixel in one region, all of its nearest neighbors will be found in the same region, and the two regions may end up with completely different shading values. This phenomenon can be found in Chen and Koltun's results in Fig. 6, as their method promotes only local consistency. In their shading result on the first row, even though the cushion on the sofa should have similar shading to the sofa and the wall, they have totally different shading values.

In order to avoid such global inconsistency, we define another constraint $f_g^N(S_B)$, which promotes global consistency:

$$f_g^N(S_B) = \sum_{p \in \mathcal{P}_N} \left(S_B(p) - \sum_{q \in \mathcal{N}_g(p)} w_{pq}^N S_B(q) \right)^2, \tag{8}$$

where $\mathcal{N}_g(p)$ is a set of global k-nearest neighbors for each pixel p. To find $\mathcal{N}_g(p)$, we simply measure the Euclidean distance between the surface normals at p and other pixels without considering their spatial locations, so that the resulting $\mathcal{N}_g(p)$ can include spatially distant pixels. With the two constraints, we define the constraint $f^N(S_B)$ as:

$$f^N(S_B) = f_l^N(S_B) + \lambda_g^N f_g^N(S_B), \tag{9}$$

where λ_g^N is the relative weight for f_g^N. We set $k = 20$ for both local and global consistency constraints.

Sub-sampling for Efficiency and Noise Handling. It can be time-consuming to find k-nearest neighbors and apply $f^N(S_B)$ for every pixel in an image. Moreover, depth images from commercial RGB-D cameras are often severely noisy as shown in Fig. 2a. We may apply a recent depth map denoising method, but there can still remain significant errors around depth discontinuities causing a noisy normal map (Fig. 2c).

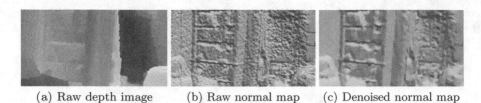

(a) Raw depth image   (b) Raw normal map   (c) Denoised normal map

Fig. 2. Depth images from commercial RGB-D cameras often suffer from severe noise, which is difficult to remove using a denoising method

To improve the efficiency and avoid noisy normals, we propose a sub-sampling based strategy for building $\mathcal{P}_N$. Specifically, we divide an image into a uniform grid. In each grid cell, we measure the variance of the surface normals in a local window centered at each pixel. Then, we choose a pixel with the smallest variance. This is because complex scene geometry is more likely to cause severe depth noise, so we would better choose points in a smooth region with low variance. We also find the nearest neighbors for $\mathcal{N}_l(p)$ and $\mathcal{N}_g(p)$ from $\mathcal{P}_N$ to avoid noisy normals and accelerate the nearest neighbor search. While we use the constraint $f^N(S_B)$ only for sub-sampled pixel positions, information on the sampled positions can be propagated to neighboring pixels during the optimization due to the constraint $f^P(S_B)$, which is described next.

5.2 Local Propagation Constraint $f^P(S_B)$

Since we use subsampled pixel positions for the constraint $f^N(S_B)$, other pixels do not have any shading constraint. To properly constrain such pixels, we propagate the effects of $f^N(S_B)$ to neighboring pixels using two local smoothness constraints on shading. Specifically, we define $f^P(S_B)$ as:

$$f^P(S_B) = f^P_{lap}(S_B) + \lambda^P_N f^P_N(S_B), \tag{10}$$

where $f^P_{lap}(S_B)$ is based on the structure of the base layer B, and $f^P_N(S_B)$ is based on surface normals.

Since all the textures are already separated out to T and we assume that R_B is piecewise constant, we can safely assume that small image derivatives in B are from the shading layer S_B. Then, S_B can be approximated in a small local window as:

$$S_B(p) \approx aB(p) + b, \tag{11}$$

where $a = \frac{1}{B_f - B_b}$ and $b = \frac{-B_b}{B_f - B_b}$, and B_f and B_b are two primary colors in the window. This approximation inspires us to use the matting Laplacian [27] to propagate information from the sub-sampled pixels to their neighbors in a structure-aware manner. Specifically, we define the first constraint for propagation using the matting Laplacian as follows:

$$f^P_{lap}(S_B) = \sum_k \sum_{(i,j) \in \omega_k} w^{lap}_{ij}(S_B(i) - S_B(j))^2, \tag{12}$$

where ω_k is the k-th local window. w_{ij}^{lap} is the (i, j)-th matting Laplacian element, which is computed as:

$$w_{ij}^{lap} = \sum_{k|(i,j)\in\omega_k} \left\{ \delta_{ij} - \frac{1}{|\omega_k|} \left(1 + \left(B(i) - \mu_k^B \right) \left(\Sigma_k^B + \frac{\epsilon}{|\omega_k|} I_3 \right)^{-1} \left(B(j) - \mu_k^B \right) \right) \right\}, \tag{13}$$

where ϵ is a regularizing parameter, and $|\omega_k|$ is the number of pixels in the window ω_k. δ_{ij} is Kronecker delta. μ_k^B and Σ_k^B are the mean vector and covariance matrix of B in ω_k, respectively. I_3 is a 3×3-identity matrix.

This constraint is based on the key advantage of removing textures from the input image. With the original image I, because of textures, information at sample points cannot be propagated properly while being blocked by edges introduced by textures. In contrast, by removing textures from the image, we can effectively propagate shading information using the structure of the base image B, obtaining higher quality shading results.

The second local smoothness constraint $f_N^P(S_B)$ is based on surface normals. Even if surface normals are noisy, they still provide meaningful geometry information for smooth surfaces. Thus, we formulate a constraint to promote local smoothness based on the differences between adjacent surface normals as follows:

$$f_N^P(S_B) = \sum_{p\in\mathcal{P}} \sum_{q\in\mathcal{N}(p)} w_{pq}^N \left(S_B(p) - S_B(q) \right)^2, \tag{14}$$

where $\mathcal{P}$ is a set of all pixels in the image and $\mathcal{N}(p)$ is the set of 8-neighbors of p. w_{pq}^N is a continuous weight, which is defined using the angular distance between normal vectors at p and q:

$$w_{pq}^N = \exp\left(-\frac{1 - \langle N(p), N(q) \rangle^2}{\sigma_n^2} \right), \tag{15}$$

where we set $\sigma_n = 0.5$. w_{pq}^N becomes close to 1 if the normals $N(p)$ and $N(q)$ are similar to each other, and becomes small if they are different.

Fig. 3 shows the effect of the constraint $f^P(S_B)$. The local propagation constraint enables shading information obtained from the LLE-based constraints to be propagated to other pixels, which results in clear shading near edges.

5.3   Reflectance Constraint $f^R(R_B)$

The constraint $f^R(R_B)$ is based on a simple assumption, which is used by many Retinex-based approaches [6, 12, 28, 29]: if two neighboring pixels have the same chromaticity, their reflectance should be the same as well. Based on this assumption, previous methods often use a constraint defined as:

$$f^R(R_B) = \sum_{p\in\mathcal{P}} \sum_{q\in\mathcal{N}(p)} w_{pq}^R \left(R_B(p) - R_B(q) \right)^2. \tag{16}$$

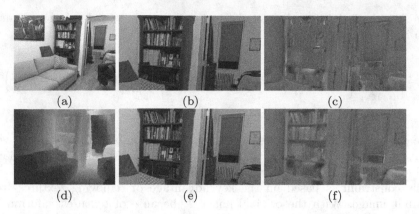

(a)   (b)   (c)

(d)   (e)   (f)

Fig. 3. Effect of the local propagation constraint $f^P(S_B)$. (a,d) Input RGB and depth images. (b-c) Reflectance and shading results without $f^P(S_B)$. (e-f) Reflectance and shading results with $f^P(S_B)$. Without the constraint, shading of pixels which have not been sampled for normal based constraint $f^N(S_B)$ are solely determined by the reflectance constraint through the optimization process. As a result, (c) shows artifacts on the bookshelves due to the inaccurate reflectance values.

The weighting function w_{pq}^R is a positive constant if the difference between the chromaticity at p and q is smaller than a certain threshold, and zero otherwise. For this constraint, it is critical to use a good threshold, but finding a good threshold is non-trivial and can be time consuming [29].

Instead of using a threshold, we use a continuous weight $w_{pq}^{R'}$, which involves chromaticity difference between two pixels p and q in the form of angular distance between two directional vectors:

$$w_{pq}^{R'} = \exp\left(-\frac{1 - \langle C(p), C(q)\rangle^2}{\sigma_c^2}\right)\left\{1 + \exp\left(-\frac{B(p)^2 + B(q)^2}{\sigma_i^2}\right)\right\}, \quad (17)$$

where chromaticity $C(p) = B(p)/|B(p)|$ is a normalized 3D vector consisting of RGB color channels. We set $\sigma_c^2 = 0.0001, \sigma_i^2 = 0.8$. The first exponential term measures similarity between $C(p)$ and $C(q)$ using their angular distance. The term becomes 1 if $C(p) = C(q)$ and becomes close to 0 if $C(p)$ and $C(q)$ are different from each other, so that consistency between neighboring pixels can be promoted only when $C(p)$ and $C(q)$ are close to each other. The second exponential term is a darkness weight. Due to the nature of imaging sensors, dark pixels suffer from noise more than bright pixels, causing severe chromaticity noise in dark regions such as shadows (Fig. 4). Thus, the second term gives larger weights to dark pixels to overcome such chromaticity noise. Using the weight $w_{pq}^{R'}$, our constraint $f^R(R_B)$ is defined as:

$$f^R(R_B) = \sum_{p \in \mathcal{P}} \sum_{q \in \mathcal{N}(p)} w_{pq}^{R'} (R_B(p) - R_B(q))^2. \quad (18)$$

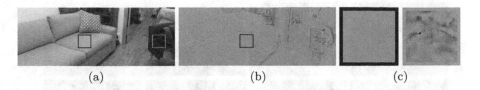

(a)   (b)   (c)

Fig. 4. Comparison of chromaticity noise between a bright region (black box) and a dark region (green box). (a) Input image. (b) Chromaticity of the input image. (c) Magnified views of two regions.

5.4 Optimization

To simplify the optimization, we take the logarithm to our model as done in [29, 12, 14]. Then, we get $\log B(p) = s_B(p) + r_B(p)$ where $s_B(p) = \log S_B(p)$ and $r_B(p) = \log R_B(p)$. We empirically found that proposed constraints could also represent the similarities between pixels in the logarithmic domain, even for the LLE weights. Thus, we approximate the original energy function (Eq. (3)) as:

$$f(s_B) = f^N(s_B) + \lambda^P f^P(s_B) + \lambda^R f^R(\log B(p) - s_B(p)). \qquad (19)$$

As all the constraints f^N, f^P, and f^R are quadratic functions, Eq. (19) is a quadratic function of s_B. We minimize Eq. (19) using a conjugate gradient method. We used $\lambda^P = \lambda^R = 4, \lambda_g^N = 1$, and $\lambda_N^P = 0.00625$.

6 Results

For evaluation, we implemented our method using Matlab, and used the structure-texture separation code of the authors [25] for decomposition of B and T. For a 624×468 image, decomposition of B and T takes about 210 seconds, and decomposition of S and R takes about 150 seconds on a PC with Intel Core i7 2.67GHz CPU, 12GB RAM, and Microsoft Windows 7 64bit OS.

For evaluation, we selected 14 images from the NYU dataset [30], which provides 1,400 RGB-D images. When selecting images, we avoided images which do not fit our Lambertian surface assumption, e.g., images with glossy surfaces such as a mirror or a glass. Fig. 5 shows some of the selected images. For other images and their corresponding results, we refer the readers to our supplementary material. It is worth mentioning that, while Chen and Koltun [14] used the synthetic dataset of [31] to quantitatively evaluate their approach, in our evaluation, we did not include such quantitative evaluation. This is because the synthetic dataset of [31] was not generated for the purpose of intrinsic image decomposition benchmark, so its ground truth reflectance and shading images are not physically correct in many cases, such as shading of messy hairs and global illumination.

In our image model $I(p) = S_B(p) \cdot R_B(p) \cdot T(p)$, texture T can contain not only reflectance textures, but also shading textures caused by subtle and complex geometry changes, which are often not captured in a noisy depth map. In this

Fig. 5. Test images from the NYU dataset [30]

paper, we do not further decompose T into reflectance and shading textures. Instead, for visualization and comparison, we consider T as a part of the reflectance layer R, i.e., $R(p) = R_B(p) \cdot T(p)$ and $S(p) = S_B(p)$. That is, every reflectance result in this paper is the product of the base reflectance layer R_B and the texture layer T.

We evaluated our method using qualitative comparisons with other methods. Fig. 6 shows results of three other methods and ours. The conventional color Retinex algorithm [32] takes a single RGB image as an input. This method highly depends on its reflectance smoothness constraint, which can be easily discouraged by rich textures. Thus, its shading results contain a significant amount of textures, which should be in the reflectance layers (e.g., patterned cushion in the sofa scene).

Barron and Malik [13] jointly estimate a refined depth map and spatially varying illumination, and obtain a shading image from that information. Thus, their shading results in Fig. 6 do not contain any textures on them. However, their shading results are over-smoothed on object boundaries because of their incorrect depth refinement (e.g., the chair and bucket in the desk scene).

The results of Chen and Koltun [14] show more reliable shading results than [32, 13], even though they do not use any explicit modeling for textures. This is because of their effective shading constraints based on depth cues. However, as mentioned in Sec. 2, due to the lack of global consistency constraints, their shading results often suffer from the global inconsistency problem (e.g., the chair in the kitchen scene). On the contrary, our method produces well-decomposed textures (e.g., cushion in the sofa scene) and globally consistent shading (e.g., the chair and the bucket in the desk scene) compared to the other three methods.

To show the effect of our texture filtering step, we also tested our algorithm without texture filtering (Fig. 7). Thanks to our non-local shading constraints, the shading results are still globally consistent (Fig. 7b). However, the input image without texture filtering breaks the Mondrian-like image assumption, so lots of reflectance textures remain in the shading result. This experiment shows that our method fully exploits properties of the texture filtered base image, such as piecewise-constant reflectance and texture-free structure information.

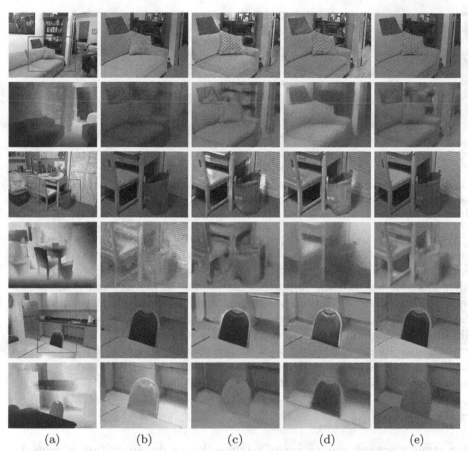

(a)   (b)   (c)   (d)   (e)

Fig. 6. Decomposition result comparison with other methods. (a) Input. (b) Retinex [32]. (c) Barron and Malik [13]. (d) Chen and Koltun [14]. (e) Ours.

(a)   (b)   (c)

Fig. 7. Decomposition results without and with the texture filtering step. (a) Input image. (b) Reflectance and shading results without texture filtering step. (c) Reflectance and shading results with texture filtering step.

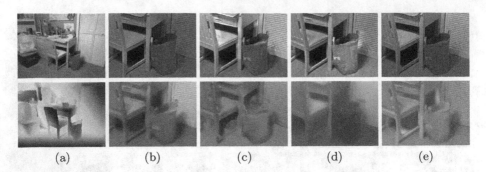

| (a) | (b) | (c) | (d) | (e) |

Fig. 8. Decomposition results of other methods using a texture-filtered input. (a) Input base image. (b) Retinex [32]. (c) Barron and Malik [13]. (d) Chen and Koltun [14]. (e) Ours.

We also conducted another experiment to clarify the effectiveness of our decomposition step. This time, we fed texture-filtered images to previous methods as their inputs. Fig. 8 shows texture filtering provides some improvements to other methods too, but the improvements are not as big as ours. Retinex [32] benefited from texture filtering, but the method has no shading constraints and the result still shows globally inconsistent shading (the bucket and the closet). Big improvements did not happen with recent approaches [13, 14] either. [13] strongly uses its smooth shape prior, which causes over-smoothed shapes and shading in regions with complex geometry. In the result of [14], globally inconsistent shading still remains due to the lack of global consistency constraints.

7   Applications

One straightforward application of intrinsic image decomposition is material property editing such as texture composition. Composing textures into an image naturally is tricky, because it requires careful consideration of spatially varying illumination. If illumination changes such as shadows are not properly handled, composition results may look too flat and artificial (Fig. 9b). Instead, we can first decompose an image into shading and reflectance layers, and compose new textures into the reflectance layer. Then, by recombining the shading and reflectance layers, we can obtain a more naturally-looking result (Fig. 9c).

| (a) Original image | (b) Naive copy & paste | (c) Our method |

Fig. 9. Texture composition

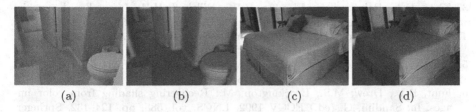

| (a) | (b) | (c) | (d) |

Fig. 10. Image relighting. (a, c) Original images. (b, d) Relighted images.

Another application is image relighting (Fig. 10). Given an RGB-D input image, we can generate a new shading layer using the geometry information obtained from the depth information. Then, by combining the new shading layer with the reflectance layer of the input image, we can produce a relighted image.

8 Conclusions

Although intrinsic image decomposition has been extensively studied in computer vision and graphics, the progress has been limited by the nature of natural images, especially rich textures. In this work, we proposed a novel image model, which explicitly models textures for intrinsic image decomposition. With explicit texture modeling, we can avoid confusion on the smoothness property caused by textures and can use simple constraints on shading and reflectance components. To further constrain the decomposition problem, we additionally proposed a novel constraint based on surface normals obtained from an RGB-D image. Assuming Lambertian surfaces, we formulated our surface normal based constraints using a LLE framework [8] in order to promote both local and global consistency of shading components.

In our experiments, we assumed textures to be a part of reflectance for the purpose of comparison with other methods. However, textures may be caused by either or both of reflectance and shading, as we mentioned in Introduction. As future work, we plan to further decompose textures into reflectance and shading texture layers using additional information such as surface geometry.

Acknowledgements. We would like to thank the anonymous reviewers for their constructive comments. This work was supported in part by IT/SW Creative Research Program of NIPA (2013-H0503-13-1013).

References

1. Yu, Y., Malik, J.: Recovering photometric properties of architectural scenes from photographs. In: Proc. of SIGGRAPH, pp. 207–217. ACM (1998)
2. Laffont, P.Y., Bousseau, A., Paris, S., Durand, F., Drettakis, G., et al.: Coherent intrinsic images from photo collections. ACM Transactions on Graphics 31(6) (2012)

3. Khan, E.A., Reinhard, E., Fleming, R.W., Bülthoff, H.H.: Image-based material editing. ACM Transactions on Graphics 25(3), 654–663 (2006)
4. Land, E.H., McCann, J.J.: Lightness and retinex theory. Journal of the Optical Society of America 61(1) (1971)
5. Barrow, H.G., Tenenbaum, J.M.: Recovering intrinsic scene characteristics from images. Computer Vision Systems (1978)
6. Funt, B.V., Drew, M.S., Brockington, M.: Recovering shading from color images. In: Sandini, G. (ed.) ECCV 1992. LNCS, vol. 588, pp. 124–132. Springer, Heidelberg (1992)
7. Kimmel, R., Elad, M., Shaked, D., Keshet, R., Sobel, I.: A variational framework for retinex. International Journal of Computer Vision 52, 7–23 (2003)
8. Roweis, S.T., Saul, L.K.: Nonlinear dimensionality reduction by locally linear embedding. Science 290(5500), 2323–2326 (2000)
9. Weiss, Y.: Deriving intrinsic images from image sequences. In: Proc. of ICCV (2001)
10. Matsushita, Y., Lin, S., Kang, S.B., Shum, H.-Y.: Estimating intrinsic images from image sequences with biased illumination. In: Pajdla, T., Matas, J(G.) (eds.) ECCV 2004, Part II. LNCS, vol. 3022, pp. 274–286. Springer, Heidelberg (2004)
11. Laffont, P.Y., Bousseau, A., Drettakis, G.: Rich intrinsic image decomposition of outdoor scenes from multiple views. IEEE Transactions on Visualization and Computer Graphics 19(2) (2013)
12. Lee, K.J., Zhao, Q., Tong, X., Gong, M., Izadi, S., Lee, S.U., Tan, P., Lin, S.: Estimation of intrinsic image sequences from image+depth video. In: Fitzgibbon, A., Lazebnik, S., Perona, P., Sato, Y., Schmid, C. (eds.) ECCV 2012, Part VI. LNCS, vol. 7577, pp. 327–340. Springer, Heidelberg (2012)
13. Barron, J.T., Malik, J.: Intrinsic scene properties from a single RGB-D image. In: Proc. of CVPR (2013)
14. Chen, Q., Koltun, V.: A simple model for intrinsic image decomposition with depth cues. In: Proc. of ICCV (2013)
15. Bousseau, A., Paris, S., Durand, F.: User-assisted intrinsic images. ACM Transactions on Graphics 28(5) (2009)
16. Kwatra, V., Han, M., Dai, S.: Shadow removal for aerial imagery by information theoretic intrinsic image analysis. In: International Conference on Computational Photography (2012)
17. Perona, P., Malik, J.: Scale-space and edge detection using anisotropic diffusion. IEEE Transactions on Pattern Analysis and Machine Intelligence 12(7), 629–639 (1990)
18. Rudin, L., Osher, S., Fatemi, E.: Nonlinear total variation based noise removal algorithms. Physica D 60(1-4), 259–268 (1992)
19. Tomasi, C., Manduchi, R.: Bilateral filtering for gray and color images. In: Proc. of ICCV (1998)
20. Buades, A., Coll, B., Morel, J.M.: A non-local algorithm for image denoising. In: Proc. of CVPR (2005)
21. Farbman, Z., Fattal, R., Lischinski, D., Szeliski, R.: Edge-preserving decompositions for multi-scale tone and detail manipulation. ACM Transactions on Graphics 27(3), 67:1–67:10 (2008)
22. Xu, L., Lu, C., Xu, Y., Jia, J.: Image smoothing via L0 gradient minimization. ACM Transactions on Graphics 30(6), 174:1–174:12 (2011)
23. Subr, K., Soler, C., Durand, F.: Edge-preserving multiscale image decomposition based on local extrema. ACM Transactions on Graphics 28(5), 147:1–147:9 (2009)
24. Xu, L., Yan, Q., Xia, Y., Jia, J.: Structure extraction from texture via relative total variation. ACM Transactions on Graphics 31(6), 139:1–139:10 (2012)

25. Karacan, L., Erdem, E., Erdem, A.: Structure-preserving image smoothing via region covariances. ACM Transactions on Graphics 32(6), 176:1–176:11 (2013)
26. Tuzel, O., Porikli, F., Meer, P.: Region covariance: A fast descriptor for detection and classification. In: Leonardis, A., Bischof, H., Pinz, A. (eds.) ECCV 2006. LNCS, vol. 3952, pp. 589–600. Springer, Heidelberg (2006)
27. Levin, A., Lischinski, D., Weiss, Y.: A closed-form solution to natural image matting. IEEE Transactions on Pattern Analysis and Machine Intelligence 30(2), 228–242 (2008)
28. Shen, L., Yeo, C.: Intrinsic images decomposition using a local and global sparse representation of reflectance. In: Proc. of CVPR (2011)
29. Zhao, Q., Tan, P., Dai, Q., Shen, L., Wu, E., Lin, S.: A closed-form solution to retinex with nonlocal texture constraints. IEEE Transactions on Pattern Analysis and Machine Intelligence 34(7) (2012)
30. Silberman, N., Hoiem, D., Kohli, P., Fergus, R.: Indoor segmentation and support inference from RGBD images. In: Fitzgibbon, A., Lazebnik, S., Perona, P., Sato, Y., Schmid, C. (eds.) ECCV 2012, Part V. LNCS, vol. 7576, pp. 746–760. Springer, Heidelberg (2012)
31. Butler, D.J., Wulff, J., Stanley, G.B., Black, M.J.: A naturalistic open source movie for optical flow evaluation. In: Fitzgibbon, A., Lazebnik, S., Perona, P., Sato, Y., Schmid, C. (eds.) ECCV 2012, Part VI. LNCS, vol. 7577, pp. 611–625. Springer, Heidelberg (2012)
32. Grosse, R., Johnson, M.K., Adelson, E.H., Freeman, W.T.: Ground truth dataset and baseline evaluations for intrinsic image algorithms. In: Proc. of ICCV (2009)

Multi-level Adaptive Active Learning for Scene Classification

Xin Li and Yuhong Guo

Department of Computer and Information Sciences
Temple University
Philadelphia, PA 19122, USA
{xinli,yuhong}@temple.edu

Abstract. Semantic scene classification is a challenging problem in computer vision. In this paper, we present a novel multi-level active learning approach to reduce the human annotation effort for training robust scene classification models. Different from most existing active learning methods that can only query labels for selected instances at the target categorization level, i.e., the scene class level, our approach establishes a semantic framework that predicts scene labels based on a latent object-based semantic representation of images, and is capable to query labels at two different levels, the target scene class level (abstractive high level) and the latent object class level (semantic middle level). Specifically, we develop an adaptive active learning strategy to perform multi-level label query, which maintains the default label query at the target scene class level, but switches to the latent object class level whenever an "unexpected" target class label is returned by the labeler. We conduct experiments on two standard scene classification datasets to investigate the efficacy of the proposed approach. Our empirical results show the proposed adaptive multi-level active learning approach can outperform both baseline active learning methods and a state-of-the-art multi-level active learning method.

Keywords: Active Learning, Scene Classification.

1 Introduction

Scene classification remains one of the most challenging problems in computer vision field. Different from the classification tasks in other fields such as NLP, where the meanings of features (e.g., words) are perceivable by human beings, the low-level features of an image are primarily built on some signal responses or statistic information of mathematical transformations. Though these low-level features are useful and powerful as proved by numerous works for decades, the *semantic gap* between the semantically non-meaningful low-level features and the high-level abstractive scene labels becomes a bottleneck for further improving scene classification performance. Recent advances on scene classification [24, 19] and other related tasks such as semantic segmentation [29, 3, 12] and object detection/recognition [32, 11, 5] have demonstrated the importance of exploiting

D. Fleet et al. (Eds.): ECCV 2014, Part VII, LNCS 8695, pp. 234–249, 2014.

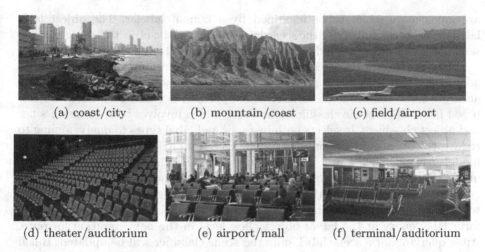

(a) coast/city   (b) mountain/coast   (c) field/airport

(d) theater/auditorium   (e) airport/mall   (f) terminal/auditorium

Fig. 1. Examples of ambiguous scene categories. *(a)-(c)* are confusing examples of outdoor scenes and *(d)-(e)* are examples of indoor scenes.

semantic information and extracting high-level scene label structures, where a scene label (e.g., coast) can be viewed as a semantic concept comprising of a set of important high level visual objects (e.g., sky, sand and sea). The work in [14] particularly demonstrated the strength of predicting scene labels based on the high-level object-based representations of images. However, this work requires supervised training of object detectors, which can significantly increase the demand for human annotation effort. Moreover, to produce a good scene classification model, a sufficient amount of target scene labels need to be acquired as well, which induces expensive human annotation cost. In this work, we address the important problem of reducing human annotation effort for learning scene classification models.

Active learning is a well studied technique for reducing the cost of manual annotations by performing selective instance sampling. In contrast to "passive" learning where the learner uses randomly generated labeled instances, "active" learners iteratively select the most informative instances to label in an interactive learning process [25]. Traditional active learners query labels for the selected instance at the target prediction label level, which however is not the best strategy in many cases of scene classification tasks. Scene labels are highly abstractive and semantic labels. Without accurately identifying their high level object-based semantic representations, some scene labels can be very difficult to be distinguished from each other even by a human labeler in many scenarios. For example, it is hard to tell for a human labeler whether the image in Figure 1(b) is indeed a mountain scene or a coast scene; similarly, it is hard to tell whether the image in Figure 1(e) is the seating area of a mall or an airport terminal. From Figure 1 we can see that such ambiguities exist not only among outdoor scenes but also in indoor scenes. However, the objects contained in these images are much more easier to be identified by a human labeler. The object level labels may successfully infer the scene labels based on the object-based statistical semantic scene structure induced from the labeled data.

Based on these observations, in this paper we develop a novel multi-level adaptive active learning approach to reduce the annotation effort of learning accurate scene classification models. This approach is based on a latent object-based hierarchical scene classification model, which involves both scene classifier and object classifiers. It selects both instance and label types to query, aiming to reduce the overall prediction uncertainty of the multi-class scene classification model over all labeled and unlabeled instances. By default, it performs label query at the target scene class level and selects instance based on a maximum conditional mutual information criterion. But whenever an "unexpected" target scene label is returned by the labeler in a given iteration, it will switch to perform label query at the latent object class level in the next iteration for once. After querying for a scene label, only the scene classifier will be updated. But if an object label is queried, both object and scene classifiers will be updated. We conduct experiments on two standard scene classification datasets to investigate the efficacy of the proposed approach. Our empirical results show the proposed adaptive multi-level active learning approach can outperform a few baseline active learning methods and a state-of-the-art multi-level active learning method.

2 Related Work

In this section, we present a brief review over the related scene classification and active learning works developed in computer vision field.

Scene classification has long gained its popularity in the literature. Previous works on scene classification can be categorized into two main groups: data representation centered methods and classification model centered methods. In the first group, mid-level representations built from low-level features such as SIFT [17] or HOG [2] features have been exploited for scene classification. For example, [4] introduces a bag-of-words (BoW) model based on low-level features to represent a natural scene image. [13] proposes a spatial pyramid matching model to further improve the BoW model by taking the spatial relationship between the visual words into account. [33] proposes a novel holistic image descriptor for scene classification. More recent efforts have centered on representing a scene with semantically meaningful information rather than statistic information of low-level hand-designed features. [24] proposes an image representation based on discriminative scene regions detected using a latent SVM model. [14] proposes an object-centered approach called object bank, where each image is represented as the response map to a large number of pre-trained generic object detectors. Our classification model shares similarity with this work on using the presence of objects as attributes for scene classification. However, the object bank method requires supervised training of a large number of object detectors which is extremely expensive in terms of annotation cost, while the object classifiers in our model are learned on the fly in a semi-supervise manner and require very limited annotations. Moreover, the object detectors of the object bank model take the whole image as input, while our object classifiers pursue patch-based training. Another work [22] also proposes an attribute based scene representation which contains binary attributes to describe the intra- and inter-class scene variations. But similar to the object bank method, their attribute learning is quite expensive and they predict the presence of attributes using the sliding window technique which further increases the computational cost.

For methods centered on classification model development, we would like to mention a few works with widely used techniques [19, 23, 20]. In [19], a deformable part-based model (DPM) has been applied to address scene categorization. [23] proposes a prototype based model for indoor scenes that captures the characteristic arrangements of scene components. [20] proposes a latent structural SVM for the reconfigurable version of a spatial bag of words model. These methods also demonstrate the usefulness of exploiting mid-level representations for scene classification. Nevertheless, all these methods are passive learning methods and require a large number of labeled instances for training.

Active learning methods have been widely used in computer vision field to reduce human labeling efforts in image and video annotation [10, 34], retrieval [31], recognition [7–9] and segmentation [29]. These active learning methods iteratively select the most informative instance to annotate according to a given instance selection criterion. Recently, some researchers have observed that exploiting single criterion for instance selection lacks the capacity of handling different active learning scenarios, and an adaptive active learning strategy that integrates strengths of different instance selection criteria has been proposed in [15]. Nevertheless, all these active learning methods are limited to querying labels in the target prediction label space, and lack sufficient capacity of handling the highly semantic scene classification problems and exploiting advanced scene classification models, especially when the scene images are ambiguous to categorize as demonstrated in Figure 1. Our proposed active learning approach will address the limitation of these current methods by exploiting a latent object-based scene classification model and performing multi-level adaptive label querying at both the scene class level and the object class level.

There are a number of existing active learning methods that query the labelers for information beyond the target image labels. For example, [18] considers attributed based prediction models and asks users for inputs on the attribute level to improve the class predictions, while assuming fixed attribute configurations for each give image class label. [30] treats the overall object classification problem as a multi-instance learning problem and considers the same type of labels at two levels, instance level (segments) and bag level (images). These works [18, 30] nevertheless are still limited to exploiting the same type of standard queries, while another few works [1, 21, 27, 11] have exploited semantic or multiple types of queries. [1, 21] introduces a new interactive learning paradigm that allows the supervisor to additionally convey useful domain knowledge using *relative* attributes. [27] presents an active learning framework to simultaneously learn appearance and contextual models for scene understanding. It explores three different types of questions: regional labeling questions, linguistic questions and contextual questions. However, it does not handle scene classification problems but evaluate the approach regarding the region labels. [11] presents an active learning approach that selects image annotation requests among both object category labels and the object-based attribute labels. It shares similarity with our proposed approach in querying at multi-levels of label spaces, but it treats image labels and attribute labels in the same way and involves expensive computations. Nevertheless, these active learning works tackle object recognition problems using pre-fixed selection criteria. Our proposed approach on the other hand uses an adaptive multi-level active learning strategy to optimize a latent object-based hierarchical scene classification model.

3   Proposed Method

In this section, we first establish the hierarchical semantic scene classification model based on latent object level representations in Section 3.1 and then present our multi-level adaptive active learning method in Section 3.2.

3.1   Hierarchical Scene Classification Model

Learning mid-level representations that capture semantic meanings has been shown to be incredibly useful for computer vision tasks such as scene classification and object recognition. In this work, we treat object category values as high level scene attributes, and use a hierarchical model for scene classification that has a mid-level object representation layer. The work flow of our approach has four stages: Firstly, we preprocess each image into a bag of patches and a bag of low-level feature vectors can be produced from the patches. For the sake of computational efficiency, we only used aligned non-overlapping patches. We expect each patch presents information at the local object level. Secondly, we perform unsupervised clustering over the patches using a clustering method K-Medoids and then assign an object *class name* to each patch cluster by querying the object level labels for the center patch in each cluster. Thirdly, we train a set of binary object classifiers based on these named clusters of patches using the one-vs-all scheme. Then for each image, its mid-level object-based representation can be obtained by applying these object classifiers over its patches. That is, each image will be represented as a binary indicator vector, where each entry of the vector indicates the presence or absence of the corresponding object category in the image. Figure 2 presents examples of this mid-level object-based representation of images. Finally, a multi-class scene classifier is trained based on the mid-level representation of labeled images. To further improve the scene classifier, we have also considered using hybrid features to train the scene classifier. That is, we train the scene classifier based on both the mid-level representation features and the low-level features of the labeled images. This turns out to be more robust for scene classification than using the mid-level representation alone. More details will be discussed in the experimental section.

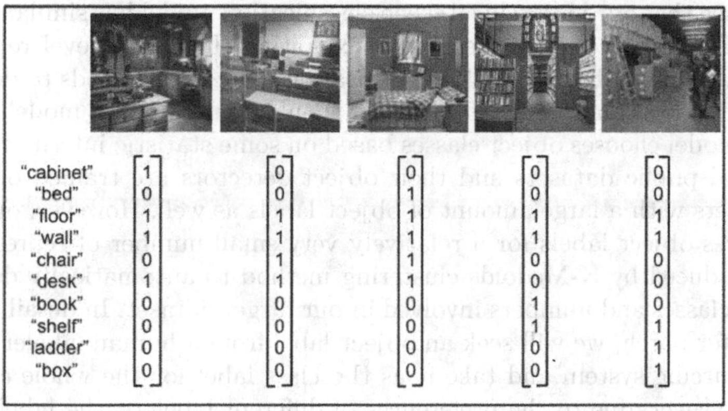

"cabinet"	1	0	0	0	0
"bed"	0	0	1	0	0
"floor"	1	1	1	1	1
"wall"	1	1	1	1	1
"chair"	0	1	1	0	0
"desk"	1	1	1	0	0
"book"	0	0	0	1	0
"shelf"	0	0	0	1	1
"ladder"	0	0	0	0	1
"box"	0	0	0	0	1

Fig. 2. Examples of the mid-level semantic representation employed in our scene classification model. Each 1 value indicates the presence of an object and each 0 value indicates the absence of an object in a given image.

Our system uses logistic regression as the classification model at both object and scene levels. Given the patch *labels* produced by clustering, for each object class, we have a set of binary labeled patches $\{(\tilde{\mathbf{x}}_i, \tilde{z}_i)\}_{i=1}^{N_o}$ with $\tilde{z}_i \in \{+1, -1\}$. We then train a probabilistic binary logistic regression classifier for each object class to optimize a ℓ_2-norm regularized log-likelihood function

$$\min_{\mathbf{u}} \quad -C \sum_{i=1}^{N_o} \log P(\tilde{z}_i | \tilde{\mathbf{x}}_i) + \frac{1}{2} \mathbf{u}^T \mathbf{u} \tag{1}$$

where

$$P(\tilde{z}_i | \tilde{\mathbf{x}}_i) = \frac{1}{1 + \exp(-\tilde{z}_i \tilde{\mathbf{x}}_i^T \mathbf{u})} \tag{2}$$

For scene classification, given the labeled data $\mathcal{L} = \{(\mathbf{z}_i, y_i)\}_{i=1}^{N}$, where $\mathbf{z}_i$ is the mid-level indicator representation vector for the i-th image $\mathcal{I}_i$, and y_i is its scene class label, we train a multinomial logistic regression model as the scene classifier. Specifically, we perform training by minimizing a ℓ_2-norm regularized negative log-likelihood function

$$\min_{\mathbf{w}} \quad -C \sum_{i=1}^{N} \log P(y_i | \mathbf{z}_i) + \frac{1}{2} \mathbf{w}^T \mathbf{w} \tag{3}$$

where

$$P(y_i = c | \mathbf{z}_i) = \frac{\exp(\mathbf{z}_i^T \mathbf{w}_c)}{\sum_{c'} \exp(\mathbf{z}_i^T \mathbf{w}_{c'})} \tag{4}$$

The minimization problems in both (1) and (3) above are convex optimization problems, and we employ the trust region newton method developed in [16] to perform training.

We can see that our hierarchical scene classification model has similar capacity with the object bank method regarding exploiting the object-level representations of images. For object-based representation models, one needs to determine what object classes and how many of them should be used in the model. The object bank model chooses object classes based on some statistic information drew from several public datasets and their object detectors are trained on several large datasets with a large amount of object labels as well. However, our model only requires object labels for a relatively very small number of representative patches produced by K-Medoids clustering method to automatically determine the object classes and numbers involved in our target dataset. In detail, for each cluster center patch, we will seek an object label from a human labeler through a crowd-sourcing system and take it as the class label for the whole cluster of patches. However, due to the preferences of different labelers, the labels can be provided at different granularity levels, e.g., "kid" vs "sitting kid". Moreover, typos may exist in the given labels, e.g., "groound" vs "ground". We thus apply some word processing technique [28] on the collected object labels. When the given label is a phrase, we will not process it as a new category if one of its component words is already a category keyword. Hence "sitting kid" will not be taken as a category if "kid" is already one. After object labels being purified, we merge the clusters with the same object labels and produce the final object classes and number for the given data. In our experiments, the numbers of object classes resulted range from 20 to 50, which fits into the principle of Zipf's Law and implies that a small proportion of object classes account for the majority of object occurrences.

3.2   Multi-level Adaptive Active Learning

Let $\mathbf{z}_i$ denote the mid-level feature vector for image $\mathcal{I}_i$, $Y = \{1 \dots K_y\}$ denote the scene class label space, $\mathcal{L} = \{(\mathbf{z}_1, y_1), \dots, (\mathbf{z}_N, y_N)\}$ denote the set of labeled instances, and $\mathcal{U}$ denote the large pool of unlabeled instances. After initializing our training model based on the small number of labeled instances, we perform multi-level active learning in an iterative fashion, which involves two types of iterations, *scene level iterations* and *object level iterations*. In a *scene level iteration*, it selects the most informative unlabeled instance to label at the scene class level, while in an *object level iteration*, it selects the most informative unlabeled instance to label at the object class level. An adaptive strategy is used to perform switch between these two types of iterations.

Scene Level Iteration. In such an iteration, we select the most informative unlabeled instance to label based on a well-motivated utility measure, named maximum conditional mutual information (MCMI), which maximizes the amount of information we gain from querying the selected instance:

$$\mathbf{z}^* = \arg\max_{\mathbf{z} \in \mathcal{U}} (H(\mathcal{L}) - H(\mathcal{L} \cup (\mathbf{z}, y))) \tag{5}$$

where the data set entropy is defined as

$$H(\mathcal{L}) = - \sum_{i=1}^{|\mathcal{L} \cup \mathcal{U}|} \sum_{l=1}^{|Y|} P_{\mathcal{L}}(y_i = l | \mathbf{z}_i) \log P_{\mathcal{L}}(y_i = l | \mathbf{z}_i) \qquad (6)$$

which measures the total entropy of all labeled and unlabeled instances. $P_{\mathcal{L}}(y|\mathbf{z})$ denotes the probability estimate produced by the classification model that is trained on the labeled data $\mathcal{L}$. Note the first entropy term $H(\mathcal{L})$ remains to be a constant for all candidate instances and can be dropped from the instance selection criterion, which leads to the selection criterion below:

$$\mathbf{z}^* = \arg\min_{\mathbf{z} \in \mathcal{U}} H(\mathcal{L} \cup (\mathbf{z}, y)) \qquad (7)$$

Though Equation (7) provides a principled instance selection criterion, it is impossible to compute given the true label y is unknown for the unlabeled query instance $\mathbf{z}$. We hence adopt the "optimistic" strategy proposed in [6] to pursue an alternative optimistic selection criterion below:

$$(\mathbf{z}^*, l^*) = \arg\min_{\mathbf{z} \in \mathcal{U}} \min_{l \in \mathcal{Y}} H(\mathcal{L} \cup (\mathbf{z}, l)) \qquad (8)$$

which selects the candidate instance $\mathbf{z}^*$ and its a label option l^* that leads to the smallest total prediction uncertainty over all instances. Once the true label y^* of the select instance $\mathbf{z}^*$ being queried, we added $(\mathbf{z}^*, y^*)$ into the labeled set $\mathcal{L}$ and retrain the scene classifier. This optimistic selection strategy however requires retraining the scene classifier for $O(|\mathcal{U}| \times |\mathcal{Y}|)$ times to make the instance selection decision: For each of the $|\mathcal{U}|$ unlabeled instances, one scene classifier needs to be trained for each of its $|\mathcal{Y}|$ candidate labels. The computational cost can be prohibitive on large datasets. To compensate this drawback, one standard way is to use random sub-sampling to select a subset of instances and label classes to reduce the candidate set in Equation (8).

Object Level Iteration. Querying labels at the object class level raises more questions. First, what, image vs patch, should be presented to the human labeler? What information should we query? A naive idea is to present a patch to the human labeler and query the object class label of the patch. However, it will be very difficult to select the right patch that contains a perceivable and discriminative object. Hence, instead of presenting patches to the annotators, we present a whole image to the labeler and ask whether the image contains a particular set of selected objects. Such specific questions will be easy to answer and will not lead to any ambiguities.

Next, we need to decide which image and what objects to query. We employ a most uncertainty strategy and select the most uncertain image (with the maximum entropy) to query under the current scene classification model:

$$\mathbf{z}^* = \arg\max_{\mathbf{z} \in \mathcal{U}} - \sum_{l=1}^{|Y|} P_{\mathcal{L}}(y = l | \mathbf{z}) \log P_{\mathcal{L}}(y = l | \mathbf{z}) \qquad (9)$$

For the selected image $\mathbf{z}^*$, we then select the top M most important objects regarding the most confident scene label $\hat{l}^*$ of $\mathbf{z}^*$ under the current scene classifier to query (We used $M = 5$ in our experiments later). Specifically, $\hat{l}^*$ will be determined as $\hat{l}^* = \arg\max_l P_{\mathcal{L}}(l|\mathbf{z}^*)$. Then we choose M objects that correspond to the largest M entries of the weight parameter vector $|\mathbf{w}_{\hat{l}^*}|$ under the current multi-class scene classifier. Our query questions submitted to the annotators will be in a very specific form: "Does object o_i appear in this image?" We will ask M such questions, one for each selected object.

The last challenge in the object level iteration is on updating the scene classification model after the selected object labels being queried. If the answer for a question is "No", we simply re-label all patches of the selected image as negative samples for that object class, and retrain the particular object classifier if needed. On the other hand, if the answer for a question is "Yes", it means at least one patch in this image should have a positive label for the particular object class. We hence assign the object label to the most confident patch within the selected image under the current particular object classifier. Then we will refine our previous unsupervised patch clustering results by taking the newly gathered patches into account. Our clustering refine scheme is very simple. Given the previous clustering result with K clusters, we set the new labeled patch as a new cluster center and perform K-Medoids updates with $K + 1$ clusters. Note two of these $K + 1$ clusters share the same object label and we will merge them after the end of the clustering process. Finally, all object classifiers will be updated based on the new clustering results. Consequently, the mid-level representations of each labeled image changes as well, and the scene classifier needs to be updated with the new mid-level features.

Adaptive Active Learning Strategy. The last question one needs to answer to produce an active learning algorithm is how do we decide which type of iterations to pursue. We employ an adaptive strategy to make this decision: By default, we will perform active learning with scene level iterations, as most traditional active learners pursued. In each such iteration, an instance $\mathbf{z}^*$ and its optimistic l^* will be selected, and its true label y^* will be queried. However, once we found the true label y^* is different from the optimistic guess l^*, which means the strategy in the scene level iteration has been misled under the current scene classifier, we will then switch to the object level iteration in the next iteration to gather more information to strengthen the scene classification model from its foundation. We will switch back to the traditional scene label iteration after that. The overall multi-level adaptive active learning algorithm is summarized in *Algorithm 1*.

4   Experimental Results

We investigate the performance of the proposed active learning approach for scene classification on two standard challenging datasets, Natural Scene dataset and MIT Indoor Scene dataset. Natural scene dataset is a subset of the LabelMe

---

Algorithm 1. Multi-level Adaptive Active Learning

1: **Input**: Labeled set $\mathcal{L}$, unlabeled set $\mathcal{U}$, and record set $\mathcal{V} = \emptyset$;
2:     M: number of objects to query on each image,
3:     K: number of patch clusters.
4: **Procedure**:
5: Apply K-Medoids clustering on patches $\{\tilde{\mathbf{x}}_i \in \mathcal{L}\}$.
6: Query object labels for each cluster center patch.
7: Merge clusters with the same object labels.
8: Train object classifiers based on the clusters.
9: Obtain mid-level representation for each image $\mathbf{z} \in \mathcal{L} \cup \mathcal{U}$.
10: Train a scene classifier on $\mathcal{L}$.
11: Set itype = 1. %scene level=1, object level = 0
12: **repeat**
13:    **if** itype == 1 **then**
14:       Select $(\mathbf{z}^*, l^*)$ from the unlabeled set $\mathcal{U}$ based on Equation (8)
          and purchase its true label y^*.
15:       Drop $\mathbf{z}^*$ from $\mathcal{U}$ and add $(\mathbf{z}^*, y^*)$ into $\mathcal{L}$.
16:       Retrain the scene classifier on the updated $\mathcal{L}$.
17:       **if** $y^* \neq l^*$ **then**
18:          Set itype =0.
19:       **end if**
20:    **else**
21:       Select $\mathbf{z}^* \in \mathcal{U} \setminus \mathcal{V}$ according to Equation (9).
22:       Predict most confident scene label $\hat{l}^*$ for $\mathbf{z}^*$.
23:       Query the top M most important objects based on the absolute
          weight values $|\mathbf{w}_{\hat{l}*}|$ for scene class $\hat{l}^*$.
24:       Update the clustering result if necessary.
25:       Update object classifiers.
26:       Add $\mathbf{z}^*$ into $\mathcal{V}$.
27:       Update the mid-level representation for all images.
28:       Update scene classifier on $\mathcal{L}$.
29:       Set itype =1.
30:    **end if**
31: **until** run out of money or achieve the aim

---

dataset, which contains 8 scene categories (coast, forest, highway, inside city, mountain, open country, street, and tall building) and each category has more than 250 images. We randomly selected 100 images from each category and pooled them together into a training set and used the rest as the test set. We further randomly selected 5 images per category (40 in total) as the initial labeled set. MIT indoor scene dataset contains 67 indoor categories and a total of 15, 620 images. The number of images varies across categories, but there are at least 100 images per category. We randomly selected 50 images per category to form the training set and the rest are used for testing. Within the training set, 2 images are randomly selected from each category as labeled instances and the rest images are pooled together as unlabeled instances.

The natural scene dataset has object level annotations available to use and the MIT indoor scene dataset also has object level annotations for a proportion of its images. We thus simulated the human annotators' answers based on these available object level annotations for our multi-level active learning. For the MIT indoor scene dataset, we further preprocessed it by discarding the categories that contain less than 50 annotated images (at the object level). After this preprocessing, only 15 categories were left. We produced all non-overlapping patches in size of 16×16 pixels that cover each image. We used the 128-dimension SIFT feature as the low-level features in our experiments.

In our experiments, we compared the proposed *Multi-Level Adaptive active learning (MLA)* method to three baselines: (1) *Single-Level Active learning (SLA)* method, which is a variant of MLA that only queries the scene labels; (2) *Single-Level Random sampling (SLR)* method, which randomly selects an image from the unlabeled pool in each iteration and queries its scene label; and (3) *Multi-Level Random sampling (MLR)* method, which randomly selects an image from the unlabeled pool in each iteration and then randomly chooses to query its object labels or scene label with equal probability. Moreover, we have also compared to the method, Active Learning with Object and Attribute annotations *(ALOA)*, developed in [11]. This *ALOA* method is the state-of-the-art active learner that utilizes both attribute and image labels. We used $K = 200$ (for the K-Medoids clustering) and $M = 5$ for the proposed and the baseline methods. For the trade-off parameters C in Eq.(1) and Eq. (3), we set C as 10 for the object classifiers and 0.1 for the scene classifier, aiming to avoid overfitting for the scene classifier with limited labeled data at the scene level. Starting from the initial randomly selected labeled data, we ran each active learning method for 100 iterations, and recorded their performance in each iteration. We repeated each experiment 5 times and reported the average results and standard deviations.

Figure 3 presents the comparison results in terms of scene classification accuracy on the MIT Indoor scene dataset and the Natural scene dataset. For the proposed approach *MLA* and the baselines *SLA, MLR, SLR*, we experimented two different ways of learning scene classifiers.[1] A straightforward way is to learn the scene classifier based on the mid-level semantic representation produced by the object classifiers. Alternatively, we have also investigated learning the scene classifier based on *hybrid* features by augmenting the mid-level representation with the low-level SIFT features. Such a mechanism was shown to be effective in [26]. Specifically, we built a 500-words codebook with K-Means clustering over the SIFT features and represented each image as a 500-long vector with vector quantization. This low-level representation together with the mid-level representation form the hybrid features of images for scene classification. The comparison results based only on mid-level representation are reported on the left column of Figure 3 for the two datasets respectively; and the comparison results based on the hybrid features are reported on the right column of Figure 3. We can see in terms of scene classification accuracy, our proposed method *MLA* beats all other comparison methods, especially the baselines, across most of the comparison

---

[1] The *ALOA* from [11] works in a different mechanism with a latent SVM classifier.

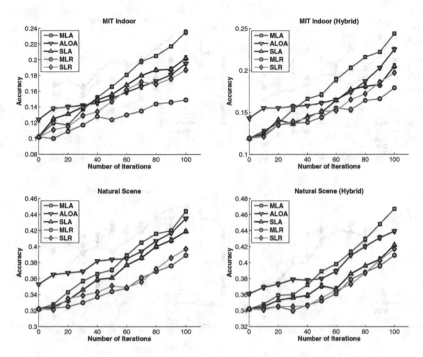

Fig. 3. The average and standard deviation results in terms of scene classification accuracy on both MIT Indoor scene dataset and Natural Scene dataset

range, except at the very beginning. At the beginning of the active learning process, $ALOA$ produces the best performance with very few labeled images. Given that $ALOA$ [11] uses the state-of-the-art latent SVM classifier, and our approach uses a simple logistic regression model, this seems reasonable. But the gap between $ALOA$ and the proposed MLA quickly degrades with the active learning process; after a set of iterations, MLA significantly outperforms $ALOA$. This demonstrates that our proposed multi-level adaptive active learning strategy is much more effective and it is able to collect most useful label information that makes a simple logistic regression classifier to outperform the state-of-the-art latent SVM classifier. Among the three baseline methods, SLA always performs the best. On MIT-Indoor dataset, it even outperforms $ALOA$ when only semantic representation is used. This suggests the MCMI instance selection strategy we employed in the scene level iterations is very effective. On the other hand, the random sampling methods MLR and SLR produce very poor performance. Another interesting observation is that at the start of active learning, though we only have very few labeled instance available for each category, the accuracy of our latent object-based hierarchical scene classification model already reaches around 12% on 15-category MIT indoor scene subset and reaches around 34% on Natural scene dataset. This demonstrates the mid-level representation is very descriptive and useful for abstractive scene classification. By comparing the two versions of results across columns, we can see that with hybrid features, the

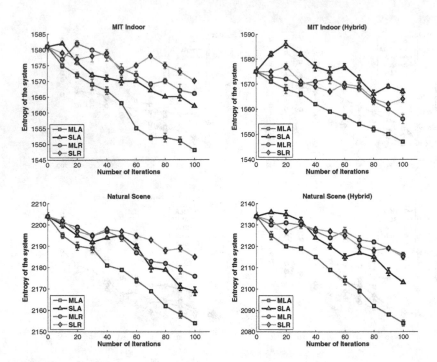

Fig. 4. The entropy reduction results on both MIT Indoor Scene dataset and Natural Scene dataset

proposed *MLA* produces slightly better results, which suggests that low-level features and mid-level representation features can complement each other.

In addition to scene classification accuracy, we have also measured the performance of the comparison methods in terms of system entropy (i.e., data set entropy). We recorded the reduction of the system entropy with the increasing number of labeled instances. The *ALOA* method from [11] uses a Latent SVM model, the system entropy of which is contributed by both the image classifier and the model's inner attribute classifiers. However, the entropies of all other methods are only associated with the target image label predictions, which makes the computed entropy of *ALOA* and others not comparable. Therefore, we only consider the other four methods in this experimental setting. The results are reported in Figure 4. It is easy to see that the proposed *MLA* method reduces the entropy much quickly than other baselines, which verifies the effectiveness of our proposed adaptive active learning strategy. The curve of *MLA* is monotone decreasing, indicating that every query is helpful in terms of entropy reduction. The curves of the other baselines nevertheless have fluctuations. Among them, *SLA* is almost always the runner-up except on the MIT indoor dataset with hybrid features. By comparing the two versions of results across columns, we can see the system entropy with hybrid features is relatively lower than its counterpart with mid-level semantic representation alone, which again suggests that the

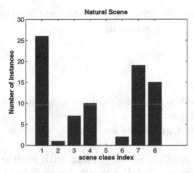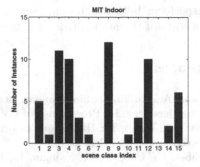

Fig. 5. Distribution of queried instances in scene label space for the proposed approach on MIT Indoor and Natural Scene datasets

low-level features can provide augmenting information for the mid-level semantic representations.

Finally, we collected the number of queries in each scene category on the two datasets for the proposed approach and presented the results in Figure 5. We can see, obviously the instances are not selected according to a uniform distribution across categories. The total numbers of scene level label queries among the 100 iterations are 65 and 80 on the MIT Indoor and Natural scene datasets respectively. The remaining querying effort is on the object-level annotations. On the MIT indoor dataset, the ratio between the numbers of queries on scene labels and object annotations is about 2 : 1. In contrast, this ratio is 4 : 1 on the Natural scene dataset. This observation indicates that our model can adaptively switch query levels based on the complexity of the data. When the object layout is easy, it will put more effort on querying scene labels; when the scene becomes complicated and ambiguous, it will ask more questions about object annotations.

5   Conclusions

In this paper, we developed a novel multi-level active learning approach to reduce the human annotation effort for training semantic scene classification models. Our idea was motivated by the facts that latent object-based semantic representations of images are very useful for scene classification, and the scene labels are difficult to distinguish from each other in many scenarios. We hence built a semantic framework that learns scene classifiers based on latent object-based semantic representations of images, and then proposed to perform active learning with two different types of iterations, the scene level iteration (abstractive high level) and the latent object level iteration (semantic middle level). We employed an adaptive strategy to automatically perform switching between these two types active learning iterations. We conducted experiments on two standard scene classification datasets, the MIT Indoor scene dataset and the Natural Scene dataset, to investigate the efficacy of the proposed approach. Our empirical results showed the proposed adaptive multi-level active learning approach can outperform both traditional baseline single level active learning methods and the state-of-the-art multi-level active learning method.

References

1. Biswas, A., Parikh, D.: Simultaneous active learning of classifiers & attributes via relative feedback. In: Proceedings of CVPR (2013)
2. Dalal, N., Triggs, B.: Histograms of oriented gradients for human detection. In: Proceedings of CVPR (2005)
3. Farabet, C., Couprie, C., Najman, L., LeCun, Y.: Scene parsing with multiscale feature learning, purity trees,and optimal covers. CoRR abs/1202.2160 (2012)
4. Fei-Fei, P.L., Perona: A bayesian hierarchical model for learning natural scene categories. In: Proceedings of CVPR (2005)
5. Gould, S., Gao, T., Koller, D.: Region-based segmentation and object detection. In: Proceedings of NIPS (2009)
6. Guo, Y., Greiner, R.: Optimistic active learning using mutual information. In: Proceedings of IJCAI (2007)
7. Jain, P., Kapoor, A.: Active learning for large multi-class problems. In: Proceedings of CVPR (2009)
8. Joshi, A., Porikli, F., Papanikolopoulos, N.: Multi-class active learning for image classification. In: Proceedings of CVPR (2009)
9. Kapoor, A., Grauman, K., Urtasun, R., Darrell, T.: Active learning with gaussian processes for object categorization. In: Proceedings of ICCV (2007)
10. A., Kapoor, G.H., Akbarzadeh, A., Baker, S.: Which faces to tag: Adding prior constraints into active learning. In: Proceedings of ICCV (2009)
11. Kovashka, A., Vijayanarasimhan, S., Grauman, K.: Actively selecting annotations among objects and attributes. In: Proceedings of ICCV (2011)
12. Kumar, M., Koller, D.: Efficiently selecting regions for scene understanding. In: Proceedings of CVPR (2010)
13. Lazebnik, S., Schmid, C., Ponce, J.: Beyond bags of features: Spatial pyramid matching for recognizing natural scene categories. In: Proceedings of CVPR (2006)
14. Li, L., Su, H., Xing, E., Fei-Fei, L.: Object bank: A high-level image representation for scene classification & semantic feature sparsification. In: Proceedings of NIPS (2010)
15. Li, X., Guo, Y.: Adaptive active learning for image classification. In: Proceedings of CVPR (2013)
16. Lin, C., Weng, R., Keerthi, S.: Trust region newton method for logistic regression. J. Mach. Learn. Res. 9 (June 2008)
17. Lowe, D.: Distinctive image features from scale-invariant keypoints. Int. J. Comput. Vision 60(2) (November 2004)
18. Mensink, T., Verbeek, J., Csurka, G.: Learning structured prediction models for interactive image labeling. In: Proceedings of CVPR (2011)
19. Pandey, M., Lazebnik, S.: Scene recognition and weakly supervised object localization with deformable part-based models. In: Proceedings of ICCV (2011)
20. Parizi, S., Oberlin, J., Felzenszwalb, P.: Reconfigurable models for scene recognition. In: Proceedings of CVPR (2012)
21. Parkash, A., Parikh, D.: Attributes for classifier feedback. In: Fitzgibbon, A., Lazebnik, S., Perona, P., Sato, Y., Schmid, C. (eds.) ECCV 2012, Part III. LNCS, vol. 7574, pp. 354–368. Springer, Heidelberg (2012)

22. Patterson, G., Hays, J.: Sun attribute database: Discovering, annotating, and recognizing scene attributes. In: Proceeding of CVPR (2012)
23. Quattoni, A., Torralba, A.: Recognizing indoor scenes. In: Proceedings of CVPR (2009)
24. Sadeghi, F., Tappen, M.F.: Latent pyramidal regions for recognizing scenes. In: Fitzgibbon, A., Lazebnik, S., Perona, P., Sato, Y., Schmid, C. (eds.) ECCV 2012, Part V. LNCS, vol. 7576, pp. 228–241. Springer, Heidelberg (2012)
25. Settles, B.: Active Learning. Synthesis digital library of engineering and computer science. Morgan & Claypool (2011)
26. Sharmanska, V., Quadrianto, N., Lampert, C.H.: Augmented attribute representations. In: Fitzgibbon, A., Lazebnik, S., Perona, P., Sato, Y., Schmid, C. (eds.) ECCV 2012, Part V. LNCS, vol. 7576, pp. 242–255. Springer, Heidelberg (2012)
27. Siddiquie, B., Gupta, A.: Beyond active noun tagging: Modeling contextual interactions for multi-class active learning. In: Proceedings of CVPR (2010)
28. Jones, K.S., Willett, P.: Readings in Information Retrieval. Morgan Kaufmann Publishers Inc. (1997)
29. Vezhnevets, A., Buhmann, J., Ferrari, V.: Active learning for semantic segmentation with expected change. In: Proceedings of CVPR (2012)
30. Vijayanarasimhan, S., Grauman, K.: Multi-level active prediction of useful image annotations for recognition. In: Proceedings of NIPS (2008)
31. Vijayanarasimhan, S., Grauman, K.: Large-scale live active learning: Training object detectors with crawled data and crowds. In: Proceedings of CVPR (2011)
32. Wang, Y., Mori, G.: A discriminative latent model of object classes and attributes. In: Daniilidis, K., Maragos, P., Paragios, N. (eds.) ECCV 2010, Part V. LNCS, vol. 6315, pp. 155–168. Springer, Heidelberg (2010)
33. Wu, J., Rehg, J.: CENTRIST: A Visual Descriptor for Scene Categorization. IEEE Transactions on PAMI 33 (2011)
34. Yan, A.R., Yang, L., Hauptmann: Automatically labeling video data using multi-class active learning. In: Proceedings of ICCV (2003)

Graph Cuts for Supervised Binary Coding

Tiezheng Ge[1,*], Kaiming He[2], and Jian Sun[2]

[1] University of Science and Technology of China
[2] Microsoft Research

Abstract. Learning short binary codes is challenged by the inherent discrete nature of the problem. The graph cuts algorithm is a well-studied discrete label assignment solution in computer vision, but has not yet been applied to solve the binary coding problems. This is partially because it was unclear how to use it to learn the encoding (hashing) functions for out-of-sample generalization. In this paper, we formulate supervised binary coding as a single optimization problem that involves both the encoding functions and the binary label assignment. Then we apply the graph cuts algorithm to address the discrete optimization problem involved, with no continuous relaxation. This method, named as Graph Cuts Coding (GCC), shows competitive results in various datasets.

1 Introduction

Learning binary compact codes [32] has been attracting growing attention in computer vision. In the application aspect, binary encoding makes it feasible to store and search large-scale data [32]; in the theory aspect, the studies on binary encoding have been advancing the investigation on the nontrivial discrete-valued problems, e.g., [14,36,19,18,35,10,25,23,21,28,13]. Binary coding solutions (e.g., [10]) can also facilitate the research on non-binary coding problems (e.g., [8,9,24]).

Recent studies [36,18,35,10,25,23,21,28,13] mostly formulate binary encoding as optimization problems with several concerns. The Hamming distance [14] between the codes should preserve the similarity among the data, whereas the bits of the codes should be informative for better data compression. Besides, the encoding functions (also known as hashing functions) are expected to be simple, e.g., to be linear functions or simple kernel maps [19,21]. If available, supervised/semi-supervised information [18,35,25,21,28] should also be respected. The formulations of these concerns lead to nontrivial optimization problems.

A main challenge in the optimization comes from the binarization of the encoding functions f, e.g., given by sign(f) or its equivalence. Various optimization techniques have been adopted, including spectral relaxation [36,35], coordinate descent [18], procrustean quantization [10], concave-convex optimization [25], sigmoid approximation [21], and stochastic gradient descent [28]. Despite the different strategies, these methods mainly focus on the optimization *w.r.t.* the

---

* This work was done when Tiezheng Ge was an intern at Microsoft Research.

D. Fleet et al. (Eds.): ECCV 2014, Part VII, LNCS 8695, pp. 250–264, 2014.

continuous parameters of the encoding function f. However, the discrete nature of the problem is often overlooked.

Nevertheless, discrete label assignment problems [5,4] are widely involved in computer vision, *e.g.*, in image segmentation [5], stereo matching [29], and many other applications [20,4,1,31,27,12]. The assignment problems are often formulated as energy minimization on a graph structure. The Graph Cuts algorithm [5,4] is a well investigated solution to this problem.

Though the graph cuts algorithm is an effective solution to discrete label assignment problems, it has not been applied to binary encoding. This is partially because the graph cuts algorithm can only give solutions to a finite set of samples, but make no prediction for the unseen ones (known as "out-of-sample" generalization). To take advantage of graph cuts, we also need to include the encoding functions in the optimization.

In this paper, we propose a binary coding method driven by graph cuts. We mainly focus on the supervised scenario as in [18,35,25,21]. We formulate supervised binary coding as an optimization problem. Unlike most existing methods that only involves the parameterized encoding functions f, we further incorporate the binary codes as auxiliary variables in the optimization. Our objective function fits the binary codes to the supervision, and also controls the loss between the binary codes and sign(f). Then we can separate the binary label assignment as a sub-problem in the optimization and solve it via the graph cuts algorithm [5,4]. In experiments, this Graph Cuts Coding (GCC) method gives competitive results in various datasets.

Our method provides a novel way of addressing the inherent issue of discreteness in binary encoding. While most existing methods (*e.g.*, [36,35,25,21]) address this issue by kinds of continuous relaxation or gradient descent, our graph cuts solution focuses more closely on the binary nature. We are not the first to consider binary coding via a "*graph*" structure, but to the best of our knowledge, ours is the first method that uses the classical "*graph cuts*" algorithm [5,4] to solve this problem. In the work of Spectral Hashing (SH) [36], it has been pointed out that the SH problem is equivalent to "graph partitioning". However, the presented solution to SH in [36] is based on continuous spectral relaxation. The work of Anchor Graph Hashing (AGH) [23] has also considered a graph structure, but has pointed out that the usage of a graph is challenged by the "out-of-sample" generalization. AGH addresses this issue via continuous relaxation, rather than the discrete graph cuts.

2 Related Work

Our work is related to two seemingly unrelated areas in computer vision: binary coding and graph cuts.

Learning Binary Codes. Earlier methods for binary encoding are randomized solutions such as Locality-Sensitive Hashing (LSH) [14,19]. Recent studies on binary encoding resort to optimization. In several supervised methods like

Binary Reconstructive Embedding (BRE) [18], Semi-Supervised Hashing (SSH) [35], Minimal Loss Hashing [25], and Kernel-based Supervised Hashing [21], the energy function minimizes the discrepancy between the data similarities and the Hamming distances of sign(f). These methods optimize the energy function *w.r.t.* the continuous parameters of the encoding function f. This is often addressed by gradient descent and/or continuous relaxation.

Graph Cuts. In computer vision, the graph cuts algorithm [5,4] is a fast and effective solution to binary/multi-label assignment problems. We refer to [3] for a comprehensive introduction. The graph cuts algorithm has been applied in image segmentation [5], image restoration [5], stereo matching [29], texture synthesis [20], image stitching [1], image enhancement [31], image retargeting [27], image inpainting [12], and so on. The graph cuts algorithm is usually used to minimize an energy in a form as [5]:

$$\mathcal{E}(\mathcal{I}) = \sum_i \mathcal{E}_u(\mathcal{I}_i) + \sum_{(i,j)} \mathcal{E}_p(\mathcal{I}_i, \mathcal{I}_j). \tag{1}$$

Here $\mathcal{I}$ are the labeling of the image pixels, *e.g.*, 0/1 in binary segmentation. $\mathcal{E}_u$ is a unary term (also called the data term) that depends on a single pixel, and $\mathcal{E}_p$ is a pairwise term (also called binary/smoothness term) that depends on two pixels. The graph cuts solver is based on the max-flow/min-cut [4], in which no continuous relaxation is needed. Graph cuts can also be used to solve higher-order energies [3].

3   Graph Cuts for Supervised Binary Coding

3.1   Formulations

We denote the data sets as $\mathbf{X} = \{\mathbf{x}_1, ..., \mathbf{x}_n\}$ that contains n training samples in $\mathbb{R}^d$. We first discuss the case of the linear encoding function $f(\mathbf{x}) = \mathbf{w}^T\mathbf{x} - b$, where $\mathbf{w}$ is a d-by-1 vector and b is a scalar. We will discuss the kernelized cases later.

Existing binary coding methods [14,36,19,18,35,10,25,23,21,28,30] mostly compute a single bit $y \in \{-1, 1\}$ by taking the sign of $f(\mathbf{x})$. However, in our *training procedure*, we allow y to be different from sign($f(\mathbf{x})$). We treat the binary code y as an auxiliary variable, and control its deviation from sign($f(\mathbf{x})$) by a loss function. This makes the energy function more flexible. As an overview, we minimize an energy function in the form of:

$$\min_{\mathbf{W,b,Y}} E_0(\mathbf{W}, \mathbf{b}, \mathbf{Y}) + \lambda E_1(\mathbf{Y}) \tag{2}$$

$$\text{s.t.} \quad y = 1 \text{ or } -1.$$

Here $\mathbf{W} = [\mathbf{w}_1, ..., \mathbf{w}_B]^T$ and $\mathbf{b} = [b_1, ..., b_B]^T$ are the parameters of the encoding functions $\{f_1, ..., f_B\}$ if B bits are given. $\mathbf{Y}$ is an n-by-B matrix with each row being the B bits of a sample vector $\mathbf{x} \in \mathbf{X}$. The values of $\mathbf{Y}$ are in either -1 or 1. λ is a weight.

In our optimization, y need not be the same as $\text{sign}(f(\mathbf{x}))$, and the term $E_0(\mathbf{W}, \mathbf{b}, \mathbf{Y})$ is used to measure the loss between each y and $f(\mathbf{x})$. The term $E_1(\mathbf{Y})$ is used to fit the codes to the supervision. Note the auxiliary variable $\mathbf{Y}$ is only used in the training procedure. After training, all the data and queries are still encoded using $\text{sign}(f(\mathbf{x}))$ with the optimized $\{\mathbf{W}, \mathbf{b}\}$.

We design the energy based on the following concerns: (i) each encoding function should maximize the margin of each bit; (ii) the encoded bits should respect the supervision; and (iii) the bits should be as independent as possible. We incorporate all concerns in a single energy function.

Encoding Functions with Maximal Margins

We regard each encoding function f_k ($k = 1, ..., B$) as a classifier trained for the n samples in $\mathbf{X}$ and their n labels $\mathbf{y}_k$. Here the n-dimensional vector $\mathbf{y}_k$ is the k-th column of $\mathbf{Y}$ (the k-th bits of all samples). In this paper, we expect each classifier to maximize the margin between the positive/negative samples as in SVM [6][1]. A binary SVM classifier can be formulated as minimizing this energy function [11]:

$$\frac{1}{2c}\|\mathbf{w}_k\|^2 + \mathcal{L}(\mathbf{y}_k, f_k(\mathbf{X})), \tag{3}$$

where $\mathcal{L}(\mathbf{y}_k, f_k(\mathbf{X})) = \sum_i \max(0, 1 - y_{k,i} f_k(\mathbf{x}_i))$ represents the hinge loss, and c is a parameter in SVM controlling the soft margin.

We put all B encoding functions together and aggregate their costs as:

$$E_0(\mathbf{W}, \mathbf{b}, \mathbf{Y}) = \sum_k^B \frac{1}{2c}\|\mathbf{w}_k\|^2 + \mathcal{L}(\mathbf{y}_k, f_k(\mathbf{X}))$$

$$= \frac{1}{2c}\|\mathbf{W}\|_F^2 + \mathcal{L}(\mathbf{Y}, \mathbf{f}(\mathbf{X})), \tag{4}$$

where $\| \cdot \|_F$ is the Frobenius norm.

In the viewpoint of classification, this energy maximizes the margin between the positive/negative samples for each bit. But in the viewpoint of binary encoding, this energy measures the loss $\mathcal{L}$ between $\mathbf{Y}$ and the encoded values $\mathbf{f}(\mathbf{X})$.

Respecting the Supervision

We suppose the supervision is provided as an n-by-n affinity matrix S as in [18,35,25,21]. For example, in KSH [21] it uses $S_{ij} = 1$ if the pair $(\mathbf{x}_i, \mathbf{x}_j)$ are

---

[1] However, as we will introduce, the graph cuts solution does not require a specific form in this term. If only this term is an unary term (i.e., it does not involve any pair-wise relation between samples), the graph cuts solution should apply.

denoted as similar, $S_{ij} = -1$ if dissimilar, and $S_{ij} = 0$ if unknown. To respect the supervision, we consider to minimize an energy as:

$$-\sum_{k}^{B}\sum_{i}^{n}\sum_{j}^{n} S_{ij} y_{k,i} y_{k,j}$$
$$= -tr(\mathbf{Y}^{\mathrm{T}}\mathbf{S}\mathbf{Y}). \tag{5}$$

where $tr(\cdot)$ is the trace. Intuitively, if $S_{ij} = 1$, then this energy favors $y_{k,i}=y_{k,j}$ (note y is either -1 or 1); if $S_{ij} = -1$, then it favors $y_{k,i} \neq y_{k,j}$.

If our optimization problem only has the terms in Eqn.(4) and (5), it will trivially produce B identical encoding functions, because both Eqn.(4) and (5) just simply aggregate B energy functions that share the same form. Next we introduce a term to avoid this trivial case.

Bits Independence

We expect all the encoding functions to be independent to each other so as to avoid the trivial case. Ideally, we would like to have a constraint as: $\frac{1}{n}\mathbf{Y}^{\mathrm{T}}\mathbf{Y} = I$ where I is a B-by-B unit matrix. This constraint was first considered in Spectral Hashing (SH) [36]. But this leads to a challenging constrained discrete optimization problem, which was continuous-relaxed in [36]. Here we instead consider a regularization of minimizing $\|\mathbf{Y}^{\mathrm{T}}\mathbf{Y} - nI\|_{\mathrm{F}}^2$. We expand it and omit the constant terms[2], and show it is equivalent to minimizing:

$$\|\mathbf{Y}^{\mathrm{T}}\mathbf{Y}\|_{\mathrm{F}}^2, \tag{6}$$

We put Eqn.(5) and (6) together:

$$E_1(\mathbf{Y}) = -tr(\mathbf{Y}^{\mathrm{T}}\mathbf{S}\mathbf{Y}) + \gamma\|\mathbf{Y}^{\mathrm{T}}\mathbf{Y}\|_{\mathrm{F}}^2, \tag{7}$$

where γ is a weight. E_1 is the energy that involves the variable $\mathbf{Y}$ only.

The Energy Function

Considering Eqn.(4) and (7), we minimize this problem:

$$\min_{\mathbf{W},\mathbf{b},\mathbf{Y}} \frac{1}{2c}\|\mathbf{W}\|_{\mathrm{F}}^2 + \mathcal{L}(\mathbf{Y}, \mathbf{f}(\mathbf{X})) - tr(\mathbf{Y}^{\mathrm{T}}\mathbf{S}\mathbf{Y}) + \gamma\|\mathbf{Y}^{\mathrm{T}}\mathbf{Y}\|_{\mathrm{F}}^2, \tag{8}$$

$$\text{s.t. } y_{k,i} = 1 \text{ or } -1, \quad \forall k, i.$$

where we have empirically set the parameter λ in Eqn.(2) as 1. The variables to be optimized are $\mathbf{W}$, $\mathbf{b}$, and $\mathbf{Y}$. Here we explicitly treat $\mathbf{Y}$ as variables to be optimized, whereas many previous works (e.g., [18,35,25,21]) only involve $\mathbf{W}$ and $\mathbf{b}$. As such, our energy function allows to directly assign binary values y to the data during the training procedure.

---

[2] $\|\mathbf{Y}^{\mathrm{T}}\mathbf{Y} - nI\|_{\mathrm{F}}^2 = \|\mathbf{Y}^{\mathrm{T}}\mathbf{Y}\|_{\mathrm{F}}^2 - 2n\, tr(\mathbf{Y}^{\mathrm{T}}\mathbf{Y}I) + n^2\|I\|_{\mathrm{F}}^2 = \|\mathbf{Y}^{\mathrm{T}}\mathbf{Y}\|_{\mathrm{F}}^2 - 2n\|\mathbf{Y}\|_{\mathrm{F}}^2 + n^2\|I\|_{\mathrm{F}}^2 = \|\mathbf{Y}^{\mathrm{T}}\mathbf{Y}\|_{\mathrm{F}}^2 + const.$

3.2   Graph Cuts for One Bit

We optimize the energy (3.1) by iteratively solving two sub-problems: (i) fix $\mathbf{Y}$, update $\{\mathbf{W}, \mathbf{b}\}$; and (ii) fix $\{\mathbf{W}, \mathbf{b}\}$, update $\mathbf{Y}$. The first sub-problem is equivalent to solving B independent binary SVM classifiers as in Eqn.(3). The second sub-problem is a binary assignment problem involving $\mathbf{Y}$. We sequentially solve each bit with the remaining bits fixed. Formally, at each time we update the n-by-1 vector $\mathbf{y}_k$ with the rest $\{\mathbf{y}_{k'}; k' \neq k\}$ fixed. Then we update each bit iteratively.

We show that the problem involving $\mathbf{y}_k$ can be presented as a graph cuts problem: it only involves unary terms and pairwise terms. For the ease of presentation we denote $\mathbf{z} \triangleq \mathbf{y}_k$. With $\{\mathbf{W}, \mathbf{b}\}$ and the rest $\{\mathbf{y}_{k'} \mid k' \neq k\}$ fixed, we will show that optimizing (3.1) $w.r.t.$ $\mathbf{z}$ is equivalent to minimizing:

$$E(\mathbf{z}) = \sum_i \mathcal{E}_\mathrm{u}(z_i) + \sum_{(i,j)} \mathcal{E}_\mathrm{p}(z_i, z_j)$$

$$\text{s.t.} \quad z_i = 1 \text{ or } -1, \quad i = 1, ...n, \tag{9}$$

where "$\sum_{(i,j)}$" sums all possible pairs of (i, j) and $i \neq j$. Here $\mathcal{E}_\mathrm{u}$ represents the unary term, and $\mathcal{E}_\mathrm{p}$ represents the pairwise term as in Eqn.(1).

It is easy to show the unary term in Eqn.(9) is:

$$\mathcal{E}_\mathrm{u}(z_i) = \begin{cases} \max(0, 1 - f_k(\mathbf{x}_i)) & \text{if } z_i \text{ is } 1 \\ \max(0, 1 + f_k(\mathbf{x}_i)) & \text{if } z_i \text{ is -1} \end{cases}. \tag{10}$$

To compute the pairwise term, we need to express the contribution of $\mathbf{z}$ to E. Denote $\mathbf{Y}'$ as the concatenation of $\{\mathbf{y}_{k'} \mid k' \neq k\}$, which is an $n \times (B\text{-}1)$ matrix. Note only E_1 contributes to the pairwise term[3]. With some algebraic operations[4] we can rewrite Eqn.(7) as:

$$E_1 = \mathbf{z}^\mathrm{T}(2\gamma \mathbf{Y}'\mathbf{Y}'^\mathrm{T} - \mathbf{S})\mathbf{z} + const, \tag{11}$$

where the constant is independent of $\mathbf{z}$. Denote $\mathbf{Q} = 2\gamma \mathbf{Y}'\mathbf{Y}'^\mathrm{T} - \mathbf{S}$, then the contribution of $\mathbf{z}$ to E_1 is $\sum_{(i,j)} 2Q_{ij} z_i z_j$. As such, the pairwise term is:

$$\mathcal{E}_\mathrm{p}(z_i, z_j) = \begin{cases} 2Q_{ij} & \text{if } (z_i, z_j) = (1,1) \text{ or } (\text{-}1,\text{-}1) \\ -2Q_{ij} & \text{if } (z_i, z_j) = (1,\text{-}1) \text{ or } (\text{-}1,1) \end{cases}. \tag{12}$$

Given these definitions, Eqn.(9) is a standard energy minimization problem with unary/pairwise terms and two labels $(+1/\text{-}1)$ as in Eqn.(1).

The problem in (9) can be represented as a graph. There are n vertexes corresponding to $z_i, i = 1, ..., n$. An edge in the graph linking z_i and z_j represents

---

[3] E_1 should also contain a term in the form of an unary term. But this term is a constant due to the fact that $z^2 = 1$.

[4] $tr(\mathbf{Y}^\mathrm{T}\mathbf{S}\mathbf{Y}) = tr(\mathbf{S}\mathbf{Y}\mathbf{Y}^\mathrm{T}) = tr(\mathbf{S}(\mathbf{Y}'\mathbf{Y}'^\mathrm{T} + \mathbf{z}\mathbf{z}^\mathrm{T})) = const + \mathbf{z}^\mathrm{T}\mathbf{S}\mathbf{z}$, and $\|\mathbf{Y}^\mathrm{T}\mathbf{Y}\|_\mathrm{F}^2 = tr((\mathbf{Y}\mathbf{Y}^\mathrm{T})(\mathbf{Y}\mathbf{Y}^\mathrm{T})^\mathrm{T}) = tr((\mathbf{Y}'\mathbf{Y}'^\mathrm{T} + \mathbf{z}\mathbf{z}^\mathrm{T})(\mathbf{Y}'\mathbf{Y}'^\mathrm{T} + \mathbf{z}\mathbf{z}^\mathrm{T})^\mathrm{T}) = const + 2\mathbf{z}^\mathrm{T}\mathbf{Y}'\mathbf{Y}'^\mathrm{T}\mathbf{z}$.

Algorithm 1. Graph Cuts Coding: Training

Input: X and **S**.
Output: W and **b**.
 1: Initialize **Y** using PCA hashing on **X**.
 2: **repeat**
 3:     **for** $k = 1$ to B **do**
 4:         Train SVM using $\mathbf{y}_k$ as labels and update $\mathbf{w}_k, b_k$.
 5:     **end for**
 6:     **for** $t = 1$ to $t_{\max}$ **do**
 7:         **for** $k = 1$ to B **do**
 8:             Update $\mathbf{y}_k$ by graph cuts as in Eqn.(9).
 9:         **end for**
10:     **end for**
11: **until** convergence or max iterations reached

---

a pairwise term $\mathcal{E}_p(z_i, z_j)$. There are two extra vertexes representing the two labels, usually called the *source* and the *sink* [4]. These two vertexes are linked to each z_i, representing the unary terms.

Minimizing the energy in (9) is equivalent to finding a "cut" [5] that separates the graph into two disconnected parts. The cost of this cut is given by the sum of the costs of the disconnected edges. The graph cuts algorithm [5,4] is a solution to finding such a cut.

Theoretically, the graph cut algorithm requires the pairwise term to be "submodular" [15], that is, $\mathcal{E}_p(-1, -1) + \mathcal{E}_p(1, 1) \leq \mathcal{E}_p(-1, 1) + \mathcal{E}_p(1, -1)$. Based on Eqn.(12), the submodular condition is $Q_{ij} \leq 0$ in our case, which in fact does not always hold. However, in various applications [20,1,27,3,12] it has been empirically observed that the deviations from this condition can still produce practically good results. Furthermore, we also empirically the graph cuts algorithm works well for effectively reducing our objective function. Another choice is to apply solvers developed for nonsubmodular cases, such as the QPBO [15]. We will investigate this alternative in the future.

3.3   Algorithm Summary and Discussions

Our solution to (3.1) is described in Algorithm 1. In lines 3-5 we update $\{\mathbf{W}, \mathbf{b}\}$, and lines 6-10 we update **Y**. We set the iteration number $t_{\max}$ for updating **Y** as 2 (more iterations could still decrease the energy but training is slower). The update of **Y** is analogous to the α-expansion in multi-label graph cuts [4]. The SVM in line 4 uses the LIBLINEAR package [7], and the SVM parameter c is tuned by cross validation. From the definition of Q we empirically set $\gamma = \frac{1}{2B}$, such that S_{ij} and $\frac{1}{\gamma}(\mathbf{Y}'\mathbf{Y}'^T)_{ij}$ have similar magnitudes. We adopt the GCO[5] as the graph cuts solver to Eqn.(9). Some discussions are as follows.

---

[5] http://vision.csd.uwo.ca/code/

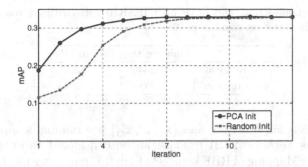

Fig. 1. The impact of initialization. The y-axis is the mean Average Precision (mAP) in the CIFAR10 dataset. See Sec. 4.1 for the experiment settings on CIFAR10. The bit number is $B=32$.

Table 1. The mAP of GCC using four kernels on CIFAR10

kernel	linear	inters.	χ^2	κ in Eqn.(13)
$B=16$	26.6	26.2	26.8	30.3
$B=32$	28.6	29.6	28.8	33.3

Initialization

To initialize $\mathbf{Y}$, we take the sign of the PCA projections of $\mathbf{X}$ (known as PCA hashing (PCAH) [35]). This works well in our experiments. But we also empirically observe that the final accuracy of our algorithm is *insensitive* to the initialization, and the initialization mainly impacts the convergence speed. To show this, we have tried to initialize each entries in $\mathbf{Y}$ fully in random. Fig. 1 shows the accuracy of using PCAH/random initializations in CIFAR10 (see the details in Sec. 4.1). We see that in both cases the final accuracy is very comparable. The random initialization also demonstrates the effectiveness of our optimization - though extremely incorrect labels are given at the beginning, our algorithm is able to correct them in the remaining iterations.

Kernelization

Our algorithm can be easily kernelized. This is achieved by a mapping function on $\mathbf{x} : \mathbb{R}^d \mapsto \mathbb{R}^D$ where D can be different from d. The mapped set is used in place of $\mathbf{X}$. We have tried the Explicit Feature Mapping [34] to approximate the intersection kernel and the Chi-squared kernel.[6] We have also tried the kernel map used in [19,21]:

$$\kappa(\mathbf{x}) = [g(\mathbf{x}, \mathbf{x'_1}), ..., g(\mathbf{x}, \mathbf{x'_D})]^\mathrm{T} \qquad (13)$$

---

[6] This can be computed via `vl_homkermap` in the VLFeat library [33].

Table 2. The training time and mAP on CIFAR10 with/without removal. The bit number is 32. The iteration number is 10.

	training time (s)	mAP
no removal	2540	33.5
with removal	605	33.3

where g is a Gaussian function, and $\{x'_1, ..., x'_D\}$ are random samples from the data (known as *anchors* [23,21]). This can be considered as an approximate Explicit Feature Mapping of RBF kernels [34]. In this paper, we use 1,000 anchors ($D = 1,000$). In Table. 1 we compare the performance of our algorithm using four kernels. It shows the kernel κ in (13) performs the best. In the rest of this paper we use this kernel.

Reduced Graph Cuts

Even though the graph cuts solver is very efficient, it can still be time-consuming because during the training stage it is run repeatedly. We propose a simplification to reduce the training time. In each time applying graph cuts to optimize one bit, we randomly set a portion of the pairwise terms in Eqn.(9) as zero. This can effectively reduce the running time because the number of edges in the graph are reduced. The removed terms are different for each bit and for each iteration, so although less information is exposed to each bit at each time, the entire optimizer is little degraded. We randomly remove 90% of pairwise terms (each sample is still connected to 10% of all the training samples). The accuracy and training speed with/without removal is in Table 2. We see that it trains faster and performs comparably. The remaining results are given with the reduced version.

4   Experiments

We compare our Graph Cuts Coding (GCC) with several state-of-the-art supervised binary coding (hashing) methods: Binary Reconstructive Embedding (BRE) [18], Semi-Supervised Hashing (SSH) [35], Minimal Loss Hashing (MLH) [25], Iterative Quantization with CCA projection (CCA+ITQ) [10], Kernel-based Supervised Hashing (KSH) [21], and Discriminative Binary Codes (DBC) [28]. We also evaluate several unsupervised binary coding methods: Locality-Sensitive Hashing (LSH) [14,2], Spectral Hashing (SH) [36], ITQ [10], Anchor Graph Hashing (AGH) [23], and Inductive Manifold Hashing (IMH) [30]. All these methods have publicly available code. Our method is implemented in Matlab with the graph cuts solver in mex. All experiments are run on a server using an Intel Xeon 2.67GHz CPU and 96 GB memory. We evaluate on three popular datasets: CIFAR10 [16], MNIST[7], and LabelMe [25].

---

[7] http://yann.lecun.com/exdb/mnist/

Table 3. The training time (single-core) on CIFAR10. All methods are using 32 bits. The GCC runs 10 iterations.

method	seconds	method	seconds
GCC	605	MLH [25]	3920
KSH [21]	483	BRE [18]	1037
DBC [28]	35	SSH [35]	3.0
KDBC [28]	56	CCA+ITQ [10]	5.3

4.1 Experiments on CIFAR10

CIFAR10 [16] contains 60K images in 10 object classes. As in previous studies of binary coding, we represent these images as 512-D GIST features [26][8]. We follow the experiment setting (and their evaluation implementation) in the KSH paper [21] and its public code. 1K images (100 per class) are randomly sampled as queries and the rest as the database. 2K images are randomly sampled from the database (200 per class) to build the pairwise supervision matrix $\mathbf{S}$: $S_{ij} = 1$ if the pair are in the same class and otherwise $S_{ij} = -1$ (0 for BRE/MLH). Our GCC and BRE/SSH/MLH/KSH accept pairwise supervision. DBC and CCA+ITQ needs explicit class labels for training. Table 3 shows the training time of several supervised methods.

Table 4 shows the results evaluated by two popular metrics: Hamming ranking and Hamming look-up [32]. The results of Hamming ranking is evaluated via the mean Average Precision (mAP), *i.e.*, the mean area under the precision-recall curve. We see that KSH [21] is very competitive and outperforms other previous methods. The GCC improves substantially upon KSH: it outperforms KSH by **3.0%** in 16 bits, **3.3%** in 32 bits, and **2.6%** in 64 bits (relative **8%-10%** improvement). Fig. 2 further shows the Hamming ranking results evaluated by the recall at the top N ranked data.

Table 4 also shows the results using Hamming look-up [32], *i.e.*, the accuracy when the Hamming distance is $\leq r$. Here we show $r = 2$. We see GCC is also superior in this evaluation setting. GCC outperforms KSH by 2.3% in 16 bits, 6.1% in 32 bits (and outperforms DBC by 4%).

Comparisons with SVM-Based Encoding Methods. Our method is partially based on SVMs (more precisely, Support Vector Classifiers or SVCs). In our SVM sub-problem, the labels $\mathbf{Y}$ directly come from the discrete graph cuts sub-problem. Consequently, throughout our optimization, the auxiliary variables $\mathbf{Y}$ are always treated as discrete in both sub-problems. There are previous solutions [22,28] that also partially rely on SVMs. However, the labels $\mathbf{Y}$ in those solutions are continuous-relaxed at some stage.

In Table 5 we compare with a method call SVM Hashing (SVMH), which was discussed in the thesis [22] of the first author of KSH [21]. If class labels are

---

[8] Actually, it is not necessary to represent them as GIST. Advanced representations such as CNN (convolutional neural networks) features [17] may significantly improve the overall accuracy of all encoding methods.

Table 4. The results on CIFAR10. On the top section are the supervised methods, and on the bottom section are the unsupervised ones. The middle column shows the Hamming ranking results evaluated by mAP. The right column shows the Hamming look-up results when the Hamming radius $r=2$. (Hamming look-up of $B = 64$ is ignored because this is impractical for longer codes [32]).

	Hamming ranking (mAP, %)			precision (%) @ $r = 2$	
B	16	32	64	16	32
GCC	**30.3**	**33.3**	**34.6**	**38.0**	**39.6**
KSH [21]	27.3	30.0	32.0	35.7	33.5
KDBC [28]	25.1	26.2	27.0	25.5	31.0
DBC [28]	23.8	26.3	28.6	29.3	35.6
CCA+ITQ [10]	21.4	21.7	23.1	23.6	27.6
MLH [25]	21.3	22.3	25.7	26.3	30.0
BRE [18]	18.7	19.5	20.1	24.2	20.7
SSH [35]	16.3	16.7	18.0	14.6	17.3
IMH [30]	18.4	19.4	20.1	21.9	25.3
ITQ [10]	16.9	17.3	17.7	24.2	18.1
AGH [23]	14.6	14.1	13.7	20.2	25.6
LSH [14]	13.4	14.2	14.7	17.6	8.5
SH [36]	13.2	13.0	13.1	19.2	21.8

Table 5. Comparisons on CIFAR10 with SVM Hashing [22] and its kernelized variant. All methods are using 10 bits. The kernel of KSVMH is the same as KSH.

method	SVMH [22]	KSVMH	KSH [21]	**GCC**
mAP	21.5	23.3	25.0	**28.2**

available, SVMH trains 10 one-vs-rest SVM classifiers, and uses the prediction functions as the encoding functions. SVMH is limited to 10 bits in CIFAR10. One can train the classifier using linear kernel or the kernel map κ. Table 5 shows the results of linear SVMH, Kernelized SVMH, KSH, and GCC (all using 10 bits for fair comparison). We see that GCC is still superior, even though the class labels are unknown to GCC. Actually, the one-vs-rest SVMs operate in a winner-take-all manner; but for binary coding or hashing, it is not sufficient to make two similar samples to be similar in just one bit. In our objective function, the term in Eqn.(5) is introduced to address this issue - it encourages as many as possible bits to be similar if two samples are similar. In our formulation, GCC is also able to produce >10 bits and shows increased performance.

More closely related to our method, DBC [28] is another method that adopts SVMs to train a classifier for each bit. However, DBC has a different objective function and applies a subgradient descent technique to solve for the labels that will be provided for SVMs. Table 4 shows that our method performs better

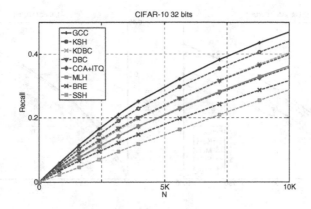

Fig. 2. The recall@N results on CIFAR10 using 32 bits. The x-axis is the number of top ranked data in Hamming ranking. The y-axis is the recall.

Table 6. The results on MNIST

	Hamming ranking (mAP, %)			precision (%) @ $r = 2$	
B	16	32	64	16	32
GCC	**86.3**	**88.1**	**88.9**	**87.1**	**87.5**
KSH [21]	78.9	82.4	83.7	84.1	85.8
MLH [25]	69.9	75.2	79.5	78.1	85.3
BRE [18]	52.2	59.9	62.4	65.4	79.2
DBC [28]	53.9	57.1	60.4	64.7	66.9
CCA+ITQ [10]	54.9	56.4	57.9	54.9	63.5
SSH [35]	43.2	48.6	48.7	64.8	74.3

than DBC. The original DBC in [28] uses linear encoding functions, so for fair comparison, we have also tested its kernelized version using the same kernel map κ as we use. We term this as kernelized DBC (KDBC) in Table 4. We see that our method also outperforms KDBC using the same kernel map. These experiments indicate the performance of GCC is not simply due to the SVMs.

4.2 Experiments on MNIST

The MNIST dataset has 70K images of handwritten digits in 10 classes. We represent each image as a 784-D vector concatenating all raw pixels. We randomly sample 1K vectors (100 per class) as queries and use the rest as the database. 2K vectors (200 per class) are sampled from the database as the training data.

We compare with the supervised methods in Table 6 (the unsupervised methods perform worse, *e.g.*, than KSH, and so are ignored). We find that KSH still outperforms other previous methods substantially, and GCC improves on KSH by considerable margins.

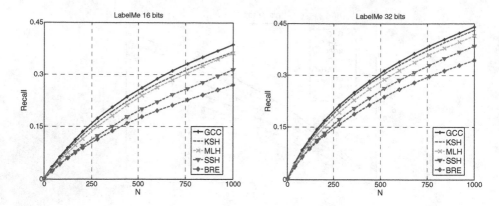

Fig. 3. The results on LabelMe using 16 and 32 bits. The x-axis is the number of top ranked data in Hamming ranking. The y-axis is the recall among these data.

4.3 Experiments on LabelMe

The LabelMe dataset [25] contains 22K images represented as 512-D GIST, where each image has 50 semantic neighbors marked as the ground truth. Only pairwise similarity labels are available in this dataset. We follow the evaluation protocol as in [25]. The data are ranked by their Hamming distances to the query, and the recall at the top N ranked data is evaluated ($R@N$). In this dataset, the reduced graph cuts step in our algorithm does not remove the pairwise terms with positive labels ($S_{ij} = 1$) because they are in a small number. All the methods are trained using 2K randomly sampled images and their pairwise labels.

Fig. 3 shows the performance of the supervised methods. Because only pairwise labels are available, the CCA+ITQ and DBC methods which need class-wise labels are not directly applicable. This also indicates an advantage of GCC that it does not require class-wise labels. We see that GCC is competitive. The measure $R@1000$ of GCC outperforms KSH by 2.1% when $B=16$, and 1.0% when $B=32$.

5 Discussion and Conclusion

We have presented a graph cuts algorithm for learning binary encoding functions. This is a beginning attempt to use discrete label assignment solvers in the binary encoding problems. In the formulations in this paper, a term has been introduced to measure the loss $\mathcal{L}$ between $\mathbf{y}$ and $\mathbf{f}(\mathbf{x})$. We note the loss function $\mathcal{L}$ need not be limited to the form (hinge loss) used in this paper. Our graph cuts solution is applicable for other forms of $\mathcal{L}$, and only the unary term needs to be modified. The development of a better $\mathcal{L}$ can be an open question, and we will study it as future work.

References

1. Agarwala, A., Dontcheva, M., Agrawala, M., Drucker, S., Colburn, A., Curless, B., Salesin, D., Cohen, M.: Interactive digital photomontage. In: SIGGRAPH (2004)
2. Andoni, A., Indyk, P.: Near-optimal hashing algorithms for approximate nearest neighbor in high dimensions. In: FOCS, pp. 459–468 (2006)
3. Blake, A., Kohli, P., Rother, C.: Markov random fields for vision and image processing. The MIT Press (2011)
4. Boykov, Y., Kolmogorov, V.: An experimental comparison of min-cut/max-flow algorithms for energy minimization in vision. TPAMI (2004)
5. Boykov, Y., Veksler, O., Zabih, R.: Fast approximate energy minimization via graph cuts. In: ICCV (1999)
6. Cortes, C., Vapnik, V.: Support-vector networks. Machine Learning, 273–297 (1995)
7. Fan, R.E., Chang, K.W., Hsieh, C.J., Wang, X.R., Lin, C.J.: Liblinear: A library for large linear classification. JMLR, 1871–1874 (2008)
8. Ge, T., He, K., Ke, Q., Sun, J.: Optimized product quantization for approximate nearest neighbor search. In: CVPR (2013)
9. Ge, T., He, K., Ke, Q., Sun, J.: Optimized product quantization. TPAMI (2014)
10. Gong, Y., Lazebnik, S.: Iterative quantization: A procrustean approach to learning binary codes. In: CVPR (2011)
11. Hastie, T.J., Tibshirani, R.J., Friedman, J.H.: The Elements of Statistical Learning. Springer, New York (2009)
12. He, K., Sun, J.: Statistics of patch offsets for image completion. In: Fitzgibbon, A., Lazebnik, S., Perona, P., Sato, Y., Schmid, C. (eds.) ECCV 2012, Part II. LNCS, vol. 7573, pp. 16–29. Springer, Heidelberg (2012)
13. He, K., Wen, F., Sun, J.: K-means Hashing: an Affinity-Preserving Quantization Method for Learning Binary Compact Codes. In: CVPR (2013)
14. Indyk, P., Motwani, R.: Approximate nearest neighbors: towards removing the curse of dimensionality. In: STOC, pp. 604–613 (1998)
15. Kolmogorov, V., Rother, C.: Minimizing nonsubmodular functions with graph cuts-a review. TPAMI (2007)
16. Krizhevsky, A.: Cifar-10, http://www.cs.toronto.edu/~kriz/cifar.html
17. Krizhevsky, A., Sutskever, I., Hinton, G.: Imagenet classification with deep convolutional neural networks (2012)
18. Kulis, B., Darrell, T.: Learning to hash with binary reconstructive embeddings. In: NIPS, pp. 1042–1050 (2009)
19. Kulis, B., Grauman, K.: Kernelized locality-sensitive hashing for scalable image search. In: ICCV (2009)
20. Kwatra, V., Schödl, A., Essa, I., Turk, G., Bobick, A.: Graphcut textures: image and video synthesis using graph cuts. In: SIGGRAPH, pp. 277–286 (2003)
21. Liu, W., Wang, J., Ji, R., Jiang, Y.-G., Chang, S.-F.: Supervised hashing with kernels. In: CVPR (2012)
22. Liu, W.: Large-Scale Machine Learning for Classification and Search. Ph.D. thesis, Columbia University (2012)
23. Liu, W., Wang, J., Kumar, S., Chang, S.-F.: Hashing with graphs. In: ICML (2011)
24. Norouzi, M., Fleet, D.: Cartesian k-means. In: CVPR (2013)
25. Norouzi, M.E., Fleet, D.J.: Minimal loss hashing for compact binary codes. In: ICML, pp. 353–360 (2011)

26. Oliva, A., Torralba, A.: Modeling the shape of the scene: a holistic representation of the spatial envelope. IJCV (2001)
27. Pritch, Y., Kav-Venaki, E., Peleg, S.: Shift-map image editing. In: ICCV (2009)
28. Rastegari, M., Farhadi, A., Forsyth, D.: Attribute discovery via predictable discriminative binary codes. In: Fitzgibbon, A., Lazebnik, S., Perona, P., Sato, Y., Schmid, C. (eds.) ECCV 2012, Part VI. LNCS, vol. 7577, pp. 876–889. Springer, Heidelberg (2012)
29. Scharstein, D., Szeliski, R.: A taxonomy and evaluation of dense two-frame stereo correspondence algorithms. IJCV, 7–42 (2002)
30. Shen, F., Shen, C., Shi, Q., van den Hengel, A., Tang, Z.: Inductive hashing on manifolds. In: CVPR (2013)
31. Tan, R.T.: Visibility in bad weather from a single image. In: CVPR, pp. 1–8 (2008)
32. Torralba, A.B., Fergus, R., Weiss, Y.: Small codes and large image databases for recognition. In: CVPR (2008)
33. Vedaldi, A., Fulkerson, B.: Vlfeat: An open and portable library of computer vision algorithms. In: Proceedings of the International Conference on Multimedia, pp. 1469–1472. ACM (2010)
34. Vedaldi, A., Zisserman, A.: Efficient additive kernels via explicit feature maps. TPAMI, 480–492 (2012)
35. Wang, J., Kumar, S., Chang, S.-F.: Semi-supervised hashing for scalable image retrieval. In: CVPR (2010)
36. Weiss, Y., Torralba, A., Fergus, R.: Spectral hashing. In: NIPS, pp. 1753–1760 (2008)

Planar Structure Matching
under Projective Uncertainty for Geolocation

Ang Li, Vlad I. Morariu, and Larry S. Davis

University of Maryland, College Park
{angli,morariu,lsd}@umiacs.umd.edu

Abstract. Image based geolocation aims to answer the question: where was this ground photograph taken? We present an approach to geolocalating a single image based on matching human delineated line segments in the ground image to automatically detected line segments in ortho images. Our approach is based on distance transform matching. By observing that the uncertainty of line segments is non-linearly amplified by projective transformations, we develop an uncertainty based representation and incorporate it into a geometric matching framework. We show that our approach is able to rule out a considerable portion of false candidate regions even in a database composed of geographic areas with similar visual appearances.

Keywords: uncertainty modeling, geometric matching, line segments.

1 Introduction

Given a ground-level photograph, the image geolocation task is to estimate the geographic location and orientation of the camera. Such systems provide an alternative way to localize an image or a scene when and where GPS is unavailable. Visual based geolocation has wide applications in areas such as robotics, autonomous driving, news image organization and geographic information systems. We focus on a single image geolocation task which compares a single ground-based query image against a database of ortho images over the candidate geolocations. Each of the candidate ortho images is evaluated and ranked according to the query. This task is difficult because (1) significant color discrepancy exists between cameras used for ground and ortho images; (2) the images taken at different times result in appearance difference even for the same locations (e.g. a community before and after being developed); (3) the ortho image databases usually have a very large scale, which requires efficient algorithms.

Due to the difficulty of the geolocation problem, many recent works include extra data such as georeferenced image databases [9,14], digital elevation models (DEM) [1], light detection and ranging (LIDAR) data [16], etc. Whenever photographs need to be geolocated in a new geographic area, this side data has to be acquired first. This limits the expandability of these geolocation approaches. One natural question to ask is whether we can localize a ground photograph using only widely accessible satellite images.

D. Fleet et al. (Eds.): ECCV 2014, Part VII, LNCS 8695, pp. 265–280, 2014.

Fig. 1. Geolocation involves finding the corresponding location of the ground image (on the left) in ortho images (an example on the right) ©Google

We address this geolocation task with no side data by casting it as an image matching problem. This is challenging because the camera orientation of a ground image is approximately orthogonal to that of its corresponding ortho image. Commonly used image features are not invariant to such wide camera rotation. In addition, considering the presence of color and lighting difference between ground and ortho images, color-based and intensity-based image features become unreliable for establishing image correspondence. Therefore, structural information becomes the most feasible feature for this application. We utilize linear structures – line segments – as the features to be matched between ground and ortho images.

Both ground and ortho images are projections of the 3D world. The information loss between these two images becomes an obstacle even for matching binary line segments. Instead of inferring 3D structure, we extract and match the linear structures that lie on the ground a large subset of which is visible in both ground and ortho images. The ortho images can be regarded as approximately 2D planes and we use classic line extraction algorithms to locate the extended linear structures in them. The ground images are more challenging so we ask humans annotate the ground lines for these images. This is not a burdensome task. Additionally, the horizon line is annotated by the human so we can construct its corresponding aerial view with the camera parameters known.

Based on chamfer matching [15], we derive a criterion function for matching each ortho image with the ortho-rectified view of the ground image. However, the projection matrix for transforming the ground image to its ortho view is usually numerically ill-conditioned. Even a small perturbation to the annotated end points of a line segment may result in significant uncertainty in location and orientation of the projected line segments, especially those near the horizon line. Therefore, we propose a probablistic representation of line segments by modeling their uncertainty and introduce a model of geometric uncertainty into our matching criterion. Within each ortho image, the matching scores for possible pairs of camera locations and orientations are exhaustively evaluated. This sliding window search is speeded up by means of distance transforms [7] and convolution operations.

Contributions. The main contributions of this paper include (1) an uncertainty model for line segments under projective transformations (2) a novel distance transform based matching criterion under uncertainty (3) the application of geometric matching to single image geolocation with no side data.

2   Related Work

Image Geolocation. Previous work on image geolocation can be classified into two main streams: geotagged image retrieval and model based matching. Hays et al. [9] were among the first to treat the image geolocation as a data driven image retrieval problem. Their approach is based on a large scale geotagged image database. Those images with similar visual appearance to the query image are extracted and their GPS tags are collected to generate a confidence map for possible geolocations. Li et al. [13] devised an algorithm to match low level features from large scale database to ground image features in a prioritized order specified by likelihood. Similar approaches improve the image retrieval algorithms applied to ground level image databases [5,20,24,25]. Generally, data driven approaches assume all possible views of the ground images are covered in the database. Otherwise, the system will not return a reasonable geolocation.

Apart from the retrieval-style geolocation, the other track is to match the image geometry with 3D models to estimate the camera pose. Battz et al. [1] proposed a solution to address the geolocation in mountainous terrain area by extracting skyline contours from ground images and matching them to the digital elevation models. From the 3D reconstruction viewpoint, some other approaches estimate the camera pose by matching images with 3D point cloud [10,12,19].

Few works make use of the satellite images in the geolocation task. Bansal et al. [2] match the satellite images and aerial images by finding the facade of the building and rectifying the facade for matching with the query ground images. Lin et al. [14] address the out-of-sample generalization problem suffered by data-driven methods. The core of their method is learning a cross-view feature correspondence between ground and ortho images. However, their approach still requires a considerable amount of geo-tagged image data for learning.

Our work differs from all of the above work in that our approach casts the geolocation task as a linear geometric matching problem instead of reconstructing the 3D world, and it is relatively "low-cost" using only the satellite images without the need for large labeled training sets or machine learning.

Geometric Matching. In the geometric matching domain, our approach is related to line matching and shape matching. Matching line segments has been an important problem in geometric modeling. Schmid et al. [21] proposed a line matching approach based on cross correlation of neighborhood intensity. This approach is limited by its requirement on prior knowledge of the epipolar geometry. Bay et al. [4] match line segments using color histograms and remove false correspondences by topological filtering. In recent years, line segments have been shown to be robust to matching images in poorly textured scenes [11,23]. Most of the existing works rely on local appearance-based features while our approach is completely based on matching the binary linear structures.

Our approach is motivated by chamfer matching [3], which has been widely applied in shape matching. Chamfer matching involves finding for each feature in an image its nearest feature in the other image. The computation can be efficiently achieved via distance transforms. A natural extension of chamfer matching is to incorporate the point orientation as an additional feature. Shotton et al. [22] proposed oriented chamfer matching by adding an angle difference term into their formulation and applied this technique in matching contour fragments for general object recognition. Another method for encoding the orientation is the fast directional chamfer matching proposed by Liu et al. [15]. They generalize the original chamfer matching approach by seeing each point as a 3D feature which is composed of both location and orientation. Efficient algorithms are employed for computing the 3D distance transform based on [7]. However, for geolocation, our problem is to match a small linear structures to fairly large structures that contain much noise, especially in ortho images. Our approach is carefully designed specifically for the needs of geolocation: it takes into account the projective transformations and line segments with uncertain end points as part of the matching criterion function.

Uncertainty Modeling. Uncertainty is often involved in various computer vision problems. Olson [17] proposed a probabilistic formulation for Hausdorff matching. Similar to Olsons work, Elgammal et al. [6] extended Chamfer matching to a probabilistic formulation. Both approaches consider only the problem of matching an exact model to uncertain image features, while our work handles the situation when the model is uncertain. An uncertainty model is proposed in [18] for projective transformations in multi-camera object tracking. They considered the case where the imaged point is sufficiently far from the line at infinity and provided an approximation method to compute the uncertainty under projective transformation. Our work differs in that (1) we provide an exact solution for projective uncertainty of line segments, and (2) we do not assume that line segments are far from the horizon line. To our knowledge, none of the previous work in geolocation were incorporated with uncertainty models.

3   Our Approach

A query consists of a single ground image with unknown location and orientation is provided. This ground image is then matched exhaustively to each candidate ortho images, and ortho images are ranked according to their matching scores. The ortho images are densely sampled by overlapped sliding windows over the candidate geographic areas. The scale of each ortho image can be around 10 centimeters per pixel. The ground images could be taken at any location within ortho images. Even in a 640×640 ortho image, there are over millions of possible discretized camera poses. The geolocation task is to localize the ground image into the ortho images, not necessarily the camera pose.

Fig. 2. Examples of line segments annotated in ground images ©Google

We have two assumptions here to simplify this problem. First, the camera parameter (focal length) for ground images is known, a reasonable assumption, since modern cameras store this information as part of the image metadata. Second, we assume the photographer holds the camera horizontally, i.e. the camera optical axis is approximately parallel to the ground. Camera rotation around the optical axis may happen and is handled by our solution. No restrictions assumed for the satellite cameras as long as satellite imagery is rectified to ensure linear structures remain linear, which is generally true.

3.1 Preprocessing

We reconstruct the aerial view of the ground image by estimating the perspective camera model from the manually annotated horizon line. In our matching approach, line segments are matched between ground and ortho images. Lines on the ground are most likely to be viewed in both ground and ortho images – most other lines are on the vertical surfaces that are not visible in satellite imagery – so we ask users to annotate only line segments on the ground plane in query images. Once the projection matrix is known, the problem becomes one of geometric matching between two planes.

Line Segment Labeling. Line segments in ground images are annotated by human users clicking pairs of ending points. It is affordable to incorporate such human labeling process into our geolocation solution since the annotation is inexpensive and each query image needs to be labeled only once. A person can typically annotate a query image in at most two minutes. Fig. 2 shows four ground image samples with superimposed annotated line segments.

Line segments in the ortho images are automatically detected using the approach of [8]. The detected line segments lie mostly on either the ground plane or some plane parallel to the ground, such as the roof of a building. We do not attempt to remove these non-ground lines. In fact, some of the non-ground plane lines prove useful for matching. For example, the rooflines of many buildings have the same geometry as their ground footprints. Human annotators label linear features around the bottoms of these buildings. Thus, the line segments lying on the edges of a building roof still contribute to the structure matching. Our geometric matching algorithm assumes a high level of outliers, so even if the rooflines and footprints are different the matching can still be successful.

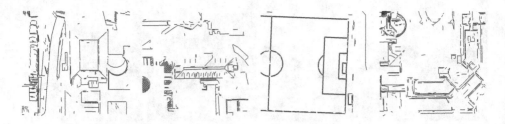

Fig. 3. Examples of line segments detected in ortho images ©Google

Aerial View Recovery. Using the computed perspective camera model, we transform the delineated ground photo line segments to an overhead view. Two assumptions are made for recovering the aerial view from ground images: (1) the camera focal length f is known, and (2) the optical axis of camera is parallel to the ground plane, i.e. the camera is held horizontally. These assumptions are not sufficient for reconstructing a complete 3D model but is sufficient for recovering the ground plane given the human annotated horizon line. The horizon line is located by finding two vanishing points, i.e. intersections of lines parallel in the real world.

Assuming the horizon line has slope angle θ, the ground image can be rotated clockwise by θ so that the horizon line becomes horizontal (the y-coordinate of rotated horizon line y_0'). The rotated coordinates are $(x', y')^\top = \mathbf{R}_\theta (x_g, y_g)^\top$ for every pixel (x_g, y_g) in the original ground image. In the world coordinate system (X, Y, Z), the camera is at the origin, facing the positive direction of the Y-axis, and the ground plane is $Z = -Z_0$. If we know pixel (x', y') is on the ground, then its corresponding world location can be computed by

$$x' = fX/Y, y' - y_0' = fZ_0/Y \Rightarrow X = x'Z_0/(y' - y_0'), Y = fZ_0/(y' - y_0') \quad (1)$$

For the ortho image, a pixel location (x_o, y_o) can be converted to world coordinates by $(X, Y) = (x_o/s, y_o/s)$ where s is a scale factor with unit 1/meter relating the pixel distance to real world distance.

3.2   Uncertainty Modeling for Line Segments

User annotations on ground images are often noisy. The two hand-selected end points could easily be misplaced by a few pixels. However, after projective transformation, even a small pertubation of one pixel can result in significant uncertainty in the location and orientation of the line segment, especially if that pixel is close to the horizon (see Fig. 5(a)). Therefore, before discussing the matching algorithm, we first study the problem of modeling the uncertainty of line segments under projective transformation to obtain a principled probabilistic description for ground based line segments. We obtain a closed form solution by assuming that the error of labeling an end point on ground images be described by a normal distribution in the original image. We first introduce a lemma which is essentially the integration of Gaussian density functions over a line segment.

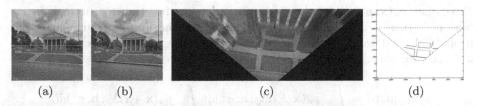

Fig. 4. Ortho view recovery: (a) the original ground image where the red line is the horizon line and the blue line is shifted 50 pixels below the red line so that the ortho-rectified view will not be too large. The blue line corresponds to the top line in the converted view (c); (b) is the same image with superimposed ground line segments; (c) is the ortho-rectified view; (d) is the corresponding linear features transformed to aerial view with field of view shown by dashed lines. The field of view (FOV) is 100 degrees which can be computed according to the focal length. ©Google

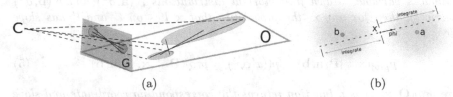

Fig. 5. (a) G is the ground image, O is the ortho-view and C is the camera. The projection from G to O results in dramatic uncertainty (b) Let a and b are centers of normal distributions. If pixel location x and the slope angle φ of the line it lies on are known, then the two end points must be on the alternative directions starting from x.

Lemma 1. *Let* $\mathbf{a}, \mathbf{b}$ *be column vectors in* $\mathbb{R}^n$ *and* $\|\mathbf{a}\| = 1$, *then*

$$\int_{t_1}^{t_2} \frac{1}{\sqrt{2\pi\sigma^2}} e^{-\frac{\|\mathbf{a}t+\mathbf{b}\|^2}{2\sigma^2}} dt$$

$$= e^{-\frac{\|\mathbf{b}\|^2 - (\mathbf{a}^\top \mathbf{b})^2}{2\sigma^2}} \cdot \frac{1}{2} \left(erf\left(\frac{t_2 + \mathbf{a}^\top \mathbf{b}}{\sqrt{2}\sigma}\right) - erf\left(\frac{t_1 + \mathbf{a}^\top \mathbf{b}}{\sqrt{2}\sigma}\right) \right) \quad (2)$$

The proof of this lemma can be found in Appendix. Using this lemma, we derive our main theorem about uncertainty modeling. A visualization of the high level idea is shown in Fig. 5(b).

Theorem 1. *Let* ℓ *be a 2D line segment whose end points are random variables drawn from normal distributions* $N(\mathbf{a}, \sigma^2)$ *and* $N(\mathbf{b}, \sigma^2)$ *respectively. Then for any point* $\mathbf{x}$, *the probability that* $\mathbf{x}$ *lies on* ℓ *and* ℓ *has slope angle* φ *is*

$$p(\mathbf{x}, \varphi | \mathbf{a}, \mathbf{b}) = e^{-\frac{\|\mathbf{x}-\mathbf{a}\|^2 - |\langle \mathbf{x}-\mathbf{a}, \Delta_\varphi \rangle|^2 + \|\mathbf{x}-\mathbf{b}\|^2 - |\langle \mathbf{x}-\mathbf{b}, \Delta_\varphi \rangle|^2}{2\sigma^2}}$$

$$\cdot \frac{1}{2} \left(1 - erf\left(\frac{\langle \mathbf{x} - \mathbf{a}, \Delta_\varphi \rangle}{\sqrt{2}\sigma}\right) erf\left(\frac{\langle \mathbf{x} - \mathbf{b}, \Delta_\varphi \rangle}{\sqrt{2}\sigma}\right) \right) \quad (3)$$

where $\Delta_\varphi = (\cos\varphi, \sin\varphi)^\top$ *is the unit vector with respect to the slope angle* φ.

Proof. Let $p_n(\mathbf{x}; \boldsymbol{\mu}, \sigma^2)$ be the probability density function for normal distribution $N(\boldsymbol{\mu}, \sigma^2)$. The probability that $\mathbf{x}$ lies on the line segment equals the probability that random variables of the two ending points are $\mathbf{x} + t_a \Delta_\varphi$ and $\mathbf{x} + t_b \Delta_\varphi$ for some $t_a, t_b \in \mathbb{R}$ and $t_a \cdot t_b \leq 0$, therefore

$$p(\mathbf{x}, \varphi | \mathbf{a}, \mathbf{b}) = \int_{-\infty}^0 p_n(\mathbf{x} + t\Delta_\varphi; \mathbf{a}, \sigma^2)dt \int_0^\infty p_n(\mathbf{x} + t\Delta_\varphi; \mathbf{b}, \sigma^2)dt$$
$$+ \int_0^\infty p_n(\mathbf{x} + t\Delta_\varphi; \mathbf{a}, \sigma^2)dt \int_{-\infty}^0 p_n(\mathbf{x} + t\Delta_\varphi; \mathbf{b}, \sigma^2)dt \qquad (4)$$

According to Lemma 1, Eq. 4 is equivalent to Eq. 3.   □

Proposition 1. *Let ℓ' be a line segment transformed from line segment ℓ in 2D space by nonsingular 3×3 projection matrix $\mathbf{P}$. If the two ending points of ℓ are random variables drawn from normal distributions $N(\mathbf{a}, \sigma^2)$ and $N(\mathbf{b}, \sigma^2)$ respectively, then for any $\mathbf{x}$, the probability that $\mathbf{x}$ lies on ℓ' and ℓ' has slope angle φ is*

$$p_{proj}(\mathbf{x}, \varphi | \mathbf{P}, \mathbf{a}, \mathbf{b}) = p((x', \varphi') = proj(\mathbf{P}^{-1}, \mathbf{x}, \varphi) | \mathbf{a}, \mathbf{b}) \qquad (5)$$

where $proj(\mathbf{Q}, \mathbf{x}, \varphi)$ is a function returns the corresponding coordinate and slope angle with respect to $\mathbf{x}$ and φ after projection transformation $\mathbf{Q}$.

The point coordinate transformed by $\mathbf{Q}$ can be obtained by homogeneous coordinate representation. For the slope angle, let $\mathbf{q}_i$ be the i-th row vector of projection matrix $\mathbf{Q}$, the transformed slope angle φ' at location $\mathbf{x} = (x, y)^\top$ is

$$\varphi' = \arctan \frac{f(\mathbf{q}_2, \mathbf{q}_3, x, y, \varphi)}{f(\mathbf{q}_1, \mathbf{q}_3, x, y, \varphi)} \qquad (6)$$

where

$$f(\mathbf{u}, \mathbf{v}, x, y, \varphi) = (u_2 v_1 - u_1 v_2)(x \sin \varphi - y \cos \varphi)$$
$$+ (u_1 v_3 - u_3 v_1) \cos \varphi + (u_2 v_3 - u_3 v_2) \sin \varphi . \qquad (7)$$

According to the above, for each pixel location in the recovered view of a ground image, the probability that the pixel lies on a line segment given a slope angle can be computed in closed form. Fig. 6 shows an example probability distribution for line segments under uncertainty. It can be observed from the plot that more uncertainty is associated with line segments farther from the camera and is resulted from a larger σ value.

3.3   Geometric Matching under Uncertainty

Our approach to planar structure matching is motivated by chamfer matching. Chamfer matching efficiently measure the similarity between two sets of image

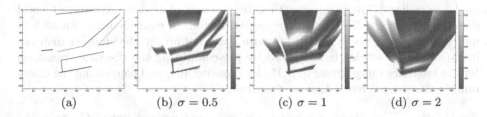

(a)   (b) $\sigma = 0.5$ (c) $\sigma = 1$ (d) $\sigma = 2$

Fig. 6. Examples of uncertainty modeling: (a) the ortho-rectified line segments (b-d) the negation of probability log map for points on lines. The probability for each pixel location is obtained by summing up the probabilities for all discretized orientations. The camera is located in the image center and faces upward.

features by evaluating the sum of distances between each feature in one image and its nearest feature in the other image [3]. More formally,

$$D_c(\mathbf{A}, \mathbf{B}) = \sum_{\mathbf{a} \in \mathbf{A}} d(\mathbf{a}, \arg\min_{\mathbf{b} \in \mathbf{B}} d(\mathbf{a}, \mathbf{b})) \tag{8}$$

where $\mathbf{A}, \mathbf{B}$ are two sets of features, and $d(\cdot, \cdot)$ is the distance measure for a feature pair. Commonly, feature sets contain only the 2D coordinates of points, even if those points are sampled from lines that also have an associated orientation. Oriented chamfer matching (OCM) [22] makes use of point orientation by modifying the distance measure to include the sum of angle differences between each feature point and its closest point in the other image. Another way to incorporate orientation is directional chamfer matching (DCM) [15] which defines features to be, more generally, points in 3D space (x-y coordinates and orientation angle). This approach uses the same distance function as the original chamfer matching but has a modified feature distance measure. We follow the DCM method [15] to define our feature space. In our case, point orientation is set to the slope angle of the line it lies on.

Notations. All of the points in our formulation are in the 3D space. A point feature is defined as $\mathbf{u} = (\mathbf{u}_l, u_\phi)$ where $\mathbf{u}_l$ represents the 2D coordinates in real world and u_ϕ is the orientation associated with location $\mathbf{u}_l$. $\mathbf{G}_p$ is the set of points $\{\mathbf{g}\}$ in the ground image with uncertainty modeled by probability distribution $p(\cdot)$. $\mathbf{O}$ is the set of points in the ortho image. $\mathbf{L}_G$ is the set of annotated line segments in the ground image. A line segment is defined as $\ell = (\mathbf{a}_\ell, \mathbf{b}_\ell)$ where $\mathbf{a}_\ell$ and $\mathbf{b}_\ell$ are the end points of ℓ. For any line segment ℓ and an abitrary line segment $\hat{\ell}$ in the feature space, $p(\hat{\ell}|\ell)$ is the confidence of $\hat{\ell}$ by observing ℓ.

Distance Metric. The feature distance for $\mathbf{u}, \mathbf{v}$ is defined as

$$d(\mathbf{u}, \mathbf{v}) = \|\mathbf{u} - \mathbf{v}\|_g = \|\mathbf{u}_l - \mathbf{v}_l\|_2 + |u_\phi - v_\phi|_a \tag{9}$$

where $\|\mathbf{u}_l - \mathbf{v}_l\|_2$ is the Euclidean distance between 2D coordinates in meters and $|u_\phi - v_\phi|_a = \lambda \min(|u_\phi - v_\phi|, \pi - |u_\phi - v_\phi|)$ is the smallest difference between two angles in radians. The parameter λ relates the unit of angle to the unit of world distance. We choose $\lambda = 1$ so that π angle difference is equivalent to around 3.14 meters in the real world. For this feature space definition, the chamfer distance in Eq. 8 can be efficiently computed by pre-computing the distance transform for the reference image (refer to [7,15] for more details) and convolving the query image with the reference distance transform.

Formulation. The distance function for matching ground image $\mathbf{G}_p$ to ortho image $\mathbf{O}$ is formulated as

$$D(\mathbf{G}_p, \mathbf{O}) = D_m(\mathbf{G}_p, \mathbf{O}) + D_\times(\mathbf{G}_p, \mathbf{O}) \tag{10}$$

where D_m is the probablistic chamfer matching distance and $D_\times$ is a term penalizing line segment crossings. The probablistic chamfer matching distance is defined as

$$D_m(\mathbf{G}_p, \mathbf{O}) = \frac{1}{|\mathbf{L}_G|} \sum_{\ell \in \mathbf{L}_G} \int p(\hat{\ell}|\ell) \int p(\mathbf{g}|\hat{\ell}) \left(\min_{\mathbf{o} \in \mathbf{O}} \|\mathbf{g} - \mathbf{o}\|_g \right) d\mathbf{g} d\hat{\ell} . \tag{11}$$

The marginal distribution $\int p(\hat{\ell}|\ell)p(\mathbf{g}|\hat{\ell})d\hat{\ell} = p(\mathbf{g}|\ell)$ is the probability that point $\mathbf{g}_l$ lies on line segment ℓ with slope angle g_ϕ. Eq. 11 is equivalent to

$$D_m(\mathbf{G}_p, \mathbf{O}) = \frac{1}{|\mathbf{L}_G|} \sum_{\ell \in \mathbf{L}_G} \int p(\mathbf{g}|\ell) \left(\min_{\mathbf{o} \in \mathbf{O}} \|\mathbf{g} - \mathbf{o}\|_g \right) d\mathbf{g} \tag{12}$$

whose discrete representation is

$$D_m(\mathbf{G}_p, \mathbf{O}) = \sum_{\mathbf{g}} p'(\mathbf{g}|\mathbf{L}_G) \left(\min_{\mathbf{o} \in \mathbf{O}} \|\mathbf{g} - \mathbf{o}\|_g \right) \tag{13}$$

where $p'(\mathbf{g}|\mathbf{L}_G) = \frac{1}{|\mathbf{L}_G|} \sum_{\ell \in \mathbf{L}_G} \frac{p(\mathbf{g}|\ell)}{\sum_{\mathbf{g}} p(\mathbf{g}|\ell)}$ is the probability of points lying on the structure and each line segment equally contributes to the distance value. In fact, Eq. 12 is equivalent to the original chamfer matching (Eq. 8) if no uncertainty is present.

Intersections between ortho line segments and ground line segments indicate low matching quality. Therefore, we add an additional term into our formulation to penalize camera poses that result in too many line segment intersections. The cross penalty for line segments is defined as

$$D_\times(\mathbf{G}_p, \mathbf{O}) = \frac{\sum_{\ell \in \mathbf{L}_G} \int p(\hat{\ell}|\ell) \sum_{\mathbf{o} \in \mathbf{O}} \int p(\mathbf{g}|\hat{\ell})|g_\phi - o_\phi|_a \delta(\mathbf{g}_l - \mathbf{o}_l) d\mathbf{g} d\hat{\ell}}{\sum_{\ell \in \mathbf{L}_G} \int p(\hat{\ell}|\ell) \sum_{\mathbf{o} \in \mathbf{O}} \int p(\mathbf{g}|\hat{\ell}) \delta(\mathbf{g}_l - \mathbf{o}_l) d\mathbf{g} d\hat{\ell}} \tag{14}$$

where $\delta(\cdot)$ is the delta function. This function is is a normalized summation of angle differences for all intersection locations, which are point-wise equally weighted. Because $\int p(\hat{\ell}|\ell)p(\mathbf{g}|\hat{\ell})d\hat{\ell} = p(\mathbf{g}|\ell)$, the function is equivalent to

$$D_\times(\mathbf{G}_p, \mathbf{O}) = \frac{\sum_{\ell \in \mathbf{L}_G} \int p(\mathbf{g}|\ell) \sum_{\mathbf{o} \in \mathbf{O}} |g_\phi - o_\phi|_a \delta(\mathbf{g}_l - \mathbf{o}_l) d\mathbf{g}}{\sum_{\ell \in \mathbf{L}_G} \int p(\mathbf{g}|\ell) \sum_{\mathbf{o} \in \mathbf{O}} \delta(\mathbf{g}_l - \mathbf{o}_l) d\mathbf{g}} \tag{15}$$

whose equivalent discrete formulation is

$$D_\times(\mathbf{G}_p, \mathbf{O}) = \frac{\sum_\mathbf{g} p'(\mathbf{g}|\mathbf{L}_G) \sum_{\mathbf{o}\in\mathbf{O}} |g_\phi - o_\phi|_a \delta[\mathbf{g}_l - \mathbf{o}_l]}{\sum_\mathbf{g} p'(\mathbf{g}|\mathbf{L}_G) \sum_{\mathbf{o}\in\mathbf{O}} \delta[\mathbf{g}_l - \mathbf{o}_l]} \tag{16}$$

where $p'(\mathbf{g}|\mathbf{L}_G)$ is defined in Eq.3.3 and $\delta[\cdot]$ is the discrete delta function.

Hypothesis Generation. Given a ground image $\mathbf{G}_p$, the score for ortho image $\mathbf{O}_i$ corresponds to one of the candidate geolocations. is evaluated as the minumum possible distance, so the estimated fine camera pose within ortho image $\mathbf{O}_i$ is

$$\hat{\mathbf{x}}_i = \hat{\mathbf{x}}(\mathbf{O}_i, \mathbf{G}_p) = \arg\min_{\mathbf{x}_l, x_\phi} D(\mathbf{R}_{x_\phi}\mathbf{G}_p + \mathbf{x}_l, \mathbf{O}_i) \tag{17}$$

where $\mathbf{R}_\alpha$ is the rotation matrix corresponded to angle α.

3.4 Implementation Remarks

The two distance functions can be computed efficiently based on distance transforms in which the orientations are projected into 60 uniformly sampled angles and the location of each point is at the pixel level. Firstly, probability $p(\mathbf{g}|\boldsymbol{\ell})$ can be computed in closed form according to Proposition 1. So the distribution $p'(\mathbf{g}|\mathbf{L}_G)$ can be pre-computed for each ground image. Based on 3D distance transform [15], Eq. 13 can be computed with a single convolution operation. The computation of Eq. 16 involves delta functions, which is essentially equivalent to a binary indicator mask for an ortho image: $M_\mathbf{O}(\mathbf{x}) = 1$ means there exists a point $\mathbf{o} \in \mathbf{O}$ located at coordinate $\mathbf{x}$ and 0 means there is no feature at this position. Such indicator mask can be directly obtained. So we compute for every orientation φ and location $\mathbf{x}$ a distance transform $A_\varphi(\mathbf{x}) = \sum_{\mathbf{o}\in\mathbf{O}\wedge\mathbf{o}_l=\mathbf{x}} |\varphi - o_\phi|_a$. The denominator of Eq. 16 can be computed directly by convolution, while the numerator needs to be computed independently for each orientation. For a discretized orientation θ, a matrix is defined $W(\mathbf{g}) = p'(\mathbf{g}|\mathbf{L}_G)M_\mathbf{O}(\mathbf{g}_l)$ for all $\mathbf{g}$ such that $g_\phi = \theta$ and otherwise $W(\mathbf{g}) = 0$. Convolving matrix W with the distance transform A_θ will achieve partial summation of Eq. 16. Summing them up for all orientations gives the numerator in Eq. 16.

4 Experiment

4.1 Experimental Setup

Dataset. We build a data set from Google Maps with an area of around $1km \times 1km$. We randomly extract 35 ground images from Google Street View together with their ground truth locations. Each ground image is a 640×640 color image. Field of view information is retrieved. A total of 400 satellite images are extracted using a sliding window within this area. Each ortho photo is also a 640×640 color image. The scale of ortho images is 0.1 meters per pixel. We use 10 ground images for experiments on the uncertainty parameter σ and the remaining 25 ground images are used for testing. Example ground and satellite images are shown in Fig. 7. Geolocation in this dataset is challenging because most of the area share highly similar visual appearance.

Fig. 7. Example ground images (upper) and ortho images (lower) from our dataset. The ground image can be taken anywhere within one of the satellite images. ©Google

Evaluation Criterion. Three quantitative criteria are employed to evaluate the experiments. First, we follow previous work [14] by using curves on *percentage of ranked candidate* vs. *percentage of correctly localized images*. By ranking all the ortho images in descending order of their matching scores, *percentage of ranked candidates* is the percentage of top ranked images in all of the ortho images and *percentage of correctly located images* is the percentage of all the queries whose ground truth locations are among the corresponding top ranked candidate images. Second, we obtain a overall score by counting the area under this curve (AUC). A higher overall score generally means more robustness in the algorithm. Third, we look into the *percentage of correctly localized images* among 1%, 2%, 5% and 10% top ranked locations.

Parameter Selection. Intuitively, σ represents the pixelwise variance of the line segment end points, so it should not be more than several pixels. We randomly pick 10 ground images and 20 ortho images including all ground-truth locations to compose training set for tuning σ. The geolocation performance over a set of σ values ranged from 0 to 3 with a step 0.5 are evaluated and shown in Fig. 8(a) where $\sigma = 0$ means no uncertainty model is used. The peak is reached when the σ is between 1.5 and 2. Therefore, we fix $\sigma = 2$ in all of the following experiment.

4.2   Results

Our geometric matching approach returns distance values densely cover every pixel and each of the 12 sampled orientations in each ortho image. The minimum distance is picked as the score of an ortho image. Therefore, our approach not only produces ranking among hundreds of ortho images but also shows possible camera locations and orientations.

We compare our approach with two existing matching methods i.e. oriented chamfer matching [22] and directional chamfer matching [15]. To study the effectiveness of our uncertainty models, we also evaluate these methods with uncertainty model embedded. DCM is equivalent to the first term D_m in our formulation. OCM is to find the nearest feature in the other image and compute the sum of pixel-wise distance and the angle differences to the same pixel. We apply our uncertainty model into their formulation in a similar way as the probablistic chamfer matching distance does. Thus, in total we have six approaches

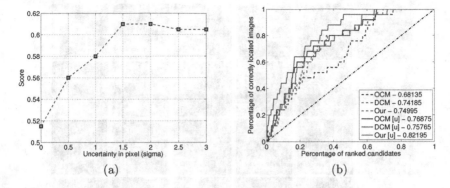

(a)   (b)

Fig. 8. (a) Geolocation AUC score under different uncertainty variances σ where $\sigma = 0$ represents the approach without uncertainty modeling. (b) Performance curve for six approaches: the ortho images are ranked in ascending order. The x-axis is the number of selected top ranked ortho images and the y-axis is the total number of ground image queries whose true locations are among these selected ortho images. The overall AUC scores are shown in the legend where "[u]" means "with uncertainty modeling". The black dash-dot line indicates chance performance.

Table 1. Comparison among oriented chamfer matching [22], directional chamfer matching [15] and our approach. The uncertainty model is evaluated for each method. For each evaluation criterion, the highest score is highlighted in red and the second one highlighted in blue. Our uncertainty based formulation is top among all these methods. Both of the three methods can be improved by our uncertainty model. OCM boosts its performance when incorporated with our probablistic representation.

Method	w/o uncertainty			w/ uncertainty		
	OCM	DCM	our	OCM	DCM	our
Top 1%	0.08	0.00	0.00	0.04	0.00	0.12
Top 2%	0.08	0.04	0.08	0.04	0.04	0.20
Top 5%	0.16	0.12	0.12	0.20	0.12	0.32
Top 10%	0.24	0.24	0.28	0.28	0.28	0.44
Score(AUC)	0.6814	0.7419	0.7500	0.7688	0.7577	0.8219

in our comparison. Their performance curves are shown in Fig. 8(b). Over 90% of the ground queries can be correctly located when half of the ortho images are rejected. Numerical results are in Table 1. While our approach significantly outperforms at any percentage of retrieved images, our performance improvement is particularly large for top ranked images.

Four successfully localized queries are shown in Fig. 9. For these ground images, the ground truth locations are included in the top 5 ranked candidate ortho images out of 400. From this visualization, few labeling errors can be noticed from miss-alignment between ortho images and rectified line segments. Among these top responses, most false alarms are building roofs. A common property is that they have relatively denser line features. Another issue is the line detection

Fig. 9. Four queries successfully geolocated within top five candidates are shown. The leftmost column is the ground image with annotated line segments. For each query, top five scoring ortho images are shown in ascending order of their rank. Ground-truths are highlighted by green bounding boxes. For each ortho image, blue lines are automatically detected and red lines are parsed from ortho-rectified ground images. Green cross indicates the most probable camera location within that ortho image.

in ortho images does not handle shadows well. Most linear structures in these shadow areas are not detected.

5   Conclusion

We investigated the single image geolocation problem by matching human annotated line segments in the ground image to automatically detected lines in the ortho images. An uncertainty model is devised for line segments under projective transformations. Using this uncertainty model, ortho-rectified ground images are matched to candidate ortho images by distance transform based methods. The experiment has shown the effectiveness of our approach in geographic areas with similar local appearances.

Acknowledgement. This material is based upon work supported by United States Air Force under Contract FA8650-12-C-7213 and by the Intelligence Advanced Research Projects Activity (IARPA) via Air Force Research Laboratory. The U.S. Government is authorized to reproduce and distribute reprints for Governmental purposes notwithstanding any copyright annotation thereon. Disclaimer: The views and conclusions contained herein are those of the authors and should not be interpreted as necessarily representing the official policies or endorsements, either expressed or implied, of IARPA, AFRL, or the U.S. Government.

References

1. Baatz, G., Saurer, O., Köser, K., Pollefeys, M.: Large scale visual geo-localization of images in mountainous terrain. In: Fitzgibbon, A., Lazebnik, S., Perona, P., Sato, Y., Schmid, C. (eds.) ECCV 2012, Part II. LNCS, vol. 7573, pp. 517–530. Springer, Heidelberg (2012), http://dx.doi.org/10.1007/978-3-642-33709-3_37
2. Bansal, M., Sawhney, H.S., Cheng, H., Daniilidis, K.: Geo-localization of street views with aerial image databases. In: ACM Int'l Conf. Multimedia (MM), pp. 1125–1128 (2011), http://doi.acm.org/10.1145/2072298.2071954
3. Barrow, H.G., Tenenbaum, J.M., Bolles, R.C., Wolf, H.C.: Parametric correspondence and chamfer matching: Two new techniques for image matching. In: Proceedings of the 5th International Joint Conference on Artificial Intelligence, IJCAI 1977, vol. 2, pp. 659–663. Morgan Kaufmann Publishers Inc., San Francisco (1977), http://dl.acm.org/citation.cfm?id=1622943.1622971
4. Bay, H., Ferrari, V., Van Gool, L.: Wide-baseline stereo matching with line segments. In: IEEE Computer Society Conference on Computer Vision and Pattern Recognition, CVPR 2005, vol. 1, pp. 329–336 (June 2005)
5. Chen, D., Baatz, G., Koser, K., Tsai, S., Vedantham, R., Pylvanainen, T., Roimela, K., Chen, X., Bach, J., Pollefeys, M., Girod, B., Grzeszczuk, R.: City-scale landmark identification on mobile devices. In: 2011 IEEE Conference on Computer Vision and Pattern Recognition (CVPR), pp. 737–744 (November 2011)
6. Elgammal, A., Shet, V., Yacoob, Y., Davis, L.: Exemplar-based tracking and recognition of arm gestures. In: Proceedings of the 3rd International Symposium on Image and Signal Processing and Analysis, ISPA 2003, vol. 2, pp. 656–661 (September 2003)
7. Felzenszwalb, P.F., Huttenlocher, D.P.: Distance transforms of sampled functions. Theory of Computing 8(19), 415–428 (2012), http://www.theoryofcomputing.org/articles/v008a019
8. von Gioi, R., Jakubowicz, J., Morel, J.M., Randall, G.: Lsd: A fast line segment detector with a false detection control. IEEE Trans. Pattern Analysis and Machine Intelligence (PAMI) 32(4), 722–732 (2010)
9. Hays, J., Efros, A.A.: im2gps: estimating geographic information from a single image. In: IEEE Conf. Computer Vision and Pattern Recognition (CVPR) (2008)
10. Irschara, A., Zach, C., Frahm, J.M., Bischof, H.: From structure-from-motion point clouds to fast location recognition. In: IEEE Conf. Computer Vision and Pattern Recognition (CVPR), pp. 2599–2606 (June 2009)
11. Kim, H., Lee, S.: Wide-baseline image matching based on coplanar line intersections. In: 2010 IEEE/RSJ International Conference on Intelligent Robots and Systems (IROS), pp. 1157–1164 (October 2010)
12. Li, Y., Snavely, N., Huttenlocher, D., Fua, P.: Worldwide pose estimation using 3D point clouds. In: Fitzgibbon, A., Lazebnik, S., Perona, P., Sato, Y., Schmid, C. (eds.) ECCV 2012, Part I. LNCS, vol. 7572, pp. 15–29. Springer, Heidelberg (2012), http://dx.doi.org/10.1007/978-3-642-33718-5_2
13. Li, Y., Snavely, N., Huttenlocher, D.P.: Location recognition using prioritized feature matching. In: Daniilidis, K., Maragos, P., Paragios, N. (eds.) ECCV 2010, Part II. LNCS, vol. 6312, pp. 791–804. Springer, Heidelberg (2010), http://dl.acm.org/citation.cfm?id=1888028.1888088
14. Lin, T.Y., Belongie, S., Hays, J.: Cross-view image geolocalization. In: IEEE Conf. Computer Vision and Pattern Recognition (CVPR). Portland, OR (June 2013)

15. Liu, M.Y., Tuzel, O., Veeraraghavan, A., Chellappa, R.: Fast directional chamfer matching. In: IEEE Conf. Computer Vision and Pattern Recognition (CVPR) (2010)
16. Matei, B., Vander Valk, N., Zhu, Z., Cheng, H., Sawhney, H.: Image to lidar matching for geotagging in urban environments. In: IEEE Workshop on Applications of Computer Vision (WACV), pp. 413–420 (January 2013)
17. Olson, C.: A probabilistic formulation for hausdorff matching. In: Proceedings of 1998 IEEE Computer Society Conference on Computer Vision and Pattern Recognition, pp. 150–156 (June 1998)
18. Sankaranarayanan, A.C., Chellappa, R.: Optimal multi-view fusion of object locations. In: Proceedings of the 2008 IEEE Workshop on Motion and Video Computing, WMVC 2008, pp. 1–8. IEEE Computer Society, Washington, DC (2008), http://dx.doi.org/10.1109/WMVC.2008.4544048
19. Sattler, T., Leibe, B., Kobbelt, L.: Fast image-based localization using direct 2d-to-3d matching. In: IEEE Int'l Conf. Computer Vision (ICCV), pp. 667–674 (November 2011)
20. Schindler, G., Brown, M., Szeliski, R.: City-scale location recognition. In: IEEE Conf. Computer Vision and Pattern Recognition (CVPR), pp. 1–7 (2007), http://www.cs.bath.ac.uk/brown/location/location.html
21. Schmid, C., Zisserman, A.: Automatic line matching across views. In: Proceedings of the 1997 Conference on Computer Vision and Pattern Recognition (CVPR 1997), pp. 666–. IEEE Computer Society, Washington, DC (1997), http://dl.acm.org/citation.cfm?id=794189.794450
22. Shotton, J., Blake, A., Cipolla, R.: Multiscale categorical object recognition using contour fragments. IEEE Trans. Pattern Analysis and Machine Intelligence (PAMI) 30(7), 1270–1281 (2008)
23. Wang, L., Neumann, U., You, S.: Wide-baseline image matching using line signatures. In: 2009 IEEE 12th International Conference on Computer Vision, pp. 1311–1318 (September 2009)
24. Zamir, A., Shah, M.: Image geo-localization based on multiple nearest neighbor feature matching using generalized graphs. IEEE Trans. Pattern Analysis and Machine Intelligence (PAMI) (2014)
25. Zheng, Y.T., Zhao, M., Song, Y., Adam, H., Buddemeier, U., Bissacco, A., Brucher, F., Chua, T.S., Neven, H.: Tour the world: Building a web-scale landmark recognition engine. In: IEEE Conf. Computer Vision and Pattern Recognition (CVPR), pp. 1085–1092 (2009)

Active Deformable Part Models Inference*

Menglong Zhu, Nikolay Atanasov, George J. Pappas, and Kostas Daniilidis

GRASP Laboratory, University of Pennsylvania
3330 Walnut Street, Philadelphia, PA 19104, USA**

Abstract. This paper presents an active approach for part-based object detection, which optimizes the order of part filter evaluations and the time at which to stop and make a prediction. Statistics, describing the part responses, are learned from training data and are used to formalize the part scheduling problem as an *offline* optimization. Dynamic programming is applied to obtain a policy, which balances the number of part evaluations with the classification accuracy. During inference, the policy is used as a look-up table to choose the *part order* and the *stopping time* based on the observed filter responses. The method is faster than cascade detection with deformable part models (which does not optimize the part order) with negligible loss in accuracy when evaluated on the PASCAL VOC 2007 and 2010 datasets.

1 Introduction

Part-based models such as deformable part models (DPM) [7] have become the state of the art in today's object detection methods. They offer powerful representations which can be learned from annotated datasets and capture both the appearance and the configuration of the parts. DPM-based detectors achieve unrivaled accuracy on standard datasets but their computational demand is high since it is proportional to the number of parts in the model and the number of locations at which to evaluate the part filters. Approaches for speeding-up the DPM inference such as cascades, branch-and-bound, and multi-resolution schemes, use the responses obtained from initial part-location evaluations to reduce the future computation. This paper introduces two novel ideas, which are missing in the state-of-the-art methods for speeding up DPM inference.

First, at each location in the image pyramid, a part-based detector has to make a decision: whether to evaluate more parts and in what order or to stop and predict a label. This decision can be treated as a *planning problem*, whose

---

* Electronic supplementary material -Supplementary material is available in the online version of this chapter at http://dx.doi.org/10.1007/978-3-319-10584-0_19. Videos can also be accessed at http://www.springerimages.com/videos/978-3-319-10583-3

** Financial support through the following grants: NSF-IIP-0742304, NSF-OIA-1028009, ARL MAST CTA W911NF-08-2-0004, ARL Robotics CTA W911NF-10-2-0016, NSF-DGE-0966142, NSF-IIS-1317788 and TerraSwarm, one of six centers of STARnet, a Semiconductor Research Corporation program sponsored by MARCO and DARPA is gratefully acknowledged.

D. Fleet et al. (Eds.): ECCV 2014, Part VII, LNCS 8695, pp. 281–296, 2014.
© Springer International Publishing Switzerland 2014

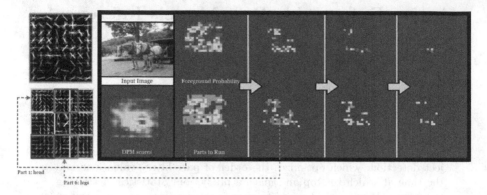

Fig. 1. Active DPM Inference: A deformable part model trained on the PASCAL VOC 2007 horse class is shown with colored root and parts in the first column. The second column contains an input image and the original DPM scores as a baseline. The rest of the columns illustrate the ADPM inference which proceeds in rounds. The foreground probability of a horse being present is maintained at each image location (top row) and is updated sequentially based on the responses of the part filters (high values are red; low values are blue). A policy (learned off-line) is used to select the best sequence of parts to apply at different locations. The bottom row shows the part filters applied at consecutive rounds with colors corresponding to the parts on the left. The policy decides to stop the inference at each location based on the confidence of foreground. As a result, the complete sequence of part filters is evaluated at very few locations, leading to a significant speed-up versus the traditional DPM inference. Our experiments show that the accuracy remains unaffected.

state space consists of the set of previously used parts and the confidence of whether an object is present or not. While existing approaches rely on a predetermined sequence of parts, our approach optimizes the order in which to apply the part filters so that a minimal number of part evaluations provides maximal classification accuracy at each location. Our second idea is to use a decision loss in the optimization, which quantifies the trade-off between false positive and false negative mistakes, instead of the threshold-based stopping criterion utilized by most other approaches. These ideas have enabled us to propose a novel object detector, Active Deformable Part Models (ADPM), named so because of the active part selection. The detection procedure consists of two phases: an off-line phase, which learns a part scheduling policy from training data and an online phase (inference), which uses the policy to optimize the detection task on test images. During inference, each image location starts with equal probabilities for object and background. The probabilities are updated sequentially based on the responses of the part filters suggested by the policy. At any time, depending on the probabilities, the policy might terminate and predict either a background label (which is what most cascaded methods take advantage of) or a positive label. Upon termination all unused part filters are evaluated in order to obtain the complete DPM score. Fig. 1 exemplifies the inference process.

We evaluated our approach on the PASCAL VOC 2007 and 2010 datasets [5] and achieved state of the art accuracy but with a 7 times reduction in the number of part-location evaluations and an average speed-up of 3 times compared to the cascade DPM [6]. This paper makes the following **contributions** to the state of the art in part-based object detection:

1. We obtain an active part selection policy which optimizes the order of the filter evaluations and balances number of evaluations with the classification accuracy based on the scores obtained during inference.
2. The ADPM detector achieves a significant speed-up versus the cascade DPM without sacrificing accuracy.
3. The approach is independent of the representation. It can be generalized to any classification problem, which involves a linear additive score and uses several parts (stages).

2   Related Work

We refer to work on object detection that optimizes the inference stage rather than the representations since our approach is representation independent. We show that the approach can use the traditional DPM representation [7] as well as lower-dimensional projections of its filters. Our method is inspired by an acceleration of the DPM object detector, the cascade DPM [6]. While the sequence of parts evaluated in the cascade DPM is predefined and a set of thresholds is determined empirically, our approach selects the part order and the stopping time at each location based on an optimization criterion. We find the closest approaches to be [21,24,9,12]. Sznitman et al. [21] maintain a foreground probability at each stage of a multi-stage ensemble classifier and determine a stopping time based on the corresponding entropy. Wu et al. [24] learn a sequence of thresholds by minimizing an empirical loss function. The order of applying ensemble classifiers is optimized in Gao et al. [9] by myopically choosing the next classifier which minimizes the entropy. Karayev at el. [12] propose anytime recognition via Q-learning given a computational cost budget. In contrast, our approach optimizes the stage order and the stopping criterion jointly.

Kokkinos [13] used Branch-and-Bound (BB) to prioritize the search over image locations driven by an upper bound on the classification score. It is related to our approach in that object-less locations are easily detected and the search is guided in location space but with the difference that our policy proposes the next part to be tested in cases when no label can yet be given to a particular location. Earlier approaches [15,17,14] relied on BB to constrain the search space of object detectors based on a sliding window or a Hough transform but without deformable parts. Another related group of approaches focuses on learning a sequence of object template tests in position, scale, and orientation space that minimizes the total computation time through a coarse-to-fine evaluation [8,18].

The classic work of Viola and Jones [22] introduced a cascade of classifiers whose order was determined by importance weights, learned by AdaBoost. The approach was studied extensively in [2,3,10,16,25]. Recently, Dollar et al. [4] introduced cross-talk cascades which allow detector responses to trigger or suppress the evaluation of weak classifiers in the neighboring image locations. Weiss et al. [23] used structured prediction cascades to optimize a function with two objectives: pose refinement and filter evaluation cost. Sapp et al. [20] learn a cascade of pictorial structures with increasing pose resolution by progressively filtering the pose-state space. Its emphasis is on pre-filtering structures rather than part locations through max-margin scoring so that human poses with weak individual part appearances can still be recovered. Rahtu et al. [19] used general "objectness" filters in a cascade to maximize the quality of the locations that advance to the next stage. Our approach is also related to and can be combined with active learning via Gaussian processes for classification [11].

Similarly to the closest approaches above [6,13,21,24], our method aims to balance the number of part filter evaluations with the classification accuracy in part-based object detection. The novelty and the main advantage of our approach is that in addition it optimizes the part filter ordering. Since our "cascades" still run only on parts, we do not expect the approach to show higher accuracy than structured prediction cascades [20] which consider more sophisticated representations that the pictorial structures in the DPM.

3   Technical Approach

The state-of-the-art performance in object detection is obtained by star-structured models such as DPM [7]. A star-structured model of an object with n parts is formally defined by a $(n + 2)$-tuple $(F_0, P_1, \ldots, P_n, b)$, where F_0 is a root filter, b is a real-valued bias term, and P_k are the part models. Each part model $P_k = (F_k, v_k, d_k)$ consists of a filter F_k, a position v_k of the part relative to the root, and the coefficients d_k of a quadratic function specifying a deformation cost of placing the part away from v_k. The object detector is applied in a sliding-window fashion to each location x in an image pyramid, where $x = (r, c, l)$ specifies a position (r, c) in the l-th level (scale) of the pyramid. The space of all locations (position-scale tuples) in the image pyramid is denoted by $\mathcal{X}$. The response of the detector at a given root location $x = (r, c, l) \in \mathcal{X}$ is:

$$score(x) = F_0' \cdot \phi(H, x) + \sum_{k=1}^{n} \max_{x_k} \left(F_k' \cdot \phi(H, x_k) - d_k \cdot \phi_d(\delta_k) \right) + b,$$

where $\phi(H, x)$ is the histogram of oriented gradients (HOG) feature vector at location x and $\delta_k := (r_k, c_k) - (2(r, c) + v_k)$ is the displacement of the k-th part from its anchor position v_k relative to the root location x. Each term in the sum above implicitly depends on the root location x since the part locations x_k are chosen relative to it. The score can be written as:

$$score(x) = \sum_{k=0}^{n} m_k(x) + b, \tag{1}$$

where $m_0(x) := F_0' \cdot \phi(H, x)$ and for $k > 0$, $m_k(x) := \max_{x_k} \left(F_k' \cdot \phi(H, x_k) - d_k \cdot \phi_d(\delta_k) \right)$. From this perspective, there is no difference between the root and the parts and we can think of the model as one consiting of $n + 1$ parts.

3.1 Score Likelihoods for the Parts

The object detection task requires labeling every $x \in \mathcal{X}$ with a label $y(x) \in \{\ominus, \oplus\}$. The traditional approach is to compute the complete score in (1) at every position-scale tuple $x \in \mathcal{X}$. In this paper, we argue that it is not necessary to obtain all $n+1$ part responses in order to label a location x correctly. Treating the part scores as noisy observations of the true label $y(x)$, we choose an effective order in which to receive observations and an optimal time to stop. The stopping criterion is based on a trade-off between the cost of obtaining more observations and the cost of labeling the location x incorrectly.

Formally, the part scores $m_0, \ldots, m_n$ at a fixed location x are random variables, which depend on the input image, i.e. the true label $y(x)$. To emphasize this we denote them with upper-case letters M_k and their realizations with lower-case letters m_k. In order to predict an effective part order and stopping time, we need statistics which describe the part responses. Let $h^\oplus(m_0, m_1, \ldots, m_n)$ and $h^\ominus(m_0, m_1, \ldots, m_n)$ denote the joint probability density functions (pdf) of the part scores conditioned on the true label being positive $y = \oplus$ and negative $y = \ominus$, respectively. We make the following assumption.

Assumption. *The responses of the parts of a star-structured model with a given root location $x \in \mathcal{X}$ are independent conditioned on the the true label $y(x)$, i.e.*

$$h^\oplus(m_0, m_1, \ldots, m_n) = \prod_{k=0}^n h_k^\oplus(m_k),$$
$$h^\ominus(m_0, m_1, \ldots, m_n) = \prod_{k=0}^n h_k^\ominus(m_k), \tag{2}$$

where $h_k^\oplus(m_k)$ is the pdf of $M_k \mid y = \oplus$ and $h_k^\ominus(m_k)$ is the pdf of $M_k \mid y = \ominus$.

We learn non-parametric representations for the $2(n+1)$ pdfs $\{h_k^\oplus, h_k^\ominus\}$ from an annotated set D of training images. We emphasize that the above assumption does not always hold in practice but simplifies the representation of the score likelihoods significantly[1] and avoids overfitting. Our algorithm for choosing a part order and a stopping time can be used without the independence assumption. However, we expect the performance to be similar while an unreasonable amount of training data would be required to learn a good representation of the joint pdfs. To evaluate the fidelity of the decoupled representation in (2) we computed correlation coefficients between all pairs of part responses (Table 1) for the classes in the PASCAL VOC 2007 dataset. The mean over all classes, 0.23, indicates a weak correlation. We observed that the few highly correlated parts have identical appearances (e.g. car wheels) or a spatial overlap.

To learn representations for the score likelihoods, $\{h_k^\oplus, h_k^\ominus\}$, we collected a set of scores for each part from the the training set D. Given a positive example $I_i^\oplus \in D$ of a particular DPM component, the root was placed at the scale and position x^* of the top score within the ground-truth bounding box. The

---

[1] Removing the independence assumption would require learning the 2 joint $(n+1)$ dimensional pdfs of the part scores in (2) and extracting the $2(n+1)$ marginals and the $2(n+1)(2^n - 1)$ conditionals of the form $h(m_k \mid m_I)$, where $I \subseteq \{0, \ldots, n\} \setminus \{k\}$.

Table 1. Average correlation coefficients among pairs of part responses for all 20 classes in the VOC 2007 dataset

aero	bike	bird	boat	bottle	bus	car	cat	chair	cow	table	dog	horse	mbike	person	plant	sheep	sofa	train	tv	**mean**
0.36	0.37	0.14	0.18	0.24	0.29	0.40	0.16	0.13	0.17	0.44	0.11	0.23	0.21	0.14	0.21	0.26	0.22	0.24	0.20	0.23

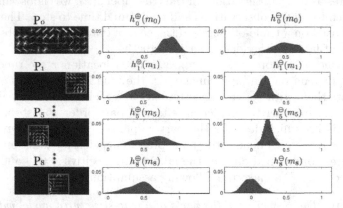

Fig. 2. Score likelihoods for several parts from a car DPM model. The root (P_0) and three parts of the model are shown on the left. The corresponding positive and negative score likelihoods are shown on the right.

response m_0^i of the root filter was recorded. The parts were placed at their optimal locations relative to the root location x^* and their scores m_k^i, $k > 0$ were recorded as well. This procedure was repeated for all positive examples in D to obtain a set of scores $\{m_k^i \mid \oplus\}$ for each part k. For negative examples, x^* was selected randomly over all locations in the image pyramid and the same procedure was used to obtain the set $\{m_k^i \mid \ominus\}$. Kernel density estimation was applied to the score collections in order to obtain smooth approximations to $h_k^\oplus$ and $h_k^\ominus$. Fig. 2 shows several examples of the score likelihoods obtained from the part responses of a car model.

3.2 Active Part Selection

This section discusses how to select an ordered subset of the $n + 1$ parts, which when applied at a given location $x \in \mathcal{X}$ has a small probability of mislabeling x. The detection at x proceeds in rounds $t = 0, \ldots, n+1$. The DPM inference applies the root and parts in a predefined topological ordering of the model structure. Here, we do not fix the order of the parts a priori. Instead, we select which part to run next *sequentially*, depending on the part responses obtained in the past. The part chosen at round t is denoted by $k(t)$ and can be any of the parts that have not been applied yet. We take a Bayesian approach and maintain a probability $p_t := \mathbb{P}(y = \oplus \mid m_{k(0)}, \ldots, m_{k(t-1)})$ of a positive label at location x conditioned on the part scores from the previous rounds. The state at time t consists of a binary vector $s_t \in \{0,1\}^{n+1}$ indicating which parts have already been used and the information state $p_t \in [0,1]$. Let $S_t := \{s \in \{0,1\}^{n+1} \mid \mathbf{1}^T s = t\}$ be the set[2] of possible values for s_t. At the start of a detection, $s_0 = \mathbf{0}$ and $p_0 = 1/2$, since no parts have been used and we have an uninformative prior for the true label.

Suppose that part $k(t)$ is applied at time t and its score is $m_{k(t)}$. The indicator vector s_t of used parts is updated as:

$$s_{t+1} = s_t + e_{k(t)}. \tag{3}$$

Due to the independence of the score likelihoods (2), the posterior label distribution is computed using Bayes rule:

$$p_{t+1} = \frac{h_{k(t)}^{\oplus}(m_{k(t)})}{h_{k(t)}^{\oplus}(m_{k(t)}) + h_{k(t)}^{\ominus}(m_{k(t)})} p_t. \tag{4}$$

In this setting, we seek a conditional plan π, which chooses which part to run next or stops and decides on a label for x. Formally, such a plan is called a *policy* and is a function $\pi(s,p) : \{0,1\}^{n+1} \times [0,1] \to \{\ominus, \oplus, 0, \ldots, n\}$, which depends on the previously used parts s and the label distribution p. An admissible policy does not allow part repetitions and satisfies $\pi(\mathbf{1},p) \in \{\ominus, \oplus\}$ for all $p \in [0,1]$, i.e. has to choose a label after all parts have been used. The set of admissible policies is denoted by Π.

Let $\tau(\pi) := \inf\{t \geq 0 \mid \pi(s_t, p_t) \in \{\ominus, \oplus\}\} \leq n+1$ denote the stopping time of policy $\pi \in \Pi$. Let $\hat{y}_\pi \in \{\ominus, \oplus\}$ denote the label guessed by policy π after its termination. We would like to choose a policy, which decides *quickly* and *correctly*. To formalize this, define the probability of making an error as $Pe(\pi) := \mathbb{P}(\hat{y}_\pi \neq y)$, where y is the hidden correct label of x.

Problem (Active Part Selection). *Given $\epsilon > 0$, choose an admissible part policy π with minimum expected stopping time and probability of error bounded by ϵ:*

$$\begin{aligned} \min_{\pi \in \Pi} \quad & \mathbb{E}[\tau(\pi)] \\ s.t. \quad & Pe(\pi) \leq \epsilon, \end{aligned} \tag{5}$$

where the expectation is over the label y and the part scores $M_{k(0)}, \ldots, M_{k(\tau-1)}$.

Note that if ϵ is chosen too small, (5) might be infeasible. In other words, even the best sequencing of the parts might not reduce the probability of error sufficiently. To avoid this issue, we relax the constraint in (5) by introducing a Lagrange multiplier $\lambda > 0$ as follows:

$$\min_{\pi \in \Pi} \quad \mathbb{E}[\tau(\pi)] + \lambda Pe(\pi). \tag{6}$$

---

[2] *Notation:* $\mathbf{1}$ denotes a vector with all elements equal to one, $\mathbf{0}$ denotes a vector with all elements equal to zero, and e_i denotes a vector with one in the i-th component and zero everywhere else.

The Lagrange multiplier λ can be interpreted as a cost paid for choosing an incorrect label. To elaborate on this, we rewrite the cost function as follows:

$$\mathbb{E}\left[\tau + \lambda \mathbb{E}_y\left[\mathbb{1}_{\{\hat{y}\neq y\}} \mid M_{k(0)}, \ldots, M_{k(\tau-1)}\right]\right]$$

$$= \mathbb{E}\left[\tau + \lambda \mathbb{1}_{\{\hat{y}\neq \oplus\}} \mathbb{P}\left(y = \oplus \mid M_{k(0)}, \ldots, M_{k(\tau-1)}\right)\right.$$

$$\left. + \lambda \mathbb{1}_{\{\hat{y}\neq \ominus\}} \mathbb{P}\left(y = \ominus \mid M_{k(0)}, \ldots, M_{k(\tau-1)}\right)\right]$$

$$= \mathbb{E}\left[\tau + \lambda p_\tau \mathbb{1}_{\{\hat{y}=\ominus\}} + \lambda(1 - p_\tau)\mathbb{1}_{\{\hat{y}=\oplus\}}\right].$$

The term λp_τ above is the cost paid if label $\hat{y} = \ominus$ is chosen incorrectly. Similarly, $\lambda(1 - p_\tau)$ is the cost paid if label $\hat{y} = \oplus$ is chosen incorrectly. To allow flexibility, we introduce separate costs λ_{fp} and λ_{fn} for false positive and false negative mistakes. The final form of the **Active Part Selection** problem is:

$$\min_{\pi \in \Pi}\ \mathbb{E}\left[\tau + \lambda_{fn}p_\tau \mathbb{1}_{\{\hat{y}=\ominus\}} + \lambda_{fp}(1 - p_\tau)\mathbb{1}_{\{\hat{y}=\oplus\}}\right]. \tag{7}$$

Computing the Part Selection Policy. Problem (7) can be solved using Dynamic Programming [1]. For a fixed policy $\pi \in \Pi$ and a given initial state $s_0 \in \{0, 1\}^{n+1}$ and $p_0 \in [0, 1]$, the value function:

$$V_\pi(s_0, p_0) := \mathbb{E}\left[\tau + \lambda_{fn}p_\tau \mathbb{1}_{\{\hat{y}=\ominus\}} + \lambda_{fp}(1 - p_\tau)\mathbb{1}_{\{\hat{y}=\oplus\}}\right],$$

is a well-defined quantity. The *optimal* policy π^* and the corresponding *optimal* value function are obtained as:

$$V^*(s_0, p_0) = \min_{\pi \in \Pi} V_\pi(s_0, p_0),$$

$$\pi^*(s_0, p_0) = \arg\max_{\pi \in \Pi} V_\pi(s_0, p_0).$$

To compute π^* we proceed backwards in time. Suppose that the policy has not terminated by time $t = n + 1$. Since there are no parts left to apply the policy is forced to terminate. Thus, $\tau = n + 1$ and $s_{n+1} = 1$ and for all $p \in [0, 1]$ the optimal value function becomes:

$$V^*(1, p) = \min_{\hat{y}\in\{\ominus,\oplus\}}\left\{\lambda_{fn}p\mathbb{1}_{\{\hat{y}=\ominus\}} + \lambda_{fp}(1 - p)\mathbb{1}_{\{\hat{y}=\oplus\}}\right\}$$

$$= \min\{\lambda_{fn}p, \lambda_{fp}(1 - p)\}. \tag{8}$$

The intermediate stage values for $t = n, \ldots, 0$, $s_t \in S_t$, and $p_t \in [0, 1]$ are:

$$V^*(s_t, p_t) = \min\left\{\lambda_{fn}p_t, \lambda_{fp}(1 - p_t),\right. \tag{9}$$

$$\left. 1 + \min_{k\in\mathcal{A}(s_t)} \mathbb{E}_{M_k} V^*\left(s_t + e_k, \frac{h_k^\oplus(M_k)p_t}{h_k^\oplus(M_k) + h_k^\ominus(M_k)}\right)\right\},$$

where $\mathcal{A}(s) := \{i \in \{0, \ldots, n\} \mid s_i = 0\}$ is the set of available (unused) parts[3]. The optimal policy is readily obtained from the optimal value function. At stage t, if the first term in (9) is smallest, the policy stops and chooses $\hat{y} = \ominus$; if the second term is smallest, the policy stops and chooses $\hat{y} = \oplus$; otherwise, the policy chooses to run the part k, which minimizes the expectation.

Alg. 1 summarizes the steps necessary to compute the optimal policy π^* using the score likelihoods $\{h_k^\oplus, h_k^\ominus\}$ from Sec. 3.1. The one dimensional space $[0, 1]$ of label probabilities p can be discretized into d bins in order to store the function π returned by Alg. 1. The memory required is $O(d2^{n+1})$ since the space $\{0, 1\}^{n+1}$ of used-part indicator vectors grows exponentially with the number of parts. Nevertheless, in practice the number of parts in a DPM is rarely more than 20 and Alg. 1 can be executed.

Algorithm 1. Active Part Selection

1: **Input:** Score likelihoods $\{h_k^\ominus, h_k^\oplus\}_{k=0}^n$ for all parts, false positive cost λ_{fp}, false negative cost λ_{fn}

2: **Output:** Policy $\pi : \{0, 1\}^{n+1} \times [0, 1] \to \{\ominus, \oplus, 0, \ldots, n\}$

3:

4: $S_t := \{s \in \{0, 1\}^{n+1} \mid \mathbf{1}^T s = t\}$

5: $\mathcal{A}(s) := \{i \in \{0, \ldots, n\} \mid s_i = 0\}$ for $s \in \{0, 1\}^{n+1}$

6:

7: $V(\mathbf{1}, p) := \min\{\lambda_{fn} p, \lambda_{fp}(1 - p)\}, \quad \forall p \in [0, 1]$

8: $\pi(\mathbf{1}, p) := \begin{cases} \ominus, & \lambda_{fn} p \leq \lambda_{fp}(1 - p) \\ \oplus, & \text{otherwise} \end{cases}$

9:

10: **for** $t = n, n-1, \ldots, 0$ **do**

11:     **for** $s \in S_t$ **do**

12:         **for** $k \in \mathcal{A}(s)$ **do**

13:             $Q(s, p, k) := \mathbb{E}_{M_k} V\left(s + e_k, \frac{h_k^\oplus(M_k)p}{h_k^\oplus(M_k) + h_k^\ominus(M_k)}\right)$

14:         **end for**

15:         $V(s, p) := \min\left\{\lambda_{fn} p, \lambda_{fp}(1 - p), 1 + \min_{k \in \mathcal{A}(s)} Q(s, p, k)\right\}$

16:         $\pi(s, p) := \begin{cases} \ominus, & V(s, p) = \lambda_{fn} p, \\ \oplus, & V(s, p) = \lambda_{fp}(1 - p), \\ \arg\min_{k \in \mathcal{A}(s)} Q(s, p, k), & \text{otherwise} \end{cases}$

17:     **end for**

18: **end for**

19: **return** π

3.3 Active DPM Inference

A policy π is obtained *offline* using Alg. 1. During inference, π is used to select a sequence of parts to apply at each location $x \in \mathcal{X}$ in the image pyramid. Note that the labeling of each location is treated as an independent problem. Alg. 2 summarizes the ADPM inference process.

---

[3] Each score likelihood was discretized using 201 bins to obtain a histogram. Then, the expectation in (9) was computed as a sum over the bins. Alternatively, Monte Carlo integration can be performed by sampling from the Gaussian mixtures directly.

Algorithm 2. Active DPM Inference

1: **Input**: Image pyramid, model $(F_0, P_1, \ldots, P_n, b)$, score likelihoods $\{h_k^{\ominus}, h_k^{\oplus}\}_{k=0}^n$ for all parts, policy π
2: **Output**: $score(x)$ at all locations $x \in \mathcal{X}$ in the image pyramid
3:
4: **for** $x \in 1 \ldots |\mathcal{X}|$ **do**   ▷ All image pyramid locations
5:     $s_0 := 0$; $p_0 = 0.5$; $score(x) := 0$
6:     **for** $t = 0, 1, \ldots, n$ **do**
7:         $k := \pi(s_t, p_t)$ ▷ Lookup next best part
8:         **if** $k = \oplus$ **then**   ▷ Labeled as foreground
9:             **for** $i \in \{0, 1, \ldots, n\}$ **do**
10:                 **if** $s_t(i) = 0$ **then**
11:                     Compute score $m_i(x)$ for part i ▷ $O(|\Delta|)$
12:                     $score(x) := score(x) + m_i(x)$
13:                 **end if**
14:             **end for**
15:             $score(x) := score(x) + b$ ▷ Add bias to final score
16:             break;
17:         **else if** $k = \ominus$ **then**   ▷ Labeled as background
18:             $score(x) := -\infty$
19:             break;
20:         **else**   ▷ Update probability and score
21:             Compute score $m_k(x)$ for part k ▷ $O(|\Delta|)$
22:             $score(x) := score(x) + m_k(x)$
23:             $p_{t+1} := \dfrac{h_k^{\oplus}(m_k(x))p_t}{h_k^{\oplus}(m_k(x)) + h_k^{\ominus}(m_k(x))}$
24:             $s_{t+1} = s_t + e_k$
25:         **end if**
26:     **end for**
27: **end for**

At the start of a detection at location x, $s_0 = \mathbf{0}$ since no parts have been used and $p_0 = 1/2$ assuming an uninformative label prior (LN. 5). At each round t, the policy is queried to obtain either the next part to run or a predicted label for x (LN. 7). Note that querying the policy is an $O(1)$ operation since it is stored as a lookup table. If the policy terminates and labels $y(x)$ as foreground (LN. 8), all unused part filters are applied in order to obtain the final discriminative score in (1). On the other hand, if the policy terminates and labels $y(x)$ as background, no additional part filters are evaluated and the final score is set to $-\infty$ (LN. 18). In this case, our algorithm makes computational savings compared to the DPM. The potential speed-up and the effect on accuracy are discussed in the Sec. 4. Finally, if the policy returns a part index k, the corresponding score $m_k(x)$ is computed by applying the part filter (LN. 21). This operation is $O(|\Delta|)$, where Δ is the space of possible displacements for part k with respect to the root location x. Following the analysis in [6], searching over the possible locations for part k is usually no more expensive than evaluating its linear filter F_k once. This is the case because once F_k is applied at some location x_k, the resulting response $\Phi_k(x_k) = F_k' \cdot \phi(H, x_k)$ is cached to avoid recomputing it later. The score m_k of part k is used to update the total score at x (LN. 22). Then, (3) and (4) are used to update the state (s_t, p_t) (LN. 23 - 24). Since the policy lookups and the state updates are all of $O(1)$ complexity, the worst-case complexity of Alg. 2 is $O(n|\mathcal{X}||\Delta|)$. The average running time of our algorithm depends on the total number of score m_k evaluations, which in turn depends on the choice of the parameters λ_{fn} and λ_{fp} and is the subject of the next section.

4   Experiments

4.1   Speed-Accuracy Trade-Off

The accuracy and the speed of the ADPM inference depend on the penalty, λ_{fp}, for incorrectly predicting background as foreground and the penalty, λ_{fn}, for incorrectly predicting foreground as background. To get an intuition, consider making both λ_{fp} and λ_{fn} very small. The cost of an incorrect prediction will be negligible, thus encouraging the policy to sacrifice accuracy and stop immediately. In the other extreme, when both parameters are very large, the policy will delay the prediction as much as possible in order to obtain more information.

To evaluate the effect of the parameter choice, we compared the average precision (AP) and the number of part evaluations of Alg. 2 to those of the traditional DPM as a baseline. Let R_M be the total number of score $m_k(x)$ evaluations for $k > 0$ (excluding the root) over all locations $x \in \mathcal{X}$ performed by method M. For example, $R_{DPM} = n|\mathcal{X}|$ since the DPM evaluates all parts at all locations in $\mathcal{X}$. We define the **relative number of part evaluations** (RNPE) of ADPM versus method M as the ratio of R_M to R_{ADPM}. The AP and the RNPE versus DPM of ADPM were evaluated on several classes from the PASCAL VOC 2007 training set (see Fig. 3) for different values of the parameter $\lambda = \lambda_{fn} = \lambda_{fp}$. As expected, the AP increases while the RNPE decreases, as the penalty of an incorrect declaration λ grows, because ADPM evaluates more parts. The dip in RNPE for very low λ is due to fact that ADPM starts reporting many false-positives. In the case of a positive declaration all $n + 1$ part responses need to be computed which reduces the speed-up versus DPM.

To limit the number of false positive mistakes made by the policy we set $\lambda_{fp} > \lambda_{fn}$. While this might hurt the accuracy, it will certainly result in less positive declarations and in turn significantly less part evaluations. To verify this intuition we performed experiments with $\lambda_{fp} > \lambda_{fn}$ on the VOC 2007 training set. Table 2 reports the AP and the RNPE versus DPM from a grid search over the parameter space. Generally, as the ratio between λ_{fp} and λ_{fn} increases, the RNPE increases while the AP decreases. Notice, however, that the increase in RNPE is significant, while the hit in accuracy is negligible.

In sum, λ_{fp} and λ_{fn} were selected with a grid search in parameter space with $\lambda_{fp} > \lambda_{fn}$ using the training set. Choosing different values for different classes should improve the performance even more.

4.2   Results

In this section we compare ADPM[4] versus two baselines, the DPM and the cascade DPM (Cascade) in terms of average precision (AP), relative number of

---

[4] ADPM source code is available at: http://cis.upenn.edu/~menglong/adpm.html

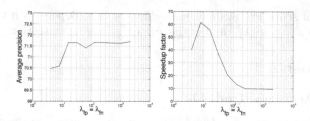

Fig. 3. Average precision and relative number of part evaluations versus DPM as a function of the parameter $\lambda = \lambda_{fn} = \lambda_{fp}$ on a log scale. The curves are reported on the bus class from the VOC 2007 **training** set.

Table 2. Average precision and relative number of part evaluations versus DPM obtained on the bus class from VOC 2007 **training** set. A grid search over $(\lambda_{fp}, \lambda_{fn}) \in \{4, 8, \ldots, 64\} \times \{4, 8, \ldots, 64\}$ with $\lambda_{fp} \geq \lambda_{fn}$ is shown.

	Average Precision						RNPE vs DPM				
$\lambda_{fp}/\lambda_{fn}$	4	8	16	32	64	$\lambda_{fp}/\lambda_{fn}$	4	8	16	32	64
4	70.3					4	40.4				
8	70.0	71.0				8	80.7	61.5			
16	69.6	71.1	71.5			16	118.6	74.5	55.9		
32	70.5	70.7	71.6	71.6		32	178.3	82.1	59.8	37.0	
64	67.3	69.6	71.5	71.6	71.4	64	186.9	96.4	56.2	34.5	20.8

Table 3. Average precision (AP) and relative number of part evaluations (RNPE) of DPM versus ADPM on all 20 classes in VOC 2007 and 2010

VOC2007	aero	bike	bird	boat	bottle	bus	car	cat	chair	cow	table	dog	horse	mbike	person	plant	sheep	sofa	train	tv	**mean**
DPM RNPE	102.8	106.7	63.7	79.7	58.1	155.2	44.5	40.0	58.9	71.8	69.9	49.2	51.0	59.6	45.3	49.0	62.6	68.6	79.0	100.6	**70.8**
DPM AP	33.2	60.3	10.2	16.1	27.3	54.3	58.2	23.0	20.0	24.1	26.7	12.7	58.1	48.2	43.2	12.0	21.1	36.1	46.0	43.5	**33.7**
ADPM AP	33.5	59.8	9.8	15.3	27.6	52.5	57.6	22.1	20.1	24.6	24.9	12.3	57.6	48.4	42.8	12.0	20.4	35.7	46.3	43.2	**33.3**
VOC2010	aero	bike	bird	boat	bottle	bus	car	cat	chair	cow	table	dog	horse	mbike	person	plant	sheep	sofa	train	tv	**mean**
DPM RNPE	110.0	100.8	47.9	98.8	111.8	214.4	75.6	202.5	150.8	147.2	62.4	126.2	133.7	187.1	114.4	59.3	24.3	131.2	143.8	106.0	**117.4**
DPM AP	45.6	49.0	11.0	11.6	27.2	50.5	43.1	23.6	17.2	23.2	10.7	20.5	42.5	44.5	41.3	8.7	29.0	18.7	40.0	34.5	**29.6**
ADPM AP	45.3	49.1	10.2	12.2	26.9	50.6	41.9	22.7	16.5	22.8	10.6	19.7	40.8	44.5	36.8	8.3	29.1	18.6	39.7	34.5	**29.1**

Table 4. Average precision (AP), relative number of part evaluations (RNPE), and relative wall-clock time speedup (Speedup) of ADPM versus Cascade on all 20 classes in VOC 2007 and 2010

VOC2007	aero	bike	bird	boat	bottle	bus	car	cat	chair	cow	table	dog	horse	mbike	person	plant	sheep	sofa	train	tv	**mean**
Cascade RNPE	5.93	5.35	9.17	6.09	8.14	3.06	5.61	4.51	6.30	4.03	4.83	7.77	3.61	6.67	17.8	9.84	3.82	2.43	2.89	6.97	**6.24**
ADPM Speedup	3.14	1.60	8.21	4.57	3.36	1.67	2.11	1.54	3.12	1.63	1.28	2.72	1.07	1.50	3.59	6.15	2.92	1.10	1.11	3.26	**2.78**
Cascade AP	33.2	60.8	10.2	16.1	27.3	54.1	58.1	23.0	20.0	24.2	26.8	12.7	58.1	48.2	43.2	12.0	20.1	35.8	46.0	43.4	**33.7**
ADPM AP	31.7	59.0	9.70	14.9	27.5	51.4	56.7	22.1	20.4	24.0	24.7	12.4	57.7	48.5	41.7	11.6	20.4	35.9	45.8	42.8	**33.0**
VOC2010	aero	bike	bird	boat	bottle	bus	car	cat	chair	cow	table	dog	horse	mbike	person	plant	sheep	sofa	train	tv	**mean**
Cascade RNPE	7.28	2.66	14.80	7.83	12.22	5.47	6.29	6.33	9.72	4.16	3.74	10.77	3.21	9.68	21.43	12.21	3.23	4.58	3.98	8.17	**7.89**
ADPM Speedup	2.15	1.28	7.58	5.93	4.68	2.79	2.28	2.44	3.72	2.42	1.52	2.76	1.57	2.93	4.72	8.24	1.42	1.81	1.47	3.41	**3.26**
Cascade AP	45.5	48.9	11.0	11.6	27.2	50.5	43.1	23.6	17.2	23.1	10.7	20.5	42.4	44.5	41.3	8.7	29.0	18.7	40.1	34.4	**29.6**
ADPM AP	44.5	49.2	9.5	11.6	25.9	50.6	41.7	22.5	16.9	22.0	9.8	19.8	41.1	45.1	40.2	7.4	28.5	18.3	38.0	34.5	**28.8**

Table 5. An example demonstrating the computational time breakdown during inference of ADPM and Cascade on a single image. The number of part evaluations (PE) and the inference time (in sec) is recorded for the PCA and the full-dimensional stages. The results are reported once without and once with cache use. The number of part evaluations is independent of caching.

	PCA no cache	PCA cache	PE	Full no cache	Full cache	PE	Total no cache	Total cache	Total PE
CASCADE	4.34s	0.67s	208K	0.13s	0.08s	1.1K	4.50s	0.79s	209K
ADPM	0.62s	0.06s	36K	0.06s	0.04s	0.6K	0.79s	0.19s	37K

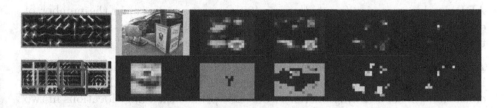

Fig. 4. Illustration of the ADPM inference process on a car example. The DPM model with colored root and parts is shown on the left. The top row on the right consists of the input image and the evolution of the positive label probability (p_t) for $t \in \{1, 2, 3, 4\}$ (high values are red; low values are blue). The bottom row consists of the full DPM $score(x)$ and a visualization of the parts applied at different locations at time t. The pixel colors correspond to the part colors on the left. In this example, despite the car being heavily occluded, ADPM converges to the correct location after four iterations.

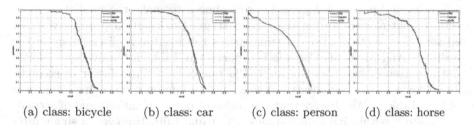

(a) class: bicycle   (b) class: car   (c) class: person   (d) class: horse

Fig. 5. Precision recall curves for bicycle, car, person, and horse classes from VOC 2007. Our method's accuracy ties with the baselines.

part evaluations (RNPE), and relative wall-clock time speedup (Speedup). Experiments were carried out on all 20 classes in the PASCAL VOC 2007 and 2010 datasets. Publicly available PASCAL VOC 2007 and 2010 DPM and Cascade models were used for all three methods. For a fair comparison, ADPM changes only the part order and the stopping criterion of the original implementations.

ADPM vs DPM: The inference of ADPM on two input images is shown in detail in Fig. 1 and Fig. 4. The probability of a positive label p_t (top row) becomes more contrasted as additional parts are evaluated. The locations at which the algorithm has not terminated decrease rapidly as time progresses. Visually, the locations with a maximal posterior are identical to the top scores obtained by the DPM. The order of parts chosen by the policy is indicative of their informativeness. For example, in Fig. 4 the wheel filters are applied first which agrees with intuition. In this example, the probability p_t remains low at the correct location for several iterations due to the occlusions. Nevertheless, the policy recognizes that it should not terminate and as it evaluates more parts, the correct location of the highest DPM score is reflected in the posterior.

ADPM was compared to DPM in terms of AP and RNPE to demonstrate the ability of ADPM to reduce the number of part evaluations with minimal loss in accuracy irrespective of the features used. The parameters were set to $\lambda_{fp} = 20$ and $\lambda_{fn} = 5$ for all classes based on the analysis in Sec. 4.1. Table 3 shows that ADPM achieves a significant decrease (90 times on average) in the number of evaluated parts with negligible loss in accuracy. The precision-recall curves of the two methods are shown in Fig. 5 for several classes.

ADPM vs Cascade: The improvement in detection speed achieved by ADPM is demonstrated via a comparison to Cascade in terms of AP, RNPE, and wall-clock time (in sec). During inference, Cascade prunes the image locations in two passes. In the first pass, the locations are filtered using the PCA filters and the low-scoring ones are discarded. In the second pass, the remaining locations are filtered using the full-dimensional filters. To make a fair comparison, we adopted a similar **two-stage** approach. An **additional** policy was learned using PCA score likelihoods and was used to schedule PCA filters during the first pass. The locations, which were selected as foreground in the first stage, were filtered again, using the original policy to schedule the full-dimensional filters. The parameters λ_{fp} and λ_{fn} were set to 20 and 5 for the PCA policy and to 50 and 5 for the full-dimensional policy. A higher λ_{fp} was chosen to make the prediction more precise (albeit slower) during the second stage. Deformation pruning was not used for either method. Table 4 summarizes the results. A discrepancy in the speedup of ADPM versus Cascade is observed in Table 4. On average, ADPM is 7 times faster than Cascade in RNPE but only 3 times faster in seconds. A breakdown of the computational time during inference on a single image is shown in Table 5. We observe that the ratios of part evaluations and of seconds are consistent within individual stages (PCA and full). However, a single filter evaluation during the full-filter stage is significantly slower than one during the PCA stage. This does not affect the cumulative RNPE but lowers the combined seconds ratio. While ADPM is significantly faster than Cascade during the PCA stage, the speedup (in sec) is reduced during the slower full-dimensional stage.

5   Conclusion

This paper presents an active part selection approach which substantially speeds up inference with pictorial structures without sacrificing accuracy. Statistics learned from training data are used to pose an optimization problem, which balances the number of part filter convolution with the classification accuracy. Unlike existing approaches, which use a pre-specified part order and hard stopping thresholds, the resulting part scheduling policy selects the part order and the stopping criterion adaptively based on the filter responses obtained during inference. Potential future extensions include optimizing the part selection across scales and image positions and detecting multiple classes simultaneously.

References

1. Bertsekas, D.P.: Dynamic Programming and Optimal Control, vol. 1. Athena Scientific (1995)
2. Bourdev, L., Brandt, J.: Robust object detection via soft cascade. In: IEEE Computer Society Conference on Computer Vision and Pattern Recognition, CVPR 2005, vol. 2, pp. 236–243. IEEE (2005)
3. Brubaker, S.C., Wu, J., Sun, J., Mullin, M.D., Rehg, J.M.: On the design of cascades of boosted ensembles for face detection. IJCV 77(1-3), 65–86 (2008)
4. Dollár, P., Appel, R., Kienzle, W.: Crosstalk cascades for frame-rate pedestrian detection. In: Fitzgibbon, A., Lazebnik, S., Perona, P., Sato, Y., Schmid, C. (eds.) ECCV 2012, Part II. LNCS, vol. 7573, pp. 645–659. Springer, Heidelberg (2012)
5. Everingham, M., Van Gool, L., Williams, C., Winn, J., Zisserman, A.: The Pascal Visual Object Classes (VOC) Challenge. IJCV 88(2), 303–338 (2010)
6. Felzenszwalb, P.F., Girshick, R.B., McAllester, D.: Cascade object detection with deformable part models. In: CVPR, pp. 2241–2248. IEEE (2010)
7. Felzenszwalb, P.F., Girshick, R.B., McAllester, D., Ramanan, D.: Object detection with discriminatively trained part-based models. PAMI 32(9), 1627–1645 (2010)
8. Fleuret, F., Geman, D.: Coarse-to-fine face detection. IJCV (2001)
9. Gao, T., Koller, D.: Active classification based on value of classifier. In: NIPS (2011)
10. Gualdi, G., Prati, A., Cucchiara, R.: Multistage particle windows for fast and accurate object detection. PAMI 34(8), 1589–1604 (2012)
11. Kapoor, A., Grauman, K., Urtasun, R., Darrell, T.: Gaussian processes for object categorization. IJCV (2010)
12. Karayev, S., Fritz, M., Darrell, T.: Anytime recognition of objects and scenes. In: IEEE Conference on Computer Vision and Pattern Recognition (CVPR) (oral, to appear, 2014)
13. Kokkinos, I.: Rapid deformable object detection using dual-tree branch-and-bound. In: NIPS (2011)
14. Lampert, C.H.: An efficient divide-and-conquer cascade for nonlinear object detection. In: CVPR. IEEE (2010)
15. Lampert, C.H., Blaschko, M.B., Hofmann, T.: Beyond sliding windows: Object localization by efficient subwindow search. In: CVPR, pp. 1–8. IEEE (2008)
16. Lehmann, A., Gehler, P.V., Van Gool, L.J.: Branch&rank: Non-linear object detection. In: BMVC (2011)
17. Lehmann, A., Leibe, B., Van Gool, L.: Fast prism: Branch and bound hough transform for object class detection. IJCV 94(2), 175–197 (2011)
18. Pedersoli, M., Vedaldi, A., Gonzalez, J.: A coarse-to-fine approach for fast deformable object detection. In: CVPR, pp. 1353–1360. IEEE (2011)
19. Rahtu, E., Kannala, J., Blaschko, M.: Learning a category independent object detection cascade. In: ICCV (2011)
20. Sapp, B., Toshev, A., Taskar, B.: Cascaded models for articulated pose estimation. In: Daniilidis, K., Maragos, P., Paragios, N. (eds.) ECCV 2010, Part II. LNCS, vol. 6312, pp. 406–420. Springer, Heidelberg (2010)

21. Sznitman, R., Becker, C., Fleuret, F., Fua, P.: Fast object detection with entropy-driven evaluation. In: CVPR (June 2013)
22. Viola, P., Jones, M.: Rapid object detection using a boosted cascade of simple features. In: CVPR. IEEE (2001)
23. Weiss, D., Sapp, B., Taskar, B.: Structured prediction cascades. arXiv preprint arXiv:1208.3279 (2012)
24. Wu, T., Zhu, S.-C.: Learning near-optimal cost-sensitive decision policy for object detection. In: 2013 IEEE International Conference on Computer Vision (ICCV), pp. 753–760. IEEE (2013)
25. Zhang, Z., Warrell, J., Torr, P.H.: Proposal generation for object detection using cascaded ranking svms. In: CVPR, pp. 1497–1504. IEEE (2011)

Simultaneous Detection and Segmentation

Bharath Hariharan[1], Pablo Arbeláez[1,2], Ross Girshick[1], and Jitendra Malik[1]

[1] University of California, Berkeley
[2] Universidad de los Andes, Colombia
{bharath2,arbelaez,rbg,malik}@eecs.berkeley.edu

Abstract. We aim to detect all instances of a category in an image and, for each instance, mark the pixels that belong to it. We call this task Simultaneous Detection and Segmentation (SDS). Unlike classical bounding box detection, SDS requires a segmentation and not just a box. Unlike classical semantic segmentation, we require individual object instances. We build on recent work that uses convolutional neural networks to classify category-independent region proposals (R-CNN [16]), introducing a novel architecture tailored for SDS. We then use category-specific, top-down figure-ground predictions to refine our bottom-up proposals. We show a 7 point boost (16% relative) over our baselines on SDS, a 5 point boost (10% relative) over state-of-the-art on semantic segmentation, and state-of-the-art performance in object detection. Finally, we provide diagnostic tools that unpack performance and provide directions for future work.

Keywords: detection, segmentation, convolutional networks.

1 Introduction

Object recognition comes in many flavors, two of the most popular being object detection and semantic segmentation. Starting with face detection, the task in object detection is to mark out bounding boxes around each object of a particular category in an image. In this task, a predicted bounding box is considered a true positive if it overlaps by more than 50% with a ground truth box, and different algorithms are compared based on their precision and recall. Object detection systems strive to find every instance of the category and estimate the spatial extent of each. However, the detected objects are very coarsely localized using just bounding boxes.

In contrast, semantic segmentation requires one to assign a category label to all pixels in an image. The MSRC dataset [30] was one of the first publicly available benchmarks geared towards this task. Later, the standard metric used to evaluate algorithms in this task converged on pixel IU (intersection over union): for each category, this metric computes the intersection over union of the predicted pixels and ground truth pixels over the entire dataset. This task deals with "stuff" categories (such as grass, sky, road) and "thing" categories (such as cow, person, car) interchangeably. For things, this means that there is no notion

D. Fleet et al. (Eds.): ECCV 2014, Part VII, LNCS 8695, pp. 297–312, 2014.
© Springer International Publishing Switzerland 2014

of object instances. A typical semantic segmentation algorithm might accurately mark out the dog pixels in the image, but would provide no indication of how many dogs there are, or of the precise spatial extent of any one particular dog.

These two tasks have continued to this day and were part of the PASCAL VOC challenge [11]. Although often treated as separate problems, we believe the distinction between them is artificial. For the "thing" categories, we can think of a unified task: detect all instances of a category in an image and, for each instance, correctly mark the pixels that belong to it. Compared to the bounding boxes output by an object detection system or the pixel-level category labels output by a semantic segmentation system, this task demands a richer, and potentially more useful, output. Our aim in this paper is to improve performance on this task, which we call **Simultaneous Detection and Segmentation** (SDS).

The SDS algorithm we propose has the following steps (Figure 1):

1. **Proposal Generation:** We start with category-independent bottom-up object proposals. Because we are interested in producing segmentations and not just bounding boxes, we need *region* proposals. We use MCG [1] to generate 2000 region candidates per image. We consider each region candidate as a putative object hypothesis.
2. **Feature Extraction:** We use a convolutional neural network to extract features on each region. We extract features from both the bounding box of the region as well as from the region foreground. This follows work by Girshick *et al.* [16] (R-CNN) who achieved competitive semantic segmentation results and dramatically improved the state-of-the-art in object detection by using CNNs to classify region proposals. We consider several ways of training the CNNs. We find that, compared to using the same CNN for both inputs (image windows and region masks), using separate networks where each network is finetuned for its respective role dramatically improves performance. We improve performance further by training both networks jointly, resulting in a feature extractor that is trained end-to-end for the SDS task.
3. **Region Classification:** We train an SVM on top of the CNN features to assign a score for each category to each candidate.
4. **Region Refinement:** We do non-maximum suppression (NMS) on the scored candidates. Then we use the features from the CNN to produce category-specific coarse mask predictions to refine the surviving candidates. Combining this mask with the original region candidates provides a further boost.

Since this task is not a standard one, we need to decide on evaluation metrics. The metric we suggest in this paper is an extension to the bounding box detection metric. It has been proposed earlier [31,32]. Given an image, we expect the algorithm to produce a set of object hypotheses, where each hypothesis comes with a predicted *segmentation* and a score. A hypothesis is correct if its *segmentation* overlaps with the *segmentation* of a ground truth instance by more than 50%. As in the classical bounding box task, we penalize duplicates. With this labeling, we compute a precision recall (PR) curve, and the average precision

(AP), which is the area under the curve. We call the AP computed in this way AP^r, to distinguish it from the traditional bounding box AP, which we call AP^b (the superscripts r and b correspond to region and bounding box respectively). AP^r measures the accuracy of segmentation, and also requires the algorithm to get each instance separately and completely. Our pipeline achieves an AP^r of 49.5% while at the same time improving AP^b from 51.0% (R-CNN) to 53.0%.

One can argue that the 50% threshold is itself artificial. For instance if we want to count the number of people in a crowd, we do not need to know their accurate segmentations. On the contrary, in a graphics application that seeks to matte an object into a scene, we might want extremely accurate segmentations. Thus the threshold at which we regard a detection as a true positive depends on the application. In general, we want algorithms that do well under a variety of thresholds. As the threshold varies, the PR curve traces out a PR surface. We can use the volume under this PR surface as a metric. We call this metric AP^r_{vol} and AP^b_{vol} respectively. AP^r_{vol} has the attractive property that an AP^r_{vol} of 1 implies we can perfectly detect and precisely segment all objects. Our pipeline gets an AP^r_{vol} of 41.4%. We improve AP^b_{vol} from 41.9% (R-CNN) to 44.2%.

We also find that our pipeline furthers the state-of-the-art in the classic PASCAL VOC semantic segmentation task, from 47.9% to 52.6%. Last but not the least, following work in object detection [18], we also provide a set of diagnostic tools for analyzing common error modes in the SDS task. Our algorithm, the benchmark and all diagnostic tools are publicly available at http://www.eecs.berkeley.edu/Research/Projects/CS/vision/shape/sds.

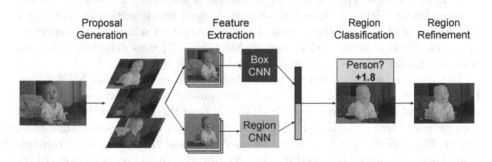

Fig. 1. Overview of our pipeline. Our algorithm is based on classifying region proposals using features extracted from both the bounding box of the region and the region foreground with a jointly trained CNN. A final refinement step improves segmentation.

2   Related Work

For semantic segmentation, several researchers have tried to use activations from off-the-shelf object detectors to guide the segmentation process. Yang *et al.* [32] use object detections from the deformable parts model [13] to segment the image, pasting figure-ground masks and reasoning about their relative depth ordering.

Arbeláez et al. [2] use poselet detections [4] as features to score region candidates, in addition to appearance-based cues. Ladicky et al. [22] use object detections as higher order potentials in a CRF-based segmentation system: all pixels in the foreground of a detected object are encouraged to share the category label of the detection. In addition, their system is allowed to switch off these potentials by assigning a true/false label to each detection. This system was extended by Boix et al. [3] who added a global, image-level node in the CRF to reason about the categories present in the image, and by Kim et al. [20] who added relationships between objects. In more recent work, Tighe et al. [31] use exemplar object detectors to segment out the scene as well as individual instances.

There has also been work on localizing detections better using segmentation. Parkhi et al. use color models from predefined rectangles on cat and dog faces to do GrabCut and improve the predicted bounding box [26]. Dai and Hoiem generalize this to all categories and use instance and category appearance models to improve detection [7]. These approaches do well when the objects are coherent in color or texture. This is not true of many categories such as people, where each object can be made of multiple regions of different appearance. An alternative to doing segmentation *post facto* is to use segmentation to generate object proposals which are then classified. The proposals may be used as just bounding boxes [27] or as region proposals [6,1]. These proposals incorporate both the consistency of appearance in an object as well as the possibility of having multiple disparate regions for each object. State-of-the-art detection systems [16] and segmentation systems [5] are now based on these methods.

In many of these approaches, segmentation is used only to localize the detections better. Other authors have explored using segmentation as a stronger cue. Fidler et al. [14] use the output of a state-of-the-art semantic segmentation approach [5] to score detections better. Mottaghi [25] uses detectors based on non-rectangular patches to both detect and segment objects.

The approaches above were typically built on features such as SIFT[24] or HOG[8]. Recently the computer vision community has shifted towards using convolutional neural networks (CNNs). CNNs have their roots in the Neocognitron proposed by Fukushima [15]. Trained with the back-propagation algorithm, LeCun [23] showed that they could be used for handwritten zip code recognition. They have since been used in a variety of tasks, including detection [29,28] and semantic segmentation [12]. Krizhevsky et al. [21] showed a large increase in performance by using CNNs for classification in the ILSVRC challenge [9]. Donahue et al. [10] showed that Krizhevsky's architecture could be used as a generic feature extractor that did well across a wide variety of tasks. Girshick et al. [16] build on this and finetune Krizhevsky's architecture for detection to nearly double the state-of-the-art performance. They use a simple pipeline, using CNNs to classify bounding box proposals from [27]. Our algorithm builds on this system, and on high quality region proposals from [1].

3 Our Approach

3.1 Proposal Generation

A large number of methods to generate proposals have been proposed in the literature. The methods differ on the type of outputs they produce (boxes vs segments) and the metrics they do well on. Since we are interested in the AP^r metric, we care about segments, and not just boxes. Keeping our task in mind, we use candidates from MCG [1] for this paper. This approach significantly outperforms all competing approaches on the object level Jaccard index metric, which measures the average best overlap achieved by a candidate for a ground truth object. In our experiments we find that simply switching to MCG from Selective Search [27] improves AP^b slightly (by 0.7 points), justifying this choice.

We use the proposals from MCG as is. MCG starts by computing a segmentation hierarchy at multiple image resolutions, which are then fused into a single multiscale hierarchy at the finest scale. Then candidates are produced by combinatorially grouping regions from all the single scale hierarchies and from the multiscale hierarchy. The candidates are ranked based on simple features such as size and location, shape and contour strength.

3.2 Feature Extraction

We start from the R-CNN object detector proposed by Girshick et al. [16] and adapt it to the SDS task. Girshick et al. train a CNN on ImageNet Classification and then finetune the network on the PASCAL detection set. For finetuning they took bounding boxes from Selective Search, padded them, cropped them and warped them to a square and fed them to the network. Bounding boxes that overlap with the ground truth by more than 50% were taken as positives and other boxes as negatives. The class label for each positive box was taken to be the class of the ground truth box that overlaps the most with the box. The network thus learned to predict if the bounding box overlaps highly with a ground truth bounding box. We are working with MCG instead of Selective Search, so we train a similar object detection network, finetuned using bounding boxes of MCG regions instead of Selective Search boxes.

At test time, to extract features from a bounding box, Girshick et al. pad and crop the box, warp it to a square and pass it through the network, and extract features from one of the later layers, which is then fed into an SVM. In this paper we will use the penultimate fully connected layer.

For the SDS task, we can now use this network finetuned for detection to extract feature vectors from MCG bounding boxes. However these feature vectors do not contain any information about the actual region foreground, and so will be ill-equipped to decide if the region overlaps highly with a ground truth segmentation or not. To get around this, we start with the idea used by Girshick et al. for their experiment on semantic segmentation: we extract a second set of features from the region by feeding it the cropped, warped box, but with the background of the region masked out (with the mean image.) Concatenating these two feature vectors together gives us the feature vector we use. (In their experiments Girshick *et al.* found both sets of features to be useful.) This method of extracting features out of the region is the simplest way of extending the object detection system to the SDS task and forms our baseline. We call this feature extractor **A**.

The network we are using above has been finetuned to classify bounding boxes, so its use in extracting features from the region foreground is suboptimal. Several neurons in the network may be focussing on context in the background, which will be unavailable when the network is fed the region foreground. This suggests that we should use a different network to extract the second set of features: one that is finetuned on the kinds of inputs that it is going to see. We therefore finetune another network (starting again from the net trained on ImageNet) which is fed as input cropped, padded bounding boxes of MCG regions with the background masked out. Because this region sees the actual foreground, we can actually train it to predict region overlap instead, which is what we care about. Therefore we change the labeling of the MCG regions to be based on segmentation overlap of the region with a ground truth region (instead of overlap with bounding box). We call this feature extractor **B**.

The previous strategy is still suboptimal, because the two networks have been trained in isolation, while at test time the two feature sets are going to be combined and fed to the classifier. This suggests that one should train the networks jointly. We formalize this intuition as follows. We create a neural network with the architecture shown in Figure 2. This architecture is a single network with two pathways. The first pathway operates on the cropped bounding box of the region (the "box" pathway) while the second pathway operates on the cropped bounding box with the background masked (the "region" pathway). The two pathways are disjoint except at the very final classifier layer, which concatenates the features from both pathways. Both these pathways individually have the same architecture as that of Krizhevsky *et al.* Note that both **A** and **B** can be seen as instantiations of this architecture, but with different sets of weights. **A** uses the same network parameters for both pathways. For **B**, the box pathway gets its weights from a network finetuned separately using bounding box overlap, while the region pathway gets its parameters from a network finetuned separately using region overlap.

Instead of using the same network in both pathways or training the two pathways in isolation, we now propose to train it as a whole directly. We use segmentation overlap as above. We initialize the box pathway with the network finetuned on boxes and the region pathway with the network finetuned on regions, and then finetune the entire network. At test time, we discard the final classification layer and use the output of the penultimate layer, which concatenates the features from the two pathways. We call this feature extractor **C**.

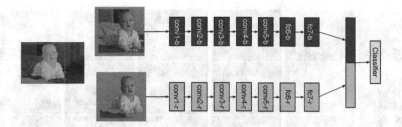

Fig. 2. Left: The region with its bounding box. Right: The architecture that we train for **C**. The top pathway operates on cropped boxes and the bottom pathway operates on region foregrounds.

3.3 Region Classification

We use the features from the previous step to train a linear SVM. We first train an initial SVM using ground truth as positives and regions overlapping ground truth by less than 20% as negative. Then we re-estimate the positive set: for each ground truth we pick the highest scoring MCG candidate that overlaps by more than 50%. Ground truth regions for which no such candidate exists (very few in number) are discarded. We then retrain the classifier using this new positive set. This training procedure corresponds to a multiple instance learning problem where each ground truth defines a positive bag of regions that overlap with it by more than 50%, and each negative region is its own bag. We found this training to work better than using just the ground truth as positives.

At test time we use the region classifiers to score each region. Because there may be multiple overlapping regions, we do a strict non-max suppression using a region overlap threshold of 0. This is because while the bounding box of two objects can in fact overlap, their pixel support in the image typically shouldn't. Post NMS, we work with only the top 20,000 detections for each category (over the whole dataset) and discard the rest for computational reasons. We confirmed that this reduction in detections has no effect on the AP^r metric.

3.4 Region Refinement

We take each of the remaining regions and refine its support. This is necessary because our region candidates have been created by a purely bottom-up, class agnostic process. Since the candidate generation has not made use of category-specific shape information, it is prone to both undershooting (*i.e.* missing some part of the object) and overshooting (*i.e.* including extraneous stuff).

We first learn to predict a coarse, top-down figure-ground mask for each region. To do this, we take the bounding box of each predicted region, pad it as for feature extraction, and then discretize the resulting box into a 10×10 grid. For each grid cell we train a logistic regression classifier to predict the probability that the grid cell belongs to the foreground. The features we use are the features extracted from the CNN, together with the figure-ground mask of the region

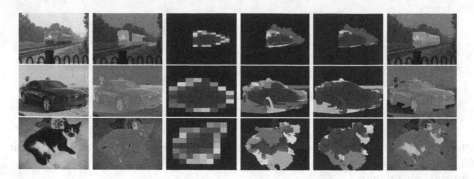

Fig. 3. Some examples of region refinement. We show in order the image, the original region, the coarse 10×10 mask, the coarse mask projected to superpixels, the output of the final classifier on superpixels and the final region after thresholding. Refinement uses top-down category specific information to fill in the body of the train and the cat and remove the road from the car.

discretized to the same 10×10 grid. The classifiers are trained on regions from the training set that overlap by more than 70% with a ground truth region.

This coarse figure-ground mask makes a top-down prediction about the shape of the object but does not necessarily respect the bottom-up contours. In addition, because of its coarse nature it cannot do a good job of modeling thin structures like aircraft wings or structures that move around. This information needs to come from the bottom-up region candidate. Hence we train a second stage to combine this coarse mask with the region candidate. We project the coarse mask to superpixels by assigning to each superpixel the average value of the coarse mask in the superpixel. Then we classify each superpixel, using as features this projected value in the superpixel and a 0 or 1 encoding if the superpixel belongs to the original region candidate. Figure 3 illustrates this refinement.

4   Experiments and Results

We use the segmentation annotations from SBD [17] to train and evaluate. We train all systems on PASCAL VOC 2012 train. For all training and finetuning of the network we use the recently released Caffe framework [19].

4.1   Results on AP^r and AP^r_{vol}

Table 1 and Table 2 show results on the AP^r and the AP^r_{vol} metrics respectively on PASCAL VOC 2012 val (ground truth segmentations are not available for test). We compute AP^r_{vol} by averaging the AP^r obtained for 9 thresholds.

1. **$\mathbf{O_2P}$** uses features and regions from Carreira *et al.* [5], which is the state-of-the-art in semantic segmentation. We train region classifiers on these features and do NMS to get detections. This baseline gets a mean AP^r of 25.2% and a mean AP^r_{vol} of 23.4%.

2. **A** is our most naive feature extractor. It uses MCG candidates and features from the bounding box and region foreground, using a single CNN finetuned using box overlaps. It achieves a mean AP^r of 42.9% and a mean AP^r_{vol} of 37.0%, a large jump over O_2P. This mirrors gains in object detection observed by Girshick *et al.* [16], although since O_2P is not designed for this task the comparison is somewhat unfair.

3. **B** is the result of finetuning a separate network exclusively on region foregrounds with labels defined by region overlap. This gives a large jump of the AP^r metric (of about 4 percentage points) and a smaller but significant jump on the AP^r_{vol} metric of about 2.5 percentage points.

4. **C** is the result of training a single large network with two pathways. There is a clear gain over using two isolated networks: on both metrics we gain about 0.7 percentage points.

5. **C+ref** is the result of refining the masks of the regions obtained from **C**. We again gain 2 points in the AP^r metric and 1.2 percentage points in the AP^r_{vol} metric. This large jump indicates that while MCG candidates we start from are very high quality, there is still a lot to be gained from refining the regions in a category specific manner.

A paired sample t-test indicates that each of the above improvements are statistically significant at the 0.05 significance level.

The left part of Figure 5 plots the improvement in mean AP^r over **A** as we vary the threshold at which a detection is considered correct. Each of our improvements increases AP^r across all thresholds, indicating that we haven't overfit to a particular regime.

Clearly we get significant gains over both our naive baseline as well as O2P. However, prior approaches that reason about segmentation together with detection might do better on the AP^r metric. To see if this is the case, we compare to the SegDPM work of Fidler *et al.* [14]. SegDPM combined DPMs [13] with O_2P [5] and achieved a 9 point boost over DPMs in classical object detection. For this method, only the bounding boxes are available publicly, and for some boxes the algorithm may choose not to have associated segments. We therefore compute an upper bound of its performance by taking each detection, considering all MCG regions whose bounding box overlaps with the detection by more than 70%, and selecting the region which best overlaps a ground truth.

Since SegDPM detections are only available on PASCAL VOC2010 val, we restrict our evaluations only to this set. Our upper bound on SegDPM has a mean AP^r of **31.3**, whereas **C**+ref achieves a mean AP^r of **50.3**.

4.2 Producing Diagnostic Information

Inspired by [18], we created tools for figuring out error modes and avenues for improvement for the SDS task. As in [18], we evaluate the impact of error modes by measuring the improvement in AP^r if the error mode was corrected. For localization, we assign labels to detections under two thresholds: the usual strict

Table 1. Results on AP^r on VOC2012 val. All numbers are %.

	O_2P	A	B	C	C+ref
aeroplane	56.5	61.8	65.7	67.4	**68.4**
bicycle	19.0	43.4	**49.6**	**49.6**	49.4
bird	23.0	46.6	47.2	49.1	**52.1**
boat	12.2	27.2	30.0	29.9	**32.8**
bottle	11.0	28.9	31.7	32.0	**33.0**
bus	48.8	61.7	66.9	65.9	**67.8**
car	26.0	46.9	50.9	51.4	**53.6**
cat	43.3	58.4	69.2	70.6	**73.9**
chair	4.7	17.8	19.6	**20.2**	19.9
cow	15.6	38.8	42.7	42.7	**43.7**
diningtable	7.8	18.6	22.8	22.9	**25.7**
dog	24.2	52.6	56.2	58.7	**60.6**
horse	27.5	44.3	51.9	54.4	**55.9**
motorbike	32.3	50.2	52.6	53.5	**58.9**
person	23.5	48.2	52.6	54.4	**56.7**
pottedplant	4.6	23.8	25.7	24.9	**28.5**
sheep	32.3	54.2	54.2	54.1	**55.6**
sofa	20.7	26.0	**32.2**	31.4	32.1
train	38.8	53.2	59.2	62.2	**64.7**
tvmonitor	32.3	55.3	58.7	59.3	**60.0**
Mean	25.2	42.9	47.0	47.7	**49.7**

Table 2. Results on AP^r_{vol} on VOC2012 val. All numbers are %.

	O_2P	A	B	C	C+ref
aeroplane	46.8	48.3	51.1	**53.2**	52.3
bicycle	21.2	39.8	42.1	42.1	**42.6**
bird	22.1	39.2	40.8	42.1	**42.2**
boat	13.0	25.1	27.5	27.1	**28.6**
bottle	10.1	26.0	26.8	27.6	**28.6**
bus	41.9	49.5	53.4	53.3	**58.0**
car	24.0	39.5	42.6	42.7	**45.4**
cat	39.2	50.7	56.3	57.3	**58.9**
chair	6.7	17.6	18.5	19.3	**19.7**
cow	14.6	32.5	36.0	36.3	**37.1**
diningtable	9.9	18.5	20.6	21.4	**22.8**
dog	24.0	46.8	48.9	49.0	**49.5**
horse	24.4	37.7	41.9	**43.6**	42.9
motorbike	28.6	41.1	43.2	43.5	**45.9**
person	25.6	43.2	45.8	47.0	**48.5**
pottedplant	7.0	23.4	24.8	24.4	**25.5**
sheep	29.0	43.0	44.2	44.0	**44.5**
sofa	18.8	26.2	29.7	29.9	**30.2**
train	34.6	45.1	48.9	49.9	**52.6**
tvmonitor	25.9	47.7	48.8	49.4	**51.4**
Mean	23.4	37.0	39.6	40.2	**41.4**

threshold of 0.5 and a more lenient threshold of 0.1 (note that this is a threshold on region overlap). Detections that count as true positives under the lenient threshold but as false positives under the strict threshold are considered mislocalizations. Duplicate detections are also considered mislocalizations. We then consider the performance if either a) all mislocalized instances were removed, or b) all mislocalized instances were correctly localized and duplicates removed.

Figure 4 shows how the PR curve for the AP^r benchmark changes if mislocalizations are corrected or removed for two categories. For the person category, removing mislocalizations brings precision up to essentially 100%, indicating that mislocalization is the predominant source of false positives. Correcting the mislocalizations provides a huge jump in recall. For the cat category the improvement provided by better localization is much less, indicating that there are still some false positives arising from misclassifications.

We can do this analysis for all categories. The average improvement in AP^r by fixing mislocalization is a measure of the impact of mislocalization on performance. We can also measure impact in this way for other error modes: for instance, false positives on objects of other similar categories, or on background [18]. (For defining similar and non-similar categories, we divide object categories into "animals", "transport" and "indoor" groups.) The left subfigure in Figure 6 shows the result of such an analysis on our best system (C+ref). The dark blue bar shows the AP^r improvement if we remove mislocalized detections and the light blue bar shows the improvement if we correct them. The other two bars show the improvement from removing confusion with similar categories and background. Mislocalization has a huge impact: it sets us back by about 16 percentage points. Compared to that confusion with similar categories or background is virtually non-existent.

We can measure the impact of mislocalization on the other algorithms in Table 1 as well, as shown in Table 3. It also shows the upper bound AP^r achievable when all mislocalization is fixed. Improvements in the feature extractor improve the upper bound (indicating fewer misclassifications) but also reduce the gap due to mislocalization (indicating better localization). Refinement doesn't change the upper bound and only improves localization, as expected.

To get a better handle on what one needs to do to improve localization, we considered two statistics. For each detection and a ground truth, instead of just taking the overlap (i.e. intersection over union), we can compute the pixel precision (fraction of the region that lies inside the ground truth) and pixel recall (fraction of the ground truth that lies inside the region). It can be shown that having both a pixel precision > 67% and a pixel recall > 67% is guaranteed to give an overlap of greater than 50%. We assign detection labels using pixel precision or pixel recall using a threshold of 67% and compute the respective AP. Comparing these two numbers then gives us a window into the kind of localization errors: a low pixel precision AP indicates that the error mode is overshooting the region and predicting extraneous background pixels, while a low pixel recall AP indicates that the error mode is undershooting the region and missing out some ground truth pixels.

The second half of Figure 6 shows the difference between pixel precision AP (AP^{pp}) and pixel recall AP (AP^{pr}). Bars to the left indicate higher pixel recall AP, while bars to the right indicate higher pixel precision AP. For some categories such as person and bird we tend to miss ground truth pixels, whereas for others such as bicycle we tend to leak into the background.

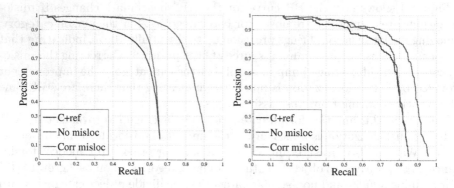

Fig. 4. PR on person(left) and cat(right). Blue is **C**+ref. Green is if an oracle removes mislocalized predictions, and red is if the oracle corrects our mislocalizations.

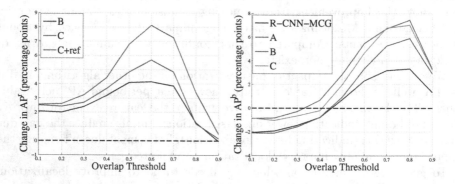

Fig. 5. Left: Improvement in mean AP^r over **A** due to our 3 variants for a variety of overlap thresholds. We get improvements for all overlap thresholds. Right: A similar plot for AP^b. Improvements are relative to R-CNN with Selective Search proposals [16]. As the threshold becomes stricter, the better localization of our approach is apparent.

4.3   Results on AP^b and AP^b_{vol}

Comparison with prior work is easier on the classical bounding box and segmentation metrics. It also helps us evaluate if handling the SDS task also improves performance on the individual tasks. To compare on AP^b, we retrain our final region classifiers for the bounding box detection task. This is because the ranking of regions based on bounding box overlap is different from that based on

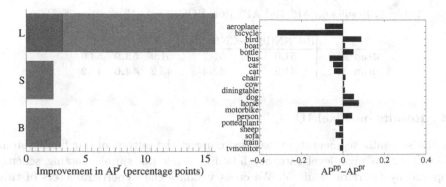

Fig. 6. Left: Impact of the three kinds of false positives on mean AP^r. L : mislocalization, B : detection on background, and S : misfirings on similar categories. Right: Disambiguating between two kinds of mislocalizations. Bars to the left mean that we frequently overshoot the ground truth, while bars to the right mean that we undershoot.

Table 3. Maximum achievable AP^r (assuming perfect localization) and loss in AP^r due to mislocalization for all systems

	A	B	C	C+ref
AP Upper bound	63.0	65.0	65.4	65.5
Loss due to mislocalization	20.1	18.0	17.7	15.8

segmentation overlap. As in [16], we use ground truth boxes as positive, and MCG boxes overlapping by less than 50% as negative. At test time we do not do any region refinement.

We add two baselines: R-CNN is the system of Girshick *et al.* taken as is, and R-CNN-MCG is R-CNN on boxes from MCG instead of Selective Search. Note that neither of these baselines uses features from the region foreground.

Table 4 shows the mean AP^b and AP$^b_{vol}$. We get improvements over R-CNN on both AP^b and AP$^b_{vol}$, with improvements on the latter metric being somewhat larger. The right half of Figure 5 shows the variation in AP^b as we vary the overlap threshold for counting something as correct. We plot the improvement in AP^b over vanilla R-CNN. We do worse than R-CNN for low thresholds, but are much better for higher thresholds. This is also true to some extent for R-CNN-MCG, so this is partly a property of MCG, and partly a consequence of our algorithm's improved localization. Interestingly, **C** does worse than **B**. We posit that this is because now the entire network has been finetuned for SDS.

Finally we evaluated **C** on PASCAL VOC 2012 test. Our mean AP^b of **50.7** is an improvement over the R-CNN mean AP^b of **49.6** (both without bounding box regression), and much better than other systems, such as SegDPM [14] (**40.7**).

310   B. Hariharan et al.

Table 4. Results on AP^b and AP^b_{vol} on VOC12 val. All numbers are %.

	R-CNN[16]	R-CNN-MCG	A	B	C
Mean AP^b	51.0	51.7	51.9	**53.9**	53.0
Mean AP^b_{vol}	41.9	42.4	43.2	**44.6**	44.2

4.4 Results on Pixel IU

For the semantic segmentation task, we convert the output of our final system (**C**+ref) into a pixel-level category labeling using the simple pasting scheme proposed by Carreira *et al.* [5]. We cross validate the hyperparameters of this pasting step on the VOC11 segmentation Val set. The results are in Table 5. We compare to O_2P [5] and R-CNN which are the current state-of-the-art on this task. We advance the state-of-the-art by about 5 points, or 10% relative.

To conclude, our pipeline achieves good results on the SDS task while improving state-of-the-art in object detection and semantic segmentation. Figure 7 shows examples of the output of our system.

Table 5. Results on Pixel IU. All numbers are %.

	O_2P [5]	R-CNN [16]	**C**+ref
Mean Pixel IU (VOC2011 Test)	47.6	47.9	**52.6**
Mean Pixel IU (VOC2012 Test)	47.8	-	**51.6**

Fig. 7. Top detections: 3 persons, 2 bikes, diningtable, sheep, chair, cat. We can handle uncommon pose and clutter and are able to resolve individual instances.

Acknowledgments. This work was supported by ONR MURI N000141010933, a Google Research Grant and a Microsoft Research fellowship. We thank the NVIDIA Corporation for providing GPUs through their academic program.

References

1. Arbeláez, P., Pont-Tuset, J., Barron, J., Marques, F., Malik, J.: Multiscale combinatorial grouping. In: CVPR (2014)
2. Arbeláez, P., Hariharan, B., Gu, C., Gupta, S., Malik, J.: Semantic segmentation using regions and parts. In: CVPR (2012)
3. Boix, X., Gonfaus, J.M., van de Weijer, J., Bagdanov, A.D., Serrat, J., Gonzàlez, J.: Harmony potentials. IJCV 96(1) (2012)
4. Bourdev, L., Maji, S., Brox, T., Malik, J.: Detecting people using mutually consistent poselet activations. In: Daniilidis, K., Maragos, P., Paragios, N. (eds.) ECCV 2010, Part VI. LNCS, vol. 6316, pp. 168–181. Springer, Heidelberg (2010)
5. Carreira, J., Caseiro, R., Batista, J., Sminchisescu, C.: Semantic segmentation with second-order pooling. In: Fitzgibbon, A., Lazebnik, S., Perona, P., Sato, Y., Schmid, C. (eds.) ECCV 2012, Part VII. LNCS, vol. 7578, pp. 430–443. Springer, Heidelberg (2012)
6. Carreira, J., Sminchisescu, C.: Constrained parametric min-cuts for automatic object segmentation. In: CVPR (2010)
7. Dai, Q., Hoiem, D.: Learning to localize detected objects. In: CVPR (2012)
8. Dalal, N., Triggs, B.: Histograms of oriented gradients for human detection. In: CVPR (2005)
9. Deng, J., Berg, A., Satheesh, S., Su, H., Khosla, A., Fei-Fei, L.: ImageNet Large Scale Visual Recognition Competition 2012 (ILSVRC 2012) (2012), http://www.image-net.org/challenges/LSVRC/2012/
10. Donahue, J., Jia, Y., Vinyals, O., Hoffman, J., Zhang, N., Tzeng, E., Darrell, T.: Decaf: A deep convolutional activation feature for generic visual recognition. arXiv preprint arXiv:1310.1531 (2013)
11. Everingham, M., Van Gool, L., Williams, C.K.I., Winn, J., Zisserman, A.: The Pascal Visual Object Classes (VOC) Challenge. IJCV 88(2) (2010)
12. Farabet, C., Couprie, C., Najman, L., LeCun, Y.: Learning hierarchical features for scene labeling. TPAMI 35(8) (2013)
13. Felzenszwalb, P.F., Girshick, R.B., McAllester, D., Ramanan, D.: Object detection with discriminatively trained part-based models. TPAMI 32(9) (2010)
14. Fidler, S., Mottaghi, R., Yuille, A., Urtasun, R.: Bottom-up segmentation for top-down detection. In: CVPR (2013)
15. Fukushima, K.: Neocognitron: A self-organizing neural network model for a mechanism of pattern recognition unaffected by shift in position. Biological Cybernetics 36(4) (1980)
16. Girshick, R., Donahue, J., Darrell, T., Malik, J.: Rich feature hierarchies for accurate object detection and semantic segmentation. In: CVPR (2014)
17. Hariharan, B., Arbelaez, P., Bourdev, L., Maji, S., Malik, J.: Semantic contours from inverse detectors. In: ICCV (2011)
18. Hoiem, D., Chodpathumwan, Y., Dai, Q.: Diagnosing error in object detectors. In: Fitzgibbon, A., Lazebnik, S., Perona, P., Sato, Y., Schmid, C. (eds.) ECCV 2012, Part III. LNCS, vol. 7574, pp. 340–353. Springer, Heidelberg (2012)
19. Jia, Y.: Caffe: An open source convolutional architecture for fast feature embedding (2013), http://caffe.berkeleyvision.org/
20. Kim, B.-S., Sun, M., Kohli, P., Savarese, S.: Relating things and stuff by high-order potential modeling. In: Fusiello, A., Murino, V., Cucchiara, R. (eds.) ECCV 2012 Ws/Demos, Part III. LNCS, vol. 7585, pp. 293–304. Springer, Heidelberg (2012)

21. Krizhevsky, A., Sutskever, I., Hinton, G.E.: Imagenet classification with deep convolutional neural networks. In: NIPS (2012)
22. Ladický, L., Sturgess, P., Alahari, K., Russell, C., Torr, P.H.S.: What, where and how many? Combining object detectors and CRFs. In: Daniilidis, K., Maragos, P., Paragios, N. (eds.) ECCV 2010, Part IV. LNCS, vol. 6314, pp. 424–437. Springer, Heidelberg (2010)
23. LeCun, Y., Boser, B., Denker, J.S., Henderson, D., Howard, R.E., Hubbard, W., Jackel, L.D.: Backpropagation applied to handwritten zip code recognition. Neural Computation 1(4) (1989)
24. Lowe, D.G.: Distinctive image features from scale-invariant keypoints. IJCV 60(2) (2004)
25. Mottaghi, R.: Augmenting deformable part models with irregular-shaped object patches. In: CVPR (2012)
26. Parkhi, O.M., Vedaldi, A., Jawahar, C., Zisserman, A.: The truth about cats and dogs. In: ICCV (2011)
27. van de Sande, K.E., Uijlings, J.R., Gevers, T., Smeulders, A.W.: Segmentation as selective search for object recognition. In: ICCV (2011)
28. Sermanet, P., Eigen, D., Zhang, X., Mathieu, M., Fergus, R., LeCun, Y.: Overfeat: Integrated recognition, localization and detection using convolutional networks. In: ICLR (2014)
29. Sermanet, P., Kavukcuoglu, K., Chintala, S., LeCun, Y.: Pedestrian detection with unsupervised multi-stage feature learning. In: CVPR (2013)
30. Shotton, J., Winn, J.M., Rother, C., Criminisi, A.: *TextonBoost*: Joint appearance, shape and context modeling for multi-class object recognition and segmentation. In: Leonardis, A., Bischof, H., Pinz, A. (eds.) ECCV 2006, Part I. LNCS, vol. 3951, pp. 1–15. Springer, Heidelberg (2006)
31. Tighe, J., Niethammer, M., Lazebnik, S.: Scene parsing with object instances and occlusion handling. In: ECCV (2010)
32. Yang, Y., Hallman, S., Ramanan, D., Fowlkes, C.C.: Layered object models for image segmentation. TPAMI 34(9) (2012)

Learning Graphs to Model Visual Objects across Different Depictive Styles

Qi Wu, Hongping Cai, and Peter Hall

Media Technology Research Centre, University of Bath, United Kingdom

Abstract. Visual object classification and detection are major problems in contemporary computer vision. State-of-art algorithms allow thousands of visual objects to be learned and recognized, under a wide range of variations including lighting changes, occlusion, point of view and different object instances. Only a small fraction of the literature addresses the problem of variation in depictive styles (photographs, drawings, paintings *etc.*). This is a challenging gap but the ability to process images of all depictive styles and not just photographs has potential value across many applications. In this paper we model visual classes using a graph with multiple labels on each node; weights on arcs and nodes indicate relative importance (salience) to the object description. Visual class models can be learned from examples from a database that contains photographs, drawings, paintings *etc.* Experiments show that our representation is able to improve upon Deformable Part Models for detection and Bag of Words models for classification.

Keywords: Object Recognition, Deformable Models, Multi-labeled Graph, Graph Matching.

1 Introduction

Humans posses a remarkable capacity: they are able to recognize, locate and classify visual objects in a seemingly unlimited variety of depictions: in photographs, in line drawings, as cuddly toys, in clouds. Computer vision algorithms, on the other hand, tend to be restricted to recognizing objects in photographs alone, albeit subject to wide variations in points of view, lighting, occlusion, *etc.* There is very little research in computer vision on the problem of recognizing objects regardless of depictive style; this paper makes an effort to address that problem.

There are many reasons for wanting visual class objects that generalise across depictions. One reason is that computer vision should not discriminate between visual class objects on the basis of their depiction - a face is a face whether photographed or drawn. A second reason for being interested in extending the gamut of depictions available to computer vision is that not all visual objects exist in the real world. Mythological creatures, for example, have never existed but are recognizable nonetheless. If computer vision is to recognize such visual objects, it must emulate the human capacity to disregard depictive style with respect to recognition problems. The final reason will consider here is to note

D. Fleet et al. (Eds.): ECCV 2014, Part VII, LNCS 8695, pp. 313–328, 2014.
© Springer International Publishing Switzerland 2014

Fig. 1. Learning a model to recognize objects. Our proposed multi-labeled graph modelling method shows significant improvement for recognizing objects depicted in variety styles. The green boxes are estimated by using DPM [10], the red are predicted from our system. The text above the bounding box displays the predicted class category over a 50-classes dataset.

that drawings, paintings, *etc.* are models of objects: they are abstractions. This is obvious when one considers a child's drawing of a car in which all four wheels are shown – the child draws what they know of a car, not what is seen. In addition, a line drawing, for example, is much more compact in terms of information content than a photograph – drawings are abstractions in the sense that a lot of data is discarded, but information germane to the task of recognition is (typically) kept. This suggests that visual class models used in computer vision should exhibit a similarly high degree of abstraction.

The main contribution of this paper is to provide a modeling schema (a framework) for visual class objects that generalises across a broad collection of depictive styles. The main problem the paper addresses is this: ***how to capture the wide variation in visual appearance exhibited by visual objects across depictive styles***. This variation is typically much wider than for lighting and viewpoint variations usually considered for photographic images. Indeed, if we consider different ways to depict an object (or parts of an object) there is good reason to suppose that the distribution of corresponding features form distinct clusters. Its effect can be seen in Figure 1 where the currently accepted state-of-art method for object detection fails when presented with artwork. The same figure highlights our contribution by showing our proposal is able to locate (and classify) objects regardless of their depictive style.

The remainder of this paper first outlines the relevant background (Sec. 2), showing that our problem is hardly studied, but that relevant prior art exists for us to build upon. Sec. 3 describes our modeling schema, and in particular introduces the way in which we account for the wide variation in feature distributions, specifically - ***the use of multi-labels to represent visual words that exists in possibly discontinuous regions of a feature space.*** A visual class model (*VCM*) is now a graph with *multi-labeled nodes* and *learned weights*. Such novel visual class models can be learned from examples via an efficient algorithm we have designed (Sec. 4), and experimentally (Sec. 5) are shown to outperform state-of-art deformable part models at detection tasks, and state-of-art BoW methods for classification. The paper concludes, in Sec. 6, and points to future developments and applications.

2   Related Work

Modeling visual object classes is an interesting open question of relevance to many important computer vision tasks such as object detection and classification. Of the many approaches to visual object classification, the bag-of-words (BoW) family [7, 19, 23, 22] is arguably the most popular and successful. It models visual object classes via histograms of "visual words", *i.e.* words being clusters in feature space. Although the BoW methods address many difficult issues, they tend to generalise poorly across depictive styles. The explanation for this is the formation of visual codewords in which clustering assumes low variation in feature appearance. To overcome this drawback, researchers use alternative low-level features that do not depend on photometric appearance, *e.g.*, edgelets [26, 12] and region shapes [15, 17]. However, even these methods do not generalise well. We argue that no single "monolithic" feature will cover all possible appearances of an object (or part), when depictive styles are considered. Rather, we expand the variation of a local feature appearance from different depiction sources by multi-labelling model graph nodes.

Deformable models of various types are widely used to model the object for detection tasks, including several kinds of deformable template models [4, 5] and a variety of part-based models [1, 6, 9–11, 13, 20]. In the constellation models from [11], parts are constrained to be in a sparse set of locations, and their geometric arrangement is captured by a Gaussian distribution. In contrast, pictorial structure models [9, 10, 13] define a matching problem where parts have an individual match cost in a dense set of locations, and their geometric arrangement is captured by a set of 'springs' connecting pairs of parts. In those methods, the Deformable Part-based Model (DPM) [10] is the most successful one. It describes an object detection system based on mixtures of multi-scale deformable part models plus a root model. By modeling objects from different views with distinct models, it is able to detect large variations in pose. However, when the variance comes from local parts, *e.g.* the same object depicted in different styles, it does not generalize well; this is exactly the problem we address.

Cross-depiction problems are comparably less well-explored. Edge-based HoG was explored in [16] to retrieve photographs with a hand sketch query. Li *et al* [21] present a method for the representation and matching of sketches by exploiting not only local features but also global structures, through a star graph. Matching visually similar images has been addressed using self-similarity descriptors [25], and learning the most discriminant regions with exemplar SVM is also capable of cross-depiction matching [27]. These methods worked well for matching visually similar images, but neither are capable of modeling object categories with high diversity. The work most similar to own in motivation and method is a graph based approach proposed in [32]. They use a hierarchical graph model to obtain a coarse-to-fine arrangement of parts, whereas we use a single layer. They use qualitative shape as node label; we use multiple labels, each a HOG features.

In summary, the problem of cross-depiction classification is little studied. We learn a graph with multi-labeled nodes and employ a learned weight vector to encode the importance of nodes and edges similarities. Such a model is unique as

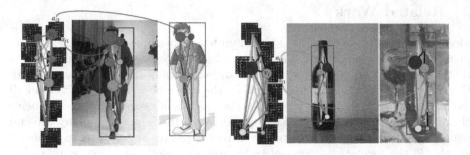

Fig. 2. Our multi-labeled graph model with learned discriminative weights, and detections for both photos and artworks. The model graph nodes are multi-labeled by attributes learned from different depiction styles (feature patches behind the nodes in the figure). The learned weight vector encodes the importance of the nodes and edges. In the figure, bigger circles represent stronger nodes, and darker lines denote stronger edges. And the same color of the nodes indicates the matched parts.

far as we know. We now describe the class model in greater detail: the formulation of the model, how to learn it, and its value to the problem of cross-depiction detection and classification.

3   Models

Our model of a visual object class is based around a graph of nodes and edges. Like Felzenszwalb *et al* [10], we label nodes with descriptions of object parts, but we differ in two ways. Unlike them, we label parts with multiple attributes, to allow for cross-depiction variation. Second, we differ in using a graph that defines the spatial relationship between node pairs using edge labels, rather than a star-like structure in which nodes are attached to a root. Furthermore, we place weights on the graph which are automatically learned using a method due to [3]. These weights can be interpreted as encoding relative salience. Thus a weighted, multi-labeled graph describes objects as seen from a single viewpoint. To account for variation in points of view we follow [10, 14, 8] who advocate using distinct models for each pose. They refer to each such model as a *component*, a term we borrow in this paper and which should not be confused with the *part* of an object.

We solve the problem of inter-depictive variation by using *multi-labeled* nodes to describe objects parts. These multiple attributes are learned from different depictive styles of images, which are more effective than attempting to characterize all attributes in a monolithic model, since the variation of local feature is much wider than the changes usually considered for photographic images, such as lighting changes *etc*. Moreover, it does not make sense that the parts of an object should be weighted equally during the matching for a part-based model. For example, for a person model, the head part should be weighted more than other parts like limbs and torso, because it is more discriminative than other parts in the matching - a person's arms are easily confused with a quadruped's forelimbs, but the head part's features are distinctive. Beside the discrimination of node appearance, the relative location, edges, should be also weighted according to its rigidity. For instance, the edges between the head and shoulder should be more rigid than the edges between two deformable arms. Hence, in our model, a weight vector β is learned automatically to encode the importance of node and edge similarity. We refer to it as the *discriminative weight* formulation for a part based model. This advantage will be demonstrated with evidence in the experimental section.

3.1   A Multi-labeled Graph Model

A *multi-labeled graph* is defined as $G^* = (V^*, E^*, A^*, B^*)$, where V^* represents a set of nodes, E^* a set of edges, A^* a set of multi-labeled attributes of the nodes and B^* a set of attributes of edges. Specifically, $V^* = \{v_1^*, v_2^*, ..., v_n^*\}$, n is the number of nodes. $E^* = \{e_{12}^*, ..., e_{ij}^*, ..., e_{n(n-1)^*}\}$ is the set of edges. $A^* = \{A_1^*, A_2^*, ..., A_n^*\}$ with each $A_i^* = \{a_{i1}^*, a_{i2}^*, ..., a_{ic_i}^*\}$ consists of c_i attributes. It is easy to see that a standard graph G is a special case of our defined *multi-labeled graph*, which restricts $c_i = 1$.

A visual object class model $M = < G^*, \beta >$ for an object with n parts is formally defined by a multi-labeled model graph G^* with n nodes and $n \times (n-1)$ directed edges. And the weight vector $\beta \in \mathcal{R}^{n^2 \times 1}$ encodes the importance of nodes and edges of the G^*. Both the model graph G^* and the weights vector β are learned from a set of labeled example graphs. Figure 2 shows two example models with their detections from different depictive style. The learning process depends on scoring and matching, so a description is deferred to Section 4.

We define a score function between a visual class model, G^*, and a putative object represented as a standard graph G, following [3]. The definition is such that the absence of the *VCM* in an image yields a very low score. Let Y be a binary assignment matrix $Y \in \{0, 1\}^{n \times n'}$ which indicates the nodes correspondence between two graphs, where n and n' denote the number of nodes in G^* and G, respectively. If $v_i^* \in V^*$ matches $v_a \in V$, then $Y_{i,a} = 1$, and $Y_{i,a} = 0$ otherwise. The scoring function is defined as the sum of nodes similarities (which indicate the local appearance) and the edges similarities (which indicate the spatial structure of the objects) between the visual object class and the putative object.

$$S(G^*, G, Y) = \sum_{Y_{i,a} = 1} S_V(A_i^*, a_a) + \sum_{\substack{Y_{i,a} = 1 \\ Y_{j,b} = 1}} S_E(b_{ij}^*, b_{ab}), \qquad (1)$$

where, because we use multi-labels on nodes we define

$$S_V(A_i^*, a_a) = \max_{p \in \{1, 2, ..., c_i\}} S_A(a_{ip}^*, a_a), \qquad (2)$$

with a_{ip}^*, the p_{th} attribute in $A_i^* = \{a_{i1}^*, a_{i2}^*, ..., a_{ip}^*, ...a_{ic_i}^*\}$, and S_A is the similarity measure between attributes.

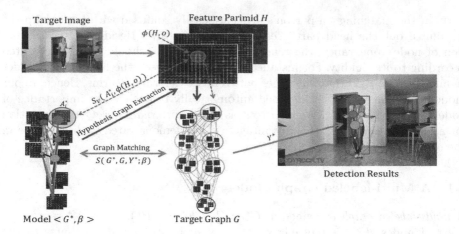

Fig. 3. Detection and matching process. A graph G will be firstly extracted from the target image based on input model $< G^*, \beta >$, then the matching process is formulated as a graph matching problem. The matched subgraph from G indicates the final detection results. $\phi(H, o)$ in the figure denotes the attributes obtained at position o.

To introduce the weight vector β into scoring, like [3], we parameterize Eq. 1 as follows. Let $\pi(i) = a$ denote an assignment of node v_i^* in G^* to node v_a in G, i.e. $Y_{i,a} = 1$. A joint feature map $\Phi(G^*, G, Y)$ is defined by aligning the relevant similarity values of Eq. 1 into a vectorial form as:

$$\Phi(G^*, G, Y) = [\cdots ; S_V(A_i^*, a_{\pi(i)}); \cdots ; S_E(b_{ij}^*, b_{\pi(i)\pi(j)}); \cdots]. \tag{3}$$

Then, by introducing weights on all elements of this feature map, we obtain a discriminative score function:

$$S(G^*, G, Y; \beta) = \beta \cdot \Phi(G^*, G, Y), \tag{4}$$

which is the score of a graph (extracted from the target image) with our proposed model $< G^*, \beta >$, under the assignment matrix Y.

3.2   Detection and Matching

To detect an instance of a visual class model (*VCM*) in an image we must find the standard graph in an image that best matches the given *VCM*. More exactly, we seek a subgraph of the graph G, constructed over a complete image, and is identified by the assignment matrix Y^+. We use an efficient approach to solve the problem of detection, which is stated as solving

$$Y^+ = \arg\max_Y S(G^*, G, Y; \beta), \tag{5a}$$

$$s.t. \sum_{i=1}^{n} Y_{i,a} \leq 1, \sum_{a=1}^{n'} Y_{i,a} \leq 1 \tag{5b}$$

where Eq.(5b) includes the matching constrains - only one node can match with at most one node in the other graph. To solve the NP-hard programming in Eq.5 efficiently, Torresani *et al.* [29] propose a decomposition approach for graph matching. The idea is to decompose the original problem into several simpler subproblems, for which a global maxima is efficiently computed. Combining the maxima from individual subproblems will then provide a maximum for the original problem. We make use of their general idea in an algorithm of our own design that efficiently locates graphs in images.

The graph G in Eq.(5a) is extracted from the target image as follows. First a dense multi-scale feature pyramid, H, is computed. Next a coarse-to-fine matching strategy is employed to locate each node of the *VCM* at k most possible locations in the image, based on the nodes similarity function S_V of Eq.(2). These possible locations are used to create a graph of the image. The 'image graph' is fully connected; corresponding features from H label the nodes; spatial attributes label the edges. This creates graph G.

Having found G the next step is to find the optimal subgraph by solving Eq. 5. During this step, we constrain the node v_i^* of the model graph G^* to be assigned (via Y) only to one of the k nodes it was associated with. In our experiments, to balance the matching accuracy and computational efficiency, we set $k = 10$. The optimal assignment matrix Y^+ between the model $< G^*, \beta >$ and the graph G, computed through Eq. (5), returns a detected subgraph of G that indicates the parts of the detected object. A detection and matching process is illustrated in Fig 3.

3.3   Mixture Models at Model Level

Our model also can be mixed using *components* as defined above and used in [10, 14, 8], so that different point of view (front/side) or poses (standing /sitting people) can be taken into account. A mixture model with m components is defined by a m-tuple, $\mathcal{M} = M_1, ..., M_m$, where $M_c =< G_c^*, \beta_c >$ is the multi-labeled *VCM* for the c-th component. To detect objects using a mixture model we use the matching algorithm described above to find the best matched subgraph that yields higher scoring hypothesis independently for each component.

4   Learning Models

Given images labeled with n interest points corresponding to n parts of the object, we consider learning a multi-labeled graph model G^* and weights β that together represent a visual class model. Because structure does not depend on fine-level details, we do not (nor should we) train an ssvm using depiction-specific features. The model learning framework is shown in Figure 4.

4.1   Learning the Model Graph G^*

For the convenience of description, consider a class-specific reference graph $G^\triangle$ (note that a reference graph is not created but is a mathematical convenience

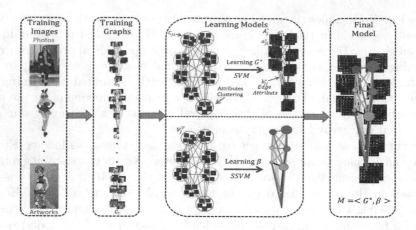

Fig. 4. Learning a class model, from left to right. (a): An input collection (different depictions) used for training. (b): Extract training graphs. (c): Learning models in two steps, one for G^*, one for β. (d): Combination as final class model.

only, see [3] for details) and a labeled training graph set $T = (< G_1, y_1 >, ..., < G_l, y_l >)$ obtained from the labeled images. In each $< G_i, y_i > \in T$, we have n nodes, $n \times (n-1)$ edges and their corresponding attributes, defined as $G_i = (V_i, E_i, A_i, B_i)$, and y_i is an assignment matrix that denotes the matching between the training graph and the reference graph $G^\triangle$. Then, a sequence of nodes which match the same reference node $v_j^\triangle \in G^\triangle$ are collected over all the graphs in T. We define these nodes as $V_j^T = \{v_{j,1}^T, v_{j,2}^T, ..., v_{j,l}^T\}$ in which $v_{j,i}$ means the j-th node in training graph G_i. Then, the corresponding attributes set A_j^T can be extracted from the corresponding G_i to be used to learn the model graph G^* via the following process.

To learn a node V_j^* in the model graph G^*, there are l positive training nodes V_j^T with their attributes A_j^T. All the attributes in A_j^T are labeled according to depictive styles. Instead of manually labelling the style for each image, we use K-means clustering based on chi-square distance to build c_j clusters automatically, C_{ji} denotes the i-th cluster for A_j^T, and attributes in the same cluster indicate the similar depictive styles. Accordingly, the attributes A_j^* for the node $V_j^* \in G^*$ actually include c_j elements, $A_j^* = \{a_{j1}^*, a_{j2}^*, ..., a_{jc_j}^*\}$. For each a_{ji}^*, it is learned by minimizing the following objective function:

$$E(a_{ji}^*) = \frac{\lambda}{2} \|a_{ji}^*\|^2 + \frac{1}{N} \sum_{s=1}^{N} \max\{0, 1 - f(a_s) < a_{ji}^*, a_s >\} \qquad (6)$$

from N example pairs $(a_s, f(a_s))$, $s = 1, ..., N$, where

$$f(a_s) = \begin{cases} 1 & \text{if } a_s \in C_{ji} \\ -1 & \text{if } a_s \in \mathcal{N}_j \end{cases} \qquad (7)$$

where $\mathcal{N}_j$ is the negative sample sets for the node V_j^* and a_s is a node attributes from the training set. In our experiments, we use all the attributes that are in T

but do not belong to A_j^T, and the background patch attributes to build the negative samples set. Hence, this learning process transfers to an SVM optimization problem, which is solved by using stochastic gradient descent [28]. Edges E^* and corresponding attributes B^* also can be learned in a similar way. We account for different depictive styles by constructing a distinct SVM for each one; so in effect the multi-labeled nodes in G^* are in fact multiple SVMs.

4.2 Learning the Weights β

The aim of this step is to learn a weight vector β to produce best matches of the reference graph $G^\triangle$ with the training examples $T = (< G_1, y_1 >, ..., < G_l, y_l >)$ of the class. Let $\hat{y}$ denote the optimal matching between the reference graph $G^\triangle$ and a training graph $G_i \in T$ given by

$$\hat{y}(G_i; G^\triangle, \beta) = \underset{y \in Y(G_i)}{\arg\max} \, S(G^\triangle, G_i, y; \beta), \tag{8}$$

where $Y(G_i) \in \{0,1\}^{n \times n'}$ defines the set of possible assignment matrix for the input training graph G_i. Inspired by the max-margin framework [30] and following [3], we learn the parameter β by minimizing the following objective function:

$$L_T(G^\triangle, \beta) = r(G^\triangle, \beta) + \frac{C}{l} \sum_{i=1}^{l} \Delta(y_i, \hat{y}(G_i; G^\triangle), \beta). \tag{9}$$

In this objective function r is a regularization function, $\Delta(y, \hat{y})$ a loss function, drives the learning process by measuring the quality of a predicted matching $\hat{y}_i$ against its ground truth y_i. The parameter C controls the relative importance of the loss term.

Cho et al. [3] propose an effective framework to transform the learning objective function in Eq. (9) into a standard formulation of the structured support vector machine (SSVM) by assuming the node and edge similarity functions are dot products of two attributes vectors. It is solved by using the efficient cutting plane method proposed by Joachims et al. [18], giving us the weight vector β to encode the importance of nodes and edges.

4.3 Features

Node Attributes. In our proposed model, we used a 31-d Histogram of Oriented Gradients (HOG) descriptor, following [10], which computes both directed and undirected gradients as well as a four dimensional texture-energy feature.

Edge Attributes. Considering an edge e_{ij} from node v_i to node v_j with polar coordinates (ρ_{ij}, θ_{ij}). We convert these distances and orientations to histogram features so that it can be used within dot products as in [3]. Two histograms (one for the length L_{ij}, and one for the angle P_{ij}) are built and concatenated to quantize the edge vectors, $b_{i,j} = [L_{ij}; P_{ij}]$. For length, we use uniform bins of size n_L in the log space with respect to the position of v_i, making the histogram

Fig. 5. Our photo-art dataset, containing 50 object categories. Each category is displayed with one art image and one photo image.

more sensitive to the position of nearby points. The log-distance histogram L_{ij} is constructed on the bins by a discrete Gaussian histogram centred on the bins for ρ_{ij}. For angle, we use uniform bins of size $2\pi/n_P$. The polar histogram P_{ij} is constructed on it in a similar way, except that a circular Gaussian histogram centered on the bin for $\theta_{i,j}$ is used. In this work, we used $n_L = 9, n_P = 18$.

5   Experimental Evaluation

Our class model has the potential to be used in many applications, here we demonstrate it in the task of cross-depiction detection and classification. Although there are several challenging object detection and classification datasets such as PASCAL VOC, ETHZ-shape classes and Caltech-256, most of the classes in these datasets do not contain objects that are depicted in different styles, such as painting, drawing and cartoons. Therefore, we augment photo images of 50 object categories, which frequently appear in commonly used datasets, to cover the large variety of art works. Each class contains around 100 images with different instances and approximately half of the images in each class are artworks and cover a wide gamut of style. Examples of each class are shown in figure 5.

5.1   Detection

In the detection task, we split the image set for each object class into two random partitions, 30 images for training (15 photos and 15 art) and the rest are used for testing. The dataset contains the groundtruth for each image in the form of bounding boxes around the objects. During the test, the goal is to predict the bounding boxes for a given object class in a target image (if any). The red bounding boxes in Fig. 1 are predicted in such way. In practice the detector outputs a set of bounding boxes with corresponding scores, and a precision-recall curve across all the test sets is obtained. We score a detector by the average precision (AP), which is defined as the area under the precision-recall curve across a test set, mAP(mean of the AP) is the average AP over all objects.

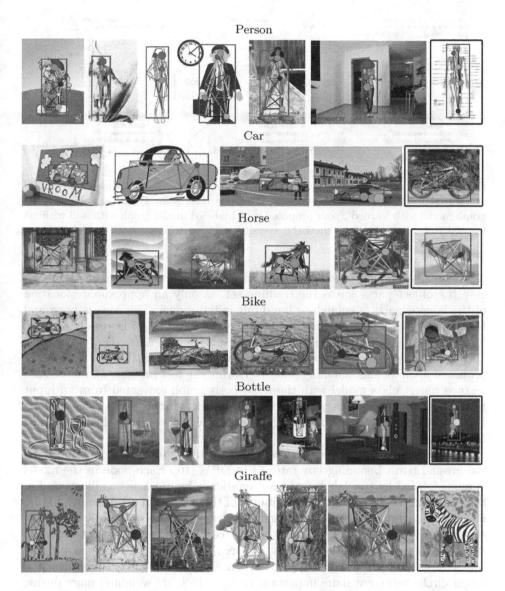

Fig. 6. Examples of high-scoring detections on our cross-depictive style dataset, selected from the top 20 highest scoring detections in each class. The framed images (last one in each row) illustrate false positives for each category. In each detected window, the object is matched with the learned model graph. In the matched graph, each node indicates a part of the object, and larger circles represent greater importance of a node, and darker lines denote stronger relationships.

Since our learning process (in Sec. 4) needs pre-labeled training graphs, n distinctive key-points have to be identified in the target images. In our experiment, we set $n = 8$. In order to ease the labelling process, rather than using

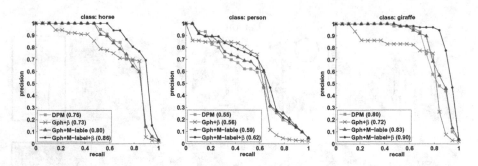

Fig. 7. Precision/Recall curves for models trained on the horse, person and giraffe categories of our cross-domain dataset. We show results for DPM, a single labeled graph model with learned β, our proposed multi-labeled model graph with and without learned β. In parenthesis we show the average precision score for each model.

the manually labeling process, we instead use a pre-trained DPM model to locate the object parts across the training set, as only an approximate location of the labeled parts is enough to build our initial model. This idea is borrowed from [34], which uses a pictorial structure [24] to estimate 15 key-points for the further learning of a 2.5D human action graph for matching. Also notice that DPM is only used to ease the training data labelling process, it is not used in our proposed learning and matching process. During the test process, we match each learned object class model with the hypothesis graph extracted from an input test image, as detailed illustrated in Sec 3.2. The detection score is computed via Eq. (5) and the predicted bounding box is obtained by covering all the matched nodes.

We trained a two component model, where the '*component*' is decided by the ground truth bounding box ratio as in DPM [10]. Each node in the model is multi-labeled by two labels (split automatically by *K-means* as illustrated in Sec. 4.1), that correspond to the attributes of the photo and art domains. Figure 6 shows some detections we obtain using our learned models. These results show that the proposed model can detect objects correctly across different depictive styles, including photos, oil paintings, children's drawings, stick-figures and cartoons. Moreover, the detected object parts are labeled by the graph nodes, and larger circles represent more important nodes, which are weighted more during the matching process, via β.

We evaluated different aspects of our system and compared them with a state-of-art method, DPM [10], which is a star-structured part-based model defined by a 'root' filter plus a set of parts filters. A two component DPM model is trained for each class following the setting of [10]. To evaluate the contribution of the mixture model and the importance of the weight β, we also implemented other two methods, multi-labeled graph without weight (Graph+M-label) and single-labeled graph with weight (Graph+β). The weight β can not be used on the DPM model, because it encodes no direct relation between nodes under the root.

Table 1. Detection results on our cross-depictive style dataset (50 classes in total): average precision scores for each class of different methods, DPM, a single labeled graph model with learned β, our proposed multi-labeled model graph with and without learned β. The mAP (mean of average precision) is shown in the last column.

	us-flag	bat	beer-mug	boom-box	butterfly	camel	wagon	crab	globe	eiffel-tower	elephant	fried-egg	frying-pan	giraffe	goldfish	hamburger	head-phones
DPM[10]	.871	.338	**.956**	.859	.718	.797	.897	.640	.961	.952	.853	.618	.757	.803	.901	.809	.808
G+β	.743	.343	.729	.683	.375	.420	.662	.633	.846	.798	.538	.627	.733	.716	.556	.650	.669
G+ml	.913	.423	.947	.913	.757	.816	.914	.723	.932	.971	.875	.778	.812	.831	.913	.883	.853
G+ml+β	**.917**	**.456**	.954	**.929**	**.839**	**.881**	**.942**	**.741**	**.993**	**.981**	**.887**	**.851**	**.838**	**.907**	**.962**	**.908**	**.879**

	horse	balloon	hourglass	skeleton	ice-cream	ketch	laptop	lightbulb	mandolin	menorah	bike	palm-tree	penguin	person	pyramid	refrigerator	rotary-phone
DPM[10]	.764	**.955**	.925	**.985**	.816	.905	.926	.751	.385	.882	.975	.899	.735	.554	**.840**	.731	.900
G+β	.733	.755	.881	.926	**.930**	.718	.780	.705	.487	.879	.933	.794	.599	.555	.719	.561	.713
G+ml	.799	.899	.953	.956	.894	.929	.954	.725	.415	.901	.996	.921	.742	.587	.760	.788	.916
G+ml+β	**.860**	.930	**.956**	.968	.911	**.976**	**.964**	**.807**	.491	**.933**	**.997**	**.936**	**.825**	**.616**	.808	**.820**	**.928**

	starfish	sunflower	superman	swan	teapot	teddy	teepee	tower-pisa	umbrella	wash-machine	watch	windmill	bottle	zebra	car	face	mAP
DPM[10]	.922	.881	.720	.923	.968	.962	.807	.924	.957	.736	.889	.892	.914	.948			.835
G+β	.713	.766	.584	.723	.632	.814	.872	.849	.724	.974	.744	.739	.639	.751	.851	.790	.711
G+ml	.942	.903	.758	.859	.992	.985	.922	.981	.794	.982	.774	.899	.911	.961	.965	.886	.858
G+ml+β	**.965**	**.923**	.791	.915	**.993**	**.991**	**.944**	**.991**	.898	**.985**	**.794**	**.965**	**.956**	**.973**	**.974**	.899	**.891**

Table 1 compares the detection results of using different models on our dataset. Our system achieves the best AP scores in 42 out of the 50 categories. DPM wins 7 times. Furthermore, our final mAP (.891) outperforms DPM (.835) by more than 5%. Figure 7 summarizes the results of different models applied on the person, horse and giraffe categories, chosen because these object classes appear commonly in many well-known detection datasets. The PR-curve of other classes can be found in the supplementary material. We see that the use of our multi-labeled graph model can significantly improve the detect accuracy. Further improvements are obtained by using discriminative weights β.

Our system is implemented by matlab, running on a Core i7 CPU@2.67GHz×8 machine. The average training time for a single class is 4 to 5 minutes (parts labelling process is not included). The average testing time of a single image is 4.5 to 5 minutes, since the graph matching takes long time.

5.2 Classification

Our proposed model can also be adapted for classification. Training requires of learning a class model, exactly the same procedure as in the previous section. The testing process determines the class by choosing the class which has the best matching score with the query image.

Using our dataset we conduct experiments designed to test how well our proposed class model generalised across depictive styles. Like the detection experiments, we randomly split the image set for each object class into two partitions, 30 images for training (15 photos and 15 artworks) and the rest are used for

Table 2. Comparison of classification results for different test cases and methods

Methods	Art	Photos
BoW[31]	69.47 ± 1.1	80.38 ± 1.1
DPM[10]	80.29 ± 0.9	85.22 ± 0.6
Our	**89.06 ± 1.2**	**90.29 ± 1.3**

testing. Unlike from the detection task, we test on photos and artworks separately to compare the performance on these two domains. The classification accuracy is determined as the average over 5 random splits.

For comparison with alternative visual class models we compare with two other methods: BoW and DPM. BoW classifier is chosen because it performs well and will help us assess the performance of such a popular approach to the problem of cross-depiction classification. We follow Vedaldi *et al* [31] using dense-sift features [2] and K-means ($K = 1000$) for visual word dictionary construction. Finally, it uses a SVM for classification. The second is the DPM [10], adapted to classification.

Classification accuracy of different methods in various testing cases, are shown in table 2. It shows that our method outperforms the BoW and DPM method in all cases, especially when the test set are artworks only. Our multi-labeled modelling method effectively train nodes of the graph in separately depictive styles and then combine them in a mixture model to global optimization. Experimental results clearly indicate that our mixture model outperforms state of the art methods which attempt to characterize all depiction styles in a monolithic model. We also made tests on some of the cross-domain literature we cited such as [25, 32] and a method that is not depend on photometric appearance, using the edgelets [12]. A mixture-of-parts method [33] is also tested. But none of them work well on such a high-variety depiction dataset. We report DPM and BoW only because they consistently out-perform those methods.

6   Conclusion

There is a deep appeal in not discriminating between depictive styles, but instead considering images in any style, not just because it echoes an impressive human ability but also because it opens new applications. Our paper provides evidence that multi-label nodes are useful representations in coping with features that exhibit very wide, possibly discontinuous distributions. There is no reason to believe that such distributions are confined to the problem of local feature representation in art and photographs; it could be an issue in many cross-domain cases. For the future work, we want to more fully investigate the way in which the distribution of the description of a single object part is represented.

Acknowledgements. We thank the EPSRC for supporting this work through grant EP/K015966/1.

References

1. Amit, Y., Trouvé, A.: Pop: Patchwork of parts models for object recognition. IJCV (2004)
2. Bosch, A., Zisserman, A., Muoz, X.: Image classification using random forests and ferns. In: ICCV (2007)
3. Cho, M., Alahari, K., Ponce, J.: Learning graphs to match. In: ICCV (2013)
4. Cootes, T.F., Edwards, G.J., Taylor, C.J., et al.: Active appearance models. TPAMI (2001)
5. Coughlan, J., Yuille, A., English, C., Snow, D.: Efficient deformable template detection and localization without user initialization. In: CVIU (2000)
6. Crandall, D., Felzenszwalb, P., Huttenlocher, D.: Spatial priors for part-based recognition using statistical models. In: CVPR (2005)
7. Csurka, G., Dance, C.R., Fan, L., Willamowski, J., Bray, C.: Visual categorization with bags of keypoints. In: ECCV (2004)
8. Dong, J., Xia, W., Chen, Q., Feng, J., Huang, Z., Yan, S.: Subcategory-aware object classification. In: CVPR (2013)
9. Felzenszwalb, P.F., Huttenlocher, D.P.: Pictorial structures for object recognition. IJCV (2005)
10. Felzenszwalb, P., Girshick, R., McAllester, D., Ramanan, D.: Object detection with discriminatively trained part-based models. TPAMI (2010)
11. Fergus, R., Perona, P., Zisserman, A.: Object class recognition by unsupervised scale-invariant learning. In: CVPR (2003)
12. Ferrari, V., Jurie, F., Schmid, C.: From images to shape models for object detection. IJCV (2010)
13. Fischler, M.A., Elschlager, R.: The representation and matching of pictorial structures. IEEE Transactions on Computers (1973)
14. Gu, C., Arbeláez, P., Lin, Y., Yu, K., Malik, J.: Multi-component models for object detection. In: Fitzgibbon, A., Lazebnik, S., Perona, P., Sato, Y., Schmid, C. (eds.) ECCV 2012, Part IV. LNCS, vol. 7575, pp. 445–458. Springer, Heidelberg (2012)
15. Gu, C., Lim, J.J., Arbeláez, P., Malik, J.: Recognition using regions. In: CVRP (2009)
16. Hu, R., Collomosse, J.: A performance evaluation of gradient field hog descriptor for sketch based image retrieval. CVIU (2013)
17. Jia, W., McKenna, S.: Classifying textile designs using bags of shapes. In: ICPR (2010)
18. Joachims, T., Finley, T., Yu, C.N.J.: Cutting-plane training of structural svms. Machine Learning (2009)
19. Lazebnik, S., Schmid, C., Ponce, J.: Beyond bags of features: Spatial pyramid matching for recognizing natural scene categories. In: CVPR (2006)
20. Leibe, B., Leonardis, A., Schiele, B.: Robust object detection with interleaved categorization and segmentation. IJCV (2008)
21. Li, Y., Song, Y.Z., Gong, S.: Sketch recognition by ensemble matching of structured features. In: BMVC (2013)
22. Perronnin, F., Sánchez, J., Mensink, T.: Improving the fisher kernel for large-scale image classification. In: Daniilidis, K., Maragos, P., Paragios, N. (eds.) ECCV 2010, Part IV. LNCS, vol. 6314, pp. 143–156. Springer, Heidelberg (2010)
23. Russakovsky, O., Lin, Y., Yu, K., Fei-Fei, L.: Object-centric spatial pooling for image classification. In: Fitzgibbon, A., Lazebnik, S., Perona, P., Sato, Y., Schmid, C. (eds.) ECCV 2012, Part II. LNCS, vol. 7573, pp. 1–15. Springer, Heidelberg (2012)

24. Sapp, B., Toshev, A., Taskar, B.: Cascaded models for articulated pose estimation. In: Daniilidis, K., Maragos, P., Paragios, N. (eds.) ECCV 2010, Part II. LNCS, vol. 6312, pp. 406–420. Springer, Heidelberg (2010)

25. Shechtman, E., Irani, M.: Matching local self-similarities across images and videos. In: CVPR (2007)

26. Shotton, J., Blake, A., Cipolla, R.: Multiscale categorical object recognition using contour fragments. TPAMI (2008)

27. Shrivastava, A., Malisiewicz, T., Gupta, A., Efros, A.A.: Data-driven visual similarity for cross-domain image matching. ACM Transaction of Graphics (TOG) (2011)

28. Singer, Y., Srebro, N.: Pegasos: Primal estimated sub-gradient solver for svm. In: ICML (2007)

29. Torresani, L., Kolmogorov, V., Rother, C.: Feature correspondence via graph matching: Models and global optimization. In: Forsyth, D., Torr, P., Zisserman, A. (eds.) ECCV 2008, Part II. LNCS, vol. 5303, pp. 596–609. Springer, Heidelberg (2008)

30. Tsochantaridis, I., Joachims, T., Hofmann, T., Altun, Y.: Large margin methods for structured and interdependent output variables. JMLR (2005)

31. Vedaldi, A., Fulkerson, B.: VLFeat: An open and portable library of computer vision algorithms (2008)

32. Wu, Q., Hall, P.: Modelling visual objects invariant to depictive style. In: BMVC (2013)

33. Yang, Y., Ramanan, D.: Articulated pose estimation with flexible mixtures-of-parts. In: CVPR (2011)

34. Yao, B., Fei-Fei, L.: Action recognition with exemplar based 2.5D graph matching. In: Fitzgibbon, A., Lazebnik, S., Perona, P., Sato, Y., Schmid, C. (eds.) ECCV 2012, Part IV. LNCS, vol. 7575, pp. 173–186. Springer, Heidelberg (2012)

Analyzing the Performance of Multilayer Neural Networks for Object Recognition

Pulkit Agrawal, Ross Girshick, and Jitendra Malik

University of California, Berkeley
{pulkitag,rbg,malik}@eecs.berkeley.edu

Abstract. In the last two years, convolutional neural networks (CNNs) have achieved an impressive suite of results on standard recognition datasets and tasks. CNN-based features seem poised to quickly replace engineered representations, such as SIFT and HOG. However, compared to SIFT and HOG, we understand much less about the nature of the features learned by large CNNs. In this paper, we experimentally probe several aspects of CNN feature learning in an attempt to help practitioners gain useful, evidence-backed intuitions about how to apply CNNs to computer vision problems.

Keywords: convolutional neural networks, object recognition, empirical analysis.

1 Introduction

Over the last two years, a sequence of results on benchmark visual recognition tasks has demonstrated that convolutional neural networks (CNNs) [6,14,18] will likely replace engineered features, such as SIFT [15] and HOG [2], for a wide variety of problems. This sequence started with the breakthrough ImageNet [3] classification results reported by Krizhevsky et al. [11]. Soon after, Donahue et al. [4] showed that the same network, trained for ImageNet classification, was an effective blackbox feature extractor. Using CNN features, they reported state-of-the-art results on several standard image classification datasets. At the same time, Girshick et al. [7] showed how the network could be applied to object detection. Their system, called R-CNN, classifies object proposals generated by a bottom-up grouping mechanism (e.g., selective search [23]). Since detection training data is limited, they proposed a transfer learning strategy in which the CNN is first pre-trained, with supervision, for ImageNet classification and then fine-tuned on the small PASCAL detection dataset [5]. Since this initial set of results, several other papers have reported similar findings on a wider range of tasks (see, for example, the outcomes reported by Razavian et al. in [17]).

Feature transforms such as SIFT and HOG afford an intuitive interpretation as histograms of oriented edge filter responses arranged in spatial blocks. However, we have little understanding of what visual features the different layers of a CNN encode. Given that rich feature hierarchies provided by CNNs are likely to emerge as the prominent feature extractor for computer vision models over

D. Fleet et al. (Eds.): ECCV 2014, Part VII, LNCS 8695, pp. 329–344, 2014.

the next few years, we believe that developing such an understanding is an interesting scientific pursuit and an essential exercise that will help guide the design of computer vision methods that use CNNs. Therefore, in this paper we study several aspects of CNNs through an empirical lens.

1.1   Summary of Findings

Effects of Fine-Tuning and Pre-training. Girshick et al. [7] showed that supervised pre-training and fine-tuning are effective when training data is scarce. However, they did not investigate what happens when training data becomes more abundant. We show that it is possible to get good performance when training R-CNN from a random initialization (i.e., without ImageNet supervised pre-training) with a reasonably modest amount of detection training data (37k ground truth bounding boxes). However, we also show that in this data regime, supervised pre-training is still beneficial and leads to a large improvement in detection performance. We show similar results for image classification, as well.

ImageNet Pre-training Does not Overfit. One concern when using supervised pre-training is that achieving a better model fit to ImageNet, for example, might lead to higher generalization error when applying the learned features to another dataset and task. If this is the case, then some form of regularization during pre-training, such as early stopping, would be beneficial. We show the surprising result that pre-training for longer yields better results, with diminishing returns, but does *not* increase generalization error. This implies that fitting the CNN to ImageNet induces a general and portable feature representation. Moreover, the learning process is well behaved and does not require ad hoc regularization in the form of early stopping.

Grandmother Cells and Distributed Codes. We do not have a good understanding of mid-level feature representations in multilayer networks. Recent work on feature visualization, (e.g., [13,26]) suggests that such networks might consist mainly of "grandmother" cells [1,16]. Our analysis shows that the representation in intermediate layers is more subtle. There are a small number of grandmother-cell-like features, but most of the feature code is distributed and several features must fire in concert to effectively discriminate between classes.

Importance of Feature Location and Magnitude. Our final set of experiments investigates what role a feature's spatial location and magnitude plays in image classification and object detection. Matching intuition, we find that spatial location is critical for object detection, but matters little for image classification. More surprisingly, we find that feature magnitude is largely unimportant. For example, binarizing features (at a threshold of 0) barely degrades performance. This shows that sparse binary features, which are useful for large-scale image retrieval [8,24], come "for free" from the CNN's representation.

2   Experimental Setup

2.1   Datasets and Tasks

In this paper, we report experimental results using several standard datasets and tasks, which we summarize here.

Image Classification. For the task of image classification we consider two datasets, the first of which is PASCAL VOC 2007 [5]. We refer to this dataset and task by "PASCAL-CLS". Results on PASCAL-CLS are reported using the standard average precision (AP) and mean average precision (mAP) metrics.

PASCAL-CLS is fairly small-scale with only 5k images for training, 5k images for testing, and 20 object classes. Therefore, we also consider the medium-scale SUN dataset [25], which has around 108k images and 397 classes. We refer to experiments on SUN by "SUN-CLS". In these experiments, we use a non-standard train-test split since it was computationally infeasible to run all of our experiments on the 10 standard subsets proposed by [25]. Instead, we randomly split the dataset into three parts (train, val, and test) using 50%, 10% and 40% of the data, respectively. The distribution of classes was uniform across all the three sets. We emphasize that results on these splits are only used to support investigations into properties of CNNs and not for comparing against other scene-classification methods in the literature. For SUN-CLS, we report 1-of-397 classification accuracy averaged over all classes, which is the standard metric for this dataset. For select experiments we report the error bars in performance as mean $\pm$ standard deviation in accuracy over 5 runs (it was computationally infeasible to compute error bars for all experiments). For each run, a different random split of train, val, and test sets was used.

Object Detection. For the task of object detection we use PASCAL VOC 2007. We train using the trainval set and test on the test set. We refer to this dataset and task by "PASCAL-DET". PASCAL-DET uses the same set of images as PASCAL-CLS. We note that it is standard practice to use the 2007 version of PASCAL VOC for reporting results of ablation studies and hyperparameter sweeps. We report performance on PASCAL-DET using the standard AP and mAP metrics. In some of our experiments we use only the ground-truth PASCAL-DET bounding boxes, in which case we refer to the setup by "PASCAL-DET-GT".

In order to provide a larger detection training set for certain experiments, we also make use of the "PASCAL-DET+DATA" dataset, which we define as including VOC 2007 trainval union with VOC 2012 trainval. The VOC 2007 test set is still used for evaluation. This dataset contains approximately 37k labeled bounding boxes, which is roughly three times the number contained in PASCAL-DET.

2.2   Network Architecture and Layer Nomenclature

All of our experiments use a single CNN architecture. This architecture is the Caffe [9] implementation of the network proposed by Krizhevsky et al. [11]. The layers of the CNN are organized as follows. The first two are subdivided into four sublayers each: convolution (conv), $\max(x, 0)$ rectifying non-linear units (ReLUs), max pooling, and local response normalization (LRN). Layers 3 and 4 are composed of convolutional units followed by ReLUs. Layer 5 consists of convolutional units, followed by ReLUs and max pooling. The last two layers are fully connected (fc). When we refer to conv-1, conv-2, and conv-5 we mean the output of the max pooling units following the convolution and ReLU operations (also following LRN when applicable).[1] For layers conv-3, conv-4, fc-6, and fc-7 we mean the output of ReLU units.

2.3   Supervised Pre-training and Fine-Tuning

Training a large CNN on a small dataset often leads to catastrophic overfitting. The idea of supervised *pre-training* is to use a data-rich auxiliary dataset and task, such as ImageNet classification, to initialize the CNN parameters. The CNN can then be used on the small dataset, directly, as a feature extractor (as in [4]). Or, the network can be updated by continued training on the small dataset, a process called *fine-tuning*.

For fine-tuning, we follow the procedure described in [7]. First, we remove the CNN's classification layer, which was specific to the pre-training task and is not reusable. Next, we append a new randomly initialized classification layer with the desired number of output units for the target task. Finally, we run stochastic gradient descent (SGD) on the target loss function, starting from a learning rate set to 0.001 (1/10-th the initial learning rate used for training the network for ImageNet classification). This choice was made to prevent clobbering the CNN's initialization to control overfitting. At every 20,000 iterations of fine-tuning we reduce the learning rate by a factor of 10.

3   The Effects of Fine-Tuning and Pre-training on CNN Performance and Parameters

The results in [7] (R-CNN) show that supervised pre-training for ImageNet classification, followed by fine-tuning for PASCAL object detection, leads to large gains over directly using features from the pre-trained network (without fine-tuning). However, [7] did not investigate three important aspects of fine-tuning: (1) What happens if we train the network "from scratch" (i.e., from a random initialization) on the detection data? (2) How does the amount of fine-tuning data change the picture? and (3) How does fine-tuning alter the network's parameters? In this section, we explore these questions on object detection and image classification datasets.

---

[1] Note that this nomenclature differs slightly from [7].

Table 1. Comparing the performance of CNNs trained from scratch, pre-trained on ImageNet, and fine-tuned. PASCAL-DET+DATA includes additional data from VOC 2012 trainval. (Bounding-box regression was not used for detection results.)

SUN-CLS			PASCAL-DET			PASCAL-DET+DATA		
scratch	pre-train	fine-tune	scratch	pre-train	fine-tune	scratch	pre-train	fine-tune
40.4 ± 0.2	53.1 ± 0.2	56.8 ± 0.2	40.7	45.5	54.1	52.3	45.5	59.2

3.1 Effect of Fine-Tuning on CNN Performance

The main results of this section are presented in Table 1. First, we focus on the detection experiments, which we implemented using the open source R-CNN code. All results use features from layer fc-7.

Somewhat surprisingly, it's possible to get reasonable results (40.7% mAP) when training the CNN from scratch using only the training data from VOC 2007 trainval (13k bounding box annotations). However, this is still worse than using the pre-trained network, directly, without fine-tuning (45.5%). Even more surprising is that when the VOC 2007 trainval data is augmented with VOC 2012 data (an additional 25k bounding box annotations), we are able to achieve a mAP of 52.3% from scratch. This result is almost as good as the performance achieved by pre-training on ImageNet and then fine-tuning on VOC 2007 trainval (54.1% mAP). These results can be compared to the 30.5% mAP obtained by DetectorNet [21], a recent detection system based on the same network architecture, which was trained from scratch on VOC 2012 trainval.

Next, we ask if ImageNet pre-training is still useful in the PASCAL-DET +DATA setting? Here we see that even though it's possible to get good performance when training from scratch, pre-training still helps considerably. The final mAP when fine-tuning with the additional detection data is 59.2%, which is 5 percentage points higher than the best result reported in [7] (both without bounding-box regression). This result suggests that R-CNN performance is not data saturated and that simply adding more detection training data without any other changes may substantially improve results.

We also present results for SUN image classification. Here we observe a similar trend: reasonable performance is achievable when training from scratch, however initializing from ImageNet and then fine-tuning yields significantly better performance.

3.2 Effect of Fine-Tuning on CNN Parameters

We have provided additional evidence that fine-tuning a discriminatively pre-trained network is very effective in terms of task performance. Now we look inside the network to see how fine-tuning changes its parameters.

To do this, we define a way to measure the class selectivity of a set of filters. Intuitively, we use the class-label entropy of a filter given its activations, above a threshold, on a set of images. Since this measure is entropy-based, a low value

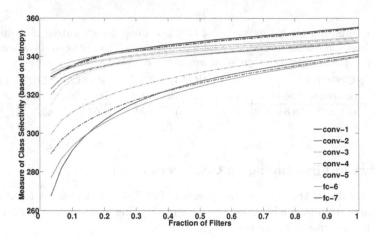

Fig. 1. PASCAL object class selectivity plotted against the fraction of filters, for each layer, before fine-tuning (dash-dot line) and after fine-tuning (solid line). A lower value indicates greater class selectivity. Although layers become more discriminative as we go higher up in the network, fine-tuning on limited data (PASCAL-DET) only significantly affects the last two layers (fc-6 and fc-7).

Table 2. Comparison in performance when fine-tuning the entire network (ft) versus only fine-tuning the fully-connected layers (fc-ft)

SUN-CLS		PASCAL-DET		PASCAL-DET+DATA	
ft	fc-ft	ft	fc-ft	ft	fc-ft
56.8 ± 0.2	56.2 ± 0.1	54.1	53.3	59.2	56.0

indicates that a filter is highly class selective, while a large value indicates that a filter fires regardless of class. The precise definition of this measure is given in the Appendix.

In order to summarize the class selectivity for a *set* of filters, we sort them from the most selective to least selective and plot the average selectivity of the first k filters while sweeping k down the sorted list. Figure 1 shows the class selectivity for the sets of filters in layers 1 to 7 before and after fine-tuning (on VOC 2007 trainval). Selectivity is measured using the ground truth boxes from PASCAL-DET-GT instead of a whole-image classification task to ensure that filter responses are a direct result of the presence of object categories of interest and not correlations with image background.

Figure 1 shows that class selectivity increases from layer 1 to 7 both with and without fine-tuning. It is interesting to note that entropy changes due to fine-tuning are only significant for layers 6 and 7. This observation indicates that fine-tuning only layers 6 and 7 may suffice for achieving good performance when fine-tuning data is limited. We tested this hypothesis on SUN-CLS and PASCAL-DET by comparing the performance of a fine-tuned network (ft) with

Table 3. Performance variation (% mAP) on PASCAL-CLS as a function of pre-training iterations on ImageNet. The error bars for all columns are similar to the one reported in the 305k column.

layer	5k	15k	25k	35k	50k	95k	105k	195k	205k	305k
conv-1	23.0	24.3	24.4	24.5	24.3	24.8	24.7	24.4	24.4	24.4 ± 0.5
conv-2	33.7	40.4	40.9	41.8	42.7	43.2	44.0	45.0	45.1	45.1 ± 0.7
conv-3	34.2	46.8	47.0	48.2	48.6	49.4	51.6	50.7	50.9	50.5 ± 0.6
conv-4	33.5	49.0	48.7	50.2	50.7	51.6	54.1	54.3	54.4	54.2 ± 0.7
conv-5	33.0	53.4	55.0	56.8	57.3	59.2	63.5	64.9	65.5	65.6 ± 0.3
fc-6	34.2	59.7	62.6	62.7	63.5	65.6	69.3	71.3	71.8	72.1 ± 0.3
fc-7	30.9	61.3	64.1	65.1	65.9	67.8	71.8	73.4	74.0	74.3 ± 0.3

a network which was fine-tuned by only updating the weights of fc-6 and fc-7 (fc-ft). These results, in Table 2, show that with small amounts of data, fine-tuning amounts to "rewiring" the fully connected layers. However, when more fine-tuning data is available (PASCAL-DET+DATA), there is still substantial benefit from fine-tuning all network parameters.

3.3 Effect of Pre-training on CNN Parameters

There is no single image dataset that fully captures the variation in natural images. This means that all datasets, including ImageNet, are biased in some way. Thus, there is a possibility that pre-training may eventually cause the CNN to overfit and consequently hurt generalization performance [22]. To understand if this happens, in the specific case of ImageNet pre-training, we investigated the effect of pre-training time on generalization performance both with and without fine-tuning. We find that pre-training for longer improves performance. This is surprising, as it shows that fitting more to ImageNet leads to better performance when moving to the other datasets that we evaluated.

We report performance on PASCAL-CLS as a function of pre-training time, without fine-tuning, in Table 3. Notice that more pre-training leads to better performance. By 15k and 50k iterations all layers are close to 80% and 90% of their final performance (5k iterations is only ~1 epoch). This indicates that training required for generalization takes place quite quickly. Figure 2 shows conv-1 filters after 5k, 15k, and 305k iterations and reinforces this observation. Further, notice from Table 3 that conv-1 trains first and the higher the layer is the more time it takes to converge. This suggests that a CNN, trained with backpropagation, converges in a layer-by-layer fashion. Table 4 shows the inter-action between varied amounts of pre-training time and fine-tuning on SUN-CLS and PASCAL-DET. Here we also see that more pre-training prior to fine-tuning leads to better performance.

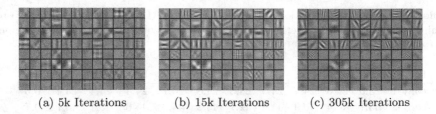

(a) 5k Iterations   (b) 15k Iterations   (c) 305k Iterations

Fig. 2. Evolution of conv-1 filters with time. After just 15k iterations, these filters closely resemble their converged state.

Table 4. Performance variation on SUN-CLS and PASCAL-DET using features from a CNN pre-trained for different numbers of iterations and fine-tuned for a fixed number of iterations (40k for SUN-CLS and 70k for PASCAL-DET)

	50k	105k	205k	305k
SUN-CLS	53.0 ± 0.2	54.6 ± 0.1	56.3 ± 0.2	56.6 ± 0.2
PASCAL-DET	50.2	52.6	55.3	55.4^2

4   Are there Grandmother Cells in CNNs?

Neuroscientists have conjectured that cells in the human brain which only respond to very specific and complex visual stimuli (such as the face of one's grandmother) are involved in object recognition. These neurons are often referred to as *grandmother cells* (GMC) [1,16]. Proponents of artificial neural networks have shown great interest in reporting the presence of GMC-like filters for specific object classes in their networks (see, for example, the cat filter reported in [13]). The notion of GMC like features is also related to standard feature encodings for image classification. Prior to the work of [11], the dominant approaches for image and scene classification were based on either representing images as a bag of local descriptors (BoW), such as SIFT (e.g., [12]), or by first finding a set of mid-level patches [10,20] and then encoding images in terms of them. The problem of finding good mid-level patches is often posed as a search for a set of high-recall discriminative templates. In this sense, mid-level patch discovery is the search for a set of GMC templates. The low-level BoW representation, in contrast, is a *distributed code* in the sense that a single feature by itself is not discriminative, but a group of features taken together is. This makes it interesting to investigate the nature of mid-level CNN features such as conv-5.

For understanding these feature representations in CNNs, [19,26] recently presented methods for finding locally optimal visual inputs for individual filters. However, these methods only find the best, or in some cases top-k, visual inputs

---

[2] A network pre-trained from scratch, which was different from the one used in Section 3.1, was used to obtain these results. The difference in performance is not significant.

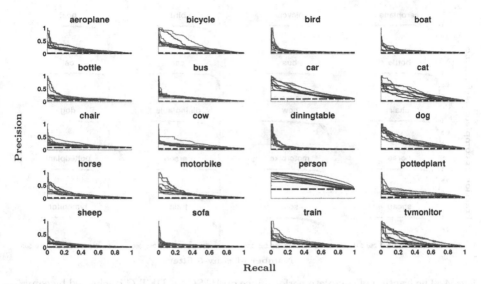

Fig. 3. The precision-recall curves for the top five (based on AP) conv-5 filter responses on PASCAL-DET-GT. Curves in red and blue indicate AP for fine-tuned and pre-trained networks, respectively. The dashed black line is the performance of a random filter. For most classes, precision drops significantly even at modest recall values. There are GMC filters for classes such as bicycle, person, car, cat.

that activate a filter, but do not characterize the *distribution* of images that cause an individual filter to fire above a certain threshold. For example, if it is found that the top-10 visual inputs for a particular filter are cats, it remains unclear what is the response of the filter to other images of cats. Thus, it is not possible to make claims about presence of GMC like filters for cat based on such analysis. A GMC filter for the cat class, is one that fires strongly on *all* cats and nothing else. This criteria can be expressed as a filter that has high *precision* and high *recall*. That is, a GMC filter for class C is a filter that has a high average precision (AP) when tasked with classifying inputs from class C versus inputs from all other classes.

First, we address the question of finding GMC filters by computing the AP of individual filters (Section 4.1). Next, we measure how distributed are the feature representations (Section 4.2). For both experiments we use features from layer conv-5, which consists of responses of 256 filters in a 6×6 spatial grid. Using max pooling, we collapse the spatial grid into a 256-D vector, so that for each filter we have a single response per image (in Section 5.1 we show that this transformation causes only a small drop in task performance).

4.1   Finding Grandmother Cells

For each filter, its AP value is calculated for classifying images using class labels and filter responses to object bounding boxes from PASCAL-DET-GT. Then,

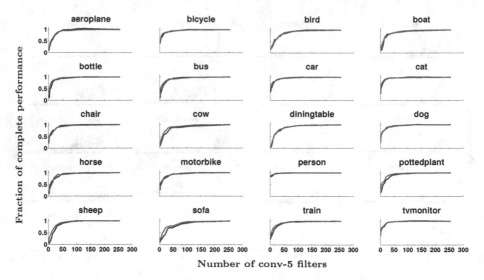

Fig. 4. The fraction of complete performance on PASCAL-DET-GT achieved by conv-5 filter subsets of different sizes. Complete performance is the AP computed by considering responses of all the filters. Notice, that for a few classes such as person and bicycle only a few filters are required, but for most classes substantially more filters are needed, indicating a distributed code.

for each class we sorted filters in decreasing order of their APs. If GMC filters for this class exist, they should be the top ranked filters in this sorted list. The precision-recall curves for the top-five conv-5 filters are shown in Figure 3. We find that GMC-like filters exist for only for a few classes, such as bicycle, person, cars, and cats.

4.2   How Distributed are the Feature Representations?

In addition to visualizing the AP curves of individual filters, we measured the number of filters required to recognize objects of a particular class. Feature selection was performed to construct nested subsets of filters, ranging from a single filter to all filters, using the following greedy strategy. First, separate linear SVMs were trained to classify object bounding boxes from PASCAL-DET-GT using conv-5 responses. For a given class, the 256 dimensions of the learnt weight vector (w) is in direct correspondence with the 256 conv-5 filters. We used the magnitude of the i-th dimension of w to rank the importance of the i-th conv-5 filter for discriminating instances of this class. Next, all filters were sorted using these magnitude values. Each subset of filters was constructed by taking the top-k filters from this list.[3] For each subset, a linear SVM was trained using only the responses of filters in that subset for classifying the class under consideration.

---

[3] We used values of $k \in \{1, 2, 3, 5, 10, 15, 20, 25, 30, 35, 40, 45, 50, 80, 100, 128, 256\}$.

Table 5. Number of filters required to achieve 50% or 90% of the complete performance on PASCAL-DET-GT using a CNN pre-trained on ImageNet and fine-tuned for PASCAL-DET using conv-5 features

	perf.	aero	bike	bird	boat	bottle	bus	car	cat	chair	cow	table	dog	horse	mbike	person	plant	sheep	sofa	train	tv
pre-train	50%	15	3	15	15	10	10	3	2	5	15	15	2	10	3	1	10	20	25	10	2
fine-tune	50%	10	1	20	15	5	5	2	2	3	10	15	3	15	10	1	5	15	15	5	2
pre-train	90%	40	35	80	80	35	40	30	20	35	100	80	30	45	40	15	45	50	100	45	25
fine-tune	90%	35	30	80	80	30	35	25	20	35	50	80	35	30	40	10	35	40	80	40	20

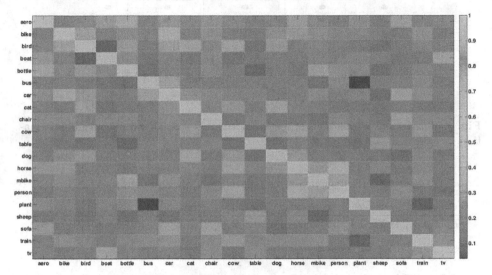

Fig. 5. The set overlap between the 50 most discriminative conv-5 filters for each class determined using PASCAL-DET-GT. Entry (i, j) of the matrix is the fraction of top-50 filters class i has in common with class j (Section 4.2). Chance is 0.195. There is little overlap, but related classes are more likely to share filters.

The variation in performance with the number of filters is shown in Figure 4. Table 5 lists the number of filters required to achieve 50% and 90% of the complete performance. For classes such as persons, cars, and cats relatively few filters are required, but for most classes around 30 to 40 filters are required to achieve at least 90% of the full performance. This indicates that the conv-5 feature representation is distributed and there are GMC-like filters for only a few classes. Results using layer fc-7 are presented in the the supplementary material. We also find that after fine-tuning, slightly fewer filters are required to achieve performance levels similar to a pre-trained network.

Next, we estimated the extent of overlap between the filters used for discriminating between different classes. For each class i, we selected the 50 most discriminative filters (out of 256) and stored the selected filter indices in the set S_i. The extent of overlap between class i and j was evaluated by $|S_i \cap S_j|/N$, where $N = |S_i| = |S_j| = 50$. The results are visualized in Figure 5. It can be

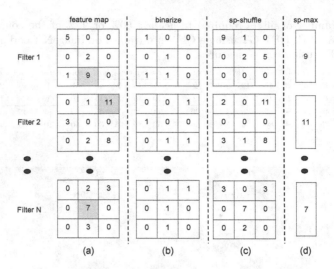

Fig. 6. Illustrations of ablations of feature activation spatial and magnitude information. See Sections 5.1 and 5.2 for details.

Table 6. Percentage non-zeros (sparsity) in filter responses of CNN

conv-1	conv-2	conv-3	conv-4	conv-5	fc-6	fc-7
87.5 ± 4.4	44.5 ± 4.4	31.8 ± 2.4	32.0 ± 2.7	27.7 ± 5.0	16.1 ± 3.0	21.6 ± 4.9

seen that different classes use different subsets of conv-5 filters and there is little overlap between classes. This further indicates that intermediate representations in the CNN are distributed.

5   Untangling Feature Magnitude and Location

The convolutional layers preserve the coarse spatial layout of the network's input. By layer conv-5, the original 227×227 input image has been progressively downsampled to 6×6. This feature map is also sparse due to the $\max(x, 0)$ non-linearities used in the network (conv-5 is roughly 27% non-zero; sparsity statistics for all layers are given in Table 6). Thus, a convolutional layer encodes information in terms of (1) which filters have non-zero responses, (2) the magnitudes of those responses, and (3) their spatial layout. In this section, we experimentally analyze the role of filter response magnitude and spatial location by looking at ablation studies on classification and detection tasks.

5.1   How Important is Filter Response Magnitude?

We can asses the importance of magnitude by setting each filter response x to 1 if $x > 0$ and to 0 otherwise. This binarization is performed prior to using the responses as features in a linear classifier and leads to loss of information contained in the magnitude of response while still retaining information about which filters fired and where they fired. In Tables 7 and 8 we show that binarization leads to a negligible performance drop for both classification and detection.

For the fully-connected layers (fc-6 and fc-7) PASCAL-CLS performance is nearly identical before and after binarization. This is a non-trivial property since transforming traditional computer vision features into short (or sparse) binary codes is an active research area. Such codes are important for practical applications in large-scale image retrieval and mobile image analysis [8,24]. Here we observe that sparse binary codes come essentially "for free" when using the representations learned in the fully-connected layers.

5.2   How Important is Response Location?

Now we remove spatial information from filter responses while retaining information about their magnitudes. We consider two methods for ablating spatial information from features computed by the convolutional layers (the fully-connected layers do not contain *explicit* spatial information).

The first method ("sp-max") simply collapses the $p \times p$ spatial map into a single value per feature channel by max pooling. The second method ("sp-shuffle") retains the original distribution of feature activation values, but scrambles spatial correlations between columns of feature channels. To perform sp-shuffle, we permute the spatial locations in the $p \times p$ spatial map. This permutation is performed independently for each network input (i.e., different inputs undergo different permutations). Columns of filter responses in the same location move together, which preserves correlations between features within each (shuffled) spatial location. These transformations are illustrated in Figure 6.

Table 7. Effect of location and magnitude feature ablations on PASCAL-CLS

layer	no ablation (mAP)	binarize (mAP)	sp-shuffle (mAP)	sp-max (mAP)
conv-1	25.1 ± 0.5	17.7 ± 0.2	15.1 ± 0.3	25.4 ± 0.5
conv-2	45.3 ± 0.5	43.0 ± 0.6	32.9 ± 0.7	40.1 ± 0.3
conv-3	50.7 ± 0.6	47.2 ± 0.6	41.0 ± 0.8	54.1 ± 0.5
conv-4	54.5 ± 0.7	51.5 ± 0.7	45.2 ± 0.8	57.0 ± 0.5
conv-5	65.6 ± 0.6	60.8 ± 0.7	59.5 ± 0.4	62.5 ± 0.6
fc-6	71.7 ± 0.3	71.5 ± 0.4	-	-
fc-7	74.1 ± 0.3	73.7 ± 0.4	-	-

Table 8. Effect of location and magnitude feature ablations on PASCAL-DET

	no ablation (mAP)	binarize (mAP)	sp-max (mAP)
conv-5	47.6	45.7	25.4

For image classification, damaging spatial information leads to a large difference in performance between original and spatially-ablated conv-1 features, but with a gradually decreasing difference for higher layers (Table 7). In fact, the performance of conv-5 after sp-max is close to the original performance. This indicates that a lot of information important for classification is encoded in the activation of the filters and not necessarily in the spatial pattern of their activations. Note, this observation is not an artifact of small number of classes in PASCAL-CLS. On ImageNet validation data, conv-5 features and conv-5 after sp-max result into accuracy of 43.2 and 41.5 respectively. However, for detection sp-max leads to a large drop in performance. This may not be surprising since detection requires spatial information for precise localization.

6   Conclusion

To help researchers better understand CNNs, we investigated pre-training and fine-tuning behavior on three classification and detection datasets. We found that the large CNN used in this work can be trained from scratch using a surprisingly modest amount of data. But, importantly, pre-training significantly improves performance and pre-training for longer is better. We also found that some of the learnt CNN features are grandmother-cell-like, but for the most part they form a distributed code. This supports the recent set of empirical results showing that these features generalize well to other datasets and tasks.

Acknowledgments. This work was supported by ONR MURI N000141010933. Pulkit Agrawal is partially supported by a Fulbright Science and Technology fellowship. We thank NVIDIA for GPU donations. We thank Bharath Hariharan, Saurabh Gupta and João Carreira for helpful suggestions.

References

1. Barlow, H.: Single units and sensations: A neuron doctrine for perceptual psychology? Perception (1972)
2. Dalal, N., Triggs, B.: Histograms of oriented gradients for human detection. In: CVPR, pp. 886–893 (2005)
3. Deng, J., Dong, W., Socher, R., Li, L.J., Li, K., Fei-Fei, L.: ImageNet: A Large-Scale Hierarchical Image Database. In: CVPR 2009 (2009)
4. Donahue, J., Jia, Y., Vinyals, O., Hoffman, J., Zhang, N., Tzeng, E., Darrell, T.: Decaf: A deep convolutional activation feature for generic visual recognition. arXiv preprint arXiv:1310.1531 (2013)
5. Everingham, M., Van Gool, L., Williams, C.K.I., Winn, J., Zisserman, A.: The pascal visual object classes (voc) challenge. IJCV 88(2) (2010)
6. Fukushima, K.: Neocognitron: A self-organizing neural network model for a mechanism of pattern recognition unaffected by shift in position. Biological Cybernetics 36(4), 193–202 (1980)
7. Girshick, R., Donahue, J., Darrell, T., Malik, J.: Rich feature hierarchies for accurate object detection and semantic segmentation. In: CVPR (2014)

8. Gong, Y., Lazebnik, S.: Iterative quantization: A procrustean approach to learning binary codes. In: 2011 IEEE Conference on Computer Vision and Pattern Recognition (CVPR), pp. 817–824. IEEE (2011)
9. Jia, Y.: Caffe: An open source convolutional architecture for fast feature embedding (2013), http://caffe.berkeleyvision.org/
10. Juneja, M., Vedaldi, A., Jawahar, C.V., Zisserman, A.: Blocks that shout: Distinctive parts for scene classification. In: Proceedings of the IEEE Conf. on Computer Vision and Pattern Recognition (CVPR) (2013)
11. Krizhevsky, A., Sutskever, I., Hinton, G.E.: Imagenet classification with deep convolutional neural networks. In: NIPS (2012)
12. Lazebnik, S., Schmid, C., Ponce, J.: Beyond bags of features: Spatial pyramid matching for recognizing natural scene categories. In: 2006 IEEE Computer Society Conference on Computer Vision and Pattern Recognition, vol. 2, pp. 2169–2178. IEEE (2006)
13. Le, Q., Ranzato, M., Monga, R., Devin, M., Chen, K., Corrado, G., Dean, J., Ng, A.: Building high-level features using large scale unsupervised learning. In: International Conference in Machine Learning (2012)
14. LeCun, Y., Boser, B., Denker, J.S., Henderson, D., Howard, R.E., Hubbard, W., Jackel, L.D.: Backpropagation applied to handwritten zip code recognition. Neural Computation 1(4) (1989)
15. Lowe, D.G.: Distinctive image features from scale-invariant keypoints. International Journal of Computer Vision 60, 91–110 (2004)
16. Quiroga, R.Q., Reddy, L., Kreiman, G., Koch, C., Fried, I.: Invariant visual representation by single neurons in the human brain. Nature 435(7045), 1102–1107 (2005), http://www.biomedsearch.com/nih/Invariant-visual-representation-by-single/15973409.html
17. Razavian, A.S., Azizpour, H., Sullivan, J., Carlsson, S.: Cnn features off-the-shelf: an astounding baseline for recognition. CoRR abs/1403.6382 (2014)
18. Rumelhart, D.E., Hinton, G.E., Williams, R.J.: Learning internal representations by error propagation. Parallel Distributed Processing 1, 318–362 (1986)
19. Simonyan, K., Vedaldi, A., Zisserman, A.: Learning local feature descriptors using convex optimisation. IEEE Transactions on Pattern Analysis and Machine Intelligence (2014)
20. Singh, S., Gupta, A., Efros, A.A.: Unsupervised discovery of mid-level discriminative patches. In: Fitzgibbon, A., Lazebnik, S., Perona, P., Sato, Y., Schmid, C. (eds.) ECCV 2012, Part II. LNCS, vol. 7573, pp. 73–86. Springer, Heidelberg (2012), http://arxiv.org/abs/1205.3137
21. Szegedy, C., Toshev, A., Erhan, D.: Deep neural networks for object detection. In: NIPS (2013)
22. Torralba, A., Efros, A.A.: Unbiased look at dataset bias. In: 2011 IEEE Conference on Computer Vision and Pattern Recognition (CVPR), pp. 1521–1528. IEEE (2011)
23. Uijlings, J., van de Sande, K., Gevers, T., Smeulders, A.: Selective search for object recognition. IJCV (2013)
24. Weiss, Y., Torralba, A., Fergus, R.: Spectral hashing. In: Advances in Neural Information Processing Systems, pp. 1753–1760 (2009)
25. Xiao, J., Hays, J., Ehinger, K.A., Oliva, A., Torralba, A.: Sun database: Large-scale scene recognition from abbey to zoo. In: CVPR, pp. 3485–3492 (2010)
26. Zeiler, M.D., Fergus, R.: Visualizing and understanding convolutional networks. CoRR abs/1311.2901 (2013)

Appendix: Estimating a Filter's Discriminative Capacity

To measure the discriminative capacity of a filter, we collect filter responses from a set of N images. Each image, when passed through the CNN produces a $p \times p$ heat map of scores for each filter in a given layer (e.g., $p = 6$ for a conv-5 filter and $p = 1$ for an fc-6 filter). This heat map is vectorized into a vector of scores of length p^2. With each element of this vector we associate the image's class label. Thus, for every image we have a score vector and a label vector of length p^2 each. Next, the score vectors from all N images are concatenated into an Np^2-length score vector. The same is done for the label vectors.

Now, for a given score threshold τ, we define the *class entropy of a filter* to be the entropy of the normalized histogram of class labels that have an associated score $\geq \tau$. A low class entropy means that at scores above τ, the filter is very class selective. As this threshold changes, the class entropy traces out a curve which we call the *entropy curve*. The *area under the entropy curve* (AuE), summarizes the class entropy at all thresholds and is used as a measure of discriminative capacity of the filter. The lower the AuE value, the more class selective the filter is. The AuE values are used to sort filters in Section 3.2.

Learning Rich Features from RGB-D Images
for Object Detection and Segmentation

Saurabh Gupta[1], Ross Girshick[1], Pablo Arbeláez[1,2], and Jitendra Malik[1]

[1] University of California, Berkeley
[2] Universidad de los Andes, Colombia
{sgupta,rbg,arbelaez,malik}@eecs.berkeley.edu

Abstract. In this paper we study the problem of object detection for RGB-D images using semantically rich image and depth features. We propose a new geocentric embedding for depth images that encodes height above ground and angle with gravity for each pixel in addition to the horizontal disparity. We demonstrate that this geocentric embedding works better than using raw depth images for learning feature representations with convolutional neural networks. Our final object detection system achieves an average precision of 37.3%, which is a 56% relative improvement over existing methods. We then focus on the task of instance segmentation where we label pixels belonging to object instances found by our detector. For this task, we propose a decision forest approach that classifies pixels in the detection window as foreground or background using a family of unary and binary tests that query shape and geocentric pose features. Finally, we use the output from our object detectors in an existing superpixel classification framework for semantic scene segmentation and achieve a 24% relative improvement over current state-of-the-art for the object categories that we study. We believe advances such as those represented in this paper will facilitate the use of perception in fields like robotics.

Keywords: RGB-D perception, object detection, object segmentation.

1 Introduction

We have designed and implemented an integrated system (Figure 1) for scene understanding from RGB-D images. The overall architecture is a generalization of the current state-of-the-art system for object detection in RGB images, R-CNN [16], where we design each module to make effective use of the additional signal in RGB-D images, namely pixel-wise depth. We go beyond object detection by providing pixel-level support maps for individual objects, such as tables and chairs, as well as a pixel-level labeling of scene surfaces, such as walls and floors. Thus our system subsumes the traditionally distinct problems of object detection and semantic segmentation. Our approach is summarized below (source code is available at http://www.cs.berkeley.edu/~sgupta/eccv14/).

RGB-D Contour Detection and 2.5D Region Proposals: RGB-D images enable one to compute depth and normal gradients [18], which we combine

D. Fleet et al. (Eds.): ECCV 2014, Part VII, LNCS 8695, pp. 345–360, 2014.

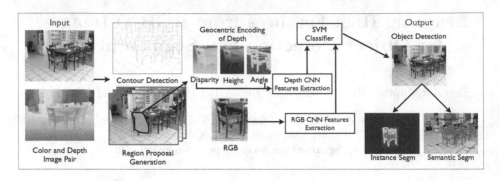

Fig. 1. Overview: from an RGB and depth image pair, our system detects contours, generates 2.5D region proposals, classifies them into object categories, and then infers segmentation masks for instances of "thing"-like objects, as well as labels for pixels belonging to "stuff"-like categories.

with the structured learning approach in [9] to yield significantly improved contours. We then use these RGB-D contours to obtain 2.5D region candidates by computing features on the depth and color image for use in the Multiscale Combinatorial Grouping (MCG) framework of Arbeláez *et al.* [1]. This module is state-of-the-art for RGB-D proposal generation.

RGB-D Object Detection: Convolutional neural networks (CNNs) trained on RGB images are the state-of-the-art for detection and segmentation [16]. We show that a large CNN pre-trained on RGB images can be adapted to generate rich features for depth images. We propose to represent the depth image by three channels (horizontal disparity, height above ground, and angle with gravity) and show that this representation allows the CNN to learn stronger features than by using disparity (or depth) alone. We use these features, computed on our 2.5D region candidates, in a modified R-CNN framework to obtain a 56% relative improvement in RGB-D object detection, compared to existing methods.

Instance Segmentation: In addition to bounding-box object detection, we also infer pixel-level object masks. We frame this as a foreground labeling task and show improvements over baseline methods.

Semantic Segmentation: Finally, we improve semantic segmentation performance (the task of labeling all pixels with a category, but not differentiating between instances) by using object detections to compute additional features for superpixels in the semantic segmentation system we proposed in [18]. This approach obtains state-of-the-art results for that task, as well.

1.1   Related Work

Most prior work on RGB-D perception has focussed on semantic segmentation [3,18,23,30,33], *i.e.* the task of assigning a category label to each pixel. While this is an interesting problem, many practical applications require a richer understanding of the scene. Notably, the notion of an object instance is missing from such an output. Object detection in RGB-D images [20,22,25,35,38], in contrast, focusses on instances, but the typical output is a bounding box. As Hariharan *et al.* [19] observe, neither of these tasks produces a compelling output representation. It is not enough for a robot to know that there is a mass of 'bottle' pixels in the image. Likewise, a roughly localized bounding box of an individual bottle may be too imprecise for the robot to grasp it. Thus, we propose a framework for solving the problem of instance segmentation (delineating pixels on the object corresponding to each detection) as proposed by [19,36].

Recently, convolutional neural networks [26] were shown to be useful for standard RGB vision tasks like image classification [24], object detection [16], semantic segmentation [13] and fine-grained classification [11]. Naturally, recent works on RGB-D perception have considered neural networks for learning representations from depth images [4,6,34]. Couprie *et al.* [6] adapt the multiscale semantic segmentation system of Farabet *et al.* [13] by operating directly on four-channel RGB-D images from the NYUD2 dataset. Socher *et al.* [34] and Bo *et al.* [4] look at object detection in RGB-D images, but detect small prop-like objects imaged in controlled lab settings. In this work, we tackle uncontrolled, cluttered environments as in the NYUD2 dataset. More critically, rather than using the RGB-D image directly, we introduce a new encoding that captures the geocentric pose of pixels in the image, and show that it yields a substantial improvement over naive use of the depth channel.

2   2.5D Region Proposals

In this section, we describe how to extend multiscale combinatorial grouping (MCG) [1] to effectively utilize depth cues to obtain 2.5D region proposals.

2.1   Contour Detection

RGB-D contour detection is a well-studied task [9,18,29,33]. Here we combine ideas from two leading approaches, [9] and our past work in [18].

In [18], we used *gPb-ucm* [2] and proposed local geometric gradients dubbed NG_-, NG_+, and DG to capture convex, concave normal gradients and depth gradients. In [9], Dollár *et al.* proposed a novel learning approach based on structured random forests to directly classify a pixel as being a contour pixel or not. Their approach treats the depth information as another image, rather than encoding it in terms of geocentric quantities, like NG_-. While the two methods perform comparably on the NYUD2 contour detection task (maximum F-measure point in the red and the blue curves in Figure 3), there are differences in the the type of contours that either approach produces. [9] produces better localized contours that capture fine details, but tends to miss normal discontinuities that [18] easily finds (for example, consider the contours between the walls and the ceiling in left part of the image Figure 2). We propose a synthesis of the two approaches that combines features from [18] with the learning framework from [9]. Specifically, we add the following features.

Normal Gradients: We compute normal gradients at two scales (corresponding to fitting a local plane in a half-disk of radius 3 and 5 pixels), and use these as additional gradient maps.

Geocentric Pose: We compute a per pixel height above ground and angle with gravity (using the algorithms we proposed in [18]. These features allow the decision trees to exploit additional regularities, for example that the brightness edges on the floor are not as important as brightness edges elsewhere.

Richer Appearance: We observe that the NYUD2 dataset has limited appearance variation (since it only contains images of indoor scenes). To make the model generalize better, we add the soft edge map produced by running the RGB edge detector of [9] (which is trained on BSDS) on the RGB image.

2.2 Candidate Ranking

From the improved contour signal, we obtain object proposals by generalizing MCG to RGB-D images. MCG for RGB images [1] uses simple features based on the color image and the region shape to train a random forest regressors to rank the object proposals. We follow the same paradigm, but propose additional geometric features computed on the depth image within each proposal. We compute: (1) the mean and standard deviation of the disparity, height above ground, angle with gravity, and world (X, Y, Z) coordinates of the points in the region; (2) the region's (X, Y, Z) extent; (3) the region's minimum and maximum height above ground; (4) the fraction of pixels on vertical surfaces, surfaces facing up, and surfaces facing down; (5) the minimum and maximum standard deviation along a direction in the top view of the room. We obtain 29 geometric features for each region in addition to the 14 from the 2D region shape and color image already computed in [1]. Note that the computation of these features for a region decomposes over superpixels and can be done efficiently by first computing the first and second order moments on the superpixels and then combining them appropriately.

2.3 Results

We now present results for contour detection and candidate ranking. We work with the NYUD2 dataset and use the standard split of 795 training images and 654 testing images (we further divide the 795 images into a training set of 381 images and a validation set of 414 images). These splits are carefully selected such that images from the same scene are only in one of these sets.

Contour Detection: To measure performance on the contour detection task, we plot the precision-recall curve on contours in Figure 3 and report the standard maximum F-measure metric (F_{max}) in Table 1. We start by comparing the performance of [18] (Gupta *et al.* CVPR [RGBD]) and Dollár *et al.* (SE [RGBD]) [9]. We see that both these contour detectors perform comparably in terms of F_{max}. [18] obtains better precision at lower recalls while [9] obtains better precision in the high recall regime. We also include a qualitative visualization of the

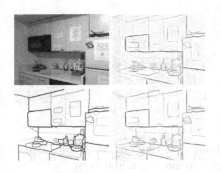

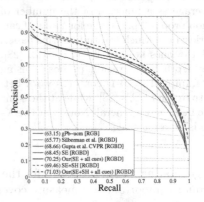

Fig. 3 legend:
- (63.15) gPb-ucm [RGB]
- (65.77) Silberman et al. [RGBD]
- (68.66) Gupta et al. CVPR [RGBD]
- (68.45) SE [RGBD]
- (70.25) Our(SE + all cues) [RGBD]
- (69.46) SE+SH [RGBD]
- (71.03) Our(SE+SH + all cues) [RGBD]

Fig. 2. Qualitative comparison of contours: Top row: color image, contours from [9], bottom row: contours from [18] and contours from our proposed contour detector

Fig. 3. Precision-recall curve on boundaries on the NYUD2 dataset

Table 1. Segmentation benchmarks on NYUD2. All numbers are percentages.

		ODS (F_{max})	OIS (F_{max})	AP
gPb-ucm	RGB	63.15	66.12	56.20
Silberman et al. [33]	RGB-D	65.77	66.06	-
Gupta et al. CVPR [18]	RGB-D	68.66	71.57	62.91
SE [9]	RGB-D	68.45	69.92	67.93
Our(SE + normal gradients)	RGB-D	69.55	70.89	69.32
Our(SE + all cues)	RGB-D	70.25	71.59	69.28
SE+SH [10]	RGB-D	69.46	70.84	71.88
Our(SE+SH + all cues)	RGB-D	71.03	72.33	73.81

contours to understand the differences in the nature of the contours produced by the two approaches (Figure 2).

Switching to the effect of our proposed contour detector, we observe that adding normal gradients consistently improves precision for all recall levels and F_{max} increases by 1.2% points (Table 1). The addition of geocentric pose features and appearance features improves F_{max} by another 0.6% points, making our final system better than the current state-of-the-art methods by 1.5% points.[1]

Candidate Ranking: The goal of the region generation step is to propose a pool of candidates for downstream processing (*e.g.*, object detection and segmentation). Thus, we look at the standard metric of measuring the coverage of ground truth regions as a function of the number of region proposals. Since we

---

[1] Dollár *et al.* [10] recently introduced an extension of their algorithm and report performance improvements (SE+SH[RGBD] dashed red curve in Figure 3). We can also use our cues with [10], and observe an analogous improvement in performance (Our(SE+SH + all cues) [RGBD] dashed blue curve in Figure 3). For the rest of the paper we use the Our(SE+all cues)[RGBD] version of our contour detector.

Fig. 4. Region Proposal Quality: Coverage as a function of the number of region proposal per image for 2 sets of categories: ones which we study in this paper, and the ones studied by Lin *et al.* [28]. Our depth based region proposals using our improved RGB-D contours work better than Lin *et al.*'s [28], while at the same time being more general. Note that the X-axis is on a *log* scale.

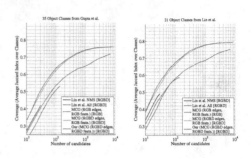

are generating region proposals for the task of object detection, where each class is equally important, we measure coverage for K region candidates by

$$\text{coverage}(K) = \frac{1}{C} \sum_{i=1}^{C} \left(\frac{1}{N_i} \left(\sum_{j=1}^{N_i} \max_{k \in [1...K]} O\left(R_k^{l(i,j)}, I_j^i \right) \right) \right), \quad (1)$$

where C is the number of classes, N_i is the number of instances for class i, $O(a, b)$ is the intersection over union between regions a and b, I_j^i is the region corresponding to the jth instance of class i, $l(i, j)$ is the image which contains the jth instance of class i, and R_k^l is the kth ranked region in image l.

We plot the function coverage(K) in Figure 4 (left) for our final method, which uses our RGB-D contour detector and RGB-D features for region ranking (black). As baselines, we show regions from the recent work of Lin *et al.* [28] with and without non-maximum suppression, MCG with RGB contours and RGB features, MCG with RGB-D contours but RGB features and finally our system which is MCG with RGB-D contours and RGB-D features. We note that there is a large improvement in region quality when switching from RGB contours to RGB-D contours, and a small but consistent improvement from adding our proposed depth features for candidate region re-ranking.

Since Lin *et al.* worked with a different set of categories, we also compare on the subset used in their work (in Figure 4 (right)). Their method was trained specifically to return candidates for these classes. Our method, in contrast, is trained to return candidates for generic objects and therefore "wastes" candidates trying to cover categories that do not contribute to performance on any fixed subset. Nevertheless, our method consistently outperforms [28], which highlights the effectiveness and generality of our region proposals.

3   RGB-D Object Detectors

We generalize the R-CNN system introduced by Girshick *et al.* [16] to leverage depth information. At test time, R-CNN starts with a set of bounding box proposals from an image, computes features on each proposal using a convolutional neural network, and classifies each proposal as being the target object class or not with a linear SVM. The CNN is trained in two stages: first, pretraining it on a large set of labeled images with an image classification objective, and then finetuning it on a much smaller detection dataset with a detection objective.

We generalize R-CNN to RGB-D images and explore the scientific question: Can we learn rich representations from depth images in a manner similar to those that have been proposed and demonstrated to work well for RGB images?

3.1   Encoding Depth Images for Feature Learning

Given a depth image, how should it be encoded for use in a CNN? Should the CNN work directly on the raw depth map or are there transformations of the input that the CNN to learn from more effectively?

We propose to encode the depth image with three channels at each pixel: horizontal disparity, height above ground, and the angle the pixel's local surface normal makes with the inferred gravity direction. We refer to this encoding as HHA. The latter two channels are computed using the algorithms proposed in [18] and all channels are linearly scaled to map observed values across the training dataset to the 0 to 255 range.

The HHA representation encodes properties of geocentric pose that emphasize complementary discontinuities in the image (depth, surface normal and height). Furthermore, it is unlikely that a CNN would automatically learn to compute these properties directly from a depth image, especially when very limited training data is available, as is the case with the NYUD2 dataset.

We use the CNN architecture proposed by Krizhevsky et al. in [24] and used by Girshick et al. in [16]. The network has about 60 million parameters and was trained on approximately 1.2 million RGB images from the 2012 ImageNet Challenge [7]. We refer the reader to [24] for details about the network. Our hypothesis, to be borne out in experiments, is that there is enough common structure between our HHA geocentric images and RGB images that a network designed for RGB images can also learn a suitable representation for HHA images. As an example, edges in the disparity and angle with gravity direction images correspond to interesting object boundaries (internal or external shape boundaries), similar to ones one gets in RGB images (but probably much cleaner).

Augmentation with Synthetic Data: An important observation is the amount of supervised training data that we have in the NYUD2 dataset is about one order of magnitude smaller than what is there for PASCAL VOC dataset (400 images as compared to 2500 images for PASCAL VOC 2007). To address this issue, we generate more data for training and finetuning the network. There are multiple ways of doing this: mesh the already available scenes and render the scenes from novel view points, use data from nearby video frames available in the dataset by flowing annotations using optical flow, use full 3D synthetic CAD objects models available over the Internet and render them into scenes. Meshing the point clouds may be too noisy and nearby frames from the video sequence maybe too similar and thus not very useful. Hence, we followed the third alternative and rendered the 3D annotations for NYUD2 available from [17] to generate synthetic scenes from various viewpoints. We also simulated the Kinect quantization model in generating this data (rendered depth images are converted to quantized disparity images and low resolution white noise was added to the disparity values).

3.2   Experiments

We work with the NYUD2 dataset and use the standard dataset splits into *train*, *val*, and *test* as described in Section 2.3. The dataset comes with semantic segmentation annotations, which we enclose in a tight box to obtain bounding box annotations. We work with the major furniture categories available in the dataset, such as chair, bed, sofa, table (listed in Table 2).

Experimental Setup: There are two aspects to training our model: finetuning the convolutional neural network for feature learning, and training linear SVMs for object proposal classification.

Finetuning: We follow the R-CNN procedure from [16] using the Caffe CNN library [21]. We start from a CNN that was pretrained on the much larger ILSVRC 2012 dataset. For finetuning, the learning rate was initialized at 0.001 and decreased by a factor of 10 every 20k iterations. We finetuned for 30k iterations, which takes about 7 hours on a NVIDIA Titan GPU. Following [16], we label each training example with the class that has the maximally overlapping ground truth instance, if this overlap is larger than 0.5, and *background* otherwise. All finetuning was done on the *train* set.

SVM Training: For training the linear SVMs, we compute features either from pooling layer 5 (*pool5*), fully connected layer 6 (*fc6*), or fully connected layer 7 (*fc7*). In SVM training, we fixed the positive examples to be from the ground truth boxes for the target class and the negative examples were defined as boxes having less than 0.3 intersection over union with the ground truth instances from that class. Training was done on the *train* set with SVM hyper-parameters $C = 0.001$, $B = 10$, $w_1 = 2.0$ using liblinear [12]. We report the performance (detection average precision AP^b) on the *val* set for the control experiments. For the final experiment we train on *trainval* and report performance in comparison to other methods on the *test* set. At test time, we compute features from the *fc6* layer in the network, apply the linear classifier, and non-maximum suppression to the output, to obtain a set of sparse detections on the test image.

3.3   Results

We use the PASCAL VOC box detection average precision (denoted as AP^b following the generalization introduced in [19]) as the performance metric. Results are presented in Table 2. As a baseline, we report performance of the state-of-the-art non-neural network based detection system, deformable part models (DPM) [14]. First, we trained DPMs on RGB images, which gives a mean

Table 2. Control experiments for object detection on NYUD2 *val* **set.** We investigate a variety of ways to encode the depth image for use in a CNN for feature learning. Results are AP as percentages. See Section 3.2.

	A	B	C	D	E	F	G	H	I	J	K	L
	DPM	DPM	CNN	CNN	CNN	CNN	CNN	CNN	CNN	CNN	CNN	CNN
finetuned?			no	yes	no	yes	yes	yes	yes	yes	yes	yes
input channels	RGB	RGBD	RGB	RGB	disparity	disparity	HHA	HHA	HHA	HHA	HHA	RGB+HHA
synthetic data?								2x	15x	2x	2x	2x
CNN layer			fc6	fc6	fc6	fc6	fc6	fc6	fc6	pool5	fc7	fc6
bathtub	0.1	12.2	4.9	5.5	3.5	6.1	20.4	20.7	20.7	11.1	19.9	**22.9**
bed	21.2	56.6	44.4	52.6	46.5	63.2	60.6	67.2	**67.8**	61.0	62.2	66.5
bookshelf	3.4	6.3	13.8	19.5	14.2	16.3	20.7	18.6	16.5	20.6	18.1	**21.8**
box	0.1	0.5	1.3	1.0	0.4	0.4	0.9	1.4	1.0	1.0	1.1	**3.0**
chair	6.6	22.5	21.4	24.6	23.8	36.1	38.7	38.2	35.2	32.6	37.4	**40.8**
counter	2.7	14.9	20.7	20.3	18.5	32.8	32.4	33.6	36.3	24.1	35.0	**37.6**
desk	0.7	2.3	2.8	6.7	1.8	3.1	5.0	5.1	7.8	4.2	5.4	**10.2**
door	1.0	4.7	10.6	14.1	0.9	2.3	3.8	3.7	3.4	2.8	3.3	**20.5**
dresser	1.9	23.2	11.2	16.2	3.7	5.7	18.4	18.9	**26.3**	13.1	24.7	26.2
garbage-bin	8.0	26.6	17.4	17.8	2.4	12.7	26.9	29.1	16.4	21.4	25.3	**37.6**
lamp	16.7	25.9	13.1	12.0	10.5	21.3	24.5	26.5	23.6	22.3	23.2	**29.3**
monitor	27.4	27.6	24.8	32.6	0.4	5.0	11.5	14.0	12.3	17.7	13.5	**43.4**
night-stand	7.9	16.5	9.0	18.1	3.9	19.1	25.2	27.3	22.1	25.9	27.8	**39.5**
pillow	2.6	21.1	6.6	10.7	3.8	23.4	35.0	32.2	30.7	31.1	31.2	**37.4**
sink	7.9	**36.1**	19.1	6.8	20.0	28.5	30.2	22.7	24.9	18.9	23.0	24.2
sofa	4.3	28.4	15.5	21.6	7.6	17.3	36.3	37.5	39.0	30.2	34.3	**42.8**
table	5.3	14.2	6.9	10.0	12.0	18.0	18.8	22.0	22.6	21.0	22.8	**24.3**
television	16.2	23.5	29.1	31.6	9.7	14.7	18.4	23.4	26.3	18.9	22.9	**37.2**
toilet	25.1	48.3	39.6	52.0	31.2	**55.7**	51.4	54.2	52.6	38.4	48.8	53.0
mean	8.4	21.7	16.4	19.7	11.3	20.1	25.2	26.1	25.6	21.9	25.3	**32.5**

AP^b of 8.4% (column A). While quite low, this result agrees with [32].[2] As a stronger baseline, we trained DPMs on features computed from RGB-D images (by using HOG on the disparity image and a histogram of height above ground in each HOG cell in addition to the HOG on the RGB image). These augmented DPMs (denoted RGBD-DPM) give a mean AP^b of 21.7% (column B). We also report results from the method of Girshick *et al.* [16], without and with fine tuning on the RGB images in the dataset, yielding 16.4% and 19.7% respectively (column C and column D). We compare results from layer *fc6* for all our experiments. Features from layers *fc7* and *pool5* generally gave worse performance.

The first question we ask is: Can a network trained only on RGB images can do anything when given disparity images? (We replicate each one-channel disparity image three times to match the three-channel filters in the CNN and scaled the input so as to have a distribution similar to RGB images.) The RGB network generalizes surprisingly well and we observe a mean AP^b of 11.3% (column E). This results confirms our hypothesis that disparity images have a similar structure to RGB images, and it may not be unreasonable to use an ImageNet-

---

[2] Wang *et al.* [37] report impressive detection results on NYUD2, however we are unable to compare directly with their method because they use a non-standard train-test split that they have not made available. Their baseline HOG DPM detection results are significantly higher than those reported in [32] and this paper, indicating that the split used in [37] is substantially easier than the standard evaluation split.

trained CNN as an initialization for finetuning on depth images. In fact, in our experiments we found that it was always better to finetune from the ImageNet initialization than to train starting with a random initialization.

We then proceed with finetuning this network (starting from the ImageNet initialization), and observe that performance improves to 20.1% (column F), already becoming comparable to RGBD-DPMs. However, finetuning with our HHA depth image encoding dramatically improves performance (by 25% relative), yielding a mean AP^b of 25.2% (column G).

We then observe the effect of synthetic data augmentation. Here, we add 2× synthetic data, based on sampling two novel views of the given NYUD2 scene from the 3D scene annotations made available by [17]. We observe an improvement from 25.2% to 26.1% mean AP^b points (column H). However, when we increase the amount of synthetic data further (15× synthetic data), we see a small drop in performance (column H to I). We attribute the drop to the larger bias that has been introduced by the synthetic data. Guo *et al.*'s [17] annotations replace all non-furniture objects with cuboids, changing the statistics of the generated images. More realistic modeling for synthetic scenes is a direction for future research.

We also report performance when using features from other layers: *pool5* (column J) and *fc7* (column K). As expected the performance for *pool5* is lower, but the performance for *fc7* is also lower. We attribute this to over-fitting during finetuning due to the limited amount of data available.

Finally, we combine the features from both the RGB and the HHA image when finetuned on 2× synthetic data (column L). We see there is consistent improvement from 19.7% and 26.1% individually to 32.5% (column L) mean AP^b. This is the final version of our system.

We also experimented with other forms of RGB and D fusion - early fusion where we passed in a 4 channel RGB-D image for finetuning but were unable to obtain good results (AP^b of 21.2%), and late fusion with joint finetuning for RGB and HHA (AP^b of 31.9%) performed comparably to our final system (individual finetuning of RGB and HHA networks) (AP^b of 32.5%). We chose the simpler architecture.

Test Set Performance: We ran our final system (column L) on the *test* set, by training on the complete *trainval* set. Performance is reported in Table 3. We compare against a RGB DPM, RGBD-DPMs as introduced before. Note that our RGBD-DPMs serve as a strong baseline and are already an absolute 8.2% better than published results on the B3DO dataset [20] (39.4% as compared to 31.2% from the approach of Kim *et al.* [22], detailed results are in the supplementary material). We also compare to Lin *et al.* [28]. [28] only produces 8, 15 or 30 detections per image which produce an average F_1 measure of 16.60, 17.88 and 18.14 in the 2D detection problem that we are considering as compared to our system which gives an average F_{max} measure of 43.70. Precision Recall curves for our detectors along with the 3 points of operation from [28] are in the supplementary material.

Fig. 5. Output of our system: We visualize some true positives (column one, two and three) and false positives (columns four and five) from our bed, chair, lamp, sofa and toilet object detectors. We also overlay the instance segmentation that we infer for each of our detections. Some of the false positives due to mis-localization are fixed by the instance segmentation.

Result Visualizations: We show some of the top scoring *true positives* and the top scoring *false positives* for our bed, chair, lamp, sofa and toilet detectors in Figure 5. More figures can be found in the supplementary material.

4   Instance Segmentation

In this section, we study the task of instance segmentation as proposed in [19,36]. Our goal is to associate a pixel mask to each detection produced by our RGB-D object detector. We formulate mask prediction as a two-class labeling problem (foreground versus background) on the pixels within each detection window. Our proposed method classifies each detection window pixel with a random forest classifier and then smoothes the predictions by averaging them over superpixels.

4.1   Model Training

Learning Framework: To train our random forest classifier, we associate each ground truth instance in the *train* set with a detection from our detector. We select the best scoring detection that overlaps the ground truth bounding box by more than 70%. For each selected detection, we warp the enclosed portion of the associated ground truth mask to a 50×50 grid. Each of these 2500 locations (per detection) serves as a training point.

We could train a single, monolithic classifier to process all 2500 locations or train a different classifier for each of the 2500 locations in the warped mask. The first option requires a highly non-linear classifier, while the second option suffers from data scarcity. We opt for the first option and work with random forests [5], which naturally deal with multi-modal data and have been shown to work well with the set of features we have designed [27,31]. We adapt the open source random forest implementation in [8] to allow training and testing with on-the-fly feature computation. Our forests have ten decision trees.

Features: We compute a set of feature channels at each pixel in the original image (listed in supplementary material). For each detection, we crop and warp the feature image to obtain features at each of the 50×50 detection window locations. The questions asked by our decision tree split nodes are similar to those in Shotton *et al.* [31], which generalize those originally proposed by Geman *et al.* [15]. Specifically, we use two question types: *unary questions* obtained by thresholding the value in a channel relative to the location of a point, and *binary questions* obtained by thresholding the difference between two values, at different relative positions, in a particular channel. Shotton *et al.* [31] scale their offsets by the depth of the point to classify. We find that depth scaling is unnecessary after warping each instance to a fixed size and scale.

Testing: During testing, we work with the top 5000 detections for each category (and 10000 for the chairs category, this gives us enough detections to get to 10% or lower precision). For each detection we compute features and pass them through the random forest to obtain a 50×50 foreground confidence map. We unwarp these confidence maps back to the original detection window and accumulate the per pixel predictions over superpixels. We select a threshold on the soft mask by optimizing performance on the *val* set.

4.2   Results

To evaluate instance segmentation performance we use the region detection average precision AP^r metric (with a threshold of 0.5) as proposed in [19], which extends the average precision metric used for bounding box detection by replacing bounding box overlap with region overlap (intersection over union). Note that this metric captures more information than the semantic segmentation metric as it respects the notion of instances, which is a goal of this paper.

We report the performance of our system in Table 3. We compare against three baseline methods: 1) *box* where we simply assume the mask to be the box for the detection and project it to superpixels, 2) *region* where we average the region proposals that resulted in the detected bounding box and project this to superpixels, and 3) *fg mask* where we compute an empirical mask from the set of ground truth masks corresponding to the detection associated with each ground

Table 3. *Test* **set results for detection and instance segmentation on NYUD2:** First four rows correspond to box detection average precision, AP^b, and we compare against three baselines: RGB DPMs, RGBD-DPMs, and RGB R-CNN. The last four lines correspond to region detection average precision, AP^r. See Section 3.3 and Section 4.2.

	mean	bath tub	bed	book shelf	box	chair	count -er	desk	door	dress -er	garba -ge bin	lamp	monit -or	night stand	pillow	sink	sofa	table	tele vision	toilet
RGB DPM	9.0	0.9	27.6	9.0	0.1	7.8	7.3	0.7	2.5	1.4	6.6	22.2	10.0	9.2	4.3	5.9	9.4	5.5	5.8	34.4
RGBD-DPM	23.9	19.3	56.0	17.5	0.6	23.5	24.0	6.2	9.5	16.4	26.7	26.7	34.9	32.6	20.7	22.8	34.2	17.2	19.5	45.1
RGB R-CNN	22.5	16.9	45.3	28.5	0.7	25.9	30.4	9.7	16.3	18.9	15.7	27.9	32.5	17.0	11.1	16.6	29.4	12.7	27.4	44.1
Our	37.3	44.4	71.0	32.9	1.4	43.3	44.0	15.1	24.5	30.4	39.4	36.5	52.6	40.0	34.8	36.1	53.9	24.4	37.5	46.8
box	14.0	5.9	40.0	4.1	0.7	5.5	0.5	3.2	14.5	26.9	32.9	1.2	40.2	11.1	6.1	9.4	13.6	2.6	35.1	11.9
region	28.1	32.4	54.9	9.4	1.1	27.0	21.4	8.9	20.3	29.0	37.1	26.3	48.3	38.6	33.1	30.9	30.5	10.2	33.7	39.9
fg mask	28.0	14.7	59.9	8.9	1.3	29.2	5.4	7.2	22.6	33.2	38.1	31.2	54.8	39.4	32.1	32.0	36.2	11.2	37.4	37.5
Our	32.1	18.9	66.1	10.2	1.5	35.5	32.8	10.2	22.8	33.7	38.3	35.5	53.3	42.7	31.5	34.4	40.7	14.3	37.4	50.5

truth instance in the *training* set. We see that *our* approach outperforms all the baselines and we obtain a mean AP^r of 32.1% as compared to 28.1% for the best baseline. The effectiveness of our instance segmentor is further demonstrated by the fact that for some categories the AP^r is better than AP^b, indicating that our instance segmentor was able to correct some of the mis-localized detections.

5   Semantic Segmentation

Semantic segmentation is the problem of labeling an image with the correct category label at each pixel. There are multiple ways to approach this problem, like that of doing a bottom-up segmentation and classifying the resulting superpixels [18,30] or modeling contextual relationships among pixels and superpixels [23,33].

Here, we extend our approach from [18], which produces state-of-the-art results on this task, and investigate the use of our object detectors in the pipeline of computing features for superpixels to classify them. In particular, we design a set of features on the superpixel, based on the detections of the various categories which overlap with the superpixel, and use them in addition to the features preposed in [18].

5.1   Results

We report our semantic segmentation performance in Table 4. We use the same metrics as [18], the frequency weighted average Jaccard Index $fwavacc^3$, but also report other metrics namely the average Jaccard Index ($avacc$) and average Jaccard Index for categories for which we added the object detectors ($avacc^*$).

---

[3] We calculate the pixel-wise intersection over union for each class independently as in the PASCAL VOC semantic segmentation challenge and then compute an average of these category-wise IoU numbers weighted by the pixel frequency of these categories.

Table 4. Performance on the 40 class semantic segmentation task as proposed by [18]: We report the pixel-wise Jaccard index for each of the 40 categories. We compare against 4 baselines: previous approaches from [33], [30], [18] (first three rows), and the approach in [18] augmented with features from RGBD-DPMs ([18]+DPM) (fourth row). Our approach obtains the best performance *fwavacc* of 47%. There is an even larger improvement for the categories for which we added our object detector features, where the average performance *avacc** goes up from 28.4 to 35.1. Categories for which we added detectors are shaded in gray (avacc* is the average for categories with detectors).

	wall	floor	cabinet	bed	chair	sofa	table	door	window	book shelf	picture	counter	blinds	desk	shelves
[33]-SC	60.7	77.8	33.0	40.3	32.4	25.3	21.0	5.9	29.7	22.7	35.7	33.1	40.6	4.7	3.3
[30]	60.0	74.4	37.1	42.3	32.5	28.2	16.6	12.9	27.7	17.3	32.4	38.6	26.5	10.1	6.1
[18]	67.6	81.2	44.8	57.0	36.7	40.8	28.0	13.0	33.6	19.5	41.2	52.0	44.4	7.1	4.5
[18]+DPM	66.4	81.5	43.2	59.4	41.1	45.6	30.3	14.2	33.2	19.6	41.5	51.8	40.7	6.9	9.2
Ours	68.0	81.3	44.9	65.0	47.9	47.9	29.9	20.3	32.6	18.1	40.3	51.3	42.0	11.3	3.5

	curtain	dresser	pillow	mirror	floor mat	clothes	ceiling	books	fridge	tele vision	paper	towel	shower curtain	box	white board
[33]	27.4	13.3	18.9	4.4	7.1	6.5	73.2	5.5	1.4	5.7	12.7	0.1	3.6	0.1	0.0
[30]	27.6	7.0	19.7	17.9	20.1	9.5	53.9	14.8	1.9	18.6	11.7	12.6	5.4	3.3	0.2
[18]	28.6	24.3	30.3	23.1	26.8	7.4	61.1	5.5	16.2	4.8	15.1	25.9	9.7	2.1	11.6
[18]+DPM	27.9	29.6	35.0	23.4	31.2	7.6	61.3	8.0	14.4	16.3	15.7	21.6	3.9	1.1	11.3
Ours	29.1	34.8	34.4	16.4	28.0	4.7	60.5	6.4	14.5	31.0	14.3	16.3	4.2	2.1	14.2

	person	night stand	toilet	sink	lamp	bathtub	bag	other str	other furntr	other prop	fwavacc	avacc	mean (maxIU)	pixacc	avacc*
[33]-SC	6.6	6.3	26.7	25.1	15.9	0.0	0.0	6.4	3.8	22.4	38.2	19.0	-	54.6	18.4
[30]	13.6	9.2	35.2	28.9	14.2	7.8	1.2	5.7	5.5	9.7	37.6	20.5	21.4	49.3	21.1
[18]	5.0	21.5	46.5	35.7	16.3	31.1	0.0	7.9	5.7	22.7	45.2	26.4	29.1	59.1	28.4
[18]+DPM	2.2	19.9	46.5	45.0	31.3	21.5	0.0	9.3	4.7	21.8	45.6	27.4	30.5	60.1	31.0
Ours	0.2	27.2	55.1	37.5	34.8	38.2	0.2	7.1	6.1	23.1	47.0	28.6	31.3	60.3	35.1

As a baseline we consider [18] + DPM, where we replace our detectors with RGBD-DPM detectors as introduced in Section 3.3. We observe that there is an increase in performance by adding features from DPM object detectors over the approach of [18], and the *fwavacc* goes up from 45.2 to 45.6, and further increase to 47.0 on adding our detectors. The quality of our detectors is brought out further when we consider the performance on just the categories for which we added object detectors which on average goes up from 28.4% to 35.1%. This 24% relative improvement is much larger than the boost obtained by adding RGBD-DPM detectors (31.0% only a 9% relative improvement over 28.4%).

Acknowledgements. This work was sponsored by ONR SMARTS MURI N00014-09-1-1051, ONR MURI N00014-10-1-0933 and a Berkeley Fellowship. The GPUs used in this research were generously donated by the NVIDIA Corporation. We are also thankful to Bharath Hariharan, for all the useful discussions. We also thank Piotr Dollár for helping us with their contour detection code.

References

1. Arbeláez, P., Pont-Tuset, J., Barron, J., Marques, F., Malik, J.: Multiscale combinatorial grouping. In: CVPR (2014)
2. Arbeláez, P., Maire, M., Fowlkes, C., Malik, J.: Contour detection and hierarchical image segmentation. TPAMI (2011)

3. Banica, D., Sminchisescu, C.: CPMC-3D-O2P: Semantic segmentation of RGB-D images using CPMC and second order pooling. CoRR abs/1312.7715 (2013)
4. Bo, L., Ren, X., Fox, D.: Unsupervised Feature Learning for RGB-D Based Object Recognition. In: ISER (2012)
5. Breiman, L.: Random forests. Machine Learning (2001)
6. Couprie, C., Farabet, C., Najman, L., LeCun, Y.: Indoor semantic segmentation using depth information. CoRR abs/1301.3572 (2013)
7. Deng, J., Berg, A., Satheesh, S., Su, H., Khosla, A., Fei-Fei, L.: ImageNet Large Scale Visual Recognition Competition 2012 (ILSVRC 2012) (2012), http://www.image-net.org/challenges/LSVRC/2012/
8. Dollár, P.: Piotr's Image and Video Matlab Toolbox (PMT), http://vision.ucsd.edu/~pdollar/toolbox/doc/index.html
9. Dollár, P., Zitnick, C.L.: Structured forests for fast edge detection. In: ICCV (2013)
10. Dollár, P., Zitnick, C.L.: Fast edge detection using structured forests. CoRR abs/1406.5549 (2014)
11. Donahue, J., Jia, Y., Vinyals, O., Hoffman, J., Zhang, N., Tzeng, E., Darrell, T.: Decaf: A deep convolutional activation feature for generic visual recognition. In: ICML (2014)
12. Fan, R.E., Chang, K.W., Hsieh, C.J., Wang, X.R., Lin, C.J.: LIBLINEAR: A library for large linear classification. JMRL (2008)
13. Farabet, C., Couprie, C., Najman, L., LeCun, Y.: Learning hierarchical features for scene labeling. TPAMI (2013)
14. Felzenszwalb, P., Girshick, R., McAllester, D., Ramanan, D.: Object detection with discriminatively trained part based models. TPAMI (2010)
15. Geman, D., Amit, Y., Wilder, K.: Joint induction of shape features and tree classifiers. TPAMI (1997)
16. Girshick, R., Donahue, J., Darrell, T., Malik, J.: Rich feature hierarchies for accurate object detection and semantic segmentation. In: CVPR (2014)
17. Guo, R., Hoiem, D.: Support surface prediction in indoor scenes. In: ICCV (2013)
18. Gupta, S., Arbeláez, P., Malik, J.: Perceptual organization and recognition of indoor scenes from RGB-D images. In: CVPR (2013)
19. Hariharan, B., Arbeláez, P., Girshick, R., Malik, J.: Simultaneous detection and segmentation. In: Fleet, D., Pajdla, T., Schiele, B., Tuytelaars, T. (eds.) ECCV 2014, Part VII. LNCS, vol. 8695, Springer, Heidelberg (2014)
20. Janoch, A., Karayev, S., Jia, Y., Barron, J.T., Fritz, M., Saenko, K., Darrell, T.: A category-level 3D object dataset: Putting the kinect to work. In: Consumer Depth Cameras for Computer Vision (2013)
21. Jia, Y.: Caffe: An open source convolutional architecture for fast feature embedding (2013), http://caffe.berkeleyvision.org/
22. Soo Kim, B., Xu, S., Savarese, S.: Accurate localization of 3D objects from RGB-D data using segmentation hypotheses. In: CVPR (2013)
23. Koppula, H., Anand, A., Joachims, T., Saxena, A.: Semantic labeling of 3D point clouds for indoor scenes. In: NIPS (2011)
24. Krizhevsky, A., Sutskever, I., Hinton, G.E.: ImageNet classification with deep convolutional neural networks. In: NIPS (2012)
25. Lai, K., Bo, L., Ren, X., Fox, D.: A large-scale hierarchical multi-view rgb-d object dataset. In: ICRA (2011)
26. LeCun, Y., Boser, B., Denker, J.S., Henderson, D., Howard, R.E., Hubbard, W., Jackel, L.D.: Backpropagation applied to handwritten zip code recognition. Neural Computation (1989)

27. Lim, J.J., Zitnick, C.L., Dollár, P.: Sketch tokens: A learned mid-level representation for contour and object detection. In: CVPR (2013)
28. Lin, D., Fidler, S., Urtasun, R.: Holistic scene understanding for 3D object detection with RGBD cameras. In: ICCV (2013)
29. Ren, X., Bo, L.: Discriminatively trained sparse code gradients for contour detection. In: NIPS (2012)
30. Ren, X., Bo, L., Fox, D.: RGB-(D) scene labeling: Features and algorithms. In: CVPR (2012)
31. Shotton, J., Fitzgibbon, A.W., Cook, M., Sharp, T., Finocchio, M., Moore, R., Kipman, A., Blake, A.: Real-time human pose recognition in parts from single depth images. In: CVPR (2011)
32. Shrivastava, A., Gupta, A.: Building part-based object detectors via 3D geometry. In: ICCV (2013)
33. Silberman, N., Hoiem, D., Kohli, P., Fergus, R.: Indoor segmentation and support inference from RGBD images. In: Fitzgibbon, A., Lazebnik, S., Perona, P., Sato, Y., Schmid, C. (eds.) ECCV 2012, Part V. LNCS, vol. 7576, pp. 746–760. Springer, Heidelberg (2012)
34. Socher, R., Huval, B., Bath, B.P., Manning, C.D., Ng, A.Y.: Convolutional-recursive deep learning for 3D object classification. In: NIPS (2012)
35. Tang, S., Wang, X., Lv, X., Han, T.X., Keller, J., He, Z., Skubic, M., Lao, S.: Histogram of oriented normal vectors for object recognition with a depth sensor. In: Lee, K.M., Matsushita, Y., Rehg, J.M., Hu, Z. (eds.) ACCV 2012, Part II. LNCS, vol. 7725, pp. 525–538. Springer, Heidelberg (2013)
36. Tighe, J., Niethammer, M., Lazebnik, S.: Scene parsing with object instances and occlusion ordering. In: CVPR (2014)
37. Wang, T., He, X., Barnes, N.: Learning structured hough voting for joint object detection and occlusion reasoning. In: CVPR (2013)
38. Ye, E.S.: Object Detection in RGB-D Indoor Scenes. Master's thesis, EECS Department, University of California, Berkeley (January 2013),
http://www.eecs.berkeley.edu/Pubs/TechRpts/2013/EECS-2013-3.html

Scene Classification via Hypergraph-Based Semantic Attributes Subnetworks Identification

Sun-Wook Choi, Chong Ho Lee, and In Kyu Park

Department of Information and Communication Engineering
Inha University, Incheon 402-751, Korea
swchoi@inhaian.net, {chlee,pik}@inha.ac.kr

Abstract. Scene classification is an important issue in computer vision area. However, it is still a challenging problem due to the variability, ambiguity, and scale change that exist commonly in images. In this paper, we propose a novel hypergraph-based modeling that considers the higher-order relationship of semantic attributes in a scene and apply it to scene classification. By searching subnetworks on a hypergraph, we extract the interaction subnetworks of the semantic attributes that are optimized for classifying individual scene categories. In addition, we propose a method to aggregate the expression values of the member semantic attributes which belongs to the explored subnetworks using the transformation method via likelihood ratio based estimation. Intensive experiment shows that the discrimination power of the feature vector generated by the proposed method is better than the existing methods. Consequently, it is shown that the proposed method outperforms the conventional methods in the scene classification task.

Keywords: Scene classification, Semantic attribute, Hypergraph, SVM.

1   Introduction

Scene understanding still remains a challenging problem in computer vision field. Among particular topics in scene understanding, image classification including scene and object classification has become one of the major issues. Over the past decade, numerous techniques have been proposed to classify scene images into appropriate categories.

Most of the existing high-level image classification techniques are performed in the transformed domain from the original image. Popular approaches employ the statistics of local feature such as histogram of textons [15] and bag-of-words (BoW) [6,24]. In the BoW model, local features obtained from an image are first mapped to a set of predefined visual words, which is done by vector quantization of the feature descriptors using a clustering technique such as K-means. The image is then represented by a histogram of visual words occurrence. The BoW model has demonstrated remarkable performance in challenging image classification tasks when it is combined with the well known classification techniques such as the support vector machine (SVM) [9,12,28].

D. Fleet et al. (Eds.): ECCV 2014, Part VII, LNCS 8695, pp. 361–376, 2014.

However, the conventional methods using low-level feature have a few limitations. First, although the visual words are more informative than individual image pixels, they still lack explicit semantic meanings.

Second, the visual words are occasionally polysemous, so it is possible to have different semantic meanings even though we have the identical visual word [25].

To overcome the limitations, several techniques have been proposed so far. Bosch *et al.* utilizes the intermediate-level representation to shows the improved classification performance [3]. However, the intermediate-level image representation technique is yet not free from the problem of visual words' ambiguity, *i.e.* *polysemy* and *synonymy* [25].

Recently, in order to utilize the higher-level contextual information for scene classification, semantic attribute is investigated actively. This technique alleviates the effect of the *polysemy* and *synonymy* problems if it is combined with the contextual information correctly [19,22,25]. Note that the semantic attributes in a scene are intuitive. Usually, they represent individual objects in the scene as well as the particular parts of them. In general, these semantic attributes show higher-order relationship between each other, which can be usually observed in real scenes. For example, a 'street' scene can be thought of as a combination of a 'building', 'road', and 'car'. However, the existing techniques using high-level semantic attributes do not exploit the higher-order relationship adequately but treat the semantic attributes independently. Furthermore, it is noticeable that some semantic attributes co-occur frequently while some other semantic attributes rarely appear together in a certain scene. We can represent the co-occurrence as the relation of semantic attributes. The interaction (relations) of semantic attributes provides strong contextual information about a scene. Based on this idea, we attempt to exploit the higher-order interaction of semantic attributes for the scene classification problem.

Generally, a graph-based modeling technique is can be considered to deal with the interaction between attributes. However, typical graph-based models use formulation that involve only single pairwise interactions and are not sufficient to model the higher-order interaction. To overcome this limitation, we can consider a hypergraph-based technique to model the higher-order interaction.

A hypergraph is a generalization of the conventional graph structure in which a set of nodes is defined as hyperedge [26]. Unlike the conventional graph model, a hypergraph contains the summarized local grouping information represented by hyperedges. In the hypergraph model, it is possible to construct various combinations of hyperedges using different sets of attributes. These hyperedges co-exist in a hypergraph and provide complementary information for the target data. In this context, the hyperedges are regarded as subnetworks of attributes. This property is beneficial to model the co-occurrence patterns of semantic attributes in scene images.

In this paper, we propose a hypergraph-based scene modeling and learning method for scene classification. By employing the hypergraph learning, we can search important subnetworks on the efficiently from the interaction network of the semantic attributes. Overall process of proposed method for scene

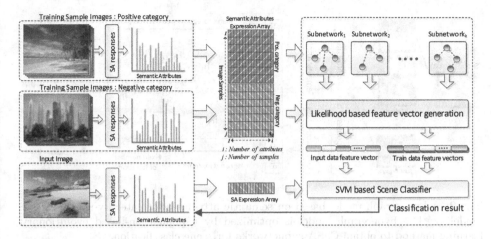

Fig. 1. Overall process of proposed method. Given training images and an input image, expression arrays of semantic attributes are calculated from responses of semantic attributes for each image. Then, for each scene category, category-specific semantic attribute (CSSA) subnetworks are obtained by proposed hypergraph based method. New feature vectors are generated by aggregation method from explored subnetworks and then input image is classified based on the newly generated feature vector with a SVM based scene classifier.

classification is depicted in Fig. 1. The main contributions of this paper are summarized as follows.

1. In order to take account the higher-order interaction of semantic attributes in scene classification, we propose a novel scene classification method based on the hypergraph model and efficient learning technique to create the category-specific hypergraph suitable for scene classification problem.
2. We propose another novel method to generate aggregated feature vector from the hypergraph suitable for discriminative model. The newly generated feature vector not only reduces the dimension of the feature space, but also alleviates the measurement noise of semantic attributes expression and therefore. This enables us to obtain a robust feature vector.

2 Hypergraph-Based Scene Modeling

In order to model a particular scene category using a hypergraph, we use the co-occurrence pattern of semantic attributes obtained from either the training sample images in the scene category or the text-based annotation of scene images. For example, when we build the hypergraph of the 'coast' category, we can get hyperedges from the training sample images I included in the category. Assuming that the number of training sample images is six, the set of semantic attributes S is generated for the 'coast' category as follows.

$$S = \{s_1('sky'),\ s_2('water'),\ s_3('sand'),\ s_4('boat'),\ s_5('tree'),\ s_6('rock')\}. \quad (1)$$

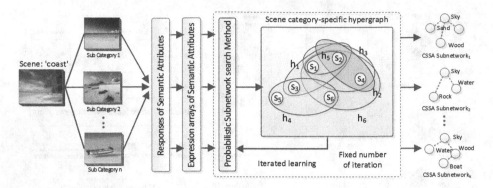

Fig. 2. A hypergraph model based on semantic attributes for category-specific scene modeling. The hypergraph model is optimized by a population-based evolutionary learning method to obtain CSSA subnetworks for scene classification.

We consider these semantic attributes S as the set of nodes of a graph. The Hyperedges E can be obtained from the image set I as follows.

$$E = \{e_1 = \{s_1, s_2, s_3\}, e_2 = \{s_2, s_4\}, e_3 = \{s_1, s_2, s_4\}, \\ e_4 = \{s_3, s_5, s_6\}, e_5 = \{s_1, s_2\}, e_6 = \{s_1, s_2, s_4, s_6\}\}. \tag{2}$$

The hypergraph $H = (S, E)$ consists of the set of nodes S and the set of hyperedges E. As in the example above, we can build a hypergraph for the certain scene category by combining the hyperedges obtained from its training sample images. Due to this characteristic, the hypergraph can be represented by the population which consists of the hyperedge. Here, each hyperedge is considered as each individual of the population.

As shown in Eq. (2), a hypergraph can model edges including an arbitrary number of attributes. Based on this property of a hypergraph, we can model each scene category by means of a hypergraph. However, even though the hypergraph model represents a certain scene category very well, it is yet still insufficient for the scene classification task. This is because the relative distribution between the desired category to be classified (denoted as 'positive category' in Fig. 1) and other categories (denoted as 'negative category' in Fig. 1) is not considered when building hyperedges of a hypergraph. Therefore, a generation of appropriate hypergraph for a scene classification task means that it is a searching process of suitable hyperedges to represent the characteristics of the target category efficiently as well as to consider the discrimination capability from other categories.

For this reason, a learning process is required to refine the initial hypergraph. In our approach, we employ the population-based learning model based on [29]. Here, the hypergraph H is re-defined as $H = (S, E, W)$ where S, E, and W are a set of vertices (semantic attributes), hyperedges, and weights of each hyperedge, respectively. That is, the re-defined hypergraph adds weight terms to the original hypergraph. Each vertex corresponds to a particular semantic attribute while each hyperedge represents the relational combination of more than two vertices with its own weight. The number of vertices in a hyperedge is called the cardinality or the order of a hyperedges, in which k-hyperedge denotes a hyperedge with k vertices.

Since the hypergraph with the weight term can be regarded as a probabilistic associative memory model to store segments of a given data set $D = \{x^{(n)}\}_{n=1}^{N}$ i.e. $\mathbf{x} = \{x_1, x_2, ..., x_m\}$ as in [29], a hypergraph can retrieve a data sample after the learning process. When $I(x^{(n)}, E_i)$ denotes a function which yields the combination or concatenation of elements of E_i, then the energy of a hypergrpah is defined as follows.

$$\varepsilon(\mathbf{x}^{(n)}; W) = -\sum_{i=1}^{|E|} w_i^{(k)} I(\mathbf{x}^{(n)}, E_i) \qquad (3)$$

$$\text{where} \quad I(\mathbf{x}^{(n)}, E_i) = x_{i1}^{(n)} x_{i2}^{(n)} ... x_{ik}^{(n)}.$$

In Eq. (3), $w_i^{(k)}$ is the weight of the i-th hyperedges E_i with k-order, $\mathbf{x}^{(n)}$ means the n-th stored pattern of data, and E_i is $\{x_{i1}, x_{i2}, ..., x_{ik}\}$. Then, the probability of the data generated by a hypergraph $P(D|W)$ is given as a Gibbs distribution as follows.

$$P(D|W) = \prod_{n=1}^{N} P(\mathbf{x}^{(n)}|W), \qquad (4)$$

$$P(\mathbf{x}^{(n)}|W) = \frac{1}{Z(W)} exp(-\varepsilon(\mathbf{x}^{(n)}; W)), \qquad (5)$$

where $Z(W)$ is a partition function, which is formulated as follows.

$$Z(W) = \sum_{\mathbf{X}^{(m)} \subset D} \exp \left\{ \sum_{i=1}^{|E|} w_i^{(k)} I(\mathbf{x}^{(m)}, E_i) \right\}. \qquad (6)$$

That is, a hypergraph is represented with a probability distribution of the joint variables with weights as parameters when we consider attributes in data as random variables.

Considering that learning of a hypergraph is to select hyperedges with a higher weight, it can be formulated as the process for maximizing log-likelihood. Learning from data is regarded as maximizing probability of weight parameter of a hypergraph for given data D. In this context, the probability of a weight set of hyperedges $P(W|D)$ is defined as follows.

$$P(W|D) = \frac{P(D|W)P(W)}{P(D)}. \qquad (7)$$

According to Eq. (5) and Eq. (7), the likelihood is defined as

$$\prod_{n=1}^{N} P(\mathbf{x}^{(n)}|W)P(W) = \left(\frac{P(W)}{Z(W)} \right)^N \exp \left\{ -\sum_{n=1}^{N} \varepsilon(\mathbf{x}^{(n)}; W) \right\}. \qquad (8)$$

Ignoring $P(W)$, maximizing the argument of exponential function is equivalent to obtaining maximum log likelihood as follows.

$$
\arg\max_W \left[\log\left\{ \prod_{n=1}^{N} P(\mathbf{x}^{(n)}|W) \right\} \right]
$$
$$
= \arg\max_W \{ \sum_{n=1}^{N} \sum_{i=1}^{|E|} w_i^{(k)} I(\mathbf{x}^{(n)}, E_i) - N \log Z(W) \}.
$$

(9)

More detail derivation of the log-likelihood are shown in [29]. A likelihood function can be maximized by exploring different hyperedge compositions which can reveal the distribution of given data better. Now, the problem is converted to finding appropriate combination of optimal hyper edges (or feature subsets). In other words, this is equivalent to exploring a suitable hyperedge-based population for a scene classification.

In general, exploring optimal feature subsets from a high-dimensional feature space is an NP-complete problem since it is impractical to explore the entire feature space. In this paper, we propose a sub-optimal hypergraph generation method to maximize the discrimination power from the perspective of Kleinberg's stochastic discrimination (SD) [13]. Based on the central limit theorem, the SD theory proves it theoretically and demonstrated experimentally that it is possible to generate a strong classifier by producing and combining many weak classifiers based on randomly sampled feature subsets. However, in order to approximate the actual distribution of data, it requires repeated random sampling process for an entire feature space as many as possible. For an efficient search, we use a heuristic search based on a population-based evolutionary computation technique as illustrated in Fig. 2. The details will be explained in the following section.

3   Learning of a Hypergraph for Scene Classification

To learn the hyper graph, we use a population-based evolutionary learning method. In this method, the variation, evaluation, and selection are performed iteratively. In the proposed learning method, a hyperedge is weighted by (i) the amount of higher-order dependency and (ii) the discrimination power between different categories. As the population changes in the learning procedure, the hypergraph structure evolves by removing hyperdges with relatively low weight and by replacing them with new hyperedges with relatively high weight. Filtering is subsequently performed for each hyperedge to have optimal elements.

In general, features on search space have the equivalent selection probability under the uniform distribution. However, it is inefficient because features used in classification do not have equivalent discriminative power. Furthermore, in the scene classification problem, it has the characteristic that the occurrence probability of each feature in the entire feature space is very sparse. Therefore, we need to adjust selection probability of each feature based on the importance of each feature.

Algorithm 1. Two-step sub-optimal hypergraph learning algorithm (Step 1)

Input: Expression array A of semantic attributes
Output: Candidate group of attribute subsets g

1: $\omega(s^i) \leftarrow$ Weight calculation of each attribute s^i by Student's t-test.
2: $g \leftarrow$ Generate a fixed number of m semantic attribute subsets randomly
   from original semantic attribute space based on the weight $\omega(s^i)$.
3: **repeat**
4:     (a) $f(g^k) \leftarrow$ Calculate a fitness value of the subset g^k.
5:     (b) Sort semantic attribute subsets g^k in descending order based on fitness
       values of $f(g^k)$ given by Eq. (10).
6:     (c) Remove the bottom 30%, and then replace with newly created subsets.
7: **until** (Predetermined number of learning.)

Algorithm 2. Two-step sub-optimal hypergraph learning algorithm (Step 2)

Input: Candidate group of semantic attribute subsets g
Output: Sub-optimized subsets $\hat{g}$

1: **for** k = 1 to $|g|$ **do** : for each subset
2:     Sort member attributes s^i in descending order based on the abs. t-test
       score of s^i.
3:     Add the 1st ranked s^i to empty set $\hat{g}^k$, then calculate the discriminative
       power d^k.
4:     **repeat**
5:         (a) $\hat{g}^k = \hat{g}^k \cup \{s^i\}$: Add the next ranked s^i to subset $\hat{g}^k$.
6:         (b) Evaluate the discriminative power d^k of $\hat{g}^k$.
7:     **until** (The new d^k is less than the previous d^k.)
8: **end for**

To solve this problem, we propose a probabilistic subnetworks search method that can sample the feature subsets efficiently based on the importance of each feature. In order to generate subnetworks of semantic attributes for scene classification using the probabilistic subnetworks search method, first, we need to measure the importance of each feature. This can be measured by the degree of association with the target category. In case of continuous data with a small number of samples, we can consider to use Student's t-test for two-class problem [8]. Using the t-test, we can get P-value which is the rejection probability of the null hypothesis $H_0 : \mu_p = \mu_n$ assuming that the mean of each population belonging to the positive category and negative category is equal. P-value has high rejection probability of the null hypothesis when its value is close to 0. This means that the distribution pattern of each class is very different. In other words, the discriminative power of each feature is strong. In order to accommodate this to the selection probability of semantic attribute s_i, we use the value of $1 - p(s_i)$ where $p(s_i)$ is a P-value of s_i. Strictly speaking, it is not the probability score, but it has the property that the selection capability becomes high when it close to 1 and vice versa.

The subnetworks search process based on the selection probability of semantic attributes is shown in Algorithm 1. At the beginning of the search, we create the predefined number of subsets (m=1000), then obtain the fitness values of each subset. Among various techniques, we use Hotelling's T^2-test [21] used in multivariate test to obtain a robust fitness value with fast speed. Note that Hotelling's T^2-test is a generalization of Student's t-test that is used in multivariate hypothesis testing. It is suitable for assessing the statistically higher-order relationship of semantic attributes composing the subset, since it can consider the correlation and interdependence between the component of subset.

Hotelling's T^2-test score for generated subsets is calculated as follows.

$$T^2 = \frac{n_p n_n}{n_p + n_n}(\mathbf{\overline{A}^P} - \mathbf{\overline{A}^n})\mathbf{S}^{-1}(\mathbf{\overline{A}^P} - \mathbf{\overline{A}^n})^\top, \tag{10}$$

where n_c is the number of samples belongs to each category c, $\overline{A}^c$ is the mean expression value of semantic attributes s_j^p and s_j^n belongs to each category. $\mathbf{S}$ is the pooled variance-covariance matrix of semantic attributes.

In the probabilistic subnetworks search method, subsets are generated through the search process as shown in Algorithm 1 using a fitness function based on the Hotelling's T^2-test. Then, filtering is performed for each subset to have sub-optimal member attributes that maximizing discriminative power through the incremental learning as shown in Algorithm 2. The sub-optimal subsets obtained from the search process are regarded as subnetworks because its member attributes are likely to interact each other. Finally, these subnetworks are hyperedges which build the learned hypergraph.

4 Feature Vector Generation Based on Likelihood Ratio

In order to use the learned hypergraph for scene classification, we employ a discriminative model. When using a discriminative model, the parameter learning is relatively simpler than a generative model. In addition, it has an advantage of an ease to utilize well-known classification methods such as support vector machine (SVM) that are known to show relatively superior classification capability in many fields.

For using the discriminative model, we need generation of feature vectors from a learned hypergrpah. Each hyperedge constituting the hypergraph includes multiple semantic attributes as shown in Fig. 2. Thus, it is impossible to apply to the classification model directly. For this, we propose a method based on the likelihood ratio to aggregate the expression values of each member attribute to make up the hyperedges from the original expression data.

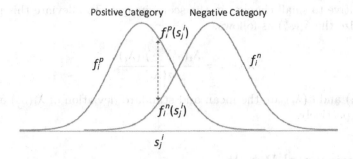

Fig. 3. Likelihood estimation for each semantic attribute

Given a expression vector $\mathbf{s}_j = (s_j^1, s_j^2, ..., s_j^n)$ which contains the expression levels of the member semantic attributes, we estimate the aggregate value of g_j^k (k-th subnetworks of sample j) as follows.

$$\text{aggregated value of } g_j^k = \frac{1}{|g_j^k|} \sum_{i=1}^{n} \lambda_i(s_j^i), \qquad (11)$$

where $\lambda_i(s_j^i)$ is the likelihood ratio between positive and negative categories for the semantic attributes. The likelihood ratio $\lambda_i(s_j^i)$ is given by

$$\lambda_i(s_j^i) = \frac{f_i^p(s_j^i)}{f_i^n(s_j^i)}, \qquad (12)$$

where $f_i^p(s)$ is the conditional probability density function (PDF) of the expression value of each semantic attribute under positive category, and $f_i^n(s)$ is the conditional PDF under negative category. The ratio $\lambda_i(s_j^i)$ is a probabilistic indicator that tells us which category is more likely based on the expression value s_j^i of the i-th member attribute.

We combine the evidence from all the member attributes to infer the aggregated value of $g_j^k = \frac{1}{|g_j^k|} \sum_{i=1}^{n} \lambda_i(s_j^i)$. The proposed approach is similar to the method of computing the relative support for the two different categories based on a naive Bayes model.

In order to compute the likelihood ratio value $\lambda_i(s_j^i)$ (see Fig. 3), we need to estimate the PDF $f_i^c(s)$ for each category. We assume that the expression level of semantic attributes under category c follows the Gaussian distribution with the mean and the standard deviation, μ_i^c and σ_i^c, respectively. These parameters are estimated based on all retrieval images that correspond to the category c. The estimated PDFs can then be used for computing the likelihood ratio. In general, we often do not have enough training image set for a reliable estimation of the PDFs $f_i^p(s)$ and $f_i^n(s)$. This may make the computation of the likelihood ratios sensitive to small changes in the scene images. To alleviate this problem, we normalize the $\lambda_i(s_j^i)$ as follows.

$$\hat{\lambda}_i(s_j^i) = \frac{\lambda_i(s_j^i) - \mu(\lambda_i)}{\sigma(\lambda_i)}, \tag{13}$$

where $\mu(\lambda_i)$ and $\sigma(\lambda_i)$ are the mean and standard deviation of $\lambda_i(s_j^i)$ across all images, respectively.

5   Experimental Result

5.1   Dataset

To evaluate the performance of the proposed method, three popular datasets are tested, i.e., Scene-15 [14], Sun-15 [28], and UIUC-sports dataset [18].

Scene-15 dataset [14] consists of 15 different scene categories. Each category consists of 200 to 400 grayscale images. The images are collected from the Google image search, the COREL collection, and personal photographs.

Sun-15 dataset consists of 15 different scene categories as the same with the Scene-15 dataset. We newly created this dataset from the SUN-397 dataset [28]. The SUN-397 dataset originally contains 397 scene categories. However, in this paper, we obtained the same categories only with the Scene-15 dataset from the original dataset.

UIUC-sports dataset [18] consists of 8 sports event categories. Each sports event category is organized as follows: rowing, badminton, polo, bocce, snowboarding, croquet, sailing, and rock climbing. Images are divided into easy and medium grade according to the human subject judgement.

For a fair comparison, we follow the original experimental setup applied in [10,14]. In the experiment, 100 images per category are randomly sampled as training images and remaining images are used as test images. In case of UIUC-sports dataset, 70 images per category are randomly sampled as training images, and the remaining images are used as test images. One-versus-all strategy is used because the scene classification is a multi-class problem and the evaluated performance is reported as the average classification rate on the all categories.

5.2   Measuring Expressions of Semantic Attributes

In order to obtain semantic attributes from scene images, we employ two approaches. First approach is the semantic attribute (SA) proposed in [25]. For this, four different types of local image features are used in this experiments as in [25]: SIFT [20], LAB [17], Canny edge [4], and Texton filterbanks [16].

We measure expression values of 67 semantic attributes based on the SA as in [25] from each scene image : local scene attributes (e.g. building, street, tree), shape attributes (e.g. box, circle, cone), materials (e.g. plastic, wood, stone), and objects (*e.g.* car, chair, bicycle). We learn a set of independent attribute classifiers using support vector machine (SVM) with Bhattacharyya kernel following the procedure in [25]. In order to measure the expression of each semantic attributes, non-negative SVM scores, which are obtained from results of a sigmoid function of the original SVM decision values, are used. The measured expression of each semantic attribute has a value between 0 and 1.

The other approach is the object bank (OB) proposed in [19]. The OB is obtained from an object filter response. The object responses are obtained by running a bunch of object filters across an image at various locations and scales by using the sliding window approach. Each filter is an object detector trained from images with similar view point. The models based on deformable part are applied for the object detector where six parts are used [11,19].

We measure expression values of 177 semantic attributes (objects) based on the OB as in [19] from each scene image. These 177 semantic attributes are determined from the popular image dataset such as ESP [1], LabelME [23], ImageNET [7], and Flickr! web site. After ranking the objects according to their frequencies in each of these datasets, the intersection set of the most frequent 1000 objects is obtained as the 177 semantic attributes. To train each of the 177 semantic attribute detectors, 100-200 images and their object bounding box information from the ImageNet dataset are used. In the training, a generalization of SVM called latent variable SVM (LSVM) is used for the semantic attribute detector [11]. In order to measure the expression of each semantic attribute, we follow the same procedure as in the SA case.

5.3   Discriminative Model Based Scene Classification

For scene classification, we use a SVM classifier with exponential chi-square kernel which is well-known to be suitable for the histogram-based image classification. The exponential chi-square kernel can be obtained as follows.

$$k_{chi-square}(x, y) = exp\left(-\frac{\gamma}{2} \sum_{i=1}^{n} \frac{(x_i - y_i)^2}{x_i + y_i}\right), \tag{14}$$

where γ is a scaling parameter.

The SVM-based scene classifier implemented by using LIBSVM [5]. One-versus-all strategy is used for a multi-class classification and the evaluated performance is reported as the average classification rate on the all categories. The final classification performance was obtained by average result of 50 times repeated experiments.

5.4   Comparative Results

Fig. 4 shows the performance evaluation results of the proposed methods compared with the existing methods in each semantic attribute approach. (Each semantic attribute approach is referred to as SA and OB, respectively.) As shown in Fig. 4, the proposed hypergraph-based method with the likelihood-ratio-based

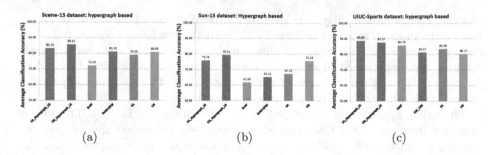

(a)   (b)   (c)

Fig. 4. Comparison of scene image classification performance with the hypergraph-based method with likelihood-ratio-based feature vector: (a) Scene-15 dataset (b) Sun-15 dataset (c) UIUC-Sports dataset

feature vector achieved outstanding performance compared with the existing methods on Scene-15, Sun-15, and UIUC-sports dataset.

In Scene-15 dataset experiment, the BoW model showed an improved performance when combined with spatial pyramid method (SPM) [14]. The methods marked as SA [25] and OB [19] are semantic-attribute-based scene classification approach in which each attribute considered individually. In the experiment, these methods showed better classification performance than the existing BoW model. However they showed lower classification result than the BoW+SPM model. On the other hand, the proposed method showed an improved result more than 4.5% compared to the results of the SA and OB considering each semantic attribute individually, even though it was not combined with the SPM unlike those in the original experiments [25,19].

In Sun-15 dataset experiment, the proposed method with the SA showed an improved result more than 10.6% compared to the result of the BoW+SPM. Especially, the proposed method with the OB showed a significantly improved result more than 14.2% compared to the result of the BoW+SPM. We can see that the method using only the Object Bank method also showed greatly improved result than existing methods. This result means that it is very important what semantic attributes are used for scene classification and how the semantic attributes are obtained from scene images.

In UIUC-sports dataset experiment, the proposed method showed an improved result more than 2.98% and 7.51% compared to the results of the HMP [2] and HIK-CBK [27], respectively. Also, in comparison with the result considering each semantic attribute individually, the proposed method showed a better result. Interestingly, unlike the previous experiments, we can see that the results using the SA-based feature vector showed better performance compared to the OB-based feature vector. We can analyze the results based on the discriminative power evaluation of feature vector. As shown in Fig. 5 (c) and Fig. 5 (f), the discriminative power of the generated feature vector based on the SA is more powerful than the generated feature vector based on the OB. More detail, the average discriminative power of top 10 features based on the SA (17.21) is bigger than the average discriminative power of top 10 features based on the OB

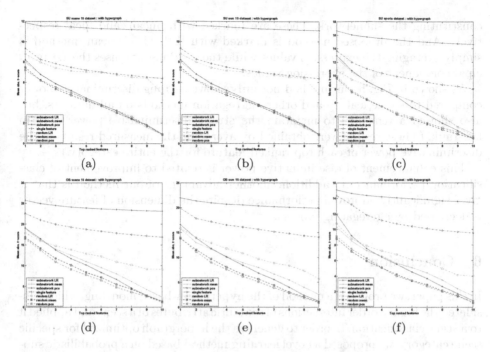

Fig. 5. Discriminative power comparison of the generated feature vectors from the SA- and OB-based semantic attributes subnetworks via the hypergraph-based method with likelihood ratio: (a) Scene-15 dataset (SA) (b) Sun-15 dataset (SA) (c) UIUC-Sports dataset (SA) (d) Scene-15 dataset (OB) (e) Sun-15 dataset (OB) (f) UIUC-Sports dataset (OB)

(15.01). Therefore, we can infer that the discriminative power of the feature vector may affect the classification performance.

Interestingly, in all experiments, we can see that the existing methods combined with the SPM were improved. We can analyze that it is a result of utilizing spatial context information. Therefore, we can expect to be able to achieve more improved performance when the subnetwork employed our method is combined with the SPM.

Previously, we analyzed that the reason why the proposed method can obtain competitive classification performance is that the discriminative power of the created feature vector by our method is strong. In order to verify this, we measured the discriminative power of feature vectors created by each method. In Fig. 5, the x-axis means rank of feature, y-axis means average absolute t-score of each feature. The discriminative power was measured using a mean absolute t-score of the top 10 features.

For a comparison, we also demonstrated a discriminative power of single semantic attribute and a discriminative power of feature vector generated from randomly selected subsets. (They are marked with single and random, respectively.) Furthermore, we compared experimental results for analyzing any difference due to the aggregation method of expression values of member attributes constituting the subnetwork. These are marked with 'mean' and 'pca' respectively. And the proposed method is marked with 'LR'. The 'mean' method is simply averaging the expression values while the 'pca' method uses the 1st principal component of the expression values.

As shown in Fig. 5, our method not only showed strong discriminative power compared to single feature and other aggregation methods on all datasets, but also showed a tendency to maintain the strong discriminative power even in low-rank. (These results were obtained by averaging the measured results of the discriminative power of each top ranked feature for the entire category.)

This enhancement of discriminative power is related to improvement of classification performance. In addition, another advantage of our method is that it gives significantly improved performance despite the dimension of feature vector is decreased by aggregating process.

6   Conclusion

In this paper, we proposed a method of the hypergraph-based modeling, which considered the higher-order interactions of semantic attributes of a scene and applied it to a scene classification. In order to generate the hypergraph optimized for specific scene category, we proposed a novel learning method based on a probabilistic subnetworks searching and also proposed a method to generate a aggregated feature vector from the expression values of the member semantic attributes that belongs to the searched subnetworks via likelihood-based estimation.

To verify the competitiveness of the proposed method, we showed that the discrimination power of the feature vector generated by the proposed method was better than existing methods through experiments. Also, in scene classification experime9nt, the proposed method showed an outstanding classification performance compared with the conventional methods. Thus, we could regard that the consider of the higher-order interaction of the semantic attributes may have an affect on the improvement of the scene classification performance.

Acknowledgement. This research was supported by NAVER Labs and Inha University Research Grant.

References

1. von Ahn, L.: Games with a purpose. Computer 39(6), 92–94 (2006)
2. Bo, L., Ren, X., Fox, D.: Hierarchical Matching Pursuit for Image Classification: Architecture and Fast Algorithms. MIT Press (2011)
3. Bosch, A., Zisserman, A., Muñoz, X.: Scene classification using a hybrid Generative/Discriminative approach. IEEE Trans. on Pattern Analysis and Machine Intelligence 30(4), 712–727 (2008)
4. Canny, J.: A computational approach to edge detection. IEEE Trans. on Pattern Analysis and Machine Intelligence 8(6), 679–698 (1986)

5. Chang, C.C., Lin, C.J.: LIBSVM: a library for support vector machines. ACM Trans. on Intelligent Systems and Technology 2(3), 27:1–27:27 (2011)
6. Csurka, G., Dance, C.R., Fan, L., Willamowski, J., Bray, C.: Visual categorization with bags of keypoints. In: Proc. of ECCV Workshop on Statistical Learning in Computer Vision, pp. 1–22 (May 2004)
7. Deng, J., Dong, W., Socher, R., Li, L.J., Li, K., Fei-Fei, L.: ImageNet: a large-scale hierarchical image database. In: Proc. of IEEE Conference on Computer Vision and Pattern Recognition, pp. 248–255 (June 2009)
8. Ding, C., Peng, H.: Minimum redundancy feature selection from microarray gene expression data. Journal of Bioinformatics and Computational Biology 3(2), 185–205 (2005)
9. Everingham, M., Van Gool, L., Williams, C., Winn, J., Zisserman, A.: The PAS-CAL visual object classes challenge 2007 (VOC 2007) results (2007), http://pascallin.ecs.soton.ac.uk/challenges/VOC/voc2007/
10. Fei-Fei, L., Perona, P.: A bayesian hierarchical model for learning natural scene categories. In: Proc. of IEEE International Conference on Computer Vision, vol. 2, pp. 524–531 (October 2005)
11. Felzenszwalb, P., McAllester, D., Ramanan, D.: A discriminatively trained, multiscale, deformable part model. In: Proc. of IEEE Conference on Computer Vision and Pattern Recognition, pp. 1–8 (June 2008)
12. Griffin, G., Holub, A., Perona, P.: Caltech-256 object category dataset. Tech. Rep. 7694 (March 2007)
13. Kleinberg, E.M.: Stochastic discrimination. Annals of Mathematics and Artificial Intelligence 1, 207–239 (1990)
14. Lazebnik, S., Schmid, C., Ponce, J.: Beyond bags of features: Spatial pyramid matching for recognizing natural scene categories. In: Proc. of IEEE Conference on Computer Vision and Pattern Recognition, pp. 2169–2178 (June 2006)
15. Leung, T., Malik, J.: Representing and recognizing the visual appearance of materials using three-dimensional textons. International Journal of Computer Vision 43(1), 29–44 (2001)
16. Leung, T., Malik, J.: Representing and recognizing the visual appearance of materials using three-dimensional textons. International Journal of Computer Vision 43(1), 29–44 (2001)
17. Lew, M.S.: Principles of visual information retrieval. Springer, London (2001)
18. Li, L.J., Fei-Fei, L.: What, where and who? classifying event by scene and object recognition. In: Proc. of IEEE International Conference on Computer Vision, pp. 1–8 (October 2007)
19. Li, L.J., Su, H., Xing, E., Fei-Fei, L.: Object bank: A high-level image representation for scene classification and semantic feature sparsification. In: Advances in Neural Information Processing Systems, pp. 1378–1386. MIT Press (2010)
20. Lowe, D.G.: Distinctive image features from scale-invariant keypoints. International Journal of Computer Vision 60(2), 91–110 (2004)
21. Lu, Y., Liu, P.Y., Xiao, P., Deng, H.W.: Hotelling's t2 multivariate profiling for detecting differential expression in microarrays. Bioinformatics 21(14), 3105–3113 (2005)
22. Rasiwasia, N., Vasconcelos, N.: Holistic context models for visual recognition. IEEE Transactions on Pattern Analysis and Machine Intelligence 34(5), 902–917 (2012)
23. Russell, B.C., Torralba, A., Murphy, K.P., Freeman, W.T.: LabelMe: a database and web-based tool for image annotation. International Journal of Computer Vision 77(1-3), 157–173 (2008)

24. Sivic, J., Zisserman, A.: Video google: A text retrieval approach to object matching in videos. In: Proc. of IEEE International Conference on Computer Vision, vol. 2, pp. 1470–1477 (October 2003)
25. Su, Y., Jurie, F.: Improving image classification using semantic attributes. International Journal of Computer Vision 100(1), 59–77 (2012)
26. Voloshin, V.I.: Introduction to graph and hypergraph theory. Nova Science Publishers, Hauppauge (2009)
27. Wu, J., Rehg, J.: Beyond the euclidean distance: Creating effective visual codebooks using the histogram intersection kernel. In: Proc. of IEEE International Conference on Computer Vision, pp. 630–637 (September 2009)
28. Xiao, J., Hays, J., Ehinger, K., Oliva, A., Torralba, A.: SUN database: Large-scale scene recognition from abbey to zoo. In: Proc. of IEEE Conference on Computer Vision and Pattern Recognition, pp. 3485–3492 (2010)
29. Zhang, B.T.: Hypernetworks: A molecular evolutionary architecture for cognitive learning and memory. IEEE Computational Intelligence Magazine 3(3), 49–63 (2008)

OTC: A Novel Local Descriptor for Scene Classification

Ran Margolin, Lihi Zelnik-Manor, and Ayellet Tal

Technion Haifa, Israel

Abstract. Scene classification is the task of determining the scene type in which a photograph was taken. In this paper we present a novel local descriptor suited for such a task: *Oriented Texture Curves* (OTC). Our descriptor captures the texture of a patch along multiple orientations, while maintaining robustness to illumination changes, geometric distortions and local contrast differences. We show that our descriptor outperforms all state-of-the-art descriptors for scene classification algorithms on the most extensive scene classification benchmark to-date.

Keywords: local descriptor, scene classification, scene recognition.

1 Introduction

Scene classification addresses the problem of determining the scene type in which a photograph was taken [6,18,21,27] (e.g. kitchen, tennis court, playground). The ability to recognize the scene of a given image can benefit many applications in computer vision, such as content-based image retrieval [32], inferring geographical location from an image [8] and object recognition [22].

Research on scene classification has addressed different parts of the scene classification framework: low-level representations, mid-level representations, high-level representations and learning frameworks.

Works on low-level representations focus on designing an appropriate local descriptor for scene classification. Xiao et al. [34] investigate the benefits of several well known low-level descriptors, such as HOG [2], SIFT [17] and SSIM [26]. Meng et al. [18] suggest the *Local Difference Binary Pattern* (LDBP) descriptor, which can be thought of as an extension of the LBP [20].

Mid-level representations deal with the construction of a global representation from low-level descriptors. Such representations include the well known bag-of-words (BoW) [29] and its extension to the *Spatial Pyramid Matching* (SPM) scheme [13], which by including some spatial considerations, has been shown to provide good results [34,18,13]. Karpac et. al [11] suggest the use of Fisher kernels to encode both the local features as well as their spatial layout.

High-level representations focus on the addition of semantic features [12,31] or incorporating an unsupervised visual concept learning framework [14]. The use of more sophisticated learning frameworks for scene classification include sparse coding [35], hierarchical-learning [27] and deep-learning [4,7].

D. Fleet et al. (Eds.): ECCV 2014, Part VII, LNCS 8695, pp. 377–391, 2014.

In this paper, we focus on low-level representations for scene classification. We propose a novel local descriptor: *Oriented Texture Curves* (OTC). The descriptor is based on three key ideas. (i) A patch contains different information along different orientations that should be captured. For each orientation we construct a curve that represents the color variation of the patch along that orientation. (ii) The shapes of these curves characterize the texture of the patch. We represent the shape of a curve by its shape properties, which are robust to illumination differences and geometric distortions of the patch. (iii) Homogeneous patches require special attention to avoid the creation of false features. We do so by suggesting an appropriate normalization scheme. This normalization scheme is generic and can be used in other domains.

Our main contributions are two-fold. First, we propose a novel descriptor, OTC, for scene classification. We show that it achieves an improvement of 7.35% in accuracy over the previously top-performing descriptor, HOG2x2 [5]. Second, we show that a combination between the HOG2x2 descriptor and our OTC descriptor results in an 11.6% improvement in accuracy over the previously top-performing scene classification feature-based algorithm that employs 14 descriptors [34].

2   The OTC Descriptor

Our goal is to design a descriptor that satisfies the following two attributes that were shown to be beneficial for scene classification [34].

- **Rotational-Sensitivity:** Descriptors that are not rotationally invariant provide better classification than rotationally invariant descriptors [34]. This is since scenes are almost exclusively photographed parallel to ground. Therefore, horizontal features, such as railings, should be differentiated from vertical features, such as fences. This is the reason why descriptors, such as HOG2x2 [5] and Dense SIFT [13], outperform rotationally invariant descriptors, such as Sparse SIFT [30] and LBP [20,1].

- **Texture:** The top-ranking descriptors for scene classification are texture-based [34]. Furthermore, a good texture-based descriptor should be robust to illumination changes, local contrast differences and geometric distortions [19]. This is since, while different photographs of a common scene may differ in color, illumination or spatial layout, they usually share similar, but not identical, dominant textures. Thus, the HOG2x2 [5], a texture-based descriptor, was found to outperform all other non-texture based descriptors [34].

In what follows we describe in detail the OTC descriptor, which is based on our three key ideas and the two desired attributes listed above. In Section 2.1, we suggest a rotationally-sensitive patch representation by way of multiple curves. The curves characterize the information contained along different orientations of a patch. In Section 2.2 we propose a novel curve representation that is robust

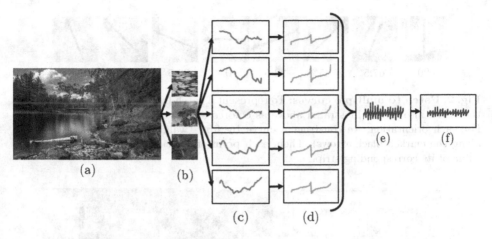

Fig. 1. OTC overview: Given an image (a), patches are sampled along a dense grid (b). By traversing each patch along multiple orientations, the patch is represented by multiple curves (c). Each curve is characterized by a novel curve descriptor that is robust to illumination differences and geometric distortions (d). The curve descriptor are then concatenated to form a single descriptor (e). Finally, the OTC descriptor is obtained by applying a novel normalization scheme that avoids the creation of false features while offering robustness to local contrast differences (f).

to illumination differences and geometric distortions. Lastly, we concatenate the obtained multiple curve descriptors into a single descriptor and suggest a novel normalization scheme that avoids the creation of false features in the descriptors of homogeneous patches (Section 2.3). An overview of our framework is illustrated in Figure 1.

2.1   Patch to Multiple Curves

Our first goal is to describe the texture of a given patch. It has been shown that different features exhibit different dominant orientations [19]. Thus, by examining a patch along different orientations, different features can be captured.

To do so, we divide an $N \times N$ patch P into N strips along different orientations (in practice, 8), as shown in Figure 2. For each orientation θ, an N-point sampled curve c_θ is constructed. The ith sampled point along the oriented curve c_θ is computed as the mean value of its ith oriented strip $S_{\theta,i}$:

$$c_\theta(i) = \frac{1}{|S_{\theta,i}|} \sum_{x \in S_{\theta,i}} P(x) \quad 1 \leq i \leq N, \tag{1}$$

$|S_{\theta,i}|$ denoting the number of pixels contained within strip $S_{\theta,i}$. For an RGB colored patch, $C_\theta(i)$ is computed as the mean RGB triplet of its ith oriented strip $S_{\theta,i}$. Note that by employing strips of predefined orientations, regardless of the input patch, we effectively enforce the desired property of rotational-sensitivity.

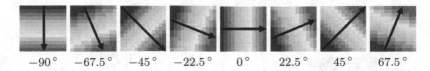

$$-90° \qquad -67.5° \qquad -45° \qquad -22.5° \qquad 0° \qquad 22.5° \qquad 45° \qquad 67.5°$$

Fig. 2. Patch to multiple curves: To represent a patch by multiple curves, we divide the patch into strips (illustrated above as colored strips) along multiple orientations. For each orientation, we construct a curve by first "walking" across the strips (i.e. along the marked black arrows). Then, each point of the curve is defined as the mean value of its corresponding strip.

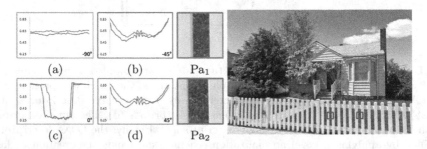

Fig. 3. Illumination differences and geometric distortions: (a-d) Curves obtained along four orientations of two very similar patches, Pa$_1$ & Pa$_2$ (blue for Pa$_1$ and red for Pa$_2$). The generated curves are different due to illumination and geometric differences between the patches. Thus, a more robust curve representation is required.

2.2 Curve Descriptor

Our second goal is to construct a discriminative descriptor that is robust to illumination differences and geometric distortions. An example why such robustness is needed is presented in Figure 3. Two patches were selected. The patches are very similar but not identical. Differences between them include their illumination, the texture of the grass, the spacing between the white fence posts, and their centering. This can be seen by observing their four curves (generated along four orientations) shown on the left. The differences in illumination can be observed by the difference in heights of the two curves (i.e. the more illuminated patch Pa$_1$ results in a higher curve than Pa$_2$). The geometric differences between the two patches can be observed in Figure 3(c). Due to the difference in spacing between the white fence posts, the drop of the red curve is to the left of the drop of the blue curve. We hence conclude that these curves are not sufficiently robust to illumination differences and geometric distortions.

Looking again at Figure 3, it can be seen that while the curves are different, their *shapes* are highly similar. To capture the shape of these curves we describe each curve by its gradients and curvatures. For a gray-level patch, for each curve c_θ we compute its forward gradient $c'_\theta(i)$ and an approximation of its curvature $c''_\theta(i)$ [3] as:

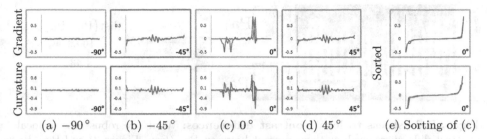

(a) $-90°$ (b) $-45°$ (c) $0°$ (d) $45°$ (e) Sorting of (c)

Fig. 4. Gradients and Curvatures: The resulting gradients and curvatures of the four curves in Figure 3 (a-d). While offering an improvement in terms of robustness to illumination differences, this representation is still sensitive to geometric distortions (c). By applying a sorting permutation, robustness to such distortions is enforced (e).

$$c'_\theta(i) = c_\theta(i+1) - c_\theta(i) \qquad\qquad 1 \leq i < N \qquad\qquad (2)$$

$$c''_\theta(i) = c'_\theta(i+1) - c'_\theta(i) \qquad\qquad 1 \leq i < (N-1). \qquad\qquad (3)$$

For RGB curves, we define the forward RGB gradient between two points as the L_2 distance between them, signed according to their gray-level gradient:

$$C'_\theta(i) = sign\{c'_\theta(i)\} \cdot ||C_\theta(i+1) - C_\theta(i)||_2 \qquad 1 \leq i < N \qquad (4)$$

$$C''_\theta(i) = C'_\theta(i+1) - C'_\theta(i) \qquad\qquad 1 \leq i < (N-1). \qquad (5)$$

The resulting gradients and curvatures of the four curves shown in Figure 3 are presented in Figure 4(a-d). While offering an improvement in robustness to illumination differences, the gradients and curvatures in Figure 4(c) still differ. The differences are due to geometric differences between the patches (e.g. the centering of the patch and the spacing between the fence posts). Since scenes of the same category share similar, but not necessarily identical textures, we must allow some degree of robustness to these types of geometric distortions.

A possible solution to this could be some complex distance measure between signals such as dynamic time warping [24]. Apart from the computational penalty involved in such a solution, employing popular mid-level representations such as BoW via K-means is problematic when the centroids of samples are ill-defined. Another solution that has been shown to provide good results are histograms [2,10,17]. While histogram-based representations perform well [19], they suffer from two inherent flaws. The first is quantization error, which may be alleviated to some degree with the use of soft-binning. The second flaw concerns weighted histograms, in which two different distributions may result in identical representations.

Instead, we suggest an alternative orderless representation to that of histograms, which involves applying some permutation π to each descriptor C'_θ and C''_θ. Let dsc_1 and dsc_2 denote two descriptors (e.g. those presented in Figure 4(c)-top in red and blue). The permutation we seek is the one that minimizes the L_1 distance between them:

$$\pi = \arg\min_{\hat{\pi}} \{||\hat{\pi}(dsc_1) - \hat{\pi}(dsc_2)||_1\}. \qquad (6)$$

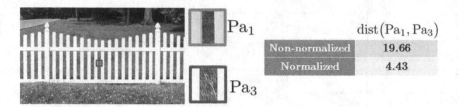

Fig. 5. Robustness to local contrast differences: We desire robustness to local contrast differences, such as those present between Pa_1 (from Figure 3) and Pa_3. By applying a normalization scheme, robustness to such differences is obtained.

A solution to Equation (6) is found in the following theorem, for which we provide proof in Appendix A.

Theorem 1. *The permutation that minimizes the L_1 distance between two vectors (descriptors) is the sorting permutation π_{sort}.*

That is to say, we sort each gradient (or curvature) in a non-decreasing manner. Sorting has been previously used to achieve rotational invariance [33,16]. Yet, since our curves are constructed along predefined orientations, we maintain the desired attribute of rotational-sensitivity, while achieving robustness to geometric distortions. Figure 4(e) illustrates the result of sorting the gradients and curvatures shown in Figure 4(c). It is easy to see that this results in a very similar response for both patches.

2.3   H-bin Normalization

Thus far, we have constructed a robust curve representation. Keeping in mind our goal of a patch descriptor, we proceed to concatenate the sorted gradients and curvatures:

$$OTC_{\text{No-Norm}} = \left\{ \pi_{sort}(C'_{\theta_1}), \pi_{sort}(C''_{\theta_1}), \ldots, \pi_{sort}(C'_{\theta_8}), \pi_{sort}(C''_{\theta_8}) \right\}. \qquad (7)$$

While offering a patch descriptor that is robust to illumination differences and geometric distortions, the descriptor still lacks robustness to local contrast differences. An example of such differences is illustrated in Figure 5. A similar patch to that sampled in Figure 3 is sampled from a different image. The patches differ in their local contrast, therefore they are found to have a large L_1 distance.

To support robustness to local contrast differences, we wish to normalize our descriptor. The importance of an appropriate normalization scheme has been previously stressed [2]. Examples of normalization schemes include the well known L_1 and L_2 norms, the overlapping normalization scheme [2] and the L_2-Hys normalization [17]. Unfortunately, these schemes fail to address the case of a *textureless* patch. Since the OTC descriptor is texture-based, textureless patches result in a descriptor that contains mostly noise. Examples of such patches can be found in the sky region in Figure 3.

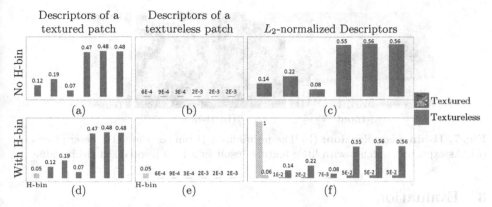

Fig. 6. H-bin normalization scheme: Under previous normalization schemes, descriptors of textureless patches (b) are stretched into false features (c)-blue. By adding a low-valued bin, prior to normalization (d-e), false features are avoided (f)-blue. In case of a descriptor of a textured patch (d), the small value hardly affects the normalized result ((f)-red compared to (c)-red). The added H-bin may be thought of as a measure of homogeneity.

The problem of normalizing a descriptor of a textureless patch is that its noisy content is stretched into false features. An example of this can be seen in Figure 6. The descriptors of a textured patch and a textureless patch are shown in Figure 6(a-b). Applying L_2 normalization to both descriptors results in identical descriptors (Figure 6(c)).

To overcome this, we suggest a simple yet effective method. For each descriptor, we add a small-valued bin (0.05), which we denote as the *Homogeneous-bin* (H-bin). While the rest of the descriptor measures the features within a patch, the H-bin measures the lack of features therein. We then apply L_2 normalization. Due to the small value of the H-bin, it hardly affects patches that contain features. Yet, it prevents the generation of false features in textureless patches. An example can be seen in Figure 6. An H-bin was added to the descriptor of both textured and textureless patches (Figure 6(d-e)). After normalization, the descriptor of the textured patch is hardly affected ((f)-red compared to (c)-red). Yet, the normalized descriptor of the textureless patch retains its low valued features. This is while indicating the presence of a textureless patch by its large H-bin (Figure 6(f)-blue). In Figure 7(b) we present the H-bins of the L_2-normalized OTC descriptors of Figure 7(a). As expected the sky region is found as textureless, while the rest of the image is identified as textured.

Thus, the final OTC descriptor is obtained by:

$$\text{OTC} = \frac{\{\text{H-bin}, \text{OTC}_{\text{No-Norm}}\}}{\left\|\{\text{H-bin}, \text{OTC}_{\text{No-Norm}}\}\right\|_2}. \tag{8}$$

(a) Input	(b) H-bin

Fig. 7. H-bin visualization: (b) The normalized H-bins of the OTC descriptors of (a). As expected, patches with little texture result in a high normalized H-bin value.

3   Evaluation

Benchmark: To evaluate the benefit of our OTC descriptor, we test its performance on the SUN397 benchmark [34], the most extensive scene classification benchmark to-date. The benchmark includes 397 categories, amounting to a total of $108,574$ color images, which is several orders of magnitude larger than previous datasets. The dataset includes a widely diverse set of indoor and outdoor scenes, ranging from elevator-shafts to tree-houses, making it highly robust to over-fitting. In addition, the benchmark is well defined with a strict evaluation scheme of 10 cross-validations of 50 training images and 50 testing images per category. The average accuracy across all categories is reported.

OTC Setup: To fairly evaluate the performance of our low-level representation, we adopt the simple mid-level representation and learning scheme that were used in [34]. Given an image, we compute its OTC descriptors on a dense 3×3 grid (images were resized to contain no more than 300^2 pixels). Each descriptor is computed on a 13×13 sized patch, resulting in a total length of $\underbrace{8}_{orientations} \times (\underbrace{12}_{gradient} + \underbrace{11}_{curvature}) = $ 184 values per patch. After adding the H-bin and normalizing, our final descriptors are of length 185. The local OTC descriptors are then used in a 3-level Spatial Pyramid Matching scheme (SPM) [13] with a BoW of 1000 words via L_1 K-means clustering. Histogram intersection [13] is used to compute the distance between two SPMs. Lastly, we use a simple 1-vs-all SVM classification framework.

In what follows we begin by comparing the classification accuracy of our OTC descriptor to state-of-the-art descriptors and algorithms (Section 3.1). We then proceed in Section 3.2 to analyze its classification performance in more detail.

3.1   Benchmark Results

To demonstrate the benefits of our low-level representation we first compare our OTC descriptor to other state-of-the-art low-level descriptors with the common mid-level representation and a 1-vs-all SVM classification scheme of [34].

In Table 1(left) we present the top-four performing descriptors on the SUN397 benchmark [34]: (1) *Dense SIFT* [13]: SIFT descriptors are extracted on a dense grid for each of the HSV color channels and stacked together. A 3-level SPM mid-level representation with a 300 BoW is used. (2) *SSIM* [26]: SSIM descriptors are extracted on a dense grid and quantized into a 300 BoW. The χ^2 distance is used to compute the distance between two spatial histograms. (3) *G-tex* [34]: Using the method of [9], the probability of four geometric classes are computed: ground, vertical, porous and sky. Then, a texton histogram is built for each class, weighted by the probability that it belongs to that geometric class. The histograms are normalized and compared with the χ^2 distance. (4) *HOG2x2* [5]: HOG descriptors are computed on a dense grid. Then, 2×2 neighboring HOG descriptors are stacked together to provide enhanced descriptive power. Histogram intersection is used to compute the distance between the obtained 3-level SPMs with a 300 BoW.

As shown in Table 1, our proposed OTC descriptor significantly outperforms previous descriptors. We achieve an improvement of 7.35% with a 1000 BoW and an improvement of 3.98% with a 300 BoW (denoted OTC-300).

Table 1. SUN397 state-of-the-art performance: *Left:* Our OTC descriptor outperforms all previous descriptors. *Right:* Performance of more complex state-of-the-art algorithms. Our simple combination of OTC and HOG2x2 outperforms most of the state-of-the-art algorithms.

Descriptors		Algorithms	
Name	Accuracy	Name	Accuracy
Dense SIFT [13]	21.5	ML-DDL [27]	23.1
SSIM [26]	22.5	S-Manifold [12]	28.9
G-tex [34]	23.5	**OTC**	**34.56**
HOG2x2 [5]	27.2	contextBow-m+semantic [31]	35.6
OTC-300	31.18	14 Combined Features [34]	38
OTC	**34.56**	DeCAF [4]	40.94
		OTC + HOG2x2	**49.6**
		MOP-CNN [7]	51.98

Since most recent works deal with mid-level representations, high-level representations and learning schemes, we further compare in Table 1(right) our descriptor to more complex state-of-the-art scene classification algorithms: (1) *ML-DDL* [27] suggests a novel learning scheme that takes advantage of the hierarchical correlation between scene categories. Based on densely sampled SIFT descriptors a dictionary and a classification model are learned for each hierarchy (3 hierarchies are defined for the SUN397 dataset [34]). (2) *S-Manifold* [12] suggests a mid-level representation that combines the SPM representation with a semantic manifold [25]. Densely samples SIFT descriptors are used as local descriptors. (3) *contextBoW-m+semantic* [31] suggests both mid-level and high-level representations in which pre-learned context classifiers are used to construct multiple context-based BoWs. Five local features are used (four low-level and one high-level): SIFT, texton filterbanks, LAB color values, Canny edge detection and the inferred semantic classification. (4) *14 Combined Features* [34] combines the distance kernels obtained by 14 descriptors (four of which appear in Table 1(left)). (5,6) *DeCAF* [4] & *MOP-CNN* [7] both employ a deep convolutional neural network.

In Table 1(right) we show that by simply combining the distance kernels of our OTC descriptor and those of the HOG2x2 descriptor (at a 56-44 ratio), we outperform most other more complex scene classification algorithms. A huge improvement of 11.6% over the previous top performing feature-based algorithm is achieved. A nearly comparable result is achieved when compared to MOP-CNN that is based on a complex convolutional neural network.

For completeness, in Table 2 we compare our OTC descriptor on two additional smaller benchmarks: the 15-scene dataset [13] and the MIT-indoor dataset [23]. In both benchmarks, our simplistic framework outperforms all other descriptors in similar simplistic frameworks. Still, several state-of-the-art complex methods offer better performance than our framework. We believe that incorporating our OTC descriptor into these more complex algorithms would improve their performance even further.

Table 2. 15-scene & MIT-indoor datasets: Our OTC descriptor outperforms previous descriptors and is comparable with several more complex methods

15-scene		MIT-indoor	
Name	Accuracy	Name	Accuracy
SSIM [26]	77.2	SIFT [13]	34.40
G-tex [34]	77.8	Discriminative patches [28]	38.10
HOG2x2 [5]	81.0	**OTC**	**47.33**
SIFT [13]	81.2	Disc. Patches++ [28]	49.40
OTC	**84.37**	ISPR + IFV [15]	68.5
ISPR + IFV [15]	91.06	MOP-CNN [7]	68.88

3.2   Classification Analysis

In what follows we provide an analysis of the classification accuracy of our descriptor on the top two hierarchies of the SUN397 dataset. The 1st level consists of three categories: indoor, outdoor nature and outdoor man-made. The 2nd level consists of 16 categories (listed in Figure 9).

In Figure 8(left) we present the confusion matrix on the 1st level of the SUN397 dataset for which an impressive 84.45% success rate is achieved (comparison to other methods is shown later). Studying the matrix, confusion is mostly apparent between indoor & outdoor man-made scenes and within the two types of outdoor scenes. Misclassification between indoor and outdoor man-made scenes is understandable, since both scene types consist of similar textures such as straight horizontal and vertical lines, as evident by comparing the image of the Bookstore scene to that of the Fire-escape (Figure 8(top-right)). Differences between outdoor nature scenes and outdoor man-made scenes are often contextual, such as the Pasture and Racecourse images shown in

Figure 8(bottom-right). Thus, it is no surprise that a texture-based classification may confuse between the two.

The 2nd level confusion matrix is displayed in Figure 9. Our average success rate is 57.2%. Most confusions occur between categories of similar indoor or outdoor settings. Furthermore, we note that the two categories with the highest errors are Commercial Buildings and House, Garden & Farm. The former is

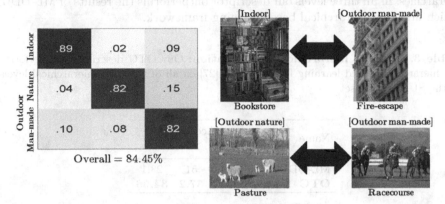

.89	.02	.09
.04	.82	.15
.10	.08	.82

Overall = 84.45%

Fig. 8. 1st level confusion matrix: *Left:* The confusion matrix of our OTC descriptor on the 1st level of the SUN397 dataset shows that most misclassifications occur between indoor & outdoor man-made scenes, and within the two types of outdoor scenes. *Right:* Images in which the classification was mistakingly swapped.

	S&D	Work	H&H	Tr	S&L	Cult	W,I,S	M,Sk	F&J	MM	Tr	HB	Pk	Ind	HG&F	CB
Shopping & Dining	.52	.09	.06	.05	.05	.10	.01			.01	.02	.02	.01		.02	.04
Workplace	.08	.50	.11	.06	.05	.08	.01		.01	.01	.02	.01	.02	.01	.02	.03
Home & Hotel	.05	.10	.58	.05	.06	.08	.01			.01	.01	.01	.01		.02	.02
Transportation	.05	.08	.05	.65	.06	.05	.01			.01		.01			.01	.01
Sports & Leisure	.05	.08	.06	.05	.59	.06	.01			.01	.01	.04			.01	.01
Cultural	.08	.09	.08	.04	.05	.53	.01	.01			.01	.02	.02	.01	.02	.03
Water, Ice, Snow	.01	.01			.01	.01	.66	.06	.06	.03	.03	.02	.04	.01	.03	.01
Mountains, Sky					.01	.01	.12	.63	.06	.03	.01	.02	.02	.03	.02	.02
Forests & Jungle	.01	.01			.01	.01	.06	.04	.66	.02	.03	.03	.06	.02	.03	.02
Man-made elements	.01	.01	.01		.01	.01	.08	.04	.08	.53	.04	.04	.06	.02	.04	.03
Transportation	.01	.02	.01	.02	.02	.02	.05	.01	.03	.03	.54	.04	.08	.03	.04	.05
Historical Buildings	.02	.01	.01	.01	.01	.03	.03	.02	.03	.03	.05	.53	.04	.04	.06	.08
Parks	.01	.01	.01	.01	.03	.01	.05	.02	.05	.03	.04	.03	.60	.02	.06	.03
Industrial	.02	.02	.01	.01	.01	.05	.04	.03	.03	.07	.07	.05		.51	.03	.05
House, Garden & Farm	.02	.02	.02	.01	.01	.02	.04	.02	.08	.04	.04	.05	.07	.02	.49	.06
Commercial Buildings	.04	.03	.03	.01	.02	.04	.01	.01	.02	.02	.04	.09	.05	.03	.07	.49

Overall=57.2%

Fig. 9. 2nd level confusion matrix: The confusion matrix of our OTC descriptor on the 2nd level of the SUN397 dataset shows that most confusions occur between categories of similar indoor or outdoor settings. Furthermore, most confusions occur between classes of semantic differences such as Home & Hotel and Workplace. These understandable misclassifications further confirm the strength of our OTC descriptor at capturing similar textures.

mostly confused with Historical Buildings and the latter with Forests & Jungle. These understandable semantic confusions further confirm the robustness of the classification strength of our OTC descriptor.

Lastly, we compare in Table 3 the average classification accuracy of our OTC descriptor on each of the three hierarchical levels, to that of ML-DDL [27]. ML-DDL is the best performing algorithm to reports results on the different hierarchies. In all three levels our descriptor outperforms the results of ML-DDL, which utilizes a hierarchical based learning framework.

Table 3. SUN397 hierarchical classification: Our OTC descriptor outperforms the hierarchical based learning framework of [27] on all of the three hierarchical levels of the SUN397 dataset

Name	Accuracy		
	1st	2nd	3rd
ML-DDL [27]	83.4	51	23.1
OTC	**84.45**	**57.2**	**34.56**

4   Conclusion

We presented the OTC descriptor, a novel low-level representation for scene classification. The descriptor is based on three main ideas. First, representing the texture of a patch along different orientations by the shapes of multiple curves. Second, using sorted gradients and curvatures as curve descriptors, which are robust to illumination differences and geometric distortions of the patch. Third, enforcing robustness to local contrast differences by applying a novel normalization scheme that avoids the creation of false features.

Our descriptor achieves an improvement of 7.35% in accuracy over the previously top-performing descriptor, on the most extensive scene classification benchmark [34]. We further showed that a combination between the HOG2x2 descriptor [5] and our OTC descriptor results in an 11.6% improvement in accuracy over the previously top-performing scene classification feature-based algorithm that employs 14 descriptors.

A   Proof of Theorem 1

Theorem 1. *The permutation that minimizes the L_1 distance between two vectors (descriptors) is the sorting permutation π_{sort}.*

Proof. Let $\acute{a}_{1 \times N}$ and $\acute{b}_{1 \times N}$ be two vectors of length N. We apply permutation π_b that sorts the elements of $\acute{b}_{1 \times N}$ to both vectors $\acute{a}_{1 \times N}$ and $\acute{b}_{1 \times N}$. Note that applying this permutation to both vectors $\left(a_{1 \times N} = \pi_b(\acute{a}_{1 \times N}), b_{1 \times N} = \pi_b(\acute{b}_{1 \times N})\right)$

does not change their L_1 distance.

Proof by induction on the length of the vectors, N:
For the basis of the induction let $N = 2$. Let x_i denote the ith element in vector x. Below we provide proof for the case of $a_1 \leq a_2$ (Recall that $b_1 \leq b_2$). A similar proof can be done for $a_2 \leq a_1$.
We show that $\underbrace{|b_1 - a_1| + |b_2 - a_2|}_{LH} \leq \underbrace{|b_1 - a_2| + |b_2 - a_1|}_{RH}$:

$$(b_1 \leq b_2 \leq a_1 \leq a_2): LH = a_1 + a_2 - b_1 - b_2 = RH \tag{9}$$

$$(b_1 \leq a_1 \leq b_2 \leq a_2): LH = a_1 - b_2 + a_2 - b_1 \underbrace{\leq}_{a_1 \leq b_2} = b_2 - a_1 + a_2 - b_1 = RH \tag{10}$$

$$(b_1 \leq a_1 \leq a_2 \leq b_2): LH = a_1 - b_1 + b_2 - a_2 \underbrace{\leq}_{a_1 \leq a_2} a_2 - b_1 + b_2 - a_1 = RH \tag{11}$$

$$(a_1 \leq b_1 \leq b_2 \leq a_2): LH = b_1 - a_1 + a_2 - b_2 \underbrace{\leq}_{b_1 \leq b_2} b_2 - a_1 + a_2 - b_1 = RH \tag{12}$$

$$(a_1 \leq b_1 \leq a_2 \leq b_2): LH = b_1 - a_1 + b_2 - a_2 \underbrace{\leq}_{b_1 \leq a_2} a_2 - a_1 + b_2 - b_1 = RH \tag{13}$$

$$(a_1 \leq a_2 \leq b_1 \leq b_2): LH = b_1 + b_2 - a_1 - a_2 = RH \tag{14}$$

Now suppose that the theorem holds for $N < K$. We prove that it holds for $N = K$.

First, we prove that given a permutation π that minimizes $||b - \pi(a)||_1 \Rightarrow \pi$ is the sorting permutation π_{sort}.
Let π be some permutation applied to a, so that a minimal L_1 distance is achieved:

$$\pi = \arg\min_{\pi} \{||b - \pi(a)||_1\}. \tag{15}$$

Let $x_{i:j}$ denote a sub-vector of a vector x from index i to index j.
We can decompose $D = ||b - \pi(a)||_1$ into $D = \underbrace{||b_1 - \pi(a)_1||_1}_{D_1} + \underbrace{||b_{2:K} - \pi(a)_{2:K}||_1}_{D_{2:K}}$.
The minimality of D infers the minimality of $D_{2:K}$. Otherwise, a smaller L_1 distance can be found by reordering the elements of $\pi(a)_{2:K}$, contradicting the minimality of D. Following our hypothesis, we deduce that $\pi(a)_{2:K}$ is sorted. Specifically $\pi(a)_2 = \min\{\pi(a)_{2:K}\}$.
Similarly, by decomposing D into $D = \underbrace{||b_{1:(K-1)} - \pi(a)_{1:(K-1)}||_1}_{D_{1:(K-1)}} + \underbrace{||b_K - \pi(a)_K||_1}_{D_K}$
we deduce that $\pi(a)_1 = \min\{\pi(a)_{1:(K-1)}\} \leq \pi(a)_2$.
This implies, that $\pi(a)$ is sorted and that $\pi = \pi_{sort}$.

Next, we prove the other side, i.e. if $\pi = \pi_{sort} \Rightarrow \pi$ minimizes $||b - \pi(a)||_1$.
Assume to the contrary that there exists a non-sorting permutation $\pi_{min} \neq \pi_{sort}$

that can achieve a minimal L_1 distance D', which is smaller than $D = ||b - \pi_{sort}(a)||_1$. Then, there must be at least two elements $\pi_{min}(a)_i > \pi_{min}(a)_j$ that are out of order (i.e. $i < j$).
We can decompose D' into:

$$D' = \sum_{k \neq i,j} |b_k - \pi_{min}(a)_k| + ||(b_i, b_j) - (\pi_{min}(a)_i, \pi_{min}(a)_j)||_1. \qquad (16)$$

$$(17)$$

Yet, as proved in the basis of our induction, the following inequality is true:

$$||(b_i, b_j) - (\pi_{min}(a)_i, \pi_{min}(a)_j)||_1 \underbrace{<}_{\pi_{min}(a)_j < \pi_{min}(a)_i} ||(b_i, b_j) - (\pi_{min}(a)_j, \pi_{min}(a)_i)||_1. \qquad (18)$$

Therefore, a smaller L_1 distance can be achieved (by reordering $\pi_{min}(a)_i$ and $\pi_{min}(a)_j$), contradicting the assumption that D' is minimal. Thus, no other permutation can achieve a smaller L_1 distance than the sorting permutation (i.e. π_{sort} is the permutation the minimizes $||b - \pi_{sort}(a)||_1$). ☐

References

1. Ahonen, T., Matas, J., He, C., Pietikäinen, M.: Rotation invariant image description with local binary pattern histogram fourier features. In: Salberg, A.-B., Hardeberg, J.Y., Jenssen, R. (eds.) SCIA 2009. LNCS, vol. 5575, pp. 61–70. Springer, Heidelberg (2009)
2. Dalal, N., Triggs, B.: Histograms of oriented gradients for human detection. In: CVPR, vol. 1, pp. 886–893 (2005)
3. Do, C., Manfredo, P.: Differential geometry of curves and surfaces, vol. 2. Prentice-Hall Englewood Cliffs (1976)
4. Donahue, J., Jia, Y., Vinyals, O., Hoffman, J., Zhang, N., Tzeng, E., Darrell, T.: Decaf: A deep convolutional activation feature for generic visual recognition. In: International Conference on Machine Learning, pp. 647–655 (2014)
5. Felzenszwalb, P.F., Girshick, R.B., McAllester, D., Ramanan, D.: Object detection with discriminatively trained part-based models. PAMI 32(9), 1627–1645 (2010)
6. Gao, T., Koller, D.: Discriminative learning of relaxed hierarchy for large-scale visual recognition. In: ICCV, pp. 2072–2079 (2011)
7. Gong, Y., Wang, L., Guo, R., Lazebnik, S.: Multi-scale orderless pooling of deep convolutional activation features. CoRR (2014)
8. Hays, J., Efros, A.A.: Im2gps: estimating geographic information from a single image. In: CVPR, pp. 1–8 (2008)
9. Hoiem, D., Efros, A.A., Hebert, M.: Recovering surface layout from an image. IJCV 75(1), 151–172 (2007)
10. Koenderink, J.J., Van Doorn, A.J.: The structure of locally orderless images. IJCV 31(2-3), 159–168 (1999)
11. Krapac, J., Verbeek, J., Jurie, F.: Modeling spatial layout with fisher vectors for image categorization. In: ICCV, pp. 1487–1494 (2011)
12. Kwitt, R., Vasconcelos, N., Rasiwasia, N.: Scene recognition on the semantic manifold. In: Fitzgibbon, A., Lazebnik, S., Perona, P., Sato, Y., Schmid, C. (eds.) ECCV 2012, Part IV. LNCS, vol. 7575, pp. 359–372. Springer, Heidelberg (2012)

13. Lazebnik, S., Schmid, C., Ponce, J.: Beyond bags of features: Spatial pyramid matching for recognizing natural scene categories. In: CVPR, pp. 2169–2178 (2006)
14. Li, Q., Wu, J., Tu, Z.: Harvesting mid-level visual concepts from large-scale internet images. In: CVPR, pp. 851–858 (2013)
15. Lin, D., Lu, C., Liao, R., Jia, J.: Learning important spatial pooling regions for scene classification. In: CVPR (2014)
16. Liu, L., Fieguth, P., Kuang, G., Zha, H.: Sorted random projections for robust texture classification. In: ICCV, pp. 391–398 (2011)
17. Lowe, D.G.: Object recognition from local scale-invariant features. In: ICCV, vol. 2, pp. 1150–1157 (1999)
18. Meng, X., Wang, Z., Wu, L.: Building global image features for scene recognition. Pattern Recognition 45(1), 373–380 (2012)
19. Mikolajczyk, K., Schmid, C.: A performance evaluation of local descriptors. PAMI 27(10), 1615–1630 (2005)
20. Ojala, T., Pietikainen, M., Maenpaa, T.: Multiresolution gray-scale and rotation invariant texture classification with local binary patterns. PAMI 24(7), 971–987 (2002)
21. Oliva, A., Torralba, A.: Modeling the shape of the scene: A holistic representation of the spatial envelope. IJCV 42(3), 145–175 (2001)
22. Oliva, A., Torralba, A.: The role of context in object recognition. Trends in Cognitive Sciences 11(12), 520–527 (2007)
23. Quattoni, A., Torralba, A.: Recognizing indoor scenes. In: CVPR (2009)
24. Rabiner, L.R., Juang, B.H.: Fundamentals of speech recognition. Prentice Hall (1993)
25. Rasiwasia, N., Vasconcelos, N.: Scene classification with low-dimensional semantic spaces and weak supervision. In: CVPR, pp. 1–6 (2008)
26. Shechtman, E., Irani, M.: Matching local self-similarities across images and videos. In: CVPR, pp. 1–8 (2007)
27. Shen, L., Wang, S., Sun, G., Jiang, S., Huang, Q.: Multi-level discriminative dictionary learning towards hierarchical visual categorization. In: CVPR, pp. 383–390 (2013)
28. Singh, S., Gupta, A., Efros, A.A.: Unsupervised discovery of mid-level discriminative patches. In: Fitzgibbon, A., Lazebnik, S., Perona, P., Sato, Y., Schmid, C. (eds.) ECCV 2012, Part II. LNCS, vol. 7573, pp. 73–86. Springer, Heidelberg (2012)
29. Sivic, J., Zisserman, A.: Video google: A text retrieval approach to object matching in videos. In: ICCV, pp. 1470–1477 (2003)
30. Sivic, J., Zisserman, A.: Video data mining using configurations of viewpoint invariant regions. In: CVPR, p. I-488 (2004)
31. Su, Y., Jurie, F.: Improving image classification using semantic attributes. IJCV 100(1), 59–77 (2012)
32. Vogel, J., Schiele, B.: Semantic modeling of natural scenes for content-based image retrieval. IJCV 72(2), 133–157 (2007)
33. Wang, Z., Fan, B., Wu, F.: Local intensity order pattern for feature description. In: ICCV, pp. 603–610 (2011)
34. Xiao, J., Hays, J., Ehinger, K.A., Oliva, A., Torralba, A.: Sun database: Large-scale scene recognition from abbey to zoo. In: CVPR, pp. 3485–3492 (2010)
35. Yang, J., Yu, K., Gong, Y., Huang, T.: Linear spatial pyramid matching using sparse coding for image classification. In: CVPR, pp. 1794–1801 (2009)

Multi-scale Orderless Pooling
of Deep Convolutional Activation Features

Yunchao Gong[1], Liwei Wang[2], Ruiqi Guo[2], and Svetlana Lazebnik[2]

[1] University of North Carolina, Chapel Hill, USA
yunchao@cs.unc.edu
[2] University of Illinois, Urbana-Champaign, USA
{lwang97,guo29,slazebni}@illinois.edu

Abstract. Deep convolutional neural networks (CNN) have shown their promise as a universal representation for recognition. However, global CNN activations lack geometric invariance, which limits their robustness for classification and matching of highly variable scenes. To improve the invariance of CNN activations without degrading their discriminative power, this paper presents a simple but effective scheme called *multi-scale orderless pooling* (MOP-CNN). This scheme extracts CNN activations for local patches at multiple scale levels, performs orderless VLAD pooling of these activations at each level separately, and concatenates the result. The resulting MOP-CNN representation can be used as a generic feature for either supervised or unsupervised recognition tasks, from image classification to instance-level retrieval; it consistently outperforms global CNN activations without requiring any joint training of prediction layers for a particular target dataset. In absolute terms, it achieves state-of-the-art results on the challenging SUN397 and MIT Indoor Scenes classification datasets, and competitive results on ILSVRC2012/2013 classification and INRIA Holidays retrieval datasets.

1 Introduction

Recently, deep convolutional neural networks (CNN) [1] have demonstrated breakthrough accuracies for image classification [2]. This has spurred a flurry of activity on further improving CNN architectures and training algorithms [3,4,5,6,7], as well as on using CNN features as a universal representation for recognition. A number of recent works [8,9,10,11,12] show that CNN features trained on sufficiently large and diverse datasets such as ImageNet [13] can be successfully transferred to other visual recognition tasks, e.g., scene classification and object localization, with a only limited amount of task-specific training data. Our work also relies on reusing CNN activations as off-the-shelf features for whole-image tasks like scene classification and retrieval. But, instead of simply computing the CNN activation vector over the entire image, we ask whether we can get improved performance by combining activations extracted at multiple *local* image windows. Inspired by previous work on spatial and feature space pooling of local descriptors [14,15,16], we propose a novel and simple pooling

D. Fleet et al. (Eds.): ECCV 2014, Part VII, LNCS 8695, pp. 392–407, 2014.

scheme that significantly outperforms global CNN activations for both supervised tasks like image classification and unsupervised tasks like retrieval, even without any fine-tuning on the target datasets.

Image representation has been a driving motivation for research in computer vision for many years. For much of the past decade, orderless bag-of-features (BoF) methods [15,17,18,19,20] were considered to be the state of the art. Especially when built on top of locally invariant features like SIFT [21], BoF can be, to some extent, robust to image scaling, translation, occlusion, and so on. However, they do not encode global spatial information, motivating the incorporation of loose spatial information in the BoF vectors through spatial pyramid matching (SPM) [14]. Deep CNN, as exemplified by the system of Krizhevsky et al. [2], is a completely different architecture. Raw image pixels are first sent through five convolutional layers, each of which filters the feature maps and then max-pools the output within local neighborhoods. At this point, the representation still preserves a great deal of global spatial information. For example, as shown by Zeiler and Fergus [22], the activations from the fifth max-pooling layer can be reconstructed to form an image that looks similar to the original one. Though max-pooling within each feature map helps to improve invariance to small-scale deformations [23], invariance to larger-scale, more global deformations might be undermined by the preserved spatial information. After the filtering and max-pooling layers follow several fully connected layers, finally producing an activation of 4096 dimensions. While it becomes more difficult to reason about the invariance properties of the output of the fully connected layers, we will present an empirical analysis in Section 3 indicating that the final CNN representation is still fairly sensitive to global translation, rotation, and scaling. Even if one does not care about this lack of invariance for its own sake, we show that it directly translates into a loss of accuracy for classification tasks.

Intuitively, bags of features and deep CNN activations lie towards opposite ends of the "orderless" to "globally ordered" spectrum for visual representations. SPM [14] is based on realizing that BoF has insufficient spatial information for many recognition tasks and adding just enough such information. Inspired by this, we observe that CNN activations preserve too much spatial information, and study the question of whether we can build a more orderless representation on top of CNN activations to improve recognition performance. We present a simple but effective framework for doing this, which we refer to as *multi-scale orderless pooling* (MOP-CNN). The idea is summarized in Figure 1. Briefly, we begin by extracting deep activation features from local patches at multiple scales. Our coarsest scale is the whole image, so global spatial layout is still preserved, and our finer scales allow us to capture more local, fine-grained details of the image. Then we aggregate local patch responses at the finer scales via VLAD encoding [16]. The orderless nature of VLAD helps to build a more invariant representation. Finally, we concatenatenate the original global deep activations with the VLAD features for the finer scales to form our new image representation.

Section 2 will introduce our multi-scale orderless pooling approach. Section 3 will present a small-scale study suggesting that CNN activations extracted

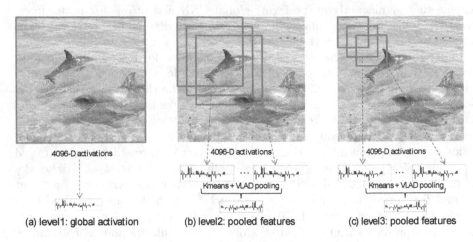

Fig. 1. Overview of multi-scale orderless pooling for CNN activations (MOP-CNN). Our proposed feature is a concatenation of the feature vectors from three levels: (a) Level 1, corresponding to the 4096-dimensional CNN activation for the entire 256×256 image; (b) Level 2, formed by extracting activations from 128×128 patches and VLAD pooling them with a codebook of 100 centers; (c) Level 3, formed in the same way as level 2 but with 64×64 patches.

at sub-image windows can provide more robust and discriminative information than whole-image activations, and confirming that MOP-CNN is more robust in the presence of geometric deformations than global CNN. Next, Section 4 will report comprehensive experiments results for classification on three image datasets (SUN397, MIT Indoor Scenes, and ILSVRC2012/2013) and retrieval on the Holidays dataset. A sizable boost in performance across these popular benchmarks confirms the promise of our method. Section 5 will conclude with a discussion of future work directions.

2   The Proposed Method

Inspired by SPM [14], which extracts local patches at a single scale but then pools them over regions of increasing scale, ending with the whole image, we propose a kind of "reverse SPM" idea, where we extract patches at multiple scales, starting with the whole image, and then pool each scale without regard to spatial information. The basic idea is illustrated in Figure 1.

Our representation has three scale levels, corresponding to CNN activations of the global 256×256 image and 128×128 and 64×64 patches, respectively. To extract these activations, we use the Caffe CPU implementation [24] pre-trained on ImageNet [13]. Given an input image or a patch, we resample it to 256×256 pixels, subtract the mean of the pixel values, and feed the patch through the network. Then we take the 4096-dimensional output of the seventh (fully connected) layer, after the rectified linear unit (ReLU) transformation, so that all the values are non-negative (we have also tested the activations before ReLU and found worse performance).

For the first level, we simply take the 4096-dimensional CNN activation for the whole 256×256 image. For the remaining two levels, we extract activations for all 128×128 and 64×64 patches sampled with a stride of 32 pixels. Next, we need to pool the activations of these multiple patches to summarize the second and third levels by single feature vectors of reasonable dimensionality. For this, we adopt Vectors of Locally Aggregated Descriptors (VLAD) [16], which are a simplified version of Fisher Vectors (FV) [15]. At each level, we extract the 4096-dimensional activations for respective patches and, to make computation more efficient, use PCA to reduce them to 500 dimensions. We also learn a separate k-means codebook for each level with $k = 100$ centers. Given a collection of patches from an input image and a codebook of centers c_i, $i = 1, \ldots, k$, the VLAD descriptor is constructed by assigning each patch p_j to its nearest cluster center $NN(p_j)$ and aggregating the residuals of the patches minus the center:

$$x = [\sum_{j:NN(p_j)=c_1} p_j - c_1, \quad \sum_{j:NN(p_j)=c_2} p_j - c_2, \quad \cdots \quad \sum_{j:NN(p_j)=c_k} p_j - c_k].$$

Following [16], we power- and L2-normalize the pooled vectors. However, the resulting vectors still have quite high dimensionality: given 500-dimensional patch activations p_j (after PCA) and 100 k-means centers, we end up with 50,000 dimensions. This is too high for many large-scale applications, so we further perform PCA on the pooled vectors and reduce them to 4096 dimensions. Note that applying PCA after the two stages (local patch activation and global pooled vector) is a standard practice in previous works [25,26]. Finally, given the original 4096-dimensional feature vector from level one and the two 4096-dimensional pooled PCA-reduced vectors from levels two and three, we rescale them to unit norm and concatenate them to form our final image representation.

3   Analysis of Invariance

We first examine the invariance properties of global CNN activations vs. MOP-CNN. As part of their paper on visualizing deep features, Zeiler and Fergus [22] analyze the transformation invariance of their model on five individual images by displaying the distance between the feature vectors of the original and transformed images, as well as the change in the probability of the correct label for the transformed version of the image (Figure 5 of [22]). These plots show very different patterns for different images, making it difficult to draw general conclusions. We would like to conduct a more comprehensive analysis with an emphasis on prediction accuracy for entire categories, not just individual images. To this end, we train one-vs-all linear SVMs on the original training images for all 397 categories from the SUN dataset [27] using both global 4096-dimensional CNN activations and our proposed MOP-CNN features. At test time, we consider four possible transformations: translation, scaling, flipping and rotation (see

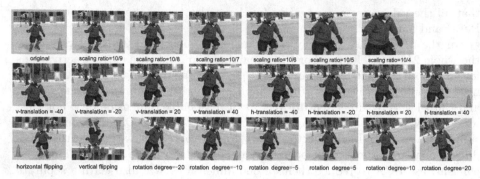

Fig. 2. Illustration of image transformations considered in our invariance study. For scaling by a factor of ρ, we take crops around the image center of $(1/\rho)$ times original size. For translation, we take crops of 0.7 times the original size and translate them by up to 40 pixels in either direction horizontally or vertically (the translation amount is relative to the normalized image size of 256×256). For rotation, we take crops from the middle of the image (so as to avoid corner artifacts) and rotate them from -20 to 20 degrees about the center. The corresponding scaling ratio, translation distance (pixels) and rotation degrees are listed below each instance.

Figure 2 for illustration and detailed explanation of transformation parameters). We apply a given transformation to all the test images, extract features from the transformed images, and perform 397-way classification using the trained SVMs. Figure 3 shows classification accuracies as a function of transformation type and parameters for four randomly selected classes: arrival gate, florist shop, volleyball court, and ice skating. In the case of CNN features, for almost all transformations, as the degree of transformation becomes more extreme, the classification accuracies keep dropping for all classes. The only exception is horizontal flipping, which does not seem to affect the classification accuracy. This may be due to the fact that the Caffe implementation adds horizontal flips of all training images to the training set (on the other hand, the Caffe training protocol also involves taking random crops of training images, yet this does not seem sufficient for building in invariance to such transformations, as our results indicate). By contrast with global CNN, our MOP-CNN features are more robust to the degree of translation, rotation, and scaling, and their absolute classification accuracies are consistently higher as well.

Figure 4 further illustrates the lack of robustness of global CNN activations by showing the predictions for a few ILSVRC2012/2013 images based on different image sub-windows. Even for sub-windows that are small translations of each other, the predicted labels can be drastically different. For example, in (f), the red rectangle is correctly labeled "alp," while the overlapping rectangle is incorrectly labeled "garfish." But, while picking the wrong window can give a bad prediction, picking the "right" one can give a good prediction: in (d), the whole image is wrongly labeled, but one of its sub-windows can get the correct label – "schooner." This immediately suggests a sliding window protocol at test time: given a test image, extract windows at multiple scales and locations, compute

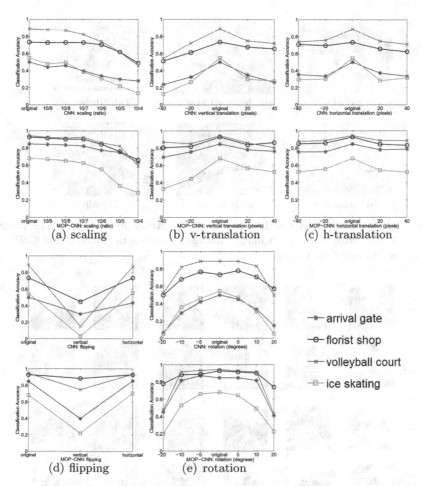

(a) scaling   (b) v-translation   (c) h-translation

(d) flipping   (e) rotation

Fig. 3. Accuracies for 397-way classification on four classes from the SUN dataset as a function of different transformations of the test images. For each transformation type (a-e), the upper (resp. lower) plot shows the classification accuracy using the global CNN representation (resp. MOP-CNN).

their CNN activations and prediction scores, and look for the window that gives the maximum score for a given class. Figure 5 illustrates such a "scene detection" approach [28,27] on a few SUN images. In fact, it is already common for CNN implementations to sample multiple windows at test time: the systems of [2,8,24] can take five sub-image windows corresponding to the center and four corners, together with their flipped versions, and average the prediction scores over these ten windows. As will be shown in Table 4, for Caffe, this "center+corner+flip" strategy gets 56.30% classification accuracy on ILSVRC2012/2013 vs. 54.34% for simply classifying global image windows. An even more recent system, Over-Feat [12], incorporates a more comprehensive multi-scale voting scheme for classification, where efficient computations are used to extract class-level activations

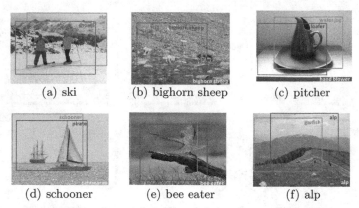

(a) ski   (b) bighorn sheep   (c) pitcher

(d) schooner   (e) bee eater   (f) alp

Fig. 4. Classification of CNN activations of local patches in an image. The ground truth labels are listed below each image. Labels predicted by whole-image CNN are listed in the bottom right corner.

(a)

(b)

(c)

(d)

Fig. 5. Highest-response windows (in red) for (a) basilica, (b) control tower, (c) boardwalk, and (d) tower. For each test image resampled to 256×256, we search over windows with widths 224, 192, 160, and 128 and a stride of 16 pixels and display the window that gives the highest prediction score for the ground truth category. The detected windows contain similar structures: in (a), (b) and (d), the top parts of towers have been selected; in (c), the windows are all centered on the narrow walkway.

at a denser sampling of locations and scales, and the average or maximum of these activations is taken to produce the final classification results. With this scheme, OverFeat can achieve as high as 64.26% accuracy on ILSVRC2012/2013, albeit starting from a better baseline CNN with 60.72% accuracy.

While the above window sampling schemes do improve the robustness of prediction over single global CNN activations, they all combine activations (classifier responses) from the final prediction layer, which means that they can only be used

Table 1. A summary of baselines and their relationship to the MOP-CNN method

pooling method / scale	multi-scale	concatenation
Average pooling	Avg (multi-scale)	Avg (concatenation)
Max pooling	Max (multi-scale)	Max (concatenation)
VLAD pooling	VLAD (multi-scale)	**MOP-CNN**

following training (or fine-tuning) for a particular prediction task, and do not naturally produce feature vectors for other datasets or tasks. By contrast, MOP-CNN combines activations of the last fully connected layer, so it is a more generic representation that can even work for tasks like image retrieval, which may be done in an unsupervised fashion and for which labeled training data may not be available.

4   Large-Scale Evaluation

4.1   Baselines

To validate MOP-CNN, we need to demonstrate that a simpler patch sampling and pooling scheme cannot achieve the same performance. As simpler alternatives to VLAD pooling, we consider **average pooling**, which involves computing the mean of the 4096-dimensional activations at each scale level, and **maximum pooling**, which involves computing their element-wise maximum. We did not consider standard BoF pooling because it has been demonstrated to be less accurate than VLAD [16]; to get competitive performance, we would need a codebook size much larger than 100, which would make the quantization step prohibitively expensive. As additional baselines, we need to examine alternative strategies with regards to pooling across scale levels. The **multi-scale** strategy corresponds to taking the union of all the patches from an image, regardless of scale, and pooling them together. The **concatenation** strategy refers to pooling patches from three levels separately and then concatenating the result. Finally, we separately examine the performance of individual scale levels as well as concatenations of just pairs of them. In particular, **level1** is simply the 4096-dimensional global descriptor of the entire image, which was suggested in [8] as a generic image descriptor. These baselines and their relationship to our full MOP-CNN scheme are summarized in Table 1.

4.2   Datasets

We test our approach on four well-known benchmark datasets:

SUN397 [27] is the largest dataset to date for scene recognition. It contains 397 scene categories and each has at least 100 images. The evaluation protocol involves training and testing on ten different splits and reporting the average classification accuracy. The splits are fixed and publicly available from [27]; each has 50 training and 50 test images.

MIT Indoor [29] contains 67 categories. While outdoor scenes, which comprise more than half of SUN (220 out of 397), can often be characterized by global scene statistics, indoor scenes tend to be much more variable in terms of composition and better characterized by the objects they contain. This makes the MIT Indoor dataset an interesting test case for our representation, which is designed to focus more on appearance of sub-image windows and have more invariance to global transformations. The standard training/test split for the Indoor dataset consists of 80 training and 20 test images per class.

ILSVRC2012/2013 [30,31], or ImageNet Large-Scale Visual Recognition Challenge, is the most prominent benchmark for comparing large-scale image classification methods and is the dataset on which the Caffe representation we use [24] is pre-trained. ILSVRC differs from the previous two datasets in that most of its categories focus on objects, not scenes, and the objects tend to be highly salient and centered in images. It contains 1000 classes corresponding to leaf nodes in ImageNet. Each class has more than 1000 unique training images, and there is a separate validation set with 50,000 images. The 2012 and 2013 versions of the ILSVRC competition have the same training and validation data. Classification accuracy on the validation set is used to evaluate different methods.

INRIA Holidays [32] is a standard benchmark for image retrieval. It contains 1491 images corresponding to 500 image instances. Each instance has 2-3 images describing the same object or location. A set of 500 images are used as queries, and the rest are used as the database. Mean average precision (mAP) is the evaluation metric.

4.3   Image Classification Results

In all of the following experiments, we train classifiers using the linear SVM implementation from the INRIA JSGD package [33]. We fix the regularization parameter to 10^{-5} and the learning rate to 0.2, and train for 100 epochs.

Table 2 reports our results on the SUN397 dataset. From the results for baseline pooling methods in (a), we can see that VLAD works better than average and max pooling and that pooling scale levels separately works better than pooling them together (which is not altogether surprising, since the latter strategy raises the feature dimensionality by a factor of three). From (b), we can see that concatenating all three scale levels gives a significant improvement over any subset. For reference, Part (c) of Table 2 gives published state-of-the-art results from the literature. Xiao et al. [27], who have collected the SUN dataset, have also published a baseline accuracy of 38% using a combination of standard features like GIST, color histograms, and BoF. This baseline is slightly exceeded by the level1 method, i.e., global 4096-dimensional Caffe activations pre-trained on ImageNet. The Caffe accuracy of 39.57% is also comparable to the 40.94% with an analogous setup for DeCAF [8].[1] However, these numbers are still worse than the 47.2% achieved by high-dimensional Fisher Vectors [34] – to our knowledge, the state of the art on this dataset to date. With our MOP-CNN pooling scheme, we are able to achieve

---

[1] DeCAF is an earlier implementation from the same research group and Caffe is its "little brother." The two implementations are similar, but Caffe is faster, includes support for both CPU and GPU, and is easier to modify.

Table 2. Scene recognition on SUN397. (a) Alternative pooling baselines (see Section 4.1 and Table 1); (b) Different combinations of scale levels – in particular, "level1" corresponds to the global CNN representation and "level1+level2+level3" corresponds to the proposed MOP-CNN method. (c) Published numbers for state-of-the-art methods.

	method	feature dimension	accuracy
(a)	Avg (Multi-Scale)	4,096	39.62
	Avg (Concatenation)	12,288	47.50
	Max (Multi-Scale)	4,096	43.51
	Max (Concatenation)	12,288	48.50
	VLAD (Multi-Scale)	4,096	47.32
(b)	level1	4,096	39.57
	level2	4,096	45.34
	level3	4,096	40.21
	level1 + level2	8,192	49.91
	level1 + level3	8,192	49.52
	level2 + level3	8,192	49.66
	level1 + level2 + level3 (MOP-CNN)	12,288	**51.98**
(c)	Xiao et al. [27]	–	38.00
	DeCAF [8]	4,096	40.94
	FV (SIFT + Local Color Statistic) [34]	256,000	47.20

cathedral (-16%)   ocean (-2%)   snow mountain (+0%)

church (-8%)   cockpit (-2%)   chalet (-2%)

Van Interior (+56%)   Video store (+48%)   Shopping mall (+42%)

Florist shop (+56%)   Playroom (+48%)   Volleyball court (+42%)

Fig. 6. SUN classes on which MOP-CNN gives the biggest decrease over the level1 global features (top), and classes on which it gives the biggest increase (bottom)

Table 3. Classification results on MIT Indoor Scenes. (a) Alternative pooling baselines (see Section 4.1 and Table 1); (b) Different combinations of scale levels; (c) Published numbers for state-of-the-art methods.

	method	feature dimension	accuracy
(a)	Avg (Multi-Scale)	4,096	56.72
	Avg (Concatenation)	12,288	65.60
	Max (Multi-Scale)	4,096	60.52
	Max (Concatenation)	12,288	64.85
	VLAD (Multi-Scale)	4,096	66.12
(b)	level1	4,096	53.73
	level2	4,096	65.52
	level3	4,096	62.24
	level1 + level2	8,192	66.64
	level1 + level3	8,192	66.87
	level2 + level3	8,192	67.24
	level1 + level2 + level3 (MOP-CNN)	12,288	**68.88**
(c)	SPM [14]	5,000	34.40
	Discriminative patches [35]	–	38.10
	Disc. patches+GIST+DPM+SPM [35]	–	49.40
	FV + Bag of parts [36]	221,550	63.18
	Mid-level elements [37]	60,000	64.03

51.98% accuracy with feature dimensionality that is an order of magnitude lower than that of [34]. Figure 6 shows six classes on which MOP-CNN gives the biggest improvement over level1, and six on which it has the biggest drop. For classes having an object in the center, MOP-CNN usually cannot improve too much, or might hurt performance. However, for classes that have high spatial variability, or do not have a clear focal object, it can give a substantial improvement.

Table 3 reports results on the MIT Indoor dataset. Overall, the trends are consistent with those on SUN, in that VLAD pooling outperforms average and max pooling and combining all three levels yields the best performance. There is one interesting difference from Table 2, though: namely, level2 and level3 features work much better than level1 on the Indoor dataset, whereas the difference was much less pronounced on SUN. This is probably because indoor scenes are better described by local patches that have highly distinctive appearance but can vary greatly in terms of location. In fact, several recent methods achieving state-of-the-art results on this dataset are based on the idea of finding such patches [37,36,35]. Our MOP-CNN scheme outperforms all of them – 68.88% vs. 64.03% for the method of Doersch et al. [37].

Table 4 reports results on ILSVRC2012/2013. The trends for alternative pooling methods in (a) are the same as before. Interestingly, in (b) we can see that, unlike on SUN and MIT Indoor, level2 and level3 features do not work as well as level1. This is likely because the level1 feature was specifically trained on ILSVRC, and this dataset has limited geometric variability. Nevertheless, by combining the three levels, we still get a significant improvement. Note that directly running the full pre-trained Caffe network on the global features from the validation set gives 54.34% accuracy (part (c) of Table 4, first line), which is higher than our level1

Table 4. Classification results on ILSVRC2012/2013. (a) Alternative pooling baselines (see Section 4.1 and Table 1); (b) Different combinations of scale levels; (c) Numbers for state-of-the-art CNN implementations. All the numbers come from the respective papers, except the Caffe numbers, which were obtained by us by directly testing their full network pre-trained on ImageNet. "Global" corresponds to testing on global image features, and "Center+Corner+Flip" corresponds to averaging the prediction scores over ten crops taken from the test image (see Section 3 for details).

	method	feature dimension	accuracy
(c)	Avg (Multi-Scale)	4096	53.34
	Avg (Concatenation)	12,288	56.12
	Max (Multi-Scale)	4096	54.37
	Max (Concatenation)	12,288	55.88
	VLAD (Multi-Scale)	4,096	48.54
(b)	level1	4,096	51.46
	level2	4,096	48.21
	level3	4,096	38.20
	level1 + level2	8,192	56.82
	level1 + level3	8,192	55.91
	level2 + level3	8,192	51.52
	level1 + level2 + level3 (MOP-CNN)	12,288	57.93
(c)	Caffe (Global) [24]	–	54.34
	Caffe (Center+Corner+Flip) [24]	–	56.30
	Krizhevsky et al. [2]	–	59.93
	Zeiler and Fergus (6 CNN models) [22]	–	64.00
	OverFeat (1 CNN model) [12]	–	**64.26**
	OverFeat (7 CNN models) [12]	–	**66.04**

accuracy of 51.46%. The only difference between these two setups, "Caffe (Global)" and "level1," are the parameters of the last classifier layer – i.e., softmax and SVM, respectively. For Caffe, the softmax layer is jointly trained with all the previous network layers using multiple random windows cropped from training images, while our SVMs are trained separately using only the global image features. Nevertheless, the accuracy of our final MOP-CNN representation, at 57.93%, is higher than that of the full pre-trained Caffe CNN tested either on the global features ("Global") or on ten sub-windows ("Center+Corner+Flip").

It is important to note that in absolute terms, we do not achieve state-of-the-art results on ILSVRC. For the 2012 version of the contest, the highest results were achieved by Krizhevsky et al. [2], who have reported a top-1 classification accuracy of 59.93%. Subsequently, Zeiler and Fergus [22] have obtained 64% by refining the Krizhevsky architecture and combining six different models. For the 2013 competition, the highest reported top-1 accuracies are those of Sermanet et al. [12]: they obtained 64.26% by aggregating CNN predictions over multiple sub-window locations and scales (as discussed in Section 3), and 66.04% by combining seven such models. While our numbers are clearly lower, it is mainly because our representation is built on Caffe, whose baseline accuracy is below that of [2,22,12]. We believe that MOP-CNN can obtain much better

Table 5. Image retrieval results on the Holidays dataset. (a) Alternative pooling baselines (see Section 4.1 and Table 1); (b) Different combinations of scale levels; (c) Full MOP-CNN descriptor vector compressed by PCA and followed by whitening [38], for two different output dimensionalities; (c) Published state-of-the-art results with a compact global descriptor (see text for discussion).

	method	feature dimension	mAP
(a)	Avg (Multi-Scale)	4,096	71.32
	Avg (Concatenation)	12,288	75.02
	Max (Multi-Scale)	4,096	76.23
	Max (Concatenation)	12,288	75.07
	VLAD (Multi-Scale)	4,096	78.42
(b)	level1	4,096	70.53
	level2	4,096	74.02
	level3	4,096	75.45
	level1 + level2	8,192	75.86
	level1 + level3	8,192	78.92
	level2 + level3	8,192	77.91
	level1 + level2 + level3 (MOP-CNN)	12,288	78.82
(c)	MOP-CNN + PCA + Whitening	512	78.38
	MOP-CNN + PCA + Whitening	2048	**80.18**
(d)	FV [16]	8,192	62.50
	FV + PCA [16]	256	62.60
	Gordo et al. [39]	512	78.90

performance when combined with these better CNN models, or by combining multiple independently trained CNNs as in [22,12].

4.4 Image Retrieval Results

As our last experiment, we demonstrate the usefulness of our approach for an *unsupervised* image retrieval scenario on the Holidays dataset. Table 5 reports the mAP results for nearest neighbor retrieval of feature vectors using the Euclidean distance. On this dataset, level1 is the weakest of all three levels because images of the same instance may be related by large rotations, viewpoint changes, etc., and global CNN activations do not have strong enough invariance to handle these transformations. As before, combining all three levels achieves the best performance of 78.82%. Using aggressive dimensionality reduction with PCA and whitening as suggested in [38], we can raise the mAP even further to 80.8% with only a 2048-dimensional feature vector. The state of the art performance on this dataset with a compact descriptor is obtained by Gordo et al. [39] by using FV/VLAD and discriminative dimensionality reduction, while our method still achieves comparable or better performance. Note that it is possible to obtain even higher results on Holidays with methods based on inverted files with very large vocabularies. In particular, Tolias et al. [40] report 88% but their representation would take more than 4 million dimensions per image if expanded into an explicit feature vector, and is not scalable to large datasets. Yet further improvements may be possible by adding techniques such as query expansion and

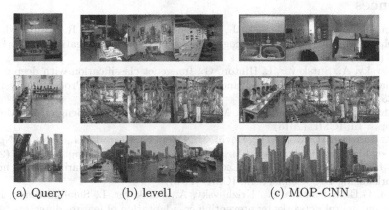

   (a) Query   (b) level1   (c) MOP-CNN

Fig. 7. Image retrieval examples on the Holiday dataset. Red border indicates a ground truth image (i.e., a positive retrieval result). We only show three retrieved examples per query because each query only has one to two ground truth images.

geometric verification, but they are not applicable for generic image representation, which is our main focus. Finally, we show retrieval examples in Figure 7. We can clearly see that MOP-CNN has improved robustness to shifts, scaling, and viewpoint changes over global CNN activations.

5 Discussion

This paper has presented a multi-scale orderless pooling scheme that is built on top of deep activation features of local image patches. On four very challenging datasets, we have achieved a substantial improvement over global CNN activations, in some cases outperforming the state of the art. These results are achieved with the same set of parameters (i.e., patch sizes and sampling, codebook size, PCA dimension, etc.), which clearly shows the good generalization ability of the proposed approach. As a generic low-dimensional image representation, it is not restricted to supervised tasks like image classification, but can also be used for unsupervised tasks such as retrieval.

Our work opens several promising avenues for future research. First, it remains interesting to investigate more sophisticated ways to incorporate orderless information in CNN. One possible way is to change the architecture of current deep networks fundamentally to improve their holistic invariance. Second, the feature extraction stage of our current pipeline is somewhat slow, and it is interesting to exploit the convolutional network structure to speed it up. Fortunately, there is fast ongoing progress in optimizing this step. One example is the multi-scale scheme of Sermanet et al. [12] mentioned earlier, and another is DenseNet [41]. In the future, we would like to reimplement MOP-CNN to benefit from such architectures.

Acknowledgments. Lazebnik's research was partially supported by NSF grants 1228082 and 1302438, the DARPA Computer Science Study Group, Xerox UAC, Microsoft Research, and the Sloan Foundation. Gong was supported by the 2013 Google Ph.D. Fellowship in Machine Perception.

References

1. LeCun, Y., Boser, B., Denker, J., Henderson, D., Howard, R., Hubbard, W., Jackel, L.: Handwritten digit recognition with a back-propagation network. In: NIPS (1990)
2. Krizhevsky, A., Sutskever, I., Hinton, G.: Imagenet classification with deep convolutional neural networks. In: Advances in Neural Information Processing Systems, vol. 25, pp. 1106–1114 (2012)
3. Goodfellow, I., Warde-Farley, D., Mirza, M., Courville, A., Bengio, Y.: Maxout networks. In: ICML (2013)
4. Le, Q., Ranzato, M., Monga, R., Devin, M., Chen, K., Corrado, G., Dean, J., Ng, A.: Building high-level features using large scale unsupervised learning. In: ICML (2012)
5. Wan, L., Zeiler, M., Zhang, S., Lecun, Y., Fergus, R.: Regularization of neural networks using DropConnect. In: ICML (2013)
6. Hinton, G.E., Srivastava, N., Krizhevsky, A., Sutskever, I., Salakhutdinov, R.R.: Improving neural networks by preventing co-adaptation of feature detectors. Arxiv preprint arXiv:1207.0580 (2012)
7. Simonyan, K., Vedaldi, A., Zisserman, A.: Deep fisher networks for large-scale image classification. In: Proceedings Advances in Neural Information Processing Systems (NIPS) (2013)
8. Donahue, J., Jia, Y., Vinyals, O., Hoffman, J., Zhang, N., Tzeng, E., Darrell, T.: Decaf: A deep convolutional activation feature for generic visual recognition. arXiv preprint arXiv:1310.1531 (2013)
9. Girshick, R., Donahue, J., Darrell, T., Malik, J.: Rich feature hierarchies for accurate object detection and semantic segmentation. arXiv preprint arXiv:1311.2524 (2013)
10. Oquab, M., Bottou, L., Laptev, I., Sivic, J., et al.: Learning and transferring mid-level image representations using convolutional neural networks. In: CVPR (2014)
11. Razavian, A., Azizpour, H., Sullivan, J., Carlsson, S.: CNN features off-the-shelf: An astounding baseline for recognition. In: CVPR 2014 DeepVision Workshop (2014)
12. Sermanet, P., Eigen, D., Zhang, X., Mathieu, M., Fergus, R., LeCun, Y.: Overfeat: Integrated recognition, localization and detection using convolutional networks. arXiv preprint arXiv:1312.6229 (2013)
13. Deng, J., Dong, W., Socher, R., Li, L.J., Li, K., Fei-Fei, L.: ImageNet: A large-scale hierarchical image database. In: CVPR (2009)
14. Lazebnik, S., Schmid, C., Ponce, J.: Beyond bags of features: Spatial pyramid matching for recognizing natural scene categories. In: CVPR (2006)
15. Perronnin, F., Dance, C.R.: Fisher kernels on visual vocabularies for image categorization. In: CVPR (2007)
16. Jégou, H., Douze, M., Schmid, C., Pérez, P.: Aggregating local descriptors into a compact image representation. In: CVPR, pp. 3304–3311 (2010)
17. Wang, J., Yang, J., Yu, K., Lv, F., Huang, T., Gong, Y.: Locality-constrained linear coding for image classification. In: CVPR (2010)
18. Csurka, G., Dance, C., Fan, L., Willamowski, J., Bray, C.: Visual categorization with bags of keypoints. In: ECCV Workshop on Statistical Learning in Computer Vision (2004)
19. Sivic, J., Zisserman, A.: Video Google: A text retrieval approach to object matching in videos. In: ICCV (2003)
20. Grauman, K., Darrell, T.: The pyramid match kernel: Discriminative classification with sets of image features. In: ICCV, pp. 1458–1465 (2005)
21. Lowe, D.G.: Distinctive image features from scale-invariant keypoints. IJCV 60(2), 91–110 (2004)

22. Zeiler, M.D., Fergus, R.: Visualizing and understanding convolutional neural networks. arXiv preprint arXiv:1311.2901 (2013)
23. Lee, H., Grosse, R., Ranganath, R., Ng, A.Y.: Convolutional deep belief networks for scalable unsupervised learning of hierarchical representations. In: ICML, pp. 609–616 (2009)
24. Jia, Y.: Caffe: An open source convolutional architecture for fast feature embedding (2013), http://caffe.berkeleyvision.org/
25. Perronnin, F., Sánchez, J., Mensink, T.: Improving the Fisher kernel for large-scale image classification. In: Daniilidis, K., Maragos, P., Paragios, N. (eds.) ECCV 2010, Part IV. LNCS, vol. 6314, pp. 143–156. Springer, Heidelberg (2010)
26. Perronnin, F., Liu, Y., Sánchez, J., Poirier, H.: Large-scale image retrieval with compressed Fisher vectors. In: CVPR (2010)
27. Xiao, J., Hays, J., Ehinger, K.A., Oliva, A., Torralba, A.: SUN database: Large-scale scene recognition from abbey to zoo. In: CVPR, 3485–3492 (2010)
28. Pandey, M., Lazebnik, S.: Scene recognition and weakly supervised object localization with deformable part-based models. In: ICCV, pp. 1307–1314 (2011)
29. Quattoni, A., Torralba, A.: Recognizing indoor scenes. In: CVPR (2009)
30. Deng, J., Berg, A., Satheesh, S., Su, H., Khosla, A., Fei-Fei, L.: Large scale visual recognition challenge (2012),
    http://www.image-net.org/challenges/LSVRC/2012/
31. Russakovsky, O., Deng, J., Huang, Z., Berg, A., Fei-Fei, L.: Detecting avocados to zucchinis: what have we done, and where are we going? In: ICCV (2013)
32. Jegou, H., Douze, M., Schmid, C.: Hamming embedding and weak geometric consistency for large scale image search. In: Forsyth, D., Torr, P., Zisserman, A. (eds.) ECCV 2008, Part I. LNCS, vol. 5302, pp. 304–317. Springer, Heidelberg (2008)
33. Akata, Z., Perronnin, F., Harchaoui, Z., Schmid, C., et al.: Good practice in large-scale learning for image classification. PAMI (2013)
34. Sanchez, J., Perronnin, F., Mensink, T., Verbeek, J.: Image Classification with the Fisher Vector: Theory and Practice. IJCV 105(3), 222–245 (2013)
35. Singh, S., Gupta, A., Efros, A.A.: Unsupervised discovery of mid-level discriminative patches. In: Fitzgibbon, A., Lazebnik, S., Perona, P., Sato, Y., Schmid, C. (eds.) ECCV 2012, Part II. LNCS, vol. 7573, pp. 73–86. Springer, Heidelberg (2012)
36. Juneja, M., Vedaldi, A., Jawahar, C.V., Zisserman, A.: Blocks that shout: Distinctive parts for scene classification. In: CVPR (2013)
37. Doersch, C., Gupta, A., Efros, A.A.: Mid-level visual element discovery as discriminative mode seeking. In: NIPS (2013)
38. Jégou, H., Chum, O.: Negative evidences and co-occurences in image retrieval: The benefit of PCA and whitening. In: Fitzgibbon, A., Lazebnik, S., Perona, P., Sato, Y., Schmid, C. (eds.) ECCV 2012, Part II. LNCS, vol. 7573, pp. 774–787. Springer, Heidelberg (2012)
39. Gordo, A., Rodrıguez-Serrano, J.A., Perronnin, F., Valveny, E.: Leveraging category-level labels for instance-level image retrieval. In: CVPR (2012)
40. Tolias, G., Avrithis, Y., Jégou, H.: To aggregate or not to aggregate: selective match kernels for image search. In: ICCV (2013)
41. Iandola, F., Moskewicz, M., Karayev, S., Girshick, R., Darrell, T., Keutzer, K.: DenseNet: Implementing efficient convnet descriptor pyramids. arXiv preprint arXiv:1404.1869 (2014)

Expanding the Family of Grassmannian Kernels: An Embedding Perspective

Mehrtash T. Harandi, Mathieu Salzmann, Sadeep Jayasumana, Richard Hartley, and Hongdong Li

Australian National University, Canberra, ACT 0200, Australia
NICTA*, Locked Bag 8001, Canberra, ACT 2601, Australia

Abstract. Modeling videos and image-sets as linear subspaces has proven beneficial for many visual recognition tasks. However, it also incurs challenges arising from the fact that linear subspaces do not obey Euclidean geometry, but lie on a special type of Riemannian manifolds known as Grassmannian. To leverage the techniques developed for Euclidean spaces (*e.g.*, support vector machines) with subspaces, several recent studies have proposed to embed the Grassmannian into a Hilbert space by making use of a positive definite kernel. Unfortunately, only two Grassmannian kernels are known, none of which -as we will show- is *universal*, which limits their ability to approximate a target function arbitrarily well. Here, we introduce several positive definite Grassmannian kernels, including universal ones, and demonstrate their superiority over previously-known kernels in various tasks, such as classification, clustering, sparse coding and hashing.

Keywords: Grassmann manifolds, kernel methods, Plücker embedding.

1 Introduction

This paper introduces a set of positive definite kernels to embed Grassmannians (*i.e.*, manifolds of linear subspaces that have a nonlinear Riemannian structure) into Hilbert spaces, which have a more familiar Euclidean structure. Nowadays, linear subspaces are a core representation of many visual recognition techniques. For example, several state-of-the-art video, or image-set, matching methods model the visual data as subspaces [5,7,22,23,10]. Linear subspaces have also proven a powerful representation for many other computer vision applications, such as chromatic noise filtering [21] and domain adaptation [4].

Despite their success, linear subspaces suffer from the drawback that they cannot be analyzed using Euclidean geometry. Indeed, subspaces lie on a special type of Riemannian manifolds, the Grassmann manifold, which has a nonlinear structure. As a consequence, popular techniques developed for Euclidean

* NICTA is funded by the Australian Government as represented by the Department of Broadband, Communications and the Digital Economy, as well as by the Australian Research Council through the ICT Centre of Excellence program.

D. Fleet et al. (Eds.): ECCV 2014, Part VII, LNCS 8695, pp. 408–423, 2014.

spaces do not apply. Recently, this problem has been addressed by embedding the Grassmannian into a Hilbert space. This can be achieved either by tangent space approximation of the manifold, or by exploiting a positive definite kernel function to embed the manifold into a reproducing kernel Hilbert space (RKHS). In either case, any existing Euclidean technique can then be applied to the embedded data, since Hilbert spaces obey Euclidean geometry. Recent studies, however, report superior results with RKHS embedding over flattening the manifold using its tangent spaces [5,23,9]. Intuitively, this can be attributed to the fact that a tangent space is a first order approximation to the true geometry of the manifold, whereas, being higher-dimensional, an RKHS has the capacity of better capturing the nonlinearity of the manifold.

While RKHS embeddings therefore seem preferable, their applicability is limited by the fact that only very few positive definite Grassmannian kernels are known. Indeed, in the literature, only two kernels have been introduced to embed Grassmannians into RKHS: the Binet-Cauchy kernel [24] and the projection kernel [5]. The former is a homogeneous second order polynomial kernel, while the latter is a linear kernel. As simple (low-order) polynomial kernels, they are limited in their ability to closely approximate arbitrary functions. In contrast, universal kernels provide much better generalization power [19,13].

In this paper, we introduce a set of new positive definite Grassmannian kernels, which, among others, includes universal Grassmannian kernels. To this end, we start from the perspective of the two embeddings from which the Binet-Cauchy and the projection kernels are derived: the Plücker embedding and the projection embedding. These two embeddings yield two distance functions. We then exploit the properties of these distances, in conjunction with several theorems analyzing the positive definiteness of kernels, to derive the ten new Grassmannian kernels summarized in Table 1.

Our experimental evaluation demonstrates the benefits of our Grassmannian kernels for classification, clustering, sparse coding and hashing. Our results show that our kernels outperform the Binet-Cauchy and projection ones for gender and gesture recognition, pose categorization and mouse behavior analysis.

2   Background Theory

In this section, we first review some notions of geometry of Grassmannians and then briefly discuss existing positive definite kernels and their properties. Throughout the paper, we use bold capital letters to denote matrices (*e.g.*, X) and bold lower-case letters to denote column vectors (*e.g.*, x). I_p is the $p \times p$ identity matrix. $\|X\|_F = \sqrt{\text{Tr}\left(X^T X\right)}$ indicates the Frobenius norm, with $\text{Tr}(\cdot)$ the matrix trace.

2.1   Grassmannian Geometry

The space of p-dimensional linear subspaces of $\mathbb{R}^d$ for $0 < p < d$ is not a Euclidean space, but a Riemannian manifold known as the Grassmannian $\mathcal{G}(d, p)$ [1].

Table 1. The proposed Grassmannian kernels and their properties

Kernel	Equation	Cond.	Properties
Polynomial	$k_{p,bc}(\boldsymbol{X},\boldsymbol{Y}) = \left(\beta + \left|\det\left(\boldsymbol{X}^T\boldsymbol{Y}\right)\right|\right)^{\alpha}$	$\beta > 0$	pd
	$k_{p,p}(\boldsymbol{X},\boldsymbol{Y}) = \left(\beta + \left\|\boldsymbol{X}^T\boldsymbol{Y}\right\|_F^2\right)^{\alpha}$	$\beta > 0$	pd
RBF	$k_{r,bc}(\boldsymbol{X},\boldsymbol{Y}) = \exp\left(\beta\left|\det\left(\boldsymbol{X}^T\boldsymbol{Y}\right)\right|\right)$	$\beta > 0$	pd, universal
	$k_{r,p}(\boldsymbol{X},\boldsymbol{Y}) = \exp\left(\beta\left\|\boldsymbol{X}^T\boldsymbol{Y}\right\|_F^2\right)$	$\beta > 0$	pd, universal
Laplace	$k_{l,bc}(\boldsymbol{X},\boldsymbol{Y}) = \exp\left(-\beta\sqrt{1 - \left|\det(\boldsymbol{X}^T\boldsymbol{Y})\right|}\right)$	$\beta > 0$	pd, universal
	$k_{l,p}(\boldsymbol{X},\boldsymbol{Y}) = \exp\left(-\beta\sqrt{p - \left\|\boldsymbol{X}^T\boldsymbol{Y}\right\|_F^2}\right)$	$\beta > 0$	pd, universal
Binomial	$k_{bi,bc}(\boldsymbol{X},\boldsymbol{Y}) = \left(\beta - \left|\det\left(\boldsymbol{X}^T\boldsymbol{Y}\right)\right|\right)^{-\alpha}$	$\beta > 1$	pd, universal
	$k_{bi,p}(\boldsymbol{X},\boldsymbol{Y}) = \left(\beta - \left\|\boldsymbol{X}^T\boldsymbol{Y}\right\|_F^2\right)^{-\alpha}$	$\beta > p$	pd, universal
Logarithm	$k_{log,bc}(\boldsymbol{X},\boldsymbol{Y}) = -\log\left(2 - \left|\det\left(\boldsymbol{X}^T\boldsymbol{Y}\right)\right|\right)$	–	cpd
	$k_{log,p}(\boldsymbol{X},\boldsymbol{Y}) = -\log\left(p + 1 - \left\|\boldsymbol{X}^T\boldsymbol{Y}\right\|_F^2\right)$	–	cpd

We note that in the special case of $p = 1$, the Grassmann manifold becomes the projective space $\mathbb{P}^{d-1}$, which consists of all lines passing through the origin. A point on the Grassmann manifold $\mathcal{G}(p,d)$ may be specified by an arbitrary $d \times p$ matrix with orthogonal columns, i.e., $\boldsymbol{X} \in \mathcal{G}(d,p) \Rightarrow \boldsymbol{X}^T\boldsymbol{X} = \boldsymbol{I}_p{}^1$.

On a Riemannian manifold, points are connected via smooth curves. The distance between two points is defined as the length of the shortest curve connecting them on the manifold. The shortest curve and its length are called geodesic and geodesic distance, respectively. For the Grassmannian, the geodesic distance between two points $\boldsymbol{X}$ and $\boldsymbol{Y}$ is given by

$$\delta_g(\boldsymbol{X},\boldsymbol{Y}) = \|\Theta\|_2 , \tag{1}$$

where Θ is the vector of principal angles between $\boldsymbol{X}$ and $\boldsymbol{Y}$.

Definition 1 (Principal Angles). *Let $\boldsymbol{X}$ and $\boldsymbol{Y}$ be two matrices of size $d \times p$ with orthonormal columns. The principal angles $0 \leq \theta_1 \leq \theta_2 \leq \cdots \leq \theta_p \leq \pi/2$ between two subspaces* span($\boldsymbol{X}$) *and* span($\boldsymbol{Y}$) *are defined recursively by*

---

[1] A point on the Grassmannian $\mathcal{G}(p,d)$ is a subspace spanned by the columns of a $d \times p$ full rank matrix and should therefore be denoted by span($\boldsymbol{X}$). With a slight abuse of notation, here we call $\boldsymbol{X}$ a Grassmannian point whenever it represents a basis for a subspace.

$$\cos(\theta_i) = \max_{\boldsymbol{u}_i \in \text{span}(\boldsymbol{X})} \max_{\boldsymbol{v}_i \in \text{span}(\boldsymbol{Y})} \boldsymbol{u}_i^T \boldsymbol{v}_i \tag{2}$$

$$\text{s.t.} \qquad \|\boldsymbol{u}_i\|_2 = \|\boldsymbol{v}_i\|_2 = 1$$

$$\boldsymbol{u}_i^T \boldsymbol{u}_j = 0, \; j = 1, 2, \cdots, i-1$$

$$\boldsymbol{v}_i^T \boldsymbol{v}_j = 0, \; j = 1, 2, \cdots, i-1$$

In other words, the first principal angle θ_1 is the smallest angle between any two unit vectors in the first and the second subspaces. The cosines of the principal angles correspond to the singular values of $\boldsymbol{X}^T \boldsymbol{Y}$ [1]. In addition to the geodesic distance, several other metrics can be employed to measure the similarity between Grassmannian points [5]. In Section 3, we will discuss two other metrics on the Grassmannian.

2.2 Positive Definite Kernels and Grassmannians

As mentioned earlier, a popular way to analyze problems defined on a Grassmannian is to embed the manifold into a Hilbert space using a valid Grassmannian kernel. Let us now formally define Grassmannian kernels:

Definition 2 (Real-valued Positive Definite Kernels). *Let* $\mathcal{X}$ *be a nonempty set. A symmetric function* $k : \mathcal{X} \times \mathcal{X} \to \mathbb{R}$ *is a positive definite (**pd**) kernel on* $\mathcal{X}$ *if and only if* $\sum_{i,j=1}^{n} c_i c_j k(x_i, x_j) \geq 0$ *for any* $n \in \mathbb{N}$, $x_i \in \mathcal{X}$ *and* $c_i \in \mathbb{R}$.

Definition 3 (Grassmannian Kernel). *A function* $k : \mathcal{G}(p, d) \times \mathcal{G}(p, d) \to \mathbb{R}$ *is a Grassmannian kernel if it is well-defined and* pd. *In our context, a function is well-defined if it is invariant to the choice of basis, i.e.,* $k(\boldsymbol{X}\boldsymbol{R}_1, \boldsymbol{Y}\boldsymbol{R}_2) = k(\boldsymbol{X}, \boldsymbol{Y})$, *for all* $\boldsymbol{X}, \boldsymbol{Y} \in \mathcal{G}(d, p)$ *and* $\boldsymbol{R}_1, \boldsymbol{R}_2 \in \text{SO}(p)$, *where* $\text{SO}(p)$ *denotes the special orthogonal group.*

The most widely used kernel is arguably the Gaussian or radial basis function (RBF) kernel. It is therefore tempting to define a Radial Basis Grassmannian kernel by replacing the Euclidean distance with the geodesic distance. Unfortunately, although symmetric and well-defined, the function $\exp(-\beta \delta_g^2(\cdot, \cdot))$ is not *pd*. This can be verified by a counter-example using the following points on $\mathcal{G}(3, 2)^2$:

$$\boldsymbol{X}_1 = \begin{bmatrix} 1 & 0 \\ 0 & 1 \\ 0 & 0 \end{bmatrix}, \; \boldsymbol{X}_2 = \begin{bmatrix} -0.0996 & -0.3085 \\ -0.4967 & -0.8084 \\ -0.8622 & 0.5014 \end{bmatrix}, \; \boldsymbol{X}_3 = \begin{bmatrix} -0.9868 & 0.1259 \\ -0.1221 & -0.9916 \\ -0.1065 & -0.0293 \end{bmatrix}, \; \boldsymbol{X}_4 = \begin{bmatrix} 0.1736 & 0.0835 \\ 0.7116 & 0.6782 \\ 0.6808 & -0.7301 \end{bmatrix}.$$

The function $\exp(-\delta_g^2(\cdot, \cdot))$ for these points has a negative eigenvalue of -0.0038.

Nevertheless, two Grassmannian kernels, *i.e.*, the Binet-Cauchy kernel [24] and the projection kernel [5], have been proposed to embed Grassmann manifolds into RKHS. The Binet-Cauchy and projection kernels are defined as

$$k_{bc}^2(\boldsymbol{X}, \boldsymbol{Y}) = \det(\boldsymbol{X}^T \boldsymbol{Y} \boldsymbol{Y}^T \boldsymbol{X}), \tag{3}$$

$$k_p(\boldsymbol{X}, \boldsymbol{Y}) = \|\boldsymbol{X}^T \boldsymbol{Y}\|_F^2. \tag{4}$$

---

[2] Note that we rounded each value to its 4 most significant digits.

Property 1 (Relation to Principal Angles). Both k_p and k_{bc} are closely related to the principal angles between two subspaces. Let θ_i be the ith principal angle between $\boldsymbol{X}, \boldsymbol{Y} \in \mathcal{G}(p, d)$, *i.e.*, by SVD, $\boldsymbol{X}^T \boldsymbol{Y} = \boldsymbol{U} \boldsymbol{\Gamma} \boldsymbol{V}^T$, with Γ a diagonal matrix with elements $\cos \theta_i$. Then

$$k_p(\boldsymbol{X}, \boldsymbol{Y}) = \left\| \boldsymbol{X}^T \boldsymbol{Y} \right\|_F^2 = \mathrm{Tr} \left(\boldsymbol{U} \boldsymbol{\Gamma} \boldsymbol{V}^T \boldsymbol{V} \boldsymbol{\Gamma} \boldsymbol{U}^T \right) = \mathrm{Tr} \left(\Gamma^2 \right) = \sum_{i=1}^{p} \cos^2(\theta_i) \,.$$

Similarly, one can show that $k_{bc}^2(\boldsymbol{X}, \boldsymbol{Y}) = \prod\limits_{i=1}^{p} \cos^2(\theta_i)$.

3 Embedding Grassmannians to Hilbert Spaces

While k_p and k_{bc}^2 have been successfully employed to transform problems on Grassmannians to Hilbert spaces [5,7,23], the resulting Hilbert spaces themselves have received comparatively little attention. In this section, we aim to bridge this gap and study these two spaces, which can be explicitly computed. To this end, we discuss the two embeddings that define these Hilbert spaces, namely the Plücker embedding and the projection embedding. These embeddings, and their respective properties, will in turn help us devise our set of new Grassmannian kernels.

3.1 Plücker Embedding

To study the Plücker embedding, we first need to review some concepts of exterior algebra.

Definition 4 (Alternating Multilinear Map). *Let $\boldsymbol{V}$ and $\boldsymbol{W}$ be two vector spaces. A map $g : \underbrace{\boldsymbol{V} \times \cdots \times \boldsymbol{V}}_{k \text{ copies}} \to \boldsymbol{W}$ is multilinear if it is linear in each slot, that is if*

$$g(\boldsymbol{v}_1, \cdots, \lambda \boldsymbol{v}_i + \lambda' \boldsymbol{v}_i', \cdots, \boldsymbol{v}_k) = \lambda g(\boldsymbol{v}_1, \cdots, \boldsymbol{v}_i, \cdots, \boldsymbol{v}_k) + \lambda' g(\boldsymbol{v}_1, \cdots, \boldsymbol{v}_i', \cdots, \boldsymbol{v}_k) \,.$$

Furthermore, the map g is alternating if, whenever two of the inputs to g are the same vector, the output is 0. That is, if $g(\cdots, \boldsymbol{v}, \cdots, \boldsymbol{v}, \cdots) = 0$, $\forall \boldsymbol{v}$.

Definition 5 (k^{th} Exterior Product). *Let $\boldsymbol{V}$ be a vector space. The kth exterior product of $\boldsymbol{V}$, denoted by $\bigwedge^k \boldsymbol{V}$ is a vector space, equipped with an alternating multilinear map $g : \underbrace{\boldsymbol{V} \times \cdots \times \boldsymbol{V}}_{k \text{ copies}} \to \bigwedge^k \boldsymbol{V}$ of the form $g(\boldsymbol{v}_1, \cdots, \boldsymbol{v}_k) = \boldsymbol{v}_1 \wedge \cdots \wedge \boldsymbol{v}_k$, with $\wedge$ the wedge product.*

The wedge product is supercommutative and can be thought of as a generalization of the cross product in $\mathbb{R}^3$ to an arbitrary dimension. Importantly, note that the kth exterior product $\bigwedge^k \boldsymbol{V}$ is a vector space, that is

$$\bigwedge^k \boldsymbol{V} = \mathrm{span} \left(\{ \boldsymbol{v}_1 \wedge \boldsymbol{v}_2 \wedge \cdots \wedge \boldsymbol{v}_k \} \right), \ \forall \boldsymbol{v}_i \in \boldsymbol{V} \,.$$

The Grassmannian $\mathcal{G}(d,p)$ can be embedded into the projective space $\mathbb{P}(\bigwedge^p \mathbb{R}^d)$ as follows. Let X be a point on $\mathcal{G}(p,d)$ described by the basis $\{x_1, x_2, \cdots, x_p\}$, i.e., $X = \mathrm{span}\,(\{x_1, x_2, \cdots, x_p\})$. The Plücker map of X is given by:

Definition 6 (Plücker Embedding). *The Plücker embedding* $P : \mathcal{G}(p,d) \to \mathbb{P}(\bigwedge^p \mathbb{R}^d)$ *is defined as*

$$P(X) = [x_1 \wedge x_2 \wedge \cdots \wedge x_p]\,, \tag{5}$$

where X *is the subspace spanned by* $\{x_1, x_2, \cdots, x_p\}$.

Example 1. Consider the space of two-dimensional planes in $\mathbb{R}^4$, i.e., $\mathcal{G}(2,4)$. In this space, an arbitrary subspace is described by its basis $\mathbf{B} = [w_1|w_2]$. Let e_i be the unit vector along the ith axis. We can write $w_j = \sum_{i=1}^{4} a_{j,i} e_i$. Then

$$
\begin{aligned}
P(\mathbf{B}) = {}& \Big(\sum_{i=1}^{4} a_{1,i} e_i \Big) \wedge \Big(\sum_{i=1}^{4} a_{2,j} e_j \Big) \\
= {}& (a_{1,1}a_{2,2} - a_{1,2}a_{2,1})(e_1 \wedge e_2) + (a_{1,1}a_{2,3} - a_{1,3}a_{2,1})(e_1 \wedge e_3) \\
& + (a_{1,1}a_{2,4} - a_{1,4}a_{2,1})(e_1 \wedge e_4) + (a_{1,2}a_{2,3} - a_{1,3}a_{2,2})(e_2 \wedge e_3) \\
& + (a_{1,2}a_{2,4} - a_{1,4}a_{2,2})(e_2 \wedge e_4) + (a_{1,3}a_{2,4} - a_{1,4}a_{2,3})(e_3 \wedge e_4)\,.
\end{aligned}
$$

Hence, the Plücker embedding of $\mathcal{G}(2,4)$ is a 6-dimensional space spanned by $\{e_1 \wedge e_2, e_1 \wedge e_3, \cdots, e_3 \wedge e_4\}$. A closer look at the coordinates of the embedded subspace reveals that they are indeed the minors of all possible 2×2 submatrices of $\mathbf{B}$. This can be shown to hold for any d and p.

Proposition 1. *The Plücker coordinates of* $X \in \mathcal{G}(d,p)$ *are the* $p \times p$ *minors of the matrix* X *obtained by taking* p *rows out of the* d *possible ones.*

Remark 1. The space induced by the Plücker map of $\mathcal{G}(p,d)$ is $\binom{p}{d}$-dimensional.

To be able to exploit the Plücker embedding to design new kernels, we need to define an inner product over $\mathbb{P}(\bigwedge^p \mathbb{R}^d)$. Importantly, to be meaningful, this inner product needs to be invariant to the specific realization of a point on $\mathcal{G}(p,d)$ (recall that, e.g., swapping two columns of a specific realization $X \in \mathcal{G}(d,p)$ still corresponds to the same point on $\mathcal{G}(d,p)$). Furthermore, we would also like this inner product to be efficient to evaluate, thus avoiding the need to explicitly compute the high-dimensional embedding. Note in particular that, for vision applications, the dimensionality of $\mathbb{P}(\bigwedge^p \mathbb{R}^d)$ becomes overwhelming and hence explicitly computing the embedding is impractical. To achieve these goals, we rely on the following definition and theorem:

Definition 7 (Compound Matrices). *Given a* $d \times p$ *matrix* A, *the matrix whose elements are the minors of* A *of order* q *arranged in a lexicographic order is called the* q^{th} *compound of* A, *and is denoted by* $C_q(A)$.

Theorem 1 (Binet-Cauchy Theorem). *Let* A *and* B *be two rectangular matrices of size* $d \times p_1$ *and* $d \times p_2$, *respectively. Then,* $C_q(A^T B) = C_q(A)^T C_q(B)$.

Therefore, for $X, Y \in \mathbb{R}^{d \times p}$, we have $\mathrm{Tr}\left(C_p(X)^T C_p(Y)\right) = \mathrm{Tr}\left(C_p(X^T Y)\right) = \det\left(X^T Y\right)$.

Since, for $X \in \mathcal{G}(p, d)$, $C_p(X)$ stores all $p \times p$ minors and hence conveys the Plücker coordinates of X, this would suggest defining the inner product for the Plücker embedding as $\det(X^T Y)$. This is indeed what was proposed in [5,24] where $\det(\cdot)$ was used as a linear kernel. However, while $\det(X^T Y)$ is invariant to the action of $\mathrm{SO}(p)$, it is not invariant to the specific realization of a subspace. This can be simply verified by permuting the columns of X, which does not change the subspace, but may change the sign of $\det(\cdot)$. Note that this sign issue was also observed by Wolf *et al.* [24]. However, this problem was circumvented by considering the second-order polynomial kernel k_{bc}^2.

In contrast, here, we focus on designing a valid inner product that satisfies this invariance condition. To this end, we define the inner product in $\mathbb{P}(\bigwedge^p \mathbb{R}^d)$ as $\langle X, Y \rangle_P = |P(X)^T P(Y)| = \left| \det\left(X^T Y\right) \right|$. This inner product induces the distance

$$\delta_{bc}^2(X, Y) = \|P(X) - P(Y)\|^2 = 2 - 2\left| \det\left(X^T Y\right) \right|. \tag{6}$$

Clearly, if $\{\theta_i\}_{i=1}^p$ is the set of principal angles between two Grassmannian points X and Y, then $\langle X, Y \rangle_P = \prod_{i=1}^p \cos(\theta_i)$, which is invariant to the specific realization of a subspace since $0 \leq \theta_i \leq \pi/2$.

In the following, we show that the Plücker embedding has the nice property of being closely related to the true geometry of the corresponding Grassmannian:

Theorem 2 (Curve Length Equivalence). *The length of any given curve is the same under δ_{bc} and δ_g up to a scale of $\sqrt{2}$.*

Proof. Given in supplementary material.   □

3.2   Projection Embedding

We now turn to the case of the projection embedding. Note that this embedding has been better studied than the Plücker one [8].

Definition 8 (Projection Embedding). *The projection embedding $\Pi : \mathcal{G}(p, d) \to \mathrm{Sym}(d)$ is defined as*

$$\Pi(X) = XX^T. \tag{7}$$

The projection embedding $\Pi(\cdot)$ is a diffeomorphism from a Grassmann manifold onto the idempotent symmetric matrices of rank p, *i.e.*, it is a one-to-one, continuous, differentiable mapping with a continuous, differentiable inverse [3]. The space induced by this embedding is a smooth, compact submanifold of $\mathrm{Sym}(d)$ of dimension $d(d - p)$. Since $\Pi(X)$ is a symmetric $d \times d$ matrix, a natural choice of inner product is $\langle X, Y \rangle_\Pi = \mathrm{Tr}\left(\Pi(X)^T \Pi(Y)\right) = \|XY\|_F^2$. This inner product can be shown to be invariant to the specific realization of a subspace, and induces the distance

$$\delta_p^2(X, Y) = \|\Pi(X) - \Pi(Y)\|_F^2 = 2p - 2\|X^T Y\|_F^2.$$

Due to space limitation, we do not discuss the properties of the projection embedding, such as isometry [3] and length of curves [6]. We refer the reader to [8] for a more thorough discussion of the projection embedding.

4   Grassmannian Kernels

From the discussion in Section 3, k_{bc}^2 and k_p, defined in Eq. 4 and Eq. 3, can be seen to correspond to a homogeneous second order polynomial kernel in the space induced by the Plücker embedding and to a linear kernel in the space induced by the projection embedding, respectively. In this section, we show that the inner products that we defined in Section 3 for the Plücker and projection embeddings can actually be exploited to derive many new Grassmannian kernels, including universal kernels and conditionally positive definite kernels. In the following, we denote by $k_{.,bc}$ and $k_{.,p}$ kernels derived from the Plücker embedding (Binet-Cauchy kernels) and from the projection embedding, respectively.

4.1   Polynomial Kernels

Given an inner product, which itself defines a valid linear kernel, the most straightforward way to create new kernels is to consider higher degree polynomials. Such polynomial kernels are known to be pd. Therefore, we can readily define polynomial kernels on the Grassmannian as

$$k_{p,bc}(\boldsymbol{X}, \boldsymbol{Y}) = \left(\beta + \left| \det \left(\boldsymbol{X}^T \boldsymbol{Y} \right) \right| \right)^\alpha, \quad \beta > 0, \tag{8}$$

$$k_{p,p}(\boldsymbol{X}, \boldsymbol{Y}) = \left(\beta + \left\| \boldsymbol{X}^T \boldsymbol{Y} \right\|_F^2 \right)^\alpha, \quad \beta > 0. \tag{9}$$

Note that the kernel used in [24] is indeed the homogeneous second order $k_{p,bc}$ with $\alpha = 2$ and $\beta = 0$.

4.2   Universal Grassmannian Kernels

Although often used in practice, polynomial kernels are known not to be universal [19]. This can have a crucial impact on their representation power for a specific task. Indeed, from the *Representer Theorem* [16], we have that, for a given set of training data $\{x_j\}$, $j \in \mathbb{N}_n$, $\mathbb{N}_n = \{1, 2, \cdots, n\}$ and a pd kernel k, the function learned by any algorithm can be expressed as

$$\hat{f}(x_*) = \sum_{j \in \mathbb{N}_n} c_j k(x_*, x_j). \tag{10}$$

Importantly, only *universal kernels* have the property of being able to approximate any target function f_t arbitrarily well given sufficiently many training samples. Therefore, k_p and k_{bc}^2 may not generalize sufficiently well for certain problems. In the following, we develop several universal Grassmannian kernels. To this end, we make use of negative definite kernels and of their relation to pd ones. Let us first formally define negative definite kernels.

Definition 9 (Real-valued Negative Definite Kernels). *Let $\mathcal{X}$ be a nonempty set. A symmetric function $\psi : \mathcal{X} \times \mathcal{X} \to \mathbb{R}$ is a negative definite (nd) kernel on $\mathcal{X}$ if and only if $\sum_{i,j=1}^{n} c_i c_j k(x_i, x_j) \leq 0$ for any $n \in \mathbb{N}$, $x_i \in \mathcal{X}$ and $c_i \in \mathbb{R}$ with $\sum_{i=1}^{n} c_i = 0$.*

Note that, in contrast to positive definite kernels, an additional constraint of the form $\sum c_i = 0$ is required in the negative definite case.

The most important example of *nd* kernels is the distance function defined on a Hilbert space. More specifically:

Theorem 3 ([9]). *Let $\mathcal{X}$ be a nonempty set, $\mathcal{H}$ be an inner product space, and $\psi : \mathcal{X} \to \mathcal{H}$ be a function. Then $f : (\mathcal{X} \times \mathcal{X}) \to \mathbb{R}$ defined by $f(x_i, x_j) = \|\psi(x_i) - \psi(x_j)\|_{\mathcal{H}}^{2}$ is negative definite.*

Therefore, being distances in Hilbert spaces, both δ_{bc}^2 and δ_p^2 are *nd* kernels. We now state an important theorem which establishes the relation between *pd* and *nd* kernels.

Theorem 4 (Theorem 2.3 in Chapter 3 of [2]). *Let μ be a probability measure on the half line $\mathbb{R}_+$ and $0 < \int_0^{\infty} t d\mu(t) < \infty$. Let $\mathcal{L}_\mu$ be the Laplace transform of μ, i.e., $\mathcal{L}_\mu(s) = \int_0^{\infty} e^{-ts} d\mu(t)$, $s \in \mathbb{C}_+$. Then, $\mathcal{L}_\mu(\beta f)$ is positive definite for all $\beta > 0$ if and only if $f : \mathcal{X} \times \mathcal{X} \to \mathbb{R}_+$ is negative definite.*

The problem of designing a *pd* kernel on the Grassmannian can now be cast as that of finding an appropriate probability measure μ. Below, we show that this lets us reformulate popular kernels in Euclidean space as Grassmannian kernels.

RBF Kernels. Grassmannian RBF kernels can be obtained by choosing $\mu(t) = \delta(t - 1)$ in Theorem 4, where $\delta(t)$ is the Dirac delta function. This choice yields the Grassmannian RBF kernels (after discarding scalar constants)

$$k_{r,bc}(\boldsymbol{X}, \boldsymbol{Y}) = \exp\left(\beta |\det\left(\boldsymbol{X}^T \boldsymbol{Y}\right)|\right), \quad \beta > 0, \tag{11}$$

$$k_{r,p}(\boldsymbol{X}, \boldsymbol{Y}) = \exp\left(\beta \|\boldsymbol{X}^T \boldsymbol{Y}\|_F^2\right), \quad \beta > 0. \tag{12}$$

Note that the RBF kernel obtained from the projection embedding, *i.e.* $k_{r,p}$, was also used by Vemulapalli *et al.* [23]. However, the positive definiteness of this kernel was neither proven nor discussed.

Laplace Kernels. The Laplace kernel is another widely used Euclidean kernel, defined as $k(\boldsymbol{x}, \boldsymbol{y}) = \exp(-\beta \|\boldsymbol{x} - \boldsymbol{y}\|)$. To obtain Laplace kernels on the Grassmannian, we make use of the following theorem for *nd* kernels.

Theorem 5 (Corollary 2.10 in Chapter 3 of [2]). *If $\psi : \mathcal{X} \times \mathcal{X} \to \mathbb{R}$ is negative definite and satisfies $\psi(\boldsymbol{x}, \boldsymbol{x}) \geq 0$ then so is ψ^α for $0 < \alpha < 1$.*

As a result, both $\delta_p(\cdot,\cdot)$ and $\delta_{bc}(\cdot,\cdot)$ are nd by choosing $\alpha = 1/2$ in Theorem 5. By employing either $\delta_p(\cdot,\cdot)$ or $\delta_{bc}(\cdot,\cdot)$ along with $\mu(t) = \delta(t-1)$ in Theorem 4, we obtain the Grassmannian Laplace kernels

$$k_{l,bc}(\boldsymbol{X},\boldsymbol{Y}) = \exp\left(-\beta\sqrt{1 - |\det\left(\boldsymbol{X}^T\boldsymbol{Y}\right)|}\right), \quad \beta > 0, \tag{13}$$

$$k_{l,p}(\boldsymbol{X},\boldsymbol{Y}) = \exp\left(-\beta\sqrt{p - \|\boldsymbol{X}^T\boldsymbol{Y}\|_F^2}\right), \quad \beta > 0. \tag{14}$$

As shown in [19], the RBF and Laplace kernels are universal for $\mathbb{R}^d, d > 0$. Since the Plücker and projection embeddings map to Euclidean spaces, this property clearly extends to the Grassmannian RBF and Laplace kernels.

Binomial Kernels. By choosing $\mu(t) = \exp(-\beta_0 t)u(t)$, where $u(t)$ is the unit (or Heaviside) step function, *i.e.*, $u(t) = \int_{-\infty}^{t} \delta(x)\mathrm{d}x$, we obtain the Grassmannian binomial kernels

$$k_{b,bc}(\boldsymbol{X},\boldsymbol{Y}) = \frac{1}{\beta - |\det\left(\boldsymbol{X}^T\boldsymbol{Y}\right)|}, \quad \beta > 1, \tag{15}$$

$$k_{b,p}(\boldsymbol{X},\boldsymbol{Y}) = \frac{1}{\beta - \|\boldsymbol{X}^T\boldsymbol{Y}\|_F^2}, \quad \beta > p. \tag{16}$$

Note that the generating function μ is a valid measure only for $\beta_0 > 0$. This translates into the constraints on β given in Eq. 15 and Eq. 16.

A more general form of binomial kernels can be derived by noting that, if $k(\cdot,\cdot) : \mathcal{X} \times \mathcal{X} \to \mathbb{R}_+$ is pd, then so is $k^\alpha(\cdot,\cdot)$, $\alpha > 0$ (see Proposition 2.7 in Chapter 3 of [2]). This lets us define the Grassmannian kernels

$$k_{bi,bc}(\boldsymbol{X},\boldsymbol{Y}) = \left(\beta - |\det\left(\boldsymbol{X}^T\boldsymbol{Y}\right)|\right)^{-\alpha}, \quad \beta > 1, \alpha > 0, \tag{17}$$

$$k_{bi,p}(\boldsymbol{X},\boldsymbol{Y}) = \left(\beta - \|\boldsymbol{X}^T\boldsymbol{Y}\|_F^2\right)^{-\alpha}, \quad \beta > p, \alpha > 0. \tag{18}$$

To show that the binomial kernels are universal, we note that

$$(1-t)^{-\alpha} = \sum_{j=0}^{\infty} \binom{-\alpha}{j}(-1)^j t^j, \quad \text{with} \quad \binom{\alpha}{j} = \prod_{i=1}^{j}(\alpha - i + 1)/i.$$

It can be seen that $\binom{-\alpha}{j}(-1)^j > 0$, which implies that both $k_{bi,bc}$ and $k_{bi,p}$ have non-negative and full Taylor series. This, as was shown in Corollary 4.57 of [19], is a necessary and sufficient condition for a kernel to be universal.

4.3   Conditionally Positive Kernels

Another important class of kernels is the so-called conditionally positive definite kernels [2]. Formally:

Definition 10 (Conditionally Positive Definite Kernels). *Let $\mathcal{X}$ be a nonempty set. A symmetric function $\psi : \mathcal{X} \times \mathcal{X} \to \mathbb{R}$ is a conditionally positive definite (cpd) kernel on $\mathcal{X}$ if and only if $\sum_{i,j=1}^{n} c_i c_j k(x_i, x_j) \geq 0$ for any $n \in \mathbb{N}$, $x_i \in \mathcal{X}$ and $c_i \in \mathbb{R}$ with $\sum_{i=1}^{n} c_i = 0$.*

The relations between *cpd* kernels and *pd* ones were studied by Berg *et al.* [2] and Schölkopf [15] among others. Before introducing *cpd* kernels on the Grassmannian, we state an important property of *cpd* kernels.

Proposition 2 ([15]). *For a kernel algorithm that is translation invariant, one can equally use* cpd *kernels instead of* pd *ones.*

This property relaxes the requirement of having *pd* kernels for certain types of kernel algorithms. A kernel algorithm is translation invariant if it is independent of the position of the origin. For example, in SVMs, maximizing the margin of the separating hyperplane between two classes is independent of the position of the origin. As a result, one can seamlessly use a *cpd* kernel instead of a *pd* kernel in SVMs. To introduce *cpd* kernels on Grassmannians, we rely on the following proposition:

Proposition 3 ([2]). *If $f : \mathcal{X} \times \mathcal{X} \to \mathbb{R}_+$ is nd then $-\log(1 + f)$ is cpd.*

This lets us derive the Grassmannian *cpd* kernels

$$k_{log,bc}(\boldsymbol{X}, \boldsymbol{Y}) = -\log\left(2 - \det\left(\boldsymbol{X}^T \boldsymbol{Y}\right)\right), \tag{19}$$

$$k_{log,p}(\boldsymbol{X}, \boldsymbol{Y}) = -\log\left(p + 1 - \left\|\boldsymbol{X}^T \boldsymbol{Y}\right\|_F^2\right). \tag{20}$$

The ten new kernels derived in this section are summarized in Table 1. Note that given the linear *Plücker* and *projection* kernels, *i.e.*, $k_{lin,bc}(\boldsymbol{X}, \boldsymbol{Y}) = |\det(\boldsymbol{X}^T \boldsymbol{Y})|$ and $k_{lin,p}(\boldsymbol{X}, \boldsymbol{Y}) = \|\boldsymbol{X}^T \boldsymbol{Y}\|_F^2$, it is possible to obtain the polynomial and Gaussian extensions via standard kernel construction rules [17]. However, our approach lets us derive many other kernels in a principled manner by, *e.g.*, exploiting different measures in Theorem 4. Nonetheless, here, we confined ourselves to deriving kernels corresponding to the most popular ones in Euclidean space, and leave the study of additional kernels as future work.

5   Experimental Evaluation

In this section, we compare our new kernels with the baseline kernels k_{bc}^2 and k_p using three different kernel-based algorithms on Grassmannians: kernel SVM, kernel k-means and kernelized Locality Sensitive Hashing (kLSH). Additional results using kernel sparse coding are given in supplementary material. In our experiments, unless stated otherwise, we obtained the kernel parameters (*i.e.*, β for all kernels except the logarithm ones and α for the polynomial and binomial cases) by cross-validation.

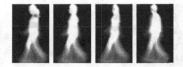

Fig. 1. GEI samples from CASIA [26]

Table 2. Gender recognition. Accuracies on the CASIA gait dataset [26].

kernel	k_{bc}^2	$k_{p,bc}$	$k_{r,bc}$	$k_{l,bc}$	$k_{bi,bc}$	$k_{log,bc}$
SVM	76.8% ± 9.1	84.1% ± 7.2	85.8% ± 4.6	84.5% ± 4.5	**86.4% ± 4.4**	82.7% ± 7.4
GGDA[7]	83.7% ± 3.7.	89.0% ± 3.7	88.3% ± 3.6	88.0% ± 3.6	**89.4% ± 3.1**	84.9% ± 3.5

kernel	k_p	$k_{p,p}$	$k_{r,p}$	$k_{l,p}$	$k_{bi,p}$	$k_{log,p}$
SVM	83.7% ± 4.3	**89.3% ± 5.8**	88.2% ± 5.8	87.6% ± 5.5	88.7% ± 5.1	85.8% ± 8.3
GGDA[7]	90.3% ± 4.7	**93.5% ± 2.7**	91.3% ± 3.8	91.0% ± 3.8	91.1% ± 3.1	89.7% ± 3.6

5.1 Gender Recognition from Gait

We first demonstrate the benefits of our kernels on a binary classification problem on the Grassmannian using SVM and the Grassmannian Graph-embedding Discriminant Analysis (GGDA) proposed in [7]. To this end, we consider the task of gender recognition from gait (*i.e.*, videos of people walking). We used Dataset-B of the CASIA gait database [26], which comprises 124 individuals (93 males and 31 females). The gait of each subject was captured from 11 viewpoints. Every video is represented by a gait energy image (GEI) of size 32×32 (see Fig. 1), which has proven effective for gender recognition [25].

In our experiment, we used the videos captured with normal clothes and created a subspace of order 3 from the 11 GEIs corresponding to the different viewpoints. This resulted in 731 points on $\mathcal{G}(3, 1024)$. We then randomly selected 20 individuals (10 male, 10 female) as training set and used the remaining individuals for testing. In Table 2, we report the average accuracies over 10 random partitions. Note that for the SVM classifier, all new kernels derived from the Plücker embedding outperform k_{bc}^2, with highest accuracy obtained with the binomial kernel. Similarly, all new projection kernels outperform k_p, and the polynomial kernel achieves the overall highest accuracy of 89.3%. For GGDA, bar the case of $k_{log,p}$, all new kernels also outperform previously-known ones.

5.2 Pose Categorization

As a second experiment, we evaluate the performance of our kernels on the task of clustering on the Grassmannian using kernel k-means. To this end, we used the CMU-PIE face dataset [18], which contains images of 67 subjects with 13 different poses and 21 different illuminations (see Fig. 2 for examples). From each image, we computed a 2×2 spatial pyramid of LBP [14] histograms and concatenated them to form a 232 dimensional descriptor. For each subject,

Fig. 2. Sample images from CMU-PIE

Fig. 3. Sample images from the mouse behavior dataset [11]

Table 3. Pose categorization. Clustering accuracies on the CMU-PIE dataset.

kernel	k_{bc}^2	$k_{p,bc}$	$k_{r,bc}$	$k_{l,bc}$	$k_{bi,bc}$	$k_{log,bc}$
accuracy	70.3%	72.2%	**78.9%**	74.8%	78.5%	72.2%
NMI	0.763	0.779	**0.803**	0.786	0.798	0.772
kernel	k_p	$k_{p,p}$	$k_{r,p}$	$k_{l,p}$	$k_{bi,p}$	$k_{log,p}$
accuracy	77.1%	79.9%	80.9%	79.8%	**82.9%**	74.4%
NMI	0.810%	0.817	0.847	0.843	**0.853**	0.812

we collected the images acquired with the same pose, but different illuminations, in an image set, which we then represented as a linear subspace of order 3. This resulted in a total of $67 \times 13 = 871$ Grassmannian points on $\mathcal{G}(3, 232)$. We used 10 samples from each pose to compute the kernel parameters.

The goal here is to cluster together image sets representing the same pose. To evaluate the quality of the clusters, we report both the clustering accuracy and the Normalized Mutual Information (NMI) [20], which measures the amount of statistical information shared by random variables representing the cluster distribution and the underlying class distribution of the data points. From the results given in Table 3, we can see that, with the exception of $k_{log,p}$, the new kernels in each embedding outperform their respective baseline, k_p or k_{bc}^2. For the Binet-Cauchy kernels, the maximum accuracy (and NMI score) is reached by the RBF kernel. The overall maximum accuracy of 82.9% is achieved by the projection-based binomial kernel.

We also evaluated the intrinsic k-means algorithm of [22]. This algorithm achieved 67.7% accuracy and an NMI score of 0.75. Furthermore, intrinsic k-means required $9766s$ to perform clustering on an i7 machine using Matlab. On the same machine, the runtimes for kernel k-means using $k_{r,bc}$ and $k_{bi,p}$ (which achieve the highest accuracies in Table 3) were $3.1s$ and $2.5s$, respectively. This clearly demonstrates the benefits of RKHS embedding to tackle clustering problems on the Grassmannian.

5.3   Mouse Behavior Analysis

Finally, we utilized kernelized Locality-Sensitive Hashing (kLHS) [12] to perform recognition on the 2000 videos of the mice behavior dataset [11]. The basic idea of

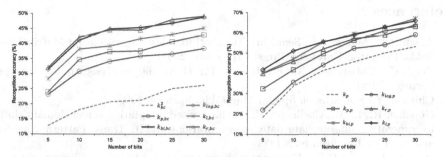

Fig. 4. Video hashing. Approximate nearest-neighbor accuracies for kernels derived from (**left**) the Plücker and (**right**) the projection embeddings.

kLSH is to search for a projection from an RKHS to a low-dimensional Hamming space, where each sample is encoded with a b-bit vector called the hash key. The approximate nearest-neighbor to a query can then be found efficiently in time sublinear in the number of training samples.

The mice dataset [11] contains 8 behaviors (*i.e.*, *drinking, eating, grooming, hanging, rearing, walking, resting* and *micro-movement of head*) of several mice with different coating colors, sizes and genders (see Fig. 3 for examples). In each video, we estimated the background to extract the region containing the mouse in each frame. These regions were then resized to 48×48, and the video represented with an order 6 subspace, thus yielding points on $\mathcal{G}(6, 2304)$. We randomly chose 1000 videos for training and used the remaining 1000 videos for testing. We report the average recognition accuracy over 10 random partitions.

Fig. 4 depicts the recognition accuracies of the new and baseline kernels as a function of the number of bits b. For the Plücker embedding kernels, the gap between our RBF kernel and k_{bc}^2 reaches 23% for a hash key of size 30. For the same hash key size, the projection-based heat kernel outperforms k_p by more than 14%, and thus reaches the overall highest accuracy of 67.2%.

6   Conclusions and Future Work

We have introduced a set of new positive definite kernels to embed Grassmannian into Hilbert spaces, which have a more familiar Euclidean structure. This set includes, among others, universal Grassmannian kernels, which have the ability to approximate general functions. Our experiments have demonstrated the superiority of such kernels over previously-known Grassmannian kernels, *i.e.*, the Binet-Cauchy kernel [24] and the projection kernel [5]. It is important to keep in mind, however, that choosing the right kernel for the data at hand remains an open problem. In the future, we intend to study if searching for the best probability measure in Theroem 4 could give a partial answer to this question.

References

1. Absil, P.A., Mahony, R., Sepulchre, R.: Optimization Algorithms on Matrix Manifolds. Princeton University Press, Princeton (2008)
2. Berg, C., Christensen, J.P.R., Ressel, P.: Harmonic Analysis on Semigroups. Springer (1984)
3. Chikuse, Y.: Statistics on Special Manifolds. Springer (2003)
4. Gopalan, R., Li, R., Chellappa, R.: Unsupervised adaptation across domain shifts by generating intermediate data representations. IEEE Trans. Pattern Analysis and Machine Intelligence (2014)
5. Hamm, J., Lee, D.D.: Grassmann discriminant analysis: a unifying view on subspace-based learning. In: Proc. Int. Conference on Machine Learning (ICML), pp. 376–383 (2008)
6. Harandi, M., Sanderson, C., Shen, C., Lovell, B.C.: Dictionary learning and sparse coding on grassmann manifolds: An extrinsic solution. In: Proc. Int. Conference on Computer Vision (ICCV) (December 2013)
7. Harandi, M.T., Sanderson, C., Shirazi, S., Lovell, B.C.: Graph embedding discriminant analysis on Grassmannian manifolds for improved image set matching. In: Proc. IEEE Conference on Computer Vision and Pattern Recognition (CVPR), pp. 2705–2712 (2011)
8. Helmke, U., Hüper, K., Trumpf, J.: Newtons's method on Grassmann manifolds. Preprint: [arXiv:0709.2205] (2007)
9. Jayasumana, S., Hartley, R., Salzmann, M., Li, H., Harandi, M.: Kernel methods on the Riemannian manifold of symmetric positive definite matrices. In: CVPR, pp. 73–80 (2013)
10. Jayasumana, S., Hartley, R., Salzmann, M., Li, H., Harandi, M.: Optimizing over radial kernels on compact manifolds. In: Proc. IEEE Conference on Computer Vision and Pattern Recognition (CVPR) (June 2014)
11. Jhuang, H., Garrote, E., Yu, X., Khilnani, V., Poggio, T., Steele, A.D., Serre, T.: Automated home-cage behavioural phenotyping of mice. Nature Communications 1, 68 (2010)
12. Kulis, B., Grauman, K.: Kernelized locality-sensitive hashing. IEEE Trans. Pattern Analysis and Machine Intelligence 34(6), 1092–1104 (2012)
13. Micchelli, C.A., Xu, Y., Zhang, H.: Universal kernels. Journal of Machine Learning Research 7, 2651–2667 (2006)
14. Ojala, T., Pietikainen, M., Maenpaa, T.: Multiresolution gray-scale and rotation invariant texture classification with local binary patterns. IEEE Trans. Pattern Analysis and Machine Intelligence 24(7), 971–987 (2002)
15. Scholkopf, B.: The kernel trick for distances. In: Proc. Advances in Neural Information Processing Systems (NIPS), pp. 301–307 (2001)
16. Schölkopf, B., Herbrich, R., Smola, A.J.: A generalized representer theorem. In: Helmbold, D.P., Williamson, B. (eds.) COLT/EuroCOLT 2001. LNCS (LNAI), vol. 2111, pp. 416–426. Springer, Heidelberg (2001)
17. Shawe-Taylor, J., Cristianini, N.: Kernel Methods for Pattern Analysis. Cambridge University Press (2004)
18. Sim, T., Baker, S., Bsat, M.: The cmu pose, illumination, and expression database. IEEE Trans. Pattern Analysis and Machine Intelligence 25(12), 1615–1618 (2003)
19. Steinwart, I., Christmann, A.: Support vector machines. Springer (2008)
20. Strehl, A., Ghosh, J., Mooney, R.: Impact of similarity measures on web-page clustering. In: AAAI Workshop on Artificial Intelligence for Web Search, pp. 58–64 (2000)

21. Subbarao, R., Meer, P.: Nonlinear mean shift over Riemannian manifolds. Int. Journal of Computer Vision 84(1), 1–20 (2009)
22. Turaga, P., Veeraraghavan, A., Srivastava, A., Chellappa, R.: Statistical computations on Grassmann and Stiefel manifolds for image and video-based recognition. IEEE Trans. Pattern Analysis and Machine Intelligence 33(11), 2273–2286 (2011)
23. Vemulapalli, R., Pillai, J.K., Chellappa, R.: Kernel learning for extrinsic classification of manifold features. In: Proc. IEEE Conference on Computer Vision and Pattern Recognition (CVPR), pp. 1782–1789 (2013)
24. Wolf, L., Shashua, A.: Learning over sets using kernel principal angles. Journal of Machine Learning Research 4, 913–931 (2003)
25. Yu, S., Tan, T., Huang, K., Jia, K., Wu, X.: A study on gait-based gender classification. IEEE Trans. Image Processing (TIP) 18(8), 1905–1910 (2009)
26. Zheng, S., Zhang, J., Huang, K., He, R., Tan, T.: Robust view transformation model for gait recognition. In: International Conference on Image Processing (ICIP), pp. 2073–2076 (2011)

Image Tag Completion by Noisy Matrix Recovery

Zheyun Feng[1], Songhe Feng[2], Rong Jin[1], and Anil K. Jain[1]

[1] Michigan State University
[2] Beijing Jiaotong University
{fengzhey,rongjin,jain}@cse.msu.edu, shfeng@bjtu.edu.cn

Abstract. It is now generally recognized that user-provided image tags are incomplete and noisy. In this study, we focus on the problem of *tag completion* that aims to simultaneously enrich the missing tags and remove noisy tags. The novel component of the proposed framework is a noisy matrix recovery algorithm. It assumes that the observed tags are independently sampled from an unknown tag matrix and our goal is to recover the tag matrix based on the sampled tags. We show theoretically that the proposed noisy tag matrix recovery algorithm is able to simultaneously recover the missing tags and de-emphasize the noisy tags even with a limited number of observations. In addition, a graph Laplacian based component is introduced to combine the noisy matrix recovery component with visual features. Our empirical study with multiple benchmark datasets for image tagging shows that the proposed algorithm outperforms state-of-the-art approaches in terms of both effectiveness and efficiency when handling missing and noisy tags.

Keywords: Tag completion, noisy tag matrix recovery, matrix completion, missing/noisy tags, image tagging, image annotation, tag ranking.

1   Introduction

With the ever-growing popularity of digital photography and social media, the number of images with user-provided tags available over the internet has increased dramatically in the last decade. However, many user-provided tags are incomplete or inaccurate in describing the visual content of images [24], making them difficult to be utilized for tasks such as tag based image retrieval and tag recommendation [15,16,27]. This is particularly true for images extracted from social media [16,27], where in most cases, only a few tags are provided for each image and some of them are noisy. In this work, we develop an effective algorithm that can simultaneously recover the missing tags and remove or down weight the noisy tags which are irrelevant to the visual content of images.

We refer to our problem as *tag completion* [7] to distinguish it from previous image tagging work. *Image annotation* [9,11] automatically assigns images with appropriate keywords. As state-of-the-art image annotation approach, search based algorithms [9,11] rely on the quality of tags assigned to training images [9].

D. Fleet et al. (Eds.): ECCV 2014, Part VII, LNCS 8695, pp. 424–438, 2014.

Tag recommendation suggests candidate tags to annotators in order to improve the efficiency and quality of the tagging process [14]. It usually identifies missing tags by topic models (e.g. *Latent Dirichlet Allocation* (LDA)) [2,14], but does not address the noisy tag problem. *Tag refinement* applies various techniques (e.g. topic model, tag propagation, sparse training and partial supervision [6,17,25]) to select a subset of user-provided tags based on image features and tag correlation [26]. Although it is able to handle noisy tags, it does not explicitly address the missing tag problem. Unlike most existing studies, the tag completion problem studied in this work simultaneously addresses the challenges of missing and noisy tags [7].

Since the tags of each image can be viewed as a mixture of topics and each topic follows a multinomial distribution over the vocabulary [2,14,25], we use a maximum likelihood component to ensure the learned tag probability matrix to be consistent with the observed tags. To simultaneously address the problem of missing and noisy tags, we assume that the observed tags are sampled independently from a low rank tag matrix; our goal is to recover the tag matrix from the noisy observations. By enforcing the recovered matrix to be low rank, we are able to effectively capture the correlation among different tags, which turns out to be the key in filling out missing tags and down weighting noisy ones [4,19,23]. This is in contrast to the existing studies for tag completion [15,18,24,27] where no principled approach is presented to capture the dependence among tags, which, however in our opinion, is the key issue to the tag completion problem. We refer to the proposed approach as tag completion by noisy matrix recovery, or **TCMR** for short.

We note that although low rank matrix recovery is closely related to topic model that has been applied to many image tag related problems [14,25], it has three novel contributions. First, unlike most existing topic models [1] that need to solve a non-convex optimization problem, the proposed TCMR solves a convex optimization problem and therefore is computationally more efficient. We have shown theoretically that under favorable conditions, the proposed TCMR is guaranteed to recover most of the missing tags even when the user-provided tags are noisy. This is in contrast to most topic models that do not come with theoretical support. Besides, TCMR further improves the performance by effectively exploiting the statistical dependence between image features and tags via a graph Laplacian [26,27], which reduces the impact of incomplete and noisy tags by assigning high weights to tags that are consistent with image features, and low weights to those which are not. Finally, our work is closely related to the theory of matrix completion and recovery [4,5]. Unlike existing studies on matrix completion/recovery, a maximum likelihood estimation is used in this work to recover the underlying low rank tag matrix, adding more complexity to both optimization and analysis.

The paper is organized as follows. Section 2 reviews the related work. Section 3 introduces the noisy matrix recovery and TCMR. Section 4 presents the theoretical support of TCMR. Section 5 summarizes the experimental results, and Section 6 concludes this work with future directions.

2 Related Work

Image Tag Completion. There are only a few studies fitting the category of tag completion with both incomplete and noisy tags. [27] proposes a data-driven framework for tag ranking that optimizes the correlation between visual cues and assigned tags. [16] removes the noisy tags based on the visual and semantic similarities, and expands the observed tags with their synonyms and hypernyms using WordNet. [24] proposes to search for the optimal tag matrix that is consistent with both observed tags and visual similarity. [18] formulates tag completion into a non-negative data factorization problem. [15] exploits sparse learning techniques to reconstruct the tag matrix. None of these studies provides any theoretical guarantee for their approaches. Matrix decomposition is adopted in [3,21,26] to handle both missing and noisy tags. The key limitation of these approaches is that they require a full observed matrix with a small number of errors, making it inappropriate for tag completion.

Low Rank Matrix Recovery. Low rank matrix recovery has been applied in many applications [4,21], including visual recovery [19,21], multilabel classification [3], tag refinement [26], etc. Since the function of matrix rank is non-convex, a popular approach is to replace it with the nuclear norm, the tightest convex relaxation for matrix rank [4,5,26]. Using the nuclear norm regularization, it is possible to accurately recover a low rank matrix from a small fraction of its entries [5] even if they are corrupted with noise [4,10]. Various algorithms [10,12,21,26] have been developed to solve the related optimization problem. Instead of the ℓ_1-norm loss [10,26], squared loss [23] and max-margin factorization model [19] used in most studies on matrix completion/recovery, a maximum likelihood estimation is used in our work to recover the underlying tag matrix.

3 Image Tag Completion by Noisy Matrix Recovery (TCMR)

In this section, we first describe a noisy matrix recovery framework for tag completion and then discuss how to incorporate visual features into the matrix recovery framework.

3.1 Noisy Matrix Recovery

Let m be the number of unique tags, and $\mathcal{D} = \{\mathbf{d}_1, \cdots, \mathbf{d}_n\}$ be a collection of n tagged images, where $\mathbf{d}_i = (d_{i,1}, \cdots, d_{i,m})$ is the tag vector for the i-th image with $d_{i,j} = 1$ when tag j is assigned to the image and zero, otherwise. For the simplicity of analysis, in this study, we assume that all the images have the same number of assigned tags, denoted by m_*[1].

---

[1] This assumption is only for the convenience of analysis, and does not affect the algorithm. When different number of tags are observed, we apply the weighting technique [22] to handle the variation in the number of tags.

Following the idea of language models [1,2], we assume that all the observed tags in each image are drawn independently from a fixed but unknown multinomial distribution. Let $\mathbf{p}_i = (p_{i,1}, \cdots, p_{i,m})$ be the multinomial distribution used to generate tags in $\mathbf{d}_i$. We use $P = (\mathbf{p}_1, \cdots, \mathbf{p}_n)$ to represent the multinomial distributions for all the images. Our goal is to accurately recover the multinomial distribution P from a limited number of observed tags in $\mathcal{D}$. In general, this is impossible since the number of parameters to be estimated is significantly larger than the number of observed tags. To address this challenge, we follow the key assumption behind most topic models [23,26], *i.e.* tags of any image are sampled from a mixture of a small number of multinomial distributions. A direct implication of this assumption is that matrix P has to be of low rank, the foundation for the theory of low rank matrix recovery [5].

Before presenting our algorithm and analysis, we first introduce the notation that will be used throughout this paper. We use $Q_{*,i}$ to represent the i-th column of matrix Q, $|Q|_F$, $|Q|_{tr}$ and $|Q|_*$ to represent the Frobenius norm, nuclear (trace) norm and spectral norm of matrix Q, respectively. $|Q|_1$ is used to represent the ℓ_1 norm of matrix Q, *i.e.*, $|Q|_1 = \sum_{i,j} |Q_{i,j}|$, and $|\mathbf{v}|_\infty$ is used to represent the infinity norm of vector $\mathbf{v}$, *i.e.*, $|\mathbf{v}|_\infty = \max_i |v_i|$. We also use $\mathbf{e}_i \in \{0,1\}^n$ to represent the i-th canonical basis for $\mathbb{R}^n$, and $\mathbf{1} \in \mathbb{R}^m$ to represent a vector with all its entries being 1.

The proposed approach combines the idea of maximum likelihood estimation, a common approach for topic model, and the theory of low rank matrix recovery. It aims to recover the multinomial probability matrix P by solving the following optimization problem

$$\min_{Q \in \Delta} \quad \mathcal{L}(Q) := \underbrace{-\sum_{i=1}^{n} \sum_{j=1}^{m} \frac{d_{i,j}}{m_*} \log Q_{i,j}}_{:=E_1} + \underbrace{\varepsilon |Q|_{tr}}_{:=E_2}, \tag{1}$$

where domain $\Delta = \{Q \in (0,1)^{m \times n} : Q_{*,i}^\top \mathbf{1} = 1, i \in [1,n]\}$, and ε is a regularization parameter. We denote by $\hat{Q}$ the optimal solution to (1). Term E_1 in (1) ensures the learned probability matrix $\hat{Q}$ to be consistent with the observed tag matrix, and term E_2 ensures that $\hat{Q}$ is of low rank and therefore all image tags are sampled from a mixture of a small number of multinomial distributions.

3.2   Incorporating Visual Features

The limitation of the noisy matrix recovery method in (1) is that it fails to exploit visual features, an important hint for accurate tag prediction. So we next modify (1) to incorporate visual features.

Let $X = (\mathbf{x}_1, \cdots, \mathbf{x}_n)^\top$ include the visual features of all images, where vector $\mathbf{x}_i \in \mathbb{R}^d$ represents the visual content of the ith image. Let $W = [w_{i,j}]_{n \times n}$ be the pairwise similarity matrix, where $w_{i,j}$ is the visual similarity between images $\mathbf{x}_i$ and $\mathbf{x}_j$, *i.e.*, $w_{i,j} = \exp\left(-d(\mathbf{x}_i, \mathbf{x}_j)^2/\sigma^2\right)$ if $j \in N_k(i)$ or $i \in N_k(j)$, where $N_k(i)$ denotes the index set for the k nearest neighbors of the ith image,

k is empirically set $k = 0.001n$, $d(\mathbf{x}_i, \mathbf{x}_j)$ represents the distance between $\mathbf{x}_i$ and $\mathbf{x}_j$, and σ is the average distance. We adopt χ distance if $\mathbf{x}_i$ is histogram features and ℓ_2 distance, otherwise. Using matrix W, we can measure the consistency between the estimated tag probability matrix Q and visual similarities by $\sum_{i,j=1}^{n} W_{i,j}|Q_{*,i} - Q_{*,j}|^2 = Tr(Q^\top L Q)$, where $L = \text{diag}(W^\top \mathbf{1}) - W$ is the graph Laplacian. By minimizing $Tr(Q^\top L Q)$, we ensure that the recovered probability matrix Q to be consistent with visual features.

By combining the noisy matrix recovery component with the component of visual features, we recover the tag probability matrix Q by solving the following optimization problem

$$\min_{Q \in \Delta} \quad -\sum_{i=1}^{n} \sum_{j=1}^{m} \frac{d_{i,j}}{m_*} \log Q_{i,j} + \frac{\alpha}{n} Tr(Q^T L Q) + \beta |Q|_{tr}, \tag{2}$$

where both α and β are regularization terms. By minimizing the objective in (2), we are able to simultaneously fill out the missing tags and filter out/down weight the noisy tags.

3.3 Implementation

Incorporation with Irrelevant Tags. Regarding the fact that the initially unobserved tags are with a small probability relevant to the associated image, we also maximize the likelihood of their irrelevance, and the objective in (2) becomes

$$\min_{Q \in \Delta} \quad -\sum_{i,j=1}^{n,m} \left[\frac{d_{i,j}}{m_*} \log Q_{i,j} + \frac{1 - d_{i,j}}{m - m_*} \log(1 - Q_{i,j}) \right] + \frac{\alpha}{n} Tr(Q^T L Q) + \beta |Q|_{tr}, \tag{3}$$

where Δ is defined in (1).

Efficient Solution of the Proposed Algorithm. We incorporate several heuristics to improve the computational efficiency. First, we adopt one projection paradigm that has been successfully applied to metric learning [8]. The key idea is to ignore the domain constraint $Q \in \Delta$ during the iteration, and only project the solution Q into Δ at the end of optimization. As a result, we only need to solve an unconstrained optimization problem. Second, we adopt the extended gradient method in [12]. To this end, we rewrite the objective function in (2) as $\mathcal{L}(Q) = f(Q) + \varepsilon |Q|_{tr}$. Given the current solution Q_{k-1}, we update the solution Q_k by solving the following optimization problem

$$\arg\min_{Q} P_{t_k}(Q, Q_{k-1}) = \frac{1}{2} \left| Q - \left(Q_{k-1} - \frac{1}{t_k} \nabla f(Q_{k-1}) \right) \right|_F^2 + \frac{\varepsilon}{t_k} |Q|_{tr}. \tag{4}$$

where t_k is the step size for the kth iteration. The detailed algorithm for solving the unconstrained version of (2) can be found in [12].

4   Theoretical Guarantee of TCMR

The following theorem bounds the difference between P and the recovered probability matrix $\hat{Q}$.

Theorem 1. *Let r be the rank of matrix P, and N be the total number of observed tags. Let $\hat{Q}$ be the optimal solution to (1). Assume $N \geq \Omega(n \log(n+m))$, and denote by μ_- and μ_+ the lower and upper bounds for the probabilities in P. Then we have, with a high probability*

$$\frac{1}{n}|\hat{Q} - P|_1 \leq O\left(\frac{rn\theta^2 \log(n+m)}{N}\right), \quad \text{where } \theta^2 := \frac{\mu_+|P\mathbf{1}|_\infty}{n\mu_-^2} \leq \frac{\mu_+^2}{\mu_-^2}. \tag{5}$$

It is clear that the recovery error is $O(rn \log(n + m)/N)$, implying that the tag matrix can be accurately recovered when $N \geq \Omega(rn \log(n + m))$. This is consistent with the standard results in matrix completion [13]. The impact of low rank assumption is analyzed in Section 4.1. We note that unlike standard matrix completion theory where observed entries are sampled uniformly at random from a given matrix, in topic model, each observed tag is sampled from an unknown multinomial distribution. This difference makes the square loss inappropriate for topic model, leading to additional challenges in analyzing the recovery property for topic model.

We now proceed to present a sketch of the proof. More details can be found in the supplementary document. Define matrix M as

$$M := \sum_{i=1}^{n}\left(\frac{1}{m_*}\mathbf{d}_i - \mathbf{p}_i\right)\mathbf{e}_i^\top = \sum_{i=1}^{n}\frac{1}{m_*}\mathbf{d}_i\mathbf{e}_i^\top - P, \tag{6}$$

where $\mathbf{e}_i \in \{0,1\}^n$ is the canonical base for $\mathbb{R}^n$. Since the occurrence of each tag in $\mathbf{d}_i$ is sampled according to the underlying multinomial distribution $\mathbf{p}_i$, it is easy to verify that $\mathbb{E}[M] = 0$.

Before presenting our analysis, we need two supporting lemmas that are important to our analysis.

Lemma 1. *Let $P \in \Delta$ and $Q \in \Delta$ be two probability matrices. We have*

$$\sum_{i=1}^{n}\sum_{j=1}^{m}\frac{|P_{i,j} - Q_{i,j}|^2}{Q_{i,j}} \geq \sum_{i=1}^{n}\sum_{j=1}^{m}|P_{i,j} - Q_{i,j}| = |P - Q|_1. \tag{7}$$

Lemma 2. *([13]) Let $Z_1, \cdots, Z_n$ be independent random matrices with dimension $m_1 \times m_2$ that satisfy $\mathbb{E}[Z_i] = 0$ and $|Z_i|_* \leq U$ almost surely for some constant U, and all $i = 1, \cdots, n$. Define*

$$\sigma_Z = \max\left\{\left|\frac{1}{n}\sum_{i=1}^{n}\mathbb{E}[Z_iZ_i^\top]\right|_*, \left|\frac{1}{n}\sum_{i=1}^{n}\mathbb{E}[Z_i^\top Z_i]\right|_*\right\}. \tag{8}$$

Then, for all $t > 0$, with a probability $1 - e^{-t}$, we have

$$\left|\frac{1}{n}\sum_{i=1}^{n}Z_i\right|_* \leq 2\max\left\{\sigma_Z\sqrt{\frac{t + \log(m_1 + m_2)}{n}}, U\frac{t + \log(m_1 + m_2)}{n}\right\}. \tag{9}$$

The following theorem is the key to our analysis. It shows that the estimation error $|P - Q|_1$, measured by ℓ_1 norm, will be small when P can be well approximated by a low rank matrix.

Theorem 2. *Let $\hat{Q}$ be the optimal solution to (1). If $\varepsilon \geq |M|_*/\mu_-$, where M is defined in (6), then*

$$|\hat{Q} - P|_1 \leq \min_{Q \in \Delta} \left\{ \frac{1}{\mu_-} |Q - P|_F^2 + 16\varepsilon^2 \mu_+ rank(Q) \right\}. \tag{10}$$

To utilize Theorem 2 for bounding the difference between P and $\hat{Q}$, we need to bound $|M|_*$. The theorem below bounds $|M|_*$ by using Lemma 2.

Theorem 3. *Define γ as*

$$\gamma := \frac{2}{\mu_-} \max \left(\frac{t + \log(m + n)}{m_*}, \sqrt{\max(1, |P\mathbf{1}|_\infty) \frac{t + \log(n + m)}{m_*}} \right). \tag{11}$$

With a probability $1 - e^{-t}$, we have $|M|_* \leq \gamma \mu_-$.

Combining Theorems 2 and 3, we have the following result for recovering the probability matrix P.

Corollary 1. *Set $\varepsilon = \gamma$. With a probability at least $1 - e^{-t}$, we have*

$$|\hat{Q} - P|_1 \leq \min_{Q \in \Delta} \left\{ |Q - P|_F^2/\mu_- + 16\gamma^2 \mu_+ rank(Q) \right\}. \tag{12}$$

Furthermore, let $\hat{P}$ be the best rank-r approximation of P. We have, with a probability $1 - e^{-t}$

$$|\hat{Q} - \hat{P}|_1 \leq |P - \hat{P}|_F^2/\mu_- + 16\gamma^2 \mu_+ r. \tag{13}$$

We now come to the proof of Theorem 1. When the rank of P is r, using Corollary 1, we have, with a high probability, $|\hat{Q} - P|_1 \leq 16\gamma^2 \mu_+ r$. If $|P\mathbf{1}|_\infty \geq 1$ and $m_* \geq O(\log(m + n))$, we have

$$\gamma = O\left(\frac{1}{\mu_-} \sqrt{|P\mathbf{1}|_\infty \frac{\log(n + m)}{m_*}} \right) \tag{14}$$

and therefore, with a high probability, we have

$$\frac{1}{n} |\hat{Q} - P|_1 \leq O\left(\frac{r \log(n + m)}{m_*} \frac{\mu_+ |P\mathbf{1}|_\infty}{\mu_-^2} \right) \leq O\left(\frac{rn \log(n + m)}{N} \frac{\mu_+ |P\mathbf{1}|_\infty}{n\mu_-^2} \right) \tag{15}$$

where N is the number of observed tags. This immediately implies Theorem 1.

4.1 Impact of Low Rank Assumption on Recovery Error

In order to see the impact of low rank assumption, let us consider the maximum likelihood estimation of multinomial distribution. Since tags for different images are sampled independently, we only need to consider one image at each time. Let $\mathbf{p}$ be the underlying multinomial distribution to be estimated, and let $\mathbf{d}$ be the image tag vector comprised of m_* words sampled from $\mathbf{p}$. We estimate $\mathbf{p}$ by the simple maximum likelihood estimation, *i.e.*,

$$\min_{\mathbf{p}\in[\mu_-,\mu_+]^m:\mathbf{p}^\top\mathbf{1}=1} -\sum_{i=1}^{n} d_i \log p_i, \tag{16}$$

where m is the number of unique tags, n is the number of images, μ_- and μ_+ are the lower and upper bounds for the probabilities in matrix $P = (\mathbf{p}_1, \cdots, \mathbf{p}_n)$.

Theorem 4. *Define* $\mathbf{z} = \mathbf{d}/m_* - \mathbf{p}$. *Let* $\hat{\mathbf{q}}$ *be the optimal solution to (16). Then*

$$|\mathbf{p} - \hat{\mathbf{q}}|_1 \le (\mu_+^2/\mu_-^2)|\mathbf{z}|_2^2.$$

Theorem 5. *With a probability* $1 - 2e^{-t}$,

$$|\mathbf{z}|_2 \le \sqrt{\frac{t + \log m}{\mu_- m_*}}|\mathbf{p}|_2.$$

Following the concentration inequality for vectors in Theorem 5, we bound $|\mathbf{z}|_2$. Then by combining Theorems 4 and 5, we have, with a probability $1 - 2e^{-t}$,

$$|\mathbf{p} - \hat{\mathbf{q}}|_1 \le \frac{\mu_+^2|\mathbf{p}|_2^2}{\mu_-^4}\frac{2(t + \log m)}{m_*} \tag{17}$$

By applying the above result to matrix P and taking the union bound, we have, with probability $1 - e^{-t}$,

$$\frac{1}{n}|P - \hat{Q}|_1 \le \frac{\mu_+^2}{\mu_-^4}\max_{1\le i\le n}|\mathbf{p}_i|_2^2 \frac{2n(t + \log m + \log n)}{|\Omega|}. \tag{18}$$

We now compare the bound in (18) to that in (5). It is easy to verify that $|\mathbf{p}_i|_2^2/\mu_-^2 \ge m$ for any $\mathbf{p}_i$. Hence, the net effect of the bound in (5) is to replace m with r, which is exactly the impact of low rank assumption.

5 Experiments

5.1 Datasets and Experimental Setup

Four benchmark datasets are used to evaluate our proposed algorithm. ESP Game dataset was collected for a collaborative image labeling task and consists of images including logos, drawings and personal photos. IAPR TC12 dataset consists of images of actions, landscapes, animals and many other contemporary life, and its tags are extracted from the text captions accompanying each image. Both Mir Flickr and NUS-WIDE datasets [7] include images crawled from Flickr, together with users provided tags. ESP Game and IAPR TC12 are collaboratively human labeled and thus relatively clean, while Mir Flickr and NUS-WIDE are automatically crawled from social media and hence pretty noisy. A bag-of-words model based on densely sampled SIFT descriptors is used to represent the visual content in Mir Flickr, ESP Game and IAPR TC12 datasets[2]. In NUS-WIDE dataset, visual content are represented by six low-level features, including color information, edge distribution and wavelet texture [7].

To evaluate the proposed approach for tag completion, we divide the original tag matrix Y into two parts: the observed tag matrix (*i.e.* training set) D and the left as evaluation ground truth (*i.e.* testing set). We create the observed tag matrix by randomly sampling a subset of tags from D for each image. The number of observed tags m_* is set to 3 for Mir Flickr and 4 for other datasets throughout this section unless it is specified otherwise. To guarantee that the evaluation is meaningful, we ensure that each image has at least one evaluation tag by filtering out images with too few tags and tags associated with only a few images. As a result of this filtering step, Mir Flickr has $5,231$ images with 372 tags, ESP Game has $10,450$ images with 265 tags, IAPR TC12 has $12,985$ images with 291 tags, and NUS-WIDE has $20,968$ images with 420 tags. Detailed statistics about the refined datasets are listed in the supplementary document. All the hyper parameter values used in TCMR, *e.g.* ε, α, β, and the parameter values in the baselines are determined by cross-validation.

Following [15], we evaluate the tag completion accuracy by the *average precision @N (AP@N)*. It measures the average percentage of the top N recovered tags that are correct. Note that a tag is correctly recovered if it is included in the original tag matrix Y but not observed in D. We also use *average recall (AR@N)* to measure the percentage of correct tags that are recovered by a computational algorithm out of all ground truth tags, and *coverage (C@N)* to measure the percentage of images with at last one correctly recovered tag. Both the mean and standard deviation of evaluation metrics over 20 experimental trials are reported in this paper.

5.2   Comparison to State-of-the-Art Tag Completion Methods

We first compare our proposed TCMR algorithm[3] to several state-of-the-art tag completion approaches: (1) LRES [26], tag refinement towards low-rank, content-tag prior and error sparsity, (2) TMC [24] that searches for the optimal

---

[2] The features were obtained from
http://lear.inrialpes.fr/people/guillaumin/data.php. More detailed description about Mir Flickr, ESP Game and IAPR TC12 can also be found at this site.
[3] The source code can be downloaded from our website
http://www.cse.msu.edu/~fengzhey/downloads/src/tcmr.zip

tag matrix consistent with both the observed tags and visual similarity, (3) MC-1 [3] which applies low rank matrix completion to the concatenation of visual features and assigned tags, (4) FastTag [6] that co-regularizes two simple linear mappings in a joint convex loss function, (5) LSR [15] that optimally reconstructs each image and each tag with remaining ones under constraints of sparsity. We also compare the proposed approach with three state-of-the-art image annotation algorithms that are designed for clean tags: (6) TagProp [11], (7)RKML [9], a kernel metric learning algorithm, and (8) vKNN, a nearest neighbor voting algorithm.

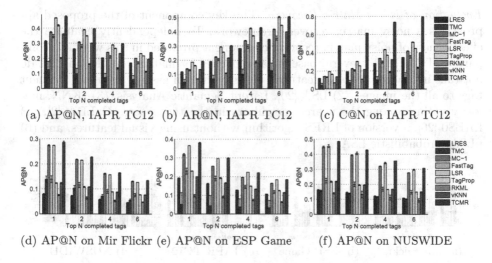

(a) AP@N, IAPR TC12   (b) AR@N, IAPR TC12   (c) C@N on IAPR TC12

(d) AP@N on Mir Flickr (e) AP@N on ESP Game   (f) AP@N on NUSWIDE

Fig. 1. Tag completion performance of TCMR and state-of-the-art baselines

Figs. 1 (a), (b), and (c) show the results for the IAPR TC12 dataset measured by $AP@N$, $AR@N$ and $C@N$, respectively. Figs. 1 (d), (e), and (f) show the results of $AP@N$ for the three remaining datasets; the results of the other two metrics can be found in the supplementary document. We observe that overall, the proposed TCMR and LSR yield significantly better performance than the other approaches in comparison. TCMR performs significantly better than LSR in terms of $C@N$. In particular, TCMR recovers at least one correct tag out of the top six predicted tags for 80% of the images while the other approaches are only able to recover at least one correct tag for less than 50% of the images, indicating that the proposed algorithm is more effective in recovering relevant tags for a wide range of images, an important property for image tag completion algorithm. We also observe that TCMR performs slightly better than LSR in terms of $AP@N$ when the number of predicted tags N is small.

Table 1 summarizes the running time of all algorithms in comparison. We observe that although TCMR is not as efficient as several baselines, it is more efficient than LSR which yields similar performance as TCMR in multiple cases. The high computational cost of LSR is due to the fact that it has to train a different model for each instance, which does not scale well to large datasets.

Table 1. Running time (seconds) for tag completion baselines. All algorithms are run in Matlab on an AMD 4-core @2.7GHz and 64GB RAM machine.

	LRES	TMC	MC-1	FastTag	LSR	TagProp	RKML	vKNN	TCMR
MirFlickr	5.6e2	4.7e3	8.6e2	1.4e3	6.2e3	2.5e2	3.0e2	2.1e2	1.3e3
ESP Game	3.4e2	5.8e3	1.0e3	8.6e2	1.3e4	6.7e2	1.3e3	4.3e2	5.9e3
IAPR TC12	5.2e2	1.2e4	1.7e3	1.6e3	1.6e4	1.1e3	1.5e3	1.0e3	9.4e3
NUS-WIDE	6.8e3	2.9e4	1.8e3	2.6e3	2.8e4	1.5e3	3.8e3	1.2e3	1.9e4

Evaluation of Noisy Matrix Recovery. The key component of the proposed approach is a noisy matrix recovery framework. To independently evaluate the effectiveness of noisy matrix recovery component proposed in this work, we compare it (TCMR0) to several baseline approaches for matrix completion that do not take into account visual features: (1) Freq, which assigns the most frequent tags to all the images, (2) LSA [20], Latent Semantic Analysis, (3) tKNN, majority voting among the nearest neighbors in the tag space, (4) LDA [2], (5) LRES0 [26], a version of LRES algorithm without using visual features, and (6) pLSA, probabilistic LSA.

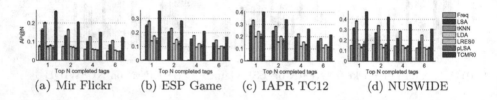

(a) Mir Flickr   (b) ESP Game   (c) IAPR TC12   (d) NUSWIDE

Fig. 2. *AP@N* for different topic models and matrix completion algorithms

Fig. 2 compares the tag completion performance without using visual features. We observe that the proposed noisy matrix recovery algorithm performs significantly better than the other baseline methods, implying that it can successfully capture the important dependency among tags. We also observe that a simple tKNN algorithm works better than the topical models (LSA, LDA and pLSA), suggesting that directly applying a topical model may not be appropriate for the tag completion problem.

From Figs. 1 and 2, we observe that TMC and RKML perform much worse than the other algorithms in comparison, while LSA and tKNN perform quite good. Accordingly, we exclude TMC and RKML, and include LSA and tKNN in the following evaluation cases.

Sensitivity to the Number of Observed Tags. We also examine the sensitivity of the proposed TCMR to the number of initially observed tags by comparing it to the baseline algorithms on IAPR TC12 and NUS-WIDE datasets. To make a meaningful evaluation, we only keep images with 6 or more tags for IAPR TC12 dataset, and images with 9 or more tags for NUS-WIDE dataset. As before, we divide the tags into testing and training sets, and randomly sample m_* tags for each image from the training tag set to create the partially observed tag matrix, where the number of sampled tags m_* is varied. We evaluate the tag completion performance on the testing tag sets.

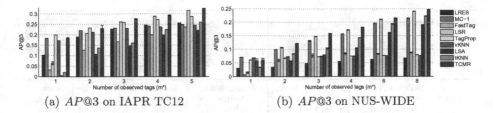

(a) $AP@3$ on IAPR TC12   (b) $AP@3$ on NUS-WIDE

Fig. 3. Tag completion performance (AP@3) with varied number of observed tags

Fig. 3 shows the influence of the number of partially observed tags to the final tag completion performance measured by $AP@3$; results of the metric $AR@5$ are reported in the supplementary document. We observe that the performance of all algorithms improves with increasing number of observed tags. We also observe that when the number of observed tags is 3 or larger, TCMR and LSR perform significantly better than the other baseline approaches. When the number of observed tags is small (*i.e.* 1 or 2), TCMR performs significantly better than LSR, indicating that the proposed algorithm is noticeably effective even when the number of observed tags is small.

Sensitivity to Noise. To evaluate the sensitivity to noise, we conduct experiments with noisy observed tags on datasets IAPR TC12 and NUS-WIDE. To generate noisy tags, we replace some of the sampled tags with the incorrect ones that are chosen uniformly at random from the vocabulary. The percentage of noisy tags among the total observed ones in the whole gallery is varied from 0 to 0.9. To ensure there are a sufficient number of noisy tags as well as sufficient number of images, we set m_*, the number of sampled tags, to be 8 for NUS-WIDE dataset and to be 4 for IAPR TC12 dataset in this experiment.

Fig. 4 shows the tag completion performance for different algorithms using noisy observed tags. It is not surprising to observe that the performance of all algorithms in comparison degrades with increasing amounts of noise. We also

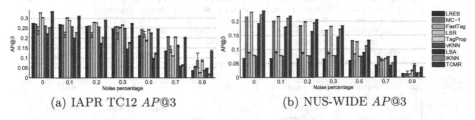

(a) IAPR TC12 $AP@3$ (b) NUS-WIDE $AP@3$

Fig. 4. Comparison of tag completion performance ($AP@3$)using noisy observed tags

Table 2. Examples of tag completion results generated by some baseline algorithms and the proposed TCMR. The observed tags in red italic font are noisy tags, and others are randomly sampled from the ground truth tags. The completed tags are ranked based on the recovered scores in descending order, and the correct ones are highlighted in blue bold font.

Ground truth	building, front, group, people, palm, lawn, tree, square, statue	boy, cap, hair, house, power, pole, roof, sky, shirt, sweater, terrain, tree	bank, bush, helmet, jacket, life, people, river, rock, tree	balcony, door, entrance, car, flag, front, lamp, house, sky, window	bed, brick, curtain, leg, man, short, sweater, wall, woman
Observed tags	lawn, people, square, *cloud*	cap, terrain, sky, *meadow*	life, river tree, *llama*	balcony, car, window, *water*	curtain, wall, *floor, team*
LSER	**people**, bike, **wall**, cloud, **square**, **tree**, house, **lawn, palm**	**terrain, sky**, **hair, sweater**, **roof**, mountain, **wall**, meadow, **cap**, trouser	**tree, river**, **life, helmet**, **rock**, woman, llama, **jacket**, gravel, **people**	**entrance, car**, **front, balcony**, water, **window**, building, people, harbour, **sky**	woman, **wall**, table, room, hand, **curtain**, floor, team, person, front
MC-1	**people, square**, cloud, **lawn**, **tree, sky**, **building**, **front**, wall	**sky**, meadow, **terrain, cap**, **wall**, mountain, man, **house**, woman, **hair**	**tree, river**, **life**, man, llama, wall, **people**, front, mountain, sky	**window, car**, **balcony**, water, man, **front**, building, wall, **house**, woman	**wall, curtain**, floor, team, window, room, **man**, table, front, **bed**
FastTag	**tree**, tourist, footpath, shirt, **river, group**, woman, tile, **people**	wall, **boy**, desk, meadow, mountain, girl, **hair**, tee-shirt, plane, fence	**life**, mountain, **people, front**, tourist, railing, **river**, llama, **tree, wall**	building, **front**, **house, car**, grey, **window**, rail, **balcony**, street, photo	**wall**, room, table, window, **bed, curtain**, hand, night, cup, towel
LSR	**sky, square**, **building**, **people, tree**, house, **lawn**, street, cloud	**house, sky**, hill, **boy**, grey, **jacket, tree**, **terrain**, cloud, landscape	**bank, jacket**, **river, helmet**, **bush**, tourist, boat, mountain, **tree, people**	**front, building**, **house, wall**, **sky**, cliff, **door, window**, street, man	**wall**, room, **window, front**, uniform, **bed**, table, jersey, **short**, round
TagProp	**people, tree**, **square**, house, **front**, wall, tourist, man, **woman**	wall, **woman**, man, **sky**, front, **sweater, hair**, mountain, table, desert	**people, tree**, woman, front, man, **rock**, wall, **river**, sky, mountain	**wall, front**, man, building, woman, table, people, **house**, **sky, entrance**	front, **woman**, **wall**, table, **man**, house, room, people, tree, window
vKNN	**tree, wall**, house, **people, sky**, **woman**, bike, **front, square**	**sweater**, desert, **sky**, landscape, **terrain, hair**, mountain, **wall**, cloud, front	**people, tree**, **helmet, front**, **river, bush**, **woman, life**, sky, man	**front**, building, people, **house**, **entrance, sky**, wall, **balcony**, tree, **window**	room, **woman**, table, front, house, **wall**, **man**, chair, window, child
LSA	**people**, cloud, **square**, roof, **group**, meadow, **building**, tower, landscape	**sky**, meadow, cloud, **hair**, **roof**, road, short, **tree**, woman, **boy**	**tree, bush**, lake, palm, meadow, **river**, tourist, slope, building, grass	**car, window**, street, **house**, building, room, **lamp, front**, **bed**, bush	**wall**, room, table, **bed**, window, hair, girl, wood, boy, **curtain**
tKNN	**people, square**, cloud, **lawn**, **sky, tree**, mountain, street, **building**	**sky**, meadow, **terrain, cap**, **people**, cloud, hill, mountain, road, **tree**	**tree, river**, **life, bush**, **house, sky**, **building**, man, **people, bank**	**window, car**, **balcony, wall**, **house, front**, building, **bed**, room, **curtain**	**wall, floor**, **curtain**, room, **bed**, front, window, girl, team, **brick**
TCMR	**people, square**, **lawn, sky**, **building**, **tree**, cloud, street, **palm**	**sky, terrain**, **cap, boy**, hill, **house, hair**, landscape, **sweater**, cloud	**tree, river**, **life**, boat, **jacket, bank**, llama, **helmet**, **rock**, mountain	**car, window**, **balcony, door**, building, **wall**, **front, house**, water, **sky**	**wall, floor**, **curtain, bed**, **brick**, room, window, front, table, team

observe that LSR seems to be significantly sensitive to the noise in the observed tags than the proposed TCMR algorithm. In particular, we find that TCMR outperforms LSR significantly when the percentage of noisy tags is large. The contrast is particularly obvious for the IAPR TC12 dataset, where LSR starts to perform worse than several other baselines when the noise level is above 50%. Besides, all algorithms reduce their performance dramatically as the noise level increases from 70% to 90%. This is not surprising because at the 90% noise level, a number of images do not have accurate observed tags for training the model, especially for the NUS-WIDE dataset whose originally assigned tags are pretty noisy. However, the proposed TCMR algorithm is overwhelmingly better in this case, especially on IAPR TC12, indicating that it is more powerful in recovering expected tags from severely noisy tagged images. Table 2 shows the tag completion results of exemplar images by different algorithms, where both partially true and noisy tags are observed.

6   Conclusions

We have proposed a robust yet efficient image tag completion algorithm (TCMR), which is capable of simultaneously fill in the missing tags and remove/down weight the noisy tags. TCMR introduces a noisy matrix recovery procedure that captures the underlying dependency by enforcing the recovered matrix to be of low rank. Besides, a graph Laplacian based on the image visual features is also applied to ensure the recovered tag matrix is consistent with the visual content. Experiments over four different scaled image datasets demonstrate the effectiveness and efficiency of the proposed TCMR algorithm by comparing it to state-of-the-art tag completion approaches. In the future, we plan to improve the tag completion performance by incorporating the visual features a more effectively, and adopting more efficient nuclear norm optimization procedure.

Acknowledgement. This work was partially supported by Army Research Office (W911NF-11-1-0383).

References

1. Blei, D.M.: Probabilistic topic models. Communications of the ACM (2012)
2. Blei, D.M., Ng, A.Y., Jordan, M.I., Lafferty, J.: Latent dirichlet allocation. Journal of Machine Learning Research (2003)
3. Cabral, R.S., la Torre, F.D.D., Costeira, J.P., Bernardino, A.: Matrix completion for multi-label image classification. In: NIPS, pp. 190–198 (2011)
4. Candès, E.J., Plan, Y.: Matrix completion with noise. Proceedings of the IEEE 98(6), 925–936 (2010)
5. Candès, E.J., Recht, B.: Exact matrix completion via convex optimization. Foundations of Computational Mathematics 9(6), 717–772 (2009)
6. Chen, M., Zheng, A., Weinberger, K.Q.: Fast image tagging. In: ICML (2013)
7. Chua, T.S., Tang, J., Hong, R., Li, H., Luo, Z., Zheng, Y.T.: Nus-wide: A real-world web image database from national university of singapore. In: CIVR (2009)

8. Davis, J.V., Kulis, B., Jain, P., Sra, S., Dhillon, I.S.: Information-theoretic metric learning. In: ICML, pp. 209–216 (2007)
9. Feng, Z., Jin, R., Jain, A.K.: Large-scale image annotation by efficient and robust kernel metric learning. In: ICCV (2013)
10. Ganesh, A., Wright, J., Li, X., Candès, E.J., Ma, Y.: Dense error correction for low-rank matrices via principal component pursuit. In: ISIT (2010)
11. Guillaumin, M., Mensink, T., Verbeek, J., Schmid, C.: Tagprop: Discriminative metric learning in nearest neighbor models for image annotation. In: ICCV (2009)
12. Ji, S., Ye, J.: An accelerated gradient method for trace norm minimization. In: ICML, pp. 457–464. ACM (2009)
13. Koltchinskii, V., Lounici, K., Tsybakov, A.B.: Nuclear-norm penalization and optimal rates for noisy low-rank matrix completion. The Annals of Statistics (2011)
14. Krestel, R., Fankhauser, P., Nejdl, W.: Latent dirichlet allocation for tag recommendation. In: ACM Conference on Recommender Systems, pp. 61–68. ACM (2009)
15. Lin, Z., Ding, G., Hu, M., Wang, J., Ye, X.: Image tag completion via image-specific and tag-specific linear sparse reconstructions. In: CVPR (2013)
16. Liu, D., Hua, X.S., Wang, M., Zhang, H.J.: Image retagging. In: Proceedings of the International Conference on Multimedia, pp. 491–500. ACM (2010)
17. Liu, D., Yan, S., Hua, X.S., Zhang, H.J.: Image retagging using collaborative tag propagation. IEEE Transactions on Multimedia 13(4), 702–712 (2011)
18. Liu, X., Yan, S., Chua, T.S., Jin, H.: Image label completion by pursuing contextual decomposability. TOMCCAP, 21:1–21:20 (2012)
19. Loeff, N., Farhadi, A.: Scene discovery by matrix factorization. In: Forsyth, D., Torr, P., Zisserman, A. (eds.) ECCV 2008, Part IV. LNCS, vol. 5305, pp. 451–464. Springer, Heidelberg (2008)
20. Monay, F., Gatica-Perez, D.: On image auto-annotation with latent space models. In: ACM International Conference on Multimedia, pp. 275–278. ACM (2003)
21. Mu, Y., Dong, J., Yuan, X., Yan, S.: Accelerated low-rank visual recovery by random projection. In: CVPR, pp. 2609–2616. IEEE Computer Society (2011)
22. Negahban, S., Wainwright, M.J.: Restricted strong convexity and weighted matrix completion: Optimal bounds with noise. JMLR 13, 1665–1697 (2012)
23. Tian, Q., Aggarwal, C., Qi, G.J., Ji, H., Huang, T.S.: Exploring context and content links in social media: A latent space method. PAMI 34(5), 850–862 (2012)
24. Wu, L., Jin, R., Jain, A.K.: Tag completion for image retrieval. PAMI 35(3) (2013)
25. Xu, H., Wang, J., Hua, X.S., Li, S.: Tag refinement by regularized lda. In: ACM International Conference on Multimedia, pp. 573–576. ACM (2009)
26. Zhu, G., Yan, S., Ma, Y.: Image tag refinement towards low-rank, content-tag prior and error sparsity. In: International Conference on Multimedia. ACM (2010)
27. Zhuang, J., Hoi, S.C.H.: A two-view learning approach for image tag ranking. In: WSDM, pp. 625–634 (2011)

ConceptMap:
Mining Noisy Web Data for Concept Learning

Eren Golge and Pinar Duygulu

Bilkent University, 06800 Cankaya, Turkey

Abstract. We attack the problem of learning concepts automatically from noisy Web image search results. The idea is based on discovering common characteristics shared among subsets of images by posing a method that is able to organise the data while eliminating irrelevant instances. We propose a novel clustering and outlier detection method, namely Concept Map (CMAP). Given an image collection returned for a concept query, CMAP provides clusters pruned from outliers. Each cluster is used to train a model representing a different characteristics of the concept. The proposed method outperforms the state-of-the-art studies on the task of learning from noisy web data for low-level attributes, as well as high level object categories. It is also competitive with the supervised methods in learning scene concepts. Moreover, results on naming faces support the generalisation capability of the CMAP framework to different domains. CMAP is capable to work at large scale with no supervision through exploiting the available sources.

Keywords: Weakly-labelled data, Clustering and outlier detection, Semi-supervised model learning, ConceptMap, Attributes, Object detection, Scene classification.

1 Introduction

The need for manually labelled data continues to be one of the most important limitations in large scale recognition. Alternatively, images are available on the Web in huge amounts. This fact recently attracted many researchers to build (semi-)automatic methods to learn from web data collected for a given concept. However, there are several challenges that makes the data collections gathered from web different from the hand crafted datasets. Images on the web are "in the wild" inheriting all types of challenges due to variations and effects. Since usually images are gathered based on the surrounding text, the collection is very noisy with several visually irrelevant images as well as variety of images corresponding to different characteristic properties of the concept (Figure1).

For the queried data for automatic learning of concepts, we propose a novel method to obtain a representative groups with irrelevant images removed. Our intuition is that, given a concept category by a query, although the list of images returned include irrelevant ones, there will be common characteristics shared among subset of images. Our main idea is to obtain visually coherent subsets, that are possibly corresponding to semantic sub-categories, through clustering and to build models for each sub-category (see Figure2). The model for each concept category is then a collection of multiple models, each representing a different aspect.

D. Fleet et al. (Eds.): ECCV 2014, Part VII, LNCS 8695, pp. 439–455, 2014.

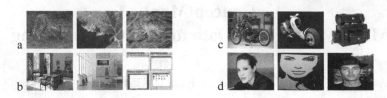

Fig. 1. Example Web images collected for query keywords (a) spotted, (b) office, (c) motorbikes, (d) Angelina Jolie. Even in the relevant images, the concepts are observed in different forms requiring grouping and irrelevant ones to be eliminated.

To retain only the relevant images that describe the concept category correctly, during clustering we need to remove outliers, i.e. irrelevant ones. The outliers may resemble to each other while not being similar to the correct category resulting in a **outlier cluster**. Alternatively, outlier images could be mixed with correct category images inside **salient clusters** corresponding to relevant ones. These images, that we refer to as **outlier elements**, should also be removed for the quality data for learning.

We propose a novel method **Concept Maps (CMAP)** for which organises the data by purifying it not only from outlier clusters but also from outlier elements in salient clusters. CMAP captures category characteristics through organising the set of given instances into sub-categories pruned from irrelevant instances. It is a generic method that could be applied on any type of concept from low-level attributes to high level object and scene categories as well as faces.

Contributions:

- We attack the problem of building a general framework to learn visual concepts by only query concept, through exploiting large volumes of weakly labelled data on the web.
- Unlike most of the recent studies that focus on learning specific types of categories from noisy images downloaded from web (such as objects [17,33], scenes[55], attributes[53,18], and faces [2,43,20]) we propose a general framework which is applicable to many domains from low level attributes to high level concepts.
- We aim to learn models that have the ability to categorise images and regions across datasets without being limited to a single source of data.
- As in [33,5] we address three main challenges in learning visual concepts from noisy web results: (i) **Irrelevant images** returned by the search engines due to keyword based queries on the noisy textual content. (ii) **Intra-class variations** within a category resulting in multiple groups of relevant images. (iii) **Multiple senses** of the concept. (5) We aim to answer not only "which concept is in the image?", but also "where the concept is?" as in [5] . Local patches are considered as basic units to solve the localisation as well as to eliminate background regions.
- We use only visual informations extracted from the images gathered for a given query word, and do not require any other additional knowledge such as surrounding text, metadata or GPS-tags [48,3,23].
- The collection returned from web is used in its **pure** form without requiring any prior supervision (manual or automatic) for organisation of the data [3,48,33].

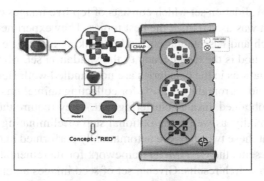

Fig. 2. Overview of our framework for concept learning shown on example concept "Red". Images are collected from web for a given keyword. Concept Map (CMAP) organises the data into clusters which are pruned from outlier elements inside salient clusters and outlier clusters. each cluster is then used as a sub-model for learning and localising the concept in a given image possibly from a different collection.

2   Related Work

Our work is related to several studies in the literature from different perspectives. We try to discuss the most relevant ones by grouping them into three categories. Reviewing the huge literature on object and scene recognition is far from the scope of this study.

Learning Attributes: The use of attributes has been the focus of many recent studies [15,29,6]. Most of the methods learn attributes in a supervised way [16,31] with the goal of describing object categories. Not only semantic attributes, but classemes [52] and implicit attributes [46] have also been studied. We focus on attribute learning independent of object categories and learn different intrinsic properties of semantic attributes through models obtained from separate clusters that are ultimately combined in a single semantics. Learning semantic appearance attributes, such as colour, texture and shape, on ImageNet dataset is attacked in [47] relying on image level human labels using AMT for supervised learning. We learn attributes from real world images collected from web with no additional human effort for labelling. Another study on learning colour names from web images is proposed in [53] where a pLSA based model is used for representing the colour names of pixels. Similar to ours, the approach of Ferrari and Zisserman [18] considers attributes as patterns sharing some characteristic properties where basic units are the image segments with uniform appearance. We prefer to work on patch level alternative to pixel level which is not suitable for region level attributes such as texture; image level which is very noisy; or segment level which is difficult to obtain clearly.

Learning Object Categories from Noisy Web Data: Several recent studies tackle the problem of building qualified training sets by using images returned from image search engines[17,3,1,13,33,48]. Fergus et al. [17] propose a pLSA based method in which the spatial information is also incorporated in the model. They collected noisy images from

Google as well as a validation set which consists of top five images collected in different languages which was used to pick the best topics. They experimented classification on subsets of Caltech and Pascal datasets, and re-ranking of Google results. The main drawback of the method is the dependency to the validation set. Moreover, the results indicate that the variations in the categories are not handled well. Berg and Forsyth [3] use visual features and surrounding the text for collecting animal images from web. Visual exemplars are obtained through clustering text. They require the relevant clusters to be identified manually, as well as an optional step of eliminating irrelevant images in clusters. Note that these two steps are automatically performed in our framework. Li and Fei-Fei [33] presents the OPTIMOL framework for incrementally learning object categories from web search results. Given a set of seed images a non parametric latent topic model is applied to categorise collected web images. The model is iteratively updated with the newly categorised images. To prevent over specialised results, a set of cache images with high diversity are retained at each iteration. While the main focus is on the analysis of the generated collection, they also compared the learned models on the classification task on the dataset provided in [17]. The validation set is used to gather the seed images. The major drawback of the method is the high dependency to the quality of the seed images and the risk for concept drift during iterations. Schroff et al. [48] first filters out the abstract images (drawings, cartoons, etc.) from the resulting set of images collected through text and image search in Google for a given category. Then, they use text and metadata surrounding the images to re-rank the images. Finally they train a visual classifier by sampling from the top ranked images as positives and random images from other categories as negatives. Their method highly depends on the filtering and text-based re-ranking as shown with the lower performances obtained by visual only based classifier. Berg and Berg [1] find iconic images that are the representatives of the collection given a query concept. First they select the images with objects are distinct from background. Then, the high ranked images are clustered using k-medoids to consider centroid images as iconic. Due to the elimination of several images in the first step it is likely that helpful variations in the dataset are removed. Moreover, clustering does not handle the images in outlier clusters to be chosen as iconic. NEIL is the most similar study to ours [5]. Similar to CMAP in NEIL multiple sub-models are learned automatically for each concept. It works on attributes, objects and scenes as well and localises objects in the images. CMAP differentiates from NEIL in some aspects. We also perform experiments on recognition of faces which was not handled in NEIL. Unlike NEIL where a single type of representation is used to describe attributes, objects and scenes, we use different descriptors for each although not specialised and can be replaced with others. However, this distinction also allows us to consider faces and possibly the videos in the future. The second difference lies in the organisation of the data for learning sub-models. High computational power required for NEIL, as well as the additional knowledge discovered and the iterative process required for learning makes it difficult to compare.

Learning Face Name Associations: Learning the faces associated with the name has been studied recently[2,43,19,21,20,42,49]. We focus on the task of learning faces given a single query name. Unlike [43,19] where a single densest component is sought in the similarity graph - which corresponds to the most similar subset of faces-, we seek for multiple subgroups that represents different characteristics of the people.

Learning Discriminative Patches: Our method is also related to the recently emerged studies in discovering discriminative patches. [34] [50] [27] [50,9,8,25,10,26,35,7]. In these studies weakly labeled datasets are leveraged for learning visual patches that are representative and discriminative. We aim to discover the patches or the entire images representing the collected data in the best way. However, we also want to keep the variations in the concept for allowing intra-class variations and multiple senses to be modelled through different sub-groups. We want to learn the characteristics of the concepts independent of other concepts, and don't consider discriminative characteristics.

3   Concept Maps

We propose CMAP which is inspired from the well-known Self Organizing Maps (SOM) [28]. In the following, SOM will be revisited briefly, and then CMAP will be described.

Revisiting Self Organizing Maps (SOM): Intrinsic dynamics of SOM are inspired from developed animal brain where each part is known to be receptive to different sensory inputs and which has a topographically organized structure[28]. This phenomena, i.e. "receptive field" in visual neural systems [24], is simulated with SOM, where neurons are represented by weights calibrated to make neurons sensitive to different type of inputs. Elicitation of this structure is furnished by competitive learning approach.

Consider input $X = \{x_1, .., x_M\}$ with M instances. Let $N = \{n_1, ..., n_K\}$ be the locations of neuron units on the SOM map and $W = \{w_1, ..., w_K\}$ be the associated weights. The neuron whose weight vector is most similar to the input instance x_i is called as the winner and denoted by $\hat{v}$. Weights of the winner and units in the neighbourhood are adjusted towards the input at each iteration t with delta learning rule.

$$w_j^t = w_j^{t-1} + h(n_i, n_{\hat{v}} : \epsilon^t, \sigma^t)[x_i - w_j^{t-1}] \tag{1}$$

Update step is scaled by the window function $h(n_i, n_{\hat{v}} : \epsilon^t, \sigma^t)$ for each SOM unit, inversely proportional to the distance to the winner (Eq.2). Learning rate ϵ is a gradually decreasing value, resulting in larger updates at the beginning and finer updates as the algorithm evolves. σ^t defines the neighbouring effect so with the decreasing σ, neighbour update steps are getting smaller in each epoch. Note that, there are different alternatives for update and windows functions in SOM literature.

$$h(n_i, n_{\hat{v}} : \epsilon^t, \sigma^t) = \epsilon^t \exp \frac{-||n_j - n_{\hat{v}}||^2}{2\sigma t^2} \tag{2}$$

Clustering and Outlier Detection with CMAP: We introduce excitation scores $E = \{e_1, e_2, \ldots, e_K\}$ where e_j, the score for neuron unit j, is updated as in Eq.3.

$$e_j^t = e_j^{t-1} + \rho^t(\beta_j + z_j) \tag{3}$$

As in SOM, window function is getting smaller with each iteration. z_j is the activation or win count for the unit j, for one epoch. ρ is learning solidity scalar that represents the decisiveness of learning with dynamically increasing value, assuming that later stages of the algorithm has more impact on the definition of salient SOM units. ρ is equal to the inverse of the learning rate ϵ. β_j is the total measure of the activation of jth unit in an epoch, caused by all the winners of the epoch but the neuron itself (Eq.4).

$$\beta_j = \sum_{\hat{v}=1}^{u} h(n_j, n_{\hat{v}}) z_{\hat{v}} \tag{4}$$

At the end of the iterations, normalized e_j is a quality value of a unit j. Higher value of e_j indicates that total amount of excitation of the unit j in whole learning period is high thus it is responsive to the given class of instances and it captures notable amount of data. Low excitation values indicate the contrary. CMAP is capable of detecting outlier units via a threshold θ in the range $[0, 1]$.

Let $C = \{c_1, c_2, \ldots, c_K\}$ be the cluster centres corresponding to each unit. c_j is considered to be a **salient cluster** if $e_j \geq \theta$, and an **outlier cluster** otherwise.

The excitation scores E are the measure for saliency of neuron units in CMAP. Given the data belonging to a category, we expect that data is composed of sub-categories that share common properties. For instance `red` images might include tones to be captured by clusters but they are supposed to share a common characteristics of being red. For the calculation of the excitation scores we use individual activations of the units as well as the neighbouring activations. Individual activations measure being a salient cluster corresponding to a particular sub-category, such as `lighter red`. Neighbourhood activations count the saliency in terms of the shared regularity between sub-categories. If we don't count the neighbourhood effect, some unrelated clusters would be called salient, e.g. noisy white background patches in `red` images.

Outlier instances in salient clusters (**outlier elements**) should also be detected. After the detection of outlier neurons, statistics of the distances between neuron weight w_i and its corresponding instance vectors is used as a measure of instance divergence. If the distance between the instance vector x_j and its winner's weight $\hat{w}_i$ is more than the distances of other instances having the same winner, x_j is raised as an outlier element. We exploit box plot statistics, similar to [39]. If the distance of the instance to its cluster's weight is more than the upper-quartile value, then it is an outlier. The portion of the data, covered by the upper whisker is decided by τ.

CMAP provides good basis of cleansing of poor instances whereas computing cost is relatively smaller since an additional iteration after clustering phase is not required. All the necessary information (excitation scores, box plot statistics) for outliers is calculated at runtime of learning. Hence, CMAP is suitable for large scale problems.

CMAP is also able to estimate number of intrinsic clusters of the data. We use PCA as a simple heuristic for that purpose, with defined variance ν to be retained by the selected first principle components. Given data, principle components describing the data with variance ν is used as the number of clusters for the further processing of CMAP. If we increase ν, CMAP latches more clusters.

$$Num.Clusters = \max_q \left(\frac{\sum_{i=1}^{q} \lambda_i}{\sum_{j=1}^{p} \lambda_j} \leq \nu \right) \tag{5}$$

q is the number of top principle components selected after PCA and p is the dimension of instance vectors. λ is the eigenvalue of corresponding component.

Discussion of Other Methods on Outlier Detection with SOM: [37,38] utilise the habitation of the instances. Frequently observed similar instances excites the network to learn some regularities and divergent instances are observed as outliers. [22] benefits from weights prototyping the instances in a cluster. Thresholded distance of instances to the weight vectors are considered as indicator of being outlier. In [56], aim is to have different mapping of activated neuron for the outlier instances. The algorithm learns the formation of activated neurons on the network for outlier and inlier items with no threshold. It suffers from the generality, with its basic assumption of learning from network mapping. LTD-KN [51] performs Kohonen learning rule inversely. An instance activates only the winning neuron as in the usual SOM, but LTD-KN updates winning neuron and its learning windows decreasingly.

These algorithms only eliminate outlier instances ignoring outlier clusters unlike CMAP. Another difference of CMAP is the computation cost. Most of outlier detection algorithms model the data and iterate over the data again to label outliers. CMAP has the ability to detect outlier clusters and the items in the learning phase. Thus, there is no need for a further iteration, it is all done in a single pass in our method.

Algorithm 1. CMAP

```
 1  In the real code we use vectorized implementation whereas we write down iterative pseudo-code for the favour of simplicity.
    Input: X, θ, τ, K, T, ν, σ^init, ε^init
    Output: OutlierUnits, Mapping, W
 2  set each item z_i in Z to 0
 3  u ← estimateUnitNumber(X, variation)
 4  W ← randomInit(u)
 5  while t ≤ T do
 6      ε^t ← computeLearningRate(t, ε^init)
 7      ρ^t ← 1/ε^t
 8      set each item β_i in B to 0
 9      select a batch set X^t ⊂ X with K instances
10      for each x_i ∈ X do
11          ŵ_i^t ← findWinner(x_i, W)
12          v̂ ← min_j(||x_i − w_j||)
13          increase win count z_ŵt ← z_ŵi^t + 1
14          increase win count z_v̂ ← z_v̂ + 1
15          for each w_k ∈ W do
16              β_k^t = β_k^t + h(n_k, n_v̂)
17              w_k = w_k + h(n_k, n_v̂)||x_i − w_v̂||
18          end
19      end
20      for each w_j ∈ W do
21          e_j^t = e_j^{t−1} + ρ^t(β_j^t + z_j)
22      end
23      t ← t + 1
24  end
25  W_out ← thresholding(E, θ)
26  W_in ← W \ W_out
27  Mapping ← findMapping(W_in, X)
28  Whiskers ← findUpperWhiskers(W_in, X)
29  X_out ← findOutlierIns(X, W_in, Whiskers, τ)
30  return W_out, X_out, Mapping, W
```

---

4   Concept Learning with CMAP

We utilise the clusters, that are obtained through CMAP as presented above, for learning sub-models in concepts. We exploit the proposed framework for learning of attributes, scenes, objects and faces. Each task requires the collection of data, clustering and outlier detection with CMAP, and training of sub-models from the resulting clusters. In the following, first we will describe the attribute learning, and then describe the differences in learning other concepts. Implementation details are presented in Section5.

Learning Low-Level Attributes: Most of the methods require learning of visual attributes from labelled data, and cannot eliminate human effort. Here, we describe our method in learning attributes from web data without any supervision.

We collect web images through querying colour and texture names. The data is weakly labelled, with the labels given by queries. Hence, there are irrelevant images in the collection, as well as images with a tiny portion corresponding to the query keyword.

Each image is densely divided into non-overlapping fixed-size patches to sufficiently capture the required information. We assume that the large volume of the data itself is sufficient to provide instances at various scales and illuminations, and therefore we did not perform any scaling or normalisation. The collection of all patches extracted from all images for a single attribute is then given to CMAP to obtain clusters which are likely to capture different characteristics of the attribute as removing the irrelevant image patches.

Each cluster obtained through CMAP is used to train a separate classifier. Positive examples are selected as the members of the cluster and negative instances are selected among the outliers removed by CMAP and also elements from other categories.

Learning Scene Categories: To show CMAP capability on higher level concepts, we target scene categories. In this case, we use the entire images as instances, and aim to discover groups of images each representing a different property of the scene, at the same time by eliminating the images that are either spurious. These clusters are then used as models similar to the attribute learning.

Learning Object Categories: In the case of objects, we detect salient regions on each image via [11], to eliminate background noise. Then these salient regions are fed into CMAP framework for clustering.

Learning Faces: We address the problem of learning faces associated with a name -which is generally referred to face naming in the literature-, through finding salient clusters in the set of images collected from web through querying the name. Here, the clusters are likely to correspond to different poses and possibly different hair and make-up style differences as well as ageing effects. Note that this task is not the detection of faces, but recognition of faces for a given name. We detect the faces in the images, and only use a single face with the highest confidence for each image.

5   Experiments

5.1   Qualitative Evaluation of Clusters

As Figure3 depicts, CMAP captures different characteristics of concepts in separate salient clusters, while eliminating outlier clusters that group irrelevant images coherent among themselves, as well as outlier elements wrongly mixed with the elements of salient clusters . On more difficult tasks of grouping objects and faces, CMAP is again successful in eliminating outlier elements and outlier clusters as shown in Figure4.

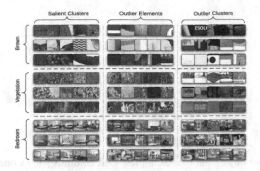

Fig. 3. For colour and texture attributes *brown* and *vegetation* and scene concept *bedroom*, randomly sampled images detected as (i) elements of **salient clusters**, (ii) elements of **outlier clusters**, and (iii) **outlier elements** in salient clusters. CMAP detects different shades of "Brown" and eliminates some superiors elements belonging the different colors. For the "Vegetation" and "Bedroom", CMAP again divides the visuals elements with respect to structural and angular properties. Especially for "bedroom", each cluster is able to capture different view-angle of the images as it successfully removes outlier instances with some of little mistakes that are belonging to the label but not representative (circular bed in very shiny room) for the concept part.

5.2 Implementation Details

Parameters of CMAP are tuned on a small held-out set gathered for each concept class for color, texture, and scene. Best ν is selected by the optimal Mean Squared Error and threshold parameters are tuned by cross-validation accuracies. Figure5 depicts the effect of parameters θ, τ and ν. For each parameter the other two are fixed at the optimum value.

We use LINLINEAR library [14] for L1 norm SVM classifiers. SVM parameters are selected with 10-fold cross validation.

CMAP implementation is powered by CUDA environment. Matrix operations observed for each iteration is kernelized by CUDA codes. It provides good reduction in time, especially if the instance vectors are long and the data is able to fit into GPU memory. Hence, we are able to execute all the optimization in GPU memory. Otherwise some dispatching overhead is observed between GPU and global memory that sometimes hinge the efficiency.

5.3 Attribute Learning

Datasets and Representation: We collected images from Google for 11 distinct colours as in [53] and 13 textures. We included the terms "colour" and "texture" in the queries, such as "red colour", or "wooden texture". For each attribute, 500 images are collected. In total we have 12000 web images. Each image is divided into 100x100 non-overlapping patches. Unlike [53], we didn't apply gamma correction. For colour concepts we use 10x20x20 bins Lab colour histograms and for texture concepts we use BoW representation for densely sampled SIFT [36] features with 4000 words. We keep

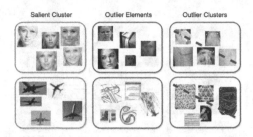

Fig. 4. CMAP results for object and face examples. Left columns shows one example of salient cluster. Middle column shows outlier instances captured from salient clusters. Right column is the detected outlier clusters.

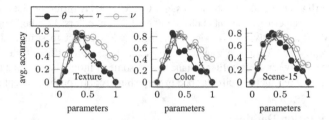

Fig. 5. Effect of parameters on average accuracy. For each parameter, the other two are fixed at their optimal values. θ is outlier cluster threshold, ν is PCA variation used for the estimation of number of clusters, τ is the upper whisker threshold for the outliers in salient clusters.

the feature dimensions high to utilise from the over-complete representations of the instances with L1 norm linear SVM classifier.

Attribute Recognition on Novel Images: The goal of this task is to label a given image with a single attribute name. Although there may be multiple attributes in a single image, for being able to compare our results on benchmark data-sets we consider one attribute label per image. For this purpose, first we divide the test images into grids in three levels using spatial pyramiding [32]. Non-overlapping patches (with the same size of training patches) are extracted from each grid of all three levels. Recall that, we have multiple classifiers for each attribute trained on different salient clusters. We run all the classifiers on each grid for all patches. Then, we have a vector of confidence values for each patch, corresponding to each particular cluster classifier. We sum those confidence vectors of each patch in the same grid. Each grid at each level is labelled by the maximum confidence classifier among all the outputs for the patches. All of those confidence values are then merged with a weighted sum to a label for the entire image. $D^i = \sum_{l=1}^{3} \sum_{n=1}^{N_l} \frac{1}{2^{3-l}} h_i e^{-(\hat{x}-x)/2\sigma^2}$ Here, N_l is the grid number for level l and h_i is the confidence value for grid i. We include a Gaussian filter, where $\hat{x}$ is center of the image and x is location of the spatial pyramid grid, to give more priority to the detections around the center of the image for reducing noisy background effect.

For evaluation we use three different datasets. The first dataset is Bing Search Images curated by ourselves from the top 35 images returned with the same queries we used for initial images. This set includes 840 images in total for testing. Second dataset is Google Colour Images [53] previously used by [53] for learning colour attributes. Google Colour Images includes 100 images for each color name. We used the whole data-sets only for testing of our models learned on a possibly different set that we collected from Google, contrary to [53]. The last dataset is sample annotated images from ImageNet [47] for 25 attributes. To test the results on a human labelled dataset, we use Ebay dataset provided by [53] which has labels for the pixels in cropped regions. It includes 40 images for each colour name.

Figure 6 compares the overall accuracy of the proposed method (**CMAP**) with three other methods on the task of attribute learning. As the baseline (**BL**), we use all the images returned for the concept query to train a single model. As expected, the performance is very low suggesting that a single model trained by crude noisy web images performs poorly and the data should be organised to train at least some qualified models from coherent clusters in which representative images are grouped. As two other methods for clustering the data, we used k-means (**KM**) and original SOM algorithm (**SOM**) with optimal cluster number, decided by cross-validation of whole pipeline, and again train a model for each cluster. The low results support the need for pruning of the data through outlier elimination. Results show that, CMAP's clusters are able to detect coherent and clean representative data groups so we train less number of classifiers by eliminating outlier clusters but those classifiers better in quality and also, on novel test sets with images having different characteristics than the images used in training, CMAP can still perform very well on learning of attributes.

Our method is also utilised for retrieving images on EBAY dataset as in [53]. [53] learns the models from web images and apply the models to another set so both method study a similar problem. We utilise CMAP with patches obtained from the entire images (**CMAP**) as well as from the masks provided by [53] (**CMAP-M**). As shown in Figure6 Right, even without masks CMAP is comparable to the performance of the PLSA based method of [53], and with the same setting CMAP outperforms the PLSA based method with significant performance difference.

On ImageNet dataset, we obtained 37.4% accuracy compared to 36.8% of Russakovsky and Fei-Fei[47]. It is also significant that, our models trained from different source of information are better to generalized for some of worse performance classes (rough, spotted, striped, wood) of [47]. Recall that we globally learn the attribute models from web images, not from any partition of the ImageNet. Thus, it is encouraging to observe better results in such a large data-set against [47]'s attribute models trained by a sufficiently large training subset.

Attribute Based Scene Recognition: While the results on different datasets support the ability of our approach to be generalised to different datasets, we also perform experiments to understand the effect of the learned attributes on a different task, namely for classification of scenes using entirely different collections. Experiments are performed on MIT-indoor [45], and Scene-15 [32] datasets. MIT-indoor has 67 different indoor scene with 15620 images with at least 100 images for each category and we use

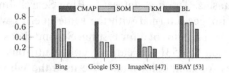 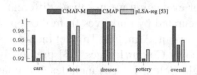

Fig. 6. Left: Attribute recognition performances on novel images compared to other methods. **Right:** Equal Error Rates on EBAY dataset for image retrieval using the configuration of [53]. CMAP does not utilise the image masks used in [53], while CMAP-M does.

100 images from each class to test our results. Scene-15 is composed by 15 different scene categories. We use 200 images from each category for our testing. MIT-indoor is extended and even harder version of Scene-15 with many additional categories.

We again get the confidence values for each grid in three levels of the spatial pyramid on the test images. However, rather than using a single value for the maximum classifier output, we keep the confidence values for all the classifiers for each grid. We concatenate these vectors for all grids in all levels to get a single feature vector of size $3xNxK$ for the image, which is then used for scene classification. Here N is the number of grids at each level, and K is the number of different concepts. Note that, while the attributes are learned in an unsupervised way, in this experiment scene classifiers are trained on the datasets provided (see next section for automatic scene concept learning).

As shown in Table 1, our method for scene recognition with learned attributes (**CMAP-A**), performs competitively with [34] while using shorter feature vectors in relatively cheaper environment, and outperforms the others. Comparisons with [45] show that using the visual information acquired from attributes is more descriptive in the cluttered nature of MIT-indoor scenes. For instance, "bookstore" images has very similar structural layout to "clothing store" images, but they are more distinct with colour and texture information around the scene. Attribute level features do not create this much difference for Scene-15 data-set since images include some obvious statistical differences.

5.4 Learning Concepts for Scene Categories

As an alternative to recognising scenes through the learned attributes, we directly learn higher level concepts for scene categories. We call this method as **CMAP-S**. Specifically, we perform testing for scene classification for 15 scene categories on [32] and MIT-indoor [45] data-sets, but learn the scene concepts directly from the images collected from Web through querying for the names of the scene concepts used in these datasets. That is, we do not use any manually labelled training set (or training subset of the benchmark data-sets), but directly the crude web images which are pruned and organised by CMAP, in contrast to comparable fully supervised methods. As shown in Table 1, our method is competitive with the state-of-the-art studies without requiring any supervised training.

We then made a slight change on our original CMAP-S implementation by using the hard-negatives of previous iteration as a negative set of next iteration (we refer to this new method as **CMAP-S-HM**). We relax the memory needs with less but strong

Table 1. Comparison of our methods on scene recognition in relation to state-of-the-art studies on MIT-Indoor [45] and Scene-15 [32] datasets

-	CMAP-A	CMAP-S	CMAP-S+HM	Li et al. [34] VQ	Pandey et al. [44]	Kwitt et al. [30]	Lazebnik et al. [32]	Singh et al. [50]
MIT-indoor [45]	46.2%	40.8%	41.7%	47.6%	43.1%	44%	-	38%
Scene-15 [32]	82.7%	80.7%	81.3%	82.1%	-	82.3%	81%	77%

negative instances. As the results in Table 1 and Figure 7 show, we achieve better perfor-mances in Scene-15 than the state-of-the-art studies with this simple addition, still with-out requiring any supervisory input. However, on a harder MIT-indoor dataset, without using attribute information, low-level features are not very distinctive.

In order to understand the effect of discriminative visual features, which aim to cap-ture representative and discriminative mid-level features, we also compare our method with the work of Singh et al. [50]. As seen in Table 1, our performances are better than both their reported results on MIT-indoor, and our implementation on Scene-15.

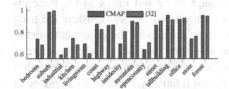

	CMAP	[17]	[33]		CMAP	[17]	[33]
airplane	0.63	0.51	0.76	car	0.97	0.98	0.94
face	0.67	0.52	0.82	guitar	**0.89**	0.81	0.60
leopard	0.76	0.74	0.89	motorbike	**0.98**	0.98	0.67
watch	**0.55**	0.48	0.53	overall	**0.78**	0.72	0.75

Fig. 7. Left: Comparisons on Scene-15 dataset. Overall accuracy is 81.3% for CMAP-S+HM , versus 81% for [32] . Classes "industrial", "insidecity", "opencountry" results very noisy set of web images, hence trained models are not strong enough as might be observed from the chart. **Right:** Classification accuracies of our method in relation to [17] and [33].

5.5   Learning Concepts of Object Categories

We learn object concepts from Google web images used in [17] and compare our results with [17] and [33] (see Figure 7 Right). [17] provides a data-set from Google with 7 classes and total 4088 gray scale images, 584 images in average for each class with many "junk" images in each class as they indicated. They test their results in a manually selected subset of Caltech Object data-set. Because of its raw nature of the Google images and adaptation to the Caltech subset, it is a good experimental ground for our pipeline.

Salient regions extracted from images are represented with 500 word quantized SIFT [36] vector with additional 256 dimension LBP [40] vector. In total we aggregated a 756 dimension vector representation for each salient region. At the final stage of learning with CMAP, we learn L2 norm, linear SVM classifiers for each cluster with negatives are gathered from other classes and the global outliers. For each learning iteration, we also apply hard mining to cull highest rank negative instances in the amount 10 times of salient instances in the cluster. All pipeline hyper-parameters are tuned via the val-idation set provided by [17]. Given a novel image, learned classifiers are passed over the image with gradually increasing scales, up to a point where the maximum class confidences are stable. Among class confidences, maximum confidence indicates the final prediction for that image. We observe 6.3 salient clusters in average for all classes and 69.4 instances for each salient clusters. That is, CMAP eliminates 147 instances for each class as supposedly outlier instances. Results support that elimination of "junk" images gives significant improvements, especially for the noisy classes in [17].

5.6 Learning Faces

We use FAN-large [41] face data-set for testing our method in face recognition problem. We use Easy and Hard subsets with the names accommodating more than 100 images (to have fair testing results). Our models are trained over web images queried from Bing Image search engine for the same names. All the data preprocessing and the feature extraction flow follow the same line of [41], that is owned from [12]. However, [41] trains the models and evaluates the results at the same collection.

We retrieve the top 1000 images from Bing results. Face are detected and face with the highest confidence is extracted from each image to be fed into CMAP. Face instances are clustered and spurious face instances are pruned. Salient clusters are used for learning SVM models for each cluster in the same settings of the object categories. For our experiments we used two different face detectors. One is cascade classifier of [54] implemented in OpenCV library [4] and another is [57] with more precise detection results, even the OpenCV implementation is very fast relatively. Results are depicted at Table2 with two different face detection method and baseline result with models trained on raw Bing images for each person.

Table 2. Face learning results with detecting faces using OpenCV(CMAP-1) and [57](CMAP-2)

Method	GBC+CF(half)[41]	CMAP-1	CMAP-2	BaseLine
Easy	0.58	0.63	0.66	0.31
Hard	0.32	0.34	0.38	0.18

6 Conclusion

We propose Concept Maps for weakly supervised learning of visual concepts from large scale noisy web data. Multiple classifiers are built for each concept from clusters pruned from outliers, to have each classifier sensitive to a different visual variation. Our experiments show that we are able to capture low level attributes on novel images and have a good basis for higher level recognition tasks like scene recognition with inexpensive setting. We also show that we can directly learn scene concepts with the proposed framework. Going further, we show that CMAP is able to learn object and face categories from noisy web data. We are able to learn in an unsupervised way from the weakly-labeled web results and test on different datasets usually with different characteristics than the web data. Comparisons with the state-of-the-art studies in all tasks show that our method achieves better or similar results to the other methods which use the same/similar web data for training or which require supervision. As the future work, this framework will be extended to learn concepts from videos.

References

1. Berg, T.L., Berg, A.C.: Finding iconic images. In: IEEE Computer Society Conference on Computer Vision and Pattern Recognition Workshops, CVPR Workshops 2009, pp. 1–8. IEEE (2009)
2. Berg, T.L., Berg, A.C., Edwards, J., Maire, M., White, R., Teh, Y.W., Learned-Miller, E.G., Forsyth, D.A.: Names and faces in the news. In: IEEE Conference on Computer Vision and Pattern Recognition (CVPR), vol. 2, pp. 848–854 (2004)
3. Berg, T.L., Forsyth, D.A.: Animals on the web. In: 2006 IEEE Computer Society Conference on Computer Vision and Pattern Recognition, vol. 2, pp. 1463–1470. IEEE (2006)
4. Bradski, G.: Dr. Dobb's Journal of Software Tools
5. Chen, X., Shrivastava, A., Gupta, A.: Neil: Extracting visual knowledge from web data. In: Proc. 14th International Conference on Computer Vision, vol. 3 (2013)
6. Choi, J., Rastegari, M., Farhadi, A., Davis, L.S.: Adding unlabeled samples to categories by learned attributes. In: CVPR (2013)
7. Couzinié-Devy, F., Sun, J., Alahari, K., Ponce, J.: Learning to estimate and remove non-uniform image blur. In: 2013 IEEE Conference on Computer Vision and Pattern Recognition (CVPR), pp. 1075–1082. IEEE (2013)
8. Doersch, C., Gupta, A., Efros, A.A.: Mid-level visual element discovery as discriminative mode seeking. In: Advances in Neural Information Processing Systems, pp. 494–502 (2013)
9. Doersch, C., Singh, S., Gupta, A., Sivic, J., Efros, A.A.: What makes paris look like paris? ACM Transactions on Graphics (TOG) 31(4), 101 (2012)
10. Endres, I., Shih, K.J., Jiaa, J., Hoiem, D.: Learning collections of part models for object recognition. In: 2013 IEEE Conference on Computer Vision and Pattern Recognition (CVPR), pp. 939–946. IEEE (2013)
11. Erdem, E., Erdem, A.: Visual saliency estimation by nonlinearly integrating features using region covariances. Journal of Vision 13(4), 1–20 (2013)
12. Everingham, M., Sivic, J., Zisserman, A.: Hello! my name is... buffy–automatic naming of characters in tv video (2006)
13. Fan, J., Shen, Y., Zhou, N., Gao, Y.: Harvesting large-scale weakly-tagged image databases from the web. In: CVPR, pp. 802–809 (2010)
14. Fan, R.E., Chang, K.W., Hsieh, C.J., Wang, X.R., Lin, C.J.: Liblinear: A library for large linear classification. The Journal of Machine Learning Research 9, 1871–1874 (2008)
15. Farhadi, A., Endres, I., Hoiem, D.: Attribute-centric recognition for crosscategory generalization (2010)
16. Farhadi, A., Endres, I., Hoiem, D., Forsyth, D.: Describing objects by their attributes. In: CVPR (2009)
17. Fergus, R., Fei-Fei, L., Perona, P., Zisserman, A.: Learning object categories from google's image search. In: Tenth IEEE International Conference on Computer Vision, ICCV 2005, vol. 2, pp. 1816–1823. IEEE (2005)
18. Ferrari, V., Zisserman, A.: Learning visual attributes. In: NIPS (2008)
19. Guillaumin, M., Mensink, T., Verbeek, J., Schmid, C.: Automatic face naming with caption-based supervision. In: IEEE Conference on Computer Vision and Pattern Recognition, CVPR 2008, pp. 1–8. IEEE (2008)
20. Guillaumin, M., Mensink, T., Verbeek, J., Schmid, C.: Face recognition from caption-based supervision. International Journal of Computer Vision 96(1), 64–82 (2012)
21. Guillaumin, M., Verbeek, J., Schmid, C.: Multiple instance metric learning from automatically labeled bags of faces. In: Daniilidis, K., Maragos, P., Paragios, N. (eds.) ECCV 2010, Part I. LNCS, vol. 6311, pp. 634–647. Springer, Heidelberg (2010)

22. Harris, T.: A kohonen som based, machine health monitoring system which enables diagnosis of faults not seen in the training set. In: Neural Networks. IJCNN 1993, Nagoya (1993)
23. Hays, J., Efros, A.A.: Im2gps: estimating geographic information from a single image. In: IEEE Conference on Computer Vision and Pattern Recognition, CVPR 2008, pp. 1–8. IEEE (2008)
24. Hubel, D.H., Wiesel, T.N.: Receptive fields, binocular interaction and functional architecture in the cat's visual cortex. The Journal of Physiology 160(1), 106 (1962)
25. Jain, A., Gupta, A., Rodriguez, M., Davis, L.S.: Representing videos using mid-level discriminative patches. In: 2013 IEEE Conference on Computer Vision and Pattern Recognition (CVPR), pp. 2571–2578. IEEE (2013)
26. Juneja, M., Vedaldi, A., Jawahar, C., Zisserman, A.: Blocks that shout: Distinctive parts for scene classification. In: 2013 IEEE Conference on Computer Vision and Pattern Recognition (CVPR), pp. 923–930. IEEE (2013)
27. Kim, G., Torralba, A.: Unsupervised detection of regions of interest using iterative link analysis. In: NIPS, vol. 1, pp. 2–4 (2009)
28. Kohonen, T.: Self-organizing maps. Springer (1997)
29. Kumar, N., Berg, A.C., Belhumeur, P.N., Nayar, S.K.: Attribute and simile classifiers for face verification. In: ICCV (2009)
30. Kwitt, R., Vasconcelos, N., Rasiwasia, N.: Scene recognition on the semantic manifold. In: Fitzgibbon, A., Lazebnik, S., Perona, P., Sato, Y., Schmid, C. (eds.) ECCV 2012, Part IV. LNCS, vol. 7575, pp. 359–372. Springer, Heidelberg (2012)
31. Lampert, C.H., Nickisch, H., Harmeling, S.: Learning to detect unseen object classes by between-class attribute transfer. In: IEEE Conference on Computer Vision and Pattern Recognition, CVPR 2009, pp. 951–958. IEEE (2009)
32. Lazebnik, S., Schmid, C., Ponce, J.: Beyond bags of features: Spatial pyramid matching for recognizing natural scene categories. In: 2006 IEEE Computer Society Conference on Computer Vision and Pattern Recognition, vol. 2, pp. 2169–2178. IEEE (2006)
33. Li, L.J., Fei-Fei, L.: Optimol: automatic online picture collection via incremental model learning. International Journal of Computer Vision 88(2), 147–168 (2010)
34. Li, Q., Wu, J., Tu, Z.: Harvesting mid-level visual concepts from large-scale internet images. In: CVPR (2013)
35. Li, Q., Wu, J., Tu, Z.: Harvesting mid-level visual concepts from large-scale internet images. In: 2013 IEEE Conference on Computer Vision and Pattern Recognition (CVPR), pp. 851–858. IEEE (2013)
36. Lowe, D.G.: Distinctive image features from scale-invariant keypoints. International Journal of Computer Vision 60(2), 91–110 (2004)
37. Marsland, S., Nehmzow, U., Shapiro, J.: A model of habituation applied to mobile robots (1999)
38. Marsland, S., Nehmzow, U., Shapiro, J.: Novelty Detection for Robot Neotaxis. In: Proceedings 2nd NC (2000)
39. Muñoz, A., Muruzábal, J.: Self-organizing maps for outlier detection. Neurocomputing 18(1), 33–60 (1998)
40. Ojala, T., Pietikainen, M., Maenpaa, T.: Multiresolution gray-scale and rotation invariant texture classification with local binary patterns. IEEE Transactions on Pattern Analysis and Machine Intelligence 24(7), 971–987 (2002)
41. Özcan, M., Luo, J., Ferrari, V., Caputo, B.: A large-scale database of images and captions for automatic face naming. In: BMVC, pp. 1–11 (2011)
42. Ozkan, D., Duygulu, P.: A graph based approach for naming faces in news photos. In: 2006 IEEE Computer Society Conference on Computer Vision and Pattern Recognition, vol. 2, pp. 1477–1482. IEEE (2006)

43. Ozkan, D., Duygulu, P.: Interesting faces: A graph-based approach for finding people in news. Pattern Recognition 43(5), 1717–1735 (2010)
44. Pandey, M., Lazebnik, S.: Scene recognition and weakly supervised object localization with deformable part-based models. In: ICCV (2011)
45. Quattoni, A., Torralba, A.: Recognizing indoor scenes. In: CVPR (2009)
46. Rastegari, M., Farhadi, A., Forsyth, D.: Attribute discovery via predictable discriminative binary codes. In: Fitzgibbon, A., Lazebnik, S., Perona, P., Sato, Y., Schmid, C. (eds.) ECCV 2012, Part VI. LNCS, vol. 7577, pp. 876–889. Springer, Heidelberg (2012)
47. Russakovsky, O., Fei-Fei, L.: Attribute learning in large-scale datasets. In: Kutulakos, K.N. (ed.) ECCV 2010 Workshops, Part I. LNCS, vol. 6553, pp. 1–14. Springer, Heidelberg (2012)
48. Schroff, F., Criminisi, A., Zisserman, A.: Harvesting image databases from the web. IEEE Transactions on Pattern Analysis and Machine Intelligence 33(4), 754–766 (2011)
49. Simonyan, K., Parkhi, O.M., Vedaldi, A., Zisserman, A.: Fisher vector faces in the wild. In: Proc. BMVC, vol. 1, p. 7 (2013)
50. Singh, S., Gupta, A., Efros, A.A.: Unsupervised discovery of mid-level discriminative patches. In: Fitzgibbon, A., Lazebnik, S., Perona, P., Sato, Y., Schmid, C. (eds.) ECCV 2012, Part II. LNCS, vol. 7573, pp. 73–86. Springer, Heidelberg (2012)
51. Theofilou, D., Steuber, V., Schutter, E.D.: Novelty detection in a kohonen-like network with a long-term depression learning rule. Neurocomputing 52(54), 411–417 (2003)
52. Torresani, L., Szummer, M., Fitzgibbon, A.: Efficient object category recognition using classemes. In: Daniilidis, K., Maragos, P., Paragios, N. (eds.) ECCV 2010, Part I. LNCS, vol. 6311, pp. 776–789. Springer, Heidelberg (2010)
53. Van De Weijer, J., Schmid, C., Verbeek, J., Larlus, D.: Learning color names for real-world applications. IEEE Image Processing (2009)
54. Viola, P., Jones, M.: Rapid object detection using a boosted cascade of simple features. In: Proceedings of the 2001 IEEE Computer Society Conference on Computer Vision and Pattern Recognition, CVPR 2001, vol. 1, p. I-511. IEEE (2001)
55. Yanai, K., Barnard, K.: Probabilistic web image gathering. In: Proceedings of the 7th ACM SIGMM International Workshop on Multimedia Information Retrieval, pp. 57–64. ACM (2005)
56. Ypma, A., Ypma, E., Duin, R.P.: Novelty detection using self-organizing maps. In: Proc. of ICONIP 1997 (1997)
57. Zhu, X., Ramanan, D.: Face detection, pose estimation, and landmark localization in the wild. In: 2012 IEEE Conference on Computer Vision and Pattern Recognition (CVPR), pp. 2879–2886. IEEE (2012)

Shrinkage Expansion Adaptive Metric Learning

Qilong Wang[1,3], Wangmeng Zuo[2], Lei Zhang[3], and Peihua Li[1]

[1] School of Information and Communications Engineering,
Dalian University of Technology, China
[2] School of Computer Science and Technology, Harbin Institute of Technology, China
[3] Department of Computing, Hong Kong Polytechnic University, Hong Kong
{csqlwang,cswmzuo}@gmail.com, cslzhang@comp.polyu.edu.hk,
peihuali@dlut.edu.cn

Abstract. Conventional pairwise constrained metric learning methods usually restrict the distance between samples of a similar pair to be lower than a fixed upper bound, and the distance between samples of a dissimilar pair higher than a fixed lower bound. Such fixed bound based constraints, however, may not work well when the intra- and inter-class variations are complex. In this paper, we propose a shrinkage expansion adaptive metric learning (SEAML) method by defining a novel shrinkage-expansion rule for adaptive pairwise constraints. SEAML is very effective in learning metrics from data with complex distributions. Meanwhile, it also suggests a new rule to assess the similarity between a pair of samples based on whether their distance is shrunk or expanded after metric learning. Our extensive experimental results demonstrated that SEAML achieves better performance than state-of-the-art metric learning methods. In addition, the proposed shrinkage-expansion adaptive pairwise constraints can be readily applied to many other pairwise constrained metric learning algorithms, and boost significantly their performance in applications such as face verification on LFW and PubFig databases.

Keywords: Shrinkage-expansion rule, adaptive bound constraints, pairwise constrained metric learning, face verification.

1 Introduction

Distance metric learning aims to learn an appropriate distance metric by taking advantages of the intrinsic structure of training data. Numerous metric learning methods have been proposed for a variety of computer vision applications such as face verification [10,17,27], object classification [26], image annotation [7,33], and visual tracking [21], etc. The information conveyed by training data can be generally represented as triplet and pairwise constraints. Triplet constraints based metric learning approaches, including large margin nearest neighbor (LMNN) [35], BoostMetric [31] and FrobMetric [30], restrict that for each triplet the distance between a pair of samples from the same class should be smaller than the distance between a pair of samples from different classes. Pairwise constraints are more pervasive in metric learning. In many applications such as face verification, only pairwise constraints are available from the training data. For example, under the restricted setting of the LFW face database [15], the only known information is whether a pair of face images is matched or not.

D. Fleet et al. (Eds.): ECCV 2014, Part VII, LNCS 8695, pp. 456–471, 2014.

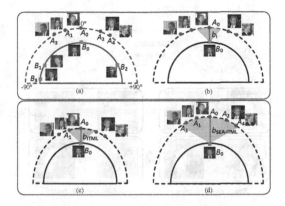

Fig. 1. An illustrative example of face verification by ITML and SEA-ITML. (a) The face image manifolds of two persons with pose variations. (b) The verification results with the decision threshold b_I before metric learning. $A_1 \sim A_4$ are all wrongly verified to be dissimilar with A_0 . (c) The verification results with the decision threshold b_{ITML} after metric learning by ITML [6] with fixed bound constraints. A_1 now is correctly verified, but $A_2 \sim A_4$ are still wrongly verified. (d) The verification results with the decision threshold $b_{SEA-ITML}$ after metric learning by ITML with the proposed shrinkage expansion adaptive constraints (SEA-ITML). $A_1 \sim A_4$ can all be correctly verified.

Most pairwise constrained metric learning methods restrict the distance between samples of a similar pair to be lower than a fixed upper bound and the distance between samples of a dissimilar pair higher than a fixed lower bound. Davis et al. [6] proposed an information theoretic metric learning (ITML) method, which restricts that the distances for all similar pairs should be smaller than an upper bound u and the distances for all dissimilar pairs should be larger than a lower bound l. Guillaumin et al. [10] learned a Mahalanobis distance metric via discriminative linear logistic regression. This method intends to find a bound b so that all distances of similar pairs can be smaller than those of dissimilar pairs. Li et al. [22] learned a second-order discriminant function instead of Mahalanobis distance for verification problem. They confined the function values of all similar pairs to be smaller than -1 and those of all dissimilar pairs larger than 1.

The above fixed bound based constraints may fail to learn effective metrics when the intra- and inter-class variations are complex. In face recognition or verification, it is commonly accepted that the face images of a person with pose and lighting variations are in a nonlinear manifold [12]. The face manifolds of different persons are similar, while the challenge lies in that the intra-class variation of face images is often very complex. Figure 1 (a) illustrates the face manifolds of two persons, Bush ($A_0 \sim A_4$) and Blair ($B_0 \sim B_3$). Figure 1 (b) illustrates the face verification results before metric learning. To avoid false acceptance, the decision threshold can be set as b_I based on the distance between A_0 and B_0. One can see that although A_0 and B_0 can be correctly verified as different subjects by b_I, $A_1 \sim A_4$ will be wrongly verified as different subjects from A_0 since their distances to A_0 are higher than b_I. Figure 1 (c) illustrates the verification results after metric learning by using the well-known ITML [6]. We can see that the manifolds shrink along the horizontal direction while keeping unchanged

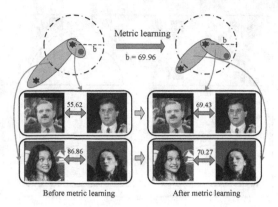

Fig. 2. A real failure case of face verification on the LFW database by conventional methods which only use a threshold b to decide if the pair is a match or non-match after metric learning. By the proposed SEAML, we can classify the pair by exploiting the shrinkage-expansion property of its sample distance, and thus both the two pairs can be correctly classified.

in the vertical direction. This time A_1 can be correctly verified by using the decision threshold b_{ITML}; however, the other images $A_2 \sim A_4$ still cannot be correctly verified.

To tackle the above mentioned problem, in this paper we propose a self-adaptive shrinkage-expansion rule based on the original Euclidean distances of the pairs, which relaxes the fixed bound based constraints by shrinking the distances between samples of similar pairs and expanding the distances between samples of dissimilar pairs. The details can be found in Section 3.1. As illustrated in Figure 1 (d), by means of SEA-ITML (i.e., ITML with the proposed shrinkage-expansion adaptive constraints; please refer to Section 3.3 for details), $A_1 \sim A_4$ all can be correctly verified by using the decision threshold $b_{SEA-ITML}$, improving significantly the verification performance. According to our experiments, ITML [6] with the proposed pairwise constraints can boost its verification performance from 76.2% to 82.4% and from 69.3% to 77.8% on the LFW and PubFig face databases, respectively (please refer to Section 5 for details). Since ITML and SEA-ITML use the same regularization and loss terms, the benefit shall be owed to that the proposed shrinkage-expansion adaptive constraints is more effective to learn the desired metrics from data with complex distributions.

Another distinct advantage of the proposed shrinkage expansion adaptive metric learning (SEAML) method is that the shrinkage-expansion adaptive constraints suggest a novel paradigm to assess the similarity between a pair of samples. Given a pair of samples, conventional metric learning approaches usually compute their Mahalanobis distance d, and judge if they are from the same class based on whether d is lower or higher than the decision threshold b. Different from these approaches, SEAML learns a Mahalanobis distance metric to shrink the distances between samples of similar pairs and expand the distances between samples of dissimilar pairs. Thus, SEAML allows us to make the decision by considering both b and the changes between the distances before and after metric learning. Figure 2 shows two pairs of images from the LFW face database. After metric learning, the Mahalanobis distance of a similar (dissimilar) pair is still higher (lower) than the threshold $b = 69.96$. With the conventional decision paradigm, these two pairs would be misclassified. Fortunately, one can observe that after metric learning, the distance of the similar pair shrinks from 86.86 to 70.27, while the distance of the dissimilar pair expands from 55.62 to 69.43. Thus, when the distance between samples of a pair is close to the decision threshold b, we can classify the pair according to the shrinkage-expansion property of its sample distance. In this way, both the two pairs in Figure 2 can be correctly classified by the proposed SEAML method. The details of the verification rule will be given in Section 4.

Our extensive experimental results on 12 UCI datasets [2], LFW [15] and PubFig [19] face databases show that SEAML outperforms many state-of-the-art metric learning methods. The rest of this paper is organized as follows. In Section 2, we review the literature related to our work. Section 3 presents the proposed shrinkage expansion adaptive metric learning framework and we introduce a novel verification paradigm of SEAML in Section 4. In Section 5, we show experimental results of the proposed method on both classification and face verification tasks. Finally, we conclude our paper in Section 6.

2   Related Work

Most of the existing metric learning methods learn metrics with triplet or pairwise constraints. The classical triplet constrained metric learning method LMNN [35] has shown powerful classification capability with the k nearest neighbor (kNN) classifier. Motivated by LMNN, Shen et al. [31] used the exponential loss instead of hinge loss in LMNN, resulting in a BoostMetric method. Based on LMNN and BoostMetric, Shen et al. [30] proposed the FrobMetric method, which utilizes the Frobenius norm regularizer to make metric learning more efficient and scalable. For kNN classification, the proposed SEAML shares similar philosophy to LMNN [35], BoostMetric [31] and FrobMetric [30]. For each triplet $(\mathbf{x}_i, \mathbf{x}_j, \mathbf{x}_k)$ (the class label of $\mathbf{x}_i$ is the same as that of $\mathbf{x}_j$ but different from that of $\mathbf{x}_k$), methods in [30,31,35] restrict that the learned distance $D_{\mathbf{M}}(\mathbf{x}_i, \mathbf{x}_j)$ between $\mathbf{x}_i$ and $\mathbf{x}_j$ should be smaller than the distance $D_{\mathbf{M}}(\mathbf{x}_i, \mathbf{x}_k)$ between $\mathbf{x}_i$ and $\mathbf{x}_k$. From the perspective of the proposed SEAML, this triplet constraint can be regarded as that $D_{\mathbf{M}}(\mathbf{x}_i, \mathbf{x}_k)$ is used as a locally adaptive upper bound of $D_{\mathbf{M}}(\mathbf{x}_i, \mathbf{x}_j)$, or $D_{\mathbf{M}}(\mathbf{x}_i, \mathbf{x}_j)$ is used as a locally adaptive lower bound of $D_{\mathbf{M}}(\mathbf{x}_i, \mathbf{x}_k)$. However, [30,31,35] cannot be applied to tasks where only pairwise constraints are available [28]. Unlike [30,31,35], SEAML uses the Euclidean distance of a pair to adaptively set the lower and upper bounds, and thus can work in more general cases.

Some pairwise constrained metric learning methods [8,9,11] also need the label information of each sample. Neighborhood components analysis [9] learns a metric for nearest neighbor classifier (NNC) by finding a linear transformation of input data such that the average leave-one-out classification performance is maximized in the transformed space. Globerson et al. [8] proposed to learn a metric by maximizing the distances between different classes while collapsing the intra-class distances to zero. Huang et al. [11] proposed an ensemble metric learning method that restricts the intra-class distances to be smaller than inter-class distances. Similar to triplet constrained metric learning methods, they work in a fully supervised learning manner.

Although many pairwise constrained metric learning approaches, such as ITML [6], LDML [10], work in a weakly supervised manner, these methods adopt the fixed bound based constraints, making them less effective when the intra- and inter-class variations are complex. To the best of our knowledge, thus far only Li et al. [23] relaxed the fixed bound problem by learning a locally adaptive decision function to distinguish similar pairs and dissimilar ones. The proposed SEAML method in this paper is essentially different from the method in [23]. First, SEAML uses a shrinkage-expansion rule to set the adaptive pairwise constraints. Second, it suggests a novel verification paradigm by considering both the decision threshold and the shrinkage-expansion property of the distance with the learned metric. Finally, SEAML learns a Mahalanobis distance metric while [23] learns a second-order decision function. In recent years, some multiple metrics learning methods [29,34] have been proposed to handle data with complex distributions. They are distinctly different from SEAML which learns a single metric but with adaptive constraints. One may refer to [3] for more details on the recent progresses on metric learning.

3   Shrinkage Expansion Adaptive Metric Learning

In Section 3.1, we first introduce the formulation of shrinkage-expansion adaptive pairwise constraints, resulting in a shrinkage expansion adaptive metric learning (SEAML) framework. In Section 3.2, we substantiate a SEAML algorithm by using the squared Frobenius norm (F-norm) regularizer and the hinge loss, which can be efficiently optimized by alternating between SVM training [4] and projection on the cone of all positive semidefinite (PSD) matrices. Section 3.3 shows that the proposed shrinkage-expansion rule can be flexibly embedded into many existing pairwise-based metric learning methods, such as ITML [6].

3.1   Shrinkage-Expansion Adaptive Constraints

Denote the set of similar pairs by $\mathcal{S} = \{(\mathbf{x}_i, \mathbf{x}_j) : \mathbf{x}_i \text{ and } \mathbf{x}_j \text{ belong to the same class }\}$, and the set of dissimilar pairs by $\mathcal{D} = \{(\mathbf{x}_i, \mathbf{x}_j) : \mathbf{x}_i \text{ and } \mathbf{x}_j \text{ belong to different classes}\}$. Metric learning aims to learn a PSD matrix $\mathbf{M} \in \mathbb{R}^{d \times d}$ which characterizes the Mahalanobis distance:

$$D_{\mathbf{M}}(\mathbf{x}_i, \mathbf{x}_j) = (\mathbf{x}_i - \mathbf{x}_j)^T \mathbf{M}(\mathbf{x}_i - \mathbf{x}_j). \tag{1}$$

To learn a proper Mahalanobis distance metric, conventional pairwise constraints usually require that the learned distances of similar pairs should be lower than some fixed upper bound u, while those of dissimilar pairs should be higher than some fixed lower bound l, which can be formulated as:

$$D_{\mathbf{M}}(\mathbf{x}_i, \mathbf{x}_j) \leq u \quad (\mathbf{x}_i, \mathbf{x}_j) \in \mathcal{S}, \tag{2}$$
$$D_{\mathbf{M}}(\mathbf{x}_i, \mathbf{x}_j) \geq l \quad (\mathbf{x}_i, \mathbf{x}_j) \in \mathcal{D}.$$

The above fixed bound based constraints may not work well for data with complex distributions, as discussed in Section 1. To address this issue, we propose to relax the fix bound based constraints by introducing an adaptive shrinkage-expansion rule to design pairwise constraints. Given a similar/dissimilar pair $(\mathbf{x}_i, \mathbf{x}_j)$, the Euclidean distance $D_{ij} = D_{\mathbf{I}}(\mathbf{x}_i, \mathbf{x}_j)$ is used as a reference to guide the shrinkage/expansion, and thus the adaptive upper/lower bound can be defined as a function of D_{ij}, i.e., $f(D_{ij})$. One obvious principle for the design of $f(D_{ij})$ is : the larger the distance of a similar pair, the more $f(D_{ij})$ should shrink from D_{ij}, while the smaller the distance of a dissimilar pair, the more $f(D_{ij})$ should expand from D_{ij}. Based on this principle, we define the following shrinkage-expansion rule to compute the adaptive upper/lower bounds for similar/dissimilar pairs:

$$f_s(D_{ij}) = D_{ij} - (D_{ij}^{(\frac{1}{N_s})}/D_c) \quad (\mathbf{x}_i, \mathbf{x}_j) \in \mathcal{S}.$$
$$f_d(D_{ij}) = D_{ij} + (D_c/D_{ij}^{(\frac{1}{N_d})}) \quad (\mathbf{x}_i, \mathbf{x}_j) \in \mathcal{D}. \tag{3}$$

where $D_c \geq 1$ is a constant. $N_s \geq 1$ and $N_d \geq 1$ are scale factors which control the level of shrinkage and expansion, respectively.

From Eq. (3), we can see that the larger the N_s, the slower $f_s(D_{ij})$ will shrink, while the larger the N_d, the faster $f_d(D_{ij})$ will expand. In this paper, we set D_c as the maximal distance (denoted by D_{max}) among all pairs used in training data and set $N_s = 1$ and $N_d = 1/log(\frac{D_c}{D_c-2})$. N_d is abbreviated as n in the following Eq. (4). Thus, we obtain the following shrinkage-expansion adaptive constraints:

$$f_s(D_{ij}) = D_{ij} - (D_{ij}/D_{max}) \quad (\mathbf{x}_i, \mathbf{x}_j) \in \mathcal{S}.$$
$$f_d(D_{ij}) = D_{ij} + (D_{max}/\sqrt[n]{D_{ij}}) \quad (\mathbf{x}_i, \mathbf{x}_j) \in \mathcal{D}. \tag{4}$$

We set $N_s = 1$ to ensure that $f_s(D_{ij})$ can shrink the fastest (note that $N_s < 1$ cannot guarantee $f_s(D_{ij})$ to be always positive). We set $N_d = 1/log(\frac{D_c}{D_c-2})$ to ensure rapid expansion of $f_d(D_{ij})$, while it allows us to automatically distinguish similar and dissimilar pairs by D_c, i.e., $f_s(D_{ij}) < D_c$ and $f_d(D_{ij}) > D_c$, $\forall(i,j)$. In our experiments, it is found that when the constant $D_c > 2$, it has little influence on the classification and verification performance.

The proposed shrinkage-expansion rule can adaptively determine the pairwise constraints, and thus can effectively distinguish between similar pairs and dissimilar pairs. Based on the proposed shrinkage-expansion rule, we can formulate the SEAML framework as follows:

$$\min_{\mathbf{M}, \boldsymbol{\xi}} r_1(\mathbf{M}) + C \cdot r_2(\boldsymbol{\xi}) \tag{5}$$
$$\text{s.t. } D_{\mathbf{M}}(\mathbf{x}_i, \mathbf{x}_j) \leq f_s(D_{ij}) + \xi_{ij} \quad (\mathbf{x}_i, \mathbf{x}_j) \in \mathcal{S},$$
$$D_{\mathbf{M}}(\mathbf{x}_i, \mathbf{x}_j) \geq f_d(D_{ij}) - \xi_{ij} \quad (\mathbf{x}_i, \mathbf{x}_j) \in \mathcal{D},$$
$$\xi_{ij} \geq 0, \forall(i,j), \mathbf{M} \succeq 0.$$

where r_1 is the regularizer on $\mathbf{M}$, r_2 is the loss term on $\boldsymbol{\xi}$, and ξ_{ij} is introduced as the soft penalty on the pairwise inequality constraint. Many existing regularizers (e.g., squared F-norm and LogDet divergence) and loss functions (e.g., hinge loss and logistic loss) can be used in the proposed SEAML framework.

3.2   SEAML with Squared F-Norm Regularizer

The studies in [18] have shown that the squared F-norm regularizer can achieve good performance in object recognition, and it is strictly convex. On the other hand, it is known that the hinge loss has good generalization performance and it is adopted in LMNN and SVM. Thus, we adopt the squared F-Norm regularizer and hinge loss function in the proposed SEAML framework, resulting in the following metric learning model:

$$\min_{\mathbf{M}, \boldsymbol{\xi}} \tfrac{1}{2}\|\mathbf{M}\|_F^2 + C\sum_{ij}\xi_{ij} \tag{6}$$
$$\text{s.t. } D_{\mathbf{M}}(\mathbf{x}_i, \mathbf{x}_j) \leq f_s(D_{ij}) + \xi_{ij} \ (\mathbf{x}_i, \mathbf{x}_j) \in \mathcal{S},$$
$$D_{\mathbf{M}}(\mathbf{x}_i, \mathbf{x}_j) \geq f_d(D_{ij}) - \xi_{ij} \ (\mathbf{x}_i, \mathbf{x}_j) \in \mathcal{D},$$
$$\xi_{ij} \geq 0, \forall(i, j), \ \mathbf{M} \succcurlyeq 0.$$

We can rewrite Eq. (6) as follows:

$$\min_{\mathbf{M}, \boldsymbol{\xi}} \tfrac{1}{2}\|\mathbf{M}\|_F^2 + C\sum_{ij}\xi_{ij} \tag{7}$$
$$\text{s.t. } l_{ij}D_{\mathbf{M}}(\mathbf{x}_i, \mathbf{x}_j) \geq f(D_{ij}, l_{ij}) - \xi_{ij},$$
$$\xi_{ij} \geq 0, \forall(i, j), \ \mathbf{M} \succcurlyeq 0.$$

where $l_{ij} = -1$, $f(D_{ij}, l_{ij}) = -f_s(D_{ij})$ if $(\mathbf{x}_i, \mathbf{x}_j) \in \mathcal{S}$ and $l_{ij} = 1$, $f(D_{ij}, l_{ij}) = f_d(D_{ij})$ if $(\mathbf{x}_i, \mathbf{x}_j) \in \mathcal{D}$. For simplicity, hereafter $f(D_{ij}, l_{ij})$ is abbreviated as f_{ij}.

Let $\mathbf{Z}_{ij} = (\mathbf{x}_i - \mathbf{x}_j)(\mathbf{x}_i - \mathbf{x}_j)^T$. We can rewrite Eq. (1) in the form of inner product: $D_{\mathbf{M}}(\mathbf{x}_i, \mathbf{x}_j) = \langle \mathbf{Z}_{ij}, \mathbf{M} \rangle = tr(\mathbf{Z}_{ij}\mathbf{M})$. Then, the Lagrange function of Eq. (7) can be expressed as follows:

$$\mathcal{L}(\mathbf{M}, \mathbf{Y}, \boldsymbol{\beta}, \boldsymbol{\gamma}, \boldsymbol{\xi}) = \tfrac{1}{2}\|\mathbf{M}\|_F^2 + C\sum_{ij}\xi_{ij} - \langle \mathbf{Y}, \mathbf{M} \rangle$$
$$- \sum_{ij}\beta_{ij}[l_{ij}\langle \mathbf{Z}_{ij}, \mathbf{M} \rangle - f_{ij} + \xi_{ij}] - \sum_{ij}\gamma_{ij}\xi_{ij} \tag{8}$$
$$\text{s.t. } \beta_{ij} \geq 0, \ \gamma_{ij} \geq 0, \ \xi_{ij} \geq 0 \ \forall(i, j), \ \mathbf{M}, \mathbf{Y} \succcurlyeq 0.$$

where β_{ij}, γ_{ij}, and $\mathbf{Y}$ are the Lagrange multipliers. Based on the Karush-Kuhn-Tucker (KKT) conditions, we obtain the Lagrange dual problem of Eq. (7):

$$\max_{\mathbf{Y}, \boldsymbol{\beta}} -\tfrac{1}{2}\|\sum_{ij}\beta_{ij}l_{ij}\mathbf{Z}_{ij} + \mathbf{Y}\|_F^2 + \sum_{ij}f_{ij}\beta_{ij} \tag{9}$$
$$\text{s.t. } 0 \leq \beta_{ij} \leq C, \forall(i, j), \ \mathbf{Y} \succcurlyeq 0.$$

Please refer to the supplementary material for the detailed deduction of the Lagrange dual.

The problem in Eq. (9) involves the joint optimization of PSD matrix $\mathbf{Y}$ and vector $\boldsymbol{\beta}$, which can be solved by iterating between two procedures. First, by fixing $\mathbf{Y}$, the subproblem in Eq. (9) can be reformulated as a quadratic programming (QP) problem:

$$\max_{\boldsymbol{\beta}} -\tfrac{1}{2}\sum_{ij}\sum_{pq}\beta_{ij}\beta_{pq}l_{ij}l_{pq}\langle \mathbf{Z}_{ij}, \mathbf{Z}_{pq} \rangle + \sum_{ij}g_{ij}\beta_{ij}$$
$$\text{s.t. } 0 \leq \beta_{ij} \leq C, \forall(i, j). \tag{10}$$

where $g_{ij} = f_{ij} - l_{ij}(\langle \mathbf{Z}_{ij}, \mathbf{Y} \rangle)$. Clearly, we can use the off-the-shelf SVM solver [4] to obtain the optimal solution to the subproblem on β. After updating β, the subproblem on $\mathbf{Y}$ can be reformulated as the projection of $\hat{\mathbf{Y}}$ on the cones of PSD matrices:

$$\min_{\mathbf{Y}} \tfrac{1}{2} \|\mathbf{Y} - \hat{\mathbf{Y}}\|_F^2 \tag{11}$$
$$\text{s.t. } \mathbf{Y} \succeq 0.$$

where $\hat{\mathbf{Y}} = -\sum_{ij} \beta_{ij} l_{ij} \mathbf{Z}_{ij}$. Let $\hat{\mathbf{Y}} = \mathbf{U}\boldsymbol{\Sigma}\mathbf{V}^T$ be the SVD of $\hat{\mathbf{Y}}$, where $\boldsymbol{\Sigma}$ is the diagonal matrix of eigenvalues, and $\mathbf{U}$ is an orthonormal matrix consisting of the corresponding eigenvectors. The closed form solution of $\mathbf{Y}$ can then be represented as $\mathbf{Y} = \mathbf{U}\boldsymbol{\Sigma}_+\mathbf{V}^T$, where $\boldsymbol{\Sigma}_+ = \max(\mathbf{0}, \boldsymbol{\Sigma})$.

We iteratively update β and $\mathbf{Y}$ until the convergence of the objective function. Based on [5], it is guaranteed that the proposed alternating minimization approach would make the objective function in Eq. (9) converge to the global optimum. Finally, the learned matrix $\mathbf{M}$ can be obtained by $\sum_{ij} \beta_{ij} l_{ij} \mathbf{Z}_{ij} + \mathbf{Y}$. The proposed SEAML algorithm is summarized in Algorithm 1. The time complexity of training in SEAML is $O(L(dN^2 + d^3))$, where L is the iteration number, d is the feature dimension, and N is the number of pairs.

3.3 ITML with Shrinkage-Expansion Adaptive Constraints

The proposed shrinkage-expansion adaptive constraints can be flexibly embedded into many pairwise constrained metric learning methods by substituting the original fixed bound based constraints with the adaptive pairwise constraints suggested in Section 3.1. As an example, we embed the shrinkage-expansion adaptive constraints into ITML [6], and call the resulting model SEA-ITML:

$$\min_{\mathbf{M},\boldsymbol{\xi}} D_{ld}(\mathbf{M}, \mathbf{M}_0) + \gamma D_{ld}(diag(\boldsymbol{\xi}), diag(\boldsymbol{\xi}_0)) \tag{12}$$
$$\text{s.t. } D_{\mathbf{M}}(\mathbf{x}_i, \mathbf{x}_j) \leq f_s(D(\mathbf{x}_i, \mathbf{x}_j)) + \xi_{ij} \quad (\mathbf{x}_i, \mathbf{x}_j) \in \mathcal{S},$$
$$D_{\mathbf{M}}(\mathbf{x}_i, \mathbf{x}_j) \geq f_d(D(\mathbf{x}_i, \mathbf{x}_j)) - \xi_{ij} \quad (\mathbf{x}_i, \mathbf{x}_j) \in \mathcal{D},$$
$$\xi_{ij} \geq 0, \forall(i, j), \mathbf{M} \succeq 0.$$

where D_{ld} is the LogDet divergence [16] between matrices.

Apparently, the SEA-ITML model in Eq. (12) is an instantiation of the proposed SEAML framework with the LogDet regularizer. SEA-ITML can be solved using the same algorithm of ITML, and thus SEA-ITML has the same complexity as ITML [6]. It is mentionable that SEA-ITML can achieve much better performance than the original ITML method. Moreover, SEA-ITML performs much better than most of state-of-the-art metric learning methods.

4   A Novel Verification Paradigm with SEAML

Thanks to the proposed shrinkage-expansion rule, the shrinkage-expansion property of the distance before and after metric learning is also an important cue when SEAML is applied to verification. In the training stage, a decision threshold b and a critical

---

Algorithm 1. Algorithm of Shrinkage-Expansion Adaptive Metric Learning (SEAML)

Input: A set of pairwise training data points $\{(\mathbf{x}_i, \mathbf{x}_j, l_{ij}) | \forall (i,j)\}$ with label l, the trade off parameter C, $\mathbf{Y}_0 = \mathbf{I}$, $t = 0$.

1: **while** Not Converge **do**
2:    Fix $\mathbf{Y}_t$ and solve the subproblem Eq. (10) on $\boldsymbol{\beta}^t$ by SVM solver.
3:    Compute $\hat{\mathbf{Y}} = -\sum_{ij} \beta_{ij}^t l_{ij} \mathbf{Z}_{ij}$
4:    Fix $\boldsymbol{\beta}^t$ and solve the subproblem Eq.(11) to update $\mathbf{Y}_t$: $\mathbf{Y}_t = \mathbf{U}\boldsymbol{\Sigma}_+\mathbf{V}^T$, where $\hat{\mathbf{Y}} = \mathbf{U}\boldsymbol{\Sigma}\mathbf{V}^T$ is the SVD of $\hat{\mathbf{Y}}$ and $\boldsymbol{\Sigma}_+ = max(\boldsymbol{\Sigma}, \mathbf{0})$.
5:    $t = t + 1$.
6: **end while**
7: Obtain the solution $\boldsymbol{\beta}^* = \boldsymbol{\beta}^t$ and $\mathbf{Y}^* = \mathbf{Y}^t$.
8: $\mathbf{M} = \sum_{ij} \beta_{ij}^* l_{ij} \mathbf{Z}_{ij} + \mathbf{Y}^*$.

Output: M

---

value δ can be determined from the training data. First, like the traditional verification paradigm, we can find a decision threshold b on the training data using the methods suggested in [10,17,38]. Then, for all training pairs, given decision threshold b and an initialization of δ (e.g., $\delta = 0$), if the absolute value of the difference between the Mahalanobis distance of training pair $(\mathbf{x}_i, \mathbf{x}_j)$ and b is smaller than δ, we adjust its label based on the following paradigm:

$$(\mathbf{x}_i, \mathbf{x}_j) \in \begin{cases} \mathcal{S} & \text{if } D_{ij} - D_{ij}^M \geq 0, \\ \mathcal{D} & \text{if } D_{ij} - D_{ij}^M < 0. \end{cases} \tag{13}$$

where D_{ij} and D_{ij}^M denote the Euclidean distance and the Mahalanobis distance of pair $(\mathbf{x}_i, \mathbf{x}_j)$, respectively. Finally, we can search an optimal solution of δ within a range on the training data. For example, we let $\delta \in [0, 3]$ and set the step size as 0.15.

In the test stage, we take advantage of a two-step strategy to verify if a test pair is similar or dissimilar with the decision threshold b and optimal δ. In the first step, the label of the test pair $(\mathbf{x}_z, \mathbf{x}_k)$ is decided by comparing the Mahalanobis distance with the threshold b. In the second step, if the Mahalanobis distance D_{zk}^M of the pair $(\mathbf{x}_z, \mathbf{x}_k)$ is close to b (i.e., $|D_{zk}^M - b| \leq \delta$), we adjust its label by using Eq. (13). The novel verification paradigm can improve more than 1% the verification performance.

5 Experiments

In this section, we evaluate the proposed method on both classification and face verification problems. The proposed SEAML and SEA-ITML have two tradeoff parameters, i.e., C and γ. Similar to ITML [6] and LMNN [35], these two parameters are tuned via three-fold cross validation in the classification experiments on the UCI datasets. In face verification, we set $C = 1$ and $\gamma = 1$ throughout our experiments. The Matlab code can be downloaded at http://www4.comp.polyu.edu.hk/~cslzhang/code/ SEAML.rar.

5.1 Classification Results on the UCI Datasets

We first evaluate the classification performances of SEAML and SEA-ITML on 12 datasets from the UCI machine learning repository [2]. These datasets are widely used to evaluate the classification performance of metric learning methods such as ITML [6], DML-eig [38], etc. Table 1 summarizes the 12 UCI datasets. The k nearest neighbor (kNN) classifier is used for classification, and we set $k = 3$ for all the datasets. We compare SEAML and SEA-ITML with the baseline algorithm without metric learning (i.e., kNN with standard Euclidean distance), and three state-of-the-art metric learning methods: ITML [6], LMNN [35] and DML-eig [38]. The hyper-parameters in ITML and LMNN are tuned via three-fold cross validation, and the classification results of DML-eig are cropped from the original paper [38].

We run the experiments 100 times. In each run, we randomly split each dataset into a training subset and a test subset. The numbers of samples in the training and test subsets are shown in Table 1. The experimental results by averaging over the 100 runs are reported in Table 2. One can see that SEAML and SEA-ITML achieve the best or the second best classification rate on almost every dataset, and they have the best and the second best average rank, outperforming DML-eig, ITML and LMNN.

5.2 Face Verification on LFW

Experimental Setting. In this subsection, we evaluate the proposed SEAML and SEA-ITML methods for face verification on the Labeled Faces in the Wild (LFW) database [15]. LFW is a challenging database designed for studying the unconstrained face verification problem. It contains 13,233 face images from 5,749 persons. Figure 3 shows some samples of similar and dissimilar pairs. There are two commonly used test protocols on LFW: image restricted and image unrestricted protocols. Under the image restricted protocol, the identities of the training images are ignored. The only available information is whether each pair of training images are from the same subject or not. The performance of a face verification algorithm is evaluated by 10-fold cross-validation, and each fold contains a subset of 300 positive and 300 negative image pairs.

To be consistent with the experimental settings used in most of state-of-the-art metric learning methods [10,17,22,38], we adopt the image restricted protocol with the face images aligned by the funneling method [13]. We represent face images by using

Table 1. Summary of the UCI datasets used in the experiment

	Wine	Iris	Segment.	Optdigits	Letter	Sonar	Waveform	Diabetes	Iono.	Breast	Face	Cardi.
# Classes	3	3	7	10	26	2	3	2	2	2	40	10
# Samples for Training	125	105	1617	1934	16000	188	3500	538	176	398	280	1914
# Samples for Test	53	45	693	946	4000	20	1500	230	175	171	120	212
Dimension	13	4	19	64	16	60	21	8	34	30	64	21

Table 2. Classification rates (%) on the UCI databases. The best and second best results on each dataset are highlighted in red and blue, respectively.

Method	Wine	Iris	Segment.	Optdigits	Letter	Sonar	Waveform	Diabetes	Iono.	Breast	Face	Cardi.	Ave. Rank
Baseline	94.24	94.89	94.28	98.33	95.54	79.58	81.13	68.91	81.73	93.53	93.33	75.34	**5.92**
ITML	96.18	95.56	94.98	98.54	97.22	85.14	84.06	70.04	85.52	93.18	97.58	80.1	**4.67**
LMNN	96.92	95.78	96.31	98.63	96.55	88.43	81.39	70.3	87.41	94.65	97.92	80.79	**3.17**
DML-eig	98.65	96.89	97.03	98.55	96.14	86.5	84.67	72.29	83.74	96.47	98.33	79.71	**2.83**
SEA-ITML	97.79	96.94	96.87	98.74	97.81	87.97	84.54	71.56	86.67	96.37	97.62	80.37	**2.5**
SEAML	98.54	97.13	97.21	98.67	97.77	88.67	85.02	71.94	86.81	95.75	97.89	80.31	**1.92**

Similar pairs   Dissimilar pairs

Fig. 3. Some examples of face image pairs in the LFW face database [15]. Left: four similar pairs; Right: four dissimilar pairs.

their SIFT features [25] provided by [10], where 128 dimensional SIFT descriptors are extracted on three scales and at 9 fiducial points (corners of the mouth, eyes, and nose) detected by a facial feature detector. Finally, each face is represented by a 3,456 dimensional SIFT feature vector. This dimensionality is rather too high for stable metric learning. Therefore, to be consistent with [10,38], principal component analysis (PCA) is applied to project each SIFT feature vector into a d-dimensional subspace. Then a $d \times d$ PSD matrix is learned as the metric matrix for face verification.

Dimension of Principal Components. The dimension d of principal components has an important impact on the verification performance of metric learning algorithms. Figure 4 shows the verification accuracy of SEAML, ITML [6], LDML [10] and DML-eig [38] with various dimensions of principal components. We can see that SEAML performs the best under all dimensions, while DML-eig performs the second best. With the increase of dimension, ITML, LDML, and DML-eig achieve their best results at dimension 55, 35, and 100, respectively. Their performance will then drop rapidly. Unlike the other methods, the verification accuracy of the proposed SEAML increases stably with the increase of PCA dimension until 170, and its verification accuracy only drops slightly (about 0.6%) when d is 200. In summary, SEAML has not only better verification accuracy than the competing methods, but also more robustness to the feature dimension. This validates that the proposed shrinkage-expansion adaptive constraints are effective in improving the accuracy and stability of metric learning.

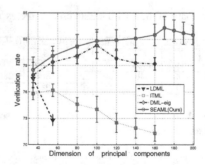

Fig. 4. Comparison of LDML, ITML, DML-eig and SEAML in face verification under different dimensions of SIFT features

Comparison with State-of-the-Arts. We compare SEAML with 13 state-of-the-art methods [1,6,10,14,17,19,20,22,23,28,32,36,38] under the same protocol of image restricted setting. Note that LMNN is not compared because it requires triplet constraints which are not applicable to the LFW database under restricted setting.

In Table 3, we first compare SEAML with those metric learning based methods using the SIFT features. Clearly, SEAML and SEA-ITML outperform all the other metric learning methods, validating the effectiveness of the proposed shrinkage-expansion adaptive pairwise constraints. Besides SIFT features, we also evaluate SEAML using the attribute features provided by [19] (please refer to Section 5.3 for more information of attribute features). With the attribute features, SEAML and SEA-ITML achieve a similar verification rate of 85.8%, outperforming state-of-the-art metric learning methods, such as LDML [10](83.4%), ITML [6] (84.0%) and KissMe [17] (84.6%). SEAML and SEA-ITML also perform slightly better than the Attribute and Simile classifiers (85.3%) [19], which achieves state-of-the-art performance using the SVM based method.

In Table 4, we evaluate SEAML by combining the SIFT and Attribute features, and compare it with those state-of-the-art non-metric learning methods or metric learning methods with multiple features. We can see that the verification accuracy (87.5%) of SEAML is the second highest, the same as Fisher vector face (87.5%) [32]. Kindly note that [32] uses much more complicated strategies, including Fisher vector based face representation and discriminative dimensionality reduction, joint distance-similarity metric learning and horizontal flipping. The method in [23] reports the best accuracy (89.6%). This method employs a learned second-order decision functions solved by kernel SVM (may suffer from high memory burden in large scale problem) for verification and it combines SIFT with complex hierarchical Gaussianization (HG) vector features [39].

Table 3. Verification accuracies (%) of competing metric learning methods on the LFW-funneled database under the image restricted protocol. (Symbol "-" means that the result is not available.)

Metric learning with single feature		
Method	SIFT	Attributes
LDML [10]	77.5 ± 0.5	83.4
ITML [10]	76.2 ± 0.5	84.0
LDA-based [36]	79.4 ± 0.2	–
DML-eig [38]	81.3 ± 2.3	–
SODFML [22]	81.0	–
KissMe [17]	80.5	84.6
SEA-ITML	82.4 ± 1.7	85.8
SEAML	83.2 ± 1.2	85.8

Table 4. Comparison with state-of-the-art results on the LFW-funneled database under the image restricted protocol

Method	Features	Accuracy (%)
MERL+Nowark [28]	SIFT and geometry	76.2 ± 0.6
V1-like/MKL [14]	V1-like features	79.4 ± 0.5
MRF-MLBP [1]	Multi-scale LBP	79.1 ± 0.2
APEM(fusion) [20]	Dense SIFT + LBP	84.1 ± 1.2
Attr.& sim. classifiers [19]	Attributes	85.3
DML-eig combined [38]	SIFT + LBP + TPLBP + FPLBP	85.7 ± 0.6
Fisher vector face [32]	Dense SIFT	87.5 ± 1.5
Li et al. [23]	SIFT + HG vector features	89.6
SEA-ITML	SIFT + Attributes	87.2 ± 1.7
SEAML	SIFT + Attributes	87.5 ± 1.3

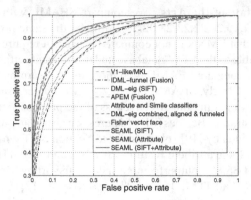

V1–like/MKL
IDML–funnel (Fusion)
DML–eig (SIFT)
APEM (Fusion)
Attribute and Simile classifiers
DML–eig combined, aligned & funneled
Fisher vector face
SEAML (SIFT)
SEAML (Attribute)
SEAML (SIFT+Attribute)

Fig. 5. ROC curves of various methods on the restricted LFW-funneled database

In Figure 5, we plot the ROC curves of various methods on the restricted LFW-funneled dataset. We can see that SEAML and Fisher vector face show comparable performance and they outperform the other competing methods. The experimental results clearly demonstrated that the proposed SEAML method can learn effective metrics from training data with complex structures and distributions.

5.3   Face Verification on PubFig

Experimental Setting. The Public Figures (PubFig) [19] face database shares similar philosophy with LFW. It is also a large, real-world face database collected from the internet, consisting of 58,797 images from 200 people. PubFig is a very challenging database with large face variations in pose, expression, lighting, scene, camera, and so on. Like LFW, PubFig provides an evaluation platform for face verification: 20,000 pairs of images from 140 people are divided into 10 cross-validation folds, and each fold consists of 1,000 intra and 1,000 extra pairs from disjoint sets of 14 people. Some illustrative examples of similar and dissimilar pairs are shown in Figure 6.

Unlike most of the existing face databases which use handcrafted features to represent face images, PubFig provides high-level semantic features which contain 73 kinds of attributes, such as hair, glass, age, race, smiling and so on. All attributes are computed by the effective attribute classifiers [19]. These attribute features allow the elaboration of semantic description which are more robust against large image variations, and can lead to good verification performance. In this section, to be consistent with [6,10,17,19,35], we use these high-level semantic features to evaluate SEAML and SEA-ITML.

Comparison with State-of-the-Arts. Apart from the baseline with Euclidean distance, we compare SEAML and SEA-ITML with ITML [6], LMNN [35], LDML [10], KissMe [17] and SVM [19]. The results of these competing methods are obtained from [17], and they are all metric learning based methods except for SVM. Kindly note that the publically reported results on the PubFig dataset are not as many as those on the LFW dataset, and the compared results here are the best ones in literature.

Fig. 6. Examples of similar and dissimilar pairs in the PubFig face database [19]

The verification results (Equal Error Rate, EER) of the competing methods are listed in Table 5. One can see that SEAML and SEA-ITML are the best two methods. LDML, KissMe and SVM also perform well. ITML does not perform well on this dataset and its EER (69.3%) is even worse than the baseline with Euclidean distance. However, by adopting the proposed shrinkage-expansion adaptive constraints into ITML, the resulting SEA-ITML method can achieve an EER of 77.8%. This further validates the effectiveness of the proposed shrinkage-expansion adaptive constraints in improving the verification performance of pairwise constrained metric learning methods.

Table 5. Verification performance on the PubFig face database. All methods use the attribute features provided by [19]. The reported results of all compared methods are copied from [17].

Method	EER
L_2 (Euclidean distance)	72.5%
ITML	69.3%
LMNN	73.5%
LDML	77.6%
KissMe	77.6%
SVM	77.6%
SEA-ITML	77.8%
SEAML	78.6%

6 Conclusion

In this paper, we presented a novel metric learning framework, namely shrinkage expansion adaptive metric learning (SEAML). With the proposed shrinkage-expansion adaptive pairwise constraints, SEAML can learn more effectively the distance metrics from data with complex distributions, and endow a new paradigm to determine whether a pair is matched or not by considering both the decision threshold and the change of matching distances before and after metric learning. Moreover, the proposed shrinkage-expansion rule can be embedded into many existing pairwise constrained metric learning methods (e.g., ITML [6]), and improve much their performance. Experimental results on the UCI datasets, the LFW and PubFig face databases validated that SEAML outperforms many state-of-the-art metric learning algorithms. In the future work, we will investigate how to adopt a low rank regularizer [37,24] in the SEAML framework to further improve its robustness against the feature dimension and computational efficiency. We are also interested in studying a flexible scheme which can learn optimized parameters of proposed shrinkage-expansion adaptive constraints.

Acknowledgements. This work is supported by the Hong Kong RGC GRF grant (PolyU 5313/13E), NSFC grants (61271093, 60973080, 61170149), the program of MoE (NCET-12-0150), and the Fundamental Research Funds for the Central Universities (DUT13RC(3)02).

References

1. Arashloo, S.R., Kittler, J.: Efficient processing of MRFs for unconstrained-pose face recognition. In: BTAS (2013)
2. Asuncion, A., Newman, D.: UCI machine learning repository (2007),
   http://www.ics.uci.edu/~mlearn/MLRepository.html
3. Bellet, A., Habrard, A., Sebban, M.: A survey on metric learning for feature vectors and structured data. arXiv 1306.6709 (2013)
4. Chang, C.C., Lin, C.J.: Libsvm: A library for support vector machines. ACM Trans. Intell. Syst. Technol. 2(3), 1–27 (2011)
5. Csiszár, I., Tusnády, G.: Information geometry and alternating minimization procedures. Statistics and Decisions (1984)
6. Davis, J.V., Kulis, B., Jain, P., Sra, S., Dhillon, I.S.: Information-theoretic metric learning. In: ICML (2007)
7. Feng, Z., Jin, R., Jain, A.: Large-scale image annotation by efficient and robust kernel metric learning. In: ICCV (2013)
8. Globerson, A., Roweis, S.: Metric learning by collapsing classes. In: NIPS (2005)
9. Goldberger, J., Roweis, S., Hinton, G., Salakhutdinov, R.: Neighbourhood components analysis. In: NIPS (2004)
10. Guillaumin, M., Verbeek, J., Schmid, C.: Is that you? metric learning approaches for face identification. In: ICCV (2009)
11. Huang, C., Zhu, S., Yu, K.: Large scale strongly supervised ensemble metric learning, with applications to face verification and retrieval. arXiv 1212.6094 (2012)
12. Huang, D., Storer, M., De la Torre, F., Bischof, H.: Supervised local subspace learning for continuous head pose estimation. In: CVPR (2011)
13. Huang, G.B., Jain, V., Learned-Miller, E.: Unsupervised joint alignment of complex images. In: ICCV (2007)
14. Huang, G.B., Jones, M.J., Learned-Miller, E.: LFW results using a combined Nowak plus MERL recognizer. In: Real-Life Images Workshop at the ECCV (2008)
15. Huang, G.B., Ramesh, M., Berg, T., Learned-Miller, E.: Labeled faces in the wild: A database for studying face recognition in unconstrained environments. Tech. rep., University of Massachusetts, Amherst (2007)
16. James, W., Stein, J.: Estimation with quadratic loss. In: Berkeley Symposium on Mathematical Statistics and Probability (1961)
17. Kostinger, M., Hirzer, M., Wohlhart, P., Roth, P.M., Bischof, H.: Large scale metric learning from equivalence constraints. In: CVPR (2012)
18. Kulis, B., Saenko, K., Darrell, T.: What you saw is not what you get: Domain adaptation using asymmetric kernel transforms. In: CVPR (2011)

19. Kumar, N., Berg, A.C., Belhumeur, P.N., Nayar, S.K.: Attribute and simile classifiers for face verification. In: ICCV (2009)
20. Li, H., Hua, G., Lin, Z., Brandt, J., Yang, J.: Probabilistic elastic matching for pose variant face verification. In: CVPR (2013)
21. Li, X., Shen, C., Shi, Q., Dick, A., van den Hengel, A.: Non-sparse linear representations for visual tracking with online reservoir metric learning. In: CVPR (2012)
22. Li, Z., Cao, L., Chang, S., Smith, J.R., Huang, T.S.: Beyond mahalanobis distance: Learning second-order discriminant function for people verification. In: CVPR Workshops (2012)
23. Li, Z., Chang, S., Liang, F., Huang, T.S., Cao, L., Smith, J.R.: Learning locally-adaptive decision functions for person verification. In: CVPR (2013)
24. Lim, D., Mcfee, B., Lanckriet, G.R.: Robust structural metric learning. In: ICML (2013)
25. Lowe, D.G.: Distinctive image features from scale-invariant keypoints. Int. J. Comput. Vision 60(2), 91–110 (2004)
26. Mensink, T., Verbeek, J., Perronnin, F., Csurka, G.: Metric learning for large scale image classification: Generalizing to new classes at near-zero cost. In: Fitzgibbon, A., Lazebnik, S., Perona, P., Sato, Y., Schmid, C. (eds.) ECCV 2012, Part II. LNCS, vol. 7573, pp. 488–501. Springer, Heidelberg (2012)
27. Mignon, A., Jurie, F.: Pcca: A new approach for distance learning from sparse pairwise constraints. In: CVPR (2012)
28. Nowak, E., Jurie, F.: Learning visual similarity measures for comparing never seen objects. In: CVPR (2007)
29. Parameswaran, S., Weinberger, K.: Large margin multi-task metric learning. In: NIPS (2010)
30. Shen, C., Kim, J., Wang, L.: A scalable dual approach to semidefinite metric learning. In: CVPR (2011)
31. Shen, C., Kim, J., Wang, L., van den Hengel, A.: Positive semidefinite metric learning with boosting. In: NIPS (2009)
32. Simonyan, K., Parkhi, O.M., Vedaldi, A., Zisserman, A.: Fisher Vector Faces in the Wild. In: BMVC (2013)
33. Verma, Y., Jawahar, C.V.: Image annotation using metric learning in semantic neighbourhoods. In: Fitzgibbon, A., Lazebnik, S., Perona, P., Sato, Y., Schmid, C. (eds.) ECCV 2012, Part III. LNCS, vol. 7574, pp. 836–849. Springer, Heidelberg (2012)
34. Weinberger, K.Q., Saul, L.K.: Fast solvers and efficient implementations for distance metric learning. In: ICML (2008)
35. Weinberger, K., Blitzer, J., Saul, L.: Distance metric learning for large margin nearest neighbor classification. In: NIPS (2006)
36. Wolf, L., Hassner, T., Taigman, Y.: Descriptor based methods in the wild. In: Real-Life Images Workshop at the ECCV (2008)
37. Ying, Y., Huang, K., Campbell, C.: Sparse metric learning via smooth optimization. In: NIPS (2009)
38. Ying, Y., Li, P.: Distance metric learning with eigenvalue optimization. J. Mach. Learn. Res. 13(1), 1–26 (2012)
39. Zhou, X., Cui, N., Li, Z., Liang, F., Huang, T.S.: Hierarchical gaussianization for image classification. In: ICCV (2009)

Salient Montages from Unconstrained Videos

Min Sun, Ali Farhadi, Ben Taskar, and Steve Seitz

University of Washington, Seattle, WA, USA

Abstract. We present a novel method to generate salient montages from unconstrained videos, by finding "montageable moments" and identifying the salient people and actions to depict in each montage. Our method addresses the need for generating concise visualizations from the increasingly large number of videos being captured from portable devices. Our main contributions are (1) the process of finding salient people and moments to form a montage, and (2) the application of this method to videos taken "in the wild" where the camera moves freely. As such, we demonstrate results on head-mounted cameras, where the camera moves constantly, as well as on videos downloaded from YouTube. Our approach can operate on videos of any length; some will contain many montageable moments, while others may have none. We demonstrate that a novel "montageability" score can be used to retrieve results with relatively high precision which allows us to present high quality montages to users.

Keywords: video summarization, video saliency detection.

1 Introduction

Video is increasingly easy to capture and store. The advent of wearable devices like GoPro cameras is accelerating this trend, allowing us to capture hours at a time in a hands-free manner. While the vast majority of this footage is unlikely to be interesting or useful, the hope is that if something interesting *does* happen, we will have recorded it, and be able to generate an *at-a-glance* visualization. Finding those interesting moments, however, is like looking for a needle in a haystack, and motivates the need for video search and summarization research.

Finding semantically interesting moments via automated means is extremely challenging. Instead, we seek to find moments that *look interesting*, and, in particular, produce high quality photo montages fully automatically (see Fig. 1). Each montage captures a *stroboscopic* image of a person performing an action, with the same person shown multiple times in the same image as if a strobe light had flashed multiple times during the same exposure. Pioneered in the 19th century by Etienne-Jules Marey, stroboscopic images provide a fascinating "time-lapse" view of an action in a single image. While Marey's work required a special chronophotographic gun, modern solutions [1,31,17,41] enable similar results with regular photos via algorithmic means. These techniques require as input several photos or a short video clip comprising the *montageable* event. The camera must remain still or only pan slowly in order to create effective montages.

Nevertheless, most videos do not satisfy these constraints; Hence, automatically producing montages from unconstrained videos is extremely challenging.

D. Fleet et al. (Eds.): ECCV 2014, Part VII, LNCS 8695, pp. 472–488, 2014.
© Springer International Publishing Switzerland 2014

Fig. 1. Given a video (click to watch on Youtube: link) captured by a head-mounted camera (top row), we first automatically identify montageable moments (highlighted by the color-coded bounding boxes) containing the salient person (the little girl in pink) and ignore irrelevant frames. A set of salient montages ordered by our novel montageability scores is generated automatically. Here we show four typical examples.

For example, such videos often contain crowded scenes with many people (see Fig. 4(b)). Existing methods lack the information to select the salient person to depict. Moreover, when the camera moves freely and/or the depth variation of the scene is large (see the playground scene in Fig. 1), global registration methods will fail; hence, low-level motion cues become unreliable.

In this work, we propose a novel, human-centric method to produce montages from unconstrained videos, by finding "montageable moments" and identifying salient people and actions to depict in each montage. Our contribution is not the compositing algorithm itself, which builds upon [1], but (1) the process of finding salient people and moments to form a montage, and (2) the application of this method to videos "in the wild." As such, we demonstrate results on videos from head-mounted cameras, where the camera moves constantly, as well as on videos downloaded from YouTube. The videos from head-mounted camers are particularly challenging since they are unedited and include many irrelevant moments due to motion blur from fast camera movement, self-occlusion from the wearer, and a lot of moments when the wearer is simply navigating the terrain (see Fig. 3). Our approach overcomes all these challenges and can operate on videos many minutes or hours long; some will contain many montageable moments, while others may have none. For this application, we specifically aim to achieve high precision (i.e., a small number of "great" summaries rather than summarizing every moment) from a large number of user videos. Note that high precision is important in many problems such as recommender systems [7].

Our approach is based on (1) clustering people tracklets into "places" (see color-coded boxes in Fig. 1-Top), (2) identifying the most salient people in each place (the little girl in Fig. 1-A), and (3) evaluating the montageability of the people tracklets in each place to select a few hypotheses (four selected person instances in Fig. 1-A). Two key enablers are a new poselet-based human detection and tracking method, and a novel tracklet-based saliency detector. The latter is based on random forests trained on gaze tracking data collected from other videos. We show that this tracklet saliency method outperforms prior saliency techniques for this task. For the third step, we minimize a montageability function that considers the scene complexity and registration quality for all human hypotheses in the place. Finally, we use a novel "montageability" score to rank the quality of the montages, which allows us to present high quality composites to users (see montages in Fig. 1-Bottom).

2   Related Work

In this section, we review related work in video summarization, video saliency detection, and person tracking.

Video Summarization: There is a large literature on video summarization (see review [4]), including techniques for sampling important frames [28,22,25,15,33,21] or generating montages. In the following, we discuss the ones most relevant to our method. Aner and Kender [2] automatically generate montages by taking a background reference frame and projecting foreground regions into it. Liu et al. [26] automatically extract panoramas from Youtube videos. However, they assume a panning camera and focus on short clips with few objects. [36,37] focus on extracting highlights from webcams or surveillance cameras and generate synopses which show several spatially non-overlapping actions from different times of the video. However, they assume the camera is stationary so that low-level motion cues can be reliably used to search for salient regions in time and space. Several methods [14,18] involving user interaction have also been proposed in the graphics and HCI communities. All of these methods focus on short clips and assume the camera is mostly stationary. To the best of our knowledge, our method is the first to handle any video, even these captured by a wearable camera.

Saliency Detection: Many methods have been proposed to detect salient regions from video. However, most methods [8,16,30,39,38] rely on low-level appearance and motion cues as inputs. A few methods [19,13,38] include information about face, people, or context. Among them, [38] is the state-of-the-art video saliency detector, since it explicitly models the conditional saliency between consecutive frames. However, they have focused primarily on TV series that typically do not contain many people. Unlike our method, they only keep a few candidate regions per frame and do not explicitly solve the person association problem (tracking).

Tracking Humans: Many tracking systems are based on linking candidate human hypotheses [35,43,32]. However, these systems obtain inferior performance due to severe body part articulation and camera motion in unconstrained videos. Other works address these issues [12,6] relying on supervoxel and/or long-term point trajectories which are computational expensive to obtain. Our system tracks pre-defined poselets to increase the accuracy without applying additional process (e.g., supervoxel).

3   Our Approach

Videos captured by casual users with smartphones or head mounted cameras are challenging because they typically contain significant camera motion and shake, inconsistent framing and composition, and a lot of redundant content. We posit

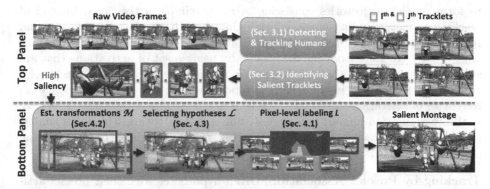

Fig. 2. Detailed system overview (click to watch raw video on Youtube: link). Top panel shows the steps toward identifying salient tracklets (Sec. 3.1 and 3.2), where each tracklet consists of color coded hypotheses. Bottom panel shows the steps toward generating a salient montage (Sec. 4). The color in the pixel-level labeling L indicates the source images indexed by color as well.

that the interesting moments in such videos typically involve people, and we focus on extracting person-centric montages that capture their salient actions. We address this goal by identifying salient people in an unconstrained video (Fig. 2-Top) and then generating montages composed of their salient actions (Fig. 2-Bottom). The overview of our approach is depicted in Fig. 2. We first describe how to identify salient people in an unconstrained video.

Our selection process begins with detecting and tracking all the people in the video, followed by choosing a few salient ones using motion, pose, composition and other cues. Although human detection and tracking are well-studied, our videos pose unique challenges to the state-of-the-art methods, which we address below.

3.1 Detecting and Tracking Humans

Detecting and tracking humans is critical for our application, since low-level motion cues are unreliable for segmenting out foreground objects due to severe camera motions in unconstrained videos. One of the primary challenges for human detection is high variation in pose and occlusion patterns in unconstrained videos. We found the poselet detector [5] to be robust and particularly useful for our approach. The poselet detector provides human hypotheses (a bounding box represents the extent of a whole human body) along with poselet activations (a poselet is a group of body parts such as left-arm, lower body, etc.), which we use to make tracking more precise. For simplicity, the human hypothesis and poselet activation are referred to as hypothesis and activation, respectively.

Detection by Poselet Trajectories. For each frame, we begin by matching poselet templates to HOG features [9] extracted at multiple scales and locations to compute poselet activations. However, we do not directly convert these activations into human hypotheses. We track the activations across nearby frames to form poselet trajectories consisting of more reliable activations. Instead of tracking poselet bounding-boxes, which include both background and foreground regions, we track the foreground region of each poselet[1] using a median flow tracker [20]. We start from the first frame by using a set of activations that are sufficiently trackable in the next frame. We repeat the process and form poselet trajectories as detailed in the technical report [40]. At the end of this stage we have a set of activations (original + tracked) in our poselet trajectories, which we spatially group into human hypotheses using a Hough voting scheme [3] similar to [5]. We have shown in Table 1(a) that this process significantly increases the detection accuracy.

Tracking by Poselet Association. Given hypotheses with their poselet activations at each frame, we form tracklets (i.e., a set of hypotheses of the same individual in different frames) by associating hypotheses at consecutive frames. Standard tracking by detection approaches associate hypotheses across neighboring frames by using the location and appearance information in a coarse bounding box representing the extent of a human. We, however, proceed to associate hypotheses using their poselet activation as descriptors. Note that robust hypotheses association is crucial for avoiding identity switch in a tracklet or tracklets drifting to background regions.

Poselet-Based Similarity. We divide each poselet into 4 by N square cells[2], where 8×3 L_1 normalized color-histogram in Lab space are extracted from each cell. For each hypothesis, we concatenate the poselet histogram following a predefined order to generate hypothesis histogram a. The poselet-based similarity of a pair of hypotheses i and j in two consecutive frames $(t, t + 1)$ is defined using the cosine similarity $sim_{ij} = \frac{a_i^T a_j}{\|a_i\|\|a_j\|}$. Although the similarity helps us avoid associating hypotheses with dissimilar poselet activations, it is insufficient to avoid associating false hypotheses fired at non-distinctive background regions. We address this problem by defining a more robust "relative similarity".

Relative Similarity. We utilize the smoothness prior on hypotheses locations within each tracklet (i.e., the locations of hypotheses at consecutive frames should be close) to define *relative similarity*. For each hypothesis i at frame t, a subset of hypotheses C at $t + 1$ are selected as the candidate set satisfying the smoothness prior if every hypothesis in C at least has ρ spatial overlap with hypothesis i. We define the relative similarity γ_{ij} of a pair of hypotheses i and j as the ratio between sim_{ij} and $\max_{j' \in C'} sim_{ij'}$, where C' is the complement of C. Note that $\max_{j' \in C'} sim_{ij'}$ will be high for a hypothesis i fired on a non-distinctive background region. As a result, false hypotheses fired at non-distinctive background regions tend to have small relative similarity.

Given the relative similarity between candidate pairs of hypotheses, we formulate the hypotheses association problem as a network flow problem and solve it approximated using a dynamic programming algorithm [35]. For simplicity,

---

[1] Foreground mask of each poselet is included in the poselet detector.

[2] N depends on the aspect ratio of the poselet.

the costs of the links in the network are the same if the relative similarity γ_{ij} is greater or equal to a threshold σ; otherwise, the costs are infinite. Finally, the network flow problem is efficiently solved to generate tracklets $\{T_k\}_k$ indexed by the tracklet index k. Each tracklet $T_k = \{j\}$ consists of a set of human hypotheses, where j is the hypothesis index. In Table 1(a), we demonstrate that our poselet-based method is much more reliable than the state-of-the-art method [35]. An ablation analysis also reveals that all components in our human detection and tracking system jointly contribute to the superior performance.

3.2   Learning Saliency from Gaze

Recall that it is important for our application to infer the salient people that the cameraman intends to capture, since there can be an unknown number of people (see Fig. 2 and 4(b)) in an unconstrained video. Given the tracklets, we aim to predict which one corresponds to a person performing salient actions. We train a predictor to generate a tracklet-based saliency score using multiple cues. To train our predictor, we asked the authors of the videos to watch them while recording eye gaze using a commodity gaze sensor (http://www.mygaze.com). We then used the gaze data as a measurement of ground truth saliency. We identify the person being salient in each frame when the gaze falls on a ground truth human annotation (see Fig. 3). We find that gaze tracks from the person who captured the video are much more informative as compared to a viewer who is unfamiliar with the event and people in it. Hence, we do not have such training data for videos from Youtube.

Our tracklet-based saliency score is built on top of a hypothesis-based saliency score. Here, we define a hypothesis-based saliency model which considers location, motion, and pose information of the hypotheses. Our training data consists of ground truth human annotations with binary "saliency" labels derived from gaze (at test time, we only have predicted human detections, and no gaze information). We train a random forest classifier to predict the saliency label and use the response of the classifier as the saliency score $s \in [0, 1]$ for each hypothesis using the following types of features.

Camera Centric Features. We define the camera centric features e as the location and relative height of the hypothesis with respect to the frame height. Hence, the model can learn the preferred location and scale of a salient person. For example, a salient person shouldn't be too small or too off-center. The feature also includes the Euclidean distance of the person's bounding box centroid to the frame center, which is typically used to model gaze in ego-centric videos [10,23].

Person Motion Features. We define the height changes $hr = h_t/h_{t+1}$ and motion direction (du, dv) in pixels between a pair of hypotheses (indices omitted) in two consecutive frames t and $t + 1$ as the basic motion features $b = [hr, du, dv]$. This allows the classifiers to differentiate forward/backward and lateral motions, respectively. Our full motion features include motion uniqueness u derived from

b and e (camera centric features) as follows (similar to the visual uniqueness measure in [34]),

$$u_i = \sum_j \|b_i - b_j\|^2 \cdot \omega(e_i, e_j) \; where \; \omega(e_i, e_j) = \tfrac{1}{Z_i} \exp(-\tfrac{1}{2\sigma_p^2} \|e_i - e_j\|^2) \;, \quad (1)$$

where i, j are indices for hypotheses in the same frame, and Z_i is the normalization term. Hypothesis i has unique motion if its motion b_i is very different from the motion b_j of hypotheses at nearby location and scale (i.e., $e_i \sim e_j$).

Pose Features. Pose provides a strong cue to determine an action. We use the raw poselet activation scores for each hypothesis as a coarse surrogate for pose.

Tracklet-Level Aggregation. The hypothesis-based saliency prediction is combined to produce the tracklet saliency score s_k (*s-score*) by summing up constituent scores $\{s_i\}_{i \in T_k}$, where T_k is a tracklet consisting of a set of hypotheses and k is the tracklet index. In Table 1(b), we show that our tracklet-based saliency measure is more accurate in identifying salient people than a state-of-the-art video saliency estimator [38].

4   Salient Montages

Given the human tracklets with their saliency scores $\{(s_k, T_k)\}_k$, we aim to generate salient montages ranked by their quality. In order to handle videos with various length, we first divide the tracklets into groups. There are multiple ways to generate groups. We use SIFT [27] point matching to find a group that is likely to contain tracklets appearing in physically nearby "places" (see technical report [40] for details).

Next, we introduce a unified model to (1) find a montageable moment in each group, (2) generate a montage for each group, and (3) rank the montages based on tracklet saliency and how visually pleasing they are. The overview of steps to generate salient montages is depicted in Fig. 2-Bottom.

4.1   Model

Our goal is to form a montage I_m from source images $\{I_i\}_{i \in \mathcal{L}}$, where the labeling space $\mathcal{L}$ is defined as the union set of hypotheses in all tracklets (i.e., $\cup_k \{i\}_{i \in T_k}$). Note that here we use the same index for both the source images and hypotheses for simplicity. This means that our model uses all hypotheses as candidate source images to generate a salient montage. More formally, we need to choose a source image index i, and a correspondence location $\hat{p}$ in the source image I_i for every pixel location p in the montage. Given i and $\hat{p}$, we assign the RGB value ($I_i(\hat{p})$) of the source image to the RGB value ($I_m(p)$) of the montage. We define a pixel-level labeling variable L, where $i = L(p)$ denotes the source image index chosen at pixel location p in the montage. We also define a transformation M_i aligning the montage coordinate to the i source image coordinate such that $\hat{p} = M_i(p)$. The following montageability cost $C(L, \mathcal{M})$ (similar to [1]) is used to select the optimal pixel-level labeling L and transformations $\mathcal{M} = \{M_i\}_{i \in \mathcal{L}}$,

$$\min_{L,\mathcal{M}} C(L,\mathcal{M}) = \min_{L,\mathcal{M}} \sum_p C_d(p, L(p); \mathcal{M}) + \sum_{p,q} C_I(p, q, L(p), L(q); \mathcal{M}) , \quad (2)$$

where C_d is the data term which encourages salient actions in source images to be selected, and C_I is the seam term considering color and gradient matching for reducing visual artifacts.

Instead of requiring users' annotations as in [1], we use the hypotheses locations and tracklet saliency to define the data term.

Saliency-Based Data Term. Intuitively, we should include a hypothesis depicting a salient action in the montage. The cost of "not" including a pixel corresponding to hypothesis i in the montage depends on its saliency as follows,

$$C_d(p, \ell \neq i; \mathcal{M}) \propto \mathbf{s}_{k(i)} \cdot m_i(M_i(p)) , \quad (3)$$

where $\mathbf{s}_{k(i)}$ is the s-score of tracklet k containing hypothesis i, and $m_i(M_i(p))$ is the estimated probability that pixel $M_i(p)$ corresponds to hypothesis i (see technical report [40] for more details). The final cost of pixel p assigned to hypothesis ℓ is defined as,

$$C_d(p, \ell; \mathcal{M}) = \lambda_d \max_{i \neq \ell} \mathbf{s}_{k(i)} \cdot m_i(M_i(p)) , \quad (4)$$

where we take the maximum cost of $i \neq \ell$, and λ_d is used to balance the seam term.

Seam Term. Our seam term in color and gradient domains is defined as,

$$C_I(p, q, L(p), L(q); \mathcal{M}) = ||I_{L(p)}(\hat{p}) - I_{L(q)}(\hat{p})|| + ||I_{L(p)}(\hat{q}) - I_{L(q)}(\hat{q})|| \quad (5)$$
$$+ ||\nabla I_{L(p)}(\hat{p}) - \nabla I_{L(q)}(\hat{p})|| + ||\nabla I_{L(p)}(\hat{q}) - \nabla I_{L(q)}(\hat{q})|| ,$$

where $\nabla I_i(p)$ is a 6-component color gradient (in RGB) of the source image i at pixel location p, both $\hat{p} = M_{L(p)}(p)$ and $\hat{q} = M_{L(q)}(q)$ are the transformed locations.

Before detailing how to solve Eq. 2 to obtain optimal labeling L^* and transformation $\mathcal{M}^*$, we discuss a way to rank montages from different groups of tracklets using a novel score derived from our model.

Montageability Score. The minimum cost $C(L^*, \mathcal{M}^*)$ in Eq. 2 cannot be used to compare montages from different groups since the values are not normalized. To overcome this problem, we define a novel montageability score as,

$$V_{\mathcal{L}} = \frac{\min_{i \in \mathcal{L}}(C(L=i, \mathcal{M}^*))}{C(L^*, \mathcal{M}^*)} \quad (6)$$

where $L = i$ denotes $L(p) = i$ for all p which is a degenerate solution when only the i source image is used. The minimal degenerate solution is used to normalize the minimum cost so that this score is always larger than one. The larger the score, the better the quality of the montage with respect to the best degenerate solution. A very high score typically means many non-overlapping salient actions can be selected to reach a relatively low cost ($C(L^*, \mathcal{M}^*)$) compared to the best degenerate solution which only selects the most salient action.

Unique Properties. Our model differs from [1] in two more ways: (1) both our data and seam terms depend on the transformation $\mathcal{M}$, and (2) our labeling space $\mathcal{L} = \cup_k \{i; \ i \in T_k\}$ is very large ($\sim 1K$) since it is the union of all hypotheses within each group. Due to these properties, it is challenging to jointly optimize transformations $\mathcal{M}$ and pixel-level labeling L. However, we observe that, when $\mathcal{M}$ is given and $\mathcal{L}$ is small, we can solve Eq. 2 using graph-cut efficiently. To this end, we first estimate $\mathcal{M}^*$ and obtain a small pruned set of hypotheses $\hat{\mathcal{L}}$ as the labeling space for computing the montage. A detailed overview of these steps is depicted in Fig. 2-Bottom. We describe each step in detail next.

4.2   Estimating Transformations

We propose to search for transformations so that a maximum number of spatially non-overlapping hypotheses exist (implicitly reducing the cost of the data term). This is to ensure that many salient actions can be shown in the montage without blocking each other. We start by matching pairs of source images in $F = \cup_k \{f(i)\}_{i \in T_k}$, where $f(i)$ denotes the source image index that hypothesis i appeared in. We introduce the f index here since many hypotheses appear in the same source image in practice. To efficiently match relevant pairs of images, we evenly divide all images into 1000 segments in time. All pairs within each segment and pairs across a few pairs of segments are matched (see technical report [40] for details). For each pair of images, we obtain sparse [27] and dense SIFT correspondences [24]. Given the correspondences between $\hat{f}$ and $f(i)$, we can estimate an initial 2D affine transformation $\hat{M}_{i,\hat{f}}$ to warp hypothesis i to frame $\hat{f}$ using correspondences surrounding the bounding box of the i hypothesis. The initial 2D affine transformation $\hat{M}_{i,\hat{f}}$ is then refined using Lucas-Kanade template matching [29][3]. Given the set of valid transformations $\hat{\mathcal{M}} = \{\hat{M}_{i,f}\}$, we calculate the binary connection matrix $Q = \{q_{i,f}\}$ such that $q_{i,f} = 1$ if $\hat{M}_{i,f}$ is valid. Next, we select the central image $f_c = \arg\max_f \sum_{i \in J_f} q_{i,f}$, where J_f is a set of mutually non-overlapping hypotheses at the f image coordinate (see technical report [40] for details). Finally, we obtain the transformation as $M_i^* \equiv \hat{M}_{i,f_c}$. Note that some of the hypotheses cannot be warped to the central image f_c due to limitations of existing registration methods. These hypotheses are removed from consideration in the next step.

---

[3] We remove pairs with transformations that have matrix condition larger than 1.25 to avoid bad registrations.

Fig. 3. Our data and annotations: the top row shows challenging frames from ego-centric videos: fast camera motion, wearer self-occlusion, and navigation moment. The middle row shows the ground truth person annotations (bounding boxes with person identity indices) and ground truth gaze (green dots). The bottom row shows ground truth salient people (red bounding boxes) and ground truth gaze (green dots). When bounding boxes overlap (bottom row, middle frame) we resolve ambiguity by minimizing identity switches.

1: **Given:** $R = \{r_{ij}\}$, and K pairs of tracklet and s-score $\{(T_k, s_k)\}$ sorted from high to low saliency.
2: **Return:** a set of highly salient and mutually montageable hypotheses $\hat{\mathcal{L}}$ such that $r_{ij} = 1; \forall i, j \in \hat{\mathcal{L}}$
3: Initialize $\hat{\mathcal{L}}$ and $\mathcal{N}$ as empty.
4: Set tracklet index $k = 1$ to start with the most salient tracklet
5: **repeat**
6:    Select $i = \arg\max_{i \in T_k} r_i$, where $r_i = \sum_{j \notin \mathcal{N}} r_{ij}$.
7:    **if** $r_i \neq 0$ **then**
8:      Add i into $\hat{\mathcal{L}}$.
9:      Add $J = \{j; r_{ij} = 0\}$ into $\mathcal{N}$.
10:     Remove i and J from $\{T_k\}$.
11:   **end if**
12:   **if** T_k is empty or $r_i = 0$ **then**
13:    **repeat**
14:      k=k+1, which selects the next most salient tracklet.
15:    **until** T_k is not empty or $k > K$.
16:   **end if**
17: **until** $k > K$.

Algorithm 1. Greedy Hypotheses Selection

4.3   Selecting Hypotheses

Recall that the number of hypotheses is typically too large for Eq. 2 to be solved efficiently. Hence, we need to select a small set of hypotheses $\hat{\mathcal{L}}$. We use the montageability score $V_{\{i,j\}}$ (defined in Eq. 6) of a pair of hypotheses (i, j) to decide if the pair is preferred to be jointly selected. If the montageability score $V_{\{i,j\}}$ is larger than β, we set $r_{ij} = 1$ which indicates that a pair of hypotheses (i, j) should be jointly selected. Given $R = \{r_{ij}\}$, the goal is to select a set of salient and mutually montageable hypotheses $\hat{\mathcal{L}}$ (i.e., $r_{ij} = 1$ for all $i, j \in \hat{\mathcal{L}}$) such that $\sum_{i \in \hat{\mathcal{L}}} s_{k(i)}$ is maximized. In this way, we select as many salient hypotheses as possible by maintaining montageability. We greedily select a set of mutually montageable hypotheses $\hat{\mathcal{L}}$ using Algorithm 1. The algorithm proceeds down the list of tracklets sorted by s-score and adds those that are mutually montageable with currently selected ones. Note that we are implicitly reducing the cost of data term by maximizing the saliency of the selected hypotheses, and reducing the cost of the seam term by selecting mutually montageable set of hypotheses.

Once there are at least two selected hypotheses in $\hat{\mathcal{L}}$, we solve Eq. 2 to obtain L^* and generate the salient montage. We apply the same process for all groups, and use the montageability scores to retrieve salient montages with good quality.

Table 1. (a) Tracking results: mean average precision (mAP) comparison of different human detection and tracking system. 'Our3" is our full poselet-based system. 'Our2" is our system without the poselet-based relative similarity. "Our1" is our system also without detection by poselet trajectories (i.e., linking person bounding boxes from poselet detectors.). (b) Ranking results: Weighted Spearman's footrule for rank error comparison. Our method (Our) achieves the smallest error except in "B1". On four videos, our average errors are lower than five. On average, our error is almost half of the [38]. C.C. denotes Camera Centric. B denotes beach. F denotes ferry. SS denotes seaside. CS denotes campsite. LS denotes lakeside. PG denotes Playground.

(a)	mAP	(b)	B1	B2	F	SS	CS	LS1	LS2	LS3	PG1	PG2	Avg.
[35]	5.09%	Our	38.51	**40.36**	**5.43**	**3.85**	**3.30**	**11.77**	**2.95**	**3.38**	**7.33**	**7.38**	**12.42**
Our1	9.28%	C. C. Feat.	45.06	44.39	16.73	18.39	4.75	13.09	5.18	5.92	14.69	11.24	17.95
Our2	17.70%	Raw Det. Score	139.27	195.77	22.57	13.75	7.53	37.21	13.78	10.45	16.03	11.19	46.75
Our3	**18.80%**	Video Saliency [38]	**33.93**	55.13	15.06	5.17	13.29	38.80	18.98	4.34	27.43	21.81	23.39

5   Experiments

We evaluate our method on two types of videos. The first type includes unedited videos captured by two people using a head mounted camera (www.looxcie.com), where the camera center roughly follows the wearers' visual attention. The second type of videos are downloaded from Youtube. These are a mixture of edited and unedited videos captured mostly from hand-held devices. Both datasets are publicly available (see technical report [40] for details). We demonstrate that our method can handle both types of videos using the same settings.

In detail, we demonstrate that (1) our poselet-based people detection and tracking system outperforms the state-of-the-art method [35], (2) our saliency prediction method outperforms the state-of-the-art saliency detector [38], and (3) visually pleasing salient montages can be retrieved with high precision.

5.1   Family Outing Dataset

We collected a "family outing" dataset which contains 10 unedited videos with a total length of 2.25 hours (243K frames). The videos include events in playgrounds, parks, lakeside, seaside, etc. These ego-centric videos are challenging for tracking and registration due to fast camera motion, self-occlusion from the wearer, and moments when the wearer is navigating the terrain (see Fig. 3-Top). We demonstrate that it is possible to generate impressive montages from these challenging videos. For training and evaluation, we collect ground truth human bounding boxes and gaze data from the camera wearers (see Fig. 3-Middle). We ask users on Amazon Mechanical Turk to annotate at least the three most salient people (if possible) for each frame using the video annotation system [42]. We also ask the camera wearers to watch the videos and record their gaze using a commodity gaze tracker. We use the gaze data from the camera wearer to assign a ground truth binary "salient" label to each human annotation, assuming gaze reveals the salient subjects in the videos (see Fig. 3-Bottom).

Detecting and Tracking Humans. We optimize the parameters of our system on one video (Playground 1) and evaluate the performance on the remaining 9 videos. In Table 1 (a), we compare the detection accuracy using hypotheses in tracklets. Our full poselet-based method ("Our3") achieves a significant 13.71% improvement in mean average precision compared to [35] using the state-of-the-art human detector [11]. We also conduct an ablation analysis by removing components in our system one at a time (see Sec. 3.1 for the components). Our system without the poselet-based relative similarity ("Our2") becomes slightly worse than the full system. By further removing the detection by poselet trajectories, our system ("Our1") becomes much worse than the full system but is still better than [35].

Salient People Prediction. It is critical for our method to discover the salient people in order to generate montages relevant to the camera wearer. Therefore, after we obtain tracklets, we need to rank the saliency of each tracklet. Given the ground truth salient label for each human annotation, we can generate the ground truth rank of the tracklets by counting the number of times the hypotheses in each tracklet overlapped[4] with the salient human annotation. Similarly, using the predicted s-scores **s** of each tracklet, we can also rank the tracklets. We conduct a leave-one-out cross-validation experiment by training the random forest classifier using nine videos and evaluating on the remaining one. Given the predicted rank and the ground truth rank, we calculate the weighted Spearman's footrule on the top 10 predicted tracklets to measure rank error as follows:

$$\frac{1}{W} \sum_{i=1}^{10} \|i - \rho(i)\| \cdot w_i \quad where \ w_i = \frac{1}{i}, \ W = \sum_{i=1}^{10} w_i \ , \qquad (7)$$

where i is the rank of the predicted tracklet, $\rho(i)$ is the ground truth rank of the ith predicted tracklet, and w_i is the weight of each rank, which emphasizes the error of tracklets with higher predicted rank. We compare our prediction using all the features with three baseline methods: (1) ranking using the raw sum of detection scores for each tracklet, (2) our method using only the camera centric features, and (3) ranking each tracklet using state-of-the-art video saliency detector [38]. For each frame, the video saliency detector generates a saliency probability map. We assign the median of the saliency probability within a bounding box as the saliency score for each hypothesis. Then we rank each tracklet using the sum of the saliency scores. A detailed rank error comparison is shown in Table 1 (b). Our method using all features significantly outperforms other baselines in 9 out of 10 videos, and our average rank error (12.42) is almost half of the error of [38].

Given the s-score of each tracklet, we generate montages as described in Sec. 4. We now discuss some interesting cases below.

Camera Motion and Scene Depth Variation. The montage A in Fig. 1 shows a little girl on a slide. Due to the lateral camera motion and the depth

---

[4] If the intersection area over the union area is bigger than 0.25, we consider two bounding boxes overlapping. If a salient human annotation is overlapping with more than one hypotheses, we consider only the tightest hypothesis.

(a) Playground2 (Youtube link)   (b) Beach2 (Youtube link)   (c) Lakeside1 (Youtube link)

Fig. 4. Montages from the family outing dataset. In each example, we show the montage and the selected frames overlaid with the hypotheses indicated by red bounding boxes.

variation in the scene, it is extremely challenging to register these four images using a global transformation. Hence, typical methods [38,26] will fail. In contrast, our method can generate an impressive montage conveying the action. A similar result is shown in Fig. 4(a).

Crowded Scenes. Videos often contain crowded scenes with multiple people. Fig. 4(b) shows that our method can select the most salient person in a crowd. A similar result is shown in Fig. 4(c).

Our method generates on average about 18.1 montages per video in this dataset. Fig. 1 shows a set of montages our method retrieved to capture an afternoon at the playground. A lot more impressive salient montages and a video are included in the technical report [40].

5.2   Youtube Dataset

We downloaded videos from Youtube following two procedures. First, we searched for less edited family outing videos using keywords such as "family outing", "playground" and "park". Then, we manually selected the first 6 less edited videos (an average of 10.4 minutes per video) and refer them as "Youtube outing dataset". Second, we searched for three queries: "obstacle course", "parkour", and "skateboarding", and downloaded the top three ranked creative commons licensed videos for each query. These nine videos (an average of 4.8 minutes per video) are referred to as "Youtube motion dataset". Note that videos in the motion data are typically edited.

Our method generalizes well to the Youtube outing dataset which is similar to the family outing dataset. Examples are shown in Fig. 5. We also achieve encouraging results on the Youtube motion dataset. Despite the fast motion and frame cuts, our system works reasonably well and generates fairly impressive results (Fig. 6). Please see technical report for more salient montages.

5.3   Retrieving Good Montages

In order to evaluate how well our method can automatically retrieve good montages, we ask human subjects to classify montages into *good*, *reasonable*, and

(a) Youtube link   (b)Youtube link   (c) Youtube link

Fig. 5. Montages from the Youtube outing dataset. In panel (a), the most salient person is successfully selected. In panel (b,c), little kids are reliably detected and tracked.

(a) Youtube link   (b) Youtube link   (c) Youtube link

Fig. 6. Montages from the Youtube motion dataset. Our system nicely handles the fast motion in obstacle course, parkour, and skateboarding.

bad ones. Good results are the ones without clear artifacts on the foreground objects and the actions are easy to understand, reasonable results are the ones with small artifacts on the foreground objects but the actions are still easy to understand, and bad results are the ones with either significant artifacts or the actions are not easy to understand. The raw distribution of good, reasonable, and bad montages are shown in Fig. 7. We evaluate how well our montageability score retrieves good montages. We achieve mean average precisions of 55%, 62%, and 78% compared to 44%, 58%, and 68% for a baseline method using only s-scores[5] on the family outing[6], Youtube outing, and Youtube motion[7] datasets. We also evaluate our recall rate on the challenging ego-centric family outing dataset. We ask a human subject to count the number of montageable moments where there is a (not necessary salient) moving person not severely occluded by other objects or scene structures. Our system achieves an average recall of about 30%. Note that the low recall is fine for our application since, similar to a recommender system [7], we aim at showing users a few salient montages rather than all montageable moments which often might be boring.

---

[5] For each montage, we sum the s-scores of the selected hypotheses for ranking.

[6] One video generates less than 10 montages and it was not included.

[7] Four videos generate less than 10 montages and they were not included.

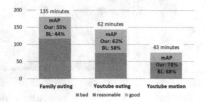

Fig. 7. Distribution of good, reasonable, and bad montages, where x axis is the number of montages. On top of each bar, we show the total length of videos in each dataset. The mean average precision (mAP) comparison between our method and the baseline (BL) method for retrieving good montages is overlaid on the bar plot.

Fig. 8. Failure cases. We show both the montage and the selected frames overlaid with the hypotheses indicated by red (correct ones) and blue (missing or incorrect ones) boxes. See technical report [40] for more analysis.

5.4 Analysis of Failure Cases

Our automatic system inevitably returns some failure cases. Fig. 8-Left shows a typical failure case due to bad localization since the person appears in a rare pose. Fig. 8-Right shows a typical failure case where unselected people (depicted by a blue bounding box) in the scene are cut in half. A more robust tracking system and a montageability function incorporates information of unselected hypotheses can potentially resolve these cases. Finally, our system will not retrieve salient moments which are not montageable (e.g., severe camera translation).

Implementation Details. Finally, we describe how we set the parameters in each component. We set all parameters for human detection and tracking on one video (Playground 1): minimal spatial overlap is set to $\rho = 0.25$, and the threshold for relative similarity is set to $\sigma = 1.5$. The bandwidth of motion uniqueness σ_p, the weight λ_d to balance the data and seam terms, and the threshold for montageability score β are empricially set to 5, 0.2, and 1.7, respectively. Our current Matlab implementation takes about 2 hours to process a 20 minutes video in family outing dataset on a single 8 cores machine.

6 Conclusion

We believe our method is the first to demonstrate the ability to automatically generate high quality montages from unconstrained videos. Our results on videos captured by wearable cameras are especially impressive due to the challenging conditions for tracking and registration methods to work reliably. In the future, we aim at inferring high-level semantic information in order to enable better prediction and understanding of "interesting moments".

Acknowledgement. We thank Microsoft, Google, Intel, the TerraSwarm research center, NSF IIS-1338054, NSF IIS-1218683, ONR N00014-13-1-0720, and ONR MURI N00014-10-1-0934 for supporting this research.

References

1. Agarwala, A., Dontcheva, M., Agrawala, M., Drucker, S., Colburn, A., Curless, B., Salesin, D., Cohen, M.: Interactive digital photomontage. In: ACM SIGGRAPH (2004)
2. Aner, A., Kender, J.R.: Video summaries through mosaic-based shot and scene clustering. In: Heyden, A., Sparr, G., Nielsen, M., Johansen, P. (eds.) ECCV 2002, Part IV. LNCS, vol. 2353, pp. 388–402. Springer, Heidelberg (2002)
3. Ballard, D.H.: Generalizing the hough transform to detect arbitrary shapes. Pattern Recognition 13(2), 111–122 (1981)
4. Borgo, R., Chen, M., Daubney, B., Grundy, E., Heidemann, G., Hoferlin, B., Hoferlin, M., Janicke, H., Weiskopf, D., Xie, X.: A survey on video-based graphics and video visualization. In: EUROGRAPHICS (2011)
5. Bourdev, L., Malik, J.: Poselets: Body part detectors trained using 3D human pose annotations. In: ICCV (2009)
6. Chen, S., Fern, A., Todorovic, S.: Multi-object tracking via constrained sequential labeling. In: CVPR (2014)
7. Cremonesi, P., Koren, Y., Turrin, R.: Performance of recommender algorithms on top-n recommendation tasks. In: Proceedings of the Fourth ACM Conference on Recommender Systems, pp. 39–46. ACM, New York (2010)
8. Cui, X., Liu, Q., Metaxas, D.: Temporal spectral residual: fast motion saliency detection. ACM Multimedia (2009)
9. Dalal, N., Triggs, B.: Histograms of oriented gradients for human detection. In: CVPR (2005)
10. Fathi, A., Li, Y., Rehg, J.M.: Learning to recognize daily actions using gaze. In: Fitzgibbon, A., Lazebnik, S., Perona, P., Sato, Y., Schmid, C. (eds.) ECCV 2012, Part I. LNCS, vol. 7572, pp. 314–327. Springer, Heidelberg (2012)
11. Felzenszwalb, P.F., Girshick, R.B., McAllester, D.: Discriminatively trained deformable part models, release 5,
    http://www.cs.berkeley.edu/~rbg/latent/voc-release5.tgz
12. Fragkiadaki, K., Zhang, W., Zhang, G., Shi, J.: Two-granularity tracking: Mediating trajectory and detection graphs for tracking under occlusions. In: Fitzgibbon, A., Lazebnik, S., Perona, P., Sato, Y., Schmid, C. (eds.) ECCV 2012, Part V. LNCS, vol. 7576, pp. 552–565. Springer, Heidelberg (2012)
13. Goferman, S., Zelnik-Manor, L., Tal, A.: Contextaware saliency detection. TPAMI (2012)
14. Goldman, D., Curless, B., Salesin, D., Seitz, S.: Schematic storyboarding for video visualization and editing. In: SIGGRAPH (2006)
15. Gong, Y., Liu, X.: Video summarization using singular value decomposition. In: CVPR (2000)
16. Guo, C., Ma, Q., Zhang, L.: Spatio-temporal saliency detection using phase spectrum of quaternion fourier transform. In: CVPR (2008)
17. Irani, M., Anandan, P., Hsu, S.: Mosaic-based representations of video sequences and their applications. In: ICCV (1995)
18. Joshi, N., Metha, S., Drucker, S., Stollnitz, E., Hoppe, H., Uyttendaele, M., Cohen, M.F.: Cliplets: Juxtaposing still and dynamic imagery. In: UIST (2012)

19. Judd, T., Ehinger, K., Durand, F., Torralba, A.: Learning to predict where humans look. In: ICCV (2009)
20. Kalal, Z., Mikolajczyk, K., Matas, J.: Tracking-learning-detection. TPAMI (2011)
21. Khosla, A., Hamid, R., Lin, C.J., Sundaresan, N.: Large-scale video summarization using web-image priors. In: CVPR (2013)
22. Lee, Y.J., Ghosh, J., Grauman, K.: Discovering important people and objects for egocentric video summarization. In: CVPR (2012)
23. Li, Y., Fathi, A., Rehg, J.M.: Learning to predict gaze in egocentric video. In: ICCV (2013)
24. Liu, C., Yuen, J., Torralba, A., Sivic, J., Freeman, W.T.: SIFT flow: Dense correspondence across different scenes. In: Forsyth, D., Torr, P., Zisserman, A. (eds.) ECCV 2008, Part III. LNCS, vol. 5304, pp. 28–42. Springer, Heidelberg (2008)
25. Liu, D., Hua, G., Chen, T.: A hierarchical visual model for video object summarization. TPAMI (2010)
26. Liu, F., Hen Hu, Y., Gleicher, M.: Discovering panoramas in web video. ACM Multimedia (2008)
27. Lowe, D.G.: Object recognition from local scale-invariant features. In: ICCV (1999)
28. Lu, Z., Grauman, K.: Story-driven summarization for egocentric video. In: CVPR (2013)
29. Lucas, B.D., Kanade, T.: An iterative image registration technique with an application to stereo vision. In: Imaging Understanding Workshop (1981)
30. Mahadevan, V., Vasconcelos, N.: Spatiotemporal saliency in dynamic scenes. TPAMI (2010)
31. Massey, M., Bender, W.: Salient stills: Process and practice. IBM Systems Journal 35(3&4), 557–574 (1996)
32. Milan, A., Schindler, K., Roth, S.: Detection- and trajectory-level exclusion in multiple object tracking. In: CVPR (2013)
33. Ngo, C., Ma, Y., Zhan, H.: Video summarization and scene detection by graph modeling. In: CSVT (2005)
34. Perazzi, F., Krahenbuhl, P., Pritch, Y., Hornung, A.: Saliency filters: Contrast based filtering for salient region detection. In: CVPR (2012)
35. Pirsiavash, H., Ramanan, D., Fowlkes, C.: Globally-optimal greedy algorithms for tracking a variable number of objects. In: CVPR (2011)
36. Pritch, Y., Rav-Acha, A., Gutman, A., Peleg, S.: Webcam synopsis: Peeking around the world. In: ICCV (2007)
37. Rav-Acha, A., Pritch, Y., Peleg, S.: Making a long video short. In: CVPR (2006)
38. Rudoy, D., Goldman, D.B., Shechtman, E., Zelnik-Manor, L.: Learning video saliency from human gaze using candidate selection. In: CVPR (2013)
39. Seo, H., Milanfar, P.: Static and space-time visual saliency detection by self-resemblance. Journal of Vision (2009)
40. Sun, M., Farhadi, A., Seitz, S.: Technical report of salient montage from unconstrained videos,
    http://homes.cs.washington.edu/~sunmin/projects/at-a-glace/
41. Sunkavalli, K., Joshi, N., Kang, S.B., Cohen, M.F., Pfister, H.: Video snapshots: Creating high-quality images from video clips. IEEE Transactions on Visualization and Computer Graphics 18(11), 1868–1879 (2012)
42. Vondrick, C., Patterson, D., Ramanan, D.: Efficiently scaling up crowdsourced video annotation. IJCV, 1–21
43. Yang, B., Nevatia, R.: An online learned crf model for multi-target tracking. In: CVPR (2012)

Action-Reaction:
Forecasting the Dynamics of Human Interaction*

De-An Huang and Kris M. Kitani

Carnegie Mellon University, Pittsburgh, PA 15213 USA

Abstract. Forecasting human activities from visual evidence is an emerging area of research which aims to allow computational systems to make predictions about unseen human actions. We explore the task of activity forecasting in the context of dual-agent interactions to understand how the actions of one person can be used to predict the actions of another. We model dual-agent interactions as an optimal control problem, where the actions of the initiating agent induce a cost topology over the space of reactive poses – a space in which the reactive agent plans an optimal pose trajectory. The technique developed in this work employs a kernel-based reinforcement learning approximation of the soft maximum value function to deal with the high-dimensional nature of human motion and applies a mean-shift procedure over a continuous cost function to infer a smooth reaction sequence. Experimental results show that our proposed method is able to properly model human interactions in a high dimensional space of human poses. When compared to several baseline models, results show that our method is able to generate highly plausible simulations of human interaction.

1 Introduction

It is our aim to expand the boundaries of human activity analysis by building intelligent systems that are not only able to classify human activities but are also capable of mentally simulating and extrapolating human behavior. The idea of predicting unseen human actions has been studied in several contexts, such as early detection [17], activity prediction [22], video gap-filling [2] and activity forecasting [9]. The ability to predict human activity based on visual

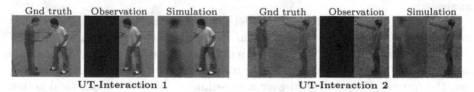

Gnd truth   Observation   Simulation   Gnd truth   Observation   Simulation

UT-Interaction 1   UT-Interaction 2

Fig. 1. Examples of ground truth, observation, and our simulation result

---

* Electronic supplementary material -Supplementary material is available in the online version of this chapter at http://dx.doi.org/10.1007/978-3-319-10584-0_32. Videos can also be accessed at http://www.springerimages.com/videos/978-3-319-10583-3

D. Fleet et al. (Eds.): ECCV 2014, Part VII, LNCS 8695, pp. 489–504, 2014.

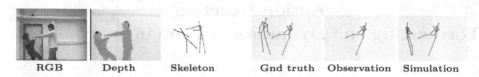

RGB   Depth   Skeleton   Gnd truth   Observation   Simulation

Fig. 2. Left three are the RGB, depth, and tracked skeleton images of SBU dataset. Right three images show our ground truth, observation, and simulation.

observations of the world is essential for advances in domains such as assistive robotics [10], human-robot interaction [7], robust surveillance [2], and smart coaching systems. For example, in the context of video surveillance, it is often the case that human activities are not fully visible to the camera due to occlusion, and in extreme cases parts of the activity may fall *outside* of the field of view (e.g., two people fighting at the periphery of the screen). A human observer however, can extrapolate what is happening despite large amounts of missing data. By observing a single person punching something outside of the field of view, we can visualize with high accuracy how the opponent has been hit. The important point being that humans have the ability to leverage contextual information to make very accurate predictions despite large amounts of visual occlusion. In this work, we aim to build a system that is able to predict and more importantly *simulate* human behavior in both space and time from partial observations.

We simplify our target domain by focusing on understanding and simulating dual-agent interaction. Traditionally dual-agent interactions (e.g.., hugging, pushing) have been represented as a joint phenomenon, where observations from both people are used as features to recognize human interactions from video [22,2,21,8,26]. Alternatively, human interactions can also be modeled as a dependent process, where one person is reacting to the actions of an initiating agent. In this work we model dual-agent interaction as a reactive control system, where the actions of the initiating agent induces a cost topology over the space of reactive poses – a space in which the reactive agent plans an optimal pose trajectory. This alternative representation of human interaction is a fundamentally new way of modeling human interactions for vision-based activity analysis.

The use of a decision-theoretic model for vision-based activity analysis has been proposed previously by Kitani *et al.* [9], where a cost function was learned over a low-dimensional 2D floor plane (with only 4 possible actions) for a single agent. While their work highlighted the importance of decision-theoretic modeling, the framework was defined over a low-dimensional state space (and action space) and was limited by the assumption of a single agent acting in a static world. In reality, the world is not static and people interact with each other. Additionally, if we desire to model human pose, the state space through which a person moves is extremely high-dimensional. To give an example, the pose space used in this work is a 819 dimensional HOG feature space, where both the state and action space are extremely large. In this scenario, it is no longer feasible to use the discrete state inference procedure used in [9].

In this work, we aim to go beyond a two dimensional state space and forecast dual-agent activities in a high-dimensional pose space. In particular, we introduce kernel-based reinforcement learning [18] to handle the high-dimensionality of human pose. Furthermore, we introduce an efficient mean-shift inference procedure [4] to find an optimal pose trajectory in the continuous cost function space. In comparative experiments, the results verify that our inference method is able to effectively represent human interactions. Furthermore, we show how this procedure proposed for 2D dual-agent interaction forecasting can also be applied to 3D skeleton pose data. Our final qualitative experiment also shows how the proposed model can be used for human pose analysis and anomaly detection.

Interestingly, the idea of generating a reactive pose trajectory has been explored largely in computer graphics; a problem known as interactive control. The goal of interactive control is to create avatar animations in response to user input [12,15]. Motion graphs [11] created from human motion data are commonly used, and the motion synthesis problem is transformed into selecting proper sequences of nodes. However, these graphs are discrete and obscure the continuous properties of motion. In response, a number of approaches have been proposed to alleviate this weakness and perform continuous control of character [24,13,14]. It should be noted that all of the interactive control approaches focus on synthesizing animations in response to a clearly defined mapping [11,15] from the user input to pose. In contrast, we aim to simulate human reaction based only on visual observations, where the proper reaction is non-obvious and must be learned from the data.

2   Dual Agent Forecasting

Our goal is to build a system that can simulate human reaction based only on visual observations. As shown in Figure 1, the ground truth consists of both the true reaction $g = [g^1 \cdots g^T]$ on the left hand side (LHS) and the observation $o = [o^1 \cdots o^T]$ of the initiating agent on the right hand side (RHS). In training time, M demonstrated interaction pairs g_m and o_m are provided for us to learn the cost topology of human interaction. At test time, only the actions of the initiating agent o (observation) on the RHS is given. We perform inference over the learned cost function to obtain an optimal reaction sequence x.

2.1   Markov Decision Processes

In this work, we model dual-agent interaction as a Markov decision process (MDP) [1]. At each time step, the process is in some state c, and the agent may choose any action a that is available in state c. The process responds by moving to a new state c' at the next time step. The MDP is defined by an initial state distribution $p_0(c)$ a transition model $p(c'|c,a)$ and a reward function $r(c,a)$, which is equivalent to the negative cost function. Given these parameters, the goal of *optimal control* is to learn the optimal policy $\pi(a|c)$, which encodes the distribution of action a to take when in state c that can maximize the expected

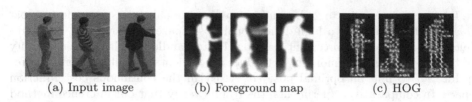

| (a) Input image | (b) Foreground map | (c) HOG |

Fig. 3. HOG features in (c) are our 819 dimensional states, which are the HOG responses of the input images weighted by the probability of foreground maps in (b)

reward (minimize the expected cost). In this work, the actions are *deterministic* because we assume humans have perfect control over their body where one action will deterministically bring the pose to the next state. Therefore, $p(c'|c,a)$ concentrates on a single state $c' = c_a$ and is zero for other states.

2.2 States and Actions

States. We use a HOG [6] feature of the whole image as a compact state representation, which does not contain the redundant textural information in the raw images. Some visualizations are shown in Figure 3. Note that only the poses on the left hand side (LHS) are referred as states, while poses on the right hand side (RHS) are our observations. We further make two changes to adapt HOG feature to our current application, pose representation. First, the HOG is weighted by probability of foreground (PFG) of the corresponding image because we are only interested in the human in the foreground. The PFG is computed by median filtering followed by soft thresholding. Second, we average the gradient in the 2×2 overlapping cells in HOG to reduce its dimension. This results in a continuous high-dimensional vector of 819 dimensions (64×112 bounding box).

Actions. Even with a continuous state space, a discrete set of actions is still more efficient to solve the MDP when possible [14]. Furthermore, there are actually many redundant actions for similar states that can be removed [23]. To alleviate redundancy, we perform k-means clustering on all the training frames on the LHS to quantize the continuous state space into K discrete states. For each cluster c ($c = 1$ to K), we will refer to the cluster center X_c as the HOG feature of quantized state c. The kth action is defined as going from a quantized state c to the kth nearest state, which gives us a total K actions. In the rest of the paper, we will fix this quantization. Given a new pose vector (HOG feature) x on the LHS, it is quantized to state c if X_c is the closest HOG feature to x.

2.3 Inverse Optimal Control over Quantized State Space

In this work, we model dual-agent interaction as an optimal control problem, where the actions of the initiating agent induce a cost topology over the space of reactive poses. Given M demonstrated interaction pair o_m (Observation) and g_m (true reaction), we leverage recent progress in inverse optimal control (IOC) [27] to recover a discretized approximation of the underlying cost topology.

In contrast to optimal control in Section 2.1, the cost function is not given in IOC and has to be derived from demonstrated examples [16]. We make an important assumption about the form of the cost function, which enables us to translate from visual observations to a single cost for reactive poses. The reward (negative cost) of a state c and an action a:

$$r(c, a; \boldsymbol{\theta}) = \boldsymbol{\theta}^{\top} \boldsymbol{f}(c, a), \tag{1}$$

is assumed to be a weighted combination of feature responses $\boldsymbol{f}(c, a) = [f_1(c, a) \cdots f_J(c, a)]^{\top}$, where each $f_j(c, a)$ is the response of a type of feature extracted from the video, such as the velocity of the agent's center of mass, and $\boldsymbol{\theta}$ is a vector of weights for each feature. By learning these parameters $\boldsymbol{\theta}$, we are learning how the actions of the initiating agent affect the reaction of the partner. For example, a feature such as moving forward will have a high cost for punching interactions because moving forward increases the possibility of being hit by the punch. In this case, the punching activity induces a high cost on moving forward and implies that this feature should have a high weight in the cost function. This explicit modeling of human interaction dynamics via the cost function sets our approach apart from traditional human interaction recognition models.

In this work, we apply the maximum entropy IOC approach [27] on the quantized states to learn a discretized approximation of the cost function. In this case, for a pose sequence $\boldsymbol{x} = [x^1 \cdots x^T]$ on the LHS, we quantize it into sequence $\boldsymbol{c} = [c^1 \cdots c^T]$ of quantized states defined in Section 2.2. In the maximum entropy framework [27], the distribution over a sequence $\boldsymbol{c}$ of quantized states and the corresponding sequence $\boldsymbol{a}$ of actions is defined as:

$$P(\boldsymbol{c}, \boldsymbol{a}; \boldsymbol{\theta}) = \frac{\prod_t e^{r(c^t, a^t)}}{Z(\boldsymbol{\theta})} = \frac{e^{\sum_t \boldsymbol{\theta}^{\top} \boldsymbol{f}(c^t, a^t)}}{Z(\boldsymbol{\theta})}, \tag{2}$$

where $\boldsymbol{\theta}$ are the weights of the cost function, $\boldsymbol{f}(c^t, a^t)$ is the corresponding vector of features of state c^t and action a^t, and $Z(\boldsymbol{\theta})$ is the partition function.

In the training step, we quantize M training pose sequences $\boldsymbol{g}_1 \cdots \boldsymbol{g}_M$ on the LHS to get the corresponding sequences $\boldsymbol{c}_1 \cdots \boldsymbol{c}_M$ of quantized states. We then recover the reward function parameters $\boldsymbol{\theta}$ by maximizing the likelihood of these sequences under the maximum entropy distribution (2). We use exponentiated gradient descent to iteratively maximize the likelihood. The gradient can be shown to be the difference between the *empirical* mean feature count $\bar{\mathbf{f}} = \frac{1}{M} \sum_{m=1}^{M} \boldsymbol{f}(\boldsymbol{c}_m, \boldsymbol{a}_m)$, the average feature counts over the demonstrated training sequences, and the *expected* mean feature count $\hat{\mathbf{f}}_\theta$, the average feature counts over the sequences generated by the parameter $\boldsymbol{\theta}$. With step size η, we update $\boldsymbol{\theta}$ by $\boldsymbol{\theta}^{t+1} = \boldsymbol{\theta}^t e^{\eta(\bar{\mathbf{f}} - \hat{\mathbf{f}}_\theta)}$. In order to compute the expected feature count $\hat{\mathbf{f}}_\theta$, we use a two-step algorithm similar to that described in [9] and [27].

Backward Pass. In the first step, current weight parameters $\boldsymbol{\theta}$ is used to compute the expected reward $V^{(t)}(c)$ to the goal from any possible state c at any time step t. The expected reward function $V^{(t)}(c)$ is also called the *value*

Algorithm 1. Backwards pass	**Algorithm 2.** Forward pass
$V^{(T)}(c) \leftarrow 0$	$D^{(1)}(c) \leftarrow \frac{1}{K}$
for $t = T - 1, \ldots, 2, 1$ **do**	**for** $t = 1, 2, \ldots, T - 1$ **do**
$\quad V^{(t)}(c) = \text{soft max}_a \, r(c, a; \boldsymbol{\theta}) + V^{(t+1)}(c_a)$	$\quad D^{(t+1)}(c_a) \mathrel{+}= \pi_\theta^{(t)}(a|c)D^{(t)}(c)$
$\quad \pi_\theta^{(t)}(a|c) \propto e^{V^{(t)}(c_a)-V^{(t)}(c)}$	**end for**
end for	$\hat{\mathbf{f}}_\theta = \sum_t \sum_c \sum_a \boldsymbol{f}^{(t)}(c, a)D^{(t)}(c)$

function in reinforcement learning. The maximum entropy policy is $\pi_\theta^{(t)}(a|c) \propto e^{V^{(t)}(c_a)-V^{(t)}(c)}$, where c is the current state, a is an action, and c_a is the state we will get by performing action a at state c. In other words, the probability of going to a state c_a from c is exponentially proportional to the increase of expected reward or value. The algorithm is summarized in Algorithm 1.

Forward Pass. In the second step, we propagate an uniform initial distribution $p_0(c) = \frac{1}{K}$ according to the learned policy $\pi_\theta^{(t)}(a|c)$, where K is the number of states (clusters). We do not assume c^1 is known as in [9] and [27]. In this case, we can compute the *expected state visitation count* $D^{(t)}(c)$ of state c at time step t. Therefore, the expected mean feature count can be computed by $\hat{\mathbf{f}}_\theta = \sum_t \sum_c \sum_a \boldsymbol{f}^{(t)}(c, a)D^{(t)}(c)$. The algorithm is summarized in Algorithm 2.

2.4   Features for Human Interaction

According to (1), the features define the expressiveness of our cost function and are crucial to our method in modeling dynamics of human interaction. Now we describe the features we use in our method. In this work, we assume that the pose sequence $o = [o^1 \cdots o^T]$ of the initiating agent is observable on the RHS. For each frame t, we compute different features $\boldsymbol{f}^{(t)}(c, a)$ from the sequence o.

Cooccurrence. Given a pose o^t on the RHS, we want to know how often a state c occurs on the LHS. This provides a strong clue for simulating human interaction. For example, when the hand of the pose o^t is reaching out, there is a high chance that the hand of the reacting person is also reaching out in response. This can be captured by the cooccurrence of reaching out poses on both LHS and RHS. Therefore, the cooccurrence feature $f_1^{(t)}(c, a) = P(c|o^t)$ is the posterior state distribution given the observation on the RHS. We estimate this distribution by discrete approximation. We quantize the observed pose o^t to observable quantized state c_o^t by k-means clustering as in Section 2.2, but now the quantization is on the RHS rather than the LHS. We approximate $P(c|o^t)$ by $P(c|c_o^t)$, which can be estimated by histogram density estimation.

Transition Probability. We want to know what actions will occur at a state c, which model the probable transitions between consecutive states. For example, at a state c that the agent is moving forward, transition to a jumping back state is less likely. Therefore, the second feature is the transition probability $f_2^{(t)}(c, a)$ $= P(c_a|c)$, where c_a is the state we will get to by performing action a at state

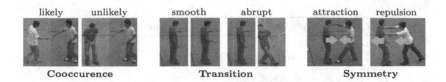

Fig. 4. We use statistics of human interaction as our features for the cost function

c. We accumulate the transition statistics from the M training sequences c_m of quantized states on the LHS. This feature is independent of time step t.

Centroid Velocity. We use centroid velocities to capture the movements of people when they are interacting. For example, it is unlikely that the centroid position of human will move drastically across frames and actions that induce high centroid velocity should be penalized. Therefore, we define the feature *smoothness* as $f_3^{(t)}(c, a) = 1 - \sigma(|v(c, a)|)$, where $\sigma(\cdot)$ is the sigmoid function, and $v(c, a)$ is the centroid velocity of action a at state c. Only the velocity along the x-axis is used. In addition, the relative velocity of the interacting agents gives us information about the current interaction. For example, in the hugging activity, the interacting agents are approaching each other and will have centroid velocities of opposite directions. Therefore, we define the feature *attraction* as $f_4^{(t)}(c, a) = \mathbb{1}(v_o^t \times v(c, a) < 0)$, where $\mathbb{1}(\cdot)$ is the indicator function, and v_o^t is the centroid velocity of the initiating agent at time t. This feature will be one if the interacting agents are moving in a symmetric way. We also define the complementary feature *repulsion* as $f_5^{(t)}(c, a) = \mathbb{1}(v_o^t \times v(c, a) > 0)$ to capture the opposite case when the agents are repulsive to each other.

2.5   Quantized State Inference

Given a set of demonstrated interactions, we can learn a discretized approximation of the underlying cost function by the IOC algorithm presented in Section 2.3. At test time, only the pose sequence of the initiating agent o_{test} on the RHS is observable. We first compute the features $f^{(t)}(c, a)$ under the observation o_{test}, and weight the features by the learned weight parameters θ to get the reward function (negative cost) $r(c, a; \theta) = \theta^\top f(c, a)$. This gives us the approximated cost topology induced by o_{test}, the pose sequence of the initiating agent.

In discrete Markov decision process, inferring the most probable sequence is straightforward: First, we fix the induced $r(c, a; \theta)$ and perform one round of backwards pass (Algorithm 1) to get the discrete value function $V^{(t)}(c)$. At each time step t, the most probable state is the state with the highest value. However, the result depends highly on the selection of K in this case. If we choose K too large, the $O(K^2T)$ Algorithm 1 becomes computational prohibited. Furthermore, the histogram based estimations become unreliable. On the other hand, if we choose K too small, the quantization error can be large.

Algorithm 3. Extended Mean Shift Inference

Compute $V^{(t)}(c)$ by Algorithm 1
$x^1 = X_{c^*}$, where $c^* = \arg\max_c V^{(1)}(c)$
for $t = 2, \ldots, T$ **do**
    $x_0 = x^{t-1}$, $w_c = V^{(t)}(c)$
    while not converged **do**
        $x_{i+1} = \frac{1}{C_h} \sum_{c=1}^K X_c w_c K_h(x_i, X_c)$, where $C_h = \sum_{c=1}^K w_c K_h(x_i, X_c)$
    end while
    $x^t = x_{converged}$
end for

2.6 Kernel-Based Reinforcement Learning

In order to address the problems of discretizing the state space, we introduce kernel-based reinforcement learning (KRL) [18] to our problem. Based on KRL, the value function $V_h^{(t)}(x)$ for any pose x in the *continuous* state space is assumed to be a weighted combination of value functions $V^{(t)}(c)$ of the quantized states. This translate our inference from discrete to continuous state space. At each time step t, the value function of a continuous state x is:

$$V_h^{(t)}(x) = \frac{\sum_{c=1}^K K_h(x, X_c) V^{(t)}(c)}{\sum_{c=1}^K K_h(x, X_c)}, \tag{3}$$

where X_c is the HOG feature of the quantized state c, and $K_h(\cdot, \cdot)$ is a kernel function with bandwidth h. In this work, we use the normal kernel.

The advantage of KRL is two-fold. First, it guarantees the smoothness of our value function. Second, we have the value function on the continuous space. Therefore, even with smaller K, we can still perform continuous inference. Furthermore, this formulation allows us to perform efficient optimization for x with maximal $V_h^{(t)}(x)$ as we will show in the next section.

2.7 Extended Mean Shift Inference

Now that we have the value function $V_h^{(t)}(x)$ on the continuous state space, we want to find the pose x^* with the highest value. In contrast to optimization in the discretized space, it is infeasible to enumerate the values of all the states in continuous space. We leverage the property of human motion to simplify the optimization problem. Since human motion is smooth and will not change drastically across frames, the optimal next pose should appear in a local neighborhood of the current pose. This restricts our search space of optimal pose to a local neighborhood. In addition, we leverage the resemblance of our formulation in (3) to the well-studied *kernel density estimation* (KDE) in statistics, which has also achieved considerable success in the area of object tracking [3]. To optimize the density in KDE, the standard approach is to apply the mean shift procedure, which will converge robustly to the local maximum of the density function.

Our formulation allows us to leverage the similarity of our problem to KDE and apply the extended mean shift framework proposed in [3] to perform efficient inference. As shown in [3], the maximization of a function of the form

$$\frac{\sum_{c=1}^{K} w_c K_h(x, X_c)}{\sum_{c=1}^{K} K_h(x, X_c)} \tag{4}$$

can be done efficiently by the extended mean shift iterations

$$x_{i+1} = \frac{\sum_{c=1}^{K} X_c w_c G_h(x_i, X_c)}{\sum_{c=1}^{K} w_c G_h(x_i, X_c)} \tag{5}$$

until convergence, where G_h is the negative gradient of K_h. In normal kernel, G_h and K_h has the same form [4]. Therefore, we can replace G_h in (5) by K_h.

Our goal is to find the pose x that maximize the value function $V_h^{(t)}(x)$ locally. In this case, the expression in (3) will have the exact same form to optimize in (4) if we define $w_c = V^{(t)}(c)$. Therefore, we derive our final extended mean shift update rule by scaling $V^{(t)}(c)$ linearly to $[0, 1]$ as w_c. The algorithm is summarized in Algorithm 3. The mean shift iterations is performed at each time step, where the update is initialize by the pose of the last frame x^{t-1}, and the converged result is taken as x^t. In our experiments, the first frame x^1 is initialized by the quantized state with the highest value.

3   Experiments

Our goal is to build intelligent systems that are capable of mentally simulating human behavior. Given two people interacting, we observe only the actions of the initiator on the right hand side (RHS) and attempt to forecast the reaction on the left hand side (LHS). For video in which the initiator is on the LHS, we flip the video to put the initiator on the RHS. Since we do not have access to the ground truth distribution over all possible reaction trajectories, we measure how well the learned policy is able to describe the single ground truth trajectory. For interaction videos, we use videos from three datasets, *UT-Interaction 1*, *UT-Interaction 2* [20], and *SBU Kinect Interaction Dataset* [25] where the UTI datasets consist of only RGB videos, and SBU dataset consists of RGB-D (color plus depth) human interaction videos. In each interaction video, we occlude the ground truth reaction $g = [g^1 \cdots g^T]$ on the LHS, observe $o = [o^1 \cdots o^T]$ the action of the initiating agent on the RHS, and attempt to forecast g. For experiments, we will first evaluate which model provides the best representation for human reaction. Then we will evaluate the features of the cost function.

3.1   Metrics

We compare the ground truth sequence with the learned policy using two metrics. The first one is probabilistic, which measures the probability of performing the ground truth reaction under the learned policy. A higher probability means the learned policy is more consistent with the ground truth reaction sequence. We use the Negative Log-Likelihood (NLL):

$$-\log P(\boldsymbol{g}|\boldsymbol{o}) = -\sum_t \log P(g^t|g^{t-1}, \boldsymbol{o}), \tag{6}$$

as our probabilistic metric. For discrete models, the ground truth reaction sequence is quantized into a sequence $\boldsymbol{c}$ of quantized states. The probability is evaluated by $P(g^t|g^{t-1}, \boldsymbol{o}) = P(c^t|c^{t-1}, \boldsymbol{o})$. For our continuous model, $P(g^t|g^{t-1}, \boldsymbol{o})$ are interpolated according to (3). The second metric is deterministic, which directly measure the physical HOG distance (or joint distance for skeleton video) of the ground truth reaction $\boldsymbol{g}$ and the reaction simulated by the learned policy. The deterministic metric is the average frame distance:

$$\frac{1}{T-1} \sum_t ||g^t - x^t||^2 \tag{7}$$

where x^t is the resulting reaction pose at frame t. The distance is not computed for the last frame because the reward function $r(c, a)$ is not defined.

3.2 Evaluating the Interaction Model

For model evaluation, we select three baselines to compare with the proposed method. The first baseline is the per frame nearest neighbor (NN) [5], which only uses the *cooccurrence* feature at each frame *independently* and does not take into account the effect of consecutive states. For each observation o^t, we find the LHS quantized state with the highest cooccurrence. That is $c_{NN}^t = \arg\max_c P(c|c_o^t) \approx P(c|o^t)$, where c_o^t is the observable quantized state of o^t.

The second baseline is the hidden Markov model (HMM) [19], which has been widely used to recover hidden time sequences. HMM is defined by the transition probabilities $P(c^t|c^{t-1})$ and emission probabilities $P(o^t|c^t)$, which are equivalent to our *transition* and *cooccurrence* features. However, the weights for these two features are always the same in HMM, while our algorithm learns the optimal feature weights $\boldsymbol{\theta}$. The likelihood is computed by the forward algorithm and the resulting state sequence c_{HMM} is computed by the Viterbi algorithm.

Table 1. Average frame distance (AFD) and NLL per activity category for UTI

(a)AFD	NN[5]	HMM[19]	MDP[9]	Proposed
shake	5.35	5.21	4.68	**3.14**
hug	4.00	4.06	3.74	**2.88**
kick	6.17	6.16	5.33	**3.96**
point	3.62	3.62	3.31	**2.45**
punch	5.10	4.99	4.23	**3.03**
push	4.90	4.91	4.01	**3.24**

(b)NLL	NN[5]	HMM[19]	MDP[9]	Proposed
shake	651.04	**473.91**	862.81	476.10
hug	751.46	608.81	958.49	**487.21**
kick	382.62	**263.08**	550.52	282.36
point	577.22	426.40	750.11	**374.73**
punch	353.85	260.72	483.01	**257.06**
push	479.33	357.00	561.01	**320.92**

Fig. 5. Forecasting result of UTI dataset 1. The RHS is the observed initiator, and the LHS is the simulated reaction of the proposed method. The activity is shaking hands.

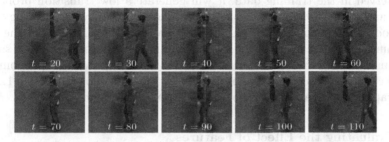

Fig. 6. Forecasting result of UTI dataset 2. The RHS is the observed initiator, and the LHS is the simulated reaction of the proposed method. The activity is hugging.

The third baseline is the discrete state inference in Section 2.5. This can be seen as applying the discrete Markov decision process (MDP) inference used in [9] to a quantized state space. We will refer to this baseline as MDP. The likelihood for MDP is computed by $\prod_t \pi_\theta^{(t)}(a^t|c^t)$, the stepwise product of the policy executions. We follow [9] and produce the probabilistic-weighted output.

We first evaluate our method on *UT-Interaction 1*, and *UT-Interaction 2* [20] datasets, which consist of RGB videos only, and some examples have been shown in Figure 1. The UTI datsets consist of 6 actions: hand shaking, hugging, kicking, pointing, punching, pushing. Each action has a total of 10 sequences for both datasets. We use 10-fold evaluation as in [2]. We use $K = 100$ in the experiments. We now evaluate which method can best simulate human reaction.

The average NLL and frame distance per activity for each baseline is shown in Table 1. It can be seen that, optimal control based methods (MDP and proposed) outperform the other two baselines in terms of frame distance. In addition, the proposed mean shift inference achieves the lowest frame distance for all activities and significantly outperforms other baselines because we use kernel-based reinforcement learning to alleviate quantization error and the mean shift inference ensures the smoothness of the resulting reaction trajectory. It should be noted that although the MDP is able to achieve lower frame distance than NN and HMM, the NLL is higher. This is because the performance of discretized inference can be affected significantly by unseen data. For example, if a transition is

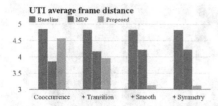 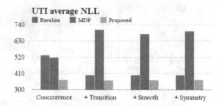

Fig. 7. Ablative analysis shows that the proposed method continually outperforms the baselines and verifies the effectiveness of our features

not observed in the training data, it will generate a low transition probability feature and induce a high cost in the IOC framework. This will make the overall likelihood of the ground truth significantly lower (a high NLL). On the other hand, our kernel-based reinforcement learning framework interpolates a smooth value function over the continuous state space and alleviates this phenomenon. The effectiveness of our approach is verified by the NLL shown in Table 1. Some visualization of the results are shown in Figure 5 and Figure 6.

3.3   Evaluating the Effect of Features

As noted in Section 2.4, the features define the expressiveness of our cost function, and are essential for us to model the dynamics of human interaction. In the previous section, we have shown that the proposed method is the best interaction model. We now evaluate the effects of different features for our model.

The average NLL and frame distance for the entire UTI dataset (1 and 2) using different features are shown in Figure 7. The performances of baselines and MDP are also shown for reference. It should be note that because centroid-based features (smooth, attraction, repulsion) cannot be easily integrated into baselines NN and HMM, the performances of HMM still only use the first two features in the *+Smooth* and *+Symmetry* columns. It can be seen that adding more features help our method to learn a policy that is more consistent with the ground truth, and significantly outperforms other baselines because our kernel-based reinforcment learning and mean-shift framework provides an efficient way for inference over a continuous space and ensures the smoothness of the result.

3.4   Extension to 3D Pose Space

To show that our method can also work in 3D pose space (not just 2D), we evaluate our method on *SBU Kinect Interaction Dataset* [25], in which interactions performed by two people are captured by a RGB-D sensor and tracked skeleton positions at each frame are provided. In this case, the state space becomes a 15×3 (joint number times x, y, z) dimensional continuous vector. We use $K = 50$ for

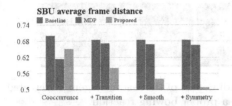
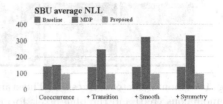

Fig. 8. Ablative analysis shows the effectiveness of our features and verifies that our 2D interaction forecasting framework can also be applied to 3D skeleton data

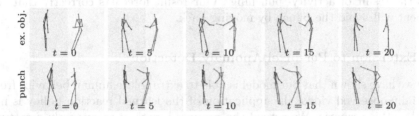

Fig. 9. Forecasting result of SBU dataset. The red skeleton is the initiating agent (observation), and the blue skeleton is our simulation result. Top row shows a result of activity exchaging object, and the bottom row shows a result of acitivity punching.

the actions because the dataset contains less frames per video compared to the UT-Interaction datasets. The SBU dataset consists of 8 actions: approaching, departing, kicking,pushing, shaking hands, hugging, exchanging object, punching. The first two actions (approaching & departing) are excluded from our experiments because the initiating agent has no action and provides no information for forecasting. 7 participants performed activities in the dataset and results in 21 video sets, where each set contains videos of a pair of different people performing all interactions. We use 7-fold evaluation, in which videos of one participants are held out for one fold. The average NLL and frame distance per activity are shown in Table 2. Again, the proposed model achieves the best performance on both frame distance and NLL. The feature evaluation results are shown in Figure 8. It can be seen that adding more features is beneficial for modelling the dynamics of human interaction. A visualization of the results are shown in Figure 9. The top row of the figure shows the result of activity 'exchanging object'. It can be seen that, the forecasting result (blue skeleton) raises his hand to catch the object

Table 2. Average frame distance (AFD) and NLL per activity category for SBU dataset

(a)AFD	NN[5]	HMM[19]	MDP[9]	Proposed
kick	0.855	0.824	0.875	**0.660**
push	0.575	0.559	0.573	**0.413**
shake	0.551	0.537	0.503	**0.389**
hug	0.768	0.751	0.690	**0.504**
exchange	0.755	0.742	0.724	**0.574**
punch	0.700	0.692	0.633	**0.510**

(b)NLL	NN[5]	HMM[19]	MDP[9]	Proposed
kick	107.17	92.89	308.85	**74.65**
push	143.46	139.84	399.56	**99.06**
shake	187.11	183.14	381.97	**120.89**
hug	166.06	169.62	284.24	**112.21**
exchange	133.87	124.95	309.43	**87.87**
punch	111.81	111.05	306.11	**78.98**

Fig. 10. Anomaly detection results. The standing part of the reacting agent is detected as anomalous (red) and the blue pixels form a proper bowing reaction.

provided by the initiating agent (red skeleton). The bottom row of the figure shows the result of activity 'punching'. Our result forecasts correctly that the opponent will avoid the punch by moving back.

3.5   Extension to Per-pixel Anomaly Detection

While we have shown that our model is able to extrapolate human behavior from a partially observed video, the application of the learned reaction policy is not limited to this scenario. We extend the proposed method to *anomaly detection*. We address this problem by comparing the simulated probability of foreground (PFG) map and the PFG map of the testing sequence. We downloaded four Karate bowing videos from YouTube. We train our model on three of the videos and test on the remaining one. We synthesize a anomalous reaction by shifting the LHS of the testing video 20 frames forward temporally. The visual anomaly detection result is shown in Figure 10. The anomalous part of the body pose is labeled as red and the normal parts of the pose are shown in blue. This visual feedback can be used in training scenarios for social interaction or sports.

4   Conclusions

We have presented a fundamentally new way of modeling human interactions for vision-based activity analysis. While interactions have traditionally been modeled as a joint phenomenon for recognition, we treat human interactions as a dependent process and explicitly model the interactive dynamics of human interaction. We have pushed beyond previous optimal control approaches for low-dimensional spaces and have introduced kernel-based reinforcement learning and mean-shift procedure to tackle the high-dimensional and continuous nature of human poses. Experimental results verified that our proposed method is able to generate highly plausible simulations of human reaction and outperforms several baseline models. Furthermore, we have shown successful extensions to 3D skeleton pose data and an application to the task of pose-based anomaly detection.

Acknowledgement. This research was sponsored in part by the Army Research Laboratory (W911NF-10-2-0061) and by the National Science Foundation (Purposeful Prediction: Co-robot Interaction via Understanding Intent and Goals).

References

1. Bellman, R.: A Markovian decision process. Journal of Mathematics and Mechanics 6(5), 679–684 (1957)
2. Cao, Y., Barrett, D.P., Barbu, A., Narayanaswamy, S., Yu, H., Michaux, A., Lin, Y., Dickinson, S.J., Siskind, J.M., Wang, S.: Recognize human activities from partially observed videos. In: CVPR (2013)
3. Comaniciu, D., Ramesh, V., Meer, P.: Real-time tracking of non-rigid objects using mean shift. In: CVPR (2000)
4. Comaniciu, D., Meer, P.: Mean shift: A robust approach toward feature space analysis. IEEE Trans. Pattern Anal. Mach. Intell. 24(5), 603–619 (2002)
5. Cover, T.M., Hart, P.E.: Nearest neighbor pattern classification. IEEE Transactions in Information Theory IT-13(1), 21–27 (1967)
6. Dalal, N., Triggs, B.: Histograms of oriented gradients for human detection. In: CVPR (2005)
7. Dragan, A.D., Lee, K.C.T., Srinivasa, S.S.: Legibility and predictability of robot motion. In: ACM/IEEE International Conference on Human-Robot Interaction (2013)
8. Gaur, U., Zhu, Y., Song, B., Chowdhury, A.K.R.: A "string of feature graphs" model for recognition of complex activities in natural videos. In: ICCV (2011)
9. Kitani, K.M., Ziebart, B.D., Bagnell, J.A., Hebert, M.: Activity forecasting. In: Fitzgibbon, A., Lazebnik, S., Perona, P., Sato, Y., Schmid, C. (eds.) ECCV 2012, Part IV. LNCS, vol. 7575, pp. 201–214. Springer, Heidelberg (2012)
10. Koppula, H.S., Saxena, A.: Anticipating human activities using object affordances for reactive robotic response. In: RSS (2013)
11. Kovar, L., Gleicher, M., Pighin, F.: Motion graphs. In: SIGGRAPH 2002 Conference Proceedings. Annual Conference Series, pp. 473–482. ACM Press/ACM SIGGRAPH (2002)
12. Lee, J., Chai, J., Reitsma, P.S.A., Hodgins, J.K., Pollard, N.S.: Interactive control of avatars animated with human motion data. ACM Trans. Graph. 21(3), 491–500 (2002)
13. Lee, Y., Wampler, K., Bernstein, G., Popovic, J., Popovic, Z.: Motion fields for interactive character locomotion. ACM Trans. Graph. 29(6), 138 (2010)
14. Levine, S., Wang, J.M., Haraux, A., Popovic, Z., Koltun, V.: Continuous character control with low-dimensional embeddings. ACM Trans. Graph. 31(4), 28 (2012)
15. McCann, J., Pollard, N.S.: Responsive characters from motion fragments. ACM Trans. Graph. 26(3), 6 (2007)
16. Ng, A.Y., Russell, S.: Algorithms for inverse reinforcement learning. In: ICML (2000)
17. Nguyen, M.H., la Torre, F.D.: Max-margin early event detectors. In: CVPR (2012)
18. Ormoneit, D., Sen, S.: Kernel based reinforcement learning. Machine Learning 49(2-3), 161–178 (2002)
19. Rabiner, L.R., Juang, B.H.: An introduction to hidden Markov models. ASSP Magazine (1986)
20. Ryoo, M.S., Aggarwal, J.K.: UT-Interaction Dataset, ICPR contest on Semantic Description of Human Activities (SDHA) (2010),
   http://cvrc.ece.utexas.edu/SDHA2010/Human_Interaction.html
21. Ryoo, M.S., Aggarwal, J.K.: Spatio-temporal relationship match: Video structure comparison for recognition of complex human activities. In: ICCV (2009)

22. Ryoo, M.S.: Human activity prediction: Early recognition of ongoing activities from streaming videos. In: ICCV (2011)
23. Safonova, A., Hodgins, J.K.: Construction and optimal search of interpolated motion graphs. ACM Trans. Graph. 26(3), 106 (2007)
24. Treuille, A., Lee, Y., Popovic, Z.: Near-optimal character animation with continuous control. ACM Trans. Graph. 26(3), 7 (2007)
25. Yun, K., Honorio, J., Chattopadhyay, D., Berg, T.L., Samaras, D.: Two-person interaction detection using body-pose features and multiple instance learning. In: CVPRW (2012)
26. Zhang, Y., Liu, X., Chang, M.-C., Ge, W., Chen, T.: Spatio-temporal phrases for activity recognition. In: Fitzgibbon, A., Lazebnik, S., Perona, P., Sato, Y., Schmid, C. (eds.) ECCV 2012, Part III. LNCS, vol. 7574, pp. 707–721. Springer, Heidelberg (2012)
27. Ziebart, B., Maas, A., Bagnell, J., Dey, A.: Maximum entropy inverse reinforcement learning. In: AAAI (2008)

Creating Summaries from User Videos*

Michael Gygli[1,2], Helmut Grabner[1,2], Hayko Riemenschneider[1],
and Luc Van Gool[1,3]

[1] Computer Vision Laboratory, ETH Zurich, Switzerland
[2] upicto GmbH, Zurich, Switzerland
[3] K.U. Leuven, Belgium
{gygli,grabner,hayko,vangool}@vision.ee.ethz.ch

Abstract. This paper proposes a novel approach and a new benchmark
for video summarization. Thereby we focus on user videos, which are raw
videos containing a set of interesting events. Our method starts by segmenting the video by using a novel "superframe" segmentation, tailored
to raw videos. Then, we estimate visual interestingness per superframe
using a set of low-, mid- and high-level features. Based on this scoring,
we select an optimal subset of superframes to create an informative and
interesting summary. The introduced benchmark comes with multiple
human created summaries, which were acquired in a controlled psychological experiment. This data paves the way to evaluate summarization
methods objectively and to get new insights in video summarization.
When evaluating our method, we find that it generates high-quality results, comparable to manual, human-created summaries.

Keywords: Video analysis, video summarization, temporal segmentation.

1 Introduction

With the omnipresence of mobile phones and other consumer oriented camera
devices, more and more video data is captured and stored. To find and access relevant videos then quickly becomes a challenge. Moreover, the easier and cheaper
video acquisition becomes, the more casual and sloppy the average quality typically gets. The automated production of good video summaries, that capture
the important information and are nice to watch, can mitigate both issues.

One way of coping with the search challenge is visual indexing, where keyframes are selected such that they best summarize the
video [28,5,1,13,18,15,16]. Keyframes are typically extracted using change detection [5] or clustering based on low-level features [1] or objects [18]. Others
resort to web priors to find important frames within a video [15,16,20]. While
keyframes are a helpful way of indexing videos, they are limited in that all motion
information is lost. That limits their use for certain retrieval tasks (e.g. when
looking for a nice panning shot from the top of the Eiffel tower), but renders

---

* Electronic supplementary material -Supplementary material is available in the online
version of this chapter at http://dx.doi.org/10.1007/978-3-319-10584-0_33.
Videos can also be accessed at http://www.springerimages.com/videos/978-3-
319-10583-3

D. Fleet et al. (Eds.): ECCV 2014, Part VII, LNCS 8695, pp. 505–520, 2014.
© Springer International Publishing Switzerland 2014

them even less useful for improving the viewing experience. Therefore, video skimming, *i.e.* replacing the video by a shorter compilation of its fragments, seems better suited for such goals. This is however a challenging task, especially for user videos, as they are unstructured, range over a wide variety of content and what is important often depends on a semantic interpretation.

Early work on the summarization of edited videos, such as tv news, is by Smith and Kanade [26], who detect camera motion, shot boundaries and faces, among other things, to create an automatic summary. Liu *et al.* [21] proposed a framework to summarize BBC rushes based on low-level cues, that clusters frames and uses image saliency and the visual differences between frames to score them. Ejaz *et al.* [5] follow a very similar approach to score frames, but use a non-linear fusion scheme. Several approaches target video summarization on a semantic level [22,19,18,9], but as the reliable detection of high-level information, such as objects, is still an open research problem, many of them take user annotations (*e.g.* object bounding boxes) as input [19,22,9].

Probably the most related work to ours are the recent works done at UT Austin [18,22]. They summarize long, raw, egocentric videos into keyframes [18] or skims [22], using an object-centered approach. In order to find important objects in a video, [18] uses object segmentations and a set of object-centered features, while [22] analyzes how objects link a set of events in a story. The usefulness of their approach was confirmed in a human study, were subjects were asked to compare the proposed summaries to several baselines.

In contrast to [18,22] we introduce a more generic algorithm that summarizes any type of video (static, egocentric or moving), while taking into account cinematographic rules. Thereby we focus on user videos, which we define as unedited video data, that was taken with a purpose. Such video data often contains a set of interesting events, but is raw and therefore often long, redundant and contains parts of bad quality. Our goal is therefore different from [18,22], who summarize video from wearable cameras, which often run for hours. Since user videos contain a wide range of content, solely relying on object-centric features, as in [18], is insufficient in our case. Therefore we propose new features better suited for the task of summarizing user videos.

Rather than manually evaluating the produced summaries, as [18,22], we introduce a new benchmark of user videos ranging over different categories. We evaluate our method using multiple 'ground truth' summaries per video, which we acquired in a study in collaboration with perception psychologists. This data allows to assess the performance of any summarization algorithm in a fast and repeatable manner.

We make the following contributions:

i) **Superframes.** A novel approach for motion-based video over-segmentation using insights from editing theory (Sec. 3). As these superfames have their boundaries aligned with positions appropriate for a cut, they create an aesthetic summary when combined.

ii) **Summarization of User Videos.** A new method to estimate the interestingness of superframes and selecting a summary from them using a 0/1-

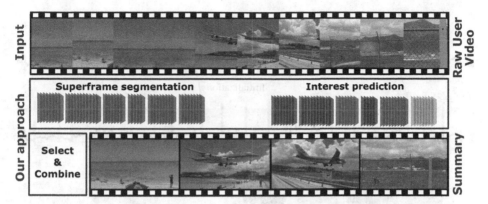

Fig. 1. Overview of our approach. First, we segment the video into superframes (cuttable segments). Then, we predict the interestingness (using low-level features and face/person, landmark detectors and motion features) for each superframe. From these, we select an optimal subset.

knapsack optimization. With this formulation the interestingness contained in the final summary is maximized, while remaining within a desired time budget (Sec. 5).

iii) **The *SumMe* Benchmark.** A new, publicly available dataset of user videos that allows for an objective and repeatable evaluation of video summarization methods. To the best of our knowledge, it is the first that is annotated with human scores for video segments rather than keyframes and that allows for an automatic evaluation of different methods[1] (Sec. 6).

2 Overview

An overview of our approach to create an *automatic summary* is shown in Fig. 1. We start by over-segmenting a video $\mathcal{V}$ into superframes $\mathcal{S}$ (Sec. 3). Superframes are sets of consecutive frames where start and end are aligned with positions of a video that are appropriate for a cut. Therefore, an arbitrary order-preserving subset can be selected from them to create an automatic summary. Inspired by a recent work on human interest in images [11], we then predict an interestingness score $I(S_j)$ for each superframe (Sec. 4). For this purpose, we use a combination of low-level image features, motion features, as well as face/person and landmark detectors. Finally, we select an optimal subset of $\mathcal{S}$, such that the interestingness in the final summary is maximized (Sec. 5).

3 Superframe Segmentation

Traditional video summarization methods are focused on edited videos, such as news stories, sport broadcasts or movies. As these videos are edited, they consist

---

[1] Dataset and evaluation code are available on:
www.vision.ee.ethz.ch/~gyglim/vsum/

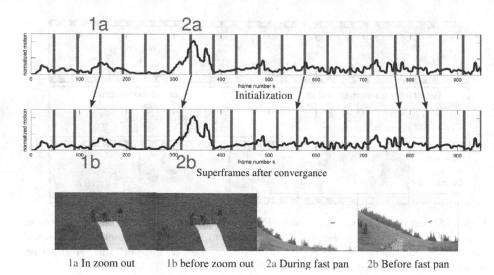

1a In zoom out   1b before zoom out   2a During fast pan   2b Before fast pan

Fig. 2. Superframe segmentation illustration. Superframes are initialized with a uniform length and then iteratively adapted to the motion. This leads to segments which have boundaries with less motion and often enclose a distinct event.

of a set of short shots. In order to segment such a video, it is sufficient to use shot detection, *e.g.* based on changes in the color histogram [26]. As we focus on largely unedited user videos, which often only contain one single shot, such an approach cannot be used in our case. This problem was also targeted earlier by [22], who proposed to classify frames from egocentric videos into *static, in transit* or *head movement*, in order to segment a video into shots. This method is however only applicable for egocentric videos and leads to shots of about 15 seconds, which is much longer than what people typically choose to summarize a video (see Fig. 3). A more general option would be to cut the video into segments of fixed length, but such arbitrarily cut shots would not correspond to logical units of the videos. In addition, this would lead to disrupting cuts, as humans are irritated by abrupt motion changes caused by cuts [24, p. 161].

As a remedy, editing guidelines propose to cut when there is no motion (or else, the motion speed and direction of two neighboring shots is matched) [24, p. 158-161]. We design a subshot segmentation that incorporates this idea. We term these segments superframes, in analogy to superpixels, and propose an approach inspired by recent work in image segmentation [2].

We define an energy function $E(\mathcal{S}_j)$ that is a measure of quality of a superframe $\mathcal{S}_j$ as

$$E(\mathcal{S}_j) = \frac{1}{1 + \gamma C_{cut}(\mathcal{S}_j)} \cdot P_l(|\mathcal{S}_j|), \tag{1}$$

where C_{cut} is the cut cost and P_l is a length prior for the superframes. $|\cdot|$ denotes the length of a superframe. The parameter γ controls the influence between the cut cost and the length prior, where a lower γ leads to more uniform superframes. The cut cost is defined as

$$C_{cut}(\mathcal{S}_j) = m_{in}(\mathcal{S}_j) + m_{out}(\mathcal{S}_j) \tag{2}$$

where $m_{in}(\mathcal{S}_j)$ and $m_{out}(\mathcal{S}_j)$ are the estimated motion magnitude in the first and last frame of the superframe. We compute $m_{in}(\mathcal{S}_j)$ and $m_{out}(\mathcal{S}_j)$ by taking the mean magnitude of the translation, which we estimate by tracking points in the video using KLT. This cost is lower for superframes that have their boundaries aligned with frames containing little or no motion.

The length prior P_l is learnt by fitting a log-normal distribution to a histogram of segment lengths of the human created summary selections (*cf.* Sec. 6). In Fig. 3 we show the prior learnt on the complete dataset. The prior serves as a regularization of the superframes, similar to the shape term in [2].

We optimize the energy of Eq. (1) locally by hill-climbing optimization. First, the superframes are initialized evenly distributed over the video/shot, using the segment length $|\mathcal{S}_j| = \arg\max_l(P_l)$. Then,

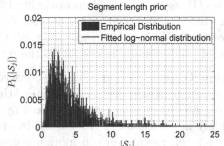

Fig. 3. Distribution of segment lengths. We show the distribution of segment lengths as selected by the study subjects and the fitted log-normal distribution. On the whole dataset we find $\arg\max_l(P_l) = 1.85$.

we iteratively update the boundaries between two superframes to optimize Eq. (1), which leads to segments that have their boundaries aligned to positions suitable for a cut. This optimization is done in a coarse to fine manner, where a boundary movement by δ frames is proposed. The movement is accepted, if it increases the mean score of Eq. (1), of the two affected superframes. We start from an initial δ and iteratively update until the algorithm converges. Then, δ is decreased by one frame and the optimization is re-executed. Fig. 2 illustrates this process. As this optimization is local, only a few iterations are needed until it converges (typically less than 10).

4   Per-frame Interestingness

We compute an interestingness score i_k for each frame v_k, as a weighted sum of features that have been found to be related to interestingness [11,18]. Thereby we combine low-level information, such as the aesthetic quality (contrast, etc.) and spatio-temperal saliency, with high-level features such as, motion classification and person and landmark detection.

Attention. We use the approach of [5] to predict a human attention score based on spatial [12] and temporal saliency (temporal gradients). As [5] we combine the scores with a non-linear fusion scheme and take the attention score as a single feature in our approach.

Aesthetics/Quality. To predict the aesthetic quality of a frame we compute colorfulness [3], contrast [14] and the distribution of edges [14].

Presence of Landmarks. Landmarks are often of high interest [11]. This is particularly true in holiday videos and has already been exploited in [20] to predict the interestingness of video frames. We follow this idea and use the framework of [8] to classify the scene in a frame as famous or non-famous, based on the presence of famous buildings.

Faces/Persons. As previous works [26,18], we detect prominent faces or persons in a frame and use them as features for summarization. We detect faces using the algorithm of [27] and persons using [6]. Given a detection, we take the relative area of the bounding box *w.r.t.* to the frame size as a feature score.

Follow Object. Similar to [18] we observe that moving cameras contain implicit information on an objects/events interestingness. A typical pattern in user videos is that an object of interest is tracked by the camera (the movie makers keep it roughly in the center of the video). In order to classify such a motion pattern, we build on recent work in motion segmentation. We separate a set of sparse motion tracks into segments using [4]. Thereby the number of motion segments is automatically determined. From a given segmentation, we find the foreground segment by assuming that it is approximately centered in the frame and spatially compact. Specifically, we take $\arg\min_{\mathbf{O}} \sum \|(\mu_{\mathbf{o_i}} - \mathbf{c})\sigma_{\mathbf{o_i}}\|$ as the foreground segment, where $\mathbf{O}$ is the set of motion segments and the sum is taken over the set of frames a segment is visible. $\mu_{\mathbf{o_i}}$ and $\sigma_{\mathbf{o_i}}$ are the mean and standard deviation of the x- and y-coordinates of the points in segment o_i and $\mathbf{c}$ is the center point of the frame. The background is taken to be the largest remaining motion segment. Given this separation, we estimate a translational motion model for foreground and background. We annotated a set of videos containing 32 *follow object* motion patterns and computed background and foreground motion magnitude m_b, m_f. From these, we use kernel density estimation over vectors $\mathbf{x} = [m_b, m_b - m_f]$ in order to estimate $P(\mathbf{x}|\mathbf{y} = follow\ object)$, $P(\mathbf{y} = follow\ object)$ and $P(\mathbf{x})$. Using Bayes theorem we compute then $P(\mathbf{y} = follow\ object|\mathbf{x})$ and use this probability as a feature.

Combination of Features. We combine the above features with a linear model, where we regress the weights $\mathbf{w}$. A frame v_k has an interestingness score i_k

$$i_k = w_0 + \sum_{i=1}^{N} w_i \cdot u_i + \sum_{i=1}^{N} \sum_{j=i+1}^{N} w_{i,j} \cdot u_i u_j, \tag{3}$$

where u_i is the score of feature i. We use unary and pairwise terms as [18], since such a model is able to capture interactions between features, while it remains sufficiently simple to avoid overfitting and allows for fast training.

We estimate **w** using least-squares and the annotated dataset from Sec. 6. As training ground truth we use a score computed by taking the fraction of selections over views for each frame (examples of such scores are shown in of Fig. 7 as 'human selection'). We randomly sample 100 frames from each training video and concatenate them. This way, all videos have the same importance in the learning process. As we randomly sample frames, we repeat this process 50 times and average the resulting weight vectors.

The interestingness score of a superframe S_i is simply a sum over the interestingness of its frames:

$$I(S_i) = \sum_{k=n}^{m} i_k, \tag{4}$$

where n and m are start and end frame of superframe S_i. We also tried other scoring methods, such as taking the maximum or including cluster size, but found this simple sum to work best.

5 Selecting an Optimal Summary

Given the set of superframes S, we want to find a subset with a length below a specified maximum L_s, such that the sum of the interestingness scores is maximized. Formally, we want to solve the following optimization problem:

$$\underset{\mathbf{x}}{\text{maximize}} \sum_{i=1}^{n} x_i I(S_i)$$

$$\text{subject to} \sum_{i=1}^{n} x_i |S_i| \leq L_s, \tag{5}$$

where $x_i \in \{0, 1\}$ and $x_i = 1$ indicates that a superframe is selected. Under the assumption of independence between the scores $I(S_i)$, this maximization is a standard 0/1-knapsack problem, where $I(S_i)$ is the value of an item and its length $|S_i|$ its weight. This problem can be solved globally optimal with dynamic programming in pseudo-polynomial time $\mathcal{O}(nL_s)$ [10], with $n = |S|$.

In this optimization, we do not explicitly account for the possibility that superframes contain redundant information. We also ran experiments where we clustered the superframes beforehand and used an uncorrelated subset of superframes in the optimization to explicitly enforce diversity for the final summary. This however led to no significant improvement, suggesting that study participants choose *interesting* over *representative* parts. Furthermore user videos rarely contain multiple interesting, but redundant events (*i.e.* from our experience it is not necessary to explicitly filter out duplicates).

6 The SumMe Benchmark

We introduce a benchmark that allows for the automatic evaluation of video summarization methods. Previous approaches generated video summaries and then let humans assess their quality, in one of the following ways:

Table 1. The videos in the *SumMe* dataset. We show consistency and the distribution of segment lengths for each video. The analysis of the consistency (Sec. 6.2) shows that there are certain individual differences but humans still generally agree on what parts of a video are interesting.

Name	Camera	Length	# of subj.	Summary length [%]	Segments avg. #	avg. length	human consistency f-measure	Cronb. α
Base jumping	egocentric	2m39s	18	13.8±2.0	5.7±2.2	4.5s	0.26	0.77
Bike Polo	egocentric	1m43s	15	12.3±3.4	3.9±1.4	3.8s	0.32	0.83
Scuba	egocentric	1m14s	17	13.2±2.0	3.5±1.3	3.4s	0.22	0.70
Valparaiso Downhill	egocentric	2m53s	15	13.6±1.9	7.7±4.0	4.2s	0.27	0.80
Bearpark climbing	moving	2m14s	15	14.4±1.0	5.1±2.2	4.7s	0.21	0.61
Bus in Rock Tunnel	moving	2m51s	15	12.8±3.3	5.7±2.7	4.7s	0.20	0.57
Car railcrossing	moving	2m49s	16	13.2±2.0	4.9±2.0	5.4s	0.36	0.78
Cockpit Landing	moving	5m2s	15	12.8±2.6	7.3±2.9	6.7s	0.28	0.84
Cooking	moving	1m27s	17	13.8±1.3	3.2±1.1	4.3s	0.38	0.91
Eiffel Tower	moving	3m20s	15	11.8±2.9	5.5±2.3	4.6s	0.31	0.80
Excavators river cross.	moving	6m29s	15	14.0±1.2	9.9±4.7	6.9s	0.30	0.63
Jumps	moving	0m39s	15	14.4±1.0	2.9±1.1	2.4s	0.48	0.87
Kids playing in leaves	moving	1m46s	15	13.2±2.4	4.2±2.5	4.6s	0.29	0.59
Playing on water slide	moving	1m42s	15	12.6±2.8	5.2±3.2	3.2s	0.20	0.56
Saving dolphins	moving	3m43s	15	13.9±1.3	6.9±2.9	6.6s	0.19	0.21
St Maarten Landing	moving	1m10s	17	13.9±1.1	2.8±1.6	4.8s	0.50	0.94
Statue of Liberty	moving	2m36s	17	10.7±3.5	3.1±2.4	7.5s	0.18	0.56
Uncut Evening Flight	moving	5m23s	15	12.1±2.5	6.3±3.1	7.6s	0.35	0.85
paluma jump	moving	1m26s	15	12.9±1.9	3.1±1.2	4.6s	0.51	0.91
playing ball	moving	1m44s	16	13.9±1.7	4.7±2.5	4.3s	0.27	0.68
Notre Dame	moving	3m12s	15	12.9±2.0	7.6±3.8	4.1s	0.23	0.63
Air Force One	static	2m60s	15	14.0±1.5	5.3±3.0	6.2s	0.33	0.85
Fire Domino	static	0m55s	15	14.0±1.7	4.0±2.0	2.2s	0.39	0.85
car over camera	static (mostly)	2m26s	15	12.4±2.5	4.7±2.7	5.0s	0.35	0.84
Paintball	static (mostly)	4m16s	17	11.5±3.3	5.2±2.2	6.6s	0.40	0.87
Mean		2m40s	16	13.1±2.4	5.1±3.0	4.9s	0.31	0.74

i) Based on a set of predefined criteria [25]. The criteria may range from counting the inclusion of predefined important content, the degree of redundancy, summary duration, etc.

ii) Humans are shown two different summaries and are asked to select the better one [18,22]. Typically, the summaries are compared to some baseline such as uniform sampling or k-means clustering.

These evaluation methods are problematic, as they are expensive and time consuming as they rely on human judges for *each* evaluation. The evaluation of the method of [22], for example, required one full week of human labor. Both approaches are discriminative, *i.e.* they help to tell which summary is better than another, but fail to show what a good summary should look like.

Rather than using the above approaches, we let a set of study subjects generate their own summaries. This was done in a controlled psychological experiment, as described in the next section. We collected multiple summaries for each videos, as there is no true answer for a correct summarization, but rather multiple possible ways. With these human summaries, referred to as *human selections*, we can compare any method that creates an *automatic summary* in a repeatable and efficient way. Such automatic vs. human comparison has already been used successfully for keyframes [1,15]. Khosla *et al.* [15] showed that comparing automatic keyframe summaries to human keyframe selections yields ratings comparable to letting humans directly judge the automatic summaries.

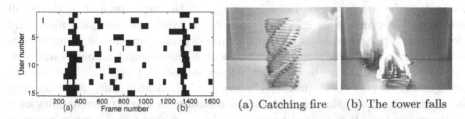

(a) Catching fire   (b) The tower falls

Fig. 4. Consistency of human selections. We show the human selections for the video "Fire Domino", a typical video from our dataset. The selection of a frame is marked in **black**. As one can see, there is a high consistency among the study participants. They consistently selected the two main events (a) and (b) of the video.

6.1 Setup

The *SumMe* dataset consists of 25 videos covering holidays, events and sports. They are raw or minimally edited user videos, *i.e.* they have a high compressibility compared to already edited videos. The length of the videos ranges from about 1 to 6 minutes (Overview in Tab. 1).

Given a video, the study subjects were asked to produce a summary that contains most of its important content, *i.e.* that best summarizes the input video. They could use a simple interface that allows to watch, cut and edit a video. We required the summary length L_s to be $5\% \leq L_s \leq 15\%$ to ensure that the input video is indeed summarized rather than being slightly shortened. The videos were shown in random order and the audio track was not included to ensure that the subjects chose based on visual stimuli. A total of 19 male and 22 female subjects, with varying educational background, participated in the study. Ages were ranging from 19 to 39 and all had normal or corrected vision. Each video was summarized by 15 to 18 different people. The total user time of the study amounts to over 40 hours.

An example from our dataset is shown in Fig. 4. The complete experimental data including verbatim instructions, user interface and the human selections can be found in the supplementary material.

6.2 Human Consistency

In this section we analyze the human selection results in terms of the consistency among the participants.

To assert the consistency of human selections, we propose the use of the pairwise f-measure between them. We will use same consistency measure to evaluate the performance of automatic summaries in Sec. 7. For a human selection i, it is defined as follows:

$$\bar{F}_i = \frac{1}{N-1} \sum_{j=1, j \neq i}^{N} 2\frac{p_{ij}r_{ij}}{p_{ij} + r_{ij}}, \tag{6}$$

where N is the number of human subjects, p_{ij} is the precision and r_{ij} the recall of human selection i using selection j as ground truth. We compute recall and precision on a per-frame basis. This procedure of averaging pairwise comparisons accounts for individual differences in the way humans select segments and was also successfully used in the Berkeley Segmentation Dataset [23]. The dataset has a mean of $\bar{F} = 0.31$ (min. 0.18, max. 0.51). Additionally we computed the Cronbach alpha, which is a standard measure to assess the reliability of a psychometric test. It is defined as $\alpha = \frac{N\bar{r}}{1+(N-1)\bar{r}}$, where $\bar{r}$ is the mean pairwise correlation between all human selections. The dataset has a mean of $\alpha = 0.74$ (min. 0.21, max. 0.94). Ideally α is around 0.9, while $\alpha > 0.7$ is the minimum for a good test [17, p. 11, 13].

To summarize, we showed that the most of the videos have a good consistency and it is thus appropriate to train and evaluate computational models on them. This is particularly true, since we use pairwise scores rather than one single reference summary. Generally, we observe the consistency depends on the diversity within a video. Videos that do not have a set of clearly separable events have lower consistency than videos with a set of visually and semantically dissimilar events.

7   Experiments

We evaluate our method using the new benchmark and the f-measure defined in Eq. (6). We compare our method to a random, uniform and clustering baseline, as well as a recent method based on visual attention [5]. Further, we compare to the individual human summaries. Ideally, a computer generated summary is as consistent as the best human summary selection. In addition, we also investigate the influence on the performance of the main steps in our pipeline. The results described here are summarized in Tab. 2.

Implementation Details. We kept all parameters fixed for all results. When estimating P_l and $\mathbf{w}$ we used leave-one training. In the superframe segmentation, we set the initial delta $\delta = 0.25s$ and the $\gamma = 1$ for all videos. For the interestingness estimation, we computed all image features sparsely every 5th frame, but processed all frames for motion features. We normalized the feature scores per video to zero mean and unit variance. For the *Follow object* feature, we used a Gaussian kernel with a window size $h = 10$ in the kernel density estimation.

7.1   Dataset Scores

We characterize the dataset by computing random scores and the upper bound (Tab. 2). The upper bound is defined as the highest reachable score for this dataset, given the human selection and the pairwise f-measure. It would only be 1.0, if all humans summary selection would be exactly the same.

Table 2. Quantitative results. We show f-measures at 15% summary length for our approach, the baselines and the human selections. We highlight the **best** and second best computational method. Our method consistently shows a high performance scoring higher than the worst human per video.

	Videoname	Random	Upper bound	Worst	Mean	Best	Uniform	Cluster.	Att.[5]	Ours
		Dataset		Humans			Computational methods			
ego.	Base jumping	0.144	0.398	0.113	0.257	0.396	_0.168_	0.109	**0.194**	0.121
	Bike Polo	0.134	0.503	0.190	0.322	0.436	0.058	_0.130_	0.076	**0.356**
	Scuba	0.138	0.387	0.109	0.217	0.302	0.162	0.135	**0.200**	_0.184_
	Valparaiso Downhill	0.142	0.427	0.148	0.272	0.400	0.154	0.154	_0.231_	**0.242**
moving	Bearpark climbing	0.147	0.330	0.129	0.208	0.267	0.152	_0.158_	**0.227**	0.118
	Bus in Rock Tunnel	0.135	0.359	0.126	0.198	0.270	_0.124_	0.102	0.112	**0.135**
	Car railcrossing	0.140	0.515	0.245	0.357	0.454	0.146	_0.146_	0.064	**0.362**
	Cockpit Landing	0.136	0.443	0.110	0.279	0.366	0.129	_0.156_	0.116	**0.172**
	Cooking	0.145	0.528	0.273	0.379	0.496	_0.171_	0.139	0.118	**0.321**
	Eiffel Tower	0.130	0.467	0.233	0.312	0.426	0.166	_0.179_	0.136	**0.295**
	Excavators river crossing	0.144	0.411	0.108	0.303	0.397	0.131	_0.163_	0.041	**0.189**
	Jumps	0.149	0.611	0.214	0.483	0.569	0.052	_0.298_	0.243	**0.427**
	Kids playing in leaves	0.139	0.394	0.141	0.289	0.416	**0.209**	_0.165_	0.084	0.089
	Playing on water slide	0.134	0.340	0.139	0.195	0.284	_0.186_	0.141	0.124	**0.200**
	Saving dolphines	0.144	0.313	0.095	0.188	0.242	_0.165_	**0.214**	0.154	0.145
	St Maarten Landing	0.143	0.624	0.365	0.496	0.606	0.092	0.096	**0.419**	_0.313_
	Statue of Liberty	0.122	0.332	0.096	0.184	0.280	_0.143_	0.125	0.083	**0.192**
	Uncut Evening Flight	0.131	0.506	0.206	0.350	0.421	0.122	0.098	**0.299**	_0.271_
	paluma jump	0.139	0.662	0.346	0.509	0.642	_0.132_	0.072	0.028	**0.181**
	playing ball	0.145	0.403	0.190	0.271	0.364	**0.179**	_0.176_	0.140	0.174
	Notre Dame	0.137	0.360	0.179	0.231	0.287	0.124	_0.141_	0.138	**0.235**
static	Air Force One	0.144	0.490	0.185	0.332	0.457	0.161	0.143	_0.215_	**0.318**
	Fire Domino	0.145	0.514	0.170	0.394	0.517	0.233	**0.349**	_0.252_	0.130
	car over camera	0.134	0.490	0.214	0.346	0.418	0.099	_0.296_	0.201	**0.372**
	Paintball	0.127	0.550	0.145	0.399	0.503	0.109	0.198	_0.281_	**0.320**
	mean	0.139	0.454	0.179	0.311	0.409	0.143	0.163	0.167	0.234
	relative to upper bound	31 %	100 %	39 %	68 %	90 %	31 %	36 %	37 %	52 %
	relative to average human	45 %	146 %	58 %	100 %	131 %	46 %	53 %	54 %	75 %

Additionally, we measure the "human performance", which is the average f-measure of one humans to all the others. We show the worst, average and best scores of the human selections in Tab. 2. The "worst human" score is computed using the summary which is the least similar to the rest of the summaries. The more similar a human selection is to all the others, the higher the score. The best human score is the mean f-measure of the most similar summary $w.r.t.$ all the others, $i.e.$ it mostly contains parts that were selected by many humans.

7.2 Baselines

We compare our approach to the following baselines:

Uniform Sampling. We uniformly select K segments of length $\arg\max_l(P_l)$, such that the final summary length is $\leq L_s$ (15% of the input).

Clustering. We computed color histograms with 16^3 dimensions for each frame and averaged these per superframe. Then, we clustered the superframes with [7], using the affinity of [18]. Given this clustering, we use the cluster centers as candidates for the final summary and select a subset using Eq. (5).

Visual Attention. Recently [5] proposed an approach for keyframe selection based on the principles of human attention (*cf.* Sec. 4). As this method produces keyframes, we selected K segments of length $\arg\max_l(P_l)$ around the highest scored frames, such that the final summary is of length L_s (15% of the input video).

7.3   Results

As can be see from Tab. 2, our method outperforms all baselines. Our method has an average performance of 52%, while the strongest baseline reaches 37%, relative to the upper bound. If we compare to the human consistency (the human 'performance'), we can see that our method even outperforms, on average, the worst human of each video. Furthermore it reaches a performance comparable to the average human summary in many cases. Our method is able to find the important segments of a video and to produce an informative summary from them. The proposed features capture the central aspects of a video.

The highest average performance is achieved on static cameras. This is not surprising as in such a setting simple features are often sufficient to find an event of interest (*e.g.* temporal gradients). While our method performs well in all settings (static, moving and egocentric), it has a low performance for certain videos, *e.g.* the video "Base jumping". This video contains fast motion and subtle semantics that define important events of the video, such as opening the parachute or the landing. These are difficult to capture based on the used image and motion features, which leads to a low performance for this video.

In Fig. 5 we show the quantitative performance over the whole video for different summarization ratios and a visualization of a few automatic summaries in Fig. 7. We refer the reader to the supplementary material for quantitative and especially qualitative results on all videos.

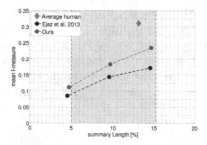

Fig. 5.   Quantitative results. We compare our method (red) to the visual attention [5] baseline (**black**) and the average human performance (green) over the entire dataset. Automatic summaries are computed for lengths ≤ 5%, 10% and 15%.

7.4   Performance of the Individual Components

Interestingness. We investigate the importance and reliability of the individual interestingness features. In Fig. 6a we show the performance gain by adding a feature to the set of used features (the difference in performance of (not) using a feature). As could be expected, general features perform best, as they can potentially help on all videos. Somewhat surprisingly, a feature as simple as colorfulness leads to a high performance gain. Additionally, we observe a large improvement by using the detection of landmarks and a camera that *follows* a moving *object*. This is despite the fact, that only a fraction of videos contains either of these. However, if *e.g.* a landmark appears in the video, this is a strong indicator that such a part should be selected for a summary. When combining

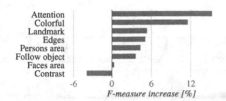

(a) **Feature performance.** We show the increase in performance by adding a feature to the set of used features.

	mean f-measure	
Segmentation	per frame	per segment
Single frame	0.217 (70%)	0.035 (10%)
Fixed length	0.222 (72%)	0.151 (44%)
Clustering	0.228 (73%)	0.155 (45%)
Superframes	0.234 (75%)	0.170 (49%)

(b) **Temporal segmentation:** We report the performance of different temporal segmentations. Percent scores are relative to the average human.

Fig. 6. Weights and performance of the individual steps in the pipeline (See text)

the individual features , they can predict what parts of a video should be selected for the automatic summary (see performance in Tab. 6b). However, the features cannot capture what is interesting in all cases. Lacking a temporal smoothing the scores are often noisy and, when selecting frames based on this score, create disruptive segments. We target these problems by temporal smoothing, as we discuss in the following.

Superframes. We analyze the performance gain by using temporal segmentation (Tab. 6b). Instead of using per-frame interestingness scores, we compute a score per temporal window. We compare the proposed superframes to segments of fixed length, where we set the length to the optimal value according to the length prior P_l. As an additional baseline we use clustering to select keyframes (k-means) and use these as centers to create segments, which partition the video into shots (with segment boundaries in the middle between two keyframes). Each segment is scored according to Eq. (4) and the summary is optimized using Eq. (5), such that the final summary length maximally 15% of the initial video. As we want to analyze the quality of the created segments, we report f-measure on the per-frame and also on the segment level. To compute recall and precision of segments, we compute the intersection over union of the segments and threshold it at 0.25.

As expected, smoothing over a temporal neighborhood leads to an increased performance, especially on the segment level. While the main aim of the superframes is to produce aesthetically pleasing summaries, we can observe that using these motion aligned segments yields a better performance. This indicates that using such a grouping is indeed more semantically logical. For qualitative differences in the produced summaries, we refer the reader to the videos in the supplementary material or on our website.

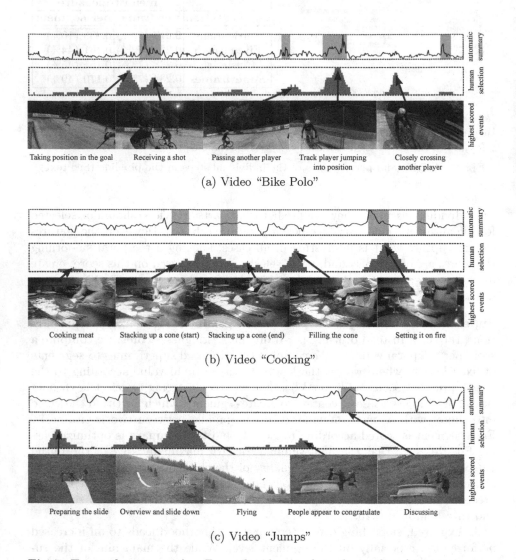

(a) Video "Bike Polo"

(b) Video "Cooking"

(c) Video "Jumps"

Fig. 7. Example summaries. For each video we show the predicted interestingness score (**black**) and the selected segments (green) on top. In the middle we show the human scores (red). The human score is computed as the ratio of selections over views, per frame. Peaks in the human score indicate that this part was often selected by humans, while a peak in the **interestingness score** indicates a high prediction for this part. Our method correctly selects the most important events and produces a compact and interesting summary from them. The superframe segementation ensures that the cuts between the segments are smooth. **Best viewed in color.** All generated summaries are given in the supplementary material.

8   Conclusion

In this work we proposed a novel temporal superframe segmentation for user videos and a method to produce informative summaries from them. To score the superframes we proposed a set of interestingness features and showed that they capture what is important well. With the use of a 0/1-knapsack formulation, we optimized the interestingness of the final summary, while remaining within a given time budget.

The evaluation of our method shows that it is generally able to create good automatic summaries, often reaching the performance of humans. Nonetheless, video summarization is still in its beginnings. The contribution of our benchmark with multiple human summaries per video makes it possible to gain additional insights into what humans rate as important. This will help develop new features and methods in the future.

Acknowledgements. We thank Michel Druey and the Varcity team for fruitful discussions and help. This work was supported by the European Research Council (ERC) under the project VarCity (#273940) and the Swiss CTI under project no. 15769.1.

References

1. de Avila, S.E.F., Lopes, A.P.B., da Luz Jr., A., de A. Araújo, A.: VSUMM: a mechanism designed to produce static video summaries and a novel evaluation method. Pattern Recognition Letters (2011)
2. Van den Bergh, M., Boix, X., Roig, G., de Capitani, B., Van Gool, L.: SEEDS: Superpixels extracted via energy-driven sampling. In: Fitzgibbon, A., Lazebnik, S., Perona, P., Sato, Y., Schmid, C. (eds.) ECCV 2012, Part VII. LNCS, vol. 7578, pp. 13–26. Springer, Heidelberg (2012)
3. Datta, R., Joshi, D., Li, J., Wang, J.Z.: Studying aesthetics in photographic images using a computational approach. In: Leonardis, A., Bischof, H., Pinz, A. (eds.) ECCV 2006. LNCS, vol. 3953, pp. 288–301. Springer, Heidelberg (2006)
4. Dragon, R., Ostermann, J., Van Gool, L.: Robust Realtime Motion-Split-And-Merge for Motion Segmentation. In: Weickert, J., Hein, M., Schiele, B. (eds.) GCPR 2013. LNCS, vol. 8142, pp. 425–434. Springer, Heidelberg (2013)
5. Ejaz, N., Mehmood, I., Wook Baik, S.: Efficient visual attention based framework for extracting key frames from videos. Signal Processing: Image Communication (2013)
6. Felzenszwalb, P.F., Girshick, R.B., McAllester, D., Ramanan, D.: Object detection with discriminatively trained part based models. PAMI (2010)
7. Frey, B.J., Dueck, D.: Clustering by passing messages between data points. Science (2007)
8. Gammeter, S., Bossard, L., Quack, T., Van Gool, L.: I know what you did last summer: object-level auto-annotation of holiday snaps. In: ICCV (2009)
9. Goldman, D., Curless, B.: Schematic storyboarding for video visualization and editing. ACM Trans. on Graphics (2006)

10. Goodrich, M.T., Tamassia, R.: Algorithm Design: Foundation, Analysis and Internet Examples. John Wiley & Sons (2006)
11. Gygli, M., Grabner, H., Riemenschneider, H., Nater, F., Van Gool, L.: The interestingness of images. In: ICCV (2013)
12. Hou, X., Harel, J., Koch, C.: Image signature: Highlighting sparse salient regions. PAMI (2012)
13. Huang, T., Mehrotra, S.: Adaptive key frame extraction using unsupervised clustering. In: Proc. Image Processing (1998)
14. Ke, Y., Tang, X., Jing, F.: The design of high-level features for photo quality assessment. In: CVPR (2006)
15. Khosla, A., Hamid, R., Lin, C., Sundaresan, N.: Large-Scale Video Summarization Using Web-Image Priors. In: CVPR (2013)
16. Kim, G., Sigal, L., Xing, E.P.: Joint Summarization of Large-scale Collections of Web Images and Videos for Storyline Reconstruction. In: CVPR (2014)
17. Kline, P.: The handbook of psychological testing. Psychology Press (2000)
18. Lee, Y.J., Ghosh, J., Grauman, K.: Discovering important people and objects for egocentric video summarization. In: CVPR (2012)
19. Liu, D., Hua, G., Chen, T.: A hierarchical visual model for video object summarization. PAMI (2010)
20. Liu, F., Niu, Y., Gleicher, M.: Using Web Photos for Measuring Video Frame Interestingness. In: IJCAI (2009)
21. Liu, Z., Zavesky, E., Shahraray, B.: Brief and high-interest video summary generation: evaluating the AT&T labs rushes summarizations. In: ACM WS on Video Summarization (2008)
22. Lu, Z., Grauman, K.: Story-Driven Summarization for Egocentric Video. In: CVPR (2013)
23. Martin, D., Fowlkes, C., Tal, D., Malik, J.: A database of human segmented natural images and its application to evaluating segmentation algorithms and measuring ecological statistics. In: ICCV (2001)
24. Mascelli, J.V.: The five C's of cinematography. Cine/Grafic Publications (1965)
25. Over, P., Smeaton, A.F., Awad, G.: The TRECVID 2008 BBC rushes summarization evaluation. In: Proc. ACM WS on Video Summarization (2008)
26. Smith, M., Kanade, T.: Video skimming and characterization through the combination of image and language understanding. In: Proc. on Content-Based Access of Image and Video Database (1998)
27. Viola, P., Jones, M.: Robust real-time face detection. IJCV (2004)
28. Wolf, W.: Key frame selection by motion analysis. Acoustics, Speech, and Signal Processing (1996)

Spatiotemporal Background Subtraction Using Minimum Spanning Tree and Optical Flow*

Mingliang Chen[1], Qingxiong Yang[1,**], Qing Li[1], Gang Wang[2],
and Ming-Hsuan Yang[3]

[1] Department of Computer Science
Multimedia software Engineering Research Centre (MERC)
City University of Hong Kong, Hong Kong, China
MERC-Shenzhen, Guangdong, China
[2] Nanyang Technological University, Singapore
[3] University of California, Merced

Abstract. Background modeling and subtraction is a fundamental research topic in computer vision. Pixel-level background model uses a Gaussian mixture model (GMM) or kernel density estimation to represent the distribution of each pixel value. Each pixel will be process independently and thus is very efficient. However, it is not robust to noise due to sudden illumination changes. Region-based background model uses local texture information around a pixel to suppress the noise but is vulnerable to periodic changes of pixel values and is relatively slow. A straightforward combination of the two cannot maintain the advantages of the two. This paper proposes a real-time integration based on robust estimator. Recent efficient minimum spanning tree based aggregation technique is used to enable robust estimators like M-smoother to run in real time and effectively suppress the noisy background estimates obtained from Gaussian mixture models. The refined background estimates are then used to update the Gaussian mixture models at each pixel location. Additionally, optical flow estimation can be used to track the foreground pixels and integrated with a temporal M-smoother to ensure temporally-consistent background subtraction. The experimental results are evaluated on both synthetic and real-world benchmarks, showing that our algorithm is the top performer.

Keywords: Background Modeling, Video Segmentation, Tracking, Optical Flow.

1 Introduction

Background modeling is one of the most extensively researched topics in computer vision. It is normally used as a fundamental pre-processing step in many

* This work was supported in part by a GRF grant from the Research Grants Council of Hong Kong (RGC Reference: CityU 122212), the NSF CAREER Grant #1149783 and NSF IIS Grant #1152576.
** Corresponding author.

D. Fleet et al. (Eds.): ECCV 2014, Part VII, LNCS 8695, pp. 521–534, 2014.
© Springer International Publishing Switzerland 2014

vision tasks, including video-surveillance, teleconferencing, video editing, human-computer interface, *etc.* It has recently experienced somewhat of a new era, as a result of publically available benchmarks for performance evaluation. These benchmarks simplify the comparison of a new algorithm against all the state-of-the-art algorithms. Both artificial pixel-level evaluation data sets [5] and real-world region-level data sets obtained by human experts [11] are available for comprehensive evaluation.

This paper focuses on traditional background subtraction problem with the assumption of a static video camera. There are significant publications on this topic, and can be classified into three broad categories: pixel-level background subtraction [9], [27], [8] [12], [33], [7], [10], region-level background subtraction [23], [15], [31], [14], frame-level background subtraction [32] and hybrid background subtraction [29] [28], [26], [13].

It is well understood that pixel-based models like mixture of Gaussians fail in sudden illumination changes. Region-based models on the other hand are more robust to these changes and tend to be vulnerable to periodic changes of pixel values. This paper proposes a way to synergistically combine the two to create a state-of-the-art background subtraction system.

The Gaussian mixture background model [27] is adopted in this paper. It is used to obtain an initial background estimate at each individual pixel location. Efficient minimum spanning tree (**MST**) based aggregation technique [30] is then integrated with a robust estimator - M-smoother to refine the initial estimates for a spatially-consistent background subtraction solution. The refined background estimates are then used to update the Gaussian mixture models to model stochastic changes in the value of each pixel. The updated Gaussian mixture models are thus robust to both periodic and sudden changes of pixel values. Note that comparing with the original Gaussian mixture background model [27], the extra computational cost is the **MST** based M-smoother, which is indeed extremely efficient. It takes about 6 ms to process a QVGA (320×240) color image on a single core CPU. Optical flow estimation is further employed to extend the proposed **MST** based M-smoother to the temporal domain to enhance temporal consistency. Although optical flow estimation is traditionally believed to be slow, recent fast nearest neighbor field [3] based optical flow algorithms like EPPM [2] enables the whole background subtraction pipeline to run in near realtime on state-of-the-art GPU.

The paper is organized as follows: Section 2 gives a brief overview of the Gaussian mixture background model adopted in the paper and the details of the proposed background modeling and subtraction algorithms. Section 3 reports results supporting the claims that the algorithm is currently the strongest available on standard benchmarks [5], [11]. Section 4 concludes.

2   Background Subtraction

A brief overview of Gaussian mixture background model is given in Sec. 2.1 and the proposed Spatially-consistent and temporally-consistent Background Models are presented in Sec. 2.2 and 2.3, respectively.

2.1   Gaussian Mixture Background Model

Stauffer and Grimson [27] propose to model the values of an image pixel as a mixture of Gaussians for background estimation. A pixel is considered to be background only when at least one of the Gaussians of the mixture includes its pixel value with sufficient and consistent evidence. The probability of observing a pixel value I_p^t at pixel p for frame t can be represented as follows

$$P(I_p^t) = \sum_{k=1}^{K} w_k^t \cdot \eta(I_p^t, \mu_k^t, \Sigma_k^t), \tag{1}$$

where η is a Gaussian probability density function

$$\eta(I_p^t, \mu_k^t, \Sigma_k^t) = \frac{1}{(2\pi)^{\frac{n}{2}} |\Sigma_k^t|^{\frac{1}{2}}} exp\left(-\frac{1}{2}(I_p^t - \mu_k^t)^T (\Sigma_k^t)^{-1}(I_p^t - \mu_k^t)\right), \tag{2}$$

μ_k^t and Σ_k^t are the mean value and the covariance matrix of the k-th Gaussian in the mixture at time t, respectively.

Each pixel has a total of K different Gaussian distributions. To adapt to illumination changes, the new pixel values from the following frames will be used to update the mixture model, as long as they can be represented by a major component of the model.

To handle background changes, Shimada et al. [26] propose to leverage information from a future period with an acceptable delay as 33 milliseconds (the duration of just one video frame). The use of the information observed in future image frames was demonstrated to improve the accuracy by about 30%.

2.2   Spatially-Consistent Background Modeling Based on Minimum Spanning Tree

The bidirectional GMM [26] has been demonstrated to be a very effective background model while being very efficient. However, each pixel is processed independently and thus is less robust to noise. Region-based background model uses local texture information around a pixel to suppress the noise but is relatively slow and vulnerable to periodic changes of pixel values.

This section assumes that connected pixels with similar pixel values shall have similar background estimates, and thus spatially-consistent background segmentation can be obtained. The similarity between every two pixels is then defined using the minimax path [24] between the two pixels by treating the video frame as a connected, undirected graph $G = (V, E)$. The vertices V are all the image pixels and the edges E are all the edges between the nearest neighboring pixels. Minimax path can identify region boundaries without high contrast and will not cross the boundary of thin-structured homogeneous object; and thus can preserve details. Additionally, minimax path can be efficiently extracted with the use of a minimum spanning tree (**MST**) [16]. Recent study show that a minimum spanning tree can be extracted from an 8-bit depth image in time linear in the number of image pixel [1].

Let $d(p, q)$ denote the minimax path between a pair of node $\{p, q\}$ for the current frame I^t and $b_p^t = \{0, 1\}$ denote the corresponding binary background estimates at pixel p obtained from Gaussian mixture background model. Minimax path $d(p, q) (= d(q, p))$ is then employed in a robust estimator - M-smoother [6] to handle outliers in the coarse estimates from mixture of Gaussians. The refined background estimates is

$$b_p^{t,spatial} = \arg\min_i \sum_{q \in I^t} exp(-\frac{d(p, q)}{\sigma})|i - b_q^t|^\alpha. \tag{3}$$

When $\alpha = 1$, Eq. (3) is indeed a weighted median filter that utilize the minimax path length and thus is aware of the underlying regularity of the video frame. Because $b_p^t = \{0, 1\}$, $(b_p^t)^\alpha = b_p^t$ and

$$b_p^{t,spatial} = \begin{cases} 1 \text{ if } \sum_{q \in I^t} exp(-\frac{d(p,q)}{\sigma}) \cdot b_q^t > \sum_{q \in I^t} exp(-\frac{d(p,q)}{\sigma}) \cdot |1 - b_q^t|, \\ 0 \text{ else.} \end{cases} \tag{4}$$

Let $\mathcal{B}^t$ denote an image whose pixel value is (b_q^t) at pixel q and $\mathcal{F}^t$ denote an image whose pixel value is $|1 - b_q^t|$ at pixel q for frame t. Let

$$\mathcal{B}_p^{t,\downarrow} = \sum_{q \in I^t} exp(-\frac{d(p, q)}{\sigma})\mathcal{B}_q^t \tag{5}$$

and

$$\mathcal{F}_p^{t,\downarrow} = \sum_{q \in I^t} exp(-\frac{d(p, q)}{\sigma})\mathcal{F}_q^t \tag{6}$$

denote the weighted aggregation result of image $\mathcal{B}^t$ and $\mathcal{F}^t$, respectively. Eq. (4) becomes

$$b_p^{t,spatial} = \begin{cases} 1 \text{ if } \mathcal{B}_q^{t,\downarrow} > \mathcal{F}_q^{t,\downarrow}, \\ 0 \text{ else.} \end{cases} \tag{7}$$

The new background estimate $b_p^{t,spatial}$ obtained from the proposed MST-based M-smoother will be used with the original estimate b_p^t to adjust the K Gaussian distributions, and the only difference is that the distributions will remain unchanged if either $b_p^{t,spatial}$ or b_p^t classifies pixel p as a foreground pixel. The noisy contribution from background pixel values for updating distributions can be significantly reduced using the spatially-consistent background estimates. As shown in Fig. 1 (b), part of the moving vehicle on the bottom right will be continuously detected as the background using Gaussian Mixture Model by adding foreground colors as new Gaussian distributions. Proposed MST-based M-smoother uses b_p^{new} as a new constrain to update Gaussian distributions and thus can correct most of the errors as can be seen in Fig. 1 (c).

(a)Video frame   (b)Mixture of Gaussians[27]   (c)Spatially-consistent

Fig. 1. Spatially-consistent background subtraction. (a) is a video frame extracted from the SABS data set [5] and (b) and (c) are foreground masks obtained from Gaussian mixture background model and the proposed spatially-consistent background model, respectively.

A Linear Time Solution. According to Eq. (7), the main computational complexity of the proposed proposed M-smoother resides in the weighted aggregation step in Eq. (5) and (6). The brute-force implementation of the nonlocal aggregation step is very slow. Nevertheless, the recursive matching cost aggregation solution proposed in [30] can be adopted:

$$\mathcal{B}_p^{t,\downarrow} = exp(-\frac{d(P(p),p)}{\sigma}) \cdot \mathcal{B}_{P(p)}^{t,\downarrow} + \left(1 - exp(-\frac{2 * d(p, P(p))}{\sigma})\right) \cdot \mathcal{B}_p^{t,\uparrow}, \quad (8)$$

where $P(p)$ denote the parent of node p, and

$$\mathcal{B}_p^{t,\uparrow} = \mathcal{B}_p^t + \sum_{P(q)=p} exp(-\frac{d(p,q)}{\sigma}) \cdot \mathcal{B}_q^{t,\uparrow}. \quad (9)$$

Note that for 8-bit depth images, $d(P(p),p) \in [0, 255]$ and $d(p,q) \in [0, 255]$ (when $P(q) = p$) and thus $exp(-\frac{d(P(p),p)}{\sigma})$ and $exp(-\frac{d(p,q)}{\sigma})$ can be extracted from a single lookup table and $\left(1 - exp(-\frac{2*d(p,P(p))}{\sigma})\right)$ can be extracted from another. Let T_1 and T_2 denote the two lookup tables, Eq. (8) and (9) can be written as

$$\mathcal{B}_p^{t,\downarrow} = T_1[d(P(p),p)] \cdot \mathcal{B}_{P(p)}^{t,\downarrow} + T_2[d(p, P(p))] \cdot \mathcal{B}_p^{t,\uparrow}, \quad (10)$$

$$\mathcal{B}_p^{t,\uparrow} = \mathcal{B}_p^t + \sum_{P(q)=p} T_1[d(p,q)] \cdot \mathcal{B}_q^{t,\uparrow}. \quad (11)$$

The computational complexity is now straightforward. Only a total of two addition operations and three multiplication operations are required at each pixel location; and thus is extremely efficient.

2.3 Temporally-Consistent Background Modeling Based on Optical Flow

This section extends the spatially-weighted M-smoother proposed in Sec. 2.2 to the temporal domain as follows:

$$b_p^{t,temporal} = \arg\min_i \sum_{j=1}^{t} \sum_{q_j \in I^j} W(p, q_j) |i - b_{q_j}^j|, \tag{12}$$

where the similarity measurement

$$W(p, q_j) = \begin{cases} 1 \text{ if } q_j \text{ is the correct correspondence of } p \text{ in frame } j, \\ 0 \text{ else.} \end{cases} \tag{13}$$

$W(p, q_j)$ is obtained directly from optical flow estimation with the assumption that the background estimate for the same object appearing in difference video frames should be identical. Theoretically, the most robust optical flow should be employed to obtain the best performance. However, most of the optical flow algorithms are slow. According to Middlebury benchmark statistics, an optical flow algorithm takes around 1 minute to process a VGA resolution video frame. As a result, to ensure practicality, EPPM [2] which is currently fastest optical flow algorithm is used in this paper. Although it is not the top performer on standard benchmarks, EPPM significantly improves the accuracy of the proposed background subtraction algorithm as discussed in Section 3.

Let $\Delta_p^{t,j}$ denote the motion vector between pixel p in frame t and its the correspondence pixel $p_j = p + \Delta_p^{t,j}$ in frame j and

$$v_p^t = \sum_{j=1}^{t} |b_{p+\Delta_p^{t,j}}^j|, \tag{14}$$

Eq. (12) can be simplified as follows:

$$b_p^{t,temporal} = \arg\min_i \sum_{j=1}^{t} |i - b_{p+\Delta_p^{t,j}}^j|, \tag{15}$$

$$= \begin{cases} 1 \text{ if } v_p^t > \frac{t}{2}, \\ 0 \text{ else.} \end{cases} \tag{16}$$

The direct implementation of Eq. (15) is extremely slow as optical flow estimation will be required between any two video frames, that is optical flow estimation are required for a total of $\frac{t(t-1)}{2}$ image pairs to obtain the motion vectors $\Delta_p^{t,j}$ for $j \in [1, t-1]$. In practice, a recursive implementation is used to approximate v_p^t in Eq. (14) so that optical flow estimation is required only between every two successive frames:

$$v_p^t = v_{p+\Delta_p^{t,t-1}}^{t-1} + |b_p^t|. \tag{17}$$

Spatiotemporal Background Modeling. A spatiotemporal background modeling solution can be directly obtained from Eq. (15) by replacing b_p^t with the spatially-consistent background estimates $b_p^{t,spatial}$ (from Section 2.2) in Eq. (17):

$$v_p^t = v_{p+\Delta_p^{t,t-1}}^{t-1} + |b_p^{t,spatial}|. \tag{18}$$

3 Experimental Results

In this section, the effectiveness of the proposed background subtraction method is experimentally verified for a variety of scenes using two standard benchmarks that use both artificial pixel-level evaluation data set [5] and real-world region-level data set obtained by human experts [11]. Visual or quantitative comparisons with the traditional model and recent methods are presented.

3.1 Evaluation Data Sets

Two public benchmarks containing both artificial and real-world scenes with different types of challenges were used for performance evaluation.

The first benchmark is SABS (Stuttgart Artificial Background Subtraction) [5], which is used for pixel-level evaluation of background models. Six artificial data sets used this benchmark cover a wide range of detection challenges. The *Dynamic Background* data set contains periodic or irregular movement in background such as waving trees or traffic lights; the *Bootstrapping* data set has no initialization data, thus subtraction starts after the first frame; the gradual scene change by varying the illumination constantly requires the segmentation when the contrast between background and foreground decreases in the *Darkening* data set; suddenly change are simulated in the *Light Switch* data set; the *Noisy Night* data set is severely affected by sensor noise which need to be coped with. Each data set contains 600 frames with the exception of *Darkening* and *Bootstrapping* both having 1400 frames. The sequences have a resolution of 800×600 pixels and are captured from a fixed viewpoint.

The second benchmark is ChangeDetection [11], which provide a realistic, camera-captured (no CGI), diverse set of videos. The real data sets used in this benchmark are representative of typical indoor and outdoor visual data captured today in surveillance, smart environment, and video database scenarios. A total of 31 video sequences with human labeled ground truth are used for testing. Similar to SABS benchmark, the video sequences are separated into six categories based on different types of challenges. The *Baseline* category represents a mixture of mild challenges typical of the other categories; The *Dynamic Background* category depicts outdoor scenes with strong (parasitic) background motion; The *Camera Jitter* category contains videos captured by unstable (e.g., vibrating) cameras; The *Shadows* category contains videos exhibiting strong as well as faint shadows; The *Intermittent Object Motion* category contains videos with scenarios known for causing "ghosting" artifacts in the detected motion, *i.e.*, objects move, then stop for a short while, after which they start moving again; The *Thermal* category contains videos captured by far-infrared cameras that result in typical thermal artifacts.

3.2 Evaluation Metric

The performance of an algorithm is evaluated on pixel-level, and the segmentation result of each pixel is a binary classification. The evaluation metric considers TP, FP and FN factors, where TP and FP denotes correctly and incorrectly classified foreground pixels respectively, FN denotes foreground pixels in GT are incorrectly classified background pixels. It also uses the F1-measure, a balance measure between precision and recall rate:

$$Precision = \frac{TP}{TP + FP}, Recall = \frac{TP}{TP + FN}, \tag{19}$$

$$F_1 = 2 \frac{Recall \cdot Precision}{Recall + Precision}. \tag{20}$$

The F1-Measures (averaged over sequence) and Precision-recall charts of the performance of the approach with varying threshold will be computed and compared with respect to different data sets.

3.3 Evaluation on SABS Benchmark

This section reports performance evaluation of proposed background subtraction algorithm on SABS benchmark [5]. The maximal F-measure of the proposed spatially-consistent background model and the extended spatiotemporal background model are presented and compared with nine other background models reported to the benchmark in Table 1.

The proposed models clearly outperform all the other models on this benchmark. The proposed spatially-consistent background model outperforms the latest bidirectional Case-based background model [26] in almost every data set as can be seen in table 1. Additionally, the extended spatiotemporal background model outperforms all the other models under all types of challenges.

The corresponding recall precision curves with respect to different challenges are presented in Fig. 2. As can be seen, the proposed spatiotemporal consistent background model obtains the highest recall ratio under the same precision level. The proposed spatiotemporal background model clearly outperforms the others under three challenges: dynamic background (*Dynamic Background* data set), sudden illumination changes (*Light Switch* data set) and sensor noise (*Noisy Night* data set). Note that region-based background models are fragile to the first challenge while pixel-level background models are not robust to last two; the proposed models synergistically combine the two to cope with all the challenges.

Table 1. F-measures for the $SABS$ benchmark [5]. The best and the 2th best performers are shown in red color and blue color, respectively. The last column presents the average F-measures. Note that the proposed spatially-consistent background subtraction algorithm outperforms the others on average, and the extended spatiotemporal algorithm outperforms all the other on all the six data sets with different types of challenges.

Approach	Basic	Dynamic Background	Bootstrap	Darkening	Light Switch	Noisy Night	Average
McFarlane[20]	0.614	0.482	0.541	0.496	0.211	0.203	0.425
Stauffer[27]	0.800	0.704	0.642	0.404	0.217	0.194	0.494
Oliver[22]	0.635	0.552	-	0.300	0.198	0.213	0.380
McKenna[21]	0.522	0.415	0.301	0.484	0.306	0.098	0.354
Li[18]	0.766	0.641	0.678	0.704	0.316	0.047	0.525
Kim[17]	0.582	0.341	0.318	0.342	-	-	0.396
Zivkovic[33]	0.768	0.704	0.632	0.620	0.300	0.321	0.558
Maddalena[19]	0.766	0.715	0.495	0.663	0.213	0.263	0.519
Barnich[4]	0.761	0.711	0.685	0.678	0.268	0.271	0.562
AtsushiShimada[26]	0.723	0.623	0.708	0.577	0.335	0.475	0.574
Proposed (spatial)	0.764	0.747	0.669	0.672	0.364	0.519	0.623
Proposed (spatiotemporal)	0.813	0.788	0.736	0.753	0.515	0.680	0.714

3.4   Evaluation on ChangeDetection Benchmark

This section evaluates the proposed method using a real-world region-level benchmark - *ChangeDetection* with data sets obtained by human experts. Due to the lack of pixel-level accuracy in the ground-truth labels, a post-processing step like median filter is normally required for all background subtraction algorithms. As a result, the MST-based M-smoother proposed in Sec. 2.2 were applied to our background subtraction results as a post-processing step.

Table 2 presents the detailed evaluation results of the proposed background subtraction models on different types of challenges in terms of F-measure. Note that the proposed methods outperform the state of the art on this benchmark, especially when the *Shadow* category is excluded. The performance of the proposed models is good for most of the categories, especially on *Baseline, Camera Jitter, Intermittent Object Motion* and *Thermal* categories. Both of the proposed models are the either the best or second best performer on these four categories. Some of the extracted foreground mask are presented in Fig. 3 for visual evaluation.

The performance of the proposed method is surprisingly low on the *Shadow* category as visible in Table 2 and Fig. 4. This is because as we believe that *shadow deserves to be processed separately* and thus is not considered in the proposed background models. The performance on *Shadow* category can be greatly improved with the use of an existing shadow detection algorithm like [25].

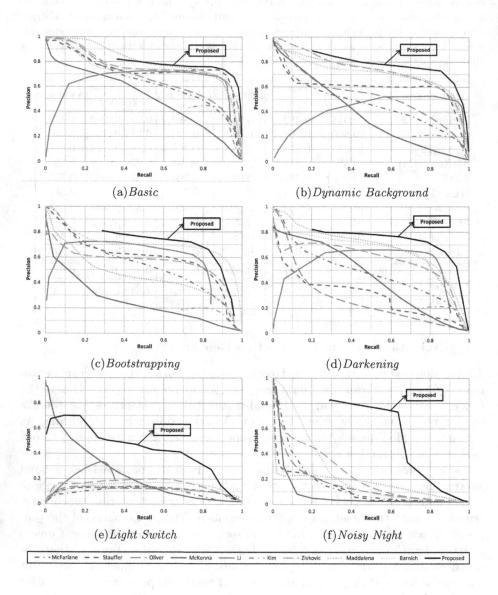

(a) *Basic*

(b) *Dynamic Background*

(c) *Bootstrapping*

(d) *Darkening*

(e) *Light Switch*

(f) *Noisy Night*

Fig. 2. Precision-recall charts for SABS benchmark [5] with different challenges. The dark solid curve presents the performance of the proposed spatiotemporal background subtraction algorithm. Note that it outperforms all the others overall.

Table 2. F-measures for *ChangeDetection* benchmark. The best and the 2th best performers are shown in red color and blue color, respectively. The last two columns present the average F-measures including and excluding the *Shadow* category. Note that the proposed spatially-consistent background subtraction algorithm is comparable to the state-of-the-art algorithms, and the extended spatiotemporal algorithm outperforms all the others on average when shadows detection is required. However, the improvement is not significant. This is mainly because shadow modeling is not included in the proposed algorithms as we believe that shadow detection deserves to be considered separately. The improvement over the current state of the art is more significant when the *Shadow* category is excluded as shown in the last column.

Approach	Baseline	Dynamic Background	Camera Jitter	Intermittent Object Motion	Shadow	Thermal	Average (Shadow)	(no Shadow)
PBAS-PID	0.9248	0.7357	0.7206	0.6267	0.8617	0.7622	0.7720	0.7540
DPGMM	0.9286	0.8137	0.7477	0.5418	0.8127	0.8134	0.7763	0.7690
Spectral-360	0.9330	0.7872	0.7156	0.5656	0.8843	0.7764	0.7770	0.7556
CwisarD	0.9075	0.8086	0.7814	0.5674	0.8412	0.7619	0.7780	0.7654
GPRMF	0.9280	0.7726	0.8596	0.4870	0.8889	0.8305	0.7944	0.7755
Proposed (spatial)	0.9250	0.7882	0.7413	0.6755	0.7606	0.8423	0.7888	0.7945
Proposed (spatiotemporal)	0.9345	0.8193	0.7522	0.6780	0.7764	0.8571	0.8029	0.8082

3.5   Computational Cost

This section reports the computational cost of the proposed background modeling and subtraction algorithms in Table 3. The proposed approach are tested on a laptop computer with a 2.3 GHz Intel Core i7 CPU and 4 GB memory. Similar to [26], the runtime of the proposed algorithms were evaluated with respect to GMM [27]. Comparing to the bidirectional GMM [26], the main additional cost of the proposed spatially-consistent background model is the use of the proposed MST-based M-smoother. Luckily, the computational complexity of this M-smoother is extremely low as has been analysis in Sec. 2.2. The total computational cost is higher than [26] but has a higher performance. The computational cost of proposed spatiotemporally-consistent background model is much higher due to the use of optical flow which is known to be slow. Nevertheless, near real-time performance (over 12 frames per second) can be obtained for QVGA-resolution videos when a state-of-the-art GPU is available.

Table 3. Computational cost of the proposed background modeling algorithms for QVGA-resolution videos (milliseconds/frame)

Method	GMM [27]	Bidirectional GMM [26]	Proposed (spatial)	Proposed (spatiotemporal)	
		CPU		CPU	GPU
Time	12	5	15	982	83

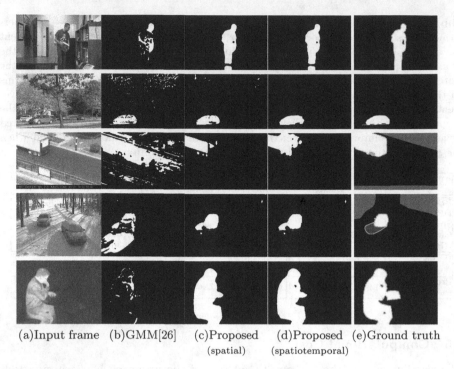

(a)Input frame   (b)GMM[26]   (c)Proposed   (d)Proposed   (e)Ground truth
                                (spatial)   (spatiotemporal)

Fig. 3. Visual comparison using foreground mask. From top to bottom: video frames extracted *Baseline, Dynamic Background, Camera Jitter, Intermittent Object Motion* and *Thermal* categories. (a) are the video frames extracted from different categories, (b) to (d) are the corresponding foreground masks obtained from GMM, proposed spatially-consistent and spatiotemporally-consistent background models, respectively and (e) are the ground-truth masks. As can be seen, the proposed extensions obviously outperforms the original GMM algorithm.

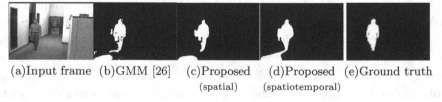

(a)Input frame   (b)GMM [26]   (c)Proposed   (d)Proposed   (e)Ground truth
                                (spatial)   (spatiotemporal)

Fig. 4. Visual comparison on *Shadow* category using foreground mask. GMM and the proposed background models do not detect shadows and thus cannot separate shadow from foreground.

4 Conclusions

In this paper, a background modeling and subtraction algorithm based on **MST** and optical flow estimation was proposed. The **MST** is used to form an efficient weighted M-smoother to enhance the spatial consistency while optical flow estimation is used to track the motion of image pixels to extend the proposed **MST** based M-smoother to the temporal domain.

Our algorithm is outperforming all other algorithms on both *SABS* and *ChangeDetection* benchmarks, but there is space left for improvement. For instance, our algorithm simply adopts the currently fastest optical flow algorithm [2] to ensure that the proposed algorithm is practical. However, other optical flow algorithms that are relatively slow but more accurate have not yet tested. They can potentially increase the performance of the proposed spatiotemporal background subtraction algorithm. Another question that was left for further study is how to adjust the algorithm for a moving camera.

References

1. Bao, L., Song, Y., Yang, Q., Yuan, H., Wang, G.: Tree filtering: Efficient structure-preserving smoothing with a minimum spanning tree. IEEE Transactions on Image Processing (2014)
2. Bao, L., Yang, Q., Jin, H.: Fast edge-preserving patchmatch for large displacement optical flow. In: CVPR (2014)
3. Barnes, C., Shechtman, E., Finkelstein, A., Goldman, D.: Patchmatch: a randomized correspondence algorithm for structural image editing. TOG (2009)
4. Barnich, O., Droogenbroeck, M.V.: Vibe: A powerful random technique to estimate the background in video sequences. In: IEEE Int. Conf. on Acoustics, Speech and Signal Processing (2009)
5. Brutzer, S., Hoferlin, B., Heidemann, G.: Evaluation of background subtraction techniques for video surveillance. In: CVPR (2011)
6. Chu, C., Glad, I., Godtliebsen, F., Marron, J.: Edgepreserving smoothers for image processing. Journal of the American Statistical Association (1998)
7. Comaniciu, D., Zhu, Y., Davis, L.: Sequential kernel density approximation and its application to real-time visual tracking. PAMI 30(7), 1186–1197 (2008)
8. Elgammal, A.M., Duraiswami, R., Harwood, D., Davis, L.S.: Background and foreground modeling using non-parametric kernel density estimation for visual surveillance. Proceedings of the IEEE (2002)
9. Elgammal, A., Harwood, D., Davis, L.: Non-parametric model for background subtraction. In: Vernon, D. (ed.) ECCV 2000. LNCS, vol. 1843, pp. 751–767. Springer, Heidelberg (2000)
10. Elqursh, A., Elgammal, A.: Online moving camera background subtraction. In: Fitzgibbon, A., Lazebnik, S., Perona, P., Sato, Y., Schmid, C. (eds.) ECCV 2012, Part VI. LNCS, vol. 7577, pp. 228–241. Springer, Heidelberg (2012)
11. Goyette, N., Jodoin, P.M., Porikli, F., Konrad, J., Ishwar, P.: changedetection.net: A new change detection benchmark dataset. In: IEEE Workshop on Change Detection at CVPR (2012)
12. Han, B., Comaniciu, D., Davis, L.: Sequential kernel density approximation through mode propagation: Applications to background modeling. In: ACCV (2004)

13. Han, B., Davis, L.S.: Density-based multifeature background subtraction with support vector machine. PAMI 34(5), 1017–1023 (2012)
14. Han, B., Davis, L.: Adaptive Background Modeling and Subtraction: A Density-Based Approach with Multiple Features. CRC Press (2010)
15. Heikkila, M., Pietikainen, M.: A texture-based method for modeling the background and detecting moving objects. PAMI 28(4), 657–662 (2006)
16. Hu, T.: The maximum capacity route problem. Operations Research (1961)
17. Kim, K., Chalidabhongse, T., Harwood, D., Davis, L.: Real-time foreground-background segmentation using codebook model. Real-Time Imaging 11(3) (2005)
18. Li, L., Huang, W., Gu, I., Tian, Q.: Foreground object detection from videos containing complex background. In: Int. Conf. on Multimedia, pp. 2–10 (2003)
19. Maddalena, L., Petrosino, A.: A self-organizing approach to background subtraction for visual surveillance applications. IEEE Transactions on Image Processing 17(7) (2008)
20. McFarlane, N., Schofield, C.: Segmentation and tracking of piglets in images. Machine Vision and Applications 8(3), 187–193 (1995)
21. McKenna, S.J., Jabri, S., Duric, Z., Rosenfeld, A., Wechsler, H.: Tracking groups of people. Computer Vision and Image Understanding 80(1) (2000)
22. Oliver, N., Rosario, B., Pentland, A.: A bayesian computer vision system for modeling human interactions. PAMI 22(8), 831 (2000)
23. Parag, T., Elgammal, A.M., Mittal, A.: A framework for feature selection for background subtraction. In: CVPR (2006)
24. Pollack, M.: The maximum capacity through a network. Operations Research (1960)
25. Prati, A., Mikic, I., Trivedi, M., Cucchiara, R.: Detecting moving shadows: Formulation, algorithms and evaluation. PAMI 25(7), 918–924 (2003)
26. Shimada, A., Nagahara, H., Taniguchi, R.: Background modeling based on bidirectional analysis. In: CVPR, pp. 1979–1986 (2013)
27. Stauffer, C., Grimson, E.: Adaptive background mixture models for real-time tracking. In: CVPR, pp. 2246–2252 (1999)
28. Tanaka, T., Shimada, A., Taniguchi, R.-I., Yamashita, T., Arita, D.: Towards robust object detection: Integrated background modeling based on spatio-temporal features. In: Zha, H., Taniguchi, R.-I., Maybank, S. (eds.) ACCV 2009, Part I. LNCS, vol. 5994, pp. 201–212. Springer, Heidelberg (2010)
29. Toyama, K., Krumm, J., Brumitt, B., Meyers, B.: Wallflower: Principle and practice of background maintenance. In: ICCV (1999)
30. Yang, Q.: A non-local cost aggregation method for stereo matching. In: CVPR, pp. 1402–1409 (2012)
31. Yoshinaga, S., Shimada, A., Nagahara, H., Taniguchi, R.-I.: Object detection using local difference patterns. In: Kimmel, R., Klette, R., Sugimoto, A. (eds.) ACCV 2010, Part IV. LNCS, vol. 6495, pp. 216–227. Springer, Heidelberg (2011)
32. Zhang, S., Yao, H., Liu, S.: Dynamic background modeling and subtraction using spatio-temporal local binary patterns. In: ICIP (2008)
33. Zivkovic, Z., Heijden, F.: Efficient adaptive density estimation per image pixel for the task of background subtraction. Pattern Recognition Letters 27, 773–780 (2006)

Robust Foreground Detection Using Smoothness and Arbitrariness Constraints

Xiaojie Guo[1], Xinggang Wang[2], Liang Yang[1,3], Xiaochun Cao[1,*], and Yi Ma[4]

[1] State Key Laboratory of Information Security, IIE, Chinese Academy of Sciences
[2] Department of EI, Huazhong University of Science and Technology, China
[3] School of Information Engineering, Tianjin University of Commerce, China
[4] School of Information Science and Technology, ShanghaiTech University, China
xj.max.guo@gmail.com, xgwang@hust.edu.cn,
{yangliang,caoxiaochun}@iie.ac.cn, mayi@shanghaitech.edu.cn

Abstract. Foreground detection plays a core role in a wide spectrum of applications such as tracking and behavior analysis. It, especially for videos captured by fixed cameras, can be posed as a component decomposition problem, the background of which is typically assumed to lie in a low dimensional subspace. However, in real world cases, dynamic backgrounds like waving trees and water ripples violate the assumption. Besides, noises caused by the image capturing process and, camouflage and lingering foreground objects would also significantly increase the difficulty of accurate foreground detection. That is to say, simply imposing the correlation constraint on the background is no longer sufficient for such cases. To overcome the difficulties mentioned above, this paper proposes to further take into account foreground characteristics including 1) the smoothness: the foreground object should appear coherently in spatial domain and move smoothly in temporal, and 2) the arbitrariness: the appearance of foreground could be with arbitrary colors or intensities. With the consideration of the smoothness and the arbitrariness of foreground as well as the correlation of (static) background, we formulate the problem in a unified framework from a probabilistic perspective, and design an effective algorithm to seek the optimal solution. Experimental results on both synthetic and real data demonstrate the clear advantages of our method compared to the state of the art alternatives.

1 Introduction

Foreground detection is fundamental to numerous computer vision applications like tracking [26,17] and behavior analysis [4], as the foreground is usually of more interest and matters more than the background to further analysis. The problem of foreground detection can be viewed as a decomposition of a video into the foreground component and the background. From this view of point, it can be achieved through either foreground or background modeling, which

---

* Corresponding author.

D. Fleet et al. (Eds.): ECCV 2014, Part VII, LNCS 8695, pp. 535–550, 2014.

mainly derives object detector based, motion based, and background construction based approaches. Object detectors are generally built by offline training [21] or online learning [1], which perform as classifiers to determine whether a target region (often searched by a sliding window) belongs to the foreground or the background. But, most of offline trained detectors are based on separate datasets, which would be insufficiently discriminative for different cases and thus lead to poor performance. The online learned ones require an initialization by manually labeling at the start of a video, which limits the applicability in automated systems. As for motion-based methods [20,3,19], they avoid such training and learning phases by exploiting motion patterns to classify pixels into different groups. This kind of methods can deal with the cases in the presence of camera motion, but the objects are assumed to move regularly [20,3] in respective regions, which is often violated in practical situations.

Alternatively, constructing the background that is always present, seems to be more simple and easier than modeling the foreground that may be of diverse appearance and complex motion. Background subtraction [8] is probably the most straightforward method in this category. The difference image can be obtained by subtracting the reference background from the current frame in a pixel-wise manner, which is the etymology of background subtraction. If the absolute difference exceeds a threshold, the pixel in question is declared to belong to the foreground. Temporal average and median filtering are two of classical background subtraction methods. These approaches are simple and efficient, but extremely sensitive because it assumes a static background with well behaved objects. In practice, this is almost never the case. To remedy the sensitivity, simple Gaussian [24] is proposed to represent each background pixel using a Gaussian model, the pixel is determined to be the background if it falls into a deviation around the mean, otherwise the foreground. A more robust strategy [18] is to record the possible values of each pixel of the background image over time by a mixture of Gaussians. Instead of modeling the feature vectors of each pixel by a mixture of several Gaussians, Elgammal *et al.* [5] try to evaluate the probability of a background pixel using a nonparametric kernel density estimation based on very recent historical samples in the image sequence. In order to achieve the quick adaptation to changes in the scene and low false positive rates, they design a scheme to combine the results of the short-term and long-term background models for better updating decisions. Maddalena and Petrosino [12] propose an approach based on self organization through artificial neural networks, which claims to be robust to multiple situations such as gradual illumination changes.

Although the methods mentioned above provide promising progresses in foreground detection, they are rarely aware of the intensive global correlation of background across different frames. By considering the correlation (low rank) prior, it is natural to formulate the background as a linearly correlated model, which turns out to be a classic problem of learning a low dimensional linear model from high dimensional data. Mathematically, let $O \in \mathcal{R}^{m \times n}$ be the observation matrix containing n frames. Each column of O corresponds to a vectorized frame that has m pixels. O can be decomposed into two components, *i.e.* $O = B + R$, where $B \in \mathcal{R}^{m \times n}$ and $R \in \mathcal{R}^{m \times n}$ denote the background and the residual, respectively. Consequently, the objective can be designed as:

$$\underset{B,R}{\operatorname{argmin}} \operatorname{rank}(B) + \alpha \Upsilon(R), \quad \text{s.t.} \quad O = B + R, \tag{1}$$

where $\operatorname{rank}(B)$ computes the rank of B and is usually substituted by the nuclear norm, *i.e.* $\|B\|_*$, to make it convex and computationally tractable, and α is the weight with respect to $\Upsilon(R)$ that acts as the regularizer on the residual. If $\Upsilon(R) \doteq \|R\|_0$ is employed, Eq. (1) becomes the problem of Robust PCA (RPCA) that is designed to be robust to sparse outliers with arbitrary magnitudes, where $\| \cdot \|_0$ denotes the ℓ^0 norm. But the problem is intractable and extremely difficult to approximate due to the non-convexity of ℓ^0. Alternatively, ℓ^1 norm can be employed as the convex surrogate of ℓ^0, which is optimal for Laplacian distribution. Based on the convex relaxation, many solutions have been investigated [2,28]. Moreover, the online extensions [7,25] broaden the applicable range of RPCA for the tasks with the requirement of incremental processing. Based on the advanced solutions and extensions, plenty of interesting applications have been developed [14,27]. Equivalently, B can be replaced with UV^T, where $U \in \mathcal{R}^{m \times r}$ and $V \in \mathcal{R}^{n \times r}$ (usually $r \ll \min\{m, n\}$). That is to say, the rank of UV^T is guaranteed to be never over r, thus the rank term can be discarded. By casting the problem into probabilistic models, [22,13,23,6] have proven to be effective to solve this problem.

However, in real world cases, only imposing the global correlation constraint on the background component is inadequate, as the dynamic background, like waving trees and water ripples, breaks the low rank assumption, and the noise caused by the image capturing process, and the camouflage also significantly increase the difficulty of accurately detecting foregrounds. Actually, some useful properties of foreground could be exploited jointly with the correlation of background for improving the performance. Specifically, the foreground should appear coherently in space and move smoothly in time. We call this property the smoothness. [29] and [23] utilize Markov Random Field (MRF) constraints directly on the foreground support to guarantee the spatial and temporal smoothness, which provide desirable results but with relatively high computational complexities. Instead, we propose a more efficient solution than MRF by using a total variation (TV) regularizer [15]. In addition, the appearance of foreground could be with any values. Even though the background is unknown in advance, the residual caused by foreground distributes the same as the foreground. That is to say, R caused by foreground is more like uniformly distributed than either Gaussian or Laplacian. We name this characteristic of foreground the arbitrariness. In this work, we focus on how to harness the arbitrariness and the smoothness of foreground and the global correlation of background for boosting the performance of foreground detection.

The main contributions of this paper can be summarized as follows:

- Our framework harnesses three priors, including the arbitrariness of foreground appearance, the spatial-temporal smoothness of foreground, and the correlation of background, in a unified fashion.

- We design an effective and efficient algorithm to seek the optimal solution of the associated optimization problem based on Augmented Lagrangian Multiplier with Alternating Direction Minimizing (ALM-ADM) strategy. Extensive experiments are conducted to demonstrate the efficacy of our method.

2   Our Method

2.1   Problem Formulation

Recall that each element $O_{ij}(i = 1, 2, ..., m; j = 1, 2, ...n)$ of the observation matrix O can be modeled as $O_{ij} = U_i V_j^T + R_{ij}$, where U_i and V_i are the ith row vectors of U and V, respectively. Since a foreground pixel can be any value within a bounded range, the corresponding residual falls into $[-U_i V_j^T, 255 - U_i V_j^T]$ (the arbitrariness). Thus, we can assume they follow the uniform distribution $\frac{1}{256}$. As for the residuals caused by the other factors, we simply assume they (approximately) follow a Gaussian distribution $\mathcal{N}(0, \sigma^2)$[5]. Let π^u and π^g be the percentages of foreground and the other, respectively, which we actually do not know in advance. As a result, each R_{ij} can be seen as a sample from a mixture model of distributions with probability $p(R_{ij}) = \pi^g \mathcal{N}(R_{ij}|0, \sigma^2) + \pi^u \frac{1}{256}$, where $\pi^g + \pi^u = 1$. Then the likelihood of O can be written as:

$$p(O|U, V, \Theta) = \prod_{i,j} p(O_{ij}|U_i V_j^T, \Theta) = \prod_{i,j} \left(\pi^g \mathcal{N}(O_{ij}|U_i V_j^T, \sigma^2) + \frac{\pi^u}{256} \right), \quad (2)$$

where $\Theta = \{\sigma^2, \pi^g, \pi^u\}$ is a parameter vector. The negative log-likelihood functional of Eq. (2) is given as follows:

$$\mathcal{L}(U, V, \Theta) = -\sum_{i,j} \log \left(\pi^g \mathcal{N}(O_{ij}|U_i V_j^T, \sigma^2) + \frac{\pi^u}{256} \right). \quad (3)$$

By applying Lemma 1 on $\mathcal{L}(U, V, \Theta)$, we have:

$$\mathcal{C}(U, V, \Theta, \Phi) = \sum_{i,j} \Phi_{ij}^g (\log \Phi_{ij}^g - \log \pi^g \mathcal{N}(O_{ij}|U_i V_j^T, \sigma^2)) + \Phi_{ij}^u (\log \Phi_{ij}^u - \log \frac{\pi^u}{256}), \quad (4)$$

with an additional variable (hidden parameter) Φ.

Lemma 1. *(Commutativity of Log-Sum operations. [11]) Given two functions $\pi_k(x) > 0$ and $p_k(x) > 0$, we have:*

$$-\log \sum_{k=1}^{K} \pi_k(x) p_k(x) = \min_{\Phi(x) \in \Delta_+} -\sum_{k=1}^{K} \Phi_k(x) \log(\pi_k(x) p_k(x)) + \sum_{k=1}^{K} \Phi_k(x) \log \Phi_k(x),$$

where $\Phi(x) = \{\Phi_1(x), \Phi_2(x), , ..., \Phi_K(x)\}$ are hidden parameters, and $\Delta_+ = \{\Phi(x) : 0 < \Phi_k(x) < 1, and \sum_{k=1}^{K} \Phi_k(x) = 1\}$ is a convex relaxation of a characteristic function decomposition.

---

[5] Although these residuals may be not pure Gaussian, our method can effectively handle this issue thanks to the smoothness, which will be demonstrated in Sec. 3.

As can be seen from Eq. (4), minimizing $\mathcal{C}(\boldsymbol{U},\boldsymbol{V},\Theta,\Phi)$ will give a minimizer of $\mathcal{L}(\boldsymbol{U},\boldsymbol{V},\Theta)$, which can be processed easily and efficiently as it becomes a quadratic function by interchanging the logarithm and summation operations. The following propositions further show good properties of $\mathcal{C}(\boldsymbol{U},\boldsymbol{V},\Theta,\Phi)$ that inspire the design of our method.

Proposition 1. *Both* $\mathcal{C}(\boldsymbol{U},\boldsymbol{V},\Theta,\Phi)$ *and* $\mathcal{L}(\boldsymbol{U},\boldsymbol{V},\Theta)$ *have the same global minimizer* $(\boldsymbol{U}^*,\boldsymbol{V}^*,\Theta^*)$ *if* $\Phi \in \Delta_+$.

Moreover, if the following Alternating Direction Minimizing (ADM) strategy is employed to minimize $\mathcal{C}(\boldsymbol{U},\boldsymbol{V},\Theta,\Phi)$:

$$\Phi^{t+1} = \underset{\Phi \in \Delta_+}{\arg\min}\, \mathcal{C}(\boldsymbol{U}^t,\boldsymbol{V}^t,\Theta^t,\Phi);$$
$$(\boldsymbol{U}^{t+1},\boldsymbol{V}^{t+1},\Theta^{t+1}) = \underset{\boldsymbol{U},\boldsymbol{V},\Theta}{\arg\min}\, \mathcal{C}(\boldsymbol{U},\boldsymbol{V},\Theta,\Phi^{t+1}), \tag{5}$$

the energy of $\mathcal{L}(\boldsymbol{U},\boldsymbol{V},\Theta)$ will gradually decrease as the two steps iterate (Proposition 2). That is to say, the local convergence of the problem is guaranteed.

Proposition 2. *The sequence* $(\boldsymbol{U}^t,\boldsymbol{V}^t,\Theta^t)$ *computed by (5) leads to*

$$\mathcal{L}(\boldsymbol{U}^{t+1},\boldsymbol{V}^{t+1},\Theta^{t+1}) \leq \mathcal{L}(\boldsymbol{U}^t,\boldsymbol{V}^t,\Theta^t). \tag{6}$$

We observe that the foreground objects, such as cars and pedestrians, should appear to be spatially coherent and move smoothly in temporal. Thus, imposing a temporal-spatial smoothness constraint on foreground would boost the performance of foreground detection. Let us here revisit the model of the observed matrix $\boldsymbol{O}$ from another viewpoint, *i.e.* $\boldsymbol{O} = \mathcal{P}_\Omega(\boldsymbol{B}) + \mathcal{P}_{\Omega^\perp}(\boldsymbol{F})$, where $\mathcal{P}_\Omega(\cdot)$ is the orthogonal projection operator on the support $\Omega \in \{0,1\}^{m\times n}$, and $\Omega^\perp \in \{0,1\}^{m\times n}$ stands for the complementary support of Ω. Based on the above observation, it is intuitive to enforce the temporal-spatial smoothness on the support Ω (or $\Omega^\perp$ equivalently). But, the binary support is unknown in advance, that is to say, directly operating on the unknown binary support is extremely difficult. Moreover, the residual reflects the difference between the observation and the background, rather than the support of foreground object. Therefore, it is still improper to impose the temporal-spatial smoothness on the residual component $\boldsymbol{R}$ without assumptions.

Alternatively, as we have introduced, the hidden variable Φ can perform as the term with the smoothness property. In this work, we only take into account Φ^g because Φ^u performs actually the same as Φ^g due to $\Phi^g + \Phi^u = 1$. Please consider an extreme case that if the Gaussian function of mean 0 and variance σ^2 goes to 0 infinitesimally, each Φ^g_{ij} equals to 1 if $\boldsymbol{O}_{ij} = \boldsymbol{U}_i\boldsymbol{V}_j^T$, otherwise 0. For our problem, we relax the restrict binary requirement of support to a continuous value range $(0,1)^6$, in which σ^2 controls the width of the interface between 0

---

[6] The reason why the range is $(0,1)$ instead of $[0,1]$ is to satisfy $\Phi \in \Delta_+$ introduced in Lemma 1. This can be easily done by adding a very small $\epsilon = 10^{-7}$ to Φ^u and Φ^g, then normalizing them by letting their summation be 1.

and 1. As a consequence, the regularization of smoothness on foreground can be achieved by imposing the anisotropic total variation on Φ^g, which is defined as:

$$\|\Phi^g\|_{tv} = \sum_{i,j} |[D_h\Phi^g]_{ij}| + |[D_v\Phi^g]_{ij}| + |[D_t\Phi^g]_{ij}|, \tag{7}$$

where D_h, D_v and D_t are the forward finite difference operators in horizontal, vertical and temporal directions, respectively. By slightly transforming the form of (7), we have $\|\Phi^g\|_{tv} = \|D\Phi^g\|_1$, where $D = [D_h^T, D_v^T, D_t^T]^T$.

By putting all the concerns aforementioned together, we can naturally formulate the problem of robust foreground detection in the following shape:

$$\min_{U,V,\Theta,\Phi} \mathcal{C}(U, V, \Theta, \Phi) + \lambda\|D\Phi^g\|_1, \tag{8}$$

where λ is the weight of the smoothness regularizer.

2.2   Optimization

As can be seen from Eq. (8), it is difficult to directly optimize because the total variation regularizer breaks the linear structure of Φ^g. To efficiently and effectively solve the problem, we introduce two auxiliary variables to make the problem separable, which gives the following constraint minimizing problem:

$$\min_{U,V,\Theta,\Phi} \mathcal{C}(U, V, \Theta, \Phi) + \lambda\|T\|_1, \quad \text{s.t.}\quad W = \Phi^g, T = DW. \tag{9}$$

For the above constraint minimizing problem, the penalty technique [10] can be adopted to change the constraint problem (9) into the unconstraint one in the following shape:

$$\begin{cases} \mathcal{Q}(U, V, \Theta, \Phi, T, W) = \mathcal{C}(U, V, \Theta, \Phi) + \lambda\|T\|_1 + \dfrac{\mu}{2}\|W - \Phi^g\|_F^2 \\ \quad + <X, W - \Phi^g> + \dfrac{\mu}{2}\|T - DW\|_F^2 + <Y, T - DW>, \end{cases} \tag{10}$$

where $\|\cdot\|_F$ denotes the Frobenius norm, $< \cdot, \cdot >$ represents matrix inner product, X and Y are the Lagrangian multipliers, and μ is a positive penalty scalar. Below are the solutions of the sub-problems based on the ADM strategy.

Φ **Sub-problem:** For computing $\hat{\Phi}_{ij}^{u\,(t+1)}$, we take derivative of $\mathcal{Q}$ with respect to Φ_{ij}^u with the unrelated terms fixed and set it to zero, then obtain:

$$\hat{\Phi}_{ij}^{u\,(t+1)} = \underset{\Phi_{ij}^u}{\arg\min}\, \mathcal{Q}(U^{(t)}, V^{(t)}, \Theta^{(t)}, \Phi^u, \Phi^{g(t)}, T^{(t)}, W^{(t)}) = \frac{\pi^{u(t)}}{256\exp(1)}. \tag{11}$$

Similarly, the problem corresponding to $\hat{\Phi}_{ij}^g$ turns out to be:

$$
\begin{cases}
\hat{\Phi}_{ij}^{g\ (t+1)} = \underset{\Phi_{ij}^g}{\arg\min}\ \mathcal{Q}(\boldsymbol{U}^{(t)},\boldsymbol{V}^{(t)},\Theta^{(t)},\Phi^{u(t+1)},\Phi^g,\boldsymbol{T}^{(t)},\boldsymbol{W}^{(t)}) \\[2mm]
\qquad = \underset{\Phi_{ij}^g}{\arg\min}\ -\Phi_{ij}^g\log\dfrac{\pi^{g(t)}}{\sqrt{2\pi\sigma^{2(t)}}}\exp\Big(\dfrac{-(O_{ij}-\boldsymbol{U}_i^{(t)}\boldsymbol{V}_j^{(t)T})^2}{2\sigma^{2(t)}}\Big) \\[4mm]
\qquad\quad +\ \Phi_{ij}^g\log\Phi_{ij}^g + \dfrac{\mu^{(t)}}{2}(\boldsymbol{W}_{ij}^{(t)}-\Phi_{ij}^g)^2 + \boldsymbol{X}_{ij}^{(t)}\Phi_{ij}^g,
\end{cases} \tag{12}
$$

However, the quadratic term in (12), i.e. $\frac{\mu^{(t)}}{2}(\boldsymbol{W}_{ij}^{(t)}-\Phi_{ij}^g)^2$, destroys the closed form solution of Φ_{ij}^g. For addressing this difficulty, we introduce pixel-wise weights $\eta_{ij}^{(t)}$ such that $\eta_{ij}^{(t)} = \frac{\boldsymbol{W}_{ij}^{(t)}-\Phi_{ij}^{g(t)}}{2}$ to approximate the original quadratic term. That is to say, we replace $\frac{\mu^{(t)}}{2}(\boldsymbol{W}_{ij}^{(t)}-\Phi_{ij}^g)^2$ with $\mu^{(t)}\eta_{ij}^{(t)}(\boldsymbol{W}_{ij}^{(t)}-\Phi_{ij}^g)$. Thus, the solution of (12) can be easily computed by:

$$
\hat{\Phi}_{ij}^{g\ (t+1)} = \frac{\pi^{g(t)}\exp\Big(\dfrac{-(O_{ij}-\boldsymbol{U}_i^{(t)}\boldsymbol{V}_j^{(t)T})^2}{2\sigma^{2(t)}}\Big)}{\sqrt{2\pi\sigma^{2(t)}}\exp\big(1-\mu^{(t)}\eta_{ij}^{(t)}-\boldsymbol{X}_{ij}^{(t)}\big)}. \tag{13}
$$

The final $\Phi_{ij}^{u(t+1)}$ and $\Phi_{ij}^{g(t+1)}$ are obtained by enforcing their summation to be 1, thus we have:

$$
\Phi_{ij}^{u(t+1)} = \frac{\sqrt{2\pi\sigma^{2(t)}}\pi^{u(t)}\exp\big(-\mu^{(t)}\eta_{ij}^{(t)}-\boldsymbol{X}_{ij}^{(t)}\big)}{\sqrt{2\pi\sigma^{2(t)}}\pi^{u(t)}\exp\big(-\mu^{(t)}\eta_{ij}^{(t)}-\boldsymbol{X}_{ij}^{(t)}\big)+256\pi^{g(t)}\exp\Big(\dfrac{-(O_{ij}-\boldsymbol{U}_i^{(t)}\boldsymbol{V}_j^{(t)T})^2}{2\sigma^{2(t)}}\Big)},
$$

$$
\Phi_{ij}^{g(t+1)} = \frac{256\pi^{g(t)}\exp\Big(\dfrac{-(O_{ij}-\boldsymbol{U}_i^{(t)}\boldsymbol{V}_j^{(t)T})^2}{2\sigma^{2(t)}}\Big)}{\sqrt{2\pi\sigma^{2(t)}}\pi^{u(t)}\exp\big(-\mu^{(t)}\eta_{ij}^{(t)}-\boldsymbol{X}_{ij}^{(t)}\big)+256\pi^{g(t)}\exp\Big(\dfrac{-(O_{ij}-\boldsymbol{U}_i^{(t)}\boldsymbol{V}_j^{(t)T})^2}{2\sigma^{2(t)}}\Big)}. \tag{14}
$$

Θ **Sub-problem:** Here, we focus on updating the parameters of the mixed model including σ^2, π^g and π^u. The update can be directly calculated via setting the derivatives of $\mathcal{Q}$ with respect to σ^2, π^g and π^u, respectively, to be zero. More specifically, each of σ^2, π^g and π^u updates via:

$$
\pi^{g(t+1)} = \frac{\sum_{ij}\Phi_{ij}^{g(t+1)}}{mn}, \qquad \pi^{u(t+1)} = \frac{\sum_{ij}\Phi_{ij}^{u(t+1)}}{mn},
$$

$$
\sigma^{2(t+1)} = \frac{\sum_{ij}\Phi_{ij}^{g(t+1)}(O_{ij}-\boldsymbol{U}_i\boldsymbol{V}_j)^2}{\sum_{ij}\Phi_{ij}^{g(t+1)}}. \tag{15}
$$

T Sub-problem: By discarding the constant terms, its closed form solution can be found by:

$$\begin{cases} \boldsymbol{T}^{(t+1)} = \underset{\boldsymbol{T}}{\operatorname{argmin}} \, \mathcal{Q}(\boldsymbol{U}^{(t)}, \boldsymbol{V}^{(t)}, \Theta^{(t+1)}, \Phi^{(t+1)}, \boldsymbol{T}, \boldsymbol{W}^{(t)}) \\[2mm] \quad = \underset{\boldsymbol{T}}{\operatorname{argmin}} \, \lambda \|\boldsymbol{T}\|_1 + \dfrac{\mu^{(t)}}{2} \|\boldsymbol{T} - \boldsymbol{DW}^{(t)}\|_F^2 + <\boldsymbol{Y}^{(t)}, \boldsymbol{T} - \boldsymbol{DW}^{(t)}> \\[2mm] \quad = \mathcal{S}_{\frac{\lambda}{\mu^{(t)}}} (\boldsymbol{DW}^{(t)} - \dfrac{\boldsymbol{Y}^{(t)}}{\mu^{(t)}}), \end{cases} \tag{16}$$

where $\mathcal{S}_{\varepsilon > 0}(\cdot)$ represents the shrinkage operator, the definition of which on scalars is: $\mathcal{S}_\varepsilon(x) = \operatorname{sgn}(x) \max(|x| - \varepsilon, 0)$. The extension of the shrinkage operator to vectors and matrices is simply applied element-wisely.

W Sub-problem: As can be seen below, the W sub-problem is a classic least squares problem, thus the optimal $\boldsymbol{W}^{(t+1)}$ can be calculated easily.

$$\begin{cases} \boldsymbol{W}^{(t+1)} = \underset{\boldsymbol{W}}{\operatorname{argmin}} \, \mathcal{Q}(\boldsymbol{U}^{(t)}, \boldsymbol{V}^{(t)}, \Theta^{(t+1)}, \Phi^{(t+1)}, \boldsymbol{T}^{(t+1)}, \boldsymbol{W}) \\[2mm] \quad = \underset{\boldsymbol{W}}{\operatorname{argmin}} \, \dfrac{\mu^{(t)}}{2} \|\boldsymbol{W} - \Phi^{g(t+1)}\|_F^2 + <\boldsymbol{X}^{(t)}, \boldsymbol{W} - \Phi^{g(t+1)}> \\[2mm] \quad + \dfrac{\mu^{(t)}}{2} \|\boldsymbol{T}^{(t+1)} - \boldsymbol{DW}\|_F^2 + <\boldsymbol{Y}^{(t)}, \boldsymbol{T}^{(t+1)} - \boldsymbol{DW}> . \end{cases} \tag{17}$$

Traditionally, the optimal estimation of $\boldsymbol{W}^{(t+1)}$ can be simply obtained by computing $(\boldsymbol{I} + \boldsymbol{D}^T \boldsymbol{D})^{-1}(\boldsymbol{D}^T(\boldsymbol{T}^{(t+1)} + \frac{\boldsymbol{Y}^{(t)}}{\mu^{(t)}}) + \Phi^{g(t+1)} - \frac{\boldsymbol{X}^{(t)}}{\mu^{(t)}})$. But, due to the size of matrix $(\boldsymbol{I} + \boldsymbol{D}^T \boldsymbol{D})$, it is computationally expensive to compute its inverse. Thanks to the block circulant structure of the matrix, it can be efficiently and exactly solved through applying 3D FFT on it, like:

$$\boldsymbol{W}^{(t+1)} = \mathcal{F}^{-1}\left(\frac{\mathcal{F}(\boldsymbol{D}^T(\boldsymbol{T}^{(t+1)} + \frac{\boldsymbol{Y}^{(t)}}{\mu^{(t)}}) + \Phi^{g(t+1)} - \frac{\boldsymbol{X}^{(t)}}{\mu^{(t)}})}{1 + |\mathcal{F}(\boldsymbol{D}_h)|^2 + |\mathcal{F}(\boldsymbol{D}_v)|^2 + |\mathcal{F}(\boldsymbol{D}_t)|^2} \right), \tag{18}$$

where $\mathcal{F}(\cdot)$ and $\mathcal{F}^{-1}(\cdot)$ stand for the 3D Fourier transform and the inverse 3D Fourier transform operators, respectively. $|\cdot|^2$ is the element-wise square and the division also performs element-wisely. Notice that the denominator in (18) only needs to be computed once.

U-V Sub-problem: In this sub-problem, we jointly seek the optimal solutions for $\boldsymbol{U}^{(t+1)}$ and $\boldsymbol{V}^{(t+1)}$. By keeping the elements related to $\boldsymbol{U}$ and $\boldsymbol{V}$ and dropping the others, the sub-problem can be rewritten as:

$$\begin{cases} (\boldsymbol{U}^{(t+1)}, \boldsymbol{V}^{(t+1)}) = \underset{\boldsymbol{U}, \boldsymbol{V}}{\operatorname{argmin}} \, \mathcal{Q}(\boldsymbol{U}, \boldsymbol{V}, \Theta^{(t+1)}, \Phi^{(t+1)}, \boldsymbol{T}^{(t+1)}, \boldsymbol{W}^{(t+1)}) \\[2mm] = \underset{\boldsymbol{U}, \boldsymbol{V}}{\operatorname{argmin}} \sum_{ij} \dfrac{\Phi_{ij}^{g(t+1)}}{2\sigma^{2(t+1)}} (\boldsymbol{O}_{ij} - \boldsymbol{U}_i \boldsymbol{V}_j^T)^2 = \underset{\boldsymbol{U}, \boldsymbol{V}}{\operatorname{argmin}} \|\Omega \odot (\boldsymbol{O} - \boldsymbol{UV}^T)\|_F^2, \end{cases} \tag{19}$$

Algorithm 1. Robust Foreground Detection

Input: The observation O
Initialization: Randomly initialize $U^{(0)}$, $V^{(0)}$, $\Phi^{g(0)} = a\mathbf{1}, a \in (0,1)$,
$\pi^{g(0)} \in (0,1)$ and $\sigma^2 > 0$. Set $T^{(0)}$, $W^{(0)}$, $X^{(0)}$, $Y^{(0)}$ to be zero matrices.
$\Phi^{u(0)} = \mathbf{1} - \Phi^{g(0)}$, $\pi^{u(0)} = 1 - \pi^{g(0)}$. Compute $|\mathcal{F}(D_h)|^2$, $|\mathcal{F}(D_v)|^2$ and
$|\mathcal{F}(D_t)|^2$, $\mu^{(0)} = 0.1$, $\rho = 1.25$, $t = 0$.
while *not converged* **do**
    Update $\Phi^{(t+1)}$ via Eq. (14);
    Update $\Theta^{(t+1)}$ via Eq. (15);
    Update $T^{(t+1)}$ via Eq. (16);
    Update $W^{(t+1)}$ via Eq. (18);
    Update $U^{(t+1)}$ and $V^{(t+1)}$ via the rules introduced in [16];
    Update $X^{(t+1)}$, $Y^{(t+1)}$ and $\mu^{(t+1)}$ via Eq. (20);
    $t = t + 1$;
end
Output: Optimal solution $(U^{(t)}, V^{(t)}, \Phi^{(t)}, \Theta^{(t)})$.

---

where $\odot$ represents the Hadamard product of two matrices, Ω performs as a weight matrix[7] and $\Omega_{ij} = \sqrt{\Phi_{ij}^{g(t+1)}/(2\sigma^{2(t+1)})}$. We can see that (19) is actually the weighted ℓ^2 low rank matrix factorization problem. The update of U and V can follow the rules introduced in existing methods, such as WLRA [16].

Besides, there are two multipliers and μ need to be updated, which can be simply done via:

$$X^{(t+1)} = X^{(t)} + \mu^{(t)}(W^{(t+1)} - \Phi^{g(t+1)}),$$
$$Y^{(t+1)} = Y^{(t)} + \mu^{(t)}(T^{(t+1)} - DW^{(t+1)}), \mu^{(t+1)} = \min\{\rho\mu^{(t)}, \zeta\}, \quad (20)$$

where $\rho > 1$ is a constant, and ζ is a predefined threshold (*e.g.* 10).

For clarity, we summarize the whole procedure of optimization in Algorithm 1. The algorithm terminates when $\|\Phi^{g(t+1)} - \Phi^{g(t)}\|_F \leq \delta\|\Phi^{g(t)}\|_F$ with $\delta = 10^{-3}$, or the maximal number of iteration is reached. Please notice that, as the elements in Φ^u are real numbers rather than binaries, but very close to either 0 or 1. For foreground detection, the binary mask is required. To this end, we simply predefine a threshold (0.9 for all of experiments) to binarize Φ^u.

3 Simulations and Experiments

To quantitatively and qualitatively evaluate the performance of our proposed method, we conduct simulations on synthetic data and experiments on real sequences in this section. The simulations concentrate on revealing the effect of parameters involved in Algorithm 1, the convergence with random initializations

---

[7] By a slight abuse of notations, we reuse the notation Ω to represent the weight matrix for being consistent with the concept of support.

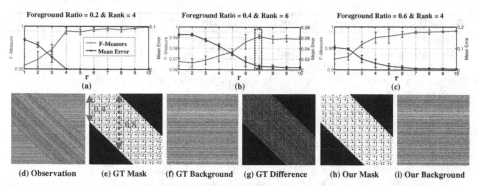

Fig. 1. The effect of parameter r. (a)-(c) are the results with respect to (Foreground Ratio: 0.2, Ground Truth Rank: 4), (0.4, 6) and (0.6, 4), respectively. (d)-(i) correspond to one trial of the case bounded by the dashed box in (b). The recovered background (i) is with only 0.0083 Mean Error and the estimated mask (g) is with 0.9906 F-Measure.

Fig. 2. Sample images from each sequence of the Star dataset

and the robustness to different types of noise, such as Speckle, Gaussian, Salt & Pepper and Poisson. We also perform experiments on real videos, allowing us to compare against a large number of alternative approaches.

Parameter Effect. There are two parameters, *i.e.* λ and r, involved in our algorithm. In this part, we focus on evaluating the effect of r with $\lambda = 5$ fixed, while the effect of λ is tested latter together with the robustness to different noises. To better visualize the data, the observation is composed of 1D images. The background matrix is generated via $B_0 = U_0 V_0^T$, where both U_0 and V_0 are $1000 \times Rank$ (an example background matrix is shown in Fig. 1 (f) corresponding to the case bounded by the dashed box in Fig. 1 (b)), and the observation (Fig. 1 (d)) is obtained by adding the foreground with a mask (Fig. 1 (e)) to the background. The foreground on each column shifts downward for 1 pixel per column. The foreground ratio controls the foreground width, taking the case with foreground ratio 0.4 for example (Fig. 1 (e)), the maximal width in the observation is actually 0.8. In addition, the entries in both the background and the foreground are sampled from the uniform distribution $[0, 255]$. To quantitatively reveal the recovery performance of both the background and the foreground mask, we employ Mean Error[8] and F-Measure[9] as our metrics. For each certain foreground ratio and r, we independently execute the algorithm for 10 times, and the average results are reported in Fig. 1 (a)-(c), as can be seen

---

[8] Mean Error is computed via computing the mean of the absolute sum of pixel-wise differences between the recovered background and the ground truth.

[9] F-Measure is defined as 2·precision·recall/(precision+recall).

from which, we find that as r increases to the ground truth rank, the F-Measure and the Mean Error sharply increases and decreases, respectively. After that, the performance changes very smoothly in a relatively large range, which indicates the insensitivity of r. For the rest experiments, we set $r = 7$.

Performance Comparison on Real Sequences. We here compare our method against numerous state of the art approaches, *i.e.* GMM [18], SOBS [12], DP-GMM [6], PCP [2], DECOLOR [29] and GRASTA [7], on the dataset Star [9]. The Star contains 9 real world videos, which has a variety of scenarios including WaterSurface (*WS: outdoor, dynamic background, lingering person*), Curtain (*Cur: indoor, light switch, people*), Fountain (*Fou: outdoor, dynamic background, people*), Hall (*Hal: indoor, static background, crowd*), Lobby (*Lob: indoor, light switch, people*), Escalator (*Esc: indoor, dynamic background, crowd*), BootStrap (*BS: indoor, static background, crowd*) and Trees (*Tre: outdoor, dynamic background, cars*). Sample images from each sequence of Star are provided in Fig. 2. In the comparison, we fix $\lambda = 5$, which is suggested by the Robustness analysis detailed latter. As for the other competitors, the codes are downloaded from the authors' websites and the parameters are all set as default. Please note that, for PCP and GRAST, the raw results are the residuals instead of the masks, so the post processing of binarization is essential to give the final foreground masks. To this end, we assume the absolute residuals in each frame satisfy a Gaussian distribution $\mathcal{N}(\tilde{\eta}, \tilde{\sigma})$. Therefore, we adaptively compute the threshold $t = \tilde{\eta} + \tilde{\sigma}$. With the threshold, the estimation of the mask is done via: if the absolute residual is larger than t, then the mask is 1, otherwise 0. The performance comparison in terms of F-Measure is given in Table 1, as can be viewed from which, our method performs stably and robustly for every sequence with high F-Measure. The average F-Measure of our method over the whole dataset is the clear evidence demonstrating the proposed method significantly outperforms the others. Figure 3 displays the changes of Φ^u (mask), without loss of generality, on the sequence of WaterSurface, as our algorithm iterates. Figure 3 (c)-(g) reveal that the estimation gradually eliminates the noise and becomes stable. From Fig. 3 (h), we observe that the final mask obtained by our method is very close to the GT mask. Note that, although the F-Measure of DE-COLOR is slightly behind our method, its computational cost is much higher than ours, please see the comparison in the next paragraph.

Table 1. Performance comparison in terms of F-Measure

method	WS	Cur	Fou	Hal	SM	Lob	Esc	BS	Tre	mean
GMM [18]	.7948	.7580	.6854	.3335	.5363	.6519	.1388	.3838	.0757	.4842
SOBS [12]	.8247	.8178	.6554	.5943	.6677	.6489	.5770	.6019	.6960	.6760
DP-GMM [6]	**.9090**	.8203	.7049	.5484	.6522	.5794	.5055	.6024	.7567	.6754
PCP [2]	.4137	.6193	.5679	.5917	.7234	.6989	.6728	.6582	.3406	.5874
DECOLOR [29]	.8866	.8255	**.8598**	.6424	.6525	.6149	**.6994**	.5869	**.8096**	.7308
GRASTA [7]	.7310	.6591	.3786	.5817	.7142	.5550	.4697	.6146	.2504	.5505
Our Method	.8796	**.8976**	.7544	**.6673**	**.7407**	**.8029**	.6353	**.6841**	.6779	**.7489**

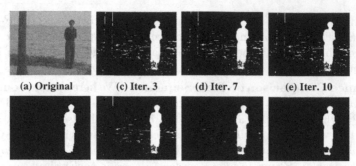

(a) Original   (c) Iter. 3   (d) Iter. 7   (e) Iter. 10

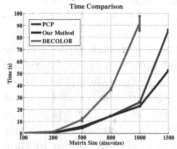

(b) GT Mask   (f) Iter. 15   (g) Iter. 24   (h) Final Mask

Fig. 3. Mask Evolution. (a) the original frame. (b) the Ground Truth (GT) mask. (c)-(g) are the estimations of the 3th, 7th, 10th, 15th and 24th iterations, respectively. (h) is the final mask. Lighter colors in (c)-(g) indicate higher possibilities of being foreground, while darker ones stand for lower.

Time Comparison. We here provide a comparison of time among our method,

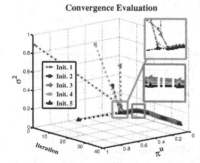

Fig. 4. Time Comparison

PCP [2] and DECOLOR [29], which are all implemented in Matlab (the core part of DE-COLOR is implemented in C++). The time comparison is conducted on a PC running Windows 7 32bit operating system with Intel Core i7 3.4 GHz CPU and 4.0 GB RAM. As can be seen from Fig. 4, as the matrix size increases, the time required by DECOLOR quickly grows up. In contrast with DECOLOR, PCP and our method are much lighter. For instance, in the case of the matrix size with 1000×1000, both PCP and our method spend about $24s$ while DECOLOR costs about $90s$. Please notice that, the computational time of DECOLOR with respect to 1500×1500 is not provided in Fig. 4, since DECOLOR runs out of memory. In other words, our method requires less memories than DECOLOR. For the larger matrix (1500×1500), as shown in the picture, the time load of PCP becomes much heavier than that of our method.

Convergence. The initialization of $U^{(0)}$, $V^{(0)}$, $\Phi^{g(0)}$, $\pi^{g(0)}$ and σ^2 in Algorithm 1 is random. To reveal the proposed algorithm can converge efficiently and stably with random initializations, we test 5 different initializations on, without loss of generality, the WS sequence. It is hard to visualize data with dimensions more than 3. Therefore, in Fig. 5, we choose π^u, σ^2 and iteration number to show, which is also capable to reflect the converging trend and speed of Algorithm 1. The initializations are indeed scattered in the σ^2-π^u plane at the beginning of loop, as shown in Fig. 5. Rapidly, within only 3 iterations, the 5 curves

Fig. 5. Convergence Evaluation

are gathering as shown in the upper $(4\times)$ zoomed in patch. At the 5th iteration, we can see, from the lower $(16\times)$ zoomed in patch, that the algorithm gives almost the same estimations of σ^2 and π^u for different cases. In all the experiments present in this paper, we set the maximal number of iteration to 35, which works sufficiently well.

Robustness to Noise. Although we simply assume the residual caused by the factors expect for the foreground satisfies a Gaussian distribution, the smoothness can make the algorithm survives from various noise types. This part aims to demonstrate the robustness of our method to different types of noise including Speckle, Gaussian, Salt & Pepper and Poisson with different levels. The upper row of Figure 6 shows the F-Measures with respect to different types of noise. As can be seen in Fig. 6 (a), as λ increases to 10, the speckle noise variance that our method can handle reaches 0.03. But when $\lambda = 30$, the performance drops because the results are over smoothed, which is further confirmed by the rest cases. Figure 6 (b) corresponds to the white Gaussian noise, from which we can find that the proposed algorithm robustly processes the noise on the 0.0125 level using a large value range of λ. Even though Salt & Pepper noise heavily deviates from the Gaussian assumption, Figure 6 (c) shows that, by setting $\lambda = 5$, our method is robust to process the case with 15% pixels polluted by such noise. The reason why the F-Measure decreases as the λ increases from 5 is that the smoothness makes masks dilated or eroded. For the Poisson noise, the results given in Fig. 6 (d) demonstrate the robustness of our method to the 10^{10} scale with λ under 10. Since the definitions of these noises are different, so are the noise levels. The lower row of Fig. 6 offers the visual results corresponding to the cases marked by the dashed green boxes in the upper row, from which we

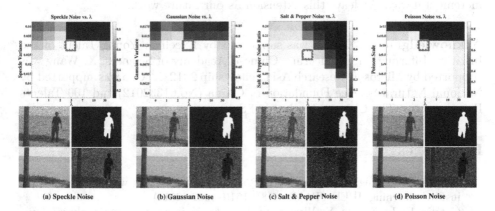

(a) Speckle Noise   (b) Gaussian Noise   (c) Salt & Pepper Noise   (d) Poisson Noise

Fig. 6. Robustness to different noise types with varying λ values. The upper row gives the F-Measures, while the lower row shows four groups of visual results corresponding to the cases marked by green dashed boxes. Each group has four sub-images: the sample input (top-left), the estimated foreground mask (top-right), the recovered background (bottom-left) and the noise component (bottom-right). The noise level differs for different types of noises, please refer to their definitions.

can see that even though the input images are severely perturbed by noises, our method can robustly recover the backgrounds, the foreground masks and the noise components. Please zoom in to see more details.

4   Conclusion and Future Work

In real world scenarios, foreground detection is difficult as videos may contain not only static backgrounds, but also noises, dynamic backgrounds and camouflage foregrounds. In this paper, we have shown how to harness three structural priors of the background and foreground, including the arbitrariness of foreground appearance, the spatial-temporal smoothness of foreground, and the correlation of background, for robustly detecting foreground objects, which are achieved by assuming the foreground satisfies the uniform distribution, smoothing the foreground via total variation regularization, and imposing the correlation constraint on the background, respectively. We have formulated the problem in a unified optimization framework and proposed a novel ALM-ADM based algorithm to effectively and efficiently seek the optimal solution. The effect of parameters, the convergence and the robustness to noises of the proposed algorithm have been analyzed. Besides, compared to the state of the art alternatives, the experimental results on real sequences have demonstrated the clear advantages of the proposed method in terms of accuracy, robustness and efficiency.

Currently, our algorithm processes sequences in a batch fashion. For applications with the online requirement, it is more desirable to design its online version, which actually can be done by reconstructing a new coming frame using the existing background model, referring to the foreground mask of the latest frame to achieve the temporal smoothness, and then updating the model in an incremental way. We leave this extension as our future work.

Acknowledgment. X. Guo was supported by Excellent Young Talent of the Institute Information Engineering, Chinese Academy of Sciences. X. Wang was supported by Microsoft Research Asia Fellowship 2012. X. Cao was supported by National Natural Science Foundation of China (No.61332012) and 100 Talents Programme of The Chinese Academy of Sciences.

References

1. Babenko, B., Yang, M., Belongie, S.: Robust object tracking with online multiple instance learning. IEEE TPAMI 33(8), 1619–1632 (2011)
2. Candès, E., Li, X., Ma, Y., Wright, J.: Robust principal component analysis? Journal of the ACM 58(3), 1–37 (2011)
3. Cremers, D., Soatto, S.: Motion competition: A variational approach to piecewise parametric motion segmentation. IJCV 62(3), 249–265 (2005)
4. Cristani, M., Raghavendra, R., Bue, A.D., Murino, V.: Human behavior analysis in video surveillance: a social signal processing perspective. Neurocomputing 100, 86–97 (2013)

5. Elgammal, A., Duraiswami, R., Harwood, D., Davis, L.: Background and foreground modeling using nonparametric kernel density estimation for visual surveillance. Proceedings of IEEE 90(7), 1151–1163 (2002)
6. Haines, T., Xiang, T.: Background subtraction with dirichlet process mixture models. IEEE TPAMI (2014)
7. He, J., Balzano, L., Szlam, A.: Incremental gradient on the grassmannian for online foreground and background separation in subsampled video. In: CVPR, pp. 1568–1575 (2012)
8. Lee, D.: Effective gaussian mixture learning for video background subtraction. IEEE TPAMI 27(5), 827–832 (2005)
9. Li, L., Huang, W., Gu, I., Tian, Q.: Statistical modeling of complex backgrounds for foreground object detection. IEEE TIP 13(11), 1459–1472 (2004)
10. Lin, Z., Chen, M., Wu, L., Ma, Y.: The augmented lagrange multiplier method for exact recovery of corrupted low-rank matrices. Tech. Rep. UILU-ENG-09-2215, UIUC Technical Report (2009)
11. Liu, J., Tai, X., Huang, H., Huan, Z.: A weighted dictionary learning model for denoising images corrupted by mixed noise. IEEE TIP 22(3), 1108–1120 (2013)
12. Maddalena, L., Petrosino, A.: A self-organizing approach to background subtraction for visual surveillance applications. IEEE TIP 17(7), 1168–1177 (2008)
13. Meng, D., De la Torre, F.: Robust matrix factorization with unknown noise. In: ICCV, pp. 1337–1344 (2013)
14. Peng, Y., Ganesh, A., Wright, J., Xu, W., Ma, Y.: Rasl: Robust alignment by sparse and low-rank decomposition for linearly correlated images. IEEE TPAMI 34(11), 2233–2246 (2012)
15. Rudin, L., Osher, S., Fatemi, E.: Nonlinear total variation based noise removal algorithms. Physica D: Nonlinear Phenomena 60(1), 259–268 (1992)
16. Srebro, N., Jaakkola, T.: Weighted low-rank approximations. In: ICML, pp. 720–727 (2003)
17. Stalder, S., Grabner, H., Van Gool, L.: Cascaded confidence filtering for improved tracking-by-detection. In: Daniilidis, K., Maragos, P., Paragios, N. (eds.) ECCV 2010, Part I. LNCS, vol. 6311, pp. 369–382. Springer, Heidelberg (2010)
18. Stauffer, C., Grimson, W.: Adaptive background mixture models for real-time tracking. In: CVPR, pp. 246–252 (1999)
19. Vidal, R.: Subspace clustering. IEEE Signal Processing Magazine 28(2), 52–68 (2011)
20. Vidal, R., Ma, Y.: A unified algebraic approach to 2-D and 3-D motion segmentation. In: Pajdla, T., Matas, J. (eds.) ECCV 2004. LNCS, vol. 3021, pp. 1–15. Springer, Heidelberg (2004)
21. Viola, P., Jones, M., Snow, D.: Detecting pedestrians using patterns of motion and appearance. IJCV 63(2), 153–161 (2005)
22. Wang, N., Yao, T., Wang, J., Yeung, D.-Y.: A probabilistic approach to robust matrix factorization. In: Fitzgibbon, A., Lazebnik, S., Perona, P., Sato, Y., Schmid, C. (eds.) ECCV 2012, Part VII. LNCS, vol. 7578, pp. 126–139. Springer, Heidelberg (2012)
23. Wang, N., Yeung, D.: Bayesian robust matrix factorization for image and video processing. In: ICCV, pp. 1785–1792 (2013)
24. Wren, C., Azarbayejani, A., Darrell, T., Pentland, A.: Pfinder: Realtime tracking of the human body. IEEE TPAMI 19(7), 780–785 (1997)
25. Xu, J., Ithapu, V., Mukherjee, L., Rehg, J., Singh, V.: GOSUS: Grassmanian online subspace updates with strutured-sparsity. In: ICCV, pp. 3376–3383 (2013)

26. Yilmaz, A., Javed, O., Shah, M.: Object tracking: A survey. ACM Computing Surveys 38(4), 1–45 (2006)
27. Zhang, Z., Ganesh, A., Liang, X., Ma, Y.: Tilt: Transform invariant low-rank textures. IJCV 99(1), 1–24 (2012)
28. Zhou, T., Tao, D.: Godec: Randomized low-rank & sparse matrix decomposition in noisy case. In: ICML, pp. 33–40 (2011)
29. Zhou, X., Yang, C., Yu, W.: Moving object detection by detecting contiguous outliers in the low-rank representation. IEEE TPAMI 35(3), 597–610 (2013)

Video Object Co-segmentation by Regulated Maximum Weight Cliques

Dong Zhang[1], Omar Javed[2], and Mubarak Shah[1]

[1] Center for Research in Computer Vision, UCF, Orlando, FL 32826
[2] SRI International, Princeton, NJ 08540
{dzhang,shah}@eecs.ucf.edu, omar.javed@sri.com

Abstract. In this paper, we propose a novel approach for object co-segmentation in arbitrary videos by sampling, tracking and matching object proposals via a Regulated Maximum Weight Clique (RMWC) extraction scheme. The proposed approach is able to achieve good segmentation results by pruning away noisy segments in each video through selection of object proposal tracklets that are spatially salient and temporally consistent, and by iteratively extracting weighted groupings of objects with similar shape and appearance (with-in and across videos). The object regions obtained from the video sets are used to initialize per-pixel segmentation to get the final co-segmentation results. Our approach is general in the sense that it can handle multiple objects, temporary occlusions, and objects going in and out of view. Additionally, it makes no prior assumption on the commonality of objects in the video collection. The proposed method is evaluated on publicly available multi-class video object co-segmentation dataset and demonstrates improved performance compared to the state-of-the-art methods.

Keywords: Video Segmentation, Cosegmentation.

1 Introduction and Related Work

Our goal is to discover and segment objects from a video collection in an unsupervised manner. We compensate for the lack of supervision by exploiting commonality of objects in video collection (if it exists) to build better object segmentation models. Unsupervised segmentation of object classes from video collection has applications in large scale video tagging and retrieval, generation of training sets for supervised learning, and forensic video analysis.

Video co-segmentation is a natural extension of image co-segmentation, for which there is a large body of prior work ([20,12,18]). Image co-segmentation was introduced by Rother et al. [20]. Later, image based object co-segmentation was proposed by [26], which introduced the use of object proposals ([5,1]) for segmenting similar object from image pairs. The co-segmentation idea was extended to handle multiple object classes ([13]) and to work in more general internet collections where all images did not share the same object [21].

There is a large body of prior work on single video segmentation techniques ([10,9,19,27]). In general these techniques use appearance information of the

D. Fleet et al. (Eds.): ECCV 2014, Part VII, LNCS 8695, pp. 551–566, 2014.

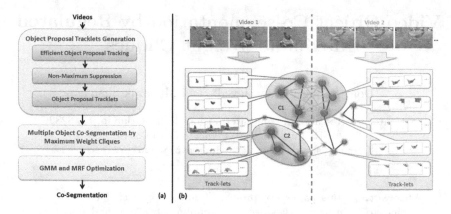

Fig. 1. (a) Shows the framework of the proposed method. (b) Shows the formulation of the Regulated Maximum Weight Cliques (RMWC) for object proposal tracklets. In this example, we generate 'object proposal' tracklets for two videos and use weighted nodes to represent them. Edges are built between similar nodes, and there are two types of edges (intra-video edges: red; inter-video edges: orange). In this example, the first two maximal cliques which have highest weights are obtained ($C1$ and $C2$). $C1$ contains all the segments for 'chicken' from two videos and $C2$ contains all the segments for 'turtle' in video 1.

videos to group the pixels in a spatio-temporal graph and/or employ motion segmentation techniques to separate objects by using motion cues. There are also several methods ([16,17,29]) designed for primary video object segmentation in single videos through use of the 'objectness' ([1]) measure. However, all of these methods use information extracted from one video for its segmentation and there is no cross-video knowledge transfer.

A related problem of object discovery has been studied in computer vision for images ([14,23,24]) and videos ([28,30]). These methods either use graph based clustering of low-level image features or generative models, such as Latent Dirichlet Allocation (LDA), to learn the distribution of class of image regions based on visual words.

Recently, a few methods have been proposed for video co-segmentation ([3,22,4]). The method in [3] attempts to segment the common region from a pair of videos and model the problem as a common foreground and background separation. It represents the video pair by super-voxels and proposes a motion-based video grouping method in order to find common foreground regions. It employs Gaussian mixture models to characterize the common object appearance. The work by Rubio et al. ([22]) aims at segmenting the same object (or objects belonging to the same class) moving in a similar manner from two or more videos. The method starts with grouping the pixels in video frames at two levels: the higher levels consists of space-time tubes and the lower level consists of within frame region segments; an initial foreground and background labeling is generated to construct the probabilistic distribution of the feature vectors of tubes and regions; and a probabilistic framework is employed to get the final co-segmentation results. Both [3] and [22] use strong assumptions of a single class of object common to all videos. Chiu and Fritz ([4]) proposed multi-class video object co-segmentation and also provided a publicly available dataset (MOViCS) with ground truth. In this work, a non-parametric Bayesian model for co-segmentation is used, which is based on a video segmentation prior. This method does not use restrictive assumptions on the number of object classes per frame or requirements on commonality of object in all videos. However, the method groups dense image patches to obtain segments, and can potentially yield noisy results. We provide a comparison of ([4]) results with our Regulated Maximum Weight Clique (RMWC) based method.

Fig.1 shows an illustration of the proposed approach. Compared to the existing video co-segmentation methods, the proposed approach has the following advantages:

1. The proposed method employs object tracklets to obtain spatially salient and temporally consistent object regions for co-segmentation, while most of previous co-segmentation methods simply use pixel-level or region-level features to perform clustering. The perceptual grouping of pixels before matching reduces segment fragmentation and leads to a simpler matching problem.

2. The proposed approach does not rely on approximate solutions for object groups. The grouping problem is modeled as a Regulated Maximum Weight Clique (RMWC) problem for which an optimal solution is available. The use of only the salient object tracklets for grouping keeps the computational cost low.

3. Unlike the state-of-the-art single video object segmentation method ([29]), the proposed method can handle occlusions of objects, or objects going in and out of videos because the object tracklets are temporally local and there is no requirement for the object to continuously remain in the field of view of the video. Furthermore, there is no limitation on the number of object classes in each video and the number of common object classes in the video collection. Therefore the proposed approach can be used to extract objects in an unsupervised fashion from general video collections.

4. The proposed method is different from Maximum Weight Clique Problem which has already been explored in video object segmentation [17], in a way that the clique weights of the proposed method is not simply defined as the summation of node weights, but regulated by the intra-clique consistency term. Therefore, the extracted cliques have more global consistency, and similar objects from different videos are accurately grouped.

In Section 2, we describe our Regulated Maximum Weighted Clique (RMWC) based video co-segmentation approach. In section 3, we present the performance evaluation of the proposed algorithm. In Section 4., the paper is concluded.

2   Regulated Maximum Weight Clique Based Video Co-segmentation

2.1   The Framework

The proposed method consists of 2 stages: (1) Object Tracklets Generation: In this stage, we generate a number of object proposals ([5]) for each frame and use each of them as a starting point, and track the object proposals backward and forward throughout the whole video sequence. We generate reliable tracklets from the track set (those with high similarity over time) and perform non-maxima suppression to remove noisy or overlapping proposals. **(2)** Multiple Objects Co-Segmentation by Regulated Maximum Weight Cliques: A graph is generated by representing each tracklet as a node from all videos in the collection. The nodes of the graph are weighted by their appearance and motion scores, and edges are weighted by tracklet similarity. Edges with weight below a threshold are removed. A Regulated Maximum Weight Clique extraction algorithm is used to find objects ranked by score which is a combination of intra-group consistency and *Video Object Scores*. The object regions obtained from the video sets are used to initialize per-pixel segmentation [8] to get the final co-segmentation results.

2.2   Object Tracklets Generation

In this stage, the method in [5] is employed to generate a number of object proposals (which are likely to be 'object regions' in each frame). And each of the object proposals has a **Video Object Score**, S^{object}, which is a combination of motion and appearance information:

$$S^{object}(x) = A(x) + M(x), \tag{1}$$

in which x is an object proposal. $A(x)$ is the appearance score (which is the objectness score defined by [5]). The appearance objectness score is high for regions that have a well defined closed boundary in space, different appearance from its surrounds and is salient [5]. $M(x)$ is the motion score (which is defined in [29] as the average Frobenius norm of optical flow gradient around the boundary of object proposal).

Efficient Object Proposal Tracking. We track every object proposal from each frame backward and forward to form a number of tracks for the object proposals (please see Fig.2).

A combined color, location, and shape similarity function is employed for object proposal tracking:

$$S^{simi}(x_m, x_n) = S^{app}(x_m, x_n) \cdot S^{loc}(x_m, x_n) \cdot S^{shape}(x_m, x_n), \tag{2}$$

in which x_m and x_n are object proposals from frame m and n respectively, S^{app} is the appearance similarity, S^{loc} is the location similarity which computes the overlap ratio between two regions, and S^{shape} is the shape similarity between the object proposals. Color histograms are used to model appearance. The descriptor for estimating shape similarity is computed by representing the contour of a region in normalized polar coordinates and sampling it from 0 to 360 degrees to form a vector. Dot products of descriptors are used for computing both shape similarity and appearance similarity.

Once the similarity function is defined, a simple greedy tracking method is employed to track large number of object proposals. By using the similarity scores defined in Eq.2, for a specific object proposal in the frame, the most similar object proposal in adjacent frame is selected to be the tracked proposal. The reason to use this method is mainly due to efficiency. As shown in Fig.2, the similarity matrices between all object proposals in adjacent frames are pre-computed. Based on the greedy method, tracking a specific object proposal to the next frame equals to finding the index of max value in a specific row of the similarity matrix. Thus this tracking process is computationally economical.

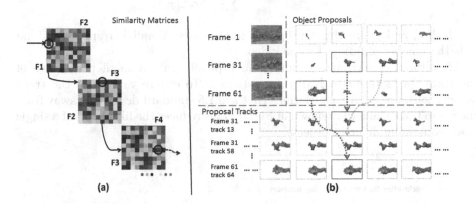

Fig. 2. Object Proposal Tracking. (a) Shows the similarity matrices between F1 (frame 1) and F2, F2 and F3, and F3 and F4. It also shows an example for tracking a specific object proposal (the 4th in F1): it finds the largest item from row 4 of similarity matrix F1 and F2 (the 1st item in this example); then it finds the largest item from row 1 of similarity matrix F2 and F3; and so on. Note that, only 10 object proposals (the matrices are 10 by 10) are shown in this figure for simplicity, but hundreds of objects proposals are used in the experiments. (b) Shows some object proposal tracks. In this example, several object proposals are generated for frame 31, and the object proposal shown in red box is tracked backward and forward to form a track throughout all the video frames. The same process is repeated for other object proposals (in orange and purple boxes as another two examples). This process is repeated for all the frames.

Non-maximum Suppression for Object Proposal Tracks. One can sample a large number of proposals per frame and, therefore, generate a larger number of tracks for an input video. Specifically, for a video that has F frames and each frame has N object proposals, $F \times N$ tracks could be obtained, since we generate tracks for each proposal. However, many of the object samples are overlapping and therefore their tracks are similar. A non-maximum suppression (NMS) ([7]) scheme is used to prune near duplicate tracks. For each object proposal track $X = \{x_1, ..., x_i, ...x_F\}$, an overall *Video Object Score* is computed as:

$$S^{object}(X) = \sum_{i=1}^{F}(S^{object}(x_i)), \tag{3}$$

where i is the frame index, and F is the number of frames.

Next, the track that has highest score is selected and all other tracks which have high overlap ratio $R^{overlap}$ with the selected track are removed. The value 0.5 is used for $R^{overlap}$, as suggested in ([7])). After that, the track with the second highest score among the surviving tracks is selected and the process is repeated. The process is continued iteratively until all tracks have been processed. The overlap ratio between two tracks X and Y is defined as:

$$R^{overlap}(X,Y) = \frac{\sum_{i=1}^{F}(x_i \cap y_i)}{\sum_{i=1}^{F}(x_i \cup y_i)},$$ (4)

in which x_i and y_i are object proposals in the track X and Y respectively, and F is the number of frames for the video.

After the non-maximum suppression, typically only a small percentage of the total tracks (prior to NMS) are retained. To ensure validity of the track associations, we remove associations that are 1.5 standard deviations away from the mean track similarity (shown in Fig.3). This reduces the likelihood of a single track containing different objects.

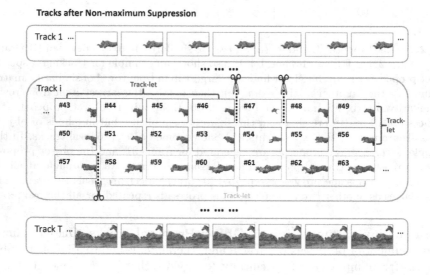

Fig. 3. Tracklet Splitting. In this example, after the Non-Maximum Suppression, there are T object proposal tracks selected. Track i is shown as an example to generate the object proposal tracklets. There are several adjacent frames which are not very similar compared to other adjacent frame pairs, therefore, they are split and several tracklets are generated (red, orange and purple).

2.3 Multiple Object Co-segmentation by Regulated Maximum Weight Cliques

Once object tracklets from the video collection have been obtained (Section 2.2), the next step is to discover salient object groupings in the video collection. We formulate the grouping problem as a Regulated Maximum Weight Clique Problem.

Clique Problems. Let $G = (V, E, W)$ be an undirected graph, where V is the set of vertices, E is the set of edges and W is a set of weights for each vertex. A clique is a complete subgraph of G, i.e. one whose vertices are pairwise adjacent. A **Maximal Clique** is a complete subgraph that is not contained in any other complete subgraph ([15]). **Finding All Maximal Cliques** from a graph is NP-hard and Bron-Kerbosch Algorithm ([2]) which has the worst case time complexity $O(3^{(n/3)})$ is known to be the most efficient algorithm in practice ([25]). The **Maximum Clique** Problem is to find maximum complete subgraph of G. The **Maximum Weight Clique** Problem deals with finding the clique which has maximum weight.

Problem Constraints. We use the following constraints for co-segmenting the objects from videos: **1)** The object proposal tracklets for the same class of objects should have similar appearance both within a video and across videos; however, due to the illumination differences across videos, for building color histograms in LAB space ([6]), the L channel (which represents the brightness) is only used for tracklets from the same video (intra-video edges), but a, b channels are used for tracklets from both same (intra-video edges) and different videos (inter-video edges). **2)** The shape of the same object would not change significantly during the same video, so the shape similarity is also used for building the edges for tracklets of the same objects in a video. **3)** The dominant objects should have high *Video Object Scores*, and **4)** the tracklets generated by an object should have low appearance variation. Based on these constraints, the graph is built as illustrated in Fig.1.

Graph Structure. The co-segmentation problem is formulated into a Regulated Maximum Weight Cliques Problem by denoting the object proposal tracklets to be the nodes. Based on constraints 1 and 2, edges are built between tracklets. There are two types of edges: intra-video edges and inter-video edges. The intra-video edge values are computed as a combined color histogram similarity in LAB color space and shape similarity:

$$E(X, Y) = (shape(X) \cdot shape(Y)^T) \cdot$$
$$\prod_{i=\{L,a,b\}} (hist(LAB_i(X)) \cdot hist(LAB_i(Y))^T), \qquad (5)$$

where $shape(X)$ and $shape(Y)$ are the shape descriptors (Sec.2.2) for object proposal tracklet X and Y respectively. The nearest two object proposals in the two tracklets are selected to represent the shapes of the tracklets.

And the inter-video edge values are computed as color histogram similarity of $\{a, b\}$ channels in LAB color space:

$$E(X,Y) = \prod_{i=\{a,b\}} (hist(LAB_i(X)) \cdot hist(LAB_i(Y))^T). \tag{6}$$

After computing the edges, the weak edges are removed (by a threshold).

Regulated Maximum Weight Clique Extraction. Based on constraint 3 and according to Equation 1, the weight of a node (object proposal tracklet) is computed as:

$$W(X) = \sum_{i=1}^{f} (S^{object}(x_i)), \tag{7}$$

in which f is the number of object proposals in this tracklet. $W(X)$ is the sum up of the *Video Object Score* of all object proposals contained in this tracklet.

Based on constraint 4, the weight of a clique is defined as:

$$W(C) = \Gamma_{hist}(C) \cdot \sum_{i=1}^{n(C)} (W(X_i)), \tag{8}$$

in which $C = \{X_1, ..., X_{n(C)}\}$ is a clique, X_i is a node (tracklet) contained in this clique, $n(C)$ is the number of nodes in this clique, and $\Gamma_{hist}(C)$ is the color histogram consistency regulator which computes the mean color histogram consistency of all the object proposals contained in the clique:

$$\Gamma_{hist}(C) = \frac{\sum_{i=1}^{f(C)} \sum_{(j=1 \wedge j \neq i)}^{f(C)} (hist(x_i) \cdot hist(x_j)^T)}{f^2(C) - f(C)}, \tag{9}$$

in which x_i and x_j are object proposals in clique C, $f(c)$ is the number of object proposals in this clique, and $hist(\cdot)$ is the $\{a, b\}$ channel color histogram in LAB space.

By this formulation, the clique that has the highest score represents the object with largest combined score of inter-object consistency and objectness. This problem is different from Maximum Weight Clique problem and can not be solved by standard methods ([15,11]), because the clique weights are not simply defined as the summation of node weights and the weights varies over iterations as we extract objects one by one. Therefore, we call this as **Regulated Maximum Weight Cliques Problem**. Note that, we want to retrieve all Regulated Maximum Weighted Cliques as possible objects. This is achieved through iteratively finding and removing the Regulated Maximum Weight Cliques from the graph to get a ranked list of cliques (i.e. objects).

A modified version of Bron-Kerbosch Algorithm ([2]) which also has a worst-case complexity of $O(3^{(n/3)})$ is proposed to solve this problem:

Step 1, Apply Bron-Kerbosch Algorithm to find all the maximal cliques from the graph;

Step 2, Compute the weight of each clique in linear time;

Step 3, Find the clique with the highest weight and remove all the nodes associated with this clique, update the clique structures and recompute the weights. This process could be performed for multiple times in order to extract multiple object groupings from the videos.

Note that, the high-complexity doesn't prohibit the use of this algorithm. The object tracklets generation stage removes most of the spurious tracklets. For videos evaluated in this paper, the maximum clique extraction process took less than a second on a standard laptop. The object regions obtained from the video sets are used to initialize per-pixel segmentation [8] to get the final co-segmentation results.

3   Experiments

The proposed method was tested on the video co-segmentation dataset (MOViCS dataset ([4])) and was compared with several other methods. The results show that it performs better both qualitatively and quantitatively. Detailed analysis is presented to show that the co-segmentation method produces better segmentation results by using information from multiple videos. Results also show that the proposed method could handle occlusions on which the state-of-the-art single video object segmentation method fails.

3.1   MOViCS Dataset

To the best of our knowledge, MOViCS dataset ([4]) is the only video co-segmentation dataset which has the ground truth annotations for quantitative analysis. It contains 4 video sets which totally has 11 videos, 5 frames of each video have pixel-level annotations for the object labels.

Experimental Setup. Following the setup in [4], the intersection-over-union metric is employed to quantify the results: $M(S, G) = \frac{S \cup G}{S \cap G}$, where S is a set of segments and G is the ground truth. The co-segmentation score for a set of video is defined as $Score_j = \max_i M(S_i, G_j)$, where S_i denotes all segments grouped into an object class i. And a single average score is defined for all object classes as: $Score = \frac{1}{C} \sum_j Score_j$, where C is the number of object classes in the ground truth.

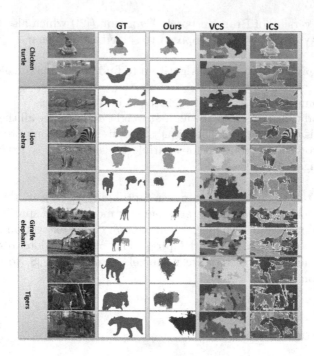

Fig. 4. Video Co-Segmentation Results on MOViCS Dataset. Each row is the results of a video in MOViCS dataset. Column 1 is one original frame from the video; column 2 ('GT') is the ground truth for co-segmentation, red regions correspond to the first object in the video set and green regions correspond to the second object in the video set; column 3 ('Ours') is the results of the proposed method, red and green regions correspond to the first and second objects in the video set and blue region corresponds to the third object; column 4 ('VCS') and 5 ('ICS') are the results of video co-segmentation method from [4] and [13] respectively. Row 1 and 2 are for 'chicken&turtle' video set, row 3-6 are for 'lion&zebra' video set, row 7 and 8 are for 'giraffe&elephant' video set and row 9-11 are for 'tigers' video set. Please refer to supplementary material for more detailed results.

Comparisons with State-of-the-art Methods. The proposed method is compared with several state-of-the-art Co-Segmentation methods, see Table 1 (the results of VCS [4] and ICS [13] are obtained from [4]). As mentioned in Section 2.3, we use a threshold to remove the weak edges, here we show the results by using a single threshold for all video sets (see column 'Ours1'), and also using optimal thresholds for different video sets (in column 'Ours2'). Qualitative results on this dataset are shown in Fig.4.

The evaluation shows that the proposed method improves on the state of the art. The average improvement is more than 20%. From Fig.4, we can see that ours are the only results which are visually very similar to the ground truth. Unlike prior methods, our method does not have the propensity for breaking objects into a number of fragments and the method also produces better contours for the objects. The only video in which the object regions are not accurately segmented is the 3rd video in video set 'tigers'. This is due to the large difference in appearance of animals from other two videos and qualitatively our method is still the best for this video set.

Table 1. Quantitative comparisons with the state of the art on MOViCS dataset. 'Ours1' shows results of using a single threshold (0.65) for removing the edges, and 'Ours2' shows results of using different thresholds for each video sets (the thresholds are [0.65 0.86 0.45 0.65] for these four video sets respectively.)

Video Set	Ours1	Ours2	VCS [4]	ICS [13]
Chicken&turtle	**0.860**	**0.860**	0.65	0.08
Zebra&lion	**0.588**	**0.636**	0.48	0.23
Giraffe&elephant	**0.528**	**0.639**	0.52	0.07
Tiger	**0.336**	**0.336**	0.30	0.30
Overall	**0.578**	**0.617**	0.49	0.17

Fig. 5. Advantages of the Proposed Video Co-Segmentation Method. Row 1 and row 2 show sample frames from two videos respectively. Row 3 and 4 are the video co-segmentation results of the proposed method for these two videos. Red regions correspond to the first object and green regions correspond to the second object. Row 5 and 6 are the segmentation results of applying the method separately to each video. Blue and dark red regions correspond to the first objects, and pink and orange regions correspond to the second objects.

Advantages of Video Co-segmentation Method. Fig.5 shows how the Co-Segmentation framework help the segmentation results for each video. In this example, we have two videos, if the proposed method is applied to these two videos, the segmentation results are shown in row 3 and 4; if the proposed method is applied separately for each video, the segmentation results are shown in row 5 and 6. It is quite clear that the Co-Segmentation method not only helps to relate the object labels (red regions for the giraffe in row 3 and 4), but also helps to get more accurate segmentation results (video 2 helps video 1 to get better segments for giraffe in row 3; without video 2, it could only get poor segmentation of giraffe in row 5).

Advantages over Single Video Object Segmentation Method. Fig.6 shows the comparisons between the proposed method (VOCS) and the state-of-the-art single video object segmentation (SVOS) method ([29]). Results show that the proposed method could segment objects by using information from other videos (row 2 and 5 in the figure), in contrast, single video object segmentation method mistakenly merges two objects together if they have similar motions (row 3 and 6 in the figure). Also, the proposed method is able to handle occlusions well (row 8 in the figure), while the single video object segmentation method generates wrong labels when there are occlusions of the objects (row 9 in the figure). We compared video object segmentation results quantitatively on MOViCS dataset in Table 2. We observe that, if there are two or more objects appearing in the video, or there are occlusions (e.g. 'elephant_giraffe_all2') of the objects, or the objects do not appear in all the frames (e.g. 'lion_zebra_all1'), the proposed method works much better than single video object segmentation method; if there is only one object in the video, the single video object segmentation method sometimes works better (e.g. 'tiger1_all8' results).

Table 2. Quantitative Comparison of Single Video Object Segmentation (SVOS) with Video Object Co-Segmentation (VOCS)

Video Name (Object)	SVOS ([29])	VOCS
ChickenNew (chicken)	0.740	**0.857**
Chicken_on_turtle (chicken)	0.306	**0.823**
Chicken_on_turtle (turtle)	0.563	**0.807**
Elephant_giraffe_all1 (giraffe)	0.570	**0.680**
Elephant_giraffe_all2 (giraffe)	0.122	**0.557**
Elephant_giraffe_all2 (elephant)	0.085	**0.557**
Lion_zebra2 (lion)	0.254	**0.817**
Lion_zebra2 (zebra)	0.510	**0.619**
Lion_zebra_all1 (lion)	0.391	**0.727**
Lion_zebra_all1 (zebra)	**0.529**	0.361
Lion_zebra_all2 (lion)	**0.883**	0.830
Lion_zebra_all2 (zebra)	0.000	**0.547**
Zebra_grass (zebra)	0.403	**0.508**
Tiger1_all8 (tiger)	**0.494**	0.428
Tiger1_all9 (tiger)	**0.841**	0.522
Tiger1_all10 (tiger)	0.384	**0.637**

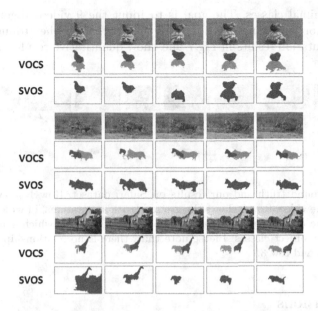

Fig. 6. Comparison between the proposed method (VOCS) and Single Video Object Segmentation (SVOS) method ([29]). Three groups of results are shown here. In each of them, the first rows (row 1, 4 and 7) are sample frames from the videos; the second rows (row 2, 5 and 8) are results of the proposed method; and the third rows (row 3, 6 and 9) are results of the single video object segmentation method. For the results, the red regions correspond to the first objects and green regions correspond to the second objects. Since the single video object segmentation method only extract primary objects from the videos, only red regions could be shown in the results.

Table 3. Quantitative results on Safari dataset

Object:	Buffalo	Elephant	Giraffe	Lion	Sheep
Baseline [4]	0.686	0.266	0.024	0.302	0.048
Ours	**0.869**	**0.353**	0.024	**0.317**	**0.363**

3.2 Safari Dataset

Since video object co-segmentation problem is new and there is only one publicly available dataset with ground truth, we collected another challenging dataset (named 'Safari dataset'[1]) by getting new videos and also reusing some videos from MOViCS dataset. We annotated the key frames. The new dataset will be made publicly available. This Safari dataset is challenging, since the Safari contains 5 classes of animals and a total of 9 videos. For each animal class, Safari dataset has a video which only contains this class. Other videos contain

---

[1] http://crcv.ucf.edu/projects/video_object_cosegmentation/

two of the animal classes. The goal is to input the 9 videos together and do co-segmentation simultaneously for all of them. We show the ground truth and our co-segmentation results in Fig.7 and show quantitative results in Table 3.

Fig. 7. The ground truth and our results on Safari dataset. Row 1 shows one frame from each of the video. Row 2 shows the ground truth annotations, in which same color represents same object class. And row 3 shows our results, in which same color also represents same object classes. Please note that, there is no relationship between the colors of row 2 and row 3.

4   Conclusions

This paper formulates the video object discovery and co-segmentation problem into a Regulated Maximum Weight Clique (RMWC) Problem and solves it using a modified version of Bron-Kerbosch Algorithm. The success of the proposed method relies on i) use of the objectness measure to obtain spatially coherent region proposals, ii) tracking of region proposals, which selects proposals with consistent appearance and smooth motion over time, and iii) using different weighting functions for within video and across video matching for graph construction, which results in improved grouping. Experimental results shows that the method outperforms the state-of-the-art video co-segmentation methods.

Acknowledgments. This work was supported by the Intelligence Advanced Research Projects Activity (IARPA) via Department of Interior National Business Center contract number D11PC20066. The U.S. Government is authorized to reproduce and distribute reprints for Governmental purposes notwithstanding any copyright annotation thereon. Disclaimer: The views and conclusions contained herein are those of the authors and should not be interpreted as necessarily representing the official policies or endorsements, either expressed or implied, of IARPA, DoI/NBC, or the U.S.Government.

References

1. Alexe, B., Deselares, T., Ferrari, V.: Measuring the objectness of image windows. PAMI (2012)
2. Bron, C., Kerbosch, J.: Algorithm 457: finding all cliques of an undirected graph. Communications of the ACM 16(9), 575–577 (1973)

3. Chen, D.J., Chen, H.T., Chang, L.W.: Video object cosegmentation. In: ACM MM, pp. 805–808 (2012)
4. Chiu, W.C., Fritz, M.: Multi-class video co-segmentation with a generative multi-video model. In: CVPR (2013)
5. Endres, I., Hoiem, D.: Category independent object proposals. In: Daniilidis, K., Maragos, P., Paragios, N. (eds.) ECCV 2010, Part V. LNCS, vol. 6315, pp. 575–588. Springer, Heidelberg (2010)
6. Fairchild, M.D.: Color appearance models. John Wiley & Sons (2013)
7. Felzenszwalb, P.F., Girshick, R.B., McAllester, D., Ramanan, D.: Object detection with discriminatively trained part-based models. PAMI 32(9), 1627–1645 (2010)
8. Fulkerson, B., Vedaldi, A., Soatto, S.: Class segmentation and object localization with superpixel neighborhoods. In: ICCV, pp. 670–677. IEEE (2009)
9. Galasso, F., Iwasaki, M., Nobori, K., Cipolla, R.: Spatio-temporal clustering of probabilistic region trajectories. In: ICCV, pp. 1738–1745. IEEE (2011)
10. Grundmann, M., Kwatra, V., Han, M., Essa, I.: Efficient hierarchical graph based video segmentation. In: CVPR (2010)
11. Jain, B., Obermayer, K.: Extending bron kerbosch for solving the maximum weight clique problem. arXiv preprint arXiv:1101.1266 (2011)
12. Joulin, A., Bach, F., Ponce, J.: Discriminative clustering for image co-segmentation. In: CVPR, pp. 1943–1950. IEEE (2010)
13. Joulin, A., Bach, F., Ponce, J.: Multi-class cosegmentation. In: CVPR, pp. 542–549. IEEE (2012)
14. Kim, G., Torralba, A.: Unsupervised detection of regions of interest using iterative link analysis. In: NIPS (2009)
15. Kumlander, D.: A new exact algorithm for the maximum-weight clique problem based on a heuristic vertex-coloring and a backtrack search. In: Proc. 5th Int. Conf. on Modelling, Computation and Optimization in Information Systems and Management Sciences, pp. 202–208 (2004)
16. Lee, Y., Kim, J., Grauman, K.: Key-segments for video object segmentation. In: ICCV, pp. 1995–2002. IEEE (2011)
17. Ma, T., Latecki, L.: Maximum weight cliques with mutex constraints for video object segmentation. In: CVPR, pp. 670–677. IEEE (2012)
18. Mukherjee, L., Singh, V., Peng, J.: Scale invariant cosegmentation for image groups. In: CVPR, pp. 1881–1888. IEEE (2011)
19. Ochs, P., Brox, T.: Object segmentation in video: a hierarchical variational approach for turning point trajectories into dense regions. In: ICCV, pp. 1583–1590. IEEE (2011)
20. Rother, C., Minka, T., Blake, A., Kolmogorov, V.: Cosegmentation of image pairs by histogram matching-incorporating a global constraint into mrfs. In: CVPR, pp. 993–1000. IEEE (2006)
21. Rubinstein, M., Joulin, A., Johannes, K., Liu, C.: Unsupervised joint object discovery and segmentation in internet images. In: CVPR (2013)
22. Rubio, J.C., Serrat, J., López, A.: Video co-segmentation. In: Lee, K.M., Matsushita, Y., Rehg, J.M., Hu, Z. (eds.) ACCV 2012, Part II. LNCS, vol. 7725, pp. 13–24. Springer, Heidelberg (2013)
23. Russell, B.C., Freeman, W.T., Efros, A.A., Sivic, J., Zisserman, A.: Using multiple segmentations to discover objects and their extent in image collections. In: CVPR, vol. 2, pp. 1605–1614. IEEE (2006)
24. Sivic, J., Russell, B.C., Efros, A.A., Zisserman, A., Freeman, W.T.: Discovering objects and their location in images. In: ICCV, vol. 1, pp. 370–377. IEEE (2005)

25. Tomita, E., Tanaka, A., Takahashi, H.: The worst-case time complexity for generating all maximal cliques and computational experiments. Theoretical Computer Science 363(1), 28–42 (2006)
26. Vicente, S., Rother, C., Kolmogorov, V.: Object cosegmentation. In: CVPR, pp. 2217–2224. IEEE (2011)
27. Xu, C., Xiong, C., Corso, J.J.: Streaming hierarchical video segmentation. In: Fitzgibbon, A., Lazebnik, S., Perona, P., Sato, Y., Schmid, C. (eds.) ECCV 2012, Part VI. LNCS, vol. 7577, pp. 626–639. Springer, Heidelberg (2012)
28. Yuan, J., Zhao, G., Fu, Y., Li, Z., Katsaggelos, A.K., Wu, Y.: Discovering thematic objects in image collections and videos. IEEE Transactions on Image Processing 21(4), 2207–2219 (2012)
29. Zhang, D., Javed, O., Shah, M.: Video object segmentation through spatially accurate and temporally dense extraction of primary object regions. In: CVPR (2013)
30. Zhao, G., Yuan, J., Hua, G.: Topical video object discovery from key frames by modeling word co-occurrence prior. In: CVPR (2013)

Dense Semi-rigid Scene Flow Estimation from RGBD Images [*]

Julian Quiroga[1,3], Thomas Brox[2], Frédéric Devernay[1], and James Crowley[1]

[1] PRIMA team, INRIA Grenoble, France
{firstname.lastname}@inria.fr
[2] Department of Computer Science, University of Freiburg, Germany
brox@cs.uni-freiburg.de
[3] Departamento de Electrónica, Pontificia Universidad Javeriana, Colombia
quiroga.j@javeriana.edu.co

Abstract. Scene flow is defined as the motion field in 3D space, and can be computed from a single view when using an RGBD sensor. We propose a new scene flow approach that exploits the local and piecewise rigidity of real world scenes. By modeling the motion as a field of twists, our method encourages piecewise smooth solutions of rigid body motions. We give a general formulation to solve for local and global rigid motions by jointly using intensity and depth data. In order to deal efficiently with a moving camera, we model the motion as a rigid component plus a non-rigid residual and propose an alternating solver. The evaluation demonstrates that the proposed method achieves the best results in the most commonly used scene flow benchmark. Through additional experiments we indicate the general applicability of our approach in a variety of different scenarios.

Keywords: motion, scene flow, RGBD image.

1 Introduction

The 3D motion field of a scene is useful for several computer vision applications, such as action recognition, interaction, or 3D modeling on nonrigid objects. One group of methods uses a stereo or multi-view camera system, where both scene flow and depth are estimated from the images, while a second group uses RGBD images as input. In the latter case, the depth given by the sensor may be used directly for scene flow estimation. In this paper, we present a new formulation for this second group.

The two main questions for scene flow estimation from RGBD images are: (a) how to fully exploit both sources of data, and (b) which motion model should be used to compute a confident scene flow. When both intensity and depth are

---

[*] This work was supported by a collaborative research program between Inria Grenoble and University of Freiburg. We gratefully acknowledge partial funding by CMIRA 2013 (Region Rhône-Alpes), GDR ISIS (CNRS), and COLCIENCIAS (Colombia).

D. Fleet et al. (Eds.): ECCV 2014, Part VII, LNCS 8695, pp. 567–582, 2014.

provided, there is not a consensus on how to combine these two sources of information most effectively. A straightforward approach would compute the optical flow from RGB images and infer the scene flow from the depth data. It is also possible to generate colored 3D point clouds and try to find out the 3D motion vectors consistent with the input data. However, it is not mandatory to explicitly represents points in 3D to solve for the scene flow: the scene structure can be represented in the image domain, where color and depth data can be coupled using a projective function. This way, depth changes influence the motion in the image domain and consistency constraints can be formulated jointly over the color and depth images. This is the approach we follow in this work. It gives us access to some of the powerful tools developed for 2D motion estimation.

The second question has been addressed less. Scene flow estimation using intensity and depth is an ill-posed problem and regularization is needed. Usually, the 3D motion vector of each point is solved to minimize color and intensity constraints in a *data term* and the whole 3D motion field is regularized to get spatially smooth solutions while preserving discontinuities. Since depth data is available, a weighted regularization can be used to preserve motion discontinuities along depth edges, where independent motions are probable to appear. However, solving for a piecewise smooth solution of the 3D motion field may not be the best choice for some motions of interest. For example, a 3D rotation of a rigid surface induces a great variety of 3D motions that are hardly well regularized by such an approach. A similar issue occurs when the RGBD sensor is moving with respect to the scene.

In this work, we take advantage of the fact that most real scenes can be well modeled as locally or piecewise rigid, i.e., the scene is composed of 3D independently rigid components. The main contribution of this paper is the definition of an over-parametrized framework for scene flow estimation from RGBD images. We model the scene flow as a vector field of rigid body motions. This representation helps the regularization process which, instead of directly penalizing variations in the 3D motion field, encourages piecewise smooth solutions of rigid motions. Moreover, the proposed rigid body approach can be constrained in the image domain to fully exploit intensity and depth data. This formulation is flexible enough to support different data constraints and regularization strategies, and it can be adapted to more specialized problems. By using the same general framework, it is possible to model the scene flow as a global rigid motion plus a non-rigid residual, which is particularly useful when estimating the motion of deformable objects in conjunction with a moving camera.

2   Related Work

Scene flow was first introduced by Vedula [18] as the 3D motion field of the scene. Since this seminal work several approaches have been proposed to compute the 3D motion field. If a stereo or multi-view camera system is available, the scene flow can be computed by enforcing consistency with the observed optical flows [18], by a decoupled [21] or joint [1,8] estimation of structure and motion, or by assuming a local rigidity of the scene [19]. In this work we assume that a depth sensor is available and the estimation of the structure is not needed. The first work using intensity and depth was by Spies *et al.* [16], where the optical flow formulation by Horn and Schunck [7] is extended to include depth data. In this approach, depth data is used simply as an additional channel in the variational formulation of the optical flow. The range flow is estimated using the observed data and enforced to be smooth. However, the scene is assumed to be captured by an orthographic camera and there is no coupling between optical and range flows. The coupling issue can be solved as in [10], where the scene flow is directly solved using the depth data to constrain the 3D motion in the image domain. However in that work, the depth data is not fully exploited since there is no range flow constraint. Similar to [16], this method suffers from the early linearization of the constancy constraints and from over-smoothing along motion boundaries because of the L^2-regularization. Quiroga *et al.* [12] define a 2D warping function to couple image motion and 3D motion, allowing for a joint local constraint of the scene flow on intensity and depth data. Although the method is able to deal with large displacements, it fails on untextured regions and more complex motions, such as rotations.

In order to solve for dense scene flow, a regularization procedure is required. Usually, the 3D motion field is assumed to be piecewise smooth, and total variation (TV) is used as regularizer. The work by Herbst [6] follows this idea, but as [16], it lacks a coupling between optical and range flows, and the regularization is done on the optical flow rather than on the scene flow. In [13], a variational extension of [12] is presented. A weighted TV is applied on each component of the 3D motion field, aiming to preserve motion discontinuities along depth edges.

All these methods assume spatial smoothness of the scene flow, which is a reasonable assumption for translational motions but not for rotations. Under a rotation, even close scene points present different 3D motions. In case of a moving camera the regularization of the motion field can be a challenge. In this work, we use an over-parametrization of the scene flow, where each scene point is allowed to follow a rigid body motion. This way, the regularization can be done on a field of rigid motions, favoring piecewise solutions, which is a better choice for real scenes. A similar idea is presented in [14], where a regularization of a field of rigid motions is proposed. Our approach differs from that work in three ways. First, we use a more compact representation of the rigid-body motion via the 6-parameter twist representation, instead of a $\mathbb{R}^{12}$ embedding. Second, our approach solves and regularizes the rigid motion field at the same time. Finally, we decouple the regularization of the rotational and translational fields, which simplifies the optimization and allows the use of different TV strategies on each field. Similar to [12], we use a depth-based weighting function to avoid penalization along surface discontinuities.

In an alternative approach, Hadfield and Bowden [5] estimate the scene flow using particle filtering in a 3D colored point cloud representation of the scene. In that approach, a large set of motion hypotheses must be generated and tested for each 3D point, leading to high computational costs. We rather use the 2D parametrization provided by RGBD sensors to formulate an efficient 3D motion exploration. As done in [12], we define a warping function to couple the twist motion and the optical flow. A very similar warp is presented in [9] to solve for a global rigid motion from RGBD images. In our approach, we use the warping function to locally constrain the rigid motion field in the image domain. The global rigid motion estimation can be seen as a particular case of the proposed formulation. Moreover, unlike [9], we define a depth consistency constraint to fully exploit both sources of data. Thus, we can solve for the local twist motion that best explains the observed intensity and depth data, gaining robustness under noise. The local solver, in conjunction with the TV regularization of the twist field, provides an adjustable combination between local and piecewise rigidity.

As we present in the experiments, this framework is flexible enough to estimate a global rigid body motion or to solve for a general 3D motion field in challenging setups. This way, we are able to model the motion of the scene as a global rigid motion and a non-rigid residual.

3   Scene Motion Model

We parameterize every visible 3D point into the image domain $\Omega \subset \mathbb{R}^2$. The projection $\pi : \mathbb{R}^3 \to \mathbb{R}^2$ maps a 3D point $\mathbf{X} = (X, Y, Z)$ onto a pixel $\mathbf{x} = (x, y)$ on Ω by:

$$\pi(\mathbf{X}) = \left(f_x \frac{X}{Z} + c_x, f_y \frac{Y}{Z} + c_y \right)^T, \tag{1}$$

where f_x and f_y are the focal lengths of the camera and (c_x, c_y) its principal point. The inverse projection $\pi^{-1} : \mathbb{R}^2 \times \mathbb{R} \to \mathbb{R}^3$ back-projects an image point to the 3D space for a given depth z, as follows:

$$\pi^{-1}(\mathbf{x}, z) = \left(z \frac{x - c_x}{f_x}, z \frac{y - c_y}{f_y}, z \right)^T. \tag{2}$$

We will use $\mathbf{X}$ or $\pi^{-1}(\mathbf{x}, z)$ as the 3D representation of image point $\mathbf{x}$.

The scene flow $\mathbf{v}(\mathbf{x}) : \Omega \to \mathbb{R}^3$ is defined as the 3D motion field describing the motion of every visible 3D point between two time steps accordingly

$$\mathbf{X}_{t+1} = \mathbf{X}_t + \mathbf{v}(\mathbf{x}_t). \tag{3}$$

3.1   Twist Motion Field

Instead of directly representing the elements of the motion field as 3D vectors, we use an over-parametrized model to describe the motion of every point as a rigid transformation. The group action of a rigid body transformation can be written as $T(\mathbf{X}) = \mathbf{R}\mathbf{X} + \mathbf{t}$, where $\mathbf{t} \in \mathbb{R}^3$ is a translation, and $\mathbf{R} \in SO(3)$ is a rotation matrix. Using homogeneous coordinates, a 3D point $\tilde{\mathbf{X}} = (\mathbf{X}, 1)^T$ is transformed into $\tilde{\mathbf{X}}'$ accordingly to

$$\tilde{\mathbf{X}}' = \mathbf{G}\tilde{\mathbf{X}}, \quad \text{with} \quad \mathbf{G} = \begin{pmatrix} \mathbf{R} & \mathbf{t} \\ \mathbf{0}_{1 \times 3} & 1 \end{pmatrix} \in SE(3). \tag{4}$$

Since **G** has only 6 degrees of freedom, a more convenient and compact representation is the 6-parameter twist. Every rigid motion can be described as a rotation around a 3D axis $\omega = (\omega_X, \omega_Y, \omega_Z)^T$ and a translation $\tau = (\tau_x, \tau_y, \tau_z)^T$ along this axis. Therefore it can be shown that for any arbitrary $\mathbf{G} \in SE(3)$ there exists an equivalent $\xi \in \mathbb{R}^6$ twist representation. A twist $\xi = (\tau, \omega)$ can be converted into the **G** representation with the following exponential map:

$$\mathbf{G} = e^{\hat{\xi}} = \mathbf{I} + \hat{\xi} + \frac{(\hat{\xi})^2}{2!} + +\frac{(\hat{\xi})^3}{3!} + \cdots, \tag{5}$$

where

$$\hat{\xi} = \begin{pmatrix} \hat{\omega} & \tau \\ \mathbf{0}_{1\times 3} & 1 \end{pmatrix}, \quad \text{with} \quad \hat{\omega} = \begin{pmatrix} 0 & -\omega_Z & \omega_Y \\ \omega_Z & 0 & -\omega_X \\ -\omega_Y & \omega_X & 0 \end{pmatrix}. \tag{6}$$

Correspondingly, for each $\mathbf{G} \in SE(3)$ there exist a twist representation given by the logarithmic map via $\xi = \log(\mathbf{G})$; see [11] for more details. The motion of the scene is embedded in a *twist motion field* $\xi(\mathbf{x}) : \Omega \to \mathbb{R}^6$, where the motion of every 3D point between two time steps is given by:

$$\tilde{\mathbf{X}}_{t+1} = e^{\hat{\xi}(\mathbf{x}_t)}\tilde{\mathbf{X}}_t. \tag{7}$$

3.2 Twist Motion on the Image

For every time t the scene is registered as an RGBD image $\mathbf{S}_t(\mathbf{x}) = \{I_t(\mathbf{x}), Z_t(\mathbf{x})\}$ where images $I(\mathbf{x})$ and $Z(\mathbf{x})$ provide color and depth, respectively, for every point $\mathbf{x} \in \Omega$. Under the action of a twist ξ between t and $t + 1$, the motion of a 3D point induces an *image flow* (u, v). We define the warping function $\mathbf{W}(\mathbf{x}, \xi) : \mathbb{R}^2 \times \mathbb{R}^6 \to \mathbb{R}^2$ that maps each non-occluded pixel onto its new location after the rigid motion. The warping function is defined as:

$$\mathbf{W}(\mathbf{x}, \xi) = \pi\left(e^{\hat{\xi}}\tilde{\mathbf{X}}\right), \quad \text{with} \quad \tilde{\mathbf{X}} = \begin{pmatrix} \pi^{-1}(\mathbf{x}, Z(\mathbf{x})) \\ 1 \end{pmatrix}. \tag{8}$$

Let $S^k(\mathbf{x})$ be a component of the RGBD image (e.g. brightness or depth) evaluated at $\mathbf{x} \in \Omega$ and let $\rho_{S^k}(\mathbf{x}, \xi)$ be a robust error function between $S_t^k(\mathbf{x})$ and $S_{t+1}^k(\mathbf{W}(\mathbf{x}, \xi))$. Every twist motion vector ξ is solved to minimize one or several consistency functions $\rho_{S^k}(\mathbf{x}, \xi)$. Optimization problems on manifolds such as $SE(3)$ can be solved by calculating incremental steps in the tangent space to the manifold. Considering that an initial estimate ξ is known, the goal at each optimization step is to find the increment $\Delta\xi$ which (approximately) minimizes $\rho_{S^k}(\mathbf{x}, \xi)$. Since $SE(3)$ is a Lie group (not an Euclidean space) with the composition as operation, the exponential and logarithmic functions are used to update the current estimate ξ with the new increment $\Delta\xi$ according to $\xi \leftarrow \log(e^{\Delta\xi}e^{\hat{\xi}})$ [11]. The iterative solution requires a linearization of the warping function. Given the initial estimate ξ, the image point $\mathbf{x}$ becomes $\mathbf{x}_\xi = \mathbf{W}(\mathbf{x}, \xi)$ and the warping function satisfies:

$$\mathbf{W}(\mathbf{x}, \log(e^{\Delta\xi}e^{\hat{\xi}})) = \mathbf{W}(\mathbf{x}_\xi, \Delta\xi) = \mathbf{x}_\xi + \delta\mathbf{x}(\mathbf{x}_\xi, \Delta\xi), \tag{9}$$

where $\delta\mathbf{x}(\mathbf{x}_\xi, \Delta\xi)$ is the image flow induced by the increment $\Delta\xi$, which is given by $\delta\mathbf{x}(\mathbf{x}_\xi, \Delta\xi) = \pi(e^{\Delta\xi}\tilde{\mathbf{X}}_\xi) - \pi(\tilde{\mathbf{X}}_\xi)$, with $\tilde{\mathbf{X}}_\xi = \left(\pi^{-1}(\mathbf{x}_\xi, Z(\mathbf{x}_\xi)), 1\right)^T$. Assuming a small rotation increment, the exponential function is approximated as $e^{\Delta\xi} \approx \mathbf{I} + \hat{\Delta\xi}$. Therefore for a small increment $\Delta\xi$ the warping function can be well approximated by the following linear version:

$$\mathbf{W}(\mathbf{x}, \log(e^{\hat{\Delta\xi}}e^{\hat{\xi}})) = \mathbf{W}(\mathbf{x}, \xi) + \mathbf{J}(\mathbf{x}_\xi)\Delta\xi, \tag{10}$$

where $\mathbf{J}(\mathbf{x}_\xi)$ is the Jacobian matrix, given by:

$$\mathbf{J}(\mathbf{x}_\xi) = \begin{pmatrix} \frac{f_x}{Z(\mathbf{x}_\xi)} & 0 & -\frac{x_\xi}{Z(\mathbf{x}_\xi)} & -\frac{x_\xi y_\xi}{f_y} & \frac{f_x + x_\xi^2}{f_y} & -\frac{y_\xi f_x}{f_y} \\ 0 & \frac{f_y}{Z(\mathbf{x}_\xi)} & -\frac{y_\xi}{Z(\mathbf{x}_\xi)} & -\frac{f_y + y_\xi^2}{f_x} & \frac{x_\xi y_\xi}{f_x} & \frac{x_\xi f_y}{f_x} \end{pmatrix}. \tag{11}$$

4   Scene Flow Formulation

Given two pairs of RGBD images $\{I_1, Z_1\}$ and $\{I_2, Z_2\}$ the goal is to solve for the scene flow field that best explains the observed data. Due to vanishing gradients, the aperture problem and outliers, this motion computation is an ill-posed problem that cannot be solved independently for each point. Therefore, a smoothness in the motion field must be assumed. In our formulation, we consider only spatial smoothness, but it can be extended to temporal smoothness. In general, we solve for the twist field ξ minimizing the following energy:

$$E(\xi) = E_D(\xi) + \alpha E_S(\xi), \tag{12}$$

where the data term $E_D(\xi)$ measures how consistent is the estimated twist-based model with the observed color and depth data, and the smoothness term favors piecewise smooth fields while preserving discontinuities.

4.1   Data Term

The warping function (8) enables the formulation of consistency constraints for the twist field in the image domain. Using the gray value image we define a *brightness constancy assumption*:

$$I_2(\mathbf{W}(\mathbf{x}, \xi)) = I_1(\mathbf{x}), \tag{13}$$

and a *gradient constancy assumption*:

$$I_2^g(\mathbf{W}(\mathbf{x}, \xi)) = I_1^g(\mathbf{x}). \tag{14}$$

where $I^g(\mathbf{x}) = |\nabla I(\mathbf{x})|$. The gradient assumption reduces the effect of brightness changes. We use the gradient magnitude since it is invariant to rotation. The estimated twist motion should satisfy these constraints for most points.

On the other hand, the surface changes under the twist action. This variation must be consistent with the observed depth data. Therefore we define a *depth variation constraint* given by:

$$Z_2(\mathbf{W}(\mathbf{x}, \xi)) = Z_1(\mathbf{x}) + \delta_Z(\mathbf{x}, \xi), \tag{15}$$

where $\delta_Z(\mathbf{x}, \xi)$ is the depth variation induced on the 3D point $\pi^{-1}(\mathbf{x}, Z_1(\mathbf{x}))$ by the twist ξ, obtained from the third component of the 3D vector:

$$\delta_{\mathbf{3D}}(\mathbf{x}, \xi) = \left(e^{\hat{\xi}} - \mathbf{I}_{4\times 4}\right)\tilde{\mathbf{X}} \quad \text{with} \quad \tilde{\mathbf{X}} = \begin{pmatrix} \pi^{-1}(\mathbf{x}, Z_1(\mathbf{x})) \\ 1 \end{pmatrix}. \tag{16}$$

This equation enforces the consistency between the motion captured by the depth sensor and the estimated motion.

Without regularization, equations (13), (14) and (15) alone are not sufficient to constrain the twist motion for a given point since there is an infinite number of twists that satisfy these constraints. However, real scenes are locally rigid and it is possible to solve for a local twist explaining the observed motion. We formulate the twist motion estimation as a local least-square problem by writing the data term as follows:

$$E_D(\xi) = \sum_{\mathbf{x}} \sum_{\mathbf{x}' \in N_{\mathbf{x}}} \Psi\left(\rho_I^2(\mathbf{x}', \xi(\mathbf{x})) + \gamma \rho_g^2(\mathbf{x}', \xi(\mathbf{x}))\right) + \lambda \Psi\left(\rho_Z^2(\mathbf{x}', \xi(\mathbf{x}))\right), \tag{17}$$

where $N_{\mathbf{x}}$ is an image neighborhood centered on $\mathbf{x}$, and with the brightness, gradient and depth residuals, respectively given by:

$$\rho_I(\mathbf{x}, \xi) = I_2(\mathbf{W}(\mathbf{x}, \xi)) - I_1(\mathbf{x}), \tag{18}$$

$$\rho_g(\mathbf{x}, \xi) = I_2^g(\mathbf{W}(\mathbf{x}, \xi)) - I_1^g(\mathbf{x}), \tag{19}$$

$$\rho_Z(\mathbf{x}, \xi) = Z_2(\mathbf{W}(\mathbf{x}, \xi)) - (Z_1(\mathbf{x}) + \delta_Z(\mathbf{x}, \xi)). \tag{20}$$

Constant γ balances brightness and gradient residuals, while λ weights intensity and depth terms. We use the robust norm $\Psi(s^2) = \sqrt{s^2 + \varepsilon^2}$, which is a differentiable approximation of the L^1 norm, to cope with outliers due to occlusion and non-rigid motion components in $N_{\mathbf{x}}$.

4.2 Smoothness Term

A twist motion field ξ can be decomposed into a rotational field ω, with $e^{\hat{\omega}} : \Omega \to SO(3)$, and a 3D motion field $\tau : \Omega \to \mathbb{R}^3$. Since they are decorrelated by nature, we regularize each field independently using weighted Total Variation (TV), which allows piecewise smooth solutions while preserving motion discontinuities.

Regularization of the fields ω and τ poses different challenges. Elements of τ lie in the Euclidean space $\mathbb{R}^3$ and the problem corresponds to a vector-valued function regularization. Different TV approaches can be used to regularize τ, as described in [4]. Particularly the channel-by-channel L^1 norm has been successfully used for optical flow [22]. We define the weighted TV of τ as:

$$\mathbf{TV}_c(\tau) = \sum_{\mathbf{x}} c(\mathbf{x}) \|\nabla \tau(\mathbf{x})\|, \tag{21}$$

where $\|\nabla \tau\| := |\nabla \tau_X| + |\nabla \tau_Y| + |\nabla \tau_Z|$ and $c(\mathbf{x}) = e^{-\beta |\nabla Z_1(\mathbf{x})|^2}$. The weighting function c helps preserve motion discontinuities along edges of the 3D surface. Moreover, the L^1 norm can be replaced by the Huber norm [23] to reduce the staircasing effect. Efficient solvers for both norms are presented in [3].

Elements of ω are rotations in the Lie group $SO(3)$ embedded in $\mathbb{R}^3$ through the exponential map, and the regularization has to be done on this manifold. In order to apply a TV regularization, a notion of variation should be used for elements of $SO(3)$. Given two points $e^{\hat{\omega}_1}, e^{\hat{\omega}_2} \in SO(3)$ the residual rotation can be defined as $e^{-\hat{\omega}_1} e^{\hat{\omega}_2}$. The product in logarithmic coordinates can be expressed as $e^{\hat{\omega}_1} e^{\hat{\omega}_1} = e^{\mu(\hat{\omega}_1, \hat{\omega}_2)}$, where the mapping μ can be expanded in a Taylor series around the identity, using the Baker-Campbell-Hausdorff formula:

$$\mu(\hat{\omega}_1, \hat{\omega}_2) = \hat{\omega}_1 + \hat{\omega}_2 + \frac{1}{2}[\hat{\omega}_1, \hat{\omega}_2] + O(|(\hat{\omega}_1, \hat{\omega}_2)|^3), \tag{22}$$

where $[\cdot, \cdot]$ is the Lie bracket in $so(3)$. Close to the identity, (22) is well approximated by its first-order terms, so that for small rotations the variation measure can be defined as the matrix subtraction in $so(3)$, or equivalently, as a vector difference for the embedding in $\mathbb{R}^3$. Accordingly, the derivative matrix $\mathbf{D}\omega := (\nabla \omega_X, \nabla \omega_Z, \nabla \omega_Z)^T : \Omega \to \mathbb{R}^{3 \times 2}$ approximates the horizontal and vertical point-wise variations of ω on the image. Following [4], we define the TV as the sum over the largest singular value σ_1 of the derivative matrix:

$$\mathbf{TV}_\sigma(\omega) = \sum_{\mathbf{x}} c(\mathbf{x}) \, \sigma_1(\mathbf{D}\omega(\mathbf{x})) \ . \tag{23}$$

This TV approach supports a common edge direction for three components, which is a desirable properties for the regularization of the field of rotations. Moreover, deviations are less penalized with respect to other measures (e.g. Frobenius norm [14]) and efficient solvers are available. However, this TV definition approximates the real structure of the manifold yielding to a biased measures far from the identity. The more the rotation is away from the identity, the more its variations in $SO(3)$ are penalized as is shown hereinafter. Given two rotations $\omega_1 = \theta_1 \overleftarrow{\omega_1}$ and $\omega_2 = \theta_2 \overleftarrow{\omega_2}$, with θ the angle and $\overleftarrow{\omega}$ the unitary axis vector of the rotation, and writing $\theta_2 = \theta_1 + \delta\theta$, leads to $\omega_2 - \omega_1 = \theta_1(\overleftarrow{\omega_2} - \overleftarrow{\omega_1}) - \delta\theta\overleftarrow{\omega_2}$. This linearly dependent penalization usually is not a problem, since large rotations imply larger motion on the image. Thus, a stronger regularization can be reasonable. Moreover, large rotation caused by a global motion of the scene or the camera can be optimized separately and compensated, as we show in Sec. 4.4. Optionally, this over-penalization can be removed by expressing each rotation as $\omega = \theta\overleftarrow{\omega}$ and applying a vectorial TV on $\overleftarrow{\omega}$ and a scalar TV on θ. In our approach, the full smoothing term is given by:

$$E_S(\xi) = \mathbf{TV}_c(\tau) + \mathbf{TV}_\sigma(\omega). \tag{24}$$

4.3 Optimization

The proposed energy (12) is minimized by decomposing the optimization into two simpler problems. We use the variable splitting method [20] with auxiliary variable χ, and the minimization problem becomes:

$$\min_{\xi,\chi} E_D(\xi) + \frac{1}{2\kappa} \sum_{\mathbf{x}} |\xi(\mathbf{x}) - \chi(\mathbf{x})|^2 + \alpha E_S(\chi), \tag{25}$$

where κ is a small numerical variable. Note that the linking term between ξ and χ is the distance on the tangent space at the identity in $SE(3)$. The solution of (25) converges to that of (12) as $\kappa \to 0$. Minimization of this energy is performed by alternating the two following optimization problems:

i. For fixed χ, estimate ξ that minimizes (25). This optimization problem can be solved point-wise by minimizing:

$$\frac{1}{2\kappa} |\xi - \chi|^2 + \sum_{\mathbf{x}' \in N_{\mathbf{x}}} \Psi \left(\rho_I^2 + \gamma \rho_g^2 \right) + \lambda \Psi \left(\rho_Z^2 \right), \tag{26}$$

where the parameters $(\mathbf{x}', \xi)$ are considered implicit. This energy can be linearized around an initial estimate $\hat{\xi}$, using a first-order Taylor series expansion:

$$\frac{1}{2\kappa} \left| \log(e^{\Delta\hat{\xi}} e^{\hat{\xi}}) - \chi \right|^2 + \sum_{\mathbf{x}' \in N_{\mathbf{x}}} \Psi \left(|\rho_I + \mathbf{I}_{\mathbf{x}} \mathbf{J} \Delta\xi|^2 + \gamma |\rho_G + \mathbf{I}_{\mathbf{x}}^g \mathbf{J} \Delta\xi|^2 \right)$$
$$+ \lambda \Psi \left(|\rho_Z + (\mathbf{Z}_{\mathbf{x}} \mathbf{J} - \mathbf{K}) \Delta\xi|^2 \right). \tag{27}$$

where $\mathbf{I}_{\mathbf{x}}$, $\mathbf{I}_{\mathbf{x}}^g$ and $\mathbf{Z}_{\mathbf{x}}$ are the row vector gradients of $\mathbf{I}_2(\mathbf{x})$, $\mathbf{I}_2^g(\mathbf{x})$ and $\mathbf{Z}_2(\mathbf{x})$, respectively, and $\mathbf{J}$ is the Jacobian (11) of the warp, all evaluated at $\mathbf{x}_\xi = \mathbf{W}(\mathbf{x}, \xi)$. The 1×6 vector $\mathbf{K}$ is defined as $\mathbf{K} = \mathbf{D} \left([\mathbf{X}_\xi]_\times | \mathbf{I}_{3\times 3} \right)$ with $\mathbf{D} = (0, 0, 1)$ isolating the third component and $[\cdot]_\times$ the cross product matrix. Finding the minimum of (27) requires an iterative approach. Taking the partial derivative with respect to $\Delta\xi$ and setting it to zero, the increment $\Delta\xi$ can be computed as:

$$\Delta\xi = -\mathbf{H}^{-1} \left[\sum_{\mathbf{x}' \in N_{\mathbf{x}}} \left\{ \Psi' \left(\rho_I^2 + \gamma \rho_G^2 \right) \left[(\mathbf{I}_{\mathbf{x}} \mathbf{J})^T \rho_I + \gamma (\mathbf{I}_{\mathbf{x}}^g \mathbf{J})^T \rho_G \right] \right. \right.$$
$$\left. \left. + \lambda \Psi' \left(\rho_Z^2 \right) (\mathbf{Z}_{\mathbf{x}} \mathbf{J} - \mathbf{K})^T \rho_Z \right\} + \frac{1}{\kappa} \log \left((e^{\hat{\xi}})^{-1} e^{\hat{x}} \right) \right], \tag{28}$$

where Ψ' is the derivative of the robust norm, which is evaluated at the current estimate $\hat{\xi}$. The 6×6 matrix $\mathbf{H}$ is the Gauss-Newton approximation of the Hessian matrix and is given by:

$$\mathbf{H} = \sum_{\mathbf{x}' \in N_{\mathbf{x}}} \Psi' \left(\rho_I^2 + \gamma \rho_G^2 \right) \left[(\mathbf{I}_{\mathbf{x}} \mathbf{J})^T (\mathbf{I}_{\mathbf{x}} \mathbf{J}) + \gamma (\mathbf{I}_{\mathbf{x}}^g \mathbf{J})^T (\mathbf{I}_{\mathbf{x}}^g \mathbf{J}) \right]$$
$$+ \lambda \Psi' \left(\rho_Z^2 \right) (\mathbf{Z}_{\mathbf{x}} \mathbf{J} - \mathbf{K})^T (\mathbf{Z}_{\mathbf{x}} \mathbf{J} - \mathbf{K}) + \frac{1}{2\kappa} \mathbf{I}_{6\times 6}. \tag{29}$$

ii. For fixed $\xi = (\omega, \tau)$, compute $\chi = (\varpi, \pi)$ that minimizes:

$$\left\{ \mathbf{TV}_c(\pi) + \frac{\eta}{2} \sum_{\mathbf{x}} |\pi(\mathbf{x}) - \tau(\mathbf{x})|^2 \right\} + \left\{ \mathbf{TV}_\sigma(\varpi) + \frac{\eta}{2} \sum_{\mathbf{x}} |\varpi(\mathbf{x}) - \omega(\mathbf{x})|^2 \right\} \quad (30)$$

where $\eta = (\kappa\alpha)^{-1}$. Each side of equation (30) corresponds to a vectorial image denoising problem with a TV-L^2 model (ROF model). Efficient primal-dual algorithms exist for solving both problems. The left side is solved component-wise using the first-order primal-dual algorithm [3]. For the right side we use the vectorial approach [4] which allows an optimal coupling between components. A small modification is necessary in both cases to include the weighting function.

4.4 Scene Flow with Camera Motion Estimation

In many applications, the sensor itself moves relative to the observed scene and causes a dominant global motion in the overall motion field. In this situation, compensating for the motion of the camera can simplify the estimation and regularization of the scene flow. Moreover, for 3D reconstruction of deformable objects, the camera motion is needed to register partial 3D reconstructions. Therefore, we consider splitting the motion of the scene into a globally rigid component $\xi_R = (\tau_R, \omega_R) \in \mathbb{R}^6$, capturing the camera motion relative to the dominant object/background, plus a non-rigid residual field $\xi = (\tau, \omega)$. We assume that a large part of the scene follows the same rigid motion. Accordingly, the scene flow is defined as the composition $\chi = \log(e^{\hat{\xi}} + e^{\hat{\xi}_R} - \mathbf{I}_{4 \times 4})$, and the estimation problem is formulated as:

$$\min_{\chi} \; E_{\mathbf{Rig}}(\chi) + E_{\mathbf{Res}}(\chi), \quad (31)$$

with $E_{\mathbf{Rig}}(\chi)$ and $E_{\mathbf{Res}}(\chi)$ the rigid and non-rigid energies, respectively. It is worth noting that the separation of the camera motion is *in addition* to the framework presented above, i.e., the non-rigid part can still deal with local motion.

Rigid Energy. The camera motion can be estimated using the data term (17), by considering every pixel (or a subset of Ω) to solve for a unique twist ξ_R. Accordingly, the rigid component of the energy is defined as:

$$E_{\mathbf{Rig}}(\chi) = \sum_{\mathbf{x}} \Psi \left(\rho_I^2(\mathbf{x}, \chi) + \gamma\rho_g^2(\mathbf{x}, \chi) \right) + \lambda\Psi \left(\rho_Z^2(\mathbf{x}, \chi) \right). \quad (32)$$

Non-rigid Residual Energy. The residual motion can be computed following (12), with the non-rigid energy given by:

$$E_{\mathbf{Res}}(\chi) = E_D(\chi) + \alpha E_S(\chi). \quad (33)$$

We minimize (31) by an iterative, alternating estimation of ξ_R and ξ:

a. Given a fixed ξ, solve for ξ_R that minimizes $E_{\mathbf{Rig}}(\chi)$. This is done by iteratively applying (28) and (29), with a zero auxiliary flow.

b. Given a fixed ξ_R, solve for ξ that minimizes $E_{\mathbf{Res}}(\chi)$. This is done by iterating steps **i** and **ii** in Sec. 4.3.

5 Experiments

5.1 Implementation Details

In order to compute the scene flow, the proposed method assumes that a pair of calibrated RGBD images is provided. Regardless of the depth sensor, depth data is always processed in cm and RGB color images are transformed to intensity images and normalized. For all the experiments $\alpha = 10$, $\beta = 1$, $\gamma = 0.1$ and $\lambda = 0.1$. For each scene a depth range is defined and only pixels having a valid depth measure inside the range are taken into account for the data term and final measurements. However, all pixels are considered in the regularization.

We use a multi-scale strategy in order to deal with larger motions. We construct an image pyramid with a downsampling factor of 2. We apply a Gaussian anti-aliasing filter to the intensity image and the pyramid is built using bicubic downsampling. For the depth image, a 5×5 median filter is used and the pyramid is constructed by averaging pixels in non-overlapped neighborhoods of 2×2, where only pixels with a valid depth measure are used. Having a pyramid with levels $l = \{0, 1, ..., L\}$, with 0 the original resolution, the computation is started at level L an the estimated twist field is directly propagated to the next lower level. The camera matrix is scaled at each level by the factor 2^l. The neighborhood $N_{\mathbf{x}}$ is defined as a $N \times N$ centering window. At each level we perform M loops consisting of $M_{\mathbf{GN}} = 5$ iterations of the Gauss-Newton procedure followed by $M_{\mathbf{TV}} = 50$ iterations of the TV solver. The constant κ is styled at each scale.

5.2 Middlebury Datasets

The Middlebury stereo dataset [15] is commonly used as benchmark to compare scene flow methods [1,8,5,13]. Using images of one of these datasets is equivalent to a fixed camera observing an object moving in X direction. As in [5,13], we take images 2 and 6 as the first and second RGBD image, respectively, and use the ground truth disparity map of each image as depth channel. Stereo-based methods [1,8] do not assume RGBD images and simultaneously estimate the optical flow and disparity maps by considering images 2, 4, 6 and 8 of each dataset. The ground truth for the scene corresponds to the camera motion along the X axis, while the optical flow is given by the disparity map. The scene flow error is measured in the image domain using root mean squared error (RMS) and the average angle error (AAE) of the optical flow. In order to compare with optical flow methods, we include results for the scene flow inferred using LDOF [2] and the depth data, as is described in [5]. Results and comparison for Teddy and Cones datasets are shown in Table 1, where stereo methods are denoted with

Table 1. Middlebury dataset: errors on the optical flow extracted from the scene flow (except for [2], which is an optical flow method). See Sec. 5.2 for details.

	Views	Teddy		Cones	
		RMS	AAE	RMS	AAE
Semi-rigid Scene Flow (ours)	1	0.49	0.46	0.45	0.37
Hadfield and Bowden [5]	1	0.52	1.36	0.59	1.61
Quiroga *et al.* [13]	1	0.94	0.84	0.79	0.52
Brox and Malik [2] + depth	1	2.11	0.43	2.30	0.52
Basha *et al.* [1]	2	0.57	1.01	0.58	0.39
Huguet and Devernay [8]	2	1.25	0.51	1.10	0.69

2 views. In this experiment, we used a 5-level pyramid, with $M = 5$, $N = 3$ and for each level l, we set $\kappa = 10^4 10^{-l}$. A non-optimized implementation of our method processes each dataset in about 60 sec. The proposed approach outperforms previous methods. Because the 3D motion field resulting from camera translation is constant, Middlebury datasets are not well suited to fully evaluate the performance of scene flow methods.

5.3   Scene Flow from RGBD Data

We performed further experiments on more complex scenes using two RGBD sensors: the Microsoft Kinect for Xbox and the Asus Xtion Pro Live. We consider three different setups: i) a fixed camera, ii) a moving camera observing a rigid scene and iii) a moving camera capturing deformable objects. In each case, we show the input images, the optical flow, and one or more components of the scene flow. To give an idea of the motion, the average of the two input RGB images is shown. The optical flow is visualized using the Middlebury color code [15]. For the scene flow, we show each component using a cold-to-warm code, where green color is zero motion, and warmer and colder colors represent positive and negative velocities, respectively.

In the first experiment, the Kinect sensor is fixed to compute the scene flow from two sequences (Fig. 1). The top row shows the deformation of a poster, which produces a non-uniform deformation. The proposed method is able to capture the poster deformation, thus it is possible to accurately estimate the changes in depth when the poster is folded. The gradient constancy constraint plays an important role here, since the sensor applies automatic white balancing. The bottom images show a motion performed with arms and hands. While hands are rotating inwards, the elbows lift, and a region of both arms remains almost still. This composite motion generates a discontinuous optical flow, which is well estimated by our method. Moreover, it can be seen that small rotations and articulated motions are well described for the proposed motion model.

The second experiment considers a static scene observed by a moving camera. We use Teddy images of the RGBD dataset [17]. Unlike the Middlebury dataset, this scene presents a changing 3D motion field due to the translation and rotation

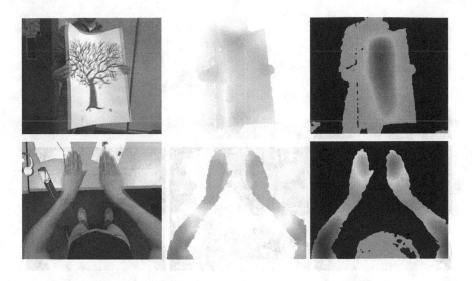

Fig. 1. Scene flow estimation with a fixed camera. a) *Left*: Input images. b) *Middle*: Optical flow c) *Right*: Z-component of the scene flow.

Fig. 2. Camera motion. *From left to the right*: a) Input images. b) Optical flow of the rigid motion estimation. c) Optical flow using the proposed method. d) Optical flow by the scene flow method [13]. Results of the proposed method are clearly more accurate than those of [13].

of the sensor. We first estimate a single rigid motion as is presented in Sec. 4.4. We estimate the parameters using every second pixel with a range between 50 cm and 150 cm from the sensor. At each level of the pyramid we run 100 iterations. This result is taken as baseline and compared in Figure 2 with resulting optical flows of our method and the dense estimation provided by [13]. The proposed method produces a close estimation of the camera motion without assuming a global rigidity of the scene. In contrast, the direct regularization on the scene flow components, as is performed in [13], fails to capture the diversity of 3D motions introduced by the camera rotation.

In the last experiment, a moving Asus Xtion camera observes a non-rigid scene. To estimate the rigid and non-rigid components we perform 3 rounds of

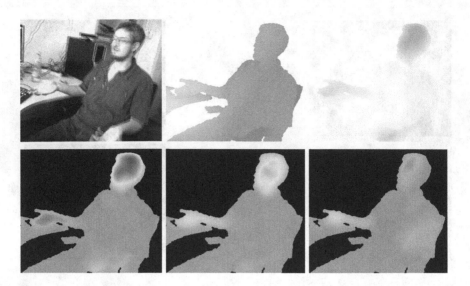

Fig. 3. Motion estimation with a moving camera. *Top, from left to right*: a) Input images. b) Optical flow of the global rigid motion. c) Optical flow of the non-rigid residual. *Bottom, from left to right*: (X, Y, Z) components of the non-rigid 3D motion.

alternation at each level of the pyramid. As is shown in Figure 3, the proposed approach allows the joint estimation of both components. Particularly, it is possible to compute the motion of both hands and the rotation of the face while the camera is turning. Capturing the motion of thin objects, as the fingers of the left hand, is a challenge since depth data is incomplete and very noisy in this area.

The size of the local neighborhood was kept fixed for all the scales and for every position on the image. Results could be improved by adjusting the size of the window using the depth data, in order to get a constant resolution.

6   Summary

We have presented a new method to compute dense scene flow from RGBD images by modeling the motion as a field of rigid motions. This allows for piecewise smooth solutions using TV regularization on the parametrization. We have decoupled the regularization procedure for the rotational and translational part and proposed some approximations to simplify the optimization. Future advances on manifold regularization may provide even more accurate and faster solvers that can be used with our parameterization. In order to fully exploit both intensity and depth data, we constrain the rigid body motion in the image domain. This way, we can solve for the local rigid motion as an iteratively reweighted least squares problem. The proposed approach provides an adjustable combination between local and piecewise rigidity, which, in conjunction with a global rigid estimation, is able to capture the motion in real world scenes.

References

1. Basha, T., Moses, Y., Kiryati, N.: Multi-view scene flow estimation: A view centered variational approach. In: Conference on Computer Vision and Pattern Recognition, pp. 1506–1513 (2010)
2. Brox, T., Malik, J.: Large displacement optical flow: Descriptor matching in variational motion estimation. IEEE Transactions on Pattern Analysis and Machine Intelligence 33(3), 500–513 (2011)
3. Chambolle, A., Pock, T.: A first-order primal-dual algorithm for convex problems with applications to imaging. Journal of Mathematical Imaging and Vision 40(1), 120–145 (2011)
4. Goldluecke, B., Strekalovskiy, E., Cremers, D.: The natural vectorial total variation which arises from geometric measure theory. SIAM Journal on Imaging Sciences 5(2), 537–563 (2012)
5. Hadfield, S., Bowden, R.: Scene particles: Unregularized particle-based scene flow estimation. IEEE Transactions on Pattern Analysis and Machine Intelligence 36(3), 564–576 (2014)
6. Herbst, E., Ren, X., Fox, D.: RGB-D flow: Dense 3-D motion estimation using color and depth. In: International Conference on Robotics and Automation (ICRA), pp. 2276–2282 (2013)
7. Horn, B.K., Schunck, B.G.: Determining optical flow. Artificial Intelligence 17, 185–203 (1981)
8. Huguet, F., Devernay, F.: A variational method for scene flow estimation from stereo sequences. In: International Conference on Computer Vision, pp. 1–7 (2007)
9. Kerl, C., Sturm, J., Cremers, D.: Robust odometry estimation for RGB-D cameras. In: International Conference on Robotics and Automation (ICRA), pp. 3748–3754 (2013)
10. Letouzey, A., Petit, B., Boyer, E.: Scene flow from depth and color images. In: British Machine Vision Conference, BMVC 2011 (2011)
11. Murray, R.M., Sastry, S.S., Zexiang, L.: A Mathematical Introduction to Robotic Manipulation, 1st edn. CRC Press, Inc., Boca Raton (1994)
12. Quiroga, J., Devernay, F., Crowley, J.: Scene flow by tracking in intensity and depth data. In: Computer Vision and Pattern Recognition Workshops (CVPRW), pp. 50–57 (2012)
13. Quiroga, J., Devernay, F., Crowley, J.: Local/global scene flow estimation. In: International Conference on Image Processing (ICIP), pp. 3850–3854 (2013)
14. Rosman, G., Bronstein, A.M., Bronstein, M.M., Tai, X.-C., Kimmel, R.: Group-valued regularization for analysis of articulated motion. In: Fusiello, A., Murino, V., Cucchiara, R. (eds.) ECCV 2012 Ws/Demos, Part I. LNCS, vol. 7583, pp. 52–62. Springer, Heidelberg (2012)
15. Scharstein, D., Szeliski, R.: High-accuracy stereo depth maps using structured light. In: Conference on Computer Vision and Pattern Recognition, vol. 1, pp. 195–202 (2003)
16. Spies, H., Jahne, B., Barron, J.: Dense range flow from depth and intensity data. In: International Conference on Pattern Recognition, vol. 1, pp. 131–134 (2000)
17. Sturm, J., Engelhard, N., Endres, F., Burgard, W., Cremers, D.: A benchmark for the evaluation of RGB-D slam systems. In: International Conference on Intelligent Robot Systems (IROS), pp. 573–580 (2012)
18. Vedula, S., Baker, S., Rander, P., Collins, R.: Three-dimensional scene flow. In: International Conference on Computer Vision, vol. 2, pp. 722–729 (1999)

19. Vogel, C., Schindler, K., Roth, S.: 3D scene flow estimation with a rigid motion prior. In: International Conference on Computer Vision, pp. 1291–1298 (2011)
20. Wang, Y., Yang, J., Yin, W., Zhang, Y.: A new alternating minimization algorithm for total variation image reconstruction. SIAM J. Img. Sci. 1(3), 248–272 (2008)
21. Wedel, A., Rabe, C., Vaudrey, T., Brox, T., Franke, U., Cremers, D.: Efficient dense scene flow from sparse or dense stereo data. In: Forsyth, D., Torr, P., Zisserman, A. (eds.) ECCV 2008, Part I. LNCS, vol. 5302, pp. 739–751. Springer, Heidelberg (2008)
22. Wedel, A., Pock, T., Zach, C., Bischof, H., Cremers, D.: An improved algorithm for TV-l^1 optical flow. In: Cremers, D., Rosenhahn, B., Yuille, A.L., Schmidt, F.R. (eds.) Visual Motion Analysis. LNCS, vol. 5604, pp. 23–45. Springer, Heidelberg (2009)
23. Werlberger, M., Trobin, W., Pock, T., Wedel, A., Cremers, D., Bischof, H.: Anisotropic Huber-L1 Optical Flow. In: Proceedings of the British Machine Vision Conference (BMVC) (2009)

Video Pop-up: Monocular 3D Reconstruction of Dynamic Scenes*

Chris Russell**, Rui Yu**, and Lourdes Agapito

University College London
http://www0.cs.ucl.ac.uk/staff/lagapito/research/youtube3d

Abstract. Consider a video sequence captured by a single camera observing a complex dynamic scene containing an unknown mixture of multiple moving and possibly deforming objects. In this paper we propose an unsupervised approach to the challenging problem of simultaneously segmenting the scene into its constituent objects and reconstructing a 3D model of the scene. The strength of our approach comes from the ability to deal with real-world dynamic scenes and to handle seamlessly different types of motion: rigid, articulated and non-rigid. We formulate the problem as hierarchical graph-cut based segmentation where we decompose the whole scene into background and foreground objects and model the complex motion of non-rigid or articulated objects as a set of overlapping rigid parts. We evaluate the motion segmentation functionality of our approach on the Berkeley Motion Segmentation Dataset. In addition, to validate the capability of our approach to deal with real-world scenes we provide 3D reconstructions of some challenging videos from the *YouTube-Objects* dataset.

1 Introduction

With the emergence of video cameras on phones and laptops and the rise of video libraries (e. g. *YouTube Action, YouTube Objects*) the use of 3D information for recognition tasks has experienced a resurgence. While structure from motion (sƒm) techniques exist that can reliably reconstruct a static scene, most scenes of interest contain multiple moving objects or even articulated or non-rigid objects. Motion segmentation and non-rigid scene reconstruction from monocular video have become more important than ever. This paper proposes a refocusing of 3D reconstruction towards reconstructing videos of dynamic scenes.

Multibody sƒm and non-rigid structure from motion (NRSƒm) have addressed some of the limitations of sƒm and have seen sustained progress in dealing with dynamic scenes [21,25] or creating vivid life-like reconstructions of deformable objects [12]. However, they remain far behind their rigid counterparts. Multibody sƒm approaches can segment the scene into multiple rigidly moving objects,

---

* This research was funded by the European Research Council under the ERC Starting Grant agreement 204871-HUMANIS.

** The first two authors assert equal contribution and joint first authorship.

D. Fleet et al. (Eds.): ECCV 2014, Part VII, LNCS 8695, pp. 583–598, 2014.

part − segmentation object − segmentation 3D − reconstruction

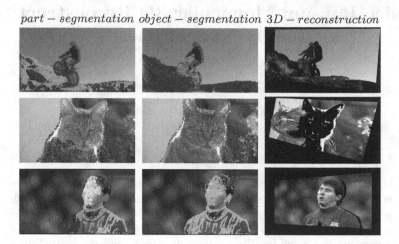

Fig. 1. Segmentation and 3D reconstruction results of two dynamic sequences of the *Youtube-Objects* Dataset [23] and a football sequence downloaded from YouTube. **Left:** segmentation into *parts* (rigid models). **Centre:** segmentation into *objects*. **Right:** densified 3D video pop-up from a novel viewpoint. The *motorbike* sequence, acquired with a moving camera, shows articulated motion. The *cat* sequence is a non-rigid sequence occluding a static background. Bottom row shows a reconstruction of football footage. For videos see the project website http://www0.cs.ucl.ac.uk/staff/lagapito/research/youtube3d.

however they cannot deal simultaneously with the presence of deformable or articulated objects in the scene. Although NRS*f*M algorithms can reconstruct a single pre-segmented deformable surface moving in front of a camera [12,33], they require manual segmentation of the scene into background and foreground.

Piecewise approaches to non-rigid and articulated reconstruction have been successfully applied to explain the complex motion of 2D tracks on a single non-rigid surface or an articulated object as a network of *overlapping* parts [9,26,33]. However, if applied to an entire scene with foreground/background objects occluding one another, depth boundaries between objects would not be respected and neighbouring models in the image would be forced to overlap irrespective of whether or not they belong to the same physical object.

Contributions: The main contribution of this paper is to offer a solution to the problem of *scene reconstruction* for real-world dynamic monocular videos that deals seamlessly with the presence of non-rigid, articulated or pure rigid motion. In an entirely unsupervised approach, we reorganise/segment the scene into a constellation of object parts, recognise which parts are likely to constitute objects, join them together, and reconstruct the scene. We offer solutions to some of the problems of previous approaches to dynamic scene reconstruction: *(i)* Our approach is able to adapt the topology of the neighbourhood graph by breaking edges where necessary to preserve boundaries between objects. In this way our approach can deal with an entire scene where objects might occlude one another and not just pre-segmented objects; *(ii)* Our work results in a hierarchical approach to dynamic scene analysis. At the higher level of the hierarchy the scene is explained as a set of *objects* that are detached from the background and from each other. At the lower level of the hierarchy, each *object* can be explained as a set of overlapping *parts* that can model more complex motion.

2 Related Work

Most works in dynamic scene reconstruction [7,10,27,21] follow a pipeline approach where first feature point tracks or dense optical flow is estimated, followed by a motion segmentation step to cluster trajectories into different independent motions before 3D reconstruction is applied independently to each of the objects. The first approach to **multibody reconstruction** [7] extended the classic affine factorisation algorithm for static scenes [30] to the case of multiple independently moving rigid objects. While the original approach [7] was unable to deal with dependencies in the motions it was later extended to deal with degenerate [38] and articulated motions [32,36]. More recent approaches to multibody s*f*M such as Ozden *et al.* [21] are able to perform simultaneous tracking, segmentation and reconstruction of a few feature points on realistic sequences. Roussos *et al.* [25] proposed a dense approach to multibody s*f*M in which depth values are estimated for every pixel in the image. However, none of these approaches can deal with non-rigidity or articulation in each of the objects which are assumed to be rigid.

Providing robust solutions to **video and motion segmentation** is a fundamental problem in computer vision and often a preliminary step towards 3D reconstruction. A wealth of motion segmentation algorithms for multi-rigid scenes have been proposed including algebraic frameworks such as GPCA [34] and methods that can deal with noise and outliers [24]. Motion segmentation has also been cast as a motion subspace clustering problem, first applied to the affine camera case [8,15] and later extended to the case of perspective scenes [18]. Approaches such as Brox and Malik's [6] exploit the consistency of point trajectories over time and can deal with non-rigid motion. On the other hand, superpixel [11] and supervoxel [35] methods for video segmentation can produce high quality video over-segmentations that respect object boundaries, are temporally consistent and are aligned with objects. However, since their aim is to segment non-rigid and articulated objects as a single segment, they are not appropriate for piecewise 3D reconstruction.

Non-rigid structure from motion (NRS*f*M) approaches reconstruct 3D models of non-rigid objects from monocular video, typically by fitting a global low-rank shape model [31,22] to 2D tracks. Piecewise reconstruction has also been successfully applied to NRS*f*M [26,33] and articulated reconstruction [9] by fitting local models. However all existing methods can only reconstruct a single presegmented object and can not resolve entire scenes.

Our approach is most closely related to the paradigm of *multiple model fitting* where tracks, that might contain outliers, belong to an unknown number of models. The assignment of tracks to models and the estimation of model parameters is then optimised jointly [14,26] to minimise a geometric cost subject to the constraint that neighbouring tracks must belong to the same model. The cost also incorporates a minimum description length (MDL) cost that prefers sparse solutions. The cost function is optimised by alternating between a discrete graph-cuts algorithm to solve the labelling problem and continuous optimisation to update the model parameters. This approach has previously been applied to computer vision problems such as stereo [2]; motion segmentation [14]; 3D reconstruction of non-rigid [26] and articulated objects [9]; and multi-body reconstruction [25].

Our approach departs from previous work in geometric multiple model fitting in multiple ways: *(i)* Our model offers segmentation at two granularities: object-level and part-level. At the object-level, we segment the scene into a small number of disjoint *objects*. At the part-level, objects are further divided into a set of overlapping parts; *(ii)* Our model uses a combination of appearance and geometry cues for segmentation which encourages salient foreground objects to be separated accurately from the background even when the motion is not distinctive enough; *(iii)* Our geometric cost uses a perspective camera model and is able to deal with perspective effects and incomplete tracks.

3   Simultaneous Segmentation and Reconstruction

We consider a monocular video sequence, possibly downloaded from the web, captured by a single camera observing a complex dynamic scene that contains an unknown mixture of multiple moving and possibly deforming objects. First, we extract a set $\mathcal{T} = [1, \ldots, T]$ of feature point tracks using Sundaram *et al.*'s publicly available code [29]. Although the tracker aims to provide long-term video correspondences, the length of tracks is variable and not all points tracked are visible in all the frames. We make no assumptions about the number of objects in the scene or their motions which could be rigid, articulated or non-rigid. Our goal is to estimate the 3D coordinates for all feature points in every frame.

3.1   Piecewise Reconstruction with Overlapping Models

The works [26,9] proposed a novel piecewise approach to the problem of 3D reconstruction of non-rigid objects. Rather than attempting to reconstruct objects by fitting a global low-rank shape model [31,22] that is sufficiently expressive to capture deformations, but sufficiently low-rank to discourage overfitting, they automatically segmented the object to be reconstructed into a set of parts, each of which could be expressed by a simple model – either local rigid reconstructions [9] or local quadratic deformations [26]. By forcing these parts to overlap, and to agree about the reconstruction of the region of overlap, per part depth/scale and sign-flip ambiguities can be resolved. Figure 2 shows an illustration of the segmentation of an articulated object into overlapping rigid parts.

The problem was formulated as a labelling one where the assignment of tracks to models and the fitting of models to tracks were jointly optimised to minimise a geometric fitting cost subject to the spatial constraint that neighbouring tracks should also belong to the same model.

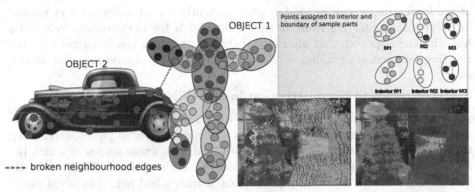

Fig. 2. Left: Conceptual illustration of our approach to 3D reconstruction of complex dynamic scenes. The image shows a person occluding a car. In the original neighbourhood graph, some point-tracks on the car are path connected with tracks on the person. Our approach reasons about object boundaries by adapting the neighbourhood, and breaking edges where necessary to detach parts from other occluding objects. **Top Right:** Illustration of the concept of overlapping models and *interior points* [26]. A tracked point belongs to the interior of a model (points with the same colour) if all its neighbours also belong to that model (though not necessarily as interior points). **Bottom right:** Real world example of segmentation into parts (left) and two objects and background (right).

Assignment of Point Tracks to Models. Let $\mathcal{T}$ refer to a set of point tracks and $\mathcal{M}$ a set of models. We use the notation $\mathbf{x} = \{\mathbf{x}_1, \mathbf{x}_2, \ldots \mathbf{x}_T\}$ to refer to a labelling, where $\mathbf{x}_i$ is the *set* of models assigned to track i. Assuming a known topology, or graph, which connects tracks together in a neighbourhood structure $\mathcal{N}$, the following objective was proposed by [9,26]

$$C(\mathbf{x}) = \sum_{i \in T} \sum_{m \in \mathbf{x}_i} U_i(m) + \mathrm{MDL}(\mathbf{x}) \tag{1}$$

where tracks are allowed to belong to multiple models in $\mathcal{M}$. The unary term $U_i(m)$ is the cost of assigning track i to model m and the term $\mathrm{MDL}(\mathbf{x})$ is a label cost that encourages sparse solutions. In [9] local rigid models were used where each model was parameterised with the rotation and translation associated with a rigid motion and the unary cost $U_i(m)$ was defined as the image reprojection error under orthographic projection for that point given the model parameters. The optimisation of (1) was subject to the constraint that each track must be an interior point of some model i.e. that for every track there is a model such that that track and all its neighbours belong to that model (Figure 2 illustrates the concept of *interior point*), or more formally $\forall i \exists \alpha : \alpha = I_i$ and

$$I_i = \alpha \rightarrow \forall j \in N_i, \alpha \in \mathbf{x}_j \tag{2}$$

where $\mathbf{I} = \{I_1, I_2 \ldots I_T\}$ refers to the assignment of each track i to the interior of one model I_i and N_i is the neighbourhood of track i. Russell *et al.* [26] showed how this problem could be formulated as a labelling problem over the assignment

of tracks to the interior of models and efficiently solved using a novel variant
of α-expansion. Starting from an excess of models the optimisation followed a
hill climbing approach that alternates between assigning tracks to models, and
refitting the models to minimise the geometric error (image reprojection error).

3.2   Obstacles to Reconstruction in the Wild

Although these multiple model fitting approaches based on overlapping models
do provide a robust approach to non-rigid [26] and articulated [9] reconstruction,
they have shortcomings. First, they cannot deal with whole scenes in which the
neighbourhood graph maintains connections between tracks of different objects
(see Figure 2) – the constraints (2) combined with a bad neighbourhood structure can force parts to straddle multiple objects, leading to an error that can not
be recovered from. Secondly, the unary terms of [9,26] minimise a geometric cost
based on multiview affine factorisation. Therefore, they have difficulty dealing
with incomplete tracks. In real-world videos, tracks are likely not to persist for
a large number of frames. Finally, a further limitation of the above approaches
comes from the fact that only motion cues are used for the segmentation. Combining motion and appearance cues is useful to encourage object boundaries to
be respected. Besides, these cues complement each other particularly if there are
frames in the sequence with small motion.

The main contribution of our work is to offer solutions to these three limitations: *(i)* Our approach adapts the topology of the neighbourhood graph by
breaking edges where necessary to preserve boundaries between objects. This
allows our approach to deal with complete video footage where objects might
occlude one another and not just singular pre-segmented objects. *(ii)* Our geometric unary cost is based on frame-to-frame fundamental matrices, an approach
that leads itself naturally to handling incomplete tracks. *(iii)* Our data term
combines geometric and appearance costs. We use the saliency score provided
by [28] to encourage parts of similar saliency to belong to the same object.

4   Scene Reconstruction with an Adaptive Neighbourhood

We propose a novel cost that allows us to modify the topology of the original
neighbourhood by deleting edges between point tracks that belong to different
physical objects, and should not overlap. Our new cost has four terms

$$C(\mathbf{x}) = E_{data} + E_{edge\_break} + E_{sparse} + E_{mdl} \tag{3}$$

$$= \sum_{i \in \mathcal{T}} \sum_{m \in \mathbf{x}_i} U_i(m) + \sum_{i \in \mathcal{T}} \sum_{j \in N_i} d_{i,j} \Delta(j \notin N'_i) \tag{4}$$

$$+ \sum_{m \neq n \in \mathcal{M}} \Delta(\exists i : I_i = m, n \in \mathbf{x}_i) + \mathrm{MDL}(\mathbf{x}) \tag{5}$$

where as before $\mathbf{x}_i$ is the *set* of models that point i belongs to; $\Delta(\cdot)$ is the indicator
function, taking value 1 if the statement is true and 0 otherwise; and N'_i the modified

neighbourhood of track i. This optimisation is subject to the constraints that every track i belongs to the interior of one model I_i, or more formally

$$\forall i, I_i = \alpha \rightarrow \forall j \in N_i', \alpha \in \mathbf{x}_j \tag{6}$$

We now describe in detail each term of our cost function.

4.1 Unary Costs (E_{data})

Our unary term is the sum of two costs i.e. $U_i(m) = G_i(m) + P_i(m)$, that encourage tracks that both move consistently as a rigid object and have similar saliency scores, to belong to the same model. The geometric term $G_i(m)$ evaluates the cost of assigning track i to a rigid model m as the deviation from the epipolar geometry across all pairs of consecutive frames. The second term $P_i(m)$ computes a saliency score for each pixel in every frame and encourages tracks with similar saliency scores, to belong to the same model.

Rigidity Term G_i. Given a set of point tracks assigned to the same rigid part, we parameterise the rigid model m associated with them as a set of $F - 1$ fundamental matrices $\mathbf{F}_m = \{\mathbf{F}_m^{1,2}, \ldots, \mathbf{F}_m^{f,f+1}, \ldots, \mathbf{F}_m^{F-1,F}\}$ for every pair of consecutive frames in the sequence $f = \{1, \ldots, F - 1\}$. The cost of associating track i to a specific rigid model m is the Sampson error [13] added over all pairs of fundamental matrices

$$G_i(m) = \sum_{f < F} \gamma^{-1} (u_i^{f+1^T} \mathbf{F}_m^{f,f+1} u_i^f)^2 \tag{7}$$

where u_i^f encodes the homogeneous image coordinates of track i in frame f and u_i^{f+1} its corresponding position in frame $f + 1$ and γ is the Sampson weight [13]. This cost is summed over all frames in which the track is visible. To estimate the fundamental matrices, we use the eight-point algorithm embedded in a Ransac scheme followed by non-linear refinement of (7). This fitting cost has several clear advantages over the affine factorisation cost used by [9]. First, it allows to model perspective effects which are often present in unconstrained videos and to perform perspective reconstruction given an estimate of the camera calibration matrix. Second, it behaves better in the presence of missing data or short tracks, as it computes frame-to-frame geometric costs only for the frames where the track is visible rather than the multiframe factorisation cost of [9].

Saliency Term. The work [28] provides a fully unsupervised method for object detection in an image I, using a novel saliency map S_I. While [28] made use of both the statistics taken from a large corpus of unlabelled images, and from the image itself, we only make use of the statistics of the single image (this measure is termed *within image saliency* in [28]). We compute saliency maps S_{I_f} for each frame f in the video sequence and define the saliency cost $P_i(m)$ of point i belonging to model m as the distance from the mean saliency of model m

$$P_i(m) = \lambda_s \sum_{f \leq F} (S_{I_f}(i) - \bar{S}_m)^2 \tag{8}$$

where $\bar{S}_m$ is the mean saliency of all tracks that currently belong to model m, $S_{I_f}(i)$ is the saliency score of point i in frame f and λ_s a weight on the importance of this term.

4.2 Topologically Adaptive Neighbourhood (E_{edge_break})

The cost (1) proposed in [26] was internally represented as a local MDL prior defined over the set of interior labels present in a local neighbourhood, and took the cost

$$\sum_{i \in \mathcal{T}} \sum_{m:\exists j \in N_i \cap m = I_j} U_i(m) \tag{9}$$

As discussed, in order to separate connected objects from one another, we wish to discard edges from the neighbourhood N_i with a per edge cost of $d_{i,j}$. As such, the new cost will be of the form

$$\sum_{i \in \mathcal{T}} \sum_{m:\exists j \in N_i \cap m = I_j} \min \left(\sum_{j:I_j=m} d_{i,j}, U_i(m) \right) \tag{10}$$

Here, the weights $d_{i,j}$ are found by passing the distance between points i and j in the image and velocity spaces through a sigmoid function.

4.3 Overlap Sparsity Term (E_{sparse})

By itself, discarding edges from the neighbourhood graph improves the quality of the parts found, and allows more objects to be found. However, it does not correctly separate objects from the background. In almost all sequences, we find that one or two ambiguous tracks exist that could be easily explained as either object or background parts. These ambiguous tracks act as junctions, or regions of overlap between foreground and background objects, connecting the two and making it impossible to distinguish between foreground and background.

To eliminate this leaking, we introduce a novel sparsity term that penalises the total number of models that overlap and encourages regions with limited overlap to disconnect. We formulate this penalty as a count of the number of pairs of models (m, n) such that there exists a track belonging to the interior of model m and also to model n, i.e.

$$\sum_{m \neq n \in \mathcal{M}} \Delta(\exists i : I_i = m, n \in \mathbf{x}_i) \tag{11}$$

As this cost does not depend on the number of tracks in the region of overlap, it dominates in small regions of overlap or where the cost of discarding edges is small, and is ignored elsewhere.

5   Efficient Optimisation

As with other multiple model fitting approaches [9,14,26], we initialise with an excess of models which are generated by sampling randomly groups of ten feature tracks and computing the frame-to-frame fundamental matrices using the eight-point algorithm [13]. We then optimise the cost (3) using a hill-climbing approach alternating between: *(i)* fixing the parameters $\mathbf{F}_m$ and optimising the labelling that assigns tracks to a set of parts (models) $\mathbf{x} = \{\mathbf{x}_1, \mathbf{x}_2, \ldots \mathbf{x}_T\}$ and *(ii)* fixing the labelling and optimising $\mathbf{F}_m$ for all models.

Alpha expansion [5] finds a local optimum of a difficult to optimise cost function by iteratively moving from a current labelling to the lowest-cost solution obtained by relabelling some of the variables as α. Finding an optimal move is formulated as a pseudo Boolean optimisation [3] and solved using graph-cuts [4]. We follow [26] in considering expansion moves over the interior of labels. We use $A \in 2^T$ to refer the found expansion move, with A_i taking value 1 if variable I_i transitions to label α in the move, and 0 otherwise. Unlike [26] we will need to explicitly keep track of whether or not tracks belong to models at all (either as interior or boundary tracks) and for a particular expansion move on label α this will be done by means of binary variables $M_i^\alpha = 1$ if $\alpha \in \mathbf{x}_i$ and a complementary set of variables M_i^β, such that $\beta \neq \alpha$ and $M_i^\beta = 0$ if $\beta \in \mathbf{x}_i$.

Optimisation of the costs E_{data} and E_{mdl} can be done using the techniques of [26]. We now deal with the modifications to the optimisation required by the terms E_{break} and E_{sparse}. Although exact optimisation of either of these costs is relatively straightforward, optimising both together is challenging, and we make use of the convex-concave procedure (CCP) [37,20], and find an optimisable cost that is tight at the current location, but an over-estimate elsewhere.

5.1   Exactly Optimising E_{break}

We can rewrite cost (10) in terms of the auxiliary variables

$$\sum_{i \in \mathcal{T}} \sum_{\substack{\beta \in \mathcal{M} \\ \beta \neq \alpha}} \sum_{j:I_j=\beta} \min_{M_i^\beta} \left(A_j d_{i,j} (1 - M_i^\beta) + U_i(\beta)(1 - M_i^\beta) \right) \qquad (12)$$

$$+ \sum_{i \in \mathcal{T}} \sum_{j:I_j=\alpha} \min_{M_i^\alpha} \left((1 - A_j) d_{i,j} M_i^\alpha + U_i(\alpha) M_i^\alpha \right) \qquad (13)$$

This change can been seen as a robustification of the local co-occurrence potentials of [26] analogous to the robust Pn model [16]. As with the Pn potentials, it can be formulated as a graph-cut problem simply by adjusting the edge weights used as shown in Figure 3, left and centre left.

5.2   Approximately Minimising E_{sparse}

For the following section it is more convenient to use sets to describe which points belong to which models. We use $\mathbf{M}^\beta$ to refer to the set of points belonging to

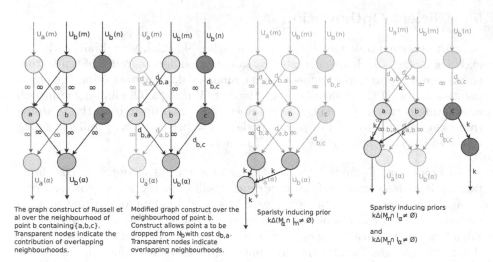

Fig. 3. Graph constructs. Of the main graph construct repeated in all subfigures, the top row contains all auxiliary variables indicating if tracks, a, b or c belong to model m or n. The middle row contains the standard expansion variables which govern whether or not a variable transitions to the interior of model α, while the bottom row indicates if a variable belongs to model α.

model β, $\mathbf{I}^\beta$ for the interior of model β, $\mathbf{M}^\beta_{\text{last}}$ for the region (fixed throughout the move) that was assigned to model β by the previous move, and $\mathbf{I}^\beta_{\text{last}}$ for points previously belonging to the interior of model β. Performing an expansion move on label α, we have three cases to consider:

1. The cost is a direct function of the interior labels $\mathbf{I}^\alpha$
2. The cost depends on tracks in the boundary of points belonging α: $\mathbf{M}^\alpha \setminus \mathbf{I}^\alpha$
3. The cost is not a function of α and depends on: $\mathbf{I}^\beta \cap \mathbf{M}^\gamma$, where $\beta, \gamma \neq \alpha$.

For an expansion move on label α, $\mathbf{I}^\alpha$ is monotone increasing while $\mathbf{I}^\beta$ is monotone decreasing. If one of either the sparsity costs, or the edge breaking of the previous subsection was not used, the labelling of $\mathbf{M}^\alpha$ and $\mathbf{M}^\beta$ would also be guaranteed to be monotone increasing/decreasing, but together the situation is more complex. In the following discussion, we artificially constrain the set of possible moves of $\mathbf{M}^\beta$ to be monotone decreasing, and allow $\mathbf{M}^\alpha$ to change arbitrarily. Let us deal with these costs by turn:

Interior of α cost: We consider the localised MDL costs

$$\Delta(\mathbf{M}^\beta_{\text{last}} \cap \mathbf{I}^\alpha \neq \emptyset) + \Delta(\mathbf{I}^\beta \neq \emptyset) - 1. \tag{14}$$

This cost is 1 if $\mathbf{I}^\alpha$ expands into $\mathbf{M}^\beta_{\text{last}}$ without completely removing model β (which can only be done by making sure no tracks belong to the interior of model β) and 0 otherwise. Clearly this is an over-estimate as the true $\mathbf{M}^\beta$ in the set of all moves considered is always smaller than $\mathbf{M}_{\text{last}}^{\beta}$, and tight at the current location. As this cost is simply two MDL costs defined over subregions of the graph, it can be optimised using the techniques of [17]. As these move costs satisfy the CCP criteria, they reduces the original cost function.

Boundary of α cost: A similar argument can be made for the above cost. Instead of directly optimising it, we solve the over-approximation

$$\Delta(\mathbf{M}^{\alpha} \cap \mathbf{I}_{\text{last}}^{\beta} \neq \emptyset) + \Delta(\mathbf{I}^{\beta} \neq \emptyset) - 1. \tag{15}$$

This can be formulated as a local MDL prior over the auxiliary variable of the previous section and an MDL cost over label β. What is more interesting is the quality of the approximation of these terms. If we assume that all tracks belonging to the same model at every iteration of graph-cuts are path-connected[1], and if no edges are discarded[2] then the over-estimate is tight. There are 3 straightforward cases to consider:

1. No variables in $\mathbf{M}_{\text{last}}^{\beta}$ are in $\mathbf{I}^{\alpha}$. Here the cost is trivially correct.
2. No variable belongs to $\mathbf{M}^{\beta}$. Again, the cost is trivially correct.
3. At least one variable i belongs to $\mathbf{I}^{\alpha}$ and $\mathbf{M}_{\text{last}}^{\beta}$, and one variable j belongs to $\mathbf{I}^{\beta}$. As i and j are path-connected in $\mathbf{M}_{\text{last}}^{\beta}$, and for any possible move variables in $\mathbf{M}_{\text{last}}^{\beta}$ must either stay as variable β or move to label α, we have a chain of variables $\{i, k, l, \dots j\}$ belonging to either $\mathbf{I}^{\alpha}$ or $\mathbf{I}^{\beta}$ such that $i \in N_{\text{k}}, k \in N_{\text{l}}, l \in \dots N_{\text{j}}$. As $i \in \mathbf{I}^{\alpha}, j \in \mathbf{I}^{\beta}$, there must be at least one pair where $k \in N_{\text{l}}, k \in \mathbf{I}^{\alpha}$ and $l \in \mathbf{I}^{\beta}$ – and the cost is tight. $\square$

Although the proof does not hold where edges are discarded it does provide intuition as to how alpha-expansion minimises the cost. In the first iterations, regions are swept out without breaking all edges, and finding solutions with excessive overlap between models. In subsequent iterations, the region belonging to the boundaries of models contracts cleanly separating parts.

Costs not dependent on α: The local co-occurrence potentials considered here, fall into the class of potentials that can not be exactly optimised by an expansion move over label α. Instead we follow the strategy of [17] and optimise the cost

$$0.5\Delta(\mathbf{I}^{\gamma} \cap \mathbf{M}_{\text{last}}^{\beta} \neq \emptyset) + 0.5\Delta(\mathbf{I}_{\text{last}}^{\gamma} \cap \mathbf{M}^{\beta} \neq \emptyset) \tag{16}$$

5.3   Merging Parts into Objects: Object-Level Segmentation

The final result of our scene segmentation algorithm is the labelling $\mathbf{x}$ which assigns each feature track to a set of rigid parts. Figure 6 shows some results of the part segmentation (second row) for five videos of the Berkeley Motion Segmentation Dataset [6]. To segment the scene into objects we label connected components of overlapping parts as object detections.

---

[1] In practice this is almost always true, due to the regularisation caused by overlapping models or pairwise terms.

[2] Again, most edges are not discarded. The majority of models that would overlap without edge discardation, continue overlapping in the solution found.

Fig. 4. Reconstruction results for a cat sequence of the *Youtube-Objects* Dataset [23]

Table 1. Evaluation results on the Berkeley Motion Segmentation Dataset using the metrics of [6] *Fayad et al.* shows performance without discarding edges, this the same optimisation as in [9,26].

	Density	overall error	average error	over-segmentation	extracted objects
First 10 frames(26 sequences)					
Brox Malik	3.34%	7.75%	25.01%	0.54	24
Fayad *et al.*	3.28%	15.23%	51.89%	0.23	7
Our method	3.28%	8.00%	25.46%	1.00	22
First 50 frames(15 sequences)					
Brox Malik	3.27%	7.13%	34.76%	0.53	9
Fayad *et al.*	3.25%	24.95%	63.67%	0.20	0
Our method	3.25%	5.93%	27.84%	3.70	13
First 200 frames(7 sequences)					
Brox Malik	3.43%	7.64%	31.14%	3.14	7
Fayad *et al.*	3.42%	28.81%	66.78%	0.29	0
Our method	3.42%	13.28%	39.86%	8.60	4

6 3D Reconstruction

The optimisation of our cost function results in the labelling of rigid models or parts. Using the information about the regions of overlap and the saliency scores, we also have a decomposition of the scene into different objects. In addition, our optimisation estimates model parameters for each rigid model m. Each rigid model is parameterised as the set of fundamental matrices $\mathbf{F}_m$ that describe the epipolar geometry between every pair of consecutive frames.

The 3D reconstruction of each object is then carried out using a piecewise rigid reconstruction approach. For each object we have a list of its constituent parts and a rigid model (set of fundamental matrices) for each of part. First each part is reconstructed independently using the estimated fundamental matrices $\mathbf{F}_m$. If the calibration of the camera is known, each fundamental matrix can be decomposed into the relative rotation and translation between frames and

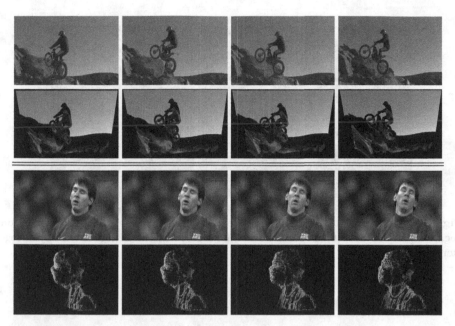

Fig. 5.   Top: Reconstruction results for a motorbike sequence *Youtube-Objects* Dataset [23]. **Bottom:** Sparse reconstruction of football footage, showing both the assignment of tracks to parts and the quality of reconstruction before densification.

an initial estimate of the shape is obtained using the DLT algorithm [13]. The shape and motion parameters are then refined using the sparse implementation of bundle adjustment [19]. If the camera calibration is unknown the shape is initialized using a factorization algorithm followed by per-frame motion estimation using the PnP algorithm [13]. A final refinement of the shape, motion and focal length parameters is then carried out via bundle adjustment.

Aligning Overlapping Segments: Objects are segmented as a set of overlapping parts that require a final *stitching* step using the areas of overlap to enforce global consistency on the 3D surface. As we use a perspective camera model, the only existing ambiguity between parts is a depth/scale ambiguity which can be resolved by enforcing that tracks belonging to two or more parts should be reconstructed at the same depth by each part model.

Depth-Map Densification: Our reconstruction algorithm is based on sparse feature tracks. To densify the 3D reconstruction, we apply Gaussian filtering on the sparse 3D tracks in xy-RGB image space using the fast implementation of [1] that performs filtering using the permutohedral lattice. Regions of the video far from any tracks in the xy-RGB space are assigned to a flat background billboard.

Fig. 6. Motion segmentation results on five sample sequences of the Berkeley Motion Segmentation Dataset [6]. **Second row:** Part segmentation. **Third row:** Object segmentation.

7   Experimental Results

Since we recover both a segmentation of the scene into multiple moving objects and a 3D model for each object, we evaluate both of these steps independently.

Evaluation of the Motion Segmentation Step: We evaluate the results of our *object-level* segmentation on the Berkeley Motion Segmentation Dataset using the tracks and evaluation tool proposed in [6]. Table 1 shows a comparison between the scores of our approach and the results from Brox and Malik's motion segmentation algorithm [6]. The results show that our method exhibits comparable performance to [6]. While our *over-segmentation* error is higher than [6], the *overall error* and *average error* are very close, and in some cases lower. Although our algorithm can be used for motion segmentation exclusively, it is geared towards 3D reconstruction of complex dynamic scenes. Providing object boundaries are respected, our 3D reconstruction method is unharmed by a slight over-segmentation given that we perform piecewise reconstruction. The same set of parameters was used for all the experiments. The results of Fayad *et al.* [9] show how our algorithm would perform without the novel edge breaking and sparsity terms. Objects are never discovered in sequences longer than 10 frames, and in the majority of the 10 frame long sequences no objects are discovered.

Evaluation of the 3D Reconstruction: We demonstrate our approach on videos from the *Youtube-Objects* Dataset [23]. These are unconstrained real-world videos downloaded from YouTube, with the purpose of object detection in video [23]. Figure 1 shows reconstructions of a *cat*, a *motorbike*, and a *footballer*. We show the decomposition into *parts*, *objects* and a 3D model of the objects from a novel viewpoint for one frame. Figures 4 and 5 show 3D reconstructions for further frames of the three sequences. Our algorithm shows a good segmentation of the scenes and a convincing 3D reconstruction of these challenging videos.

8   Conclusion

In this paper we propose a fully unsupervised approach to the challenging problem of simultaneously segmenting a dynamic scene into its constituent objects and reconstructing a 3D model of the scene. We focus on the reconstruction of real-world videos downloaded from the web or acquired with a single camera observing a complex dynamic scene containing an unknown mixture of multiple moving and possibly deforming objects. Our results show examples of segmentation and 3D reconstruction on videos from the *Youtube Objects* dataset.

References

1. Adams, A., Baek, J., Davis, A.: Fast high-dimensional filtering using the permutohedral lattice. In: Eurographics (2010) 595
2. Bleyer, M., Rother, C., Kohli, P.: Surface stereo with soft segmentation. In: CVPR (2010) 586
3. Boros, E., Hammer, P.L.: Pseudo-boolean optimization. Discrete Applied Mathematics, 155–225 (2002) 591
4. Boykov, Y., Kolmogorov, V.: An Experimental Comparison of Min-Cut/Max-Flow Algorithms for Energy Minimization in Vision. PAMI 26(9), 1124–1137 (2004) 591
5. Boykov, Y., Veksler, O., Zabih, R.: Fast approximate energy minimization via graph cuts. PAMI 23 (2001) 591
6. Brox, T., Malik, J.: Object segmentation by long term analysis of point trajectories. In: Daniilidis, K., Maragos, P., Paragios, N. (eds.) ECCV 2010, Part V. LNCS, vol. 6315, pp. 282–295. Springer, Heidelberg (2010) 585, 593, 594, 596
7. Costeira, J., Kanade, T.: A multi-body factorization method for motion analysis. In: ICCV, pp. 1071–1076 (1995) 585
8. Elhamifar, E., Vidal, R.: Sparse subspace clustering. In: CVPR (2009) 585
9. Fayad, J., Russell, C., Agapito, L.: Automated articulated structure and 3D shape recovery from point correspondences. In: IEEE International Conference on Computer Vision (ICCV), Barcelona, Spain (November 2011) 584, 585, 586, 587, 588, 589, 591, 594, 596
10. Fitzgibbon, A.W., Zisserman, A.: Multibody structure and motion: 3-D reconstruction of independently moving objects. In: Vernon, D. (ed.) ECCV 2000. LNCS, vol. 1842, pp. 891–906. Springer, Heidelberg (2000) 585
11. Galasso, F., Cipolla, R., Schiele, B.: Video segmentation with superpixels. In: Lee, K.M., Matsushita, Y., Rehg, J.M., Hu, Z. (eds.) ACCV 2012, Part I. LNCS, vol. 7724, pp. 760–774. Springer, Heidelberg (2013) 585
12. Garg, R., Roussos, A., Agapito, L.: Dense variational reconstruction of non-rigid surfaces from monocular video. In: CVPR (2013) 583, 584
13. Hartley, R., Zisserman, A.: Multiple View Geometry in Computer Vision. Cambridge University Press (2000) 589, 591, 595
14. Isack, H., Boykov, Y.: Energy-based geometric multi-model fitting. International Journal of Computer Vision (IJCV) 97(2) (2012) 585, 586, 591
15. Kanatani, K.: Motion segmentation by subspace separation and model selection. In: ICCV, Vancouver, Canada, vol. 2, pp. 301–306 (July 2001) 585
16. Kohli, P., Ladicky, L., Torr, P.: Robust higher order potentials for enforcing label consistency. In: CVPR (2008) 591
17. Ladický, L., Russell, C., Kohli, P., Torr, P.H.: Inference methods for crfs with co-occurrence statistics. International Journal of Computer Vision 103(2), 213–225 (2013) 593

18. Li, Z., Guo, J., Cheong, L.-F., Zhou, Z.: Perspective motion segmentation via collaborative clustering. In: ICCV (2013) 585
19. Lourakis, M.A., Argyros, A.: SBA: A Software Package for Generic Sparse Bundle Adjustment. ACM Trans. Math. Software (2009) 595
20. Narasimhan, M., Bilmes, J.A.: A submodular-supermodular procedure with applications to discriminative structure learning. arXiv preprint arXiv:1207.1404 (2012) 591
21. Ozden, K., Schindler, K., van Gool, L.: Multibody structure-from-motion in practice. IEEE Transactions on Pattern Analysis and Machine Intelligence (PAMI) (2010) 583, 585
22. Paladini, M., Del Bue, A., Xavier, J., Agapito, L., Stosic, M., Dodig, M.: Factorization for Non-Rigid and Articulated Structure using Metric Projections. IJCV (2012) 585, 586
23. Prest, A., Leistner, C., Civera, J., Schmid, C., Ferrari, V.: Learning object class detectors from weakly annotated video. In: CVPR (2012) 584, 594, 595, 596
24. Rao, S., Tron, R., Vidal, R., Ma, Y.: Motion segmentation in the presence of outlying, incomplete or corrupted trajectories. IEEE Transactions on Pattern Analysis and Machine Intelligence (PAMI) 32(10), 1832–1845 (2010) 585
25. Roussos, A., Russell, C., Garg, R., Agapito, L.: Dense multibody motion estimation and reconstruction from a handheld camera. In: ISMAR (2012) 583, 585, 586
26. Russell, C., Fayad, J., Agapito, L.: Energy based multiple model fitting for non-rigid structure from motion. In: CVPR (2011) 584, 585, 586, 587, 588, 590, 591, 594
27. Schindler, K., Suter, D., Wang, H.: A model selection framework for multibody structure-and-motion of image sequences. International Journal of Computer Vision (IJCV) 79(2), 159–177 (2008) 585
28. Siva, P., Russell, C., Xiang, T., Agapito, L.: Looking beyond the image: Unsupervised learning for object saliency and detection. In: CVPR (2013) 588, 589
29. Sundaram, N., Brox, T., Keutzer, K.: Dense point trajectories by GPU-accelerated large displacement optical flow. In: Daniilidis, K., Maragos, P., Paragios, N. (eds.) ECCV 2010, Part I. LNCS, vol. 6311, pp. 438–451. Springer, Heidelberg (2010) 586
30. Tomasi, C., Kanade, T.: Shape and motion from image streams: a factorization method - part 3 detection and tracking of point features. Technical Report CMU-CS-91-132, Computer Science Department, Carnegie Mellon University, Pittsburgh, PA (April 1991) 585
31. Torresani, L., Hertzmann, A., Bregler, C.: Non-rigid structure-from-motion: Estimating shape and motion with hierarchical priors. PAMI, 878–892 (2008) 585, 586
32. Tresadern, P., Reid, I.: Articulated structure from motion by factorization. In: CVPR, vol. 2, pp. 1110–1115 (June 2005) 585
33. Varol, A., Salzmann, M., Tola, E., Fua, P.: Template-free monocular reconstruction of deformable surfaces. In: ICCV (2009) 584, 585
34. Vidal, R., Ma, Y., Sastry, S.: Generalized principal component analysis (gpca). In: CVPR, pp. 621–628 (2003) 585
35. Xu, C., Corso, J.J.: Evaluation of super-voxel methods for early video processing. In: CVPR (2012) 585
36. Yan, J., Pollefeys, M.: A factorization-based approach for articulated non-rigid shape, motion and kinematic chain recovery from video. PAMI 30(5) (May 2008) 585
37. Yuille, A.L., Rangarajan, A.: The concave-convex procedure (cccp). In: NIPS (2002) 591
38. Zelnik-Manor, L., Irani, M.: Degeneracies, dependencies and their implications in multi-body and multi-sequence factorizations. In: CVPR, vol. 2, pp. 287–293 (June 2003) 585

Joint Object Class Sequencing and Trajectory Triangulation (JOST)

Enliang Zheng, Ke Wang, Enrique Dunn, and Jan-Michael Frahm

The University of North Carolina, Chapel Hill

Abstract. We introduce the problem of joint object class sequencing and trajectory triangulation (JOST), which is defined as the reconstruction of the motion path of a class of dynamic objects through a scene from an unordered set of images. We leverage standard object detection techniques to identify object instances within a set of registered images. Each of these object detections defines a single 2D point with a corresponding viewing ray. The set of viewing rays attained from the aggregation of all detections belonging to a common object class is then used to estimate a motion path denoted as the object class trajectory. Our method jointly determines the topology of the objects motion path and reconstructs the 3D object points corresponding to our object detections. We pose the problem as an optimization over both the unknown 3D points and the topology of the path, which is approximated by a Generalized Minimum Spanning Tree (GMST) on a multipartite graph and then refined through a continuous optimization over the 3D object points. Experiments on synthetic and real datasets demonstrate the effectiveness of our method and the feasibility to solve a previously intractable problem.

1 Introduction

Reconstruction from photo collections has attracted significant attention in the last decade, enabling systems to build 3D models from entire city datasets of millions of images[14]. Despite these advances, the current state-of-the-art methods model only static scenes. One reason for this is that in typical datasets there only exists one view of any dynamic scene object, e.g. a person or car. Hence, current techniques are not able to determine the 3D position of such objects. This situation is regarded to have a highly limited potential for reconstruction as stated by Park et al. [23] and Valmadre et al. [29].

We propose a technique to determine the 3D geometry of common dynamic object paths from temporally uncorrelated images, i.e. a set of images along a street with pedestrians walking (see Figure 1(a)). The challenges in this kind of datasets are that each instance of the object is typically only seen once in the images. Moreover, there is no temporal consistency between the observations of the different images and the capture times of the images are typically unknown. The only constraint available for our reconstruction is the fact that all observed instances of an object move along a common compact path in the 3D scene, which we call an object class trajectory. To obtain the object class

D. Fleet et al. (Eds.): ECCV 2014, Part VII, LNCS 8695, pp. 599–614, 2014.

(a)   (b)

Fig. 1. Left: 3 images of the pedestrian dataset and the output of SFM. Right: The reconstruction of two pedestrians that are captured in the single image.

trajectory our method needs to simultaneously determine the sequence of the objects along the 3D path and the 3D positions of the objects on the path. Accordingly, this can be seen as a joint object class sequencing and trajectory triangulation, which generalizes the well known sequencing problem [2,3] and the trajectory triangulation problem [29,39,23] into a common framework. In fact, our proposed framework handles both of these problems as special cases. The resulting reconstructed object class trajectory then allows us to solve the generally ill-posed 3D reconstruction of a dynamic object from a single image by constraining the reconstruction through the 3D path of the object class. An example of a single view reconstruction of two pedestrians is shown in Figure 1(b), visualizing a generic person at the correct 3D position in the reconstruction of the 3D scene.

2   Related Work

The joint object class sequencing and trajectory triangulation is closely related to 3D reconstruction from single image, which is inherently ambiguous and difficult without further assumptions. Saxena et al. [25] propose a method for reconstruction from a single image. They compute reasonable depthmaps from a single still image by using a hierarchical multi-scale Markov Random Field (MRF) that incorporates several features. The parameters of the MRF model are trained using ground truth depth. In man-made scenes with mainly orthogonal facades (called a Manhattan world [6]), 3D reconstruction from a single image can be simplified to finding 3D lines and planes within the scene. Delage et al. [9] use a MRF model to identify the different planes and edges in the scene, as well as their orientations. Then, an iterative optimization algorithm is applied to infer the planes' positions. Ramalingam et al. [24] reconstruct the 3D lines in a Manhattan scene from an image using linear programming that identifies a sufficient minimal set of least-violated line connectivity constraints. In contrast, our joint object class sequencing and trajectory triangulation targets the reconstruction of the dynamic scene parts, in particular the object class trajectory, from a set of images.

Non-rigid structure from motion (NRSFM) methods are another class of methods related to our joint object class sequencing and trajectory triangulation. They aim to recover a deforming object's structure as well as camera motion given corresponding 2D points in a sequence of images. Tomasi and Kanade [28] propose to do rigid structure from motion through matrix factorization under an affine camera assumption. As an important extension of the well-known Tomasi-Kanade factorization, the work by Bregler et al. [5] tackles the NRSFM problem by assuming an object can be represented by a linear combination of low-order shape bases. Due to the fact that the shape bases are not unique, Xiao et al. [35] proves that using only rotation constraints results in ambiguous and invalid solutions. To solve this shape ambiguity, most existing works rely on different prior knowledge specific to the problem at hand. Not until very recently, Dai et al. [7] solved the problem by introducing a prior-free method. All these methods require a certain amount of points to be available for each frame to form a shape, as their approaches require the shape to be present. In contrast, our method only requires a single point per object class instance to infer the object class trajectory and does not have any assumption about the object shape. As a dual method, Akhter et al. [1] proposed that the smooth trajectory of each point can be restricted to a low-dimensional subspace and represented by a linear combination of Discrete Cosine Transform (DCT) bases. In contrast to [7] which requires no temporal information, [1] fails completely if frames are randomly shuffled. Whereas our proposed joint object class sequencing and trajectory triangulation does not require any temporal frame information or ordering.

Park et al. [23] reconstruct the 3D trajectory from a monocular image sequence using SFM for camera registration. They represent the trajectory by a number of low-order DCT bases, similar to Akhter et al. [1]. Their method recovers accurate 3D trajectory, but with two major flaws as pointed in [29]: (1) The user needs to manually determine the number of bases for each image sequence, and (2) the accuracy of 3D trajectory reconstruction is fundamentally limited by the correlation between the trajectory of 3D points and the motions of camera centers. This high correlation of object and camera motion is commonly occurring in real captures and degrades the reconstruction results. Valmadre et al. [29] recover the trajectory by minimizing the response of the trajectory to a set of high pass filters. Their method, in contrast to Park et al. [23], requires no basis size but still suffers under the correlation between object and camera motion. Zhu et al. [39] first estimate the 3D coordinates of a few keyframes in the video sequence, and then use those key frames to constrain the 3D trajectory. All of these methods require smooth trajectories and a given temporal order of the captured frames, while our method does not need to know the temporal order in order to successfully recover the object class trajectory.

Recently Basha et al. [2,3] propose two methods that determine the temporal order photos taken by a set of cameras. In [2], they compute the partial orders for a subset of the images by analyzing the dynamic features in the subsets 2D images. The method inherently relies on two images taken from the same static camera to eliminate the uncertainty in the sequencing. Later Basha et al. [3]

propose to enforce the constraint of a known order for the images taken by each camera. Our proposed method does not need any knowledge about the image order nor does it require multiple images of a static camera.

As another class of reconstruction, 3D articulated object reconstruction given monocular image sequences has received much attention. Several particle filter approaches have been developed for 3D human tracking [27,26]. Wei et al. [32] and Valmadre et al. [31] reconstruct the 3D human poses from a small number of 2D point correspondences obtained from uncalibrated monocular images. Based on [23], Park et al. [22] reconstruct 3D articulated motion with the constraint that a trajectory remains at a fixed distance with respect to a parent trajectory. This improves the reconstructibility over their earlier approach [23], but involves solving an NP-hard quadratic programming problem. Valmadre et al. [30] develop a dynamic programming approach which scales linearly in the number of frames to overcome solving the quadratic programming problem. While the articulated motions require multiple characteristic points observed on the same object instance, our method successfully recovers the object class trajectory from observing different object instances that each determines only a single characteristic point.

3   Joint Object Class Sequencing and Trajectory Triangulation

We now detail our method for joint object class sequencing and trajectory triangulation from uncontrolled image captures, which in particular removes the constraint of known temporal camera information and known object position. To perform joint object class sequencing and trajectory triangulation from the uncontrolled image set, we proceed as follows

1. Spatially register the cameras to a common 3D coordinate system.
2. Detect object instances and estimate motion tangents from input imagery.
3. Leverage the image positions of the object instances to simultaneously
   (a) Determine a camera ordering compliant with a continuous motion of the objects along a trajectory.
   (b) Triangulate the geometry of the corresponding motion path.

Our main contribution is an algorithm for tackling challenge 3, while we exploit known methods to solve for camera registration, object detection and motion tangents in the images. Next, we introduce the above components in more detail.

3.1   Spatial Registration

The goal of the initial spatial registration in our method is to establish camera registration in a common coordinate system. Given that in all our datasets a fair portion of the images contains static background structure, we use the publicly available structure from motion tool VisualSFM by Wu [34]. It produces the camera registration and the camera calibration. See Fig. 1(a) for an example.

The obtained camera registration determines the camera center $\tilde{\mathbf{C}}_j$ of the j-th camera. Please note, we use bold font letters $\mathbf{x}$ to indicate that an entity is a vector and regular letters x for scalar values. With the known camera calibration and registration, each pixel in the camera defines a ray direction $\mathbf{r}$ in the 3D scene space. For our object class trajectory we are only interested in the ray directions $\mathbf{r}_i$ for the different object i of the desired class (for simplicity we refer in the paper to them as objects) with $i = 1, \ldots, N$, where N is the number of detected object class instances over all frames. Hence, we only aim to compute the ray directions $\mathbf{r}_i$ for pixels belonging to the different detected objects i. The ray $\mathbf{X}_i$ in the 3D space represents a 1D subspace on which the imaged object has to lie and is described by:

$$\mathbf{X}_i(t_i) = \mathbf{C}_i + t_i \cdot \mathbf{r_i}, \tag{1}$$

where $t_i \geq 0$ is the positive distance from the camera center $\mathbf{C}_i$ along the ray $\mathbf{X}_i$. In the remaining of the paper, we keep the condition $t_i \geq 0$ implicit for the purpose of concise formulation. We denote the camera centers as $\mathbf{C}_i$ with $\mathbf{C}_i = \tilde{\mathbf{C}}_j$, where $\mathbf{C}_i$ is the center of the camera j in which the object instance i is detected. Please note that if more than one object is detected in camera j, there will be multiple $\mathbf{C}_i$ with identical positions. The unknown true distance of the object instance i along ray $\mathbf{X}_i$ is denoted as $\hat{t}_i$. Once obtained, it determines the 3D object position $\hat{\mathbf{X}}_i$.

3.2   Object Detection and Motion Tangent Estimation

Our proposed joint object class sequencing and trajectory triangulation leverages the motion tangent of the object instances, which is defined as the moving direction of the dynamic object in the 3D space, so both the objects detection and motion tangents estimation are performed based on a single image. For trajectory triangulation this has historically been solved by using videos for estimating the motion tangents [37], but for our proposed joint object class sequencing and trajectory triangulation problem, temporal coherence or temporal proximity of the images cannot be assumed. Hence only motion tangent estimation based on a single image is applied. The particular choice of object and motion tangent estimation method depends on the specific object class and the scenes. We discuss our particular choices in Section 4, and for now we assume available the positions on each image defining the rays $\mathbf{X}_i$ and a coarse estimate of the motion tangent $\mathbf{d}_i$ of object i. We determine the image positions of each detected object $i = 1, \ldots, N$ by the center of the bounding box. These object detections provide us a ray $\mathbf{X}_i(t_i)$ for each object observed in a camera, with the ray describing the one-dimensional subspace in which the detected object can be placed in the 3D scene space.

3.3   Object Class Trajectory Estimation Problem

Assuming known rays $\mathbf{X}_i(t_i)$ and the motion tangents $\mathbf{d}_i$, we will now define the object class trajectory estimation problem before delving into our data representation and our estimation framework. For the ease of description, we directly leverage the rays $\mathbf{X}_i(t_i)$ of the detected objects i and do not use the camera registration directly as the latter is implicitly present in the ray.

Intuitively, an object class trajectory describes the motion along a path taken by the observed objects of the desired class through the 3D scene. A path can in general be any continuous curve in the 3D scene space. Since we only have a finite number of observations of objects along the path, we only sample a discrete set of 3D points on the path. The samples along the path are the 3D object positions $\hat{\mathbf{X}}_i$. Here, we represent the path as a combination of piecewise linear functions in between the sampled object positions $\hat{\mathbf{X}}_i$. The desired object class trajectory is the path of minimal length and it can be determined through a minimization of the cost function:

$$\min_{\mathbf{p}} \sum_{(i,j)\in\mathbf{p}} \|\hat{\mathbf{X}}_i - \hat{\mathbf{X}}_j\|_2^2 \tag{2}$$

with $\mathbf{p}$ representing the adjacency of the points defining the topology of the path, which is list of adjacency relationships between all the points $\hat{\mathbf{X}}_i$, $i = 1, \ldots, N$. While the trajectory above is based on the observed 3D object positions $\hat{\mathbf{X}}_i$, we can only observe the rays $\mathbf{X}_i(t_i)$. To determine the object class trajectory, we also need to determine the position of each object i along its viewing ray $\mathbf{X}_i(t_i)$, which defines the 3D position of the object $\hat{\mathbf{X}}_i$. We propose to find the adjacency relation by optimizing over variables $\mathbf{t} = [t_1, \ldots, t_N]$ and $\mathbf{p}$ jointly as follows,

$$\min_{\mathbf{p},\mathbf{t}} \sum_{(i,j)\in\mathbf{p}} \|\mathbf{X}_i(t_i) - \mathbf{X}_j(t_j)\|_2^2. \tag{3}$$

Given the motion tangents $\mathbf{d}_i$ estimated from the images, we can further constrain the trajectory, obtaining an optimization problem:

$$\min_{\mathbf{p},\mathbf{t}} \sum_{(i,j)\in\mathbf{p}} \|\mathbf{d}_{i,j} \times (\mathbf{X}_i(t_i) - \mathbf{X}_j(t_j))\|_2^2 + \lambda\|\mathbf{X}_i(t_i) - \mathbf{X}_j(t_j)\|_2^2, \tag{4}$$

where the operator $\times$ is the cross product, λ is a positive weight (discussed at length in Sec. 3.6). The direction $\mathbf{d}_{i,j}$ is selected from $\mathbf{d}_i$ and $\mathbf{d}_j$, as the motion tangent that is closest to the 3D motion direction $\mathbf{X}_i(t_i) - \mathbf{X}_j(t_j)$. In Eq. (4), the penalty of the first term increases if the direction of the vector $\mathbf{X}_i(t_i) - \mathbf{X}_j(t_j)$ deviates from $\mathbf{d}_{i,j}$. The optimization procedure simultaneously determines both the adjacency $\mathbf{p}$ of the rays and the positions of the objects through $\mathbf{t}$.

Traditionally, these problems have been treated separately as either a sequencing problem, where the 3D points are given and only the sequence of traversal needs to be estimated, or as a trajectory triangulation problem [23,29], where the sequence of observations for the trajectory is given and the 3D points along the trajectory need to be determined. Our proposed method generalizes these problems into a common framework to allow the simultaneous estimation of the adjacency of observations and the 3D position of the observations. In order to optimize Eq. (4), we propose a new discrete-continuous optimization strategy through the Generalized Minimum Spanning Tree (GMST).

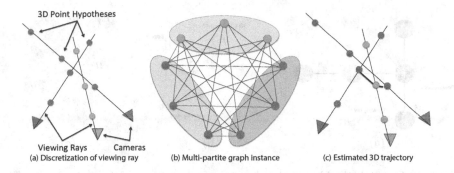

3D Point Hypotheses

Viewing Rays   Cameras
(a) Discretization of viewing ray   (b) Multi-partite graph instance   (c) Estimated 3D trajectory

Fig. 2. Illustration of GMST. See the text for more details

3.4 Generalized Trajectory Graph

To determine the object class trajectory, we conceptually have to choose for each ray $\mathbf{X}_i(t_i)$ the 3D point, and simultaneously determine the adjacency $\mathbf{p}$ representing the adjacency relations of the rays $\mathbf{X}_i(t_i)$, which defines the topology of the object class trajectory. Our discrete-continuous optimization strategy first uses a Generalized Minimum Spanning Tree (GMST) to find adjacency $\mathbf{p}$, and followed by a convex optimization over $\mathbf{t}$ with $\mathbf{p}$ being fixed.

In the discrete optimization step, we map the continuous problem of finding the 3D point along each ray to a discrete problem of selecting a 3D point out of a set of discrete 3D points. Then we determine one 3D point along each ray and the adjacency $\mathbf{p}$ by computing the (GMST) on an undirected multipartite graph $\mathcal{G}(\mathcal{V}, \mathcal{E})$ [20]. This allows us to simultaneously determine the topology and the discrete 3D object position.

An undirected multipartite graph is a graph whose vertices are partitioned into N partite sets $\{V_1, \ldots, V_N\}$ with $|V_i| = k$, while fulfilling $\mathcal{V} = V_1 \cup V_2 \cup \cdots \cup V_N$ and $V_o \cap V_p = \emptyset, \forall o \neq p$, with $o, p \in \{1, \ldots, N\}$. The multipartite graph $\mathcal{G}(\mathcal{V}, \mathcal{E})$ has only edges between the different partite sets of vertices V_o, and all edge cost are non-negative. Now we will detail on how we define the graph $\mathcal{G}(\mathcal{V}, \mathcal{E})$ for our object class trajectory estimation problem.

Each ray $\mathbf{X}_i(t)$ defines a one dimensional constraint on the 3D position of the object. We discretize the ray to obtain a discrete set of potential depth estimates. This leads to a finite set of possible 3D positions along the ray (see Figure 2(a) for an illustration), defining a finite set of 3D point hypotheses $\{\hat{\mathbf{X}}_i^o | o = 1, \ldots, k\}$, where k is the number of the discrete hypotheses along the ray. In our representation, each 3D point $\hat{\mathbf{X}}_i^o$ establishes node $V_{o,i}$ in the graph. The set of nodes $\{V_{o,i} | i = 1, \ldots, N\}$ related to the ray $\mathbf{X}_i(t)$ of object i defines a partite set of nodes V_o in the graph $\mathcal{G}(\mathcal{V}, \mathcal{E})$. Given that no nodes within a group have any connecting edges, it enforces that traversing the graph to obtain an object class trajectory, the path cannot move along a ray. This is consistent with the understanding of moving between the different instances of the object class in the scene to determine the object class trajectory.

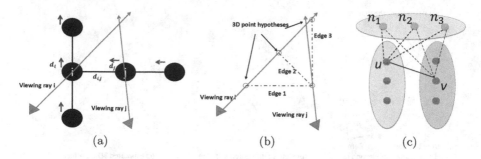

Fig. 3. In Fig. 3(a), the black nodes shows the real positions of dynamic objects. The red vector represents the direction associated with each object. In the shown example, $\mathbf{d}_{i,j}$ equals $\mathbf{d}_i$.

We now define the edge cost of the multipartite graph based on Eq. (4). The multipartite graph only has edges between the nodes from different partite sets. We define the edge direction $\mathbf{d}_{i,j}$ between any two nodes $V_{o,i}$ and $V_{p,j}$ in the partite set i and partite set j respectively, as the consistency of the 3D motion with the motion tangents $\mathbf{d}_i$ and $\mathbf{d}_j$ (see Sec. 3.2). This definition comes from the intuition that the edge direction should be compliant with the motion tangent observed in the images. Given the motion of two objects i and j and their respective motion tangents $\mathbf{d}_i$ and $\mathbf{d}_j$, it is clear that the motion between the points $\mathbf{X}_i^o$ and $\mathbf{X}_j^p$ (associated with the nodes $V_{o,i}$ and $V_{p,j}$) should be close in direction to at least one of the motion tangents $\mathbf{d}_i$ and $\mathbf{d}_j$. Therefore, we define the edge cost $e(V_{o,i}, V_{p,j})$ of the edge between the nodes $V_{o,i}$ and $V_{p,j}$ as

$$e(V_{o,i}, V_{p,j}) = \min(\|\mathbf{d}_i \times (\mathbf{X}_i^o - \mathbf{X}_j^p)\|_2^2, \|\mathbf{d}_j \times (\mathbf{X}_i^o - \mathbf{X}_j^p)\|_2^2) + \lambda\|\mathbf{X}_i^o - \mathbf{X}_j^p\|_2^2. \quad (5)$$

If only considering the first term in Eq. (5), edges with 3D motion directions that are approximately parallel to $\mathbf{d}_i$ or $\mathbf{d}_j$ have lower edge cost than 3D motion directions that are at an angle to both $\mathbf{d}_i$ and $\mathbf{d}_j$. For instance, Edge 1 and Edge 3 in Fig. 3(b) have a relatively lower cost than Edge 2 because Edge 1 is parallel to $\mathbf{d}_j$ and Edge 3 is parallel to $\mathbf{d}_i$.

3.5   GMST

A Generalized Minimum Spanning Tree (GMST) on the graph $\mathcal{G}(\mathcal{V}, \mathcal{E})$ is a tree of minimal cost that spans exactly one node from each partite set V_i. For our proposed graph, it means a GMST includes exactly one 3D point from each ray. Furthermore, GMST prefers the edge $((o,i), (p,j))$ that has small $\|\mathbf{X}_i^o - \mathbf{X}_j^p\|^2$ and is compliant with the motion tangents in the images, as those edges have lower edge cost. Accordingly, a GMST is our desired solution for estimating the object class trajectory. Notice that if we sample infinite number of 3d points along each viewing ray, the GMST problem is equivalent to the original cost function Eq. (4).

The multipartite graph defined above contains a large amount of edges, which increases the complexity of computing the GMST. We use a deterministic way introduced by Ferreira et al. [13] to remove those edges that are guaranteed not to be included in the GMST. Here we use a specific toy example in Fig. 3(c) to illustrate the method. If the cost of edge (u, v) is larger than any cost of the 6 edges (u, n_l) and (v, n_l), $l = 1, 2, 3$, the edge (u, v) is safe to be removed. A simple proof is that if edge (u, v) exists in the computed GMST, we could remove edge (u, v) and replace it by one of the 6 edges to obtain a new GMST with lower cost. Therefore, edge (u, v) can not be present in the GMST. Moreover, it is plausible to explore other ways to remove edges based on given prior information. For instance, if it is known the pairwise neighboring 3D objects are close in 3D space, we can safely remove the edges that connects two farther point hypotheses by applying a threshold.

The GMST problem was first introduced by Myung et al. [20] and was extensively studied in the past two decades [12,20,21,13,10] due to its wide applications in telecommunications, agriculture watering, and facility distribution design [20,10]. Unlike the minimum spanning tree (MST) problem, which can be solved in polynomial time, finding the GMST is proved to be NP-hard [20]. Myung et al. [20] and Feremans et al. [12] propose several integer programming formulations for the GMST problem. However, those provide no guarantee of efficiency, especially when the problem scale is large. The computational challenge of the GMST problem has led to the development of metaheuristics [21,13] that search the hypothesis space, and are empirically shown to be effective.

We exploit the state-of-the-art GRASP-based approach proposed by Ferreira et al. [13]. GRASP (Greedy Randomized Adaptive Search Procedure) is a metaheuristic that consists of iterations made up two phases: 1) solution construction and 2) solution improvement through local search. Ferreira et al. [13] proposed the method considering several solution construction algorithms, a local search procedure, and two additional mechanisms: path-relinking and iterative local search. We refer readers to their paper [13] for more details.

The output of GMST computation is the estimation of the 3D points $\widehat{\mathbf{X}}$ and the adjacency topology of the object class trajectory. Then $\mathbf{d}_{i,j}$ equals one of $\mathbf{d}_i$ and $\mathbf{d}_j$ that has smaller angle to the vector $\widehat{\mathbf{X}}_i - \widehat{\mathbf{X}}_j$,

$$\mathbf{d}_{i,j} = \underset{\mathbf{d} \in \{\mathbf{d}_i, \mathbf{d}_j\}}{\operatorname{argmax}} (|\mathbf{d} \cdot (\widehat{\mathbf{X}}_i - \widehat{\mathbf{X}}_j)|). \tag{6}$$

We fix the adjacency $\mathbf{p}$ given by the GMST, and add a final continuous refinement step for the 3D object position $\widehat{\mathbf{X}}_i$, through a convex program optimization over variable $\mathbf{t}$

$$\min_{\mathbf{t}} \sum_{(i,j) \in \mathbf{p}} \|\mathbf{d}_{i,j} \times (\mathbf{X}_i - \mathbf{X}_j)\|_2^2 + \lambda \|\mathbf{X}_i - \mathbf{X}_j\|_2^2 \tag{7}$$

3.6 Reconstructability Analysis

Now we analyze the reconstructability of the proposed method, i. e. determining under which conditions the solution of Eq. (4) generates accurate 3D points.

The direct analysis of Eq (4) is difficult, as it needs to determine in which situation the adjacency $\mathbf{p}$ with minimum cost, out of N^{N-2} possible adjacencies ([33]), corresponds to the object class trajectory. We find that having the motion tangent constraint reduces the possibility of finding the wrong adjacency $\mathbf{p}$. Hence, we focus on the reconstructability of the continuous method Eq. (7) given the adjacency $\mathbf{p}$.

Assume we already know the ground truth 3D point $\mathbf{X}_i^*$ of object i, $i = 1, \ldots, N$. Given that $\mathbf{X}_i^*$ is present on the viewing ray $\mathbf{X}_i$, we move the camera center $\mathbf{C}_i$ to $\mathbf{X}_i^*$ along the ray $\mathbf{X}_i(t)$ in direction $\mathbf{r}_i$. Then any point on the line that passes through $\mathbf{X}_i^*$ and has ray direction $\mathbf{r}_i$ can be represented as $\mathbf{X}_i(s_i) = \mathbf{X}_i^* + s_i \cdot \mathbf{r}_i$, where s_i is the signed distance (not the positive distance as defined by the t_i). Then Eq. (7) can be reformulated as:

$$\min_{\mathbf{s}} \sum_{(i,j) \in \mathbf{p}} \|\mathbf{d}_{i,j} \times (\mathbf{X}_i(s_i) - \mathbf{X}_j(s_j))\|_2^2 + \lambda \|\mathbf{X}_i(s_i) - \mathbf{X}_j(s_j)\|_2^2, \qquad (8)$$

where $\mathbf{s} = [s_1, \ldots, s_N]$. Though s_i is signed distance and t_i is positive distance, minimizing Eq. (7) and Eq. (8) still output the same 3D point positions, as long as the computed 3D points in Eq. (8) are in front of the camera centers. We will see that this is normally true, because the computed 3D points are typically close to their ground truth position if the system is well-conditioned.

We denote the solution of Eq. (8) as $\mathbf{s}^{\text{opt}}$. The true 3D points are ideally reconstructed if $\mathbf{s}^{\text{opt}} = 0$, since $\mathbf{X}_i(0)$ equals to $\mathbf{X}_i^*$ given $\mathbf{s}^{\text{opt}} = 0$. More specifically, $\mathbf{s}^{\text{opt}}$ equals the signed Euclidean distance between the 3D points produced by Eq. (7) and the ground truth X_i^*. Therefore, $\|\mathbf{s}^{\text{opt}}\|$ is the error of the estimated 3D points by Eq. 7. In the remaining of this section, we further analyze when $\|\mathbf{s}^{\text{opt}}\|$ is small to understand the quality of the estimated 3D points.

The minimum value of Eq. (8) is achieved at the point where the first derivative relative to $\mathbf{s}$ equals 0. This produces a linear equation system $\mathbf{A}\mathbf{s}^{\text{opt}} = \mathbf{b}$, where the ith row and jth column of matrix $\mathbf{A}$ is

$$A_{ij} = \begin{cases} [(\mathbf{r}_i \cdot \mathbf{d}_{i,j})\mathbf{d}_{i,j} - (1+\lambda)\mathbf{r}_i] \cdot \mathbf{r}_j & \text{if } i \neq j \text{ and } (i,j) \in \mathbf{p} \\ 0, & \text{if } i \neq j \text{ and } (i,j) \notin \mathbf{p} \\ \sum_{(i,k) \in \mathbf{p}} [1 + \lambda - (\mathbf{r}_i \cdot \mathbf{d}_{i,k})^2] & \text{if } i = j \end{cases} \qquad (9)$$

The ith element of vector $\mathbf{b}$ is

$$b_i = \sum_{(i,k) \in \mathbf{p}} (\mathbf{X}_k^* - \mathbf{X}_i^*) \cdot [(1+\lambda)\mathbf{r}_i - (\mathbf{r}_i \cdot \mathbf{d}_{i,k})\mathbf{d}_{i,k}] \qquad (10)$$

Eq. (9) and Eq. (10) have the following interesting properties:

1. If $\mathbf{b}$ is 0, $\mathbf{s}^{\text{opt}}$ equals 0, which means the solution of Eq. (7) recovers the true 3D points. There are a few situations $\mathbf{b}$ equal 0. (1) In the case of a static object $\mathbf{X}_i^* = \mathbf{X}_k^*$, $\mathbf{b}$ equals 0 based on Eq. (10). (2) Careful observation reveals that if λ is set to 0, in Eq. (10) the vector $(1+\lambda)\mathbf{r}_i - (\mathbf{d}_{i,k} \cdot \mathbf{r}_i)\mathbf{d}_{i,k}$ is perpendicular to vector $\mathbf{X}_i^* - \mathbf{X}_k^*$ (Fig. 4(a)), hence $b_i = 0$. However, we

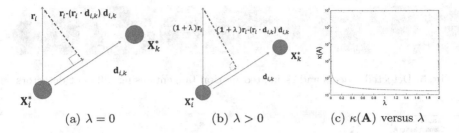

Fig. 4. Left two: Plot of Eq. (10) with $\lambda = 0$ and $\lambda > 0$. Right: $\kappa(\mathbf{A})$ given different λ.

will show that with $\lambda = 0$, the linear system $\mathbf{A}s = \mathbf{b}$ is unstable due to the high condition number of $\mathbf{A}$. (3) As shown in Fig. 4(b), as λ increases from 0, the two vectors slowly deviate from being perpendicular. Therefore, b_i is likely to be small if λ is close to 0.

2. Since we can not control 3D positions and there are typically small measurement errors in $\mathbf{d}_{ij}$, $\mathbf{b}$ does not exactly equal to 0. This can be regarded as a small disturbance of $\mathbf{b}$ around $\mathbf{0}$. For the linear system $\mathbf{A}s^{\text{opt}} = \mathbf{b}$, one can think of the condition number $\kappa(\mathbf{A})$ as being (roughly) the rate at which the solution, s^{opt}, will change with respect to a change in $\mathbf{b}$. $\kappa(\mathbf{A})$ is available as it solely depends on r_i, $\mathbf{d}_{i,j}$ and λ, but not on the ground truth 3D points $\mathbf{X}^*$. Therefore, we can roughly estimate the reliability of the reconstructed 3D points by computing $\kappa(\mathbf{A})$. Moreover, we empirically found that the condition number of matrix $\mathbf{A}$ is inversely related to λ. The condition number shown in Fig. 4(c) is computed using 100 random cameras, and averaged over 200 trials. We can see $\kappa(\mathbf{A})$ is large if λ is close to 0 and drop dramatically with small λ. Then $\kappa(\mathbf{A})$ decreases monotonically and slowly as λ increases. In our experiments, we choose $\lambda = \frac{1}{15}$ as a balance of having good chance of small $\mathbf{b}$ and the stability of the linear system.

In conclusion, if the adjacency $\mathbf{p}$ is correctly found, the reconstructabililty of the object class trajectory mainly depends on the condition number of the linear system. Given the well-conditioned system and correct motion tangent $\mathbf{d}_{i,j}$, we are able to reconstruct the 3D positions close to the ground truth.

4   Object Detector and Motion Tangent Estimation

Before presenting our experimental evaluation, we first briefly describe the particular object detectors we use in our experiments. Single image based object detection is a well studied problem in computer vision with a wide variety of method readily available [36,8,11]. Similarly, there is a large number of motion tangent estimation methods in the literature [4,16,17,19]. We opt for leveraging the method that jointly determines the face position and its motion tangent direction [38]. In our experiments, the detection threshold is set to -0.35 to avoid false detections, as the false alarm may disturb our algorithm. Our chosen

Fig. 5. Detected objects and estimated motion tangents using different detectors

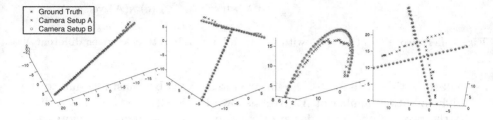

Fig. 6. Example results for line path, T-junction path, half circle and crossed paths

detectors provide a motion tangent of object i that is quantized every $\theta = 15°$ in the range of $-90°$ and $90°$.

For cars and pedestrians with small faces in the image, we default to the deformable parts detector [11,15]. We used the pre-trained model with detection threshold 0.35. The moving directions of the pedestrians and cars are estimated using the 3D point cloud (output of VisualSFM) of the background wall by assuming the dynamic objects move parallel to the wall. This is normally true for the Manhattan Scene. Some of the detection results are shown in Fig. 5.

5   Experiments

We evaluate our algorithm on both synthetic and real datasets. The GMST algorithm used in our method [13] searches the hypothesis space, which stops either the GMST cost is under a preset value or the run time reaches a preset limit. For all experiments, we use the time limit to stop searching, given the lack of an adequate *a priori* approximation of the true GMST cost for each dataset.

Table 1. The table shows the average errors. The subscript represents camera setup. The absence of asterisk represents the GMST algorithm output, and the asterisk is the refined output of Eq. (7). Notice that in ground truth 3D points, the average distance between every pair of nearest points equals 1.

	single line	T junction	double lines	half circle	sine wave	cross
error_A	0.5963	1.9688	1.5169	2.3751	2.3705	3.4111
error_A^*	0.4263	1.9148	1.4982	2.3340	2.3516	3.4030
error_B	0.2151	0.2126	0.7824	0.2281	0.2578	0.2251
error_B^*	0.0287	0.0944	0.7692	0.1074	0.2305	0.1308

Synthetic Datasets. Our first experiment uses synthetic data, with six different object class trajectory shapes on a plane, including a single line path, a T-junction path, a path with two parallel lines, a half circle path, sine wave shaped path, and two crossed path. For each of these shapes, we tested 32 instances, with each containing 50 randomly chosen object observation at different 3D positions. For more convenient error estimation during the evaluation, we normalized the 3D points so that the average distance between every pair of nearest points equals 1. The cameras are randomly generated around the 3D object points with two different configurations. In camera configuration A, all the camera centers stay in the same plane as the 3D points, which is more difficult since each viewing ray may intersect the ground truth path several times. In camera configuration B, the camera centers are set randomly off the plane, with the angle between the viewing ray and the plane being at most $10°$ and camera distance of 2-3 times the length of the path. We choose $k = 100$ uniformly distributed discrete 3D hypotheses $\mathbf{X}_i^o$ along each viewing ray $\mathbf{X}_i$ in a range that contains the ground truth 3D point. The size of the range is set as 1.5 times the length of the path. Notice that while the ground truth 3D points lie in the range, it is not guaranteed to be one of the discrete samples $\mathbf{X}_i^o$.

Errors are measured using the Euclidean distance between the estimated 3D points and the ground truth. The average errors over the 32 instances for each shape category are listed in Table 1. We report errors of the GMST output, and the errors after the continuous refinement using Eq. (7). Table 1 shows our continuous refinement always improves the reconstruction accuracy over the GMST approximation. The results demonstrate *off-plane* cameras yield improved results than *in-plane* cameras for complex paths (e.g. crossed paths), due to the multiplicity of ray-to-path intersections. In these cases the GMST solution has a more complex search space and yields a sub-optimal solution. However, the condition number of the linear system does not vary significantly across configurations. Fig. 6 shows the estimated 3D points overlaid onto the ground truth.

Real Datasets. We evaluated our method on two image datasets registered by VisualSFM [34]. The detection confidence threshold is set high in order to lower down the false alarm rate. However, a very small amount of false alarms are purged manually as it may affect the reconstruction. We sample 100 samples along the viewing ray in the range $[0, far]$, where far is estimated using the model scale. The running time for each object class trajectory is set to 3 hours.

The first dataset captures random pedestrians walking on the sidewalk, and random cars running on a lane. It contains 135 images with 82 valid car detections and 137 valid pedestrian detections. The scene and the reconstructed object class trajectory are shown in Fig. 7. The second dataset captures several people who are walking on a T-junction shaped path at the corner of a building. It contains 47 images with 66 valid detections. Using the camera positions, we convert the face directions into the global coordinate system to obtain the motion tangents $\mathbf{d}_i$ of the moving people. For illustration, we construct the background static scene using CMPMVS [18]. The general 3D human and car mesh models

Fig. 7. The left column: an aerial image showing the scene and a figure showing the cameras and reconstructed cars and pedestrians. The right four columns: four pedestrian detections (shown in yellow rectangles) and the poses of the corresponding cameras. These four pedestrians are adjacent in the reconstructed object class trajectory. Notice that the second and the third images are the same image but with different detections.

Fig. 8. Two views for each of the reconstructed results

are inserted into each of the estimated 3D positions. We show different views of the reconstructed results in Fig. 8.

6   Conclusions

We proposed a solution to the novel joint object class sequencing and trajectory triangulation problem, which allows the reconstruction of an object class trajectory from unordered images for which the capture times are unknown and there is no requirement of more than one view observing any object instance. This problem has previously been seen as highly limited in reconstructabililty. We evaluated our proposed method on synthetic and real world datasets and show promising results demonstrating the feasibility of the proposed approach to solve the joint object class sequencing and trajectory triangulation problem and in fact the first time demonstrating its solvability.

Acknowledgement. This material is based upon work supported by the National Science Foundation under Grant No. IIS-1252921 and No. IIS-1349074.

References

1. Akhter, I., Sheikh, Y.A., Khan, S., Kanade, T.: Nonrigid structure from motion in trajectory space. In: NIPS (2008)
2. Basha, T., Moses, Y., Avidan, S.: Photo sequencing. In: Fitzgibbon, A., Lazebnik, S., Perona, P., Sato, Y., Schmid, C. (eds.) ECCV 2012, Part VI. LNCS, vol. 7577, pp. 654–667. Springer, Heidelberg (2012)
3. Basha, T., Moses, Y., Avidan, S.: Space-time tradeoffs in photo sequencing. In: ICCV (2013)
4. Blanz, V., Vetter, T.: Face recognition based on fitting a 3D morphable model. PAMI (2003)
5. Bregler, C., Hertzmann, A., Biermann, H.: Recovering non-rigid 3D shape from image streams. In: CVPR (2000)
6. Coughlan, J.M., Yuille, A.L.: Manhattan world: Compass direction from a single image by bayesian inference. In: ICCV (1999)
7. Dai, Y., Li, H., He, M.: a simple prior-free method for non-rigid structure-from-motion factorization. In: CVPR (2012)
8. Dalal, N., Triggs, B.: Histograms of oriented gradients for human detection. In: CVPR (2005)
9. Delage, E., Lee, H., Ng, A.Y.: Automatic single-image 3D reconstructions of indoor manhattan world scenes. In: International Symposium on Robotics Research (2005)
10. Dror, M., Haouari, M., Chaouachi, J.: Generalized spanning trees. European Journal of Operational Research 120(3), 583–592 (2000)
11. Felzenszwalb, P.F., Girshick, R.B., McAllester, D., Ramanan, D.: Object detection with discriminatively trained part based models. PAMI (2010)
12. Feremans, C., Labbe, M., Laporte, G.: A comparative analysis of several formulations for the generalized minimum spanning tree problem. Networks (2002)
13. Ferreira, C.S., Ochi, L.S., Parada, V., Uchoa, E.: A grasp-based approach to the generalized minimum spanning tree problem (2012)
14. Frahm, J.-M., et al.: Building rome on a cloudless day. In: Daniilidis, K., Maragos, P., Paragios, N. (eds.) ECCV 2010, Part IV. LNCS, vol. 6314, pp. 368–381. Springer, Heidelberg (2010)
15. Girshick, R.B., Felzenszwalb, P.F., McAllester, D.: Discriminatively trained deformable part models, release 5,
http://people.cs.uchicago.edu/~rbg/latent-release5/
16. Gu, L., Kanade, T.: 3D alignment of face in a single image. In: CVPR (2006)
17. Jain, V., Learned-Miller, E.G.: Fddb: a benchmark for face detection in unconstrained settings. UMass Amherst Technical Report (2010)
18. Jancosek, M., Pajdla, T.: Multi-view reconstruction preserving weakly-supported surfaces. In: CVPR (2011)
19. Jones, M., Viola, P.: Fast multi-view face detection. Mitsubishi Electric Research Lab TR-20003-96 (2003)
20. Myung, Y., Lee, C., Tcha, D.: On the generalized minimum spanning tree problem. Networks (1995)
21. Oncan, T., Cordeau, J., Gilbert, L.: A tabu search heuristic for the generalized minimum spanning tree problem. European Journal of Operational Research (2008)
22. Park, H., Sheikh, Y.: 3D reconstruction of a smooth articulated trajectory from a monocular image sequence. In: ICCV (2011)

23. Park, H.S., Shiratori, T., Matthews, I., Sheikh, Y.: 3D reconstruction of a moving point from a series of 2D projections. In: Daniilidis, K., Maragos, P., Paragios, N. (eds.) ECCV 2010, Part III. LNCS, vol. 6313, pp. 158–171. Springer, Heidelberg (2010)

24. Ramalingam, S., Brand, M.: Lifting 3D manhattan lines from a single image. In: ICCV (2013)

25. Saxena, A., Chung, S.H., Ng, A.Y.: 3D depth reconstruction from a single still image. IJCV (2008)

26. Sidenbladh, H., Black, M.J., Fleet, D.J.: Stochastic tracking of 3D human figures using 2D image motion. In: Vernon, D. (ed.) ECCV 2000. LNCS, vol. 1843, pp. 702–718. Springer, Heidelberg (2000)

27. Sminchisescu, C., Triggs, B.: Kinematic jump processes for monocular 3D human tracking. In: CVPR (2003)

28. Tomasi, C., Kanade, T.: Shape and motion from image streams under orthography: a factorization method. IJCV (1992)

29. Valmadre, J., Lucey, S.: General trajectory prior for non-rigid reconstruction. In: CVPR (2012)

30. Valmadre, J., Zhu, Y., Sridharan, S., Lucey, S.: Efficient articulated trajectory reconstruction using dynamic programming and filters. In: Fitzgibbon, A., Lazebnik, S., Perona, P., Sato, Y., Schmid, C. (eds.) ECCV 2012, Part I. LNCS, vol. 7572, pp. 72–85. Springer, Heidelberg (2012)

31. Valmadre, J., Lucey, S.: Deterministic 3D human pose estimation using rigid structure. In: Daniilidis, K., Maragos, P., Paragios, N. (eds.) ECCV 2010, Part III. LNCS, vol. 6313, pp. 467–480. Springer, Heidelberg (2010)

32. Wei, X.K., Chai, J.: Modeling 3D human poses from uncalibrated monocular images. In: ICCV (2009)

33. Wikipedia: Cayley's formula, http://en.wikipedia.org/wiki/Cayley's_formula

34. Wu, C.: Visualsfm: A visual structure from motion system (2011), http://homes.cs.washington.edu/~ccwu/vsfm/

35. Xiao, J., Chai, J.-X., Kanade, T.: A closed-form solution to non-rigid shape and motion recovery. In: Pajdla, T., Matas, J. (eds.) ECCV 2004. LNCS, vol. 3024, pp. 573–587. Springer, Heidelberg (2004)

36. Zhang, J., Marszalek, M., Lazebnik, S., Schmid, C.: Local features and kernels for classification of texture and object categories: A comprehensive study. In: CVPR (2006)

37. Zhao, W., Chellappa, R., Phillips, P.J., Rosenfeld, A.: Face recognition: a literature survey. ACM Computing Surveys, CSUR (2003)

38. Zhu, X., Ramanan, D.: Face detection, pose estimation, and landmark localization in the wild. In: CVPR (2012)

39. Zhu, Y., Cox, M., Lucey, S.: 3D motion reconstruction for real-world camera motion. In: CVPR (2011)

Scene Chronology

Kevin Matzen and Noah Snavely

Cornell University, Ithaca NY
{kmatzen,snavely}@cs.cornell.edu

Abstract. We present a new method for taking an urban scene reconstructed from a large Internet photo collection and reasoning about its change in appearance through time. Our method estimates when individual 3D points in the scene existed, then uses spatial and temporal affinity between points to segment the scene into spatio-temporally consistent clusters. The result of this segmentation is a set of spatio-temporal objects that often correspond to meaningful units, such as billboards, signs, street art, and other dynamic scene elements, along with estimates of when each existed. Our method is robust and scalable to scenes with hundreds of thousands of images and billions of noisy, individual point observations. We demonstrate our system on several large-scale scenes, and demonstrate an application to time stamping photos. Our work can serve to **chronicle** a scene over time, documenting its history and discovering dynamic elements in a way that can be easily explored and visualized.

Keywords: Structure from motion, temporal reasoning, 4D modeling.

1 Introduction

In the last few years, our ability to model the world around us in 3D has greatly increased, due to the availability of vast numbers of photographs from sources such as Flickr, Facebook, and Picasa, as well as new reconstruction algorithms that can run on Internet-scale collections [1,2]. Indeed, the concept of "Internet-scale" now encompasses the scale of the world, as planet-sized reconstructions are now being built [3]. Once every stone has been turned to a point in a point cloud, does that mean the problem of 3D reconstruction is complete? While we often refer to scenes reconstructed via methods such as structure from motion (SfM) as being "static," in reality many urban scenes are quite dynamic over time scales of even a few years. Signs, lights, decorations, and street art are examples of such dynamism—they are often reconstructable with current methods, but transient in a longer-term view. Such visual elements provide opportunities for us to reconstruct and visualize our ever-changing world.

However, state-of-the-art 3D reconstruction methods remain largely agnostic to the time domain. While some systems work out of the box when applied to dynamic scenes, they usually provide an output model devoid of any temporal information, where points from different time spans simply co-exist. Other systems actively prune multiple points that occupy the same spatial location, which for time-varying scenes leads to broken reconstructions, veritable chimeras of different objects or appearances conflated in time.

Our aim is to bring temporal meaning back to these reconstructions. We propose a simple approach by which output from an existing 3D reconstruction method can be

D. Fleet et al. (Eds.): ECCV 2014, Part VII, LNCS 8695, pp. 615–630, 2014.

Fig. 1. A montage of a planar region of the 5 Pointz dataset, showing how this region has changed over time as different pieces of art have been overlaid atop one another

taken as input and segmented into distinct space-time objects, each with a specific extent in time. This method takes the web of observations and untangles it into temporally consistent components. Our approach not only augments a reconstruction with temporal information, but also leverages the time dimension as a unique signal for segmenting scenes into meaningful objects; just as object motion is an important cue for video segmentation, temporal structure is a useful cue for segmenting scenes.

Our method works by analyzing two key pieces of information: (1) the visibility relationship between images and points in a reconstruction, and (2) the timestamps on the images themselves. However, due to noise, it is difficult to use this raw information to directly reason about time. Incorrect timestamps, registration failures, uncontrolled illumination, photographer bias, sporadic temporal sampling, and photo manipulation all make temporal reasoning a challenging task. Our work in inspired by previous methods on temporal inference on 3D scenes [4,5], but our approach differs especially in *scale* and *granularity*—our method is designed for handling tens to hundreds of thousands of images sampled relatively densely in time. When reasoning about time in image collections, every observation has something to say, and so we focus on methods that are simple and highly scalable to the billions of individual observations in our datasets.

We demonstrate our method on several large-scale datasets, including dynamic city scenes, such as Times Square, as well as 5 Pointz, an outdoor street art exhibit space in NYC. Figure 1 shows a region of our 5 Pointz dataset, demonstrating the output we produce—extracted regions, sometimes overlapping in space, each with a temporal span. We use these results in two applications: a system for visualizing scenes over time, and a method for timestamping a new photo based on its contents. More broadly, we believe that our system can be used as the basis for *temporal visual discovery*—allowing one to automatically chronicle the rich visual appearance of a scene over time leveraging the wealth of online imagery, and to explore and visualize the results.

2   Related Work

Dynamic Scene Analysis. Scenes can be dynamic at many different time scales—seconds, minutes, years, decades. At video-rate time scales, there has been significant work on reconstruction of moving objects, spanning problem domains including motion capture [6], non-rigid SfM [7], scene flow methods [8,9], and video browsing [10]. Recent work has also sought to automatically *sequence* unstructured images captured over short time scales, based on motion constraints [11]. Somewhat longer time scales can be captured with time-lapse video, which only captures a single viewpoint but is especially useful for studying changes due to illumination [12,13] or long-term motions of objects [14]. Our domain of dynamic reconstruction methods from unstructured imagery at the scale of several years has received relatively little attention, but is becoming more and more feasible as the number of available images of scenes grows ever larger (imagine a future scenario where 100 years' worth of densely sampled imagery is available for any scene!)

There are a few systems that operate on unstructured imagery over large time scales. Notably, Schindler and Dellaert [5] build probabilistic temporal reconstructions of scenes from historical photo collections. By analyzing occluder-occludee relationships of buildings and considering timestamps of varying precision, they formulate a graphical model and perform joint inference to determine the most likely temporal ordering for a set of photographs, a set of improved timestamps, and temporal extents for the observed buildings. Our work differs in several key respects. First, their analysis was conducted on photo collections containing hundreds of photos, and performs an inference involving potentially expensive steps, such as an occlusion-test subroutine. In contrast, a key goal of ours is to scale to very large collections (our largest input set includes over 1 million photos). Second, we focus on more fine-grained temporal reasoning, involving photos sampled densely in time over the last ten years. We also focus primarily on changes in *appearance* (e.g., one billboard changing to another), rather than changes in geometry. Finally, their work performs an initial object segmentation based on proximity and a simple camera co-visibility metric. In our work, we integrate time-based reasoning directly into the scene segmentation, avoiding hard segmentation decisions early on.

Change Detection. A related field is that of change detection, where the goal is to identify differences between two or more 2D images or 3D scenes. Pollard and Mundy proposed a change detection method for 3D scenes observed from an aerial vehicle [15]. By building a model of occupancy and appearance over a voxel grid, they can determine if a new view was generated either by the background model or by some change. Other related work proposes geometric change detection by comparing 3D reconstructions built from video [16,17]. However, these formulations only produce differences between two points in time. Our work provides a full temporal model across a large timespan. Fard et al. proposed a method for using unstructured photo collections to monitor the progress of a building under construction by comparing 3D reconstructions to 3D building specifications [18]. In our case, however, we have no a priori scene model.

3   Overview

Our overall goal is to build a dense 3D point cloud with appearance information, e.g., using methods such as PMVS, and then to segment this reconstruction into a set of temporally coherent geometric components (corresponding to signs, billboards, storefronts, etc.), as well as estimate a time range $[t_{min}, t_{max}]$ for each component defining its temporal extent. We use the timestamps on images for this task. However, due to noise in timestamps and in our estimates of point visibility, this task is difficult to perform robustly. In addition, due to the scale of our data, we require very efficient algorithms.

Assumptions and Scene Representation. Our method makes several assumptions about the input scene. First, we apply a standard SfM and multi-view stereo (MVS) pipeline (with a few modifications) to derive an initial reconstruction from a set of photos. Hence, even for a dynamic scene, we assume we can reconstruct accurate cameras and points using SfM. This assumption relies on there being sufficient scene content that is constant over time, or at least there being sufficient continuity in a scene from one time to the next. Second, we assume that the geometry of the scene is largely static, but that the appearance can change dramatically from one time to the next. Such appearance changes are a key source of dynamism in scenes like Times Square, where storefronts, billboards, and other ads are changing, often from one week to the next. Finally, because we focus on urban scenes, we assume that the scene geometry can be well-approximated with a set of planes, as in other work on urban reconstruction [19,20].

This last assumption leads to our choice of output scene representation. We assume that the components we segment the scene into can be approximated as (not necessarily axis-aligned) planar facets—i.e., at any given time, the 3D scene is approximated by 2D planes. Further, as in Schindler et al. [5], we assume that unique objects come into existence at some time, exist for a while, then are removed or replaced permanently. Hence, each object exists for a single, contiguous span of time. If we consider a dynamic scene as a 4D space-time volume, then our planar objects form 3D space-time "cuboids" in this volume—2D in space, 1D intervals in time. Hence, our output representation consists of a set of such objects, which we refer to as "plane-time cuboids."

Space-Time Reconstruction System. Our overall pipeline is illustrated in Figure 2. We take a large collection of Internet photos of a scene, and generate a dense 3D point cloud reconstruction (Fig. 2(1)), which initially is the union of all points across time. Next, we reason about which cameras observe which points (2), and use the observation profile of each 3D point to reason about the time interval in which it existed (3). We then segment the scene into sets of points that are spatio-temporally coherent ((4) and (5)), from which we can render visualizations of each part of the scene over time (6). We now describe our space-time reconstruction and segmentation algorithm in detail.

4   Method

4.1   Dense 3D Reconstruction

Our input is a large set of photographs (tens of thousands to millions) downloaded from the Web using targeted keyword searches such as `times square`. We restrict our download to photos with timestamps (e.g., for Flickr, photos that have a `datetaken` field). Using a random subset of 20,000 photos, we build an initial SfM reconstruction using Bundler to obtain camera parameters and a sparse 3D point cloud [21]. We then use 2D-to-3D matching techniques to register the remaining photos to the reconstruction [22]. This process results in a set of reconstructed images $\mathcal{I}$, camera parameters

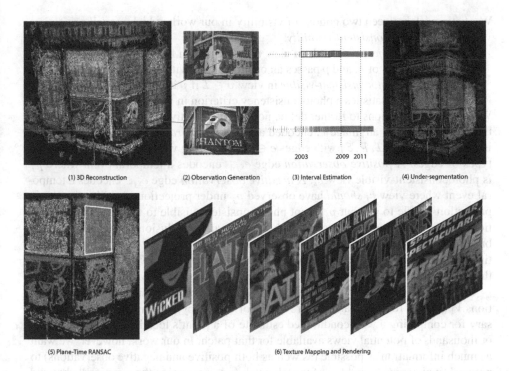

Fig. 2. System pipeline. Given a dense 3D reconstruction (1), we expand a visibility graph (2), and then use that graph to estimate per-patch time intervals (3). Using spatial and temporal cues, we construct a spatio-temporal graph and perform an undersegmentation (4). Then we fit plane-time cuboids to this graph (5) and generate texture maps for visualization (6). This example shows an exploded view of several billboards at the same location over time.

for each image, and a sparse set of 3D points. Finally, we use CMVS to factor the reconstruction into smaller components [23], then use a modified version of PMVS to generate a dense 3D point cloud [24]. PMVS contains a number of geometric filters that disallow two 3D points from occupying the same (or very similar) spatial location. We modify PMVS to remove this restriction on output geometry, as detailed in the supplemental material. The result of CMVS+PMVS is a dense set of 3D patches $\mathcal{P}$. Each patch $p \in \mathcal{P}$ is represented with a 3D position, a surface normal, and a set of images $V_{\text{PMVS}}(p) \subseteq \mathcal{I}$ in which p is deemed to be visible (as determined by high photoconsistency with a reference patch for p). One of these views is selected as a reference view.

4.2 Computing the Visibility Graph

Our system relies on a good initial estimate of the visibility of each patch p in the set of cameras, as visibility (along with timestamps on images) provides strong information about when in time a patch existed. The visibility sets V_{PMVS} produced by PMVS are very approximate, and so we expand these sets into a richer representation of visibility.

We distinguish between two notions of visibility in our work, which we call *projection-visibility* and *photoconsistent-visibility*:

- A patch p is *projection-visible* in view $v \in \mathcal{I}$ if p is in front of v, p projects inside the field of view of v, and p passes an occlusion test with other patches.
- A patch p is *photoconsistent-visible* in view $v \in \mathcal{I}$ if p is projection-visible in view v and further p satisfies a photoconsistency criterion in view v.

We use these definitions to further define notions of "positive" and "negative" observations of a patch p in an image v, encoded as a *visibility graph*. The visibility graph $\mathcal{V}$ is a bipartite graph $(\mathcal{I}, \mathcal{P}, \mathcal{E})$ with edges $e \in \mathcal{E}$ connecting views to patches. $\mathcal{V}$ has two types of edges. A *positive observation* edge e_{ij+} encodes a temporal event where p_j is photoconsistent-visible view v_i. A *negative observation* edge e_{ij-} encodes a temporal event where view v_i *should* have observed p_j under projection-visibility (i.e., p_j is projection-visible to v_i), but p_j is not photoconsistent-visible to v_i. Negative observations can occur for several reasons, including dynamic occlusion and misregistration, but more importantly, they occur when a patch does not exist at a particular point in time. These observations help us narrow down exactly when a patch *does* exist. Note that observations that are not projection-visible are treated as providing no information.

CMVS+PMVS typically produces only a small subset of possible positive observations $V_{\mathrm{PMVS}}(p)$ for each patch p, for reasons of efficiency; only a few views are necessary for computing a well-conditioned estimate of a point's location, not the hundreds or thousands of potential views available for that patch. In our work, however, we want as much information as possible (as well as both positive and negative observations) to precisely estimate $t_{\min}$ and $t_{\max}$ for each patch (i.e., answering the question "when did this patch exist?"). Therefore, we perform a visibility graph expansion step.

To do so, for each image $v \in \mathcal{I}$, we generate a depth map by projecting all reconstructed patches into v's image frame using a z-buffering algorithm. Each patch adds a 3-pixel radius contribution to the depth map. After generating this depth map, we project each patch p once more into the image; if p projects inside v's field of view and satisfies a soft depth test against this depth map, we deem p projection-consistent. We then compute a photoconsistency score by comparing a reference patch for p extracted from p's reference view (computed according to PMVS's patch extraction method) to the projection of the same oriented planar patch in v. If the normalized cross-correlation of both windows is above a threshold τ_{pos}, then a positive observation is recorded. Similarly, if the normalized cross-correlation is below a threshold τ_{neg}, then a negative observation is recorded. For all experiments, we set $\tau_{\mathrm{pos}} = 0.8$ and $\tau_{\mathrm{neg}} = -0.2$.

4.3 Initial Time Interval Estimation

The set of observations for a given patch p gives us useful information about when in time p existed, via the timestamps on images that observe p. For the segmentation step of our pipeline, we require an approximate initial time span $[t_{\min}(p), t_{\max}(p)]$, which we compute from the associated image timestamps. A natural algorithm is to simply take the minimum (earliest) and maximum (latest) positive observation timestamps as the time interval. However, this algorithm doesn't work well due to false positive observations and incorrect timestamps; surprisingly, even in a time when many cameras are networked, there are many reasons why timestamps can be wrong. We also tried or-

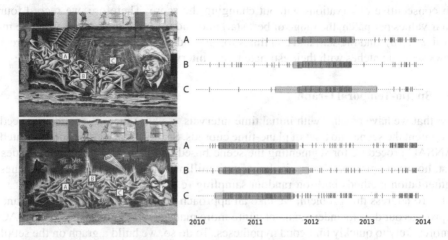

Fig. 3. Time profiles (right), for two different appearances of the same wall (left). Green (red) marks on the timeline indicate positive (negative) observations. Dark gray intervals indicate the shortest interval with the maximal F_1 score. Any interval with endpoints contained within the light gray regions will have the same F_1 score. Note the false positive red marks inside the gray intervals and the false negative green marks outside the gray intervals, as well as the very non-uniform distribution of observations, which highlight the need for robust methods.

dering positive observations by time and trimming off the bottom and top k-percentile. However, because our observations are very non-uniform samples in time (with some times much more densely sampled than others), we found that this approach also performed poorly. In general, we found that considering only positive observations was insufficient to compute robust time bounds for a patch, and we must also use negative observations.

We found it effective to formulate this problem is in terms of classification, where we wish to select a single time interval that classifies observations as being positive (inside the interval) or negative (outside the interval), with the goal of achieving both good precision and recall. Here, *precision* is the ratio of positive observations inside the interval to the total number of observations in the interval. Similarly, *recall* is the ratio of the number of positive observations in the interval to the total number of positive observations across all of time. One common way to balance these measures is to use the F_1 score, which is the harmonic mean of these two terms:

$$\text{Precision} = \frac{\#\text{TP}}{\#\text{TP} + \#\text{FP}} \quad \text{Recall} = \frac{\#\text{TP}}{\#\text{TP} + \#\text{FN}} \quad F_1 = \frac{2 \cdot \text{Precision} \cdot \text{Recall}}{\text{Precision} + \text{Recall}}$$

For each patch p, we search over all possible start and end times $t_{\min}(p)$ and $t_{\max}(p)$ (where we can limit the search to only consider the discrete set of timestamps corresponding to our observations of that patch), and select the pair defining the time interval with the maximum F_1 score. This can be computed very quickly using dynamic programming. Note that in general there is a family of intervals with the same F_1 score for a set of discrete observations, as we can vary the endpoints continuously between two consecutive observations without changing the score. Therefore, we record four scalar values per patch, the range of best start and end times for the beginning of the interval, $t_{\min}(p)$, and the start and end times for the end of the interval, $t_{\max}(p)$. Figure 3 shows several patches with their estimated time intervals.

4.4   Spatio-Temporal Graph

Now that we have patches with initial time intervals, we have the information we need to segment the scene into a set of plane-time cuboids. Section 4.5 describes our repeated RANSAC procedure for segmenting the scene based on geometric and temporal cues. First, however, our scenes are quite large, with millions of patches, and for such scenes segmentation methods built on random sampling (e.g., RANSAC) can be difficult to scale. To address this problem, we take an approach inspired by GroupSAC [25], and preprocess our data to under-segment it into more manageable chunks where RANSAC is more likely to quickly find good hypotheses. To do so, we build a graph on the set of patches where pairs of patches are connected if they have high *spatio-temporal affinity*— if they are proximate in space and time—and then compute connected components of this graph. This method is related to the object segmentation in [5], but considers time as well, and serves as a preprocess to our final segmentation algorithm.

We connect two patches p and q if they satisfy the following criteria:

- **Spatial proximity.** p and q are within a 3D distance δ_d, and have normals that differ by no more than an angle δ_θ.
- **Temporal overlap.** p and q have time observations with a high degree of overlap.
- **Common view.** p and q are seen by at least one common camera from the original PMVS reconstruction ($|V_{\mathrm{PMVS}}(p) \cap V_{\mathrm{PMVS}}(q)| > 0$).

For the temporal overlap criterion (item 2), we could use the degree of overlap in the time intervals for p and q estimated in Section 4.3 above. Instead, we found a somewhat stricter notion of temporal overlap to be useful, in particular, we use the positive observations for each patch to form an *observation profile*. For each positive observation for a patch p, we pad it by ± 1 week to form a time interval. Overlapping time intervals for a single patch are aggregated into larger time intervals. The final set of (not necessarily contiguous) time intervals forms the observation profile for p. To measure the temporal overlap of a pair of patches (p, q), we compute the size of the intersection divided by the size of the union of the two observation profiles (where here "size" means the total time mass in the intersection or union of two observation profiles). This gives us a single scalar temporal affinity score. If this score is greater than a threshold δ_t, then the pair (p, q) satisfies the temporal overlap criterion.

To efficiently evaluate the three criteria above, for each patch p, we use FLANN [26] to find spatial neighbors within a 3D distance δ_d, then prune these potential candidate neighbors by the surface normal, temporal overlap, and common view criteria. The surviving edges define a graph G_{st} whose connected components form a rough initial undersegmentation into objects, as illustrated in Figure 2(4). For all experiments, we use $\delta_\theta = 60°$, $\delta_t = 0.75$, and we manually select a per-reconstruction δ_d equal to roughly 1-2 meters. Note, an alternative to manually selecting δ_d is to geo-register the reconstruction so that it is to metric scale.

4.5   Plane-Time Clustering

Finally, we further segment each component of G_{st} from the initial spatio-temporal segmentation into a set of plane-time cuboids that represent coherent objects in the scene. We perform the segmentation by greedily and repeatedly running a special "Plane-Time RANSAC," on each component, after each round removing the induced subgraph given by the RANSAC inliers from G_{st} to form G'_{st}, and recursively applying the same procedure to the connected components of G'_{st}. We terminate the recursion if a connected component does not contain some minimum number of vertices or if we are unable to find any valid RANSAC hypotheses after some fixed number of iterations. This process is run in parallel on each connected component.

Plane-Time RANSAC combines a standard plane-fitting inlier criterion with a new time interval hypothesis criterion. In particular, the algorithm samples three patches at random from the component and fits a plane to the three samples. It also computes a time interval hypothesis by taking the union of the patches' time intervals as estimated in Section 4.3. Thus a hypothesis is a combination of a plane and a time interval. A patch is considered an inlier to this hypothesis if (1) it is within some spatial distance of the hypothesis plane, (2) its normal is within some cosine distance of the hypothesis plane, and (3) its time interval has a high degree of overlap with the hypothesis time interval. Once again, we define overlap of two time intervals to be the size of their intersection divided by the size of their union. Because the estimated patch time interval is really a family of intervals with endpoints that are allowed to vary slightly, we select the unique patch time interval that maximizes the overlap between the patch and the hypothesis. Note that when generating a hypothesis, three non-collinear points uniquely define a plane, but the normals and time intervals of the sample points themselves may not satisfy the inlier criterion for the hypothesis. We check for such cases and discard the hypothesis if any sample is not an inlier to its own hypothesis. In our experiements, RANSAC was allotted 1000 attempts to generate a hypothesis, but was limited to 100 valid hypotheses.

At termination, we have a set of plane-time cuboids (associated with each cluster), and each patch has either been assigned to a cluster or has been discarded (as not belonging to a large enough cluster). The time interval associated with each plane-time cuboid can then be transferred back to the individual patches in the cluster to obtain refined per-patch time intervals, since we assume the object represented by the cluster appears and disappears as one unit. The distance, normal, and time overlap thresholds used in all RANSAC runs are identical to their analogous counterparts in Section 4.4.

5   Experiments and Results

Datasets. We ran our pipeline on three highly dynamic datasets of urban environments from photos taken over a span of several years. TimesSquare in Manhattan contains a quarter million registered photos exhibiting a wide variety of change in appearance in terms of billboards, signs, and building facades. Akihabara in Tokyo offers a related setting where most of the dynamic content is localized to billboards and signs. However, Akihabara also contains dramatic instances where entire buildings change appearance. Finally, 5Pointz in Queens, NYC, served for several years as an outdoor

Table 1. Dataset statistics

Dataset	Photos Retrieved	Photos Registered	Patches	Positive Obs.	Negative Obs.
Times Square	1,222,792	246,218	13,590,341	5,274,437,797	12,347,622,570
5 Pointz	48,375	12,777	12,263,640	635,602,574	821,189,516
Akihabara	171,469	13,946	1,732,784	132,520,809	254,624,878

art exhibit space for graffiti artists, and offers a visually rich experience involving many pieces of art over time. In this last case, our method can be seen as a step towards automatic, distributed, art documentation. Table 1 shows the scale of these datasets.

5.1   Viewing and Rendering

Our plane-time cuboid representation provides a simple yet effective way to explore the evolution of a scene through space and time. We have created an interface where a user can explore the scene using standard 3D navigation controls, but can also move back and forth in time using a slider control.[1] At any selected time, we can render a snapshot of the scene as a point cloud using the patches that existed during that time, or can additionally render each cuboid as a texture mapped "quad." To do so, for each plane-time cuboid proxy, we generate a bounding 3D rectangle with one axis perpendicular to the scene's estimated up vector. For each camera that observes at least six patches associated with the cuboid, we apply the homography mapping image space to the quad's texture space. To enable clean blending between multiple cameras despite transient occlusions and geometric misregistration, we generate an alpha matte using Gaussian splats of uniform size centered at the projections of the positive patch observations. Examples of these quads are shown in Figures 2, 4, and 7.

4 June 2011   14 November 2013

Fig. 4. A texture mapped rendering of 5Pointz at two different points in time. Please refer to the project webpage for a video exploring all three datasets.

Our plane-time cuboids qualitatively represent meaningful semantic units. Figure 4 shows a birds-eye view of 5Pointz at two distant, visually distinct points in time. Throughout time, segments come in and out of existence, sometimes in synchrony,

---

[1] Please visit http://www.cs.cornell.edu/projects/chronology/ for videos and other visualizations.

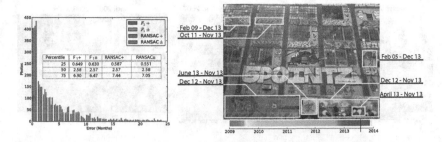

Fig. 5. 5Pointz timestamp prediction results. Positive and negative observations provide clues as to when a photo was taken. Left: histogram and statistics of errors in timestamping. Right: positive observations for a sample photo are shown in green. Several components of this scene are well-localized in time and can be used to build a timestamp scoring function. The timestamp with the highest score is marked on the timeline. We predict this photo was taken on July 25, 2013; the photo metadata indicates it was taken on August 10, 2013.

sometimes independently. It is not until the whole collection is analyzed that the behavior of the scene becomes clear. For these sorts of scenes, it would be difficult for an expert to manually analyze each photo to determine the scene's temporal structure over the span of several years. However, we can achieve our results fully automatically. Please refer to the video on our project webpage for a rich visualization of the evolution of all three scenes. Figure 7 shows a number of interesting examples of automatically recovered space-time cuboids. Of particular interest are examples with temporal cues contained within the image. For example, a poster advertising the 2008 US presidential election is estimated to exist during the election period. Anime ads found in Akihabara advertise products with recent release dates. Graffiti in 5Pointz can be matched with coarse-grained databases found online. Each of these examples gives us clues about the world's appearance at a given point in time. While it is difficult to evaluate results quantitatively, subjectively we achieve segmentations with close correspondence to temporal objects in each scene.

5.2 Timestamp Prediction

Another application of our system is for the task of predicting the date of a photo, in case a date is missing or incorrect. Our time-stamping algorithm analyzes what portions of our time-varying reconstruction are observed in a query photo, what portions are not observed, and determines a date that best fits that information.

Given a new query photo registered to the model (e.g., using 2D-to-3D matching), we use the same observation generation procedure as described in Section 4. However, we select a more conservative $\tau_{neg} = -0.5$ to obtain more confident observations. Given the positive and negative patch observations, we use a voting scheme to determine a time interval where the positive observation time intervals overlap, but where the negative time intervals do not. For each observation, we generate a start event and an end event; each event carries a vote. For a positive observation, the start event carries a vote of $+w$ and the end event carries a weight of $-w$ where w is a tunable weight, $w = 10$ in

Fig. 6. Retimestamped photos. The timeline indicates our timestamp scoring function with the given timestamp indicated in blue and our predicted timestamp indicated in pink. The originally recorded date and estimated date range as determined by manual inspection are provided above.

our experiments. For a negative observation, the start event carries a vote of -1 and the end event carries a weight of $+1$. The score for each time subinterval is computed by sorting all events by timestamp and then stepping along the timeline, accumulating the vote carried by each event. The subinterval with the maximal score is then found. To generate a single predicted timestamp, we select the midpoint of this interval.

In practice, we found that we had to consider the effect of unmodeled occlusions and its impact on negative observations. By unmodeled occlusion, we mean the effect of holes in the depth buffer used to determine projection-visibility of a point due to parts of the scene geometry not being reconstructed. While this is not as much of a concern when aggregating observations at each patch since this effect is more or less random for a given patch, it is very consistent for aggregating observations for each camera. Therefore, we only include a negative observation if at least one positive observation is in close 3D spatial proximity. This implies that we could see the surface geometry at one point in time, but we do not currently see a certain appearance in the query photo.

To evaluate this method, we conducted a timestamping experiment on 5Pointz. We selected a random 10% of registerable photos as a test set and ran our pipeline as a training stage on the remaining 90%. The test set was selected such that no photographer overlaps between training and test sets, to prevent any bias a single photographer might introduce. Note that while we measure distance to the original timestamps as ground truth, these contain noise, and so our results should be interpreted with this in mind.

We present four variations on the algorithm described above. Methods denoted F_1 use the per-patch time estimates obtained by our F_1 interval procedure before Plane-Time RANSAC segmentation is performed. Methods denoted RANSAC use per-cluster time estimates obtained via Plane-Time RANSAC. Methods denoted $+$ use only positive observations while those denoted $\pm$ use both positive and negative observations. Figure 5 shows our results as a histogram of distances between predicted and original timestamps. We observe improvement with both the F_1 and RANSAC methods after we introduce negative observations, achieving a median distance of around 2.5 months, with 25% of images having about 0.5 month distance (quite low given that all the only cue we are using is changing scene appearance). However, there is an increase in error for the 75th percentile when we move to the RANSAC methods from the F_1 methods. One explanation is that by clustering the points, we might be losing some precision

Fig. 7. An assortment of plane-time cuboids from `TimesSquare` (blue), `Akihabara` (green), and `5Pointz` (red) with texture maps and estimated time intervals produced by our system

in our time estimates; another is that we are seeing effects from noise in the original timestamps.

We also applied our timestamping method to photos from TimesSquare. Figure 6 shows examples of images that we believed to have incorrect timestamps based on the content in the scene (i.e. ads, weather, clothing), and for which our method predicted timestamps that more closely matches our belief of when these photos were taken. In general for this dataset, applying RANSAC ± resulted in a 25-50-75 percentile errors of 1.22, 5.47, and 20.1 months, respectively, indicating that this is a harder dataset for timestamping than 5Pointz.

6   Discussion and Conclusion

Our system has several limitations, some common to traditional 3D reconstruction systems and some unique to the 4D reconstruction problem. One key issue is that photo misregistration can prevent accurate timestamp estimation. If several photos are localized incorrectly in 3D due to some repeated structure in the scene, then all of the timestamps associated with those photos will contaminate their associated geometry. Since these photos themselves are in photoconsistent agreement, our system maybe decide to merge them into a single, potentially long-lasting segment. Another issue is that many structures in the real world cannot be approximated accurately using planar segments. In that case, our system often oversegments these regions into several smaller facets. An improvement would be to extend the set of models available in the RANSAC segmentation routine, or to have a more flexible geometric model that uses time as a strong segmentation cue.

Even in the scenes we studied, there were examples of changes in the physical structure of the buildings which violate our static geometry assumption. In 2009 a staircase at 5Pointz collapsed and our reconstruction captures this in its segmentation. However, since the z-buffer used in our system is time-agnostic, the projection-visible test culls potential positive observations that became visible after the staircase's removal.

The assumption that objects come into and leave existence only once can be violated. The 5Pointz dataset has at least one example where graffiti was covered up and then later restored. Both the original graffiti as well as its protective surface were reconstructed as two separate segments and the reappearance of the graffiti was suppressed.

Finally, timespan estimation is much more precise for segments that are clearly limited to some range of time in the middle of the dataset's timeline. Segments that occur very early (pre-2005) or very late (post-2013) often have no negative observations to help limit either their starting or ending points.

Conclusion. Point observations over time can play an important role in the semantic segmentation of 3D point clouds. We introduce the first fully automatic and Internet-scalable system for segmenting 3D point cloud reconstructions for scenes containing largely static geometry, but changing appearance. By leveraging a simple classification accuracy statistic, we are able to robustly estimate time intervals for each point in a reconstruction by considering both positive and negative observations, despite severe noise. Our method then leverages spatial, temporal, and co-visibility cues to segment points into spatio-temporally consistent components that we call plane-time cuboids.

The segments produced by our system often are natural units (signs, facades, art, etc.), and are useful for both visualization and time stamping applications.

Future work will involve extending state-of-the-art image-based rendering techniques into the time domain for immersive photo exploration through space and time using the plane-time cuboid proxies generated by our system. In addition, we hope to integrate our appearance-based method with modeling of larger-scale geometric changes, as well as more general types of visual changes over time [27].

Acknowledgements. This work was funded in part by NSF grants IIS-1111534 and IIS-1149393, by support from the Intel Science and Technology Center for Visual Computing, and by support from Amazon Web Services in Education.

References

1. Agarwal, S., Snavely, N., Simon, I., Seitz, S.M., Szeliski, R.: Building Rome in a day. In: ICCV (2009)
2. Frahm, J.-M., et al.: Building rome on a cloudless day. In: Daniilidis, K., Maragos, P., Paragios, N. (eds.) ECCV 2010, Part IV. LNCS, vol. 6314, pp. 368–381. Springer, Heidelberg (2010)
3. Klingner, B., Martin, D., Roseborough, J.: Street view motion-from-structure-from-motion. In: ICCV (2013)
4. Schindler, G., Dellaert, F., Kang, S.B.: Inferring temporal order of images from 3D structure. In: CVPR (2007)
5. Schindler, G., Dellaert, F.: Probabilistic temporal inference on reconstructed 3D scenes. In: CVPR (2010)
6. Shotton, J., Fitzgibbon, A., Cook, M., Sharp, T., Finocchio, M., Moore, R., Kipman, A., Blake, A.: Real-time human pose recognition in parts from single depth images. In: CVPR (2011)
7. Bregler, C., Hertzmann, A., Biermann, H.: Recovering non-rigid 3D shape from image streams. In: CVPR, pp. 690–696 (2000)
8. Vedula, S., Baker, S., Rander, P., Collins, R.T., Kanade, T.: Three-dimensional scene flow. PAMI 27(3) (2005)
9. Ulusoy, A.O., Biris, O., Mundy, J.L.: Dynamic probabilistic volumetric models. In: ICCV (2013)
10. Ballan, L., Brostow, G.J., Puwein, J., Pollefeys, M.: Unstructured video-based rendering: Interactive exploration of casually captured videos. In: SIGGRAPH (2010)
11. Basha, T., Moses, Y., Avidan, S.: Photo sequencing. In: Fitzgibbon, A., Lazebnik, S., Perona, P., Sato, Y., Schmid, C. (eds.) ECCV 2012, Part VI. LNCS, vol. 7577, pp. 654–667. Springer, Heidelberg (2012)
12. Sunkavalli, K., Matusik, W., Pfister, H., Rusinkiewicz, S.: Factored Time-Lapse Video. In: SIGGRAPH (2007)
13. Jacobs, N., Roman, N., Pless, R.: Consistent temporal variations in many outdoor scenes. In: CVPR (2007)
14. Rubinstein, M., Liu, C., Sand, P., Durand, F., Freeman, W.T.: Motion denoising with application to time-lapse photography. In: CVPR (2011)
15. Pollard, T., Mundy, J.: Change detection in a 3-D world. In: CVPR, pp. 1–6 (June 2007)
16. Taneja, A., Ballan, L., Pollefeys, M.: Image based detection of geometric changes in urban environments. In: ICCV (November 2011)

17. Taneja, A., Ballan, L., Pollefeys, M.: City-scale change detection in cadastral 3D models using images. In: CVPR (June 2013)
18. Fard, M.G., Peña-Mora, F., Savarese, S.: Monitoring changes of 3D building elements from unordered photo collections. In: ICCV Workshops (2011)
19. Sinha, S., Steedley, D., Szeliski, R.: Piecewise planar stereo for image-based rendering. In: ICCV (2009)
20. Furukawa, Y., Curless, B., Seitz, S.M., Szeliski, R.: Reconstructing building interiors from images. In: ICCV (2009)
21. Snavely, N., Seitz, S.M., Szeliski, R.: Modeling the world from Internet photo collections. IJCV 80(2), 189–210 (2008)
22. Li, Y., Snavely, N., Huttenlocher, D., Fua, P.: Worldwide pose estimation using 3D point clouds. In: Fitzgibbon, A., Lazebnik, S., Perona, P., Sato, Y., Schmid, C. (eds.) ECCV 2012, Part I. LNCS, vol. 7572, pp. 15–29. Springer, Heidelberg (2012)
23. Furukawa, Y., Curless, B., Seitz, S.M., Szeliski, R.: Towards Internet-scale multi-view stereo. In: CVPR (2010)
24. Furukawa, Y., Ponce, J.: Accurate, dense, and robust multi-view stereopsis. PAMI 32(8), 1362–1376 (2009)
25. Ni, K., Jin, H., Dellaert, F.: GroupSAC: Efficient consensus in the presence of groupings. In: ICCV (2009)
26. Muja, M., Lowe, D.G.: Fast approximate nearest neighbors with automatic algorithm configuration. In: Int. Conf. on Computer Vision Theory and Application (2009)
27. Lee, Y.J., Efros, A.A., Hebert, M.: Style-aware mid-level representation for discovering visual connections in space and time. In: ICCV (2013)

Author Index